SPECIAL ALERT
Pension Protection Act of 2006

Seeking to avert a meltdown and taxpayer bailout of traditional private pension plans, Congress has passed a comprehensive pension reform bill. The mammoth Pension Protection Act of 2006 (P.L. 109-280) does not only strengthen traditional pension plans. It also extends and, in some cases, improves over 20 retirement tax-savings benefits, many of which taxpayers had come to expect as permanent; adds extensive new rules governing specific charitable donations; imposes tighter controls on exempt organizations; and impacts over a dozen other major tax provisions.

The new law passed the House by a vote of 279 to 131 on July 28. The Senate voted 93 to 5 to approve the bill on August 3. President Bush signed the bill into law on August 17.

The pension reform portion of the final bill addresses pension funding, participant education, hybrid plans, multi-employer plans, and plan terminations. This "compromise" reflects more than a year of often frequently acrimonious negotiations. The final provisions are complex, representing the first comprehensive pension legislation in more than 30 years.

STRENGTHENING TRADITIONAL PENSION PLANS

The new law identifies troubled private pension plans, helps stabilize them before employers resort to bankruptcy, and strengthens the Pension Benefit Guaranty Corporation (PBGC), the pension provider of last resort. It uses the tax law to do so by implementing a traditional carrot-and-stick approach: allowing a higher limit on the amount of employer contributions that are deductible while generally requiring higher funding levels in order to continue qualified plan tax status.

Some pension professionals are concerned that the reform bill could have the unintended consequence of encouraging employers to terminate troubled plans or reduce benefits rather than pay more into their plans to stabilize them. If this occurs, and it snowballs, the entire traditional pension system could collapse, leaving taxpayers to pick up the bill.

"This pension reform is the worst of every possible world," Rep. George Miller, D-Calif., said shortly before Congress passed the new law. Lynn Dudley of the American Benefits Council commented, "I think that the new funding provisions fail to give any incentive to stay in the system, first and foremost." This criticism goes to the heart of the dilemma now faced by corporate counsel and firms that advise them:

separating political rhetoric from fact in determining whether an employer should terminate, continue, or bolster its pension plan as the result of the new law

Roughly 44 million Americans are covered by traditional pension plans. Most are concentrated in manufacturing and other non-service industries. Many are seriously financially strapped. As pension costs have skyrocketed over recent years, many employers have abandoned traditional plans for 401(k) and other savings plans.

Deduction Limits

The new law encourages plans to create a funding cushion. Generally, under current law, an employer is allowed a tax deduction for plan contributions up to 100 percent of the plan's current liability. Contributions above that amount are subject to a 10 percent excise tax.

For plans beginning in 2006 and 2007, the new law amends Code Sec. 404 to increase the maximum deductible amount to 150 percent of current plan liabilities. After 2007, deductible contributions may be made up to an amount equal to the excess of the funding target, normal costs, and a "cushion account" equal to 50 percent of target liability plus accountability for projected compensation increases over the value of the plan assets. Plans with 100 or fewer participants get a break on computing benefit increases for highly compensated employees. The deduction limit for multiemployer plans increases to 140 percent of current liability.

The new law also increases allowable deductions for an employer that maintains both a defined contribution plan and a defined benefit plan by excluding contributions to defined benefit plans insured by the PBGC. For 2006 and later years, the contribution limits apply only if defined contributions exceed a six-percent ceiling.

Full Funding

The new law requires most pension plans to become fully funded over a seven-year period. The transition from current 90 percent funding to 100 percent full funding is gradual.

None of the funding rules apply to plan years starting before 2008. After 2007, transition rules apply to give most plans a softer landing. Plans that are not fully funded at the start of 2008 may work on meeting interim targets of 92 percent in 2008, 94 percent in 2009, and 96 percent in 2010.

Plans in existence in 2007 that have a prefunding balance may maintain a funding standard carryover balance until it reaches zero. New plans established after 2007 are not entitled to most transition rules.

An estimated 30,000 pension plans are now underfunded and will need to put more money into their plans. The Labor Department estimates that plans are currently about $450 billion underfunded.

In special airline provisions, Delta and Northwest are allowed 17 years to fully fund their plans; other airlines get 10 years.

At Risk Plans

Having an "at risk" plan will subject the employer-sponsor to even stricter funding requirements. The result will require accelerated contributions. Under the rules, a plan "at risk" is: (1) less than 80-percent funded, without regard to at-risk liabilities and (2) less than 70-percent funded counting at-risk liabilities. Transition rules apply. At risk liabilities are determined by assuming that employees eligible to retire in the next 10 years will retire as early as possible.

Benefit Limitations

Companies that are below 80-percent funded are prohibited from using credit balances for funding or making promises to provide any enhanced or new benefits. Plans that are less than 60-percent funded will be restricted from offering any lump-sum benefit payments and new accruals are frozen in those plans. Finally, payouts under nonqualified deferred compensation plans, as well as special pension plans for executives, will be restricted in the case of those severely underfunded plans, starting immediately on date of enactment.

Valuing Pension Liabilities

Measuring liabilities is critical to determining what constitutes full funding under the new law. Pension plan liabilities generally are determined by valuing a plan's current liabilities, which in turn are generally measured by benefits accrued to date. The new law brings some good and bad news into that computation.

The interest rate used for 2006 and 2007 can be based on investment grade corporate bonds. In 2008, the interest rate will be based on a three-segmented yield curve. Mortality tables are updated and use of a substitute table that reflects a plan's actual experience and projected trends is permitted.

A combination of asset valuation and liabilities determines a plan sponsor's "minimum required contribution" each year. As under current law, a failure to fund results in an excise tax equal to 10 percent of the funding deficiency.

Hybrid Plans

Rather than leave employees with no pension plan at all by pulling out of the system, some employers have been opting for hybrid "cash balance" plans—part pension and part savings plans. Congress wants to encourage this alternative. Some employers have been worried about lawsuits based on claims of age-discrimination because the conversion hurts older employees who have too few years to build up a savings nest egg. The new law insulates employers from those claims on further conversions.

Participant Education

The new law requires pension plans to educate participants about their rights and responsibilities, including investment education and the tax consequences of various payout options.

Multi-Employer Plans

The new law creates new benchmarks for identifying when a multi-employer plan is in trouble, provides additional funding rules, and describes actions trustees must take. In some cases, plans will be barred from increasing benefits if those increases would further jeopardize the health of the plan. The new law also imposes heightened notice requirements on troubled plans to keep participants fully informed.

More than nine million Americans participate in multi-employer plans, which are common in the construction, maritime and other traditionally unionized industries.

NEW AND ENHANCED RETIREMENT-SAVINGS INCENTIVES

Although new rules for defined benefit plans account for more than half of the Pension Protection Act, the new law also addresses retirement savings held in IRAs, 401(k) and other defined contribution plans. These provisions affect tens of millions more taxpayers than do the pension rules.

The provisions also may make changeovers from pension plans to 401(k) plans and IRA-type arrangements less traumatic for employers and employees alike if more employers continue to freeze or terminate existing pension plans.

The new law bolsters the future of defined contribution plans in two ways. It introduces some new and improved rules. And, it expands benefits by making permanent a long list of benefits introduced by the Economic Growth and Tax Relief Reconciliation Act of 2001 (EGTRRA) that had been scheduled to sunset after 2010. Here are the highlights.

Automatic Enrollment

The new law makes it easier for employers to automatically enroll their employees into the company's 401(k) plan. In such an arrangement, employees must affirmatively opt-out in order not to participate. Employers make default contribution decisions.

Investment Advice

The new law permits 401(k), IRA, and similar providers to offer personalized investment advice to accountholders. Generally, the investment advice arrangement must provide that any fees, including commission, received by the fiduciary advisor do not vary depending on the basis of any investment option selected or a computer model must be used.

The Bush Administration has long advocated this change. Ann Combs, Assistant Secretary of Labor, predicted several years ago that greater access to investment advice will "give workers the information they need to make better retirement decisions." On the other hand, consumer groups are worried that advisors could steer individuals to certain investments and put their own interests ahead of the best interests of accountholders.

Although 401(k) providers can give personalized investment advice to accountholders, they cannot advise employers about which funds and investments to include in their plans.

The new law directs the Treasury and the Department of Labor (DOL) to study the feasibility of applying computer model investment advice programs to IRAs and similar plans. Treasury and DOL are to complete this study "as soon as practicable after the date of enactment."

IRAs and Tax Refunds

Taxpayers will have more options when it comes to depositing their tax refunds. Under the new law, taxpayers can direct the IRS to deposit their refund into an IRA.

In May, the IRS announced that taxpayers will be able to split their refunds and deposit them into as many as three different bank accounts. The IRS expects to issue new Form 8888, for taxpayers to use to split their refunds in time for the 2007 filing season.

Military and Public Service Personnel

Individuals who are called to active military duty may make penalty-free early distributions from their IRAs, 401(k)s, and similar arrangements. The taxpayer must be a member of the Reserves who is called to active duty after September 11, 2001, and before December 31, 2007. The new law gives service personnel up to two years after the end of their active duty period to re-contribute the amounts they withdrew and avoid paying income tax on the distributions.

The new law also waives the 10-percent penalty on early distributions from a government plan for certain public safety employees. In addition, distributions from a government plan to pay for health or long-term care insurance premiums of a retired public safety officer will be excluded from income up to $3,000.

401(k) Hardship Withdrawals

The new law instructs the Treasury to issue rules within 180 days of enactment that allow 401(k) plan withdrawals for hardships and unforeseen financial emergencies with respect to any person who is listed as a beneficiary under the 401(k) plan. The Treasury rules are to be consistent with hardship withdrawals now allowed for spouses and Sec. 152 dependents.

Nonspouse Beneficiaries

A taxpayer may roll over his or her deceased spouse's interest in a qualified retirement plan, government plan, or tax sheltered annuity into an IRA. The taxpayer will not be taxed except as normal distributions are taken. The new law extends this special treatment to nonspouse beneficiaries.

This and the expanded hardship withdrawal rule for 401(k) plans are two new law provisions that may benefit same-sex couples.

Nonspouse beneficiaries will now also be able to apply for waivers of the 60-day rollover period.

Direct Plan-to-Roth IRA Rollovers

Effective for distributions after December 31, 2007, the new law will allow direct rollovers from a qualified retirement plan, tax-sheltered annuity, or governmental plan directly to a Roth IRA and will treat it as a Roth conversion if all other conversion qualifications (e.g., income below the $100,000 level before 2010) are met.

Prior to this change, savvy taxpayers had to go through a two-step process to reach the same result: first roll over the amount to a traditional IRA, and then convert the traditional IRA to a Roth.

And Much More . . .

- Waiver of excise tax on nondeductible contributions for household workers
- Notification of reduction in plan benefits
- Rollovers of after-tax annuity amounts to qualified plan

- Enhanced catch-up rules for IRAs when employer becomes bankrupt
- Use of annuity contracts for long-term care
- Combined use of defined benefit and 401(k) plans for small employers
- Reporting simplification
- New rules for Indian tribal government and church plans
- Indexed income limits for IRAs and Saver's Credit
- Reinvestment of ESOP dividends

Permanent EGTRRA Retirement Provisions

EGTRRA made many taxpayer-friendly changes to the Tax Code's retirement plan rules. It authorized catch-up contributions for older workers, increased contribution limits and benefits, made some retirement arrangements more attractive for small businesses, expanded rollover options for taxpayers with 457 and 403(b) plans, targeted relief to certain groups, and provided many other incentives. Like most of EGTRRA's provisions, the enhanced retirement savings incentives were temporary and would have ended after December 31, 2010. The new law repeals the sunset provisions in EGTRRA that apply to retirement savings. Long-range retirement planning is enhanced by making these provisions permanent.

Since 2001, taxpayers and employers have grown accustomed to the enhanced retirement savings incentives in EGTRRA. To go back to pre-EGTRRA days would be quite a jolt for many people: increased benefit limits, greater flexibility and portability, expanded savings opportunities would all disappear. The new law adds certainty to retirement planning.

These are the first incentives in EGTRRA to be made permanent—a huge win for the Bush Administration, which has lobbied since 2001 to make all of EGTRRA permanent.

EGTRRA 2010 Sunset Eliminated

The major EGTRRA retirement provisions that would be made permanent rather than sunset at the end of 2010 include:

- Permanent higher dollar amount for IRA contributions ($4,000 starting in 2006, $5,000 in 2008, inflation adjusted thereafter)
- Permanent higher dollar limits on defined contribution plans ($44,000 in 2006), elective deferrals (including $15,000 in 2006 for 401(k) plan deferrals), 457 plan deferrals ($15,000 in 2006),

SIMPLE plan contributions ($10,000 in 2006) and compensation that may be taken into account under a plan;

- Permanent increases in the annual benefit limit under a defined benefit plan ($175,000 for 2006);
- Permanent catch-up contributions for older workers ($1,000 after 2005 for IRAs, $2,500 for SIMPLE plans, $5,000 for 401(k) plans);
- Permanent faster vesting of employer matching contributions (full vesting under three- or six-year schedules);
- Permanent greater portability for 403(b) and 457 plans;
- Permanent higher deductible amounts for employer contributions to employee retirement plans (inflation-adjusted to $220,000 in 2006; 25-percent compensation deduction limit for stock bonus and profit sharing plans);
- Permanent Roth 401(k)s and 403(b)s;
- Permanent start-up tax credit for new small employer-sponsored plans (maximum $500/year for each of the first three years);
- Permanent deemed IRAs set up under an employer plan allowing separate employee contributions;
- Permanent enhanced rollover rules (including qualified plan rollovers of distributions of after-tax contributions, direct rollovers from IRAs to employer plans, and rollovers of distributions from governmental 457 plans, 403(b) plans, or cash-outs);
- Permanent ESOP enhancements; and
- Permanent modifications to the top-heavy nondiscrimination and coverage rules.

None of the post-2010 extensions appear to require any immediate action, with the exception of the Roth 401(k) option for employee-share contributions. While the Roth 401(k) option has been available since the start of 2006, many employers have not revised their plans out of concern that the expense of maintaining separate Roth accounts for employees would outweigh the benefits if further Roth contributions were not allowed after 2010. Now that the future of the Roth 401(k) is secure, many employers are expected to amend their plans by the end of this year. These rules apply equally to 403(b) plans.

The $1,000 IRA catch-up contribution amount is not adjusted for inflation. The $2,500 SIMPLE and $5,000 401(k) catch-up amounts are adjusted, in $500 increments.

The new law does not touch the maximum adjusted gross income limits for either traditional or Roth IRAs beyond which the maximum contribution levels are phased out.

EGTRRA authorized the IRS to waive the 60-day rollover rule when failure to waive the requirement would be against equity or good conscience, including casualty, disaster, or other events beyond the taxpayer's reasonable control. Before EGTRRA (and after 2010 if it were not for this legislation), the IRS could waive the 60-day rule in only two circumstances: (1) the taxpayer is performing military service in a combat zone or (2) the taxpayer is affected by a Presidentially-declared disaster.

Many of EGTRRA's retirement savings provisions were clarified by technical corrections in the Job Creation and Worker Assistance Act of 2002 (JCWA).

Planning tip. The Tax Increase Prevention and Reconciliation Act of 2005, signed into law on May 17, 2006, eliminated the $100,000 adjusted gross income ceiling for converting a traditional IRA to a Roth IRA starting in 2010.

Defined benefit plan limits. EGTRRA's "permanent extensions" are not exclusively focused on defined contribution plans. EGTRRA increased the maximum annual defined benefit plan limit. In 2001, only the lesser of 100 percent of three-year-high average compensation or $140,000 could be paid out annually. EGTRRA initially boosted it to $160,000 and indexed it for inflation in $5,000 increments; today it is $175,000. The new law makes this treatment permanent.

If benefits begin before Social Security retirement age, the dollar limit on annual benefits is subject to an actuarial reduction. Conversely, the dollar limit is increased if benefits begin after Social Security retirement age. Under EGTRRA, the dollar limit is reduced if benefits begin before 62 and increased for benefits beginning after 65. EGTRRA also increased the compensation limit that may be taken into account for determining benefits under a qualified plan. The limit reaches $200,000 in 2006 and it is indexed for inflation in $5,000 increments.

Saver's Credit

Unlike the other EGTRRA provisions that were to sunset at the end of 2010, the Saver's Credit would have ended very soon, in tax years beginning after December 31, 2006. The new law makes the Saver's Credit permanent. Under this provision, lower- and middle-income taxpayers can claim a nonrefundable tax credit for their contributions or deferrals to retirement savings plans and IRAs.

The credit amount is equal to the credit rate (50, 20, or 10 percent) times the dollar amount of qualified retirement savings contributions for the year (not to exceed $2,000), based on income and filing status.

As an enhancement to the Saver's Credit, the new law provides that the adjusted gross income amounts used to figure the amount of the credit will be adjusted for inflation starting in 2007.

Unlike other EGTRRA provisions that are made permanent, the permanent Saver's Credit is not indexed for inflation. Consequently, the value of the credit will progressively erode.

Section 529 College Savings Plans

As a last-minute addition, the new law also permanently extends the rules allowing for Sec. 529 qualified tuition programs. Starting out slowly after EGTRRA, Sec. 529 plans have taken off recently, with current taxpayer funds in those plans doubling during last year alone. The new law also adds stricter rules related to the operation of Sec. 529 plans to prevent abuse.

CCH FINANCIAL AND ESTATE PLANNING GUIDE

16th Edition

Terence Myers

Dorinda DeScherer

Sidney Kess, Consultant

CCH
a Wolters Kluwer business

First Edition May 1976—Sixteenth Edition October 2006

The *CCH Financial and Estate Planning Guide* is based, in part, on materials in the "Strategies" volume of CCH FINANCIAL AND ESTATE PLANNING. Sidney Kess and Bertil Westlin authored the First through Tenth Editions of the *Guide*.

ISBN-10: 0-8080-9078-X
ISBN-13: 978-0-8080-9078-6

4025 W. Peterson Ave.
Chicago, IL 60646-6085
1 800 248 3248
http://CCHGroup.com

Printed in the United States of America

Preface

This 16th edition of the *CCH Financial and Estate Planning Guide* continues to serve as the premier resource for financial and estate planners. This edition reflects many important changes, including the recently enacted Tax Increase Prevention and Reconciliation Act (TIPRA) (P.L. 109-222). Financial planners, estate planners, trust officers, life underwriters, attorneys, CPAs, enrolled agents, and other professionals can all benefit from the explanations and planning pointers included in this edition. The Guide also serves as a popular textbook or supplement for estate planning programs and estates and trusts courses. The broad scope of the *CCH Financial and Estate Planning Guide* reflects the fact that estate planning is an integral part of financial planning.

Updated and improved throughout are important explanations of the tax law. In addition, many of the planning pointers have been updated and expanded. Discussions of the following developments are the key additions to the 16th edition:

- The expansion of the "kiddie tax" on the investment income of children;
- The extension of capital gain treatment for qualifying dividends;
- Tough new crackdown on charitable donations of cars, planes and boats;
- IRS liberalization of "use-it-or-lose-it" rule for cafeteria plans;
- New Medicare Part D prescription drug coverage;
- Increased exemptions for gift and estate transfers; and
- IRS guidance on the new rules for deferred compensation arrangements;

Readers of this edition of the *CCH Financial and Estate Planning Guide* will find it to be a valuable resource in serving their clients.

Terence Myers
Dorinda DeScherer

October 2006

Table of Contents

Paragraph

Part I: General Principles and Techniques

Chapter 1 The Art of Financial Planning 101
Chapter 2 Estate and Client Analysis 205
Chapter 3 The Co-ownership of Property 301
Chapter 4 Lifetime Gifts to Individuals 401
Chapter 5 Charitable Giving 504
Chapter 6 The Use of Trusts 601
Chapter 7 Life Insurance 701
Chapter 8 Annuities 805
Chapter 9 Employee Benefits 901
Chapter 10 Transfers Includible in the Estate at Death 1001
Chapter 11 Wills 1101
Chapter 12 The Marital Deduction 1201
Chapter 13 Powers of Appointment 1301
Chapter 14 Selection and Appointment of Fiduciaries 1401
Chapter 15 Post-Mortem Planning 1501

Part II: Special Situations

Chapter 16 Planning for the Executive 1601
Chapter 17 Planning for the Professional 1701
Chapter 18 Closely Held Businesses—Choice of Business Form 1801
Chapter 19 Planning for the Close Corporation Owner 1901
Chapter 20 Planning for the Partner 2001
Chapter 21 Planning for the Sole Proprietor 2101
Chapter 22 Planning for the Farmer and Rancher 2201
Chapter 23 Impact of Freeze Rules on Intra-Family Transfers 2301
Chapter 24 Planning for Marriage, Divorce, or Separation 2401
Chapter 25 Planning for Couples Living Together 2501
Chapter 26 Planning for the Elderly and Disabled 2601
Chapter 27 Planning for Generation-Skipping Transfers 2701
Chapter 28 Planning for a Personal Residence 2801
Chapter 29 Medical Care by Proxy 2901
Chapter 30 College Planning 3001

Paragraph

Part III: Building the Estate

Chapter 31 Investment and Financial Planning Strategies and Vehicles 3101
Chapter 32 Family Income-Splitting Techniques 3201
Chapter 33 Year-End and New Year Tax Planning 3301
Chapter 34 Maximizing Deductions and Reducing Taxes 3401
Chapter 35 Social Security Benefits, Medicare, and Medicaid 3501

Part IV: Planning Aids

Appendix 5001
Topical Index .... Page 989

Table of Exhibits

		Page
Exhibit 1	Financial and Estate Planning Questionnaire	23
Exhibit 2	General Comparison of Sole and Joint Ownership of Property	60
Exhibit 3	Comparison of Cash Gift with Gift of Income Property for Income Tax Purposes	123
Exhibit 4	Comparison of Basic Forms of Gifts to Minors	148
Exhibit 5	Checklist of Income Tax Contribution Deduction Rules	161
Exhibit 6	Basic Types of Trusts, Their Benefits and Tax Treatment	238
Exhibit 7	Comparison of Basic Insurance Policies	277
Exhibit 8	Unified Rate Schedule for 2006 through 2009	402
Exhibit 9	Estate Owner's Confidential Data Bank	430
Exhibit 10	Comparison of Forms of Qualifying Marital Bequests	443

Part I

General Principles and Techniques

Chapter 1

The Art of Financial Planning

Overview .... ¶101
The Financial and Estate Planner .... ¶105
Staying Ahead of Tax Law Changes .... ¶110

¶101 OVERVIEW

Financial planning is the process of setting financial goals and objectives during life, designing strategies to achieve them, and monitoring progress toward achieving them. Financial planning includes investment planning, college planning, insurance planning and risk management, employee benefits planning, retirement planning, income tax planning, and estate planning. This book addresses each of these areas of financial planning and gives special emphasis to estate planning.

Estate planning is setting goals and objectives and developing strategies for disposing of assets and providing for family members, friends, and charities at death. Estate planning is a part of financial planning because estate planning goals, objectives, and strategies affect the financial planning process during life.

Although people often think of estate planning as being important for the wealthy, anyone who owns property or has money has an estate. Estate planning includes more than estate tax planning. The federal and state governments regulate the use of property. However, generally the property owner decides what to do with the property—whether to keep it, sell it, exchange it, or give it away. The property owner may devise or bequeath the property upon his or her death or allow the state to determine the property's disposition under state law.

Although a financial planner may concentrate in one of the highly interrelated areas of financial planning, the financial planner needs a working knowledge of all these areas. The goals of financial planning include avoiding potential problems and fulfilling the client's wishes. Financial planning is an art because it is a skill obtained by study and experience.

Investment planning includes developing investment strategies. These strategies could include designing a systematic investment plan and developing an asset allocation strategy. Investment planning is a major part of retirement planning. College planning includes saving and investing for future college costs of the client's children or other family members. Insurance planning and risk management include analysis and evaluation of risks, choosing which risks to insure, and obtaining the right kind of insurance to protect against such risks. Life insurance is often a major part of estate planning. Employee benefits planning includes the evaluation of group insurance plans, employee stock options, and other employee benefit programs. The financial planner should consider income taxes and estate taxes in developing employee benefit plans, investment plans, insurance plans, and retirement plans. Some strategies require the planner to consider tradeoffs between income taxes and estate and gift taxes.

Financial planning requires the client to make value judgments. The individual's personal investment philosophy toward potential returns and risks is an important consideration in making these value judgments. The individual must also consider family, emotional, and religious considerations. The financial planner should be careful not to impose his or her values, philosophy, or personal feelings upon the client. The role of the financial planner is to inform the client about alternative financial strategies and the potential consequences of those strategies.

State law, the federal estate tax, and state inheritance taxes affect any estate plan. The estate and gift tax exacts a high toll for transferring property of substantial value. The estate and gift tax is an integrated tax based on the value of the property transferred. The law allows various deductions, exclusions, and credits in computing the estate and gift tax.

Gifts and transfers at death are taxed are an integrated system with a unified estate and gift tax schedule. But, at present, this system is in a state of flux. Under the Economic Growth and Tax Relief Reconciliation Act of 2001 (EGTRRA), gift and estate taxes are being gradually reduced in stages through 2009. In 2010, the estate tax (but not the gift tax) will be repealed for one year only. Unless Congress acts, the less generous pre-EGTRRA tax structure will be reinstated in 2011 under EGTRRA's "sunset" provisions. As a result, financial planners must keep a close eye on developments in Washington and alert their clients if future tax law changes require revisions in the clients' estate plans.

One of the allowable credits against the estate tax is the unified credit that corresponds to an applicable exclusion amount. The unified tax credit is equal to the estate and gift tax rates[1] multiplied by an applicable exclusion amount. Under EGTRRA, the applicable exclusion amount[2] for estate tax purposes is equal to the following amounts for estates of decedents dying during the years indicated:

2006 and 2008	$2,000,000
2009	$3,500,000
2010	estate tax repealed for this year only
2011 and thereafter	$1,000,000

The applicable exclusion amount for gift purposes is equal to $1 million for gifts made from 2005 through 2009.[3] For gifts made in 2010 (when the estate tax has been temporarily repealed), the credit against the tentative gift tax liability will be equal to $1,000,000 multiplied by a new tax rate schedule for gifts only.

For gifts made in 2011 and thereafter, when the estate tax returns, a single $1 million exclusion will apply to both gifts and transfers at death.

Once the amount of the taxable estate or taxable gifts exceeds the applicable exclusion amount, the tax rates apply to the excess. For cumulative gifts in excess of $1 million in 2006 (the exclusion amount), the tax rate begins at 41 percent and goes to a maximum of 46 percent. For decedents dying in 2006, estates in excess of $2 million (the exclusion amount) are taxed at a flat 46 percent.[4] In 2007 through 2009, the maximum gift tax rate and the flat estate tax rate drops to 45 percent. In 2010, the maximum gift tax rate drops to 35 percent (the same as the maximum income tax rate). In 2011, when the pre-EGTRRA provisions return, the maximum rate under the unified gift and estate tax rate schedule will be 55 percent.

The financial planner and client must also consider state death and inheritance taxes. The law previously allowed a limited credit against the federal estate tax for state death and inheritance taxes.[5]

Congress repealed the state death tax credit and changed it to a deduction for the years 2005 through 2009. For 2010, of course, there is no estate tax. For years 2011 and thereafter, the state death tax credit reverts to the amount allowed prior to EGTRRA.

[1] Code Sec. 2001.
[2] Code Sec. 2010.
[3] Code Sec. 2404(a)(1).
[4] Code Sec. 2001.
[5] Code Sec. 2011.

Many states have a state inheritance tax equal to the amount previously allowed as a credit against the federal estate tax. Some practitioners call these state taxes "pick-up taxes" because they pick up the taxes the estate would otherwise pay to the federal government. The financial planner may want to check the applicable state law to determine the nature and extent of a particular state's death or inheritance tax.

The costs of the probate process exact another toll on the estate. The costs of probate vary from state to state and with the size of the estate. The principal costs are the attorney's fees and executor's fees. These fees may be based on the value of the gross estate and not on the taxable estate. Thus, exclusions and deductions from the gross estate would not reduce the amount of attorney's fees and executor's fees. The gross estate includes assets that pass to beneficiaries by operation of law, but the probate estate does not include these assets. Attorney's fees and executor's fees might be in the range of eight to nine percent for a small estate of $100,000, decreasing to about four percent for an estate of $10,000,000. Complications due to a poorly drafted will or a challenge of the competency of the testator can cause the costs to be much greater.

The estate may also incur substantial accounting fees. If the client sets up trusts, the client must pay fees for setting up the trusts and trustees' fees for administering the trusts. If the client has minor children, he or she may need to appoint a guardian in his or her will to safeguard the interests of his or her minor children. If the decedent failed to appoint a guardian, the court will appoint a guardian for minor children with no living parent. The choice of the court may not reflect the parent's wishes or values. In any case, the fees of the guardian exact another toll on the estate. In addition to the major visible costs of transferring property at death, the estate will incur miscellaneous costs such as court filing fees and routine expenses.

The estate can also incur hidden costs. If the estate must sell assets quickly, it may not receive the fair market value of the assets. The estate may have to settle accounts receivable at deep discounts.

The gross estate may include more property than the property transferred at death. Property transferred during life will be included in the decedent's gross estate if at the time of death the decedent retained a life estate in the property.[6] Revocable transfers are included in the gross estate.[7] In addition, property over which the decedent held a general power of appointment is included in the gross

[6] Code Sec. 2036.

[7] Code Sec. 2038.

estate.[8] If the decedent made a gift of any these properties within three years of the date of death, the value of these properties will be included in the gross estate.[9] Any gift of a life insurance policy within three years of the decedent's death is included in the gross estate.[10] The gift tax on any gift the decedent or the decedent's spouse made within three years of the date of death is included in the gross estate.[11]

Generally, if the decedent held property as a joint tenant with right of survivorship at the time of death, the full value of the property is included in the decedent's gross estate.[12] If the only other joint tenant is the decedent's spouse, one half of the full value of the property is included in the decedent's gross estate. The law allows an exception if the executor can prove that the surviving joint tenant contributed to the property's acquisition cost. Proving what took place perhaps years ago is difficult without access to the appropriate records. These examples are only some of the examples of how the gross estate can include property not owned by the decedent at the time of death.

The law may impose the estate tax on phantom values. Proving the fair market value of stock in a closely held corporation to an IRS agent may be quite difficult. Chances are the executor and the IRS agent will have valuations that are vastly different. If the executor does not agree with the agent's determination, the executor can request a hearing with an IRS Appeals Officer. If the executor cannot negotiate an acceptable compromise with the IRS Appeals Officer, the estate will receive a statutory notice of deficiency.[13] Such a notice allows the executor 90 days to file a petition with the U.S. Tax Court.[14]

The executor could pay the proposed tax assessment and sue for a refund in a U.S. District Court or the U.S. Court of Federal Claims. Filing an appeal of an IRS agent's determination with the IRS Appeals Division and litigating the issue can be very expensive. However, the cost of disputing a proposed tax assessment by the IRS is reduced somewhat because these costs are deductible in computing the taxable estate.[15] The executor may need to file an amended return to claim these expenses in computing the taxable estate. Thus, in effect the IRS might be paying a substantial portion of the costs incurred by the estate for challenging a proposed tax assessment.

---

[8] Code Sec. 2041.
[9] Code Sec. 2035(a).
[10] Code Secs. 2035(a)(2) and 2042.
[11] Code Sec. 2035(b).
[12] Code Sec. 2040(a).
[13] Code Sec. 6212.
[14] Code Sec. 6213.
[15] Code Sec. 2053(a).

The estate generally bears the burden of proof that the proposed IRS assessment is incorrect.[16] Although the law now allows the taxpayer to shift the burden of proof to the IRS in certain cases, meeting the requirements for shifting the burden of proof is often difficult.[17]

The executor often settles for a higher valuation than the executor believes to be fair because of the time and expense of litigation with uncertain results. The higher valuation has another effect on top of the additional tax. Higher valuations generally increase administration costs because the size of the estate often serves as a base for administration costs.

In addition, the hidden costs often continue after the probate court closes the estate. The unlimited marital deduction allows an individual to transfer the entire estate to the surviving spouse free of estate taxes.[18] However, this provision operates more as a means of estate tax deferral rather than a permanent saving of estate taxes. This result occurs because all the assets owned by the surviving spouse are included in the surviving spouse's gross estate. Unless the surviving spouse remarries and transfers assets at death to the new spouse, no marital deduction will exist upon the surviving spouse's death.

The transfer of property at death can be very expensive. The costs of transferring property at death include estate taxes, state inheritance taxes, and probate costs. The estate may also receive less than the fair market value on a sale of its assets. Cutting these costs is an ample reason for estate planning.

However, estate planning involves much more. Estate planning is concerned with providing for the welfare of individuals and the protection of their interests through trusts and other means. Estate planning is concerned with the disposition of an estate, but it also involves the acquisition and preservation of an estate during the client's life. Estate planning includes building tax-sheltered retirement benefits, a whole range of employee and executive compensation benefits, investments, and reducing the family's income tax. Thus, estate planning is an integral part of personal financial planning.

¶105 THE FINANCIAL AND ESTATE PLANNER

The estate owner is the person who must take the responsibility for planning his or her own estate. However, the estate owner will

[16] Tax Court Rule 142(a).

[17] Code Sec. 7491(a).

[18] Code Sec. 2056(a).

need professional help to do so. No one can expect a layperson to understand the complex law involving the federal income tax, estate tax, gift tax, and generation-skipping transfer tax without professional guidance. Anyone who attempts to do so is placing his or her estate plan in serious jeopardy and endangering the financial security of his or her family and others for whom he or she is responsible.

To assist individuals in planning their financial affairs and estates, the financial planner must approach estate planning with a breadth of knowledge and experience. Some financial planners may possess all of the necessary skills in formulating an estate plan. More typically, estate planning requires a team approach. Estate planning often involves accountants, appraisers, attorneys, financial planners, life underwriters, and trust officers.

Certainly, the unified credit provides an exemption from federal estate taxes for many estates. The unlimited marital deduction allows for deferral of estate taxes for married individuals until the death of the second spouse. The financial planner must consider the federal estate tax even if the client's estate is apparently not subject to the federal estate tax. The client's estate could increase significantly due to an unforeseen event. The client's marital status could change due to marriage, divorce, or the death of his or her spouse. The financial planner must ask if making full use of the unlimited marital deduction makes sense because the marital deduction only defers estate tax. If the applicable exclusion amount is insufficient to avoid all estate taxes, the financial planner should consider strategies such as lifetime gifts to take advantage of the annual exclusion from taxable gifts.[19] The financial planner must consider the need of the estate for liquidity, especially if the estate consists of valuable but illiquid assets. The financial planner or estate planning team should discuss these issues with the client. However, the client should make the decisions regarding planning options.

The financial planner must also consider state property law, family law, and probate procedures in formulating an estate plan to recommend to the client. In addition, the financial planner must examine the income tax consequences of the estate plan for the client, his or her estate, and for the family. Factors the financial planner should consider include the following:

- Basis of assets
- Legal title of assets

[19] Code Sec. 2503(b).

- Income in respect of a decedent
- Life insurance
- Retained incidents of ownership
- Assignments
- Beneficiary designations and settlement options
- Annuities
- Employee benefits
- Executive compensation
- Charitable giving
- Income splitting within the family
- Alternative minimum tax
- Income taxation of trusts

Special considerations apply to an individual who is a business owner either as a shareholder in a closely held corporation, a member of a limited liability company, a partner, or a sole proprietor. The financial planner may need to address how corporate and partnership law, securities law, and accounting practices affect the estate plan.

For tax years 2005 through 2010, the highest marginal income tax rate is 35 percent. In 2011 and thereafter, the highest marginal income tax rate will revert to the 39.6 percent rate in effect for 2000. High federal income taxes combined with high employment taxes and state income taxes have created demands on financial planners to develop strategies to minimize these taxes. Planners should be mindful of the words of Judge Learned Hand: “There is nothing sinister in so arranging one’s affairs as to keep taxes as low as possible. Everybody does so, rich or poor; and all do right. Nobody owes any public duty to pay more than the law demands; taxes are enforced exactions, not voluntary contributions.” Planners have a positive duty to maximize tax-saving opportunities that goes beyond the words of Judge Hand.

The financial planner must be aware of tax-advantage or tax-sheltered investments, including the 50-percent exclusion from gross income for gains on certain small business stock.[20] The financial planner should at least be familiar with the complex rules that limit deductions for passive losses[21] and the need for passive income to absorb passive losses. The financial planner should know the basic types of investments such as real estate, stocks and bonds, mutual funds, tax-exempt bonds, Treasury securities, annuities, and limited

[20] Code Sec. 1202.

[21] Code Sec. 469.

partnerships. The planner should know what types of assets produce net capital gains[22] taxed at lower rates.[23] Under the Tax Increase Prevention and Reconciliation Act (hereinafter "TIPRA"), the tax rate on most dividends and long-term capital gains is 15 percent through 2010. That is less than half the maximum tax rate on ordinary income.

The financial planner must also be alert to the impact of the increasingly significant alternative minimum tax (AMT). Once only a concern of the wealthy, the AMT is now affecting many middle-class individuals. This shift has occurred for a number of reasons. For example, the AMT exemptions have not kept pace with inflation. And, since the AMT applies only when it exceeds the regular income tax, the recent reduction in the regular income tax rates have placed more taxpayers in AMT territory. In any case, financial planners must be careful to consider the AMT when mapping income tax strategies.

The financial planner needs to be aware of how current economic trends, such as inflation and interest rates, affect the financial plan. While no one can predict the future with certainty, the financial planner must make a reasonable forecast of the overall economy. The financial planner must also be aware of pending tax and legal changes that could affect the financial plan. Financial planning is an ongoing process, and the financial planner should reevaluate the plan periodically in light of changing circumstances.

The financial planner also needs good human relations skills. The financial planner needs to be sensitive to the needs of the client and the client's family. In addition, the financial planner must be able to work with other professionals on the financial and estate planning team. Communication skills, especially the ability to listen intently, are very important.

No one can know everything about financial and estate planning. Perfect financial planners and perfect plans do not exist. However, the law does not require perfection. Although the financial planner may feel that he or she needs to be highly knowledgeable about all aspects of financial and estate planning, the law holds the financial planner only to a standard of reasonable skill and competence. The financial planner should make clients aware of any limitations in the financial and estate planning process. In addition, the financial planner should recognize his or her own limitations. The financial

---

[22] Code Sec. 1222.

[23] Code Sec. 1(h), as amended by the 2006 Tax Increase Prevention and Reconciliation Act (hereinafter "TIPRA"), Sec. 102.

planner should suggest the inclusion of other professionals when he or she cannot serve the client's entire needs effectively.

Financial and estate planning is often a team effort that requires the joint effort of the lawyer, the accountant, the life underwriter, the trust officer, and the investment counselor. Practitioners often recognize the need for teamwork, even with respect to clients with smaller amounts of wealth. These practitioners seek to build mutually beneficial relationships with other practitioners or informal networks. These relationships and networks allow planners to tap the specialized expertise needed to safeguard the interests of their clients and themselves in developing a plan of any complexity.

However, in the real world, cost and time factors may preclude or limit the use of a true team effort. The distinction between the separate functions of each team member is becoming less clear. Accountants are obtaining licenses to sell insurance and securities, and securities firms are acquiring accounting firms. However, financial planners who are not lawyers need to be careful not to engage in the unauthorized practice of law. For example, only a lawyer may prepare a will or trust for a client.

The public needs to have reasonable confidence in the professional competence of those holding themselves out as financial and estate planners. Most professional planners recognize the public interest involved. The big question is how best to protect the public interest: through governmental regulation, self-regulation, or some mixture of the two as one can find in the legal and accounting professions. The Certified Financial Planner Board of Standards assures some measure of competency by conferring the Certified Financial Planner™ certificant designation (CFP®) upon candidates who satisfactorily complete its requirements. The American College has a similar program in which its graduates earn the designation Chartered Financial Consultant (ChFC). In addition, the American Institute of Certified Public Accountants (AICPA) has developed the Personal Financial Specialist (CPA/PFS) designation for its members who meet its experience and education requirements.

In many cases, the accountant can best spot financial and estate planning opportunities for clients. The accountant has access to the client's books, records, and financial statements. Lawyers, life underwriters, bankers, and investment counselors may also be privy to financial conditions of their clients or prospects that present planning opportunities.

The CCH FINANCIAL AND ESTATE PLANNING GUIDE is a guide to many of these opportunities, with warning lights around the pitfalls.

This GUIDE will not tell the financial planner everything he or she needs to know, but it serves as a road map to the financial and estate planning process. It shows practical ways of building, preserving, and transferring wealth.

¶110 STAYING AHEAD OF TAX LAW CHANGES

Over the last two decades, Congress has revised the tax law many times. This level of change makes the financial planner's job much more difficult, but also much more important. Although tax laws seem to change almost every year, the financial planner can rely on some general guidelines.

A competent individual may revoke or revise a will at any time. The same rule applies to a revocable trust. Accordingly, a lawyer should draft a will and trust documents based on the current tax law. If the tax law changes, the financial planner can urge the client to review these documents. The lawyer can then make any needed revisions. A will or trust based on an anticipated change in the tax law that never materialized may lead to undesirable results. Generally, an individual should plan a will or revocable trust as though it would soon take effect.

A gift, an irrevocable trust, or a sale of property requires a different strategy. Because the client cannot change the documents after these transfers, the financial planner should conduct a careful review of tax law changes under consideration. The financial planner should communicate the likely impact of the proposed changes upon the client's financial and estate plan. However, the wise financial planner will encourage the client to make any decisions with irrevocable consequences based on anticipated changes in the tax law. The principle the financial planner should follow is to give assistance and advice, but let the client decide which steps to take.

Obvious uncertainties surround predictions of future tax rules. Therefore, the financial planner should carefully document plans and their purposes. When the financial planner considers future tax rules or deliberately ignores them, the financial planner should keep adequate documentation. File memoranda and letters to the client should fully document whether the financial planner considered future tax rules and indicate who made the final decision. The more documentation that exists, the more the financial planner will be insulated from legal liability should the client or his or her beneficiaries or heirs later allege malpractice. In addition, the more explanation given to the client, the better the opportunity the client has to evaluate the alternatives and make the best possible decisions. For example, when the financial planner makes projections of future tax consequences, the planner should inform the client that the financial planner is basing the projections on the current tax law. If possible, the financial planner should show the client additional projections based on anticipated and known tax law changes. The 2001 EGTRRA is a good case in point. EGTRRA makes numerous changes in the tax code, such as a reduction of the income tax rates, a lowering and eventual elimination of the estate tax, and a liberalization of the limits on retirement plan contributions. But, under EGTRRA's sunset provisions, these changes will vanish—and the old rules will be reinstated—after 2010. So, depending on the situation, the financial planner may want to make alternate projections based on (1) the sunsetting of the EGTRRA changes and (2) an extension of the EGTRRA changes through Congressional action.

Hindsight is 20/20 in pointing out past errors in financial and estate plans. Reconstructing the situation at the time the financial planner gave the advice is much more difficult. The financial planner should guard against potential liability with thorough documentation. Focusing on the current tax law and pointing out the changes under active consideration can help prevent future complaints. Thorough documentation also helps the client make the best possible decisions. The next chapter provides guidance on the documents the financial planner should gather in the estate planning process.

Chapter 2

Estate and Client Analysis

Overview .... ¶201
Plan Prerequisites .... ¶205
Encouraging Disclosure .... ¶210
Questionnaires .... ¶215
Planner's Checklist .... ¶220
Constructing a Plan .... ¶225

¶201 OVERVIEW

This chapter provides helpful tips and techniques for obtaining a client's financial and estate plan information. Useful checklists to help the financial planner get started are provided in Exhibit 1 at the end of the chapter.

¶205 PLAN PREREQUISITES

A financial planner cannot construct a sound financial plan on hunches. Development of a sound financial plan requires the following:

- Full disclosure by the client of all assets and liabilities.
- Determination of the client's needs and objectives, without regard to the tax consequences, and of how he or she feels about the members of his or her family, including their requirements, strengths, potentials, weaknesses, and goals.
- Full disclosure and review of any existing plan.
- Full communication between the client and the financial planner concerning the existing plan's merits and disadvantages, the options open for improving or replacing it, and the consequences of the various choices.

The financial planner can normally expect a certain reluctance on the part of the client to make the full disclosures needed. The client might fear a breach of confidence. The client may have emotional difficulties in examining his or her attitudes and feelings toward members of the family. The client might share some of the common misconceptions about financial planning and the financial planner's role. He or she might be concerned about the legitimacy of the different tax avoidance techniques. In addition, the client often has the understandable tendency to avoid facing his or her own mortality in the estate planning part of financial planning.

¶210 ENCOURAGING DISCLOSURE

The client must be able to trust the financial planner. The client must have some understanding of financial planning to provide the financial planner with necessary information. Here are some approaches that have been helpful in eliciting information.

.01 Financial Planning

Financial planning involves meeting goals and objectives through financial management. Financial planning includes such areas as investment planning, college planning, retirement planning, income tax planning, insurance planning and risk management, employee benefits planning, and estate planning. Some clients view estate planning as a separate activity, but it is an integral part of financial planning. To some, estate planning is an unpleasant activity because it is associated with death. However, the estate planner can change this attitude by pointing out that building, preserving, and transferring wealth and property are key factors in the estate planning process.

The financial planner should remind the client that proper planning can help ensure that the needs of his or her heirs will be met.

.02 Financial Disclosure

The financial planner should make clear the possible cost of nondisclosure or incomplete disclosure in terms of lost opportunities for tax savings. The financial planner should inform the client about income tax rates and credits and estate tax rates and credits.

.03 Personal Disclosures

Specific inquiries about disabled children, the marital status of children, divorces, separations, estrangements, intrafamily jealousies and the like are not likely to be as fruitful as less direct approaches. In outlining the nature of individualized planning, the financial planner might suggest hypothetical situations requiring trusts for the disabled and protection for the spendthrift. Other possible hypothetical situations include anticipating the possible adverse effects of an out-of-state or foreign divorce on a later marriage and the availability of the marital deduction, and detailing the advantages in terms of gift tax exclusions of a joint gift to a child and the child's spouse.

The hidden message is that even seemingly irrelevant matters can be pertinent to the financial and estate plan.

.04 Getting Realistic Values

Values given by clients for assets without established market values are apt to be unreliable. Clients might give lower values if estate or gift taxes are being considered than if a sale is the issue. The financial planner must clearly inform the client that fair market value, not book value or cost, is the relevant figure. If a business interest is involved, the financial planner might request an independent appraisal. If the financial planner needs insurance values, an agent or broker or the insurance company itself might supply the answers.

.05 Tax Basis of Assets

The tax basis of assets that are to be the subject of a gift will be important to both the donor and the donee. The basis of a gift to the donee is generally the same as it would be in the hands of the donor.[1] For the donee, the tax basis will provide a benchmark for measuring gain on the disposition of the gift in a taxable transaction. For the donor, the tax basis will be important in those situations where the donor is deemed to realize gain on the gift, i.e., the donee assumes or takes subject to a mortgage in excess of the donor's basis, or possibly if the gift is conditioned on the donee's payment of the gift tax (a net gift). Assets passing from a decedent receive a stepped-up basis equal to their fair market value at the date of death, or six months later if the executor elects the alternate valuation date.[2]

However, Congress repealed the stepped-up basis rules for property acquired from a decedent who dies in the year 2010 and replaced them with a modified "carryover basis" system. Under EGTRRA's sunset provision, the stepped-up basis rules will return in 2011. As a result, the carryover basis rules currently are of limited interest. However, if Congress votes to keep the estate tax repeal intact

[1] Code Sec. 1015(a).

[2] Code Sec. 1014(a).

beyond 2010, the carryover basis system will almost certainly be extended as well. Thus, it warrants a closer examination.

Under the carryover basis system, inherited property will have a basis equal to the lesser of (1) the adjusted basis of the property in the hands of the decedent, or (2) the fair market value of the property on the date of the decedent's death.[3] However, the executor may increase the basis of assets the executor chooses by up to $1,300,000.[4] The executor may increase this $1,300,000 general basis increase by the sum of any capital loss carryover[5] and the amount of any net operating loss (NOL) carryover[6] that the decedent would have available had he or she lived. In addition, the executor may increase the $1,300,000 general basis increase by the sum of any allowable losses[7] if the decedent had sold the property for its fair market value immediately before his or her death.[8]

In addition to the $1,300,000 general basis increase as adjusted for the items noted above, the law allows an additional $3,000,000 increase in basis for qualified spousal property passing to the decedent's surviving spouse.[9] Qualified spousal property includes an outright transfer of property[10] or qualified terminable interest property (QTIP).[11] An outright transfer must not terminate or fail on the lapse of time or on the occurrence or failure to occur of some event or contingency. A property interest will fail this test under the following conditions:

- An interest in the same property has passed for less than full and adequate consideration in money or money's worth from the decedent to any person other than the surviving spouse or the estate of the surviving spouse and
- By reason of its passing, such person or his or her heirs or assigns may possess or enjoy any part of the property after such termination or failure of the interest passing to the surviving spouse or
- Such interest is to be acquired for the surviving spouse pursuant to directions of the decedent, by the decedent's executor, or by a trustee of a trust[12]

A requirement that a marital bequest is subject to the surviving spouse living more than six months after the decedent's death or not dying in a common disaster will not disqualify a marital bequest from

[3] Code Sec. 1022.
[4] Code Sec. 1022(b)(2)(B).
[5] Code Sec. 1212(b).
[6] Code Sec. 172.
[7] Code Sec. 165.
[8] Code Sec. 1022(b)(2)(C).
[9] Code Sec. 1022(c).
[10] Code Sec. 1022(c)(4)(A).
[11] Code Sec. 1022(c)(3).
[12] Code Sec. 1022(c)(4)(B).

being an outright transfer. However, the surviving spouse must meet the specified contingencies.[13]

The definition of qualified terminable interest property for the basis rules closely follows the rules for the marital deduction.[14] To qualify for the spousal basis increase as under the QTIP provision, the property must pass from the decedent to the surviving spouse who must have a qualifying income interest for life in the transferred property.[15] The surviving spouse will have a qualifying income interest provided it meets both of the following conditions:

- The surviving spouse is entitled to all the income from the property, payable at least annually, or has a usufruct interest for life under Louisiana property law.
- No person has a power to appoint any part of the property to anyone other than the surviving spouse while the surviving spouse is alive.

An annuity will be treated similar to an income interest in property, regardless of whether the property from which the annuity is to be paid can be separately identified.[16]

Property passing to the surviving spouse on account of the death of a decedent who dies in 2010 may receive both the $1,300,000 general basis increase and the $3,000,000 spousal property increase. Thus, a total basis increase of $4,300,000 is possible. Increases in basis under either provision may not cause the adjusted basis of any property to exceed its fair market value on the date of the decedent's death.[17]

For the property to qualify for the general basis increase or the spousal basis increase, the decedent must have owned the property at the time of his or her death.[18] Special rules apply to jointly held property, revocable trusts, property subject to a power of appointment, and community property.

The decedent's ownership interest in property held as joint tenants with the right of survivorship will be determined using several factors. These factors include the following:[19]

- The number of joint tenants
- Whether the joint tenants are husband and wife
- The consideration the decedent furnished in acquiring the property
- How the joint tenants acquired the property

[13] Code Sec. 1022(c)(4)(C).
[14] Code Sec. 2056(b)(7).
[15] Code Sec. 1022(b)(5)(A).
[16] Code Sec. 1022(b)(5)(B).
[17] Code Sec. 1022(d)(2).
[18] Code Sec. 1022(d)(1)(A).
[19] Code Sec. 1022(d)(1)(B)(i).

If the decedent and his or her spouse are the only joint tenants, the law deems the decedent to have owned 50 percent of the property. This rule applies regardless of how the couple acquired the property and regardless of the consideration the decedent furnished, if any.[20]

In cases in which the decedent is one of three or more joint tenants, the decedent's ownership interest will be based on the decedent's proportionate contribution compared with that of the other joint tenants.[21] If the decedent and two or more other persons acquired property as joint tenants with the right of survivorship by gift, bequest, devise, or inheritance, state law will determine the decedent's share of the property interest. If state law does not specify or fix the ownership interests in such cases, the decedent's share for purposes of the basis rules will be computed by dividing the value of the property by the number of joint tenants.[22]

The decedent will be treated as owning property that he or she transferred while living to a qualified revocable trust. A revocable trust meets this definition if the decedent is deemed the owner of the trust under Code Sec. 678 because the decedent retained the power to revoke the trust.[23]

The law does not deem a decedent to own property for the purposes of the basis increase rules solely because the decedent held a power of appointment over the property at the time of his or her death.[24]

The law deems community property to have been acquired from the decedent. However, at least half of the community property must be treated as owned by and acquired from the decedent without regard to the basis rules.[25]

The law does not allow increases in basis for property the decedent acquired by gift or by a lifetime transfer for less than adequate and full consideration in money or money's worth within three years of the decedent's death.[26] However, this prohibition generally does not apply to property the decedent received from his or her spouse during this three-year period. However, the spouse must not have acquired the property in whole or in part by gift or by a lifetime transfer for less than adequate and full consideration in money or money's worth.[27]

---

[20] Code Sec. 1022(d)(1)(B)(i)(I).
[21] Code Sec. 1022(d)(1)(B)(ii).
[22] Code Sec. 1022(d)(1)(B)(i)(III).
[23] Code Sec. 1022(d)(1)(B)(ii).
[24] Code Sec. 1022(d)(1)(B)(iii).
[25] Code Sec. 1022(d)(1)(B)(iv).
[26] Code Sec. 1022(d)(1)(C)(i).
[27] Code Sec. 1022(d)(1)(C)(ii).

The increases in basis do not apply to the following properties:[28]

- Stock or securities of a foreign holding company
- Stock of a domestic international sales corporation (DISC) or a former DISC
- Stock of a foreign investment company
- Stock of a passive foreign investment company (PFIC)

An exception to the prohibition of the stock of a passive foreign investment company applies if the stock is a qualifying electing fund with respect to the decedent. To be treated as a qualified electing fund under Code Sec. 1295, the investor in the PFIC must have elected to treat the PFIC as a pass-through entity, which limits the deferral on its investment income.

The estates of nonresidents who are not citizens are allowed only a $60,000 general basis increase instead of the $1,300,000 general basis increase allowed to the estates of other decedents. In addition, the estates of nonresidents who are not citizens are not allowed the $3,000,000 spousal basis increase.[29]

In light of the upcoming carryover basis rules (for 2010 and possibly beyond), the financial planner should ascertain the client's date of acquisition and basis for each asset.

.06 Estate Planning Misconceptions

A little knowledge can be a dangerous thing, in estate planning as elsewhere. The client might have acquired views similar to these: (1) avoiding probate is always a good thing; (2) taking the full marital deduction is always advisable; (3) making lifetime gifts to children cannot hurt; (4) assigning ownership of a life insurance policy to one's spouse is always a smart move; (5) joint ownership of property is the easiest and best way of transferring property on death; (6) the only reason one might want to put property in trust for his or her spouse is if one feels that he or she will not be able to handle the funds.

If these or other misconceptions surface, the financial planner must deal with them. Even if they do not surface, the financial planner should clarify any possible preconceptions. In this way, the financial planner can often establish credibility with the client.

.07 Spouse's Possible Remarriage

The financial planner can discuss a spouse's possible remarriage after the client's death hypothetically. For example, the financial

---

[28] Code Sec. 1022(d)(1)(D).

[29] Code Sec. 1022(b)(3).

planner could explain the use of a trust for the surviving spouse's benefit. The financial planner can show how the trust would serve to relieve the surviving spouse of management responsibilities and free the spouse from the claims of creditors or the demands of relatives, while at the same time protecting the children as the ultimate beneficiaries, even if the surviving spouse should remarry.

.08 Disinheriting Children

If a parent wants to disinherit a child, perhaps the financial planner should not try to dissuade the client. However, suggesting that such feelings might be transitory would be appropriate. An estate plan is intended to stand for several years. A hasty and ill-considered disinheritance can produce severe and unimagined effects on family relationships and on the disinherited child.

¶ 215 QUESTIONNAIRES

A questionnaire is a good way to obtain pertinent information. Whether the client should complete it before, during, or after the meeting with the financial planner depends on the client and his or her relationship with the financial planner. If an established relationship exists, advance preparation of the questionnaire by the client will save time and make the meeting easier and more fruitful. The questionnaire should not touch on sensitive personal relationships and attitudes requiring special handling.

If the relationship has not been established, the financial planner should usually meet and establish a relationship with the client, raise the sensitive issues, and ask the client to complete and return the questionnaire at a later time. The financial planner should encourage the client to inquire about any items that might present problems.

In either case, the financial planner should carefully review with the client the information that the client has provided to ensure full disclosure. The following sample questionnaire is quite comprehensive.

Exhibit 1

Financial and Estate Planning Questionnaire

____

Client

____

Date

DOCUMENTS TO BE ATTACHED

		Attached or N/A
1.	Existing wills of both spouses.	☐
2.	Living wills and medical directives.	☐
3.	Gift tax returns filed by either spouse.	☐
4.	Life insurance policies.	☐
5.	Pension, profit-sharing, stock bonus or deferred compensation plans. Also, Keogh plans, traditional IRAs, Roth IRAs, SEP plans, and SIMPLE plans.	☐
6.	Buy/sell or stock redemption agreements.	☐
7.	Trust instruments.	☐
8.	Income tax returns for the past five years.	☐
9.	Business agreements and documents regarding interests in corporations, partnerships, limited liability companies, and sole proprietorships.	☐
10.	Pre- or postnuptial agreements, separation agreements, and divorce papers.	☐
11.	Instruments showing basis of assets held.	☐
12.	Instruments creating spouses' joint tenancies, tenancies by the entireties, or separate property in community property states.	☐
13.	Durable powers of attorney.	☐

FAMILY INFORMATION

1. Personal:	Client	Spouse
a. Name		
b. Home address		
c. Home phone		
d. Citizenship		
e. Employer & business address		
f. Business telephone		
g. Principal residence (indicate state and county)		
h. Other current (indicate state(s)) residences		
i. Prior residences (indicate state(s))		
j. Birth date		
k. Place of birth		
l. Social Security number		
m. Marital status		
n. If married, date and place of marriage		
o. If divorced, prior marriages (name of former spouse(s), date and place of divorce(s))		
p. If unmarried, and living with another person, name and age of that person		

2. Your Children:*

	Name and Address	Birth Date **	Social Security #***
a.			
b.			
c.			
d.			

3. Particulars regarding your grandchildren:*

	Their Parents		Names of Grandchildren	Birth Date**	Social Security #
a.	______	(1)	______	______	______
	______	(2)	______	______	______
		(3)	______	______	______
b.	______	(1)	______	______	______
	______	(2)	______	______	______
		(3)	______	______	______

* Indicate if any children or grandchildren are stepchildren, adopted children or are from a prior marriage.

** Under TIPRA, children under the age of 18 are taxed at the parental rate on investment income over $1,700 per year for tax year 2006, and this amount is indexed for inflation.

*** The taxpayer must have the dependent's Social Security number in order to claim a dependency exemption for any individual.

4. Parents:

	Husband		Wife	
Father:	______		______	
	Name		Name	
	______		______	
	Address		Address	
	______		______	
	Date of Birth	Date of Death	Date of Birth	Date of Death
Mother:	______		______	
	Name		Name	
	______		______	
	Address		Address	
	______		______	
	Date of Birth	Date of Death	Date of Birth	Date of Death

5. Other dependent persons—Names, addresses, relationships, degree of dependency, and date of birth:

____

____

6. Medical history—Please list all significant medical conditions or medical history for you and your family:

____

____

ADVISORS

Names, addresses, and telephone numbers:

1. **Attorney:** ______________________________
____

2. **Accountant:** ______________________________
____

3. **Life insurance advisor:** ______________________________
____

4. **Banker and trust officers:** ______________________________
____

5. **Stockbrokers:** ______________________________
____

6. **Executor or personal representative:** ______________________________
____

7. **Trustee:** ______________________________
____

8. **Designated guardian for children:** ______________________________
____

9. **Investment advisor:** ______________________________
____

10. **Financial planner:** ______________________________
____

11. **Physician:** ______________________________
____

12. **Clergyman:** ______________________________
____

13. **Casualty insurance agent:** ______________________________
____

14. **Appraiser:** ______________________________
____

DISTRIBUTION OBJECTIVES

1. Upon your death, how and to whom do you want your assets distributed?
   ____
   ____
   ____

2. (a) If you and your spouse both die before your children reach the age of majority, should children receive property at the age of majority or should it be held until they reach a more mature age?
   ____

   (b) Do any of your children have special educational, medical, or financial needs?
   ____

3. Is there anyone in your family whom you consider to be a good money manager?
   ____

4. Whom do you want to manage your estate from an investment standpoint?
   ____

   To whom would that person look for management help?
   ____

5. Is reducing or eliminating estate taxation of great importance to you? ________

6. Is minimizing income taxes of great importance to you? ________

7. Do you contemplate making future gifts? ________

   Furnish details: ________

8. Do you wish to make bequests to a religious organization or order or to any other charitable organization? ________ In cash or in kind? ________

   Furnish details: ________
   ____
   ____

9. If none of your children is living at the time of your spouse's death, do you want your estate to go to: Your family? ______ Spouse's family? ______ Elsewhere? ________

10. Does your spouse have employment skills? Do you expect that the survivor will work? ________

11. Will your spouse live in your present home? ________

12. Who will serve as your executor or personal representative? ________

IMPORTANT QUESTIONS

1. **Have you lived in any other state or foreign country? If so, where and for how long?**

2. **Did you or your spouse own any substantial separate property before marriage?**

3. **Have any gifts or inheritances been received by either you or you spouse separately or do you expect any in the future?**

CASH AND EQUIVALENTS

	Bank	Amount	Form of Ownership and With Whom
Bank accounts:			
Certificates of deposit:			
Other (money market funds, etc.):			

Total $____________

PERSONAL EFFECTS

	Fair Market Value
Automobiles (state whether leased or owned)	________
Household furnishings	________
Club memberships	________
Aircraft	________
Boats	________
Furs	________
Jewelry	________
Collections (Art, etc.)	________
Others (describe)	________
________	________
________	________
________	________
________	________
	________
	Total $ ________

LIFE INSURANCE POLICIES

LIFE INSURANCE PROVIDED BY EMPLOYER

	Policy # 1	Policy # 2	Policy # 3
Company			
Policy number			
Type (term, whole life, endowment, or universal life)			
If nonterm, date policy was entered into*			
Insured			
Owner			
Beneficiary			
Contingent beneficiary			
Face value			
Amount of loan**			
Settlement terms			
Employee's contribution			

OTHER LIFE INSURANCE

	Policy # 1	Policy # 2	Policy # 3
Company			
Policy number			
Type (term, whole life, universal, or variable life)			
Insured***			
Owner			
Beneficiary			
Contingent beneficiary			
Face value			
Current cash surrender value			
Amount of loan**			
Settlement terms			
Annual premium			

* Some investment-oriented policies (e.g., single premium) entered into on or after June 21, 1988, may be subject to special tax rules (under which amounts received, including loans, are treated first as income and a 10-percent penalty tax may apply).

** Interest on loans under life insurance contracts is generally not deductible after 1990.

*** Include policies on life of spouse and children.

STOCKS AND MUTUAL FUNDS

Company or Fund and Type	Ownership*	Number of Shares	Date of Purchase or Acquisition	Basis	Total Current Market Value/Listed on What Exchange

Total $____________

* Indicate restrictions on transfer if any.

TREASURY BONDS, NOTES, AND BILLS

Ownership	Date of Purchase	Cost	Maturity*	Current Yield	Current Value

Total $____________

* Final maturity for Series E savings bonds is 40 years. No interest is earned after this point.

MUNICIPAL BONDS, NOTES, AND BILLS

Issuer	AMT*	Non-AMT	Date of Purchase	Maturity	Current Value

* Private purpose municipals may be subject to the Alternative Minimum Tax (AMT).

CORPORATE BONDS AND NOTES

Issuer	Date of Purchase	Maturity	Current Value

NOTES AND MORTGAGES

Debtor	Type of Debt and Maturity	Security	Present Value

REAL ESTATE

	Property 1	Property 2
Legal description	Please Attach	
Location		
Type of property (residential, commercial, vacant land, etc.)		
Owned in names of		
Form of ownership		
Date of acquisition		
How acquired (gift, purchase, etc.)		
Cost (note cost of improvements)		
Accumulated depreciation*		
Current market value		
Encumbrances: (names of mortgagee, lienors, etc.)		
Amount		
Monthly payments (principal & interest)		
Interest rate		
Remaining period of loan		
Purpose of loan/use of $100,000 equity loan amount		
Annual interest		
Annual taxes		
Annual income (gross)*		
Annual depreciation*		
Annual costs (maintenance, etc.*)		
Annual net income*		
Farm property**		

* Income-producing property only

** Excess of value of property when put to highest and best use over value as operating farm

CLOSELY HELD BUSINESS INTERESTS

(Use separate sheet for each business interest)

Name____________________ Percent Owned____________

Type of entity: C Corporation____ Partnership____ Sole Proprietorship____
S Corporation____________________
Limited Liability Company________________

Is interest jointly owned with spouse?________________

Has your spouse participated in the business?____________

Your estimate of the fair market value of your interest ________

Your tax basis for your interest ____________________

Do you have any plans to dispose of business interest during your lifetime? ____

If so, please describe ________

What are your wishes as to disposition of ownership after death or during your lifetime:

1 Transfer to family ____________________

2 Sale to co-owner of business ________________

3 Sale to key-employee ____________________

4 Other ____________________________

Is there a buy/sell or redemption agreement? Yes ____ No ____

If "yes," please furnish copy for review.

Have you considered liquidating the corporation?________________

Please provide financial statements and tax returns for the previous five years and a copy of any buy/sell or redemption agreements.

ANNUITIES, RETIREMENT, DISABILITY, AND DEATH BENEFITS

(Include qualified plans, Keogh plans, traditional IRAs, Roth IRAs, deferred compensation plans, SEP plans, and SIMPLE plans.)

Type of Plan	Joint v. Survivor Annuity	Name of Beneficiary	Form of Payment	Present Vested Benefits

OTHER ASSETS

Description	Fair Market Value	Basis
Incentive stock options (include option price):		
Nonqualified stock options (include option price):		
Property received for services which is subject to a substantial risk of forfeiture:		
Stock appreciation rights:		
Copyrights or patents:		
Accounts receivable:		
Notes receivable:		
Archer medical savings accounts:		
Health savings accounts		
Other:		

Note: Include other assets such as a remainder, reversionary, or income interest in a trust. Also include the source and approximate amount of any expected inheritance.

LIABILITIES

(Not previously listed, e.g., mortgages on real estate)

Creditor	Secured By	Interest Rate	Date Incurred	Due Date	Repayment Schedule	Current Balance

GIFT DATA

GIFTS MADE

Have you made any gifts—other than to charities—in any one year to any one or more persons that exceeded in value $10,000* if made by you alone ($3,000 if before 1982) or $20,000* ($6,000 if before 1982) if both you and your spouse consented to gift splitting?

Yes ______ No ______

Did you make any gifts to pay for medical or education expenses?**

Yes ______ No ______

If gift tax returns were filed, please furnish Federal and State tax returns and appraisals.

If gift tax returns were not filed, describe the gift, date, fair market value, and to whom given:

____

____

Have gifts been made by creating a trust? Yes ______ No ______

If so, provide trust document.

Did you set up a *Clifford* trust before March 2, 1986?***

Yes ______ No ______

Did you set up a spousal remainder trust before March 2, 1986?***

Yes ______ No ______

Have gifts been made under the Uniform Gifts to Minors Act or the Uniform Transfers to Minors Act?

Yes ______ No ______

If you or your wife are the custodian, please give details on the property.

____

____

Have any gifts been made within the past three years?

If so, what was subject of gifts?

REMARKS

____

____

____

* The dollar values apply to gifts of a present interest. If the gift is of a future interest, the exclusions do not apply. If in doubt as to whether a gift is of a present or a future interest, so indicate in Remarks. The $10,000/ $20,000 amounts apply for transfers occurring after 1982 and before 1999. These amounts are indexed for inflation for calendar years after 1998. For tax year 2001, the amounts remained at $10,000 and $20,000 (Code Sec. 2503(b)). For tax years 2002 through 2005, the amounts are $11,000 and $22,000. For tax year 2006, the amounts are $12,000 and $24,000.

** An unlimited gift tax exclusion applies for amounts paid directly to providers for qualified medical or education expenses (Code Sec. 2503(e)).

*** Benefits for such trusts set up after March 1, 1986, have been eliminated.

ANNUAL EXPENDITURES

Auto	
Care and maintenance	$______
Insurance	______
Payments	______
Childcare	______
Clothing	______
Contributions to charity	______
Debt payments (other than mortgage)	______
Education	______
Entertainment	______
Equipment	______
Food	______
Furnishings	______
Gifts	______
Housing	
Care and maintenance	______
Mortgage	
Principal	______
Interest	______
Real estate taxes	______
Insurance	______
Interest (other than mortgage)	______
Laundry & dry cleaning	______
Life insurance premiums	______
Medical and dental care	______
Personal care	______
Personal gifts	______
Retirement plan contributions	
Qualified plan (defined contribution (401(k)) and defined benefit)	______
Keogh	______
IRA	______
SEP plan	______
SIMPLE plan	______
Telephone/Computer lines	______
Travel	______
Utilities	______
Vacation	______
Other	______
Total	$______

ANNUAL INVESTMENTS

(Exclude principal payments on home, voluntary contributions to retirement plans)

Savings accounts	$__________
CDs	__________
Stocks	__________
Bonds	__________
Mutual funds	__________
Municipals	__________
Treasuries	__________
Other	__________
Total	$__________

LIVING WILL AND MEDICAL DIRECTIVES

Do you and/or family members wish to direct medical care or removal of medical care through the use of a living will, durable power of attorney, springing power of attorney, health care proxy, or other form of medical directives?

¶ 220 PLANNER'S CHECKLIST

The estate planner takes the raw data from the questionnaire and supplements it with information gathered in personal interviews. He or she hopes thereby to touch all bases.

The following form is designed to fulfill this purpose. Here the planner can check off the documents that have been reviewed and obtain an overall picture of the assets and liabilities, gift data, cash flow, and other pertinent data.

Financial and Estate Planning Questionnaire

____
Client

____
Date of Interview

____
Interviewed by

COPIES OF DOCUMENTS THAT MUST BE REVIEWED

	Obtained
1. Existing wills of both spouses.	
2. All gift tax returns ever filed by client and/or spouse.	
3. Individual income tax returns for the past five years.	
4. Insurance policies in effect.	
5. Existing pension, profit-sharing, stock bonus, Keogh, deferred compensation or similar type plans, traditional IRAs, Roth IRAs, SEP plans, and SIMPLE plans	
6. Real estate deeds and mortgages.	
7. Trust instruments.	
8. Personal and business financial statement for the past five years.	
9. Business income tax returns for the past five years.	
10. Buy-sell or stock redemption agreements.	
11. Partnership, LLC, and/or joint venture agreements.	
12. Powers of appointment.	
13. Divorce, separation and pre-marital agreements.	
14. Instruments showing basis of assets held.	
15. Instruments creating spouses' joint tenancies or tenancies by the entirety.	
16. Living wills and medical directives.	
17. Durable powers of attorney.	

GIFTS

Lifetime Use of Unified Estate and Gift Tax Credit	Federal
Husband has used:	$______
Wife has used:	$______

Gifts After 9/8/76 and Before 1/1/77

Aggregate amount allowed
as specific exemption *

Cumulative Taxable Gifts Per Latest
Gift Tax Returns

	Federal	State
Husband:	$______	$______
Wife:	$______	$______

GIFT DATA

A. Trust created (grantor, beneficiaries, powers and rights retained, value of gift, trustee, term, reversion, present value):

____

____

B. Existing custodial accounts under Uniform Gifts to Minors Act and Uniform Transfers to Minors Act (donor, date, custodian, minor (age), value of gift, present value):

____

____

C. Substantiation of value at time of gift:

____

____

* Unified credit is reduced by 20 percent of this amount to a maximum of $6,000.

EMPLOYMENT

Current employer______________________________

Date employed ______________

Annual compensation________ Projected retirement date______________

CASH FLOW

	Currently	Projected After Client's Death	Projected for Retirement
Sources of cash:			
Compensation	$______	______	______
Dividends	______	______	______
Interest	______	______	______
Cash flow from rental property	______	______	______
Royalties	______	______	______
Keogh	______	______	______
IRA	______	______	______
SEP plan	______	______	______
SIMPLE plan	______	______	______
Income from installment sales	______	______	______
Business interests:			
__________	______	______	______
__________	______	______	______
Miscellaneous:			
Trusts	______	______	______
__________	______	______	______
__________	______	______	______
Annuities	______	______	______
Pension benefits	______	______	______
Social Security	______	______	______
__________	______	______	______
__________	______	______	______
__________	______	______	______
Total	$______	______	______

CASH FLOW

	Currently	Projected After Client's Death	Projected for Retirement
Expenditures:			
Auto			
Care and maintenance			
Insurance			
Payments			
Childcare			
Clothing			
Contributions to charity			
Debt payments (other than mortgage)			
Education			
Entertainment			
Equipment			
Food			
Furnishings			
Gifts			
Housing			
Care and maintenance			
Mortgage			
Principal			
Interest			
Real estate taxes			
Insurance			
Laundry & dry cleaning			
Life insurance premiums			
Medical and dental care			
Personal care			

CASH FLOW

	Currently	Projected After Client's Death	Projected for Retirement
Retirement plan contributions			
Qualified plan (defined contribution (401(k)) and defined benefit)			
Keogh			
IRA			
SEP plan			
SIMPLE plan			
Tax liabilities			
Telephone/ Computer lines			
Travel			
Utilities			
Vacation			
Other			
Total	$		
Excess (deficit)	$		

CLOSELY HELD BUSINESS INTERESTS

(Use separate sheet for each business interest)

Name/Taxpayer Identification Number ______________________

Business Address ______________________

Type of Entity: C Corporation ____________ Partnership ________

Sole Proprietorship ____________ S Corporation ________

Limited Liability Company ______________________

Percentage of Ownership: Self: __________ Spouse: __________

Joint: __________ Participation: __________

Others: __________ Children: __________

Buy/sell or redemption agreement? Yes _____ No _____ Details: __________

____

Code Sec. 2703 compliance? Yes _____ No _____ Details: __________

____

Client's wishes on disposition of interest ______________________

KEY-PERSON INSURANCE

EMPLOYEE	FACE VALUE	CASH VALUE

Most recent transfer of ownership equity by any owner:

Price __________ Percentage or number of shares __________

Date of transfer __________

Corporate obligations guaranteed by client ______________________

Estimate of fair market value per your analysis ______________________

Estimate of fair market value per client ______________________

Basis of securities held __________ Date acquired __________

REMARKS

____

____

TYPE OF PLAN

	Stock Bonus	Pension*	Profit-Sharing*	Individual Retirement Account	Deferred Compensation
Company______ **					
Retirement benefits					
Amount currently vested***					
Death benefits					
Disability benefits					
Beneficiary at death					
Amount of insurance excludable under Code Sec. 2042					
Employee contributions to date					
Name and address of plan administrator(s)					

* Indicate if either is a Keogh plan, SEP plan, or SIMPLE plan.

** If more than one, attach separate sheet.

*** For most workers, vesting occurs after five years on the job.

STOCK OPTIONS

	Date of Grant	Option Price	Number of Shares	Type of Option	F.M.V. at Date of Grant
Option 1	________	$________	________	________	________
Option 2	________	$________	________	________	________

	Expiration Date	How Long Exercisable by Estate	Present F.M.V.	Value: Number of Shares × (F.M.V.) Option Price
Option 1	________	$________	________	________
Option 2	________	$________	________	________

RESTRICTED PROPERTY

Description of Property Subject to Restriction	Nature of Restriction	Expected Date Such Restriction Will Lapse	Section 83(b) Election in Effect

LOCATION OF ASSETS AND DOCUMENTS

1. Safe deposit box (location of box, who has access, who has keys, in whose name is box registered): ______

2. Original current wills: ______

3. Life, health and accident insurance policies: ______

4. Long-term care insurance policies: ______

5. Securities: ______

6. Trust agreements: ______

7. Tax returns; years covered: ______

8. Contracts and business agreements: ______

9. Real estate and condominiums: ______
   a. Location and how owned: ______
   b. Deed and title policy: ______
   c. Mortgages: ______
   d. Leases: ______

10. Car titles: ______

11. Custody and other managed accounts: ______

12. Jewelry and other valuable tangibles: ______

13. Cancelled checks and stubs; period covered: ______

14. Cemetery plot (location of plot and deed; care arrangements): ______

15. Birth certificates: ______

16. Death certificates: ______

17. Marriage certificates: ______

LOCATION OF ASSETS AND DOCUMENTS

18. Divorce papers: ______________________________

____

19. Employee benefit statements: ______________________________

____

20. Employee benefit plan copies: ______________________________
21. Military discharge papers: ______________________________
22. Naturalization papers: ______________________________
23. Passports: ______________________________
24. Adoption papers: ______________________________
25. General insurance policies: ______________________________
26. Private safe (location, who has access): ______________________________
27. Firearms and registration requirements: ______________________________
28. Funeral directions: ______________________________
29. Living wills: ______________________________
30. Entitlements (Social Security, veterans, etc.): ______________________________

POWERS OF ATTORNEY outstanding, including bank accounts and safe deposit access and health care decisions. Give dates and names (obtain copies; show: attorney in fact; address; description of power; date):

____

____

MEDICAL, DISABILITY, AND LONG-TERM CARE INSURANCE

	Company	Benefits	Beneficiary
Medical			
Surgical			
Hospital			
Disability			
Long-Term Care			

¶ 225 CONSTRUCTING A PLAN

The chapters that follow deal with taking the information and developing a plan that will carry out the client's objectives in the most economical and effective way. To this end, the financial and estate planner will consider forms of property ownership, lifetime personal and charitable giving, use of trusts, life insurance, and all other matters dealing with the general principles and techniques of financial and estate planning discussed in Part I of this book. Special situations, covered in Part II, deal with planning for corporate executives, professionals, the owners of closely held businesses and others. The ways and means of building the estate are developed in Part III. A discussion of making use of the planning aids is found in Part IV.

Chapter 3

The Co-ownership of Property

Overview ....¶ 301
Evaluating Forms of Ownership of Property ....¶ 305
Joint Ownership ....¶ 310
Use of Joint Ownership with Special Types of Property ..¶ 315
Tenancy in Common ....¶ 320
Community Property ....¶ 325
Timesharing of Property ....¶ 330

¶ 301 OVERVIEW

Individuals often become involved in the co-ownership of property without fully realizing what it means in terms of loss of freedom and control, and the costs entailed. The cost is necessarily affected by tax considerations. Thus, the estate planner must take into account the direct and indirect effects of tax rules on the various forms of co-ownership.

Co-ownership, of course, may assume many different forms, some of which are beyond the scope of this chapter. The modern corporation, for example, is a form of co-ownership, as is a partnership, a cooperative apartment, a condominium, a limited liability company, or even a trust. Co-ownership might also be deemed to include ownership by different persons of qualitatively different interests in the same property such as ownership of a life or term interest by one party and a remainder interest by another party. This chapter does not address those forms of ownership. Rather, this chapter discusses the common forms of ownership in which individuals may hold their homes, their bank accounts, their securities, and their other investments. Specifically, this chapter examines what is probably the most common form of co-ownership—joint ownership or joint tenancy, with a right of survivorship. Special attention is focused on the special rule (¶ 315.02) that permits one half of spouses' jointly owned property to be excluded from the gross estate of the first to die, regardless of the amount of consideration furnished by each spouse.[1] This chapter also considers a special form of joint ownership, also with a right of survivorship, between husband and wife, known as a tenancy by the entirety. In addition, this chapter examines tenancies in common, which provide no right of survivorship. Finally, this chapter addresses community property, which is a kind of co-ownership for married couples in eight states (Arizona, California, Idaho, Louisiana, Nevada, New Mexico, Texas, and Washington). Wisconsin has adopted the Uniform Marital Property Act, which is similar to community property statutes.

Individuals who need estate planning often wait until middle age to consult an estate planner. When they do come for help, the estate planner is apt to be confronted with accomplished facts as to form of property ownership. Few individuals have property arrangements that will pass muster by estate planning tests. Assets and property rights will have been acquired in a more or less haphazard fashion, based on feelings, incomplete knowledge, custom, arrangements made by other family members, habit, and even chance. Although feelings, customs, and habits are not to be completely ignored, they do have to be recognized for what they are. The estate planner must help the client to recognize any consequences that might result from prior arrangements. The togetherness that can be symbolized by joint ownership or another person's fear of togetherness can exact a price in terms of hidden costs or loss of flexibility. Once aware of these factors, the owners might wish to modify their earlier plans, after evaluating the cost of doing so.

The first job of the estate planner is to find out exactly what forms of ownership exist. The estate planner will also want to know what the cost basis of each asset is, and what changes, if any, are desirable. The estate planner can then determine the best way to make any changes in the form of ownership. The cost of making any changes should be compared to the benefits of the changes.

The checklist at ¶ 305 sets out the steps the estate planner should generally take. The chapter later discusses in detail what needs to be done and how to do it.

¶ 305 EVALUATING FORMS OF OWNERSHIP OF PROPERTY

The following steps should be taken by estate planners in evaluating forms of property ownership:

1. **Document check.** Check all bank accounts, government bonds, listed and unlisted securities, deeds, co-op shares,

[1] Code Sec. 2040(b).

and other evidences of ownership to determine whether the particular property is held jointly with right of survivorship, as a tenancy by the entirety, as a tenancy in common, or as community property under applicable local law.

2. **Mode of acquisition.** Was property acquired in any of the forms of co-ownership by purchase, gift, or inheritance?
3. **Contributions of co-tenants.** How much did each of the co-tenants contribute, if anything, to the acquisition?
4. **Income tax consequences.** What are the income tax consequences of co-ownership, taking into account applicable local law?
5. **Severance of interests—legal feasibility.** How may a severance of a joint interest be made under state law? Can it be done unilaterally or only by mutual consent?
6. **Tax consequences of severance.** What will be the effect of the severance and termination of joint tenancies, including tenancies by the entirety, in terms of estate tax, gift tax, and income tax consequences?
7. **Fractional interest rule for spouses' jointly owned property.** Under Code Sec. 2040(b), only 50 percent of the value of jointly owned personal and real property held by the spouses in joint tenancy with right of survivorship, or as tenants by the entirety, will be included in the gross estate of the first spouse to die regardless of the consideration furnished by each spouse. However, the U.S. Court of Appeals for the Sixth Circuit has held that this rule does not apply to joint tenancies created before 1977 (¶315.02).[2]
8. **Effect of joint and mutual will.** The estate planner should check any will to determine its effect in relation to jointly owned property and the marital deduction in the light of applicable local law.
9. **Structure plan.** The estate planner should explain to the client the legal and tax consequences of the current forms of ownership, and the costs and benefits of proposed changes. The client should decide whether or not he or she wants the revisions made.

¶310 JOINT OWNERSHIP

Some use the term "joint ownership" to include tenancies in common, where each tenant owns an undivided portion of the

[2] *M. Gallenstein*, CA-6, 92-2 USTC ¶60,114.

property which he or she may freely dispose. This chapter will not quarrel with that use of the term. However, when estate planners use it, they mean a form of ownership in which the entire property passes to the survivor on the death of his or her joint tenant. This chapter also uses it to include that special form of joint tenancies between husbands and wives known as tenancies by the entirety. Although tenancies by the entirety are also characterized by a survivorship feature like that in ordinary joint tenancies, they differ from the point of view of termination. This last point will be discussed in ¶315.02.

Generally, from a purely estate planning point of view, joint tenancies or tenancies by the entirety are undesirable. They are especially undesirable where the estate is substantial and subject to a large estate tax. However, these joint tenancies can also create problems for smaller estates.

Anyone transferring property from sole ownership to joint ownership can expect to lose full control. With some types of property, an owner may be able to retain control by keeping evidence of joint ownership. However, by retaining control, the owner might make the transfer revocable or ineffective. Also, joint ownership usually involves a sharing of income from the property, which might not be desirable. Sharing the income is undesirable if the transferor needs the income. However, sharing the income might be desirable if the transferor wants to share it with the joint tenant, especially if the latter is in a lower income tax bracket. Joint ownership rules out any form of post-mortem control by the person who created the joint ownership. The survivor will have control over the property. This circumstance might not be desirable if the survivor is not able to manage the property. For example, a survivor might have difficulty managing a business interest where he or she lacks management experience or might suffer from some form of disability. Ordinarily, allowing the survivor to have control over the property is not advisable if he or she remarries and the property passes out of the family.

Joint tenancies involve a variety of estate tax, gift tax, and income tax considerations, which will be discussed later in detail.

In addition, joint tenancy is somewhat like marriage, not only in the surrender and sharing of control and income but also in its divorce and termination aspects. Indeed, modern divorce laws and procedures in some jurisdictions at least may make obtaining a divorce easier than unwinding joint ownership. The joint tenants must also consider state laws and any gift taxes that they must pay.

The idea that joint tenancies are a substitute for a will is a myth. No one can be certain that all his or her property will be in joint ownership. A last-minute inheritance, settlement, bonus, or other property bonanza always remains a possibility. Simultaneous death of the joint tenants is another possibility. The potential occurrence of any of these events makes a will an estate planning necessity.

However, joint tenancies have their place in estate planning. They combine the survivorship principle with an avoidance of probate in a way that can make this form of ownership desirable from an estate planning point of view. For example, a husband and wife with a modest joint checking or savings account should usually hold the account as joint tenants with a right of survivorship. The couple can use this form of ownership to provide the survivor with almost immediate cash for support, payment of funeral expenses, and other debts and costs demanding prompt payment. This scenario assumes that the survivor would not otherwise have such funds available. It also assumes that the amount in the joint accounts is kept large enough for the survivor's reasonably anticipated needs for current cash.

A husband and wife might also desire to put their personal residence in joint tenancy or tenancy by the entirety for the reasons described in ¶ 315.02.

Although the idea of combining survivorship, avoidance of probate, and taking care of the survivor's current cash needs via joint ownership is attractive, the estate planner should consider alternatives. Some alternatives might achieve the same purposes without some of the disadvantages of joint ownership. A revocable trust, for example, can be set up to provide the survivorship feature, avoid probate, and supply the survivor with immediate cash. At the same time, the revocable trust allows the settlor to retain control and have beneficial use of the property during his or her lifetime. However, a revocable trust is not always preferable. It carries its own limitations and disadvantages, including complying with the laws and requirements in forming it and administering it (see ¶ 630 for a full discussion of the revocable trust).

The legal and tax consequences of joint ownership of property can vary depending on the character of the property involved and local law. Exhibit 2, which follows, is designed to give the reader a general view of the advantages and disadvantages of joint ownership, compared with those of sole ownership. Following the chart, the estate tax, gift tax, income taxes, termination problems, and the use of joint ownership in special properties are considered.

Exhibit 2

General Comparison of Sole and Joint Ownership of Property

Point of Comparison	Sole Ownership	Joint Ownership
Lifetime Control	Full	Divided
Postmortem Control	Yes	No
Power to Bequeath	Full	None
Income from Property	All	Shared
Tax on Creation		
Generally	None	Possible gift tax Possible income tax
Interspousal	Not applicable	No gift tax Possible income tax
Tax on Termination		
Generally	Possible gift tax Possible income tax	Possible gift tax Possible income tax
Interspousal	Not applicable	No gift tax No income tax
Inclusion in Gross Estate		
Generally	All	All, unless survivor shows contribution
Interspousal	Not applicable	One-half
Tax on Postmortem Disposition	Full step-up in basis	No step-up for part not includible in decedent's gross estate*
Tax on Postmortem Disposition for Property Acquired from a Decedent Who Dies in 2010 Only	Limited step-up in basis	Limited step-up in basis for part deemed owned by decedent only
Cash Availability on Death of Owner	Delayed	Immediate or as soon as waiver of state tax lien obtained
Need for Will	Yes, unless statutory disposition is OK	Same as sole ownership unless no other possible property interests
Administration Expenses	Included in computing expenses and fees	Generally not included in computation
Unwinding	No special problem	Legal problems on top of tax problems
Creditors' Claims	Fully subject to	Free under some state laws

* No step-up if joint tenancy acquired by decedent by gift from his or her joint tenant within one year of death (Code Sec. 1014(e)).

.01 Estate and Death Taxes

Under Code Sec. 2040(a), the full value of jointly held property is includible in the gross estate of the first joint tenant to die unless the executor shows that some part of the property belonged to the survivor before the joint tenancy was created or that the survivor contributed to the acquisition of the property or its improvement. However, the requirement of a showing of contribution generally is not necessary in the case of a joint tenancy between spouses,[3] as discussed in detail at ¶ 315.02. Another exception to the full value rule applies if the property was acquired by gift, legacy, or inheritance. This exception will be discussed below, under the heading "Joint property acquired by gift or inheritance."

Focusing first on the exception involving contributions by the survivor, the estate planner should note the consequences of proving survivor contributions. The amount excluded from the decedent's gross estate is not merely the amount of the survivor's contribution, but rather a fractional part of the full value of the property at the time of death. The numerator of the fraction is the amount contributed, and the denominator is the full value of the property at the time the contribution was made.

> ***Example 3.1.*** Assume that a parcel of real estate is acquired for \$30,000, with Donna Cline putting up \$20,000 and Steve Henderson \$10,000. Years later, if Cline dies and the property is then worth \$90,000, \$30,000 (\$90,000 × \$10,000/\$30,000), not \$10,000, would be excludible from Cline's gross estate.

The deceased joint tenant might have given the survivor money or other property before the jointly held property was acquired. If that money or other property became the basis of the survivor's contribution, it is not counted as a contribution by the survivor. This rule applies even though the gift property appreciated in value between the time of the gift and the time of acquisition of the jointly held property.

> ***Example 3.2.*** Alice Wilson gave Bob Jenkins real estate worth \$20,000, and five years later (when the real estate was worth \$40,000), Jenkins exchanged it for real estate worth \$50,000, title being taken by Wilson and Jenkins as joint tenants. Jenkins would be considered to have made no contribution toward the acquisition of the new property. On the other hand, income earned from the property or money acquired by gift may be used as a basis for the survivor's contribution. For example, if Jenkins used accumulated rents from the property received as a

[3] Code Sec. 2040(b).

gift to acquire the new joint tenancy property, these rents would be considered a contribution by Jenkins.

If the jointly held property is mortgaged, difficult questions can arise. Is the amount of an assumed mortgage considered to be a contribution? A U.S. district court addressed this issue in a case involving an acquisition by a husband and wife. The husband put up all the cash, but both parties' names were on the mortgage. The court held that the wife contributed to the purchase price to the extent of the value of the property attributable to one-half of the amount of the mortgage assumed and paid, even though the mortgage payments were made by the husband.[4] However, that case was decided many years ago, and the value of that decision as precedent is doubtful. Obviously, it is an approach that permits estate taxes to be avoided. This makes sense if the joint liability on the mortgage is genuine at the time the mortgage is assumed or placed by the joint tenants. However, if the parties contemplate from the beginning that one or the other is to bear full responsibility and make the mortgage payments, the result could be different. The IRS, in any case, will very likely want to take a close look at the transaction to determine whether it is real or a sham, particularly where a pattern exists where one individual has made all the payments from his or her own funds. If the parties acquire property subject to an existing mortgage, the amount outstanding at the time of acquisition should have no effect in determining contributions. However, subsequent mortgage payments may affect the determination of contributions.

In all events, except for qualifying tenancies between spouses (¶ 315.02),[5] the full value of jointly held property is presumptively includible in the gross estate of the first joint tenant to die.[6] The burden is on the executor to show otherwise. The rule puts a premium on record keeping. The survivor, except as he or she may also be interested in holding estate taxes to a minimum, has no particular interest in establishing his or her contributions. Rarely can anyone predict who will die first. Because the survivor might also be interested in reducing the estate tax, both joint tenants should keep complete records of their own and their joint tenant's contributions.

During the planning stage, an estate planner might have to address an existing joint tenancy. If the client cannot prove past contributions to the estate planner's satisfaction, the client will likely have difficulty in proving them to the IRS on the death of the other joint tenant. Therefore, in computing the potential estate tax liabilities attributable to the property, the estate planner should not count

---

[4] *Bremer v. Luff*, DC NDNY, 7 FSupp. 148 (1933).

[5] Code Sec. 2040(b).

[6] Code Sec. 2040(a).

the claimed but unproven contributions of one or the other joint tenants. If the individual who originally owned all the property and who created the joint tenancy paid a gift tax, the contribution qualifies as a credit against his or her estate tax. The credit is limited to the extent that the value of the jointly held property is included in his or her gross estate.

Joint property acquired by gift or inheritance. If the joint tenants acquired the property from someone else by way of gift or inheritance, Code Sec. 2040 and the regulations thereunder provide that on the death of one of the joint tenants only the value of his or her fractional interest in the property is includible in his or her gross estate. The fractional interest is that interest specified in the gift or fixed by law. If none is specified or fixed by law, the fractional interest is determined by dividing the value of the property by the number of the joint tenants. Of course, when dealing with a tenancy by the entirety of a husband and wife, the only two tenants will be the husband and wife. As a general rule, only half of the value of the property is includible in the gross estate of the first to die (¶ 315.02).[7] Other types of joint tenancies can have more than two tenants. An individual might, for example, make a testamentary transfer of property to four grandchildren. However, if the property will have more than two owners, using a tenancy in common is usually advisable.

Suppose one of the joint tenants acquired the property by gift or inheritance as a sole owner and subsequently converted the property to joint ownership. A court has held that the rule, calling for a fractional exclusion of the total value of the property based on contributions of the survivor, does not apply to amounts contributed by the survivor for improvements.[8] Only the cost of the improvements is considered, unless the parties show that the improvements increased or decreased in value from the time made until the date of death.

Simultaneous death of joint tenants. Simultaneous death of joint tenants does not occur frequently. However, the simultaneous death of joint tenants can produce unexpected estate tax results. The Uniform Simultaneous Death Act was promulgated in 1940 and adopted by 49 states. In 1991, the Act was made part of the Uniform Probate Code Article II and the Uniform Act on Intestacy, Wills, and Donative Transfers. The Act was amended in 1993. The 1993 version of the Act has been adopted by the District of Columbia and the

---

[7] Code Sec. 2040(b).

[8] *E. Peters Est.*, CA-4, 67-2 USTC ¶ 12,497, 386 F2d 404, aff'g 46 TC 407 (Acq.), CCH Dec. 28,005.

following states: Alaska, Arizona, Arkansas, Hawaii, Kansas, Kentucky, New Mexico, North Dakota, Ohio, South Dakota, and Virginia. Most of the other states still follow the 1940 version of the Act. The Act creates a presumption of simultaneous death, absent a sufficient showing to the contrary. It also provides, in the case of a joint tenancy or tenancy by the entirety, that the property is to be distributed half to the distributees of each. In effect, the joint tenancy is treated as though it were a tenancy in common without survivorship rights.

However, the IRS has issued a contrary ruling in a situation involving the simultaneous death presumption for property held by husband and wife as tenants by the entirety. In that case, the husband had contributed the full consideration for acquiring the property. The IRS ruled that the full value of the property was includible in the husband's gross estate because he had furnished the full consideration. Half of the value of the property was includible in the wife's gross estate by reason of the Uniform Simultaneous Death Act. This half qualified for the marital deduction[9] in the husband's estate.[10]

This approach the IRS used would not apply under Code Sec. 2040(b). This section deals with spousal joint tenancies and provides that only one-half of the value of the jointly held property generally is includible in the gross estate of each (¶ 315.02). What if the IRS followed the same approach with a joint tenancy between persons other than husband and wife, where one of the tenants furnished full consideration for the acquisition? His or her gross estate would include the full value of the property, without benefit of the marital deduction;[11] and the other's gross estate would include half the value of the property. Presumably, the estate tax paid by the estate required to include the full value would be allowed as a credit against the estate tax payable by the other tenant's estate. However, no definitive ruling or case on point is available.

.02 Gift Taxes on Creation of Joint Tenancy

Creation of a joint tenancy generally gives rise to a taxable gift unless the interest acquired by each joint tenant is equal to his or her contribution to the joint interest.[12] The general rule does not apply, however, to joint tenancies or tenancies by the entirety between spouses (¶ 315.02),[13] purchases of U.S. savings bonds (¶ 315.03), joint bank accounts (¶ 315.01), and joint brokerage accounts (¶ 315.05) under special circumstances.[14]

---

[9] Code Sec. 2056(a).

[10] Rev. Rul. 66-60, 1966-1 CB 221, modified on other grounds in Rev. Rul. 76-303, 1976-2 CB 266.

[11] Code Sec. 2056(a), or Code Sec. 2040(b).

[12] Reg. § 25.2511-1(h)(5).

[13] Code Sec. 2523(a) and Reg. § 25.2511-1(h)(5).

[14] Reg. § 25.2511-1(h)(4).

Of course, not all gifts result in tax. Consider the $12,000 (for 2006 and indexed for inflation) annual gift tax exclusion,[15] the split-gift concept,[16] the marital deduction,[17] and the applicable estate and gift tax credit amount,[18] all of which are discussed in Chapter 4.

Also, in evaluating the gift tax potential, an estate planner should weigh the gift tax potential against other possibly favorable tax consequences flowing from the payment of gift taxes: (1) the gift tax paid may be excluded from the donor's gross estate if the gift is not made within three years of death;[19] and (2) the portion of the gift tax paid attributable to appreciation in the gift property increases the tax basis of the property,[20] which can increase depreciation deductions for depreciable property and reduce tax liability on the proceeds if the property is later sold.

Where an individual buys property with his or her own funds and title is taken in joint tenancy, the value of the gift is one-half of the value of the jointly held property.[21] Special rules apply where the parties are married and the property is held in a tenancy by the entirety (¶ 315.02).[22]

.03 Income Tax Consequences on Creation of Joint Tenancy

Joint ownership generally permits a splitting of income. Each joint tenant reports his or her share of the income or gain on sale on his or her own separate tax return. This splitting of income can produce overall tax savings. The shift of income from the creator of the joint tenancy reduces the creator's tax liability and might cause the remaining income taxable to the creator to be taxed at a lower rate. Where the two owners do not file a joint return, the creation of a joint tenancy can reduce the combined tax paid on the income generated by the property.

Taking into account federal rates alone, the spread between the tax bracket of the creating joint tenant and the other tenant might be substantial in view of the 35-percent top rate for 2005 through 2010. In 2011, as a result of the sunset provision of the Economic Growth and Tax Relief Reconciliation Act of 2001, the highest marginal income tax rate will revert to the 39.6 percent rate in effect for 2000. When state and local taxes are considered, the spread might be even greater.

Creation of joint interests in appreciated property affords special income-splitting opportunities. On a subsequent sale of the property

---

[15] Code Sec. 2503(b).

[16] Code Sec. 2513.

[17] Code Sec. 2523(a).

[18] Code Secs. 2010 and 2505.

[19] Code Sec. 2035(b).

[20] Code Sec. 1015(d)(6).

[21] Reg. § 25.2511-1(h)(5).

[22] Reg. § 25.2511-1(h)(5).

by the joint tenants, the gain is divided between or among the joint tenants according to their fractional interests. A possible exception to this rule could occur where the sale negotiations began before the creation of the joint interest. In that case, the IRS might want to attribute the entire gain to the creator of the joint tenancy under the step transaction doctrine and assignment of income doctrine. Substantial savings might be realized if the creator of the joint tenancy would be taxed at a 15-percent marginal rate on any gain[23] and the other tenant would be taxed at a rate of 5 percent.[24]

These income tax benefits are not available with savings bonds (¶ 315.03) and many joint savings accounts (¶ 315.01) where one joint tenant makes the purchase or deposit because the purchase or deposit is not considered a completed gift.[25]

Creation of a joint tenancy by a parent with a child under the age of 18 will not produce any significant tax savings because the child is taxed at the higher of his or her own tax rate of the parent's tax rate on unearned income in excess of $1,700 (in 2006).[26] Indeed, even if the creator of the joint tenancy with the child were a grandparent or other family member, the result would be the same. When the child attains the age of 18, the child's unearned income will be taxable at his or her own personal rate.

A joint tenancy with a spouse is not apt to be of much income tax use, at least on the federal return where income splitting is permitted on a joint return. However, many state income tax laws do not provide for income splitting on a joint return. In those states, splitting income between spouses through joint ownership can produce income tax savings.

In all cases, gift tax costs (¶ 310.02), if any, must be weighed against income tax savings.

.04 Termination of Joint Tenancies

The joint tenants themselves can end the relationship while they are alive. Death, of course, ends it automatically. A joint tenant may usually terminate regular joint tenancy unilaterally. Generally, a tenancy by the entirety may be ended only by mutual consent or by termination of the marital relationship.

Lifetime terminations. Termination during life is accomplished by dividing the property, selling it, and dividing the proceeds or by exchanging it for other property. Regardless of which method is used, gift tax liabilities are possible if the joint tenants are not

[23] Code Sec. 1(h)(1)(C).

[24] Code Sec. 1(h)(1)(B).

[25] Reg. § 25.2511-1(h)(4).

[26] Code Sec. 1(g).

married to each other.[27] A gift of the property occurs if the property or the proceeds are divided to give one of the joint tenants less than the value of his or her fractional interest in the property.

> ***Example 3.3.*** Assume that jointly held property is sold for $100,000 and each of the joint tenants, Amy Jones and Bill Davis, has a one-half interest in the property. Jones receives $60,000 and Davis receives $40,000. Davis has made a gift of $10,000 to Jones. If each had received $50,000, no gift occurs, regardless of how much each contributed to set up the joint tenancy.

From this example, one might conclude that the thing to do is to give each tenant no more than his or her fractional interest. Doing so certainly avoids the gift tax, but it overlooks two factors that the estate planner should keep in mind: (1) contributions to the acquisition and improvement of the property, and (2) survivorship value. The first factor is easy enough to handle. If the contributions have been unequal, the parties will doubtless be aware of this fact. Once the estate planner calls it to their attention, they will have the opportunity to make adjustments for this factor in effecting a division. The survivorship factor, however, could be more troublesome and less obvious in most cases. It is clear enough, however, with respect to situations where there is a wide disparity in the ages of the joint tenants. Nominal equality would not be true equality in such cases.

> ***Example 3.4.*** Assume a situation where a 90-year-old grandfather, Guy Long, owns a parcel of real estate with his 21-year-old grandson, Steve Jacobs. Measured by actuarial standards, the chances of Long's receiving the whole of the property by survivorship are slight, and a 50-50 division would hardly reflect reality.

Effect of estate taxes on terminations. The parties should also consider estate taxes in ending a joint tenancy. The estate planner should consult three particular sections of the Internal Revenue Code in advising his or her client: (1) Code Sec. 2035, concerned with transfers within three years of death, which, while no longer generally includible for estate tax purposes, are included in the estate for purposes of determining eligibility for special-use valuation of farm or business real estate, the 14-year extension for payment of estate taxes[28] and Code Sec. 303 stock redemptions;[29] (2) Code Sec. 2036, which requires inclusion in the estate of the value of any interest transferred by a decedent in which he or she retains a life interest; and (3) Code Sec. 2038, dealing with revocable transfers.

---

[27] Code Sec. 2523(a).

[28] Code Sec. 6166.

[29] Code Sec. 2035(c).

Under Code Sec. 2035, the creation of a joint tenancy will not generally result in the inclusion of the joint interest in the estate of the creator for estate tax purposes. However, if the donor is the owner of a closely held corporation, the creation of the joint tenancy could affect the ability of the donor's estate to meet the test for a Code Sec. 303 redemption of stock. This situation could occur if the donor dies within three years after creating the joint tenancy and before the creation of the joint interest. The donor's estate would be unable to meet the test imposed by Code Secs. 303 or 6166. This test requires that the closely held business interest have a value of more than 35 percent of the gross estate. The creation of a joint interest in nonbusiness property, although removing the interest created for estate tax purposes, will not be effective in terms of enabling the estate to meet the 35-percent test.[30] Although a gift within three years of death is not includible, any gift tax paid or payable thereon will be includible.[31] In other words, the gross-up rule continues to apply.

Code Sec. 2036, another provision to consider, requires inclusion in an individual's gross estate of the value of any property that he or she has at any time transferred in which he or she has retained a life interest. When jointly held property is transferred in trust, with the joint tenants reserving a life interest in the trust during their joint lives and for the life of the survivor, Code Sec. 2036 clearly applies. When one of the joint tenants dies, assuming it is the one who furnished the entire consideration for the acquisition of the property, how much of it is to be included in his or her gross estate? Only the portion representing the decedent's fractional interest in the property transferred to the trust will be includible. Rev. Rul. 69-577[32] states that where property held in a tenancy by the entirety is transferred to a trust under which each spouse reserves a joint and survivor life estate, only one-half of the value of the trust property is includible in the gross estate of each, even where the trust is irrevocable. Although the ruling dealt with spousal joint tenancies, it has application to other joint tenancies, as well.

If the joint tenants transfer the property to a trust without retaining any life interest for themselves, whether the trust was revocable or irrevocable would make a difference. If revocable, Code Sec. 2038 applies. The gross estate of the first joint tenant to die would include one half of the value of the trust property. If the trust is irrevocable, Code Sec. 2038 would not apply.

Setting up a trust that complies with the requirements of Rev. Rul. 69-577, referred to above, might be one of the best ways of ending

[30] Code Sec. 2035(c).

[31] Code Sec. 2035(b).

[32] 1969-2 CB 173.

an unwanted joint tenancy. The trust must dispose of any property left in the trust after the two life interests have ended. The trustee should consider possible gift tax liabilities in making the disposal. The interest disposed of is called a remainder interest. The IRS has tables for determining the value of such interests. The values vary depending on the ages of the life tenants. If both life tenants are young, the remainder interest will have little value for gift tax purposes. If they are both old, a gift tax liability is possible. The dimensions of it will vary depending on the value of the trust property and available exemptions and exclusions. If the potential liability is significant, the settlor should reserve a power to appoint the remainder among the descendants. In such a case, no completed gift will occur that would cause a gift tax liability.[33]

Income tax consequences. Income tax consequences must be considered when a joint tenancy is terminated. Each joint tenant, on termination during his or her life by a sale or exchange to an outsider, might realize taxable gain or loss on the transaction. Gain or loss is determined by the difference between what is received by each joint tenant in relation to the tax basis for his or her fractional interest in the property.[34] Generally, where the property was acquired for consideration, the cost, less depreciation, if any, allocated to the joint tenants according to their respective fractional interests in the property, will determine their tax basis.[35] If the property was acquired by the joint tenants as a gift from a third party, the donor's adjusted basis increased for any gift tax paid due to the appreciation in the property determines basis.[36] If the property was acquired from a decedent, the fair market value of the property includible in the decedent's gross estate determines basis.[37]

How the survivor is taxed. When a joint tenancy is automatically terminated by death, the survivor becomes the sole owner. From that time on, the survivor is taxable on all of the income generated by the property. If he or she sells or exchanges the property, special rules apply for computing the gain or loss. These rules depend on how the survivor's tax basis is computed.

If the property is includible in the gross estate of the decedent, its basis is the fair market value at the date of death[38] or six months later,[39] if the executor elects the alternate valuation date.[40] To the extent that the property was not includible in the deceased joint tenant's gross estate, the survivor's basis is his or her cost if he or

[33] Reg. § 25.2511-2(b).
[34] Code Sec. 1001(a).
[35] Code Sec. 1011(a).
[36] Code Sec. 1015.
[37] Code Sec. 1014(a).
[38] Code Sec. 1014(a)(1).
[39] Code Sec. 1014(a)(2).
[40] Code Sec. 2032.

she bought it or contributed to its purchase. Property acquired from a decedent who dies in 2010 will not necessarily receive a basis equal to its fair market value on the date of the decedent's death. Rather, such property will generally have a basis equal to the lower of the basis of the property in the hands of the decedent or the property's fair market value on the date of the decedent's death. The executor may allocate a general increase in basis of up to $1,300,000.[41] In addition, the law allows an additional basis increase of up to $3,000,000 for property that passes to a surviving spouse.[42] See ¶210 for additional details on the basis rules for property acquired from a decedent who dies in 2010 under the Economic Growth and Tax Relief Reconciliation Act of 2001.

If depreciable property is involved, and is includible in the gross estate of the deceased joint tenant, the survivor's basis generally must be reduced by any depreciation deductions allowed the survivor before the joint tenant's death.[43]

Of course, if the survivor keeps the property, it would be includible in his or her gross estate. However, a special estate tax credit for property previously taxed may be available if the survivor dies within 10 years of the death of the former joint tenant in whose estate the property had been included and taxed.[44]

Conversion to a tenancy in common. One of the ways in which the survivorship feature of a joint tenancy may be eliminated and the tenancy terminated is to have the tenants join in transferring the property to themselves as tenants in common. No gain or loss will be recognized on such a transfer.[45] As long as the proportional interests are not disturbed, the joint tenants will not incur any gift tax liability. If the joint tenancy is between spouses, the unlimited marital deduction[46] avoids gift tax whether or not the proportional interests are disturbed. In addition, no sale occurs for income tax purposes.

¶315 USE OF JOINT OWNERSHIP WITH SPECIAL TYPES OF PROPERTY

The rules dealing with joint tenancies can vary depending on the type of property held in joint ownership. The paragraphs that follow deal with these differences as they affect different types of property commonly encountered in estate planning.

---

[41] Code Sec. 1022(b).

[42] Code Sec. 1022(c).

[43] Code Sec. 1014(b)(9).

[44] Code Sec. 2013.

[45] See Rev. Rul. 56-437, 1956-2 CB 507, involving a joint tenancy in stock.

[46] Code Sec. 2523(a).

.01 Bank Accounts

Almost everyone has a joint bank account with another person such as a spouse, child, sibling, grandparent, or fianceé. Some people might have more accounts, many of them joint, than they can count. Rarely will anybody call a lawyer to determine if he or she should consider special factors in opening an account. The individual goes to a bank and says he or she wants to open up a joint account. He or she receives some papers by a bank clerk to fill out, gives the bank some cash or a check, and receives a statement which may read "Pay to John or Jane or Survivor." If he is John, he is fairly sure that clause means that when Jane dies, he will receive what is in the account. However, he does not have the faintest idea of what it means in terms of income tax, gift tax, and estate tax consequences. In fact, he would be quite surprised to discover that it has any such consequences.

Joint accounts can be highly convenient, but they are also fraught with many potential dangers. What are the advantages of joint accounts? They are obviously very convenient for married couples. They also are convenient for an incapacitated senior family member who needs the assistance of a junior family member to make withdrawals to pay for the senior's living expenses. The survivorship feature offers the opportunity of avoiding probate. This advantage can assure a continued source of funds for a surviving spousal joint tenant following the death of the other spouse. Absent a joint account, the survivor could be low on funds pending settlement of the estate.

However, joint accounts also have disadvantages. A spouse named as a joint tenant could withdraw funds from the account and place the withdrawn funds in his or her own account, consume them, or give them away. The incapacitated senior family member might not want the funds in the joint account to go to the child who is the named joint tenant, but to be shared equally by that child and his or her other children who were not named as joint tenants. However, the funds go to the named joint tenant by operation of law. The discussion that follows examines the legal consequences of joint accounts.

Some states have laws spelling out the legal consequences of joint accounts. Most states leave it to the deposit agreement to define the rights of the joint holders of the account. The legal relationship can directly affect the various consequences. Although the legal relationship can vary, depending on state law and deposit agreement variations, joint accounts generally fall into one of three basic categories:

1. **Joint tenancy with immediate vesting.** Each joint owner, on the creation of the account, acquires an interest

in one-half of the funds deposited, and cannot withdraw more than his or her half without accounting to the other.

2. **Revocable account.** Each joint account holder may withdraw the full amount on deposit without accounting to the other.
3. **Convenience account.** One individual deposits all the funds and has the sole right to the funds while both are alive. The other individual may make deposits and withdrawals only as the agent for the other individual.

All three types provide for survivorship. In the case of the convenience account, the individual supplying the funds receives the funds if he or she is the survivor. On the other hand, if the other account holder survives, whether or not he or she receives the funds depends on the deposit agreement and local law.

Personal checking accounts are not apt to be of great concern to the estate planner because the amount in the account at any one time is probably not much more than one month's bills or living expenses. Savings accounts are likely to be more significant. In addition, time deposits, certificates of deposit, and money market accounts might be even more important. In a climate of economic uncertainty, the desire for security lures money into bank deposits. The deposits can be sizable, and the income tax, gift tax, and estate tax consequences equally large.

Income tax consequences. With respect to the vested-rights type of account, because each account holder owns half of the amount on deposit, each account holder is entitled to and should report half of the interest income. Income tax savings are possible if one joint tenant is in a lower bracket than the one furnishing the funds. Unearned income in excess of $1,700 (in 2006) of a child under the age of 18 is taxable at the higher of the child's tax rate or the parent's top tax rate.[47] If the depositors are husband and wife, and they file a joint return, they will receive no income-splitting advantage.

With respect to two other types of accounts, direct authority is scarce. However, the income would seem to be reportable on the basis of the amount earned by the funds contributed by each. If one furnishes all the deposits, he or she is chargeable with all the income. However, the bank will report all of the interest income on a Form 1099-INT to the one whose Social Security number is on the account. If a taxpayer receives a Form 1099-INT that includes an amount received as a nominee for the other joint tenant, the taxpayer who

[47] Code Sec. 1(g).

received the Form 1099-INT must report the full amount shown as interest on the Form 1099-INT on his or her income tax return. The taxpayer then shows a subtotal of all interest income. Below that subtotal, the taxpayer should write "Nominee Distribution" and the amount that belongs to the other joint tenant. The taxpayer then subtracts that amount from the interest income subtotal. The taxpayer must also file a Form 1099-INT, along with a Form 1096, for the interest earned by the other joint tenant. The joint tenant who received the interest as a nominee must give the other joint tenant a copy of Form 1099-INT. The joint tenant who received the interest income as a nominee should be listed as the payer and the other joint tenant as the recipient. If the other joint tenant is the taxpayer's spouse, the taxpayer does not have to file an additional Form 1099-INT for interest received as a nominee for his or her spouse.[48]

Ordinarily, the Social Security number of any one of the joint tenants is sufficient. However, if the choice is between adult and minor, the adult's number should be used. For a joint account of a husband and wife, in determining the number to be used, primary consideration should be given to who owns the funds in the account. If the funds are mixed, the Social Security number of either spouse may be used.[49]

Gift tax consequences. Where one owner funds a vested-rights joint account, a gift occurs of one-half of the deposit on the opening of the account. A gift could also occur on withdrawal if one joint tenant withdraws more than his or her half, unless the withdrawal is for the benefit of the other joint tenant.

With a revocable account, no gift occurs on opening the account, but a gift occurs when the joint tenant who did not contribute funds withdraws funds.[50] With a convenience account, no gift occurs on opening the account or when withdrawals are made as the agent of the joint tenant who made the deposit. However, a gift occurs if the agent withdraws funds and uses them for his or her own purpose, even with the consent of the principal.

If there is a gift, the $12,000 (for 2006 and indexed for inflation) annual gift tax exclusion,[51] applicable credit amount (unified credit),[52] and the marital deduction[53] can reduce or eliminate actual liability. For 2005 through 2009, the applicable exclusion amount for gift tax purposes is $1,000,000. This amount is not indexed for

---

[48] IRS Publication 550 "Investment Income and Expenses."

[49] Rev. Proc. 77-28, 1977-2 CB 537.

[50] Reg. § 25.2511-1(h)(4).

[51] Code Sec. 2503(b).

[52] Code Secs. 2010 and 2505.

[53] Code Sec. 2523(a).

inflation. Large deposits, especially time deposits, proposed or in place, can pose special problems and should be watched carefully.

Estate tax consequences. The pertinent estate tax regulation provides that a decedent's gross estate presumptively includes, under Code Sec. 2040(a), the value of property held jointly at the time of the decedent's death by the decedent and another person(s) with the right of survivorship.[54] It then defines property held jointly as including a deposit of money in the name of the decedent and any other person and payable to either or survivor. Thus, with respect to a bank deposit that meets precisely the definition in that regulation, the entire balance in the account at the time of the death of one of the joint tenants will be includible in his or her gross estate. This result holds true unless the executor is able to prove that some or all of the account is attributable to deposits the survivor made.[55] A revocable account would seem to be within reach of the regulation, although the exact words "payable to either or survivor" might not be used because the whole is payable to either or survivor.

Authority is lacking on the type of account that gives each joint tenant a vested right in half of the balance. As against the bank, either joint tenant may be able to withdraw the full amount. However, as between the parties themselves, if one withdraws more than his or her share, that joint tenant would be accountable to the other joint tenant. One could argue if under state law and the deposit agreement only one-half of such accounts belongs to each joint tenant, only one-half should be includible in the gross estate of the first to die.

With the convenience account, the full amount in the account should be includible in the gross estate of the principal and none in the gross estate of the agent. However, an estate planner should exercise caution. Determining the ownership of the funds depends on the facts and circumstances and applicable local law.

Estate tax consequences as to joint accounts of spouses are discussed at ¶ 315.02.

When the death of one joint tenant appears imminent, a more or less popular tactic is to withdraw the funds in anticipation of death. Although the other joint tenant could withdraw the entire amount, the more common approach is for the one who is ill to sign a withdrawal slip and deliver it to the other joint tenant. As a general rule, Code Sec. 2035 no longer requires inclusion in the gross estate of transfers made within three years of death. (Or, if the amount

---

[54] Reg. § 20.2040-1.

[55] Code Sec. 2040(a).

involved does not exceed the $11,000 (for 2005 and indexed for inflation) annual gift tax exclusion,[56] no gift tax is due.)

Code Sec. 2040, as noted under the regulation, refers to joint property held at the time of death. If the account is closed out by the survivor-to-be before the death of the other joint tenant, the amount will likely not be included in the decedent's gross estate. However, the U.S. Tax Court has held that if the account is not terminated under state law, the move is ineffective.[57]

Record keeping. Record keeping is important if substantial sums are to be maintained in bank accounts of individuals whose estates are expected to be subject to estate taxes. One way to make a record is to note on check stubs or other records who deposited what amount and who withdrew what amount. Alternatively, the parties might open two joint accounts.

> ***Example 3.5.*** Don James and Sandra Smith open two joint accounts with a written arrangement that James is to make deposits and withdrawals only in account A and Smith is to do so only in account B. They preserve the record of the agreement and comply with its terms.

.02 Property Owned by Married Couples

One-half of the value of any property held by a husband and wife as joint tenants with a right of survivorship, or as tenants by the entirety, is includible in the gross estate of the first to die, regardless of which spouse furnished the original consideration.[58] However, the U.S. Court of Appeals for the Sixth Circuit has held that this rule does not apply to joint tenancies created before 1977. See discussion below under the heading "Estate tax consequences."

Planning considerations. As a general rule, an individual should not create a joint interest in property with his or her spouse. If the individual wishes, he or she can transfer the property by will to the spouse rather than creating a joint tenancy, and do so with the assurance that the unlimited marital deduction[59] will exclude the entire value from estate tax. In the meantime, control of the property is retained for life. Of course, joint ownership has the advantage of avoiding probate, which might be an important consideration.

The couple should also consider the income tax consequences in addition of eliminating the probate advantage of joint ownership by spouses.

---

[56] Code Sec. 2503(b).

[57] *H.W. Grant Est.*, 1 TC 731, CCH Dec. 13,026.

[58] Code Sec. 2040(b).

[59] Code Sec. 2056(a).

If sole ownership is retained and transferred to the surviving spouse at death, the surviving spouse will have a stepped-up basis equal to the fair market value of the property at death (or six months later if the alternate valuation date is elected).[60] This benefit could be worth more than the probate savings of joint ownership.

Example 3.6. Janet and Ted Hansen are married. Janet buys a home, which the couple will occupy as their principal residence, for $150,000 in September 1980. She takes title in joint names with a right of survivorship. On Janet's death in 2002, the home has a fair market value of $1,000,000. On a sale by Ted at that price in 2006, his tax basis for computing gain would be $500,000 as to the half passing to him by reason of survivorship[61] and $75,000 as to the half which he acquired by gift[62] when the property was placed in both names in 1980. He would, thus, realize a taxable gain of $175,000 ($1,000,000 – $575,000 (basis) – $250,000 (amount excluded as sales proceeds from a residence under Code Sec. 121)) (¶ 2820). If Janet and Ted owned the home as community property, all of the residence would receive a step-up in basis on Janet's death.[63]

If Janet had taken title in her own name and devised the property to Ted, on her death the basis of the property in Ted's hands would be $1,000,000 and no gain would be realized on a sale at that price. The savings in income taxes, would need to be weighed against possible administration costs resulting from sole ownership.

The stepped-up basis rules are repealed for decedents who die in 2010. They are replaced by rules that allow the executor to increase the basis of estate property by up to $1,300,000[64] and up to an additional $3,000,000 for property passing to a surviving spouse.[65]

Life expectancy factors, the relative size of the estates, and other factors should also be considered before placing property in joint tenancy or in the name of only one of the spouses.

In many cases where joint tenancies between spouses exist, the couple should consider terminating an existing joint interest and vesting the entire ownership in one of the spouses. Such a termination could provide income tax benefits on the death of the spouse who owns the property. The unlimited marital deduction[66] allows a termination of a joint interest without considering gift tax consequences.

---

[60] Code Sec. 1014(a).
[61] Code Sec. 1014(a).
[62] Code Sec. 1015.
[63] Code Secs. 1014(a) and 1014(b)(6).
[64] Code Sec. 1022(b).
[65] Code Sec. 1022(e).
[66] Code Sec. 2523(a).

Still, placing property in joint tenancy could have important beneficial side effects where an individual owns a closely held business. The estate must meet percentage tests if the estate of the first joint tenant to die includes a closely held business and the benefits of any of the following provisions are sought: (1) special use valuation under Code Sec. 2032A; (2) an extension of time to pay estate taxes attributable to the closely held business under Code Sec. 6166; or (3) a redemption of corporate stock under Code Sec. 303 (with respect to a closely held business in the corporate form.

A business owner can remove one-half of nonbusiness property from his or her gross estate by placing it in joint tenancy. Thus, one-half of the value is removed from the owner's gross estate. This reduction in value can help meet the percentage tests, if it occurs more than three years before death.[68] However, placing the business interest in joint tenancy would likely be a mistake. Doing so would reduce the amount of the business interest in the estate and make satisfying the percentage tests more difficult.

> ***Example 3.7.*** John Cooper owns stock in a closely held corporation with a fair market value of $575,000. His gross estate is $2,000,000, all of which is held in his own name. His adjusted gross estate is estimated to be $1,900,000. He wishes to give $900,000 to his wife, Sara, and the residue, after payment of taxes, to a trust for the benefit of children of a prior marriage. Under these circumstances, if he were to make such disposition by will, his estate would not qualify for the benefits of either the Code Sec. 6166 extension of time to pay estate tax or a Code Sec. 303 redemption. If, however, more than three years before his death he placed $900,000 of nonbusiness property in joint ownership with his wife, his adjusted gross estate would be reduced to $1,450,000 ($1,900,000 – ($900,000 × 1/2)), and the closely held business would meet the 35-percent-of-adjusted-gross-estate test.

If the property placed in joint tenancy had increased significantly in value at a pace greater than that shown by the other assets in the estate, the estate might have a problem in satisfying the tests. Thus, the selection of property with relatively less appreciation potential is a factor the estate planner should consider.

Income tax consequences. Income tax considerations are usually of little importance in connection with a personal residence, which ordinarily produces no income. However, income tax considerations might assume significance if the parties file separate returns

[68] Code Sec. 2035(c).

and one spouse pays all the real estate taxes and mortgage interest and, thus, is entitled to the deductions.[69] Even with income-producing property, income taxes will ordinarily be of no consequence if the parties file a joint return. If separate returns are filed, income-splitting and the splitting of deductions might produce some current income tax savings. On the other hand, the filing of separate returns could increase the couple's overall tax liability.

On the sale or exchange of property held by husband and wife as joint tenants or tenants by the entirety, the gain or loss of each is determined by the difference between the tax basis of each spouse and his or her share of the proceeds or property received in exchange.[70]

Gift tax consequences. The creation of a joint interest either by one spouse acting alone or by both spouses is free of gift tax consequences by reason of Code Sec. 2523(d), which qualifies the transfer for the marital deduction. However, the estate planner should check state tax consequences because not all states have similar provisions.

Termination of joint ownership of property by sale, exchange, or otherwise is without gift tax consequences no matter how the property or the proceeds are divided.

Transfer of a jointly held interest in property from one spouse to another in a divorce settlement may escape gift tax either by reason of the marital deduction[71] (if the transfer takes place before termination of the marriage by divorce), or if the transfer is incident to the divorce it is deemed made in consideration of money or money's worth. The latter occurs if the transfer is made (1) under a written agreement in settlement of marital or support rights and the divorce takes place within the three-year period beginning one year before the agreement is entered into;[72] (2) under a divorce decree settling property rights if required by state law;[73] (3) in consideration of relinquishment of support rights;[74] or (4) for property or cash of equal value.

Without a transfer, a joint tenancy (or a tenancy by the entirety) between husband and wife will be converted into a tenancy in common on divorce. (See ¶ 310.04 for treatment of such conversion; see Chapter 24 on the subject of divorce in terms of financial planning.)

Estate tax consequences. As to joint tenancies and tenancies by the entirety, only one-half of the value of the jointly held property

---

[69] Code Secs. 163 and 164.

[70] Code Sec. 1001(a).

[71] Code Sec. 2523(a).

[72] Code Sec. 2516.

[73] *C. Harris*, 50-2 USTC ¶ 10,786, 340 US 106.

[74] Rev. Rul. 68-379, 1968-2 CB 414.

is includible in the gross estate of the first to die, regardless of contribution to acquisition costs.[75]

To the extent that property held by spouses as joint tenants, or as tenants by the entirety is includible in the gross estate of the first to die, it qualifies for the estate tax marital deduction.[76]

The U.S. Court of Appeals for the Sixth Circuit has held that the one-half inclusion rule of Code Sec. 2040(b) does not apply to joint tenancies created before 1977.[77] Under the court's view, such joint tenancies are subject to the general rule of Code Sec. 2040(a) under which the full value of the property is included in the decedent's gross estate if the survivor made no contribution. The *Gallenstein* decision has been followed by the U.S. Court of Appeals for the Fourth Circuit.[78] The U.S. Tax Court also cited the *Gallenstein* decision as support for a decision that was appealable to the U.S. Court of Appeals for the Ninth Circuit.[79]

The IRS acquiesced to the U.S. Tax Court's decision in *T. Hahn,* so the IRS will no longer argue that Code Sec. 2040(b)(1) applies to joint interests created before January 1, 1977, where the deceased joint tenant died after December 31, 1981. Rather, these joint tenancies will be subject to the contribution rule of Code Sec. 2040(a) as it stood before the amendments to Code Sec. 2040(b) in 1981. Therefore, a surviving spouse who did not contribute toward the purchase of the jointly held property will receive a step-up in basis equal to the full value of the property.

Because of the acquiescence of the IRS to the U.S. Tax Court's decision in *Hahn,* which cited *Gallenstein, Gallenstein* is a landmark decision. Surviving joint tenants who made no contributions can receive substantial income tax savings through a step-up in basis to the fair market value of the jointly held property at the date of the decedent's death. Such individual would wind up with a stepped-up basis in 100 percent of the property[80] rather than a step-up in only 50 percent of the property.[81] However, the surviving spouse in any case receives a stepped-up basis for 100 percent of the property held as community property.[82] Indeed, the court's decision in *Gallenstein* eliminated a capital gain of over $1.75 million for the surviving spouse. However, the step up in basis for property passing from an individual who dies in 2010 is subject to an aggregate limit of $1,300,000[83] and an additional $3,000,000 for property passing to a surviving spouse.[84]

---

[75] Code Sec. 2040(b).

[76] Code Sec. 2056(a).

[77] *M. Gallenstein*, CA-6, 92-2 USTC ¶60,114.

[78] *J. Patten*, 97-2 USTC ¶60,279.

[79] *T. Hahn*, 110 TC 140 (March 4, 1998).

[80] Code Secs. 1014(a) and 2040(a).

[81] Code Secs. 1014(a) and 2040(b).

[82] Code Secs. 1014(a) and 1014(b)(6).

[83] Code Sec. 1022(b).

[84] Code Sec. 1022(c).

In situations where the *Gallenstein* rule applies, the higher inclusion in the decedent's gross estate should not increase the estate tax because of the unlimited marital deduction.[85]

The court's decision could also affect an estate's qualification for special use valuation,[86] deferral of tax on closely held business interests,[87] redemptions to pay death taxes,[88] and the qualified family-owned business deduction.[89] The qualified family-owned business deduction is repealed for estates of decedents who die after 2003 and before 2011. Qualification for these benefits involves a test geared to a percentage of the gross estate, which would be higher as a result of the full inclusion.

Special considerations involving the residence. Joint ownership of the personal residence frequently involves nontax considerations. Joint ownership might be influenced by psychological and emotional factors having to do with each spouse's contribution to the maintenance of the home. The couple will usually want the surviving spouse to have continued occupancy of the residence. Family tradition and community custom of joint ownership can also play a part. Also, joint ownership can serve to insulate this important asset from the claims of creditors of either spouse. Nontax factors such as these can result in placing the residence in joint ownership despite possible adverse tax consequences. The $250,000 exclusion from gain on the sale of a principal residence by individuals,[90] can help diminish or eliminate the effect of the loss of a step-up in basis of one-half of property held in joint ownership on the death of the first joint tenant to die (¶ 2820). For decedents dying in 2010, the limited exclusion of gain from the sale of a principal residence will be applicable to a decedent's principal residence that is sold by the decedent's estate, any individual who acquired the residence from the decedent as a result of his or her death, or a trust established by the decedent that was a qualified revocable trust immediately prior to the decedent's death.

.03 U.S. Savings Bonds

A common asset found in estates of all sizes is the U.S. savings bond. Currently, only Series EE and Series I bonds may be purchased for cash. Series EE bonds are issued at a 50-percent discount from face value. The Series E bond, issued before January 1, 1980, was originally issued at 75 percent of face value. In all other respects, the E and EE bonds are identical.

---

[85] Code Sec. 2056(a).
[86] Code Sec. 2032A.
[87] Code Sec. 6166.
[88] Code Sec. 303.
[89] Code Sec. 2057.
[90] Code Sec. 121.

Series I bonds are issued at face value and accrue interest based on the rate of inflation. Interest is compounded semiannually. Series I bonds issued in January 2003 or earlier may be cashed in at any time after six months of issue. Series I bonds issued in February 2003 or later may be cashed in at any time after 12 months from the date of issue.

The yield on Series EE bonds is fixed periodically by the government. Because the income accrues, the redemption value increases monthly. Final maturity of Series EE bonds does not extend beyond 40 years. (Note: Prior to September 1, 2004 Series EE bonds could be exchanged tax free for Series HH bonds at any time up to one year after final maturity. This is no longer an option.)

The bonds are issued in one simple form of co-ownership: "A or B," which means that the Treasury will pay either A or B on presentation of the bond. If either A or B dies, the survivor is the sole owner.

However, they are also issued in beneficiary form. This form reads, "A payable on death to B." This form means that, during A's life, the government will pay only A. On A's death, the government will pay only B, unless A, during his or her lifetime, has substituted another as beneficiary. Thus, the interest of the beneficiary resembles a contingent future interest more than a present co-ownership interest.

Income tax consequences. Taxation of the interest on Series H and HH bonds is straightforward. It is taxable to the co-owners on a cash basis when received. The taxation of Series E, Series EE, and Series I bonds is a bit complicated.

The owners of Series E, Series EE and Series I bonds do not have to report the annual appreciation in their value until the bonds are redeemed or they have matured, unless the owners elect to report the appreciation on an annual basis.

The election, once made, applies to all Series E, Series EE and Series I bonds owned, as well as to any subsequently acquired and any other similar obligations sold on a discount basis.

The appreciation or interest is taxable to the co-owner who furnished the consideration, even though he or she permits the other co-owner to redeem the bonds (whether at or before their maturity) and retain the entire proceeds.[91] If the noncontributing co-owner surrenders the bond for reissue in his or her own name, the contributing co-owner must include the appreciation to the date of reissue in his or her gross income.[92] However, if the bond is reissued in the sole name

[91] Rev. Rul. 54-143, 1954-1 CB 12.

[92] Rev. Rul. 55-278, 1955-1 CB 471.

of the contributing co-owner, he or she need not include the appreciation in his or her gross income in the year of reissue.[93]

Savings bonds are an attractive investment for children under the age of 18. By having a child purchase Series EE or Series I bonds that mature after the child reaches 18, the rule that taxes a child's unearned income in excess of $1,700 (in 2006) at the higher of the child's rate or the parent's top rate is avoided.[94] When the bonds mature, the interest will be taxed at the child's tax rate.

Savings bonds can also be a tax-free way to pay for a child's college education. The interest on EE bonds issued after 1989 and on Series I bonds might escape tax altogether under Code Sec. 135 if the taxpayer pays for qualified higher education expenses (for the taxpayer, his or her spouse, or his or her dependents) in the year the bonds are redeemed, and his or her modified adjusted gross income does not exceed certain limits that are annually adjusted for inflation. The purchaser must be at least 24 years old before the date the bonds are issued. These bonds may be purchased in sole ownership form or in co-ownership form with a spouse.

An individual may purchase up to $30,000 face amount of Series EE or Series I savings bonds in one calendar year. The main attraction of such bonds is that annual appreciation can be deferred until the bonds are redeemed or matured. In addition, savings bonds are exempt from state and local income taxes.

> **Planning pointer.** Series E savings bonds reach their final maturity after 40 years. If the taxpayer has elected to defer reporting the interest, the entire accrued interest becomes taxable in the year of maturity. However, if the taxpayer exchanges the E bonds for HH bonds, the deferred interest need not be reported until the HH bonds are redeemed. Bonds held *more than* 40 years from the date of issuance may not be exchanged for HH bonds.

Gift tax consequences. The creation of co-ownership in savings bonds is free of gift tax. When a bond is bought in co-ownership form, the purchaser can cash in the bond and recover his or her money. Therefore, a completed gift has not occurred. The gift occurs when the noncontributing owner cashes the bond without obligation to account to his or her benefactor,[95] or when the bond is reissued in the sole name of the noncontributor. The $12,000 (for 2006 and indexed for inflation) annual gift tax exclusion is available for such

[93] Rev. Rul. 68-61, 1968-1 CB 346.

[94] Code Sec. 1(g) and Rev. Proc. 2002-70, IRB 2002-46, 845 (November 18, 2002).

[95] Rev. Rul. 55-278, 1955-1 CB 471.

gifts of present interests.[96] If the co-owners are married, the unlimited marital deduction is available.[97]

Only one way of giving away a U.S. savings bond will be recognized for federal tax purposes. The bond must be redeemed and reissued in the name of the donee—mere delivery is not sufficient.[98]

Estate tax consequences. The estate tax consequences of co-ownership of savings bonds is nothing exceptional. The bond's redemption value at the estate tax valuation date will be includible in the gross estate of the first co-owner to die, except to the extent the executor is able to show that the survivor contributed to the purchase[99] or the co-owners were married. In the latter case, only one-half of the value generally is includible in the gross estate of the first to die,[100] and that half qualifies for the marital deduction.[101]

.04 Safe Deposit Boxes

Many individuals hold safe deposit boxes in joint ownership, or at least as joint lessees. A joint safe deposit box does not transform sole ownership of the contents into joint ownership. All that is involved in a joint safe deposit box is joint access to the contents. If joint ownership is desired, the owner of each item must transfer it into joint ownership in a way that satisfies the local legal requirements. Generally, one can do so by a written transfer specifying who is transferring what to whom, in what form of ownership, and for how much, if anything. The transferor must deliver the instrument, or copy, to the co-owner. The co-owner must accept the transfer. The parties should also check to see if they must comply with any special local requirements.

.05 Securities

Joint ownership of securities (stocks and bonds) involves special legal factors, which differ from those involved in joint ownership of other types of property. The differences flow primarily from variations in local law. Superimposed on local law, are the stock exchange and brokerage house rules, some of which may stem from federal securities laws. In addition, the formal account agreements between brokerage houses and their customers might affect ownership rights. No special tax rules apply to joint ownership of securities.

One of the unique aspects of joint ownership of securities arises out of joint brokerage accounts. These aspects usually concern the

---

[96] Code Sec. 2503(b).

[97] Code Sec. 2523(a).

[98] *E.G. Chandler*, 73-1 USTC ¶12,902, 410 US 257.

[99] Code Sec. 2040(a).

[100] Code Sec. 2040(b).

[101] Code Sec. 2056(a).

formal agreement between the co-owners of the securities in the account and the broker. They often provide for survivorship. In some cases, the securities themselves will be registered in the names of the co-owners. For example, "A and B as joint tenants, with right of survivorship, and not as tenants in common," is one of the most common forms of registration. More often, however, the securities in the account will be registered in street name, that is, the name of a person designated by the broker. A street name account can involve legal risks for the customers if the brokerage house should go out of business or declare bankruptcy.

The Securities Investor Protection Corporation (SIPC) offers significant insurance protection in such instances. In any event, with the ordinary street name registration, either of the co-owners may deal with the broker as though he or she were the sole owner, which is not always possible if securities are registered in joint names.

Income tax consequences. If the securities are registered in joint names, interest, dividends, and capital gains and losses from the securities are generally allocable to each joint owner, proportionate to his or her fractional interest under local law. If a parent buys stock and has it registered in the parent's name and the child's name as joint tenants, the dividends and capital gains and losses are split between them. This approach can achieve the tax savings possible in income splitting between senior family members and junior members in lower brackets, without a complete transfer of the income-producing property, but only if the child is 18 or older.[102]

The same income tax consequences should apply where securities are registered in a street name if, under local law, each co-owner is entitled to an equal share of income. The IRS has not issued a ruling directly on the point, but a ruling on gift tax consequences might create some doubts. In general, the gift tax ruling provides that the creation of a street name account by a party who furnishes all the money results in no gift to the other.[103] If no gift occurs, the other owner's right to income could be called in question.

No income-splitting advantage usually accrues to married couples holding securities in joint ownership because they normally file joint returns. In those states having income tax laws that do not permit married couples to file joint state income tax returns, joint ownership might produce state income tax savings. For a high-income individual within range of the alternative minimum tax, joint ownership with someone other than his or her spouse could

---

[102] Code Sec. 1(g).

[103] Rev. Rul. 69-148, 1969-1 CB 226.

not only offer basic income-tax-splitting advantages, but it could also push him or her out of range of the alternative minimum tax.

Gift tax consequences. The general rules relating to gift taxes on creation and termination of joint ownership apply to securities transactions except for street name accounts. With the latter type of account, the IRS has adopted the position that no gift occurs when one of the co-owners of the account contributes cash or securities to the account.[104] A gift occurs only when the noncontributing co-owner takes cash or securities out of the account for his or her own benefit. If the contributing co-owner withdraws everything that is in the account and closes it, and has the securities transferred to his or her own name, no gift occurs. If the account is closed and the noncontributing co-owner receives something, to that extent a gift occurs.

If the co-owners contemplate that they will make contributions to a joint street name account, the determination of whether a gift occurs on termination can prove to be most troublesome. Part of the difficulty is that income and capital charges attributable to the contributions of each owner would apparently not enter into valuation of the gift. Furthermore, separating these items might be difficult. The better way to handle the situation might be to set up two separate joint accounts, preferably with different brokerage houses. Each person would limit his or her contributions to one of the accounts.

In accordance with the general rules governing joint ownership between spouses, the creation and termination of joint ownership of securities between spouses is without gift tax consequences.[105]

Estate tax consequences. The general estate tax rules are fully applicable to joint ownership of securities. The practical aspects of record keeping can take on an added dimension if a person with a joint brokerage account has been actively trading over the years and the other joint tenant has been a frequent contributor. Tracing and allocation can be most difficult, if not impossible without complete records.

¶ 320 TENANCY IN COMMON

In a tenancy in common, each tenant or co-owner owns an undivided interest in the property. The size of that interest, measured as a fractional part of the whole, can vary from slightly above zero percent to slightly below 100 percent. In most cases, the ownership interest will be proportional to the number of co-tenants. For example, two

[104] Rev. Rul. 69-148, 1969-1 CB 226.

[105] Code Sec. 2523.

co-tenants will usually each have a 50-percent undivided interest. Each co-tenant is entitled to a proportionate share of the income, if any. Each co-tenant may sell that portion, give it away, or dispose of it by will. (If there is no will, it will pass to the co-tenant's heirs by operation of law.)

For tax purposes, each co-tenant's share of the property is generally treated as though it were owned by him or her separately. A tenancy in common can be used for intrafamily income-splitting purposes. A father could, for example, put an apartment house that he owns into a tenancy in common with his children. He might wish to undertake this transaction when he has exhausted depreciation deductions. At that point, the tax shelter is gone and he is beginning to be taxed on the income at a higher rate. However, if the property is income-producing, income-shifting will not be achieved if the co-tenant is under the age of 18, because the unearned income of a minor under 18 in excess of $1,700 a year (for 2006) is taxed at the higher of the child's tax rate or the parents' tax rate.[106]

A gift will occur on the creation of a tenancy in common to the extent that tenants who have not contributed anything receive something, or to the extent that those who have contributed something receive a greater share than their contributions warrant. A discount from fair market value may be allowed because of the donee's partially locked-in position.[107] A gift could also occur on termination of the tenancy. For example, if the entire property is sold and one co-tenant receives more than his proportionate share of the proceeds, a gift occurs for the difference. The unlimited marital deduction permits creation and termination of tenancies in common between spouses without gift tax.[108]

When a tenant in common sells his or her interest, he or she will ordinarily realize gain or loss as though he or she held the property in separate ownership.[109] Tenants in common, generally, have a right, through appropriate procedures, to bring about a partition sale. Often, at such a sale, the property may be repurchased by those tenants who prefer to remain with the property. The IRS has ruled that in a situation where property owned by six tenants in common was sold at a partition sale and then repurchased by five of them, no sale occurred by the five, but the sixth did make a sale.[110]

When a co-tenant dies, the fair market value of his or her interest will be includible in his or her gross estate.[111] Here, as under

---

[106] Code Sec. 1(g) and Rev. Proc. 2002-70, IRB 2002-46, 845 (November 18, 2002).

[107] *J. Propstra*, CA-9, 82-2 USTC ¶ 13,475, 680 F2d 1248.

[108] Code Sec. 2523.

[109] Code Sec. 1001(a).

[110] Rev. Rul. 55-77, 1955-1 CB 339.

[111] Code Sec. 2033.

Propstra,[112] a discount should be allowable for the partially locked-in position of the interest. A partition sale may be held to unlock the interest, but a sale under those circumstances is not likely to command a fair market value price.

¶ 325 COMMUNITY PROPERTY

Eight states—Arizona, California, Idaho, Louisiana, Nevada, New Mexico, Texas, and Washington—have a form of co-ownership of property known as community property. Wisconsin has adopted the Uniform Marital Property Act, which is similar to community property statutes. While the details of the system can vary from state to state, with certain common exceptions, all property acquired by a husband and wife during their marriage, while they are domiciled in one of the community property states, is community property. It belongs to each of the marriage partners, share and share alike. They share not only in the physical property acquired but also in the income from the property and their salaries, wages, and other compensation for services.

At the same time, each spouse might still have separate property. They may also hold property between them in joint tenancy. Generally, they may adjust their property interests between their community and separate property. An estate planner should understand these basic factors about community property rules.

.01 In General

In general, community property assets retain that character even after the parties have moved to a noncommunity property state. However, they may adjust their property rights between themselves. Thus, couples living in a community property state might have acquired a community property bank account. When they move into a separate property state and take the proceeds of the account with them, the money still retains its character as community property. If they invest it in real estate in their new state, the real estate may be viewed as community property.[113]

On the other hand, generally, when a couple moves from a separate property state to a community property state, the personal property they acquired in the former state, whether tangible or intangible (such as stocks and bonds), retains its character as separate, joint, or other form of ownership. Any real estate acquired in a separate property state will retain the form of ownership assigned to it.

---

[112] CA-9, 82-2 USTC ¶ 13,475, 680 F2d 1248.

[113] Rev. Rul. 72-443, 1972-2 CB 531.

The distinction between what is his, hers, and theirs for any couple who has been domiciled in a community property state becomes very important from a tax standpoint. These basic general rules will afford some help in drawing the distinction:

- Property acquired before marriage or before becoming domiciled in a community property state retains the form of ownership it had when acquired—separate, joint, or other.
- Property acquired during the marriage by gift or inheritance by one of the parties retains the character in which it was acquired.
- Earnings of the spouses during marriage are community property.
- Property purchased with community property is community property, and property purchased with separate property is separate property.
- Property purchased with commingled community and separate property, so that the two cannot be separated, is community property.
- Compensation for personal injuries is generally treated as separate property.

Estate tax considerations. Married couples domiciled in a community property state may each have their own separate property in addition to their community property. They may also own property as joint tenants with right of survivorship, or as tenants in common. Their noncommunity property for estate tax purposes will receive the same treatment in community property states that it does in separate property states.

Community property calls for special treatment and rules. Community property is includible in the gross estate of the first to die only to the extent of the decedent's interest. This interest is ordinarily one-half of its value, but a discount may be allowed because of the lock-in effect. See *J. Propstra*[114] where a 15-percent discount was allowed in valuing real estate. This rule applies even though the survivor earned all the community property. Community property qualifies for the marital deduction.[115]

Community property includible in a decedent's gross estate may be offset only by expenses, claims, and deductions applicable to that particular property.

---

[114] CA-9, 82-2 USTC ¶13,475, 680 F2d 1248.

[115] Code Sec. 2056(a).

One of the basic choices that the estate planner and his or her clients have in a community property state is whether to hold property jointly or in community property form. With joint property or community property, only one-half is includible in the gross estate of the first to die,[116] where it can be sheltered by the marital deduction.[117] Jointly held property is not subject to probate, while community property is subject to probate. However, this advantage might be more than offset by basis considerations. In the case of community property, the surviving spouse receives a full step-up in basis in the entire property if at least one-half of the whole property is includible in the deceased spouse's gross estate.[118] By contrast, with joint property, only one-half of the property gets a stepped-up basis.[119] For decedents dying in 2010, the step up in basis is limited to $1,300,000 plus $3,000,000 for property received by a surviving spouse. However, the surviving spouse's one-half share of community property will generally be deemed to have been acquired from the decedent.

What happens when the survivor dies? With community property, the first spouse might have placed his or her share of the community property in a trust for the benefit of the survivor for life. The trust might allow the surviving spouse limited access to the principal of the trust if such access became necessary.[120] Thus, the surviving spouse might have essentially the same financial security that would have been possible had the survivor owned the property outright. On the survivor's death, the remainder of the estate could be made to pass to the couple's children or other beneficiaries without being taxed as part of the survivor's estate. If the couple used joint ownership, whatever was left of the property at the time of the survivor's death would be includible in the survivor's gross estate.

The special provision for the valuation of real estate used in farming or other closely held business provides for equal treatment of community and individually owned realty.[121]

Of course, the estate planner should consider other factors. State inheritance or estate taxes could be a factor. The estate planner should also consider the unified credit against the estate tax.[122] For example, if what is left in the estate of the surviving spouse after administration expenses and other deductions is less than the amount that the available unified credit will offset, the second tax potential with jointly held property would be of no real consequence.

---

[116] Code Sec. 2040(b).

[117] Code Sec. 2056(a).

[118] Code Secs. 1014(a) and 1014(b)(6).

[119] Code Sec. 1014(a).

[120] Code Sec. 2041(b)(1)(A).

[121] Code Sec. 2032A(e)(10).

[122] Code Sec. 2010.

If this amount will not be offset by the unified credit, the estate planner and his or her clients should give serious thought to community property estate planning.

Gift tax considerations. No gift occurs when property earned or acquired by one spouse becomes community property. Even if a gift occurred, the unlimited marital deduction would bar a gift tax.[123] While a conversion of separate property to community property might be a gift, it will be tax free. In addition, if community property is converted into separate or joint property, the conversion will be free of gift tax consequences.

If both husband and wife join in making a gift of community property to someone else, such as a member of the family, both spouses would be subject to gift tax liability on the gift of their half interests. Of course, each spouse is allowed the $12,000 (for 2006 and indexed for inflation) annual gift tax exclusion.[124]

.02 Interest in Qualified Plan

In a community property state, does an employee's spouse have a community interest in the employee's participation in a qualified employee benefit plan? The U.S. Supreme Court addressed this issue in *Boggs v. Boggs*.[125] The Court held that the Employee Retirement Income Security Act of 1974 (ERISA)[126] pre-empts state law that allowed a nonparticipant spouse to make a testamentary transfer of her rights in a joint and survivor annuity to her sons. The Court also ruled that ERISA pre-empted a state law claim by the sons to an IRA and ESOP transferred to them by their mother in the testamentary transfer. The Court stated that ERISA conferred pension plan beneficiary status on a nonparticipant spouse only to the extent that a covered plan required a survivor's annuity, or when a qualified domestic relations order (QDRO) awards the spouse an interest in a participant's benefits. The Court's ruling is contrary to the usual rule that state law determines property rights. However, when the state law conflicts with federal law, the federal law will control. Thus, nothing should be included in a nonparticipant spouse's gross estate for his or her interest in undistributed pension benefits covered by ERISA. If the nonparticipant spouse has an interest in a pension not covered by ERISA, the nonpartcipant spouse's interest in the account, as defined by local law, would be included in his or her gross estate.[127]

---

[123] Code Sec. 2523(a).
[124] Code Sec. 2503(b).
[125] 520 U.S. 833 (1997), rev'g 82 F. 3d 90.
[126] 29 USC § 1001 et seq.
[127] Code Sec. 2033.

.03 Life Insurance

Life insurance merits special attention. Life insurance involves complex rules that are not the same in all states. Different questions can arise as to whether the proceeds are to be treated as separate property or as community property under a state's community property laws. The answer might depend on when, where, and how the policy was acquired; who paid the premiums and when; and other factors. Once this question is answered under state law, federal estate tax law determines the extent to which the proceeds are includible in the gross estate and, if includible, whether the marital deduction[128] is available.

If the policy was purchased in a community property state and premiums were paid with community property, the couple was at all times domiciled in a community property state, the insured retained incidents of ownership in the policy, and the policy proceeds are subject to the community property claim of the surviving spouse, only the decedent's community property share, one-half of the proceeds, is included in his or her gross estate.[129]

If the policy, at its inception, was not subject to community property rules, conflicting views exist. Texas holds that if the policy was not community property at inception, it will not be converted to community property by the fact that later premiums are paid with community property. However, the proceeds are subject to the community estate's right of reimbursement for the return of community funds used to pay premiums.[130] If the insured retains incidents of ownership, the full value of the proceeds will be includible in his or her estate less one-half the amount of premiums paid out of community funds. California follows a different rule, under which the percentages of premiums paid with community property funds and those paid with separate property are computed. The proceeds are then divided up into community and separate property in accordance with those percentages.

To avoid this type of complication, the policy owner should consider assigning the policy and all incidents of ownership to the beneficiary, usually, the spouse. In drawing the assignment, the attorney should use precise language to indicate clearly that the policy owner intends to make a transfer of full ownership and all incidents thereof.

¶ 330 TIMESHARING OF PROPERTY

Multiple ownership and/or use of property is what is involved in timesharing. It has been applied to condominiums, townhouses,

---

[128] Code Sec. 2056(a).

[129] Reg. § 20.2042-1(b)(2).

[130] Rev. Rul. 80-242, 1980-2 CB 276.

hotels, motels, single family detached homes, campgrounds, and even boats and yachts. It may be used with new construction or with respect to conversion of existing structures. It can exist in projects devoted solely to timesharing as well as those with both timesharing and non-timesharing properties.

Usually, a vacation home sits idle much of the time. Yet taxes, mortgage payments, insurance, and maintenance costs continue full-time. The timeshare purchaser has all these costs pro-rated. He or she buys an interest or a right to use the property, but he or she pays only for a specified time. Further, the timesharing facility might have recreational amenities infrequently found in single vacation homes.

Thus, timesharing permits individuals to enjoy vacation facilities that they might not otherwise be able to afford. If affordable, owning all of the property might be considered uneconomical in terms of its projected use.

From a legal standpoint, four different types of timesharing arrangements are available:

1. **Time span ownership (TSO).** Each purchaser receives a deed to an undivided interest in a parcel of real estate as a tenant in common with all other purchasers. At common law, a tenant in common has the right to partition of the property. Therefore, the deed or agreement accompanying it should contain an enforceable waiver of the right of partition, because partition could destroy the timesharing arrangement.
2. **Interval estate.** A purchaser receives a deed for an estate for years in a particular unit over a recurring period and also receives a vested remainder in fee. Thus, the purchaser has an undivided interest in the unit in fee as a tenant in common with all other purchasers. To avoid merger of the estate for years and the remainder, because the purchaser owns both, the timesharing declaration must contain an express statement that it is the intent of the parties that the two estates remain separate and not merge.
3. **Statutory.** Statutes in some states create timesharing arrangements that allow ownership of a particular week or weeks in perpetuity.
4. **Licensing.** The licensor retains fee title and the purchaser/licensee has a bare right to use under specified terms.

The purchaser's title under the first three forms is insurable, as is the mortgagee's title under these arrangements.

Timesharing is an area where a need for consumer protection exists. The states of Massachusetts, Rhode Island, and Wisconsin have adopted the Model Real Estate Time-Share Act. It has also influenced legislation in other states.

The Federal Trade Commission (FTC) has two rules applicable to right-to-use plans but not to ownership timesharing. One gives the purchaser the right to assert claims and defenses against the holder in due course of notes given on an installment sale that he or she could assert against the seller. The other provides for a cooling-off period on door-to-door sales, which gives the purchaser a three-day rescission right.

Chapter 4

Lifetime Gifts to Individuals

Overview .... ¶401
Tax Factors .... ¶405
Basic Strategies in Lifetime Giving .... ¶410
Direct and Indirect Gifts .... ¶415
Gifts in Trust .... ¶420
Gifts to Minors .... ¶425
Gifts Within Three Years of Death .... ¶430

¶401 OVERVIEW

One of the things an estate planner looks for in analyzing a client's estate is whether a program of lifetime gifts to individuals is advisable. Lifetime giving is part of the estate planner's stock in trade. Planned gifts can provide income tax and estate tax savings. However, estate planners should not place estate and income tax savings before more pressing practical realities. Once these practical realities are resolved and a client begins to make gifts of money and other property, tax factors take on more importance.

No one should give money or other property away that he or she might need in case of a disaster or for normal living expenses. The ability to afford the gift should be the number one consideration.

Next, the estate planner should consider the donor's needs and desires. What satisfaction does the donor seek from the gift? Is the objective to escape from the management of the property? Does the donor hope to see the property used and enjoyed as he or she thinks it should be? Does the donor seek the secrecy that might be possible with a lifetime gift but impossible with a bequest? Does the donor hope that the gift will promote in the donee a sense of financial maturity or in some other way help in the donee's personal growth? The donor should consider what the real needs of the donee are, what the donee's level of maturity and responsibility is, and many other factors. These are factors that have very little, if anything, to do with tax savings. Nevertheless, they are important, perhaps even more important than tax factors.

Lifetime gifts are also a way of avoiding probate and eliminating the costs of bequests. Therefore, gifts help to conserve the estate over and above possible tax savings.

Gifts can flow from mixed motives. The motives are not always altruistic, kindly, and beneficent. Sometimes the purpose might be to put the given property beyond the reach of current or future creditors. The donor must be sure that the gift does not violate the laws against fraudulent conveyances if the objective is to place the donated property beyond the reach of current creditors. Sometimes, the motive could be a desire to bend the donee to the will of the donor. At other times, the motive could be a peace offering, or fulfilling a perceived social or business obligation, or expected political gain. Gifts based primarily on such motives are not likely to be influenced by tax or estate planning considerations.

When the donor is motivated primarily by benevolence, tax considerations and estate planning considerations are likely to assume importance. To the uninitiated, this fact might seem strange. When a client comes to appreciate the tax benefits that he or she can realize by planned giving, he or she understands that tax-saving considerations and strategies permit greater beneficence than would otherwise be possible. How and under what circumstances these tax savings are possible is the subject matter of the rest of this chapter.

¶405 TAX FACTORS

.01 In General

Once the donor has considered the practical realities of giving and has found good reason for making a gift or a series of gifts, the estate planner should help the donor evaluate the tax factors. The goal is to save estate taxes and income taxes at either minimal or no gift tax cost. The estate planner must also consider the generation-skipping transfer tax, which is discussed in detail in Chapter 27, for any gifts a client makes to grandchildren or other skip persons. Few roadblocks impede the goal of achieving estate tax savings by making lifetime gifts. Individuals may reduce their estates and save estate tax by making lifetime transfers gift-tax free under the $12,000 (for 2006 and indexed for inflation) per donee annual gift tax exclusion.[1]

---

[1] Code Sec. 2503(b).

The goal of saving income taxes, on the other hand, has been marked by many obstacles.

For example, the traditional use of *Clifford* and spousal remainder trusts as income-shifting devices has been eliminated. Generally, any trust property that can revert to the donor or the donor's spouse is treated as owned by the donor, and its income is included in the donor's gross income.

The kiddie tax has also been an obstacle to achieving income tax savings in the past and will be an even greater obstacle in the future. Under this tax, a child is taxed at the higher of the child's rate or his or her parents' rate on unearned income in excess of $1,700 (for 2006).[2] The first $850 of the child's unearned income is sheltered by the standard deduction,[3] and the next $850 is taxed at 10 percent.[4] In the past, the kiddie tax applied only to children under the age of 14. However, as a result of a change made by TIPRA, the kiddie tax applies to children under the age of 18, beginning with 2006.[5]

If the child is 18 or older, unearned income in excess of $850 is taxed at the child's rate, starting at 10 percent.[6] With the top tax bracket of 35 percent through 2010, a large spread separates the lowest 10-percent bracket from the highest bracket. State and local taxes can widen the spread considerably. In addition, the parents' income might be taxed at a marginal rate even higher than the nominal top rate, due to the phaseout of the deduction for personal and dependency exemptions[7] and the limitation on itemized deductions.[8] However, the phaseout of the deduction for personal and dependency exemptions and the limitation on itemized deductions is reduced by one-third in 2006 and two-thirds in 2008, and will be repealed for tax year 2010. Thus, taxpayers can save a considerable amount of taxes by making gifts that shift income to children over age 14.

Even if the child is under age 18, parents can use strategies to reduce the effect of the kiddie tax. For example, parents could place funds in investments that are designed to produce not more than $1,700 (for 2006) of current income, $850 of which would be received tax free by the child and the balance of which would be taxed to the child at the child's rate. The parent could place the balance of the funds in growth stocks, Series EE bonds, Series I Bonds, or other assets that do not produce current income. After the child attains age 18, the parents could convert the assets to income-producing assets so that the child could gain full advantage from a low bracket.

---

[2] Code Sec. 1(g).
[3] Code Sec. 63(g).
[4] Code Secs. 1(c) and 1(g)(4).
[5] TIPRA, Sec. 510.
[6] Code Sec. 1(c).
[7] Code Sec. 151(d)(3).
[8] Code Sec. 68.

Of course, parents should consider the investment aspects in addition to tax savings in changing the investments.

The income tax brackets of estates and trusts are highly compressed. This rate compression has an impact on use of trusts as gift-giving vehicles. For example, the $12,000 (for 2006 and indexed for inflation) annual gift tax exclusion is allowed only for gifts of present interests.[9] Code Sec. 2503(c) minors' trusts and custodial gifts are considered to meet the present interest requirement even if the trustee or the custodian does not have to distribute the income until the child reaches the age of majority. Income from custodial gifts is taxed directly to the child, whereas income from a Code Sec. 2503(c) trust is taxed to the trust if accumulated and to the child if distributed.[10] Because these vehicles generally are used to accumulate income, the more compressed brackets clearly favor custodianships over Code Sec. 2503(c) trusts. In some cases, custodianships are favored over Sec. 2503(c) trusts even if the child is subject to the kiddie tax.[11]

Imputed interest on loans with interest rates below the market rate. A lender is deemed to have made a gift to a borrower on a gift loan with an interest rate that is below the market rate. The deemed interest is equal to the principal of the loan, multiplied by the difference between the stated interest rate, if any, and the applicable federal rate.[12] A gift loan is one in which the foregoing of interest occurs because of donative intent.[13] On a gift loan, the lender is deemed to have paid the foregone interest to the borrower. The interest deemed paid is considered a gift, which is subject to the gift tax. The deemed gift is eligible for the $12,000 (for 2006 and indexed for inflation) annual exclusion.[14] The borrower is deemed to have received a gift, and then the borrower is deemed to have paid the interest to the lender.[15] The borrower receives a deduction for the interest deemed paid only if it qualifies under Code Sec. 163. Generally, Code Sec. 163 disallows a deduction for personal interest.[16] The lender must recognize the imputed interest income in his or her gross income.[17] The interest deemed to have been retransferred from the borrower to the lender may not exceed the borrower's net investment income for the year.[18] However, the net investment income limitation does not apply if the loan has as one of its principal purposes the avoidance of any federal tax[19] or for any day

[9] Code Sec. 2503(b).
[10] Code Secs. 661 and 662.
[11] Code Sec. 1(g).
[12] Code Secs. 1274(d) and 7872(f).
[13] Code Sec. 7872(f)(3).
[14] Code Sec. 2503(b).
[15] Code Sec. 7872(a).
[16] Code Sec. 163(h).
[17] Code Sec. 61(a).
[18] Code Sec. 7872(d)(1)(A).
[19] Code Sec. 7872(d)(1)(B).

in which the total outstanding loans between the individuals is more than $100,000.[20] A de minimis exception provides that gift loans of $10,000 or less are not subject to the imputed interest rules unless the borrower uses the loan to purchase or carry income-producing assets.[21]

Valuation tables. Code Sec. 7520 provides tables for valuing annuities, life estates, terms for years, remainders, and reversions for purposes of federal income, and estate and gift taxation. These tables use an interest factor based on 120 percent of the federal midterm rate for the month in which the valuation date occurs. These tables are effective for valuations on or after May 1, 1989. Whether or not to make a gift currently or later depends on the trend of interest rates, and the kind of property interest being valued for gift-tax purposes. For example, if interest rates go up, then the value of life estates and term interests will also go up, but the value of future interests will go down. If interest rates go down, the value of life estates and term interests will decrease, but the value of future interests will increase.

Undervaluation penalty. Undervaluing property for estate and gift tax purposes may result in an accuracy-related penalty (¶ 1005).[22]

Special rules for spouses who are not U.S. citizens. The gift tax marital deduction does not protect gifts made to spouses who are not citizens. However, a special $100,000-a-year gift-tax exclusion applies for gifts made to such spouses.[23] This $100,000 exclusion is allowed only for transfers that would qualify for the marital deduction if the donee spouse were a U.S. citizen. This $100,000 statutory exclusion is indexed for inflation. The exclusion for the year 2006 is $120,000.

> ***Note.*** This chapter's analysis of lifetime giving to a spouse assumes that both the donor and the donee are U.S. citizens.

For a discussion of the estate tax treatment of surviving spouses who are not U.S. citizens, see ¶ 1230.

.02 Gift Taxes: The Rate, Credit, Annual and Unlimited Exclusions, Marital Deduction, and Return

A single unified rate schedule exists with respect to gifts and to estates of decedents.

For gifts made in 2006, the top marginal estate and gift tax rate is 46 percent, applicable to amounts in excess of $2,000,000. The top

[20] Code Sec. 7872(d)(1)(D).
[21] Code Sec. 7872(c)(2).
[22] Code Sec. 6662.
[23] Code Sec. 2523(i).

rate is 45 percent in 2007, 2008, and 2009, applicable to amounts in excess of $1,500,000. The estate tax is repealed for estates of decedents dying in 2010. For gifts made in 2010, the top marginal rate is 35 percent. In 2011, the rules in effect before the Economic Growth and Tax Relief Reconciliation Act of 2001 are again applicable.

How the amount of gift tax is computed. The amount of gift tax payable for any calendar year is determined by applying the unified rate schedule to the cumulative lifetime transfers for all past taxable periods and the current calendar year and then subtracting the taxes payable on all taxable gifts made in preceding calendar years and quarters.[24] Prior gifts are computed under the unified rate schedule even where the gifts were made before 1977.

The donor must file a gift tax return on Form 709.[25]

Unified Gift and Estate Tax Rates for 2005 through 2009

Size of Taxable Estate or Aggregate Taxable Gifts* I	II	Tax on Amount in Column I	Tax Rate on Excess over Column I
$ 0 to	$ 10,000	$ 0	18%
10,000 to	20,000	1,800	20
20,000 to	40,000	3,800	22
40,000 to	60,000	8,200	24
60,000 to	80,000	13,000	26
80,000 to	100,000	18,200	28
100,000 to	150,000	23,800	30
150,000 to	250,000	38,800	32
250,000 to	500,000	70,800	34
500,000 to	750,000	155,800	37
750,000 to	1,000,000	248,300	39
1,000,000 to	1,250,000	345,800	41
1,250,000 to	1,500,000	448,300	43
1,500,000 to	2,000,000	555,800	45
Over 2,000,000		780,800	46 for 2006**

* To compute estate tax, the taxable estate and post-1976 taxable gifts are combined and an offset is allowed for gift tax on post-1976 gifts.

** The top rate 45% for 2007–2009 on amounts in excess of $1,500,000.

The applicable exclusion amount. An applicable credit amount is allowed against estate and gift taxes. The applicable credit amount is equal to the estate and gift tax rates multiplied by the applicable exclusion amount. The applicable exclusion amount for

[24] Code Sec. 2502(a).

[25] Code Sec. 6019.

gifts made through 2009 is $1,000,000 and is not indexed for inflation. The applicable exclusion amount for the estate tax for the years indicated is shown in the following table.

Phase-in of Applicable Exclusion Amounts for the Estate Tax

Year	Applicable Exclusion Amount
2006, 2007, 2008	$2,000,000
2009	$3,500,000

The marginal rate of tax is 41 percent on taxable amounts in excess of $1,000,000 (for 2005) and the top rate of tax is 46 percent (for 2006). Thus, only an five percentage point difference separates the rate of tax on the smallest taxed gift and the top rate on the multimillion dollar gift.

However, a big difference in the method of calculating the two taxes operates to favor lifetime giving over testamentary transfers, if tax savings are the prime consideration. These savings occur because the gift tax is tax exclusive whereas the estate tax is tax inclusive. However, a testamentary transfer might provide more tax savings in some cases through 2009. The reason is that the applicable exclusion amount for the estate tax is greater than the applicable exclusion amount for the gift tax.

The savings of a lifetime gift over a testamentary transfer are demonstrated in the following example, which ignores both the annual gift tax exclusion[26] and gift splitting.[27]

> ***Example 4.1.*** Peter Collins has made gifts sufficient to have exhausted his applicable credit amount (unified credit) and put him in the 45% transfer tax bracket. He has $101,500 to give to his adult son, Todd. Peter wants the gift tax paid out of the $101,500, which brings the net gift down to $70,000 ($101,500/(100% + 45%)), on which the gift tax is (at the rate of 45% of the net gift) $31,500. A $101,500 transfer at death (assuming the decedent's estate remained in the 45% bracket) would cost $45,675 in transfer taxes. Todd has $70,000 left from the gift. A legatee of a bequest would be left with $55,825.

Making gifts of property with appreciation potential also excludes future appreciation from transfer tax even if the donor

[26] Code Sec. 2503(b).

[27] Code Sec. 2513.

dies within three years of making the transfer.[28] Also, lifetime gifts can produce savings and benefits for the donor and his or her family in a number of ways:

- If the donor dies within three years of the gift, any gift taxes paid on such gifts will be included in the donor's gross estate. However, if the gift occurs more than three years before the donor's death, any gift taxes paid will be excluded from the donor's gross estate.[29]
- Administration expenses will not be incurred on either the gift taxes paid or the gifted property itself.
- If the gift is to a family member in a lower income tax bracket than the donor and the gift is of income-producing property, the give will cause a reduction in family income taxes. This tax benefit will be sharply reduced if the recipient is under age 18.[30]
- The income earned on the gift property, after tax, will be excluded from the donor's gross estate.
- State death taxes will be reduced.
- If the property is of a kind that generates tax preference income[31] and causes the donor to incur alternative minimum tax liability,[32] the transfer will relieve the donor of such liability.

In addition, one should not forget that the $12,000 (for 2006) annual gift tax exclusion[33] combined with gift splitting[34] can remove up to $24,000 per year per donee from the donor's gross estate without gift tax. The amount of the annual exclusion will be adjusted for inflation, which can increase the amounts that a donor will be able to give tax free during his or her lifetime.[35]

Lifetime gifts with appreciation potential may also be encouraged in the sense that the applicable exclusion amount allows the prospective donor to make substantial gifts without incurring gift tax and without donating needed assets. The applicable exclusion amount for gift tax purposes is $1,000,000 through 2009.[36] At the same time, this action would remove asset appreciation that would otherwise generate estate tax liability.

However, lifetime interspousal gifts usually do not provide any transfer tax savings because of the unlimited marital deduction.[37] The unlimited marital deduction allows a transfer at death without

[28] Code Sec. 2035.
[29] Code Sec. 2035.
[30] Code Sec. 1(g).
[31] Code Sec. 57.
[32] Code Sec. 55.
[33] Code Sec. 2503(b).
[34] Code Sec. 2513.
[35] Code Sec. 2503(b)(2).
[36] Code Secs. 2505 and 2010(c).
[37] Code Sec. 2056(a).

incurring estate tax cost. Thus, the prospective donor spouse might prefer to retain property during life rather than giving it to his or her spouse. Among other things, retaining property rather than making an interspousal gift would guard against the possibility that a later divorce would cause the donor to regret having made the gift.

Revaluation of lifetime gifts for estate tax purposes. In *F. Smith Est.*,[38] the U.S. Tax Court held that the statute of limitations provision of Code Sec. 2504(c) applies only to revaluation of lifetime gifts for gift tax purposes. It does not bar the revaluation of lifetime gifts for estate tax purposes. This result has been overturned by the Taxpayer Relief Act of 1997, effective for gifts made after August 5, 1997. However, in order for this provision to apply, the gift in question must have been adequately disclosed. Accordingly, the gift tax statute of limitations will not run with respect to a gift that is not adequately disclosed, even if a gift tax return was filed for other transfers in the same year.

The annual exclusion. In 2006, the first $12,000 in gifts (*other than future interests*) made to any one person during each calendar year is not taxable.[39] In other words, one $12,000 exclusion per donee per year is allowed. The number of exclusions is not determined by the number of gifts, but by the number of donees.

> ***Example 4.2.*** Assume that Dan Young gives $12,000 every year to each of his four children. He could make a total of $48,000 in gifts each year to the four of them without incurring gift tax. If Dan's wife, Eve, consents to gift splitting, these amounts could be doubled. What if the couple started an ongoing gift program extending over the four-year period beginning in 2006 and ending in the year of Dan's death in 2009: $384,000 ($48,000 × 2 × 4) in gifts could be passed tax free to the children. These tax-free gifts reduce Dan's gross estate considerably. In addition, Dan has removed the appreciation of the gifted assets from his gross estate. The larger the estate, the larger the estate tax savings. On a taxable estate that would otherwise be $4 million, taking advantage of the annual exclusions totaling $384,000 saves $172,800 ($384,000 × 45%)(assuming 2009 as the year of death when the applicable exclusion amount is $3,500,000). The estate tax on $4 million would be $1,680,800, which would be reduced by the unified credit of $1,455,800, for a net estate tax liability of $225,000. The estate tax on $3,616,000 ($4,000,000 – $384,000) would be $1,508,000, which would be reduced by the unified credit of $1,455,800, for a net estate tax liability of $52,200.

[38] 94 TC 872, CCH Dec. 46,648 (Acq.).

[39] Code Sec. 2503(b).

Of course, Dan could avoid the estate tax completely by making the gifts of $384,000 and bequeathing at least $116,000 of his property to his wife Eve.[40] His taxable estate would be $3,500,000 or less, and the unified credit would offset all of his estate tax liability.

However, Dan could have made additional tax-free gifts. Using the same assumptions as above, Dan might be able to reduce the size of his gross estate by $768,000 rather than by $384,000. How? If the four children are married, and their spouses are joined as donees, the number of annual exclusions is doubled. Each year, with Eve consenting to gift splitting, $24,000 ($12,000 × 2), tax free, could be given to each of the four children and their spouses. Thus, Dan could give $192,000 ($12,000 × 2 × (4 × 2)) away each year free of gift tax. A gift to two or more persons as joint tenants, tenants by the entirety (joint tenancy between spouses not severable by either acting unilaterally), or tenants in common is considered as a gift to each tenant in proportion to his or her interest in the tenancy. The rule would similarly govern a gift to husband and wife as community property if they were living in a community property state.

Basically, as long as the donor makes outright gifts, the $12,000 (for 2006) annual gift tax exclusion usually presents no serious problems. However, a problem could arise if a question exists as to whether the gift is of a future interest.

Code Sec. 2503(b) establishes the annual exclusion and the exception of future interests. In this context, a future interest means any interest that is to commence in possession and enjoyment at some future time. Whether the interest is vested (the individual holding it or his or her heirs are certain to come into possession and enjoyment) or contingent (possession or enjoyment depends on the occurrence or nonoccurrence of certain events) does not matter. In either case, the annual exclusion is not available.

Congress's stated reasons for enacting the future-interest exception were to eliminate the difficulty of ascertaining who the eventual donees would be and the number of exclusions available. In addition, the restriction reduces the difficulty of determining the value of their individual gifts.

In any event, if a husband gives the family residence to his wife for her life, and that upon her death the house goes to the children, the gift to the children is a gift of a future interest. Therefore, the annual exclusion would not be available.

---

[40] Code Sec. 2056(a).

If an individual donates income-producing property and the gift is restricted in any way that would effectively deny the immediate commencement of an income flow to the donee, the donee might be treated as having been given a future interest. In that case, the annual exclusion is not available.

However, these situations are not the most troublesome situations involving the future interest issue. The most troublesome situation occurs when a donor transfers full title to property with strings attached. When the gift is made through a trust with restrictions on the income interest, or when the property transferred is nonincome-producing, the future-interest rule may present special problems. An examination of the trust problems is presented in connection with the discussion of trusts, generally, at ¶660. There, the use of a *Crummey* power affording a limited power of withdrawal of income or corpus by the beneficiary is discussed. This power is a means of making the annual exclusion available in cases where the trust does not provide for the mandatory distribution of income at least annually and is not a trust for a minor satisfying the requirements of Code Sec. 2503(c) (¶425.04).

Unlimited exclusion—tuition and medical care. An unlimited gift tax exclusion applies to qualifying payments of tuition or medical care.[41] This exclusion is in addition to the annual gift tax exclusion.[42] The unlimited exclusion for tuition and medical care is permitted without regard to the relationship between the donor and the donee.[43]

The exclusion for tuition is limited to direct tuition costs and does not include payments for books, supplies, dormitory fees, etc.[44]

The exclusion for medical care is not allowed for amounts reimbursed by insurance. Medical expenses are limited to those defined in Code Sec. 213(d) (i.e., those for diagnosis, cure, mitigation, treatment or prevention of disease, or for the purpose of affecting any structure or function of the body).[45]

> **Planning pointer.** Use of the unlimited tuition exclusion merits consideration by an individual with grandchildren enrolled in college or post-graduate training. The parents would likely pay for their children's tuition. Thus, this exclusion effectively allows the grandparents to transfer funds to the parents without transfer tax cost. At the same time, this move trims the donor's estate over and above the means afforded by the use of the $12,000 (for 2006) annual gift tax exclusion.

[41] Code Sec. 2503(e).

[42] Code Sec. 2503(b).

[43] Reg. § 25.2503-6(a).

[44] Reg. § 25.2503-6(b)(2).

[45] Reg. § 25.2503-6(b)(3).

The IRS has ruled privately that the tuition exclusion is available for prepayments of tuition (e.g., prepaying twelve years' worth of tuition for elementary and secondary education) if the prepayments are nonrefundable and become the sole property of the school.[46] Prepayment may be an attractive option, for example, if grandparents may not survive through a grandchild's school years. By prepaying tuition, the grandparents can effectively transfer a substantial sum to their heirs free of transfer tax.

The medical expense exclusion might be of particular value in providing care for an aged parent. If the parent is elderly or seriously ill and not covered by insurance or only inadequately covered, he or she could incur enormous charges. Even if the parent has sufficient assets to pay the charges incurred, the parent might have to sell highly appreciated assets at a substantial income tax cost to do so. Thus, the heir-apparent might pay for medical care, with the informal assurance that the appreciated assets would pass to him or her on the death of the parent. Hence, the heir-apparent would receive a stepped-up basis in the property,[47] and the parent would avoid any income tax on the appreciation up to the time of death. However, the step up in basis for a decedent dying in 2010 is limited to $1,300,000 plus $3,000,000 for property received by a surviving spouse.

Of course, such calculations and planning require considerable emotional detachment and might not always be feasible. However, Code Sec. 2503(e) allows the possibility.

The marital deduction. An unlimited marital deduction applies to lifetime gifts[48] and to testamentary transfers.[49] For a gift by one spouse to the other to qualify for the gift tax marital deduction, the following requirements must be satisfied.

- The parties must be legally married at the time the gift is made. No deduction is available for a prenuptial gift.
- The donee spouse must be a U.S. citizen.[50]
- The gift usually cannot be a terminable interest,[51] but an exception applies for qualified terminable interest property (or QTIPs).[52]

While gifts to noncitizen spouses do not qualify for a lifetime marital deduction, such gifts may qualify for a $120,000 annual exclusion for gifts made in calendar year 2006 (see discussion above at

---

[46] PLR 20060200.

[47] Code Sec. 1014(a).

[48] Code Sec. 2523(a).

[49] Code Sec. 2056(a).

[50] Code Sec. 2523(i).

[51] Code Sec. 2523(b).

[52] Code Sec. 2523(f).

¶405 under the heading "Special rules for spouses who are not citizens").[53] The $120,000 exclusion for gifts made in calendar year 2006 is the statutory $100,000 exclusion adjusted for inflation after calendar year 1998.[54] It is allowed only for transfers that would qualify for the marital deduction if the donee spouse were a U.S. citizen.[55]

A gift of a life estate to one's spouse with a general power of appointment vested in the donee spouse will qualify for the unlimited marital deduction under the following conditions:

- The spouse must have the right to receive all of the income from the entire interest or specific portion thereof for life payable at least annually.
- The donee spouse must have the power to appoint the entire interest or a specific portion thereof to himself or herself or the donee's estate.
- The power must be exercisable by the donee spouse alone and in all events during life or by will.
- The interest or the specific portion thereof subject to the power may not be subject to a power in any other person to appoint any part of the property to any person other than the donee spouse.[56]

In general, transfers of terminable interests may be considered QTIPs if the donor so elects and the spouse receives a qualifying interest for life. The interest must meet these conditions:

- The spouse must be entitled for a period measured solely by his or her life to all the income from the entire interest, or all the income from a specific portion thereof, payable annually or at more frequent intervals.
- There must not be a power in any other person (including the spouse) to appoint any of the property subject to the qualifying interest to any person other than the spouse during the spouse's life.[57]

Annuities qualify as income interests.[58] Also, a spousal joint and survivor annuity qualifies for QTIP treatment as long as only the spouses have the right to receive any payments before the death of the surviving spouse.[59] QTIP treatment applies automatically, but the donor may elect out of QTIP treatment.[60] While annuities qualify, income interests for a term of years or life estates subject to

[53] Code Secs. 2503(b) and 2523(i)(2).

[54] Code Secs. 2503(b) and 2523(i)(2).

[55] Code Sec. 2523(i).

[56] Code Sec. 2523(e).

[57] Code Secs. 2523(f) and 2056(b)(7)(B).

[58] Code Sec. 2523(f)(2)(B) and Reg. § 25.2523(f)-1(c)(3)(ii).

[59] Code Sec. 2523(f)(6)(A).

[60] Code Sec. 2523(f)(6)(B).

termination on remarriage or the occurrence of a specified event do not qualify for the marital deduction.[61] A usufruct interest for life qualifies.[62]

Property for which a QTIP election has been made is subject to transfer taxes at the earlier of: (1) the date on which the spouse disposes (either by gift, sale or otherwise) of any part of the qualifying income interest,[63] or (2) the date of the spouse's death.[64]

A transfer by the donee of any part of the income interest will trigger a tax on the entire remainder interest without benefit of the annual exclusion.[65] The life income interest qualifies for the $12,000 (for 2006) annual gift tax exclusion.[66]

If the property is not disposed of before the death of the surviving spouse, the fair market value of the property as of the date of the spouse's death or the alternate valuation date,[67] if elected, will be includible in the spouse's gross estate under Code Sec. 2044.

The additional estate taxes attributable to the taxation of the qualified terminable interest property are borne by that property.[68] Unless the spouse directs otherwise,[69] the spouse or the spouse's estate is granted a right to recover the gift tax paid on the remainder interest as a result of a lifetime transfer of the qualifying interest[70] or the estate tax paid as a result of including such property in the spouse's gross estate.[71] The spouse is also entitled to recover any penalties or interest paid that are attributable to the additional gift or estate tax.[72] However, the spouse cannot recover from the remaindermen any unified credit used to offset the tax on the transfer.

The QTIP exception does not otherwise change the terminable interest rules.

Code Sec. 2523(b)(1) provides that the marital deduction is not to be allowed if the donor retains in himself or herself or transfers or has transferred (for less than adequate and full consideration in money or money's worth) to any person other than the donee-spouse (or the estate of such spouse) an interest in the gifted property such that the donor or such person (or their heirs or assigns) may possess or enjoy any part of such property after termination of the interest of the donee-spouse. Thus, if a donor is considering giving a 15-year term

---

[61] Reg. § 25.2523(f)-1(c)(1)(i).

[62] Code Secs. 2523(f)(3) and 2056(b)(7)(B)(ii).

[63] Code Sec. 2519.

[64] Code Sec. 2044.

[65] Code Sec. 2519 and 2503(b).

[66] Code Sec. 2503(b).

[67] Code Sec. 2032(a).

[68] Code Sec. 2207A(a)(1).

[69] Code Sec. 2207A(a)(2).

[70] Code Sec. 2207A(b).

[71] Code Sec. 2207A(a)(1).

[72] Code Sec. 2207A(d).

interest in property to his or her spouse and selling the interest after that term to a third party (i.e., a real estate developer), the donor should first sell the interest following the term to the third party for adequate and full consideration in money or money's worth, and then give his or her spouse the term interest that has been retained. This procedure is preferable to the reverse procedure of making a gift to the spouse of a 15-year term interest, retaining the remainder interest, and then selling it to the third party.

If the donor follows the latter course, in making a gift of the term interest to the spouse, the donor retains a remainder or a reversionary interest. Thus, the donor would come within the terms of Code Sec. 2523(b)(1). However, if the donor first disposes of the remainder interest to a third party for adequate and full consideration in money or money's worth, the consideration takes the donor outside the terms of the provision. When the donor later transfers the full term interest to his or her spouse, the donor retains no interest. Therefore, the donor would fall outside the terms of the retained interest portion of Code Sec. 2523(b)(1).

Another type of nondeductible terminable interest occurs if the donor, instead of retaining an interest in the property itself, retains a power to appoint someone other than the spouse to possess or enjoy any part of the property after the spouse's interest terminates.[73] The power need not be a general power of appointment.

A special rule deals with tainted assets. This rule applies to a situation where a donor gives a spouse an interest in a group of assets that includes a particular asset that would be nondeductible if it passed directly from the donor. In this case, the donor must reduce the marital deduction by the value of the nondeductible asset or assets.[74]

A full life interest given to the spouse, plus a power of appointment over the remainder that is exercisable in favor of the donee-spouse or his or her estate, will qualify for the marital deduction. However, it must meet the requirements of Code Sec. 2523(e) and the related regulations. The applicable gift tax regulations in this connection closely follow the estate tax marital deduction regulations.

The estate planner and his or her client face two basic questions in connection with the unlimited marital deduction insofar as it relates to lifetime gifts:

1. To what extent is it to be used, if at all?
2. If it is to be used, should the QTIP election be made?

[73] Code Sec. 2523(b)(2).

[74] Code Sec. 2523(c).

Lifetime use of the unlimited marital deduction affords no greater transfer tax savings than if used at death. However, using the unlimited marital deduction for lifetime gifts saves administration expenses and avoids probate of the gifted assets. The donor realizes no income tax benefits, assuming the property is income-producing and the couple files a joint return. A gift could provide some intangible psychological benefits. If the marriage fails, however, the donor spouse might regret having made the gift.

The possibility exists that the donee spouse might predecease the donor spouse. In that case, the estate tax marital deduction[75] would not be available. This factor might possibly serve as an incentive to procure life insurance for the spouse. It might also encourage lifetime use of the marital deduction, at least in amounts which, together with the value of any property held by him or her as separate property, would allow full use of the unified credit available to his or her estate. It could save taxes for the donor-spouse's estate if the donee-spouse predeceased him or her and the benefit of the estate tax marital deduction were lost. It would permit the donee-spouse to make a tax-free transfer to the children or other objects of bounty that the donor and donee might agree on. However, it would not guarantee that result, as would a QTIP.

The loss could be great if the spouse squanders the gift. Therefore, the donor might want to consider ways and means of reducing or avoiding this risk of loss.

A QTIP is one way of reducing the risk of loss. A QTIP limits the possible loss to the value of a life-income interest, while guaranteeing the interest of the children or other remaindermen. However, a QTIP is not the only way of minimizing the risk of loss. A life insurance policy on the life of the donor spouse might be a way of providing the children with some protection at a smaller cost than providing the donee spouse with a QTIP interest. The children should own the policy and be its beneficiaries.

One might ask what effect, if any, the unlimited marital deduction might have on the disposition of life insurance policies owned by the insured. If the insured is to use the unlimited marital deduction, whether the insurance proceeds are includible in his or her gross estate will not matter greatly, except their inclusion might add somewhat to administration costs. Further, if the donee spouse should predecease the donor spouse, and if the donor spouse has retained the policy and names his or her estate as beneficiary, the policy proceeds at the donor's death might help to alleviate any

[75] Code Sec. 2056(a).

liquidity problems his or her estate might have. Also, retention of a cash value policy might be important in aiding the donor's own financial security during his or her lifetime. The loan value of the policy, standing by itself, could be an important asset, especially because state law often protects life insurance policies from creditors.

Under some circumstances, the donor might want to make a lifetime transfer of a policy and all incidents of ownership to his or her spouse. If the donor makes such a transfer, the donee spouse will be in a position to transfer the policy to the children or others by will if he or she predeceases the insured. While the value of the policy at the time of the death of the donee spouse would be includible in his or her gross estate, the proceeds payable on the death of the donor spouse would not be includible in the gross estate of the donee nor in the gross estate of the insured on his or her death. The course to be followed in any given situation will depend on an analysis of the facts and goals. Another possibility is to transfer the policy to an irrevocable life insurance trust. If the grantor (insured) survives for three years following the transfer, the policy proceeds would not be included in the grantor's gross estate at the time of death.[76]

As to the QTIP exception, the donor spouse must decide whether the interest is to qualify for the marital deduction. The choice is in the form of an election made after a life-income interest has been created in trust (or other qualifying) form which gives the donee-spouse a right to income payable at least annually and with no right in any person to appoint the property to anyone other than the spouse during his or her lifetime.[77] While the donor makes the formal choice by an election after the fact, sound planning dictates that the donor give careful thought to the matter before making the election.

Although one can easily conjure up reasons for the creation of a life-income interest as part of a testamentary plan, justifying the creation of such interests as part of a lifetime gift plan is more difficult. To be sure, an individual who is in business or who for other reasons does not wish to expose all of his or her assets to the claims of creditors and who has no fears as to the stability of his or her marriage might wish to give his or her spouse a life-income interest in some portion of his or her assets. Also, if an individual believes his or her spouse has only a short time to live and is fearful of estate tax consequences (with the resulting loss of the marital deduction), the transfer of a QTIP interest to the spouse might serve a very good estate planning purpose in some cases. It might enable the spouse's estate to take advantage of the available unified credit[78] to make

---

[76] Code Secs. 2035(a) and 2042.

[77] Code Sec. 2523(f)(4)(A).

[78] Code Sec. 2010.

tax-free transfers to the children or others. Otherwise, the unified credit might be wasted.

Under both the QTIP and general power exceptions to the terminable interest rule, if the life-income interest is made terminable on remarriage or on the occurrence of some other specified event, the transfer is not eligible for the marital deduction.[79]

Whether the QTIP exception to the terminable interest rule is to be elected in connection with a lifetime transfer of an interest or whether the donor-settlor decides not to make the election will generally depend on the amount of unified credit available[80] to the donor.

> ***Example 4.3.*** Hal Irving has an estate of $5,000,000 in 2006. He has available an applicable credit amount (unified credit) of $780,800 (equal to an applicable exclusion amount of $2,000,000). For business reasons, he has decided to transfer $825,000 to an irrevocable trust to pay the income, at least annually, to his spouse Linda, with the remainder to their children. He decides not to elect the life-income exception to the terminable interest rule. Use of the available unified credit avoids actual payment of gift tax. On Linda's death, the property will pass to the children tax free without being included in her gross estate. If Hal dies in 2006, by use of the unlimited marital deduction, he will be able to transfer his estate to Linda tax free. He will still have available the applicable exclusion amount of $1,175,000 ($2,000,000 – $825,000) of unused unified credit, permitting him to make a tax-free transfer to the children or others in that amount.
>
> If he had made the QTIP election, the transfer to the trust would be tax free by reason of the unlimited marital deduction. He would be assured that the trust corpus would pass to the children. However, the transfer to the children would be a taxable event and could result in actual payment of transfer taxes on Linda's death, assuming the balance of Hal's $5,000,000 estate passed to her at Hal's death and remained intact. The unified credit available to Linda might not be sufficient to avoid payment of tax. Further, the applicable credit amount (unified credit) available to Hal would have been partially wasted.

The result illustrated by the above example is that a donor should not make the QTIP election without careful calculation of the ultimate tax cost. The donor should take into account the use or loss of use of the applicable credit amount (unified credit), as well as the ultimate disposition of the property involved.

---

[79] Code Sec. 2523(b)(1) and Reg. § 25.2523(b)-1. [80] Code Secs. 2010 and 2505.

Filing of gift tax returns. An individual who makes gifts other than gifts qualifying for the marital deduction,[81] charitable deduction (other than for split gifts),[82] $12,000 (for 2006) annual exclusion, or exclusion for tuition or medical care[83] during a calendar year must file an annual gift tax return.[84] As a general rule, the return must be filed by April 15th of the calendar year following the calendar year in which the gift or gifts were made.[85] However, an extension of time to file the donor's federal income tax return also acts to extend the time for filing the donor's gift tax return.[86] Under another exception, the gift tax return for the calendar year in which the donor dies must be filed no later than the due date for filing the donor's estate tax return (including extensions).[87] In the case of split gifts, a return must be filed even though a gift tax liability does not result (i.e., where the gift is not in excess of the annual exclusions available to the donor-spouse and the consenting spouse).[88]

Savings clauses. Savings clauses attempt to place a ceiling on gift tax liability in the event the IRS or a court places a higher value on the gift than was reported. That result may be achieved in a variety of ways. The question with such clauses is whether the courts will respect them or declare them void as against public policy. If the clause attempts to revoke the gift, it probably will be voided.[89] On the other hand, if the transfer is for consideration, and the clause calls for an increase in the sales price in the event of an IRS determination that the consideration was inadequate, the courts might uphold them as valid, as was the case in *J. King*.[90]

The U.S. Tax Court held a clause void as against public policy that called for a downward adjustment in the number of shares gifted if the value of the shares was determined to exceed the valuation placed upon them by the donor. The Court held the clause void even though it also called for an upward adjustment of the number of shares in the event of too high a valuation by the donor.[91] The IRS noted that the latter was unenforceable by the donee as unsupported by consideration.[92]

.03 The Split Gift

When a married person makes a gift of his or her own property to a third person, if his or her spouse consents, that gift will be treated

[81] Code Sec. 2523.
[82] Code Sec. 2522.
[83] Code Sec. 2503(e).
[84] Code Sec. 6019.
[85] Code Sec. 6075(b)(1).
[86] Code Sec. 6075(b)(2).
[87] Code Sec. 6075(b)(3).
[88] Reg. § 25.6019-2.
[89] *F.W. Procter*, CA-4, 44-1 USTC ¶10,110, 142 F2d 824.
[90] CA-10, 76-2 USTC ¶13,165, 545 F2d 700.
[91] *C.W. Ward*, 87 TC 78, CCH Dec. 43,178.
[92] Rev. Rul. 86-41, 1986-1 CB 300.

for gift tax purposes as though each spouse made one-half of the gift. A split gift allows the gift to be taxed at a lower rate than if it had been taxed as a gift given by one spouse.

Important tax savings and/or applicable credit amount (unified credit) savings are available through the use of the split gift. For example, the amount of unified credit used on a gift of $100,000, for a donor who had made no prior taxable gifts, would be $23,800, but the unified credit used on two gifts of $50,000 each would be $21,200, for a unified credit savings of $2,600. These amounts do not take into account the annual gift tax exclusion. They focus only on the unified credit savings and assume that the donors have already used the annual exclusion by making previous gifts to the donee.

Equally important, the $12,000 annual gift tax exclusion available for 2006, and the unified credit available to each spouse can be applied jointly. The annual exclusion per donee then amounts to $24,000 instead of $12,000. If neither spouse has used his or her applicable exclusion amount, the couple theoretically could give $2,000,000, plus $24,000, to a single donee in 2006 without having to pay gift tax. Of course, using up all their applicable credit amount (unified credit) in this way would be unusual. Most couples prefer to spread the gifts over a period of years to take better advantage of the annual exclusion, but the result indicated is theoretically possible.

However, each spouse may use his or her applicable credit amount (unified credit) against only that portion of the gift that is treated as his or hers.

Gift splitting is allowed under Code Sec. 2513(a) only under the following conditions:

- Each spouse was a citizen or resident of the United States at the time the gift was made
- The parties are married at the time and, if divorced or widowed after, do not remarry during the remainder of the calendar year in which the gift was made
- Both spouses agree to split all their gifts for the calendar year

Only gifts to persons other than the donor's spouse qualify for gift splitting. If an individual makes a gift of property in part to his or her spouse and in part to others, gift splitting will be permitted for the gift to others, provided that the latter is severable and its value is ascertainable.

Both spouses must consent to gift splitting and must do so within a specific period spelled out in Code Sec. 2513(b)(2). Generally, the consents must be filed after the year in which the gifts are made and on or before the 15th day of April of the year after the gifts were made.

The IRS has ruled that once one of the spouses has filed a timely return, and the due date for filing the return has passed, the spouses may not correct a failure to treat a gift as a split gift.[93]

The actual donor must file the gift tax return. The consenting spouse, who is only a constructive donor, need not file a gift tax return if his or her portion of the gift is of a present interest and is valued at $12,000 (in 2006) or less. The consenting spouse should file a gift tax return if his or her gift might be valued at more than $12,000 or might be viewed as a gift of a future interest, thus barring use of the annual exclusion.

Either spouse may revoke his or her consent at any time up to the time the gift tax return is due, but not afterwards. Consent is irrevocable if given after the due date.[94] Effective consent makes each spouse liable for his or her own, as well as the spouse's, gift tax liability.[95] Gift splitting, then, is not something to be entered into lightly. For example, if the marriage is in trouble and a divorce or separation is possible, the consenting spouse must somehow be protected against this joint and several liability for the gift tax on this constructive gift. Even if the consenting spouse has no gift tax liability, the consenting spouse should consider the effect of losing some of his or her unified credit.

.04 Estate Tax Savings in Giving

One can save estate taxes by giving away money or property during his or her lifetime. Of course, as with almost everything else in tax law, exceptions and qualifications apply. If an individual makes a gift but retains an interest or rights in the gifted property, the property may be included in the individual's gross estate.[96] Also, if an individual owns a life insurance policy and makes a gift of it within three years of his or her death, it will be included in his or her gross estate.[97]

Apart from these broad-based exceptions, gift giving is generally an effective way of saving estate taxes. Although a donor should consider the gift tax costs, one may make gifts under the umbrella of the annual exclusion and spousal gift splitting without incurring a gift tax liability. Further, the $12,000 (for 2006) annual gift tax exclusion[98] can serve to reduce the gift tax liability on gifts to an individual donee in excess of the amount of the annual exclusion.

As previously noted, an annual gift program with multiple donees will in time permit large wealth transfers that eliminate the estate tax with no gift tax cost.

---

[93] Rev. Rul. 80-224, 1980-2 CB 281.

[94] Code Sec. 2513(c).

[95] Code Sec. 2513(d).

[96] Code Secs. 2036-2038.

[97] Code Secs. 2035(a) and 2042.

[98] Code Sec. 2503(b).

If the donated property has high appreciation potential, the estate tax savings are so much the higher. Even if the gift is taxable and the donor uses up the applicable credit amount to avoid the tax or actually pays the tax, after the applicable credit amount (unified credit) has been exhausted, the donor ordinarily will be better off. If the donor makes the gift more than three years before his or her death, any gift taxes paid will be excluded from the donor's gross estate, along with any future appreciation.[99]

The applicable exclusion amount for gift tax purposes is $1,000,000 for gifts made through 2009. This amount is not indexed for inflation. The applicable exclusion amount for estate tax purposes is $2,000,000 in 2006, 2007, and 2008; and $3,500,000 in 2009. The estate tax is repealed for decedents dying in 2010.

Assets that an individual owns might appreciate in value, if not in real terms, in nominal dollars as time goes on. Clients who are now out of reach of the estate tax could be subject to the estate tax in the future although their wealth has not increased in value in real terms. Gift tax rates in 2006 range from 41 percent to 46 percent. The estate tax rate is a flat 46 percent (assuming the full $2,000,000 exclusion amount is available). The top gift tax rate and the flat estate tax rate drops to 45 percent for 2007, 2008, and 2009. The top gift tax rate will be 35 percent in 2010 when the estate tax is repealed.

Consequently, individuals who face the prospect of having almost half of their estates taxed at their death and who are able to make gifts to family members will find that lifetime giving is an effective way to save estate taxes.

.05 Income Tax Savings in Giving

Gifts can be an effective source of income tax savings. Savings will be generated if the donor is in a higher tax bracket than is the donee. Currently, there is a large point spread between the top income tax rate and the bottom income tax rate. The spreads between the income tax rate brackets provide a strong incentive for making gifts to children (other than those who are not at least 18 years old) and other relatives (such as parents) in low tax brackets to utilize the 10-percent and 15-percent rates fully.

The traditional use of short-term *Clifford* and spousal remainder trusts has been abolished by a revision of the grantor trust rules. However, tactics are still available for the financial planner to use in assisting the client to help children and parents in low tax brackets enjoy income tax savings.

---

[99] Code Sec. 2035(b).

Grantor trust rules. The traditional use of short-term or *Clifford* trusts and spousal remainder trusts has been effectively eliminated. Code Sec. 673 provides that, for trusts created by transfers after March 1, 1986, the grantor of a trust is treated as the owner (and is taxable on the income) of any portion of the trust in which he or she has a reversionary interest in either the corpus or income, if, as of the inception of that portion, the value of the interest exceeds five percent of the value of such portion. However, this rule has one narrow exception: the grantor will not be taxable if he or she retains a reversionary interest that takes effect only on the death of a lineal descendant beneficiary under age 21. This exception, along with trusts for minors generally, is discussed below. In addition, a remainder interest in the grantor's spouse is treated as being held by the grantor, giving him or her the equivalent of a reversionary interest.

As noted above, for the grantor to be taxed on the trust income, his reversionary interest must exceed five percent of the value of the trust or trust portion at inception. This value is computed using IRS tables under Code Sec. 7520. The interest factor under these tables changes monthly. This reversion rule always had been of little practical value, but it is of even less value when interest rates are low. Thus, the rule appears to be useful only with very young beneficiaries.

The lineal descendant exception permits the grantor to retain a reversionary interest without being taxed as the grantor if the trust is for the benefit of a lineal descendant (child, grandchild, great-grandchild) and the reversion is to take place only on the death of the beneficiary before age 21.[100] This exception would seem to be of no practical value in the normal course of events where the beneficiary is likely to attain age 21.

What about a beneficiary who suffers from a terminal illness but has not reached the stage where death is imminent? The exception could be of significant tax-saving value in such case, especially if the grantor is in a combined federal, state, and local tax bracket that is 20 percentage points or more above the beneficiary's bracket. This situation would be the case for grantors in the highest income tax brackets.

An individual in a low tax bracket may nevertheless have substantial wealth and be in a position to help other family members financially through the use of a reversionary trust of short duration. The individuals to be helped might be in a higher tax bracket.

---

[100] Code Sec. 673(b).

Example 4.4. Brian and Susan Taylor are married and file a joint return for 2006 showing taxable income of $34,000, which places them in the 15% marginal tax bracket. The Taylors also have $50,000 of income that is exempt from federal, state, and local tax. The Taylors have a net worth, not including residences, of over $1,000,000. Susan's sister, Brenda Doyle, is a widow with two minor children. Doyle claims head-of-household status and has taxable income of $50,000, which places her in a marginal bracket of 25%. The Taylors wish to provide Doyle with some financial assistance, at least until the children cease to be dependent. The Taylors set up a reversionary trust for a term of 10 years, funding it at the rate of $24,000 annually with gift splitting, strategically timed at the end of one year and the beginning of the next year so that $48,000 is working for her within the first week of the trust, using tax-exempt bonds that yield 4%. When the trust is fully funded with $120,000 after four years and one week, the tax-exempt income generates $4,800 ($120,000 × 4%) annually, the equivalent of a taxable yield of $6,400 in her tax bracket.

The Taylors could retain the tax-exempt bonds themselves and make an annual gift to Susan's sister of the yield. However, the trust provides a measure of security for the sister, a commitment which would survive the death of the Taylors. At the same time, the trust funds may provide a measure of security for the Taylors to the extent that the income and corpus are placed beyond the reach of their creditors.

Other uses of trusts by individuals in low tax brackets might be possible. A young adult with significant assets might want to establish a trust to contribute to the support of grandparents whom his or her parents have been supporting, with a resulting net savings to the family as a unit. This situation might occur where the young adult's parents are in the highest marginal bracket while his or her tax rate is 15 percent. To the extent of every dollar of support furnished by the child for the grandparents, his or her parents would be relieved of a dollar of support.

Possible ways of achieving family tax savings include having a family member in a low income tax bracket make use of a reversionary trust for family welfare purposes.

Kiddie tax. Despite popular conceptions to the contrary, one can still achieve significant intra-family savings by shifting income-producing assets to children, even if the income is subject to the kiddie tax.[101] However, TIPRA has changed the ground rules for the

[101] Code Sec. 1(g).

kiddie tax. Starting in 2006, the tax applies to children under the age of 18, not 14.[102]

The kiddie tax separates a child's unearned income into three parts. For 2006, assuming the child has no earned income and no itemized deductions, the breakdown is as follows:

100% tax-free income: Unearned income up to $850, sheltered by child's special $850 standard deduction	$ 850
Income subject to tax at the 10% rate	$ 850
	Unearned income over
Net unearned income subject to tax at parental rate	$1,700

At low investment-return rates, a fairly large gift of assets can be made without coming close to the $1,700 limit.

If the child's unearned income already is substantially above the net unearned income limit, a parent can still possibly reduce overall family income taxes by making gifts of property designed to produce income or profit in the future, after the child is age 18 or over. Such gifts include the following:

- Growth stock or growth mutual funds that have low current dividends but that are expected to increase in value (and dividend yield) over the long term
- Stock in the family business, which the corporation can redeem after the child is free of the kiddie tax
- Assets that produce no income currently, but that can result in substantial gains in the future (e.g., prime raw land)
- Series EE bonds or Series I, on which the tax on accruing interest may be deferred until the bonds are redeemed

Parents may elect to include directly on their return the income of certain children who are subject to the kiddie tax. A child who is under age 18 is not required to file a return if parents elect to include the child's gross income on the parents' return.[103] The election can be made only if the child's income was more than $850 and less than $8,500 and consists of only interest, dividends, and Alaska Permanent Fund dividends; and if the child has not made estimated tax payments; and is not subject to backup withholding (see instructions to IRS Form 8814 for additional requirements). In addition to being

[102] TIPRA, Sec. 510.

[103] Code Sec. 1(g)(7).

taxed on the child's income, parents who make this election must pay an amount equal to the lesser of $85 ($850 × 10%) (2006) or 10 percent of the excess of the child's income over $850 (2006).[104] These amounts are indexed for inflation. The parents must also treat any tax-exempt interest from specified private activity bonds as a tax preference item of the parents in computing the alternative minimum tax.[105]

> **Planning pointer.** Electing out of kiddie tax simplifies tax filing chores, but it may not be a wise move. The parents' adjusted gross income will increase, which could cost the parents deductions and loss of other tax breaks under various adjusted gross income-based phaseouts. In addition, the election may increase the family's state income tax.

.06 Incomplete Gifts

No gift, no income splitting, and no gift tax occur unless the gift is complete and bona fide. The general rules for determining this require the following:

- A competent donor and donee
- A clear intent to make a gift
- An irrevocable transfer of legal title barring further control by the donor
- A delivery to the donee of the gift or of evidence of title—such as a deed or stock certificate
- Acceptance of the gift by the donee[106]

Gifts in which the donor reserves some interest in or power over the property, which result in the gifts being treated as incomplete, occur mostly in connection with transfers in trust (discussed at ¶420). However, the principles examined there usually apply to other types of gifts as well. One must be careful of gifts in which the donor retains a right to revoke the gift without the donee or anybody else having any say about it. No completed gift occurs in such a case.

A gift is not necessarily considered incomplete, however, if the donor reserves the right to reacquire the property if the donee predeceases the donor. That type of transaction is called a possibility of reverter, which reduces the gift's value, but does not make it incomplete.

Similarly, if the donor retains a life estate in the property and gives only a remainder interest, the gift would be complete. However,

---

[104] Code Sec. 1(g)(7)(B)(ii)(II).

[105] Code Sec. 57(a)(5).

[106] See *R.W. Hite, Sr., Est.*, 49 TC 580, CCH Dec. 28,871, spelling out bona fide gift requirements.

the value of the gift, for gift tax purposes, would be computed by consulting IRS valuation tables under Code Sec. 7520.

Promise of a gift. In the case of a promise that is legally enforceable under state law to transfer property for less than adequate and full consideration in money or money's worth, the promisor makes a completed gift on the date when the promise is binding and determinable in value rather than when the promised payment is actually made.[107]

Gifts by check or note. The IRS has always maintained that a gift of the donor's own check to a noncharitable donee is not complete until it is paid, certified, accepted by the drawee or negotiated to a third party for value. Until such time, the gift is revocable.[108] A gift of a check made in December of one year that did not clear until January 2 of the following year has been treated as made in the earlier year. The taxpayer established intent to make a gift, made an unconditional delivery of the check, and presented the check for payment within the earlier year and within a reasonable time of issuance in *Metzger*.[109] Based on its defeat in the Fourth Circuit, the IRS has conceded the application of the relation-back doctrine to noncharitable gifts under the circumstances of the *Metzger* decision.[110] However, in *Estate of Newman*,[111] the U.S. Court of Appeals for the District of Columbia ruled that checks written by the decedent's attorney-in-fact before the decedent's death but paid to noncharitable donees after the decedent's death were included in the decedent's gross estate. The Court reasoned that the checks were not completed gifts because the decedent had the power to revoke the gifts before the bank paid the checks. The key difference between the decisions in *Metzger* and *Newman* is that the donor was still alive at the time the bank paid checks in *Metzger* but was deceased at the time the bank paid the checks in *Newman*.

A gift of the donor's own unenforceable note is not complete until it is paid or transferred for value. This result has been upheld even where a note is secured by a real estate mortgage.[112] However, this particular ruling seems open to question. A gift of a donor's own note that is legally enforceable under state law is complete on the date when the promise is binding and determinable in value, rather than when the note is paid.[113]

---

[107] Rev. Rul. 84-25, 1984-1 CB 191.

[108] Rev. Rul. 67-396, 1967-2 CB 351; *D.F. McCarthy*, CA-7, 86-2 USTC ¶13,700, 806 F2d 129; *J.M. Gagliardi Est.*, 89 TC 1207, CCH Dec. 44,393.

[109] *A.F. Metzger Est.*, CA-4, 94-2 USTC ¶60,179.

[110] Rev. Rul. 96-56, IRB 1996-50, 7.

[111] 99-2 USTC ¶60,358, 203 F3d 53, (1999) aff'g 111 TC 81 (1998).

[112] IRS Letter Ruling 8119003, February 10, 1981.

[113] Rev. Rul. 84-25, 1984-1 CB 191.

¶410 BASIC STRATEGIES IN LIFETIME GIVING

A number of factors involved in lifetime giving suggest the existence of basic strategies. These concern whether or not a gift, made under specific circumstances, would be economically wise, how the applicable credit amount,[114] annual exclusion,[115] marital deduction,[116] and gift splitting[117] may be used to their maximum advantage, and whether a gift of cash or a gift of income-producing property should be made. This section focuses on these and other factors as they apply.

Lifetime gifts may be drawn into the donor's gross estate if he or she retains a life income interest in the gifted property[118]—an interest that does not in fact end before his or her death—or if he or she disposes of such an interest within three years of death,[119] as discussed in ¶1005.

One of the basic factors to be considered by a donor is the income tax cost of making a gift in cash as compared to a gift of income-producing property yielding the same amount as the cash gift, assuming no income tax liability on the part of the donee. The income tax cost will vary with the income tax bracket of the donor. The following table (Exhibit 3) compares the income tax cost of a yearly gift of $1,000 with that of a gift of property yielding $1,000, assuming no income tax liability for the donee. However, if the donee is under the age of 18, the first $850 of the unearned income would be tax free, the next $850 (2006) of the unearned income would be taxable at 10 percent, and the child's unearned income in excess of $1,700 (2006) would be taxable at his or her parent's top rate.[120] These amounts are indexed to inflation.

The table assumes that the donor possesses income-producing property with a high enough yield to provide sufficient income after taxes in the donor's particular bracket to enable the donor to make a gift of $1,000. Alternatively, the donor, instead of making a gift of cash, gives the donee enough income-producing property to provide the donee with $1,000 in income.

---

[114] Code Secs. 2010 and 2505.
[115] Code Sec. 2503(b).
[116] Code Sec. 2523(a).
[117] Code Sec. 2513(a).
[118] Code Sec. 2036(a).
[119] Code Sec. 2035(a).
[120] Code Sec. 1(g).

Exhibit 3

Comparison of Cash Gift with Gift of Income Property for Income Tax Purposes

Donor's Top Tax Rate	Income Needed to Net $1,000 After Taxes	Income from Gift Property	Income Kept by Donor	Donor's After-Tax Income
10%	$1,111	$1,000	$111	$100
15%	$1,176	$1,000	$176	$150
25%	$1,333	$1,000	$333	$250
28%	$1,389	$1,000	$389	$280
33%	$1,493	$1,000	$493	$330
35%	$1,538	$1,000	$538	$350

This table illustrates that, in all tax brackets, a gift of income-producing property is better than a gift of cash, from the donor's standpoint, in that the donor avoids the income tax on the income from the property.

A cash gift of $1,000 (and, indeed, a gift of as much as $12,000 or $24,000 with gift splitting[121]) may be made without gift tax in 2006,[122] while a gift of property sufficient to produce an annual yield of $1,000 might result in gift tax liability. Assuming a yield of less than 8.33 percent, a gift of more than $12,000 would be required. With gift splitting, there would be no tax unless the yield were less than 4.17 ($1,000 ÷ $24,000) percent.

.01 What Types of Property to Give

Selecting the right property for the gift is an important part of any planned gift strategy. Listing the categories of property with gift possibilities is often helpful:

- **Personal property.** Art objects, business interests, cash, certificates of deposit, contract rights, copyrights, estate and trust interests, interests in pension or profit-sharing plans, jewelry, joint property interests, mortgages (on real estate and personal property), notes, patents, receivables, securities (stocks, bonds, mutual fund shares, investment contracts, and limited partnership interests), trademarks, and personal effects, autos, and other types of tangible property.
- **Real estate.** Income-producing property, joint tenancies, leases, residences (condominiums and interests in cooperative

[121] Code Sec. 2513(a).

[122] Code Sec. 2503(b).

apartments included), vacant land, vacation homes, and various rights in real estate, including easements of access, light, and air.

- **Life insurance and annuities.** Cash values, refunds, and remainders.

In selecting gift property, these are the major general considerations:

- **Low gift tax value—high estate tax value.** Usually, an estate planner wants to help the client to reduce estate taxes at minimum gift tax cost. Thus, the client should select property that will probably have low gift tax value and high estate tax value. Property with a low present value and a high appreciation potential meets this test.
- **Appreciated property.** A gift of appreciated property from an individual in a high tax bracket to a family member in a lower tax bracket can reduce the effective cost of a gift. For example, assume that an individual owns ordinary income property that has a cost basis of $2,000 and is worth $12,000. If he or she is in the 35-percent tax bracket for 2006 and sells the property, the tax on the transaction would be $3,500. Assume that he or she gives that property to his or her parents, who are in the 15-percent bracket. If they sell the property, they will have to pay a tax of $1,500, which results in a net income tax savings of $2,000. However, sometimes retaining appreciated property until death to get a stepped-up basis[123] might be better, unless the income tax savings are offset by added estate taxes. However, for property acquired from a decedent dying in 2010, the step up in basis will be limited to $1,300,000 plus $3,000,000 for property received by a surviving spouse.
- **Property with growth potential.** The client should consider giving property that is most likely to appreciate and cause donor/parent estate tax problems if retained.
- **Assets not likely to be sold.** If the gift property is not likely to be sold by the donee at any foreseeable time, even though the property may have appreciated in value, a stepped-up basis on the death of the owner may be of little or no importance.
- **High income-producing property.** Usually, an estate planner will want to recommend that a client in a high tax bracket select a gift of high income-producing property to give to a family member in a lower bracket, as long as the donee is age 18 or older. However, if the donee is in a higher

[123] Code Sec. 1014(a).

bracket than the donor (gift from a retired parent to a middle-aged child), a gift of low-yield growth-type property might be better.

- **Property not readily subject to controlled testamentary disposition.** Property that might present problems for the executor or trustee of an estate, such as property that is difficult to value, sell, or divide up, is apt to be good for gifts.
- **Shrinking or wasting assets.** Assets that shrink in value with the passage of time, such as copyrights, patents, leaseholds, and mineral rights, are not usually good to give as gifts.

These and other factors affect the selection of specific types of property:

- **Art objects, antiques, and jewelry.** These objects are apt to be good for lifetime giving, because they fall within the scope of the sixth major general consideration listed above. They will ordinarily be frozen assets in the estate, and they can present problems of valuation. Also, they raise questions as to whether they are to be sold or retained and, if retained, to whom they should be given if not the subject of a specific legacy.
- **Business interests.** Interests in a closely held business can usually be given away without adversely affecting the donor's control. Income-splitting benefits may be achieved, especially if the business is in partnership or corporate form. Stock in an S corporation is especially good for giving because it causes corporate income to be passed through to the donees. Likewise, gifts of interests in a family limited partnership would cause income to be passed through to the donees.
- **Family residence.** A lifetime gift of the family residence to one's spouse may afford a means of enabling the donee to take advantage of the $1,000,000 applicable exclusion amount of unified credit in making gifts to children, if cash or cash equivalents are not available. A lifetime gift of the residence to a spouse may be contra-indicated if the owner-spouse has a low basis, is elderly, expects to predecease the other spouse, and has a sizable amount of appreciation in the house. Upon death, the residence would receive a stepped-up basis[124] that would eliminate all income tax liability for appreciation up to the time of death. However, for decedents dying in 2010, the step up in basis will be limited to $1,300,000 plus $3,000,000 for

[124] Code Sec. 1014(a).

property received by a surviving spouse. Both gifts and a devise of the property through a will would qualify for the marital deduction[125] and could enable the donee-spouse to take advantage of the $250,000 ($500,000 for married couples) gain exclusion for sales of principal residences (¶ 2815).[126]

- **Joint property.** Interests in jointly held property might make good gifts by the older joint tenant to the younger one. Under the general rule of Code Sec. 2040(a), the entire value of jointly held property is included in the gross estate of the first joint tenant to die unless the survivor is able to demonstrate the proportionate share of his or her contributions to the property's acquisition. Such a determination might be difficult to establish. Where property is held jointly by husband and wife, only one-half of the value of the jointly held property is includible in the gross estate of the first to die.[127]
- **Life insurance.** With the exception of policies (e.g., single premium) treated as modified endowment contracts, cash value life insurance receives favorable income tax treatment. Life insurance proceeds are also excluded from the decedent's gross estate if the policy is not payable to his or her estate and the decedent has not held any incidents of ownership in the policy in the three years before the decedent's death.[128] A life insurance trust or transfer of *all* incidents of ownership to junior family members will ensure that the client's gross estate is not unnecessarily increased by insurance proceeds (¶ 430). Given a choice between transferring property such as securities of a given value and a paid-up insurance policy of the same stated value at death, the life insurance policy generally could be given at a lower gift tax cost.
- **Nonincome-producing property.** If one transfers nonmarketable and nonincome-producing property in trust to pay income to the trust beneficiaries, the gift may not qualify for the annual exclusion because it may be treated as a gift of a future interest.[129]
- **Remainder interests.** Remainder interests are interests that grow in value as the preceding estate nears termination. Some remainder interests are therefore suitable for lifetime giving, whether the interest is deemed vested or contingent. However, the annual exclusion is not available for those gifts because they are gifts of future

[125] Code Secs. 2056(a) and 2523(a).
[126] Code Sec. 121.
[127] Code Sec. 2040(b).
[128] Code Secs. 2035(a) and 2042.
[129] Code Sec. 2503(b) and *F.A. Berzon*, 63 TC 601, CCH Dec. 33,072, aff'd by CA-2, 76-1 USTC ¶ 13,140, 534 F2d 528, involving a gift of closely held stock with a history of nonpayment of dividends.

interests.[130] Also, if the donor retains a life income interest, a gift of a remainder is not advisable because the full value of the property would be included in the decedent's gross estate.[131]

- **Securities.** Good growth stocks make good gifts, particularly during the lower periods in a bear market.
- **Zero coupon bonds.** A gift of a zero coupon bond may be effected at low gift tax cost relative to its value at maturity but exposes the donee to inclusion of interest in gross income before maturity, unless the bond is tax exempt.
- **U.S. savings bonds.** Savings bonds make good gifts, but they should be purchased so that only the donee's name appears as the owner. If the donor's name appears as co-owner, the bonds may be includible in the donor's gross estate under Code Sec. 2040. An exclusion from gross income applies to the interest on Series EE and Series I bonds issued after 1989 and redeemed to pay for college tuition.[132] However, in a twist on the usual family income-shifting strategy of giving away property, unless the bonds are bought and held in the parent's name, the special interest exclusion will not be available.[133] The exclusion is subject to a phaseout for taxpayers with high modified adjusted gross income.[134]

.02 Income Tax Basis Rules

Basis, for income tax purposes, is a broad term that marks the point of departure for computing a property owner's gain or loss on the sale of the property or for computing allowable depreciation. One of the most important estate planning factors to be weighed in deciding between lifetime gifts and testamentary transfers is the step-up in the federal income tax basis which a decedent's estate or beneficiaries receive. They take as their basis the fair market value of the property for estate tax purposes, that is, the value at the date of death or six months later if the estate is eligible for the alternate valuation date and the executor elects it.[135] Thus, any unrealized appreciation up to the time of the estate tax valuation date never becomes subject to federal income taxation. However, for decedents dying in 2010, the step up in basis will be limited to $1,300,000 plus $3,000,000 for property received by a surviving spouse.

Property acquired by lifetime gift is not so favorably treated. The donee's basis is the same as the donor's basis, with an adjustment for

[130] Code Sec. 2503(b).
[131] Code Sec. 2036(a).
[132] Code Sec. 135(a).
[133] Code Sec. 135(c)(1).
[134] Code Sec. 135(b)(2).
[135] Code Secs. 1014(a) and 2032.

gift tax paid. The adjustment is limited to the amount allocable to the net appreciation element in the gift.[136]

Where the donor's basis is higher than the fair market value of the property at the time of the gift, for the purpose of determining a loss, the donee takes the fair market value as his or her basis.[137] (However, a spousal donee takes the donor's basis under Code Sec. 1041.) The result is that the donee, on the sale of the property, will not be able to take advantage of the donor's paper loss. Thus, the donor should consider selling the property to recognize the loss, and then give the proceeds to the donee.

Generally, highly appreciated property might not be a good subject for a gift if the owner can easily hold it until his or her death. The property would then receive a step-up in basis (except as previously described for decedents dying in 2010), and the beneficiary could avoid income tax on the appreciation that occurred before the owner's death. However, the estate planner should evaluate the tradeoff between income tax savings for the donee or beneficiary and the estate tax on the property if the owner holds it until his or her death. If long-term capital gain property is involved (¶ 3101), the reduced tax rate on net capital gains might make the lifetime gift alternative more attractive than holding the property until death.

Additional advantages of a lifetime gift are explained at ¶ 405. Also, if a sale of appreciated property is necessary to meet a family member's expenses (a child's college expenses, for example), usually the owner should transfer the property to the family member as a gift (but only if the family member is 18 or older) and let the donee sell it. The gain would then be taxable at the donee's presumably lower tax rate.

If the donee can show capital losses on his or her income tax return that can be used to offset capital gains, the losses might be a factor in the decision to transfer appreciated property. This strategy might be particularly desirable if the donor can make the gift at a low or no cost in gift taxes.

At one time, one could give appreciated property to a dying person who would then bequeath the property back to the donor or the donor's spouse. As a result, the property would receive a stepped-up basis equal to its fair market value for estate tax purposes.[138] All income tax liability for appreciation up to that point would be eliminated. However, Code Sec. 1014(e) now provides that if one gives

[136] Code Sec. 1015.

[137] Code Sec. 1015(a).

[138] Code Sec. 1014(a).

property to an individual who dies within one year of the gift and the donee bequeaths the property back to the donor or the donor's spouse, the basis of the property in the hands of the original donor or his or her spouse will be the basis of the property in the hands of the decedent immediately before death. This rule applies whether the decedent was terminally ill or died unexpectedly.

The provision leaves open the possibility of obtaining a stepped-up basis by having the decedent-donee effect a testamentary transfer to persons other than the donor or his or her spouse. For example, one spouse is dying and the other spouse gives the dying spouse appreciated property. The dying spouse bequeaths the property to the couple's children. They receive a stepped-up basis. In this example, the gift to the dying spouse can be effected without gift tax cost by reason of the unlimited marital deduction. The bequest to the children may be tax free to the dying spouse's estate to the extent that unused applicable credit (unified credit) amounts are available.[139] If the applicable credit amount is exhausted, amounts in excess of the available credit may be transferred to the surviving spouse tax free under the umbrella of the unlimited marital deduction,[140] and if other appreciated property (not transferred to the dying spouse by the other spouse within one year of death) is included, the surviving spouse will get a stepped-up basis.

.03 Gifts Between Spouses

Interspousal gifts generally do not result in federal income tax savings. Interspousal gifts are, however, useful in achieving estate tax savings. The estate tax liability may be lowered by the unlimited gift tax marital deduction,[141] the unified credit[142] and the fractional interest rule[143] for property jointly owned by spouses, each of which is discussed in ¶405.02. Thus, lifetime gifts to a spouse might be indicated for these reasons:

- The unlimited gift tax marital deduction protects a gift of any amount without dilution of the applicable credit amount (unified credit).
- The gift reduces the donor's gross estate.
- The gift may enable the donee-spouse to make use of the applicable credit amount (unified credit).
- The gift operates as a hedge against the loss of the marital deduction if the donee should predecease the donor.

---

139 Code Sec. 2010.

140 Code Sec. 2056(a).

141 Code Sec. 2523(a).

142 Code Secs. 2010 and 2505.

143 Code Sec. 2040(b).

- The gift may, to some extent, serve the purpose of equalizing the estates of the spouses to reduce the tax burden on each of their estates.

On the last point, equalization may be accomplished by an equalization clause in a marital deduction bequest or by such a clause contained in a living trust.[144]

Equalization of this type is normally only resorted to where each spouse has rather substantial holdings of property. However, a couple might also move toward equalization to avoid wasting the applicable credit amount (unified credit)[145] to which each spouse is entitled.

.04 An Ongoing Program

A planned, ongoing gift program offers the greatest opportunity for reducing estate taxes at minimal gift tax cost. This type of program is designed to take maximum advantage of the $12,000 (for 2006) annual gift tax exclusion.[146] A donor should engage in an ongoing gift program only where his or her financial needs and those of his or her spouse, if married, are met. The gifts should not jeopardize his, her, or their, welfare.

The donor in that situation could make substantial gifts to his or her children or others well in excess of the amount permitted by the annual exclusion.[147] However, the donor should consider the wisdom of such a course of action on a variety of grounds. The donor should weigh the following considerations:

- The applicable credit amount[148] and the unlimited estate and gift tax marital deduction[149] might make an ongoing gift-giving program with the primary emphasis on reducing estate taxes less urgent for many estates. This consideration is especially important because the applicable exclusion amount for lifetime gifts is $1,000,000 through 2009, but the applicable exclusion amount for estate tax purposes increases from $2,000,000 in 2006 to $3,500,000 in 2009.
- A prospective donor who is married might plan to make use of the marital deduction and the applicable credit amount (unified credit) to avoid estate tax. Nevertheless, in appropriate circumstances, the prospective donor might wish to undertake an ongoing gift program with a view to reducing estate taxes of the surviving spouse's estate.

---

[144] See *C.W. Smith, Est.*, 66 TC 415, CCH Dec. 33,862 (Acq.), aff'd per curiam, CA-7, 77-2 USTC ¶ 13,215, 565 F2d 455; see also *F.L. Meeske Est.*, 72 TC 73, CCH Dec. 35,987 (Acq.) and *V.S. Laurin Est.*, 38 TCM 644, CCH Dec. 36,009(M), TC Memo. 1979-145.

[145] Code Sec. 2010.

[146] Code Sec. 2503(b).

[147] Code Sec. 2503(b).

[148] Code Sec. 2010.

[149] Code Secs. 2056(a) and 2523(a).

- An unmarried individual whose estate is large enough to generate estate tax liability might wish to consider making lifetime gifts, unless doing so would unduly reduce the individual's current economic well-being.
- The donor might question whether the donee has sufficient maturity to handle substantial amounts of money or property. While a donor could use a trust to make up for the donee's lack of maturity, the cost and other complications of a trust might act as a deterrent.
- If the donor questions the donee's maturity, the donor might want to make annual gifts in relatively small amounts as a form of test.
- Gifts in excess of the annual $12,000 (for 2006) exclusion[150] use up the applicable credit amount (unified credit)[151] and require payment of the gift tax when the credit is exhausted. This, in turn, imposes a further drain on the donor unless the gift is given in the form of a net gift. A net gift is one in which the donee agrees to pay the gift tax. The gift tax liability assumed by the donee reduces the amount of the taxable gift.[152]

  However, a net gift may involve income tax problems as discussed at ¶ 410.07. Also, under the unified estate and gift tax system, taxable lifetime gifts affect the estate tax, usually pushing the estate into higher estate tax brackets.[153]
- Unearned income of a child under the age of 18 in excess of $1,700 (2006) is taxed at the greater of the child's or parent's top rate.[154] When making gifts to such children, the donor should consider transfers of property that will generate little or no taxable income until the child reaches age 18.

For these reasons, if the financial situation of the client is strong enough, the estate planner should consider recommending a planned, ongoing gift program that makes use of the $12,000 (for 2006) annual exclusion[155] and gift splitting.[156] Also, an unlimited gift-tax exclusion applies for direct payment of tuition and medical expenses (¶ 405.02).[157]

The risk of a spouse with substantial property dying before completion of the ongoing gift program may be reduced by a gift to the other spouse. The unlimited marital deduction bars a gift tax.[158]

The estate planner should give some consideration to insurance on the life of the donor: (1) to pay for the increased estate tax liability

[150] Code Sec. 2503(b).
[151] Code Secs. 2010 and 2505.
[152] Rev. Rul. 75-72, 1975-1 CB 310.
[153] Code Sec. 2001(c).
[154] Code Sec. 1(g).
[155] Code Sec. 2503(b).
[156] Code Sec. 2513(a).
[157] Code Sec. 2503(e).
[158] Code Sec. 2523(a).

that would result from noncompletion of the program, and (2) to provide any additional liquidity that the estate might need.

The loss of gift splitting and the unlimited marital deduction on the death of the spouse engaging in the ongoing gift program might be a factor warranting insurance on the life of the other spouse.

.05 Timing Strategies

Timing is important in developing a gift strategy. The following are some key factors to consider.

Stock market low points. If gifts of securities are contemplated, the donor should make the gift at low points in the market to minimize the gift tax liability or use of the applicable credit amount.

Year-end. The law does not allow a carryover for an unused annual exclusion. Therefore, as year-end approaches, the gift situation requires review.

Deathbed of donor. As a general rule, deathbed gifts are not includible in the donor's gross estate. However, interests in property otherwise included in the value of the gross estate under Code Secs. 2036, 2037, 2038, or 2042 (or those which would have been included if the interest had been retained by the decedent) are includible.[159]

In addition, all transfers within three years of death (other than those eligible for the annual exclusion) will be included for the purpose of determining the estate's qualification for death tax redemption,[160] special use valuation,[161] deferral of estate tax payments,[162] and for the purpose of determining property subject to estate tax liens.[163]

Deathbed gifts in unlimited amounts may be made to the donor's spouse without estate or gift tax consequences under the unlimited marital deduction.[164] Gift splitting[165] may be used to take advantage of the annual exclusion. Gift splitting allows gifts of $24,000 per donee in 2006[166] without use of the unified credit. See, further, ¶ 430 for a detailed discussion of gifts made within three years of the donor's death.

Death of consenting spouse. Generally, gifts made within three years of death are not included in the decedent's gross estate. However, under Code Sec. 2035(b), any gift tax paid on gifts made by

[159] Code Sec. 2035(a).
[160] Code Sec. 303.
[161] Code Sec. 2032A.
[162] Code Sec. 6166.
[163] Code Sec. 2035(c).
[164] Code Sec. 2523(a).
[165] Code Sec. 2513(a).
[166] Code Sec. 2503(b).

the decedent or the decedent's spouse within three years of death is includible in the gross estate of the decedent.

As a result, deathbed consents of a donor's spouse can reduce the amount of the gift tax on gifts in excess of $24,000 in 2006 and will eliminate the gift tax on gifts of less than that amount. While no part of the gifts consented to would be includible in the consenting spouse's gross estate, any taxable gifts would likely be treated as part of the consenting spouse's adjusted taxable gifts for estate tax calculation purposes (¶ 1005).

.06 The Bargain-Sale Gift

Someone could own a piece of property that he or she thinks the prospective donee could put to good use. However, the property could be worth a lot more than the donor would like to give. The donor has several options in such circumstances. For one, the donor could transfer only a joint interest in the property. However, the donor would still have responsibility with respect to the property, while limiting the prospective donee's rights. These are two results the donor might not have intended. Another idea would be to sell the property for less than its fair market value (a bargain sale) to the donee.

For gift tax purposes, a bargain sale may be treated as a gift to the extent of the bargain, that is, the amount by which the property's fair market value exceeds the price paid.[167] Obviously, in the business world, a person selling at a price that could be considered a bargain is not going to incur a gift tax. However, a gift occurs where the transferor has donative intent and the sale is not an arm's-length transaction.

Even when a situation resembling giving exists, for many types of property, different individuals could have many honest differences of opinion as to what constitutes fair market value. A transaction is not necessarily a gift merely because the price is not fixed in the upper ranges of estimates of market value. Of course, if listed securities, mutual funds, or a life insurance policy is involved, the parties will have less room for differences of opinion about fair market value at the time the transaction occurs.

The part-sale, part-gift transaction results in gain or loss to the seller to the extent that the sales proceeds exceed the adjusted basis of the property allocated to the sale portion.[168] Code Sec. 267 disallows a loss deduction on transactions between certain closely related family members and some others. The buyer-donee takes the donor's basis for the gift portion, plus an adjustment for any gift tax the donor

[167] Code Sec. 2512(b).

[168] Code Sec. 1001.

pays,[169] and would add to that the amount paid to acquire the property.[170]

.07 The Net Gift Technique

The net gift technique essentially involves a gift made on condition that the donee pay the gift tax. A definitive revenue ruling, a U.S. Supreme Court decision, and a U.S. Tax Court decision now limit the technique's usefulness and value:

- Under the revenue ruling, the donor must first exhaust the unified credit (applicable credit amount) before any gift tax is payable by the donee.[171]
- Under the U.S. Supreme Court decision, when a donor makes a gift and the donee pays the federal gift tax due, the donor has taxable income to the extent that the gift tax paid exceeds the donor's adjusted basis in the gift property.[172]

  The *Diedrich* rule might adversely affect the use of the net gift technique where it might otherwise be useful. However, with appropriate tax planning, donors can reduce the impact of *Diedrich* through selection of the gift property, using property where any gift tax to be paid by the donee will not exceed the donor's basis and, if this is not possible, by taking steps to offset any income tax liability that the donor might incur.
- Under the U.S. Tax Court decision, a decedent's gross estate includes the amount of gift tax paid by donees on net gifts made by the decedent within three years of death.[173]

Only a handful of states impose gift taxes. In those states, the donee's agreement to pay the state gift tax raises the following federal and state income and gift tax issues:

- **Federal income tax.** Under the part-sale, part-gift approach of *Diedrich*, the donee's agreement to pay the state gift tax should serve to increase the donor's gain. If both the donor and donee are jointly and severally liable for the state gift tax, only one-half of the gift tax liability increases the donor's gain.
- **Federal gift tax.** The amount of the gift tax paid by the donee reduces the value of the gift for federal gift tax purposes.[174] However, if the donor and donee under state law

[169] Code Sec. 1015.

[170] Code Sec. 1012.

[171] Rev. Rul. 81-223, 1981-2 CB 189.

[172] *V.P. Diedrich*, 1982-1 USTC ¶9419, 457 US 191.

[173] *S.C. Sachs Est.*, 88 TC 769, CCH Dec. 43,823, aff'd, CA-8, 88-2 USTC ¶13,781, 856 F2d 1158.

[174] Rev. Rul. 76-49, 1976-1 CB 294 (N.Y.); Rev. Rul. 76-57, 1976-1 CB 297 (N.C.); and Rev. Rul. 76-104, 1976-1 CB 301 (Calif.).

are jointly and severally liable for the gift tax, only one-half of the gift tax paid by the donee will reduce the value of the gift.[175]

- **State income tax.** In a state with an income tax, the law would likely apply the principle of *Diedrich* to tax the donor on gain resulting from the donee's assumption of gift tax liability unless the state law otherwise provides.
- **State gift tax.** The donee's assumption of state gift tax liability should serve to reduce the value of the gift for state gift tax purposes absent any state law provision for credit against gift tax liability. In the latter case, the state might adopt a requirement of exhaustion of the credit as under federal law. A state law providing that the donee's payment or agreement to pay the state gift tax is not consideration for the gift will not reduce the value of the gift.[176]

¶415 DIRECT AND INDIRECT GIFTS

The gift tax has been given a very broad reading by the U.S. Supreme Court.[177] It applies to both direct and indirect gifts. A direct gift may be effected by the creation of a trust, the forgiveness of a debt, the assignment of a judgment, the assignment of the benefits of an insurance policy, or the transfer of cash, certificates of deposit, or federal or municipal bonds.[178] An indirect gift may be made by the payment of another person's expenses, except where a legal obligation exists to pay the expenses, e.g., a parent providing support for a minor child, or a specific exclusion applies, e.g., payment of another's tuition or medical care.[179] An interest-free loan is considered a gift.[180] A gift can be made by a transfer to one person to benefit another. For example, if A makes a transfer to B, in return for B's promise to pay C an annuity, a gift to C would occur if the annuity is equal to the value of the transfer from A to B. If B's promise is worthless, then A has made a gift to B.[181]

Creation of a family partnership interest might constitute a gift, as might a renunciation or disclaimer of a bequest or devise. Reg. § 25.2511-1(c) contains detailed provisions dealing with the gift tax consequences of such renunciations or disclaimers, but refers the reader to Code Sec. 2518 for rules relating to qualified disclaimers.

The broad reading given the gift tax by *Dickman* has, in effect, given the IRS a license to explore the outer reaches of the federal gift tax.

---

[175] Rev. Rul. 80-111, 1980-1 CB 208.

[176] Rev. Rul. 76-104, 1976-1 CB 301 (Calif.).

[177] *E.C. Dickman*, 84-1 USTC ¶13,560, 465 US 330.

[178] Reg. § 25.2511-1(a).

[179] Code Sec. 2503(e).

[180] *Dickman, supra* 179.

[181] Reg. § 25.2511-1(h)(2) and (3).

The IRS has ruled, for example, that the failure of a controlling shareholder who owns preferred stock to have the corporation declare a preferred stock dividend constitutes a gift to younger generation shareholders of the corporation to the extent of the preferred dividends foregone.[182] The ramifications of the U.S. Supreme Court's broad reading might be to bring a variety of intra-family transactions within the gift tax net. Thus, a parent allowing an adult child and his or her family to use a residence rent-free could be considered to be a gift.

In fact, nonaction has been deemed to cause a gift. In *E.W. Snyder*,[183] the U.S. Tax Court held that a taxpayer, by failing to convert noncumulative preferred stock into cumulative preferred stock, which would have entitled the taxpayer to accumulated dividends, made an indirect gift to the common shareholders.

This chapter is not intended to offer an encyclopedic treatment of the subject of indirect gifts, but simply to call attention to the basic fact that anytime someone transfers property for less than adequate and full consideration in money or money's worth, a taxable gift occurs.

¶ 420 GIFTS IN TRUST

Lifetime giving can spring from many motives. In a family, income splitting might still be among such motives, despite the compression of income tax rates. Under the assignment of income doctrine, one may not separate the dividend from the stock, the interest from the bond, the fruit from the tree, as it were. If shifting income is the goal, one must transfer the underlying property producing the income. The potential donor might not be ready to make such a transfer. The donee might not be ready for the property with all its responsibilities, either. If the donee is a minor, the donor could use one or more of the approaches discussed at ¶ 425 to accomplish the purpose, including the special types of trusts more suitable for gifts to minors.

If the donee is not a minor, some other form of trust is probably the most efficient way of splitting income and satisfying the needs of both the donor and the donee. The forms and shapes of such trusts are perhaps as varied as those who create them. Not all forms effectively shift income. Some trusts, in addition to shifting income, are effective in reducing the estate taxes of their creators. Some gifts in trust qualify for the annual exclusion. However, other gifts in trust are deemed to be gifts of future interests and thus ineligible for the exclusion.

---

[182] IRS Letter Ruling 8723007, February 18, 1987.

[183] 93 TC 529, CCH Dec. 46,137.

Chapter 6 discusses the ramifications of trusts in much greater depth. However, one point is worth noting here. Because the income tax brackets of trusts are highly compressed, trusts that accumulate income are far more costly than custodianships. The latter can accumulate income until the minor reaches the age of majority, but the income is taxed directly to the minor. The accumulation of income is treated much less favorably for a trust, however. For example, for tax years beginning in 2006, the 15-percent rate applies to a trust's taxable income up to $2,050, the 25-percent rate applies to taxable income between $2,050 and $4,850, the 28-percent rate applies to taxable income between $4,850 and $7,400, the 33-percent rate applies to taxable income between $7,400 and $10,050, and the 35-percent rate applies to taxable income over $10,050. A child who has attained age 18, on the other hand, is taxed at a rate of 10 percent on taxable income up to $7,550; at 15-percent for taxable income between $7,550 and $30,650; and at 25 percent between $30,650 and $74,200. Higher rates apply on taxable income above that amount.

¶425 GIFTS TO MINORS

An estate planner does not need to take a poll to determine that gifts from parents to children, and from grandparents to grandchildren, are the most common lifetime gifts.

Many of these gifts will be to minors. Many gifts will be made without any particular thought to legal or tax consequences, which is all right if the gifts are small. As the gifts increase in size, the donors should consider the tax and legal factors more carefully. The kiddie tax[184] has an especially severe impact on gifts to minors (¶405.05).

The tax laws are concerned with taxing gifts at every opportunity, subject to available exclusions. A gift made to a newborn infant is clearly taxable unless it falls within the $12,000 (for 2006) annual exclusion.[185] State laws, however, are concerned with the legal capacity of an infant to possess and own property, take care of it, and sell and transfer it. They are also concerned with the protection of the rights of the infant.

These state concerns are responsible, for example, for laws barring registration of securities in a minor's name; providing for the appointment of judicially supervised guardians of the property (and person) of minors; limitations on the power of a minor to contract; and many other restrictions and limitations. All of these restrictions complicate making gifts to minors and bring into play trusts,

[184] Code Sec. 1(g).

[185] Code Sec. 2503(b).

custodianships, and guardianships as vehicles for gifts to minors to help protect their interests. Each of these vehicles differs from the others in one or more respects.

Exhibit 4 (¶425.04) compares outright gifts, custodianships, guardianships, and four different types of trusts that may be used as vehicles for gifts to minors. The comparison is in terms of a variety of different legal, tax, and practical factors, all of which are developed in the more detailed discussion of each vehicle in the numbered paragraphs following the table.

.01 Factors to Consider in Choosing a Vehicle

When considering these different vehicles, the estate planner should keep the following factors in mind.

Income shifting. A family can realize limited income tax savings when a parent transfers income-producing property or money to an account in the name of a minor child, or to a custodial account, guardian, or trust for the child. Under TIPRA, if the child is under the age of 18, the child's unearned income in excess of $1,700 (for 2006) is taxed at the greater of the child's rate or the parent's top rate.[186] When the child reaches age 18, the income will no longer be taxed at the parent's rate, but the child will be without the benefit of a personal exemption and will have only $850 of standard deduction to shield unearned income (assuming the child can be claimed as a dependent). Thus, for 2006, the child will be taxable at a 10-percent rate on unearned income over $850 up to taxable income of $7,550 and at higher rates for earned income above that level. For example, a single person's taxable income between $7,550 and $30,650 is taxed at 15 percent. The rate rises to 25 percent for taxable income between $30,650 and $74,200. The maximum rate of 35 percent applies to taxable income over $336,550.

The potential 25 (35 – 10) point spread makes for considerable interest in income splitting once the child reaches age 18. The spread can be even further heightened for taxpayers caught by progressive state and local income taxes.

Consider this simple example, showing family tax savings by a transfer of $850 in income from a parent at various tax bracket levels to a minor child without other taxable income.

---

[186] Code Sec. 1(g) as amended by TIPRA, Sec. 510.

Parent's Top Tax Bracket	Family Tax Savings
25%	$213
28%	$238
33%	$281
35%	$298

Highly compressed income tax brackets of trusts. The income tax brackets of trusts are highly compressed when compared to the brackets of other categories of taxpayers. For example, for tax years beginning in 2006, the 15-percent rate applies to taxable income up to $2,050, the 25-percent rate applies to taxable income between $2,050 and $4,850, the 28-percent rate applies to taxable income between $4,850 and $7,400, the 33-percent rate applied to taxable income between $7,400 and $10,050; and the 35-percent rate applies to taxable income over $10,050.

This rate structure obviously affects the use of trusts as income-shifting vehicles. In many cases, custodial accounts may be preferable to Code Sec. 2503(c) minors' trusts. With a custodial account, the income is taxed directly to the child even though it is accumulated until the child reaches the age of majority. Income accumulated in a trust, on the other hand, would be subject to the highly compressed brackets set out above.

Income used for support. Income of a trust actually applied or distributed to the support or maintenance of a beneficiary whom the grantor of the trust is legally obligated to support or maintain is taxable to the grantor under Code Sec. 677(b). The IRS has ruled that the same rule applies to custodial accounts.[187] In addition, a guardianship may be held to be a trust under state law so that Code Sec. 677(b) would be brought into play.[188]

The amount taxable to a person obligated to support a minor is limited to the extent of his or her legal obligations under local law.[189]

The area is one in which the estate planner must watch state law developments closely. Under some circumstances, private school expenses have been considered support obligations.[190] Further, college education and, indeed, graduate school education might be deemed within the ambit of support obligations although the child may have attained adulthood.[191]

Braun was decided under New Jersey law. In New Jersey, the support obligation rests on the parent's financial circumstances,

[187] Rev. Rul. 59-357, 1959-2 CB 212.

[188] *C.P. Brooke*, CA-9, 72-2 USTC ¶9594, 468 F2d 1155.

[189] Rev. Rul. 56-484, 1956-2 CB 23.

[190] *C. Stone*, 54 TCM 462, CCH Dec. 44,181(M), TC Memo. 1987-459.

[191] *F.C. Braun, Jr.*, 48 TCM 210, CCH Dec. 41,250 (M), TC Memo. 1984-285.

education, attitudes toward education, and other factors. The cautious estate planner in other states will want to take *Braun* and *Stone* into account.

Planning pointer. The estate planner should consider the following as a means of avoiding or cushioning the danger posed by these cases:

- Discuss the cases and the risks with the client.
- Provide for payment of income to adult beneficiaries.
- Provide in the trust that income is not to be applied to any item judicially or legislatively determined to be a support obligation.
- Where possible, have grandparents fund the trusts because they would have no support obligation for higher education.
- If grandparents lack the resources, consider gifts from the parents to the grandparents who would then have funds to set up the trust. Of course, the parties must implement this plan in such a way to avoid the IRS reclassifying the transactions under the step transaction doctrine.

One should also be aware of the reach of Code Sec. 677(a). Under this provision, the grantor of a trust may be taxed on trust income used to satisfy a grantor's express or implied contractual obligation. This provision may also apply to guardianships that, under state law, are regarded as trusts. Under this section, although a parent might not have an obligation of support, trust income may be taxable to the parent-settlor if it is used to discharge an express or implied obligation of the settlor.[192] From this perspective, a parent who has assumed express (or implied) liability for his or her child's college tuition might be held taxable on trust income used to pay tuition. This result could occur although a college education, under local law, might not be within the parent's support obligation.

.02 Custodianships

All states have special laws that make gifts to minors easier and safer. The Uniform Gifts to Minors Act (UGMA) came to be adopted in almost all states. More recently, it has been superseded in many states by the Uniform Transfers to Minors Act (UTMA), which significantly broadens UGMA. For example, UTMA places no limitations on the types of property transferable. Real estate, limited partnership interests, patents, tangible personal property, and

[192] *G.B. Morrill, Jr.*, DC Me., 64-1 USTC ¶9463, 228 FSupp. 734.

other forms of property may be transferred. In addition, custodians have all powers over custodial property that unmarried adult owners have over their own property, subject to fiduciary obligations. This allows UTMA custodians to enter into a broad range of business transactions.

To advise a client on making a gift to a minor under either uniform act, the estate planner should check the exact language to be used under local law, as some variations might exist in the uniform acts from state to state. The estate planner should also check local law as to the custodian's responsibilities and duties. The Uniform Act originally set the age of majority at 21, but the age of majority has since been lowered in many states.

Both uniform acts provide for paying over the custodial property on attaining a specified age. UTMA sets the age at 21 for gift property and at 18 or other state statutory age for other property. The UGMA age has been lowered in some states. The estate planner should check applicable state law.

Income tax aspects. When a custodial account is created for a child under age 18, any unearned income over $1,700 (2006) is taxed to the child at the greater of the child's rate or the parent's marginal tax rate[193] without the benefit of a personal exemption, provided that the child is eligible to be claimed as a dependent by the parents. After making use of the benefit of a $850 standard deduction, another $850 of the child's unearned income will be taxed at the child's rate.

When the child reaches age 18, the income from the account will no longer be taxable at the parent's rate, but the child will still be without the benefit of a personal exemption. However, the $850 standard deduction may still be used to shield unearned income. Thus, for 2006, the child will be taxable at a 10-percent rate on unearned income over the $850 covered by the standard deduction up to $7,550 and at higher rates for earned income above that level. For example, a single person's taxable income between $74,200 and $154,800 is taxed at 28 percent. The rate rises to 33 percent for taxable income between $154,800 and $336,550 until it tops out at 35 percent for taxable income over $336,550.

If the income from the gift is used to discharge someone else's obligation, the income is taxable to that individual. If the income is used to satisfy a duty of support (it is used to buy blue jeans, sneakers, and lunches for the minor, for example) it is taxable to the parent or the one under a legal duty of support, regardless of whether or not he or she made the gift or is the custodian.[194]

---

[193] Code Sec. 1(g).

[194] Rev. Rul. 56-484, 1956-2 CB 23.

Planning pointer. The income tax brackets of trusts are greatly compressed, which serves to make custodial accounts far better than trusts in saving family income taxes. For example, for tax years beginning in 2006, the 15-percent rate applies to a trust's taxable income up to $2,050, the 25-percent rate applies to taxable income between $2,050 and $4,850, the 28-percent rate applies to taxable income between $4,850 and $7,400, the 33-percent rate applies to taxable income between $7,400 and $10,050, and the 35-percent rate applies to taxable income over $10,050.

Estate tax aspects. If the minor dies before the funds in the account are distributed, the amount in the fund is includible in the minor's gross estate. It is not includible in the donor's gross estate unless the donor is the custodian and dies before the minor attains the age of majority. This result, as applied to UGMA transfers, follows from federal estate tax law and should be the same with respect to UTMA transfers. A gift may not, as a general rule, be includible in the gross estate of the donor even though made within three years of the donor's death unless it is a gift of an insurance policy or otherwise falls under Code Sec. 2035 (¶430).

Except where insignificant amounts are involved, having the donor serve as custodian is not prudent and runs the risk of having the custodial funds included in his or her gross estate. The next logical candidate for the job might be the donor's spouse, the other parent of the minor beneficiary. However, Code Sec. 2041 might pose a problem. If the parent-custodian dies before the child attains the age of majority, the IRS might contend that he or she possessed a general power of appointment in that the property could be used to discharge the parent-custodian's obligation of support. Of course, in many states, a parent cannot use a minor child's money to discharge a legal obligation, and anyone living in a state where this is true would be safe in naming the nondonor spouse and parent of the minor as custodian. Reciprocal gifts made by the spouses at the same time and in the same amounts, each naming the other as custodian, run the risk of being treated as each naming himself or herself as custodian.[195] Generally, if a trustworthy aunt, uncle, or other relative is willing to serve as custodian naming that person as custodian would be safer.

Gift tax aspects. Gifts made under either uniform act qualify for the annual gift tax exclusion of $12,000 (for 2006 and indexed for

[195] *Exchange Bank & Trust Co.*, CA-FC, 82-2 USTC ¶13,505, 694 F2d 1261.

inflation),[196] or double that if the donor's spouse consents.[197] Both acts, of course, were carefully framed to ensure this result under the provisions of Code Sec. 2503(b) and (c). Just as there is an estate tax danger if a parent serves as custodian, a possible gift tax danger also exists. The danger arises because Code Sec. 2514 provides that the release of a general power of appointment is a gift. Under a somewhat strained interpretation of that section, the IRS might maintain that when a parent-custodian turns over the funds to the beneficiary when the beneficiary attains the age of majority, the parent-custodian releases a general power of appointment to use the custodial funds for support. However, such power may be negated by local law requirements. Still, this possibility offers another reason for not having a parent with a duty of support serve as custodian, whether or not the parent is the donor.

.03 Guardianships

A legal guardian may be made the recipient of a gift to a minor. The guardian has custody and management of the minor's property, and has fiduciary responsibilities akin to those of a trustee. However, the guardian does not hold legal title to the property as does a trustee. Courts have held that a court-administered guardianship may be considered a trust for the purpose of Code Sec. 677(b). Under that provision, the trust grantor is taxable on trust income used to discharge a support obligation. For example, where the father of minor children is appointed their legal guardian, he may be taxable on income used for their support, as defined by local law.[198]

Unearned income in excess of $1,700 (2006) of a minor under the age of 18 is taxed at the greater of the child's rate or the parent's marginal tax rate.[199] Once the child reaches age 18, income is taxable to the child even though accumulated and not paid to him or her or currently used for his or her benefit, aside from amounts used for support that may possibly be taxed to a parent. The guardian is under a duty to file the minor's income tax return. The property given is removed from the donor's gross estate, subject to the limited gifts-within-three-years-of-death strictures of Code Sec. 2035. The gift is treated as a gift of a present interest, for which the $11,000 (for 2005 and indexed for inflation) annual exclusion is available.[200]

A guardianship assures the minor of greater protection of his or her property rights than with even a trust or custodial account.

---

[196] Code Sec. 2503(b).

[197] Code Sec. 2513(a).

[198] *C.P. Brooke*, CA-9, 72-2 USTC ¶9594, 468 F2d 1155, aff'g DC Mont., 69-1 USTC ¶9366, 300 FSupp. 465, amending DC Mont., 68-2 USTC ¶9544, 292 FSupp. 571.

[199] Code Sec. 1(g).

[200] Code Sec. 2503(b).

Guardianships require accountings, bonding, and court supervision, the form and content varying with local law. However, a guardianship involves higher costs in the form of initial legal fees, bonding costs, guardian fees (unless a family member is appointed), and the costs of accounting and terminating the guardianship. Termination at age 21, or at an earlier age of majority, may be another negative factor when compared to trusts of possibly longer duration. Another factor meriting consideration is that when a gift is made to a guardian, one cannot provide that if the minor dies before the guardianship ends, the interest is to pass to a contingent beneficiary, as one can with a trust. Hence, if the minor lacks the capacity to make a will (as is the case in many states), upon death, the property might revert to the parent-donor. The result would be that the parent might lose the income tax and estate tax savings sought in the first instance, at least until the parent makes some further disposition of the property.

Still, a court-appointed parent-guardian would not likely be vulnerable to the arguments made in connection with custodial accounts. These include the argument that the custodial property would be includible in the gross estate of the parent-custodian predeceasing the minor or the contention that turning over the property to the minor, at the end of the guardianship, could amount to the release of a general power of appointment.

.04 Trusts for Minors

The estate planner might think of a trust for a minor as something that the estate planner is basically free to design. The trust may provide what is to be done with the trust income, whether it is to be distributed to the minor or accumulated, or both; how long the trust is to last; who is to serve as trustee (and how a successor is to be selected, if that should become necessary); when and how the principal of the trust is to be distributed; and many other details. However, the settlor should not think that, once he or she has created a trust that he or she is then free to do with it as desired. If the settlor does so, he or she will be treated as the owner for income and estate tax purposes. Still, if substantial gifts are involved, the benefits of a trust might outweigh its costs. The greatest flexibility is to be found in a broad, general type of trust suitable for adult beneficiaries, as well as for minors. This broad, general type of trust is discussed at ¶ 420. Here the focus is on two special types of trusts that are widely used as vehicles for gifts to minors. One is shaped by Code Sec. 2503(c), which deals with the availability of the $12,000 (for 2006) annual gift tax exclusion for transfers for the benefit of minors. The other is the offspring of Code Sec. 2503(b), which makes the annual exclusion available only for gifts of present interests and so mandates current income distributions from the trust, if that requirement is to be satisfied.

These two different types of trusts are examined in greater detail in the following subparagraphs. However, the essential difference lies in how the trusts distribute income and principal (corpus). The (c) type trust does not require the current distribution of income, but does require distribution of the "property and the income therefrom," a phrase discussed below, which may possibly require distribution of principal on the minor's attaining his or her majority. The (b) type trust requires current distribution of income, but does not require distribution of principal on the minor's attaining the age of majority. Trusts that accumulate income are far more costly from a tax standpoint because of the highly compressed income tax rates applicable to trusts. The estate planner should keep this rate structure in mind in choosing between a Code Sec. 2503(b) trust, which pays out income, or a Code Sec. 2503(c) trust, which may accumulate income. Likewise, the estate planner should consider income tax rates when considering a custodianship, which may accumulate income that is taxed directly to the minor on whose behalf the account is established.

Section 2503(c) trust to last during minority. Code Sec. 2503(c) gave rise to the Section 2503(c) trust. The section itself says nothing about trusts. It merely describes a specific form of transfer for the minor's benefit that will qualify as a gift of a present interest to make the $12,000 (for 2006) annual exclusion available.

The section, by its terms, provides that a gift to an individual who is not yet 21 will *not* be considered a gift of a future interest (that is, it will be considered a gift of a present interest) if the gift "property and the income therefrom": (1) may be expended by, or for the benefit of, the donee before attaining the age of 21 years, and (2) to the extent not so expended, will be paid to the donee upon reaching 21 or, if the donee dies before then, will be paid to the donee's estate or to such persons as the donee appoints under a general power of appointment. Although legal restrictions on a minor's ability to exercise the power do not affect the exclusion,[201] the donor will lose the exclusion if a provision in the document regarding the exercise of the power is more restrictive than is applicable state law.[202]

An important point to note is that the Code section does not *require* that "the property and the income therefrom" be used for the minor's benefit during minority in order for the gift to be

[201] Reg. § 25.2503-4(b).

[202] *G. Gall*, CA-5, 75-2 USTC ¶ 13,107, 521 F2d 878, aff'g DC Tex., 75-1 USTC ¶ 13,067.

regarded as a gift of a present interest, only that it *may* be. Thus, these trusts do not require the current distribution of income. However, the estate planner should remember that income actually accumulated in the trust will be taxed at the highly compressed brackets that apply for trusts, as discussed above.

Another important point is that the Code section uses the phrase "the property and the income therefrom," as above indicated. It does not refer to principal or corpus. In any case, a gift may be separated into component parts, one of which may qualify as a present interest under the statute. Accordingly, courts have held that a gift of income only may satisfy the statute and qualify as a gift of a present interest. Further, such interest will not fail to qualify because it is coupled with other interests that are future interests. Thus, courts have held that a trust that provided that all income up to the age of majority must be paid to the beneficiary or expended for the beneficiary's benefit before the age of majority, or be paid over to the beneficiary at age 21 or to the beneficiary's estate or appointee in the event of death prior to 21, qualified for the annual exclusion even though the trust also provided for further payments of income after the beneficiary attained age 21 until age 30 and did not allow the trust principal to be paid over to the trust beneficiary until age 30.[203] The IRS goes along with the determination that a gift of trust income to a minor satisfies the requirements of Code Sec. 2503(c) even though the beneficiary has no interest in the corpus at age 21.[204] *Herr* provides an important planning tool that makes the $12,000 (for 2006) annual exclusion available although corpus is not required to be distributed at age 21.

Further, Rev. Rul. 74-43[205] provides that, if the beneficiary, upon attaining the age of majority, is given a right for a limited period to require immediate distribution of the trust corpus by giving written notice to the trustee, the annual exclusion will be available. Upon failing to do so, the trust may be made to continue automatically for whatever period the donor provided in setting up the trust. Because the ruling does not address the question of whether the trustee is required to notify the beneficiary of this right, the settlor might be wise to deal with it in the trust. In fixing the time within which the beneficiary is to act, a reasonable time to reflect on the choice and to act should be allowed (e.g., 60 days were found to be reasonable in IRS Letter Ruling 8507017[206]).

---

[203] *A.I. Herr*, 35 TC 732, CCH Dec. 24,652 (Acq.), aff'd, CA-3, 62-2 USTC ¶12,079, 303 F2d 780.

[204] Rev. Rul. 68-670, 1968-2 CB 413.

[205] 1974-1 CB 285.

[206] November 19, 1984.

While a trust may delay distribution of corpus, as is shown above, the trust may also provide for the distribution of corpus and income before age 21 if that should be desired. The IRS has ruled that age 21 as referred to in Code Sec. 2503(c) is the maximum age at which the turnover must be made, not the minimum age.[207] If the sums involved are not too large, a distribution at age 18 (as a beneficiary is about to enter college, for example) might be thought appropriate.

In any event, the price to be paid for the present-interest concession is that the "property and the income therefrom" must be paid over to the donee upon turning 21 at the latest, if not sooner. If large sums are to be paid over, this requirement can be a serious, practical limitation on the use of this type of trust.

If the sums involved are not too large, the donor might want to mark the donee's coming of age by distributing the trust funds. On the other hand, the donor might feel more comfortable if the trust were to continue until age 25, or some other age. The donor may do so either by the technique used in *Herr* or pursuant to Rev. Rul. 74-43, both of which are discussed above.

[207] Rev. Rul. 73-287, 1973-2 CB 321.

Exhibit 4

Comparison of Basic Forms of Gifts to Minors

Item of Comparison	Outright Gift	Custodianship	Guardianship	Trusts: Regular	Trusts: Sec. 2503(b)	Trusts: Sec. 2503(c)
Use of Income for Minor	Generally, no	Yes	Yes	Trust controls	Mandatory distribution	Discretionary
Use of Principal for Minor	Generally, no	Yes	Yes	Trust controls	Trust controls	Discretionary
Judicial Close Supervision	No	No	Yes	No	No	No
Fiduciary Qualifications	No	Any adult or trust company	Court-approved	Donor-imposed	Donor-imposed	Donor-imposed
Risk in Donor as Fiduciary	No	Yes	No	Possibly	Possibly	Possibly
Bonding Required	No	No	Yes	Only if the donor requires bonding		
Accounting	No	Records kept; possible accounting	Yes	Generally, only private records need be kept		
Investments	Unlimited	Limited	Generally, unlimited	Generally, unlimited within donor's control		
When Minor Gets Title	Immediately	Immediately	Immediately	On termination or earlier distribution of income or principal		
When Minor Gets Possession	Immediately	Age of majority	Age of majority	Trust controls	Trust controls	Generally, age of majority
When Minor Can Dispose of Gift Property	Generally, at majority; younger for money, bank accounts and EE bonds	Age of majority	Age of majority	Trust controls	Trust controls	Generally, age of majority

Exhibit 4 (contd.)

Comparison of Basic Forms of Gifts to Minors

Item of Comparison	Outright Gift	Custodianship	Guardianship	Trusts: Regular	Trusts: Sec. 2503(b)	Trusts: Sec. 2503(c)
Fiduciary's Death	No fiduciary	Inclusion of fund in estate possible	No effect except on successor appointment	No effect, generally, if trust is irrevocable and settlor retains no interest, otherwise includible in settlor's estate		
Minor's Death	Heirs of minor take unless minor has will effective under local law			Trust controls	Trust controls	Estate of minor or appointees
Tax Liability for Distributed Income	Minor*	Minor is generally taxable* except as it is used to discharge parent's obligation of support and is taxable to parent				
Tax Liability for Undistributed Income	Minor*	Minor*	Minor*	Trust	Must* distribute	Trust
Gift Tax Annual Exclusion	Yes	Yes	Yes	If present income interest	Yes	Yes
Exclusion of Gift from Estate of Donor	Yes	Yes, except if donor-custodian dies	Yes	Yes, except if settlor dies possessing forbidden powers or rights		Yes
Cost	Generally, none or nominal	Generally, none or nominal	Legal fees and bonding costs and possible guardian's fees	Legal fees varying with complexity, size of trust and other factors, and possible trustee fees		

* Unearned income of a minor under the age of 18 in excess of $1,700 annually (2006) and indexed to inflation is taxed at the parent's top rate, assuming the parent's rate is higher than that of the child (Code Sec. 1(g)).

Income and estate tax aspects. A Code Sec. 2503(c) trust is a separate taxable entity. To the extent that income is accumulated, it is taxable to the trust. For tax years beginning in 2006, the income is taxed at the rate of 15 percent on the first $2,050 of trust income. The 25-percent rate applies to income over $2,050 and up to $4,850. Trust income between $4,850 and $7,400 is taxed at a rate of 28 percent. The 33-percent rate applies to taxable income between $7,400 and $10,050, and the 35-percent rate applies to taxable income over $10,050. Thus, accumulating income in trusts is extremely costly. A custodial account may accumulate income at far less tax cost.

Another concern of Code Sec. 2503(c) trusts is Code Sec. 677(b), under which income applied to or distributed for the support of a beneficiary whom the grantor is legally obligated to support will be taxable to the grantor. A lowered age of majority, relieving the parent-grantor of the obligation of support, might help here, as will distributions used for purposes not falling within the support obligation under local law (¶ 425).

Generally, the trust property is not includible in the donor's gross estate.

The availability of the $12,000 (for 2006) annual exclusion for Code Sec. 2503(c) trusts has already been discussed. However, gift splitting[208] is also available, making possible gifts of as much as $24,000 (for 2006) per year per donee. Transfers to a Code Sec. 2503(c) trust are permitted at annual intervals. Thus, the annual exclusion and gift splitting will, over a period of years, permit a substantial fund to be accumulated. For example, the fund would have $240,000 plus accumulated interest over a period of 10 years.

If accumulated income and corpus are to be turned over to the minor at age 21, the settlor might not want to make contributions as large as those permitted to be made tax free through use of the annual exclusion and gift splitting. If, however, the trust is to provide for distribution of income only at age 21 and retention of the corpus until a later age or for life, then the settlor might want to contribute larger sums. In such a case, separate computations would be required for the income interest and the gift of corpus, using the Code Sec. 7520 actuarial tables for the valuation of the respective interests (¶ 405). The gift of corpus would ordinarily be treated as a gift of a future interest, for which the $12,000 annual exclusion would not be available.[209]

Section 2503(b) current income trusts. If a trust requires mandatory distribution of income to the trust beneficiary, at least

---

[208] Code Sec. 2513(a).

[209] Code Sec. 2503(b).

annually, gifts to it will qualify as gifts of present interest and so become eligible for the $12,000 (for 2006) annual gift tax exclusion under Code Sec. 2503(b). Such trusts are known as Section 2503(b) trusts. Except insofar as they require mandatory distribution of income, they permit much more flexibility in structuring than either the previously discussed Section 2503(c) trust or custodianships. While one may structure a Section 2503(c) trust so that principal need not be distributed to the beneficiary, as discussed above, a custodianship requires distribution of principal and unexpended income no later than age 21. The Section 2503(b) trust has no such requirement. It may last for a lifetime or any shorter fixed term. The principal need never pass to the income beneficiary, but may go to other persons the donor-settlor designated or whom the income beneficiary may have been authorized to designate.

A Code Sec. 2503(b) trust created for a child under the age of 18 results in income in excess of $1,700 (2006) being taxed to the child at the greater of the child's rate or the parent's top rate.[210] After the child reaches age 18, unearned income in excess of $850 (2006) will be taxed at the child's rate, starting at 10 percent, except as the trust income may be taxed to the settlor-parent as having been used to discharge a parental obligation of support, as discussed at ¶ 425. These amounts are indexed to inflation.

The entire trust property is treated as a gift. The gift has two parts—an income portion and a principal or remainder portion. Only the income portion qualifies for the $12,000 annual exclusion. The other portion is a future interest and does not qualify.[211] The value of the income portion for gift tax purposes is determined on the basis of IRS tables issued pursuant to Code Sec. 7520. The value varies depending on the duration of the income interest and the federal midterm rate for the month in which the valuation occurs (¶ 405).

The $12,000 gift tax annual exclusion (doubled with gift splitting under Code Sec. 2513(a)) makes possible a substantial build-up of trust funds through an ongoing program of annual gifts without incurring any gift tax liability. The future interest portion of the gift, however, would be subject to gift tax without the benefit of the annual exclusion.

Under Code Sec. 2503(b), the present income portion retains its status as such, even though the income portion may be reduced by a power given the trustee to use principal. However, the power must be used for the income beneficiary and not for some other person.

---

[210] Code Sec. 1(g).

[211] Code Sec. 2503(b).

The IRS, in Rev. Rul. 69-344,[212] took the position that the annual $12,000 exclusion is not allowable for a gift of property in trust that provides that all income must be paid to the beneficiary but also permits principal to be invested in nonincome-producing property and life insurance policies. Caution dictates that the trust instrument should specifically deny such power to the trustee.

¶ 430 GIFTS WITHIN THREE YEARS OF DEATH

Generally, the value of gifts made within three years of the donor's death is not includible in the gross estate of the donor and any post-gift appreciation will not be subject to transfer tax. Accordingly, such property will not be considered to pass from the decedent, and the stepped-up basis of Code Sec. 1014 will not apply. The basis rules of Code Sec. 1015, which deals with the basis of gift property in the hands of the donee, will apply.

However, certain exceptions apply. Gifts of interests in property that would otherwise have been included in the gross estate under Code Sec. 2036 (retained life estate), 2037 (transfers taking effect at death), 2038 (revocable transfers) or 2042 (life insurance) or that "would have been included under any of such Code sections if such interest had been retained by the decedent" are included in the gross estate if transferred within three years of death.[213]

The quoted language is from the Code provision. It apparently is intended to mean that if the decedent within three years of death releases or transfers an interest that would have been included in his or her gross estate under any of the cited sections if he or she had retained it until death (which is the operative fact under those sections), it will be included in his or her gross estate under the exception to Code Sec. 2035. Such interests are included in the transferor's gross estate whether or not a gift tax return was required.

The value of property transferred to a donee from a decedent's revocable trust within three years of the decedent's death, and the value of property in such a trust with respect to which the decedent's power to revoke is relinquished during the three years before death, is not includible in the decedent's gross estate.[214] This provision is effective for estates of decedents dying after August 5, 1997. It codifies the holding of *H. McNeely*[215] and *E. Kisling Est.*[216]

All transfers within three years of death (other than gifts eligible for the annual gift tax exclusion) will be included for purposes of

[212] 1969-1 CB 225.
[213] Code Sec. 2035(a).
[214] Code Sec. 2035(e).
[215] CA-8, 94-1 USTC ¶ 60,155.
[216] CA-8, 94-1 USTC ¶ 60,176 (Acq.), IRB 1995-33, 4.

determining the estate's qualification for special redemption, of determining property subject to the estate tax liens, and for valuation and deferral purposes (under Code Secs. 303, 2032A, and 6166).[217]

Assume the owner of a business interest wants to meet the percentage requirements that will enable the owner's estate to take advantage of the cited Code sections. The owner might make gifts of nonbusiness property to increase the value of the business interest as a percentage of his or her adjusted gross estate. To be effective, the owner will have to make such gifts more than three years before his or her death.

Code Sec. 2035(b), the gross-up provision, continues to apply to all estates so that gift taxes paid on gifts within three years of death are includible in the donor's gross estate.

.01 Pros and Cons of Gifts Under Rule

The rule applicable to gifts made within three years of death by decedents offers these advantages:

- Any post-gift appreciation is not subject to transfer tax so that property with such appreciation potential may be a proper subject for a gift.
- State gift taxes, if any, paid or payable, may be excluded from the gross estate.
- The value of the gift is not includible in the probate estate so that all the advantages of avoiding probate attach, including savings in administration costs and the avoidance of delay and publicity.
- The unlimited marital deduction[218] permits a married individual to make a gift in an unlimited amount without incurring gift tax. The individual also may do so by will,[219] but at the price of including the bequest in the probate estate.
- If the gift is of income-producing property, post-gift income will not be includible in the donor's gross estate.
- If the donee is in a lower tax bracket than the donor, post-gift income will be taxable at a lower rate. If the donee is the donor's spouse and they file a joint return, this advantage would not be applicable.

One disadvantage is the gross-up rule,[220] which may not be a significant problem if the estate is not subject to the federal estate tax. The lifetime gift will also result in the loss of a step-up in basis at

[217] Code Sec. 2035(c).
[218] Code Sec. 2523(a).
[219] Code Sec. 2056(a).
[220] Code Sec. 2035(b).

death (limited for decedents dying in 2010).[221] If long-term capital gain property is involved (¶ 3101), the reduced tax rates on net capital gains[222] might make this loss of stepped-up basis more palatable.

If the gift is of property that, at the time the gift is made, has a fair market value in excess of the donor's adjusted basis in the property, the donee's basis will be the donor's adjusted basis increased by the gift tax on the net appreciation.[223] If the gift property further appreciates after the date of the gift, no additional gift tax is due on the appreciation and the law allows no further increase in basis.

In any case, in deciding whether to make a gift at a time when death is likely to result within three years, all of the above-mentioned factors should be taken into account. An estimate should be made of the transfer costs if a gift is not made and the property is includible in the gross estate of the deceased owner. Inclusion of the property in the owner's gross estate can result in federal estate taxes, state death taxes, additional probate costs, and other disadvantages. These negative factors might be offset in part by the benefit of receiving a stepped-up basis for appreciated property acquired from the decedent at death (limited for decedents dying in 2010).[224]

Use of durable power of attorney. In view of the advantages offered by gifts made within three years of death, a client could have incentives for deathbed giving. Once the prospective donor lapses into a state of incompetency, the estate planning opportunity will usually be lost. However, a possibility exists that the prospective donor may retain the planning opportunity through the use of a durable power of attorney. All states now recognize durable powers of attorney. If the principal so desires, the durable power of attorney should authorize the agent to make gifts. The estate planner should check applicable state law to ensure that the durable power of attorney meets all applicable requirements.

Gifts of group-term life insurance. A gift of group-term insurance might be viewed as the basis for a series of annual transfers, in which case an individual could not make a gift that would be outside the three-year rule of Code Sec. 2035. This rule draws gifts of life insurance within three years of death into the donor's gross estate. However, in Rev. Rul. 80-289,[225] the IRS held that where the employee made an assignment of his group-term policy more than three years before he died, and the employer terminated the old policy and entered into an arrangement with a new insurer within

---

[221] Code Sec. 1014(a).
[222] Code Sec. 1(h).
[223] Code Sec. 1015.
[224] Code Sec. 1014(a).
[225] 1980-2 CB 270.

three years of death, and the employee then made an assignment of the new policy to the assignee of the old policy, the policy proceeds were not includible in the decedent's gross estate.

This ruling seems to indicate that the IRS is not disposed to view group-term life insurance as annually renewable term insurance. If the IRS did so, the policy proceeds would be includible in the decedent's gross estate in any case under the theory that each year marked the commencement of a new three-year period.[226]

> **Planning pointer.** When dealing with an employee assignment of a group-term insurance policy, the assignment form should contain language such as the following: "This assignment is intended to be effective with respect to all group-term policies that the employer may later use as a replacement for the current policy."

.02 Limits of the Gross-Up Rule

The gross-up rule of Code Sec. 2035(b) is limited to federal gift taxes. Thus, in those states that impose gift taxes, deathbed gifts can serve the purpose of excluding the state gift tax paid from the decedent's gross estate.

Finally, the gross-up rule does not apply to gift taxes paid on gifts made more than three years before death.

[226] Code Secs. 2035(a) and 2042.

Chapter 5

Charitable Giving

Overview ....¶ 501
Income Tax Deduction for Charitable Contributions ......¶ 505
Estate Tax Deduction for Charitable Contributions ....¶ 510
Gifts of Charitable Remainders ....¶ 515
Charitable Gift Annuities ....¶ 520
Gifts of Life Insurance to Charity ....¶ 525
Gifts of Income to Charity—Charitable Lead Trust ....¶ 530
Contribution of Partial Interests in Property ....¶ 535

¶ 501 OVERVIEW

An individual who gives to charity can benefit himself or herself, family members, and selected charities. Generally, no one should make major gifts to charity until the individual's own financial security and the financial security of his or her family are on firm ground.

The affordability of a gift depends not on the immediate cost in property or money, but rather it depends on the after-tax cost. The major factors in determining the after-tax cost are the donor's filing status, taxable income, and overall tax rate (federal, state, and local). However, the lower rates of tax on net capital gains might somewhat dampen enthusiasm for making gifts of approved long-term capital gain property.

Finally, the significant estate tax savings possible through charitable giving are a major consideration.

.01 Various Techniques for Charitable Giving

If an individual is not ready to make an outright gift, he or she can use various ways to make a charitable contribution while retaining an interest in the property to be contributed. Yet, the donor is able to obtain a current income tax charitable deduction.[1] These ways include the following:

- A charitable remainder trust in which an income interest is retained (¶ 515.01).
- A gift of a remainder interest in a personal residence or farm (¶ 515.03).
- A gift of a lease on, an option to purchase, or an easement or remainder interest in real estate for conservation purposes (¶ 535).
- A bargain sale to charity (¶ 505.10).
- A transfer of property to charity in exchange for an annuity (¶ 520).
- A gift of life insurance to a charity (¶ 525).
- A gift of an income interest to charity through a charitable lead trust (¶ 530).

The techniques for charitable giving are many. These techniques and the special tax and practical considerations for each are developed separately in the subsequent numbered paragraphs of this chapter.

.02 Valuation Tables

The Code Sec. 7520 tables for valuing annuities, life estates, terms for years, remainders, and reversions for purposes of federal income, estate, and gift taxation use an interest factor that is based on 120 percent of the federal midterm rate for the month in which the valuation takes place. For purposes of computing the value of an income, gift, or estate tax charitable deduction, however, the taxpayer has another option. The taxpayer may base the valuation on the federal midterm rate for either of the two months preceding the month in which the transfer takes place.[2]

¶ 505 INCOME TAX DEDUCTION FOR CHARITABLE CONTRIBUTIONS

Anyone who has ever filled out Form 1040 knows that a taxpayer who itemizes deductions on Schedule A may deduct contributions to organizations operated for religious, charitable, educational, scientific, or literary purposes, or to prevent cruelty to animals or

[1] Code Sec. 170(a).

[2] Code Sec. 7520(a)(2).

children.[3] The higher the taxpayer's marginal rate, the greater the tax savings. If a contribution is also deductible under a state and/or local income tax, the value of the deduction is increased.

In preparing Form 1040, questions can arise, such as whether the taxpayer is entitled to a deduction for buying benefit tickets, raffle or bingo tickets; for out-of-pocket expenses when doing volunteer work; and for donations of old clothes. Generally, this chapter does not discuss these everyday questions. Rather, this chapter discusses situations in which clients plan charitable giving with a goal of realizing important estate and gift tax savings. A financial planner cannot find the answers to these questions about planned giving in the Form 1040 instructions.

However, clients might overlook the following two rules. First, a taxpayer may not deduct any contribution of $250 or more unless the taxpayer has written substantiation from the charity of the contribution, including a good faith estimate of the value of any good or service that has been provided to the donor in exchange for making the gift.[4] This rule is discussed in greater detail below under the heading "Substantiation Requirements." Second, charities that solicit or receive *quid pro quo* contributions in excess of $75 (i.e., payments that are partly contributions and partly consideration for goods or services from the charity, such as a compact disc supplied by listener-sponsored television station) must supply the donor with a written statement that essentially makes a good faith estimate of the deductible portion of the payment.[5] The law provides a de minimis exception for contributions of $75 or less[6] and an exception for receipt of an intangible religious benefit.[7] Charities that fail to comply are subject to penalties.[8]

Probably the first thing to do in planning a substantial gift to an organization whose exact status is not known is to ask whether it is on the Treasury list of approved charities. The financial planner might want to check the list. A potential donor might also want to check for possible violations of civil rights laws with respect to its exempt purpose.

The next step is to make sure that the gift does not violate the percentage limitations on current income tax deductions for gifts. These percentage limitations vary, depending on whether the contribution is to a public, semipublic, or private charity; consists of cash or property; is a gift for the use of one of these charities; or is a gift of

---

[3] Code Secs. 170(a) and 170(c)(2)(B).
[4] Code Sec. 170(f)(8).
[5] Code Sec. 6115(a).
[6] Code Sec. 6115(a).
[7] Code Sec. 6115(b).
[8] Code Sec. 6714.

certain types of capital gain property. Any charitable contribution that is not currently deductible because of the percentage limitations may be carried over for up to five years.[9] Hence, before any discussion of the percentage limitations themselves, an understanding of the different categories should prove helpful.

.01 Categories

Public charities. These charities are the types of organizations listed in Code Sec. 170(b)(1)(A). They generally include churches, temples, nonprofit colleges, universities and other schools, hospitals and medical research organizations, government units, private operating foundations, private distributing foundations, and private foundations maintaining a common fund. They also include a broad range of organizations not meeting specific criteria for public charities that have, over a four-year period, received a substantial amount of public support, normally one-third, excluding amounts received from their exempt function or activities.[10]

[9] Code Sec. 170(d)(1)(A).

[10] Reg. § 1.170A-9(e).

Exhibit 5

Checklist of Income Tax Contribution Deduction Rules

Form of Contribution	Amount Deductible	Maximum Deduction as % of Adjusted Gross Income
Cash or Check	100%	50% to public charities 30% to other charities
Appreciated Property		
Long-Term Capital Gain, Generally	(1) 100% of value or (2) by election, basis	(1) 30% public charities 20% other charities (2) 50% public charities 20% other charities
Short-Term Assets	Basis	Same as for cash
Inventory	Basis	Same as above
Tangible Personal Property (Long-Term), i.e., Art, Antiques, Jewels etc.	100% of value if donee's use related to charity, if not, basis	Same as above
Life Insurance	Lesser of 100% of value or basis	Generally, same as above
Intellectual property	Lesser of 100% of value or basis; see ¶505.11	Same as above
To Certain Private Foundations	Basis	20%
Bargain Sale of Appreciated Property		
Long-Term, Generally	100% bargain element, appreciation partly taxed	30% public charities 20% other charities
Short-Term, Generally	None, if sold at basis	
Tangible Personal Property	100% of bargain element	30% public charities
Future Interests	See ¶515	
Income Interests	See ¶530	
Qualified Conservation Contributions	See ¶535	

Semipublic charities. These organizations do not fall within the public-charity category, and include veterans' organizations,[11] fraternal organizations operated under a lodge system,[12] and non-profit cemetery associations.[13]

Private charities. These charities are private foundations that are not operating or distributing foundations, or those not maintaining a common fund.[14]

Contributions for the use of a charity. These contributions are limited to 30 percent of adjusted gross income, as will be noted.[15] A contribution of an income interest in property, whether or not in trust, is considered as made for the use of the charity rather than to the charity.[16] Gifts of remainder interests are generally considered as made to the charity (see ¶515 for a discussion of charitable remainders).

Capital gain property. Discussed at ¶505.09 under the context of gifts of appreciated property.

.02 Percentage Limitations

The various percentage limitations on charitable contributions are as follows.

The 50-percent limit. Generally, an individual's charitable contribution deduction for the year is limited to 50 percent of his or her adjusted gross income computed without regard to any net operating loss carryback.[17] Adjusted gross income in this sense means gross income less the deductions listed in Code Sec. 62. This 50-percent limitation applies to all contributions to public, semipublic, and private charitable organizations. In applying the limitation, however, contributions to public charities are applied first. If the 50-percent limit is used up on these contributions, no deductions are available for contributions to semipublic or private charitable organizations or for contributions for the use of any charitable organization.[18] Contributions to public charities in excess of the 50-percent limit are treated as contributions to public charities in each of the five succeeding taxable years.[19]

The 30-percent limit for certain contributions to private charities and for contributions for the use of charities. Contributions of cash and ordinary income property to semi-public and private charities and contributions for the use of any charitable

[11] Code Sec. 170(c)(3).
[12] Code Sec. 170(c)(4).
[13] Code Sec. 170(c)(5).
[14] Code Secs. 170(b)(1)(E) and 509(a).
[15] Code Sec. 170(b)(1)(B).
[16] Reg. § 1.170A-8(a)(2).
[17] Code Secs. 170(b)(1)(A) and 170(b)(1)(F).
[18] Code Sec. 170(b)(1)(B).
[19] Code Sec. 170(d)(1).

organization are limited to 30 percent of the contributor's adjusted gross income. This 30 percent limit is further reduced by the amount by which contributions to public charities exceed 20 percent of the contribution base. Thus, a taxpayer who contributes 25 percent to public charities is limited to 25 percent for the 30-percent charities.[20] Excess contributions are eligible for a five-year carryover.[21]

The 20-percent limit. Contributions of capital gain property to semipublic and private charities are limited to 20 percent of the contributor's contribution base.[22] This 20 percent is further reduced by the amount by which contributions of certain capital gain property to public charities exceed 10 percent of the contribution base.[23] Thus, for example, if such contributions equalled 18 percent of the contribution base, contributions of capital gain property to semipublic and private charities would be limited to 12 percent. However, excess contributions are eligible for a five-year carryover.[24]

The 30-percent limit. A special 30-percent limitation applies to contributions of certain capital gain property.[25] This limitation will be discussed in greater detail in ¶ 505.09. However, an individual contributing only this type of property to a public charity is generally limited to a deduction equal to 30 percent of his or her adjusted gross income. If the taxpayer contributes the property to a 20-percent charity, the limit is 20 percent.[26] Again, contributions to public charities come first. Thus, if a taxpayer uses all of the 30-percent limitation in contributions to public charities, nothing will be left for contributions to 20-percent charities.[27]

.03 Fixing the Value of Property Contributions

A deduction for a property contribution is measured by the fair market value of the property at the time of contribution,[28] subject to reduction in the case of contributions of appreciated property,[29] as discussed in ¶ 505.09. In addition, special limitations apply to certain types of property contributions, as discussed in ¶ 505.11.

Listed securities present no serious valuation problem; the value is the average between the day's high and low.[30] Other things being equal, once a taxpayer decides to give securities, the taxpayer will receive a larger deduction by donating the securities on a day in which the price is high. The stock market success formula of

[20] Code Sec. 170(b)(1)(B).
[21] Code Secs. 170(b)(1)(B) and 170(d)(1).
[22] Code Sec. 170(b)(1)(D)(i).
[23] Code Sec. 170(b)(1)(D)(i).
[24] Code Secs. 170(b)(1)(D)(ii) and 170(d)(1).
[25] Code Sec. 170(b)(1)(C)(i).
[26] Code Sec. 170(b)(1)(D)(i).
[27] Code Sec. 170(b)(1)(D)(i).
[28] Reg. § 1.170A-1(c).
[29] Code Sec. 170(e).
[30] Reg. § 20.2031-2(b).

buy low and sell high could be modified slightly for charitable contribution purposes. The formula would be give high and hold low.

Determining the fair market value of property where no public auction market exists is more difficult. The fair market value in these situations is generally defined as the price at which the property would change hands between a willing seller and a willing buyer, the buyer being under no compulsion to buy and having reasonable knowledge of the relevant facts.[31] If a financial planner is dealing with an item like a collection of stamps, sales of comparable stamp collections within a reasonable time before or after the contribution might be the best measure of value.

However, a financial planner usually must advise his or her clients about contributions of unique items such as art objects and antiques, whose value determination is more difficult. The French grid system of valuation derives the value of relatively minor works of an artist from the sales of the artist's major works. The value of real estate is one of the most difficult things to calculate. For contributions of property over $5,000, a taxpayer must attach a qualified appraisal to the return.[32] The rules relating to how to determine fair market value are discussed in IRS Publication 561, "Determining the Value of Donated Property,"[33] and in *IRS Valuation Training for Appeals Officers Coursebook,* which is published by CCH Incorporated.

.04 Substantiation Requirements

Under Code Sec. 170(f)(8), a taxpayer who makes a contribution of $250 or more may not deduct it unless the gift is substantiated by a contemporaneous written acknowledgment from the charity. A canceled check is not considered proof. Contemporaneous means on or before the earlier of the date the taxpayer files a return for the year in which the contribution is made or the due date plus extensions for the return.[34] From a practical standpoint, however, a donor should obtain written acknowledgment from the charity as soon as the donor makes each affected contribution.

The disallowance rule for unsubstantiated gifts of $250 or more applies separately to each gift.[35] Although gifts generally are not aggregated, the IRS warns that it is authorized to issue anti-abuse rules to prevent avoidance "by taxpayers writing separate smaller checks on the same date." IRS Publication No. 1171, "Charitable Contributions—Substantiation and Disclosure Requirements,"[36] provides guidance in complying with the substantiation rules.

---

[31] Reg. § 1.170A-1(c)(2).
[32] Reg. § 1.170A-13(c).
[33] Rev. October 2005.
[34] Code Sec. 170(f)(8)(C).
[35] Reg. § 1.170A-13(f)(1).
[36] Rev. July 2005.

No prescribed acknowledgment form exists. The IRS even allows acknowledgement by email.[37] However, the charity's statement must indicate the donor's name (Social Security number or taxpayer identification number (TIN) is not necessary) and provide sufficient information to substantiate the amount of the contribution. Separate acknowledgments for each $250 contribution are not necessary; the charity may furnish periodic statements substantiating such contributions.

The information that the donor must obtain from the charity depends on the type of donation:

- For gratuitous contributions of $250 or more in cash, the charity indicates the amount given and that the donor received nothing in return.
- For gratuitous contributions of $250 or more in property (or cash and property), the charity must describe, but need not value, the property and also must state that the donor received nothing in return. A charity may use an agent to solicit and process contributions of property, such as used automobiles. The agent may provide the taxpayer with the contemporaneous written acknowledgement of the contribution.[38]
- For contributions of $250 or more where the donor receives intangible religious benefits in exchange, the acknowledgment requirements generally are the same as for gratuitous contributions. However, the charity must state that the donor received an intangible religious benefit, although it need not value or describe it. An intangible religious benefit is one provided by an organization organized exclusively for religious purposes and of a type that is not generally sold outside the donative context. An example of such an intangible religious benefit is admission to a religious ceremony.[39]

Goods or services that have insubstantial value as determined under the annually indexed IRS guidelines need not be taken into account by the charity for purposes of the $250 rule. In addition, a taxpayer does not have to take into account certain annual membership benefits received from a charity for an annual payment of $75 or less.[40] Also, the cited regulations address contributions by payroll

[37] IRS Publication 1771, "Charitable Contributions—Substantiations and Disclosure Requirements" (Rev. July 2005).

[38] Rev. Rul. 2002-67, IRB 2002-47 (November 6, 2002).

[39] Reg. § 1.170A-13(f)(2).

[40] Reg. § 1.170A-13(f)(8).

and provide that for purposes of the $250 threshold, each paycheck is treated as a separate contribution.

Reg. § 1.170A-13 sets forth substantiation requirements that must be met for large gifts of property. A taxpayer must obtain a qualified appraisal and attach a summary of it (Section B, Form 8283) to the return if the claimed value of donated property (other than publicly traded securities) is over $5,000 ($10,000 in the case of nonpublicly traded stock). Briefly, the qualified appraisal must describe the property, give the date of the appraisal, the date of the contribution, and any special conditions attached to it (e.g., restrictions on donee's use), identify the appraiser and his or her qualifications, the appraised value of the property, and how that value was arrived at. The appraisal must be signed by the appraiser. The IRS has provided guidance on requesting a statement of value from the IRS for art appraised at $50,000 or more.[41] If the IRS audits a return that claims a deduction of $20,000 or more per item, the revenue agent must refer the claimed deduction to Art Appraisal Services for review by the Commissioner's Art Advisory Panel.[42]

The appraisal must be performed no earlier than 60 days before the contribution is made, and no later than the date it must be received by the donor (due date, including extensions, of the return on which the contribution is claimed).[43]

The appraiser must be qualified to make appraisals of the type of property donated and must not be the donor, the donee, a party to the transaction in which the donor acquired the property, a person employed by, or related to, any of the foregoing, a spouse of such a related party, or any person whose relationship to the donor would cause a reasonable person to question the independence of the appraisal.[44] The appraisal fee must not be based on a percentage of the appraised value.[45] However, this prohibition does not apply to fees based on a sliding scale paid to a generally recognized appraisers' association.

No deduction is allowed unless these requirements are met.[46]

.05 Overvaluation Penalty

Significant overvaluation of donated property can result in a deficiency assessment and a penalty under Code Sec. 6662. If the claimed value is 200 percent or more of the correct value,[47] the penalty is imposed at a rate of 20 percent of the underpayment attributable to the overvaluation.[48] The penalty is doubled where the

---

[41] Rev. Proc. 96-15, 1996-1 CB 627.

[42] Internal Revenue Manual 4.48.2 and 8.18.1.3.

[43] Reg. § 1.170A-13(c).

[44] Reg. § 1.170A-13(c)(5).

[45] Reg. § 1.170A-13(c)(6).

[46] Reg. § 1.170A-13(c)(2).

[47] Code Sec. 6662(e)(1)(A).

[48] Code Sec. 6662(a).

claimed value is 400 percent or more of correct value.[49] The penalty does not apply unless the underpayment of tax exceeds $5,000.[50] Moreover, the penalty does not apply if all of the following requirements are met:

1. The taxpayer proves that he or she had reasonable cause for the underpayment, and the taxpayer acted in good faith.[51]
2. The claimed value of the property was based on a qualified appraisal by a qualified appraiser.[52]
3. The taxpayer made a good faith investigation of the value of the property.[53]

Qualified appraisal and qualified appraiser have the same meanings as they do in connection with income tax charitable contribution substantiation requirements, as discussed above.[54]

.06 When the Taxpayer May Deduct the Contribution

The contribution is deductible in the year made.[55] Problems can arise if the taxpayer makes the payment by check or promissory note, or if completion of the gift is subject to the satisfaction of certain conditions.

The fact that a contribution fulfills a pledge or subscription is of no consequence, even though the obligation might be legally enforceable. When the taxpayer makes the payment is what counts. Payment by check is effective as of the date of delivery or the date of mailing, provided the check clears the bank and delivery is unconditional.[56] Contributions made by credit card are deductible in the year charged to the credit card regardless of the year in which the taxpayer pays the credit card bill.[57]

With a gift of stock, an unconditional delivery or mailing of a properly endorsed certificate is effective as of the date of delivery or mailing, provided that the certificate is received in the ordinary course of the mail.[58] However, hand delivery of the certificate is the best way of ensuring the deduction. Delivery of the stock certificate to the donor's bank or broker for transfer of the stock on the corporate books is also risky at year-end, because the contribution will be effective only when the transfer of the stock is made on the corporate books. The last event could take place after year-end and cause the gift to be deductible in the following year.

---

[49] Code Sec. 6662(h).
[50] Code Sec. 6662(e)(2).
[51] Code Sec. 6664(c)(1).
[52] Code Sec. 6664(c)(2)(A).
[53] Code Sec. 6664(c)(2)(B).
[54] Code Sec. 6664(c)(3).
[55] Code Sec. 170(a)(1).
[56] Reg. § 1.170A-1(b).
[57] Rev. Rul. 78-38, 1978-1 CB 67.
[58] Reg. § 1.170A-1(b).

A contribution in the form of a promissory note is deductible only when the note is paid, even if the note is adequately secured. Attempts on the donor's part to restrict the charity's use of the contributed property or to attach conditions to the contribution can only result in questions as to whether the taxpayer has made a completed, deductible contribution. Even if those questions are answered satisfactorily, they will raise further questions as to the value of the contributions.

.07 Loss Property

Generally, a taxpayer should not contribute property that has a fair market value that is less than his or her basis in the property. The charitable contribution deduction will be limited to the fair market value of the property without the benefit of any loss deduction.[59]

Rather, the taxpayer should sell the property, donate the proceeds of the sale to a charity, and take a loss deduction on the sale of the property. Even if the donor incurs a sales commission, the tax savings from the loss deduction will usually exceed the sales commission.

.08 Applications and Permutations of the Rules

The following subparagraphs (¶ 505.09 and ¶ 505.10) discuss applications and permutations of the basic income tax rules as applied to contributions of appreciated property and bargain sales of appreciated property. The dominant motivation for transactions of this type is often income tax savings. This chapter later examines the estate tax considerations of contributions of appreciated property. Then this chapter examines the income tax and estate tax aspects of contributions of other types of property and different methods of charitable giving.

.09 Contributions of Appreciated Property

Contributions of appreciated property are deductible, based on the property's fair market value at the time of the contribution.[60] However, such contributions are subject to special rules affecting the amount of the deduction.[61] The rules vary with the type of property (real or personal, intangible or tangible), the holding period, the kind of charity, and the use to be made of the property

Capital gain property. Contributions of appreciated property held by the donor for more than one year are generally given

---

[59] *L.M. Withers*, 69 TC 900, CCH Dec. 35,029.

[60] Reg. § 1.170A-1(c)(1).

[61] Code Sec. 170(e).

favorable tax treatment. Such property qualifies as capital gain property. With certain exceptions, and subject to contribution limits that will be discussed, the donor receives a deduction for the property's fair market value and escapes tax on the appreciation.[62]

Three different basic rules affect the contribution of the following appreciated property held long term by the donor:

1. Real estate and intangible personal property (i.e., securities, insurance policies, and other contract rights)
2. Tangible personal property (such as works of art, rare books, and antique furniture)
3. Any contribution to certain private foundations

As for real estate and intangible personal property, the donor is entitled to a deduction based on the property's fair market value at the time of the contribution. However, unless the donor makes the special election, discussed below, the deduction is generally limited to 30 percent of the donor's adjusted gross income. The 30-percent limit applies only if the donor makes the contribution to a public charity (an organization listed in Code Sec. 170(b)(1)(A)(i)-(viii) and discussed at ¶ 505). If the donor makes the contribution to a semiprivate or private charity (a 20-percent charity) the upper limit is 20 percent. The 30-percent limit is applied first. Thus, if the taxpayer exhausts the 30-percent limit by gifts to public charities, he or she has nothing left for contributions to 20-percent charities. However, excess gifts to 20-percent charities qualify for a five-year carryover.[63]

Notwithstanding the general 30-percent limitation on contributions of appreciated property, the donor may deduct up to the 50 percent ceiling if he or she elects to reduce the contribution by the amount of the appreciation. Whether a taxpayer should make this election depends on two factors:

1. The amount of appreciation
2. If the appreciation is large enough, the importance to the donor of receiving a current deduction for more than the 30-percent limit otherwise available

The top rate for most long-term capital gains is 15 percent. For individuals in the 10-percent or 15-percent ordinary income tax brackets, the top rate on most long-term capital gains is 5 percent. For tax years 2008 through 2010, individuals in the 10-percent and 15-percent tax brackets will be subject to a 0-percent rate on their

---

[62] Code Sec. 170(e)(1)(A) and Reg. § 1.170A-1(c)(1).

[63] Code Sec. 170(d)(1).

long-term capital gains. The 2-percentage point reduction in capital gains tax rates that applied to property held more than five years has been repealed.

These rates were originally scheduled to expire for tax years beginning after December 31, 2008. However, the 2006 Tax Increase Prevention and Reconciliation Act (P.L. 109-222) extends the reduced rates through 2010. After that, the 15-percent rate will revert to the 20-percent rate and the 0-percent rate will revert to the 10-percent rate. The 2-percentage point reduction in capital gains rates for property held more than five years will once again apply for tax years beginning after December 31, 2010.

The 25-percent rate still applies to the recapture of depreciation on depreciable real estate under Code Sec. 1250. In addition, the 28-percent rate still applies to capital gains on the sale or exchange of collectibles and the portion of any Code Sec. 1202 gain that is subject to tax. The tax savings from avoiding the recognition of long-term capital gains are equal to the appreciation in the property multiplied by the appropriate tax rate on long-term capital gains.

Charity bailout of closely held stock. What if a taxpayer wants to make a significant contribution to his or her favorite charity, but is short on cash? The taxpayer has a strategy available if he or she holds stock in a closely held corporation, perhaps a controlling interest. If he or she cannot or will not sell the stock, he or she might be able to work out an informal agreement with the charity. Under the agreement, the taxpayer will give the charity some portion of his or her stock. The charity then presents the stock to the corporation for redemption. The charity receives cash for the stock, and the shareholder receives a deduction for the fair market value of the stock. The IRS accepts the U.S. Tax Court holding in *D.D. Palmer*[64] to the effect that, so long as the charity is not legally bound to go through with the redemption at the time it receives the shares, the transaction is to be treated according to its form. Thus, the plan will work even though the parties had a prearranged plan of redemption.[65] The IRS argued in *G.A. Rauenhorst*[66] that it was not bound by Rev. Rul. 78-197. However, the IRS has not withdrawn or modified that ruling. The U.S. Tax Court held for the taxpayer and ruled that Rev. Rul. 78-197 was a concession by the IRS.

As long as the charity is not legally bound to redeem the shares and cannot be compelled to redeem them, a risk exists that it will not redeem them. The charity might attempt to sell the shares to realize

[64] 62 TC 684, CCH Dec., 32,739, aff'd, CA-8, 75-2 USTC ¶9726, 523 F2d 1308.

[65] Rev. Rul. 78-197, 1978-1 CB 83.

[66] 119 TC 157, CCH Dec. 54,899.

cash, or could retain the shares as a minority shareholder. As a practical matter, however, the likelihood that the charity will not redeem the shares is low. The charity is dependent on the donor and others for future contributions and will be eager to retain their goodwill. Also, the charity will be eager to realize cash. The redemption is an easier and quicker way of doing so than attempting to find a buyer for closely held stock at a price that will match the redemption price.

Tangible personal property qualifying for long-term gain. Contributions of tangible property, the sale of which would result in a long-term capital gain, are subject to different rules. The tax treatment depends on the use the charity plans to make of the property. If the use is unrelated to its purpose or function—the source of its tax-exempt status—the donor must reduce the amount of the deduction by the amount of gain that would have been long-term capital gain if the donor had sold the property for its fair market value at the time of the contribution.[67]

The Treasury regulations, in discussing related and unrelated use, offer this example:

> If a painting contributed to an educational institution is used by that organization for educational purposes by being placed in its library for display and study by art students, the use is not an unrelated use; but if the painting is sold and the proceeds used by the organization for educational purposes, the use of the property is an unrelated use.[68]

If the donor claims that the use is related and therefore, he or she need not reduce the deduction, he or she must be able to show the following:

- That the property was not, in fact, put to an unrelated use.
- That anticipating that the property would not be put to an unrelated use was reasonable.[69] A written statement made by the charity of its intended use and one related to its functions and activities, if made in good faith, should give the donor a reasonable basis for anticipation of related-use treatment.

The fact that the charity subsequently sells the contributed property does not necessarily require reduction of the contribution as having been made for an unrelated use. However, the donor must

[67] Code Sec. 170(e)(1)(B).

[68] Reg. § 1.170A-4(b)(3)(i).

[69] Reg. § 1.170A-4(b)(3)(ii).

have reasonably anticipated that the charity would use the property for a related use and not sell it.

Contributions to certain foundations. The deduction for any capital gain property contributed to certain private foundations is limited to the donor's adjusted basis in the property. A private foundation subject to this rule includes a foundation that is not a private operating foundation or a community foundation. However, the private foundation will be exempt from the special rule if within two and one-half months after the year it receives the contribution, it makes a qualifying distribution equal to the amount of the contribution.[70] In addition, a donor may deduct the fair market value of stock given to a private foundation if price quotations for the stock are readily available on an established securities market.[71] The rules governing foundations are extremely complex and technical, and this CCH FINANCIAL AND ESTATE PLANNING GUIDE covers them lightly.

Ordinary income property. The deduction for property that, if sold by the donor at fair market value, would give rise to ordinary income is limited to its adjusted basis.[72] Obviously, a donor would usually not select this type of appreciated property for a gift to charity. Included in this category of property are all sorts of real and personal property, tangible and intangible, held short-term; business inventory items; and crops. Works created by the donor, such as paintings, sculpture, books, letters, and memoranda, are in this category. In the case of a painting, for example, the deduction would be limited to the artist's cost of the canvas and paints. Conceivably, the property could be worth less than it cost to produce it, in which case the fair market value would be used to limit the deduction.

Property with both capital gain and ordinary income potential. Where a person makes a charitable contribution of property that, if sold, would result in the realization of both capital gain and ordinary income, both the capital gain and the ordinary income rules discussed above would come into play.[73] An example would be where the contribution was of income-producing real estate placed in service before 1987 and on which the taxpayer claimed accelerated depreciation deductions. Code Sec. 1250 calls for the recapture as ordinary income of accelerated depreciation over what straight-line depreciation would have been on real estate. Similar rules apply to depreciable personal property under the recapture provision of Code Sec. 1245.

---

[70] Code Secs. 170(b)(1)(E) and 170(e)(1)(B).

[71] Code Secs. 170(e)(1)(B)(ii) and 170(e)(5).

[72] Code Sec. 170(e)(1)(A).

[73] Code Sec. 170(e)(1).

Alternative minimum tax. There is no alternative minimum tax (AMT) preference for charitable contributions of appreciated property, whether real, personal, or intangible.

.10 Bargain Sales of Appreciated Property

Sometimes a charity-minded individual might have a piece of appreciated property he or she would like to contribute to charity. However, the property is worth more than the individual wants to give, and the property is not divisible. For example, a potential donor might want to recover his or her investment in the property and give only what amounts to the appreciation. A donor can achieve this result with a bargain sale to the charity.

However, a donor who makes a bargain-sale faces tax liability. The transaction would be split in two under Code Sec. 1011(b), a sale portion and a contribution portion, with the sale portion being taxable. To figure the capital gain on the sale portion, an allocation of the tax basis of the property must be made between the sale portion and the contribution portion. Follow these steps:

1. Take the tax basis of the property,
2. Multiply it by a fraction where the numerator is the sale proceeds and the denominator is the property's fair market value, and
3. Subtract (2) from the sale proceeds.

The remainder is the taxable gain on the sale portion.

Example 5.1. Jean Freer sells her college a piece of real estate for $48,000, which is her tax basis for the property. The property is worth $80,000 at current values. On the bargain sale, she makes a donation of $32,000 to her college, but will have realized capital gains, as follows:

(1) Tax basis of property	$48,000	
(2) Less: Basis allocable to sale portion	$28,800	$\$48,000 \times \dfrac{\$48,000}{\$80,000}$
(3) Taxable gain	$19,200	

If she had sold the property for $80,000, she would have realized a capital gain of $32,000 ($80,000 – $48,000). The bargain sale saves the tax on $12,800 ($32,000 – $19,200), as well as the selling expenses. Brokerage commissions at six percent would have amounted to $4,800 ($80,000 × 6%).

The contribution portion, consisting of appreciated property, is subject to the rules discussed in ¶ 505.09, dealing with gifts of appreciated property, generally.

If the property sold is subject to a mortgage, the amount of the debt, whether or not the charity assumes the mortgage, is included as part of the amount realized for tax purposes.[74] This rule not only decreases the size of the contribution, but also leaves the donor in a position where the donor is still liable for the mortgage. Most likely, if the donor were eventually called upon to pay the mortgage, this might be considered as a further contribution to the charity. However, it would generally be an unplanned, if not coerced, form of contribution, which hardly commends itself to an estate and financial planning approach.

The bargain-sale rules apply to real estate, tangible personal property that the charity can use, and intangible personal property such as stocks and bonds. However, bargain sales of securities or other forms of property that are fungible or readily divisible seldom make sense. In the case of listed stocks, for example, the donor who wants to recoup his or her investment in a block of stock can do so by selling off enough shares to become whole. Thus, the individual would be in a position to contribute the balance of the shares without having to go through a bargain sale. Still, if the individual has other holdings in the stock and he or she feels that a sale to recoup his or her investment might adversely affect the market, a bargain sale might be advisable. In other words, the estate planner and the client will have to look at the total picture before deciding which way to go.

.11 Other Special Rules

Special tax law rules apply to donations of certain types of property. For example:

Intellectual property donations. A taxpayer's deduction for the donation of "qualified intellectual property" is limited to the lesser of donor's basis or the property's fair market value at the time of the initial contribution.[75] However, subject to certain limitations, the donor can take additional deductions in the year of contribution and in succeeding years based on a sliding-scale percentage (from 100% to 10% depending on the year after the initial contribution) of the "qualified donee income" that the charitable donee receives or accrues from the contributed intellectual property.[76] An additional deduction is allowed in any year only to the extent that the

[74] Reg. § 1.1011-2(a)(3).

[75] Code Sec. 170(e)(1)(B).

[76] Code Sec. 170(m).

aggregate of the specified percentages of qualified donee income exceeds the initial deduction claimed by the donor for the intellectual property.[77]

This charitable contribution limitation and additional deductions apply to the contribution of a:

- Patent,
- Copyright (other than a copyright held by the creator of the property or by a transferee whose basis is determined by reference to the creator's basis),
- Trademark
- Trade name
- Trade secret
- Know-how
- Software (other than software that is readily available for purchase by the general public, is subject to a nonexclusive license, and has not been substantially modified),
- Similar property, or applications or registrations of such property.[78]

However, the additional deductions are not allowed for contributions to or for the use of a private foundation.[79]

Qualified donee income eligible for additional deductions is any net income properly allocable to the qualified intellectual property (as opposed to the activity in which the intellectual property is used) that is received by or accrued to the donee organization during a year. Qualified donee income does not include any income received by or accrued to the donee organization after the earlier of the tenth anniversary of the date of the contribution or the expiration of the legal life of the qualified intellectual property.

To qualify for the additional deductions, a donor must notify the donee at the time of the contribution that the donor intends to treat the contribution as a qualified intellectual property contribution.[80] According to an IRS notice, a donor will satisfy the notification requirement if the donor delivers or mails to the donee, at the time of the contribution, a written statement containing the following information:

- The name, address, and taxpayer identification number of the donor;

[77] Code Sec. 170(m)(2).

[78] Code Sec. 170(e)(10(B)(iii).

[79] Code Sec. 170(m)(9).

[80] Code Sec. 170(m)(8).

- A description with sufficient detail to identify the qualified intellectual property received by the donee;
- The date of the contribution to the donee; and
- A statement that the donor intends to treat the contribution as a qualified intellectual property contribution for purposes of Code Secs. 170(m) and 6050L.[81]

A donee that receives such notification must file a return with respect to a qualified intellectual property contribution for each taxable year showing the amount of any qualified donee income and must provide a copy of the return to the donor.[82] The amount of net income taken into account by the donor in computing the additional deductions cannot exceed the amount of income reported by the donee.

Contributions of vehicles, boats and airplanes. A donor's deduction for a contribution of a highway vehicle, boat, or airplane that is valued at more than $500 may be limited, depending on the use of the qualified vehicle by the donee organization. Moreover, no deduction is allowed unless the donor obtains a contemporaneous written acknowledgment from the donee organization and includes the acknowledgment with the tax return on which the deduction is claimed.[83] An acknowledgment is considered contemporaneous if the organization furnishes the acknowledgment to the donor no later than 30 days after the date of the sale.

For these vehicles, the acknowledgment rules *replace* the substantiation rules that generally apply for donations of more than $250.

If the donee organization sells the vehicle, the donor's deduction is generally limited to the gross proceeds received from the sale, even if that amount is less than fair market value. However, there are three exceptions: The gross proceeds limitation does not apply:

1. When there has been "significant intervening use" of the vehicle by the donee organization before the sale,
2. When the donee organization makes "material improvements" to the vehicle,
3. When there is a bargain sale or a gift of the vehicle by the donee organization to a needy individual.[84]

A "significant intervening use" means that a donee organization must actually use the donated vehicle to substantially further the

[81] Notice 2005-41, IRB 2005-23 (May 20, 2005).

[82] Code Sec. 6050L; Reg. § 1.6050L-2T.

[83] Code Sec. 170(f)(12).

[84] Notice 2005-44, IRB 2005-25, (June 30, 2005).

organization's regularly conducted activities, and the use must be significant. Incidental use by an organization is not a significant intervening use.

A "material improvement" includes a major repair or improvement that significantly increases the value of the vehicle. Cleaning, minor repairs, and routine maintenance are not considered material improvements. In addition, services such as the application of paint or other types of finishes (e.g., rustproofing or wax), removal of dents and scratches, cleaning or repair of upholstery, and installation of theft deterrent devices are not considered material improvements. To be a material improvement, an improvement may *not* be funded by an additional payment to the charity from the vehicle's donor.

In the case of a bargain sale or gift of a vehicle by a donee organization, the sale or gift must directly advance a charitable purpose of the organization to help the poor, distressed or underprivileged in need of a means of transportation. Note that this exception is not available if the organization sells the vehicle to a non-needy individual and merely applies the proceeds to the use of needy individuals.

If one of the exceptions to the gross proceeds limitations applies, the donor may deduct the fair market value of the vehicle. A qualified appraisal is required for a deduction in excess of $5,000.

If a donor donates a vehicle valued at more than $500 that is subsequently sold for $500 or less and none of the three exceptions is available, a special rule applies. The donor may deduct the lesser of (1) $500 or (2) the fair market value of the vehicle at the time of the donation. If the fair market value is $250 or more, a written acknowledgment must be obtained.

The special rules and gross proceeds limit do not apply to deductions for vehicles valued at $500 or less. However, if the donated vehicle has a claimed value of more than $250, the donor must obtain the same contemporaneous written acknowledgment that is required for all property donations of more than $250.

Acknowledgment requirements. All acknowledgments required for deductions over $500 deductions must include the following information:

- The name and taxpayer identification number of the donor,
- The vehicle identification number of the donated vehicle and
- The date of the donation.

Additional information is required depending on what happens after the vehicle is donated.

If the vehicle is sold by the donee organization and none of the three exceptions applies, the acknowledgment also must contain:

- The date the qualified vehicle was sold,
- A certification that the qualified vehicle was sold in an arm's length transaction between unrelated parties,
- A statement of the gross proceeds from the sale, and
- A statement that the deductible amount may not exceed the amount of the gross proceeds.

If the vehicle is to be sold after significant intervening use or material improvement, the acknowledgment must contain:

- A certification and detailed description of (1) the intended significant intervening use and the intended duration of the use, or (2) the intended material improvement; and
- A certification that the qualified vehicle will not be sold before completion of the use or improvement.

If the vehicle is sold and the needy individual exception applies, the acknowledgment also must contain a

- Certification that the donee organization will sell the qualified vehicle to a needy individual at a price significantly below fair market value (or, if applicable, that the organization will give the vehicle to a needy individual), and
- Certification that the sale (or gift transfer) will be in direct furtherance of the organization's charitable purpose of relieving the poor and distressed or the underprivileged who are in need of a means of transportation.

¶510 ESTATE TAX DEDUCTION FOR CHARITABLE CONTRIBUTIONS

Charitable contributions can generate not only income tax deductions, but also estate tax deductions.[85] The value of the deduction varies with the size of the taxable estate. If the estate's top bracket is 45 percent, the deduction saves 45 cents per dollar; if the estate's rate is 47 percent, there will be a savings of 47 cents on the dollar. A contribution made during the donor's lifetime, can generate both an income tax deduction and an estate tax deduction.

---

[85] Code Sec. 2055(a).

[86] Code Sec. 2036.

Both deductions can occur if the property is includible in the donor's gross estate by reason of the donor's retention of a lifetime interest[86] or powers over it,[87] or because, in the case of a gift of life insurance, it was made within three years of death.[88] If the client makes a bequest to a charity, only an estate tax deduction may be taken.

In many ways, the estate tax rules parallel the income tax rules. The rules are generally the same as to qualified recipients, the rules governing gifts of charitable remainders, and the valuation of gifts. However, a significant difference is that the estate tax rules do not contain the percentage limitations found in the income tax rules. Another difference is that the charity does not have to be a domestic charity; a contribution to a foreign charity is deductible in computing the taxable estate.[89]

The deduction is limited to the amount actually available for the charity's use. If the contribution is burdened with transmission expenses or death taxes, the deduction would be reduced accordingly.[90] The charitable deduction is not reduced by estate management expenses attributable to and paid from the charitable share.[91] However, the charitable deduction is reduced for management expenses attributable to property other than the charitable share but paid from the charitable share.[92] Management expenses are expenses incurred to manage the estate's assets such as brokerage commissions, investment advisor fees, and interest.[93] Transmission expenses are expenses other than management expenses. Examples of transmission expenses are executor's commissions, attorney's fees, and probate fees.[94] Whether the contribution is to be burdened with these charges is basically something the contributor should decide in his or her will or deed of gift. If the contributor fails to do so, local law will make the determination. A deductible charitable contribution might add to administration expenses, which will normally be deductible. If a charitable bequest is payable out of residue and the residue is chargeable with death taxes, a difficult mathematical problem arises. Every dollar of estate tax reduces the donation, which increases the estate tax and so on. Reg. § 20.2055-3(a)(2) explains that the computation can be made by the use of an algebraic formula or by trial and error. See also the instructions for Form 706, the federal estate tax return.

---

[87] Code Sec. 2041.

[88] Code Secs. 2035(a) and 2042.

[89] Code Sec. 2055(a)(2) and Reg. § 20.2055-1(a).

[90] Code Sec. 2055(c) and Reg. § 20.2055-3(b)(2).

[91] Reg. § 20.2055-3(b)(3).

[92] Reg. § 20.2055-3(b)(4).

[93] Reg. § 20.2055-3(b)(1)(i).

[94] Reg. § 20.2055-3(b)(1)(ii).

.01 The Estate Tax Deduction

Anyone with a strong aversion to paying income taxes or having his or her estate pay estate taxes can avoid them in one very simple, direct way. He can put his or her money into tax-exempt bonds, marry someone who is likely to live longer, and leave his or her spouse any amount desired and the rest to charity. This plan will result in no income taxes in life and no estate taxes in death.

.02 The Marital Deduction

A split gift to one's spouse and charity may qualify for the marital deduction. This may take the form of a qualified charitable remainder annuity trust (CRAT) or charitable remainder unitrust (CRUT) with the spouse as beneficiary, as discussed at ¶515.01, or a pooled income fund with the spouse as beneficiary, as discussed at ¶515.02.

¶515 GIFTS OF CHARITABLE REMAINDERS

An individual may be thinking of giving money or property to a charity at some future time, but might not be ready to make the gift now. The individual can make a bequest to a charity in his or her will. However, a bequest might take effect sooner or later than the testator would like. A bequest would take effect sooner than desired, if the testator would like to leave his or her spouse or other family member the benefit of the money or property after his or her death. A bequest would take effect later than desired, if the testator would prefer to make a gift to a charity during his or her life. What the individual can do is make a present gift of a remainder interest to the charity. If the individual wants to give money, he or she can so through a trust. However, one can give a remainder interest in property without using a trust. In either case, the remainder interest may be set up to take effect at the end of a term of years, on the donor's death, on the death of his or her spouse, or on the deaths of some other persons, his or her parents, for example. The longer the period before the charity comes into possession of its remainder interest, the smaller the income tax deduction.

The deduction for a gift of a remainder interest is strictly limited. If the gift is to be made through a charitable remainder trust, it must be a charitable remainder annuity trust (CRAT), a charitable remainder unitrust (CRUT), (both discussed in ¶515.01) or a pooled income fund (discussed in ¶515.02).[95]

[95] Code Sec. 2055(e)(2).

[96] Code Sec. 170(f)(3)(B)(i).

[97] Code Sec. 170(f)(3)(B)(iii).

If the gift is not to be made in trust, and if it is a gift of a charitable remainder in a personal residence or a farm, the special rules discussed in ¶ 515.03, must be observed.[96] These rules are relatively simple. A special limited dispensation exists for contributions of partial interests in real estate for conservation purposes (¶ 535).[97] If it is not a residence or farm or for conservation purposes, then the only way a deduction may be obtained is by following the complex rules applicable to CRATs, CRUTs, and pooled income funds.[98] Special considerations apply to remainder interests in tangible personal property (¶ 515.04).

.01 Charitable Remainder Trusts: Annuity Trust and Unitrust

An income, estate, or gift tax deduction for a contribution to a charitable remainder trust that has one or more noncharitable income beneficiaries is limited. The trust must qualify as either a charitable remainder annuity trust (CRAT) or a charitable remainder unitrust (CRUT) to sustain a deduction.

A CRAT provides a fixed annuity to its income beneficiaries, while a CRUT provides a form of variable annuity. They may be set up during a person's lifetime or by will. Both require that their creator set aside certain assets, with specified amounts payable either for a term of years, no more than 20, or for the life of the settlor, the settlor's spouse, or other persons named by the settlor, with the remainder to go to a qualified charity.[99] Both require that the beneficiaries be living at the time of the creation of the trust, that payments be made to the beneficiaries at least annually, and that the principal not be used for the beneficiaries, except to satisfy the specific payout requirement of the trust.[100]

Both forms of trust require a rate of return of *no less* than five percent. Moreover, the trust cannot have a maximum payout percentage in excess of 50 percent of the trust's value. In addition, the value of the charitable remainder must be at least 10 percent of the value of the property transferred to the trust.[101]

Although a CRAT and a CRUT are subject to similar rules, they do have their differences. With a CRAT, the return must be of a fixed or determinable amount and the no-less-than-five percent return is calculated on the basis of the initial net fair market value of the assets transferred to the trust.[102] With a CRUT, the return is calculated on the basis of the value of the trust assets, as determined annually.[103]

---

[98] Code Sec. 170(f)(3)(A).
[99] Code Sec. 664(d).
[100] Code Sec. 664(d).
[101] Code Sec. 664(d).
[102] Code Sec. 664(d)(1)(A).
[103] Code Sec. 664(d)(2)(A).

In other words, the beneficiary has what amounts to a variable annuity. If the trust assets are in stocks or bonds, the annuitant's payments will fluctuate with portfolio values.

With a CRAT, the annuitant *must be paid out of principal* if the trust income is insufficient to meet the payout requirement. However, a CRUT *may* (but need not) provide that, if the income is insufficient, no payment will be made out of principal and that only income must be paid. However, the trust must further provide that any deficit be made up in later years in which the trust has more than enough income to meet payout requirements.

One other important difference between a CRAT and a CRUT concerns additional contributions. Once a CRAT is set up, the law allows no further contributions to it.[104] However, with a CRUT, additional contributions may be made on specified terms and conditions.[105] The additional contributions may be made during the settlor's life or by will.[106] The IRS has issued sample forms of both types of trusts that should prove useful.

Sample provisions for charitable remainder annuity trusts are set forth in Rev. Proc. 2005-53 (inter vivos annuity trust providing for payments for one measuring life), Rev. Proc. 2003-54 (inter vivos annuity trust providing for payments for a term of years), Rev. Proc. 2003-55 (inter vivos annuity trust providing payments consecutively for two measuring lives), Rev. Proc. 2003-56 (inter vivos annuity trust providing payments currently and consecutively for two measuring lives), Rev. Proc. 2003-58 (a testamentary annuity trust providing for payments for a term of years), Rev. Proc. 2003-59 (a testamentary annuity trust providing payments consecutively for two measuring lives), and Rev. Proc. 2003-60 (a testamentary annuity trust providing payments currently and consecutively for two measuring lives).[107] Sample provisions for charitable remainder unitrusts are set out in Rev. Proc. 2005-52 (an inter vivos unitrust for one measuring life), Rev. Proc. 2005-53 (an inter vivos unitrust for a term of years), Rev. Proc. 2005-54 (an inter vivos unitrust providing payments consecutively for two measuring lives), Rev. Proc. 2005-55 (an inter vivos unitrust for payments payable currently and consecutively for two measuring lives), Rev. Proc. 2005-56 (a testamentary unitrust for one measuring life), Rev. Proc. 2005-57 (a testamentary unitrust for a term of years), Rev. Proc. 2005-58 (a testamentary unitrust providing payments consecutively for two

[104] Reg. § 1.664-2(b).

[105] Reg. § 1.664-3(b).

[106] Rev. Rul. 74-149, 1974-1 CB 157.

[107] IRB 2003-31, 230 (Aug. 4, 2003).

[108] IRB 2005-34, 326 (Aug. 22, 2005).

measuring lives), and Rev. Proc. 2005-59 (unitrust for payments payable currently and consecutively for two measuring lives).[108]

Restrictions on investments—tax-exempt securities. Reg. § 1.664-1(a)(3) states that a trust is not a charitable remainder trust if the trust restricts the trustee from investing in a manner "which could result in the annual realization of a reasonable amount of income or gain from the sale or disposition of trust assets."

To restrict a trustee to investments in tax-exempt securities might be deemed to violate the regulation. First, the IRS could question whether such investments restrict realization of a "reasonable amount of income," taking into account the fact that the yield of tax-exempt securities is apt to be less than the yield on taxable securities of equal quality. Because the trust is not taxable in any case, the charity might object to investments in tax-exempt securities. Mandatory investment in tax-exempt securities might also violate the gain portion of the quoted regulation. Of course, if tax-exempt securities are bought below par, their value is likely to increase over time. Thus, the trust would have a possibility of realizing gain. Restricting the trustee to investment in tax-exempt securities or any other types of investments that might be in violation of the regulation would not be wise.

IRS sample trusts include a provision that states that nothing in the trust instrument is to be construed to restrict the trustee from investing in a manner that results in the annual realization of a reasonable amount of income or gain.

If the trust contains such a provision and specifically authorizes the trustee to invest in tax-exempt securities, an investment in tax-exempt securities would seem not to jeopardize the status of the trust. However, as a matter of prudence, the trustee should limit such investments, especially where their yield falls short of meeting the required payout to the income beneficiaries.

Investments in real estate or growth securities would not seem to present any special problems under the regulation. Still, the trust should probably include the sample provision cited and provide specific authority to invest in real estate or growth-type securities.

Split gifts to spouse and charity. A special rule applies for interests in the same property transferred to a spouse and a charity. If an individual creates a qualified annuity or unitrust and the donor and his or her spouse are the only noncharitable beneficiaries, the spouse's interest will not be a nondeductible terminable interest.[109]

---

[109] Code Sec. 2056(b)(8).
[110] Code Sec. 2055(a).
[111] Code Sec. 2056(a).

The donor or his or her estate receives an estate or gift tax charitable contribution deduction for the charity's interest[110] and an estate or gift tax marital deduction for the spouse's interest.[111]

Code Sec. 664(d)(3) makes provision for a modified form of unitrust, sometimes referred to as an income-only option. Such a trust may provide that the trustee must pay the income beneficiary only the amount of the trust income if the income amount is below the fixed percentage yield.[112] If this income-only approach is used, the trust instrument may further contain a restoration provision. This provision allows the trust to pay any income that exceeds the amount that the specified percentage of trust assets would yield to the beneficiary to the extent that the aggregate amount paid in prior years fell short of the aggregate amount determined under the specified percentage method.[113]

Spouse's right of election. Most states prevent an individual from disinheriting a spouse by giving the spouse the right to take an elective share of the individual's estate. As a general rule, a spouse's elective share is based solely on the individual's probate estate. However, in some states, property transferred during life, including a charitable remainder trust established during a grantor's life, may be subject to a spouse's elective share.

On the other hand, the tax law provides that no amount other than annuity payments in the case of a CRAT or unitrust payments in the case of a CRUT can be paid to or for the use of any person other than a qualified charity.[114] Accordingly, the IRS says that the mere possibility that charitable remainder trust assets could be used to satisfy a spouse's elective share technically disqualifies the trust's tax exemption from the start, even if the spouse never makes an election. Moreover, disqualification of the trust technically will cause loss of income, gift, and estate tax deductions for the value of the charity's remainder interest.[115]

The IRS initially took a relatively hard line on this problem. In a revenue procedure issued in 2005, the IRS announced that it would not disqualify a trust created before June 28, 2005, merely because of the existence of a spousal right of election. However, if the spouse actually exercised the right of election, the trust would be treated as failing to qualify as of its creation. By contrast, a new trust created on

---

[112] Code Sec. 664(d)(3)(A).

[113] Code Sec. 664(d)(3)(B).

[114] Code Sec. 664(d).

[115] Rev. Proc. 2005-24, IRB 2005-16, 909 (March 30, 2005).

[116] Rev. Proc. 2005-24, IRB 2005-16, 909 (March 30, 2005).

or after June 28 2005, would escape disqualification only if the spouse irrevocably waived the right to make the election.[116]

In response to negative comments, the IRS subsequently announced that it is reconsidering the problem. Until further guidance is published regarding the effect of a spousal right of election on a trust's qualification as a CRAT or CRUT, the IRS will disregard the existence of such a right of election, even without a waiver—but only if the surviving spouse does not exercise the right of election.[117]

Thus, at least until further guidance is issued, the IRS will not disqualify a trust merely because the grantor's spouse failed to waive the right of election. However, if the spouse actually exercises the right of election, the trust will be treated as failing to qualify as of its creation. Because of this risk, a waiver is highly recommended for all trusts subject to a spouse's right of election. A waiver will provide certainty that the right of election will not disqualify the trust.

Income, estate, and gift tax consequences. Charitable remainder trusts offer several tax advantages. The transfer of appreciated property to a charitable remainder trust allows the donor to avoid the recognition of taxable gains. In addition, the transfer results in an income tax deduction for the present value of the remainder interest.[118] The transfer to the charity is deductible in arriving at taxable gifts[119] and removes the property and any future appreciation in the property from the donor's gross estate.

The value of a remainder interest under an annuity trust, for income, estate, and gift tax purposes, is the net fair market value of the property placed in trust, less the present value of the annuity,[120] computed under Code Sec. 7520 tables. The interest factor under these tables is based on 120 percent of the federal midterm rate, and that rate changes monthly.[121] For charitable transfers, the interest factor for the month of the transfer or for either of the two prior months may be used.[122] Thus, if interest rates change within this three-month time period, a taxpayer will be in a position to choose the rate that produces the maximum deduction (a lower interest rate reduces the deduction for a charitable remainder annuity trust). If two or more lives are involved, computations are based on the life contingencies of each individual.

[117] Notice 2006-15, 2006, IRB 2006-8, 501 (Feb. 3, 2006).

[118] Code Sec. 170.

[119] Code Sec. 2522.

[120] Reg. §§ 170A-6(b)(2) and 1.664-2(c).

[121] Code Sec. 7520(a)(2).

[122] Code Sec. 7520(a)(2).

The following example adapted from the regulations and making use of current Code Sec. 7520 tables contained in IRS Publication 1458 illustrates the process.

Example 5.2. Al Hamlin, who will be 50 years old on April 15, 2007 (age at nearest birthday is used), transfers $100,000 to a charitable remainder unitrust on January 1, 2007. The trust is required to pay Hamlin at the end of each year six percent of the fair market value of the assets as of the beginning of the tax year of the trust. The present value of the remainder interest is $24,974, computed as follows.

The adjusted payout is 5.660% (6% × .943396 [the present value of $1.00 payable at the end of a year using a 6% discount factor]). Table U(1), set out in IRS Publication 1458, shows the present worth of a remainder interest in a charitable remainder unitrust having various adjusted payout rates where the remainder follows a single life. The table does not show a value of 5.660%. It shows a value for adjusted payout rates of 5.6% and 5.8%. To compute the value of a remainder interest with an adjusted payout rate of 5.660%, one must interpolate as follows:

The factor in the table at 5.6% for age 50	.25283
The factor for 5.8% is	.24253
Difference	.01030

Interpolation adjustment:

$$\frac{5.660\% - 5.6\%}{5.8\% - 5.6\%} = \frac{\times}{.01030}$$

$$\times = .00309$$

Factor at 5.6% at age 50	.25283
Less: Interpolation adjustment	.00309
Interpolated factor	.24974
Present value of remainder interest ($100,000 × .24974)	$24,974

With the annuity trust, the federal midterm rate affects valuation. With the unitrust as described above, the rate of return fixed in the trust instrument affects valuation. The higher the rate, the more the life interest is worth, the less the remainder is worth, and the smaller the deduction.

A unitrust involves annual valuations of trust assets and the payout is determined by these valuations. Therefore, unless the trust has assets with established market values, a possible danger is that the trustee might manipulate the values to favor income beneficiaries. For this reason, the IRS could disallow a tax deduction on the transfer of assets with no readily ascertainable value. These assets include stock in a closely held corporation or real estate, unless the trust has an independent trustee, whom the settlor may not replace, to fix values.

If an individual contributes appreciated property to a charitable remainder trust of either type, the rules governing deductions for contributions of appreciated property generally apply, including the 30-percent adjusted gross income limitation,[123] unless the donor makes the special election to reduce the amount of the contribution to the adjusted basis in the property.[124]

Both types of trusts are expressly exempt from income taxes, even though they may have undistributed income, unless they have unrelated business taxable income.[125]

Trust beneficiaries of both types of trusts are taxed on distributions to them, under Code Sec. 664(b), as follows:

- First, as ordinary income to the extent of the trust's ordinary income for the year, and undistributed income for prior years
- Second, as capital gains to the extent of the trust's undistributed capital gains
- Third, as other income (including income exempt from tax) to the extent of such income
- Fourth, as distribution of trust principal (corpus)

For estate tax purposes, if the settlor-donor is the sole income beneficiary, the trust property's full value will be includible in the donor's gross estate because of the retained life interest,[126] but it will be fully offset by a charitable contribution deduction[127] in computing the taxable estate. If there are other beneficiaries, and they survive, the full value of the trust assets will be includible in the settlor's gross estate,[128] but the charitable contribution deduction will be reduced by the value of the remaining noncharitable beneficiaries' interests.

Accelerated charitable remainder trusts. At one time, a literal reading of the charitable remainder trust provisions led some tax practitioners to advocate the use of accelerated charitable remainder trusts. These trusts were designed to convert appreciated assets into cash while avoiding most of the tax on the appreciation.

---

[123] Code Sec. 170(b)(1)(C).
[124] Rev. Rul. 74-53, 1974-1 CB 60.
[125] Code Sec. 664(c).
[126] Code Sec. 2036(a).
[127] Code Sec. 2055(a).
[128] Code Sec. 2037(a).

For example, some taxpayers created charitable remainder unitrusts with an annual payout rate of 80 percent and funded them with highly appreciated assets that produced no income. Additionally, the trust would make no distribution in Year 1, but would sell all the trust assets at the beginning of Year 2. The proceeds from the sale would then be used to pay the required distribution for the previous year. These taxpayers treated this distribution of 80 percent of the trust assets as a nontaxable distribution of corpus under the ordering rule because the trust did not realize any income during its first year.

Current law contains two new rules designed to curb accelerated charitable remainder trusts. The first rule is a percentage payout limitation, and the second rule is a minimum charitable benefit.

1. **Percentage payout limitation.** A trust will not qualify as a charitable remainder trust if the annual payout exceeds 50 percent. In the case of a charitable remainder annuity trust, this means that the annual payout may not exceed 50 percent of the initial fair market value of the trust's assets.[129] In the case of a charitable remainder unitrust, it means that the annual payout cannot exceed 50 percent of the fair market value of the trust assets determined annually.[130] Trusts that fail the 50-percent test will be treated as complex trusts rather than charitable remainder trusts. The result will be that all of their income will be taxed to the trust beneficiaries.[131]
2. **Minimum charitable benefit.** A 10-percent minimum value requirement is also imposed on charitable remainder trusts. In the case of a charitable remainder annuity trust, the value of the remainder interest must be at least 10-percent of the initial fair market value of all property place in the trust.[132] With a charitable remainder unitrust, the 10-percent minimum applies with respect to each contribution of property to the trust.[133] Trusts not meeting the 10-percent test may qualify for relief provisions, which allow for voiding the trust, or reforming it to comply with the 10-percent rule.[134]

.02 Pooled Income Funds

An individual might want to help a charity with a gift of income-producing property, securities, or other types of property, but cannot

[129] Code Sec. 664(d)(1)(A).
[130] Code Sec. 664(d)(2)(A).
[131] Code Sec. 662(a).
[132] Code Sec. 664(d)(1)(D).
[133] Code Sec. 664(d)(2)(D).
[134] Code Sec. 2055(e)(3)(J).
[135] Code Sec. 642(c)(5).
[136] Code Sec. 170(f)(2)(A).

afford to part with all of the income for the rest of his or her life. He or she might also be concerned with providing income during a spouse's life or the life of some other person. The charitable remainder trust, either the annuity trust or the unitrust, discussed in ¶515.01, offers one solution. The pooled income fund, also a creature of the Internal Revenue Code, offers another solution.[135] The pooled income fund was framed with the idea of affording a vehicle for charitable contributions that would meet donor needs and provide a tax deduction.[136] The pooled income fund also provides guidelines and safeguards to permit the valuation of contributions and the protection of the government and the charity.

Pooled income funds involve the pooling of the contributions of several contributors to benefit both the charity and the individuals concerned. The charitable remainder trust can provide a measure of investment diversification for someone who has been locked into an investment by capital-gain tax fears. The pooled income fund should be able to do a better job of diversification because of the larger amount of money it has to invest.

Within limits, the funds themselves can set up their own rules governing the types of property or securities that they will accept. The donor, in exchange for a contribution, receives participation units, based on the value of his or her contribution and the value of units outstanding at the time.

In essence, the pooled income fund is a trust formed to pay income to noncharitable beneficiaries. If contributions to it are to qualify for income tax deductions, the trust must meet these conditions:[137]

1. The donor must retain a life income interest for himself or herself or one or more noncharitable beneficiaries.
2. The charities must have irrevocable remainder interests for which contributions are eligible for the 50-percent adjusted gross income limitation for income tax purposes (¶505).
3. All property of all donors must be commingled.
4. The trust must be maintained or controlled by the charity to which the remainder interests are contributed; however, the charity need not be a trustee.
5. The trust may not receive or invest in tax-exempt securities.
6. Neither the donor nor a noncharitable beneficiary may serve as trustee.

[137] Code Sec. 642(c)(5).

7. For each year in which a noncharitable beneficiary is entitled to receive income, he or she must receive an amount determined by the trust rate of return for that year.
8. On termination of the life interest, the remainder interest must be severed from the trust and paid to or retained for the charity's use.
9. A pooled income fund that is created after February 15, 1991, or that accepts donations after that date, must either prohibit the fund from accepting or investing in depreciable or depletable property. Alternatively, the fund may require that the trustee establish a depreciation or depletion reserve in accordance with generally accepted accounting principles.[138]

Obviously, donors who contemplate this type of gift should evaluate the qualification of the trust. They will also want to examine the trust's current rate of return over a span of years, because that might indicate the return they could expect in the future. It could also be the key to the size of the available income tax deduction.

Relationship to marital deduction. If the donor's spouse is named the sole income beneficiary of a pooled income fund, a marital deduction may be allowed for the entire value of the property as QTIP property if a proper election is made.[139] Neither the donor spouse nor the donor spouse's estate will, however, be allowed a double deduction, that is, a marital deduction for the full value of the QTIP and a charitable deduction for the remainder interest.[140] However, the estate of the donee spouse will be entitled to the charitable contribution deduction.[141]

How the deduction is figured. The charitable contribution income tax deduction is based on the present value of the remainder interest to the charity.[142] This value is determined by subtracting the value of the life interest or interests reserved from the value of the property contributed. If the fund has existed for at least three tax years immediately preceding the tax year in which the contribution is made, the value of the life interest or interests is to be computed on the basis of the highest rate of return earned by the fund in any one of the three years preceding the year of the contribution.[143] If a fund has been in existence less than three taxable years immediately preceding the taxable year in which

[138] Rev. Ruls. 90-103, 1990-2 CB 159, and 92-81, 1992-2 CB 119.

[139] Code Sec. 2056(b)(7).

[140] Code Secs. 2056(b)(9) and 2523(h).

[141] Code Sec. 2044(c).

[142] Code Sec. 170(f)(2)(A).

[143] Reg. § 1.642(c)-6(e)(3)(ii).

[144] Reg. § 1.642(c)-6(e)(4).

the transfer of property to the fund is made, the highest yearly rate of return shall be deemed to be one percentage point less than the highest annual average of the monthly rates (prescribed by Code Sec. 7520(a)(2)) for the three calendar years immediately preceding the year in which the fund is created (rounded to the nearest two tenths of one percent).[144]

Other tax factors. In general, the donor recognizes no gain or loss on a transfer of property to a pooled income fund. However, if the donor receives property from the fund, in addition to the life interest or interests, the donor will recognize gain. In addition, if the property transferred is subject to a mortgage in an amount in excess of the donor's adjusted basis, he or she will recognize gain. In the latter case, whether or not the debt is assumed, the transfer will be taxable in accordance with the bargain sale rules.[145]

The trust itself and its beneficiaries are taxable in accordance with the Code provisions applicable to estates, trusts, and beneficiaries, generally (Subchapter J of the Code). However, the rules applicable to grantor trusts[146] do not apply.[147]

Practical factors. The way in which the remainder interest is valued for the purposes of an income tax deduction might place a potential contributor in something of a dilemma. The donor would like to have both a large deduction and the prospect of a high-income yield. If past performance is any indication of future performance, however, the donor cannot have both. The fund showing the highest rate of return would provide the smallest deduction. The fundamental quandary is for the client, not the estate planner, to resolve. Nevertheless, the estate planner can help with the arithmetic and provide advice to the client.

The donor may not exit from the pooled income fund. The donor and/or the donor's beneficiaries are stuck for life in that remainder trust. Thus, the estate planner should encourage the client to diversify his or her investments.

.03 Charitable Remainder in a Personal Residence or Farm

As a general rule, one may not obtain a charitable contribution deduction for a gift of a future interest in property except through a charitable remainder trust of either the annuity or unitrust type, discussed in ¶515.01, or a pooled income fund discussed in ¶515.02.[148] One exception is the gift of a personal residence or

[145] Reg. § 1.642(c)-5(a)(3).
[146] Code Secs. 671-677.
[147] Reg. § 1.642(c)-5(a)(2).
[148] Code Sec. 170(f)(2)(A).
[149] Code Sec. 170(f)(3)(B).
[150] Reg. § 1.170A-7(b)(3).

farm.[149] An individual may contribute a residence or farm to a charity, without setting up a trust, and reserve the right to live in it or use it for the rest of his or her life (and the life of his or her spouse), or for a term of years. The donor will obtain an income tax deduction for the contribution. The gift must be irrevocable.

Personal residence for this purpose is not limited to permanent residence but also includes vacation homes and stock in a cooperative apartment used as a residence.[150]

A farm means land and improvements used by the donor or his tenant to produce crops, fruits, or other agricultural products or livestock or poultry.[151] The Code, however, provides that, in determining the value of the remainder interest in the real estate, depreciation (computed on the straight-line method) and depletion of the property are to be taken into account. The value is discounted at a six-percent annual rate, except as the Treasury might set a different rate.[152] Pursuant to this authority, the Treasury Department has indicated that rates that are adjusted monthly apply to transfers after April 30, 1989.[153]

An allocation must be made between the depreciable and nondepreciable portions of the property. The value of the nondepreciable portion will generally be computed like any other remainder interest. The value of the depreciable portion (a personal residence is not considered depreciable for other purposes if it is owner-occupied) is computed under a special formula that makes use of a table containing certain factors to be taken into account, including a depreciation adjustment factor.[154]

If a substantial part of the value lies in the depreciable portion, the depreciation factor would seriously reduce the amount of the charitable contribution deduction if the donor or his or her spouse have anything but short life expectancies. Land itself is not depreciable. However, if it is mineral land, or land that can be used as a sand or gravel pit, then depletion must be considered.[155]

Use of these types of property as charitable contributions might be indicated where the depreciation or depletion factor does not loom large; a stepped-up basis on death[156] is not a major factor (limited for property acquired from a decedent dying in 2010); the donor expects to outlive the mortality table's life expectancy; and the donor does expect the property to appreciate substantially in value by the time

---

[151] Reg. § 1.170A-7(f)(4).
[152] Code Sec. 170(f)(4).
[153] Notice 89-24, 1989-1 CB 660.
[154] Reg. §§ 1.170A-12(c) and 25.2512-5.
[155] Reg. § 1.170A-12(c).
[156] Code Sec. 1014(a).

the charity comes into possession. Use may be discouraged where the factors mentioned above do not exist.

Special consideration should be given to Code Sec. 121, which excludes up to $250,000 ($500,000 for a residence held by a married couple) of gain on the sale of the principal residence of a taxpayer who meets certain holding and use requirements (¶ 2820). For tax year 2010, this exclusion will apply to a decedent's principal residence sold by (1) the decedent's estate, (2) any individual who acquired the residence from the decedent as a result of his or her death, or (3) a trust established by the decedent that was a qualified revocable trust immediately before the decedent's death.

Under this provision, a residence with $250,000/$500,000 or more in appreciation is worth considerably more to the taxpayer or a surviving spouse if sold during life than it would be worth if the gain were taxable. This factor might provide an incentive for a lifetime sale, accompanied by other arrangements for a charitable contribution.

.04 Contributions of Future Interests in Tangible Personal Property: Art, Paintings, etc.

A person owning a painting or any other kind of tangible personal property cannot generally receive a current tax deduction for a charitable contribution of a future interest in the property.[157] A future interest is an interest that is to begin in use, possession, or enjoyment at some future time.

In other words, a person cannot obtain an income tax deduction by sending a deed to a painting to a museum if the deed states that the museum is to receive the painting on the death of the donor or after a certain number of years. A donor can, however, receive a deduction when he or she gives up the right of possession and enjoyment of the painting to the museum. When the donor gives up the right to possession of the painting, the donor receives a deduction based on the gift's then fair market value

These rules are contained in Reg. § 1.170A-5. Paragraph (a)(2) calls attention to a form of co-ownership of paintings and other works of art that might offer some interesting planning possibilities. It discusses a situation in which four individuals have an undivided one-quarter interest in a painting, and each owner is entitled to three months' possession in each year. Furthermore, each co-owner can receive a deduction on receipt by the charity of a formally executed

---

[157] Code Sec. 170(f)(3)(A).

and acknowledged deed of the gift, provided that the charitable donee's period of initial possession is not deferred more than a year.

One of the illustrations set out in paragraph (b), Example 5, suggests an interesting twist. A man gives a museum a remainder interest in a painting, reserving a life interest to himself. He then transfers his interest to his son. Because of the relationship, the transfer does not operate to give him a deduction for the remainder interest. However, when the son transfers his interest to the museum, father and son each receive a charitable contribution deduction. Of course, the amounts deductible by each will be different. This technique offers a means of deduction splitting within a family that might produce worthwhile family income tax savings in the right circumstances.

¶520 CHARITABLE GIFT ANNUITIES

Many established charities promote what are known as charitable gift annuities. In substance, money or property is exchanged for the charity's promise to pay an annuity, usually a lifetime transfer. Sometimes, an individual might set up one of these annuities through a will on behalf of another person or persons. In that case, the individual receives no income tax deduction, but his or her estate may claim an estate tax deduction.

The difference between the value of the annuity and the value of the property contributed is the amount allowed as a charitable deduction. The value of the annuity is determined under the tables issued under Code Sec. 7520. The interest factor under these tables is based on 120 percent of the federal midterm rate, which changes monthly. For charitable transfers, the interest factor for the month of the transfer or for either of the two prior months may be used.[158] Thus, if interest rates change within this three-month time period, a taxpayer will be in a position to choose the rate that produces the maximum deduction.

The annuity can provide for immediate or deferred payments. Most charities follow the recommended schedule of gift annuity rates of the American Council on Gift Annuities. Effective July 1, 2006, through June 30, 2007, the suggested rate for a single life annuity for an individual who is age 65 is 6.0 percent. The rates, of course, vary with age. The rates are revised periodically. The most current rates are available at the council's Web site: www.acga-web.org. The annuity payments are favorably taxed. A portion of each payment is non-

[158] Code Sec. 7520(a)(2).
[159] Code Sec. 72(b)(1).
[160] Code Sec. 72(b)(2).
[161] Code Sec. 72(b)(3).

taxable income to the recipient. The exclusion is computed by multiplying the amount received annually by a fraction representing the investment in the contract over the expected return over the life of the contract.[159] Once the investment in the contract is fully recovered, no further exclusion is allowed.[160] If death occurs before recovery, the unrecovered amount is allowed as a deduction on the decedent's return for his or her last taxable year.[161]

Unlike transfers to charitable remainder trusts or pooled income funds, a transfer of appreciated property in exchange for an annuity gives rise to tax liability. The gain must be specifically allocated between the gift part of the contract and the annuity. The gain is taxable to the annuitant, pro rata, over his or her life expectancy. If he or she dies prematurely, that ends the liability if he or she is the sole annuitant. If the annuity is a joint and survivor annuity, the survivor would assume the remaining liability.[162]

In determining the amount to be paid on a deferred annuity, the charity will take into account its use of the money or property before annuity payments start.

If the annuity is a two-life annuity, with the donor as the first life annuitant, a gift occurs to the survivor of the right to receive future payments. Because it is a future interest, the annual gift tax exclusion ($12,000 for 2006, indexed for inflation) is not available.[163] If the donor retains a right to revoke the survivor's annuity, no gift tax liability would occur because the gift is not a completed transfer.[164] If the donor dies before the other annuitant, the annuity's value to the survivor would be includible in the decedent's gross estate.[165] The value would be based on what it would cost to buy a comparable commercial annuity for the survivor.[166]

A spousal joint and survivor annuity automatically qualifies for the estate and gift tax marital deduction as long as only the spouses have the right to receive any payments before the death of the last spouse to die.[167]

If the donor buys a single life annuity for someone else, it is considered a gift to the other individual in the amount of the annuity's value. The annuity has no estate tax consequences when the donor dies.

---

[162] Code Sec. 691(a).

[163] Code Sec. 2503(b).

[164] Reg. § 25.2511-2(c).

[165] Code Secs. 2038(a) and 2039(a).

[166] Reg. § 20.2031-8(a).

[167] Code Secs. 2056(a), 2056(b)(7)(A), and 2056(b)(7)(C).

¶525 GIFTS OF LIFE INSURANCE TO CHARITY

Gifts of life insurance on the donor's life offer many tax, legal, and practical advantages to both donor and charity. Some of the key legal and practical advantages to the donor are as follows:

- **Avoidance of publicity.** A charitable bequest is exposed to public view. A gift of life insurance can be kept secret and avoid possible family arguments.
- **Avoidance of legal challenge.** Some state laws limit the percentage of a person's estate that may be contributed to charity by will. These restrictions appear to be inapplicable to insurance proceeds payable to a charity.
- **Simplicity.** An individual can give a life insurance policy without the legal expenses attending the drafting of a will or codicil.
- **No loss of current income.** Unlike a gift of income-producing property, with this form of gift the donor incurs no loss of income.
- **Possible increase in cash flow.** If the donor is relieved of paying premiums, he or she will experience increased cash flow. (If the donor pays the premium, he or she receives an income tax deduction for a charitable contribution, which increases his or her cash flow to a lesser degree.)

The charity receives the following advantages from a gift of life insurance over a legacy or a lifetime gift of other types of property:

- **Cash equivalent.** The charity, if given ownership of a cash value policy, can cash it in and use the proceeds for its purposes, before the donor's death.
- **Potential gain.** Life insurance can produce instant substantial gains for the charity, especially in cases where the insured dies prematurely. In addition, if the insured dies as the result of an accident and the policy contains a double indemnity rider, the charity will receive double the face value of the policy.
- **Avoidance of probate.** The charity can come into the proceeds on proof of death without the delays attending probate.
- **Loan value.** If the charity owns the policy, it can borrow against the policy's cash surrender value at low interest rates, without any obligation to repay the loan. The charity may borrow against the policy to pay premiums or for other purposes. Universal and variable life products may permit the charity to finance insurance without borrowing from the policy's cash value.

- **Conversion privileges.** As owner of the policy, the charity may convert it to a paid-up life policy for a reduced amount, with no further premiums payable. It may convert the policy to an extended term policy for the same amount to last for a predetermined time, also without further premium payment.

Now, the chapter will discuss the income and estate tax consequences of contributions of life insurance.

.01 Income Tax Consequences

Generally speaking, charitable contributions of life insurance policies on the donor's life are subject to the same rules of deductibility governing charitable contributions of other types of property.[168] The estate planner must take into particular account, however, some of the general rules as they affect contributions of life insurance.

In general terms, Code Sec. 170(f)(3) denies a charitable contribution deduction for partial interests in personal property, except where the contribution is of a fractional interest in the property *or* the transfer is made in trust and is subject to certain strict limitations. Under this section, an outright charitable contribution of a life insurance policy in which the insured reserves significant rights amounting to a partial interest would not qualify for an income tax deduction.

An income tax deduction will also be disallowed if, in connection with a transfer, the charity directly or indirectly pays premiums on any "personal benefit contract" under which the transferor, a family member or a person designated by the transferor is a direct or indirect beneficiary.[169] This deduction prohibition is intended to crack down on so-called charitable split-dollar life insurance arrangements in which a donor transfers funds to a charity, and the charity uses the funds to purchase a cash value life insurance policy that benefits both taxpayer and charity.[170]

The valuation of gifts of life insurance also presents special problems. The Treasury has no income tax regulations on the subject, but the IRS has ruled that the applicable Treasury estate and gift tax regulations may properly be used for income tax purposes.[171]

Under the gift and estate tax regulations, the policy's value is to be determined on the basis of the sale of the particular contract by the

[168] Code Sec. 170.

[169] Code Sec. 170(f)(10)(A).

[170] Notice 99-36, 1999-1 CB 1284 (June 15, 1999).

[171] Rev. Rul. 59-195, 1959-1 CB 18.

company or sales of comparable contracts sold by the company. If the contract has been in force for some time and further premiums are to be paid, the policy's value is the interpolated terminal reserve value on the date of gift (somewhat more than the cash surrender value), plus a proportionate part of the gross premium last paid before the gift, and extending for a period thereafter.

If no further premiums are to be paid on the policy (i.e., it is a single premium or paid-up policy), the value is the amount the company would charge for a single premium contract of the same amount on the life of a person of the age of the insured.[172]

In valuing payments payable on a person's death for estate and gift tax purposes, the IRS actuarial tables must generally be used. Reg. § 25.7520-3(b)(2)(iii) provides that the standard factor under Code Sec. 7520 may not be used to value a remainder or reversionary interest unless the effect of the interest will allow the beneficiary the beneficial enjoyment of the property that the law of trusts affords. An example of a case in which the donor may not use the standard factor is the funding of a trust with unproductive property. Reg. § 25.7520-3(b)(3) provides that transfers of limited property interests are not allowed to be valued using the mortality component of the tables under Code Sec. 7520 for an individual who dies or is terminally ill at the time of the gift. Rather, gifts made by individuals who are terminally ill must be valued using a mortality factor that reflects the individual's actual life expectancy.[173] An individual is considered to be terminally ill if he or she has an incurable illness or other deteriorating physical condition and has at least a 50-percent probability of dying within one year. If the individual survives for at least 18 months after the date of the gift, he or she will generally be presumed not to have been terminally ill at the time of the gift. This presumption may be rebutted with clear and convincing evidence.[174]

If this same rule were to be applied to determine value for purposes of the income tax deduction, a donor whose death appears imminent and who would be able to use the income tax deduction might want to make a charitable contribution of the policy. Perhaps the IRS would apply the rule that the value increases as death becomes imminent only to support higher gift and estate tax valuations. The IRS might not allow the higher valuation for purposes of income tax deductions. Gifts of life insurance also offer possible estate tax benefits, as discussed below.

Premiums paid by the donor, after having transferred the policy to the charity, are deductible as charitable contributions.[175]

---

[172] Reg. §§ 20.2031-8 and 25.2512-6.
[173] Reg. § 25.7520-3(b)(4).
[174] Reg. § 25.7520-3(b)(3).
[175] Code Sec. 170.

.02 Estate Tax Consequences

Life insurance proceeds payable to a named charitable beneficiary might be includible in the insured's gross estate under several provisions of the estate tax law:

- **Code Sec. 2035—transfer within three years of death.** If the insured dies within three years of the policy's transfer, the proceeds will be includible in his or her gross estate.
- **Code Sec. 2042—retained incidents of ownership or reversionary interest.** The proceeds will be includible in the insured's gross estate under Code Sec. 2042 if the insured, at the time of his or her death, possessed any incidents of ownership in the policy, or if he or she held a reversionary interest in the policy or the proceeds, and the value of the reversionary interest immediately before his or her death exceeded five percent of the value of the policy.[176]
- **Policies placed in a trust.** Life insurance policies placed in a trust for the benefit of a named charity may be includible in the insured's gross estate if the trust is revocable[177] or the insured retains a life interest[178] or a reversionary interest in the trust of more than five percent of the value of the property[179] or if, as trustee, he or she may exercise incidents of ownership.[180]

However, the estate normally would be allowed a charitable deduction,[181] which would serve to offset the amount includible. Of course, the insured can avoid inclusion altogether by transferring the policy and all incidents of ownership in it more than three years before death.

.03 Insurable Interest

The requirement of an insurable interest is a familiar concept in all insurance law. The idea is that the applicant for an insurance policy on another person's life should have an interest based on marriage, blood, or financial considerations that takes the policy out of the category of a wagering contract. If a charity were to take out a policy on an individual whose only connection with it was that he or she wanted to make a contribution, a question could arise as to whether the charity had an insurable interest.

[176] Code Sec. 2037.
[177] Code Sec. 2038.
[178] Code Sec. 2036.
[179] Code Sec. 2037.
[180] Code Sec. 2042.
[181] Code Sec. 2055(a).

For this reason, prudence suggests that the charity should never be the applicant for the policy, nor should the donor apply for the policy in the charity's name.

A possible danger occurs if a policy taken out by the insured is transferred too soon thereafter to the charity. The transaction might be viewed as prearranged, with the charity really procuring the policy. The preferred approach would be to assign a policy that has been in existence for some time. If necessary, the donor should obtain a new policy to protect the family.

¶530 GIFTS OF INCOME TO CHARITY—CHARITABLE LEAD TRUST

An individual may use a charitable remainder trust to give income-producing property to a favorite charity while retaining the income and obtain an income tax deduction for the gift. What about the individual who would like to reverse the process, give the income and keep the property?

A wealthy person who wishes to give to charity but who is also concerned with increasing the level of affluence of family members may use the charitable income trust. This trust, often called a charitable lead trust and sometimes referred to as a front trust, is designed to provide the charity with a determinable amount of income for a determinable period. At the end of the period, individual beneficiaries are to receive a remainder interest. Conceptually, it is basically the reverse of the charitable remainder trust in which individuals start out as the income beneficiaries and the charity holds a remainder interest. This distinction is not always clear. Sometimes, individuals may enjoy income interests along with the charity.

The lead trust may exist either in the form of a living trust or a testamentary trust. As a living trust, it is apt to be most valuable. It is most appropriate for use in situations where the settlor and his or her family have no immediate need for more income than they currently enjoy. They should be able and willing to forego current income for the prospect of long-term capital appreciation. In such situations, the lead trust can accomplish the following:

1. Enable the donor to carry out his or her charitable purposes and commitments over a period of years with monies that might otherwise be expended largely in taxes.
2. Enable the donor funding the trust with property with strong appreciation potential to pass the appreciation to his or her beneficiaries without gift tax cost on the appreciation.

3. Enable the donor to exclude the appreciation and gift taxes paid from his or her gross estate. This reduction in the gross estate might in turn reduce estate liquidity needs. Thus, the donor could retain illiquid assets with high yield and/or growth potential, to the ultimate benefit of the individual beneficiaries.
4. Enable the donor to keep control of the trust assets within the family. If the donor uses a closely held business interest to fund the trust, keeping control of the business will be a matter of crucial importance. Funding the trust with other types of investment property will permit the development of investment strategies that will serve family interests.

An income tax deduction based on the value of the charity's income interest under a charitable lead trust is seldom a factor in setting up such a trust. Special rules deny the donor a deduction unless the grantor is taxable on the trust income under the grantor trust rules of Code Secs. 671–677 and then only if the charity's income interest qualifies as a guaranteed annuity interest or unitrust interest.[182] However, the law does not require that the payments be at least equal to five percent of the initial or annual value of the trust as it does for the annuity trust or unitrust.[183]

If the lead trust requires qualifying payments to one or more qualified charities, the donor or his or her estate will be entitled to a gift[184] or estate tax deduction[185] at the time of the creation of the trust based on the present value of the charitable interest. This value is determined on the basis of the present value of the payments provided for in the trust instrument.

The remainder interest created when a charitable lead trust is established during the life of the settlor is subject to gift tax. The value of the gift is the value of the property transferred to the trust at the time of transfer, less the present value of the charity's "income" interest computed on the basis of Code Sec. 7520 tables. The interest factor under these tables is based on 120 percent of the federal midterm rate and it changes monthly. For charitable transfers, the interest factor for the month of the transfer or either of the two prior months may be used.[186] Thus, if interest rates change within this three-month time period, a taxpayer will be in a position to choose the rate that produces the maximum deduction.

[182] Reg. § 1.170A-6(c)(1).
[183] Code Sec. 664(d).
[184] Code Sec. 2522.
[185] Code Sec. 2055.
[186] Code Sec. 7520(a)(2).
[187] Reg. §§ 20.7520-3(b)(3) and 25.7520-3(b)(3).

The standard actuarial factors embodied in the Code Sec. 7520 tables may not be used if the grantor is terminally ill at the time of the transfer. The grantor is deemed to be terminally ill if he or she is known to have an incurable illness or deteriorating physical condition such that there is at least a 50-percent chance that he or she will die within one year. If the individual survives for at least 18 months after the date the gift is completed, however, the presumption is made that he or she was not terminally ill at the time of the gift.[187]

¶535 CONTRIBUTION OF PARTIAL INTERESTS IN PROPERTY

A deduction is allowed for gifts to charity of partial interests in property when the gift is made in trust and the trust conforms to the Code requirements governing charitable remainder trusts, more specifically annuity trusts and unitrusts, as discussed earlier.[188] A deduction is also allowable for gifts of partial interests not in trust made to a pooled income fund, as discussed at ¶515.02,[189] and for gifts of remainder interests in a personal residence or farm.[190]

With these exceptions, a charitable contribution of any interest in property that consists of less than the donor's entire interest in the property does not qualify for a deduction[191] unless it is:

- A gift of an undivided portion of the donor's entire interest.[192]
- A gift of a partial interest in property that would have been deductible if it had been made in trust.[193]
- A transfer of a work of art as to which the copyright is retained. Under Code Sec. 2055(e)(4), the work of art and the copyright are treated as separate properties for purposes of the estate and gift tax charitable deductions.

A gift of a partial interest in property will qualify for a deduction if it is the donor's entire interest in the property. An individual could hold only an income interest in property or only a remainder interest. If the individual holds only such an interest and donates it to a charity, he or she will be entitled to a charitable contribution deduction measured by the value of the interest at the time of the contribution.

[188] Code Sec. 170(f)(2)(A).
[189] Code Sec. 170(f)(2)(A).
[190] Code Sec. 170(f)(3)(B).
[191] Code Sec. 170(f)(3)(A).
[192] Code Sec. 170(f)(3)(B)(ii).
[193] Code Sec. 170(f)(3)(A).
[194] Reg. § 1.170A-7(b)(1).

A deduction is allowed for the value of a charitable contribution of an undivided portion of the donor's entire interest in property.[194]

Thus, a deduction is allowable where an individual is given an interest in an office building measured by another individual's life and he or she gives half of the interest to a charity. If an individual has a remainder interest in a testamentary trust, he or she will be allowed a deduction for a charitable contribution of a percentage interest in the remainder interest.

Reg. § 1.170A-7(b)(2) provides that a deduction is allowed for the value of a charitable contribution not in trust of a partial interest in property that is less than the donor's entire interest in the property and that would be deductible if it had been transferred in trust.

This limitation includes gifts of remainder interests by an individual who retains a life or term interest in the property. The only gifts of a remainder interest in trust that permit a charitable contribution deduction are those in which the annual dollar amount of income interest is payable in the form of a fixed annuity based on the value of the property at the time of the gift (the charitable remainder annuity trust) or in which the annual income payments are based on a fixed percentage of the net fair market value of the trust's assets at the beginning of each year (the unitrust).

.01 Income and Estate Tax Deductions for Conservation Purposes

As discussed above, a deduction is allowed for a charitable contribution, not in trust, of an undivided portion of a donor's entire interest in property. Reg. § 1.170A-7(b)(1)(ii) states that a charitable contribution of an open space easement in gross and in perpetuity is considered a contribution of an undivided portion of the entire interest of the donor in the property. The regulation defines an easement in gross as a mere personal interest in, or right to use, the land of another. It states, as an example, that a deduction is allowed for the value of a restrictive easement gratuitously conveyed to the United States in perpetuity where the donor agrees to certain restrictions. Examples include restrictions on the type and height of buildings that may be erected, the removal of trees, the erection of utility lines, the dumping of trash, and the use of signs. Special rules apply with respect to easements and remainder interests granted for conservation purposes.

---

[195] Code Sec. 170.

As a general rule, gifts of partial interests in real estate do not qualify for a charitable contribution deduction. One exception under Code Sec. 170(f)(3)(B)(iii) is a qualified conservation contribution. Code Sec. 170(h) defines a qualified conservation contribution as a contribution of a qualified real property interest to a qualified organization exclusively for conservation purposes. It then defines a qualified real property interest as either: (1) the entire interest of the donor other than a qualified mineral interest, (2) a remainder interest, or (3) a restriction (granted in perpetuity) on the use which may be made of real property.

The same contribution, if made during the donor's lifetime, can generate both an income tax deduction[195] and an estate tax deduction.[196] This situation can occur if the property is includible in the donor's gross estate by reason of the donor's retention of a lifetime interest[197] or powers over it.[198] If the contribution is made by will, only an estate tax deduction may be taken.[199]

A contribution will not qualify under this provision if the donor has reduced his or her entire interest in real property before the contribution is made. For example, the contribution would not qualify if the donor transferred part of his or her interest in the property.[200]

.02 Conservation Purposes

The term "conservation purposes" is defined to include any one (or more) of four objectives:[201]

1. The preservation of land areas for outdoor recreation by the general public or for the education of the general public.
2. The protection of a relatively natural habitat of fish, wildlife, or plants, or similar ecosystem.
3. The preservation of open space, including farmland and forest land, where such preservation: (1) is for the scenic enjoyment of the general public and will yield a significant public benefit, or (2) is pursuant to a clearly delineated federal, state or local conservation policy and will yield a significant public benefit.
4. The preservation of a historically important land area or certified historic structure.

---

[196] Code Sec. 2055.
[197] Code Sec. 2036(a).
[198] Code Sec. 2041.
[199] Code Sec. 2055.
[200] Reg. § 1.170A-14(b)(1).
[201] Code Sec. 170(h)(4).
[202] Code Sec. 170(h)(5)(B).
[203] Reg. § 1.170A-14(g)(2).
[204] Code Sec. 170(h)(3).

The conservation purpose must be protected in perpetuity to satisfy the requirement that no surface mining rights may be retained.[202] No deduction is allowed for an interest in property subject to a mortgage unless the mortgage subordinates its rights in the property to the right of the qualified organization to enforce in perpetuity the conservation purposes of the gift.[203]

Qualified organizations are limited to government and publicly supported charities or those which, if not publicly supported, are controlled by a government or publicly supported organization.[204]

The value of the conservation easement is based on sales of similar easements (e.g., to governmental bodies) if a substantial record of such sales exists. Otherwise, the conservation easement is valued indirectly as the difference between the fair market value of the property before and after the easement.[205] The before-and-after value must take into account a number of factors, such as any effect of the easement on other property owned by the donor and the likelihood that development barred by the easement would in fact have taken place (and when).

After the conservation easement is made, the donor must reduce the basis of his or her retained property by that part of the total basis allocable to the easement.[206] Basis allocable to the easement is equal to the basis of the property multiplied by the fair market value of the easement divided by the fair market value of the property before the donation of the easement.

In recent years, the IRS has initiated a crackdown on taxpayers who claim what it considers inappropriate charitable contribution deductions for cash payments or easement transfers to charitable organizations in connection with the taxpayers' purchases of real property. For example, in some cases, a charitable organization purchases property and places a conservation easement on the property. The charity then sells the property subject to the easement to the taxpayer for a price that is substantially less than the price paid by the charity for the property. As part of the sale, the taxpayer makes a second payment, designated as a charitable contribution, to the charity. The total payments from the taxpayer to the charity fully reimburse the charity for the cost of the property. The IRS says that, in appropriate cases, it will treat these transactions in accordance with their substance, rather than their form. Thus, the Service may treat the total of the buyer's payments to the charity as the purchase price

---

[205] Reg. § 1.170A-14(h)(3).

[206] Reg. § 1.170A-14(h)(3)(iii).

[207] Notice 2004-41, 2004-28 IRB 31 (June 30, 2004).

paid by the taxpayer for the property, with no amount deductible as a charitable contribution.[207]

.03 Partial Exclusion from Gross Estate for Conservation

If an executor so elects, Code Sec. 2031(c) allows an exclusion from a decedent's gross estate of up to 40 percent (the "applicable percentage") of the value of the land subject to a qualified conservation easement. Where an estate also claims a Code Sec. 2055(f) deduction with respect to the land, the qualified conservation easement exclusion is reduced by the amount of this deduction.

Phase-in of benefits. Under Code Sec. 2031(c)(3), the maximum amount that an estate may exclude as a qualified conservation easement is the lesser of the applicable percentage or the exclusion limitation. The exclusion limitation is $500,000 for decedents dying in 2002 and thereafter.

Location and use requirements. To qualify for the conservation easement exclusion, requirements relating to the location and use of the land must be met.

For estates of decedents dying before January 1, 2011, the exclusion for a qualified conservation easement is available for any otherwise qualifying real property that is located in the United States or any possession of the United States.

For estates of decedents dying after December 31, 2010, land will qualify only if it meets any of these three criteria under Code Sec. 2031(c)(8)(A):

- The land is located in or within 25 miles of a metropolitan area (as defined by the Office of Management and Budget).
- The land is in or within 25 miles of a national park or wilderness area (unless the IRS determines that such land is not under significant development pressure).
- The land is in or within 10 miles of an Urban National Forest, as designated by the Forest Service of the U.S. Department of Agriculture.

In either case, the following requirements related to family use and control must also be met:

1. The land must have been owned by the decedent or member of the decedent's family (generally defined as the decedent's spouse, parents, brothers, sisters, children, stepchildren

---

[208] Code Sec. 2031(c)(8)(A)(ii).

[209] Code Sec. 2031(c)(8)(A)(iii).

[210] Code Sec. 2031(c)(9).

and lineal descendants of these individuals) during the three-year period ending on the date of the decedent's death.[208]

2. The land must be subject to a qualified conservation easement (discussed in more detail under the heading "Qualified conversation easement," below) granted by the decedent or a member of the decedent's family.[209] An after-death easement can be placed on the property, but if this is done, the easement must be in place by the date of the election to claim the exclusion.[210]

Planning pointer. Although the current tax law rules, which were enacted as part of the Economic Growth and Tax Relief Reconciliation Act of 2001, extend the exclusion to easements on land located anywhere within the United States or its possessions, the rules will become significantly more restrictive when that law sunsets after 2010. Therefore, taxpayers who are contemplating such donations should consider whether the easements will qualify for an exclusion under the more stringent requirements. Bear in mind, too, that this is one situation where a taxpayer's heirs can engage in some after-the-fact tax planning. As noted above, qualified conservation easement can be placed on property after death.

An election to treat an easement as a qualified conservation easement for purposes of the Code Sec. 2031(c) provision is made on the decedent's estate tax return, and once made, is irrevocable.[211]

Qualified conservation easement. Under Code Sec. 2031(c)(8)(B), a qualified conservation easement must pass muster as a qualified conservation contribution, as defined in Code Sec. 170(h)(1). To meet this definition, the donated property interest must either be the donor's entire interest in the real property (other than a qualified mineral interest), or a remainder interest. The donation must also be considered to be for conservation purposes as defined in Code Sec. 170(h)(4)(A) (as listed under the heading Conservation purposes, above). However, the fourth listed objective, that of preservation of a historically important land area or certified historic structure, will not support an exclusion claimed as a qualified conservation easement. Further, certain de minimis commercial recreational activity that is consistent with the conservation purpose will not cause the property to fail to qualify for the exclusion.

[211] Code Sec. 2031(c)(6).

Exclusion amount. The exclusion amount is calculated based on the value of the property after the conservation easement has been placed on the property. In addition, the exclusion amount does not include the value of any development rights retained by the decedent. Development rights are defined as rights retained to use the land for any commercial purpose. However, development rights do not include rights that are subordinate to and directly supportive of use of the land for farming purposes, as defined in Code Sec. 2032A(e)(5).

Applicable percentage. Computation of the exclusion depends, in part, on determining an applicable percentage with respect to the property. To determine this applicable percentage, the estate initially starts out with 40 percent, then reduces this number by two percentage points for every percentage point (or fraction thereof) by which the value of the conservation easement is less than 30 percent of the value of the land.[212] For this purpose, the value of the land is determined without regard to the easement and is reduced by the value of any retained development rights.

No qualified conservation easement exclusion will be available if the value of the easement is 10 percent or less of the value of the land before the easement. Computation of the applicable percentage of an easement that would lead to an exclusion appears in the following example.

> ***Example 5.3.*** John Thomas died in 2006, owning land subject to a qualified conservation easement. He retained no development rights in the property, and the property was not mortgaged. The fair market value of the property on the date of death was $8,000,000 without the conservation easement and $6,000,000 with the easement. Thus, the value of the easement is $2,000,000, or 25% of the value of the property without the easement. The applicable percentage is 30% (40% reduced by twice the difference between 30% and 25%). While this result would yield an exclusion amount of $600,000 (30% of $2,000,000), the exclusion is limited to $500,000 because of the exclusion limitation.

To the extent that the value of the land is excluded from the decedent's gross estate, the transfer of the land subject to the conservation easement receives a carryover basis, rather than a stepped-up basis.[213]

---

[212] Code Sec. 2031(c)(2).
[213] Code Sec. 1014(a)(4).
[214] Code Sec. 2031(c)(4).

Debt-financed property. Land for which there is an acquisition indebtedness outstanding on the date of the decedent's death can qualify for the conservation easement deduction to the extent of the net equity in the property.[214]

Retained mineral rights. A contribution of a conservation easement on property qualifies for a charitable deduction for estate and income tax purposes where a mineral interest has been retained and surface mining is possible, but only if the possibility is so remote as to be negligible. Under prior law, a charitable deduction was available for such a contribution only if the mineral interests were separated from the land before June 13, 1976.

Special use valuation. The granting of a conservation easement does not affect specially-valued farm or business property under Code Sec. 2032A. Thus, the grant of such an easement is not treated as a disposition for purposes of Code Sec. 2032A(c) and does not trigger liability for the additional estate tax. Further, the existence of a qualified conservation easement does not prevent the property from subsequently qualifying for special use valuation.

> **Planning pointer.** In order to receive the conservation easement exclusion, the decedent (or his or her estate) will have to grant the easement permanently to a qualified charity. By its nature, such a transfer will lessen the value, and limit the marketability, of the land subject to the easement. Accordingly, like any other significant property transfer, the client should carefully consider the consequences of a conservation easement within the parameters of the client's total estate plan. If the grant of such an easement is consistent with this plan, it can offer a meaningful reduction of the decedent's gross estate.

> **Planning pointer.** In addition to the direct savings that a qualified conservation easement can offer by reason of reducing the gross estate, it can also help the estate qualify for the special use valuation.[215] In addition, a qualified conservation easement can help the estate qualify for the installment payment of estate taxes[216] with respect to family-owned farms and other closely held businesses. However, the land qualifying for the easement exclusion must not be special use valuation property or closely held business property. (If it is, the reduction in value of the property would make qualifying under Code Secs. 2032A or 6166 more difficult.) If, however, meeting the percentage qualifications for special use valuation and deferred payment of estate

[215] Code Sec. 2032A.

[216] Code Sec. 6166.

taxes is not a problem, granting a conservation easement will help the estate qualify for special use valuation without disrupting the operation of the family-owned business itself.

Chapter 6

The Use of Trusts

Overview .... ¶601
Trusts and Income Taxes .... ¶605
Trusts and Estate Taxes .... ¶610
Trusts and Gift Taxes .... ¶615
Types of Trusts and Special Trust Provisions .... ¶620
The Irrevocable Living Trust .... ¶625
The Revocable Living Trust .... ¶630
The Standby Trust .... ¶635
Trusts Created by Will .... ¶640
The Pourover Trust .... ¶645
Grantor Retained Interest Trust: GRIT, GRAT, and GRUT .... ¶650
The Foreign Trust .... ¶655
Special Trust Provisions to Provide Flexibility and Safety ... ¶660
Trustees—Their Selection, Responsibilities, and Powers ..... ¶665

¶601 OVERVIEW

The trust is widely used in financial and estate planning. It is simply an arrangement by which one person holds legal title to an asset and manages it for the benefit of someone else. It has, of course, many uses outside the field of financial and estate planning. One can use a trust in a business setting. For example, consider the employee benefit trust, the debtor-creditor trust, the voting trust, and the trust used in connection with sales and financing.

Given sufficient input, a trust can do almost anything that the settlor might do for himself or herself and some things that the settlor might not be able to do because of lack of a required skill, sickness, disability, distance from the scene, or death.

The ability of the trust to bridge the gap between life and death is surely one of its most remarkable characteristics. Through a trust, the settlor can rule from the grave, not in perpetuity, but for as long as the law allows. Generally, the trust may last as long as any living individuals the settlor names remain alive, and for 21 years after the last of those designated individuals dies. This rule is the rule against perpetuities in its common law form. Many states have enacted the uniform rule against perpetuities, which permits trusts to last for either the common law period or 90 years. The rule against perpetuities is a matter of state substantive law, not of tax law.

Often, a settlor will set up a trust for his or her own benefit, not necessarily for tax, but for various other reasons. The settlor might want investment management or might want to take a chance on some new business venture and use the trust to provide income in the event the venture struggles or fails. He or she might want to form a trust for the benefit of a spouse and family. A settlor might feel that, while he or she is currently able to manage his or her own finances, the future is uncertain. He or she might go off on a long trip abroad, or might have an accident, in which case a standby trust would be beneficial, to manage his or her financial affairs while he or she recovers.

A settlor usually forms a trust not so much for the settlor's own direct benefit, but for the benefit of others, such as a spouse, children, parents, or grandchildren. Often, the settlor might want to provide the beneficiaries with what he or she might regard as missing elements in their abilities, experiences, or training. This desire is clearly the case where minors or others who have been deemed legally incompetent are the intended beneficiaries. However, trusts may be created for the benefit of responsible, competent adults for the same reasons. The settlor might also want to set up a trust for the settlor's own benefit, including freedom from management burdens, freedom to move about, expert management, and other practical reasons, the most eminently practical being cash savings.

For some clients, the cash savings for the family and other benefits that can be achieved through the use of trusts to avoid probate might be important. Possible estate and gift tax savings can be even more important. However, these potential savings must be balanced against income tax costs. Trust income tax brackets are extremely compressed so that accumulated trust income is apt to be taxed at much higher rates than if it were distributed.[1]

These savings, and how, when, and for whom they might be achieved, along with the nontax benefits of trusts, constitute the

[1] Code Secs. 1(e) and 661(a).

main concern of this chapter. This chapter examines various types of trusts—living trusts (trusts that come into being while the settlor is still alive), which may be either revocable or irrevocable; testamentary trusts (created by a person's will), which are irrevocable on the death of the maker of the will; pourover trusts, which are a special kind of living trust into which estate assets may be transferred; sprinkling or discretionary trusts; foreign trusts; multiple trusts; and annuity or unitrusts trusts in which the grantor retains an interest.

Before addressing the specifics of each type of trust, this chapter will discuss the various rules that need to be taken into account in dealing with trusts. These rules include how and when trust income is taxable to the trust, the beneficiary, and the settlor, and how the settlor can keep trust property out of his or her gross estate. The gift tax aspects involved in the creation of trusts and the transfer of trust interests will also be examined.

This very brief summary provides an overview of the tax rules:

- Trusts are generally treated as separate taxable entities,[2] and they have their own limited exemptions from income tax[3] and tax brackets, which are extremely compressed when compared with the tax brackets that apply to individuals.[4]
- If the trust is one that requires all of its income to be distributed currently to the beneficiaries, the trust beneficiaries are generally taxable on the income.[5]
- If the beneficiary is under the age of 18, and either parent is alive at the end of the tax year, unearned income of the child in excess of $1,700 for 2006 is taxed at the higher of the child's rate or the parent's rate.[6] A parent may elect to include the child's income on his or her own return in some cases.[7]
- If trust income is accumulated, the trust is taxed on the income received.[8]
- The settlor (grantor) of a living trust may be taxable on the income of the trust if it can be used for his or her personal or economic benefit, now or in the future.[9]
- Trust property is not includible in the settlor's gross estate if: (1) the trust is irrevocable, and (2) the settlor does not possess any substantial rights and powers over it.[10]

---

[2] Code Sec. 641.
[3] Code Sec. 642(b).
[4] Code Sec. 1(e).
[5] Code Sec. 652(a).
[6] Code Sec. 1(g).
[7] Code Sec. 1(g)(7).
[8] Code Sec. 641(a).
[9] Code Sec. 671.
[10] Code Sec. 2038.

- Transfers to trusts are treated as gifts to the beneficiaries and are taxable or not taxable in accordance with the general gift tax rules.

A financial and estate planner should also have a general idea of what a trust looks like. The following is a description of the provisions ordinarily found in a trust:

- **Property transferred.** The property transferred is described.
- **Trustee.** The trustee is named, and, if it is a living (*inter vivos*) trust, he or she also signs the trust agreement.
- **Beneficiaries.** Both primary and contingent beneficiaries are named and the conditions under which they are to receive income or principal (corpus) are spelled out.
- **Powers.** The administrative powers of the trustee are spelled out.
- **Spendthrift provision.** This provision bars transfer of a beneficiary's interest and stipulates that it is not subject to the claims of his or her creditors.
- **Savings clause—perpetuities.** This clause provides that, anything else in the trust to the contrary notwithstanding, the trust is to terminate no later than the period allowed by the state rule against perpetuities.
- **Bond.** Normally, the appointed trustee will be exempted from having to post bond or other security. Special provision will be made as to whether the exemption extends to a successor or substitute trustee.
- **Successor.** Provides for the appointment of a successor trustee in the event of the named trustee's declining the appointment (in a testamentary trust), dying, resigning, or being incapable of serving. A corporate trustee, for example, named in a will, might decline to serve because the amount of its fee might be insufficient.
- **Trustee's fee.** Provides for the payment of a reasonable fee that is acceptable to the trustee. In some cases the provision appointing the trustee may say that he or she is to serve without fee.

An estate planner should also understand that trust law is complex and is based on the statutes and court decisions of the applicable state. Moreover, the various states do not have a uniform law of trusts. Consequently, a trust instrument should be drafted by a lawyer who knows all the applicable rules.

In the next few paragraphs this chapter gives a more detailed treatment of the income, estate, and gift tax rules than is contained in the brief summary.

.01 Marital Deduction Trusts and Nonmarital Trusts

Marital deduction trusts, along with nonmarital trusts, are discussed in Chapter 12.

.02 Generation-Skipping Trusts

Wealthy clients might wish to create trusts lasting for several generations for the purpose of reducing transfer taxes. Alternatively, they might wish to make gifts directly to members of a generation younger than that of their children (i.e., to grandchildren or great-grandchildren). Generation-skipping transfers are discussed in Chapter 27.

¶605 TRUSTS AND INCOME TAXES

Numerous tax law changes over the past several years have had a major impact on the income taxation of trusts (and estates). In short, as a result of these changes, achieving income tax savings through use of trusts is difficult. In many cases, the family tax bill could be increased if income is allowed to accumulate in a trust.

.01 Tax Considerations

The following are some of the tax considerations in using a trust.

Tax rates. The income tax brackets of trusts are greatly compressed.[11] For example, for tax year 2006, the 35-percent rate applies to taxable income over $10,050. A single individual, on the other hand, is taxed at a rate of 10 percent up to $7,550 and at a rate of 15 percent on taxable income between $7,550 and $30,650 and at 25 percent between $30,650 and $74,200 and at higher rates on taxable income above that amount. A 35% tax rate does not apply until income exceeds $336,550 for 2006. These compressed rates create difficulty in using trusts as vehicles for saving family income taxes if trust income is to be accumulated rather than distributed. On the other hand, a trust can offer family tax savings if the income will be paid out to beneficiaries who are in lower tax brackets than the grantor. Purposely setting up a trust to be a grantor trust whose income is taxed to the grantor also can yield savings in some cases, as discussed below in connection with the grantor trust rules.

[11] Code Sec. 1(e).

Short-term trusts. Use of *Clifford* trusts and spousal remainder trusts, which used to be favored tax planning devices for middle income persons, is no longer recommended. In these trusts, the grantor is taxed on the income of the trust if the grantor owns more than a five-percent remainder in the trust.[12] Nonetheless, as a result of the extremely compressed trust brackets, an individual might want to set up a short-term trust for a junior family member. This trust can produce a lower tax bill than if the trust accumulated income and it were taxed at the trust rates. Also, the senior member's payment of the income tax on the trust's income will not be regarded as a gift to the beneficiary, thereby saving transfer tax. See the discussion below of the grantor trust rules.

Estimated tax payments. Trusts must make estimated payments of income tax.[13] A grantor trust to which the residue of the decedent's estate will pass under his or her will (or, if the decedent had no will, the trust primarily responsible for paying debts, taxes, and administration expenses) is not required to pay estimated taxes for taxable years ending within two years of the decedent's death.[14] In the case of trusts making estimated payments, Code Sec. 643(g)(1) provides that if the trust's estimated tax payments for a taxable year exceed its income tax liability shown on its return for that year, the trustee may elect to assign any amount of the quarterly payments, to the extent the payments exceed the trust's tax liability, to a beneficiary or beneficiaries. Such election must be made on the income tax return of the trust which is filed within 65 days after the end of the trust taxable year.[15] If the trustee makes such an election, the amount of credits assigned to beneficiaries is considered a distribution under the 65-day rule of Code Sec. 663(b)(1). The beneficiary to whom the credit is assigned is deemed to have received a distribution on the last day of the trust year for federal income tax purposes (although the credit will be treated as received on the date the election is made for purposes of the beneficiary's estimated tax payments).

Calendar year. Trusts, other than certain charitable trusts, must use a calendar year as their tax year.[16] Thus, deferral through use of a fiscal year is not possible.

Miscellaneous deductions. The two percent of adjusted gross income floor beneath miscellaneous itemized deductions[17] applies to trusts. However, the costs paid or incurred in connection with trust

[12] Code Sec. 673(a).
[13] Code Sec. 6654(l).
[14] Code Sec. 6654(l)(2).
[15] Code Sec. 643(g)(2).
[16] Code Sec. 644.
[17] Code Sec. 67.

administration that would not have been incurred if the property were not held in trust are not subject to the two-percent AGI floor. In a case decided by the Sixth Circuit, this exception has been held to apply to investment advisory fees paid by a trust.[18] The IRS nonacquiesced in that decision and announced that it would not follow the court's reasoning outside the Sixth Circuit.[19] Subsequently, both the Federal and Fourth Circuits held that the 2 percent deduction floor does apply to investment advisory fees paid by a trust.[20] Most recently, the Tax Court, in a reported decision, once again held that investment advisory fees paid by a trust are deductible only to the extent that they exceed 2 percent of a trust adjusted gross income.[21]

Consistency requirements for beneficiaries. Beneficiaries must file their income tax returns in a manner consistent with how the trust reported their respective shares of the trust's income (Form 1041, Schedule K-1). If the beneficiaries disagree with the trust's treatment of an item or items, they must file a notice of inconsistent treatment with the IRS.

A trust can be a separate taxable entity or a conduit through which income is passed to the beneficiaries. Income generally will be taxable to the beneficiaries to the extent that the trust actually distributes the income to them or makes it available to them.[22] Income is taxable to the trust if it is accumulated by the trust;[23] however, the trust can be set up so that part of the income is taxable to the trust and part to the beneficiaries. In this way, the income may be split in at least one more portion than the number of beneficiaries. If arrangements are properly made, a client can achieve an even better result. The client can have several trusts, one for each beneficiary (see the discussion under the heading "Multiple Trust Benefits" below). However, the cost of doing this must be balanced against the potential savings given that, for tax years beginning in 2006, the lowest 15-percent bracket applies only to the first $2,050 of trust income, as discussed above.

.02 Grantor Trust Rules

The grantor may be taxed on trust income in accordance with any of the grantor trust rules set out in Code Secs. 671-677. Traditionally, these rules were viewed as a stumbling block to saving income taxes.

---

[18] *W. O'Neill, Jr. Irrevocable Trust*, CA-6, 93-1 USTC ¶50,332, 994 F2d 302, rev'g 98 TC 227.

[19] AOD 1994-006, 1994-2 CB 1.

[20] *Mellon Bank, N.A. v. U.S.*, CA-6, 265 F3d 1275 (2001); *Scott v. U.S.*, CA-4 (2003).

[21] *William L. Rudkin Testamentary Trust*, 124 TC No. 19 (2005).

[22] Code Secs. 652(a) and 662(a).

[23] Code Secs. 641(a) and 661(a).

However, with trust brackets now being highly compressed, in some cases, family savings can be realized by causing the grantor trust rules to apply. The income tax cost may be lower than if the income were taxed at the trust's rates. Additionally, payment of the income tax by the grantor will not be regarded as a taxable gift by the grantor to the beneficiary who is directly benefited by the payment. A discussion of these rules follows.

Code Sec. 673 taxes trust income to the grantor if he or she has a reversionary interest in the corpus or income that is worth more than five percent of the value of the trust at the time of the trust's inception. In addition, Code Sec. 673(c) provides that when testing for the five-percent reversionary interest, any discretionary powers are assumed to be exercised in such a way as to maximize the reversionary interest. The only exception is if the reversion is to take place on the death of the beneficiary who is an under-age-21 lineal descendant of the grantor.[24] Also, the grantor is generally treated as holding any power or interest held by his or her spouse.[25] The grantor is taxable if the income is or may be paid to the grantor or his or her spouse, accumulated for future distribution to either of them, or applied to pay premiums for life insurance on either of their lives.[26] The regulations under this section make the grantor liable if trust income is or may be used to discharge a legal obligation of the grantor or his or her spouse.[27] The only exception to this approach is in connection with the support of dependents. Here, Code Sec. 677(b) taxes the grantor only if trust income is *actually used* for the support of someone he or she is legally obligated to support. In other words, the fact that the trust income *may be* used for support is not sufficient to cause the income to be taxed to the grantor.

If the grantor can escape being taxed under Code Secs. 673 and 677, he or she might be taxed under Code Sec. 676 if he or she retains the power to revoke the trust, except under the rather remote contingency specified in Code Sec. 676(b). In addition, income may be taxed to the grantor under Code Sec. 674, if he or she retains the power to control the beneficial enjoyment of the trust property or its income, except that paragraph (b) of that section allows the grantor to retain certain specific powers. The following is a brief explanation of the Code Sec. 674 exceptions, which can be thought of as safe harbors:

- An unexercised power to apply income to the support of a dependent, but, if the income is actually applied to the

[24] Code Sec. 673(b).
[25] Code Sec. 672(e).
[26] Code Sec. 677.
[27] Reg. § 1.677(a)-1(d).

support of the dependent, it would be taxable to the grantor under Code Sec. 677(b), previously mentioned.

- Power to affect enjoyment after the death of an income beneficiary who is a lineal descendant dying before age 21 will not affect taxability during the lifetime of the income beneficiary, but will thereafter, unless relinquished.
- A power exercisable only by will. (This exception does not apply to a power to appoint income accumulated without the consent of an adverse party.)
- Power to allocate income or corpus among charitable beneficiaries.
- Power to distribute corpus: (1) to or for any beneficiary limited by a reasonably definite standard, or (2) to or for current income beneficiaries, if chargeable to their proportionate share of corpus held in trust to pay income.
- Power to withhold income temporarily, on certain specified conditions.
- Power to withhold income during period of legal disability or minority of beneficiary.
- Power to allocate receipts and disbursements between income and corpus.
- Powers of independent trustees will not cause trust income to be taxed to the grantor. This very important exception, provided by Code Sec. 674(c), permits trustees other than the grantor to pay or accumulate income and principal to trust beneficiaries under certain circumstances.

Insofar as the rules described for Code Secs. 674, 676, and 677 are concerned, if the power is exercisable by someone who is described as a nonadverse party, the rules are the same as if the power were exercisable by the grantor. A nonadverse party is simply any person who does not have a substantial beneficial interest that would be adversely affected by the exercise or nonexercise of that power which he or she possesses. A trustee is generally considered a nonadverse party[28] unless the trustee is an independent trustee within the meaning of Code Sec. 674(c).

Then, Code Sec. 675 says that the grantor will be taxable as the owner of any portion of the trust over which he or she has certain administrative powers. The first and second powers set out both deal with actions taken by the grantor or a nonadverse party without the approval of an adverse party. These powers enable anyone to dispose of income or corpus for less than full value or enable the grantor to

[28] Code Sec. 672(a) and (b).

borrow without adequate interest or security. The third power treats the grantor as owner of a trust from which he or she has directly or indirectly borrowed the corpus or income and has not completely repaid the loan before the beginning of the year. This rule does not apply, however, if the loan provides for an adequate interest rate and security and is made by a trustee unrelated and not subservient to the grantor.

There is a fourth part of Code Sec. 675. Its importance lies more in terms of what it permits the grantor (or any person, for that matter) to do without the grantor being taxed on the trust income than in terms of what it bans. It bans the exercise of power in a nonfiduciary capacity by the grantor or any person without the consent of a fiduciary in three specific areas: (1) voting stock held by the trust in a corporation in which the grantor and the trust have significant voting control, (2) controlling investments by the trust to the extent that the trust owns securities in which the grantor and the trust have significant voting control, and (3) repurchasing trust assets. However, the grantor, or any person can exercise these powers if he or she acts in a fiduciary capacity or with the consent of an independent fiduciary. A corporate fiduciary will be safest. These powers take on great importance when the grantor transfers stock in his or her closely held corporation to the trust.

Planning pointer. As noted above, sometimes setting up a trust whose income will be taxed to the grantor under the grantor trust rules will be beneficial for income tax purposes. However, such a trust poses the danger that the trust property will be included in the grantor's gross estate. Nonetheless, discrepancies between the grantor trust rules and the estate tax inclusion rules allow for the creation of defective grantor trusts. The income of a defective grantor trust is taxable to the grantor, but the trust property is not includible in the grantor's gross estate for estate tax purposes (¶610). Carefully limiting a grantor's administrative control over a trust, making the grantor's spouse a discretionary beneficiary, or giving the grantor the power to substitute property of an equivalent value are techniques for making a trust defective.

Example 6.1. Jim Green establishes a nongrantor trust for his one-year old son, Frank, on January 1, 2006, funding the trust with $200,000 in assets yielding 6%. None of the income is distributed to Frank so that it is taxable to the trust. The trust is allowed an exemption of $100. The trust's tax on $11,900 is $3,243.50.

Now, assume that the trust is a grantor trust and Green is taxed on the $12,000 of trust income at a rate of 33%

(for simplicity, ignoring the possible effect of the additional income on Green's itemized deductions and other tax benefits). The tax to Green would be $3,960, an extra tax cost of $716.50. However, a financial and estate planner cannot just look at the comparative income tax costs. A financial and estate planner also has to consider that Green, by paying the tax, in effect, will be making a tax-free gift to Frank without using any portion of his annual gift tax exclusion[29] ($12,000 for 2006 and indexed for inflation) or any of his unified credit.[30] Under this approach, at the end of the trust, more money will go to Frank than if the trust paid the income taxes (as would be the case if the trust were a nongrantor trust) without any additional transfer tax cost.

A word of caution is in order here, however. The result could be different if the trust reimburses the grantor for the income tax paid. An IRS revenue ruling makes it clear that when the grantor of a trust pays income tax on the trust's income under the grantor trust rules, the grantor is not treated as having made a gift of the amount of the tax to the trust beneficiary. However, if under the terms of the trust instrument or under applicable local law, the grantor must be reimbursed by the trust for the income tax paid by the grantor on the trust's income, the full value of the trust's assets will be includable in the grantor's gross estate under Code Sec. 2036(a)(1). On the other hand, if the trust or local law merely gives the trustee discretion to reimburse the grantor—but does not require reimbursement—the existence of that discretion (whether or not it is exercised) will not cause the value of the trust's assets to be included in the grantor's gross estate. The IRS revenue ruling applies prospectively only; the IRS will not apply the holding adversely to grantor's estates with respect to any trust created before October 4, 2004.[31]

.03 How Trust and Beneficiary Are Taxed

Generally, a trust is taxed like an individual, with certain exceptions.[32] A trust required to distribute all of its income currently, receives the equivalent of a personal exemption of $300; all other trusts are allowed only a $100 exemption.[33]

For tax years beginning in 2006, the income is taxed at the rate of 15 percent on the first $2,050 of trust income. The 25-percent rate applies to income over $2,050 up to $4,850. Trust income between $4,850 and $7,400 is taxed at the rate of 28 percent. The 33-percent

---

[29] Code Sec. 2503(b).

[30] Code Secs. 2505 and 2010.

[31] Rev. Rul. 2004-65, 2004-27 IRB 7 (July 1, 2004).

[32] Code Sec. 641(b).

[33] Code Sec. 642(b).

rate applies to taxable income between $7,400 and $10,050 and the 35-percent rate applies to taxable income over $10,050.

The deductions and credits the trust may take are normally the same as those for individuals, with some differences. Most of these are spelled out in Code Sec. 642, and flow principally from the conduit principle that applies to the taxation of trusts.

The conduit principle applies to current distributions of income. The trust reports its income, is allowed a deduction for the income distributed or required to be distributed to the beneficiary, and this income is then taxable to the beneficiary. The beneficiary is taxable on income required to be distributed to him or her whether or not he or she receives the income.[34] The fact that the income could be distributed to the beneficiary is not sufficient. If the beneficiary is to be taxed, he or she must have an enforceable right of some kind to the income. If the beneficiary has that right and he or she chooses to leave the income in the trust, the beneficiary is still taxable on it.

In effect, the trust operates as a conduit through which income, actual or phantom, is passed through to the beneficiaries. The most important concept involved in the conduit treatment of income is that of distributable net income (DNI), defined in Code Sec. 643(a). The DNI concept limits the distribution deduction allowed to the trust,[35] and also limits the amount includible in the beneficiary's gross income.[36]

Basically, DNI is taxable income, and not accounting income. The practical effect is to give the beneficiary of trust income the benefit of all trust deductions entering into the computation of taxable income. The beneficiary receives the benefit of these deductions even though the trust allows some of these deductions to be chargeable to principal or trust corpus, not to income.

For example, assume that a simple trust requires the current distribution of all income to the life beneficiary. The trust has ordinary income of $12,000, expenses of $500 chargeable to income, long-term capital gains of $4,000 allocable to principal, and $1,500 in commissions and other expenses chargeable to corpus.

The beneficiary would receive $11,500. The trust's DNI is $12,000 (capital gains are excluded from DNI under Code Sec. 643(a)(3)), less $2,000 in expenses, or $10,000. This amount is the ceiling on the amount taxable to the beneficiary. The trust's taxable income would be computed this way: $12,000 ordinary income,

[34] Code Sec. 652(a).
[35] Code Sec. 651(b).
[36] Code Sec. 652(a).

plus the long-term capital gain of $4,000 for a total of $16,000, less the trust's exemption of $300, less $2,000 in deductible expenses, less the $10,000 deductible as a distribution to the beneficiary, leaving the trust with taxable income of $3,700.

The example is that of a simple trust. The taxation of complex trusts, which may accumulate income or which may distribute principal, is much more intricate. Two different categories of distributions are recognized: (1) current income of the trust, which is required to be distributed currently; and (2) any other amounts properly paid or credited or required to be distributed by the trust for the taxable year.[37]

Those receiving or entitled to receive the first type of distribution include that amount in their own gross incomes.[38] Insofar as the second type of distribution is concerned, those receiving it are taxed only if the first type fails to exhaust the DNI of the trust.[39] Even if they are taxed, the amount taxed is often only a comparatively small portion of the entire DNI. Hence, in structuring a trust that has both high- and low-bracket beneficiaries, and consistent with the settlor's intent and desires, one would want the high-bracket beneficiaries to receive distributions of the second type.

A beneficiary receiving property from a trust takes the trust's basis,[40] and the trust's distribution deduction is limited to the lesser of the property's basis or fair market value at the time of distribution.[41] However, the trustee may elect to have the gain recognized to the trust with the result of a step-up for the beneficiary and a full distribution deduction for the trust.[42]

Trustees will have to take a close look at the trust's and the beneficiaries' comparative income tax pictures before making distributions in kind. The gain election should be considered where the trust has losses.

The income tax basis of lifetime gifts to a trust is the donor's basis increased by the gift tax attributable to unrealized appreciation.[43] This rule is explained in ¶410.

Assets passing from a decedent, when includible in the gross estate of the decedent, receive a basis equal to their value for estate tax purposes, that is, a stepped-up basis.[44] This rule is an important

---

[37] Code Sec. 661(a).
[38] Code Sec. 662(a)(1).
[39] Code Sec. 662(a)(2).
[40] Code Sec. 643(e)(1).
[41] Code Sec. 643(e)(2).
[42] Code Sec. 643(e)(3).
[43] Code Sec. 2015.
[44] Code Sec. 1014(a).

income tax planning factor in dealing with testamentary trusts. Note: The step up in basis will be limited to $1,300,000 plus $3,000,000 for property received by a surviving spouse for decedents dying in 2010.

.04 How Accumulated Income Is Taxed

The tax brackets for estates and trusts are extremely narrow. For example, for tax years beginning in 2006, trust income above $10,050 is taxed at the highest 35 percent rate. Therefore, the ability to use accumulation trusts to save income tax for well-off income beneficiaries is greatly reduced. However, sometimes one might want to accumulate trust income without any particular thought of tax consequences. A grantor might feel, for example, that the beneficiary does not need all of the income that the trust investments will generate and the beneficiary will not be able to handle it wisely if it is distributed currently. Additional nontax benefits of accumulation trusts are discussed at ¶660.

.05 Multiple Trust Benefits

Code Sec. 643(f) provides that two or more trusts will be treated as one trust if they have the same grantor(s) and substantially the same primary beneficiary(ies) and a principal purpose of the trusts is the avoidance of tax.

The following example of trusts that would not be aggregated might be helpful in avoiding Code Sec. 643(f).

> ***Example 6.2.*** Frank McGill establishes two irrevocable trusts for the benefit of his son and daughter. The son is the income beneficiary of the first trust, and the trustee (Bank of P) is required to pay all income currently to the son for life. The daughter is the remainder beneficiary and is an income beneficiary of the second trust. The trust instrument for the second trust permits the trustee (Bank of D) to accumulate or to pay income, in its discretion, to the daughter for her education, support, and maintenance. The trustee may also pay income or corpus to the son for his medical expenses. The daughter is the remainder beneficiary and will receive the trust corpus upon the son's death.

Absent rules or regulations to the contrary, financial and estate planners might also find the following strategies to be useful:

- Two or more trusts may be created by the same grantor for different beneficiaries and the trusts will be entitled to independent recognition for tax purposes.

- The U.S. Tax Court's holding in *E. Morris Trusts*,[45] in which the same grantor uses one instrument to create two or more trusts for different beneficiaries with independent interests in the trust property, might be useful in creating separate taxpaying entities.
- Code Sec. 643(f) recognizes the independence of separate trusts created by the same grantor if the trusts have different dispositive provisions, do not have substantially the same beneficiaries, and do not have tax avoidance as a principal purpose.
- Any multiple trusts used should be structured so that each trust is as different as is possible while remaining consistent with the grantor's underlying intent. The settlor should make clear the purposes for which each trust is to be established, especially where substantive, dispositive provisions are involved. If possible the beneficiaries also should be different.

  Also, nontax reasons for the trusts should be stressed. If adult children, for example, are the beneficiaries, each one might have different needs, different attitudes toward investment risk, and varying degrees of sophistication and maturity. All of these differences can be used to negate tax considerations as a principal purpose of the multiple trusts. The intent to avoid jealousies and antagonism, if a real factor, might also support the claim of nontax factors.
- The statute refers to two or more trusts. Unless the regulations take a broad view of what is a trust, a grantor might be able to make gifts, for example, to a uniform gift to minor's custodianship and to a trust for the child and not run afoul of the rules of Code Sec. 643(f). This strategy could give the grantor all of the benefits of two trusts for the same child, with attendant income-splitting possibilities. Yet, this arrangement would technically be outside the scope of the statute's definition.

.06 Trusts and S Corporations

Subject to certain exceptions, trusts may not be shareholders of an S corporation. The chief exceptions are a voting trust, a grantor trust (i.e., income from the trust is taxable to the grantor under Code Secs. 671-677), a trust in which a person other than the grantor is treated as the owner under Code Sec. 678, and a qualified subchapter S trust. In addition, an electing small business trust may be an S corporation shareholder.[46]

---

[45] 51 TC 20, CCH Dec. 29,181 (1968).

[46] Code Sec. 1361(c)(2)(A).

The electing small business trust provisions permit broader estate planning opportunities for S corporation shareholders by allowing trusts to be funded with S corporation stock. To qualify, all beneficiaries of the electing small business trust must be individuals or estates eligible to be S corporation shareholders, except that charitable organizations may hold contingent remainder interests. For a small business trust to be an eligible S corporation shareholder, interests in the trust must be acquired by reason of gift, bequest, or other nonpurchase acquisition method.[47]

Although electing small business trusts may allow broader planning opportunities, they come with a distinctly negative tax consequence. The portion of the trust that consists of S corporation stock is treated as a separate trust for purposes of computing the income tax attributable to the S corporation stock held by the trust. This portion of the trust's income, except for net capital gains, is taxed at the highest rate imposed on estates and trusts (35 percent under Code Sec. 1(e)). Net capital gains are taxed at the usual rates specified in Code Sec. 1(h).[48] The taxable income attributable to this portion includes the following: (1) the items of income, loss, or deduction allocated to the trust as an S corporation shareholder under the rules of subchapter S, (2) gain or loss from the sale of the S corporation stock, and (3) any state or local income taxes and administrative expenses of the trust properly allocable to the S corporation stock. Otherwise, allowable capital losses are allowed only to the extent of capital gains.[49]

As a general rule, if any trust, other than those types listed above, holds stock in a corporation that has made an S election, the election is automatically nullified.[50] In such cases, the corporation will be taxed as a regular C corporation. Hence, it will not be able to pass through its income and losses to its shareholders. Note, however, that there are two limited exceptions to this rule. A trust in which the grantor or another person is treated as the owner may continue as an eligible shareholder following the death of the owner, but only for two years beginning on the date of the owner's death.[51] In addition, a testamentary trust that receives S corporation stock on the death of an S corporation owner qualifies as an eligible shareholder for a two-year period beginning on the date the stock is transferred to the trust.[52]

.07 Short-Term Trusts

Both *Clifford* trusts (in which the grantor has a reversionary interest) and spousal remainder trusts created after March 1, 1986,

---

[47] Code Sec. 1361(e).
[48] Reg. § 1.641(c)-1(e)(1).
[49] Code Sec. 641(c).
[50] Code Sec. 1362(d)(2).
[51] Code Sec. 1361(c)(2)(A)(ii).
[52] Code Sec. 1361(c)(2)(A)(iii).

are impractical. Code Sec. 673 provides that grantors are taxable on trust income if either they or their spouses retained a reversionary or remainder interest in the trust property of a present value of more than five percent. An exception is provided for an interest to take effect on the death of a minor income beneficiary before age 21.[53] This contingency is highly unlikely.

The demise of *Clifford* trusts eliminated an opportunity to save family income taxes. However, as a result of the extremely compressed trust brackets, an individual might want to set up a Short-term trust for a junior family member even though the individual will be taxed on the trust's income under the grantor trust rules. This result might produce a lower tax bill than if the trust accumulated income and were taxed at the trust brackets. Also, the senior member's payment of the income tax on the trust's income will generally not be regarded as a gift to the child, thereby saving transfer tax. See the discussion above of the grantor trust rules.

.08 Alternative Minimum Tax

The alternative minimum tax (AMT)[54] is applied to estates and trusts by determining distributable net income on a minimum tax basis. The estate or trust then allocates to each beneficiary his or her proportionate share of distributable net alternative minimum taxable income (DNAMTI). Form 1041 Schedule I is to be used by a fiduciary to compute DNAMTI, the beneficiary's share of DNAMTI, and the fiduciary's share of alternative minimum tax.

¶610 TRUSTS AND ESTATE TAXES

An estate planner should answer a couple of questions regarding the effect of estate taxes on trust assets. The first question is "Will the trust property be included in the gross estate of the settlor (grantor) or in the gross estate of one or more of the trust beneficiaries?" The second question is "Will exclusion from the settlor's gross estate really make a difference in the taxable estate?"

An estate planner should not exert much effort to keep trust property out of the settlor's gross estate or out of another individual's gross estate if its inclusion in the gross estate will not cause any estate tax. If its inclusion in the gross estate will cause no tax, the estate planner must determine whether keeping the trust property out of the estate to avoid probate and its attendant expenses is worthwhile. Costs vary from state to state, depending principally on the fees,

[53] Code Sec. 673(b).

[54] Code Sec. 55.

if any, to be paid to the executor of the estate and his or her legal counsel.

A living (*inter vivos*) trust is one that takes effect during the settlor's lifetime. Whether property held in such a trust will be includible in the settlor's gross estate depends on whether the settlor is willing to give up all of his or her interests in the trust property and personal control over it.[55]

If the settlor is willing to part with the trust property forever and have nothing further to do with it and its administration, the property will not be included in his or her gross estate. An exception applies if the property consists of life insurance on the life of the settlor and he or she dies within three years of transferring it to the trust.[56] In such a case, the proceeds will be includible in the settlor's gross estate.

Most settlors, however, are reluctant to sever themselves from any substantial part of their property, permanently, and absolutely, to save estate taxes. These people are not concerned with the hereafter; they are concerned with the present. They want a regular check coming from the trust, or to be able to terminate the trust if it does not seem to be working out the way they intended. In addition, the settlor might want to designate which beneficiaries are to receive distributions, when they are to receive them, or for what purpose they may receive them. In all of these circumstances, the property is includible in the settlor's gross estate.[57]

Problems arise with living trusts only in the situations between the two extremes. In these cases, the settlor is not entirely separated from the trust property. Whether the settlor has retained enough control over it or benefit from it to warrant its inclusion in his or her gross estate is not clear. Ultimately, the trust settlor must choose between enjoyment and control of the property, or his or her estate's ability to exclude the property from the gross estate.

The underlying tax policy is reflected in and implemented by an array of Code sections. The essence of these provisions is that, if the settlor wants to keep the trust property out of his or her gross estate, he or she should observe the following rules:

- **Power to revoke or change.** The settlor should not, under *any* circumstances, be caught with a power to revoke, alter, amend, or terminate the trust. If the settlor does have such power, he or she should give it up more than three years before death.[58]

---

[55] Code Sec. 2038.

[56] Code Secs. 2035(a) and 2042.

[57] Code Sec. 2041.

[58] Code Secs. 2035 and 2038.

- **Retained life interest.** The settlor should not retain a life interest in the possession or enjoyment of, or the right to, the income from the property or the right, either alone or with anyone else, to dictate who is going to enjoy or possess the property or its income.[59] Neither should the settlor retain voting rights in stock in a controlled corporation transferred to a trust.[60]
- **Reversionary interest.** A settlor should not form a trust so that someone else can get the property only if he or she survives the settlor while the settlor keeps a reversionary interest proving to be worth more than five percent of the value of the property when the settlor dies. This value is determined by mortality tables and actuarial principles. Reversionary interest is broadly defined to include a *possibility* that the property might return to the settlor or his or her estate or that the settlor might control its disposition.[61] If the settlor has such an interest, he or she should give it up more than three years before death.[62]
- **Power to direct disposition.** The settlor should not retain a general power of appointment, as defined in Code Sec. 2041. Briefly, that power permits its holder to control the disposition of the property in his or her own favor, or that of his or her estate or his or her creditors. However, Code Sec. 2041 has exceptions that allow the holder to use trust property for his or her own benefit if the power is limited by an ascertainable standard relating to his or her health, education, support, or maintenance. Incidentally, Code Sec. 2041 deals not only with the situation where the settlor is the holder of a general power of appointment, but also with those cases where that power is held by anyone else. The trust property is includible in the holder's gross estate, no matter who the settlor is, if he or she still holds that power when he or she dies or had released it some time before his or her death so that it would be includible in his or her gross estate under any one of the Code sections mentioned in paragraphs 1 to 3, above.
- **Power over insurance policy.** If an insurance policy is to be part of the trust property, the insured should not designate the estate as the beneficiary. If someone else is named as beneficiary, the insured should not retain any incidents of ownership in the policy; otherwise the proceeds will be includible in his or her gross estate under Code Sec. 2042. A transfer of the policy or incidents of ownership within three years of death will result in inclusion of the proceeds

[59] Code Sec. 2036(a).

[60] Code Sec. 2036(b).

[61] Code Sec. 2037.

[62] Code Secs. 2035 and 2037.

in the decedent's gross estate.[63] On the other hand, if a trust applies for a new policy of life insurance on the settlor's life, the proceeds may be excludable even if the settlor dies within three years, provided that the trustees were not required to buy the policy by the settlor. This topic is discussed in more depth at ¶ 735, where insurance trusts are discussed.

- **Retention of any interest—the catchall.** The settlor should not retain any interest in the property at the time of his or her death.[64] Generally, one must check local law to determine whether the settlor held any interest in the property.
- **Transfers within three years of death.** As a general rule, transfers within three years of death are not includible in the transferor's gross estate. However, interests in property otherwise includible in the gross estate under any one or more of Code Secs. 2036-2038 or 2042 (or those that would have been included if the interest had been retained by the decedent) will be included in the transfer's gross estate if the transferor dies within three years of the transfer.[65]

Despite this rather formidable lineup of barriers to prevent the trust property from being kept out of the settlor's gross estate, the settlor can still exclude it from his or her gross estate through careful planning. All of the interests and powers mentioned in the first six paragraphs above refer to interests or powers possessed at death. Hence, the mere fact that the settlor possesses any of these interests or powers at the time he or she forms the trust does not automatically cause the trust property to be included in the settlor's gross estate. The settlor must relinquish such powers or interests before his or her death. If the settlor waits too long, i.e., until within three years of death, then the property may be includible in his or her gross estate under Code Sec. 2035, just discussed.

The settlor should also consider the gift considerations discussed in Chapter 4 and the tax factors in ¶ 405. Deductions are also allowed that operate in favor of the settlor and his or her estate. If the settlor is married, he or she has the marital deduction available.[66] The charitable deduction is also available.[67] If the settlor wants to give a spouse the entire estate or something less than the entire estate and the rest to a qualified charity, the estate will be free of federal estate taxes. Also, life insurance proceeds may be excluded under Code Sec. 2042 if properly handled. Further, any tentative estate tax liability may be offset by the unified credit,[68] so that no estate tax actually need be paid.

---

[63] Code Sec. 2035(a).
[64] Code Sec. 2033.
[65] Code Sec. 2035(a) and (d).
[66] Code Sec. 2056(a).
[67] Code Sec. 2055(a).
[68] Code Sec. 2010.

If the estate will have no tax liability after the unified credit despite the inclusion of the trust property in the gross estate, the more immediate concern is apt to be to make sure that the settlor retains control over the trust property. However, if the settlor is making a lifetime transfer to a trust, he or she needs to look to the effect of inclusion of the property not merely on the basis of its current value, but also in terms of its appreciation potential. If the appreciation potential is such as to provide estate tax exposure when death is likely to occur (based on reasonable assumptions as to the life expectancy of the settlor), the settlor might prefer to surrender control over the property.

.01 Retention of Beneficial Enjoyment or Management or Administrative Powers

The basic test of whether a retained power will result in the inclusion of the property subject to the power in the holder's gross estate is whether it affects the beneficial enjoyment of the property. As a general rule, mere administrative or management powers do not affect beneficial enjoyment. Whether a given power is merely administrative or affects beneficial enjoyment is not always clear.

State law is the first thing to consult. Because federal tax law is also involved, these questions most frequently arise in the federal courts. The U.S. Supreme Court has ruled that federal courts are bound only by decisions of the highest state court on the interpretation of state law.[69] The result is that federal decisions, either applying state law as laid down by the state's highest court or supplying their own interpretations of state law, become the principal benchmarks for determining which powers are administrative or managerial.

However, Congress can and has over turned such court decisions. For example, an amendment to Code Sec. 2036 effectively reversed a decision of the U.S. Supreme Court construing the cited section before amendment. The decision was *M. Byrum*,[70] which held that Byrum's retention of the voting rights to the stock transferred to the trust did not constitute retained enjoyment of the stock within the meaning of Code Sec. 2036(a)(1). Congress provided that the amendment applies only to retained voting rights in a controlled corporation, that is, one in which the decedent or his or her relatives owned or had the power to vote at least 20 percent of the total combined voting power of all classes of stock.[71]

[69] *H. Bosch Est.*, 67-2 USTC ¶12,491, 387 US 456, 87 SCt 1776.

[70] 72-2 USTC ¶12,859, 408 US 125, 92 SCt 2382, reh'g den'd, 409 U.S. 898.

[71] Code Sec. 2036(b).

Congress also provided that indirect transfers might result in inclusion and that the relinquishment of retained voting rights within three years of death might result in inclusion under Code Sec. 2035.

In any case, the reversal of *Byrum* is hardly complete. *Byrum* still seems to stand for the proposition that the retained right under Code Sec. 2036 must be a legally enforceable right, and not a *de facto* right.

According to the regulations and the U.S. Tax Court, if the grantor reserved the power to discharge a trustee and appoint himself or herself as trustee, he or she is considered as having the power held by the trustee.[72] At one time, the IRS took the position[73] that a reservation by a grantor of a power to remove a trustee at will and appoint another trustee is equivalent to reservation of the trustee's powers. After defeat on this issue in the U.S. Tax Court[74] and in the Eighth Circuit,[75] the IRS reconsidered its stance. The IRS revoked Rev. Rul. 79-353. The IRS ruled in Rev. Rul. 95-58[76] that a grantor's reservation of an unqualified power to remove a trustee and appoint an individual or corporate successor trustee that is not related or subordinate to the grantor within the meaning of Code Sec. 672(c), is not considered a reservation of the trustee's discretionary powers of distribution over the trust property.

> **Planning pointer.** Allowing a grantor to replace a trustee is useful for dealing with such situations as (1) a move by the beneficiary to a distant location that would make the beneficiary's contact with the trust department impractical, or (2) a takeover of the trust company by an out-of-state entity.

.02 Safeguards

When the settlor, as an individual and not as a trustee, reserves administrative powers, the trust should be precise about the fact that these powers are to be exercised in a fiduciary capacity. At the same time, however, one would not want to have the settlor placed in the position of being treated as a fiduciary *for all purposes* or to have attributed to him or her substantive or dispositive powers. That fact, too, should be made clear in the trust instrument or related documents.

The trust instrument could include a clause declaring void any powers given a trustee or retained by the settlor if they could result in adverse estate tax consequences. While the IRS has ruled that such

[72] Reg. §§ 20.2036-1(b)(3) and 20.2038-1(a)(3).

[73] Rev. Rul. 79-353, 1979-2 CB 325.

[74] *H. Wall Est.*, CCH Dec. 49,330.

[75] *J. Vak Est.*, 92-2 USTC ¶ 60,110, 973 F2d 1409 (CA-8, 1992) rev'g and rem'g 62 TCM 942.

[76] 1995-2 CB 191.

a provision does not help,[77] the courts might uphold it if valid under state law.[78]

¶ 615 TRUSTS AND GIFT TAXES

A transfer to a personal trust involves a gift. The subject of gifts and gift taxes is generally covered in Chapter 4. This chapter simply calls attention to the fact that, in the case of a transfer to a trust, the trust beneficiaries, rather than the trust or trustee, are the donees. This factor takes on special importance in applying the annual gift tax exclusion ($12,000 for 2006, indexed for inflation).[79] It means that instead of only one available annual exclusion or twice this amount if the donor's spouse consents to gift splitting under Code Sec. 2513, as would be the case if the gift were considered as made to the trustee, the number of annual exclusions available equals the number of trust beneficiaries.

Of course, the annual gift tax exclusion is not available except for gifts of present interests.[80] However, if the trust beneficiary is given a *Crummey* power (see ¶ 660.04), the present interest requirement may be satisfied. Such powers allow the beneficiary to make a withdrawal from the trust in amounts up to the amount of the annual gift tax exclusion during a limited period. The annual exclusion may also be used for a gift of an income interest in a trust if the trust requires the income of the trust to be distributed at least annually. Such a gift of an income interest is valued using the tables in Reg. § 25.2512-5. If, in the trustee's discretion, the income may either be distributed currently or accumulated, the annual exclusion may not be used except for a trust for a minor that meets all the Code Sec. 2503(c) requirements. Trusts for minors are separately discussed at ¶ 425.

Transfers of nonincome-producing property to a trust pose special problems in connection with the availability of the annual gift tax exclusion for gifts of income interests. This problem is apt to be particularly acute when stock is transferred to the trust in a situation where the company has a history of nonpayment of dividends. The problem, however, is not limited to transfers of such property.

Two questions are relevant: (1) Has there been a transfer of a present income interest in the nonincome-producing property? and if that question can be answered affirmatively, (2) Is the value of that

---

[77] Rev. Rul. 65-144, 1965-1 CB 442.

[78] *Miami Beach First National Bank* (DC Fla.), 1970-1 USTC ¶ 12,681, rev'd on other grounds (CA-5) 71-1 USTC ¶ 12,774).

[79] Code Sec. 2503(b).

[80] Code Sec. 2503(b).

interest ascertainable? The IRS has occasionally conceded that the present interest requirement may be satisfied in these situations, but, it has ruled that the annual gift tax exclusion is not allowed because the value of the interest is unascertainable. The U.S. Tax Court has sided with the IRS in *Berzon* and *Rosen*.[81] However, *Rosen* was reversed by the U.S. Court of Appeals for the Fourth Circuit,[82] which held that the taxpayer could use actuarial tables to value the income interest in a stock that had not paid dividends for a considerable period. To cloud the issue further, the Eighth Circuit followed the IRS and the U.S. Tax Court decisions.[83]

In this uncertain state of affairs, with the odds favoring the IRS and the U.S. Tax Court positions, if a donor wants to be certain of obtaining the annual gift tax exclusion, he or she should avoid transferring nonincome-producing property. If is the donor has no choice of property, perhaps the exclusion can be salvaged in either of two ways:

1. The transferor could give the income beneficiary a *Crummey* power to withdraw income or principal in a specific amount up to the amount of the annual gift tax exclusion with a limited time for exercise of the power. The transferor should consider limiting the right to withdraw principal annually to the greater of $5,000 or five percent of principal to keep the principal from being includible in the beneficiary's gross estate.[84]
2. The transferor could give the beneficiary a right to require that nonincome-producing property be converted into income-producing property.

In the case of stock, persuading the corporation to pay nominal dividends before and after transfer to the trust will not work.[85]

¶620 TYPES OF TRUSTS AND SPECIAL TRUST PROVISIONS

Trusts have many varied uses and purposes in estate planning. Regardless of the other purposes they may serve, trusts can provide one or more qualifications for managing assets that the trust

[81] *F. Berzon*, 63 TC 601, CCH Dec. 33,072, acq. 1975-2 CB 1, aff'd (CA-2) 76-1 USTC ¶13,140, 534 F2d 528; and *L. Rosen*, 48 TC 834, CCH Dec. 28,601.

[82] 68-2 USTC ¶12,539, 397 F2d 245.

[83] *L.H. Stark*, 73-1 USTC ¶12,921, 477 F2d 131, aff'g (DC Mo.) 72-2 USTC ¶12,877, 345 FSupp. 1263.

[84] Code Sec. 2041(b)(2).

[85] *E.M. Morgan*, 42 TC 1080, CCH Dec. 26,971, aff'd per curiam (CA-4) 66-1 USTC ¶12,367, 353 F2d 209.

beneficiaries lack or that the trust settlor perceives they lack. The beneficiaries could lack prudence, maturity, management or investment skill and experience, physical capacity, mental competence, sufficient interest, or adequate time.

Other uses and purposes for trusts include insulating trust assets from the claims of creditors of a business, accumulating funds for special purposes, or serving as a parental substitute in financial matters.

In addition to these purposes, settlors might also form trusts to save income taxes and/or estate taxes. Many settlors also want to avoid probate.

To carry out the purposes of the individual creating the trust, special trust provisions are often required. Some provisions can be useful with all types of trusts; some provisions are useful for a particular type of trust only. A revocable trust, where the settlor retains the right to amend the trust, may be adapted to changing circumstances as they unfold. Changing an irrevocable trust is impossible. Therefore, the settlor must be careful to build sufficient flexibility into the trust to permit reasonable adaptation to altered circumstances. Special provisions that might be useful in various types of trusts are discussed at ¶660. Trusts for minors are discussed in connection with the discussion of gifts to minors at ¶425. Life insurance trusts are discussed in connection with the broad topic of life insurance in estate planning in Chapter 7, and the marital deduction trust and the nonmarital trust for the surviving spouse are discussed in Chapter 12. Trusts that qualify to hold S corporation stock are discussed at ¶1945. Generation skipping trusts are discussed in Chapter 27.

Exhibit 6, at ¶625, compares eight basic types of trusts in terms of essential characteristics, nontax benefits, and tax treatment (income, estate, and gift taxes).

¶625 THE IRREVOCABLE LIVING TRUST

The irrevocable living trust has many features that promote its use as an estate-planning tool. It can save income taxes for the family, help build an estate, protect the family's assets and beneficiaries, save estate taxes in both the estate of the settlor and the estate or estates of the life beneficiaries, and avoid probate. As with many of life's good things, however, there is a price.

The price for saving income and estate taxes and avoiding probate is making an irrevocable transfer of property to the trust. Generally, the settlor must maintain a hands-off position forevermore. The client must decide if the price is right or too high for the benefits. The client should especially consider the prospective estate tax savings.

The client should also consider the benefits of avoiding probate. Although an irrevocable trust can be used to avoid probate, it is not the only trust with that benefit. The revocable trust also has that feature (¶ 630), but it does not carry the income and estate tax benefits of the irrevocable trust.

Is probate really worth avoiding? Probate is generally not as burdensome as many clients believe. The Uniform Probate Code, adopted in a number of states, as well as other reform measures, have significantly improved the probate process. Still, probate generally has these disadvantages:

- **Publicity.** Dispositions made by will are public documents. Details about the deceased's financial affairs are in the records, as well as the size of the estate, the names of the recipients, what they receive, and on what terms. An irrevocable living trust generally keeps these matters secret, although leaks are always possible. Questions can also arise concerning the interpretation of trust provisions, which could bring the trust into the public courts where it might become a matter of public record. Furthermore, clearing title to property might demand disclosure. In general, however, one can expect less publicity by avoiding probate.
- **Delay.** Probate is bound to involve a certain amount of delay. Therefore, if the beneficiaries need to receive cash quickly, special steps to prevent delay must be taken.
- **Costs.** The greater the value of the property includible in the probate estate, the bigger the fees of the executor and his or her legal counsel. Setting up an irrevocable trust usually involves legal expenses and trustees' fees, but they are not apt to be as high as those involved in probate.

In addition, the probate court might be required to appoint appraisers and guardians if the interests of minor children are involved, each of which can be a further drain on the estate.

The irrevocable trust offers the possibility of saving income tax where the trust income is to be paid to beneficiaries who are in lower tax brackets than the grantor. If trust income is to be accumulated, income tax savings generally will not be realized if the income is taxed to the trust under the highly compressed trust tax brackets.[86]

[86] Code Sec. 1(e).

However, in some cases, savings can be realized if the trust is purposely set up to fail the grantor trust rules and the income is taxed to the grantor. Such a move also results in gift tax savings in that the benefit of income taxes paid by the grantor is generally not treated as a gift to the beneficiary. These points are discussed at ¶ 605.

To achieve the estate tax savings, the settlor must keep the trust property out of his or her gross estate by complying with all the applicable rules discussed at ¶ 610. Briefly, the settlor must not retain a life interest in the property or control its enjoyment,[87] possess a reversionary interest worth more than five percent of the value of the property at the time of his or her death,[88] possess the power to alter, terminate, or revoke the trust,[89] possess a general power of appointment,[90] possess an incident of ownership in any insurance policy on his or her life naming the trust as beneficiary,[91] or transfer life insurance on his or her own life to the trust within three years of death.[92]

When a settlor forms an irrevocable trust, he or she could be liable for gift tax. The settlor makes a gift of a present interest in the income of the trust and a gift of a future interest in the principal or corpus. A *Crummey* power to withdraw income or principal (see ¶ 660.04) given to trust beneficiaries may operate to convert a future interest into a present interest. The annual gift tax exclusion ($12,000 for 2006 and indexed for inflation) is available for gifts of present interests.[93] The trust beneficiaries are the donees, and the donor may claim the exclusion for each gift made to each donee. The exclusion amount may be doubled if the donor is married and his or her spouse consents to gift splitting.[94] In addition, the donor and his or her spouse may use the unified credit[95] to reduce any gift tax for gifts of present interests and gifts of future interests. For tax years through 2009, the applicable credit amount for gift tax purposes will be based on an applicable exclusion amount of $1,000,000. This $1,000,000 applicable exclusion amount is not indexed for inflation. The gifts are to be valued in accordance with the rules discussed in Chapter 4.

---

[87] Code Sec. 2036.
[88] Code Sec. 2037.
[89] Code Sec. 2038.
[90] Code Sec. 2041.
[91] Code Sec. 2042.
[92] Code Sec. 2035.
[93] Code Sec. 2503(b).
[94] Code Sec. 2513.
[95] Code Secs. 2010 and 2505.

Exhibit 6

Basic Types of Trusts, Their Benefits and Tax Treatment

Trust Type	Characteristics	Nontax Benefits	Tax Treatment: Income	Tax Treatment: Estate	Tax Treatment: Gift
1) Irrevocable Living	Settlor gives up property forever.	Supervised control and investment; avoids probate.	Currently distributed. Is taxed to beneficiary. Accumulated, first to trust, then to beneficiary on distribution subject to special rule.	Not taxable in settlor's estate unless life insurance on his or her life transferred within 3 years of death. Can avoid tax on life beneficiary's death.	Taxable to settlor. Annual exclusion available for present gift of income interest, not remainder.
2) Revocable Living	Settler can revoke. May be funded or unfunded.	Same as [1].	Taxable to settlor.	Includible in settlor's estate.	No liability.
3) Testamentary	Created by will.	Supervised control and investment.	Same as [1].	Includible in estate of creator. Can avoid tax on death of life beneficiary.	No liability.
4) Grantor Retained Interest Trust ("GRIT", "GRAT" [1], and "GRUT" [2])	Grantor reserves a qualified term interest in the form of an annuity or unitrust under Code Sec. 2702, after which principal passes to remaindermen.	Often negligible.	Taxable to settlor (grantor).	Not taxable in grantor's estate unless grantor dies within reserved income term, subject to special rules under Code Sec. 2702 (see Chapter 23).	Tax based on value of remainder at time of creation of trust. Special rules apply (see Chapter 23).
5) Standby	Generally revocable, but may be irrevocable on settler's permanent disability.	Supervised control and investment on settlor's disability or absence.	Taxable to settlor.	Includible in settlor's estate.	No liability.
6) Pourover	Living trust, revocable or irrevocable, funded or unfunded.	Receptacle for employee benefits, life insurance proceeds, estate assets.	Taxable to settlor.	Same as [1] or [2] depending on revocability.	Same as [1] or [2] depending on revocability.

[1] Grantor retained annuity trust

[2] Grantor retained unitrust

¶630 THE REVOCABLE LIVING TRUST

The revocable living trust is a useful estate planning tool offering these advantages:

- Avoids the publicity, the expenses, and the delays of probate
- Avoids the interruption of income for family members on the death of the settlor or on his or her becoming disabled or incompetent
- Permits the settlor to see the trust in operation and to make changes as experience and changed circumstances suggest
- Serves as a receptacle for estate assets and death benefits from qualified employee benefit plans and insurance on the life of the settlor
- Can bring together scattered assets in two or more states or jurisdictions by placing title in the trustee and avoiding administration of the individual's estate (particularly real estate) in different places
- Makes selecting the law that is to govern the trust easier than if the settlor attempted to do so through a will
- Enables a going business to continue without interruption
- Facilitates gifts to charities in states where restrictions apply to charitable bequests
- Relieves the settlor of burdens of investment management
- May authorize the trustee to advance funds to the settlor's executor for certain purposes or to buy assets from the executor at a fixed price, and so help avoid the forced sale of estate assets at depressed prices
- Can be less vulnerable to attack on the grounds of the settlor's capacity, fraud, and duress than a will or will-created trust would be
- Requires less accounting, administration, and judicial supervision than a trust created by will
- Bars a surviving spouse's statutory right in some states to share in his or her deceased spouse's property
- Places the property beyond the reach of the settlor's creditors, at least in some states

A revocable living trust provides no income tax savings for the settlor. Code Sec. 676 makes the settlor taxable on the income of a revocable living trust. However, on the settlor's death without the trust having been revoked, the trust becomes irrevocable. The beneficiaries are then entitled to whatever income tax savings may be open to the beneficiaries of an irrevocable trust. If the settlor has formed several trusts, the beneficiaries will have all the advantages of multiple trusts, provided care has been taken to avoid having the multiple trusts treated as one for tax purposes.

The settlor's estate will not derive any tax benefits. Code Sec. 2038 makes the property of a revocable trust includible in the settlor's gross estate. However, the settlor can establish the trust so as to avoid a second estate tax on the deaths of its prime beneficiaries. If they are merely given a life interest with a limited right to principal subject to an ascertainable standard, upon their deaths, the remaining principal may pass to other beneficiaries tax free. However, this approach is subject to considerable restriction under the generation-skipping transfer tax, as discussed in Chapter 27.

In general, a revocable living trust provides no immediate income tax or first-generation estate tax advantages. However, because the transfers to the trust are revocable, the settlor avoids any liability for gift tax.

Having listed the advantages of the revocable living trust in general terms, this chapter will now take a closer look at some of these items, and also examine some problem areas.

The revocable trust saves future probate costs but at the expense of present costs of setting up and funding the trust. Another expense is the current trustee's fee. A revocable trust does not have the same income and estate tax pressures as does an irrevocable trust to have an independent (often paid) trustee. However, one can assume that the trustee will have to be paid, just as an executor will take commissions.

In some localities, a trust company, acting as the trustee of a revocable trust, will want extra compensation of as much as one full executor's commission on the death of the settlor for the extra work required. This compensation includes the handling of post-mortem income of the trust and estate tax planning. Also, normally, one can expect an accounting for the trust on the death of the settlor. This accounting will involve legal and accounting fees. The revocable trust could save some filing fees. If minors are involved, the revocable trust might reduce guardian's fees, because they are usually measured by the size of the probate estate.

One of the advantages of a revocable trust is that the settlor can locate it in a state whose laws are favorable. If that state happens to be a state other than that in which probate is required, the probate proceedings could become complicated, causing delay and added expense. The settlor should pay particular attention to any legal formalities of execution under the laws of the state chosen to establish the trust.

In making a choice, the settlor should consider creditors' rights, any right of election a surviving spouse may have, the state rule against perpetuities, powers of appointment and their exercise, the capacity of beneficiaries to take, the allocation of estate taxes, and, if the state is a community property state, the impact of community property laws.

Also, the estate could have practical problems where a revocable trust is located in one state and a probate estate in another state. These problems are compounded if the trust and estate have different fiduciaries.

If the trust authorizes the trustee to advance funds to the executor for specific purposes, problems could occur if the funds are not used for the stated purposes. The trust should provide safeguards for such an event.

As a general rule, if a trust, other than a voting trust, grantor trust, Code Sec. 678 trust (i.e., one where a person other than the grantor is taxable as the owner), qualified subchapter S trust, or an electing small business trust, holds stock of an S corporation, the S election will be nullified.[96] A trust in which the grantor or another person is treated as the owner may continue as an eligible shareholder following the death of the owner, but only for two years beginning on the date of the owner's death.[97] An estate, on the other hand, may hold such stock indefinitely without destroying the election.[98]

The settlor should also consider the possibility that he or she might become incapable of effective revocation. In that case, the settlor might want to provide that the trust is to become irrevocable.

In sum, the revocable living trust offers numerous advantages, but it is not without its problems and pitfalls. The estate planner can avoid many of these problems by careful draftsmanship and special handling. The will should be coordinated with the trust instrument. Generally, the trust and estate should have common fiduciaries. If the settlor has assets scattered in different jurisdictions, the estate planner should pay particular attention to the problems likely to arise. An estate planner might want to advise the settlor to have separate revocable trusts in separate jurisdictions, especially if real estate is involved. The estate planner will need to check out the law in the various jurisdictions involved. Also, the settlor might want to give the trustee authority to shift the trust's situs and to transfer assets, and to give him or her power to administer assets outside the jurisdiction.

---

[96] Code Sec. 1362(d).

[97] Code Sec. 1361(c)(2)(A)(ii).

[98] Code Sec. 1361(b)(1).

¶635 THE STANDBY TRUST

A special kind of trust, known as the standby trust, merits the estate planner's consideration. This type of trust stands in readiness to take over and manage trust assets when the settlor is no longer able to manage for himself or herself. It may provide for a takeover upon the settlor's physical or mental disability or when he or she is away on a trip or otherwise unable to manage his or her affairs. It is not especially designed to save taxes, although it can be structured to do so. Instead, its best use is to help the ailing client avoid cumbersome and expensive incompetency proceedings under state law. The standby trust can preserve the client's assets while providing the financial structure to help him or her meet personal needs.

A standby trust is usually revocable at the beginning, but it may be made to become irrevocable upon the settlor's suffering permanent mental disability. Absent such provision, on the settlor's suffering such disability, a court might appoint a guardian who could exercise the power to revoke for the settlor with attending tax and dispositive consequences.

An estate planner should always check local law to find out if, when, and how standby trusts are permitted.

¶640 TRUSTS CREATED BY WILL

A trust may be created in accordance with instructions contained in a person's will. Such trusts are known as testamentary trusts. Testamentary trusts are for the individual who is unable or unwilling to part with certain property while he or she is alive, not even in a revocable trust. Such a person wants the control that a trust can give for what he or she conceives to be the best interests of his or her beneficiaries in the long or short run.

While the testamentary trust does not result in any immediate estate or income tax savings when the will is executed or takes effect, it ultimately can result in tax savings. The trust can protect the trust property from successive estate tax levies as it passes from one beneficiary to another, from the surviving spouse, to the children, and even to the grandchildren. However, the generation-skipping transfer tax limits one's ability to pass assets to successive generations without incurring additional transfer tax (Chapter 27).

The most common example of the estate-tax-saving trust is the bypass trust, also called the credit shelter trust. Part of the estate owner's property is bequeathed to the surviving spouse either outright or in a trust that qualifies for the marital deduction.[99] The rest (often an amount equal to the applicable exclusion amount under Code Sec. 2010 (exemption equivalent) available to the estate owner) is put into a bypass trust that pays the surviving spouse income for life. The bypass trust might also permit use of the principal (corpus) for the survivor's defined and ascertainable needs, but it carefully avoids giving the surviving spouse too much control or rights in the trust property. In this way, the property will not be includible in the surviving spouse's gross estate and can pass estate-tax free to the beneficiary or beneficiaries next in line.[100] If there are multiple beneficiaries, the estate planner might want to set up multiple trusts. The client should have enough money or property involved to warrant the added expense, and the estate planner should be able to project worthwhile income tax savings for those concerned (¶ 605).

The settlor might also want to allow the trustee to accumulate income and use it for specific purposes spelled out in the trust. Flexibility can be most important in a testamentary trust, and the estate planner will want to consider the use of a number of special provisions discussed at ¶ 660 designed to impart flexibility to meet changes in the circumstances of the beneficiaries.

An estate planner should remember something very important in connection with testamentary trusts. A testamentary trust can make provisions for a trust beneficiary that he could not make for himself or herself, if he or she were to set up a trust, without running into income and estate tax complications. For example, if a beneficiary created his or her own trust and retained the income rights, the trust property would be includible in his or her gross estate under Code Sec. 2036. If, under the terms of this trust, income may be used to pay insurance premiums on the settlor's life or that of the spouse, the income would be taxable to the settlor under Code Sec. 677. The settlor would also be treated as the owner of the policy and the proceeds would be includible in his or her gross estate. However, neither of these consequences would result if he or she occupied the position of beneficiary of a testamentary trust.

¶ 645 THE POUROVER TRUST

The pourover trust, as its name suggests, is a trust into which assets are poured from another source. The pourover may be from the settlor's will or from a source completely outside the testamentary estate. It is most useful as a receptacle for benefits from qualified

[99] Code Sec. 2056.

[100] Code Sec. 2041(b)(1).

employee benefit plans, Keogh plans, IRAs, or insurance proceeds. Also, it may receive assets from other trusts or estates.

The trust may be either revocable or irrevocable, with all the attendant advantages and disadvantages of either. If the trust is revocable, the settlor, after seeing it in operation and noting changes in circumstances, may make appropriate changes and adjustments. If it is irrevocable, then change is barred, and the settlor will want to build into the trust enough flexibility to permit the trustee to adjust to changed conditions.

In both revocable and irrevocable forms the settlor avoids probate of the trust property, reduces publicity, and might reduce the costs, delays, and inconvenience of probate.

The pourover trust is apt to be especially useful where it is made to receive insurance proceeds exempt from estate taxes under Code Sec. 2042, employee benefits, or IRA benefits. Code Sec. 2042 exempts the proceeds of a life insurance policy payable to a beneficiary other than the insured's estate, provided the insured retained no incidents of ownership in the policy at the time of his or death and did not transfer them within three years of death.[101]

The pourover trust can be used to take advantage of this exemption. It can also save a second tax on these assets. If they were made payable directly to an individual, what remained of them would be taxable as part of the individual's estate. With the pourover trust, this tax may be avoided by giving the prime beneficiary only a life interest and by directing payment of what is left to others on the prime beneficiary's death.

Where the client wants benefits payable to several beneficiaries, the trust form will normally be the most effective way of making distributions in accordance with the wishes of the settlor and the needs of the beneficiaries. In this respect, the estate planner will want to build into the trust provisions, such as those discussed in ¶660, which will permit the desired flexibility.

The pourover trust is helpful not only where there are multiple beneficiaries but also where there are multiple assets. It permits the bringing together of these assets in one place and the development of a plan that coordinates and makes use of them in a way that is most likely to further the objectives of the settlor and the interests of the family. It also has the advantage of the revocable trust in bringing together trust assets in different jurisdictions, as noted at ¶630. However, an estate planner needs to note possible problems as well.

---

[101] Code Sec. 2035(a).

When pourover trusts first appeared on the scene, the courts were troubled by them. The main problem concerned pourovers from wills. Nearly all states now have statutes that, in one form or another, uphold the validity of pourovers. Nevertheless, an estate planner should be familiar with some of the problems, especially because the statutes may leave some of them unresolved.

When used with a will, one might view the pourover trust as involving a testamentary disposition of property. One then has the problem of observance of the formalities required to make testamentary dispositions. Courts have long recognized that a will may incorporate another document by reference. The other document would then become a part of the will. The testator does not want the pourover trust to be incorporated into the will. Rather, the testator prefers that the two documents be kept separate. Notwithstanding this difficulty, the courts have been able to sustain pourovers on the basis of incorporation-by-reference. Implicit in the incorporation-by-reference theory is a requirement that the trust be in existence when the testator executes the will. Also, problems will arise under this doctrine if the trust is revocable or subject to amendment after the date the testator executes his or her will.

Against this background, one can better understand the purpose of the Uniform Testamentary Additions to Trust Act, which is in force in a number of states. Its main section provides (emphasis supplied) as follows:

> *Section 1. Testamentary Additions to Trusts.*— A devise or bequest, the validity of which is determinable by the law of this state, may be made by a will to the trustee or trustees of a trust established *or to be established* by the testator or by the testator and some other person or persons or by some other person or persons (including a funded or unfunded life insurance trust, although the trustor has reserved any or all rights of ownership of the insurance contracts) *if the trust is identified in the testator's will and its terms are set forth in a written instrument* (other than a will) *executed before or concurrently with* the execution of the testator's will or in the valid last will of a person who has predeceased the testator (regardless of the existence, size, or character of the corpus of the trust). The devise or bequest *shall not be invalid because the trust is amendable or revocable*, or both, or *because the trust was amended after the execution of the will*

> or after the death of the testator. Unless the testator's *will provides otherwise*, the property devised or bequeathed (a) *shall not be deemed to be held under a testamentary trust* of the testator but shall become a part of the trust to which it is given and (b) shall be administered and disposed of in accordance with the provisions of the instrument or will setting forth the terms of the trust, including any amendments thereto made before the death of the testator (regardless of whether made before or after the execution of the testator's will), *and, if the testator's will so provides, including any amendments to the trust* made after the death of the testator. A revocation or termination of the trust before the death of the testator shall cause the devise or bequest to lapse.

This act provides that the validity is not affected by the fact that the trust is amended after the execution of the will. Other statutes of this type might not be so explicit. If any doubt exists about this matter and the trust is amended after the execution of the will, good practice calls for a new will or codicil. The new will or codicil should note the amendment and provide for a pourover to the amended trust.

Note also that the Uniform Act permits a bequest to a trust *to be established*, provided a written instrument exists that sets out *its* terms, before or concurrently with the execution of the will. Still, having the trust in existence before the will is executed is better practice. However, a codicil to the will picking up a trust set up after the will's execution might be sufficient.

All the care that goes into putting together a testamentary trust should go into the preparation of a pourover trust, including the consideration of those provisions discussed at ¶660 designed to give flexibility. In addition, the pourover trust should be clear whether it is to be revocable or irrevocable, and whether it may be amended by the trustee, and, if so, how and when. Also, the settlor should give consideration to the estate's tax liabilities and how they are to be handled. If the bulk of the taxable estate goes into the pourover trust, leaving the estate with insufficient assets to pay estate taxes, the trust should contain a provision for the payment of estate taxes. The trust could also provide for payment of debts and expenses of administration of the estate.

The will used in conjunction with a pourover trust merits special attention. The will should mention that heirs not mentioned in the will are provided for in the trust, if that is the case, or that the omission is intentional. A will might contain various specific legacies that may lapse and fall into the residue to be turned over to the trust. In such a case, the testator should consider having the executor turn these into cash rather than turn them over in kind to the trust, if retention, allocation, sale, or exchange might create problems for the trustee. Consideration also needs to be given to the potential problems caused by assets scattered in different jurisdictions in line with the discussion of revocable trusts (¶ 630).

The surviving spouse's election may also apply to the pourover will. He or she should be given the economic equivalent of his or her statutory share of the estate. This provision reduces the possibility of the surviving spouse renouncing the will. In addition, an alternate plan of disposition is recommended if the surviving spouse renounces the will. Also, a fail-safe provision in the will, providing alternate dispositions of the estate if the pourover trust is invalidated, may be advisable.

¶ 650 GRANTOR RETAINED INTEREST TRUST: GRIT, GRAT, AND GRUT

When a grantor retains an income interest in a trust for a term of years and designates certain specified family members (e.g., a spouse or child) to receive the remainder, the grantor is treated as having made a gift of 100 percent of the value of the property unless the retained interest is a qualified interest.[102] Two types of trusts are treated as qualified interests: (1) a grantor retained annuity trust (GRAT) in which the grantor retains the right to receive a fixed payment each year and (2) a grantor retained unitrust trust (GRUT) in which the grantor retains the right to receive a fixed percentage of the trust assets each year.

A GRAT or GRUT can save gift taxes because the value of the gift of the remainder interest is determined by subtracting the present value of the grantor's retained interest using special valuation tables (discussed at ¶ 2315). By contrast, a trust in which the grantor retains all of the income from the trust property (GRIT) will be subject to gift tax on 100 percent of the value of the trust property. (See, however, ¶ 2315.02 for a discussion of the use of a GRIT when the person designated to receive the remainder is not a designated family member

A GRAT, GRUT or GRIT can be an estate tax-saver as well. Post-transfer appreciation in the value of the trust assets will not be included in the grantor's estate, provided the grantor survives the trust term. However, if the grantor dies during the term of the trust, the trust property will be included in the grantor's estate.[103]

---

[102] Code Sec. 2702.

[103] Code Sec. 2036.

¶ 655 THE FOREIGN TRUST

Foreign trusts are apt to be unfamiliar to most estate planners. Foreign trusts have never been for every person or for every estate planner because they have required specialized expertise in their creation and use.

Discussion of foreign trusts in any depth is beyond the scope of this book. However, an estate planner should generally beware of foreign trusts for U.S. persons. The IRS will likely view them as tax dodges worthy of special scrutiny. Unless very large sums of money are involved, the complications and uncertainties associated with these trusts will likely outweigh the expected benefit.

¶ 660 SPECIAL TRUST PROVISIONS TO PROVIDE FLEXIBILITY AND SAFETY

Trusts are usually built to last for a good span of time. Many things can change in the course of time that require different approaches and responses from those contemplated when the trust was set up. If the trust is revocable, the settlor, if alive and well, can make appropriate changes in the trust. If the trust is an irrevocable living trust or a testamentary trust, the trustee could have difficulty in dealing with changing circumstances and needs of the beneficiaries. To avoid this problem, the trust should include the flexibility required to enable the trustee to develop sensible responses to new situations.

Everyone will agree to the need for flexibility in the abstract. However, in practice, the estate planner is apt to find that many clients are afraid of it. The settlor is being asked to confer a degree of discretion on a fiduciary. He or she may or may not have complete confidence in the fiduciary. If the settlor has that confidence, he or she may lack confidence in the fiduciary's durability, and he or she might be fearful of entrusting an unknown successor or substitute. The settlor might be more fearful of entrusting someone with the tools for doing what might be required than he or she is of the consequences that could result if required changes cannot be made. This problem has psychological and emotional roots. It illustrates the point that estate planning is not a pure science, providing neat and sensible property arrangements, but an art that fundamentally involves dealing with human beings in a creative way.

The following are some of the key provisions that can, if accepted by the settlor, impart flexibility and safety.

.01 Income Sprinkling Clause

Few people make up a family budget and division of income among family members to run for a year, let alone 10 or 20 years.

Family income is generally used to meet actual family needs, i.e., the needs of each family member, as they develop. Income is sprinkled where the parents think it is most needed. That is the idea of the sprinkling trust. The trustee is to function as a parental substitute, assuming that the beneficiaries are the children of the settlor, distributing income or accumulating it as he or she thinks best.

Usually, an experienced trustee given sprinkling powers is apt to follow closely the suggestions of the surviving parent as to how the sprinkling should go. When there is no surviving parent, the trustee is going to be very careful about any sort of uneven sprinkling, unless a clear family consensus develops, indisputable special circumstances justify it, or the trust itself or the will creating it explicitly authorizes it.

Generally, the spray will be what is called a horizontal one, taking in the entire family, including a surviving spouse, children, and grandchildren. One may also have a sprinkling trust set up for an individual, usually a child of the settlor, and his or her descendants. This arrangement is a vertical spray.

A well designed and administered trust with a sprinkling feature can produce family income tax savings insofar as low bracket beneficiaries are favored. Where the surviving spouse is included as a beneficiary, the trust can also produce estate tax savings to the extent that the spouse is given no more income than needed. Thus, the surviving spouse's gross estate will not be increased unnecessarily.

Because the beneficiaries have no right to income until it is allocated to them, the sprinkling feature operates as a protection against creditors.

Some of the key considerations in setting up a sprinkling arrangement are as follows:

- The trustee should be given guidelines for sprinkling, indicating, for example, the settlor's preferences and priorities both as to beneficiaries and as to the needs and purposes to be served. Perhaps, the settlor can best do this by a separate memo outside the trust instrument.
- To avoid antagonisms between siblings, consideration should be given to the adoption of separate trusts with a vertical spray only. Some inequality in the amount in each trust may be more readily tolerated when made by the settlor than would be inequality in spraying by a trustee.
- If the surviving spouse is to be included and he or she is the settlor's prime concern, the settlor should consider giving the surviving spouse a set minimum amount of income and limiting the sprinkling to the excess.

- If the sprinkling is part of a living trust, one must be concerned with the grantor-trust income tax rules of Code Secs. 671-677. Income will be taxable to the grantor if he or she is in a position to direct the spray or if the grantor or his or her spouse may benefit. An estate planner must also be concerned with the estate tax consequences of powers retained by the settlor which would throw trust assets into the settlor's gross estate under Code Secs. 2036 (retained life interest) and 2038 (power to revoke, amend, or terminate).
- The selection of an able trustee is most critical. The settlor should be sensitive to the tax ramifications, too, and generally avoid naming someone who has an interest in the trust. A corporate trustee plus a co-trustee who knows the family and family needs might be best, if the costs are acceptable.
- The settlor should consider what is to be done with excess income not needed for special educational, medical, or other needs of individual participants. Is it to be accumulated or distributed? If distributed, on what basis? It can be done on a per capita or per stirpes basis. With the first, it would be distributed evenly per capita to all in the group. On a per stirpes basis, the distribution would be to members of a subgroup. For example, assume that A and B are children of the settlor, with A having four children and B one. Per stirpes would call for a distribution of the excess income by halves, half to A's family and half to B's. The settlor should consider a weighted distribution on a per capita basis, with the more remote descendants getting a small share.
- The settlor should consider the distribution of principal to children as they come of age. Is the trust to be divided into separate shares when it makes the first distribution of principal? Is the trust to distribute the entire principal when the oldest or youngest attains a given age? Is payment to each child to be made as he or she attains a specified age? The settlor should consider the effect of the distribution scheme on the beneficiaries. When the older beneficiaries take principal out of the trust, the younger ones are left with less in the common fund to satisfy their needs. Because the expenses of administering the trust are not likely to diminish proportionately as trust assets are reduced, the younger beneficiaries in this situation may have to shoulder relatively larger administration fees.

These factors are only some of the key considerations. The most important consideration is to develop a mode of operation and distribution that reflects the objectives and desires of the settlor.

.02 Use of Principal of Trust

Almost all trusts give the trustee discretion to use the principal or corpus of the trust for the benefit of income beneficiaries on certain terms and conditions. This discretion is known as a power to invade corpus.

Ascertainable standard. A trust beneficiary will rarely be the sole trustee. However, if he or she is only a co-trustee and possesses a power to invade corpus, the trust corpus might be includible in his or her gross estate under the terms of Code Sec. 2041. To avoid inclusion, the power must be limited by a definite external or ascertainable standard. That rule has generated a lot of litigation. The safest course is to follow the Treasury regulations on the subject. As examples of powers properly limited, they cite powers for the holder's "support," "support in reasonable comfort," "maintenance in health and reasonable comfort," "support in his accustomed manner of living," "education including college and professional education," and similar formulations dealing with health, medical care, and dental care. On the other hand, the regulations state that a power to use property for the comfort, welfare, or happiness of the holder is not limited by the requisite standard.[104]

Similar considerations affect the power of invasion as it may relate to a trust's income being taxable to the settlor. Code Sec. 674 makes the income taxable to the grantor if he or she has power to control beneficial enjoyment of the income or corpus, but it excepts a power to distribute corpus if limited to a reasonably definite standard. Reg. § 1.674(b)-1(b)(5)(i) cites standards similar to those contained in the estate tax regulations as acceptable.

A similar rule will apply under Code Sec. 678 to other persons who possess a similar power.

No ascertainable standard. What provision should a trust include if a beneficiary is to serve as co-trustee and the trust permits distributions of corpus not limited by an ascertainable standard or if there is doubt as to whether distributions are so limited? The trust should prohibit the beneficiary-trustee from participating in the exercise of any discretion that might benefit him or her or anyone to whom he or she owes a legal obligation.

When there is a prime beneficiary, i.e., a surviving spouse, and secondary beneficiaries, i.e., children, one may want to permit invasion on behalf of the latter only if the security of the former is not jeopardized.

[104] Reg. § 20.2041-1(c)(2).

The trust could also provide that invasions of principal on behalf of a beneficiary, who will ultimately receive a distribution of principal, are to be regarded as an advance principal distribution.

.03 Power of Beneficiary to Withdraw Principal

A settlor might not want a beneficiary to have full control of assets. At the same time, the settlor might not want to leave the beneficiary completely at the mercy of the trustee to make payments to him or her out of corpus if the need arises. The settlor can resolve this dilemma by giving the beneficiary a right to withdraw corpus, subject to limitations. If the trust instrument has no provision that would make the trust property includible in the gross estate of the beneficiary, one will most likely want to limit the power of withdrawal to preserve the estate tax benefit.

To do so, the trust should limit the power of withdrawal in any one year to the greater of $5,000 or five percent of the value of the trust property at the time the power is exercisable.[105] The power should be noncumulative. In this way, no gift will result on the non-exercise or lapse of the power. The only amount includible in the holder's gross estate is the amount he or she was entitled to withdraw for the year in which death occurs, less any amount which he or she withdrew that year.[106]

In advising his or her client, an estate planner should also consider that under Code Sec. 678(a) the beneficiary may be deemed to be the owner of so much of the corpus as is subject to withdrawal. Hence, the beneficiary would be taxable on the income attributable to that part.

.04 Power of Withdrawal to Assure Availability of Annual Exclusion—The "*Crummey*" Power

Crummey powers are frequently used in trusts that permit the accumulation of income in order to allow contributions to the trust to satisfy the present interest requirement for the annual gift tax exclusion ($12,000 for 2006, indexed for inflation) under Code Sec. 2503(b).[107]

A *Crummey* power gives the beneficiary a limited power to withdraw income or principal or both. The beneficiary must receive proper notice of his or her right to demand a portion of the trust corpus. Generally, the power is exercisable only during a limited

[105] Code Sec. 2041(b)(2).

[106] Reg. § 20.2041-3(d)(3).

[107] *D. Clifford Crummey*, CA-9, 68-2 USTC ¶ 12,541, 397 F2d 82, aff'g 25 TCM 772, CCH Dec. 28,012(M), TC Memo. 1966-144.

period (30 days) each year. The power is noncumulative. Thus, if the beneficiary does not exercise the power in one year, the beneficiary loses the power of withdrawal for that year. The U.S. Tax Court has allowed annual gift tax exclusions for *Crummey* powers given to trust beneficiaries who held contingent remainder interests.[108] Much to the undoubted consternation of the IRS, the U.S. Tax Court, citing the *Cristofani* decision, allowed annual exclusions with respect to the unrestricted rights of each of 16 contingent beneficiaries to demand up to the then $10,000 annual exclusion amount annually from an irrevocable trust created by a grantor just three months before his death. None of the beneficiaries exercised the rights after being timely notified of their existence. None requested notification of future transfers of property to the trust. Nevertheless, the court refused to conclude that the beneficiaries and the grantor had agreed the rights would not be exercised.[109]

The power of withdrawal is generally limited to the amount excludable from gift tax under the annual exclusion ($12,000 for 2006, and indexed for inflation under Code Sec. 2503(b)). However, tying the *Crummey* power to the amount of the annual gift tax exclusion in order to assure full availability of the annual exclusion for transfers to the trust may possibly involve gift and estate tax considerations. In the prior discussion under the heading "Power of Beneficiary to Withdraw Principal" (¶660.03), reference was made to the need to limit the power to the greater of $5,000 or five percent of the trust corpus in order to avoid gift tax[110] on the lapse of the power and to avoid having the trust includible in the gross estate of the beneficiary.[111] Thus, if the trust property has a value of $240,000 or more, a *Crummey* power in an amount of $12,000 for 2006 would not make the trust includible in the beneficiary's gross estate. If one is concerned at all about possible gift tax or inclusion of the trust in the beneficiary's gross estate, one would not want to run the risk of inclusion under the five-percent test. The value of the corpus would possibly have to be $300,000 or more to allow sufficient leeway for shrinkage and inflation adjustment increases in the annual gift tax exclusion.

The $5,000 or five-percent limitation has gift tax implications that may be more important than the estate tax implications for the trust beneficiary. It also may operate to limit full funding of the trust and thinning of the estate of the grantor. For example,

---

[108] *M. Cristofani*, 97 TC 74, CCH Dec. 47,491, acq. in result only.

[109] *L. Kohlsaat Est.*, 73 TCM 2732, CCH Dec. 52,031.

[110] Code Sec. 2514(e).

[111] Code Sec. 2041(b)(2).

suppose a grantor establishes a trust in 2006 and initially funds it with an amount equal to the $12,000 annual gift tax exclusion, giving the trust beneficiary a *Crummey* power to withdraw the full amount of the trust contribution. Because the amount the beneficiary can withdraw exceed the greater of $5,000 or five percent of the trust corpus, the beneficiary will be treated as having made a taxable gift of the excess $7,000 when the *Crummey* power lapses.[112] One way to avoid this problem is to limit the grantor's contributions until the trust grows large enough to support a *Crummey* power equal to the annual exclusion. However, these limitations can be overcome by the use of a so-called hanging or pendent power. The grantor may make annual gifts to the trust to the maximum allowed by the annual gift tax exclusion ($12,000 per donee for 2006 and indexed for inflation under Code Sec. 2503(b); double with gift-splitting under Code Sec. 2513) while providing that the noncumulative power is to lapse only to the extent of the greater of $5,000 or five percent of the trust property. This plan would assure full use of the annual exclusion. The unused power would be carried over for use at some future time unless limited. The grantor will usually want to limit the future use of the carried over power in order to assure that the trust funds are primarily distributed in accordance with the terms of the trust. Ideally, the limitation should be done in such a way that it would not result in a gift tax to the holder of the power.

In Letter Ruling 8901004,[113] the IRS ruled that pendent or hanging powers are invalid where they are drafted so that the withdrawal power will continue if lapse of the power would be deemed a taxable gift by the beneficiary. According to the IRS, any attempt to make the lapse of the power subject to a condition subsequent tends to discourage enforcement of the gift tax law, and, therefore, offends public policy.

On the other hand, hanging powers that are drafted to avoid imposing what the IRS considers a condition subsequent appear to with stand IRS scrutiny. This result can be accomplished by drafting the power so that it does not refer to a "lapse" or "release." Instead, the trust can contain a provision that causes powers to lapse only in the amount permitted under Code Sec. 2514(e), or the greater of $5,000 or five percent of trust principal.

Using hanging powers might be especially appropriate where the trust owns a large policy of life insurance, demanding a large annual premium payment, and the client will need maximum use of annual exclusion gifts. The estate planner should make the client aware that

---

[112] Code Sec. 2514(e).

[113] September 16, 1988.

the IRS has not ruled definitively on the use of hanging powers and there is some risk of IRS an challenge (which may not arise for many years after the creation of the trust), and keep a record of the client's informed decision.

.05 Provisions for Beneficiaries with Disabilities

A settlor should consider the effect of disability of a trustee or beneficiary. The trust should define disability. For example, the trust might provide that a determination made by two medical doctors and submitted in writing would be sufficient. The trust should make provision for payment to a guardian of a beneficiary, if one is appointed, application of payments for his or her benefit, for depositing them in a bank account, or retaining them in the trust in a separate account.

.06 Spendthrift Provision

The whole purpose of a trust might be defeated if a beneficiary could anticipate payment of trust income and assign his or her rights to it to creditors or others before the trust distributes the income. This consideration is applicable to trusts for minors, but it is not limited to minors. Therefore, the trust may expressly provide against anticipation and assignment of income.

.07 Provisions Aimed at Cutting Costs

In structuring a trust, one should weigh the benefits against the costs involved and not extend the life of the trust to the point where the costs outweigh the benefits. This consideration is especially important where trust assets are not substantial or might be rapidly consumed. Alternatively, the trust may provide for termination by the trustee or third party when administration becomes uneconomical.

The settlor should also give thought to the use of co-trustees, and the added costs involved. This cost and other cost factors concerning fiduciaries are discussed at ¶665.

Finally, the settlor should consider express provisions to limit the compensation of trustees to reduce administrative costs. Of course, one should not specify commissions that are so low that the trustees will be unwilling to act or will soon lose interest (except perhaps in the case of close family members whose continued interest is assured).

The elimination of formal accounting is another way to reduce costs. However, some informal accounting will be required to protect beneficiaries and satisfy local law requirements.

.08 Inflation- and Recession-Proofing the Trust

Inflation- and recession-proofing a trust is not easy. When trust income declines or the income distributed loses purchasing power, provisions for the use of trust principal for the benefit of income beneficiaries will obviously help. Sprinkling provisions that allow beneficiaries' needs to be taken into account will also help.

.09 Influencing Conduct Through Trusts

Individuals traditionally have used trusts to hold and manage assets for persons who are inexperienced or otherwise incapable of handling large sums of money or other assets. Individuals can also use trusts to influence beneficiary behavior through positive and negative means that affect payments of both principal and income.

The hold-back provisions discussed below offer positive encouragement.

.10 Hold-Back Provisions

A trust often provides for the distribution of all principal and income on the occurrence of a specified event, such as the death of the principal life beneficiary or the attainment of a certain age. However, circumstances might arise in which a mandated distribution will not be in the best interest of the beneficiary. Examples of such circumstances are involvement in divorce proceedings or other litigation, terminal illness, or severe problems with alcohol or other drugs.

Because of such possibilities, the settlor should consider the use of a trust hold-back provision that will enable the trustee to withhold distributions in specified circumstances, while continuing the trust and administering it in accordance with its terms.

Some clients might wish to disinherit beneficiaries and go much further than the hold-back provisions. These clients would direct that the beneficiary be divested of any interest he or she might have in the trust in the event that the beneficiary fails to live up to certain societal norms. For example, the trust might provide that a beneficiary loses his or her interest in the trust if he or she is convicted of a drug offense or if the beneficiary in some other sense fails to measure up to other specified standards of the grantor. In this case, the trust assets could be distributed to other beneficiaries, including charities.

.11 Delayed Distribution

Going beyond positive encouragement and negative sanctions, the grantor of the trust might wish to delay the age at which the beneficiary becomes entitled to any distribution of income. Trusts often provide that the beneficiary of a trust of long duration will receive all of the income of the trust once he or she attains a specified age, for example, 25 or 30. However, trust income might itself be enough to make a young beneficiary relatively wealthy. In fact, the income could be a burden to the beneficiary by taking away any incentive on his or her part to become a productive member of society. Therefore, the estate planner and client might wish to consider delaying the receipt of income by requiring the accumulation of all trust income until the beneficiary becomes much older. Forced accumulation of income can result in higher income taxes given the highly compressed trust tax brackets, as discussed at ¶605. However, as long as the estate planner explains the potential tax cost, the client may properly create an income-accumulating trust that has as its primary goal ensuring that the beneficiaries receive their inheritances at an appropriate time.

.12 Special Powers of Appointment

A person creating a living or testamentary trust may give a trust beneficiary a power to direct who will enjoy the right to trust property. This trust is known as a power of appointment trust, and the power may be either general or special.

A general power of appointment under Code Sec. 2041 gives the holder the right to direct that property subject to the power be paid to the holder, his or her estate, his or her creditors, or the creditors of his or her estate. Under a special or limited power, however, the holder may not appoint the trust property to any of these categories. The great flexibility advantage offered by the special power is that the power-holder can alter trust ownership, as he or she deems fit, without adverse estate tax consequences to himself or herself.

Provided a power qualifies as a special one, its scope may be as narrow or as broad as the person creating the trust might wish. An example of a narrow restriction would be where the holder is given the power by will to appoint the principal of the trust created by the grantor among such of the power-holder's descendants as shall survive him or her in such amounts or proportions and outright or in further trust as the power-holder shall appoint. A broader special power of appointment would permit the holder to appoint the principal of the trust to any individual or corporation (other than the power-holder, his or her estate, his or her creditors, or the creditors of his or her estate). Whether the power is broad or narrow, its careful exercise can provide the holder with a valuable estate planning tool permitting appropriate dispositions for his or her beneficiaries. For example, instead of requiring that the trust principal pass per stirpes to the descendants of the power-holder on his or her death, exercise of a special power of appointment could permit the holder not to make payments to any child. Alternatively, the special power could allow the holder to appoint the property in further trust for the child for his or her lifetime.

¶665 TRUSTEES—THEIR SELECTION, RESPONSIBILITIES, AND POWERS

A critical choice for the trust settlor is the selection of the trustee or trustees. Probably the first qualification to consider is that the person selected must measure up to the job in a practical way. If a large part of the trust property consists of an ongoing business, for example, an individual with business experience might be preferred. If the trust property is a large portfolio of listed securities, an investment advisor, if available, might be a suitable appointee. Trustees must also meet legal qualifications. Local law requirements are usually more restrictive as to executors than they are as to trustees. Nevertheless, the estate planner should check local law, especially if the situs of the trust is to be in one state and a potential trustee is from another state.

Ability, durability, integrity, experience, judgment, understanding, and solvency are all qualities to look for whether the trust is big or small. Indeed, with a small trust, the need for care in selection will be even greater, because the beneficiaries will likely have greater needs.

Tax considerations also affect the selection of a trustee. If the settlor names himself or herself a trustee, the powers over principal and income may make the settlor taxable on trust income under Code Secs. 671-677. If a person other than the settlor is named, the estate planner should consider whether he or she will be taxable on trust income under Code Sec. 678. Under Code Sec. 678, a person other than the settlor is taxable on the trust income if he or she has the power solely by himself or herself to vest income or principal in himself or herself or has partially released such power, but retains such control as would make him or her taxable if he or she were the settlor.

The estate planner should also consider estate tax issues flowing from the Code provisions designed to include in an individual's gross estate property that he or she is able to control or to enjoy beneficially (¶610). The estate planner needs to look at whether the possession of powers within the reach of one or more of those sections will bring the property into the trustee's gross estate.

Trustee's fees are also a matter of practical concern. This issue might involve the question of whether to select a corporate or individual trustee, as well as whether to use co-trustees. Both topics are separately discussed below. Cost considerations might lead the settlor to use an individual as trustee while the trust is largely unfunded, and to add a corporate trustee and possibly an individual co-trustee when full funding takes place. Similar considerations are applicable to a living trust so long as it is revocable, or while it merely serves as a standby trust, with the settlor serving as trustee. When some event occurs that makes the trust irrevocable or the standby becomes effective, the settlor might wish to switch to a paid trustee. The client might be able to bargain with the trustee on commission rates that are lower than those provided under state law. Agreements to limit the compensation of trustees of testamentary trusts are best secured during the client's lifetime.

.01 Corporate or Individual Trustee?

The estate planner does not need to discuss with the client whether to use a corporation or an individual as a trustee until the trust assets are sufficient to warrant consideration by a corporate trustee. A corporate trustee, depending on locality, might not be willing to serve as a trustee unless the trust assets are substantial. For example, a corporate trustee might not be willing to serve as trustee unless the trust assets are worth at least $500,000.

Apart from cost factors and the personal touch, the corporate trustee is likely to be more effective than an individual. The corporate trustee is a specialist. It has experience. It is a combination of individuals. It never gets sick, and it is immortal. In dealing with the trust and beneficiaries, a corporate trustee is not distracted by emotional ties and commitments and can act impartially.

Fees for a corporate trustee, however, can be expensive. A settlor might be able to get a family member to take the job without any compensation. However, corporate trustees are in business to make money. They may have minimum fees. They may have an acceptance fee or a termination fee and sometimes both. The trustee could charge additional fees for the preparation of tax returns or beneficiary tax reports. Corporate trustees might demand extra fees if the trust has a co-trustee, on the theory that a co-trustee makes their job more difficult. These fees are all proper subjects of inquiry before making a commitment to a corporate trustee.

On the other hand, some corporate trustees will discount their regular fees if they are permitted to invest trust funds in their common funds. In such cases, the estate planner will want to know the amount of common fund management fees and expenses. The client with substantial liquid assets might be able to persuade a corporate trustee to serve for lower than ordinary rates.

The corporate trustee, however, is apt to lack that personal touch and knowledge that an individual close to the settlor and his or her family might have. Such a personal connection might be helpful in exercising discretion as to distributions to trust beneficiaries.

The combination of cost factors and lack of personal touch and knowledge are factors that argue against the corporate trustee and favor the qualified individual. The settlor might especially prefer an individual trustee if he or she anticipates few complications in the administration of the trust and the trust assets are not very substantial.

.02 Co-trustees

The ideal arrangement might seem to be to have a corporation and an individual serve as co-trustees. The individual would supply the personal touch and knowledge that the corporate trustee lacks. However, co-trusteeships can be very expensive if both are to receive full fees, especially if the corporate trustee wants additional fees because of the additional work (conferences, meetings, and delays) involved.

An arrangement might be possible in which the trust would allocate special duties and responsibilities to each co-trustee and fix reasonable compensation on that basis. Another way of approaching it might be to have the individual delegate his or her rights and powers to the corporate trustee, subject to recall at will. Alternatively, instead of having the individual appointed as trustee, he or she might simply be authorized to carry out special functions, such as advising the corporate trustee of individual needs of beneficiaries. The trust would then provide compensation for such limited functions.

If the settlor names a co-trustee, or gives an individual who is not a co-trustee certain powers, the estate planner should consider the tax consequences along the lines suggested above.

.03 Naming Alternate or Successor Trustees

The estate planner will also want to advise the settlor to consider appointing alternate or successor trustees. This consideration applies even when the settlor initially names a corporate trustee, especially if the trust is a testamentary trust. Although a corporate trustee might have given a preliminary commitment of acceptance, by the time the trust becomes operative it might not have substantial assets. Therefore, the corporate trustee might renounce the appointment.

If the trustee accepts the appointment, the trustee might later resign. If a vacancy occurs, and the trust itself makes no provision for an alternate or successor, courts of equity will find the vacuum abhorrent and will undertake to fill it on an application duly made. However, the trust will incur a legal fee for the proceeding. In addition, most likely a bond will be required. The trust would have to pay a premium for the bond.

Therefore, selecting an alternate or successor trustee is very important. The settlor should exercise the same care in selecting a successor or alternate trustee as if he or she were making the initial choice. The settlor may provide for or dispense with the requirement of a bond for an alternate or successor trustee as seems prudent.

The settlor's reservation of the right to fill a vacancy or name a successor that does not bar his or her own appointment will result in the inclusion of the trust property in his or her gross estate under Code Sec. 2036(a)(2).[114] However, a grantor's reservation of an unqualified power to remove a trustee and appoint an individual or corporate successor trustee that is not related or subordinate to the grantor within the meaning of Code Sec. 672(c) is not considered a reservation of the trustee's discretionary powers of distribution over the trust property.[115]

.04 Powers of Trustees

The trustee needs to be given sufficient power to enable him or her to carry out the purposes and objectives of the settlor. State law will spell out in considerable detail the powers with which the trustee is vested, absent anything in the trust to the contrary. The estate planner should check local law, but usually a trustee will have power to do the following:

- Retain trust property
- Sell trust property and reinvest the proceeds
- Consent to corporate adjustments
- Manage real estate
- Allocate receipts and disbursements to income or principal (corpus)
- Lend and borrow
- Settle claims
- Exercise stock options

[114] *M. Farrel Est.*, CtCls, 77-1 USTC ¶13,185, 213 CtCls 622, 533 F2d 637.

[115] *H. Wall Est.*, 101 TC 300, CCH Dec. 49,330; Rev. Rul. 95-58, 1995-2 CB 191; revoking Rev. Rul. 79-353 CB 325.

- Distribute property in kind
- File tax returns
- Exercise all powers appropriate to a trustee

The settlor will want to go beyond these statutory powers, if need be, to permit the trustee to carry out his or her objectives. The special provisions discussed in ¶ 660 suggest some of the additional powers that the settlor might want to confer. The settlor might provide the trustee with more specific powers for investment management. The settlor might do so to liberalize or limit the usual prudent-investor rule under the Uniform Prudent Investor Act. The settlor might want to confer specific authority to invest in common bank funds, mutual funds, variable annuities, or the like, in which investment decisions are in effect delegated to others. Special provisions might be necessary in relation to the holding of nonincome-producing property. In short, the purpose is to permit the trustee to carry out the goals and objectives of the settlor.

Chapter 7

Life Insurance

Overview .... ¶ 701
Types of Policies .... ¶ 705
Life Insurance Investment Yields and the Income Tax ...... ¶ 710
Life Insurance and the Estate Tax .... ¶ 715
Life Insurance and the Gift Tax .... ¶ 720
Practical Considerations Affecting Gifts of Life Insurance ... ¶ 725
Who Should Be Named Beneficiary? .... ¶ 730
The Insurance Trust .... ¶ 735
How Much Insurance? .... ¶ 740
Financed Insurance .... ¶ 745
Settlement Options or How Insurance Proceeds May Be Made Payable .... ¶ 750
Replacing Policies in Force .... ¶ 755

¶ 701 OVERVIEW

Life insurance has two major functions: (1) to replace the earning power of the family breadwinner; and (2) to provide liquidity for an estate. Estate liquidity is necessary to guard against its loss in value by the forced sale of estate assets to meet the family's current cash needs, the costs of estate administration, the federal estate tax, and state inheritance taxes.

The first function is a fairly compelling reason for heads of young families who have few assets and many long-term family responsibilities. Life insurance is the only sure way to provide a family with an instant estate upon the death of a breadwinner.

The need for liquidity is not quite as compelling. A client can provide for estate liquidity in other ways such as cash and cash equivalents. Although an estate can easily liquidate publicly traded equity securities and bonds, their values can fluctuate greatly. Neither the executor nor the beneficiaries of an estate are going to be happy if the estate is forced to sell securities at low prices just before an upturn. In any event, life insurance can eliminate the need for holding low-yield liquid investments when high-yield illiquid investments are available.

Life insurance that offers a cash value or cash accumulation feature can also serve as an investment, which is safer than are most other investments. State supervision, diversification, and professional investment management are key safety factors. A life insurance policy might guarantee a minimum return. Some newer forms of life insurance might provide higher investment returns than do those traditionally associated with whole life insurance. Life insurance can also be a tax shelter, as discussed at ¶ 710, and the proceeds are usually sheltered against the claims of creditors.

Insurance is favorably treated under death tax laws, and many states exempt insurance payable to named beneficiaries. For the rule in a particular state, see CCH STATE INHERITANCE, ESTATE AND GIFT TAX REPORTS.

The federal estate tax exempts insurance proceeds payable to beneficiaries other than the executor or administrator of the insured's estate, if the insured, at the time of death, retains no incidents of ownership in the policy.[1] This benefit is more fully discussed at ¶ 715.

Insurance also is favorably treated under both federal and state income tax laws. Many states follow the federal rule generally exempting insurance proceeds from income tax.[2]

The various settlement options available under insurance policies constitute another benefit, permitting flexibility and security for policy owners and their beneficiaries (¶ 750).

In addition, relatively low-interest loans against cash values generally offer a valuable benefit in times of tight money. However, loans from modified endowment policies may be subject to income tax, as discussed at ¶ 705.

Life insurance, as an estate planning tool, takes on added importance when business interests are involved. The role of life insurance in planning for the owner of an interest in a close corporation is discussed at ¶ 1935; in partnerships at ¶ 2015; and in sole proprietorships in Chapter 21.

Group life insurance as an employee benefit receives special treatment as discussed at ¶ 945. Life insurance for the executive is discussed at ¶ 1605.

---

[1] Code Sec. 2042(2).

[2] Code Sec. 101(a).

This chapter has a broader focus. This chapter examines life insurance in its more general aspects and applications.

.01 Understanding a Life Insurance Contract

Life insurance policies can be important assets in an individual's potential gross estate. The estate planner should review all of the client's policies and make appropriate summaries and recommendations. A review of some important provisions follows.

Assignment. The policy spells out the rules for making an assignment. Usually the life insurance company is not bound until it receives a written notice of assignment. In addition, the assignment is subject to any policy loan. This clause is important to a potential creditor who wants to lend money on the policy's security.

Beneficiary. The policy owner can designate one or more beneficiaries and can provide that payment of the proceeds shall be by a settlement option, which is other than an outright payment of the proceeds. An estate planner should always check to see whether the policy owner has made any beneficiary or settlement option irrevocable before planning or making changes. Also, the policy owner must comply with the procedural rules when changing beneficiaries.

Cash value. The policy states whether it has, or will have, any cash value. If the policy provides for a cash value, it will include a table listing the amount of cash that the owner may obtain upon a surrender of the policy. This cash value is not the same as the gift tax value of the policy, but it may be used as an estimate because cash values are usually only slightly lower than gift tax values.

Dividends. Participating policies stipulate the payment of dividends. These dividends are not like dividends on stock, but are merely the nontaxable return of some excess premiums by the insurance company. A participating policy will describe the various available dividend options that the policy owner may select. These options include the following:

- Cash payments (payment by the company)
- One-year term additions (automatic application of dividends to purchase additional one-year term coverage)
- Paid-up additions (applied to purchase additional paid-up insurance coverage)
- Dividends retained at interest (dividends held on deposit by the insurance company, which also credits interest on this amount)

- Reduced premium dividends (applied to pay for a portion of the premium that would otherwise be paid by the policy owner)

Double indemnity. This feature is a rider available for an additional premium under which the insurance company pays beneficiaries double the face amount of the policy if the insured dies as a result of an accident. The advisability of this rider is open to question. If the insured has adequate insurance, the rider is an unnecessary expense. If, however, the insured needs greater coverage, he or she should buy additional life insurance.

Extended insurance. Unlike term insurance, permanent insurance might provide that the coverage will not automatically expire if a premium is not paid on time. Instead, the insurance generally continues as term insurance for a limited period, which can sometimes run for a number of years. Generally, this option is not the preferred option when an individual decides to stop paying premiums.

Guaranteed insurability. This rider guarantees the insured the right to purchase specified amounts of additional insurance at specified times. It is normally less readily available with term policies. The rider usually specifies maximum and minimum amounts of insurance that the insured may purchase. The premium for the added coverage is based on the insured's age at the time he or she acquires the added coverage.

Living benefits. If certain requirements are satisfied, accelerated death benefits received under a life insurance contract on a terminally or chronically ill insured may be excluded from gross income. Similarly, if an assignment or sale of a policy is made to a viatical settlement provider, amounts received from the provider are excludable from gross income. Thus, an individual diagnosed with a fatal illness (one reasonably expected to cause death within 24 months) may obtain the proceeds of a life insurance contract or assign the contract's benefits to a viatical settlement provider without paying tax on the proceeds. This rule is an exception to the usual rule that life insurance proceeds must be paid by reason of death to be excluded from gross income.[3] An individual who is chronically ill, but not expected to die within 24 months, may also exclude life insurance proceeds received. However, the amount must be received under a policy provision or rider treated as a long-term insurance contract under Code Sec. 7702B (¶3420).

Payments made on a per diem or other periodic basis without regard to actual expenses are still excluded from gross income,

[3] Code Sec. 101.

but subject to the dollar cap applicable under a per diem type long-term care insurance contract (¶ 3420).

Loan values. Permanent insurance permits the policy owner to borrow up to a specified percent of the cash value, frequently 95 percent, at guaranteed interest rates. These interest rates are less than those charged by other commercial lenders. The insured may select an automatic premium loan provision, which provides that the insurance company will make loans automatically to pay any premiums that are not paid when due. This provision avoids a lapse of the policy for nonpayment of premiums.

Nonparticipating policies. Nonparticipating cash value policies provide fixed premium costs, but do not pay dividends. Usually, premium costs will be lower than are those of participating policies. In the long run, however, participating policies might prove less costly.

Ownership clause. The person owning the policy is named. The owner is usually the same as the named insured, but the owner may name another individual, a trust, or another entity. If the insured does not hold the incidents of ownership, and the proceeds are not payable to the insured's estate, the proceeds may not be included in the insured's gross estate.[4]

Paid-up insurance. Permanent insurance with cash values also contains a table showing the amount of paid-up insurance that the owner can obtain, instead of cash or extended insurance, if the owner decides to surrender the policy.

Waiver of premiums. A special rider provides that premiums will not have to be paid for the period in which the insured is disabled. With some policies, the rider is automatic and the cost is built into the annual premium. With others, it is an optional feature, the cost of which may vary depending on age, gender, the terms of the waiver, and the particular insurer. These provisions keep needed life insurance policies in force, and ease the insured's economic burden while disabled. However, the financial planner should also inquire as to the adequacy of the insured's basic disability coverage.

.02 Definition of Life Insurance

Code Sec. 7702 provides a definition of life insurance for all tax purposes—estate, gift, and income. This provision prevents thinly disguised investment vehicles from qualifying as life insurance. In the event a contract fails to meet the applicable test, the pure insurance portion of the contract (the difference between the cash

[4] Code Sec. 2042(2).

surrender value and the death benefit) will be treated as term insurance for tax purposes. The cash surrender part of such a contract will be treated as a side fund, the income of which will be taxable to the policy owner in the year the contract fails to qualify as life insurance. Not only will the income of the current year be taxable to the policyholder, but all income earned in all prior years will be taxed as ordinary income. Income in this connection is the amount by which the increase in net surrender value and the *cost of the life insurance provided* exceed the amount of the premiums paid, less any dividends credited.

The "cost of the insurance provided" is the lower of (1) the cost of individual insurance on the insured's life (regulations provide uniform premiums rates that must be used[5]), or (2) the mortality charge, if any, stated in the contract.

On the death of the insured, if the policy is disqualified, only the excess of the death benefit over the net surrender value will qualify for the exclusion from gross income under Code Sec. 101(a).

.03 Tax Treatment of Lifetime Withdrawals

Withdrawals made by a policyholder from a life insurance policy are generally taxable only to the extent that they exceed the premiums paid, minus dividends. However, withdrawals from modified endowment policies are treated as income first, then recovery of basis.

Modified endowment policies. Some of the tax advantages that generally apply to life insurance contracts do not apply to policies known as modified endowment contracts. The reason is that these contracts have too much of an investment orientation. A modified endowment contract (MEC) is defined as a policy that satisfies the definition of life insurance but fails to satisfy the seven-payment test.[6] A policy fails this test if the cumulative amount paid under the contract at any time during the first seven years exceeds the sum of the net level premiums that would have been paid on or before such time had the contract provided for paid-up future benefits after the payment of seven level premiums.[7] The amount paid in this connection is the amount of the premiums paid reduced with some exceptions by amounts received under the contract. Policies that fail the seven-payment test that were issued before June 21, 1988, and that were not later materially changed are not modified endowment contracts. Loans and distributions from these policies are subject to the same favorable tax rules that apply to regular life insurance policies.

---

[5] Reg. § 1.79-3(d)(2).

[6] Code Sec. 7702A(a).

[7] Code Sec. 7702A(b).

Modified endowment contracts are subject to income tax rules and penalties, which are different from those that apply to other life insurance contracts. Policy loans and partial withdrawals of funds are taxed to the extent of any inside income buildup within the policy.[8] Thus, policy loans and withdrawals are taxable before any tax-free return of investment is permitted from the policy. In addition, a 10-percent additional tax applies to any taxable withdrawals before age 59½, except for payments attributable to disability or for certain annuitized payments.[9] The additional tax applies as well to amounts withdrawn on termination of the policy.

The tax rules for modified endowment policies principally affect those policyholders who take out policy loans or make withdrawals before age 59½. If the insured does not contemplate such loans or withdrawals, the holder of an affected policy should be in no hurry to terminate the policy, especially if the policy itself calls for surrender charges.

¶705 TYPES OF POLICIES

An individual can choose from a wide choice of insurance policies to provide an instant estate, estate liquidity, or both. The fundamental choice is between term insurance and some form of cash value insurance, which is an investment combined with insurance.

.01 Term Insurance

Term insurance is also known as pure insurance because it does not have any investment features. Term insurance provides insurance for a stated term such as for one year or five years. The premiums might be level for the term and then increase with the next term. An individual might use a declining term policy for such things as paying a mortgage in the event of his or her death. Declining term policies usually provide for level premiums, but the insurance coverage decreases annually. The term insurance might be guaranteed renewable as long as the policy owner pays the premiums. Some term policies are also convertible, which means that the insured may convert the term policy to a cash value policy. The premiums for level term insurance are low when the insured is young, but usually increase as the insured grows older because the risk of death increases with age.

Some clients have a ready answer when confronted with the choice between term insurance and a cash value policy. They say,

[8] Code Secs. 72(e)(10), 72(e)(2)(B) and 72(e)(4)(A). [9] Code Sec. 72(v).

"Buy term (pure insurance) and invest the difference." But the choice is not that simple. Term insurance buys the greatest amount of protection per premium dollar. Term insurance will release dollars for investment in equity or high-yielding debt securities. However, term insurance carries with it uncertainties and risk. Premiums generally rise rapidly at higher age levels. The risk is that, as one ages, the policy may become too expensive, even though the insured still needs insurance protection. In the end, term might show a higher true cost of insurance than do some investment types of contracts.

Many variations exist in term policies. No policy exists that provides term insurance to age 75, which might have some cash value. Level premium term has set premiums for 10, 15, or even 20 years. Another type of term policy is renewable term to age 65. Convertible term allows the insured to change the policy to ordinary life without having to show evidence of insurability. These features, while available only on payment of an additional premium, reduce the risk of loss of insurability. Whether buying term and investing the difference will prove better over the long run depends on a number of variables:

- The soundness and the yield on the outside investment and whether it is taxable
- If it is taxable, the top tax bracket of the insured
- The premium cost and net cost, taking into account the buildup of cash value in the policy (these figures may vary depending on the company and the type of policy, whether it guarantees a fixed rate of return or allows the insured to pick from a variety of investment choices within the policy, and whether it pays dividends or is nonparticipating)
- Whether the insured lives or dies while the policies are in force

The cash buildup outside the policy adds to the insured's protection over and above the face amount of term insurance. Cash buildup within a policy of permanent insurance reduces the effective insurance coverage. This last statement is true because at the death of the insured, the typical cash value policy pays out only the policy's face amount, not the face amount plus the accumulated cash value. However, some permanent insurance policies pay the cash value of the policy in addition to the face amount of the policy.

With permanent cash value insurance, the policyholder can borrow at low interest rates for any purpose he or she sees fit. The term insurance buyer can use his or her savings, but at the cost of a lower yield on the amount borrowed. This cost might be higher than the cost of borrowing against a cash value policy.

Exhibit 7 provides an overview of different types of basic policies, their characteristics, and uses.

.02 Types of Cash Value Policies

Many different types of cash value policies are available. The most common type of cash value policy is the whole life policy or straight life policy. With this type of policy, the insured continues to pay whatever premium required at the issuance of the policy for his or her entire life up to age 95 or older. At that point, the cash value of the policy equals the face amount of the policy, and the policy is said to endow.

The whole life policy has several variations. One variation affects the payment period. The policy may endow at age 95, but the policy is paid up at an earlier age, such as age 65, 75, or 85.

Some policies make automatic adjustments or make adjustments based on factors outside the insured's control. Generally, a financial planner should base a recommendation for a client's insurance coverage on a careful review of the client's particular situation at periodic intervals. The financial planner might recommend whole life insurance, term insurance, or a combination of the two.

Conventional whole life policies. With a conventional whole life policy, the death benefits are fixed, the policy has a fixed maturity date, the policy requires fixed level premiums, and the policy provides for a fixed progression of cash values. When available, a change in the plan of insurance requires a catch-up payment in the case of additional coverage, or a refund if the insured reduces coverage.

Single-premium life insurance. Single-premium life insurance once was heavily promoted as a tax-sheltered investment. Single-premium policies issued after June 20, 1988 (or issued earlier but materially modified after June 20, 1988), are subject to the modified endowment rules discussed above (¶ 701) that affect the tax treatment of loans and withdrawals.

Single-premium policies still provide a number of advantages. They allow up-front funding of a vehicle providing tax-deferred growth. At death, the proceeds are income-tax free[10] and can also be made free of federal estate tax and state death taxes.[11] The insured can use the policy to avoid probate and to stem attacks on or elections against the insured's will. The policy can bar creditors' claims against the insured or his or her beneficiaries.

[10] Code Sec. 101(a).

[11] Code Sec. 2042.

Universal life policies. This type of policy separates the cash value element and the term protection element inherent in a whole life policy. Part of the premiums paid are invested in a cash fund; the rest are used to finance renewable term insurance. The policy does not require payment of premiums beyond the initial premiums. This provision makes such a policy the ultimate in flexible premium policies. If the insured elects not to make a premium payment, the insurance company withdraws money from the cash fund to make the payment. If the cash fund is inadequate to pay the premium, the death benefit will remain at the original level. However, if the cash fund does not increase at a pace sufficient to pay the missed premiums, the death benefit will decrease.

The real attraction of universal life was the higher yields produced in the high interest climate that once prevailed. The popularity of traditional universal life policies declined with the decline of interest rates. This scenario led to the development of a policy with a broad range of investment options that came to be known as variable universal life, or "Universal Life II" in some quarters. This type of policy combines elements of traditional universal life with elements of variable life (see below) to permit maximum flexibility with high investment potential. Two elements of traditional universal life are present: (1) the ability to alter premium amounts, and (2) the ability to change the death benefit. At the same time, the policyholder may use the policy as an investment vehicle within the limits prescribed by law. Various investment options are available (e.g., money market funds, bond funds, and stock funds). Further, investment vehicles may be split and shifted within certain parameters.

The insured bears the investment risk in these policies. Poor performance can result in a lower death benefit. Universal life policies that fail to meet the seven-payment test, discussed above, will be treated as modified endowment contracts (MECs) and be subject to the tax rules governing such contracts.

> **Planning pointer.** The flexibility of a universal life policy allows an insured to scale back premium payments to an amount just sufficient to pay the term component of the policy. However, doing so is not a good idea, except to deal with an economic emergency. If from the outset, the insured does not intend to pay premiums sufficient to build a meaningful cash fund, the universal policy is a bad choice as a vessel to purchase only term insurance. With a universal life policy, the insured pays for policy features associated with the cash fund. If the insured does not plan to use these features, he or she could likely purchase term coverage more cheaply with a term policy itself.

Variable life policies. This type of policy is a variant of regular whole life cash value insurance, with premiums on a similar scale. Such policies do not ordinarily allow the insured the degree of flexibility of the flexible premium type policies discussed above. Net premiums, after expenses, are invested in a fund or funds selected by the policyholder. If the funds earn more than a specified return, the death benefit and the cash value increase. If the funds earn less than a specified return, the death benefit and the cash value decrease. However, the death benefit never decreases below the original face amount.

The choice of funds might include stock, bond, money market, real estate, and various other combinations. In addition, the policyholder may usually switch from one fund to another at specified intervals.

Most policies allow a two-year period in which the policyholder may convert the policy to ordinary life insurance.

The big advantage of a variable life policy is that it is a tax-deferred investment permitting the investor to take advantage of a bull market in equities. The disadvantage is that the unpredictability of the stock market places the burden of investment management and the investment risk on the policyholder.

While the policy usually guarantees that the death benefit will not fall below a specified minimum amount, the guarantee might depend on the insured paying a target premium. If the insured omits payment of a premium and the fund cannot support the minimum, the insurance company may reduce the death benefit. The prospective policyholder will want to check the terms of the policy to determine the scope and effect of the death benefit guarantee.

Adjustable life policies. This type of policy permits the insured to choose between term insurance, cash value insurance, or some combination of each, as well as the amount of coverage desired. The insured can control the premium to be paid by altering the ratio of cash value to term insurance within limits set by the insurer. With each change, the premiums are fixed until the next change. The insured may change the premiums and the face amount of the policy as his or her needs and income change. The flexibility afforded broadens the appeal of this type of policy.

Modified whole life. Another type of cash value policy is modified whole life. In this type of policy, the premium is not constant; it is lower in the early years and then increases. These policies might be suitable for young families who cannot afford sufficient insurance in the early years but who might be able to pay higher premiums in later years. It also helps the insurer to sell insurance.

Economatic policies. Yet another cash value policy is known as an economatic policy. Insurance companies in the business of selling participating policies designed this type of policy. Their goal was to make their premiums more competitive with those offered by companies selling nonparticipating policies.

> ***Example 7.1.*** Fred Pillow ultimately wants $100,000 of cash value insurance. He buys an economatic policy. It is a package consisting of a whole life policy in the face amount of $65,000 with a provision that each year the dividends on the policy are to be automatically applied to the purchase of a combination of one-year term insurance and whole life insurance in an additional amount to be added to the basic policy. As a result, the amount of whole life insurance increases and the amount of one-year term decreases. In time, Pillow has a whole life policy in the amount desired. At that time, Pillow is free to exercise any one of the dividend options usually provided in a whole life participating policy.

A possible disadvantage of an economatic policy is that, in the early years, the policy does not guarantee that the dividends will be sufficient to provide the full amount of coverage desired. Also, the policy requires the automatic application of the dividends in the manner indicated. This provision deprives the insured of other dividend options until the whole life portion has reached maturity.

Split-dollar life insurance. Split-dollar life insurance is a cash value life insurance policy often used to cover the lives of key executives of a company. The individual and the company split the cost of the policy and the benefits and proceeds. The company might pay the premiums equal to the increase in the cash surrender value or the individual might pay the cost of the equivalent term insurance. Thus, the company pays the majority of the premium cost. Under a traditional split-dollar arrangement, the company is the beneficiary of the policy up to the amount of the cash surrender value (or the premiums paid by the company if greater). The individual names a beneficiary for the remainder of the death benefit. However, under an "equity" split-dollar arrangement, the death benefit that goes to the individual's beneficiary is not limited to what is left over after the company gets the cash value; the beneficiary gets a portion of the cash value as well. The company generally recovers only an amount equal to the cumulative premiums it paid. The remainder of the death benefit is paid to the beneficiary. During the life of the policy, when the cash value buildup exceeds the cumulative premiums paid by the company, the individual is considered to have an equity interest in the policy. If the policy is surrendered, the individual will receive a portion of the cash value. Split-dollar life insurance plans are not subject to the antidiscrimination rules that apply to qualified plans.

The two basic types of split-dollar life insurance plans are the endorsement method and the collateral assignment method. Under the endorsement method, the employer owns the policy and endorses the death benefits to the employee. The employer pays most or all of the premiums. The employee pays the cost of the equivalent term insurance. Under the collateral assignment method, the employee owns the policy, and the employer pays all or most of the premiums. The employee assigns a security interest in the policy to the employer in an amount that equals the premiums paid by the employer.

On September 11, 2003, the IRS issued final regulations[12] on the treatment of all split-dollar life insurance arrangements. These regulations apply to split-dollar arrangements executed or materially modified after September 17, 2003. For split-dollar arrangements entered into on or before September 17, 2003, taxpayers may continue to rely on revenue rulings as described in Cumulative Bulletin Notice 2002-8, IRB 2002-4, 398 (January 3, 2002) as long as such arrangements are not materially modified.[13]

Under the new regulations, the amount taxable to an individual under a traditional split-dollar arrangement with a company is generally determined as under prior law. This means the individual is taxed on the value of the death benefit coverage provided by the company, based on the cost of one year of term insurance. For split-dollar arrangements entered into before January 28, 2002, this cost may be determined using the PS 58 rates if a contractual arrangement between the company and the individual provides that those rates will be used.[14] For arrangements entered into on or after January 28, 2002, Table 2001 must be used to determine the cost of current life insurance protection.

While leaving the tax treatment of traditional split-dollar policies relatively intact, the final regulations substantially alter the tax treatment of equity split-dollar arrangements. The tax consequences of an equity split-dollar life insurance arrangement depends on its classification under one of two alternative regimes: (1) the economic benefit regime or (2) the loan regime.

The economic benefit regime applies when the employer is the owner of the policy. The employer is treated as providing an economic benefit to the individual employee. The economic benefit is taxable

[12] Reg. § 1.61-22 and Reg. § 1.7872-15.

[13] Rev. Rul. 2003-105, IRB 2003-40 (September 11, 2003).

[14] Notice 2002-8, 2002-4 IRB 398.

the employee as compensation. Any right or benefit in the insurance policy, such as in interest in the cash surrender value, is treated as additional compensation.

Under the loan regime the employee owns the policy and the employer pays the premiums. The employer is deemed to loan the premium payments to the employee. The loan regime applies where (1) the payment is made by the employer to the employee, (2) the payment is a loan under the tax law or a reasonable person would expect the payments to be repaid and (3) the payment is made from or secured by the death benefit or the cash surrender value of the policy. Each premium payment is treated as a seperate loan. If the loan under the split-dollar arrangement is not a below-market loan, the general rules for loans apply. The borrower may not deduct any interest paid on the split-dollar loan because it is personal interest. If the loan under the split-dollar arrangement is a below-market loan, the provisions of Code Sec. 7872 apply. However, the de minimis exception of Code Sec. 7872 does not apply to split-dollar loans. The imputed interest on a below-market loan to an employee under a split-dollar arrangement is usually taxable compensation to the employee.

The final regulations do not affect the calculation of the amount included in an employee's gross income for group term life insurance that exceeds $50,000. The amount included in the employee's gross income in such cases is still determined under Reg. § 1.79-3(d)(2).

Exhibit 7

Comparison of Basic Insurance Policies

Type	Characteristics	Uses
Whole Life	Low cost, cash value, premiums payable for lifetime (until age 95 or older).	Young single persons and young married persons for protection, with some savings, and as an emergency source of funds.
Modified Whole Life	Allows the insured to choose between term or cash value insurance or a combination of the two, and the amount of coverage.	Individuals who want a great deal of flexibility in changing their life insurance.
Economatic	Cash value insurance in which dividends are used to purchase term insurance and whole life insurance.	Individuals who want to increase their cash value insurance coverage over time.
Universal Life	Higher investment component than traditional whole life.	High-income individuals who find tax-free build-up attractive.
Variable-Universal Life	Availability of mutual fund like investments within the policy.	Individuals who want to direct their investments within a tax-sheltered environment.
Limited Payment Life	Stays in force when paid up. Builds cash and paid-up values. Less insurance payments, paid-up protection.	Good for persons with short-term high income, sports stars, entertainers. Also, high-income middle-aged individuals.
Single-Premium Life	Minimal insurance protection. Investment builds tax free.	High-income individuals who find tax-free build-up attractive and can use estate-tax-free transfer of assets.

Type	Characteristics	Uses
First-to-die	Covers more than one individual but pays on the death of the first insured only.	Used to fund buyout plans of partnerships or small corporations.
Second-to-die	Pays only on the death of the second spouse.	Used to pay estate taxes due on the death of the second spouse. Good for couples who will take advantage of the marital deduction on the death of the first spouse who need cash to pay estate taxes on the death of the second spouse.
Term	Protection only. Low cost.	Good for persons who need large amount of coverage for a short period (1-, 5-, 10-, 15-, 20-year term). Good for young married persons with growing children.
Decreasing Term	Protection reduced with time. Low cost.	Good for mortgage redemption, repayment of other loans or installment payments.
Split Dollar	Employer and employee split cost and benefits of cash value insurance.	Used for providing insurance to executives.

Vanishing premium policies. This type of contract involves the reinvestment of policy dividends so that the owner eventually will not have to pay premiums. This policy is affected by the seven-payment, net level premium test, discussed in connection with modified endowment contracts (¶ 701). For purposes of this test, the amount paid under the policy means the premiums paid "reduced by amounts received under the contract that are not received as an annuity to the extent that such amounts are not includible in gross income and are not attributable to a reduction in the originally scheduled death benefit."[15] Thus, use of dividends to reduce premiums could cause the policy to fail the test. Failure to pass the test results in the contract's being characterized as a modified endowment contract with LIFO-type tax treatment being applied to loans and other withdrawals. If the policyholder or would-be policyholder has no plans to borrow or withdraw before surrender or maturity, this unfavorable tax treatment might not be a significant factor. The vanishing premium aspect and other life insurance features, including the benefits of Code Sec. 101 (tax-free proceeds at maturity) and Code Sec. 2042 (escape from estate tax), might make the contract attractive.

Vanishing premium policies might be well suited for gifts to insurance trusts because the grantor may make gifts to each beneficiary of the full amount of the annual exclusion ($12,000 per donee per year for 2006[16] and indexed for inflation[17]) through pendent or hanging powers (¶ 660), or reduce or eliminate the beneficiaries' exposure to gift tax liability (to the extent that the value of their unexercised withdrawal powers exceeds the greater of $5,000 or five percent of trust principal in any year under Code Sec. 2041(b)(2)).

Prospective buyers of vanishing premium life insurance should know how these policies work. Strictly speaking, the obligation to pay premiums never vanishes. However, at some point, the yearly earnings from the policy's investment fund becomes sufficient to pay the premiums without future cash payments into the policy. The financial planner should inform the prospective buyer that the policy dividend rate assumed in the calculation might not be realized. A longer period than the period initially projected might be required for the owner's premium payment to vanish. Even worse, a premium that vanished earlier can reappear at a later date. If this event happens, the insured must again commence paying premiums, or lose the policy.

Joint lives. Couples use spousal or second-to-die insurance to pay the estate tax liability of the surviving spouse. No estate tax is due

---

[15] Conference Committee Report to the Technical and Miscellaneous Revenue Act of 1988 (P.L. 100-647).

[16] Code Sec. 2503(b)(1).

[17] Code Sec. 2503(b)(2).

on the death of the first spouse when the decedent transfers all property to the surviving spouse because of the unlimited marital deduction.[18] First-to-die insurance is used to fund buy-sell agreements. Both types of policies reduce premium costs.

¶ 710 LIFE INSURANCE INVESTMENT YIELDS AND THE INCOME TAX

The rate of return on conventional, cash value life insurance traditionally has been low. However, the life insurance industry has developed new forms of life insurance designed to improve the rate of return. Their goal is to make life insurance more competitive with other investment vehicles. In the process, the life insurance industry has developed universal life and other flexible premium-type policies, variable life insurance, and single premium life insurance. In any case, a financial planner should measure life insurance returns in light of the potential tax shelter that life insurance provides.

The investment growth of a life insurance policy does not completely escape tax. Proceeds paid before death can be taxable if the policy is a modified endowment contract (MEC) (¶ 701) or if the policy is not an MEC and the proceeds exceed the insured's cost. If the proceeds are received in a lump sum, the excess over cost is taxable as ordinary income. If the insured receives the proceeds in the form of payments over a specified number of years, the cost or investment in the contract is prorated over the selected income period. Only amounts received in excess of that amount are taxed in the year of receipt.

The insured uses the same approach, known as the exclusion ratio method, when the insured receives the proceeds as an annuity payable over the lifetime of the insured.

The exclusion ratio method for individuals whose annuity starting date is after 1986 compares the total amount that the individual may exclude from income to the total amount of his or her investment in the contract.[19] If the insured dies before the insured has recovered his or her investment, the unrecovered cost is allowed as a deduction on the individual's final income tax return.[20]

Special adjustments are necessary if the annuity is payable over more than one life, or if the contract guarantees a minimum number of payments or a minimum total amount to be paid.[21] Figuring the

[18] Code Sec. 2056(a).

[19] Code Sec. 72(b)(1).

[20] Code Sec. 72(b)(3).

[21] Code Sec. 72(c)(2).

taxable amounts in these special cases is complex, and one is apt to rely on the numbers furnished by the insurance company.

If a taxpayer transfers an insurance policy for consideration, the taxpayer usually must recognize gain to the extent that the consideration exceeds the taxpayer's basis in the policy. An exception applies if the transfer is by an insured who is terminally ill or chronically ill as explained below. The purchaser of a life insurance policy for valuable consideration must recognize gross income on the insured's death to the extent that the proceeds exceed the cost of the policy and the subsequent premiums paid by the purchaser.[22] However, if the policy is transferred as a gift or to a partner, partnership, or corporation as a part of a partnership or corporate buy-sell agreement, an exception applies. The insured must be a partner or shareholder of the business to meet this exception.[23] If the transfer meets this exception, then upon the death of the insured, all of the life insurance proceeds are excluded from the beneficiary's gross income under the general rule.[24]

In certain circumstances, an insured may receive the benefits of a life insurance policy while alive without having to recognize any gross income. If an individual is terminally ill or chronically ill and receives the proceeds of the policy while alive, he or she does not recognize any gross income.[25] If a terminally ill or chronically ill insured sells or assigns a life insurance policy to a viatical settlement provider, the insured recognizes no gross income.[26] A viatical settlement provider is a person engaged in the trade or business of purchasing life insurance policies on the lives of terminally ill or chronically ill individuals if the person is licensed to buy life insurance policies under such circumstances. If a state does not require licensing of viatical settlement providers, the provider must meet certain standards promulgated by the National Association of Insurance Commissioners.[27] Payments received by a chronically ill individual who is not terminally ill are excluded from gross income only to the extent used to pay for qualified long-term care services that are not covered by Medicare.[28] These rules that allow life insurance proceeds to be received tax free before death do not apply to taxpayers other than the insured if the taxpayer has an insurable interest in the insured as a director, officer, or employee of the taxpayer or if the insured has a financial interest in a trade or business of the taxpayer.[29]

A terminally ill individual is an individual whom a physician has certified as having an illness or physical condition expected to result

[22] Code Sec. 101(a)(2).
[23] Code Sec. 101(a)(2).
[24] Code Sec. 101(a)(1).
[25] Code Secs. 101(g)(1) and 101(a)(1).
[26] Code Secs. 101(g)(2)(A) and 101(a).
[27] Code Sec. 101(g)(2)(B).
[28] Code Sec. 101(g)(3)(A).
[29] Code Sec. 101(g)(5).

in death in 24 months or less after the date of certification. A chronically ill individual is one who cannot perform at least two activities of daily living for a period of at least 90 days.[30] A chronically ill individual does not include a terminally ill individual.[31]

On the insured's death, life insurance proceeds, when paid in a lump sum to the beneficiary, are exempt from income tax.[32] However, payments under settlement options will be partly taxable. The interest on proceeds left with the insurance company is taxable to the beneficiary when paid or credited.[33] If the insurance company is to make installment payments, the exempt proceeds are prorated over the anticipated installments. The excess over the amount prorated is taxable to the recipient.

Calculating the tax liabilities when a policy has more than one beneficiary or has guaranteed payments is complex. In such cases, the insurance company is generally the best source for providing accurate figures.

In general, life insurance premiums are not deductible for income tax purposes even if the policy has a bona fide business purpose.[34] However, a business may deduct premiums paid on employee-owned policies that are treated as taxable compensation to the employee.[35] This also includes a group term life insurance policy, even though the premiums paid by the employer are not included in the employee's gross income if the face amount of the policy is $50,000 or less.[36] However, the employee must recognize gross income on the value of the premiums paid by the employer for the excess of the face amount of the policy over $50,000.[37]

¶715 LIFE INSURANCE AND THE ESTATE TAX

Purchasing a $100,000 life insurance policy loses some of its luster if the most that the beneficiaries can receive is the $100,000 less the applicable estate tax. However, this situation may occur if the individual has a taxable estate that is greater than the applicable exclusion amount ($2,000,000 in 2006, 2007, and 2008; and $3,500,000 in 2009 under Code Sec. 2010(c)), apart from life insurance, and the decedent owns a $100,000 policy at the time of his or her death.

For the beneficiaries to receive the intended amount, the insured should transfer the policy and "all incidents of ownership" to the

---

[30] Code Secs. 101(g)(4)(B) and 7702B(c)(2)(A).
[31] Code Sec. 101(g)(4)(B).
[32] Code Sec. 101(a).
[33] Code Sec. 61(a) and Reg. § 1.451-2(a).
[34] Code Sec. 264(a).
[35] Code Sec. 79(a).
[36] Code Sec. 162(a).
[37] Code Sec. 79(a) and Reg. § 1.79-3(d)(2).

intended beneficiaries or to a trust. The transfer must occur more than three years before death to avoid inclusion in the gross estate under Code Sec. 2035. Then, Code Sec. 2042 takes the proceeds out of the gross estate. The transfer of the incidents of ownership can be tricky and can include a possible gift tax.

Insurance frequently is carried to make cash available for the payment of estate taxes and administration expenses. Life insurance also provides immediate funds for the beneficiaries. The insurance might be made payable to the executor of the estate or to other beneficiaries with the intention that they apply as much of the proceeds as needed to pay federal estate taxes and other designated estate expenses. To achieve this goal, the insured must not only transfer all incidents of ownership in the policy before his or her death, as already indicated, but must also make sure that the beneficiary is not under a legal obligation to make use of the insurance proceeds to pay estate taxes or other estate obligations. If he or she had such obligation, it would become an asset of the estate, taxable as such, and the objective of keeping the insurance proceeds out of the estate is frustrated. Ordinarily, this problem does not arise where the beneficiary is a living person, but it can arise where the beneficiary is a trust created by the insured.

If insurance proceeds intended for the payment of estate taxes are to be made payable to the executor, much larger amounts of insurance coverage will be required than if the proceeds were payable to another beneficiary. The insurance made payable to the executor for the purpose of paying estate taxes will itself operate to increase estate taxes and, in turn, require more insurance to pay the additional tax.

.01 Transfer of All Incidents of Ownership

To keep the insurance proceeds out of the insured's estate, he or she must name a beneficiary other than his or her executor, avoid the three-year rule of Code Sec. 2035, and surrender all incidents of ownership in the policy. Thus, the insured must assign the policy and give up all and any powers over the policy and its benefits. The term "incidents of ownership" includes the power to change the beneficiary, to surrender or cancel the policy, to assign it, to revoke an assignment, to pledge the policy for a loan, or to borrow against the cash surrender value. The regulations also include powers over the choice of settlement option, and the retention of a possible reversionary interest in the policy or its proceeds by the insured as incidents of ownership.[38]

[38] Reg. § 20.2042-1(c).

In Rev. Rul. 84-179,[39] the IRS ruled that a decedent will not be deemed to have incidents of ownership over an insurance policy on his or her life under the following conditions:

- His or her powers are held in a fiduciary capacity and are not exercisable for his or her personal benefit.
- He or she did not transfer the policy or any consideration for purchasing or maintaining it to the trust from personal assets.
- The devolution of the powers on the decedent was not part of a prearranged plan involving the decedent's participation.

However, Rev. Rul. 84-179 goes on to state that a decedent will be deemed to have incidents of ownership over an insurance policy on his or her life where his or her powers are held in a fiduciary capacity and where he or she transferred the policy or any of the consideration for purchasing and maintaining the policy to the trust. Also, where the decedent's powers could have been exercised for his or her benefit, they will constitute incidents of ownership in the policy, without regard to how the powers were acquired or whether the decedent transferred property to the trust. Thus, if the decedent reacquires powers over insurance policies in an individual capacity, the powers will constitute incidents of ownership, although the decedent is a transferee.

There are also special rules under which the controlling shareholder of a corporation holding a policy on his or her life may be treated as possessing incidents of ownership in the policy by reason of his or her ability to control the corporation. This particular aspect is discussed separately in Chapter 18, which deals with planning for the owner of an interest in a close corporation.

Special considerations apply to the transfer of interests in group-term insurance as an employee benefit. These issues are discussed in Chapter 9.

.02 Three-Year Rule

A gift of an insurance policy made by the insured within three years of death results in the entire proceeds of the policy[40] and any gift tax paid thereon[41] being included in the insured's gross estate. In addition, if a decedent transfers a life insurance policy more than three years before death but retains incidents of ownership in the policy until death or releases them within three years of death, the life insurance proceeds will be includible in the decedent's gross estate.[42]

[39] 1984-2 CB 195.

[40] Code Sec. 2035(a).

[41] Code Sec. 2035(b).

[42] Code Secs. 2042(2) and 2035(a).

The U.S. Courts of Appeals for the Sixth and Tenth Circuits have held that the gross estate does not include the proceeds of life insurance policies purchased by life insurance trusts within three years of death, provided the decedent did not possess any incidents of ownership. Both courts also held that the payment of premiums did not constitute an incident of ownership.[43] Although the insureds in these cases never actually possessed any incidents of ownership in the policies on their lives, the IRS tried to include the proceeds in their gross estates under a constructive transfer theory, as if the insureds had purchased the insurance and transferred it to the trust. Although the IRS disagrees with these cases, it announced that it would no longer litigate the issue.

Code Sec. 2035(a) says nothing about gifts of premiums on life insurance policies made within three years of death. It refers only to Code Sec. 2042, which applies only to life insurance policy proceeds. Thus, premiums paid by the insured on a life insurance policy within three years of death will not be includible in his or her gross estate under Code Sec. 2035(a). However, unfavorable consequences can occur if the insured pays premiums, as discussed below.

.03 Effects of Community Property Laws

If a decedent owned a life insurance policy as community property, the decedent's gross estate includes only one half of the proceeds whether the proceeds are payable to the estate[44] or to another beneficiary.[45]

The IRS ruled in Rev. Rul. 2003-40[46] that where a decedent purchased a life insurance policy during marriage in the state of Louisiana, named the decedent as the owner of the policy, and did not transfer ownership of the policy, the policy is presumed to be community property under Louisiana law. Therefore, one-half of the proceeds of the policy is included in the decedent's gross estate. However, if the decedent paid the premiums partly with community funds and partly with separate funds, the calculation of the amount included in the decedent's gross estate is more complex. This situation could occur if the decedent purchased the policy while single or living in a state that was not a community property state. The courts have used two alternative approaches to calculate the amount of life insurance proceeds to include in the decedent's gross estate in these circumstances.

---

[43] *J. Leder Est.*, CA-10, 90-1 USTC ¶60,001, 893 F2d 237 and *E. Headrick Est.*, CA-6, 90-2 USTC ¶60,049.

[44] Reg. § 20.2042-1(b)(2).

[45] Reg. § 20.2042-1(c)(5).

[46] IRB 2003-17, 813 (April 28, 2003).

The first approach is called the reimbursement approach. This approach is based on the inception of title doctrine and is followed in Texas, Louisiana, and New Mexico. Under the inception of title doctrine, separate property remains separate property even if the owner used community funds to pay for part of its cost. However, the marital community has a claim for reimbursement for the amount paid with community property. In such cases, the proceeds of the life insurance minus the amount paid for with community funds are included in the decedent's gross estate under Code Sec. 2042. The decedent's gross estate also includes one half of the premiums paid with community funds under Code Sec. 2033.[47] In these circumstances, an estate is not allowed a deduction under Code Sec. 2053(a) for the community's claim for reimbursement because the claim is against the insurance proceeds rather than against the estate.

The second approach is called the tracing approach. Under this approach, the amount included in the decedent's gross estate is equal to the proceeds multiplied by a fraction. The numerator of the fraction is the sum of the premiums paid with the decedent's separate funds and the decedent's one half of the premiums paid with community funds. The denominator is the total premiums paid.[48] The states of California and Washington follow the tracing approach.

¶720 LIFE INSURANCE AND THE GIFT TAX

When a person transfers a life insurance policy in a noncommercial setting, a taxable gift occurs. The value of the gift is the cost of replacing the policy, cash surrender value, or loan value. This cost is usually small compared to the value of the policy when it matures, i.e., at death or when it is paid up. The cost is derived from the interpolated reserve value at the date of the gift, plus a proportionate part of the last premium paid covering a period after the date of the gift.[49] The insurance company or its agent will be able to supply the figures on request.

Suppose the insured pays a premium on a policy where proceeds are payable to beneficiaries other than his or her estate, and the insured has no power to control the economic benefits of the policy. The insured has made a taxable gift to the beneficiaries, to the extent of the premium paid, although their right is conditioned on surviving the insured.[50]

---

[47] Rev. Rul. 80-242, 1980-2 CB 276.

[48] *Scott v. Commissioner*, 374 F 2d 154 (CA-9, 1967).

[49] Reg. § 25.2512-6(a).

[50] Reg. § 25.2511-1(h)(8).

The $12,000 annual exclusion (for 2006[51] and indexed for inflation[52]) is available for gifts of a present interest in property. An outright gift of an insurance policy will not be viewed as a gift of a future interest.[53] The same rule applies to premiums paid by the donor. Generally, a taxable gift occurs when a policy is assigned to a trust or the insured pays a premium on a policy held by a trust. The gift in such case will generally be treated as a gift of a future interest for which no annual exclusion is allowed. The law provides no exception in the case of a trust for a minor meeting the requirements of Code Sec. 2503(c), i.e., the trust may use income and corpus for the minor's benefit and pay unused amounts to the minor on attaining age 21 (¶ 425). The annual exclusion applies to both the policy itself and to premium payments. The premium payments are treated as though the money had been paid to the owner who then paid it to the insurance company.

Any unused portion of the unified credit of the insured-donor is also available to offset any gift tax liability.[54]

.01 Doubling the Unified Credit and Annual Exclusion—Split Gifts

If the donor's spouse consents to a gift of a policy or the payment of premiums, each is entitled to his or her own annual exclusion and may draw upon his or her unified credit. In addition, the couple may elect gift splitting.[55] If the couple elects gift splitting, Code Sec. 2513(a) treats the gift as made one-half by each spouse.

.02 Marital Deduction

On a gift of the policy or premiums to the donor's spouse, the unlimited marital deduction is available (¶ 405).[56] Thus, the donor does not have to rely on the annual exclusion and the unified credit.

.03 Estate Tax Consequences on Death of Owner of Policy Before or Simultaneously with Insured

When a policy owner who is not the insured dies before the insured, only the value of the policy at that time is included in the policy owner's gross estate.[57] The generally applicable estate tax rule is that the value is determined by adding to the interpolated terminal reserve (the insurer will provide the figure) at the date of the decedent's death the proportionate part of the gross premium last paid

[51] Code Sec. 2503(b)(1).
[52] Code Sec. 2503(b)(2).
[53] Reg. § 25.2503-3(a).
[54] Code Sec. 2505.
[55] Code Sec. 2513.
[56] Code Sec. 2523(a).
[57] Code Sec. 2033.

before the date of the decedent's death covering the period extending beyond that date.[58] This same rule has been applied where the insured and the owner of the policy die simultaneously.[59]

¶ 725 PRACTICAL CONSIDERATIONS AFFECTING GIFTS OF LIFE INSURANCE

Avoiding the estate tax by a timely transfer of a life insurance policy and all incidents of ownership is not especially difficult. The more difficult question for the insured might be whether or not he or she wants to give up the cash value in the policy. The insured might also have to give up the low interest loans against the cash value that become so attractive when interest rates rise.

An insured can have his or her cash and loan value, and at the same time remove much of the insurance proceeds from his or her gross estate if he or she is insurable. The insured can convert the existing policy to paid-up insurance. The proceeds of that policy would remain includible in the insured's gross estate. However, the spouse or other intended beneficiary could take out a new policy on the insured's life and finance it with the premium money no longer needed for the converted policy. However, the total death benefit coverage of both policies might be less than the amount of the single policy before conversion to paid-up insurance, even though the same number of premium dollars is paid under this new plan. Thus, the insured should check all the figures carefully before deciding.

Given a choice between policies to be gifted, low-value policies are apt to be prime candidates. Term policies, individual or group, have low gift tax values. The annual exclusion of $12,000 (for 2006[60] and indexed for inflation[61]) per donee applies to gifts of present interests.

Whether one is using the new policy approach or is assigning an existing policy, he or she must decide who is to own the policy. If an individual is the owner and dies before the insured, the value of the policy will be includible in the owner's gross estate. This result is not desirable. The insured can try two things to avoid it: (1) put ownership of the policy in a younger family member, rather than in the hands of the insured's spouse, if the spouse's life expectancy is shorter or not much longer than the insured's life expectancy; or (2) place the policy in a trust. The trust is often better (see ¶ 735 for a discussion of life insurance trusts).

---

[58] Reg. § 20.2031-8(a)(2).

[59] Rev. Rul. 77-181, 1977-1 CB 272.

[60] Code Sec. 2503(b)(1).

[61] Code Sec. 2503(b)(2).

Planning pointer. The insured's spouse owns the policy and designates the trustee of a revocable trust created by the insured as beneficiary. On the insured's death, the proceeds are paid to the trustee. Under the terms of the trust, the surviving spouse is entitled to the income for life. If the surviving spouse has the power to change the beneficiaries, but does not do so before the death of the insured, the IRS maintains the position that the surviving spouse made a gift of the proceeds, less the surviving spouse's life income interest, to the children when the insured died.[62] In addition, gift splitting will not apply because the gift took place at the exact instant of death. At that same instant of death, the marital relationship, upon which gift-splitting depends, ceased.[63]

Rather than make the spouse the policy owner and the children the beneficiaries, the spouse should be the policy owner and the beneficiary. The surviving spouse can then make gifts of the proceeds to the children to make the best use of the annual exclusion.[64]

Planning pointer. An insurance policy to be transferred might be subject to a bank loan, and the lender may be able to apply the insurance proceeds against the loan. Under the law of some states, the beneficiary may be able to compel the estate to pay him or her an amount equivalent to the insurance proceeds taken by the lender. The effect might be a windfall for the policy beneficiary, contrary to what the insured might have intended. To avoid this result, the loan agreement or the will (or both if possible) should contain appropriate provisions reflecting the intent of the borrower-testator.

¶730 WHO SHOULD BE NAMED BENEFICIARY?

The owner of a life insurance policy is free to name almost anyone as a beneficiary. The choice normally involves deciding whether to name as beneficiary the estate or executor of the insured, the trustee of a trust that the insured might have set up during his or her lifetime or in a will, or one or more individuals. This chapter does not address the naming of a charity or a corporation as a beneficiary because these issues are addressed elsewhere in this book.

If the insurance proceeds are payable to the estate or the executor, they are included in the decedent's gross estate.[65] In addition,

[62] Rev. Rul. 81-166, 1981-1 CB 477.

[63] Rev. Rul. 73-207, 1973-1 CB 409.

[64] Code Sec. 2503(b).

[65] Code Sec. 2042(1).

the proceeds become a part of the probate estate and subject to such charges as executor's commissions and attorney's fees. Because the proceeds go to pay items that are deductible from the gross estate (debts, funeral expenses, taxes, and administration expenses) the proceeds are offset by the deductions.[66] Naming the estate or executor as beneficiary will not cause any estate tax if the estate has no estate tax liability because of the marital deduction[67] and the applicable credit amount (unified credit).[68]

From a practical standpoint naming the estate as the beneficiary can make sense in some cases to provide the estate with liquidity. However, naming a responsible individual or a trustee to serve as beneficiary is preferable if the individual or trustee will make the proceeds available to meet the estate's liquidity needs. The proceeds will not be included in the probate estate and can still meet its liquidity needs.

The beneficiary or trustee could make the funds available to the estate either by lending cash or buying estate assets. If the client is not sure that he or she has an individual on whom he or she can rely, the client should use a trust, with a trustee who is authorized to help the estate and who has no adverse interest that would inhibit the trustee (i.e., the trustee is not a trust beneficiary nor related to one). However, the client should not require the trustee to help the estate. The proceeds might then be deemed to be receivable by the insured's probate estate and therefore includible in the gross estate. This result is the very thing the client wants to avoid from an estate tax standpoint. Although the estate might not be subject to the federal estate tax, state death taxes and illiquid assets might create a need for liquidity provided by life insurance. In such a case, keeping the proceeds out of the probate estate is advisable.

Once beyond the matter of supplying the estate's liquidity needs, the client should begin to think about individual needs. The client will want the proceeds to go to or be used on behalf of those whom he or she or the policy owner chooses to benefit.

Generally, the most common path for a married individual will be to name his or her spouse as the beneficiary, with the children named as contingent beneficiaries. This path avoids probate and usually avoids state death taxes. However, an assignment of the policy and all incidents of ownership to the spouse are not necessary to avoid federal estate taxes because of the unlimited marital deduction.[69]

If the children are to be named as primary, or even contingent, beneficiaries, and some of them are minors, the estate planner should

[66] Code Sec. 2053(a).

[67] Code Sec. 2056(a).

[68] Code Sec. 2010(c).

[69] Code Sec. 2056(a).

urge the client to consider guardianships. An insurance company is not likely to pay the life insurance proceeds without the appointment of a legal guardian for each minor. The requirement to name a guardian will cause additional expenses and complications.

A client should think carefully before naming specific children as beneficiaries if the client might have or adopt additional children. If a client names Tom, Dick, and Harry as beneficiaries and then Mary is born, she will be left out. Yet, Mary might have the greatest financial need.

The better way to name children as beneficiaries is to list the beneficiaries as follows: "Tom, Dick and Harry, children of the insured, and any other children of the insured hereafter born or legally adopted."

If the children of a deceased child are to take the parent's share, the beneficiary designation should also state as follows: "The children of a deceased child of the insured shall be entitled to receive their parent's share, equally." If stepchildren or children informally adopted are to be designated, they should be specifically named. The insured should not rely on their being included in a general designation of "children of the insured."

If the proceeds are substantial, using a trust as beneficiary offers many advantages, as described at ¶735. Only a trust is flexible enough to meet changing circumstances and needs. Only a trust can protect against a second estate tax when the primary beneficiary dies.

¶735 THE INSURANCE TRUST

The life insurance trust combines two pillars of estate planning—life insurance and the trust.

A life insurance trust is usually a living (inter vivos) trust, which may be revocable or irrevocable, funded or unfunded. The category also includes trusts set up by a will (testamentary trusts) to receive, hold, and distribute life insurance proceeds.

Generally, insurance trusts mean trusts that hold life insurance policies. However, insurance trusts also include trusts named as beneficiaries of policies held by others.

Naming a trust as beneficiary offers many distinct advantages, whether it owns the policies or not. Among these advantages are the following:

- Greater flexibility in handling distributions of the proceeds and income than would be possible under insurance settlement options.

- Restrictions and limitations on the use of the funds for the beneficiaries that might be included in the trust.
- Possible elimination of the inconvenience and expense of guardians for minor beneficiaries.
- Elimination of a second estate tax on the deaths of life insurance beneficiaries.
- Authorization for the accumulation of some or all of the income, subject to possible state law restrictions and limitations.
- Broad investment discretion on the trustee's part.

All of these factors are important, but the first two are very important. If the proceeds are to be used for the benefit of a surviving spouse and children, only a trust allows the use of the funds according to the needs of the individual beneficiaries. The insured will not know, for example, when the surviving spouse will remarry and no longer need the insurance money; which child will become financially independent; which child will struggle to make ends meet; which children will have their own children and which children will not have children; who will be sick, disabled, or institutionalized; and who will be able to handle money wisely. Only a trustee knows these things as they occur and can make informed, intelligent distributions and impose needed restrictions, as the insured might have done.

Setting up a trust involves legal expenses. The expenses of administering a trust include the trustee's fees and expenses, legal expenses, and accounting fees. These expenses are usually nominal before the insured dies.

Some states may require the policy owner to assign the policies to the trustee in order to have a valid trust with no other assets, rather than simply depositing the policies with the trustee. As long as the settlor retains the power to revoke the trust, the assignment does not lessen his or her practical control nor will it alter the tax consequences.

Funding a revocable insurance trust provides no income tax advantages because the trust income would be taxable to the settlor under Code Sec. 676. Thus, the settlor receives no income-splitting tax advantage in transferring income-producing property to the trust, which will use the income to pay premiums.

Still, if the trust is funded, the settlor has the opportunity to see how the trustee manages money. The settlor can make changes if he or she is dissatisfied with the performance of the trustee. With an unfunded trust, the settlor cannot evaluate the trustee's ability to manage money.

The proceeds payable to the trust can be made to qualify for the marital deduction,[70] if the settlor sets the trust up to do so. If the surviving spouse is simply given a life income interest with the remainder given to the children, the marital deduction requirements may be satisfied if certain conditions are met under the QTIP exception to the terminable interest rule.[71] See ¶ 1205 on the requirements for the marital deduction and ¶ 1215 on when a settlor might not want assets to qualify for the marital deduction.

Funding a revocable trust does not cause a completed gift. Thus, no gift tax is due on a transfer of assets to a revocable trust.

.01 The Irrevocable Trust

The irrevocable insurance trust, like a revocable trust, avoids probate, and can do all the good things that trusts generally can do in terms of protecting the interests of the beneficiaries and carrying out the settlor's directions. An irrevocable trust has the added advantage of potential estate tax savings, albeit with loss of control over the policy and a possible gift tax cost.

If the trust is unfunded, the settlor generally will later contribute funds to pay premiums on the policy. With a funded trust, the settlor transfers cash or property to the trust along with the policy, and the trust uses those resources and their earnings to pay the premiums. In either event, the premiums generally are paid with after-tax dollars. With an unfunded trust, that result is obvious. With a funded trust, the settlor is taxable on the trust income if the trust may use the income, without the approval or consent of any adverse party, to pay the insurance premiums on the lives of either the settlor or the settlor's spouse (unless the policies are payable irrevocably to a qualified charity). The trust could be funded and yet not provide for premium payments from trust income or for the beneficiary to pay the premiums from trust income. In that case, income is not taxable to the extent such payments are made by the beneficiary, or at the beneficiary's direction, out of trust income.

The fact that the income of a funded trust carrying insurance on the life of the settlor generally is taxed to the settlor, rather than to the trust, is no longer much of a tax disadvantage. The income tax brackets for trusts are now so compressed that income shifting no longer affords great tax-saving potential.

---

[70] Code Sec. 2056(a).

[71] Code Sec. 2056(b)(7).

The real value of the irrevocable trust is the avoidance of federal estate taxes, probate, and state death taxes. As for avoidance of the federal estate tax, two things to consider are (1) the insured's retention or possession of incidents of ownership in the policy on his or her life at the time of death;[72] and (2) the transfer of the policy or the relinquishment of all incidents of ownership in the policy under Code Sec. 2035 (¶430).

The first problem is not too difficult to handle if everything goes according to plan. The policy is assigned to the insurance trust together with all incidents of ownership, the insured gives up all control over the policy and the trust, and the trust beneficiary dutifully survives the settlor-insured. A problem could occur if the beneficiary does not survive, and the deceased beneficiary's interests in the policy revert to the settlor as the beneficiary's heir or trustee. See the discussion at ¶715 dealing with the ramifications of the problem under the heading, "Transfer of All Incidents of Ownership."

The safest course is to arrange things so that the settlor will never become the owner of the policy or serve as a trustee. One solution might be to appoint the insured as co-trustee, but bar the insured from exercising any rights, powers, options, or privileges with regard to the insurance. If these plans fail, the insured must again dispose of his or her after-acquired incidents of ownership as fast as possible.

As for Code Sec. 2035, no problem occurs if the insured lives three years or more after an effective transfer to the trust. If the decedent makes the transfer within three years of death, the proceeds will be includible in his or her gross estate in accordance with the rules discussed at ¶715.

Assume there are no problems in keeping the insurance proceeds out of the settlor's gross estate. Can an irrevocable trust provide other benefits? The answer is yes. The trust can save some taxes, help with any liquidity problems of the estate, provide good management, and avoid probate. The estate planner should assist the client in determining how much these benefits are worth. The estate planner should also consider the disadvantages.

How much can one save in taxes? That question is certainly relevant. Where the estate will not have an estate tax liability, because of the unlimited marital deduction,[73] the charitable deduction,[74] and the unified credit,[75] the only possible taxes are state inheritance taxes.

---

[72] Code Sec. 2042(2).
[73] Code Sec. 2056(a).
[74] Code Sec. 2055(a).
[75] Code Sec. 2010.

What are the net savings, taking into consideration gift tax liabilities, if any? An assignment of policies to an irrevocable trust constitutes a gift. The value of the gift is the cash replacement value (in technical terms, the interpolated terminal reserve), less unearned premiums. Each premium thereafter paid by the settlor is an additional gift. Usually, the trust is set up so that the annual gift tax exclusion will not be available because the gifts will be of future interests.[76]

The client can avoid some of the gift tax problems by transferring policies that have no value, such as policies from which the client has borrowed the cash values before making the gift, or group-term insurance. However, the problem of how to pay the premiums remains if the trust is unfunded. The settlor can make gifts of the annual premiums. Because gifts to a trust are not gifts of a present interest in property, they are not eligible for the annual gift tax exclusion unless the trust includes a properly drafted *Crummey* powers provision. The trust can borrow against the cash value to pay premiums.

The estate planner should also address the practical aspects associated with irrevocability. Many things can happen after an irrevocable trust is set up in a world in which almost everything else is revocable, including marriage, family relationships, values, and desires. If the trust is unfunded, the estate planner should ask who is going to pay the premiums, if the settlor cannot or will not.

Although an irrevocable life insurance trust might be an appropriate vehicle in some situations, the estate planner should advise the client of the possible consequences. Once the client sets up an irrevocable trust, the decision is irreversible.

.02 Checklist for Setting Up an Insurance Trust

1. Group life insurance should be kept out of the insured's estate. Assign the policy to an irrevocable trust and assure that the right to convert it to an individual policy is assigned.
2. The trustee's power and responsibility for premium payments in a funded trust should be clearly described: (1) using income from funding property, (2) invading principal (corpus), (3) the right to borrow against policies, and (4) notifying beneficiaries and the grantor if premium deficiencies exist.
3. The trust should allow the purchase of additional policies, if desired.

[76] Code Sec. 2503(b)(1).

4. The insured should never be a trustee of an insurance trust, except possibly as a co-trustee with no rights or powers as to the insurance. The insured should assign all rights to avoid retaining any incidents of ownership.
5. The trust beneficiary should be given some present right in the trust to take advantage of the gift tax exclusion (*Crummey* powers).
6. The trust should authorize legal proceedings by the trustee to collect proceeds. The trust should indemnify the trustee for the costs of such proceedings.
7. To avoid later problems, the estate planner should advise the client about the marital deduction rules when setting up a trust.
8. All policies in the trust should be described accurately, including number, company, face amount, and name of the insured. The grantor should initial the policy schedule, if such a schedule is attached to the trust.

¶740 HOW MUCH INSURANCE?

How much insurance should a client have? That question is one of the most important and difficult questions clients often ask an estate planner.

The estate planner must consider the client's subjective goals, present and future needs, present and future earnings, assets, liabilities, income, estate and gift taxes, and the effects of estate planning. In the end, the best answer is still an estimate. Yet, the approach to this question is clear. How much insurance is required to meet objectives and responsibilities? How much insurance can the client afford? These questions are basic. For many people, the need is likely to be greater than what they can afford. They will need to strike a balance between their needs and their ability to pay premiums. Purely subjective factors can also affect the decision. The best the estate planner can do is to help the client understand the factors to consider in the decision.

One source of difficulty is that people tend to view insurance in isolation. However, insurance is only one component of what should be an overall, integrated estate plan. Unfortunately, seldom does a client have an ideal estate plan. The client might feel a need for more insurance. However, the client might not be sure of his or her existing insurance policies or how they work. The main purpose of life insurance is to replace lost earnings in the event of a premature death. To supply that need, all one needs to do is apply the basic rule of thumb, which is 10 times earnings. If that much insurance produces too large a premium figure, the client will have to accept a lower amount of insurance. That is what insurance agents often tell the client. The client is often willing, sometimes under an insurance agent's pressure, to buy that amount of insurance.

A better way to determine life insurance needs, especially for a client with a significant estate, is as follows:

1. Gather information about the family, personal objectives, assets and liabilities, and the existing estate plan (whether it is the individual's own plan or a plan that will be supplied by state law in default of an individual plan).
2. Tally the assets and liabilities, project those values 5 or 10 years from now (anything longer is pure speculation). Compute estate taxes, state death taxes, and administration costs as if the client were to die tomorrow. If the client is married, make the computation with and without the marital deduction. Consider additional insurance for the client's spouse to cover any loss of the marital deduction. Compute estimates of Social Security benefits for previous spouse and family. Add on the debts and funeral expenses, which have to be paid within a short time after death. Add on the family's cash needs when the client dies.

   Now subtract the value of the liquid assets that will be available to satisfy the liquidity needs of the estate and the beneficiaries. The difference is an estimate of the amount of insurance required under the existing plan.
3. Assess the effect of the disposition of those liquid assets on the family income available to maintain the family's standard of living. Add back those liquid assets required to maintain living standards. The result is a closer estimate of the insurance required for this purpose.
4. Next, determine the current and future needs and important desires of the family. If the existing plan does not provide sufficient liquidity to meet those needs, the client will need additional life insurance.
5. Having determined the likely effects of the existing plan and the client's desires, make a complete analysis of the existing plan. Determine if and how the client can make better use of existing and projected assets to bring the client closer to reaching the goals for his or her family.
6. After developing a new, better insurance plan, the next step is to measure the shortfall, if any, from the desired goal. If the life insurance is still inadequate to meet the client's

goals, the estate planner can advise the client to consider the purchase of more insurance, if he or she can afford it. What kind of insurance remains to be determined. The amount will depend on the size of the shortfall, and the expected return. Estimate the added income required, and capitalize it, using a fairly conservative after-tax yield.

7. The client is not likely to acquire new assets to supply plan deficiencies quickly except by life insurance. Thus, the estate planner should consider some form of life insurance that will meet the client's objectives, if he or she should die before he or she acquires the needed assets. The estate planner might suggest new life insurance from the standpoint of type, amount, ownership, beneficiary designations, and the funds available to pay the premiums.

An estate planner should help the client explore various ways to pay for life insurance premiums. The client could use funds in a savings account, borrow against liquid assets, use personal credit, borrow on the insurance policy itself, or borrow on existing policies. An estate planner should also explore income tax saving approaches in paying for life insurance. These approaches include shifting income to a trust set up by someone other than the insured, and making gifts to family members in lower income tax brackets. The family members can use the income from the gifts to buy the life insurance. Other possibilities exist for the client who is engaged in business in the corporate or partnership form. For example, the corporation or partnership could pay the premiums. The client could transfer income-yielding stocks to the corporation to realize the benefits of the 70-percent dividends-received deduction.[77] However, the client should be careful not to have the corporation realize so much divided income that the corporation is subject to the personal holding company tax. In addition, with dividend received by individuals now being taxed at only 15 percent through 2010; there is less incentive to place common stocks in corporations. The corporation can use the higher after-tax yields to pay the life insurance premiums. In addition, the corporation could provide group insurance to the employee-shareholder at a lower after-tax cost than would be possible for an individual policy. Qualified pension and profit-sharing plans may also be the source of inexpensive insurance for participants.

These techniques are just some of the tax-saving possibilities. However, an estate planner with ingenuity and creativity can develop other tax-saving strategies.

---

[77] Code Sec. 243(a)(1).

A client can increase investment yields simply by converting assets with low yields into assets with higher yields. The estate planner might help the client discover additional sources of earned income. A competent estate planner can find a way for a client to pay for needed life insurance.

¶745 FINANCED INSURANCE

Over the years, Congress has restricted tax benefits for financed insurance and minimum deposit insurance. Congress has also restricted the deductibility of interest.

For some time, a rule has barred deductions for interest unless four of the first seven premiums were paid without borrowing. Personal interest is currently not deductible at all, except for qualified residence interest.[78]

A client may deduct interest on a life insurance loan if the client uses the loan proceeds for outside investment purposes,[79] subject to the special limitation on deductions for investment interest.[80] A client may also deduct interest on loans used for business purposes. However, the amount of business interest that is deductible on a policy covering the life of any officer, employee, or other person with a financial interest in a business is limited to the interest on the first $50,000 borrowed from or against the policy.[81] These departures do not help an individual to purchase cash value life insurance at low cost.

Another threat to financed insurance is the seven-payment test. If the policy fails this test, it will be treated as a modified endowment contract. In that case, policy loans are treated as distributions (¶701).

Financed insurance will most likely not satisfy the seven-payment test. The amount paid under this test means the premium paid under the contract "reduced by the amounts received under the contract that are not received as an annuity to the extent that such amounts are not includible in gross income and are not attributable to a reduction in the originally scheduled death benefit." Loans from a policy would seem to fall within this statement. To satisfy the seven-payment test, the premiums paid by themselves, without borrowed amounts (or dividends), would need to be sufficient to satisfy the test.

Loans and withdrawals from modified endowment policies are taxed to the extent of earnings within the policy.[82] Thus, the first

---

[78] Code Sec. 163(h).
[79] Code Secs. 163(a) and 163(h)(2)(B).
[80] Code Sec. 163(d).
[81] Code Secs. 264(a)(4) and 264(e)(1).
[82] Code Secs. 72(e)(10)(A) and 72(e)(2)(B).

amounts withdrawn or borrowed become taxable to the policyholder. Not only is the borrower denied an interest deduction, but he or she is also taxed on the amount borrowed to the extent of the earnings withdrawn.

If the policy satisfies the seven-payment test, the taxpayer/policyholder is able to escape this tax rule. However, the seven payments required without borrowing defeat the basic concept behind financed insurance or minimum deposit insurance.

¶750 SETTLEMENT OPTIONS OR HOW INSURANCE PROCEEDS MAY BE MADE PAYABLE

A life insurance policy owner does not need to worry about the beneficiary spending the entire proceeds in a short time. Instead of making the proceeds payable in one lump sum, the policy can require a series of payments. The basic settlement options are as follows:

- **Interest option.** The proceeds are left with the insurer, and the insurer pays only interest to the beneficiary for a limited period. At the end of that period, the policy owner may choose another option. A policy owner might use this option, for example, for the period while the surviving spouse with dependent children is collecting Social Security benefits. The conversion would take place when the Social Security benefits for the children end.
- **Fixed period option.** Under the fixed period option, the proceeds are payable in equal installments over a fixed period, with a guaranteed rate of interest.
- **Fixed income option.** The fixed income option provides for payment of a fixed amount for each installment. This option differs from the fixed period option because the payment is fixed instead of the period. A variation is to provide for a fixed payment for a fixed period, to a specified date, or to when the beneficiary has reached a certain age. At that time, the insurance company would pay the remaining balance under another option, including cash.
- **Life income option.** The life income option provides an annuity for life. It assures that the payments will not end before the beneficiary's death. The three types of the life income option are as follows: (1) for the life of the annuitant; (2) for the annuitant's life, with a certain number of installments guaranteed; and (3) the refund annuity option, which provides that if the annuitant dies before receiving the principal sum, the balance will be paid to a second beneficiary.

Actuarially, the payoff for the insurance company is apt to be the same. However, the individual must decide which of the options will provide the best return to the insured and to the beneficiaries. The insurance company computes the odds for the various options in terms of the monthly payoff per $1,000 of insurance proceeds. The odds vary with the insured's age, gender, and with the particular insurer.

.01 Deciding What Options to Use

The settlement options and how they work in the abstract is only one consideration. The estate planner must evaluate how they work in a practical context, when they are useful, and when they are not beneficial.

The settlement options do not describe investment yields, how insurance companies calculate the payouts, and why a lump-sum cash payment to an individual or a trust might be more advantageous. For example, insurers use different mortality tables for computing insurance premiums and for figuring the amount to be paid to a beneficiary under a settlement option. As might be expected, a person applying for life insurance is assigned a lower life expectancy (higher premium) than if he or she were applying for an annuity. The annuity payout will be less than if the insurance company used the lower life insurance expectancies. The justification offered for the disparity is that annuitants live longer. Of course, a form of adverse selection works against the insurance company. If an individual believes death is imminent, he or she will want all the insurance he or she can get today, and wants no part of a lifetime annuity. However, if an individual expects to live for a long time, he or she will prefer an annuity over life insurance.

The proceeds retained by the insurance company are not held in trust. Only a debtor-creditor relationship exists between the company and the beneficiary. Therefore, unless the insurance company operates in a state that guarantees payments, the beneficiary will likely receive little if the insurance company becomes insolvent or files bankruptcy. Generally, money due under a settlement option is not like money in a bank that is insured by the FDIC.

Because the relationship is only that of debtor and creditor, the beneficiary does not ordinarily receive the benefit of any appreciation in the retained proceeds invested by the insurer. The capital gains and interest income belong to the insurance company. However, some companies provide for the payment of excess interest under some settlement options so that the beneficiary may realize some of the investment earnings. Some policies associated with a family of mutual funds actually offer capital growth.

Settlement options should not be used to provide high yields. Providing a high yield is not their function. Neither should life insurance serve primarily as an investment. Although life insurance as an investment has some tax shelter aspects, settlement options do not include any tax shelter. The most important aspect of settlement options is safety. Despite the possibility of bankruptcy, insurance carriers over the years have been relatively safe. Legislation creating a guaranty further strengthens the safety factor.

Some of the very features that provide safety also make for rigidity. Settlement options can never provide the flexibility possible with a trust. No insurance company can stand over its thousands of beneficiaries and spread income to them according to their needs as the insured would wish. If the client wants flexibility, he or she should set up a trust.

Another factor about settlement options is that leaving proceeds with the insurance company can distort an overall estate plan. If the client has a number of insurance policies, a choice of different settlement options can produce unpredictable results. What happens if a particular policy is allowed to lapse? The client should consider how to replace the proceeds that otherwise would have gone to the beneficiaries.

An integrated, unified estate plan is usually the better way. In certain circumstances, settlement options make sense. Generally, settlement options make sense where the insurance proceeds are relatively small and are intended to provide for a single family member's limited needs. In those circumstances, a trust might be preferable in the abstract, but cost too much for the limited benefits.

.02 Settlement Options and the Marital Deduction

Settlement options pose a threat to qualifying life insurance proceeds for the marital deduction.[83] To qualify for the marital deduction, the surviving spouse must generally be the unconditional beneficiary. If the proceeds are not payable outright and the policy owner must name a successor beneficiary, the proceeds may still qualify for the marital deduction if any of the following conditions is satisfied:

- No part of any remainder interest created goes to anyone other than the surviving spouse or his or her estate.
- The beneficiary provisions meet all five of the following conditions: (1) The payments must be unconditionally payable

[83] Code Sec. 2056(a).

only to the surviving spouse; (2) interest installment payments must be payable annually, or, more frequently, no later than 13 months after the insured's death; (3) the surviving spouse must have the power to appoint all proceeds held by the insurance company in favor of himself or herself or his or her estate; (4) this power must be unconditional; and (5) no other person must have any power of appointment over any part of the proceeds that permits appointment to a person other than the surviving spouse.

- The payout is set up to qualify for the QTIP exception to the terminable interest rule,[84] as discussed at ¶1210.

The simpler way of assuring that the proceeds will qualify for the marital deduction is for the insured not to elect any settlement options. Rather, the policy should allow the proceeds to go to the survivor in a lump sum, in the expectation or hope that the survivor will choose the settlement option that the insured desired. The risk is that the surviving spouse will take the lump sum and spend it quickly.

¶755 REPLACING POLICIES IN FORCE

The reasons why replacing an existing policy with a new one is rarely in the best interest of the insured are as follows:

- The insured will have to pay new acquisition costs.
- The existing policy, because the insured will have to pay new acquisition costs and because of other factors, tends to increase in value with age.
- The new policy will most likely have to pass through a contestable period, which may already have passed with the old policy.
- Even if the replacement policy provides for dividends, it will probably be years before they match those payable under the old policy.
- If a cash value policy is cashed in and the proceeds are transferred into a replacement policy, seldom, if ever, will the new policy's cash value equal that of the old.
- If the replacement policy is of a different type from the old policy, it will not in most cases fulfill the needs that prompted the purchase of the old policy, assuming those needs remain the same.

---

[84] Code Sec. 2056(b)(7).

Some state insurance departments have adopted replacement regulations that require full disclosure of all material facts to the policyholder.

The changing circumstances of an insured, might require changes in his or her insurance portfolio. Some insurance companies have developed adjustable life, universal life, and other flexible premium policies to accommodate such changing circumstances as discussed at ¶ 705.

However, the more traditional forms of insurance provide a certain amount of flexibility similar to flexible premium policies. For example, in years when the insured might find paying premiums to be difficult, he or she may borrow against cash value at relatively low interest rates. Also, the insured can purchase the disability waiver of premium, the guaranteed increase provision, and the accidental death benefit (included in adjustable life).

Code Sec. 1035(a)(1) permits a tax-free exchange of one policy for another on the life of the same insured. For policies subject to outstanding loans, the estate planner should make sure that the loans do not result in gross income, where the loan on the old policy is extinguished. The client can avoid tax if the insurance company issues the new policy subject to a loan in the amount of the old loan, assuming the new policy has enough loan value.

Chapter 8

Annuities

Overview .... ¶801
Commercial Annuities .... ¶805
The Private Annuity .... ¶810

¶801 OVERVIEW

Life insurance provides financial security for family members and other beneficiaries in case of a premature death. However, life insurance does not provide very well for those who live beyond their life expectancy. The insurance industry offers annuities as the solution to this problem. Annuities offer protection against consuming financial resources before death.

An individual who buys an annuity is known as the annuitant. All annuities guarantee the annuitant payments at least annually for life or for a specified period. These payments consist of two parts: a return of capital and a return on capital in the form of interest or investment income. An annuity is essentially a systematic capital-consuming vehicle meant to provide the annuitant with an income for life or a specified period.

¶805 COMMERCIAL ANNUITIES

An individual can buy a commercial annuity in a variety of forms. However, two basic kinds of annuities are the fixed annuity and the variable annuity. A fixed annuity pays the annuitant fixed payments for life or a specified period. A variable annuity is essentially an annuity tied to a mutual fund. A variable annuity pays the annuitant payments that vary with investment results for life or a specified period.

An equity-indexed annuity is a hybrid annuity. It pays the annuitant a minimum fixed rate of return. In addition, it pays the annuitant a percentage of the increase in a related stock-market index.

One big weakness of the fixed annuity is that the annuity payments may not keep pace with inflation. In times of high inflation, the annuitant sees constantly rising prices while the annuity payments remain constant. During periods of low inflation, this factor is less important. When inflation was high, insurance companies developed variable annuities for individuals who were concerned about inflation eroding the purchasing power of fixed annuities. Insurance companies invest money in variable annuities in stocks, bonds, and money market instruments. Under the skilled management of the insurance company's investment advisers, the annuitant can expect a variable annuity to grow and keep ahead of inflation. However, variable annuities have more risk and may not achieve the desired result. Even if variable annuity payments do not keep pace with inflation, a guaranteed stream of depreciated dollars is better than having no income.

The advantage of equity-indexed annuities is the low risk because of the minimum guaranteed return. The disadvantage is that the potential return is less than the potential return on a variable annuity. The annuitant receives only a portion of the increase in the stock-market index to which the annuity is linked. The participation rate determines how much of the increase in the related stock-market index will be credited as interest to the annuitant. For example, if the participation rate was 75 percent and the related stock-market index increased by 10 percent, the annuitant would receive an interest rate of 7.5 percent (75% × 10%) for that period. The features, benefits, and limitations of equity-indexed annuities vary across insurance companies.

According to the NASD, sales of equity-indexed annuities have increased significantly in recent years. Equity-indexed annuities do have some risks. The minimum guaranteed rate of return is usually 90 percent of the premiums paid plus three percent annual interest. The guarantee is only as good as the insurance company that sells the annuity. Charges for an early surrender of an equity-indexed annuity may be high. Because of the growing popularity of these annuities, they are coming under increased scrutiny from regulators. Financial planners should examine equity-indexed annuities carefully before recommending them to clients. Detailed information is available at the Web site of Advantage Compendium at www.indexannuity.org.

Unless an investor has some way of retaining his or her capital and investing it in a way that beats inflation, the annuity deserves consideration. Individuals who have reason to believe that they will outlive the life expectancies in annuity mortality tables should seriously consider annuities. One of the best ways to evaluate variable annuities is to compare them to mutual funds. A financial planner should look at various kinds of annuities for clients who want to invest in an annuity.

One obvious advantage of the annuity for some individuals is that the guaranteed payments from an annuity protect a person from the inability to manage money. An annuity can also be attractive to a person who wants to provide an assured income for the life of another person.

Straight annuities pay a specified amount periodically for the life of the annuitant. Other kinds of annuities provide payments for 5, 10, 15, or 20 years. Another type of annuity pays a cash refund to the annuitant's beneficiaries.

The straight annuity provides the largest payment per dollar invested because the insurance company's obligation ceases on the annuitant's death. The longer the period of guaranteed payments, the smaller the periodic annuity payments will be. The cash refund type of annuity does not guarantee a fixed number of payments. Instead, it gives the annuitant's beneficiaries the difference, if any, between the annuitant's investment in the contract and the amount he or she received.

An insurance company computes the payments on joint and survivor annuities by taking into account the life expectancies of the annuitant and the survivor. Obviously, life expectancies of two individuals will be greater than that of one individual. Accordingly, the periodic annuity payments will be smaller.

.01 Deferred Annuities

As described above, some annuities begin paying immediately. Deferred annuities are another type of annuity. In deferred annuities, the annuitant makes a current investment in an annuity contract in return for annuity payments that begin in the future.

Withdrawals from a deferred annuity before the annuity starting date, and partial surrenders or distributions in the nature of dividends, are subject to immediate taxation.[1]

In addition, a 10-percent additional tax generally applies to premature distributions.[2] While a taxpayer can usually ask the IRS to abate tax penalties for reasonable cause, the taxpayer must find a specific exception in the Code to avoid this additional tax. Fortunately, the Code allows the taxpayer to avoid the additional tax for distributions under certain conditions. This additional tax does not

[1] Code Sec. 72(e).

[2] Code Sec. 72(q)(1).

apply to taxable amounts received after age 59½[3] or because of the annuitant's death[4] or disability.[5] Substantial equal periodic payments made over the life expectancy of the taxpayer or over the joint lives of the taxpayer and his or her designated beneficiary are not subject to the additional tax.[6] The 10-percent additional tax does not apply to investments in annuity contracts before August 14, 1982.[7] Early withdrawals may also be subject to insurance company surrender charges.

Individuals often turn to annuities for additional tax-sheltered retirement savings after exhausting their limits on qualified plans (e.g., 401(k) plans) and IRAs. Contributions to deferred annuities are not subject to limits as are contributions to IRAs or qualified plans.

Deferred annuities may be especially useful for individuals who expect to outlive their life expectancies contained in the annuity mortality tables. Annuity mortality tables assign longer life expectancies than do life insurance tables. This difference is because of the selection process involved in buying one product or the other. Annuitants are generally concerned with outliving their financial reserves. Life insurance policyholders are generally concerned with premature death and leaving their dependents in a financial bind.

If the owner of a deferred annuity dies before the annuity starting date, the beneficiary must receive the entire interest in the annuity generally within five years after the contract holder's death.[8] Alternatively, the beneficiary may receive the annuity over a period not more than the life expectancy of the beneficiary.[9] When the beneficiary receives payments based on his or her life expectancy, the payments must begin within one year of the contract holder's death.[10] If the beneficiary is a spouse, the spouse may continue the contract in the spouse's name and defer income tax.[11]

If the contract holder dies on or after the annuity starting date, the beneficiary must receive any remaining portion of the annuity interest at least as rapidly as under the method of distribution in effect at the contract holder's death.[12]

These rules do not apply to an annuity contract provided by a qualified pension plan, profit sharing plan, stock-bonus plan, Code Sec. 403(b) tax-sheltered annuity, or an annuity purchased in an IRA.

---

[3] Code Sec. 72(q)(2)(A).
[4] Code Sec. 72(q)(2)(B).
[5] Code Sec. 72(q)(2)(C).
[6] Code Sec. 72(q)(2)(D).
[7] Code Sec. 72(q)(2)(F).
[8] Code Sec. 72(s)(1)(B).
[9] Code Sec. 72(s)(2)(B).
[10] Code Sec. 72(s)(2)(C).
[11] Code Sec. 72(s)(3).
[12] Code Sec. 72(s)(1)(A).

.02 Variable Annuities Versus Mutual Funds

Variable annuities generally offer the advantages of mutual funds plus the opportunity to defer taxes. However, the fees and other charges of variable annuities and unfavorable taxation at death or lifetime sale are disadvantages.

Variable annuities and mutual funds are similar in many ways. Both provide professional management of a securities portfolio. Neither offers a guaranteed cash value. Rather, the amount the investor receives depends on the performance of the portfolio. Both charge the investor a sales charge and the costs of investment management and administration. Both allow several transfers between funds each year without charge.

The chief advantage of variable annuities over mutual funds is the opportunity for tax deferral. Investors in annuities do not pay tax on the dividends and the capital gains until they withdraw the money. The amount received over the taxpayer's basis in the annuity is subject to tax as ordinary income at a tax rate of up to 35 percent. However, the holder of a mutual fund pays taxes on any income or gain from the mutual fund in the year earned, even if the taxpayer reinvests the money in the mutual fund. The taxpayer can avoid paying current taxes on the income and gain if the mutual fund investments are in a qualified pension or profit sharing plan, a traditional IRA, a Roth IRA, a 401k plan, or a 403(b)(7) plan.

Other factors also may favor the annuity. First, a transfer between funds is not a taxable event for annuities, but it is for mutual funds. Second, investment advisory fees on variable annuities reduce the gross income received from the annuities, thereby providing a tax benefit for such fees. Investment fees on mutual funds are not tax deductible unless miscellaneous itemized deductions exceed two percent of adjusted gross income and total itemized deductions exceed the standard deduction.[13] Third, loans are available against annuity balances, although they are generally taxable distributions.[14]

The Code also treats most loans on annuities in qualified plans (e.g., a 403b plan) as distributions.[15] However, the Code allows loans for annuities in a qualified plan up to $50,000, or the greater of one half of the value of the vested benefit or $10,000.[16] The terms of the loan must require the borrower to repay the loan within five years[17] unless the borrower used the proceeds of the loan to purchase

[13] Code Secs. 67 and 212.

[14] Code Sec. 72(e)(4)(A).

[15] Code Sec. 72(p)(1).

[16] Code Sec. 72(p)(2)(A).

[17] Code Sec. 72(p)(2)(B)(i).

a principal residence.[18] If the borrower defaults on a loan payment, the entire loan balance, including accrued interest, is a deemed distribution that will subject the borrower to tax. The 10-percent additional tax also applies to the deemed distribution unless the taxpayer meets an exception. The plan administrator may allow the borrower a grace period to cure the default on the loan. The grace period may not extend beyond the last day of the calendar quarter following the calendar quarter in which the required payment was due.[19]

The maximum tax rate of 15 percent[20] for most long-term capital gains and qualified dividends is an advantage that mutual funds have over variable annuities. Income recognized from variable annuities is ordinary income subject to tax rates of up to 35 percent.[21] Annuity balances also receive unfavorable tax treatment at death because the beneficiary must recognize the appreciation as ordinary income under the income in respect of decedent rules.[22] However, the appreciation of mutual funds has escaped income tax at death because the beneficiaries receive a tax-free step-up in basis.[23] The stepped up basis rules are repealed for decedents dying in 2010. However, for decedents dying in 2010, executors may increase the basis of estate property by up to $1,300,000 and up to an additional $3,000,000 for property passing to a surviving spouse. The basis increase is limited to the fair market value of the property.[24]

Additionally, the poor liquidity and increased annual charges of variable annuities may offset the tax deferral advantages of variable annuities. Variable annuities are generally illiquid because of the 10-percent additional tax and insurance company surrender charges for early withdrawals.

.03 How Annuities Are Taxed

Annuity payments under a commercial annuity received after the annuity starting date are partly a return of capital and partly a return on capital in the form of interest or investment earnings. Interest and investment earnings are taxable, but the annuitant's return of capital is not taxable. For annuitants whose annuity contributions were tax sheltered such as in a 403b plan, all of the annuity payments received will be taxable.

The annuitant must separate each payment received. The amount not taxable is equal to an exclusion ratio multiplied by the payment. The taxable amount is equal to the payment minus

[18] Code Sec. 72(p)(2)(B)(ii).
[19] Reg. § 1.72(p)-1 Q&A 10.
[20] Code Sec. 1(h).
[21] Code Sec. 1(i).
[22] Code Sec. 691(a)(1).
[23] Code Sec. 1014(a).
[24] Code Sec. 1022.

the amount not taxable. The exclusion ratio is equal to the annuitant's investment in the contract divided by the total expected return for the life of the contract.[25] To compute the expected return, the annuitant multiplies the annual return by a multiple supplied by the appropriate Treasury table in Reg. § 1.72-9.

> ***Example 8.1.*** In 2006, Howard Gray, age 62, purchased a fixed annuity for $100,000 with funds that were not tax sheltered. The annuity will pay him $7,000 per year for life. According to the table in Reg. § 1.72-9, Howard's life expectancy is 22.5 years. Howard's exclusion ratio is 63.49% [$100,000/(22.5 × $7,000)]. When Howard receives a $7,000 payment, he will treat $4,444 ($7,000 × 63.49%) of the payment as a tax-free recovery of basis. He will include the difference of $2,556 in his gross income as ordinary income.

For individuals whose annuity starting date is after 1986, the total amount that the annuitant may exclude from gross income is limited to the investment in the contract.[26] Thus, when the annuitant reaches the point where he or she has fully recovered his or her investment in the contract, all remaining payments are fully taxable.

> ***Example 8.2.*** Assume the same facts as in Example 8.1. If Howard Gray lives for 25 years, he will have recovered $97,768 (22 × $4,444) of his $100,000 basis in the annuity after 22 years. In year 23, Howard will treat $2,232 of the $7,000 payment as a tax-free recovery of basis. His gross income from the annuity payment will be $4,768 ($7,000 – $2,232). In years 24 and 25, Howard will include all $7,000 of each payment in his gross income.

If the annuitant dies before recovering all of the investment in the contract, the Code allows an itemized deduction on the annuitant's final return for the remaining basis in the annuity.[27] The deduction is not a miscellaneous itemized deduction,[28] and therefore it is not subject to the two percent of adjusted gross income floor. For purposes of computing a net operating loss, the Code treats this deduction as though it were attributable to a trade or business.[29]

> ***Example 8.3.*** Using the same facts as Example 8.1, assume that Howard Gray died after receiving 15 annuity payments rather than living for 25 years. Howard's basis in the annuity would be $33,340 [$100,000 – (15 × $4,444)]. The executor of

---

[25] Code Sec. 72(b)(1).
[26] Code Sec. 72(b)(2).
[27] Code Sec. 72(b)(3)(A).
[28] Code Sec. 67(b)(10).
[29] Code Sec. 72(b)(3)(C).

Howard's estate may take a deduction of $33,340 on Howard's final income tax return.

The taxpayer includes payments received before the annuity starting date that are less than or equal to the increase in cash value[30] after August 13, 1982,[31] in gross income.[32] Amounts received that are greater than the increase in cash value after August 13, 1982, are a tax-free recovery of basis.[33] The taxpayer includes all additional payments in gross income after he or she has recovered all of his or her basis in the contract.

The Code provides a simplified method for assigning basis to monthly annuity payments received under a qualified plan.[34] If the primary annuitant has reached age 75 by the annuity starting date, the taxpayer may not use the simplified method unless the annuity has fewer than five years of guaranteed payments.[35] The part of the annuity payment attributable to the taxpayer's basis is equal to the basis in the contract divided by the number of anticipated payments. Based on the age of the annuitant at the annuity starting date, the annuitant assigns basis to the payments based on the number of anticipated payments. The following table from Code Sec. 72(d)(1)(B)(iii) applies to employee annuities with an annuity starting date after November 18, 1996:

Age of the annuitant on the annuity starting date is:	**The number of anticipated payments is:**
Not more than 55	360
More than 55 but not more than 60	310
More than 60 but not more than 65	260
More than 65 but not more than 70	210
More than 70	160

Example 8.4. Debra Johnson retires at age 62 and begins receiving monthly payments of $2,000 as a life annuity from her employer. Debra had contributed $130,000 to the annuity with after-tax funds. Her employer also contributed to the annuity. Debra will recover her basis over 260 months by treating $500 ($130,000/260) of each payment as a tax-free recovery of basis. She will include the remaining $1,500 of each payment in her gross income. After she has recovered all her $130,000 basis, then she will include all of the $2,000 monthly payment in her gross income.

[30] Code Sec. 72(e)(3)(A).
[31] Code Sec. 72(e)(5)(B).
[32] Code Sec. 72(e)(2)(B).
[33] Code Secs. 72(e)(2)(B) and 72(e)(3)(B).
[34] Code Sec. 72(d).
[35] Code Sec. 72(d)(1)(E).

The number of anticipated payments is different if the annuity is payable over the lives of more than one individual. The following table from Code Sec. 72(d)(1)(B)(iv) shows the number of anticipated payments based on the combined ages of the annuitants for annuities with a starting date after December 31, 1997:

If the combined ages of annuitants are:	The number of anticipated payments is:
Not more than 110	410
More than 110 but not more than 120	360
More than 120 but not more than 130	310
More than 130 but not more than 140	260
More than 140	210

Example 8.5. Dave and Gwen Fritz are ages 65 and 63, respectively. Dave has a basis of $124,000 in an annuity. His employer also contributed to the annuity. Dave begins receiving monthly payments of $4,000. The payments are for Dave's life and will continue for Gwen's life if she survives him. Dave will allocate $400 ($124,000/310) of basis to each $4,000 payment until he recovers the $124,000 investment in the contract.

¶810 THE PRIVATE ANNUITY

The private annuity resembles a commercial annuity that an insurance company might issue. However, someone not in the insurance business issues a private annuity. In addition, instead of a cash payment for the annuity, a person can acquire a private annuity in exchange for a transfer of property. The party making the promise to pay the annuity is the obligor. He or she is usually a member of the annuitant's family, typically a junior member. However, the obligor can also be someone outside the family.

A transfer of property in exchange for a private annuity is a transaction loaded with tax and practical advantages. Thus, private annuities are very useful in estate planning in the right circumstances. The important benefits are as follows:

- The annuitant removes property from his or her estate, saving not only estate taxes but administration expenses as well.
- If the annuitant transfers appreciated property, the annuitant does not have to recognize gain immediately. To obtain a commercial annuity, the transferor would first have to sell the property and pay tax on the gain. The transferor would

then have a smaller amount with which to buy the commercial annuity.

- If the property is no longer suitable for retention as an investment and the obligor wants to diversify his or her investment portfolio, the obligor may sell the property without necessarily realizing gain. The obligor would not recognize gain if the annuity promised is greater than or equal to the value of the property transferred.
- If the present value of the annuity payments equals the value of the property transferred, no gift tax will result.
- The annuity payments received will be larger than the yield of the property transferred because a part of the payments will be a return of capital.
- The reportable income factor in the annuity payments might produce less tax liability for the annuitant than the tax on the yield of the property transferred. However, the annuitant should compare the tax results carefully, especially if the property transferred is stock that pays qualified dividends. The maximum tax rate on qualified dividends is 15 percent through 2010, but the taxable portion of the annuity income is subject to a tax rate as high as 35 percent.
- To the extent that income from the property transferred (or income from a substitute property in the case of sale) becomes taxable in a lower tax bracket, the family realizes income tax savings.
- An increase in the annuitant's cash flow and its steady nature provided by the annuity payments might help the annuitant to develop a gift program that can further reduce estate administration costs.
- A transfer for a private annuity permits the owner of a closely held business to transfer interests in it to family members or key employees. The owner might realize a better return than he or she would realize on a sale to outsiders, in the sense that the present value of the annuity payments might be worth more than an outright sale for cash.
- An installment sale within the family can also defer capital gains on a sale of stock or a partnership interest. However, the installment sale gives the seller notes that will be included in his or her gross estate if the seller dies before collecting the balance on the notes. In addition, with an installment sale, the seller must recognize any depreciation recapture income in the year of sale.[36] With a private

[36] Code Sec. 453(i).

annuity, the seller recognizes depreciation recapture income as he or she receives the annuity payments.

- The annuitant avoids investment and management responsibilities with respect to the property transferred.
- A transfer in exchange for a private annuity is especially useful to a surviving spouse as a means of disposing of marital deduction property and keeping it out of the surviving spouse's estate. This strategy takes on added importance if the transfer involves business property or other investment property with high appreciation potential.

The previous discussion shows that the reduction and deferral of taxes may be an important advantage of the private annuity.

.01 Things to Watch

One of the big disadvantages of the private annuity flows from one of its main advantages. The transferor does not recognize any gain at the time of the transfer of the property because the unsecured promise to pay the annuity does not have an ascertainable fair value. The price of this tax advantage is an unsecured promise. The lack of collateral can undermine the whole arrangement for anyone relying on the annuity payments for sustenance, unless the obligor has sufficient other resources to assure satisfaction of a judgment in case of a default.

The taxpayer should exercise great care in setting up the transaction. Following are the factors to consider.

Appraisal. The parties should get an independent appraisal of the property. This appraisal will have a bearing on the economic reality of the transaction for income and gift tax purposes.

Annuitant's health. The annuitant's health might be a factor in weighing the economic reality of the transaction and could adversely affect the obligor's cost basis in determining his or her tax liability on a sale of the property. A written health report is desirable.

Insurance on obligor. The annuitant may want to take out insurance on the obligor. However, the basic annuity agreement should not mention the insurance because the IRS might construe the insurance policy as security for the obligation. A secured obligation results in adverse tax consequences.[37]

Insurance on the annuitant. The obligor may want insurance on the annuitant's life for the reasons discussed below concerning the obligor's tax consequences.

[37] *L.G. Bell Est.*, 60 TC 469 (1973) and *212 Corp.*, 70 TC 788 (1978).

Additional annuities barred. Barring the obligor by contract from issuing another annuity while one remains in force is wise.

Corporate obligor. A close corporation might issue an annuity in exchange for stock. If the annuity is worth more than the stock, the IRS might claim that the excess value is taxable as a dividend to the extent of the corporation's earnings and profits.[38]

Grantor trust rules. An individual could set up a trust and transfer property to it in exchange for an annuity. The grantor risks that the trust income might be taxable under the grantor trust rules if the trust income relates too closely to the annuity payments and it is the only source of payment.

Valuation of annuity. Taxpayers generally must determine the value of the annuity under tables issued under Code Sec. 7520. These tables use an interest rate equal to 120 percent of the federal mid-term rate in effect for the month in which the transferor exchanges property for the annuity. Low interest rates make private annuities even more attractive. See the discussion under the heading "Gift Tax" at ¶ 810.03.

.02 How the Annuitant's Income Is Taxed

Code Sec. 72 governs the income tax treatment of annuities. The annuitant excludes a portion of each year's payment from gross income. The balance is taxable as capital gain or ordinary income, or both, depending on the circumstances of the particular case. In almost all cases, the value of the property transferred exceeds its adjusted basis resulting in a gain. Thus, each year's payments will consist of (1) a return of capital excluded from gross income; (2) a gain based on the difference between the present value of the annuity (determined under Reg. § 20.2031-7) and the tax basis of the property transferred divided by the life expectancy; and (3) ordinary income (the balance of each year's payments). If the asset transferred is a capital asset, the gain will be a capital gain. After the taxpayer recognizes all the gain realized on the transfer, the taxpayer will recognize all amounts exceeding the exclusion as ordinary income. The capital gain/ordinary income distinction is extremely important. Ordinary income is subject to a top tax rate of 35 percent. The maximum rate of tax on a net capital gain is generally only 15 percent through 2010. A net capital gain is the excess of a net long-term capital gain over any net short-term capital loss.[39]

The annuitant computes the amount excluded from gross income by multiplying each year's payments by the ratio of his or her

[38] Code Sec. 301.

[39] Code Sec. 1222(11).

investment in the contract (the tax basis) divided by the total expected return. The taxpayer computes the total expected return by using a multiplier from an IRS table contained in Reg. § 1.72-9.

For individuals whose annuity starting date is after 1986, the total amount excluded from gross income may not exceed the total investment in the contract. Once the annuitant fully recovers the investment in the contract, all remaining payments are fully taxable. If payments cease before the date the annuitant has fully recovered his or her investment, the executor of the annuitant's estate may deduct the unrecovered basis as an itemized deduction on the annuitant's final income tax return.

However, individuals whose annuity starting date is before 1987 are subject to different rules. An individual may recover more than the investment in the contract free of income tax. An individual who dies before the expiration of the tabular life expectancy never recovers all of the investment. The executor of the annuitant's estate may not take a deduction on the annuitant's final income tax return for the unrecovered basis.

The Code treats any excess of the value of the property transferred over the present value of the annuity as a gift. If a gift occurs, Rev. Rul. 69-74[40] sets out an example showing how the IRS intends the rules to operate. This example gives the annuitant a break in that it does not require the annuitant to allocate any basis to the gift portion, as the law requires for a gift to a charity. The higher basis allocated to the sale portion of the transfer reduces income tax.

The exchange may trigger recapture of depreciation under Code Sec. 1250 (real estate) or under Code Sec. 1245 (in general, tangible personal property and certain other assets) and the investment credit.

.03 Gift Tax

A gift results to the extent that the fair market value of the property transferred exceeds the annuity's present value. The taxpayer generally computes the present value under IRS valuation tables issued in IRS Publication 1457 under Code Sec. 7520 (but see the discussion under the heading "When the Taxpayer Cannot Use the Tables" at ¶ 810.04).

These tables use an interest rate equal to 120 percent of the federal mid-term rate for the month in which the transfer in exchange for the annuity occurred. Low interest rates make private

---

[40] 1969-1 CB 43.

annuities even more attractive because they make transferring large amounts to children possible without adverse gift tax consequences.

Example 8.6. Frank Young, age 70, transfers land with a fair market value of $100,000 to his son Sam, during a month in which the interest factor under the Code Sec. 7520 tables is 6.0%. Frank and Sam determine the amount that Sam has to pay at the end of each year to avoid any gift tax consequences by computing the annuity factor from the remainder factor in the applicable Code Sec. 7520 table, i.e., Table S in Reg. § 20.2031-7. The remainder factor from Table S for a 70-year-old with an interest rate of 6.0% is .49007. According to Reg. § 20.2031-7(d)(2)(iv)(B), the taxpayer must convert this factor to an annuity factor by subtracting it from 1.00000 and then dividing the difference by the interest rate of 6.0%. Thus, the annuity factor is 8.4989 [(1.00000 – .49007)/.06]. Dividing $100,000 by 8.4989 shows that Sam has to make an annual payment of $11,766.23 to Frank for Frank's life to avoid any gift tax consequences.

If the annuity payments were less than $11,766.23, a gift would result from the transfer. For example, assume Sam could afford only to pay $10,000 a year. The gift from Frank to Sam would be $15,011 [$100,000 – ($10,000 × 8.4989)].

Example 8.7. Assume that the transfer from Frank Young to his son Sam takes place in a month in which the interest factor is 7.0%. In this case, the remainder factor is .44456, and the annuity factor is 7.9349 [1.0000 – .44456/.07]. Sam has to make an annual payment of $12,602.55 ($100,000/7.9349) to avoid any gift tax consequences for Frank. If the rate were 10%, the remainder factor would be .34204, and the annuity factor would be 6.5796 [(1.00000 – .34204/.10]. The annual payment would be $15,198.49 ($100,000/6.5796).

.04 When the Taxpayer Cannot Use the Tables

An annuitant who is terminally ill at the time of the transfer may not use the standard actuarial factors embodied in the Code Sec. 7520 tables. The law deems the annuitant terminally ill if he or she has an incurable illness or deteriorating physical condition with at least a 50 percent chance that he or she will die within one year. If the annuitant survives for at least 18 months after the date of the transfer, however, the law presumes that he or she was not terminally ill at the time of the transfer that gave rise to the annuity obligation. In such a case, the IRS might still consider the annuitant terminally ill at the time of the transfer. However, the IRS bears the burden of proving it by clear and convincing evidence.[41]

.05 Estate Tax

If the value of the property equals that of the annuity, and the annuitant retains no security interest in the property, the property is not includible in the annuitant's gross estate. The Code sections that might otherwise apply are not applicable because the transfer was for full and adequate consideration in money or money's worth.

If a gift results because the value of the property exceeds the value of the annuity, then the annuitant's gross estate might include the property. The annuitant's gross estate includes only the amount by which the property's fair market value at the time of death exceeds the value of the annuity at the time of the original transaction.[42] If the obligor has disposed of the property originally transferred, the different time frames and tracing problems suggest the advisability of splitting the transaction if it involves a gift. The annuitant should make one transaction as a gift and the other as an exchange of property for an annuity of equal value.

.06 Tax Consequences to the Obligor

The obligor is taxable on the income derived from the property received, but the obligor receives no deduction for any portion of the payments made to the annuitant. Rather, the payments increase the obligor's cost basis in the property.[43] His or her obligation to the annuitant is not indebtedness, and hence he or she is not entitled to an interest deduction. Neither the original issue discount rules nor Code Sec. 483, dealing with imputed interest on deferred payments, applies to Code Sec. 72 annuities.

Figuring the obligor's tax basis for the transferred property in case of a sale and for depreciation purposes involves complicated tax rules. Rev. Rul. 55-119[44] specifies these rules. For example, in measuring gain on a sale of the property before the death of the annuitant, the obligor's basis is the total of the payments made and the actuarial value of the balance of the payments. If the sale results in a gain and the annuitant thereafter dies before the annuity payments equal the basis used by the obligor in computing gain on sale, the obligor has additional gain to report. If the payments exceed such basis, a loss results. On a sale of the property after the annuitant's death, the obligor's basis equals the total amount of payments actually made.

---

[41] Reg. § 1.7520-3(b)(3).

[42] Code Sec. 2043(a).

[43] Code Sec. 1012.

[44] 1955-1 CB 352.

Chapter 9

Employee Benefits

Overview .... ¶901
Primer on Qualified Retirement Plan Rules .... ¶905
Employee Stock Ownership Plan (ESOP) Opportunities ..... ¶910
Individual Retirement Account (IRA) Opportunities .... ¶915
Profit-Sharing Plans .... ¶920
Cash or Deferred (401(k)) Arrangements .... ¶925
Pension Plans .... ¶930
Thrift and Savings Plans .... ¶935
Borrowing from the Plan .... ¶940
Group-Term and Group Permanent Life Insurance .... ¶945
Death Benefits .... ¶950
General Estate Planning Factors for Qualified Plan and IRA Benefits .... ¶955
Employee Awards .... ¶960
Health Plans .... ¶965
Below-Market Loans to Employees .... ¶970
Cafeteria Plans .... ¶975
Employer-Provided Dependent Care Assistance .... ¶980
Code Sec. 132 Fringe Benefits .... ¶985

¶901 OVERVIEW

Cash is the quintessential employee benefit, but cash alone is not sufficient to attract the best employees in today's competitive economy. Employees have come to expect a wide range of benefits as part of their total compensation package. Employers can provide many such benefits to employees on a tax-free or tax-deferred basis. The tax-favored treatment also works to the advantage of the employer. The employer can provide a lower dollar amount of benefits in lieu of additional cash compensation. The employee benefits by having more after-tax compensation than he or she would have solely from cash compensation.

Tax-free benefits generally escape payroll taxes. Another advantage is that the employer can provide such benefits to employees without raising the employee's adjusted gross income (AGI). This benefit is important because some tax benefits, such as personal and dependency exemptions and many itemized deductions, are phased out after AGI reaches certain levels.[1] However, the phaseout of the deduction for personal and dependency exemptions and the limit on itemized deductions are reduced every two years beginning in 2006 and repealed for 2010. Some other deductions are permitted only to the extent they exceed a certain percentage of AGI. For example, medical expenses are allowed as a deduction only to the extent that they exceed 7.5 percent of AGI.[2]

This chapter covers in some detail what is perhaps the biggest employee benefit of all—the qualified retirement plan. Among other things, this chapter examines the various types of plans, distribution rules, factors in borrowing from plans, and estate planning for plan benefits. This chapter also discusses other popular benefits including health plans, cafeteria plans, and dependent-care assistance.

Many of the benefits discussed in this chapter are equally suitable for both highly compensated employees and nonhighly compensated employees. However, benefits of a character primarily for highly compensated employees, such as deferred compensation and stock options, are not considered in this chapter. They are discussed at ¶ 1605.

¶ 905 PRIMER ON QUALIFIED RETIREMENT PLAN RULES

An understanding of the basic qualified retirement plan rules is essential for every financial and estate planner. First, the financial and estate planner should note that the law does not require that an employer furnish employees with any retirement benefits. However, if the employer offers a qualified retirement plan, the employer and the employees will receive significant income tax benefits. The employer receives a current deduction for contributions to the plan.[3] The plan's earnings accumulate free of current tax. Employees are

[1] Code Secs. 68 and 151(d)(3).
[2] Code Sec. 213(a).
[3] Code Sec. 404.

generally taxed on their stake in the plan only when their share is distributed to them.

While the law in this area consists of both tax and labor law provisions, the focus of this chapter is on the tax provisions, although the two sometimes overlap. The labor provisions cover notice requirements, plan administration, fiduciary responsibility, and other matters.

.01 Fundamental Aspects of Qualified Plans

Defined contribution v. defined benefit plans. While a detailed discussion of different types of retirement and benefit plans appears at ¶910 and the paragraphs that follow, an introduction to the two basic types of qualified plans will be helpful in understanding fundamental concepts. Defined contribution and defined benefit plans are the two basic types of qualified plans. All other plans essentially are hybrids of these forms. A defined contribution or individual account plan involves a fixed employer contribution.[4] The employer's contributions, together with earnings thereon, yield a retirement benefit to the employees. In this type of plan, the contribution is fixed or defined. However, the actual retirement benefit is indeterminable at the outset because the earnings on the contributions ultimately determine the retirement benefit amount. A defined contribution plan formula would be expressed, for example, as 10 percent of compensation. The employer would contribute that amount annually to the plan, and the plan would credit the contribution to a separate account maintained for a plan participant. Upon retirement, the participant is entitled to receive the amount in the account. A participant who separates from service with the employer before retirement would be entitled to receive the vested interest in the account.

The other basic plan form is a defined benefit plan. A defined benefit plan is one in which the amount of the benefit, and not the amount of contribution, is determinable at the outset.[5] Benefit formulas under defined benefit plans are generally stated either as a percentage of final or average pay, or as a percentage of pay for each year of service. For example, an employee might retire with a benefit equal to 50 percent of final pay or average pay. Alternatively, an employee might receive two percent of pay for each year of participation up to a maximum of 20 years, yielding a maximum retirement benefit of 40 percent of pay. The contribution required to produce the benefit is determined actuarially and will vary

[4] Code Sec. 414(i).

[5] Code Sec. 414(j).

depending on several factors. These factors include the amount of the benefit, the employee's age and projected length of service with the employer, and the plan's history of gains and losses, i.e., the investment success of employer contributions.

Ceilings on benefits and contributions. Code Sec. 415 limits benefits and contributions under qualified plans. If an employer maintains more than one defined-benefit plan, all the defined-benefit plans will be treated as one defined-benefit plan for purposes of determining the limitation on benefits.[6] If an employer maintains more than one defined-contribution plan, all the defined-contribution plans will be treated as one defined-contribution plan for purposes of determining the limitation on contributions and other additions.[7] The Code Sec. 415 limits governing benefits and contributions are different from the limit on the amount that an employer may deduct. Code Sec. 404 prescribes limits on the deductibility of employer contributions. While the two limits are interrelated, different rules apply to both determinations.

The Code Sec. 415 limit for defined contribution plans is expressed in terms of the maximum annual addition. The limit for 2006 is the lesser of 100 percent of compensation or $44,000.[8] The dollar limit is indexed to inflation in $1,000 increments.[9] Annual additions include employer contributions, employee contributions, and reallocated forfeitures.[10]

For 2006, the maximum annual benefit payable under a defined benefit plan is limited to the lesser of $175,000 or 100 percent of the average compensation for the three highest consecutive years.[11] The dollar limit is indexed to inflation in $5,000 increments.[12] Adjustments to the dollar limit apply for early and late retirement.[13] Also, the dollar limit is based on 10 years of plan participation.[14]

Nondiscrimination rules. A plan may not discriminate in favor of highly compensated employees as to benefits or contributions.[15] Generally, all benefits, rights, and features of a qualified plan must be made available in a nondiscriminatory way. However, a plan is not discriminatory merely because benefits or contributions bear a direct relationship to compensation.[16] Certain disparities are permitted,[17] as discussed below under the heading "Plan Integration." The nondiscrimination rules are extremely technical, and

[6] Code Sec. 415(f)(1)(A).
[7] Code Sec. 415(f)(1)(B).
[8] Code Sec. 415(c)(1).
[9] Code Sec. 415(d).
[10] Code Sec. 415(c)(2).
[11] Code Sec. 415(b)(1).
[12] Code Sec. 415(d).
[13] Code Secs. 415(b)(2)(C) and 415(b)(2)(D).
[14] Code Sec. 415(b)(5).
[15] Code Sec. 401(a)(4).
[16] Code Sec. 401(a)(5)(B).
[17] Code Sec. 401(a)(5)(C).

plans are required always to be in compliance with them. However, the IRS allows plans to be tested on one representative day of a plan year using simplified methods that do not always require total precision.[18] If the plan does not change significantly, testing need be done only once every three years.[19]

Coverage. The coverage rules require that the plan meet one of the following criteria:[20]

- At least 70 percent of the nonhighly compensated employees are covered by the plan
- The percentage of nonhighly compensated employees covered by the plan is at least 70 percent of the percentage of highly compensated employees covered by the plan
- The plan benefits such employees who qualify under a classification set by the employer and found by the IRS not to discriminate in favor of highly compensated employees, and the average benefit under the plan for nonhighly compensated employees is at least 70 percent of the benefit available for highly compensated participants

Code Sec. 401(a)(26) requires qualified plans to benefit at least 50 employees or 40 percent of all employees of the employer, whichever is less. This rule applies separately to each qualified plan of the employer, and the employer may not aggregate plans to satisfy this requirement. In certain cases, a single plan may be treated as comprising separate plans.

Participation/eligibility. Generally, an employee may not be excluded from plan coverage if the employee is at least 21 years old and has completed a year of service.[21] However, a plan may require, as a condition of participation, that an employee complete up to two years of service with the employer if the plan also gives each participant a nonforfeitable right to 100 percent of the accrued benefit under the plan when the benefit is accrued.[22] Generally, an employer may exclude part-time workers, defined as those who have worked less than 1,000 hours during a year of service.[23]

Benefit accrual. Benefit accrual is a general concept referring to the amount a participant earns under a qualified plan. A participant's accrued benefit is expressed differently depending on the type of plan under consideration. In a defined contribution plan, a participant's accrued benefit is the amount set aside in a bookkeeping

[18] Rev. Proc. 93-42, 1993-2 CB 540.

[19] Ann. 93-130, IRB 1993-31 (September 28, 1993).

[20] Code Sec. 410(b).

[21] Code Sec. 410(a)(1)(A).

[22] Code Sec. 410(a)(1)(B).

[23] Code Sec. 410(a)(3)(A).

account. In a defined benefit plan, the accrued benefit is the present value of the retirement benefit being funded.

Vesting. All qualified plans must provide that participants have a nonforfeitable right to fixed percentages of their accrued benefits after a prescribed period. Employees must always be 100 percent vested in their own contributions.[24] In general, employer contributions must vest at least as rapidly as (1) 100 percent vesting after five years of service, or (2) 20 percent after three years and 20 percent each year thereafter to achieve 100 percent vesting after seven years of service (known as seven-year graded vesting).[25] For plan years through 2010, employer matching contributions must vest as rapidly as (1) 100 percent vesting after three years of service, or (2) 20 percent after two years and 20 percent each year thereafter to achieve 100 percent vesting after six years of service. A matching contribution is an employer's contribution to a defined contribution plan on behalf of an employee due to the employee's making a contribution or an elective deferral. The purpose of this faster vesting schedule for matching contributions is to increase participation in defined contribution pension plans by lower- and middle-income employees.[26] All years of service with an employer, after the employee has attained age 18, are taken into account.[27] Special rules apply to a plan maintained pursuant to a collective bargaining agreement.

Employers may always provide more rapid vesting than the minimum vesting requirements.

Two special rules apply in the vesting area. First, top-heavy plans are subject to different vesting requirements, as discussed below.[28] Second, 100-percent vesting is triggered upon both normal retirement age[29] and plan termination, irrespective of the plan's regular vesting schedule.[30]

Funding. In a defined benefit plan, technical rules govern the manner in which benefits must be accrued and funded to ensure that requisite funds will be available when the promised benefit becomes payable.[31] These technical rules apply to a lesser extent to defined contribution (also known as money purchase) pension plans. Failure to satisfy the prescribed funding rules subjects the employer to an excise tax.[32] The employer must make the required plan contributions quarterly to satisfy the minimum funding rules.[33]

---

[24] Code Sec. 411(a)(1).
[25] Code Sec. 411(a)(2).
[26] Code Secs. 411(a)(12) and 401(m)(4)(i).
[27] Code Sec. 411(a)(4).
[28] Code Sec. 416(b).
[29] Code Sec. 411(a).
[30] Code Sec. 411(d)(3).
[31] Code Sec. 412.
[32] Code Sec. 4971.
[33] Code Sec. 412(m)(3).

Fiduciary responsibility. Both labor and tax law provisions contain a number of rules concerning fiduciary responsibility. The term "fiduciary" is broadly defined to include most persons who have an administrative or investment role in connection with a plan. Fiduciaries are subject to a knowledgeable prudent man standard, a duty to diversify investments, and detailed rules forbidding transactions between a plan and parties-in-interest, referred to as prohibited transactions. Code Sec. 4975 imposes excises taxes on disqualified persons engaging in prohibited transactions. In addition, elaborate reporting and disclosure rules govern fiduciaries both in their dealings with plan assets, governmental agencies, and plan participants.

Plan integration. Qualified plans are permitted to take into account certain benefits derived from employer contributions to Social Security when determining whether benefit or contribution levels discriminate in favor of the prohibited group.[34] The rationale for this rule is that a greater percentage of a nonhighly compensated employee's retirement benefit will be covered by Social Security.

Automatic survivor benefits. Defined benefit plans and certain defined contribution plans must provide for automatic survivor benefits. A qualified joint and survivor annuity must be provided for a participant who retires. In addition, a qualified pre-retirement survivor annuity must be provided to the surviving spouse when a vested participant dies before the annuity starting date.[35]

The participant may waive the joint and survivor annuity or the pre-retirement annuity for his or her spouse, but only if certain notice, election, and spousal consent requirements are satisfied.[36] Consent contained in a prenuptial agreement does not satisfy the consent requirement. The waiver of either type of annuity by a non-participant spouse is not a taxable transfer for gift tax purposes.[37]

A plan generally is not required to treat a participant as married unless the participant and the participant's spouse have been married throughout the one-year period ending on the earlier of (1) the participant's annuity starting date, or (2) the date of the participant's death.[38]

> ***Comment.*** The pre-retirement annuity for the surviving spouse of a participant who dies at a young age or with a very small amount of vested accrued benefits is likely to be small. If the plan provides a lump-sum pre-retirement benefit, the

[34] Code Secs. 401(a)(5)(C), 401(a)(5)(D), and 401(l).

[35] Code Sec. 401(a)(11)(A)(ii).

[36] Code Sec. 417.

[37] Code Sec. 2503(f).

[38] Code Sec. 417(d).

combined value of the lump sum and the annuity may not exceed the amount of death benefits permitted under the incidental death benefit rule.[39]

Planning pointer. The pre-retirement annuity is no substitute for life insurance. A tax-free group-term life insurance benefit[40] might be worth much more to the surviving spouse (and the family) than a small pre-retirement annuity that might not commence until the survivor reaches early retirement age (55) or later.

Top-heavy plans. More stringent rules apply for top-heavy plans, basically defined as plans in which key employees have more than 60 percent of the benefits.[41] The key additional requirements are that such plans must provide more rapid vesting[42] and minimum benefits for nonkey employees.[43]

The Economic Growth and Tax Relief Reconciliation Act of 2001 significantly modified the rules for top-heavy plans. Under the Act's definitions of top-heavy plans and key employees, fewer plans will be deemed to be top heavy. In addition, the Act adjusted the minimum benefit or contribution rules to reduce the cost to employers. The Act created a safe harbor for tax years 2002 through 2010 for 401(k) plans that meet the safe harbor requirements for the actual deferral percentage nondiscrimination test[44] and that meet the requirements for matching contributions.[45] Such 401(k) plans are specifically excluded from the definition of a top-heavy plan.[46] The Act also added a special rule for 401(k) plans not deemed to be a top-heavy under the new safe harbor but that belong to an aggregation group that is a top-heavy plan. Under these circumstances, the 401(k) plan's contributions may be taken into account in determining whether any other plan in the group meets the Code Sec. 416(c)(2) minimum distribution requirements.[47]

For years 2002 through 2010, the Act generally changed the rule for computing the present value of a participant's accrued benefit or a participant's account balance for purposes of determining whether the plan is top heavy. Under this provision, the accrued benefit or account balance is increased for distributions made to the participant during the one-year period ending on the determination date.[48] However, the Act retained the five-year lookback rule for distributions

[39] Rev. Rul. 85-15, 1985-1 CB 132.
[40] Code Sec. 79.
[41] Code Sec. 416(g)(1)(A).
[42] Code Secs. 416(a) and 416(b).
[43] Code Secs. 416(a) and 416(c).
[44] Code Sec. 401(k)(12).
[45] Code Sec. 401(m)(11).
[46] Code Sec. 416(g)(4)(H).
[47] Code Sec. 416(g)(4)(H).
[48] Code Sec. 416(g)(4).

made for a reason other than separation from service, death, or disability. For such distributions, the accrued benefit is increased for distributions made during the five-year period ending on the determination date.[49]

For plan years 2002 through 2010, a key employee is an employee who at any time during the year was one of the following:[50]

- An officer with annual compensation exceeding $140,000 (for 2006 and indexed for inflation)
- A 5-percent owner
- A 1-percent owner with annual compensation exceeding $150,000

No more than 50 employees may be treated as officers. If the employer has fewer than 50 employees, the number of officers may not exceed the greater of three employees or 10 percent of the employees.

Under the Act, for plan years 2002 through 2010, employer-matching contributions are considered when determining whether the employer has satisfied the minimum benefit requirement for a defined contribution plan. Any reduction in benefits that occurs because the employer may take matching contributions into account will not cause a violation of the contingent benefit rule of Code Sec. 401(k)(4)(A). This provision overrides a provision in Reg. § 1.416-1, Q&A M-19, which states that if an employer uses matching contributions to satisfy the minimum benefit requirement, the employer may not use such matching contributions for purposes of the Code Sec. 401(m) nondiscrimination rules. Thus, the provision under the Act allows employers to take matching contributions into account for purposes of both the nondiscrimination rules and the top-heavy rules.

The Act added a provision for determining whether a defined benefit plan meets the minimum benefit requirement for years 2002 through 2010. Under this provision, any year in which the plan is frozen is not considered a year of service for purposes of determining an employee's years of service. A plan is frozen for a year when no key employee or former key employee benefits under the plan.[51]

---

[49] Code Sec. 416(g)(3)(B).

[50] Code Sec. 416(i)(1) and Notice 2005-75, 2005-45 IRB 929 (November 3, 2005).

[51] Code Sec. 416(c)(1)(C)(iii).

Definition of highly compensated. A highly compensated employee for 2006 is one who, during 2005 or 2006:

- Was a five-percent or more owner of the employer
- Received more than $95,000 in annual compensation from the employer[52]

The threshold for being a highly compensated employee is indexed to inflation.[53]

Compensation cap. A $220,000 (for 2006) cap applies to the amount of compensation that may be taken into account for purposes of determining contributions or benefits under qualified plans and simplified employee pension plans.[54] This limit is indexed to inflation.[55]

Credit for plan start-up costs of small employers. Employers with no more than 100 employees who received at least $5,000 of compensation from the employer for the previous year may claim a tax credit for some of the costs of establishing new retirement plans in years 2002 through 2010.[56] The credit is 50 percent of the start-up costs the small employer incurs to create or maintain a new employee retirement plan.[57] The maximum amount of the credit is $500 in any one year, and an eligible employer may claim the credit for qualified costs incurred in each of the three years beginning with the tax year in which the plan becomes effective.[58] The employer may elect to claim the credit in the year immediately before the first year in which the plan is effective.[59] In addition, an eligible employer may elect not to claim the credit for a tax year.[60] A new employee retirement plan includes a defined benefit plan, a defined contribution plan, a 401(k) plan, a SIMPLE plan, or a SEP.[61] The plan must cover at least one employee who is not a highly compensated employee.[62] Qualified start-up costs include any ordinary and necessary expenses incurred to establish or administer an eligible plan or to educate employees about retirement planning.[63] The credit allowed reduces the otherwise deductible expenses to prevent a double tax benefit.[64] The credit is allowed as a part of the general business credit.[65]

---

[52] Code Sec. 414(q) and Notice 2005-75, 2005-45 IRB 929 (November 3, 2005).

[53] Code Secs. 414(q)(1) and 415(d).

[54] Code Secs. 401(a)(17)(A) and 404(l).

[55] Code Secs. 401(a)(17)(B) and 404(l).

[56] Code Secs. 45E(c)(1) and 408(p)(2)(C)(i).

[57] Code Sec. 45E(a).

[58] Code Sec. 45E(b).

[59] Code Sec. 45E(d)(3).

[60] Code Sec. 45E(e)(3).

[61] Code Sec. 45E(d)(2).

[62] Code Sec. 45E(d)(1)(B).

[63] Code Sec. 45E(d)(1)(A).

[64] Code Sec. 45E(e)(2).

[65] Code Sec. 38(b)(14).

Credit for elective deferrals and IRA contributions. For tax years through 2006, an eligible individual may claim a nonrefundable tax credit for elective deferrals and IRA contributions. An eligible individual means an individual who is at least 18 years old at the end of the tax year; is not a student as defined in Code Sec. 151(c)(4); and cannot be claimed as a dependent on another taxpayer's return.[66]

The credit is in addition to any allowable deduction or exclusion from gross income. Its purpose is to encourage taxpayers with low or moderate incomes to establish and maintain retirement savings plans. The credit will not reduce a taxpayer's basis in an annuity, endowment, or life insurance contract. The credit is equal to the applicable percentage multiplied by the amount of qualified retirement plan savings contributions for the year up to $2,000.[67]

A taxpayer must reduce the contribution amount by any distributions received from a qualified retirement plan, an eligible deferred compensation plan, and a Roth IRA other than qualified rollover contributions during the testing period.[68] Distributions received by a taxpayer's spouse are treated as received by the taxpayer for purposes of computing the credit if the couple files a joint return.[69] However, certain distributions such as loans from annuities, distributions of excess contributions, and rollover distributions from traditional IRAs are not considered distributions for purposes of computing the credit.[70] The testing period is: (1) the current tax year, (2) the two preceding tax years, and (3) the period after such tax year and before the due date for filing the income tax return, including extensions.[71]

A taxpayer's filing status and adjusted gross income (AGI) (computed without regard to the exclusions for foreign earned income, foreign housing, and income from possessions of the United States or Puerto Rico) determine the applicable percentage as shown in the following table:

Joint Return		
Over	Not Over	Applicable Percentage
$ 0	$30,000	50
30,000	32,500	20
32,500	50,000	10
50,000		0

[66] Code Sec. 25B(c).

[67] Code Sec. 25B(a).

[68] Code Sec. 25B(d)(2).

[69] Code Sec. 25B(d)(2)(D).

[70] Code Sec. 25B(d)(3)(C).

[71] Code Sec. 25B(d)(2)(B).

Head of Household

Over	Not Over	Applicable Percentage
$ 0	$22,500	50
22,500	24,375	20
24,375	37,500	10
37,500		0

Single, Surviving Spouse, or Married Filing Separately

Over	Not Over	Applicable Percentage
$ 0	$15,000	50
15,000	16,250	20
16,250	25,000	10
25,000		0

The maximum credit is 50 percent of the elective deferral or IRA contribution. The credit is completely phased out for a married couple filing a joint return with an AGI of $50,000, for heads of household with an AGI of $37,500, and for single taxpayers and married couples filing a separate return at an AGI of $25,000.[72] For tax years beginning in 2004 through 2006, the credit is limited to the excess of the sum of the regular tax liability and the alternative minimum tax over the sum of the nonrefundable tax credits allowed except for this credit, the credit for adoption expenses, and the foreign tax credit.[73] The credit is not allowed for tax years beginning after 2006.[74]

.02 Distributions from Qualified Plans

Generally, distributions must commence no later than April 1 of the year following the year in which the employee attains age 70½. An employee who is still working past age 70½ may choose to delay receipt of a distribution until April 1 of the calendar year following the calendar year in which he or she retires.[75] This alternative is not available to plan participants who are at least five-percent owners of the company, nor does it apply to required distributions from IRAs.[76]

The Economic Growth and Tax Relief Reconciliation Act of 2001 repealed the special minimum distribution rules that applied only to

[72] Code Sec. 25B(b).
[73] Code Sec. 25B(g).
[74] Code Sec. 25B(h).
[75] Code Sec. 401(a)(9)(C)(i).
[76] Code Sec. 401(a)(9)(C)(ii).

Code Sec. 457 deferred compensation plans. The repeal is effective for tax years 2002 through 2010. Thus, Code Sec. 457 plans need only satisfy the minimum distribution rules applicable to qualified plans.[77] In addition, for tax years 2002 through 2010, amounts deferred under a Code Sec. 457 plan sponsored by a state or local government are includible in the employee's gross income only when paid rather than when otherwise made available to the employee.[78] This rule applies only to governmental Code Sec. 457 plans and not to such plans sponsored by tax-exempt organizations.

If an employee chooses to delay receipt of distributions until commencement of a post-age 70½ retirement, the employee's accrued benefit must be actuarially adjusted to reflect the value of the benefits that the employee would have received if he or she had chosen to retire at age 70½ and then began receiving benefits.[79] This actuarial adjustment rule does not apply to defined contribution plans, governmental plans, or church plans.[80]

Distributions are to be made, in accordance with regulations, over a period not extending beyond the life expectancy of the employee and the employee's designated beneficiary.[81]

Final Treasury regulations issued in 2002 govern required minimum distributions from qualified plans and IRAs for Calendar years beginning on or after January 1, 2003.[82]

Minimum distributions must comply with requirements of Code Sec. 401(a)(9) and the regulations thereunder.

Calculating the required minimum distribution. The Commissioner may waive the 50-percent excise tax imposed under Code Sec. 4974 for a tax year if the payee satisfies the Commissioner that the failure to distribute the required minimum distribution was due to reasonable error and that reasonable steps are being taken to correct the error.[83] Under the regulations, taxpayers must calculate the required minimum distribution using the uniform lifetime table in situations in which the employee's spouse is not the only beneficiary or the employee's spouse is the only beneficiary and is not more than 10 years younger than the employee.[84] This table is reproduced on the following page.

---

[77] Code Sec. 457(d)(2).

[78] Code Sec. 457(a)(1)(A).

[79] Code Sec. 401(a)(9)(C)(iii).

[80] Code Sec. 401(a)(9)(C)(iv) and Conference Report to the Small Business Job Protection Act of 1996 (P.L. 104-188).

[81] Code Sec. 401(a)(9)(A).

[82] Reg. §§ 1.401(a)(9)-0 through 1.401(a)(9)-9.

[83] Reg. § 54.4974-2, Q&A 7.

[84] Reg. § 1.409(a)(9)-9, Q&A 2.

Uniform Lifetime Table

Age	Distribution Period	Age	Distribution Period?
70	27.4	93	9.6
71	26.5	94	9.1
72	25.6	95	8.6
73	24.7	96	8.1
74	23.8	97	7.6
75	22.9	98	7.1
76	22.0	99	6.7
77	21.2	100	6.3
78	20.3	101	5.9
79	19.5	102	5.5
80	18.7	103	5.2
81	17.9	104	4.9
82	17.1	105	4.5
83	16.3	106	4.2
84	15.5	107	3.9
85	14.8	108	3.7
86	14.1	109	3.4
87	13.4	110	3.1
88	12.7	111	2.9
89	12.0	112	2.6
90	11.4	113	2.4
91	10.8	114	2.1
92	10.2	115+	1.9

To calculate the required minimum distribution, the taxpayer finds the distribution period in the table based on his or her age at the end of the year. The taxpayer then divides the account balance as of December 31 of the previous year to determine the required minimum distribution. The taxpayer returns to the table each year to determine the new distribution period to use to calculate the required minimum distribution. Because the table has a distribution period of 1.9 years even for someone who is more than 115 years old, the regulations never require a taxpayer to deplete the entire balance in his or her account. Thus, the account holder may always leave some of his or her pension fund to a beneficiary.

Example 9.1. Ralph Simon had $500,000 in his defined contribution pension plan on December 31, 2005. On December 31, 2006, Simon is 73 years old. The distribution period for 2006 is 24.7 years. His required minimum distribution for 2006 is calculated as follows: $500,000 ÷ 24.7 = $20,242.91. On December 31,

2006, Simon had $560,000 in his defined contribution pension plan. His required minimum distribution for 2007 is calculated as follows: $560,000 ÷ 23.8 = $23,529.41.

The account holder does not have to designate a beneficiary to calculate the required minimum distribution. In addition, the account holder does not have to select a distribution method to compute the minimum required distribution. Only one method applies unless the spousal exception applies. As illustrated in the following example, if the designated beneficiary is the account holder's spouse and the spouse is more than 10 years younger than the account holder, the account holder may use the longer of the period determined under the uniform lifetime table or the couple's actual joint life expectancy using the joint and last survivor table in Reg. § 1.401(a)(9)-9 Q&A 3 to calculate the required minimum distribution.[85]

Example 9.2. Ron Hurst has a defined contribution pension fund with a balance of $340,000 on December 31, 2005. His wife, Gladys, is 15 years younger. On December 31, 2006, Ron is 75 years old, and Gladys is 60 years old. If Hurst used the uniform lifetime table, his required distribution period would be 22.9 years. His required minimum distribution for 2006 would be computed as follows: $340,000 ÷ 22.9 = $14,847.16. However, using the couple's actual joint life expectancy, the distribution period is 26.5 years from joint and last survivor table in Reg. § 1.401(a)(9)-9 Q&A 3. The required minimum distribution is calculated as follows: $340,000 ÷ 26.5 = $12,830.19.

Beneficiary selection. Under the final regulations, a beneficiary designation does not affect the required minimum distribution, unless the beneficiary is the account holder's spouse who is more than 10 years younger than the account holder. In addition, the account holder has no choice of distribution method other than the exception for a spouse who is more than 10 years younger than the account holder.

The term "designated beneficiary" has special meaning with respect to retirement distributions. Although the law provides a look-through rule for trusts, generally, only an individual may be a designated beneficiary.

The regulations provide a flexible approach to the designation of a beneficiary. Specifically, they allow for the selection or change of a beneficiary after the required beginning date without penalty in terms of the required minimum distribution amount. In fact, the

[85] Reg. § 1.401(a)(9)-5, Q&A 4(b).

rules allow for a change of beneficiary to be recognized up until September 30 of the calendar year following the calendar year of the account holder's death.[86] Accordingly, not only may the account holder change beneficiaries after the required beginning date, but a post-mortem beneficiary change motivated by estate planning strategies may be accomplished through a disclaimer. In a case in which the account holder has selected multiple beneficiaries and one of them is not an individual (e.g., a charity), the new regulations would also appear to allow for buying out a beneficiary who is not an individual by paying the beneficiary all benefits due it before September 30 of the calendar year following the calendar year of the account holder's death. Thus, a charity could be disregarded in determining a designated beneficiary for purposes of the distribution rules.

In addition, if the account holder's death occurs before the required beginning date and the account holder has designated a beneficiary other than his or her spouse, the life expectancy method[87] will now apply rather than the five-year rule.[88] In fact, except in the case of a contrary plan provision or election of the five-year rule, the life expectancy rule will always apply if the account holder has a designated beneficiary. Only if there was no designated beneficiary as of September 30 of the calendar year following the calendar year of the employee's death would the five-year rule apply automatically.[89]

Planning pointer. The rule allowing a change in beneficiary until September 30 of the calendar year following the calendar year of the account holder's death is very beneficial. The new rules allow a disclaimer to be coupled with use of a younger contingent beneficiary's life expectancy in the required minimum distribution calculation. Thus, the new regulations allow significant tax deferral. However, a financial and estate planner should not interpret the regulations to mean that an account holder no longer needs to select a designated beneficiary. The flexibility provided by the potential to change beneficiaries by a disclaimer is welcome, but the account holder should still designate a beneficiary.

For those who die without a designated beneficiary, the rules allow a distribution period equal to the account holder's remaining life expectancy as calculated immediately before death. For each year after the employee's death, the distribution period is reduced by one year.[90]

---

[86] Reg. § 1.401(a)(9)-4, Q&A 4.

[87] Code Sec. 401(a)(9)(B)(iii).

[88] Code Sec. 401(a)(9)(B)(ii).

[89] Reg. § 1.401(a)(9)-3, Q&A 4.

[90] Reg. § 1.401(a)(9)-5, Q&A 5.

Trust look-through rules. The final regulations provide that only individuals may be designated beneficiaries for purposes of determining the required minimum distribution.[91] However, the regulations also provide that if a trust is named as a beneficiary of a qualified plan, the beneficiaries of the trust, and not the trust itself will be treated as beneficiaries of the employee under the plan for purposes of determining the distribution period under Code Sec. 401(a)(9).[92] The trustee of the trust named as beneficiary must provide the administrator of the plan with a final list of beneficiaries of the trust, including information on contingent beneficiaries and remaindermen, as of September 30 of the calendar year following the calendar year of the employee's death. The trustee must provide this list to the plan administrator by October 31 of the calendar year following the calendar year of the employee's death.[93] Therefore, the trustee has one month after the deadline for determining designated beneficiaries to inform the administrator of the plan of the final list of beneficiaries of the trust.

QDROs. As provided under Code Sec. 401(a)(13), retirement assets may be assigned pursuant to a qualified domestic relations order (QDRO). A QDRO is an order, judgment or decree that relates to child support, alimony, or property rights of a spouse or former spouse, child, or dependent of the participant made pursuant to a state domestic relations law.[94] The regulations provide that a former spouse to whom all or a portion of the employee's benefit is payable pursuant to a QDRO will be treated as a spouse (including a surviving spouse) of the employee for purposes of Code Sec. 401(a)(9), including the minimum distribution incidental benefit requirement, regardless of whether the QDRO specifically provides that the former spouse is treated as the spouse for purposes of Code Secs. 401(a)(11) and 417.[95] This rule applies regardless of the number of former spouses an employee has who are alternate payees with respect to the employee's retirement benefits.

In addition, if a QDRO divides the individual account of an employee in a defined contribution plan into separate accounts for the employee and for the alternate payee, the required minimum distribution to the alternate payee during the employee's lifetime must still be determined using the same rules that apply to distributions to the employee. Thus, required minimum distributions to the alternate payee must commence by the employee's required beginning date. The required minimum distribution for the alternate

[91] Reg. § 1.401(a)(9)-4, Q&A 3.

[92] Reg. § 1.401(a)(9)-4, Q&A 5.

[93] Reg. § 1.401(a)(9)-4, Q&A 6.

[94] Code Sec. 414(p).

[95] Reg. § 1.401(a)(9)-8, Q&A 6.

payee during the lifetime of the employee may be determined using the uniform distribution table above. Alternatively, if the alternate payee is the employee's former spouse and is more than 10 years younger than the employee, the required minimum distribution is determined using the joint life expectancy of the employee and the alternate payee.

The Economic Growth and Tax Relief Reconciliation Act of 2001 allows QDRO-based distributions from Code Sec. 457 deferred compensation plans for distributions, transfers, and payments made in 2002 through 2010.[96] For purposes of determining whether a distribution from a Code Sec. 457 plan is pursuant to a QDRO, the special rule of Code Sec. 414(p)(11) for governmental and church plans will apply. A distribution or payment from a Code Sec. 457 plan will be treated as from a QDRO if the plan makes the payment pursuant to a domestic relations order and the order creates or recognizes the existence of an alternate payee's rights to, or assigns to an alternate payee the right to receive all or a portion of the benefits payable to the participant in the plan.[97] Rules similar to Code Sec. 402(e)(1)(A) will apply to a distribution or payment pursuant to a QDRO.

Timing of distributions. If a participant in pay status dies before his or her entire interest has been distributed, the balance must be distributed to his or her beneficiary at least as rapidly as it would have been under the method in effect at the participant's death.[98]

If distributions have not commenced before the participant's death, the balance must be distributed in five years,[99] subject to the following exceptions. First, if the employee has designated a beneficiary, distributions may be made over a period not extending beyond the beneficiary's life expectancy. Such distributions must begin not more than one year after the participant's death (or such later date as the IRS may permit).[100] Second, if the designated beneficiary is the employee's spouse, distribution need not commence until the date on which the employee would have attained age 70½.[101]

The distribution rules present opportunities for clients who have no present need for distributions to take them over longer periods. By deferring the receipt of payments, the clients derive the benefit of deferred payment of taxes and continued tax-free build-up of the funds during the deferral period. In addition, if the client or his or

---

[96] Code Secs. 414(p)(10), 414(p)(11), and 414(p)(12).

[97] Code Sec. 414(p)(11).

[98] Code Secs. 72(s)(1)(A) and 401(a)(9)(B).

[99] Code Secs. 72(s)(1)(B) and 401(a)(9)(B)(ii).

[100] Code Secs. 72(s)(2) and 401(a)(9)(B)(iii).

[101] Code Secs. 72(s)(3) and 401(a)(9)(B)(iv).

her beneficiary is in a lower tax bracket when the plan distributes the money, the recipient will realize further benefits.

In figuring the amount that must be distributed each year under the regulations, a participant's life expectancy must be recalculated annually using the uniform lifetime table. The joint life expectancy of a participant and his or her spouse who is more than 10 years younger than the participant must also be recalculated annually using the tables in Reg. § 1.409(a)(9)-9, Q&A 3.[102]

An individual who fails to take a required distribution must pay a 50-percent nondeductible excise tax on the excess of the minimum required distribution over the amount actually distributed.[103]

Additional tax on premature withdrawals. Early withdrawals from qualified plans (and Code Sec. 403(b) annuities and IRAs) are subject to a 10-percent additional tax.[104] Early withdrawals generally are distributions made before attainment of age 59½, death, or disability.[105] This additional tax is often called a penalty, but it is technically an additional tax. Unlike penalties, which a taxpayer may avoid for reasonable cause, a taxpayer must meet a specific statutory exception to avoid this additional tax. The following are exceptions to the additional tax:[106]

- A distribution that is part of a scheduled series of substantially equal periodic payments for the life of the participant (or the joint lives of the participant and the participant's designated beneficiary) or the life expectancy of the participant (or the joint life expectancies of the participant and the participant's designated beneficiary)
- A distribution to an employee after separation from service and after attainment of age 55
- A distribution that does not exceed the amount allowable as a medical expense deduction (i.e., expenses in excess of 7.5 percent of adjusted gross income) determined without regard to whether the taxpayer itemizes deductions
- Payments made to or on behalf of an alternate payee pursuant to a qualified domestic relations order (QDRO)
- Certain distributions of excess contributions to and excess deferrals under a qualified cash or deferred arrangement
- Dividend distributions under Code Sec. 404(k)

[102] Code Sec. 401(a)(9)(D).
[103] Code Sec. 4974(a).
[104] Code Sec. 72(t)(1).
[105] Code Sec. 72(t)(2)(A).
[106] Code Sec. 72(t)(2).

In the case of distributions from IRAs, the post-55, and QDRO exceptions do not apply. The exception for substantially equal payments applies to distributions from plans qualified under Code Sec. 401(a), tax-sheltered annuities, and custodial accounts only if the distribution is made after separation from service.

The 10-percent additional tax on early distributions will not apply to distributions from an IRA that are used to pay for the following:

- Health insurance premiums of an unemployed individual after separation from employment[107]
- Qualified higher education expenses[108]
- First-time homebuyer expenses[109]

The qualified higher education expense exception covers amounts withdrawn and used to pay qualified higher education expenses (tuition, fees, books and supplies) of the taxpayer, spouse, children, and grandchildren. The amount of qualified educational expenses is reduced by payments received for a student's education that are excludable from gross income (such as a qualified educational scholarship, educational allowance or payment).[110]

> **Planning pointer.** The amount that can be withdrawn from the IRA without imposition of the 10-percent additional tax is generally reduced by excludable educational payments.[111] However, this rule does not apply to excludable payments arising from a gift, bequest, devise, or inheritance.[112] Thus, planned or unplanned gratuitous payments for the student's education will not cause an otherwise qualifying educational early withdrawal to be subjected to the 10-percent additional tax.

The 10-percent additional tax on early distributions from an IRA will not apply to IRA distributions (up to $10,000) used to pay expenses incurred by qualified first-time homebuyers (¶ 2810).[113]

Tax treatment of distributions. Amounts distributed from qualified plans are subject to tax as annuities or as lump-sum distributions or may qualify for tax-free rollover treatment.[114] Each is separately discussed below. Early withdrawals are subject to a 10-percent additional tax, as discussed above. Failure to take a large enough required distribution may result in a 50-percent penalty, as discussed above.

---

107 Code Sec. 72(t)(2)(D).
108 Code Sec. 72(t)(2)(E).
109 Code Sec. 72(t)(2)(F).
110 Code Sec. 72(t)(7).
111 Code Sec. 72(t)(7)(B).
112 Code Secs. 72(t)(7)(B) and 25A(g)(2)(C).
113 Code Secs. 72(t)(2)(F) and 72(t)(8).
114 Code Sec. 408(d)(3).

Annuity rules. As a general rule, distributions are taxed under the annuity rules of Code Sec. 72. Under these rules, a portion of each payment is treated as a tax-free return of employee contributions, if applicable, and a portion of each payment is taxable. The annuity rules are discussed in detail in Chapter 8.

Lump-sum distributions. Ten-year averaging and pre-1974 capital gain treatment for lump-sum distributions generally were repealed for distributions made after 1986, and five-year averaging was generally repealed for lump-sum distributions received in tax years beginning after 1999. However, special transitional rules discussed in the next paragraph continue to apply to individuals who attained age 50 before January 1, 1986.

An individual who attained age 50 before January 1, 1986, and who receives a lump-sum distribution after 1986 is permitted (1) to make one election to use five-year forward averaging (using current tax rates) or to use ten-year averaging (using 1986 rates and the 1986 zero-bracket amount), without regard to the requirement of attainment of age 59½, and (2) to elect capital gain treatment with respect to the pre-1974 portion of a lump-sum distribution, with the capital gain being taxed at a flat rate of 20 percent. The special transitional rules may be used by any individual, trust, or estate with respect to an employee who had attained age 50 by January 1, 1986.

For purposes of the transitional rules, a lump-sum distribution is a distribution made within one taxable year of the receipt of the balance to the credit of the participant in the plan or any plan of the same type: (1) on account of the employee's death, (2) after the employee attains age 59½, (3) on account of the employee's separation from service (except in the case of a self-employed individual), or (4) on account of disability in the case of a self-employed individual.[115]

Net unrealized appreciation attributable to that part of a lump-sum distribution that consists of employer securities (other than appreciation attributable to deductible employee contributions) is excluded in figuring the tax on the lump sum. The unrealized appreciation is taxable only on a disposition of the securities in a taxable transaction. The rule also applies to distributions that would qualify as lump sums but for their failure to meet the five-year minimum participation rule.

Portability—tax-free rollovers. No current income tax is owed on eligible rollover distributions from a plan that are rolled over to another qualified plan or a traditional IRA. For distributions

[115] Code Sec. 402(d)(4)(A).

in 2002 through 2010, an eligible rollover distribution may also be rolled over into a Code Sec. 403(b) annuity or a governmental Code Sec. 457 plan. In addition, eligible rollover distributions from Code Sec. 403(b) annuities or governmental Code Sec. 457 plans made in 2002 through 2010 may be rolled over into a qualified plan.[116] An eligible rollover distribution is any distribution to an employee of part or all of his or her account balance in a qualified trust, except for the following:

- Distributions that are part of a series of substantially equal periodic payments made at least annually over the life or life expectancy of the employee (or joint lives or joint life and last survivor expectancies of employee and designated beneficiary), or a specified period of at least 10 years
- Required distributions, such as a minimum distribution required because the taxpayer has reached age 70½[117]

The nontaxable portion of a distribution, such as the part of a distribution attributable to employee after-tax contributions, is not eligible for a rollover. Generally, plan loans treated as distributions are not eligible for a rollover.

Rollover-eligible distributions can avoid current tax whether the employee uses a direct rollover to another eligible retirement plan, or takes the distribution personally and rolls it over into another eligible retirement plan within 60 days.[118] However, if a direct rollover is not used, the distribution is subject to 20-percent withholding, making it difficult for the recipient to roll over the entire amount, and thereby fully avoid tax on it.[119] Any part of an eligible rollover distribution that is not timely rolled over is subject to current taxation.[120]

The rules for eligible rollover distributions apply to the plan participants, their surviving spouses, and to spouses or former spouses if the payment is made under a qualified domestic relations order (QDRO). For eligible rollover distributions in 2002 through 2010, distributions to nonspouse beneficiaries are not eligible for rollover treatment.[121]

Eligible rollover distributions of are subject to mandatory 20-percent federal income tax withholding[122] unless the recipient elects to have the distribution paid directly to another eligible retirement plan.[123] Withholding is not required if only employer securities are distributed or $200 or less in cash is disbursed instead of fractional

[116] Code Sec. 402(c).
[117] Code Sec. 408(d)(3)(E).
[118] Code Sec. 408(d)(3).
[119] Code Sec. 3405(c)(1).
[120] Code Sec. 408(d)(1).
[121] Code Sec. 408(d)(3)(C).
[122] Code Sec. 3405(c)(1).
[123] Code Sec. 3405(c)(2).

employer securities.[124] Distributions that are not eligible rollover distributions are excepted from mandatory 20-percent withholding.

A direct rollover can be accomplished by any reasonable means, including a wire transfer or check from the old plan to the trustee (or custodian) of the transferee eligible retirement plan designated by the taxpayer. The check can be mailed to the transferee eligible retirement plan; it can even be given to the employee for delivery to the eligible retirement plan if it is made out properly to the new plan's trustee or custodian. Distributing plans must offer a direct rollover option to participants eligible to receive eligible rollover distributions; however, plans are not required to accept rollover contributions.

A plan participant may direct that only part of an eligible rollover distribution be transferred via a direct rollover to another plan. In that case, only the part that is not directly rolled over is subject to 20-percent withholding.

> **Planning pointer.** Distributions from simplified employee pension (SEP) plans are not eligible rollover distributions because each individual account in a SEP is an IRA. Therefore, SEP distributions are not subject to mandatory 20-percent withholding. However, SEP distributions can be transferred to other traditional IRA accounts via trustee-to-trustee transfers or 60-day rollovers under the usual rules that apply to traditional IRAs.

Plans are permitted to limit distributees to a single direct rollover for each eligible rollover distribution.[125] Therefore, a retiree who wants a large distribution to be transferred to more than one IRA institution may not be able to accomplish this directly. However, the retiree can achieve this goal by a direct transfer of the entire distribution to one traditional IRA. Then trustee-to-trustee transfers can be made tax free from that IRA to the others.

A surviving spouse may roll over all or a portion of any lump-sum distribution received on account of the participant's death into a traditional IRA or annuity but not into a qualified plan in which he or she is a participant. The same is true of a plan termination distribution received by the surviving spouse after the participant's death. A surviving spouse may also make a tax-free rollover of a partial distribution from a qualified plan to the same extent as a participant.

---

[124] Code Sec. 3405(e)(8).

[125] Code Sec. 408(d)(3)(B).

¶910 EMPLOYEE STOCK OWNERSHIP PLAN (ESOP) OPPORTUNITIES

Employers will want to consider the advantages an employee stock ownership plan (ESOP)[126] provides. The ESOP from the employer's standpoint is considered in some detail at ¶1920.

While employers receive significant benefits under ESOPs, the main focus here is on the benefits that employees can expect to derive from an ESOP. Like most employee benefit plans, an ESOP (under ERISA rules) is designed to benefit participating employees—generally, those who stay with the employer the longest and contribute the most to the corporation's financial success. All cash and employer stock contributed to the ESOP are allocated each year to the accounts of the participating employees under a specific formula.[127] These amounts are held in trust and administered by a trustee who is responsible for protecting the interests of the participants and their beneficiaries.

An employee's ownership generally depends on the vesting schedule adopted by the company within the limits prescribed by Code Sec. 411(a), which are the same as those available to other qualified plans (¶905).

In general, unless a participant elects otherwise with any required spousal consent, payment of benefits must commence no later than one year after the later of the close of the plan year: (1) in which the participant retires, becomes disabled or dies, or (2) that is the fifth year following the plan year in which the participant otherwise separates from service.[128] Unless the participant elects otherwise, distribution is to be made in substantially equal installments (not less frequently than annually) over a period not longer than five years.[129] Additional time to distribute is provided if the account balance is over $885,000 for 2006.[130] This amount is indexed to inflation.[131]

Distribution of an employee's vested benefits must normally be made in cash or shares of employer stock as determined by the administrator of the plan, subject to the distributee's right to demand stock, unless the charter or bylaws restrict ownership of stock to employees.[132]

The following questions and answers are designed to help in further apprising employees of ESOP rights.

---

[126] Code Sec. 4975(e)(7).
[127] Code Sec. 409(b).
[128] Code Sec. 409(o)(1)(A).
[129] Code Sec. 409(o)(1)(C).
[130] Code Sec. 409(o)(1)(C)(ii).
[131] Code Sec. 409(o)(2).
[132] Code Sec. 409(h).

Q. May an ESOP provide for the purchase of incidental life insurance whose proceeds are payable to beneficiaries of employees participating in the ESOP?

A. Yes, provided the aggregate life insurance premiums for each participant do not exceed 25 percent of the amount allocated to his or her ESOP account at any particular time. This 25-percent limit applies, regardless of the type of life insurance purchased (i.e., ordinary life, term, etc.).[133]

Q. May the employer be required to purchase the securities distributed to a participant?

A. Yes, if the securities are not readily tradable on an established market. The price is to be determined by a fair valuation formula.[134] The requirement of a put option is satisfied if the option exists for at least 60 days following distribution of the stock and if it is not exercised within such 60-day period for an additional period of at least 60 days in the following plan year.[135] An employer that is required to repurchase employer securities distributed as part of a total distribution under the put option requirements must pay the employee in substantially equal payments over a period not exceeding five years. In the case of a put option exercised as part of an installment distribution, the employer is required to repay the option price within 30 days of exercise. These last two rules apply to distributions attributable to stock acquired after 1986. Also, a plan may elect to have such rules apply to all distributions made after October 22, 1986.

Q. Must an employee be permitted to direct diversification of his or her account?

A. Effective with respect to stock acquired after 1986, ESOPs must allow qualified participants (those who have attained age 55 and have completed 10 years of participation in the plan) to direct diversification of up to 25 percent of their account balances over a six-year period (50 percent in the sixth year). The election period generally begins with the plan year during which the participant attains age 55 unless he or she has not yet completed 10 years of service, in which case the period begins in the year in which he or she completes such service.[136]

Q. May an employee who receives employer stock from an ESOP trust be required to offer to sell the stock to the employer before offering to sell it to a third party?

---

[133] Rev. Rul. 70-611, 1970-CB 89.

[134] Code Sec. 409.

[135] Code Sec. 409(h)(4).

[136] Code Sec. 401(e)(28).

A. Yes.

Q. What are some of the problems or disadvantages of an ESOP?

A.

1. In a closely held corporation, the major disadvantage of utilizing an ESOP is that a large number of minority shareholders may be created unless stock ownership is restricted to employees or the ESOP.
2. A closely held corporation might have problems of valuation. However, the corporation can overcome these problems by a specific provision or formula.
3. The corporation might have problems of compliance with SEC rules on offerings, disclosure, and stock restrictions.
4. ESOPs are intended to motivate employees and to give them a share of the ownership in their employer-corporation. In a declining market, employees might not be motivated by the potential for appreciation in the value of the stock.

¶915 INDIVIDUAL RETIREMENT ACCOUNT (IRA) OPPORTUNITIES

This paragraph examines the rules and applicable planning strategies relating to traditional IRAs—deductible and nondeductible as well as simplified employee pensions (SEPs), savings incentive match plans for employee (SIMPLE plans), and Roth IRAs.

.01 In General

For tax years 2006 and 2007, every employee or self-employed individual may contribute the lesser of 100 percent of his or her earnings or $4,000 to his or her own IRA.[137] The maximum amount that a taxpayer may contribute to his or her own IRA is increased to $5,000 for 2008 through 2010. The $5,000 limit will be adjusted for inflation in 2009 and 2010. In addition, a taxpayer who is age 50 or older may contribute an additional $1,000 for 2006 through 2010. The earnings on the contributions increase tax free until the taxpayer starts making withdrawals (normally after age 59½). However, Code Sec. 219(g) limits the deductibility of IRA contributions in the case of an active participant in a qualified retirement plan, SEP, Code Sec. 403(b) annuity, or government plan, whose adjusted gross income (AGI) exceeds certain levels. For tax years beginning in

[137] Code Sec. 219(b)(1).

2006, the deduction is phased out starting at an AGI of $75,000 (joint return), $50,000 (single, head of household, and surviving spouse returns), and $0 (married filing separate return), with complete phaseout at $10,000 over those levels. For tax years beginning after December 31, 2006, the phaseout for joint filers will begin when AGI reaches $180,000 with the phaseout complete once AGI reaches $100,000 (i.e., the phaseout range for joint filers will increase to $20,000).

Individuals denied deductions may make nondeductible contributions and achieve deferral of tax on IRA earnings.[138]

> **Planning pointer.** The phaseout amounts will reduce or eliminate IRA deductions for a good number of individuals and families. If the taxpayer faces this situation, the advisability of nondeductible investments in a traditional IRA should be seriously questioned in light of the availability of the Roth IRAs. Roth IRAs, while also not providing a deduction for contributions, give the benefit both of tax-free buildup (like a traditional IRA), and the real possibility of being able to receive the IRA funds *tax free* on retirement (¶915.04).

Spousal IRAs. A spouse who does not have earned income or who has only a small amount of earned income can nonetheless make the maximum contribution for the year, provided the other Spouse's earnings are sufficient to support the contribution generally allowed to contribute up to $4,000 for 2005 through 2007, and $5,000 for 2008 and thereafter to an IRA.[139] However, if the spouse who has earned income is an active participant in an employer-sponsored retirement plan and the couple's AGI is greater than the amount at which the phaseout begins ($75,000 for 2006), the maximum amount of the spousal IRA contribution that will be deductible will be proportionately reduced in the same way that a nonspousal IRA is reduced under current law.[140]

The limit on these spousal contributions is $4,000 for 2006 and 2007, and $5,000 for 2008 through 2010. The $5,000 limit will be adjusted for inflation in 2009 and 2010. In addition, a spouse who is age 50 or older may contribute an additional $500 for 2005 and an additional $1,000 for 2006 through 2010.

Additionally an individual will not be considered to be an active participant in an employer-sponsored plan merely because the individual's spouse was such a participant. Thus, most spouses who are not

---

[138] Code Sec. 408(o)(2)(B).

[139] Code Sec. 219(c).

[140] Code Sec. 219(g).

actually participants in an employer plan will be able to make the maximum deductible contribution to an IRA. The maximum deduction for such non-participant spouses, however, is phased out for couples with adjusted gross incomes between $150,000 and $160,000.[141]

Deemed IRAs. For tax years through 2010, if a qualified plan allows employees to make voluntary contributions to a separate account or annuity established under the plan, and under the terms of the plan the account or annuity meets the requirements for a traditional IRA or a Roth IRA, the account or annuity will be treated as an IRA and not as a qualified plan for all purposes under the Internal Revenue Code.[142] In addition, a qualified plan will not lose its qualified status solely because it establishes and maintains a deemed IRA program. This provision effectively allows employers to set up traditional IRAs or Roth IRAs for their employees without affecting any other qualified plan. The deemed IRA and contributions to it are subject to ERISA's exclusive benefit and fiduciary rules to the extent otherwise applicable to the plan. However, they are not subject to the ERISA reporting and disclosure, participation, vesting, funding, and enforcement requirements applicable to the eligible retirement plan.

Distributions. Distributions from traditional IRAs must commence by April 1 of the year following the year in which the IRA owner attains age 70½.[143] Failure to take a required distribution results in a 50 percent excise tax.[144] Final Treasury regulations[145] governing required minimum distributions from qualified plans also apply to IRAs with some modifications.[146] Taxpayers with IRAs may use the uniform distribution rules without revising their governing documents. The uniform lifetime table and more details on the distribution rules are discussed at ¶905.02.

Under the final regulations, trustees, custodians, or issuers of IRAs, must provide account holders with information regarding the minimum amount required to be distributed from the IRA each year according to guidance published in the Internal Revenue Bulletin and in tax forms and their accompanying instructions.[147] The IRS has issued guidance that requires an IRA trustee to provide a statement to the IRA owner by January 31 following the end of the calendar year if the IRA owner is alive and subject to a minimum required distribution.[148] The trustee must inform the IRA owner

[141] Code Sec. 219(g)(7).

[142] Code Sec. 408(q)(1).

[143] Code Sec. 401(a)(9)(C).

[144] Code Sec. 4974(a).

[145] Reg. §§ 1.401(a)(9)-0 through 1.401(a)(9)-9.

[146] Reg. § 1.408-8.

[147] Reg. § 1.408-8 Q&A 10.

[148] Cumulative Bulletin Notice 2002-27, IRB 2002-18, 814 (April 16, 2003).

of the required minimum distribution in accordance with two alternatives.

Under the first alternative, the IRA trustee must provide the IRA owner with a statement of the amount and date of the required minimum distribution with respect to the IRA for the calendar year. The trustee may calculate the amount of the required minimum distribution assuming that the only beneficiary of the IRA is not the spouse of the IRA owner who is more than 10 years younger than the IRA owner. The trustee may also assume that no amounts received by the IRA after December 31 of the previous year are required to be taken into account to adjust the value of the IRA as of December 31 of the previous year for purposes of calculating the required minimum distribution with respect to rollovers and trustee-to-trustee transfers.

Under the second alternative, the trustee must provide a statement to the IRA owner that a minimum distribution is required for the IRA for the calendar year and the date by which the distribution must occur and offer to provide the IRA owner, upon request, a calculation of the amount of the required minimum distribution. If the IRA owner makes a request for the calculation, the trustee must make the calculation and provide it to the IRA owner.

Under both alternatives, the trustee must inform the IRA owner that the trustee will report to the IRS that the IRA owner must receive a required minimum distribution for the calendar year. The trustee may provide the statement to the IRA owner along with the statement of the fair market value of the IRA as of December 31 of the previous year that the trustee must provide to the IRA owner by January 31 following the end of the calendar year. The trustee must report to the IRS on Form 5498, "IRA Contribution Information" that a minimum distribution is required. The trustee does not have to report the amount of the required minimum distribution to the IRS. The trustee does not have to file any reports for deceased owners of traditional IRAs or for any Roth IRAs.

The IRS clarified this guidance by providing that IRA trustees may use the first alternative for some IRA owners and the second alternative for other IRA owners. In addition, the IRA trustee may transmit the required statement electronically. The electronic transmission must comply with a reasonable and good-faith interpretation of the applicable law. The trustee may provide the information electronically only if the trustee satisfies the procedures applicable to the electronic transmission of Forms W-2, including the consent requirement described in the regulations under Code Sec. 6051.[149]

---

[149] Cumulative Bulletin Notice 2003-3, IRB 2003-2 (December 20, 2002).

Requiring custodians to inform the IRS that the IRA owner has a required minimum distribution allows the IRS to determine more easily whether account holders have taken the required minimum distribution. Account holders who do not take the required minimum distribution are subject to a 50-percent excise tax on the difference between the required minimum distribution and the actual distribution.[150] The law treats taxpayers with multiple IRAs as having one contract.[151] The required minimum distribution must be calculated separately for each IRA. However, taxpayers may take distributions from their choice of one or more of their IRAs as long as they take total distributions greater than or equal to the total required minimum distribution.[152] This rule allows holders of multiple IRAs to use lower-yielding IRAs to satisfy the minimum distribution requirements. However, distributions from Roth IRAs or Code Sec. 403(b) accounts may not be used to satisfy the required minimum distribution from IRAs.

> ***Example 9.3.*** Brad Peterson is 76 years old. He has two IRAs. On December 31, 2005, the balance in the first IRA is $180,000, and the balance in the second IRA is $120,000. His required minimum distribution for 2006 is ($180,000 + $120,000) ÷ 20.9 = $300,000 ÷ 22 = $13,636.36. Peterson should be able to take all of the required minimum distribution from either account or receive a distribution from each account as long as the total distribution is at least $13,636.36.

The reporting requirements leave some unanswered questions, however. For example, what happens if the custodian were to report, on the IRA owner's request under the second reporting alternative, a lower amount for an IRA owner's required minimum distribution than the true figure? Does the IRA owner have a duty to inform the IRS that the custodian's figures are incorrect? In the case of individuals with multiple IRAs, if required minimum distributions are paid from only one IRA rather than proportionately, will the IRS be able to coordinate those cases in which one or more of an individual's IRAs report no distributions?

The final regulations provide that the election by a surviving spouse eligible to treat an IRA as the spouse's own may be accomplished by redesignating the IRA with the name of the surviving spouse as owner rather than as beneficiary.[153] This election could be beneficial, for example, in that the surviving spouse could name

---

[150] Code Sec. 4974(a).

[151] Code Sec. 408(d)(2).

[152] Reg. § 1.408-8, Q&A 9.

[153] Reg. § 1.408-8, Q&A 5(b).

a new beneficiary. The spouse should then name a new beneficiary immediately.

If the surviving spouse contributed to the IRA or did not take the required minimum distribution for a year under Code Sec. 401(a)(9)(B) as a beneficiary of the IRA, the final regulations, treat the surviving spouse as having made a deemed election to treat the IRA as the surviving spouse's own IRA. The deemed election is permitted only if the spouse is the sole beneficiary of the account and has an unlimited right of withdrawal from it. This requirement is not satisfied if a trust is named as beneficiary of the IRA, even if the spouse is the sole beneficiary of the trust.[154]

Distributions are to be made over a period not extending beyond the life expectancy of the IRA owner and the designated beneficiary.[155] If an owner in pay status dies before his or her entire interest has been distributed, the balance must be distributed to the beneficiary at least as rapidly as it would be under the method in effect at the IRA owner's death.[156]

If distributions have not commenced before the owner's death, the balance must be distributed in five years, subject to the following exceptions.[157] First, if the owner has designated a beneficiary, distributions can be made over a period not extending beyond the life expectancy of the beneficiary. Such distributions must begin not more than one year after the owner's death (or such later date as the IRS may permit).[158] Second, if the designated beneficiary is the owner's spouse, distribution need not commence until the date on which the owner would have attained age 70½.[159]

Also, in the case of holders of multiple IRAs with different beneficiaries, funds can be left in IRAs with younger beneficiaries, thereby maximizing the total possible tax deferral, unless the needs of older beneficiaries dictate otherwise.

If an individual has made no nondeductible contributions to any IRA, the entire amount of any distribution is taxable as ordinary income. On the other hand, if an individual has made a nondeductible contribution to any IRA, special rules apply. Under the special rules, any withdrawal will be taxable on a pro rata basis taking into account the ratio of the nondeductible contributions to the entire amount in the account.

[154] Reg. § 1.408-8, Q&A 5(a) and (b).
[155] Code Sec. 401(a)(9)(A).
[156] Code Sec. 401(a)(9)(B).
[157] Code Sec. 401(a)(9)(B)(ii).
[158] Code Sec. 401(a)(9)(B)(iii).
[159] Code Sec. 401(a)(9)(B)(iv).

Example 9.4. If nondeductible contributions over five years add up to $10,000 and earnings thereon equal $5,000, there is $15,000 in the account. On a withdrawal of $1,200, the tax-free recovery of basis would be $800 and $400 would be taxable.

Another pro rata rule applies if the individual also has a deductible IRA, as shown by the following example.

Example 9.5. The nondeductible IRA is as previously described in Example 9.4. The taxpayer also has $35,000 in a deductible IRA, for a total of $50,000 in both IRAs. On a withdrawal of $1,000 from the nondeductible IRA, only one-fifth, or $200, would be deemed to come from the nondeductible IRA. To compute the taxable versus nontaxable amounts, first divide the total nontaxable amount by the total in both accounts (in this case, $10,000/$50,000 = 0.2 = 20%) Then multiply the resulting percentage by the amount of the withdrawal ($1,000 × 20% = $200). The result is $800 is taxable, and $200 is a tax-free recovery of basis.

The larger the deductible IRA in relation to the nondeductible IRA, the larger the amount of the withdrawal subject to tax. In general, withdrawals before age 59½, death or disability are subject to an additional 10-percent tax.[160] The exceptions to this rule are discussed at ¶ 905.02, under the heading "Additional tax on premature withdrawals."

State law considerations. The income tax treatment of IRA contributions and distributions by individual states varies widely and can present problems for the financial planner and the client alike.

Most states that have an income tax give their residents a deduction equivalent to the federal deduction for IRA contributions. However, some states limit the deduction to amounts less than the federal maximum deduction, and other states bar a deduction altogether.

As to distributions, while most states follow the federal approach, in many states the income tax treatment of IRA distributions is more complex. The financial planner should check applicable state law.

Selecting IRA investments. The two types of IRA investments or approaches to IRA investments are (1) individual retirement accounts with a bank or other qualified person as trustee, and (2) individual retirement annuities (nontransferable annuities issued by a life insurance company).

[160] Code Sec. 72(t).

That formal listing does not do justice to the investment opportunities open to the IRA investor. There is intense competition within the financial services industry for IRA dollars. The competition among financial institutions to provide products aimed at the IRA market has spawned a bewildering array of investment choices. The best advice is to choose investments with the best combination of expected return and risk.

Listed below is a brief summary of the types of investments offered by the various entities marketing IRAs.

Thrift institutions. The investment options that may be offered by savings and loan associations and mutual savings banks for IRA accounts are limited to fixed and variable rate certificates of deposit of varying maturities and money market accounts. The investments are protected by FDIC insurance, up to $250,000 per institution. The fees, if any, charged for opening and maintaining an IRA are relatively small.

Brokerage houses. Brokerage houses, through self-directed IRAs, offer the widest range of investment options, with some offering everything from money market funds, stocks, bonds, and mutual funds to limited partnership interests in real estate.

As long as the self-directed IRA holder keeps the same brokerage house as custodian, he or she can move his or her IRA assets among different investments to get the best return. The ability to reallocate assets offers an important advantage over investments in bank certificates, which the investor cannot dispose of without suffering interest penalties.

Self-directed IRAs, however, do not offer the assured return or safety provided in bank deposits. If the individual invests in government securities, however, at least the securities are backed by the government.

Generally, an investor will pay a price for the flexibility offered by brokerage houses. The house may exact a fee for opening the account, as well as custodial fees, possibly based on a percentage of the amount in the account, with a fixed-dollar minimum.

Zero coupon bonds. Zero coupon bonds based on underlying U.S. Treasury issues, which are often marketed by brokerage houses under such names as CATs (certificates of accrual on Treasury securities) or COUGARS (certificates on government receipts), can serve to lock in good interest rates and maximize returns on IRAs. The zero coupon bond provides the investor with a means to avoid the problem of reinvesting periodic income payments at lower yields if interest rates fall.

U.S. Treasury STRIPS (Separate Trading of Registered Income and Principal Securities) are federally sponsored zero coupon bonds. The STRIP program allows the IRA owner to purchase zero coupon bonds guaranteed by the United States Government.

The zero coupon bond's failure to produce any current income makes such bonds more volatile than ordinary bonds. Also, brokers may charge steep fees for zero coupon bonds based on underlying Treasury securities.

Mutual funds. Mutual funds are often used for IRAs. Mutual funds offer a range of investment options almost as broad as those offered by brokerage houses. Families of mutual funds range from conservative to very aggressive growth funds, plus money market funds. The IRA investor may move from one fund to another without penalty, so long as it is within the same family and maintains the same manager or trustee. FDIC insurance is lacking, but funds are available that invest in government securities. These funds might require trustee fees and charges.

Commercial banks. Commercial banks may offer certificates and FDIC insurance of up to $250,000 on principal and interest, as can thrift institutions. They may market and manage common funds for IRA customers, giving them broad investment options and flexibility. They might also offer other conveniences, such as transfers from checking accounts and direct payroll deductions.

Insurance companies. Some insurance companies, in a bid for IRAs, have set up stock equity funds, fixed-dollar or bond funds, and money market funds, in addition to their more conventional annuity plans. State regulation of insurance companies can be counted upon to provide some element of safety, but FDIC insurance, which is provided to banks, is lacking. The financial planner should check the fees and other charges.

Investment choices in times of low interest rates. IRA contributions should not be put off in anticipation of higher interest rates, but investment choices should be made accordingly. The earlier in a given year the taxpayer makes a contribution, the sooner earnings on the contribution begin to accrue on a tax-deferred basis for traditional IRAs or on a tax-free basis for Roth IRAs. Earlier contributions lead to a greater compounding of interest. Over the life of the IRA, the additional compounding can mean thousands of extra dollars.

Individuals who are anticipating a rise in interest rates might consider nonfixed investments for the short term, such as money market funds or money market-type bank accounts. When interest rates climb, the individuals can move the money to a higher yielding fixed vehicle, such as a CD.

Collectibles. Code Sec. 408(m) penalizes an IRA participant who directs his or her investments into collectibles (art works, rugs, antiques, metals, gems, stamps, coins, alcoholic beverages, and any other tangible personal property so characterized by the IRS). It also provides that, if any IRA assets are used to acquire a collectible, the amount is treated as a distribution taxable to the participant. However, IRA investments are permitted in state-issued coins and the following U.S. gold and silver coins: one-ounce, half-ounce, quarter-ounce, and tenth-of-an-ounce gold bullion coins and a one-ounce silver bullion coin. Also, IRA investments are allowed in certain platinum coins and in gold, silver, platinum, and palladium bullion. However, the bullion must be in the physical possession of the IRA trustee.

Rollovers. Qualified plan distributions may be rolled over tax free into an IRA only within 60 days of distribution (¶ 905.02).[161] However, for distributions made before 2011, the IRS may waive the 60-day rollover period if the failure to roll the funds over within 60 days is due to good cause such as a casualty or disaster.[162] An IRA-to-IRA rollover may be made without tax penalty only once a year.[163] However, an unlimited number of direct transfers from one IRA trustee to another, even if it is the same trustee, may be made without tax penalty. In either case, depending on the particular IRA, the individual might incur interest penalties and might not be able to recover prepaid fees.

.02 Simplified Employee Pension (SEP) Plans Using IRAs

A simplified employee pension (SEP) plan offers employers a simplified way of providing employees with pensions. SEPs make use of IRAs. In plans years beginning before January 1, 1997, employers could establish salary reduction SEPs, as separately discussed below.

While a SEP takes the form of an IRA, employees still can set up their own IRAs. However, participation in the SEP will cause deductions for contributions to the IRA to be phased out for participants with adjusted gross incomes above certain levels (¶ 915.01).[164]

Employer contributions are excluded from the employee's gross income and are not subject to employment taxes. Elective deferrals

---

[161] Code Sec. 408(d)(3)(A).

[162] Code Secs. 402(c)(3) and 408(d)(3).

[163] Code Sec. 408(d)(3)(B).

[164] Code Sec. 219(g).

and salary reduction contributions are also excluded from gross income, but they are subject to employment taxes.

Contributions must not discriminate in favor of highly compensated employees. Not more than $220,000 (for 2006) of compensation may be taken into account.[165] This amount is indexed to inflation.[166]

Basic advantages. SEPs offer a number of advantages:

- Low start-up costs
- Low administration costs
- Contributions need not be made to the SEP every year
- Portability of benefits
- Reduced fiduciary responsibility on the part of the employer

Disadvantages. Possibly, the biggest disadvantage of the SEP is the required inclusion of part-time or seasonal employees—those short-term employees who provide the least contribution to the company's success.[167]

Also, the employer should be made especially aware of the SEP provisions relating to vesting, withdrawals, employee coverage, and the tax consequences on distribution, all of which are separately discussed below.

IRS model SEP agreement. The IRS model Form 5305-SEP may be used by employers in establishing SEPs (Form 5305A-SEP may be used to establish salary reduction SEPs). However, employers who currently maintain any other qualified plan, or who have ever maintained a defined benefit plan, may not use Form 5305-SEP. The advantage of using the model form is that the employer is assured that the SEP meets applicable requirements without the need for an additional ruling, opinion, or determination letter from the IRS. Use of this form simplifies ERISA reporting and disclosure requirements. Basically, all the employer has to do is to provide copies of the completed form to participants and statements showing contributions made on their behalf.

Coverage. The employer must make contributions on behalf of each employee who: (1) has attained age 21, (2) has performed services for the employer during at least three of the immediately preceding five years, and (3) has received at least $450 (for 2006 and indexed to inflation[168]) in pay during the year.[169]

---

[165] Code Sec. 408(k)(3)(c).
[166] Code Secs. 401(a)(17) and 404(l).
[167] Code Sec. 408(k)(2).
[168] Code Sec. 408(k)(8).
[169] Code Sec. 408(k)(2).

Full vesting and withdrawals. All employer contributions to a participant's IRA are fully (100 percent) vested; the employee takes immediate ownership and may withdraw the contributions at any time, but subject to income tax and a special penalty tax on a premature withdrawal.

Employer deductions. The contributions made by the employer under a SEP are deductible for the year in which they are made. The amount of the deduction is limited to 25 percent of compensation paid during the SEP's plan year. An employer may use its taxable year for purposes of determining contributions to a SEP. The excess of the contribution over the 25 percent limit is carried forward and deductible in future tax years in order of time, subject to the 25-percent limit in each succeeding tax year.[170]

Distributions. SEP distributions are subject to the final regulations applicable in determining the required minimum distribution from qualified plans and IRAs. See more details and the uniform lifetime table at ¶905.02 and the IRA rules discussed at ¶915.01.

SEPs for persons past age 70½. A sole proprietor, partner, or corporate employee who is past the age of 70½ may enjoy special benefits through SEPs because SEP contributions may be made even after he or she reaches that age. However, where the SEP holder has reached age of 70½ at the time the contributions are made, distributions must commence at that time. The SEP holder may stretch out the payments by using the uniform lifetime table under the final regulations governing minimum distributions (shown and discussed at ¶905.02). Under the uniform lifetime table, an individual's life expectancy from year to year is never reduced by a full year. Therefore, SEP distributions may be stretched out far beyond the individual's life expectancy, as computed when distributions first commenced.

Salary reduction simplified employee plans (SARSEPs). In plans years beginning before January 1, 1997, an employer could establish a salary reduction (cash or deferred) arrangement as part of a SEP. Such arrangements may not be established in plan years beginning after December 31, 1996. However, SARSEPs set up before 1997 may continue to operate after 1997, subject to the same conditions and requirements that were always in place. Further, new employees hired after December 31, 1996, may participate in a SARSEP of their employer established before January 1, 1997.

---

[170] Code Sec. 404(h)(1)(C).

The maximum annual elective deferral under a SARSEP is $15,000 for 2006 through 2010. The $15,000 limit is indexed for inflation beginning in 2007. This limit applies to total elective deferrals under all plans.

The election to have amounts contributed to a SEP or received in cash is available only if at least 50 percent of the employees of the employer who are eligible to participate elect to have amounts contributed to the SEP.[171] In addition, the election is available only to employers that did not have more than 25 employees who were eligible to participate (or who would have been required to be eligible if a SEP was maintained) at any time during the prior taxable year.[172]

The highly compensated employees may not defer more than 1.25 times the average deferral percentage for all other employees who participate.[173]

For purposes of meeting the participation requirements as to elective (salary reduction) arrangements, an individual who is eligible is deemed to receive an employer contribution.

The attractive feature of a salary reduction SEP, from the employer's standpoint, is that the cost to the employer is limited to the cost of administering the plan. Indeed, to the extent that owners are able to participate, their tax savings through elective deferrals can go a long way toward offsetting the after-tax cost of administration. The latter involves a minimal amount of paperwork and bookkeeping.

Elective contributions are excludable from employees' gross income, but they are subject to FICA and FUTA taxes.

The employer is deemed to make the contributions that are produced by salary reductions. Accordingly, the employer receives a deduction.

.03 SIMPLE Retirement Accounts

The savings incentive match plans for employees (SIMPLE plans) (¶ 925.02) are intended to encourage employers, who currently do not maintain a qualified plan for their employees, to set up a SIMPLE plan. These plans can either be set up as an IRA (discussed here), or as a 401(k) cash or deferred plan (discussed at ¶ 925).

Employers with 100 or fewer employees who received at least $5,000 in compensation from the employer in the preceding year

[171] Code Sec. 408(k)(6)(A)(ii).

[172] Code Sec. 408(k)(6)(B).

[173] Code Sec. 408(k)(6)(A)(iii).

may adopt a SIMPLE plan, if they do not maintain another qualified plan. A SIMPLE plan allows employees to make elective contributions of up to $10,000 in 2006.[174] The limit is indexed for inflation in $500 increments for years 2006 through 2010. Employers must make matching contributions.[175] Assets in the account are not taxed until they are distributed to an employee, and employers generally may deduct contributions to employees' accounts. In addition, a SIMPLE plan is not subject to the nondiscrimination rules (including top-heavy provisions) or other complex requirements applicable to qualified plans.

SIMPLE plans must be open to all employees who meet the $5,000 compensation qualification,[176] and all employer contributions to an employee's SIMPLE account are immediately vested.[177]

Employees covered by a SIMPLE plan may make elective contributions in greater amounts than they could contribute to traditional IRAs. Unlike contibutions to a traditional IRA, the employee's SIMPLE elective contributions must be set up as a percentage of compensation, rather than a flat dollar amount.[178]

Employers must use one of two contribution formulas. First, under the matching contribution formula, the employer is generally required to match employee contributions, on a dollar-for-dollar basis, to a maximum of three percent of the employee's compensation for the year. (However, if the employer satisfies certain notice requirements to employees, in two out of five years, the employer may choose to match only a maximum of one percent of each employee's compensation.[179]) Alternatively, the employer may make a nonelective contribution of two percent of compensation for each eligible employee who earned at least $5,000 in compensation for the year.[180]

> **Planning pointer.** While the SIMPLE IRA plan may be an attractive alternative for a small employer that wants to avoid the administrative complexity associated with other types of qualified plans, those other qualified plans allow greater yearly elective contributions ($15,000 in 2006 and years thereafter).[181]

Clearly, having a qualified retirement plan is a good thing for employees. However, employees need to be aware that they will incur a 25 percent additional tax if they withdraw funds from the SIMPLE plan during their first two years of participation.[182]

[174] Code Sec. 408(p)(2)(A).
[175] Code Sec. 408(p)(2)(A)(iii).
[176] Code Sec. 408(p)(4).
[177] Code Sec. 408(p)(3).
[178] Code Sec. 408(p)(2)(A)(ii).
[179] Code Sec. 408(p)(2)(C).
[180] Code Sec. 408(p)(2)(B).
[181] Code Sec. 401(g)(1)(B).
[182] Code Sec. 72(t)(6).

A participant in a SIMPLE plan may use the minimum required distribution rules that apply to other qualified plans. See ¶ 905.02 for the uniform distribution period table and ¶ 915.01 for how these rules affect distributions from IRAs.

.04 Roth IRAs

Although the maximum permissible contribution to a Roth IRA is not deductible,[183] distributions from the account are received *tax free* if certain requirements are met.[184] The maximum amount that a taxpayer may contribute to a Roth IRA is $4,000 for 2006 and 2007, and $5,000 for 2008 through 2010. The $5,000 limit will be adjusted for inflation in 2009 and 2010. In addition, taxpayers who are at least 50 years old may contribute an additional $1,000 for 2006 through 2010. With a traditional IRA, distributions related to deductible contributions are fully taxed as ordinary income, while nondeductible contributions are taxed as annuity payments (nontaxable return of contributions; ordinary income tax on earnings).

Distributions from a Roth IRA are tax-free to the extent they represent nondeductible contributions to the account. To qualify for tax-free distribution treatment of earnings, the Roth IRA distributions must satisfy a five-year holding period, and must also meet the following requirements:[185]

- The distribution is made on or after the date the individual attains age 59½,
- The distribution is made to a beneficiary (or the individual's estate) on or after the individual's death,
- The distribution is attributable to the individual being disabled, or
- The distribution is a qualified special purpose distribution defined as a qualified first-time homebuyer distribution.[186]

Nonqualifying distributions are treated as coming first from nondeductible contributions. Therefore, distributions become taxable only after all contributions have been recovered.

Unlike a traditional IRA, distributions from a Roth IRA do not have to commence by April 1 in the calendar year in which the individual reaches age 70½.[187]

[183] Code Sec. 408A(c).
[184] Code Sec. 408A(d).
[185] Code Sec. 408A(d)(2)(A).
[186] Code Secs. 408A(d)(2)(A)(iv), 408(d)(5), and 72(t)(2)(F).
[187] Code Sec. 408A(c)(5).

Contributions. A Roth IRA also has the advantage that, unlike traditional IRAs, an individual may still contribute to a Roth IRA after he or she reaches age 70½.[188]

An individual's ability to contribute to a Roth IRA is phased out for single individuals with modified adjusted gross income (AGI) between $95,000 and $110,000, for joint filers with AGI between $150,000 and $160,000, and for a married individual filing a separate return between $0 and $10,000.[189]

Rollovers and conversions. Amounts in a traditional IRA may be rolled over into a Roth IRA and entitled to later tax-free distributions under the Roth IRA rules, if the individual meets both of the following requirements:[190]

- The individual's modified AGI for the year does not exceed $100,000, and
- The individual is not married and filing separately.

If both of the above requirements are met, the 10-percent additional tax will not apply. However, the regular income tax that would have been due if the IRA account balance had been distributed upon retirement must still be paid.

For tax years beginning after 2009, the 2006 Tax Increase Prevention and Reconciliation Act (P.L. 109-222) eliminates the income limit on Roth IRA conversions. In addition, married taxpayers filing seperately will be permitted to make Roth IRA conversions.

Pros and cons of Roth IRAs. Roth IRAs offer financial planners and their clients attractive tax benefits and a good measure of flexibility. However, Roth IRAs also have disadvantages. Accordingly, the following list notes the advantages and disadvantages of Roth IRAs, as contrasted with those of traditional IRAs.

Advantages of Roth IRAs

- If the relevant qualifications are met, qualified distributions from Roth IRAs are not taxable.[191]
- Particularly if the accumulation period is long, the gain from the tax-exempt treatment of the Roth IRA distributions should outweigh the tax deductions allowed for contributions to a traditional IRA. This possibility will be enhanced where high-appreciation potential investments (such as growth-oriented mutual funds) are housed in the Roth IRA.

---

[188] Code Sec. 408A(c)(4).

[189] Code Sec. 408A(c)(3).

[190] Code Sec. 408A(c)(3)(B).

[191] Code Sec. 408A(d)(1).

- The primary tax benefit flowing from the Roth IRA (contributions that will later produce tax-free distributions) does not begin to be phased out until single individuals have modified AGI of at least $95,000 and married taxpayers filing jointly have modified AGI of at least $150,000. The primary benefit associated with traditional IRAs (deductible contributions that will later produce taxable distributions) begins to be phased out, for taxpayers who are active participants in a qualified plan, at the modified AGI levels for the years and filing status indicated below:[192]

Year	Single, Head of Household, and Surviving Spouse	Married Filing Jointly	Married Filing Separately
2006	50,000	75,000	0
2007 and later	50,000	80,000	0

- Unlike a traditional IRA, the law does not require that distributions from a Roth IRA begin in the year in which the individual attains age 70½.[193]
- Also, unlike a traditional IRA, contributions to a Roth IRA may continue after the individual reaches age 70½.[194]
- If a Roth IRA distribution has met the requirements so that it is tax free when received, the distribution would not increase the income base for taxation of Social Security benefits.[195] Depending on the amount of income that the individual receives in addition to the Social Security benefits (¶ 3505), this advantage could be significant.
- Under the ordering rules that determine taxation of withdrawals from Roth IRAs that are not qualified distributions, amounts that do not exceed the individual's accumulated contributions in the account may be withdrawn tax free.[196] These ordering rules differ from the rules applicable to ordinary IRAs that require early withdrawals to be taxed as income and subject to the 10-percent additional tax. Consequently, Roth IRAs give the owner the flexibility to meet unexpected financial emergencies without an immediate tax disadvantage. However, withdrawing money from a tax-advantaged IRA is not something to be done lightly. Taking the money out early forfeits the tax-free build-up on the contributions. Additionally, once accumulated

[192] Code Sec. 219(g).
[193] Code Sec. 408A(c)(5).
[194] Code Sec. 408A(c)(4).
[195] Code Sec. 86.
[196] Code Sec. 408A(d)(4)(B).

Roth IRA contributions are withdrawn, the taxpayer may not contribute them back to the account. However, the individual may continue to make the maximum yearly contributions to the account as long as he or she is eligible to do so.

Disadvantages of Roth IRAs

- No current deduction is allowed for amounts contributed to a Roth IRA.[197] This aspect compares unfavorably with a traditional IRA deduction, which reduces the initial cost of the contribution.[198]
- The advantage to be gained from the tax-free distributions from Roth IRAs might not outweigh the lost deductions for contributions, particularly if the number of years to accumulate the benefits is not great. In addition, the individual might be in a lower tax bracket at retirement than when the individual made the contributions.
- While new contributions to Roth IRAs are likely to be advantageous, the same might not be true of rollovers from traditional IRAs to Roth IRAs. A taxpayer must pay tax on the rollover to the extent that the amount exceeds the taxpayer's basis, if any, in the traditional IRA.[199] The higher the tax bracket a taxpayer is in, the less likely the conversion will be beneficial.
- Some individuals might not feel comfortable with trading the up-front tax advantage available with a traditional, deductible IRA, for the future tax benefit promised by a Roth IRA. Congress may amend the tax law, and nothing can prevent a later Congress from reducing or eliminating the benefits of a Roth IRA.

¶920 PROFIT-SHARING PLANS

Profit-sharing plans offer very attractive tax advantages:

- The employer makes contributions to the plan for the future benefit of employees, but the employer receives a current deduction.
- Employer contributions are not taxable to the employee when made. Thus, all of the contribution is invested.
- Income earned on invested contributions (both employer and employee), earnings on earnings, and realized appreciation are not taxed while they are in the plan.

[197] Code Sec. 408A(c)(1).

[198] Code Sec. 219(a).

[199] Code Sec. 408A(d)(3)(A)(i).

- When the employee receives distributions on retirement, he or she receives favorable tax treatment under the annuity rules (or, if eligible, the lump-sum distribution rules), as discussed at ¶905.02. If the employee takes a distribution in employer stock that has appreciated in value over the plan's basis, he or she pays no tax at all on the appreciation until he or she sells it (unless he or she elects otherwise).

From the employer's standpoint, one of the key features of a profit-sharing plan is that it allows excellent cost control. Also, contributions are permitted by the employer, even in the absence of profits.

.01 Making Plans Effective

Financial planners do not have to be pension and profit-sharing experts. However, they should be legitimately concerned with measures that can serve to make profit-sharing plans more effective instruments for attaining both company and employee objectives. Some of the ideas the financial planner should explore are listed below.

Individual investment choice. The law recognizes individual account plans in which the participant is permitted to exercise independent control over the assets in his or her individual account. In these cases, the individual is not regarded as a fiduciary and the other fiduciaries are not liable for any loss that results from control by the participant or beneficiary. With this approach, the employee is placed in essentially the same position he or she would be in if the employee received cash and was left to invest it. However, the employee has the enormous benefit of the tax shelter offered by the plan.

Under Department of Labor regulations, a plan sponsor can be held liable for imprudent investment decisions by participants of individual retirement account plans unless the plan offers a broad range of investment alternatives.

Choice of funds. Different investment funds are set up within the plan and the plan gives the participant a choice among various funds. For example, the employee might have a choice of bonds, common stock, balanced or venture funds, or some combination of these funds.

Access to cash. A profit-sharing plan may make benefits available to participants after a relatively brief deferral period (as little as two years). However, a 10-percent additional tax is imposed on early withdrawals.[200]

[200] Code Sec. 72(t).

Pension floor. A supplemental defined benefit pension plan can be used to provide a floor for retirement benefits. This defined benefit plan puts part of the risk of the profit-sharing plan's poor performance on the company. This will work, however, only where the company is able and willing to assume the risk. The use of a simplified employee pension (SEP) plan is another possibility to be considered.

Minimum guarantees by company. Some companies, in lieu of adopting a supplemental defined benefit plan, guarantee a minimum annual contribution to the profit-sharing plan out of accumulated earnings in years in which the company has no profits.

Another possibility is for the company to guarantee investment performance up to a set amount.

.02 Incidental Insurance

Profit-sharing plans are looked upon as primarily a source of benefits for the participant while he or she is alive. However, the trust may buy insurance on the life of the participant, provided that the insurance is merely incidental. The insurance is considered incidental in the case of a profit-sharing plan if the aggregate life insurance premiums for each participant are less than one-half the total contributions standing to his or her credit at any specific time. The plan must require that, on retirement, the policy either be distributed to the participant or be converted by the trustee into cash to provide periodic payments.

The premiums paid by the company for incidental insurance are deductible by it, and only the pure insurance portion of the premiums, determined under a special rate table, is taxable to the participant.[201] The participant may be able to exclude the insurance proceeds from his or her gross estate if the policy meets the requirements of Code Sec. 2042.

¶925 CASH OR DEFERRED (401(k)) ARRANGEMENTS

Code Secs. 401(k) and 402(a)(8) permit employers to establish cash or deferred arrangements (often referred to as 401(k)s) as part of a qualified plan. Under a 401(k) plan, the employee is given a choice of receiving cash, making a contribution, or having one made by the employer to a qualified plan and deferring tax on the amount contributed.

---

[201] Reg. § 1.79-3(d)(2).

.01 In General

The plan may be in the form of a salary reduction agreement. For example, under such an agreement, an employee could elect to reduce his or her current compensation or forego a raise and have the amounts foregone contributed to the plan on his or her behalf. This particular feature makes the 401(k) so attractive to employers. Employers may adopt a 401(k) plan without added payroll costs other than the costs of setting up and administering the plan.

The 401(k) plan also has advantages for the employee. A 401(k) plan permits employees to provide for their own retirement with pretax dollars, rather than after-tax dollars. The income generated by their contributions also avoids current taxation. The employees who choose contributions to the plan receive less current cash, but they pay correspondingly lower taxes. By choosing a contribution, employees who would have saved a like amount in the absence of a plan can receive more spendable cash. The employee may change his or her choice of cash or contribution annually, as his or her needs and circumstances change.

Cap on deferrals. An aggregate cap applies to elective deferrals for all plans in which an employee participates. The cap is $15,000 in 2006 through 2010. The $15,000 limit is indexed for inflation in $500 increments in 2007 through 2010. This cap does not bar matching contributions by the employer up to maximum contributions in the aggregate of $44,000 in 2006 by the employer and employee.[202] This limit is indexed for inflation.[203]

Qualification requirements. In general, a Code Sec. 401(k) arrangements must be part of a plan that meets the general requirements for plan qualification (or a plan intended to be a qualified plan). It must also meet special tests that prevent deferrals of highly compensated employees from exceeding a certain level determined with reference to deferrals by nonhighly compensated employees.

Hardship withdrawals. Hardship withdrawals are permitted only if the participant has an immediate and heavy financial need and other resources are not reasonably available to meet the need. In addition, the plan or other legally enforceable agreement must prohibit the employee from making any contribution to the plan or any other plan maintained by the employer for at least six months after the employee receives a hardship withdrawal.[204]

---

[202] Code Sec. 415(c)(1) and Cumulative Bulletin Notice 2005-75, IRB 2005-45 IRB 929 (November 3, 2005).

[203] Code Sec. 415(d).

[204] Reg. § 1.401(K)-1(d)(3)(iv)(E)(2).

Wide availability. Tax-exempt organizations may establish 401(k)s for their employees.[205] Rural cooperatives and Indian tribal governments may also establish 401(k)s, but state and local governments (and their political subdivisions) still may not set up cash or deferred plans.[206]

The Economic Growth and Tax Relief Reconciliation Act of 2001 repealed the "same desk" rule for distributions from 401(k) plans, 403(b) plans, and 457 plans for distributions through 2010. Under the same desk rule, the law treated a participant as not having separated from service if the employee retained the same job for a new employer following a liquidation, merger, or acquisition. Under current rules, an employee will not be prevented from receiving distributions if he or she continues the same job for a different employer following a liquidation, merger, or acquisition.[207]

.02 SIMPLE 401(k) Plans

An employer that does not employ more than 100 employees or maintain another qualified plan may set up a savings incentive match plan for employees (SIMPLE plan) as part of a 401(k) arrangement. SIMPLE plans in the form of an IRA are discussed at ¶ 915.03.

Under a SIMPLE 401(k) plan, the nondiscrimination rules (including the top-heavy rules), do not apply, provided that each of the following three requirements is met:[208]

1. Elective deferrals made by the employee in a year do not exceed $10,000 in 2006. This $10,000 limit is indexed for inflation in $500 increments through 2010. These deferrals must be computed as a percentage of compensation, not as a fixed dollar amount.
2. The employer makes contributions matching the employee's elective deferrals up to a maximum of three percent of employee compensation. Alternatively, the employer may make a nonelective contribution of two percent of compensation for each eligible employee who earned at least $5,000 from the employer for the year.
3. No other contributions are made under the arrangement.

Employer contributions must be immediately vested in the employees' accounts.

[205] Code Sec. 401(k)(4)(B)(i).

[206] Code Secs. 401(k)(4)(B)(ii) and 401(k)(4)(B)(iii).

[207] Code Secs. 401(k)(2)(B)(i), 403(b)(7)(A)(ii), 403(b)(11)(A), and 457(d)(1)(A)(ii).

[208] Code Sec. 401(k)(11).

Planning pointer. SIMPLE 401(k) plans may be an attractive alternative for small employers that want to set up a qualified plan because they lack the administrative complexity that is normally present. However, under a regular 401(k) plan, participants may contribute a greater amount each year than may SIMPLE plan participants.

Employers should also note that unlike SIMPLE IRA plans, SIMPLE 401(k) plans are not allowed to reduce matching contributions below three percent by reason of the two of five year rule (¶915.03).

If the SIMPLE plan rules encourage the establishment of retirement plans by employers that otherwise would not have done so, the SIMPLE plan will certainly be advantageous to employees. However, employees should know that they will incur an additional tax of 25 percent[209] if they withdraw funds from the SIMPLE plan during their fist two years of participation.

¶930 PENSION PLANS

The three basic types of pension plans are as follows:

- A defined-benefit plan, which promises fixed or determinable benefits
- A target plan, which aims at providing a certain benefit but does not promise it
- A money purchase plan, in which there are fixed employer contributions and the participant gets whatever benefit his or her pension account will buy

All three may be viewed as a way of spreading an employee's compensation over his or her lifetime, including the period after retirement. A tax-qualified pension plan offers all the well-known tax advantages of any qualified plan:

- The employer receives a current tax deduction for contributions to the plan.
- The employee is not currently taxed.
- The pension fund grows in a tax-sheltered environment, and benefit distributions receive favorable tax treatment.

From the employer's point of view, pension plans have always involved a long-term commitment to support the plan financially in good times and bad so long as the plan continues. A financially

[209] Code Sec. 72(t)(6).

healthy employer with confidence in future strength is most likely to make the commitment. Terminating pension plans is difficult. The excise tax on reversions is generally 50 percent.[210] This tax is reduced to 20 percent if a qualified replacement plan is set up and maintained.[211] These cost factors encourage the adoption of profit-sharing plans, cash or deferred plans, including salary reduction plans, stock bonus plans, ESOPs, thrift plans, and IRAs. However, none of these plans offers a perfect solution to satisfy the needs of both the company and the employee.

The defined benefit plan still has an important role in some situations. It can provide a benefit based upon 100 percent of average compensation for the highest three years, whereas a profit-sharing plan is basically a plan based on average earnings over the employee's career. This benefit of a defined-benefit plan might be especially important for shareholders-executives in closely held corporations.

The future of defined benefit plans must rest on holding costs in check. The vital element in pension planning remains what it has always been—keeping a balance between costs and benefits on a scale the company can financially support.

The factors to be taken into account and the methods of holding down costs will vary from company to company. These factors and methods depend on the nature of the operation, the character of the work force, its age and composition, turnover, and union affiliations.

A company might decide to participate in a ready-made, master or prototype plan sponsored by a trade association, insurance company, mutual fund, or bank. If a substantial number of employees are involved, the company should most likely call in an expert or experts to tailor a plan to the company's own situation and that of its employees. The experts will marshal the facts, make the projections and actuarial assumptions for various alternatives, and leave the final decision to the company. The company might want to check what the competition is doing or has done. The following is a list of factors that will affect costs and benefits:

- **Coverage and participation.** A plan may exclude certain employees (¶905). Use of independent contractors and leased employees can also hold down costs. Although rules can cause leased employees to be treated as actual employees for employee benefit plan purposes, that is generally not the case if a leased employee works for the employer for less than one year.[212]

---

[210] Code Sec. 4980(d)(1).

[211] Code Sec. 4980(a).

[212] Code sec. 414(n).

- **Type of plan.** Money purchase and target plans, as distinguished from defined benefit plans, can limit costs.
- **Benefit formula.** A formula using a career average compensation yields lower cost than a final pay formula.
- **Incidental benefits.** A no frills approach obviously keeps down costs. Incidental benefits include disability insurance, death benefits, and health and accident benefits for retired employees.
- **Integration with Social Security.** An integrated plan begins with part of Social Security benefits as its base and supplements these benefits so that a coordinated retirement plan results. This integration also can help reduce costs.
- **Employee contributions.** Mandatory contributions can cut costs. Voluntary contributions permit an employee to increase his or her benefits.
- **Vesting formula.** Which minimum standard (¶ 905) will produce lower cost, taking into account age, composition of employees and expected rates of turnover?
- **Retirement age.** The older the retirement age up to age 65, the lower the cost of providing specific benefits. If the plan allows early retirement, reduced benefits on a sound actuarial basis might reduce cost.
- **Investment and actuarial assumptions.** All costs, liabilities, rates of interest, and other factors under the plan must be determined on the basis of actuarial assumptions and methods. Each of these assumptions must be reasonable, taking into account the experience of the plan and reasonable expectations. Alternatively, in the aggregate, the assumptions must result in a total contribution equivalent to the contribution that would be obtained if each assumption were reasonable. Further, the actuarial assumptions and methods must, in combination, offer the actuary's best estimate of anticipated experience under the plan.
- **Past service.** Providing benefits for service before the adoption of the plan obviously adds to cost. Nevertheless, providing benefits for past service might be necessary because of practical considerations. Code Sec. 415 bars the use of such service in determining the maximum benefit allowable.
- **Speed of funding.** Generally, the faster funding takes place, the lower the cost, because income of the fund accumulates tax free inside the plan and would be taxable

outside the fund. However, a cap applies to the deductible amount. In addition, a 10-percent excise tax applies to nondeductible contributions.[213]

.01 Money Purchase Plan

A money purchase pension plan calls for a specified contribution by the employer, such as a percentage of compensation of each covered employee. The plan promises no specific benefit. The employee receives whatever benefit the aggregate contributions, plus the income and gains realized, will buy at retirement. This approach, by itself, gives no recognition to past service. For this reason, employers sometimes supplement it with a unit-benefit approach that may give credit for past service.

.02 Target Plan

A target benefit plan can be described as a hybrid of a defined benefit plan and a money purchase plan. It resembles a defined benefit plan in that annual contributions are based on the amount necessary to buy specified benefits at normal retirement. It differs from a defined benefit plan, however, in that it does not promise to deliver the benefits but merely sets the specified benefit as a target. Thus, as in a money purchase plan (and a profit-sharing plan), the ultimate benefit depends on investment experience.

A contribution to a target plan, once made, is allocated to the separate accounts of the participants, as are increases or decreases in trust assets. Decreases in the trust assets are at the risk of the participants, rather than the employer. In a defined-benefit plan, the employer must make greater contributions if trust assets decrease in value. Likewise, gains in asset value are for the participants, and do not reduce the employer's contributions.

.03 Incidental Life Insurance

Pension plans are primarily for retirement benefits, but they may include incidental life insurance benefits.[214] Under regular pension plans, coverage under an ordinary (e.g., whole life policy) is considered incidental so long as the face amount of the policy does not exceed 100 times the projected monthly benefit. With money purchase pension plans, the same limitation applicable to profit-sharing plans is used. The aggregate premiums for an ordinary

---

[213] Code Sec. 4972(a).

[214] Reg. § 1.401-1(b)(1)(i).

policy must be less than one-half the amount standing to the credit of the participant at any specific time.[215]

The company may deduct the premiums paid for incidental life insurance. The pure insurance portion of the premium, determinable under a special table,[216] (see ¶ 945.01) is taxable to the participant. The participant may exclude the insurance proceeds from his or her gross estate if the policy meets the requirements of Code Sec. 2042.

¶ 935 THRIFT AND SAVINGS PLANS

Thrift plans may possess the predominant characteristics of a profit-sharing plan, a pension plan, or a stock bonus plan. All forms of thrift plans, however, have one common characteristic: the employee-participants contribute some percentage of their compensation to the plan, and the employer matches their contributions dollar-for-dollar or in some other way spelled out in the plan. The plan may or may not be tax qualified.

When the plan is tax qualified, the employer receives a current income tax deduction for its contributions to the plan, and the employee is not currently taxed. The employee's own contribution is not tax deductible but comes out of after-tax dollars. Both employer and employee contributions are free to grow within the plan without tax, and withdrawals and distributions are subject to the same rules applicable to pension, profit-sharing, and stock bonus plans.

In the typical plan, the employee is required to contribute a percentage of his or her compensation if the employee is to participate in the plan. If too high a percentage were required, the lower paid employees would be unable to participate in the plan, and only the highly compensated employee would benefit. Special, complicated nondiscrimination rules contained in Code Sec. 401(m) prevent this situation.

A savings plan differs from the type of thrift plans discussed above in that it may simply be an adjunct plan to an otherwise qualified pension, profit-sharing, or stock bonus plan, with the employee permitted to make voluntary contributions out of after-tax dollars in order to receive the tax shelter that the plan affords. Code Sec. 401(m) limits the amount of voluntary contributions the highly compensated may make depending on the contributions made by other employees.

A thrift plan may permit an employee to suspend his or her contributions temporarily without losing the right to participate in

[215] Rev. Rul. 66-143, 1966-1 CB 79 (January 1, 1966); Rev. Rul. 66-164, 1961-2 CB 99.

[216] Reg. § 1.79(3)(d)(2).

the plan. Most plans permit withdrawals while the employee is still on the job, usually with some conditions attached. Some thrift plans provide for periodic distributions at specified intervals, for example, five years. On retirement, death, or disability, the entire amount in the employee's account usually becomes payable, although the plan may provide for other types of distributions.

¶940 BORROWING FROM THE PLAN

The terms of a qualified plan may permit the plan to lend money to participants without adverse income or excise tax results, if certain requirements are met. This paragraph primarily addresses income tax factors.

In general, the law treats loans from qualified plans as distributions.[217] However, a loan will not be treated as a distribution to the extent aggregate loans to the employee do not exceed the lesser of (1) $50,000, or (2) the greater of one half of the present value of the employee's vested accrued benefit under such plans, or $10,000. The $50,000 maximum sum is reduced by the participant's highest outstanding balance during the preceding 12-month period.[218]

Plan loans generally must be repaid within five years,[219] unless the funds are used to acquire a principal residence for the participant.[220]

In addition, plan loans must be amortized in level payments, made not less frequently than quarterly over the term of the loan.[221] The deduction of interest on all loans from qualified plans is subject to the general interest deduction limitations.[222] However, interest on loans secured by elective deferrals and interest on loans to key employees are not deductible in any event.[223]

An unreasonable rate of interest may cause the plan to be disqualified.[224]

Repayments of loans, including those treated as distributions, are not considered employee contributions under the rules limiting employee contributions or limiting additions to defined contribution plans.

A pledge of the participant's interest under the plan or an agreement to pledge such interest as security for a loan by a third party, as well as a direct or indirect loan from the plan itself, is treated as a loan.[225]

---

[217] Code Sec. 72(p)(1)(A).
[218] Code Sec. 72(p)(2)(A).
[219] Code Sec. 72(p)(2)(B)(i).
[220] Code Sec. 72(p)(2)(B)(ii).
[221] Code Sec. 72(p)(2)(C).
[222] Code Sec. 163(h).
[223] Code Sec. 72(p)(3).
[224] Rev. Rul. 89-14, 1981-1 CB 111.
[225] Code Sec. 72(p)(1)(B).

The plan administrator is subject to loan reporting requirements. In addition, the employee must furnish the employer plan with information on loans.

The Economic Growth and Tax Relief Reconciliation Act of 2001 allows loans to S corporation shareholders, partners, and sole proprietors to qualify for the statutory exemption to the excise tax under the prohibited transaction rules of Code Sec. 4975. This provision is effective for loans made in 2002 through 2010. The prohibited transaction rules still apply to IRAs. If a participant fails to make a loan payment when it is due, the plan administrator may allow a cure period. The IRS limits the cure period to the last day of the calendar quarter after the calendar quarter in which the loan payment was due. if the participant does not cure the default, the entire loan balance including any accrued interest, is treated as a deemed distribution.[226]

¶ 945 GROUP-TERM AND GROUP PERMANENT LIFE INSURANCE

.01 In General

Group-term life insurance has been a valuable tax-favored employee benefit for many years. An employer may provide up to $50,000 of group-term life insurance coverage, on a tax-free basis to employees, under a plan meeting the requirements of Code Sec. 79 and the regulations thereunder. An employer may make any amounts in excess of $50,000 available on favorable terms. The plan may not discriminate in favor of key employees. If the plan discriminates in favor of key employees, the exclusion will not apply to the key employees.[227]

The cost of employer-provided group-term life insurance is treated as wages for FICA purposes to the extent the cost is includible in gross income for income tax purposes.[228]

Retired and disabled employees. The amount of coverage that an employer may provide to a disabled employee tax free is unlimited.[229] The same had been true of retirees. However, retirees are generally subject to the $50,000 ceiling, subject to a grandfather rule for retirees under a plan in existence on January 1, 1984 (or any comparable successor plan), who attained age 55 on or before that date and who either: (1) were employed by the company during 1983, or (2) retired on or before January 1, 1984 and who, when they

[226] Reg. § 1.72(p)-1 Q&A 10.

[227] Code Sec. 79(d)(1)(A).

[228] Code Sec. 3121(a)(2)(C).

[229] Code Sec. 79(b)(1).

retired, were covered by a group-term life insurance plan of the employer (or a predecessor plan).

Tax treatment to employer and employee. If the employer is not a direct or indirect beneficiary of the policy and all other Code Sec. 79 requirements are met, the employer receives a deduction for the premiums paid.[230]

As noted above, up to $50,000 of coverage may be provided tax free to the employee. However, Code Sec. 79 requires that the employee include in his or her gross income an amount equal to the cost of group-term insurance in excess of $50,000, based on the Uniform Premium Table contained in Reg. § 1.79-3(d)(2), less any amount contributed by the employee.[231] The table for insurance provided on or after July 1, 1999, is shown below.

Insurance Provided on or After July 1, 1999

Five-Year Age Bracket	Cost per $1,000 of Protection for One-Month Period
Under 25	$.05
25 to 29	.06
30 to 34	.08
35 to 39	.09
40 to 44	.10
45 to 49	.15
50 to 54	.23
55 to 59	.43
60 to 64	.66
65 to 69	1.27
70 and over	2.06

These cost-per-$1,000 figures are arbitrary and are not related to the actual premiums paid for the coverage. To illustrate how to use the premium tables, consider a key employee who is age 45 and covered by $150,000 of group-term life insurance. His or her gross income attributable to the insurance coverage over $50,000 is calculated as follows:

Step 1—Cost of insurance per $1,000 for an individual age 45 for one year ($.15 × 12) = $1.80

Step 2—Amount to be included in his or her gross income for the insurance coverage over $50,000 (100 × $1.80) = $180

This sum is added to the employee's gross income.

---

[230] Code Secs. 162(a) and 264(a)(1).

[231] Code Secs. 79(a) and 79(c).

Note that state law may decrease the $50,000 ceiling. The amount of tax-free coverage to the employee may not exceed a state ceiling.[232]

.02 Effect of Changing Insurers or Policies

Often, an employer may cancel a group-term policy with one insurance company and purchase a new policy with a new carrier, possibly one offering better service or lower rates.

Two important questions arise as the result of such change:

1. If, following the change, the insured makes a new assignment of incidents of ownership in the new policy to the assignee of the old policy, does the new assignment start a new three-year period for purposes of Code Sec. 2035? This Code section includes in the gross estate of the transferor all gifts of life insurance made within three years of death.
2. Is an assignment of all rights in a current group-term policy and also of rights under any arrangement for life insurance coverage provided by the employer effective as a present transfer of rights under a policy issued by a new carrier?

The IRS in Rev. Rul. 79-231[233] answered "yes" to the first question and "no" to the second. In 1980, the IRS revoked this ruling and gave a conditional "no" answer to the first question, while seeming to adhere to the prior "no" answer to the second question.[234]

The facts in both Rev. Rul. 79-231 and Rev. Rul. 80-289 were identical. They were as follows:

> In 1971 an employee who was insured under a group-term life insurance policy, the premiums for which were paid by the employer, assigned to his spouse all rights under the policy and under any arrangement of the employer for life insurance coverage. In 1977, the employer terminated the arrangement with one insurance carrier and entered into an arrangement with a new carrier identical in all relevant respects to the prior arrangement. Shortly thereafter and within three years of death, the employee executed an assignment of all his rights under the new policy to his spouse.

---

[232] Reg. § 1.79-1(e).

[233] 1979-2 CB 323.

[234] Rev. Rul. 80-289, 1980-2 CB 270.

Rev. Rul. 80-289 states:

> The Internal Revenue Service maintains the view that the anticipatory assignment was not technically effective as a present transfer of the decedent's rights in the policy issued by Z [the new carrier]. Nevertheless, the IRS believes that the assignment in 1977 to D's (deceased employee's) spouse, the object of the anticipatory assignment in 1971, should not cause the value of the proceeds to be includible in the gross estate of the decedent under section 2035 where the assignment was necessitated by the change of the employer's master insurance plan carrier and the new arrangement is identical in all relevant aspects to the previous arrangement with Y [the prior carrier].

Thus, the ruling appears to be based on fairly narrow grounds. Consequently, prudence suggests that assignments of group-term insurance in situations where the employer has changed carriers should follow the requirements of this ruling to the letter:

1. Following a change of carriers, the insured should make a new assignment, spelling out his or her interests in the new policy. The sooner this takes place the better.
2. The assignee should be the same person in both assignments.
3. The new group-term arrangement should be identical in all relevant respects to the prior arrangement. The ruling leaves unanswered the question of whether added amounts of coverage would affect the result. If coverage is added, the insured might make separate assignments to the same assignee of the old and new coverage, lest the new coverage be deemed to taint the entire assignment.
4. All premiums should be paid by the employer.
5. While the ruling appears to deny the effectiveness of the anticipatory assignment, it may be well to provide for an assignment of the assignor's interest in a new policy necessitated by a change of insurance carriers. Under the facts disclosed in the ruling, the anticipatory assignment was of "rights under any arrangement for life insurance coverage of the employees" of the corporation. In those terms, it was broad enough to cover both employer-provided permanent life insurance and group-term insurance. While the ruling does not state that this factor is the basis for the assignment's ineffectiveness, greater specificity might possibly

> obtain a favorable result in situations where the insured, following a change of carriers, does not get around to making a new assignment. Such anticipatory assignments are apparently not harmful, except possibly where the insured, after making the anticipatory assignment, has a change of heart and wants to make the assignment to another person.

Rev. Rul. 79-231, which contains a fairly detailed discussion of anticipatory assignment under local law, indicates that it is to be treated as a contract to assign insurance policies subsequently obtained and may be enforceable if and when a new policy is acquired. In this view, the promise becomes enforceable when the employer acquires a master policy from the new carrier.

If the insured has not made an anticipatory assignment, when a new carrier is substituted, the insured should be free to make an assignment to a different assignee. However, in doing so, the insured runs the risk of having the proceeds includible in his or her gross estate if he or she dies within three years of the new assignment.[235] The risk of that happening might in some circumstances be preferable to having the proceeds go to the first assignee.

.03 Use of a Trust for Group-Term Policy

Use of an irrevocable trust to hold a group-term policy and its proceeds can be an effective way of keeping the proceeds out of the gross estate of the insured,[236] provided the insured is able to avoid the problems associated with Code Sec. 2035 (transfers within three years of death) and its special application to group-term life insurance. The use of a trust might be desirable where substantial sums are involved, the intended beneficiaries are lacking in the necessary qualities of a trustee, and the available settlement options are deemed inadequate.

However, if a trust is to be used, the premiums paid by the employer (and any paid by the insured) will be deemed to be gifts from the insured to the trust beneficiaries. These transfers will be deemed gifts of future interests for which the gift tax annual exclusion for gifts of present interest will not be available.[237] However, the annual exclusion may be made available if the trust contains a *Crummey* power giving the beneficiary the right to withdraw trust contributions of up to the annual exclusion amount ($12,000 for 2006, indexed for inflation) each year on a noncumulative basis.

---

[235] Code Secs. 2035(a) and 2042.

[236] Code Sec. 2042.

[237] Code Sec. 2503(b).

If the trust is set up to provide the surviving spouse a life interest in the proceeds, with limited powers of invasion of principal, at the survivor's death the proceeds may pass to those given remainder interests without being included in his or her gross estate.[238]

.04 Group Permanent Life Insurance

Permanent life insurance, standing by itself, is not within the tax shelter provided by Code Sec. 79 for group-term life insurance, at least according to the IRS. However, regulations permit a policy of group-term insurance to include permanent benefits, provided a great many conditions are satisfied. Complex formulas are included for determining the amount taxable to the employee under such policies.[239]

¶ 950 DEATH BENEFITS

Estate planning factors for qualified retirement plan and IRA benefits are considered at ¶ 955. This paragraph focuses on death benefits payable outside of qualified plans. These death benefits might consist of payments that the employer has contracted to make or may be in the nature of extra compensation for services performed. The payments are generally taxable to the recipient.[240]

The employee may name the beneficiary. The employee might also be in a position to control the type and form of payment to be made to the beneficiary. He or she will, therefore, want to consider the means of control available. The employee should also consider the income tax on the beneficiary or beneficiaries to be selected, along with estate tax effects. Should the executor be named as the beneficiary of all or part of the death benefit or should beneficiaries other than the executor be named? Will enough funds be available to the executor to satisfy any liquidity requirements the estate may have? Other questions include the steps, if any, needed to protect the interests of the beneficiary. Will a trust be needed to protect his or her interests? Will a trust giving the prime beneficiary a life interest be desirable only as a means of avoiding estate taxes on the death of the prime beneficiary? Contractual death benefits are not includible in the employee's estate as annuities within the reach of Code Sec. 2039(a). On the other hand, an estate planner should consider Code Sec. 2037. That section makes lifetime transfers includible in the decedent's gross estate if the beneficiary can obtain property (death benefits) only by surviving the transferor *and* the transferor

[238] Code Sec. 2041(b).
[239] Reg. § 1.79-1(b).
[240] Code Secs. 61(a) and 691(a).

retains a reversionary interest in the property (death benefits) worth more than five percent of its value immediately before death.

The five-percent reversionary interest is of prime concern. The reversionary interest exists if there is a possibility that the beneficiary might die before the employee dies under conditions that will result in the benefits going to the employee's estate. The value of the interest is measured by IRS tables in the first instance. The values given by the tables are presumptively correct. The value varies with the age of the beneficiary.

The IRS has taken the position that, where a nonqualified death benefit is combined with a plan offering disability benefits for the employee, the death benefits are includible in the employee's gross estate as an annuity, subject to the premises of Code Sec. 2039(a). The IRS lost this argument in *W. Schelberg Est.*,[241] but won under the same facts in *J. Looney*.[242] However, for undisclosed reasons, the IRS, after its victory in *Looney*, moved to vacate the District Court's opinion, thereby providing the taxpayer in that case with a victory by default.

The victory accorded the taxpayer by the IRS following *Looney*, along with its defeat in *Schelberg*, offers an opportunity to escape the annuity pitfall, at least in factual situations identical to those in the two cited cases.

The IRS developed another technique for extracting revenue from a contractual death-benefit-only arrangement. The underlying theory is that, when an employee designates a beneficiary of the death benefit, he or she makes a gift that is perfected and complete when death occurs.[243]

The U.S. Tax Court, in *A. DiMarco Est.*,[244] expressly rejected the gift-on-death theory advanced by the IRS in Rev. Rul. 81-31.[245] In *DiMarco*, the decedent was employed by International Business Machines Corporation (IBM) and participated in its death-benefit-only plan. Under the plan, the death benefit could only be paid to a spouse, minor children, or dependent parents. The decedent-employee had no control over the beneficiary designation or the amount or timing of the payment of the death benefit, all of which were predetermined by the plan and subject to the employer's control. The decedent possessed no interest in any fund established to pay the death benefit. Indeed, the death benefit became payable out of the employer's general assets. Subsequently, the IRS conceded this issue. It revoked Rev. Rul. 81-31[246] and acquiesced in *DiMarco*.[247]

[241] CA-2, 79-2 USTC ¶13,321.
[242] DC Ga., 83-2 USTC ¶13,538.
[243] Rev. Rul. 81-31, 1981-1 CB 475.
[244] 87 TC 653, CCH Dec. 43,390 (Acq.).
[245] 1981-1 CB 475.
[246] Rev. Rul. 92-68, 1992-2 CB 257.
[247] 1990-2 CB 1.

However, the acquiescence applies only under the following conditions: (1) the employee is automatically covered by the benefit plan and has no control over its terms, (2) the employer retains the right to modify the plan, and (3) the employee's death is the event that first causes the value of the benefit to be ascertainable.

> **Planning pointer.** A carefully structured death-benefit-only plan, following the outlines of the IBM plan described above, might present a major planning opportunity. The death payments will escape both estate and gift tax, although the recipient of the death benefit will be liable for income tax on the full amount of the payments.

¶955 GENERAL ESTATE PLANNING FACTORS FOR QUALIFIED PLAN AND IRA BENEFITS

Estate planning for qualified plan and IRA benefits should take into account estate tax considerations, the gift tax consequences of choosing various forms of distributions, the treatment of life insurance provided under a qualified plan, and possible liquidity concerns. Commencement of payment of a required joint and survivor annuity automatically qualifies for estate and gift tax marital deductions,[248] as discussed in greater detail below. Apart from the required survivor annuity situation, irrevocably designating any beneficiary will constitute a gift. On the other hand, a nonparticipant spouse's consent to the naming of another beneficiary does not constitute a gift by the nonparticipant.[249] These various factors are explored below.

.01 Gift Tax Factors

The gift tax consequences of a spouse's qualified plan annuity rights and of naming nonspousal beneficiaries are discussed below.

Spouses. As a general rule, a qualified retirement plan must provide a joint and survivor annuity in the case of a married participant who retires, unless the participant's spouse consents to some other form of distribution. Plans generally must also provide a preretirement survivor annuity in the case of a vested participant who dies before the annuity starting date and who has a surviving spouse.[250] The spouse's consent also is needed in such a case to waive the annuity.[251]

The participant will generally not be treated as making a gift to his or her spouse by virtue of the spouse's right to receive either

---

[248] Code Secs. 2056 and 2523.

[249] Code Sec. 2503(f).

[250] Code Sec. 401(a)(11).

[251] Code Sec. 417.

annuity. No gift occurs provided that the spousal joint and survivor annuity automatically qualifies for the estate and gift tax marital deductions[252] as long as only the spouses have the right to receive any payments before the death of the last spouse to die. While the provision applies automatically, the executor or donor may elect not to have it apply.

Presumably, the provision also applies to a joint and survivor annuity payable to a spouse under an IRA.

Nonspousal beneficiary. Irrevocably designating a nonspousal beneficiary will constitute a gift for gift tax purposes. The gift will be of a future interest and will not qualify for the annual exclusion.[253]

Code Sec. 2503(f) makes it clear that a nonparticipant spouse does not make a gift by virtue of a waiver of his or her annuity rights.

.02 Estate Tax

Qualified plan and IRA benefits are fully includible in a participant's gross estate[254] (except for certain grandfathered benefits and possible life insurance proceeds[255]). A survivor annuity paid to a participant's surviving spouse automatically qualifies for the estate tax marital deduction[256] as long as only the spouses have the right to receive any payments before the death of the last spouse to die (for further details, see discussion above in connection with the gift tax). Presumably, the same would be true of an annuity payable under an IRA.

.03 Life Insurance Proceeds

If a qualified plan provides participants with cash value life insurance, the cash value of the policy immediately before death is not excludable from gross income under Code Sec. 101(a). However, the remaining portion of the proceeds paid to the beneficiary is excludable under Code Sec. 101(a).[257] Life insurance proceeds paid under a qualified plan would be includible in the gross estate under Code Sec. 2042, dealing with life insurance policies, rather than Code Sec. 2039.[258] Thus, the participant may be able to exclude the insurance proceeds from his or her gross estate by removing any incidents of ownership that he or she had in the policy more than three years before his or her death.[259] An actual distribution of the cash value of the policy to the participant might be the best way for

[252] Code Secs. 2056 and 2523.
[253] Code Sec. 2503(b).
[254] Code Sec. 2031.
[255] Code Sec. 2042.
[256] Code Sec. 2056.
[257] Reg. § 1.72-16(c)(2)(ii).
[258] Reg. § 20.2039-1(d).
[259] Code Secs. 2035(a) and 2042.

the participant to begin the process of having the proceeds excluded from his or her gross estate. The insured must recognize gross income to the extent, if any, that the cash received exceeds his or her adjusted basis in the policy.[260]

¶960 EMPLOYEE AWARDS

An item of tangible personal property (not cash or cash equivalents) transferred to an employee for length of service or safety achievement is excludable from gross income, subject to dollar limitations discussed below.[261] The item must be awarded as part of a meaningful presentation and under circumstances that do not create a significant likelihood of the payment of disguised compensation.[262]

Length-of-service awards qualify only if made after a minimum of five years of service.[263] Managers, administrators, clerical workers, and other professional employees are precluded from receiving qualifying safety awards because their positions do not involve safety concerns.[264]

The employer's deduction for all awards provided to the same employee generally is limited to $400.[265] The limit is $1,600 in the case of a qualified plan award,[266] defined as an award provided under an established written plan or program that does not discriminate in favor of highly compensated employees.[267] The $1,600 limit also applies in the aggregate to both types of awards.

If the award is fully deductible by the employer, then the full fair market value of the award is excludable by the employee.[268] If the deduction limit prevents a portion of the cost from being deducted by the employer, then the employee receives only a partial exclusion. In such cases, the employee must include in his or her gross income the greater of (1) the portion of the cost that is not deductible, or (2) the amount by which the item's fair market value exceeds the deduction limitation.[269]

¶965 HEALTH PLANS

An employer may provide medical benefits to employees either without charge to the employees or on an employee contribution basis. The benefits may include payment or reimbursement of medical (including dental) expenses of the employee and his or her

[260] Code Sec. 72(e).
[261] Code Secs. 74(c)(1), 162(a), and 274(j)(2).
[262] Code Sec. 274(j)(3)(A).
[263] Code Sec. 274(j)(4)(B).
[264] Code Sec. 274(j)(4)(C).
[265] Code Secs. 162(a) and 274(j)(2)(A).
[266] Code Sec. 274(j)(2)(B).
[267] Code Sec. 274(j)(3)(B).
[268] Code Sec. 74(c)(1).
[269] Code Sec. 74(c)(2).

dependents. In addition, the employer may provide payment of or reimbursement for premiums for accident and health insurance, including major medical and dental insurance, for the employee and his or her dependents.

The amounts the employer pays or reimburses for medical expenses may be completely tax free to employees[270] (including those who are retired[271] and those who have been laid off[272]) and the payments are fully deductible by the employer, assuming that total compensation is not unreasonable.[273] The benefit is especially valuable to employees because medical expenses paid by employees are deductible only to the extent that they exceed 7.5 percent of adjusted gross income[274] and because itemized deductions of any kind operate to reduce tax liability only to the extent that they exceed the standard deduction.

Self-insured medical reimbursement plans are subject to special nondiscrimination rules.[275]

One relatively new type of heath plan is worthy of particular note because it combines the ability to cover health costs on a tax-favored basis with the opportunity for tax-favored savings.

The Medicare Prescription Drug, Improvement, and Modernization Act of 2003[276] added Section 223 to the Internal Revenue Code to permit eligible individuals to establish health savings accounts (HSAs). An HSA is a tax-exempt trust or custodial account established exclusively for the purpose of paying out-of-pocket medical expenses of the account beneficiary who, for months in which contributions are made to an HSA, is covered under a high-deductible health plan.[277] HSAs can receive tax-favored contributions by or on behalf of eligible individuals, and amounts accumulated in an HSA may be distributed on a tax-free basis to pay or reimburse qualified medical expenses.

In the case of an HSA established for an employee, the employee, the employer, or both may contribute to the HSA. Employer contributions to an employee's HSA are treated as employer provided coverage for medical expenses under an accident or health plan and are excludable from the employee's gross income. The employer contributions are not subject to withholding from wages for income tax or subject to payroll taxes. An individual's own contributions to his or

[270] Code Secs. 105 and 106.

[271] Rev. Rul. 82-196, 1982-2 CB 53.

[272] Rev. Rul. 85-121, 1985-2 CB 57.

[273] Code Sec. 162(a).

[274] Code Sec. 213(a).

[275] Code Sec. 105(h).

[276] P.L. 108-173.

[277] Notice 2004-2, 2004-2 IRB 269 (December 22, 2003).

her HSA are deductible in determining adjusted gross income—that is, they are deductible "above the line," whether or not the employee itemizes deductions. However, an employee's own contributions can be made through a cafeteria plan, in which case they are treated as employer contributions that are excludable from the employee's income. Employer provided coverage under a high-deductible health plan is treated like other health plan coverage for tax purposes (see above).

The high-deductible health plan supporting an HSA may be either an insured plan or an employer-sponsored self-insured medical reimbursement plan. For 2006, in the case of individual self-only coverage, the plan must have an annual deductible of at least $1,050 and an annual cap on out-of-pocket expenses (counting deductibles, co-payments, and other amounts, but not premiums) of no more than $5,250. For family coverage, the annual deductible for 2006 must be at least $2,100 and the annual out-of-pocket expense cap cannot exceed $10,500.[278]

The amount that can be contributed to an HSA depends on the type of health plan coverage (i.e., self-only or family), the annual deductible, and the period of coverage during the year. The maximum annual contribution is the sum of limits determined separately for each month.

For 2006, the maximum monthly contribution for an individual with self-only coverage is 1/12 of the lesser of the annual deductible (minimum $1,050) or $2,700. For family coverage, the maximum monthly contribution is 1/12 of the lesser of the annual deductible (minimum $2,100) or $5,450.[279] In addition, individuals age 55 or older can make catch-up contributions in addition to their regular contributions for the year. Catch-up contributions may also be made by a spouse who is covered under an individual's HDHP and who meets the age requirements. For 2006, the catch-up contribution limit is $700 (increasing in $100 increments until it reaches $1,000 in 2009). The catch-up contribution limit is also computed on a monthly basis. So, for example, an individual who is covered by a high-deducible plan for six months during 2006 can make $350 in catch-up contributions (6/12 of $700).[280] Contributions, including catch-up contributions cannot be made by or for an individual over age 65 who is enrolled in Medicare

[278] Rev. Proc. 2005-70, 2005-47 IRB 979 (October 28, 2005).

[279] Rev. Proc. 2005-70, 2005-47 IRB 979 (October 28, 2005).

[280] Code Sec. 223(a)(3)(B).

An HSA distribution that is used exclusively to pay qualified medical expenses (i.e., medical expenses that are not covered by insurance or otherwise, including expenses for nonprescription drugs) of the account holder, his or her spouse, or dependents is excludable from income. The exclusion applies even if the account holder is not eligible to make HSA contributions at the time of the distribution—for example, if the account holder is no longer covered by a high-deductible health plan or has reached age 65 and is no longer eligible to make contributions. What's more, the exclusion applies to distributions for qualified expenses of a spouse or dependent who is not covered by the high-deductible plan.

Planning pointer. An individual can receive distributions from an HSA at any time and for any purpose. A distribution that is not used to pay qualified medical expenses is includable in the gross income of the account holder. In addition, such a distribution generally is subject to a 10 percent penalty tax. However, the penalty tax does not apply to a distribution that is made after the account holder's death or disability—or after the account holder reaches age 65. In other words, funds in an HSA that are not needed for medical expenses can serve as a tax-deferred savings account for retirement.

An employer with more than 19 employees must meet the COBRA continuation coverage requirements of Code Sec. 4980B.

To improve the portability of health insurance coverage, the Health Insurance Act of 1996[281] placed restrictions on the ability of certain group health plans to exclude individuals from coverage based on preexisting conditions or health status. Group health plans, other than government and small employer plans (plans with fewer than two current employees at the beginning of the plan year) that fail to comply with these restrictions face stiff fines.

¶970 BELOW-MARKET LOANS TO EMPLOYEES

Below-market interest loans made by the employer offer an attractive benefit to those employees to whom the loans are extended. An employer may offer loans to employees on a selective basis without meeting the nondiscrimination rules that apply to many other benefits. The loans may serve needs related to the borrower's employment or solely personal needs. For example, an employer may provide a loan to finance the purchase of company stock under a stock purchase plan or stock option. Employer loans might also provide funds for investment, college, or a home purchase.

[281] P.L. 104-191.

.01 Demand Loans v. Term Loans

The tax treatment of these loans is largely favorable for both the employer and the employee.[282] The law draws a distinction between demand loans and term loans.[283] However, some term loans may be considered demand loans.

In the case of a demand loan, the employee-borrower is treated as having paid to the employer-lender imputed interest for any day the loan is outstanding. The employer-lender is treated as having received the amount so paid as interest and as having transferred an identical amount to the borrower as wages.[284]

In other words, the employee has gross income in the amount of the value of the use of the money lent[285] and a possible interest deduction for the imputed interest.[286] However, deductions for personal interest are generally disallowed.[287] The employer receives the imputed interest as gross income and has an equivalent deduction for imputed compensation paid, subject to reasonable compensation limits.[288] The employer's real cost is the loss of the use of the money lent.

In the case of a term loan, the employer is treated as transferring to the employee, on the date of the loan, compensation in an amount equal to the excess of the amount of the loan over the present value of principal and interest (if any) due under the loan. This excess is then treated as original issue discount, and the employer and the employee are respectively treated as receiving and paying interest over the life of the loan.[289] In other words, the employee is taxed up front, but the employee's interest deductions, if any, are spread out over the term of the loan. The situation is just the opposite for the employer. Interest deductions are subject to various limitations and restrictions, including the fact that personal interest is not deductible.[290]

A compensation-related term loan is to be treated as a demand loan if the benefit derived by the employee from the interest arrangement is (1) nontransferable, and (2) conditioned on the future performance of substantial services by the employee.[291]

.02 Factors to Consider

Loans of $10,000 or less. For any day on which the amount of the loan outstanding does not exceed $10,000, no amounts are

[282] Code Sec. 7872.

[283] Code Secs. 7872(a) and 7872(b).

[284] Code Sec. 7872(a)(1).

[285] Code Sec. 61(a).

[286] Code Sec. 163.

[287] Code Sec. 163(h).

[288] Code Sec. 162(a).

[289] Code Sec. 7872(b).

[290] Code Sec. 163(h).

[291] Code Sec. 7872(f)(5).

deemed transferred by the employer to the employee-borrower and retransferred by the employee to the lender.[292]

Imputed interest rates. If the loan is for less than three years or is a demand loan, the imputed interest rate is the federal short-term rate. If the loan is for over three years but not over nine years, the federal mid-term rate is to be used. If the loan is for over nine years, the federal long-term rate applies.[293] The rates are revised monthly.[294]

Advantage of loan secured by residence. If a no-interest loan from an employer is secured by the employee's residence and otherwise meets the Code Sec. 163(h) rule for qualified residence debt, the employee may deduct the interest as an itemized deduction. Thus, the deduction for the interest would provide the employee with a tax benefit only to the extent that the employee's total itemized deductions exceed his or her standard deduction. The imputed interest deemed received is extra compensation income. Securing the loan with a mortgage against the employee's residence might be especially advantageous where the employee's itemized deductions exceed the standard deduction.

¶975 CAFETERIA PLANS

Under a Code Sec. 125 cafeteria plan, a participant may choose between two or more benefits, consisting of cash and qualified benefits. Cafeteria plans that reimburse health and dependent care costs are sometimes called flexible spending accounts. A plan must meet be in writing,[295] be maintained for the exclusive benefit of employees,[296] and must also meet various nondiscrimination requirements. First, the plan must not discriminate in favor of highly compensated employees as to eligibility to participate.[297] Second, the plan must meet a concentration test under which qualified benefits provided to key employees may not exceed 25 percent of aggregate qualified benefits provided to all employees.[298] Third, each type of benefit available or provided under a cafeteria plan is subject to its own applicable nondiscrimination rules and to any applicable concentration test.[299]

Failure to meet the eligibility discrimination tests results in highly compensated employees being taxed on the value of available taxable benefits.[300] Similarly, failure to meet the 25-percent tests

[292] Code Sec. 7872(c)(3)(A).
[293] Code Sec. 1274(d)(1)(A).
[294] Code Sec. 1274(d)(1)(B).
[295] Prop. Reg. § 1.125-1.
[296] Code Sec. 125(d)(1).
[297] Code Sec. 125(b)(1).
[298] Code Sec. 125(b)(2).
[299] Code Sec. 125(f).
[300] Code Secs. 61(a) and 125(b)(1).

results in key employees being taxed on the value of available taxable benefits.[301] Failure to meet individual nondiscrimination requirements generally results in highly compensated employees being taxed on the discriminatory excess.

A cafeteria plan may offer the following nontaxable benefits: group-term life insurance up to $50,000 (¶ 945); coverage under an accident and health plan (¶ 965); and coverage under a dependent care assistance program (¶ 980). Any such benefits chosen and received will be nontaxable if the requirements of the applicable Code sections are met.[302] A plan may also offer, as a qualified benefit, group-term life insurance in excess of $50,000.[303]

The most popular nontaxable benefits under cafeteria plans are health insurance, other medical costs, and dependent care assistance. Some cafeteria plans are known as premium-only plans (POP). A premium-only plan allows the employee to pay the employee's portion of group health insurance for the employee and/or the employee's family with tax-sheltered dollars. Many cafeteria plans allow reimbursement for medical costs and dependent care assistance in addition to the cost of group health insurance. Reimbursements from cafeteria plans are excluded from gross income and excluded from wages for employment tax purposes.

The IRS has ruled that a health flexible spending account cafeteria plan may reimburse employees for the cost of nonprescription drugs.[304] The reimbursement is nontaxable to the employee. By contrast, if an individual incurs nonprescription drug costs, except insulin, that are not reimbursed under an employee benefit plan, such costs are not deductible as an itemized deduction under Code Sec. 213.[305] The cost of food supplements, such as vitamins, that an employee takes to maintain good health is not eligible to be reimbursed under a cafeteria plan.[306] Employers may need to revise their cafeteria plans to provide for the reimbursement of nonprescription drugs if they want to provide this benefit.

A plan may offer benefits that are nontaxable by reason of employee after-tax contributions. For example, a plan may offer participants an opportunity to purchase health coverage with their own after-tax contributions.[307]

---

[301] Code Secs. 61(a) and 125(b)(2).

[302] Code Sec. 125(f) and Prop. Reg. § 1.125-1.

[303] Rev. Rul. 2003-102, IRB 2003-38 (September 22, 2003).

[304] Rev. Rul. 2003-102, IRB 2003-38 (September 3, 2003).

[305] Rev. Rul. 2003-58, IRB 2003-22 (May 15, 2003).

[306] Code Secs. 79(a) and 125(f).

[307] Prop. Reg. § 1.125-1.

A plan may not offer a benefit that defers the receipt of compensation,[308] subject to certain exceptions. One exception is that an employer may offer participants the opportunity to make elective contributions under a Code Sec. 401(k) arrangement.[309]

Under Prop. Reg. § 1.125-1, a salary reduction feature is permitted, but the employee must choose the salary reduction in advance and forfeit any unused benefits. For instance, assume an employee takes a salary reduction of $2,000 in exchange for medical reimbursement in a like amount. However, the employee incurs medical expenses of only $1,500. He or she must forfeit the unused $500. In the past, this "use-it-or-lose-it" applied strictly on a year by year basis. However, starting with the 2005 plan year, IRS rules permit a cafeteria plan to be amended to allow a grace period of up to 2½ months for tapping unused benefits from the prior plan year. If a grace period is adopted, qualified expenses incurred during the grace period may be paid or reimbursed from funds remaining in an employee's account at the end of the prior plan year.[310] A 2½ month grace period may, for example be adopted for a health or dependent care flexible spending arrangement under a cafeteria plan.

The IRS now allows tax-free payment or reimbursements for medical costs under a cafeteria plan to be made by debit cards, credit cards, and other electronic media. However, the employer must have adequate controls in place to assure that such payments or reimbursements are for medical costs only.[311]

¶980 EMPLOYER-PROVIDED DEPENDENT CARE ASSISTANCE

Code Sec. 129 provides that employees may exclude up to $5,000 of employer-provided dependent care assistance from their gross income.[312] The $5,000 limit is not indexed to inflation. For highly compensated employees to be allowed the exclusion, the employer must provide the benefits under a written nondiscriminatory plan.[313]

The dependent care may be directly provided by the employer or by a third party. Payments to anyone for whom the employee or his or her spouse may take a dependency exemption and payments to children under 19 are not eligible for the exclusion.[314] A child attains age 19 on the 19th anniversary of the date on which the child was born. For example, a child born on January 1, 1987, attains age 19 on January 1, 2006.[315]

---

[308] Code Sec. 125(d)(2)(A).

[309] Code Sec. 125(d)(2)(B).

[310] Notice 2005-42, 2005-23 IRB 1 (May 18, 2005).

[311] Rev. Rul. 2003-43, IRB 2003-21 (May 6, 2003).

[312] Code Secs. 129(a) and 129(d).

[313] Code Sec. 129(d).

[314] Code Sec. 129(c).

[315] Rev. Rul. 2003-72, IRB 2003-33 (July 18, 2003).

The amount excluded from gross income reduces the amount of expenses that qualify for the credit available under Code Sec. 21 for payments for household and dependent care services.[316]

Payments made by the employer are deductible under Code Sec. 162(a) to the extent that they are ordinary and necessary business expenses.

Code Sec. 129 plans can be tested for nondiscrimination under the Code Sec. 129 rules themselves. The penalty for failing the Code Sec. 129 test is that all highly compensated employees must include the value of any benefits they receive from the plan in their gross income.[317]

The Economic Growth and Tax Relief Reconciliation Act of 2001 added a new tax credit through 2010 for employers that provide child care benefits to employees. The credit is part of the general business credit. The credit for the employer is equal to the sum of 25 percent of the qualified child care expenditures and 10 percent of the qualified child care resources and referral expenditures.[318] The credit is limited to $150,000 per year.[319] The employer may not receive a deduction for any expenditures used as a base for the credit.[320] In addition, the employer must reduce the basis of the qualified property for expenditures claimed as a base for the credit.[321] The credit is subject to recapture if an employer terminates the child care benefits.[322]

¶985 CODE SEC. 132 FRINGE BENEFITS

Code Sec. 132 excludes certain categories (discussed below) of benefits from gross income and from employment taxes.

.01 No-Additional-Cost Service

The entire value of any no-additional-cost service provided by an employer to an employee (including an employee's spouse or dependent children) or a retiree is excludable from the employee's or retiree's gross income. The exclusion is available to highly compensated employees only if the employer meets nondiscrimination requirements.[323] The employer may incur some additional cost or loss of revenue, provided it is not substantial.[324] Also, another business with which the employer has a reciprocal written agreement may provide the services.[325] For example, two airlines may provide seats for each other's employees.

---

[316] Code Sec. 129(e)(7).
[317] Code Secs. 61(a) and 129(d)(1).
[318] Code Sec. 45F(a).
[319] Code Sec. 45F(b).
[320] Code Sec. 45F(f)(2).
[321] Code Sec. 45F(f)(1)(A).
[322] Code Sec. 45F(d).
[323] Code Sec. 132(j)(1).
[324] Code Sec. 132(b).
[325] Code Sec. 132(h)(3)(i).

Examples of such excluded services include airline, railroad, bus or subway seats, if customers are not displaced. Hotel rooms provided to employees working in the hotel business would also be excluded. Utilities may also qualify if excess capacity is available, e.g., phone services provided to phone company employees.

.02 Employee Discounts

An employee may exclude a qualified employee discount from his or her gross income.[326] The value of a discount on services provided to an employee is excluded from the employee's gross income to the extent that it does not exceed 20 percent of the selling price of the services to customers.[327] In the case of goods, the discount may not exceed the gross profit percentage of the price at which the employer offers the property for sale to customers.[328]

In either case, the property or service must be of the same type that is ordinarily sold to the public in the line of business in which the employee works. In addition, the discount must go to a current employee or retiree, the spouse or dependent child of either, or the surviving spouse or dependent child of a deceased employee.[329]

However, the discount is not excluded from the gross income of highly compensated employees unless the employer meets certain nondiscrimination requirements.[330] Also, discounts on the sale of real estate or personal property held for investment (e.g., stock) do not qualify for exclusion. If an employee receives a discount on such property, the employee must include the discount in his or her gross income.[331] For example, if a real estate broker allows a discount on the sale of real estate to a real estate salesperson, the salesperson must include the discount in his or her gross income.

To some extent, employee discounts on merchandise can be a substitute for cash compensation. To the extent that the discount is close to the employer's gross profit on the particular merchandise, it might be very steep.

The law does not limit the aggregate value of the discounts that an employee may exclude from his or her gross income. However, practical considerations might limit the ability of an employee to take full advantage of the available discounts.

---

[326] Code Sec. 132(a).
[327] Code Sec. 132(c)(1).
[328] Code Sec. 132(c)(2).
[329] Code Sec. 132(h).
[330] Code Sec. 132(j)(1).
[331] Code Secs. 61(a) and 132(c)(4).

.03 Working Condition Fringe Benefits

The fair market value of any property or services provided to an employee is excluded from the employee's income to the extent that the cost of the property or services would be deductible as ordinary and necessary business expenses if the employee had paid for such property or services[332] The nondiscrimination requirements do not apply to working condition fringe benefits.[333] Thus, a highly compensated employee may exclude working condition fringe benefits from his or her gross income even if the employer provides such benefits only for certain employees.

Examples of working condition fringe benefits include the following:

- Use of a company car or airplane for business purposes
- Subscription to publications useful for business purposes
- Use of a car by full-time salespersons
- Certain consumer product testing by employees
- A bodyguard or a car and a driver provided for security reasons
- On-the-job training
- Business travel
- Under certain circumstances, outplacement services[334]

.04 De Minimis Fringe Benefits

Property or services not otherwise tax free are excluded from an employee's gross income if their value is so small as to make accounting for the benefits unreasonable or administratively impracticable. The frequency with which similar fringe benefits (otherwise excludable as de minimis fringes) are provided by the employer is to be taken into account, among other relevant factors, in determining whether the fair market value of the property or services is so small that accounting would be unreasonable or impracticable.[335]

Examples of de minimis fringe benefits include occasional use of copying machines, supper money, taxi fare because of overtime, and holiday gifts with a low fair market value.

Subsidized eating facilities operated by the employer on or near the employer's business premises are considered de minimis if revenue from the facilities equals or exceeds direct operating costs.

[332] Code Secs. 132(a) and 132(d).
[333] Code Sec. 132(j)(1).
[334] Rev. Rul. 92-69, 1992-2 CB 51.
[335] Code Secs. 132(a) and 132(e)(1).

The employer may restrict the use of the facilities to a reasonable classification of employees, as long as the employer does not discriminate in favor of highly compensated employees.[336]

.05 Qualified Transportation Fringe Benefits

Certain employer-provided transportation fringe benefits are tax free to employees.[337] These benefits include transit passes or vouchers worth up to $105 (for 2006) a month; commuting in a commuter highway vehicle worth up to $105 (for 2006) a month; and employer-provided parking worth up to $205 (for 2006) a month at or near the employer's premises or a place from which the employee commutes by mass transit.[338] The aggregated tax-free amounts for transit passes and highway vehicle commuting may not exceed $105 a month (for 2006).[339] These amounts are indexed for inflation.[340] Employer-provided benefits above these amounts are taxable to the employee.[341]

These qualified transportation fringe benefits may not be provided on a tax-free basis to partners, two-percent S corporation shareholders, sole proprietors, or independent contractors.[342] However, the IRS said, in Notice 94-3,[343] that the de minimis and working condition fringe benefit rules apply to partners, S corporation shareholders, and independent contractors to the same extent as they did before 1993 when qualified transportation fringe benefits came into being. Therefore, these taxpayers may still exclude from their gross income employer-provided transit passes valued at no more than $21 a month, and employer-provided business-transportation-related parking (but not commuter parking) under the preexisting rules.

.06 On-Premises Athletic Facilities

The value of any on-premises athletic facilities (gym or other facilities) provided for employees, their spouses, or their dependent children is not includible in the employees' gross income.[344]

.07 Moving Expenses

Employer reimbursements of qualified job-related moving expenses are received tax free by employees.[345] To be a qualified

---

[336] Code Sec. 132(e)(2).

[337] Code Sec. 132(f)(2).

[338] Code Secs. 132(f)(1), 132(f)(2) and Rev. Proc. 2002-70, IRB 2002-46 (October 30, 2002).

[339] Code Sec. 132(f)(2)(A) and Rev. Proc. 2002-70, IRB 2002-46, (October 30, 2002).

[340] Code Sec. 132(f)(6).

[341] Code Secs. 61(a) and 132(f)(2).

[342] Code Secs. 132(f)(5)(E), 401(c), 1372(a) and Reg. § 1.132-9.

[343] 1994-1 CB 327.

[344] Code Sec. 132(j)(4).

[345] Code Sec. 132(a).

moving expense reimbursement, the moving expenses must be of a kind that would be deductible if the employee incurred them or paid them directly.[346] Moving expenses are deductible only if the new job is at least 50 miles farther from the employee's old home than the old job was from the old home.[347] In addition, the taxpayer must be a full-time employee for at least 39 weeks of the 12-month period following the move. Alternatively, the individual may perform services as a self-employed individual on a full-time basis for at least 78 weeks during the 24-month period following the move, of which at least 39 weeks must be during the 12-month period following the move.[348] Deductible moving expenses include only the cost of moving household goods and personal effects from the old residence to the new one, and the cost of traveling to the new location. Expenses for en route lodging are deductible, but the expenses of meals during the move are not deductible. Move-related expenses such as house-hunting trips, temporary living expenses, and closing costs are not deductible.[349]

.08 Qualified Retirement Planning Services

For tax years through 2010, the Economic Growth and Tax Relief Reconciliation Act of 2001 added an exclusion for qualified retirement planning services. This exclusion allows employees and their spouses to exclude from their gross income the value of qualified retirement planning services provided by employers that sponsor qualified retirement plans.[350] Qualified retirement planning services include retirement planning advice and information.[351] The exclusion applies to highly compensated employees only if the employer offers the retirement planning services to all employees of the group who normally receive information and education about the plan.[352] The exclusion does not extend to related services such as tax return preparation.

---

[346] Code Sec. 132(g).
[347] Code Sec. 217(c)(1).
[348] Code Sec. 217(c)(2).
[349] Code Sec. 217(b)(1).
[350] Code Sec. 132(a)(7).
[351] Code Sec. 132(m)(1).
[352] Code Sec. 132(m)(2).

Chapter 10

Transfers Includible in the Estate at Death

Overview .... ¶1001
The Costs of Transfer .... ¶1005

¶1001 OVERVIEW

A fundamental consideration in estate planning is how the decedent will make transfers of property owned at death and to whom. If the decedent did not make any arrangements for such transfers, state law will determine the distribution of the individual's estate.

Thus, an individual's main concern will be with giving favored heirs as much as possible, while holding transfer costs to a minimum. The toll takers along the line of transfer include federal and state tax collectors, executors or personal representatives, trustees, attorneys, appraisers, accountants, guardians, court clerks, and others. Those who perform services are entitled to the fees and charges, which the law and fair play allow them.

The federal estate tax usually will cause practitioners and their clients the greatest concern. The unlimited marital deduction[1] can completely offset estate tax liability, as discussed at ¶1005. In addition, for the unmarried and the married who do not make full use of the unlimited marital deduction, an applicable credit amount (unified credit) is available to offset or reduce federal estate tax liability. This credit has the effect of exempting from tax the first $2,000,000 in 2006, 2007, and 2008; and $3,500,000 in 2009 (see ¶405).[2] The top marginal rate is 46 percent in 2006, and 45 percent for 2007, 2008, and 2009.

---

[1] Code Sec. 2056(a).

[2] Code Sec. 2010(c).

The 46 percent (2006) toll has the estate planner looking for escapes through lifetime planning. For example, the estate planner may want to change forms of ownership of assets, unwind joint ownership arrangements, develop family gift programs, set up living trusts, plan life insurance coverage and employee benefits, and utilize family income-splitting and other techniques. In the right circumstances, a private annuity arrangement for the estate owner may be suitable. However, practical considerations limit what the estate planner can do or should do. He or she might not be able to get consent to the unwinding of joint ownership. A client's individual circumstances and the law also may shackle the estate planner. For instance, the death of a spouse will deprive the client of the marital deduction unless the client remarries.

Inevitably, transfers at death will occur and the client must face up to the costs of transfer, consisting primarily of probate costs and federal and state death taxes. The federal estate tax is repealed for estates of decedents who die in 2010. The paragraphs that follow explain how the federal estate tax works, discuss other transfer costs, and compare different modes of transfer in terms of cost.

Although this chapter, and the ones immediately following it, will discuss effective ways to reduce estate taxes, the best way for many clients to deal with the tax consequences of increased wealth will be through increased reliance on lifetime gifts, which are discussed in Chapter 4.

¶1005 THE COSTS OF TRANSFER

For many individuals the biggest cost of transferring property at death is the federal estate tax, despite the relief for married individuals provided by the unlimited marital deduction.[3] However, not every individual is married, and not every married individual is prepared to take full advantage of the unlimited marital deduction.

As a result, the federal estate tax is something to be reckoned with not only by those currently with estates within its reach, but also by those who in the foreseeable future may have estates subject to its bite. Once the decedent has exhausted possible deductions and the unified credit, the effective estate tax rate is a flat 46 percent for estates of decedents who die in 2006. Congress made many changes to the estate tax in the Economic Growth and Tax Relief Reconciliation Act of 2001.[4] However, because of the sunset provision in the law, the estate tax is repealed only for the estates of decedents who die in 2010.

[3] Code Sec. 2056(a).

[4] H.R. 1836.

The estate tax is neither a tax on the estate or a tax on the property in the estate. It is an excise tax, a tax on the right or privilege of a deceased person to transfer property to beneficiaries of the decedent's own selection or to those state law may select for the decedent. However, the estate tax is measured by the value of the taxable estate. Property includes items that few would think of as property. Property includes some property that the decedent disposed of long before death.

All the property that the decedent owned is valued at the date of death, or six months later if the executor or administrator so chooses, provided the later date reduces the value of the estate and the estate tax payable. This amount is the decedent's gross estate.[5] Then, the estate may deduct funeral expenses, debts or obligations of the estate, administration and probate costs, the fees of the personal representative (executor or administrator), attorney's fees, casualty losses during the administration of the estate, state death taxes and certain other taxes including income taxes on income received after the death of the decedent and property taxes not accrued before death.[6] The decedent's gross estate is further reduced by the amount of any bequest made to the decedent's spouse that qualifies for the marital deduction.[7] Finally, the estate may deduct any qualifying bequests to charity.[8]

The difference between the gross estate and the allowable deductions is the taxable estate.[9] Determining the estate tax under the unified estate and gift tax rate schedule is a bit more complicated. The complication comes about primarily because the tax takes into account certain lifetime transfers, plus the gift tax payable on those transfers. The estate tax is determined by applying the rate schedule to the aggregate of certain lifetime transfers and the taxable estate, and then subtracting, the gift taxes payable on those lifetime transfers. The completed lifetime transfers to be taken into account are only those made after 1976 and, by the same token, the gift tax subtraction, or offset, is limited to the tax on post-1976 gifts.[10]

For gifts made after August 5, 1997, the gift tax statute of limitations bars the IRS from revaluing any gift for estate tax purposes, as long as the gift was originally adequately disclosed. However, for prior gifts, the U.S. Tax Court has held in *F. Smith Est.*[11] that the gift tax statute of limitations provision of Code Sec. 2504(c) applies only to revaluation of lifetime gifts for gift tax

[5] Code Sec. 2031(a).

[6] Code Secs. 2053 and 2054 and the regulations thereunder.

[7] Code Sec. 2056(a).

[8] Code Sec. 2055(a).

[9] Code Sec. 2051.

[10] Code Sec. 2001(b).

[11] 94 TC 872, CCH Dec. 46,648.

purposes but does not bar the revaluation of lifetime gifts for estate tax purposes. The same result was reached by the U.S. Court of Appeals for the Eighth Circuit in *C. Evanson.*[12] As a result, the value of gifts prior to August 6, 1997, that do not have a readily determinable market value (such as traded securities) should be supported at the time of transfer by appraisals and other documents establishing fair market value.

What about transfers includible in the decedent's gross estate under one or more Code provisions, which include lifetime transfers with retained interests, rights, or powers, as detailed below? Certainly, counting such transfers twice would be unfair, once as lifetime transfers and again as part of the decedent's gross estate. Hence, they are not to be counted as lifetime transfers. However, the gift tax payable on such transfers is available as a subtraction or offset in determining the estate tax.

In addition, the gift tax paid by a spouse can be subtracted where the transfer subject to tax is included in the decedent's gross estate and is considered to have been a transfer made in part by the surviving spouse under the gift-splitting provision.[13] However, if the spouse's gift tax was offset by the unified credit (discussed below) the credit used will not be restored to the surviving spouse because the transfer involved is included in the decedent's gross estate.

One further factor affects taxable transfers made within three years of death. Generally, the transfer itself is not includible in the gross estate, but the amount of the gift tax paid on the transfer is includible. This is the so-called "gross-up" rule under Code Sec. 2035(b). The gift tax subject to the rule includes the tax paid by the decedent or his or her estate on any gift made by the decedent or his or her spouse. It does not, however, include any gift tax paid by the spouse on a gift made within three years of death that is treated as having been made one-half by the spouse, because the spouse's payment of such tax would not reduce the decedent's gross estate.

These are the basic rules. The following discussion explains how they might apply in a specific situation.

---

[12] CA-8, 94-2 USTC ¶60,174.

[13] Code Sec. 2513.

Example 10.1. Jeff Jones' estate at his death in 2006 is valued at $3,100,000. He made taxable gifts of $250,000 since 1977 and paid no gift taxes because of the unified credit. Items deductible under Code Sec. 2053 amount to $100,000 and the state death tax deduction is also $100,000. His estate has no losses. There are no charitable deductions. His wife is given a marital deduction bequest equal to the value of the adjusted gross estate less the maximum applicable exclusion amount, i.e., $2,000,000.

Gross Estate	$3,100,000
Administration Expense	100,000
State death taxes	$ 100,000
Adjusted Gross Estate	$2,900,000
Marital Deduction	900,000
Taxable Estate	$2,000,000
Taxable Gifts	250,000
Tentative Tax Base	$2,250,000
Estate Tax on Tentative Tax Base	$ 895,800
Credit for Gift Taxes Paid	0
Tax Before Applicable Credit Amount	$ 895,800
Applicable Credit Amount*	780,800
Estate Tax Payable	$ 115,000

* While, in effect, the applicable credit amount (unified credit) against the estate tax is reduced to the extent that the applicable credit amount is used against the gift tax, in order to preserve the applicable credit amount taken in computing gift taxes, it is necessary for the applicable credit amount to appear in the estate tax computation before computing the total tax liability. The total taxable gifts are added to the taxable estate in computing the tentative tax base, but the applicable credit amount used against the gift taxes is reflected as a reduction of the gift taxes payable. If the applicable credit amount did not appear in the estate tax computation, the effect would be to cancel out the effect of taking the credit in computing the gift tax.

Exhibit 8

Unified Rate Schedule for 2006 through 2009

(A) Amount subject to tax equal to or more than—	(B) Amount subject to tax less than—	(C) Tax on amount in column (A)	(D) Rate of tax on excess over amount in column (A)
—	$ 10,000	—	18%
$ 10,000	20,000	$ 1,800	20
20,000	40,000	3,800	22
40,000	60,000	8,200	24
60,000	80,000	13,000	26
80,000	100,000	18,200	28
100,000	150,000	23,800	30
150,000	250,000	38,800	32
250,000	500,000	70,800	34
500,000	750,000	155,800	37
750,000	1,000,000	248,300	39
1,000,000	1,250,000	345,800	41
1,250,000	1,500,000	448,300	43
1,500,000	2,000,000	555,800	45
2,000,000	2,500,000	780,800	46 in 2006 45 in 2007-2009

The applicable exclusion amount is $2,000,000 in 2006, 2007, and 2008 and $3,500,000 in 2009 (see ¶ 405).

.01 Other Credits Against the Estate Tax

Code Sec. 2012 allows a credit for gift taxes on pre-1977 gifts includible in the donor's gross estate. This credit does not apply to post-1976 gifts. As noted above, gift taxes paid on such gifts are subtracted in computing the estate tax.

Code Sec. 2013 provides a credit for federal estate taxes paid on prior transfers to the decedent by persons who died within 10 years before or two years after the decedent's death. The amount of the credit allowed depends on how many years the transferor predeceased the decedent.

A credit is also available for foreign death taxes, as spelled out in Code Sec. 2014.

.02 What Is Included in the Federal Gross Estate?

The federal estate tax does not allow any property exemptions as some state death taxes allow for a homestead or household goods.

Everything that normally passes for property is included. Stocks, bonds, mutual funds, notes, mortgages, bank accounts, cash, jewelry, personal effects, real estate, automobiles, furniture and furnishings, works of art, patents, copyrights, trademarks, business interests, and limited partnership investments are a part of the gross estate. In short, all property is included to the extent of the decedent's interest at the time of death.[14]

Also includible are rights and claims that one might not ordinarily think of as property. A claim for an income tax refund, a leasehold interest, an interest in a trust, a judgment that the deceased may have held against someone, a debt owed the decedent which he or she had all but forgotten, and other like items are included.

However, these things are familiar to most persons. The estate tax provisions include other things that one would not normally think of as being owned by the decedent. A brief listing of these items follows:

- The value of any property that a person has given away during his lifetime in which he retains: (1) the right to enjoy the income for life; (2) the right to designate who is to enjoy the income or the property itself; or (3) the right to vote transferred stock in a "controlled" corporation, i.e., where the decedent or his relatives own 20 percent or more of the stock.[15]
- The value of any property which a person has given away during his lifetime, but which is to become effective in possession and enjoyment by the donee only upon the donor's death and in which the donor at the time of his death retains a reversionary interest worth more than five percent of the value of the property at that time.[16]
- Property that the decedent transferred during his or her lifetime, in trust or otherwise, without adequate and full consideration, in which he or she retained the right to revoke, alter, amend or terminate the enjoyment of the property transferred.[17] This provision applies to revocable living trusts set up by the decedent.

[14] Code Sec. 2033.
[15] Code Sec. 2036.
[16] Code Sec. 2037.
[17] Code Sec. 2038.

- Annuities providing a death benefit, a refund, or survivor income.[18]
- The full value of property held by the decedent as a joint tenant with any other person (other than his or her spouse), except as it may be shown that someone else contributed part or all of the consideration for its acquisition. If it is a joint tenancy with a right of survivorship between spouses, in general, only one-half of the value is includible in the gross estate of the first to die.[19]
- The value of property subject to a general power of appointment possessed by the decedent that is, generally, property which the decedent may not have actually possessed and enjoyed but which he or she could direct to be transferred to the decedent, the decedent's estate, the decedent's creditors or the creditors of the decedent's estate.[20]
- Insurance policies on the decedent's life payable to his or her estate or as to which he or she is deemed to possess an incident of ownership such as the right to name the beneficiary, to borrow against the cash surrender value, or otherwise control the economic benefits of the policy, including, in some cases, the power to control a corporation that owns the property.[21]
- The value of any interest of the surviving spouse as dower or curtesy or any statutory substitute.[22]
- Property from which a qualified terminable interest property (QTIP) income interest was payable.[23]
- A catchall provision that brings into the gross estate property in which the decedent has any interest at the time of his or her death, to the extent of the decedent's interest.[24] Code Sec. 2033 includes everything that normally passes for property, as previously noted. For example, the regulations under this section note that a cemetery lot owned by the decedent is part of his or her gross estate, but its value is limited to the salable value of that part of the lot which is not designated for the interment of the decedent and the members of his or her family. Notes or other claims held by the decedent, according to the regulations, are likewise included even though they are canceled by the decedent's will.[25]

Code Sec. 2035(d) provides that the value of property transferred within three years of death for an adequate consideration in money or

[18] Code Sec. 2039.
[19] Code Sec. 2040(b).
[20] Code Sec. 2041.
[21] Code Sec. 2042.
[22] Code Sec. 2034.
[23] Code Sec. 2044.
[24] Code Sec. 2033.
[25] Reg. § 20.2033-1(b).

money's worth is generally not includible in the gross estate of the transferor. However, the decedent's gross estate will include interests in property that would otherwise have been included under Code Secs. 2036, 2037, 2038, or 2042 if the decedent had retained such interest.[26] For example, under Code Sec. 2042, the value of life insurance policies transferred within three years of death would be included in the decedent's gross estate.

In addition, under Code Sec. 2035(c), the value of all property transferred within three years of death (other than gifts eligible for the annual gift tax exclusion) is included for purposes of determining the estate's qualification for redemption of stock to pay death taxes, special use valuation, and 14-year deferral of payment of estate tax.[27]

Code Sec. 2035(b) includes in the gross estate any gift tax paid by the decedent or his or her estate on any gift made by the decedent or his or her spouse within three years of the decedent's death.

What must surely come across from this recital of Code provisions is that the estate tax collector is well armed. Careful planning is required to reduce or avoid the estate tax.

.03 Administration and Probate Costs

Executor's commissions are apt to account for a good chunk of the cost of transferring property on death. Generally, the testator may fix the amount of commissions or provide that no commissions are to be paid.

Most states have a statutory fee schedule for executors or personal representatives that applies, unless the will or an agreement of the parties provides otherwise. Some states call for reasonable compensation to be determined by the probate court. The statutory fees vary among the several states. Fees are usually a percentage of the estate inventory or receipts and disbursements, with higher percentages at lower brackets, ranging from five percent to seven percent or so on for the first $5,000, down to two percent to three percent on amounts above, say, $200,000, with still lower percentages on larger estates. The probate court might sometimes award additional compensation for extraordinary services.

Attorneys' fees, although usually not fixed by statute, and no longer guided by bar association fee schedules, will usually parallel those allowed the personal representative or executor. However, special services will call for special compensation, and general rules

---

[26] Code Sec. 2035(a).

[27] Code Secs. 303, 2032A and 6166.

for valuing an attorney's services will apply. An attorney's compensation will take into account, among other things, customary fees, the standing of the attorney, the time spent, the amount involved, the results obtained.

Other miscellaneous expenses include court filing fees, costs of appraisals, accounting services, and stenographic services. These expenses, however, are generally a relatively small part of the cost of administration. Overall, to be on the safe side for planning purposes, a financial and estate planner can figure on probate and administration expenses of roughly nine percent on an estate of $50,000, on down to 5.5 percent on a $1 million estate, and probably no less than 4.5 percent on the very largest estates.

The IRS, in Technical Advice Memorandum 8838009,[28] ruled that for an administration expense to be deductible, the expense must be found to be reasonable for purposes of both state probate law and federal estate tax law. Hence, the IRS may independently determine the reasonableness of an expense allowed by a state probate court. The IRS successfully advanced this point of view in *J. White.*[29]

[28] June 17, 1988.

[29] CA-2, 88-2 USTC ¶ 13,777, cert. granted 2/27/89, cert. dismissed 110 SCt 273.

Chapter 11

Wills

Overview ....¶1101
What a Will Can and Should Do ....¶1105
Will Forms and Provisions ....¶1110
Execution of the Will ....¶1115
Joint, Mutual, and Reciprocal Wills ....¶1120
Instructions and Data Sources Outside the Will ....¶1125

¶1101 OVERVIEW

Every individual has in force a legal plan for the disposition of his or her property upon death. A will sets forth the testator's plan for the disposition of his or her probate property at death. The testator might own some property that will be disposed of outside of probate. For example, the testator's interest in property owned as joint tenants with right of survivorship will pass to the other joint tenants. Pension funds, life insurance policies, and property in a living trust will pass to the named beneficiaries. A living trust can do many of the same things as a will, but not everybody has a will or an effective trust. If a person does not have either, the law steps in and disposes of the individual's property at death as it assumes the decedent would have wanted, in the light of existing family relationships. As far as a particular individual is concerned, the law's assumptions may or may not be well-founded. Even when the beneficiaries selected by law are the same as those that the individual would have chosen, there is no advantage in simply allowing the law to take its course.

On the contrary, having a will offers many advantages. A will enables an individual to decide both type and amount of property to be distributed to primary beneficiaries. A will can also specify the terms and conditions governing the distribution of property to contingent beneficiaries. Naming contingent beneficiaries is important in case the primary beneficiaries predecease the testator or the primary beneficiaries choose to disclaim property. The will should state how the testator wants any disclaimed property to be distributed. A will also allows an individual to address other estate administration matters such as appointing a guardian for minor children, selecting an executor, and directing which beneficiaries will bear the burden of the estate's debts and taxes.

An individual, for example, might be perfectly willing to have any property owned at death divided equally between the individual's surviving spouse and surviving children, if that is what applicable state law provides. However, the idea of a court-appointed guardian stepping in to control the children's share might be objectionable. The person might prefer to set up a trust, with an independent trustee, to make investments and distribute income and principal, as circumstances dictate, without having to go to court for approval and without making formal accountings. Similarly, the individual might feel that a surviving spouse's interest deserves the protection of a trust. Such provisions can be accomplished only by a properly drafted will.

Estate planning involves a great deal more than arranging for the transfer of property on the death of the owner, which is the fundamental purpose of a will. The estate planner has to do several things to help a client plan a will. The estate planner will want to look at the existing forms of ownership of property, the possibilities of lifetime personal and charitable giving, the use of living trusts, existing life insurance arrangements, qualified retirement plan and IRA benefits and beneficiary designations, and other property interests that may or may not pass under the will. If the estate owner has an interest in a closely held business, the estate planner will want to examine those interests carefully in terms of their legal and tax structure and the planning opportunities and pitfalls present in those interests.

When the estate planner has the complete picture of the individual's assets and liabilities, as well as any plans for heirs and other intended beneficiaries, then he or she can begin thinking about committing to paper, the client's will, desires, and intent. That word "intent" is most important. When an estate planner or a court looks at a will with a view to interpreting it, if there is any ambiguity in the language used, the object is to find out what the person who made the will, the testator, intended. The objective of the will draftsman should be to put into clear language what the testator really wants.

The testator's intent must be an informed intent. He or she will know better than anyone else about his or her heirs and what he or she would like for them. The testator will also know better than anyone else about his or her various property interests and their economic potential. But, chances are the testator will know little, if anything, about estate planning.

Some estate planning matters may be beyond the competence of the estate planner. In that case, the estate planner has to seek expert counsel. The point is that a will cannot adequately reflect a client's intent and consent to transfer property on death unless it is an informed consent. It cannot be an informed consent unless the estate planner tells the client what is possible, and why certain will provisions are necessary. There are shorthand terms used in wills that have become encrusted with legal meanings. Many of these terms escape the layman unless the estate planner explains them.

¶1105 WHAT A WILL CAN AND SHOULD DO

A will is a legal declaration of what an individual wants done with his or her probate property or estate upon death. From a legal standpoint, any sensible person can do almost anything with his or her probate property through a will. However, there are limitations on disinheriting a spouse, the duration of a trust, the amount that the individual may give to charity in some situations, and a few other restrictions that vary from state to state.

The important thing is not so much what the client can do but what the client should do. What should the testator think about in terms of will provisions? What types of things do not belong in a will?

A will should not merely express the testator's hopes and wishes, but it should also make positive directions and positive dispositions of property. Hopes and wishes tend to confuse things. Beneficiaries and family members might question the interpretation of a provision in the will, such as whether the testator's wish is to be taken as a command. Even if a court should conclude that the wish in question is still a wish, the parties might wish the dispute had never arisen.

Courts and lawyers refer to this sort of wishing type of language as precatory language. However, "precatory" may also connote something stronger than a wish, but less than a command or direction. In any case, wishes and precatory language are generally to be avoided, unless the wish expressed is clearly only a wish. It should not be a direction or command used to dilute or in any way modify positive directions or commands.

The will can cover a wide variety of details about what is to be done about the estate and property. Following are some of the key areas the estate owner should consider.

.01 Family Income During Administration

Getting a stream of income flowing out of an estate or trust takes time. In the meantime, the family, whose income has been shut off by the death of the family member, may suffer unless some special provision has been made or is available. If the surviving spouse already has enough cash or liquid assets, together with insurance proceeds, then income from the estate or trust during administration is less important. A joint account is almost as good a source of ready cash as a separate account, except that in most states the survivor will not be able to access the joint account until state tax waivers are presented. This process usually involves only a short delay, from a few days to two weeks. The surviving spouse will not have a liquidity problem if a living trust has been set up to deliver family income on the death of the settlor. Neither does a problem occur if, under state law, the surviving spouse is given an adequate allowance. Alternatively, the will can provide that the surviving spouse is to receive a specified amount each month, commencing with the testator's death and continuing until the estate makes a distribution of a specified amount, or trust income begins to flow. If a trust is to be used, another approach might be to provide that the estate may advance income, which accrues to the trust, to the surviving spouse while the trust is being set up.

.02 Funeral Arrangements

Funeral arrangements are best left to the discretion of the family or in special instructions addressed to the family or the executor independent of the will. The testator should leave some discretion to the family, which allows the family to accommodate unusual circumstances. If the testator inserts desired funeral arrangements into the will, the executor and surviving family members might not discover the instructions until after making funeral arrangements. In addition, a problem could arise as to the force and effect of the instructions, if they are included in the will.

.03 Tangible Personal Property

Tangible personal property includes jewelry, furniture and furnishings, cars, works of art, clothing, and basically any moveable item. Disposing of tangible personal property in a separate will provision is best, for two good reasons:

1. If the testator does not dispose of such property in a separate will provision, it will generally go into the residue of the estate, i.e., what is left after debts, administration expenses and specific bequests have been paid. Then, the executor or

personal representative might be obligated to sell these items. Selling the items could create a variety of problems, such as failure to realize true value, loss of sentimental value, and mechanics and expenses of sale.

2. If the tangible personal property is left in the residue and passed on to the legatee or legatees, they might have to pay income taxes on the amount distributed to them to the extent that the estate has distributable net income. This income tax rule does not apply to distributions of specific bequests.

The testator should make specific bequests of the more valuable items to named individuals, and include a catchall provision to take care of miscellaneous items. The testator may give the person named in the catchall specific bequest outright ownership or instruct him or her to divide the items among family members, as he or she sees fit.

.04 Legacies

There are four types of legacies to be considered: (1) gifts of specific property; (2) general gifts of money; (3) gifts of money payable out of a particular source; and (4) gifts payable out of the residue or what remains after other legacies, expenses and debts have been paid.

Different rules apply to different types of bequests, which the estate owner will want to take into account. If a bequest is of specific property, and the testator sold or otherwise disposed of the property before death, the legatee will get nothing, unless the testator makes some other provision in the will. The legatee's loss is technically known as "ademption." Similarly, if the estate owner, after having made a specific bequest of property, puts a mortgage on the property, the legatee generally takes the property subject to the mortgage. In that case, there is a partial ademption.

The other thing that the estate owner needs to know is what the law provides in the situation where the estate assets are insufficient to satisfy all of the estate's debts, costs, and bequests. The law steps in and provides an order of priority in cutting bequests, unless a will provision, called an abatement clause, directs otherwise. The bequests out of residue are the first to be cut or abated. If there is still a deficiency, the general money bequests are cut, followed by the money bequests payable out of specific sources, and then the bequests of specific property.

The estate owner should also consider the effects of inflation, deflation, and other factors resulting in growth or shrinkage of the estate, because these may affect the various legatees. If, for example, the estate is smaller than expected, those beneficiaries given cash bequests do relatively better than the residuary legatees, who are usually the testator's prime concern. On the other hand, if the estate proves to be larger than anticipated, the residuary legatees do better, and any problem is not so serious.

One way of handling the shrinkage problem is to provide that the executor is to pay cash bequests only if the estate is valued at more than a set minimum. Another way is to make the cash bequests, not in terms of fixed dollars, but in fractions of the estate, possibly not to exceed a fixed amount. If the testator is concerned about the specific legatees losing out because of inflation, the testator could use the fractional bequest approach, with any fixed-dollar limitation high enough to compensate for possible inflation.

.05 Real Estate

Real estate can present special questions. For example, will the real property be retained by the executor or sold? If it is to be sold, when and how is it to be sold? What if the real estate market at the time is soft? May the executor mortgage the property? The surviving spouse may have certain interests in real estate acquired during marriage by virtue of the common law rights of dower or curtesy or modern statutory substitutes under applicable state law. There are other considerations if an individual owns real estate outside the state of residence where the will is to be probated. Problems may arise as to rights in the property under "foreign" law, the power of the executor to deal with it, and the need for ancillary probate proceedings in the jurisdiction where the real estate is situated. The estate would also incur the added expense of such proceedings. These factors invite consideration of alternatives such as lifetime gifts, sales of the foreign real estate, and the use of trusts.

The law usually defines real estate to include not only land but also the improvements on the land. Property law has many complex rules and exceptions, most of which are of interest only to lawyers, judges, and title companies. Often, the family residence is the subject of a specific bequest to the surviving spouse. The client might want to know whether he or she should gift the residence during life, leave it to the spouse outright in the will, or in trust. Another issue is whether the surviving spouse is to be given an interest that will qualify for the marital deduction, including a QTIP interest, or a more limited interest. A more limited interest could be a nonqualifying term interest, with a remainder interest left to other family members. The testator might also leave the remainder interest to a charity, to take advantage of the special rules that apply to charitable gifts of a remainder interest in a personal residence or farm (¶515.03). Also, the estate planner should remind the client of the $250,000 exclusion of gain on the sale of a residence by the surviving spouse.[1] See Chapter 12 for a full discussion of the marital deduction.

Incidentally, condominiums and cooperative apartments merit many of the same considerations as any other type of family residence. However, their precise status as real or personal property may require expert legal counsel in some states.

Certain farm or other business real property includible in the estate may require special attention. Generally, property includible in the gross estate is valued at its fair market value for estate tax purposes. However, Code Sec. 2032A provides that an executor may *elect* to value *qualified* real property used for farming or business based on its value for current use, rather than on its highest and best use. Details of this provision are discussed in ¶ 1005.

.06 Gifts of Income

The will may provide for periodic payments of income to named beneficiaries. The will may direct the executor to buy annuities or to set up a trust for the purpose. The principal would go to others on the death of the income beneficiaries or at some earlier date fixed in the trust.

.07 Disposing of the Bulk of the Estate

After payment of debts, administration expenses, taxes, and specific legacies, the executor must dispose of the bulk of the estate called the residue or remainder. All or a good portion of it will usually go to the surviving spouse of a married testator. If it is to be shared, the executor will be directed to divide it into the fractional shares indicated for the named beneficiaries. Obviously, there will be problems in making a physical division of some types of property. And there will be uncertainties of valuation if the assets are to be distributed in kind to the beneficiaries and values have changed after their valuation for estate tax purposes. Provisions for the sale of properties to permit equal division and to avoid valuation problems are available.

Providing for contingent beneficiaries of the residuary if the primary beneficiaries do not survive the testator is important. Usually, the children of the primary beneficiary will be named contingent beneficiaries. The testator could have two or more primary beneficiaries, both of whom have children. In such a case, the will should specify whether the children of each prime beneficiary are simply to take their parent's share, divided up equally among the children of that particular parent, or whether all of the children of all of the

[1] Code Sec. 121.

deceased prime beneficiaries are to share equally in the combined shares of their deceased parents. The first is known as a per stirpes distribution; the latter, is a per capita distribution. The following example illustrates how each works.

> ***Example 11.1.*** The residue is to go to Adam and Bob in equal shares and, if either or both die before the testator, then to their children living per stirpes. Adam and Bob both die before the testator. Adam has one child, Carla; and Bob has two children, Debra and Earl. Carla gets half of the residue. Debra and Earl each get one quarter. If a per capita distribution were called for, then Carla, Debra, and Earl would each get one third.

.08 Protecting Minor Beneficiaries

A testator could make a bequest to a beneficiary who is a minor at the time of payment. In such a case, the minor must usually have a guardian appointed by the probate court to hold and manage his or her bequest during the period of minority. In some states, a will designation of a guardian of the property would be acceptable. Guardianship entails expense and usually requires judicial accounting. The age of majority for most purposes has been lowered from the formerly universally accepted 21 to 18 in almost all states. The estate planner should check applicable state law. A trust is usually preferred over a guardianship because it offers greater flexibility and control while avoiding unnecessary red tape and expense. Provision may be made for use of trust income or principal for the benefit of the minor. The trust may terminate on the minor's attaining majority or continue until a later age.

.09 Protecting Adult Beneficiaries

If one has an adult beneficiary who is incompetent, he or she has a choice between some form of guardianship (the form varies in different states) and a trust, with the latter generally being preferable. If the adult is competent, then the choice is between an outright bequest of the full amount or one payable in installments over a limited period, or the use of a trust. A trust is favored if the testator feels a trustee is needed to supply one or more attributes missing in the beneficiary. These missing attributes could include lack of money sense, lack of investment experience or judgment, and inability to resist the demands of other family members.

.10 Trust Provisions

Trusts are flexible instruments, and the testator has a great deal of leeway in deciding how and when the trust is to distribute income or principal, how long the trust is to last, what the trust is to do with income or principal left in the trust on termination, and many other details. If the trust is for the benefit of the surviving spouse and is to qualify for the marital deduction, it will have to take the form of a power-of-appointment trust, a QTIP trust, an estate trust, or a portion trust. The subject of trusts is treated extensively in Chapter 6, and the marital deduction is covered in Chapter12.

.11 Choice of the Executor or Trustee

One looks for trustworthiness, competence, availability, and cost factors when choosing an executor or trustee. Selection of trustees is discussed in Chapter 6; selection of executors is discussed in Chapter14.

.12 Business Interests

If the estate includes business interests including a sole proprietorship, a partnership interest, an interest in a closely held corporation or in a professional corporation, many different planning opportunities and pitfalls are opened up. These opportunities and pitfalls are considered in separate chapters devoted to planning for each form of business interest. See also ¶1105.05 as to business real estate.

.13 Life Insurance Interests

The will provisions, if any, dealing with life insurance should be integrated with existing insurance arrangements (Chapter 7).

.14 Payments of Death Taxes

The testator can allocate the burden of federal estate taxes and state death taxes and provide either that they are to be borne by the estate or the individual beneficiaries. If the will contains no provision for the allocation of death taxes, the executor must check state law. Many states have apportionment acts allocating the death taxes proportionately to the items generating the taxes. If the gross estate for federal estate tax purposes will consist solely of probate assets, placing the burden on some specific portion of the assets might be desirable. If the gross estate will include both probate and nonprobate assets, the testator may allocate the tax burden to the probate assets or some portion of them, to the nonprobate assets, or to both. Code Sec. 2207B provides a right of recovery from persons who received property that is includible in the gross estate under Code Sec. 2036. A will provision may waive this right of recovery provided the will specifically indicates this result and contains a specific reference to "QTIP," "QTIP trust," Code Sec. 2044, or Code Sec.

2207A. A bequest to the surviving spouse that qualifies for the marital deduction reduces the burden of federal estate taxes. Therefore, the marital deduction bequest will normally not be called upon to share in the burden of federal estate taxes under the tax apportionment provisions of the will. The testator should also consider the burden of death taxes on other beneficiaries.

.15 Survivorship

Occasionally, determining in what order the person making the will and his or her spouse died or in what order two or more beneficiaries died will be important. This issue is readily manageable if there is clear evidence of the order of deaths. Sometimes such clear evidence does not exist. The problem becomes most acute where husband and wife die near the same time and the availability of the marital deduction is an issue. That aspect is discussed in Chapter 12 on the marital deduction. Some consideration should also be given to the broader aspects, such as when a bequest is contingent on the testator's survival, or on that of a primary beneficiary. Practically all states have adopted the Uniform Simultaneous Death Act, which provides that if two persons die under circumstances such that one cannot tell who died first, each is presumed to be the survivor to his or her property. But that provision applies only when one cannot tell the order of deaths, and it does not apply if a will provides for a different presumption. Apart from the simultaneous death situation where the order of deaths cannot be determined, one should consider situations in which deaths of the individuals involved occur within a relatively short time of one another. In such a case, to avoid two probate proceedings within a short time, the estate planner might want to provide for survivorship for a specified period of time as a condition of the bequest. A marital deduction bequest conditioned on survivorship of up to six months may still qualify for the marital deduction if the spouse survives that long. But that time limitation is of no particular importance if the marital deduction is not involved. One might provide for survivorship for a more extended period as a condition of a bequest.

.16 Investment Powers

The executor has very limited power to invest unless provided for by the will. Thus, the executor's basic job is to marshal assets, liquidate them, and distribute them as fast as possible. If the executor holds on to an asset beyond a reasonable time and the estate suffers a loss, the executor can be held liable. The executor also runs a risk of liability for holding on to cash too long without putting it in an interest-bearing account. If large sums are involved beyond the current FDIC $100,000 insurance limit, maintaining many separate accounts might be inconvenient. The executor might choose to keep all the funds in one account if the financial institution provides collateral for the account. Investment in short-term government paper may be permitted as an exception to the general rule against investment. However, if the maturity dates do not conform to the estate's cash requirements, the executor may not be able to invest in such instruments. The testator will want to consider these potential problems facing the executor, and might want to give somewhat greater freedom than the law otherwise allows.

A trustee is in a different position. He or she has implied investment powers if the trust does not provide them. Some states limit trustees to a list of approved investments of a generally conservative stripe. In others, the trustee is subject to the "prudent investor rule," which establishes criteria for determining the prudence of investments by a trustee. The American Law Institute promulgated the prudent investor rule as a part of the Restatement (Third) of Trusts in 1992. Under this rule, the trustee is to evaluate the prudence of an investment based on its impact of the total investment portfolio rather than as a single investment. The trustee must consider the risk and potential return of any investment, and the trustee may invest in any asset consistent with the objectives of the trust. In addition, the trustee may delegate the investment and management functions under certain conditions. The prudent investor rule is a part of the Uniform Prudent Investor Act (UPIA) promulgated by the Uniform Law Commissioners in 1994. The District of Columbia and a majority of the states have enacted the UPIA. The UPIA is a change to the "prudent man rule," which allows investments that a prudent man would make in the management of his own affairs with the objective of preserving the corpus. The American Law Institute promulgated the prudent man rule as a part of the Restatement (Second) of Trusts in 1959. The prudent man rule is more restrictive than is the prudent investor rule. The prudent man rule may still be the standard in some states. The settlor can free a trustee of these restrictions by a provision in the trust giving the trustee broad discretion, short of investing in something illegal. How much power is given necessarily depends on the trustee selected and his or her abilities. If the trustee is strong on integrity and weak on investment experience, the trustee should consider permitting employment of a professional investment advisor. Generally, if there is any hesitancy about conferring broad investment powers, setting out investment guidelines is better than restricting the trustee unduly. The trustee needs to be able to respond to changing market conditions. The fluctuations in money market interest rates and Treasury bills that have developed in the past offer an example.

¶1110 WILL FORMS AND PROVISIONS

There is no single or standard form of will. Individuals differ, and their wills differ. The basic objective of all wills is the same—to transfer the probate property from the estate of the testator to chosen beneficiaries. To this end, wills tend to follow a common structure, with variations, additions, and subtractions appropriate for the testator and the testator's estate. A checklist of common components of a will, and some not so common components, follows.

.01 Testator's Identity

Some wills not only identify the testator by name, but also indicate family relationships, persons named in the will, and family members who are omitted. The additions might be useful, but are generally considered better left to a separate letter of instructions to the executor.

.02 Domicile

Commonly, the will declares the testator's domicile in a certain state or jurisdiction. Domicile is important in determining such things as the formal requirements of a will and its execution, property rights, rights of the surviving spouse, and other important matters. The declaration made in a will is some evidence of domicile at the time of execution and at the time of death, but it is not controlling. Still, including a declaration is a good idea, if it is made with due regard for the legal ramifications. If an individual has two or more residences in different probate court districts, the will should indicate the principal residence and district of probate.

.03 Revocation of Prior Wills and Codicils

The testator revokes prior wills and codicils. (Codicils are instruments executed with the formality of a will modifying or adding to a prior will and legally considered as forming a part of the prior will.)

.04 Funeral Directions and Disposition of Body

Funeral and burial or cremation directions are best handled outside the will, if for no other reason than that they may come too late if family members or the executor rely on the will. The same is true of any plans the testator might have for the disposition of body or organs for the use of others because of the added factor of legal complications in the disposition of the body by will. All states have adopted the Uniform Anatomical Gift Act (1968) that sets out the rules. Almost half the states have adopted the Revised Uniform Anatomical Gift Act (1987). The testator should obtain forms for such gifts from the intended donee organization.

.05 Cemetery, Monument, Memorials

The testator might make provision for perpetual care and bequests made for masses or other religious services. Designating the individual by title who holds a position in a named institution as the recipient of the bequest, i.e., the pastor of St. Mary's, rather than a named individual, is better. The named individual might not be at the institution at the time of the testator's death.

.06 Payment of Debts

This provision directs the payment of debts, funeral expenses, the costs of administration, and possibly the source from which such amounts are to be paid. The testator might also want to establish as debts items that might not otherwise qualify. For example, a loan from a child might have been made on an informal basis and the testator might wish to make formal acknowledgment. However, because debts are deductible for estate tax purposes, the IRS might suspect that the testator is using the debt to get an estate tax deduction for what is really a bequest. The will might provide that the executor is to pay all of the testator's just debts that are not barred from enforced collection by the statute of limitations.

.07 Payment of Taxes

This provision establishes the source of payment of death taxes as well as other expenses of estate administration. Often death taxes will be made payable out of the residue instead of being apportioned among all the assets includible in the taxable estate, whether passing under the will or outside the will. Examples of assets that pass outside the will are life insurance, jointly held property, and revocable living trusts. If a marital or charitable deduction gift is payable out of the residuary estate, the testator might not want the marital or charitable deduction portion of the residue to bear the tax burden, especially insofar as the marital or charitable deduction portion has not contributed to the tax burden. Also, the tax burden may operate to reduce the marital or charitable deduction and possibly increase estate taxes. By the same token, the testator might not want other assets qualifying for the marital or charitable deduction and passing to the surviving spouse or charity under other portions of the will or outside the will (but includible in the adjusted gross estate) to bear the burden of taxes not attributable to the transfer to the surviving spouse or charity. If the residue is divisible into a marital or charitable deduction portion and a nonmarital or noncharitable deduction portion, then the latter may be given the burden of death taxes. However, the testator would not want to do so if such a provision would seriously distort or impair the testator's intent to benefit the beneficiaries of the nonmarital or noncharitable share. If the latter appears likely, the testator should make some other allocation of the tax burden.

.08 Administration Expenses

A clause addressing payment of administration expenses identifies the source for payment of expenses incurred in collecting, maintaining, and distributing an estate. Examples of such expenses include executor and attorney's fees, court costs, storage costs, accountant's fees, and appraiser's fees. Administration expenses are often paid out of the residue of the estate; however, payment can be apportioned among all the assets includible in the estate. As in the case of tax payment clauses discussed above, the attorney who drafts the will must take special care to avoid erosion of the marital and charitable deduction, and possibly increasing estate taxes, when drafting an apportionment clause for administration expenses. In the absence of an apportionment clause for administration expenses, state law governs.

The U.S. Supreme Court ruled in *O. Hubert Est.*[2] that an estate did not have to reduce its marital and charitable deductions by the amount of administration expenses paid out of income generated during administration by assets allocated to a marital and charitable trust. Pursuant to *Hubert*, an executor could use the income generated by the marital or charitable assets to pay administration expenses if the use of such income was not a material limitation of the right of the surviving spouse or charity to the income and if the executor had been granted the discretion to use such income for that purpose. To pass the "material limitation" test of *Hubert*, the expenses paid had to be properly chargeable to the income generated by the marital or charitable assets under applicable state principal and income allocation rules.

However, after the decision in *Hubert*, the Treasury modified the Regulations governing the calculation of the deduction for administration expenses and the marital deduction. Reg. § 20.2055-3(b), which applies to estates of decedents dying on or after December 3, 1999, provides that the charitable deduction is reduced by the

[2] 97-1 USTC 60,261, 117 SCt 1124, aff'g CA-11, 95-2 USTC ¶ 60,209.

amount of estate transmission expenses paid from the charitable share. Estate transmission expenses are expenses arising from the decedent's death and the necessity to transfer the decedent's property to his or her beneficiaries. The charitable deduction is also reduced by estate management expenses paid from the charitable share but attributable to a property interest that is not a part of the charitable share. However, the charitable deduction is not reduced for the estate management expenses attributable to and paid from the charitable share. Estate management expenses are expenses incurred in connection with the investment of estate assets or maintenance during a period of administration.

In addition, Reg. § 20.2056(b)-4(d), which applies to estates of decedents dying on or after December 3, 1999, provides that transmission expenses paid from the marital share reduce the marital deduction. The marital deduction is not reduced for estate management expenses attributable to and paid from the marital share unless the executor deducts such expenses as an administration expense on the estate tax return. However, the marital deduction is reduced by estate management expenses paid from the marital share but attributable to a property interest that is not a part of the marital share.

.09 Personal Property

Disposing of personal property in a separate will provision is always best for the reasons mentioned in ¶ 1105. The will should note that some types or items of personal property do not belong to the testator. For example, the property might already belong to the testator's spouse. In that case, one might want to confirm such ownership in the will. If the testator lives in a community property jurisdiction, the attorney who drafts the will may use a clause recognizing the community property interest of the surviving spouse in one-half of the tangible personal property owned by the community.

.10 Legacies

Legacies fall into four basic categories: (1) bequests or devises of specific property; (2) general money bequests; (3) money bequests payable out of specific property; and (4) residuary bequests. If, at the time of the testator's death, he or she no longer owns the specific property intended to be given, the legatee takes nothing, unless the testator makes some other provision in the will. This is known as ademption. The testator can guard against ademption of a specific legacy or against ademption, generally, by providing for a cash legacy equal to the value of the property bequeathed at the time of its disposition, or the proceeds, if sold, or some other amount of cash. If estate assets are insufficient to pay all legacies, the law provides an order of priority—an order of abatement of legacies, depending on the particular types of legacy involved. (See ¶ 1105.) The testator may change this order by a provision in the will. Gifts of the residue abate first, and residuary legatees are usually the testator's prime concern. Therefore, the testator should protect against their receiving nothing because of an unforeseen shrinkage in the estate. The will may state that the legacies of those less favored by the testator are to abate first.

.11 Residuary Bequests

In most cases, residuary bequests are very important. The transfer may be of all of the residue to one named beneficiary or of fractional shares to two or more named beneficiaries. The bequest can be outright or in trust. The trust or trusts can be those created by the will. Alternatively, a living trust created during the testator's lifetime can receive the bequest. Bequests of the residue frequently involve the marital deduction, which is a subject separately treated in Chapter 12.

.12 Lapsed Legacies

What happens if a legatee is unwilling to accept a legacy, or dies before the testator, or after the testator but before a gift vests? For example, what if a gift of a remainder interest is contingent on surviving the holder of a life estate? State law will furnish an answer if the testator's will does not address this contingency. As a general rule, the lapsed legacy becomes a part of the residuary estate. If the lapse is in the residuary estate, then the property may pass under the laws of intestacy, as it would pass if there were no will. Many states have special antilapse statutes dealing with bequests to descendants or brothers or sisters of the testator. In any event, the possibility of lapse exists, and some provision, for or against, is advisable to control the situation to the testator's liking.

.13 Power of Appointment

The testator may possess a power of appointment exercisable solely by will. This is typically the case where a power of appointment marital deduction trust has been set up for the benefit of a surviving spouse. Often the person creating the power will put substantial obstacles in the way of exercising it in the hope that the named beneficiaries, on failure to exercise the power, will stand a better chance of getting the funds. Therefore, the holder of a power exercisable by will should take great care to make sure that the requirements for exercise are fully satisfied. If the holder of the power does not wish to exercise it, he or she should state so explicitly in the will.

.14 Gifts to a Class

Gifts to a class are gifts made to persons not individually named who fit a general description or class, such as children or grandchildren. The testator may include unborn persons in the class. Generally, membership in the class is determined as of the date the gift is intended to take effect. This date might be the date of the testator's death or some later date, and possibly a date before the testator's death. One will want to avoid a *direct* gift to a class because of problems in identifying the class and the possibility of lapse.

.15 Appointment of the Fiduciary

The testator appoints the person, individual or corporate, who is to serve as executor, and any successors or substitutes. The testator also makes the provision waiving the posting of a bond or other security, if that waiver is deemed prudent. A special provision for compensation of the executor may be included, usually on terms mutually agreed upon in advance by the testator and the executor. The testator may appoint more than one executor. The testator may name successors or substitutes to fill in the gaps if an executor is unable or unwilling to serve.

Chapter 14 discusses the selection and appointment of fiduciaries in detail.

.16 Survivorship

Will provisions can address two potential problems concerning survivorship: (1) establishing the order of deaths of the testator and his or her spouse or other beneficiary where there is no proof; and (2) avoiding the expense of double administration where two parties, one inheriting from the other, die within a short time of one another (see ¶ 1240, which reviews the area and suggests solutions).

.17 Disinheritance

In most states, the testator cannot completely disinherit a spouse. Children who are not mentioned or provided for may, in some states, be entitled to what they would inherit if there were no will. In other states, this rule is limited to children who are born after the will is executed. Some states have similar restrictions if the testator makes charitable bequests and makes no mention of particular classes of heirs. The person or persons being disinherited need not be named; a class designation will do. However, naming the individual and the reason, tactfully stated, for the disinheritance is good practice. Will provisions that explicitly address disinheritance can help provide a defense later to charges of fraud, undue influence, or lack of capacity to make a will.

.18 Powers Clauses

State law will give an executor certain powers without benefit of a will provision. A testator may add to or subtract from those given. One of the possible problems involved in relying on state law is that one cannot always rely on the testator to remain in that state so that the "right" state law powers will be read into the will. The better way may be for the attorney who drafts the will to select carefully the powers appropriate to the particular estate and spell them out in the will. Many administration powers can have substantial dispositive effects. No power should be included unless the testator knows what it means and what the possible effects might be, and that it is consistent with his or her basic intentions. The testator should give the fiduciary broad enough powers to be able to handle the variety of situations that can arise in the way the testator might want them handled if still alive. Instead of limiting the fiduciary with direct limitations, the better way will often be for the testator to set forth guidelines in a particular area, intended as suggestions and not commands, making such intent crystal clear. Investment powers are most important, as is apparent from the discussion at ¶ 1105.16.

If a trust is set up, dealings between the trust and the estate become another important place in which the powers of the executor and the trustee need to be structured to assure a smooth working relationship. Most likely, one will want to permit the trust to lend money to the estate and purchase estate assets. This provision might be of particular importance in supplying estate liquidity. At the same time, if the trust is to be the recipient of insurance proceeds, one must be mindful of the adverse estate tax consequences that can result if the trustee is required to make loans to the estate. In any case, the powers of the estate and the trust must be coordinated. For example, the power of the trust to lend has to be matched by a power of the executor to borrow from the trust. Special types of assets call for special types of powers. Business assets, for instance, are of this type, and the whole subject of planning for business interests is developed in Part II of this book.

If real estate is involved, a variety of powers might be appropriate, including power to foreclose, improve, manage, subdivide, insure or, perhaps, abandon the property. If there are minor or incompetent beneficiaries, the estate planner should consider other special powers, including a power to accumulate income and to make direct payments to or on behalf of the beneficiary. In short, the powers need to be commensurate with the duties and responsibilities of the fiduciary and adequate to meet the situations that might arise.

.19 Disclaimers

If there is a possibility that a disclaimer might be a useful postmortem strategy, the testator should make provision for it in the will (see ¶1525 for a discussion of disclaimers).

¶1115 EXECUTION OF THE WILL

A will speaks when its maker can no longer speak, so the voice heard must be identified as that of the maker. Property rights and human rights depend on it. To safeguard those rights, the law surrounds the execution of a will with formal requirements, which need to be carefully observed and satisfied.

The requirements might vary somewhat from state to state, but they all are intended to establish the will's validity. Specifically, these formalities establish that the testator executed the instrument in question, with full and complete knowledge that it was the testator's will, the testator meant it to be his or her last will, signed it or placed his or her mark at the end of the instrument on a certain date, and had it duly witnessed and attested. While some states might give effect to unwitnessed wills, for practical purposes, one should ignore this possibility.

The following is a more detailed model of how these general formalities break down into specifics, subject to some variations in state law that might require special attention.

.01 Declaration of Will

In the past, many wills started out with the testator saying that, "I make, publish and declare this to be my Last Will and Testament." All three verbs are important, but today many wills leave only the "declare" part up front. The recital of the "making" and the "publishing" is not essential so long as the testator executes the will and the witnesses are told that it is the will of the testator.

.02 Signature or Mark

The testator should sign the will. If the testator is unable to sign the will, he or she should place a mark where the signature should be or ask someone else to sign the will on his or her behalf and in his or her presence. The signing should be located immediately at the end of the will proper.

.03 Witnesses

At least three disinterested witnesses should be on hand to witness the execution of the will. Two witnesses may be all that are legally required in some states, but some require three. Even where only two are needed, a third witness will facilitate proof if one is later unavailable for any reason.

The witnesses generally should not be any of the following: (1) a beneficiary, executor, or trustee under the will, or the spouse or business partner of any such person; (2) an officer, director, or shareholder of a corporation that is an executor or trustee under the will, or a beneficiary; or (3) a resident of a state or political subdivision that is a beneficiary under the will if the gift might possibly reduce the resident's taxes.

.04 Publication and Attestation

The witnesses should be told that the instrument that they are called upon to witness is the testator's will, and the testator should specifically ask them to "witness the execution" of the will.

Each witness must either see the testator sign or hear the testator acknowledge that the testator's signature is already on the will. This signature should be pointed out to the witnesses and be actually seen by them. If the testator is unable to sign and someone else signs on the testator's behalf, the witnesses should observe that the person signing does so at the request of the testator and in the presence of the testator.

The witnesses, at the request of the testator and in his or her unobstructed view, should sign their names and write their addresses. In some states, the witnesses may do so independently of the attestation clause that follows. In other states, the witnesses' signatures and addresses appear only once following the attestation clause.

Each witness, the testator, and the person, if any, signing for the testator, should all be present throughout the entire proceedings for execution of the will.

.05 Date and Place

The will should fully and correctly state the place and date of its execution.

.06 Page Numbering

As a matter of practice, if not a legal requirement, the attorney should number the pages of the will consecutively, bind them together, and have the testator and witnesses initial each page.

.07 Attestation

Either as the vehicle for the attesting witnesses' signatures or as an additional provision following their signatures, an attestation clause should be set out, reciting all the formalities of publication and attestation referred to in ¶1115.04, the date of the execution of the will, and the number of pages of the will.

In some states, provision is made for an affidavit of the witnesses to be executed at, or about the time of, the will's execution. The probate court may accept this affidavit in lieu of the witnesses' making an affidavit or appearing personally when the will is probated. This affidavit eliminates difficulties of proof that might arise if at the time of probate one or more of the attesting witnesses is not available.

In some instances, the will itself and the attestation clause might contain recitals as to the testator's competence. One attestation clause recites, for example, that the testator appeared to be "of sound mind and memory and was in all respects competent to make a will." Some practitioners question whether this clause adds anything useful. If a will is to be executed by someone who is seriously ill and, perhaps, hospitalized, obtaining the opinion of the attending physician as to competency before the execution of the will would be prudent. The attorney might want to get a written statement, preferably in affidavit form, supporting the competency of the testator at the precise time of the execution of the will.

The formalities surrounding the execution of a will are of great importance and should not be regarded lightly. Each state has its own requirements, which should be followed to the letter. Once the testator has died, any technical error may invalidate the will.

¶1120 JOINT, MUTUAL, AND RECIPROCAL WILLS

Sometimes two related individuals, such as a husband and wife, have a common plan for the disposition of their property. Special problems can arise because of the marital deduction, and that aspect of joint or mutual wills is discussed in Chapter 12.

This chapter covers situations where a husband and wife are not involved, and where no marital deduction problem exists for a husband and wife. First of all, one should be able to distinguish between joint, mutual, and reciprocal wills. A joint will is a single will executed by two or more individuals. A mutual will is one made pursuant to an agreement between two or more individuals to dispose of their property in a special way. The will in such case might be a joint will or there could be separate wills. Reciprocal wills are those in which each testator names the other as his or her beneficiary, either in a joint will or in separate wills.

However appealing this kind of arrangement might appear at any given point in time, generally parties should not tie themselves together in this way. Individuals who do so run the risk of being unable to deal with changed circumstances arising upon the death of one of the parties. Such arrangements also present much greater potential for expensive legal disputes between different beneficiaries of different documents. Often, arrangements of this type are the product of fear and distrust or a kind of bartering. Each individual should be free to choose the use and disposition of his or her property as seems best under the prevailing circumstances.

Determining whether the parties are contractually bound can be troublesome. Usually, while both parties are alive, one party may revoke the agreement upon notice to the other. However, on the death of one party, the courts are more disposed to find a binding contract. If a client wants an arrangement of this type, spelling out its binding effect, if any, is important before and after the death of one of the parties.

¶1125 INSTRUCTIONS AND DATA SOURCES OUTSIDE THE WILL

A will is a marvelous device for doing the basic job it is intended to do—transfer probate property on death. It is a legal document, and it is almost invariably written by a lawyer for a layman. It tends to be in formal terms. Although some people might prefer to have it written in less formal terms, there is often a real danger in departing from tried and tested legal language. There is also a danger, in expressing wishes or offering guidance as to particular matters, lest they be taken as commands or create doubts and uncertainties about portions of the will. Some things that the testator might want to say are not appropriate. Once the will is submitted for probate, it becomes a public document, which many people can read. For these and other reasons, instructions outside the will, whether in the form of a letter or a memorandum from the testator, make a lot of sense.

Some examples of suggestions that might be appropriate include the following:

- Suggestions as to investment and whether to sell or hold securities.
- Suggestions as to special assets of the estate (works of art, stamp and coin collections and the like) in which the

testator's judgment might be better than that of anyone else in the family or one charged with the administration of the estate.

- Suggestions as to the selection of insurance options.
- Explanations of the reasons for some of the will provisions. For example, the testator might explain the use of a marital and nonmarital trust.
- An investment philosophy for the guidance of trustees or others.

In addition, the estate owner should prepare a data source list, which will facilitate the administration of his or her estate. Once completed, this information should be kept in a safe, accessible place and be periodically reviewed and updated (preferably annually). The following are forms that the estate owner can use.

Exhibit 9

Estate Owner's Confidential Data Bank

KEY ADVISORS: PERSONAL, BUSINESS, FINANCIAL, AND PROFESSIONAL

Advisor	Name	Address	Phone Number
Attorney			
Accountant			
Financial Advisor			
Banker			
Stockbroker			
Insurance Agent			
Undertaker			
Doctor			
Dentist			
Clergyman			
Employer and/or Business Associates			
Appraiser			
Other			

KEY PERSONAL PAPERS

Name	Location
Certificates: birth adoption baptismal marriage	
Will: original copy	
Brokerage Statements	
Income Tax Returns	
Gift Tax Returns	
Household Inventory	
Military Service Records	
Social Security Number and Cards	
Employment Records	
Educational Records (diplomas, transcripts)	
Medical and Health Records (medication, vaccinations)	
Cemetery Site Deed	
Divorce Decree or Separation Agreement	
Passport	
Citizenship Papers	
Organizations: professional religious fraternal union other	
Powers of Attorney	
Living Wills (Medical Directives)	
Trusts	
Others	

MEMBERS OF FAMILY

(List spouse, children, grandchildren, parents, brothers and sisters, and others who may be involved in your estate or in caring for your family after your death.)

Name	Address	Relationship	Date of Birth	Place of Birth	Marital Status	Date of Death	Place of Death

BANK DATA

	Name of Bank, Credit Union, etc.	Address	Name of Account	Account Number	Location of Bank Statements, checkbook, or key
Savings Accounts					
Checking Accounts					
Money Market Accounts					
Certificates of Deposit					
Safe Deposit					

U.S. SAVINGS BONDS

Serial No.	Names Registered	Purchase Date	Purchase Price	Maturity Date	Maturity Value	Location

STOCKS, BONDS, MUTUAL FUNDS, AND OTHER INVESTMENTS

Broker__________ Address__________ Telephone__________

Issuer	Owner (Indicate whether registered or bearer)	Description	Date of Purchase	Number of Shares	Purchase Price	Location
Stocks						
Bonds						
Mutual Funds						
Other						

OTHER PERSONAL PROPERTY
(car, jewelry, art, etc.)

Type of Property	Location	Insured		Other Comments*
		Yes	No	

* Include cost basis of items which may have appreciated in value and date acquired.

REAL ESTATE
(Include cemetery plot, condominium, and cooperative apartment)

Description and Location	Date of Purchase	Purchase Price	Title in Name of	Mortgage: Amount/ Holder	Location of Records
List separately date, cost and nature of improvements.					

OTHER ASSETS

Company Benefits	Company	Beneficiary	Administrator
Pension			
Profit-Sharing			
Traditional IRA			
Roth IRA			
Annuity			
Medical Savings Account			
Health Savings Account			
Other			

INSURANCE

Broker __________ Address __________ Telephone __________

	Company and Address	Policy Number	Location of Policy	Type of Insurance Beneficiary	Value on Natural Death	Value on Accidental Death
Life Insurance						
Health Insurance						
Disability Income Insurance						
Long-Term Care Insurance						
Health Insurance						
Home/Car Insurance						
Other						

DEBTS
(Bank, mortgage, broker, and insurance loans, installment contracts)

Creditor's Name and Address	Amount	Collateral, if any	Location of Records and Documents

Chapter 12

The Marital Deduction

Overview .... ¶ 1201
Qualifying for the Marital Deduction .... ¶ 1205
Qualifying Terminable Interest Property (QTIP) .... ¶ 1210
To What Extent Should the Marital Deduction Be Used? .... ¶ 1215
How to Make a Marital Deduction Bequest .... ¶ 1220
Use of Trusts in Marital Deduction Planning .... ¶ 1225
Alien Surviving Spouses—Qualified Domestic Trusts (QDOTs) .... ¶ 1230
Use of Disclaimers .... ¶ 1235
Common Disaster, Survivorship and Equalization Provisions .... ¶ 1240

¶ 1201 OVERVIEW

The estate of a decedent may claim a deduction, called the marital deduction, for qualifying bequests or transfers of property to a surviving spouse.[1] The deduction is unlimited. The gift tax marital deduction (¶ 405) is also unlimited.[2]

The use of this unlimited marital deduction is the primary focus of this chapter. The actual requirements for qualifying for the deduction are discussed in ¶ 1205. The special requirements for qualified terminable interest property (QTIP)[3] are discussed in ¶ 1210. The extent to which a married individual should use the marital deduction is covered in ¶ 1215. The proper forms of expressing a marital deduction disposition and the advantages and disadvantages of each are listed in ¶ 1220. The use of trusts in marital deduction planning, including the bypass nonmarital trust, is considered in ¶ 1225.

[1] Code Sec. 2056(a).
[2] Code Sec. 2523(a).
[3] Code Sec. 2056(b)(7).

Disclaimers (¶1235) and common disaster, survivorship, and equalization bequests (¶1240) are important elements to consider in marital deduction planning.

Bequests to spouses who are not citizens of the United States generally are not eligible for the estate tax marital deduction unless they are in the form of a qualified domestic trust (QDOT) as defined in Code Sec. 2056A. Such trusts are discussed in detail in ¶1230.

¶1205 QUALIFYING FOR THE MARITAL DEDUCTION

Code Sec. 2056 spells out the rules governing the allowance of the marital deduction. It allows an estate tax deduction equal to the value of property included in the deceased spouse's gross estate that actually passes to the surviving spouse and that is not a nonqualified terminable interest.

A married individual can qualify for the marital deduction easily. A married individual who tells a lawyer to draw up a will giving everything to his or her spouse if the spouse survives and, if not, to the children, creates no marital deduction problem for his or her estate. The estate will receive the full marital deduction if the spouse survives. Other problems could occur, however, which are addressed below.

On the other hand, a married individual who tells a lawyer that he or she wants his spouse to have everything, but is afraid of what the surviving spouse might do with the property, might have difficulty. The individual might be afraid the surviving spouse might remarry and the new spouse might receive a portion of the accumulated wealth. The individual cannot eliminate that risk completely and still take advantage of the marital deduction.

Property bequeathed to one's spouse without restrictions qualifies for the marital deduction. However, if a testator burdens the bequest with restrictions under which the interest in the property can be revoked and transferred to someone else upon the occurrence or nonoccurrence of a contingency, the bequest will not ordinarily qualify.

In legal terms, the bequest without restrictions is an absolute bequest of an absolute interest. The bequest with restrictions is a terminable interest. Generally, an interest is terminable if it will end or fail by reason of lapse of time or the occurrence or nonoccurrence of a specified event. An interest given a spouse that will terminate on the spouse's remarriage is terminable. A terminable interest will not qualify for the deduction if another interest in the same property passed from the decedent to another person and that person may possess the interest after termination of the spouse's interest. The reason for this rule is to prevent a deduction for property that will not be taxed in the survivor's estate.s

.01 Exceptions to the Terminable Interest Rule

The terminable interest rule has five exceptions. These exceptions ensure that the property will be taxed in the survivor's estate. Thus, the marital deduction is essentially a tax deferral mechanism.

The most important exception is the one for qualified terminable interest property (QTIP).[4] It is separately discussed in ¶ 1210.

A second exception, found in Code Sec. 2056(b)(5), is the general power of appointment exception. This provision permits a life interest arrangement to qualify, whether it is in trust or not. The surviving spouse must be entitled to all the income from the entire interest or from a specific portion thereof (payable at least annually) and must have the power to appoint the property to himself or herself (i.e., in the case of a trust, power to direct the trustee to pay him or her all of the principal) or has the power to appoint the property to his or her estate (i.e., has a general power of appointment).

A third exception to the terminable interest rule relates to a survivorship condition. Code Sec. 2056(b)(3) provides that, if the only condition of a bequest to the survivor is that he or she survive for a period not exceeding six months, the marital deduction is allowable, if he or she actually survives for the period specified.

A fourth exception to the terminable interest rule is contained in Code Sec. 2056(b)(6), and provides that a right to the payment of life insurance or annuity proceeds held by an insurer, coupled with a power of appointment in the survivor exercisable in favor of the survivor or the survivor's estate, will qualify.

The fifth exception is for a bequest to the spouse of an income interest in a charitable remainder unitrust (CRUT) or charitable remainder annuity trust (CRAT) where the spouse is the only noncharitable beneficiary (¶ 515).[5]

.02 The Joint and Mutual Wills' Disqualifying Pitfall

Sometimes a husband and wife execute joint and mutual wills under the terms of which the survivor is obligated to make bequests to certain persons. If, under state law, the survivor may not revoke

---

[4] Code Sec. 2056(b)(7).

[5] Code Sec. 2056(b)(8).

the will or make a different disposition, the bequest to the surviving spouse will be regarded as a terminable interest not qualifying for the marital deduction.[6]

To safeguard the marital deduction, each spouse must trust the other. Usually, no legal obstacle prevents the survivor from disposing of the property received under the decedent's will. Consequently, the safest procedure is for each spouse to execute a separate will, with no provision or other agreement restricting the survivor's freedom of disposition. For further safety, a cautious estate planner might recommend that each spouse execute his or her will out of the presence of the other. The estate planner might even have each spouse state affirmatively that he or she does so freely without any compulsion or undue influence of the other and without any understanding, agreement, or obligation that he or she may or may not change his or her will at any time in the future. In a really troublesome situation, both spouses might be asked to sign a statement to that effect. However, this procedure is rare and unusual. It should not be used without considering its possible negative impact. The procedure might possibly invite inquiry as to whether the couple in fact had an understanding or agreement.

¶1210 QUALIFYING TERMINABLE INTEREST PROPERTY (QTIP)

Code Sec. 2056(b)(7) allows a special form of life income interest given to a surviving spouse to qualify for the marital deduction. This interest has come to be known as a QTIP or qualifying terminable interest property. As discussed in ¶1205, a life income interest accompanied by a general power of appointment in the surviving spouse will qualify for the marital deduction. However, that requirement presents a married individual with the choice of (1) surrendering control of the ultimate disposition of the marital bequest property, or (2) surrendering the tax benefit of the marital deduction in order to assure that on the death of the surviving spouse the property will pass to children or other objects of bounty of the testator. With a QTIP arrangement, the testator can control the disposition of the remainder interest after the spouse's death.

---

[6] *D. Siegel Est.*, 67 TC 662, CCH Dec. 34,210.

Exhibit 10

Comparison of Forms of Qualifying Marital Bequests

Point of Comparison	Outright	Power of Appointment Trust	Estate Trust	QTIP Trust
Survivor's Freedom to Use and Manage Assets	Yes	No	No	No
Cost Savings: Trustee's Fees, Accountings	Yes	No	No	No
Right to Elect to Take Against Will May Be Barred	Yes	Yes	No	Yes
Protection Against:				
Survivor's Improvidence	No	Yes	Yes	Yes
Survivor's Lifetime Creditors	No	Yes	Yes	Yes
Survivor's Creditors at Death	No	Yes*	No	Yes*
Flexibility in Distributions of Income Based on Need	No	Yes	Yes	No
Flexibility in Distributions of Principal Based on Need	No	Yes	Yes	Yes
Limitation on Survivor's Right of Disposition:				
Lifetime Assignments	No	Yes	Yes	Yes
By Will	No	No	No	Yes
Mandatory Distribution of Income at Least Annually	No	Yes	No	Yes
Income Distributions Terminable on Survivor's Remarriage	No	No	Yes	No
Avoidance of Probate on Survivor's Death	No	Yes	No	Yes
Availability of Assets to Survivor's Executor	Yes	No	Yes	No
Retention of Nonincome-Producing Property in Marital Deduction Share	Yes	No	Yes	No

* Claim for estate taxes excepted.

For a life income interest to qualify for the marital deduction as a QTIP, the following conditions must be met:

- The surviving spouse must be entitled to all of the income from the property payable at least annually for his or her life.
- A QTIP interest in property not placed in trust must provide the survivor with rights to income that are sufficient to satisfy the rules applicable to marital deduction trusts.
- No one (including the spouse) may have any power to appoint any part of the property to any person other than the spouse during the spouse's life.
- The executor must elect to have the interest treated as a QTIP.

The QTIP election is generally irrevocable.[7] However, if the taxpayer provides sufficient evidence that the QTIP election was not necessary to reduce the estate tax liability to zero, the IRS will disregard the QTIP election and treat it as null and void.[8]

Annuities may qualify under regulations to be prescribed.[9] The final marital deduction regulations, discussed below, do not address the qualification for the marital deduction of annuities created by decedents dying after October 24, 1992.

Also, a spousal joint and survivor annuity automatically qualifies for the estate and gift tax marital deductions as long as only the spouses have the right to receive any payments before the death of the last spouse to die.[10] While the provision applies automatically, the executor or donor may elect not to have it apply.[11]

Property subject to the QTIP election will be subject to transfer taxes at the earlier of the date: (1) on which the spouse disposes (either by gift, sale, or otherwise) of any part of the qualifying income interest,[12] or (2) of the spouse's death (except if the spouse dies in 2010 when the estate tax is repealed for decedents dying in that year only).[13]

If the donee makes a lifetime disposition of any part of his or her life income interest, that will trigger a tax on the entire remainder,[14] actuarially valued[15] and without benefit of the annual exclusion because the remainder is not a present interest in property.[16] The

---

[7] Code Sec. 2056(f)(7)(B)(v).

[8] Rev. Proc. 2001-38, IRB 2001-24, 1335, (June 11, 2001).

[9] Reg. § 20.2056(b)-7(f).

[10] Code Sec. 2056(b)(7)(C).

[11] Code Sec. 2056(b)(7)(C)(ii).

[12] Code Secs. 2511 and 2519.

[13] Code Sec. 2044.

[14] Code Sec. 2519(a).

[15] Code Sec. 2702.

[16] Code Sec. 2503(b) and Reg. § 25.2503-3.

life income interest will be subject to the ordinary gift tax rules and will be eligible for the annual gift tax exclusion ($12,000 for 2006, indexed for inflation).[17]

If the qualifying income interest is not disposed of before death, the fair market value of the property subject to the income interest is includible in the decedent's gross estate.[18]

Additional estate taxes attributable to the taxation of the qualifying interest are borne by the property. The spouse or the spouse's estate has a right to recover the gift tax paid or the estate tax attributable to inclusion of the property in the gross estate, unless the spouse otherwise directs.[19]

.01 All Income for Life Requirement

The U.S. Court of Appeals for the Eleventh Circuit[20] and the U.S. Federal Court of Claims[21] have held that the requirement that the surviving spouse receive all of the income for life will not cause disqualification of a QTIP trust that distributed stub income (income that a trust accumulates between the date of the last distribution and the death of the surviving spouse) to someone other than the surviving spouse.

The IRS takes the position[22] that the surviving spouse will not be deemed to receive all of the income for life if the QTIP trust contains unproductive assets and the surviving spouse does not have the power to direct the trustee to convert such assets into productive assets.

Code Sec. 2056(b)(7)(B)(ii) defines a qualifying income interest for life to include property in which the surviving spouse has a usufruct interest under Louisiana law, which refers to a life estate in property.

Reg. § 20.2056(b)-7(d)(1) provides that a power under applicable state law that allows a trustee to adjust the amounts of income and principal in accordance with the trustee's duty to remain impartial between income beneficiaries and remainder beneficiaries will not be considered a power to appoint the trust property to someone other than the surviving spouse. An executor may make the QTIP election with respect to an IRA payable to a trustee as named beneficiary if the surviving spouse can force the trustee to withdraw all of the income from the IRA at least annually and pay all the income to the surviving spouse.[23]

---

[17] Code Sec. 2503(b).

[18] Code Sec. 2044.

[19] Code Sec. 2207A.

[20] *L. Shelfer Est.*, 96-2 USTC ¶ 60,238.

[21] *D. Talman, Exr.*, 97-1 USTC ¶ 60,270.

[22] IRS Technical Advice Memorandum 9717005, December 18, 1996.

[23] Rev. Rul. 2000-2, IRB 2000-3 (January 18, 2000).

.02 Other QTIP Issues

Annuities. Code Sec. 2056(b)(10) provides that, for QTIP purposes, a specific portion of property must be determined on a fractional or percentage basis. This limitation makes the treatment of annuities uncertain, because the specific portion of a trust to which an annuity relates would be identified in terms of the fixed sum payable to the surviving spouse.

The IRS has delayed issuing guidance on the deductibility of spousal annuities to which Code Sec. 2056(b)(10) applies (in general, annuities created by individuals dying after October 24, 1992).[24]

With respect to commercial annuities, a commercial annuity purchased by the decedent spouse's executor pursuant to a directive of the decedent does not qualify as QTIP. Such an annuity would be a terminable interest.[25]

Severance of elective portion. Reg. § 20.2056(b)-7(b)(2)(ii) expressly permits the elective and nonelective portions of QTIP property to be severed and held as separate trusts.

Remarriage. An individual who might be disposed to use the QTIP exception to the terminable interest rule might have second thoughts because of the fact that the interest will not qualify if it is made terminable on remarriage. In view of this consideration, he or she might be disposed to set up a trust maximizing the use of the unified credit[26] and providing the surviving spouse with income for life or until remarriage, with the remainder to the couple's children or other designated beneficiaries.

Contingent interests. Reg. § 20.2056(b)-7(d)(3) had taken the position that an income interest that is contingent on the executor making a QTIP election is not a qualified income interest for QTIP purposes, regardless of whether the QTIP election is made. The IRS's rationale for denying the deduction was that if the executor could choose not to make the QTIP election, the executor could appoint the property to someone other than the surviving spouse. However, having lost its argument in the U.S. Tax Court[27] and three U.S. Courts of Appeals,[28] the IRS issued Reg. § 20.2056(b)-7(d)(3) that provides that a surviving spouse's income interest for life, which is contingent upon the executor's QTIP election, will not fail to qualify as a QTIP.

---

[24] Reg. § 20.2056(b)-7(f).

[25] Code Sec. 2056(b)(7)(C).

[26] Code Sec. 2010.

[27] *W. Clack Est.*, 106 TC 131, CCH Dec. 51,193 Acq.

[28] *W. Robertson Est.*, CA-8, 94-1 USTC ¶ 60,153; *A. Clayton Jr., Est.*, CA-5, 92-2 USTC ¶ 60,121; *J. Spencer Est.*, CA-6, 95-1 USTC ¶ 60,188.

¶1215 TO WHAT EXTENT SHOULD THE MARITAL DEDUCTION BE USED?

The marital deduction is in the Code to be used, but it does not have to be used. Whether it is used, and to what extent, depends primarily on tax factors and secondarily on nontax factors. The testator should consider the needs and legal rights of the potential surviving spouse. At common law, a wife had dower and a husband had curtesy to the income for life from one-third of the real estate owned by the decedent spouse.

Now, most states provide a right of election to take against the will unless the decedent leaves a certain portion of the real estate to the surviving spouse. Many states also allow the right to take against the will for personal property. The rules can vary from state to state, but they are factors the testator should consider in deciding how much to devise and bequeath to the surviving spouse and in what form. This decision in turn may control the availability of the marital deduction.

The nontax factors that influence the use of the marital deduction include, but are not limited to, the following:

- Love and affection, or the lack thereof
- Confidence or lack of confidence in the judgment of one's spouse
- Fear or lack of fear of the spouse's remarriage
- Survivor's resources, both material and in terms of talent
- Possibility of inheritance from other sources
- Presence or absence of young children and their financial needs

If the only consideration were tax savings in the estate of the first spouse to die, the testator would want to use the marital deduction to the fullest extent possible. Thus, the testator would bequeath everything to his or her spouse in a marital deduction bequest. The testator should also consider the estate situation of the survivor because it will be affected by the use of the marital deduction. A tax on property qualifying for the marital deduction is only deferred until the death of the surviving spouse, to the extent that the property is not consumed or given away. If the survivor has a separate estate, it will affect the survivor's estate tax situation. The estate planner should analyze how the use of the marital deduction affects the aggregate estate taxes of both spouses.

.01 Unified Applicable Credit Amount

The unified applicable credit amount (unified credit)[29] against estate tax liability is generally an important factor in marital deduction planning. The equivalent applicable exclusion amount for the estate tax is shown below for the years indicated:

Applicable Exclusion Amount

$2,000,000 in 2006, 2007, and 2008
$3,500,000 in 2009
estate tax repealed in 2010
$1,000,000 in 2011 and thereafter

Note: For 2006, the applicable estate tax rate above the exemption amount is 46%. It drops to 47% for 2007 through 2009.[30]

These amounts assume that no lifetime use has been made of the unified credit to offset gift taxes. The applicable exclusion amount for gift tax purposes is $1,000,000, and it is not indexed for inflation.[31]

The estate planner must take into account the value of the unified credit to the client, to the client's estate, to the surviving spouse, and to the estate of the surviving spouse.

Failure to take account of the unified credit can result in its waste and cause higher taxes than might otherwise be incurred taking into account the aggregate taxes of both estates.

Maximizing the use of the unified credit, rather than maximizing the use of the marital deduction, can be the key to estate tax savings.

> ***Example 12.1.*** Charles Lloyd dies in March 2006 with an estate of $2,300,000 after payment of debts, funeral, and administration expenses. His spouse Valerie is without assets of her own. If he bequeaths the $2,300,000 to Valerie with a qualifying marital deduction bequest, his estate will incur no estate tax. But if Valerie also dies in 2006 after receiving such a bequest, having accumulated enough additional assets to offset debts, funeral expenses, and administration expenses, her estate tax before the unified credit will be $918,800 [$780,800 + ($2,300,000 − $2,000,000) × 46%)]. If she has all of her $918,800 unified credit left,[32] she will incur a federal estate tax of $138,000 ($927,800 − $780,800).[33] The same result would occur whether the bequest was an outright bequest or part outright and part by way of a marital deduction trust.

---

[29] Code Sec. 2010.
[30] Code Sec. 2001(b)(2).
[31] Code Sec. 2505(a)(1).
[32] Code Sec. 2010(c).
[33] Code Sec. 2001(c)(1).

On the other hand, if Charles bequeathed $1,000,000 to Valerie outright and placed the other $1,500,000 in a nonmarital bypass trust with the income to Valerie for life, with limited powers of invasion of corpus (if desired), and the remainder to their children, both estates would escape tax, and the children would be $138,000 richer.

A significant amount of federal estate taxes on the estate of the first spouse to die can be avoided by a combined use of the marital deduction[34] and the applicable credit amount (unified credit).[35]

Combining the marital deduction with a bypass trust geared to the applicable credit amount is certain to produce better tax results for the estates of both spouses in the aggregate than full use of the unlimited marital deduction by the first to die.

The applicable credit amount approach deprives the surviving spouse of the use of principal that would be available if the testator had made an outright marital deduction bequest. However, the testator may give his or her spouse a limited power to invade the corpus of a trust designed to take advantage of the applicable credit amount. (These trusts are also known as credit shelter trusts.) A power of invasion limited by an ascertainable standard related to health, support, and maintenance will not make the trust property includible in the gross estate of the holder.[36]

The preceding example assumed that the surviving spouse lacks other assets. If the surviving spouse possesses separate assets, the estate planner should take that factor into account in planning the use of the marital deduction.

Example 12.2. Michael Johnson has an estate of $2,500,000. His wife, Lisa, also has an estate of $2,500,000. If Michael were to leave Lisa everything at his death in 2006, his estate would escape federal estate tax, but Lisa would have an estate of $5 million, except as reduced by consumption or gifts or increased by asset appreciation. If Lisa also dies in 2006 and the full amount of $5,000,000 were taxable, the estate tax would be $1,380,000 ($2,160,800 – $780,800) ($1,485,800 – $555,800), assuming that all of her unified credit was available. If, instead of bequeathing Lisa everything, he gave her nothing and gave all of his $2,500,000 to the children, his estate tax would be $230,000 ($1,010,800 – $780,800), assuming that all of his unified credit was available, and Lisa's estate (assuming she also died in 2006) would be

[34] Code Sec. 2056(a).

[35] Code Sec. 2010.

[36] Code Sec. 2041(b)(1)(A).

similarly taxed. The aggregate taxes for both estates would be $460,000, assuming each spouse's unified credit was available at death. Thus, the estate tax savings on both estates would be $920,000 ($1,380,000 – $460,000).

The tax savings projected in Example 12.2, above, do not take into account loss of the use of money paid by the estate of the first spouse to die. The loss of the use of $230,000 for a sufficient period of time might offset the estate tax savings. When that situation can be expected to occur depends on assumptions as to yield and the surviving spouse's life expectancy. If the surviving spouse has a short life expectancy, use of the unlimited marital deduction would appear to be ill-advised. If the surviving spouse has a relatively long life expectancy, the probability is that the tax deferral obtainable by use of the unlimited marital deduction may be favored.

Three essential points emerge on the use of the unlimited marital deduction viewed strictly from the standpoint of tax factors: (1) it is never to be used without regard to the available applicable credit amount (unified credit); (2) it is never to be used without regard to the size of the survivor's estate; and (3) consideration should be given to the possibility of the survivor's ability and willingness to reduce the size of his or her estate, as discussed below.

The unlimited marital deduction applies to both lifetime gifts and to devises and bequests. The subject of interspousal lifetime gifts has already been discussed in Chapter 4. As a general rule, lifetime interspousal gifts offer no special advantage over testamentary transfers. However, a lifetime gift might serve to make available the marital deduction even though the donee spouse may predecease the donor or might aid in enabling the donor's estate to qualify for special benefits for certain business interests, as discussed below. In that case, use of the marital deduction would serve to place assets in the donee spouse's estate and prevent loss of the benefit of the applicable credit amount (unified credit) by his or her estate, assuming the estate would otherwise be without sufficient assets to use all of the available credit.

Example 12.3. Matthew Akers had an estate of $2,500,000 in 2000. His wife, Helen, had no assets. In 2000, Matthew made a lifetime gift of $1,000,000 to Helen. Helen died in 2006, bequeathing her entire $1,000,000 estate to the couple's children (assume that she consumed the earnings on the $1,000,000). Her estate is free of tax. Matthew is left in the position in which he can transfer his entire $1,500,000 estate free of estate tax. Without the lifetime gift to Helen, Matthew would be left with an estate of $2,500,000 on which, if he died in 2006, the estate tax, assuming full use of the unified credit, would be $230,000 ($1,010,800 – $780,800).

This result may be accomplished by a gift to a donee spouse on his or her deathbed. If the gift to the dying spouse consists of appreciated property, the property will receive a stepped-up basis[37] that will eliminate any income tax liability for pre-death appreciation if, as indicated, the property is devised or bequeathed by the donee spouse to the couple's children. However, for property acquired from a decedent dying in 2010, the step up in basis will be limited to $1,300,000 plus $3,000,000 for property acquired by a surviving spouse. If the property is willed to the donor spouse, however, it will not receive a stepped-up basis if the donee dies within one year of the gift.[38] If a donor gives appreciated property to an individual, and the donor or his or her spouse acquires the property again on the death of the donee within one year of the gift, the donor's basis in the property will be the decedent's adjusted basis in the property immediately before his or her death.[39]

.02 Transfer of Insurance to Spouse

Before the unlimited marital deduction,[40] one of the standard estate planning techniques was for the insured to transfer life insurance policies to the spouse, along with all incidents of ownership. The objective of this transfer was to keep the insurance proceeds out of the gross estate of the transferor-decedent.[41] That technique might not be necessary. If the decedent retains the policy and the proceeds are includible in the gross estate of the insured, no estate tax will be due in any case if the spouse is the beneficiary of the proceeds in a marital deduction bequest. A better strategy might be to retain the policy and incidents of ownership as a valuable asset in case of divorce or some other circumstance making retention desirable. Transfers of life insurance within three years of death are includible in the gross estate of the transferor-decedent.[42] Thus, if the marital deduction is not to be used, such transfer might generate estate tax liability depending on the facts (deductions and credits) involved in the particular estate.

.03 Spousal Second-to-Die Insurance

The loss of the marital deduction by reason of the spouse predeceasing the estate owner is a factor to be considered. The potential loss can be great and the insurance needs could be correspondingly

[37] Code Sec. 1014(a).
[38] Code Sec. 1014(e).
[39] Code Sec. 1014(e)(1).
[40] Code Sec. 2056(a).
[41] Code Sec. 2042.
[42] Code Sec. 2035(a).

great. Such needs can be satisfied with spousal second-to-die insurance. (¶ 705).

.04 Possible Reduction of the Survivor's Estate

As previously discussed, one of the key considerations involved in the use of the marital deduction is the probable impact on the estate tax liabilities of the survivor's estate.

The probable impact will depend in part on the extent to which the survivor consumes or otherwise disposes of the funds available to him or her. This consumption and disposition of the estate depends in part on the estimated time within which the survivor can make dispositions.

With these factors in mind, the use of the gift tax annual exclusion ($12,000 for 2006, indexed for inflation)[43] offers one way of reducing the size of the survivor's gross estate without transfer tax cost.

> ***Example 12.4.*** Harry Melton is a surviving spouse with three married children. Each married child has two children. Therefore, Melton has a total of 12 potential donees whom he could give at least $12,000 each year. Thus, Melton could give a total of $144,000 to his children and grandchildren in 2006 without incurring a gift tax liability. He could also give anyone else $12,000 without incurring a gift tax liability because the annual gift tax exclusion is not limited to gifts to family members. Moreover, he could make equivalent gifts subject to indexing adjustments in succeeding years.

Indeed, the process of reduction of a spouse's gross estate through the use of the annual exclusion may begin before the death of the first spouse to die by lifetime gifts to children or others. With gift-splitting,[44] such reductions may take place at an accelerated pace per donee per year until the time of death of the first spouse to die. For 2006, the annual exclusion for split gifts is $24,000.

Also, the private annuity remains an effective means of removing large blocks of property from an individual's gross estate. See ¶ 810 for a detailed discussion of the uses and limitations of the private annuity.

The intra-family installment sale is another possibility for reducing the survivor's gross estate.

.05 Disclaimer

From a planning standpoint, one might want to provide in the will that the surviving spouse may refuse to accept any part of the

[43] Code Sec. 2503(b).

[44] Code Sec. 2513.

marital bequest. A qualified disclaimer (¶ 1525), in effect, treats the interest disclaimed as if it had never been transferred to the disclaimant. Hence, no gift occurs from the disclaimant to the person acquiring the property as a result of the disclaimer. If the surviving spouse does not make a qualified disclaimer, he or she will then need to weigh the cost of making a lifetime gift against the cost of retaining the property and having it included in his or her gross estate. To the extent that the surviving spouse uses the annual gift tax exclusion ($12,000 for 2006, indexed for inflation)[45] or the gift is of property with potential appreciation, lifetime giving generally results in less transfer taxes than including the property in the gross estate. However, if lifetime giving will result in actual payment of tax, the value of tax deferral resulting from leaving the property in the decedent's estate needs to be weighed.

.06 Lifetime Interspousal Gifts to Qualify for Special Benefits

The unlimited marital deduction allows the use of lifetime interspousal gifts made more than three years before death as a means of qualifying the donor's estate for benefits that depend on the size and composition of the estate.[46]

> ***Example 12.5.*** Glenda Gates has a gross estate valued at $4,000,000, which includes stock in a closely held corporation valued at $900,000. She plans to bequeath one-half of her estate to her spouse and the other half to her children. Under these circumstances, the closely held stock would not meet the 35% test[47] for a Code Sec. 303 redemption. However, if she were to make a lifetime gift of $1,500,000 to her spouse more than 3 years before her death, reducing her gross estate to $2,500,000 at her death and bequeathed her spouse $250,000, the 35% test would be satisfied (.35 × $2,500,000 = $875,000).

Such gifts, if made long enough before death, will also be useful in terms of qualifying an estate for special use valuation under Code Sec. 2032A and for the benefits of Code Sec. 6166 providing for a 14-year extension of time for the payment of estate taxes attributable to the inclusion of closely held business interests in the gross estate.

While gifts made within three years of death will not, as a general rule, be included in the gross estate of the donor, such gifts will be included for the purpose of determining eligibility for the benefits of Code Secs. 303, 2032A and 6166.[48]

---

[45] Code Sec. 2503(b).
[46] Code Sec. 2035(c).
[47] Code Sec. 303(b)(2)(A).
[48] Code Sec. 2035(c).

.07 Home and Personal Effects

In a marital bequest, tax considerations are not the sole factors involved. The estate planner must always consider the human elements of estate planning. For example, each spouse might want the other spouse to have certain household and personal effects regardless of tax considerations. Usually, the spouses will want their residence to go to the survivor. The client and the estate planner should consider these human elements.

Example 12.6. Joe Cooper has an estate worth $2,000,000. His wife, Ramona, has a separate estate worth $200,000, consisting of their residence. Assume that Ramona devises the residence to Joe outright upon her death in 2006. No estate tax is due on Ramona's death because of the unlimited marital deduction[49] and the unified credit.[50] Joe dies later in 2006. If the $200,000 residence is not included in his gross estate, the estate tax would be $0 ($780,800 – $780,800), assuming that all of his unified credit is available. If the $200,000 residence is included in Joe's gross estate, the estate tax would be $92,000 ($872,800 – $780,800), assuming that all of his unified credit is available. The result of Ramona's devising the $200,000 residence to Joe is an added estate tax of $92,000. If the residence is devised to the children outright, that $92,000 is saved. Which is more important—that Joe have a residence he can call his own, or that his estate save the $92,000? That question is something for the parties themselves to answer. Alternatively, Ramona could give Joe a right of occupancy in a way that would not qualify for the marital deduction. Thus, the residence would avoid inclusion in his gross estate at his death. For income tax purposes, whoever receives the property, the spouse or the children, will obtain a step-up in basis[51] that will eliminate the income tax on the pre-death appreciation. The step up in basis is limited to $1,300,000, plus up to $3,000,000 for property acquired by a surviving spouse, for property acquired from a decedent dying in 2010 only. However, if the recipient of the house lives in it as a principal residence for at least two years of the five years before its sale, the step-up in basis might not be important because of the $250,000 ($500,000 on a joint return) exclusion available on the gain on the sale of a principal residence.[52]

[49] Code Sec. 2056(a).
[50] Code Sec. 2010.
[51] Code Sec. 1014(a).
[52] Code Sec. 121.

.08 State Death Taxes

To the extent that federal estate and gift taxes take on relatively less importance, state death taxes (and, in some states, gift taxes) can take on relatively greater importance in planning.

Historically, state death taxes have fallen into three major categories: (1) inheritance tax, (2) estate tax, and (3) estate "pick-up" tax to make maximum use of the federal credit for state death tax allowance under the federal estate tax. However, the federal credit for state death taxes was repealed for decedents dying in 2005 through 2009. Instead, Congress changed death taxes to a deduction in computing the taxable estate for decedents dying in 2005 through 2009. As a result, many states have taken steps to decouple their death taxes from the federal system.

An inheritance tax is levied on the right to *receive* property by inheritance. Beneficiaries are divided into classes according to their closeness to or remoteness from the decedent, with different exemptions and tax rates applicable to each class. In general, the closer the relationship, the lower the tax.

A few states levy an estate tax similar to the federal tax, giving a flat exemption to the estate as a whole. However, some states provide exemptions to beneficiaries by classes, totalling the exemptions and applying them to the estate as a whole.

In certain cases, insurance proceeds will enjoy substantial exemptions or be free entirely of state death taxes. Use of insurance in these states might be indicated as a means of cutting taxes even though the proceeds are includible in the gross estate for federal estate tax purposes.

State death taxes can also be avoided in states that do not tax a power of appointment in the hands of the donee unless it is exercised. In those states, a power of appointment trust qualifying for the federal marital deduction would escape state death taxes if the surviving spouse does not exercise the power given him or her.

The essential point is that an estate planner should examine state death taxes in marital deduction planning and check them for conformity or lack of conformity to federal rules.

¶1220 HOW TO MAKE A MARITAL DEDUCTION BEQUEST

There is more than one way to make a marital deduction bequest that will qualify for the marital deduction. A testator may make the bequest outright, as a direct transfer to the surviving spouse. However, the testator can also transfer property to a trust for the surviving spouse's benefit, provided the trust meets certain requirements.

Whether outright or in trust, the bequest will usually fall into basic patterns:

- **Bequest of specific property.** Outright, the bequest might be in these terms: "I give my husband the 5,000 shares of IBM common stock which I own." In trust: "I give the 5,000 shares of IBM common stock which I own to the Fidelity Trust Company of Boston, Massachusetts, as trustee under an agreement dated January 6, 2005, for the benefit of my husband, Zack."
- **Bequest of money.** "I give my husband $500,000." This type of bequest is known as a pecuniary bequest.
- **Straight fractional share of "net estate."** The net estate is technically known as the residue. It is what is left after payment of debts, administration expenses, specific bequests, and other charges not imposed on the residue. It might be worded: "I give one-third of my residuary estate, outright, to my wife."
- **Formula marital deduction bequests.** Maximizing the unified credit to which each spouse is entitled in many circumstances might produce greater estate tax savings for the estates of both than bequeathing everything to one's spouse in a marital deduction bequest. The preferred way to set aside the largest amount that can pass free of federal estate tax by way of the applicable credit amount (unified credit) (with the addition of the state death tax credit as a refinement) is by means of a formula marital deduction bequest.

Three formula clauses are commonly used: (1) the pecuniary marital deduction formula, (2) the pecuniary unified credit formula, and (3) the fractional residuary formula. These formulas have numerous variations and refinements. The basic formulas, their advantages and disadvantages, and their planning implications, are as follows.

- **Pecuniary marital deduction formula.** "I give my [husband, wife] the smallest sum of money that will minimize the federal estate tax payable with respect to my estate, provided, however, that in determining this sum, the provisions of any treaty or convention of the United States and/or of the Internal Revenue Code of 1986, as it may be amended, other than the unified credit [applicable credit amount] provisions of Section 2010 of said Code, shall not be taken into account to the extent that taking such provisions into account would increase state death taxes payable with respect to my estate." The foregoing marital deduction bequest can be made to the spouse outright or in a marital deduction trust (¶ 1225). After using this provision, the testator will dispose of his or her residuary estate, which will generally correspond to the exclusion equivalent provided by the available applicable credit amount.[53] In most cases, the testator may freely dispose of the residuary estate to a nonmarital trust or outright to beneficiaries other than his or her surviving spouse, for the full benefit of this provision to be realized.

- **Pecuniary unified credit formula (usually in trust form).** "I give my trustee, in trust, the largest amount that may pass free of federal estate tax, pursuant to the unified credit [applicable credit amount] allowable to my estate, after taking account of the value of property passing to beneficiaries under this Will or otherwise that is includible in my gross estate and does not qualify for the marital or charitable deduction." This provision also can be used to make an outright bequest to persons other than the surviving spouse. The residuary estate, under such a formula, will constitute the marital deduction amount. This disposition of the residuary estate can be outright or in a marital deduction trust (¶ 1225).
- **Fractional residuary marital deduction formula.** "I give my [husband, wife] the smallest fractional share of my residuary estate that will minimize the federal estate tax payable with respect to my estate; provided, that, in determining the size of such share, the provisions of any treaty or convention of the United States and/or of the Internal Revenue Code of 1986, as amended from time to time, providing for a credit against the federal estate tax, other than the unified credit [applicable credit amount] provisions of Section 2010 or said Code, shall not be taken into account to the extent that taking such provisions into account would increase state death taxes payable with respect to my estate." This type of bequest may be made outright to the surviving spouse or to a marital deduction trust (¶ 1225). Should this bequest be made, the balance of the residuary estate will be composed of the exemption equivalent provided by the available applicable credit amount.[54]

A formula marital deduction bequest is the only way the testator can fix precisely the exemption equivalent and obtain the optimum amount of marital deduction. Experts engage in an ongoing debate as to which of the formulas to choose. In this connection, the estate planner should consider these factors:

- Pecuniary formulas are easier to express and explain.

[53] Code Sec. 2010.

[54] Code Sec. 2010.

- Pecuniary formulas may offer greater opportunities for post-mortem estate planning if the fiduciary is given authority to select and allocate assets.
- A pecuniary bequest (whether it be pecuniary marital or pecuniary unified credit) generally freezes the value of the pecuniary share. That share of the estate that is not part of the pecuniary bequest generally obtains the benefits of appreciation and bears the risks of depreciation in estate values.
- If appreciated property is distributed in satisfaction of either of the pecuniary marital deduction bequests, the estate realizes gain measured by the difference between the estate's basis in the property and its fair market value at the date of distribution.[55]
- A fractional residuary marital bequest will cause the surviving spouse to participate in the appreciation or depreciation of estate values during administration.
- No gain (or loss) is recognized by the estate upon a distribution in satisfaction of a fractional residuary marital deduction.[56]
- The fractional residuary marital deduction can present serious administrative problems for the fiduciary, in that the fraction of the residuary estate constituting the marital deduction share must be recomputed upon every distribution of the estate. In many cases, the actual amount of estate principal and income due the marital share cannot be ascertained until the final accounting of the executor, and then only after what is often a subtle and difficult calculation.

The ultimate choice of one formula or another rests on several factors:

- Careful analysis of the testator's assets and their gain and loss potential
- Testator's preferences about his or her spouse receiving the benefits from estate appreciation (suffering a loss from estate depreciation)
- Whether the benefits and risks are to be shifted to the nonmarital share of the estate, with the hope of allocating the possible appreciation to the nonmarital disposition where it will escape estate taxation at the death of the surviving spouse
- Testator's family relationships

[55] Reg. § 1.1014-4(a)(3).

[56] Reg. § 1.1014-4(a)(3).

If, in the testator's projected estate, the realization of gains is not probable because the assets are unlikely to fluctuate in value, or if selection of assets can avoid gain, a pecuniary bequest of either kind described above may be favored.

However, if there is a good possibility of appreciation, and family relationships and other circumstances are such that a sharing of the appreciation seems desirable, the use of a fractional marital deduction might be indicated, despite the administrative difficulties.

If the surviving spouse is to receive the income of the nonmarital share for life, the use of a pecuniary marital deduction formula and the transfer of the appreciation potential to the nonmarital share might be beneficial. The loss of appreciation potential by the marital share may be offset by the gain to the nonmarital share, which will pay its income to the spouse for life and will escape estate taxation at his or her death. However, this leverage of the nonmarital share by the frozen marital share might not be advantageous: if the estate significantly depreciates in value, the nonmarital share can be destroyed.

The choice of a marital deduction formula requires a careful analysis of all of the foregoing factors.

.01 Special Handling of Life Insurance Proceeds

Many individuals retain incidents of ownership in life insurance policies on their lives for any number of reasons. Where the policy proceeds payable upon death are intended to benefit the surviving spouse, the estate tax marital deduction will be allowed if the disposition meets the requirements for the marital deduction in general.[57]

There are 10 ways of disposing of life insurance proceeds, to or for the benefit of a surviving spouse. Each of these ways will qualify for the federal estate tax marital deduction.

1. Lump-sum payment to the spouse.
2. Lump-sum payment to a trust, whose terms are such that any property included in the gross estate and passing to this trust will qualify for the federal estate tax marital deduction.
3. Lump-sum payment to the spouse, but only if the spouse survives the decedent for a stated period of time, which cannot exceed six months. If the spouse does not so survive, the proceeds are payable to someone else.

---

[57] Code Sec. 2056(b)(6); Reg. §§ 20.2056(b)-1(d)(3) and 20.2056(b)-6.

4. Lump-sum payment to the spouse, but if the decedent and the spouse die as the result of a common disaster, then the proceeds are payable to someone else. Of course, under 3 or 4, if the spouse does not survive (actually or presumptively) to become entitled to the proceeds, then the marital deduction will not be allowed.
5. Proceeds left on deposit with the insurance company, with the interest payable to the spouse for life, at least annually. The first interest payment would be made no later than 13 months after the decedent's death, with the principal fund payable to the spouse's estate.
6. Same as 5, except that, instead of the principal fund being payable to the spouse's estate, the spouse has the power to direct that the principal fund be paid to the spouse's estate. If this power is not exercised, then the principal fund is payable to someone else.
7. Same as 5, except that, instead of the principal fund being payable to the spouse's estate, the spouse has the power to withdraw all of the principal fund at any time during his or her lifetime. Any amounts not withdrawn by the time of the spouse's death are payable to someone else.
8. Proceeds payable only in annual or more frequent installments to the spouse for life, with the first installment payable no later than 13 months after the decedent's death. A specified number of payments or a minimum total amount is guaranteed. If the spouse dies before the guaranteed number of payments or minimum total amount has been paid out, then the unpaid balance is payable to the spouse's estate.
9. Same as 8, except that, instead of the insurance company having the obligation to pay the unpaid balance to the spouse's estate, the spouse has the power to withdraw the value of the remaining guaranteed payments or amount in a lump sum at any time during his or her life. If the spouse does not receive the guaranteed payments or amount before death, and does not exercise the power to withdraw the lump sum, then the unpaid balance of the guaranteed payments or amount is payable to someone else.
10. Same as 8, except that, instead of the insurance company having the obligation to pay the unpaid balance to the spouse's estate, the spouse has the power to direct that the unpaid guaranteed balance be paid to the spouse's estate. If this power is not exercised, that balance is payable to someone else.

Planning pointer. The estate planner should read all of the client's life insurance policies. All policies are not the same and contain different settlement options with different financial arrangements. In addition to tax aspects, such as the marital deduction, the estate planner should not overlook the financial aspects. How much will the beneficiary receive under each of the alternatives? Will this amount meet the beneficiary's needs? When working with life insurance policies, a knowledgeable life insurance professional should be consulted, whenever possible. His or her expertise can solve many complex life insurance problems in estate planning.

.02 Special Handling of Personal Effects

The testator should usually make a specific bequest to the surviving spouse of the personal and household items to assure their availability. Sometimes these items, although includible in the gross estate, will pass outside the will. Either way, a marital deduction fractional share formula bequest applied to the residuary estate may call for an adjustment to take into account the value of other property passing to the surviving spouse by bequest or otherwise. This other property would include personal and household items. Their value is not easily established. The surviving spouse might want the lowest possible value put upon them, while other beneficiaries might strive for the highest values.

.03 Foreign Property

If the testator holds foreign property used to satisfy the marital bequest, the foreign taxes paid will not be available as a credit to reduce the U.S. estate tax.[58] The testator should not use such property for the marital bequest. Rather, the testator should use it for nonmarital bequests where the credit for foreign death taxes is available.[59]

¶1225 USE OF TRUSTS IN MARITAL DEDUCTION PLANNING

The marital deduction bequest may be outright or in trust. A trust may be used in any situation where significant assets are involved and the testator feels that professional management and administration of the property to be bequeathed to the surviving spouse will be in his or her best interest. Also, a trust can afford protection against the demands of children, relatives, creditors, and others.

---

[58] Code Sec. 2014(b)(2).

[59] Code Sec. 2014(b).

Marital deduction trust planning often involves the coordination of a marital deduction bequest with the unified credit portion. Depending on what the needs of the surviving spouse are, the estate plans of sizeable estates often make use of trusts to carry out a marital deduction plan (¶ 1220).

The most commonly used trust in marital deduction planning has not been a marital deduction trust at all. Instead, it has been a bypass trust to hold that portion of the gross estate that is exempt from tax upon the testator's death by reason of the unified credit.[60] Frequently, this bypass trust (also known as a unified credit trust) is designed to pay the surviving spouse all of its income. However, in many other cases, it is a sprinkle trust created for the benefit of the surviving spouse and other family members.

The bypass trust is designed with two purposes in mind, either or both of which may be realized. First, if the surviving spouse is to be a beneficiary, the assets of this trust will be exempt from federal estate taxation upon the surviving spouse's death. Second, even if the spouse is not a beneficiary of the trust, the trust can be designed to take maximum benefit of estate appreciation where the testator desires that the spouse not benefit from it.

The bypass trust often is used with an outright formula marital deduction bequest. However, it can also be used in conjunction with a formula marital deduction trust, as follows:

- **Pecuniary marital deduction trust and residuary unified credit trust.** Such an arrangement allocates all of the risk of gain or loss during estate administration to the residuary unified credit trust.
- **Pecuniary applicable credit amount (unified credit) trust and residuary marital deduction trust.** Such an arrangement protects the unified credit portion from erosion resulting from depreciation, but it will not help the testator achieve the goal of allocating any gains in estate values to the nonmarital portion. All of the gains must necessarily pass to the residuary marital portion.
- **Fractional residuary marital deduction trust and balance of the residuary (the amount exempted from tax by the available applicable credit amount) also in the trust.** As stated above, this method is complicated, but it also protects the two trust shares from the wide variations in valuation that can occur if the pecuniary formulas (marital or unified credit) are used.

---

[60] Code Sec. 2010.

The following discussion assumes that the estate owner will wish both the marital and nonmarital portions of the estate to be held in trust.

If a bequest in trust to the surviving spouse is to qualify for the marital deduction, the trust must give the survivor an opportunity for ultimate control over the trust property.

In most cases, the choice will be between a power of appointment trust and a qualifying life income trust, also known as a QTIP.[61] Before creation of the QTIP, the power of appointment trust was most widely used. The QTIP might now occupy that status, but its use must be determined by rational decision, not by popularity. An estate trust also may be used (see below).

The QTIP has the basic advantage of enabling the settlor-testator to control the ultimate disposition of the property on the surviving spouse's death.

The exercise of that right where the testator has children from a prior marriage that he or she wishes to protect is understandable and should be explained to the testator's spouse. If not so explained, or where such explanation is inapplicable, the QTIP may be construed as a statement to the surviving spouse of the following: (1) the settlor-testator believes that because the property involved is his or hers, the settlor-testator is not willing to give the spouse any more than a life income interest (and such peripheral rights as the settlor-testator chooses to confer); (2) the settlor-testator is unwilling to entrust the ultimate disposition of the trust property to the surviving spouse; and (3) the settlor-testator is better able to make the decision as to ultimate disposition than is the surviving spouse.

These assumptions may be open to challenge on several grounds:

- The fact that the settlor-testator held title to the trust property does not necessarily mean that the surviving spouse is without rights in the property. For example, the surviving spouse might have rights that would be recognized on principles of equitable distribution in divorce proceedings.
- If the ultimate takers are joint lineal descendants of the spouses, the settlor-testator's capability of making a fairer or more appropriate distribution than the survivor might be an issue.
- If the ultimate disposition is to take place long after the settlor-testator has died, another issue might be whether he or she is better able to make a more appropriate disposition than the survivor.

[61] Code Sec. 2056(b)(7).

If a second marriage is involved and the settlor-testator has children or other beneficiaries from a prior marriage, the QTIP provides a useful way of safeguarding their interests while preserving the marital deduction.

The settlor-testator using a QTIP need not deprive the surviving spouse of all voice in the ultimate disposition. The survivor may be given a wide-ranging power of appointment that stops short of a general power of appointment. This power may limit possible challenges along the lines suggested above.

The choice should be a rational one, taking into account not only what may be done under the law but also what is likely to produce the better end result.

.01 QTIP Trusts

If certain conditions are met, a so-called qualified terminable interest property (QTIP) trust providing a surviving spouse with a life-income interest only may qualify for the marital deduction.[62] The Code requirements are discussed at ¶ 1210.

The most important difference between a QTIP trust and the power-of-appointment trust, described below, is the ability of the testator to control the disposition of the remainder interest in the trust after the spouse's death. This consideration is much more a personal decision than a tax decision on the part of the creator of the QTIP interest. Some of the considerations connected with this are described above.

The income payment provisions of the QTIP trust are governed by Code Sec. 2056(b)(7) and the regulations promulgated thereunder. In virtually all respects, the income to be paid to the surviving spouse must meet the same criteria as those set up with respect to power-of-appointment trusts.

Once the testator has created the dispositive pattern of a QTIP trust, the most important planning issue connected with the QTIP trust lies in the election to be made by the executor on the federal estate tax return.

The QTIP election can take place in the following contexts:

1. The testator makes a bequest of his or her entire estate (other than tangible personal property) in trust for the benefit of the surviving spouse. The executor, in this case, may elect to qualify the entire trust for the marital

[62] Code Secs. 2056(b)(7)(A) and 2056(a).

deduction, or he or she can make a partial election and qualify only part of the principal of the trust for the marital deduction. In this case, the testator does not care about the niceties of formula bequests. The task of preserving the applicable credit amount[63] is left to the executor as part of the QTIP election.

2. The testator makes a formula marital deduction bequest in which the estate is divided into an applicable credit amount trust portion (or outright bequests to persons other than the surviving spouse) and a trust portion, which is eligible for the marital deduction as the executor elects, under the QTIP provision, to so qualify it. The testator has already taken steps to reduce his or her estate tax to zero in the most efficient way, through an applicable credit amount disposition separate from the marital deduction. The executor's task is to see if he or she wishes to engage in further estate planning and to qualify the entire QTIP trust for the marital deduction, or only part of it, with the hope of avoiding greater estate tax at the surviving spouse's death.
3. The testator makes a pecuniary nonformula bequest (for example, $2 million) or a straight fractional bequest (for example, one-third of his or her residuary estate) in trust for the surviving spouse. This type of bequest is frequently made in second-marriage situations, where the testator wishes to control the disposition of the trust remainder after the spouse's death. The testator gives the executor the power under Code Sec. 2056(b)(7) to make a QTIP election as to this trust.

After the testator's death, the executor should determine whether to elect the full marital deduction under the QTIP rule.

In cases 2 and 3, above, the executor has received directions from the testator. Where the testator has selected a formula marital deduction, the executor normally will wish to qualify the entire QTIP trust for marital deduction treatment. The reason is that the testator's will containing the formula has already reduced the estate by the amount exempted under the available unified credit. On the other hand, where the testator has made a straight pecuniary bequest or fractional bequest, the testator's usual intent is also clear. The testator would want the executor to elect the entire principal of the trust to qualify for the marital deduction as QTIP.

---

[63] Code Sec. 2010.

A more difficult case is posed by the facts of case 1, above. If, for example, the testator's gross estate (exclusive of tangible personal property) is $2.5 million upon his or her death in 2006, how much should the executor elect? The executor can qualify the entire $2.5 million for the marital deduction as QTIP, but that will only defer taxation until the spouse's death. Instead, the executor, within the confines of the marital deduction trust, should make a partial election. The effect of a partial election is that only the amount of marital deduction necessary, after the application of the unified credit, will be elected. The applicable exclusion amount of the unified credit is $2,000,000 (equivalent to a unified credit of $780,800) in 2006. Thus, the marital deduction needed to reduce estate tax to zero is $500,000 ($2,500,000 – $2,000,000). In such a case, the QTIP partial election will be made as to $500,000/$2,500,000, or 20 percent of the trust assets.

The executor need not make the QTIP election for the sole purposes of preserving the applicable credit amount and minimizing the amount of estate tax to be paid on the decedent's death. In some cases, a full QTIP election would be disadvantageous. For example, where the spouse has died shortly after the testator (or is in imminent danger of death at the time the testator's executor is faced with the election), the executor should consider the potential estate tax on the estate of the survivor's spouse, and other relevant facts and circumstances, at the time the election is to be made. Consideration should also be given to a possible conflict of interest if the surviving spouse is named the executor.

.02 Power of Appointment Trusts

The most widely used trust in marital deduction planning before the creation of QTIPs was the power of appointment trust. As commonly used, it has four essential components.

1. It gives the surviving spouse a life income interest in the trust property.
2. It gives the trustee or the surviving spouse the right to use trust principal for designated purposes.
3. It gives the surviving spouse the right to provide in his or her will who is to receive the trust assets, i.e., a general power of appointment exercisable by will.
4. It provides that if the surviving spouse fails to take advantage of the right given him or her to name the beneficiaries of the trust assets, they are to go to the beneficiaries named in the trust by the spouse who is the first to die.

The following discussion provides some general comments on these typical components.

The survivor must have the right to all the income from the trust, and it must be paid to the survivor at least annually. The survivor or the trustee does not have to receive the right to use principal. If the estate planner is concerned about reducing taxes in the survivor's estate, this arrangement will be a means to do so. To hasten consumption, if desirable, consider a provision that authorizes the surviving spouse to use principal to make gifts to children and grandchildren and to pay any gift tax on such gifts.

The surviving spouse must be given a general power of appointment exercisable in favor of the surviving spouse or his or her estate (unless it is a QTIP or an estate trust), but the power need not be limited to exercise by will. A good reason exists why it is frequently so limited. It avoids having the capital gains of the trust taxable to the surviving spouse, as they would be if the survivor had a general power exercisable during the survivor's lifetime. The regulations say that the power of appointment must be exercisable by the surviving spouse "alone and in all events."[64] This requirement is probably not to be taken literally because no power would be exercisable by an incompetent. If the spouse is an incompetent, the IRS will nevertheless allow the marital deduction.[65] Nevertheless, the "alone" part must be heeded, and the "in all events" part as well, except where mental incompetence might arise.

The surviving spouse might have merely a power of appointment that he or she fails to exercise. In that case, the trust assets are includible in his or her gross estate for tax purposes, but they are not included for the purpose of calculating executor's fees. An exception would be if under the terms of the trust, the trust assets, in default of appointment, go to the survivor's estate.

.03 The Estate Trust

The estate trust is a bit unusual. It is a trust that will qualify for the marital deduction, even though it is set up so that the surviving spouse receives none of the income or principal while he or she is alive. The trust ends on the surviving spouse's death and the trust assets and accumulated income are to be paid to his or her estate at that time. Then, because they are part of the surviving spouse's estate, the survivor will be free to control their disposition by his or her will. It is not a terminable interest and so is not required to satisfy the life interest and power of appointment exception to

[64] Reg. § 20.2056(b)-5(g).

[65] Rev. Rul. 75-350, 1975-1 CB 115.

the terminable interest rule previously discussed. It qualifies for the marital deduction under the same provision as property given outright.

In the example described above is an extreme form. The surviving spouse does not have to be denied income or principal while alive. The trustee may be given discretion to make such distributions, but the surviving spouse has no right to demand them.

The estate trust is for the surviving spouse who really does not need income. The surviving spouse has either sufficient income to sustain himself or herself, or the trust distributes more income than the surviving spouse will need to live comfortably.

Distributions of income to the survivor may be based upon need, taking into account other sources of income and the survivor's standard of living. The stream of income can be terminated upon the survivor's remarriage and be allowed to accumulate for the eventual benefit of the surviving spouse's heirs.

Nothing prevents an estate trust from holding nonincome-producing property with good growth potential. Holding such property would very likely present problems with a power of appointment trust.

However, the estate planner should make certain that the applicable state law recognizes the estate trust as a valid trust. The estate planner should make sure that state law does not convert it into some other type of legal entity that will not give the surviving spouse an interest that qualifies for the marital deduction.

On the survivor's death, the estate trust encounters some other problems. In addition to the estate tax, the chances are the trust assets and accumulated income will have increased. The estate trust will cause additional administration expenses and executor's commissions, which are avoided with a power-of-appointment trust if the power is not exercised.

Another possible disadvantage of the estate trust is that if the surviving spouse remarries, on the surviving spouse's death the second spouse may be able to claim part of the trust assets as a surviving spouse.

After defining the marital share, by formula or dollar amount, language similar to the following can be used:

> The Trustee shall hold the Marital Share as the principal of a new, separate and distinct trust, for MARY'S sole benefit. This trust will be known as the Marital Trust.

The Trustee may pay over, and distribute, as much (including all or none) of the income and principal of the Marital Trust to MARY as the Trustee, in its sole discretion, considers advisable to enable MARY to maintain the standard of living which she enjoyed during my lifetime. The Trustee shall add any undistributed income to the principal of the Marital Trust annually.

Any principal, including accrued and undistributed income, remaining in the Marital Trust at MARY'S death is called the Distributive Property. The Trustee shall pay over, and distribute, the Distributive Property to the Executors or Administrators of MARY'S estate, to be held, administered, and distributed in all respects as a part thereof.

.04 The Nonmarital Trust

As stated above, the nonmarital bypass trust has become a common means of using the unified credit available at the testator's death in an economical fashion. Instead of bequeathing everything in a marital deduction bequest to one's spouse, the testator can provide a separate trust to pay all of its income to the surviving spouse for life, with the remainder to the testator's children. The surviving spouse will not possess a general power of appointment over this trust. In addition, the QTIP election is not properly made with respect to a nonmarital trust. Therefore, no part of the principal of this trust will be includible in the gross estate of the surviving spouse at death.

The nonmarital trust is not dependent upon whether the testator has selected a marital trust for the benefit of his or her spouse, or, if a marital trust has been selected, what type of trust it is. The value of the trust lies principally in its ability to provide the surviving spouse (and other family members, if desired) with a continuing source of income and limited rights to principal of the trust during the spouse's lifetime. Even if the surviving spouse's income from the marital bequest is adequate for his or her needs, a nonmarital trust for the benefit of younger family members can be structured so that the trustee can pay the spouse such part of the income or principal of the trust as the testator wishes. Thus, the nonmarital trust can be a highly effective backup measure.

The nonmarital trust generally will be structured with two prime objectives:

1. Meeting the current and long-term needs of intended beneficiaries, such as the surviving spouse, the children, or others.

2. Avoiding the inclusion of trust assets in the gross estate of the surviving spouse on his or her death.

The testator can write virtually whatever provisions he or she wishes into the nonmarital trust. The income interest of the spouse can be terminated upon remarriage. It need not even exist at all, and the estate owner's children can be made beneficiaries of the trust to the exclusion of the surviving spouse. The nonmarital trust (or its nontrust equivalent, the outright disposition of the unified credit exemption equivalent available at death) is one of the few places in estate planning where the testator can act free from the constraints of estate and gift taxes.

.05 The Portion Trust

A surviving spouse may be given a qualifying income interest in a portion of a single trust both for QTIP and general power of appointment trust purposes. The testator might do so in situations where the administrative costs of a two-trust plan do not justify its use. Another reason might be if the estate assets, if divided into two trusts, would be insufficient to induce a professional trustee to accept appointment as trustee of one or both of the trusts.

Code Sec. 2056(b)(10) limits the term "specific portion" to a fractional or percentile share of the property. It overrules case law holding that a specific portion could be identified in terms of a fixed amount of income or principal, which caused appreciation in certain marital deduction property to be includible in neither spouse's gross estate.[66]

¶ 1230 ALIEN SURVIVING SPOUSES—QUALIFIED DOMESTIC TRUSTS (QDOTS)

No marital deduction is allowed under Code Sec. 2056(d) if the surviving spouse is not a U.S. citizen, unless certain special requirements are met. The deduction is allowed if the surviving spouse becomes a U.S. citizen before the estate tax return is filed, and was a resident of the United States at all times after the decedent's death and before becoming a citizen. The deduction also is allowed for property passing to a surviving spouse who is not a U.S. citizen if the property passes in a qualified domestic trust (QDOT). Property passing to the surviving spouse is treated as passing in a QDOT if it is transferred or irrevocably assigned to a QDOT before the decedent's estate tax return is filed.

---

[66] *Northeastern Pennsylvania National Bank and Trust Co.*, SCt, 67-1 USTC ¶ 12,470, 387 US 213; *C. Alexander Est.*, 82 TC 34, CCH Dec. 40,913, aff'd without opinion, CA-4, 760 F2d 264.

A QDOT is a trust that meets the following conditions:

- The trust instrument must require that at least one of the trustees of the trust be an individual U.S. citizen or a domestic corporation. The IRS has authority to waive this requirement if local foreign law prohibits a trust from having a U.S. trustee.
- The trust instrument must provide that no distribution, other than a distribution of income, may be made from the trust unless a trustee who is an individual U.S. citizen or a domestic corporation has the right to withhold from the distribution the estate tax on the distribution.
- If the assets passing or deemed to pass under the QDOT exceed $2 million, the trust must meet certain requirements to ensure collection of the estate tax.[67]
- The executor must make an election on the estate tax return. Once made, the election is irrevocable.[68] In order to allow the estate of a decedent with a nonresident alien spouse to qualify for the marital deductions in those situations where the use of a trust is prohibited by local foreign law, the IRS has been given the authority to treat as trusts legal arrangements that have substantially the same effect as a trust, effective for decedents dying after August 5, 1997.[69]

Under Reg. § 20.2056A-2(b)(1), an interest passing in a QDOT must otherwise qualify for the marital deduction as a life estate with power of appointment, QTIP, estate trust, or lifetime beneficial interest of a charitable remainder trust (¶ 1205).

.01 Protective Election

Under Reg. § 20.2056A-3(c), an executor may make a protective QDOT election if there is a bona fide legal controversy that would render the making of the election infeasible at the time the return is filed. Reg. § 20.2056A-3(b) bars a partial QDOT election.

.02 Reformation and Transfers

If property passes to a trust that otherwise qualifies for the marital deduction but for the fact that the surviving spouse is not a U.S. citizen, under Reg. § 20.2056A-4(a) the property is treated as passing to a QDOT if the trust is reformed to meet the QDOT requirements. The reformation may occur pursuant to the decedent's will or trust agreement, or a judicial proceeding.

---

[67] Reg. § 20.2056A-2(d).

[68] Reg. § 20.2056A-3.

[69] Code Sec. 2056A(c)(3).

In addition, under Reg. § 20.2056A-4(b), property that passes to a noncitizen surviving spouse outside of a QDOT is treated as passing to a QDOT if the surviving spouse either transfers or irrevocably assigns the property to a QDOT pursuant to an assignment that is enforceable under local law before the estate tax return is filed and at a time when the QDOT election may still be made. However, the property is treated as passing from the decedent to the QDOT solely for purposes of qualifying for the marital deduction. For all other purposes, such as income, gift, estate, and generation-skipping transfer tax purposes, the proposed regulations treat the surviving spouse as the transferor of the property to the QDOT.

.03 Tax on QDOT Property

Estate tax is imposed on the value of the property remaining in a qualified domestic trust at the time of the death of the surviving spouse.[70]

Estate tax is also imposed under the following conditions:

- There is a distribution before the surviving spouse's death.[71]
- No trustee is an individual citizen or a domestic corporation.[72]
- The trust ceases to meet the requirements prescribed in Reg. § 20.2056A-2(d).[73]

Any portion of the tax imposed on a distribution that is paid out of the QDOT is treated as a distribution and, thus, is itself subject to tax.[74]

No tax is imposed on any distribution to the surviving spouse of income or on account of hardship.[75] Under Reg. § 20.2056A-5(c)(1), a distribution is made on account of hardship if the distribution is in response to an immediate substantial financial need relating to the noncitizen spouse's health, maintenance, education, or support, or the health, maintenance, education, or support of any individual whom the surviving spouse is legally obligated to support. A distribution is not considered made on account of hardship to the extent that the amount distributed may be obtained from other sources that are reasonably available to the noncitizen spouse. Assets such as closely held business interests, real estate, and tangible personal property are not considered sources that are reasonably available to the surviving spouse.

[70] Code Sec. 2056A(b)(1)(B).

[71] Code Sec. 2056A(b)(1)(A).

[72] Code Secs. 2056A(a)(1)(A) and 2056A(b)(4).

[73] Code Sec. 2056A(a)(2).

[74] Code Sec. 2056A(b)(11).

[75] Code Sec. 2056A(b)(3).

In addition, the following distributions are exempt from the estate tax under Reg. § 2056A-5(c)(3):

- Payments for ordinary and necessary expenses of the QDOT
- Payments to government authorities for income or other taxes, not the deferred estate tax, imposed on the QDOT
- Dispositions of trust assets by the trustees
- Payments by the QDOT to the surviving spouse to reimburse the spouse for income taxes attributable to amounts received from a nonassignable annuity or other arrangement transferred from the spouse to the QDOT

The tax does not apply after the surviving spouse becomes a U.S. citizen under the following conditions:

- The surviving spouse was a U.S. resident at all times after the date of the decedent's death and before becoming a U.S. citizen.
- No tax was imposed on any distribution before the surviving spouse became a U.S. citizen.
- The surviving spouse elects to treat any taxable distribution as a taxable gift. The surviving spouse may also treat any reduction in the tax imposed on a distribution because of the unified credit allowable against the decedent's estate[76] as a credit allowable to the surviving spouse for the purposes of determining the amount of the unified credit against the gift tax on gifts made by the surviving spouse in the year he or she becomes a U.S. citizen or any later year. (The applicable exclusion amount for gifts is $1,000,000, and it is not indexed for inflation.)

The amount of the estate tax is the amount equal to the tax that would have been imposed on the decedent's spouse's estate if the decedent spouse's taxable estate had been increased by the sum of the following:

1. The amount involved in the taxable event; and
2. The aggregate amount involved in previous taxable events with respect to qualified domestic trusts of the decedent; reduced by
3. The tax that would have been imposed on the decedent's estate if the decedent's taxable estate had been increased by the amount in 2.

[76] Code Sec. 2010.

For purposes of computing the amount of federal estate tax due, a credit is allowed for state or foreign death taxes paid by the surviving spouse's estate.

The estate tax imposed because of a distribution during the surviving spouse's life is due on the 15th day of the fourth month following the calendar year in which the distribution occurs. The tax imposed because of a distribution in the year in which the surviving spouse dies and the tax imposed at the death of the spouse is due on the date nine months after the surviving spouse's date of death.

The trustee is personally liable for the amount of tax imposed. A lien attaches to the property giving rise to the tax for 10 years after the taxable event.

.04 QDOT Security Rules

The IRS has issued regulations[77] regarding the security requirements that apply to QDOTs with assets in excess of $2 million. Under these rules, if the fair market value of the assets of the QDOT at the death of the first decedent exceeds $2 million, the trust instrument must require the following: (1) at least one U.S. trustee be a bank, or (2) the U.S. trustee furnish a bond or security to the IRS in an amount equal to 65 percent of the fair market value of the trust corpus, computed as of the decedent's date of death. For purposes of this $2 million threshold, the value of the surviving spouse's principal residence (to a maximum of $600,000) is excludable.

If the fair market value of the QDOT assets is $2 million or less, the QDOT does not have to meet the bank or bond requirements if, in the alternative, the trust instrument expressly provides that no more than 35 percent of the fair market value of the trust assets, determined annually, may be invested in real property that is not located in the United States.

¶1235 USE OF DISCLAIMERS

Disclaimers, discussed in detail in Chapter 15, are effective postmortem estate planning tools. The subject is discussed here because disclaimers may be used in connection with marital deduction bequests. The disclaimer would serve to keep the property bequeathed, or the part disclaimed out of the surviving spouse's estate, while at the same time serving to shift the property to the younger generation without incurring gift tax liability. A disclaimer by the surviving spouse is valid even if the will directs that the

[77] Reg. § 20.2056A-2(d).

property disclaimed passes to a trust in which he or she has an income interest limited by an ascertainable standard.

Disclaimers may also be used in favor of the surviving spouse. If the surviving spouse is given less than the unlimited marital deduction allows, the children might partially disclaim their legacies to permit the mother or father to receive a larger deductible amount. Any estate tax savings generated might ultimately benefit the children.

¶1240 COMMON DISASTER, SURVIVORSHIP AND EQUALIZATION PROVISIONS

An estate planner should also consider whether to use the marital deduction in situations where both spouses die within a short time of one another or where they die in a common disaster or where one cannot determine the order of survivorship.

> ***Example 12.7.*** Wendy Gomez dies in March 2006 with a gross estate of $2,035,000, and she bequeaths everything to her husband Max. Her estate incurs $35,000 in administration expenses. Because of the unlimited marital deduction,[78] her estate tax is zero. Two months later, Max dies. Wendy's will contained no survivorship provision. Max had an estate of his own in the amount of $800,000 before Wendy died. Now with the $2,000,000 ($2,035,000 – $35,000) he obtains from Wendy's estate, he has a gross estate of $2,800,000. Assume that debts and taxes on Max's estate were $50,000. His taxable estate is $2,750,000 ($2,800,000 – $50,000). The estate tax is $345,000 ($1,125,800 – $780,800), assuming that all of his unified credit was available.
>
> If Wendy has a survivorship provision in her will, the result will be different. Most likely it would be a provision tailored to fit Code Sec. 2056(b)(3). If the only condition attached to a bequest to the surviving spouse is that he or she survive the deceased for a period not exceeding six months, and he or she survives for that period, the marital deduction is allowable.
>
> ***Example 12.8.*** Now assume that Max dies in 2006 within six months of Wendy's death and that Wendy's will contains a six-month survivorship provision. His estate incurs $50,000 in administration expenses, and the remaining $750,000 passes to the couple's children. Max has a taxable estate of $750,000 ($800,000 – $50,000). His estate tax is zero, assuming that all

[78] Code Sec. 2056(a).

of his available unified credit is available. His taxable estate of $750,000 is less than the $2,000,000 applicable exclusion amount equivalent of the unified credit for 2006. The estate tax on Wendy's $2,000,000 estate that will pass to her children or others is $0 ($780,800 – $780,800). The estate tax savings resulting from the survivorship provision in Wendy's will are $345,000. In addition, the couple would incur lower administration expenses because the assets in Wendy's estate would not have to pass through probate twice.

In this example, Wendy failed to make use of a bypass trust giving Max a life income interest with limited powers of invasion, with the remainder to the children or others named. If she had done so, and not used the six-month survivorship provision, Max's gross estate would continue to be $800,000, because the $2,000,000 applicable exclusion amount equivalent of the unified credit on Wendy's estate would cause the entire $2,000,000 of her assets to pass to the trust. The tax on Wendy's estate would be $0 ($780,800 – $780,800).

Survivorship provisions are not as common as they once were. At least where married taxpayers are involved, the unlimited marital deduction might have rendered survivorship provisions obsolete. The unlimited marital deduction offers a precise solution to both the tax savings and the asset control problems the survivorship provisions previously addressed. If the testator's estate provides for a QTIP disposition for the surviving spouse, and the surviving spouse dies soon after the testator, the testator's executors may make an election to ensure that both the marital deduction and the preservation of assets for the testator's family are accomplished.

Because more sophisticated tools now exist to accomplish the planning purposes of survivorship provisions, estate planners should consider using these tools. Survivorship provisions are more suitable for cases in which individuals who are not husband and wife (and who are, thus, ineligible for the QTIP solution) need protection against the untoward consequences of dying within a short time of each other owning assets that otherwise might pass entirely to the other's family.

.01 Common Disaster Provisions

Code Sec. 2056(b)(3) also makes the marital deduction available if the bequest to the surviving spouse is contingent on the spouse surviving a common disaster that takes the life of the decedent, if the spouse survives the common disaster. If at the time of the final audit of the estate tax return for the decedent's estate a possibility exists that the surviving spouse might be deprived of the marital bequest by operation of the common disaster provision as given effect by local law, the marital deduction will be denied.[79] Although local law could conceivably save the marital deduction by providing a presumption of survival of a common disaster for a specified period, an estate planner might be unwise to rely on local law. From a planning standpoint, making the marital bequest available to the survivor to meet his or her actual needs and medical expenses might be desirable. Indeed, that factor might be of greater importance than possible savings in transfer costs. From this point of view, a presumption of survivorship of the common disaster on survival for a year or some other specified period that would permit the estate to provide the survivor with funds would merit consideration. Alternatively, a testator might consider a specific money bequest, not contingent on survival for any specified period.

Another important factor in connection with a common disaster provision is that it does not provide for the situation in which the spouses die within a short time of each other but not as a result of a common disaster. Accordingly, the common disaster provision may be coupled with a provision requiring survival for a period of six months or less.[80]

.02 Equalization Provisions

Where one spouse has a significantly larger estate than the other, the estate planner should consider a tax equalization clause. The objective is to have the estates of the two spouses pay the lowest aggregate amount of estate taxes by minimizing the impact of the progressive estate tax rate structure, which imposes higher rates of tax on larger taxable estates.

> ***Example 12.9.*** Gordon Cliff dies in 2006 and has a taxable estate of $2,500,000 (before application of the marital deduction), and everything is to go to Beverly, his wife, if she survives him for at least six months; otherwise, it goes to their children. Beverly also dies in 2006, within six months of Gordon. Gordon's estate tax is $230,000 ($1,010,800 – $780,800). The children, as contingent beneficiaries, would receive $2,270,000 ($2,500,000 – $230,000).
>
> If, instead of disqualifying Beverly completely, where she had no estate of her own, Gordon had bequeathed her $1,000,000, qualifying for the marital deduction, these would be the results: Gordon's estate tax would be zero because of the $2,000,000 applicable exclusion amount in 2005. Beverly's

[79] Reg. § 20.2056(b)-3(c).

[80] Reg. § 20.2056(b)-3(d), Example 2.

estate tax would also be zero. The children, despite additional administration costs, would net far more because of the tax savings provided by equalization.

The IRS, by acquiescing in *C. Smith Est.*[81] and other cases, has allowed risk-free equalization of tax by estates.[82] *Smith* involved an inter vivos pourover trust and did not contain a six-month survivorship provision. The following is the language of the *Smith* equalization provision:

> (b) There shall be allocated to the Marital Portion that percentage interest in the balance of the assets constituting the trust estate which shall, when taken together with all other interests and property that qualify for the marital deduction and that pass or shall have passed to Settlor's said wife under other provisions of this trust or otherwise, obtain for Settlor's estate a marital deduction which would result in the lowest federal estate taxes in Settlor's estate and Settlor's wife's estate, on the assumption Settlor's wife died after him, but on the date of his death and that her estate were valued as of the date on (and in the manner in) which Settlor's estate is valued for federal estate tax purposes; Settlor's purpose is to equalize, insofar as possible, his estate and her estate for federal estate tax purposes based upon said assumptions.

An equalization clause containing a six-month survivorship clause for inclusion in a will might provide as follows:

> If my said [wife, husband] shall not survive me, or, having survived me, shall not survive me by six (6) months, I GIVE to [her, him] that fraction of my residuary estate which shall, when taken together with all other interests and property that qualify for the marital deduction and that pass or shall have passed to my said [wife, husband] under other provisions of this Will or otherwise, obtain for my estate a marital deduction which would result in the lowest federal estate taxes in my estate and in my said [wife's, husband's] estate, on the assumption that my [wife, husband] died after me, but on the date of my death and that my said [wife's, husband's] estate were valued as of the date on (and in the manner in) which my estate is valued for federal estate tax purposes; my purpose is to equalize, insofar as possible, my estate and [her, his] estate for federal estate tax purposes, based upon said assumptions.

[81] CA-7, 77-2 USTC ¶13,215, 565 F2d 455.

[82] Rev. Rul. 82-23, 1982-1 CB 474.

The foregoing clause will accomplish exact equality between the estates of the testator and the surviving spouse. However, this exact equality might not be necessary, because exact equality requires that the estate of the predeceasing spouse transfer sufficient assets to the estate of the surviving spouse to equalize federal estate taxes. The purposes of equalization can also be realized if the deceased spouse transfers only so much value to the surviving spouse as to equalize the marginal estate tax rates that apply to both estates. If only marginal rates are equalized, the estate of the surviving spouse will not unnecessarily be enlarged by property that was previously administered in the predeceasing spouse's estate.

Despite the victory of the taxpayer in *Smith* and the acquiescence of the IRS in that (and similar) decisions, the benefit of equalization clauses can only be obtained (like the marital deduction itself) where the wealthier spouse dies first. Furthermore, since enactment of the unlimited marital deduction, the real usefulness of equalization between spouses may be limited to situations where the wealthier spouse (testator) leaves an outright legacy, and not a trust legacy, to the surviving spouse. Because the qualified terminable interest property (QTIP) election is now permitted, an equalization provision is not necessary in a will creating QTIP interests. The only provision needed in such a will is a simple reversal of the ordinary survivorship presumption provided under the Uniform Simultaneous Death Act.

Chapter 13

Powers of Appointment

Overview ....¶1301
General and Special Powers ....¶1305

¶1301 OVERVIEW

An individual has a power of appointment if he or she has the legal right to determine who will become the beneficial owner of property. The individual who has a power of appointment is the holder of the power. A power of appointment is not an interest in property. Therefore, the gross estate of an individual who dies holding a power of appointment does not include the value of the property subject to the power under Code Sec. 2033. However, the gross estate may include property subject to a power of appointment under Code Sec. 2041.

Estate planners use powers of appointment to give flexibility to an estate plan. When setting up an estate plan, an estate planner does so on the basis of what seems sensible at the time and as far down the road as he or she can see. However, estate planners often cannot see too far or too clearly.

Suppose an estate planner is planning an estate for a couple with young children. The husband and wife know what their current needs are and can estimate their future needs. They also know whether either one can handle money. They may have some ideas about the children's needs, but the children's needs are more uncertain.

The couple could place their children's future entirely in the hands of the surviving spouse, leaving everything to him or her, in full faith and confidence that the survivor will adequately provide for the children. Each spouse may feel that the other will make sensible judgments about the children. However, one or both spouses may not be too sure of the survivor's ability to handle an investment portfolio. Each spouse may have concerns about the impact on the children of a possible remarriage by the surviving spouse. The solution could be a trust that provides the surviving spouse with a power of appointment.

> ***Example 13.1.*** Ben Thompson sets up a testamentary trust to be funded with $1,000,000 in cash and securities. If his wife Jennifer survives him, the trust provides that she will receive the income from the trust for her life. At Jennifer's death, the remainder of the trust will go to their children David and Sara in equal shares. Ben also gives Jennifer the power to vary the trust corpus as she sees fit to provide for the needs of David and Sara.

The power given can be as broad or as narrow as the grantor desires. The power could allow the surviving spouse to exercise the power only in favor of the children. Alternatively, the power could allow the surviving spouse to exercise the power in favor of other classes of relatives such as parents, grandparents, nieces, and nephews. In its broadest terms, the power may allow the holder to appoint the trust corpus in favor of the holder or the holder's estate. However, tax considerations may affect the choice of the extent of the power. In addition, the holder does not necessarily have to be the surviving spouse.

> ***Example 13.2.*** Assume the same facts as in Example 13.1 except that Ben gives Jennifer the power to vary the trust corpus as she sees fit not only for the children's benefit, but also for Jennifer's support.

¶1305 GENERAL AND SPECIAL POWERS

The two kinds of powers of appointment are general and special. With certain exceptions, a general power of appointment "means a power which is exercisable in favor of the decedent, his estate, his creditors, or the creditors of his estate."[1] Congress believes that general powers of appointment are essentially similar to outright ownership of property. Hence, a decedent's gross estate includes property over which he or she held a general power of appointment.[2] Generally, a decedent's gross estate does not include property over which he or she held a special power of appointment.

The Code does not consider a power to be a general power of appointment if it contains one of the following provisions:

- An ascertainable standard relating to the holder's health, education, support, or maintenance that limits the holder's power to consume, invade, or appropriate the property.[3]

---

[1] Code Secs. 2041(b)(1) and 2514(c).
[2] Code Sec. 2041(a).
[3] Code Sec. 2041(b)(1)(A).

- The holder cannot exercise the power except in conjunction with the creator of the power.[4]
- The holder cannot exercise the power except in conjunction with a person having a substantial adverse interest in the property involved.[5]

Example 13.3. Wendy Emerson grants her husband, Arnold, a power of appointment over property in a trust. However, Arnold may not exercise the power without the consent of Wendy. Arnold's power is not a general power of appointment.

Example 13.4. Anthony Santamaria grants a power of appointment to his wife Antonia over property in a trust. Antonia may invade the trust corpus only to provide for her health, education, support, or maintenance. Antonia's power is not a general power of appointment.

Property subject to a general power of appointment is includible in the gross estate of the holder of the power.[6] In addition, for gift tax purposes, the Code treats the exercise or release of a general power of appointment as a transfer of the property by the holder. Code Sec. 2514(e) treats the lapse of a power of appointment as a release of the power. However, the Code does not treat a disclaimer of such power as a release.[7]

Example 13.5. Don Miller holds a general power of appointment over $500,000 of property in a trust. At Don's death, his gross estate includes the $500,000 in the trust.

Example 13.6. Debra Harrison holds a general power of appointment over $425,000 of property in a trust. Debra releases the general power of appointment. Debra has made a $425,000 taxable gift.

The estate planner can use a power of appointment with the power of appointment trust. This trust, discussed in detail at ¶1225, qualifies for the marital deduction. In order to qualify, the power of appointment must be a general power of appointment. (Of course, with a QTIP, discussed at ¶1210, the grantor does not have to give a spouse a power of appointment.)

Estate planners may also use a power of appointment in a Code Sec. 2503(c) trust for a minor, as discussed in ¶425, and in other trusts that do not provide for the mandatory distribution of income. Such powers may allow gifts to the trust to qualify for the

---

[4] Code Sec. 2041(b)(1)(C)(i).

[5] Code Sec. 2041(b)(1)(C)(ii).

[6] Code Sec. 2041.

[7] Code Sec. 2514(b).

annual exclusion ($12,000 for 2006, indexed for inflation) from taxable gifts.[8]

Powers of appointment that do not meet the Code's definition of a general power of appointment are special powers of appointment. Special powers of appointment generally are not taxable either for estate or gift tax purposes.

> ***Example 13.7.*** Patricia Nolan holds a power of appointment over $780,000 in a trust. She may invade the corpus of the trust to provide for her health and education only. At Patricia's death, the value of the trust is not included in her gross estate.

The estate planner can create the widest possible special power of appointment by using the Code definition of a general power of appointment as a guideline. The estate planner does so by providing for a power of appointment that the holder can exercise in favor of any one or more individuals, corporations, organizations or entities. However, the holder cannot exercise the power in favor of himself or herself, the holder's estate, the holder's creditors, or the creditors of the holder's estate unless the power meets one of the exceptions in the Code.

The Code provides a very helpful rule to the estate planner who is designing or reviewing a will or trust agreement. Code Sec. 2041(b)(1)(A) provides that if an ascertainable standard relating to health, education, support, or maintenance limits the holder's power to consume or appoint the property, the power is not a general power of appointment.

The use of any one or more of the four statutory standards will cause the power to be sufficiently limited for estate tax purposes. Reg. § 20.2041-1(c)(2) contains examples of other limited powers that are not general powers of appointment. These examples of safe-harbor phrases include powers exercisable for the following benefits of the holder:

- Support in reasonable comfort
- Maintenance in health and reasonable comfort
- Support in his or her accustomed manner of living
- Education, including college and professional education
- Medical, dental, hospital and nursing expenses and expenses of invalidism

Reg. § 20.2041-3(b) provides that ". . . a power which by its terms is exercisable only upon the occurrence during the decedent's lifetime

[8] Code Sec. 2503(b).

of an event or contingency which did not in fact take place or occur during such time is not a power in existence on the date of the decedent's death." The regulation provides three examples of such contingencies: attaining a certain age, surviving someone, and dying without issue.

In one case, *E. Kurz Est.*,[9] an individual was the beneficiary of two trusts, a marital trust and a nonmarital trust. During her life, she was entitled to all the income from both trusts and had an unlimited right to demand the entire principal from the marital trust. She also had a right to demand payments of up to five percent of the principal from the nonmarital trust if the principal of the marital trust had been completely exhausted. At the time of her death, each trust had assets of over $3 million.

The estate tax return for the individual's estate did not include any of the assets of the nonmarital trust, arguing that no power existed at the time of death under Reg. § 20.2041-3(b). The U.S. Tax Court disagreed and included those assets in her estate after adopting and applying the following standard for contingent powers:

> [I]f by its terms a general power of appointment is exercisable only upon the occurrence during the decedent's lifetime of an event or contingency that has no significant nontax consequence independent of the decedent's ability to exercise the power, the power exists on the date of the decedent's death, regardless of whether the event or contingency did in fact occur during such time.

Thus, the estate planner should be careful to document the significant nontax consequences of an event or contingency that allows the exercise of the power.

When a person receives a general power of appointment and may exercise it during his or her lifetime, subject to certain exceptions discussed below, the exercise takes the property out of his or her gross estate. The exercise of the power reduces the potential estate tax even if the holder exercises the power within three years of death. This provision is beneficial. A power exercisable during lifetime, as well as by will, imparts greater flexibility than if the holder could exercise the power only by will. Some individuals may oppose such flexibility. They might fear, for example, that the children of the holder would pressure the holder to exercise the power. In addition,

---

[9] 101 TC 44, CCH Dec. 49,166, aff'd, CA-7, 95-2 USTC ¶ 60,215,

they may feel that limiting the exercise of the power to appointments by will is more likely to achieve their estate planning goals.

The exercise or release of a power of appointment, even if within three years of death, will ordinarily not draw the property subject to the power into the gross estate of the decedent. However, the Code provides an exception if the power relates to property that would be includible in the decedent's gross estate under Code Sec. 2035 (transfer of life insurance within three years of death) or Code Sec. 2038 (revocable transfers). In such cases, the exercise or release of the power will cause the property to be includible in the decedent's gross estate.

In this connection, estate planners may design some powers to lapse if the holder does not exercise them within a specified period, often the calendar year. The lapse of the power is a release of the power. However, this rule applies only to the extent the holder could have appointed property in excess of the greater of $5,000 or five percent of its aggregate value.[10] This exception is a five-and-five power.

Estate planners often use a five-and-five power with a nonmarital trust. In this situation, one spouse desires to give the surviving spouse or other life beneficiary a noncumulative power of invasion of corpus without drawing the trust corpus into the gross estate of the holder.

A *Crummey* power of invasion allows the beneficiary of a trust to withdraw a contribution.[11] A *Crummey* power converts what would otherwise be a gift of a future interest in property to a present interest in property. Only present interests in property qualify for the annual exclusion ($12,000 for 2006, indexed for inflation) from taxable gifts.[12]

A lapse of a *Crummey* power of invasion may pose an estate tax problem if the *Crummey* power allows the withdrawal of the full annual exclusion or indeed any amount in excess of $5,000. The gross estate of the holder of the *Crummey* power may include the excess over $5,000 unless the five-percent rule provides relief.[13]

.01 Power of Appointment Checklist

1. Does the will or trust clearly state how the holder of the power may exercise it? In many states, the law presumes a residuary clause in a will to exercise all powers of appointment. Estate planners should consider providing that a

---

[10] Code Sec. 2514(e).

[11] *Crummey*, 68-2 USTC ¶12,541, 397 F2d 82 (9th Cir., 1968) aff'g in part and rev'g in part 25 TCM 772, Dec. 28,012(M), TC Memo 1966-144.

[12] Code Sec. 2503(b)(1).

[13] Code Sec. 2514(e).

person may exercise testamentary powers only if the will specifically refers to them. Because of differing requirements of state law, a lifetime power should be exercised in the form of a deed under the law of a specific state.

2. Does the instrument create any disguised powers? Can any beneficiary, acting as a trustee, pay principal to himself or herself unrestrained by an ascertainable standard? Does the trustee have to discharge a beneficiary's legal obligations?
3. May the holder exercise the power in another trust? Under the law of some states, a holder must exercise special powers outright unless the holder has specific authority to create a trust.
4. Does a provision for a gift terminate if the holder does not exercise the power?
5. May the holder appoint unequally among the objects of the power? May he or she exclude any or all of the objects?
6. Is a clear provision made for the payment of estate taxes on property subject to a general power? The Code provides that unless a contrary provision exists, the executor may recover the pro rata portion of the estate tax from the person receiving the appointive property.[14]
7. May the holder disclaim all powers? May the holder release or reduce the powers from general to special? Code Sec. 2518, as discussed generally in ¶ 1525, governs disclaimers. It specifically allows disclaimers of powers to be made free of gift tax. The document creating the power should provide for a method of disclaimer and for a beneficiary to limit the objects of a power to make it nontaxable.
8. If a trust provides for both a five-and-five power and a *Crummey* power, does it coordinate them?

.02 Matters to Consider before Exercising a Power of Appointment

The effective exercise of a power depends on careful observance of the requirements of the instrument creating the power. Sometimes the estate planner deliberately structures these requirements to discourage exercise or decrease the possibility of ineffective exercise, thus permitting the creator's plan of disposition to take effect.

[14] Code Sec. 2207.

Before exercising a power of appointment, the holder should carefully review the requirements of the will, trust, or other instrument conferring the power. The holder may want to consult an attorney for advice and counsel in interpreting the conditions under which he or she may exercise the power. Consulting an attorney is especially important if the holder wants to exercise the power for the holder's own benefit. Allowing the holder to invade the corpus of a trust for the holder's health, education, support, or maintenance meets the requirements of the Code for avoiding classification as a general power of appointment. However, this standard may be sufficiently vague to invite controversy with the beneficiaries of the trust or estate. The holder must strictly comply with the requirements of the power.

The holder should keep good records to document that the holder used the appointive property in accordance with the terms of the power. The holder wants to avoid controversy with beneficiaries of the trust or estate. In addition, the holder wants to be sure that the exercise of the power does not violate the limits of the power that keep the appointive property out of his or her gross estate.

If the holder of the power can exercise the power only in conjunction with one or more individuals who have an adverse interest in the property, the holder will need to secure their approval. If the adverse parties will not consent to the exercise of the power, the holder may want to explore ways of settling the dispute, including the use of a mediator.

Chapter 14

Selection and Appointment of Fiduciaries

Overview .... ¶1401
Selecting an Executor or Personal Representative ...... ¶1405
Alternate or Successor Fiduciaries .... ¶1410
Selection of Guardians .... ¶1415

¶1401 OVERVIEW

Chapter 6 discussed the selection and appointment of trustees. This chapter focuses on the selection and appointment of executors and guardians.

¶1405 SELECTING AN EXECUTOR OR PERSONAL REPRESENTATIVE

Executors are now known in some states as personal representatives. When choosing an executor, the first concern must be to find someone who is trustworthy, responsible, and capable of handling the job. The executor should also be free of possible conflicts of interest with the beneficiaries. If any potential conflict exists, the estate planner should clearly inform the client of the potential conflict. In some situations, the client may still decide to name that person as an executor. If the client's attorney can find no legal impediment, then he or she should implement the client's wishes. When a potential conflict of interest exists, a wise client should look for another candidate. Beyond avoiding potential conflicts of interest, the client should look to statutory qualifications. A nonresident individual may not be able to serve as executor. The estate planner should check state law on this point. An executor should command respect and confidence among the beneficiaries and not favor one beneficiary over another. Available time is another important factor in selection. Before a client nominates an executor in his or her will, he or she should specify the job requirements and ask for the person's consent.

A client should have a general idea of what an executor's job involves. An executor is responsible for the following:

- Gathering the assets of the estate
- Paying debts and claims against the estate
- Filing the estate tax return and estate's income tax return and paying the taxes
- Paying the estate's administration expenses
- Liquidating assets as required
- Distributing money and assets to beneficiaries
- Settling the estate

The executor must carry out all these duties and comply with legal and tax requirements, exceptions, and limitations.

An executor's job begins even before it is official. Between the testator's death and the probate of the will, the executor should be available to help the family as circumstances dictate, take steps to protect assets, and prepare for probate.

After the probate court admits the will to probate, the probate court will issue letters testamentary that give the executor the power to act on behalf of the estate. The executor must gather the assets of the estate and preserve them. The job may require detective-like skills to locate all the assets. Then the executor will want to pay the debts of the estate as quickly as possible. The executor may want to take advantage of discounts for prompt payment and avoid additional charges for interest and penalties. If the estate has business interests, the executor must do many other things. At the same time, the executor will be handling all the details of administering the estate, including the following:

- Obtaining appraisals
- Scheduling cash needs
- Preparing for sales
- Setting up the estate tax return
- Choosing the valuation date
- Filing any necessary gift tax returns
- Filing the estate's income tax returns
- Resolving any ambiguities in the will

Next, the executor makes distributions to beneficiaries. The executor must face the problems often associated with distributions, such as making an allocation of tax burdens, avoiding interest payments on cash legacies, and safeguarding distributions to minors, incompetents, charities, and others.

The will may contain a provision for a QTIP interest for the surviving spouse.[1] If so, the executor will have to make a timely election[2] for the interest to qualify for the marital deduction.[3] This election may call for the judicious exercise of discretion, taking into account several factors including projected tax results. The need for a QTIP election may have a direct bearing on the selection of the executor.

The executor has help in administering the estate. The estate attorney will be there to provide guidance. The attorney for the estate usually prepares the estate tax return (Form 706), with possible assistance from an accountant. The accountant usually prepares the income tax return (Form 1041). The accountant may also prepare schedules showing distributions to beneficiaries and allocations of estate taxes to them. Although the attorney and accountant provide valuable help, the executor retains the primary responsibility. If anything goes wrong, the court will likely hold the executor responsible. In lawyer's language, the executor is "surcharged."

The executor has plenty of room for error. In addition, fraud is always a possibility. The likelihood of error and its associated cost are less for a small estate than for a large estate. Because of the possibilities of error and fraud, the court will usually require a bond for the executor. The bond usually requires that other individuals sign as sureties. Even if the will states that the executor is to serve without bond, the probate court may require the executor and sureties to sign an unsecured paper bond.

Clients often consider a spouse or close family member as an executor. The spouse or close family member may be willing to serve without pay. However, nominating an inexperienced family member may be more problematic than nominating a professional fiduciary who will charge a fee.

.01 Corporate or Individual

The corporate fiduciary appears to have the better qualifications. A corporate fiduciary specializes in the handling of estates, has

[1] Code Sec. 2056(b)(7).

[2] Code Sec. 2056(b)(7)(B)(v).

[3] Code Sec. 2056(a).

experience, and is responsible. It has no emotional bias, is fair and impartial, is never sick, is never on vacation or abroad, and never dies.

The edge that an individual might have is familiarity with the family. That factor probably takes on more importance when the client is considering the appointment of a trustee, rather than an executor. However, familiarity with the family is still a factor the client should consider when appointing an executor.

.02 Co-executors

Co-trustees are apt to be more common than co-executors. However, sometimes a testator will feel more comfortable with two executors (an idea akin to having a co-signer on a loan). Co-executors might possibly make sense when one executor has special knowledge about the handling of certain estate assets such as business interests, works of art, or other items requiring special handling. Objections to co-executors are as follows: (1) divided authority holds the possibility of deadlocks; (2) there may be delays in getting together and approving actions to be taken; and (3) possible double fees and added costs. Unless there is a strong reason for having co-executors, one executor is generally preferable.

.03 Fees

Fees payable to executors vary in different states. When a testator names two or more executors, the total fee may be larger. In one state, if the estate is over a certain size, the law entitles each executor to a full statutory fee. However, if the estate has more than three executors, they must share the total fee. Thus, adding another executor may both increase the estate administration expenses and reduce the amount that each executor would otherwise receive. Occasionally a will directs an executor to serve without a fee. In such cases, however, the nominee generally has a right to decline to serve. Today, many trust companies will decline the appointment unless the estate assures them a certain amount in fees.

For federal estate tax purposes, administration expenses allowable by state laws, including executors' fees, are deductible from the gross estate.[4] An executor's fee is includible in the executor's gross income.[5] In many instances, the executor's income tax bracket will be lower than the lowest effective estate tax bracket. In such cases, the combined tax liability of the estate and the executor will be lower by paying the executor the statutory fee rather than leaving the executor an equivalent bequest. The estate saves more in estate taxes than the

[4] Code Sec. 2053(a)(2).

[5] Code Sec. 61(a).

executor pays in income taxes. An equivalent bequest would not be subject to income tax, but it would not be deductible from the gross estate in computing the taxable estate.

An estate must also file an income tax return (Form 1041) and pay income tax. The executor's fee is also a deductible administration expense.[6] To prevent a double deduction, the income tax deduction is not allowable unless the estate files a statement that it has not taken the same amount as an estate tax deduction. Thus, the executor should compare the tax saved by deducting administration expenses on the estate tax return to the tax saved by deducting administration expenses on the estate's income tax return.

The IRS may disallow the deduction for executors' fees if they are unreasonable.[7] Approval by a state court of competent jurisdiction is not determinative of the reasonableness of the fee for federal income tax purposes. The IRS may independently determine the reasonableness of an expense allowed by a state probate court.[8]

¶1410 ALTERNATE OR SUCCESSOR FIDUCIARIES

The executor the client names may be unable or unwilling to serve when the time comes to accept the appointment. Even if the executor accepts, the executor may later be unable or unwilling to continue to serve. Hence, a client should provide for a successor or alternate.

If the testator fails to act, the probate court will appoint someone as the administrator. Having an administrator rather than an executor may result in less effective performance and higher costs. A testator who names a successor or alternate can dispense with bonding if the testator so elects. Conceivably, a will could provide that any court-appointed administrator is to serve without bond. Although a court might give effect to this provision, writing such a provision would be ill-advised. In addition, the proceedings for the judicial appointment of an administrator involve court costs and legal expenses.

¶1415 SELECTION OF GUARDIANS

Individuals with minor children or incapacitated adult children should include a provision in their wills nominating a guardian for their children. If one parent dies or becomes incapacitated, the surviving parent usually will have custody of the children. Even if the

[6] Code Secs. 212 and 641(b).

[7] Reg. § 1.212-1(d).

[8] *J.M. White, Exr.*, CA-2, 88-2 USTC ¶13,777.

surviving parent is a non-custodial parent, the surviving parent usually receives custody of the children upon the custodial parent's death. However, in some cases the surviving parent may not receive custody if a court determines that such custody would not be in the children's best interest. Parents should also plan for the possibility of their death because of a common accident. Yet, many parents with young children have no formal instructions concerning who will take care of their children in the event of their death. If parents die without naming a guardian for their children, the court will decide whom to appoint as the guardian without knowing the parents' wishes. In such cases, the guardian the court chooses may not share the parents' values. Although the court does not have to appoint the guardian nominated by the parents, courts generally give great weight to the parents' wishes.

Parents should think carefully about whom they would want as the guardian for their children. In many cases, the parents will want a family member to be the guardian. In other cases, the parents may prefer a close friend. The parents should talk to the potential guardians to learn if they would be willing to serve. The individual(s) nominated should be of good character. Usually, the parents will want to nominate an individual who shares their basic values. The guardian should be able to get along well with the children and set a good example for them. The guardian should be healthy, both physically and emotionally. In some cases, the children's grandparents may not be physically capable of caring for small children. In short, the individual nominated should be able to act as a parent to the children.

An attorney should prepare a will or a codicil to an existing will to nominate a guardian. The parents should also nominate an alternate or successor in case the primary guardian is unable or unwilling to serve or to continue to serve.

In most cases, the parents should set up a trust to provide the financial support for the children. Parents should not ask the guardian to bear the financial burden of supporting the children. In addition, parents will want the children to have adequate financial resources for their support, health care, and education. Life insurance is a common way to provide the financial resources for the children's support in case of the parents' death. An alternative is to leave a bequest to the guardian or name the guardian as the beneficiary of a life insurance policy.

Chapter 15

Post-Mortem Planning

Overview ....¶ 1501
Income Tax Savings on Decedent's Final Return ....¶ 1505
Planning for the Estate's Liquidity ....¶ 1510
Handling Administration Expenses, Casualty Losses, and Estimated Taxes ....¶ 1515
Selecting the Valuation Date for Estate Assets ....¶ 1520
Changing the Testator's Plan ....¶ 1525
Qualified Terminable Interest Property (QTIP) Election ....¶ 1530

¶ 1501 OVERVIEW

The objective of estate planning is to improve the financial posture of the individuals involved and to protect their interests. Post-mortem planning is, strictly speaking, not estate planning. However, to the extent that the objective of minimizing estate taxes and fulfilling the wishes of the decedent can be achieved by post-mortem planning, post-mortem planning is part of the same process.

Moreover, the estate planner needs to be aware of things that he or she can do while the client is alive that will facilitate post-mortem planning. In this chapter, the focus is on post-mortem planning strategies of the executor to reduce estate taxes, income taxes, and otherwise improve the situation of the estate and its beneficiaries. This chapter also considers moves by a decedent's survivors that might operate to change the executor's plan.

¶ 1505 INCOME TAX SAVINGS ON DECEDENT'S FINAL RETURN

Following are some questions a financial planner may want to consider as a decedent's final return checklist.

.01 Should a Joint Income Tax Return Be Filed with the Surviving Spouse?

The executor or administrator may file a separate return for the decedent or elect to file a joint return with the surviving spouse if the surviving spouse has not remarried before the end of the tax year.

> **Planning pointer.** Generally, a joint return results in tax savings because of the tax rate schedule's income-splitting benefits. (In community property states, separate returns produce essentially the same tax results as joint returns.) In addition, some tax credits such as the earned income credit and the credit for child and dependent care services are not allowed on a separate return.

If the surviving spouse has not remarried and has a dependent child, the surviving spouse may file his or her income tax return using the filing status of surviving spouse (also known as widow(er) with dependent child) for the two years following the death of a spouse.[1] This filing status allows the surviving spouse to use the same tax rates as a married couple filing jointly.[2] However, it does not allow the surviving spouse an exemption for the decedent spouse.

An unabsorbed capital loss in the year of death might influence the election decision. Such a loss cannot be carried forward to the estate's income tax return. On a joint return, however, it can be applied against the surviving spouse's income. The same is true of losses suspended under passive activity rules (Chapter 24). The suspended passive losses are allowed on the decedent's final return to the extent that the basis of the property in the hands of the transferee exceeds the adjusted basis of the property immediately before the death of the decedent.[3] The unused passive losses may not be carried to the estate's income tax return.

The surviving spouse's tax year does not terminate at the decedent's death; it continues to its normal closing period. This rule affords an opportunity for the survivor to realize gains or losses and to accelerate or postpone income or deductions to minimize income taxes.

The liability on a joint return is joint and several.[4] Therefore, the election to file a joint return with the surviving spouse may subject the estate, and the surviving spouse, to additional tax liability. However, the innocent spouse rules[5] provide relief in some cases for joint and several liability.

---

[1] Code Sec. 2(a).
[2] Code Sec. 1(a).
[3] Code Sec. 469(g)(1)(C)(2).
[4] Code Sec. 6013(d)(3).
[5] Code Sec. 6015.

.02 Should Commissions of Surviving Spouse-Executor Be Waived?

A frequent question is whether an executor who is the surviving spouse should waive commissions.

The surviving spouse-executor should usually waive commissions subject to income tax, particularly when (1) he or she will otherwise receive an equivalent amount as a bequest or legacy (not taxable), and (2) the marital deduction exempts the estate from estate tax so that a deduction for the commissions is not needed. Complying with the Code and IRS guidelines on disclaimers is important to avoid incurring tax liability.

A survivor-executor has an opportunity to accelerate income to the final joint return by paying partial commissions from the estate before the close of the year in which the decedent died.

.03 Were Decedent's Medical Expenses Paid Within One Year After Death?

As a general rule, medical expenses are deductible only in the year paid.[6] However, medical expenses incurred before death and paid within one year after death may be claimed as medical deductions on the decedent's final return.[7] Moreover, medical expenses unpaid at death may be an estate tax deduction. To prevent a double deduction and to claim expenses as a deduction on the decedent's final income tax return,[8] the executor or administrator must file a waiver of right to claim the estate tax deduction.[9] Before deciding where to claim these medical deductions, the executor should compare the tax results of each approach.

> **Planning pointer.** Amounts are deductible for income tax purposes only to the extent they exceed 7.5 percent of adjusted gross income.[10] The amount deductible on an estate tax return is not subject to any limit.
>
> The executor should not claim the expenses on the estate tax return where no estate tax is payable because of the unlimited marital deduction or unified credit.

.04 Did the Decedent Constructively Receive Any Income Before Death?

One of the chief problems encountered in filing the decedent's final income tax return is the determination of what income items to

---

[6] Code Sec. 213(a).
[7] Code Sec. 213(c)(1).
[8] Code Sec. 2053(a).
[9] Code Sec. 213(c)(2).
[10] Code Sec. 2132(a).

include in it. For a cash-basis taxpayer, all income, actually or constructively received up to the time of death, must be reported.[11] (The decedent's gross income reported on his or her final return includes income constructively received before death, although actually received thereafter.) Income earned by a decedent but not included in the final income tax return because it was not actually or constructively received before death is known as income in respect of a decedent.[12] Such income is reported on the recipient's income tax return (beneficiary or estate).

> **Planning pointer.** Determining what income the decedent constructively received before death and what items constitute income in respect of a decedent is important. Determining that items of income were constructively received before death is advantageous if the decedent's marginal income tax rate is lower than the marginal rate of the beneficiary or of the estate.

.05 Did the Decedent Own Any U.S. Savings Bonds?

Series E, Series EE, and Series I bonds might constitute part of the decedent's assets. The interest income on U.S. Series E, Series EE, and Series I bonds is usually reported upon the bonds' redemption (or on redemption of Series H or HH bonds received in exchange for Series E or EE bonds). However, Code Sec. 454(a) permits an election to report as income in any one year the total increase in the value of Series E or EE bonds to date (or unreported income reflected in Series H or HH bonds received in an exchange). If the election is not made, the accrued income will be income in respect of a decedent.[13] Series I bonds are issued at their face amount. They pay a fixed interest rate plus an additional amount of interest based on the rate of inflation. A cash-basis taxpayer may defer the recognition of interest income on the Series I bonds until the earlier of their maturity date or date of disposal. A taxpayer must use the same accounting method to account for Series E, Series EE, and Series I bonds.

> **Note.** Series EE and Series HH bonds replaced Series E and Series H bonds as of January 1, 1980. Series HH bonds are available only on exchange for eligible Series E and Series EE savings bonds.

> **Planning pointer.** Reporting all of such accrued and previously unreported income on the decedent's final income tax return might be advantageous. This method is particularly advantageous if death occurred early in the final tax year

[11] Code Sec. 451(a) and Reg. § 1.451-2(a).
[12] Code Sec. 691(a).
[13] Code Sec. 691(a).

(e.g., January) before receipt of substantial taxable income. Even if the election results in the imposition of federal income taxes (interest on these bonds is exempt from state and local income taxes), the tax liability is deductible on the estate tax return.[14]

.06 Does the Survivor Qualify as a Surviving Spouse?

A qualifying surviving spouse[15] is eligible to use the joint return tax rates[16] for two years following the year of death if: (1) a dependent child resides in the survivor's household, (2) the survivor was entitled to file a joint return with the decedent for the year of death, and (3) the survivor did not remarry in the taxable year in issue.

Planning pointer. Compare the income tax brackets of the surviving spouse and the estate, and strive to maximize the benefits and advantages of joint return rates. The estate might be able to accelerate income to the surviving spouse by making distributions during the two-year period. In making the comparison, a financial planner should remember that the income tax brackets of estates are highly compressed. For example, for tax years beginning in 2006, the 15-percent rate applies to an estate's taxable income up to $2,050 and the 25-percent rate applies to taxable income between $2,050 and $4,850. The 28-percent rate applies to taxable income between $4,850 and $7,400 while the 33-percent rate applies to taxable income between $7,400 and $10,050. Finally, the 35-percent rate applies to taxable income over $10,050.

.07 Are There Any Bad Debts or Losses for Worthless Securities to Be Claimed?

If there are any debts or stocks that are worthless at the date of death, the executor should determine whether worthlessness occurred during the year of death or in a prior open year.

Planning pointer. If worthlessness occurred during prior open years, the executor should consider a refund claim. The statute of limitations for claiming a refund is seven years from the due date of the return for a claim arising from a worthless debt.[17]

¶1510 PLANNING FOR THE ESTATE'S LIQUIDITY

The estate will need cash or cash equivalents for many purposes, such as payment of debts, taxes, cash legacies, and administration expenses. With good advance planning and good luck, the estate's

---

[14] Code Sec. 2053(a).
[15] Code Sec. 2(a).
[16] Code Sec. 1(a).
[17] Code Sec. 6511(d)(1).

liquidity needs will have been provided. If these elements are missing, the estate could be in trouble. Listed in this section are five ways in which the executor may be able to solve the estate's liquidity problem.

.01 Distributions in Kind

Obviously, if the executor can distribute assets instead of cash, the cash needs of the estate will be reduced. Thus, the client's will should give the executor the required authority. The executor might be able to distribute assets in kind without express authority with the consent of all beneficiaries. However, the consent of all beneficiaries might not be sufficient grounds for a distribution in kind in the case of a cash bequest. Unless the will provides specific authority covering the cash bequest as well as all others, a single beneficiary may hold up the distribution in kind and compel a forced sale of assets at an inopportune time. If the estate would be allowed a marital deduction and the executor is planning to make a distribution in kind, special rules apply that demand attention. These rules are discussed at ¶ 1220. Also, under Code Sec. 643(e), the beneficiary receives the estate's basis in property distributed in kind, and the estate's distribution deduction is limited to the lesser of the property's basis or its fair market value. However, the executor may elect to have the gain recognized by the estate. In this case, the beneficiary receives a stepped-up basis, and the estate receives a full distribution deduction. If the estate makes this election, it applies to all distributions made during the taxable year.

An executor must look very closely at the comparative income tax situations of the estate and the beneficiaries. If the estate has capital losses, the executor should consider making the election, because the estate could use the losses to offset the gain. In making the comparison, the executor should remember that the income tax brackets of estates are highly compressed (see ¶ 1509.06). For example, for tax years beginning in 2006, the top 35% rate applies to an estate's taxable income in excess of $10,050. By comparison, the 35-percent rate applies to single taxpayers for taxable income over $336,350 for 2006.

.02 Putting Depressed Assets in Trust

A will often creates a trust, and the executor encounters a variety of assets. Some of these assets are marketable, but others are not marketable or are temporarily depressed in value. Under these circumstances, the executor should consider selling the marketable assets (for example, listed securities) and transferring the other assets to the trust. In turn, the trust would be in a better position to hold out for a sale at fair market value or for a lesser amount justifying retention. If a living trust created by the testator is in existence and is funded, a sale of estate assets to the trust might be advisable. Such a sale is especially advisable if both the trust instrument and the will contemplate and authorize the sale.

.03 Borrowing from a Beneficiary or Trust

The estate can raise cash by borrowing from a beneficiary or a trust. The trust will usually be a living trust created by the testator. While authorization in the will or trust is not required for an executor to borrow from a beneficiary or trust, express authorization in the will and trust instruments will make such borrowing easier. If the proceeds of a life insurance policy payable to the trust will be the source of the borrowed funds, the estate planner should take care to avoid an arrangement calling for mandatory lending of the funds in order to assure their exclusion from the gross estate.[18]

.04 Business Interests

The gross estate might include an interest in a closely held business, whether in corporate form or not. If such an interest represents 35 percent of the adjusted gross estate, a corporation may use a tax-favored stock redemption under Code Sec. 303 to provide the estate with liquidity. In addition, if the same percentage test is met, an installment payment of estate tax liabilities under Code Sec. 6166 (14 years) will help ease the estate's liquidity problem. These provisions are discussed in detail in Part II of this book.

.05 Minimizing Income and Estate Taxes

Techniques for minimizing income and estate taxes by the judicious use of deductions for administration expenses and losses are discussed at ¶1515. To the extent that these techniques save taxes, they reduce liquidity needs.

¶1515 HANDLING ADMINISTRATION EXPENSES, CASUALTY LOSSES, AND ESTIMATED TAXES

An executor may choose to deduct administration expenses and casualty losses either on the estate tax return[19] or on the estate's income tax return.[20] If the executor takes these deductions on the estate tax return, they reduce the estate tax at the expense of a higher income tax liability. The reverse is true if the executor takes the deductions on the income tax return.

---

[18] Reg. § 20.2042-1(b)(1).

[19] Code Secs. 2053 and 2054.

[20] Code Sec. 642(g).

Usually, the choice made by the executor will turn on the relative income and estate tax brackets. In estates not subject to the estate tax either by reason of the unified credit and/or the marital deduction or charitable deduction, the executor should take the deduction on the income tax return.

On the other hand, if the estate is subject to estate tax, the executor should compare the applicable estate and income tax rates. For 2006, the top income tax rate is 35 percent, which applies to taxable income over $10,050 for an estate. The top estate tax rate is 46 percent for 2006 and 45 percent for 2007, 2008, and 2009. The estate tax is repealed for 2010 only. In 2011 and thereafter, the top estate tax rate is 55 percent. Thus, in many instances, the estate tax deduction will produce greater savings. However, in some cases, the income tax deduction will produce slightly higher savings than the estate tax deduction.

Nevertheless, the choice between deducting these items on the income or estate tax return involves more than a comparison of the relative tax brackets and working out the arithmetic.

.01 Beneficiaries

An election one way or the other might adversely affect some estate beneficiaries and favor others. When this occurs, if the adverse effects or favoritism is substantial, costly litigation might ensue unless the parties can resolve the conflict by an adjustment.

.02 Distributions

If the estate will make distributions to beneficiaries, the comparison should be between the results taking into account the estate tax bracket and the income tax brackets of the beneficiaries, rather wthan the income tax bracket of the estate. In this connection, the income tax brackets of individuals are not nearly as compressed as those that apply to estates. For example, for tax years beginning in 2006, an estate hits the top bracket of 35 percent for taxable income over $10,050 whereas a single individual is taxed at a rate of 10 percent on taxable income up to $7,550, at a rate of 15 percent on taxable income between $7,550 and $30,650 and at 25 percent between $30,650 and $74,200 and at higher rates on taxable income above that amount.

.03 Marital Deduction

The choice of returns for the deduction can affect the marital bequest. If the will provides for a marital deduction[21] formula

[21] Code Sec. 2056(a).

bequest, a deduction taken on the estate's income tax return, rather than on the estate tax return, would increase the marital deduction.

.04 Effect on Beneficiaries of a Trust

If the estate property is placed in a trust, the executor must consider the effect of the election on the income beneficiaries and on the remaindermen. Administration expenses, casualty losses, and estate taxes paid are ordinarily charges against principal and the remaindermen. Therefore, the deduction of administration expenses and casualty losses on the estate tax return, to the extent that it reduces the estate tax, benefits the remaindermen. Deduction of those items on the income tax return of the trust benefits the income beneficiaries, at the expense of the remaindermen.

Accordingly, under local law, if the executor takes the deductions on the income tax return of the trust, the income account might be required to compensate the principal account in an amount equal to the increased estate taxes resulting from deducting the items against income. If a charity is the remainderman, the amount credited to the principal account would give rise to an additional charitable contribution deduction.[22]

.05 Special Estate Tax Factors

In some cases, the election can affect estate taxes, even where the estate makes full use of the unlimited marital deduction.[23] There might be estate tax liability if the administration expenses deducted on the income tax return, when added to certain other items, exceed the available applicable credit amount of the unified credit.[24] These other items are (1) the decedent's post-1976 adjusted taxable gift amount;[25] (2) debts that, although enforceable, are not deductible for estate tax purposes because they were not incurred for consideration in money or money's worth;[26] and (3) lifetime transfers to persons other than the decedent's spouse that are includible in the decedent's gross estate.[27]

.06 Interest Deductions

Two prime issues as to the deductibility of interest paid or incurred by an estate are (1) deductibility against income, and (2) deductibility as an administration expense against the estate tax.

As for the first issue, the disallowance of the deduction for personal interest contained in Code Sec. 163(h) applies to estates

[22] Code Sec. 2055(a).
[23] Code Sec. 2056(a).
[24] Code Sec. 2010(c).
[25] Code Sec. 2001(b)(1).
[26] Code Sec. 2053(c)(1)(A).
[27] Code Secs. 2036 and 2038.

("all taxpayers other than corporations"). Personal interest is any interest other than interest in connection with a trade or business, investment interest, interest taken into account in computing income or loss from a passive activity, qualified residence interest, and interest payable on unpaid estate taxes during which an extension of time for the payment of such tax is in effect under Code Sec. 6163 (payment of estate tax on the value of a reversionary or remainder interest in property).

Note that Code Sec. 6161 (which allows the discretionary extension of time to pay estate taxes) is not excepted from the definition of personal interest. In addition, the estates of decedents who died after December 31, 1997, may not deduct interest paid on the 14-year extension for the payment of estate taxes under Code Sec. 6166.[28] The denial of the interest deduction in such cases, as well as personal interest on any other borrowing by the estate for any legitimate purpose, obviously adds to the cost of such borrowing.

If the gross estate includes a trade or business, incorporated or unincorporated, any interest paid or incurred in connection with the estate's operation of the business would be deductible.[29]

Investment interest is deductible,[30] as noted within the exception, but deductibility is limited to the net investment income received by the estate for the year.[31] Through 2010, investment income does not include qualified dividends unless the taxpayer elects to include them and forego the reduced tax rate of 15 percent (or 5 percent if the estate is in the 15-percent bracket for ordinary income) on such qualified dividends. Long-term capital gains are not included in investment income unless the taxpayer elects to include them in investment income. Any long-term capital gains included in investment income are taxed as ordinary income.[32]

Otherwise qualifying interest paid or accrued by an estate is treated as qualified residence interest if paid in connection with a home used as a qualified residence by a beneficiary who has a present or residuary interest in the estate.[33]

As to the second issue, deductibility against the estate tax, deductibility basically hinges on the benefit to the estate.

An estate may not deduct the interest paid for the 14-year deferral of estate taxes under Code Sec. 6166 as an administration

---

[28] Code Sec. 163(h) and Committee Reports on P.L. 105-34 (Revenue Reconciliation Act of 1997).

[29] Code Secs. 162(a) and 163(h)(2)(A).

[30] Code Secs. 163(a) and 163(h)(2)(B).

[31] Code Sec. 163(d)(1).

[32] Code Sec. 163(d)(4)(B) and Temp. Reg. § 1.163(d)-IT.

[33] Code Sec. 163(h)(4)(D).

expense on the estate tax return.[34] Interest payable by an executor electing to pay estate tax in installments under other applicable Code provisions is deductible as an administration expense.[35] However, the interest is deductible only when it accrues, and the estate claims the deduction. At that time, the estate tax is recomputed. No refund will be made until the entire tax liability has been paid; interest on the refund accrues daily.[36]

In *C. Graegin Est.*,[37] the U.S. Tax Court allowed an estate to deduct currently as an administration expense the full amount of interest due 15 years later. The federal estate tax amounted to $204,000. The estate had only about $20,000 in liquid assets and the executor decided the best course was to borrow to pay the estate tax. The lender was a wholly owned subsidiary of the closely held corporation in which the decedent held stock. It agreed to loan the estate the needed $204,000 on an unsecured note bearing interest at 15 percent, the prime rate at that time, with principal and interest in a single payment due 15 years later. Prepayment of interest or principal was barred.

Tax-exempt income presents a special situation. The expenses of earning tax-exempt income are not deductible for income tax purposes,[38] but may be deducted for estate tax purposes.[39]

.07 Distributions

The executor will also want to take into account the effect of an election on income beneficiaries when he or she is required to make current distributions of income under the terms of the will or applicable state law. While the estate receives an income tax deduction for the amounts distributed,[40] the amount received by beneficiaries is taxable.[41] Thus, their tax brackets become a factor in the choice to be made. Code Sec. 642(h) provides that if, on termination of the estate, its deductions exceed the estate's gross income for the year, the excess is allowable as a deduction by the beneficiaries succeeding to the property of the estate. The terminating deductions passed through to beneficiaries apparently would be subject to the two-percent floor on Code Sec. 212 deductions and other miscellaneous itemized deductions.[42] In view of this limitation, some estates, instead of passing through terminating deductions, may be able to file amended estate tax returns and claim the amounts as administration expenses.[43]

[34] Code Sec. 2053(c)(1)(D).

[35] *C.A. Bahr Est.*, 68 TC 74, CCH Dec. 34,369 (Acq.); Rev. Rul. 78-125, 1978-1 CB 292.

[36] Rev. Rul. 80-250, 1980-2 CB 278.

[37] 56 TCM 387, CCH Dec. 45,107(M), TC Memo. 1988-477.

[38] Code Sec. 265(a).

[39] Code Sec. 2053(a).

[40] Code Sec. 661(a).

[41] Code Secs. 61(a) and 662(a).

[42] Code Sec. 67.

[43] Code Sec. 2053(a).

A decedent's estate has the right to take advantage of the 65-day rule for distributions, formerly available only to trusts. Thus, for purposes of computing the estate's income tax liability, the executor may elect to treat distributions made within 65 days after the close of its tax year as if they were made on the last day of the tax year.[44] The executor must make the election by the due date of the estate's income tax return, including extensions. The election is irrevocable.[45]

.08 Timing

The executor should also consider the timing of the payments. If the estate is on a cash basis, the executor might want to advance the date of payment of certain expenses. A provision in the will can help here, because otherwise a court order might be required.

.09 Selling Expenses of the Estate

The selling expenses of the estate are deductible against the estate tax or the income tax, but not both. This rule is made clear by Code Sec. 642(g), which bars not only double deductions but also the use of an expense as an offset against the sales price.

.10 Deductions Against Income in Respect of a Decedent

"Income in respect of a decedent" (IRD) generally refers to those amounts the decedent was entitled to as gross income, but which were not includible in his or her final income tax return (or in any prior year) under the accounting method used. IRD is taxable to the recipient under Code Sec. 691(a).

Code Sec. 691(c) allows a deduction for the federal estate tax attributable to the inclusion of income in respect of a decedent. Code Sec. 691(b) allows the IRD recipient deductions for unpaid business expenses, interest, taxes, investment expenses, and the foreign tax credit that are not allowable on the decedent's final return. These Code Sec. 691(b) deductions are known as deductions in respect of a decedent. The Code Sec. 642(g) bar on double deductions does not extend to deductions in respect of a decedent; they may be taken as both estate tax deductions and income tax deductions.

.11 Selecting a Tax Year

Although a trust must generally use the calendar year as its tax year,[46] an estate may choose a fiscal year or the calendar year as its

---

[44] Code Sec. 663(b).

[45] Reg. § 1.663(b)-2(a)(1).

[46] Code Sec. 644(a).

tax year.[47] If the estate's first income tax return is for a period of less than 12 months, the estate does not have to annualize its income.[48] The executor should choose the tax year of the estate carefully. The executor should consider the timing of the estate's expected revenues and expenses and choose the tax year that will minimize the estate's income tax liability.

.12 Estimated Payments of Income Tax

An estate must make estimated income tax payments for any taxable year ending more than two years after the date of the decedent's death.[49] An estate is subject to the same penalty for underpayment of estimated taxes as is an individual.[50] Underpayment of estimated taxes could subject the estate to the penalty for underpayment of estimated tax, and possibly subject the executor to surcharge, which is personal liability for the penalty.

Making intelligent projections of an estate's taxable income is often difficult because it requires a projection of deductible distributions to beneficiaries. The conscientious executor needs to know the income tax picture of the beneficiaries, which often becomes clear only fairly late in the estate's tax year.

> **Planning pointer.** Wills should be drafted to include exonerations for executors who cause the estate to pay the penalty for underpayment of estimated tax by reason of incorrect estimation of quarterly tax payments. This exoneration should be effective if the fiduciary undertakes to discharge his or her duty in good faith. This provision will prevent beneficiaries from taking fiduciaries to task for failure to discharge duties that are exceedingly difficult to perform.

The executor should consider claiming every administration expense deduction on the estate tax return (it can subsequently be shifted to the income tax return), because no waiver is required to support the estate tax deduction.

For estate tax purposes, administration expenses may be paid at any time during the course of the administration. Frequently, an estate will have its highest taxable income in its first full year. If so, the executor should pay these expenses during the first year in order to claim them against high income. The executor should claim any expense that is not deductible for income tax purposes (e.g., an expense relating to tax-exempt income) on the estate tax return.

---

[47] Code Sec. 441(b) and Temp. Reg. § 1.441-1T(b)(2).

[48] Reg. § 1.443-1(a)(2).

[49] Code Sec. 6654(l)(2).

[50] Code Sec. 6654(l)(1).

¶ 1520 SELECTING THE VALUATION DATE FOR ESTATE ASSETS

In general, estate assets are valued at the date of death.[51] However, an executor may elect to value all the property included in the decedent's gross estate six months later (or the date of the earlier disposition of any particular assets) under Code Sec. 2032(a) if the election will decrease both the value of the gross estate and the sum of any estate and generation-skipping transfer tax (after credits) imposed.[52]

The purpose of this election is to reduce the tax liability where there has been a shrinkage in value following death.[53] The estate may use date of death valuation or the alternate valuation date only.

.01 Use of QTIP to Qualify for Alternate Valuation

Despite the rule of Code Sec. 2032(c), discussed above, the opportunity might exist to elect the alternate valuation date where estate assets have depreciated in value and no estate tax ordinarily would be due by reason of the marital deduction.[54]

The idea would be to take steps to make sure that a small estate tax would become due without election of the alternate valuation date. The election of the alternate valuation date would reduce the gross estate and the small estate tax. Thus, it would satisfy both conditions of Code Sec. 2032(c).

How can the estate achieve this result? If the marital deduction bequest qualifies for a QTIP election,[55] the executor can make a partial QTIP election to generate a small estate tax. If the gross estate has decreased in value during the six months following the decedent's death, the alternate valuation election would then reduce the gross estate and thereby reduce the small estate tax resulting from the partial QTIP election.

In view of the above, a QTIP pecuniary marital deduction provision (with the residuary estate to pass to a nonmarital trust or to nonspouse beneficiaries) might be an attractive option. If the estate appreciates in value, date-of-death values can be chosen so that all appreciation can be allocated to the nonmarital share. If the estate depreciates, the use of the alternate valuation date will allocate all of the depreciation to the marital deduction share, thus reducing assets to be ultimately subject to tax on the spouse's death.

---

[51] Code Sec. 2031(a).

[52] Code Sec. 2032(c).

[53] Reg. § 20.2032-1.

[54] Code Sec. 2056(a).

[55] Code Sec. 2056(b)(7).

The executor should carefully analyze the decision to pay a small amount of estate tax. Depending on the state of the decedent's domicile, the payment of a small amount of federal estate tax might have to be accompanied by a much larger amount of state inheritance tax.

.02 Late-Filed Returns

Code Sec. 2032(d) provides that the alternate valuation date is permitted if elected on a late-filed estate tax return that is filed no more than one year after its due date. Further, the House Committee Report to the Tax Reform Act of 1984 (P.L. 98-369) states that the alternate valuation date must be elected on the first estate tax return filed.

¶1525 CHANGING THE TESTATOR'S PLAN

Sometimes the best laid plans do not work out. Something happens. Assets appreciate or depreciate in value. A loss occurs. An unexpected gift is received. A new family member arrives while an old one departs. Often, events move faster than one can adjust plans to the new situations. Sometimes the testator is simply neglectful. Death comes, and it is too late to change the testator's estate plan. However, those who survive can make certain changes in the plan of disposition through disclaimers, settlements, and the election to take against the will.

.01 Disclaimers

Beneficiaries are not forced to accept property bequeathed to them under another person's will. They can disclaim a bequest. Of course, no one is going to disclaim a sizable bequest unless some benefit comes from the disclaimer, if not for the disclaimant, then for others who will benefit by the disclaimer. If someone, who does not wish to accept an interest in property, makes a qualified disclaimer, the interest disclaimed will be treated for federal tax purposes as if it had never been transferred to that person.[56] The disclaimant will not be treated as having made a gift, for either gift or estate tax purposes, to the person to whom the interest passes by reason of the disclaimer.[57]

A beneficiary may make a qualified disclaimer of a beneficial interest in a decedent's IRA under Code Sec. 2518, even though, before making the disclaimer, the beneficiary received the required minimum distribution for the year of the decedent's death from the

---

[56] Code Sec. 2518(a).

[57] Reg. § 25.2518-1(b).

IRA. The beneficiary may make a qualified disclaimer under Code Sec. 2518 with respect to all or a portion of the balance of the account, except for the income attributable to the required minimum distribution that the beneficiary received. At the time of the disclaimer, the disclaimed amount and the income attributable to it must be paid to the beneficiary entitled to receive the disclaimed amount or segregated in a separate account.

An individual who disclaims his or her entire remaining interest in an IRA will not be considered a designated beneficiary of the IRA for purposes of Code Sec. 401(a)(9), if the individual makes the qualified disclaimer on or before September 30 of the calendar year following the calendar year of the decedent's death. In addition, on or before that September 30, the disclaimant must be paid the income attributable to the required minimum distribution amount, so that the disclaimant is not entitled to any further benefit in the IRA after September 30 of the calendar year following the calendar year of the decedent's death.[58]

By the surviving spouse. If the surviving spouse's qualifying marital deduction bequest gives the spouse more than he or she might need or consume, the unconsumed amount will be includible in the surviving spouse's gross estate. This situation could result in the survivor's beneficiaries receiving less than they might otherwise receive. In this type of situation, the surviving spouse might wish to disclaim all or part of the bequest. If the disclaimer will result in the bequest passing to those he or she wishes to benefit (e.g., the survivor's children), the property will never be included in the survivor's gross estate and will pass to the intended beneficiaries without gift tax liability, and possibly without any added transfer expenses. The surviving spouse may also make a valid disclaimer although the property disclaimed goes to a trust in which he or she has an income interest. However, Reg. § 25.2518-2(e)(2) requires that this result occur without the surviving spouse's direction (i.e., as a result of a provision in the decedent's will directing the disposition of any disclaimed property). In addition, the power to receive the income from the trust must be limited by an ascertainable standard.

Of course, any disclaimer of a marital deduction bequest might increase the estate tax liability of the decedent's estate unless it is in favor of a charity[59] or a sufficient amount of unified credit[60] is available to offset the liability. Even if the estate incurs additional estate tax, the disclaimer might possibly reduce the estate tax and

---

[58] Rev. Rul. 2005-36, IRB 2005-26 (June 27, 2005).

[59] Code Sec. 2055.

[60] Code Sec. 2010.

administration costs of the disclaimant's estate. These factors should be considered. A qualified disclaimer has been held to override a QTIP election.

Disclaimer in favor of surviving spouse. Sometimes when the surviving spouse is to receive a marital deduction bequest[61] that might be deemed less than adequate and there are bequests to children or other relatives, the executor might want to have the other beneficiaries disclaim their bequests, in whole or in part. The effect will be to increase the marital deduction and so reduce estate taxes. Code Sec. 2056(a) permits an estate tax marital deduction for property disclaimed by a third person that passes in favor of the surviving spouse. Children might do this for a variety of reasons, such as concern for the surviving spouse's needs. They might also do so with the reasonable hope that gifts in the amount of their disclaimed bequest will later be forthcoming. Such gifts could be made in installments to take advantage of the annual gift tax exclusion.[62] Also, they might ultimately benefit by the resulting estate tax savings.

Disclaimers by others without regard to the marital deduction. Occasionally a legatee will not need a legacy and prefer to have it go to others. A disclaimer may accomplish this purpose without incurring gift tax liability, while keeping the legacy out of the legatee's gross estate.

Powers of appointment. A general power of appointment may be the object of a disclaimer. If a decedent holds a general power of appointment at death, all the property subject to the power will be includible in his or her gross estate under Code Sec. 2041.

If an individual is given or bequeathed a general power of appointment, any exercise of that power, even within nine months, is not treated as a qualified disclaimer. Rather, it is considered an acceptance of the power's benefits. Moreover, a release of a general power of appointment is treated as a gift or bequest of the property subject to the power. However, a qualified disclaimer of the power does not trigger any tax consequences.

If the surviving spouse enjoys a power of appointment marital deduction trust, circumstances might exist in which he or she might wish to disclaim the power of appointment. The disclaimer in such case would result in the loss of the marital deduction and increase estate taxes for the decedent's estate. The survivor's interest would be converted to a life estate and would not be includible in the surviving spouse's gross estate. Depending on the factors such as the

---

[61] Code Sec. 2056(a).

[62] Code Sec. 2503(b).

survivor's age, health, the relative sizes of the survivor's gross estate and the decedent's gross estate, the disclaimer of the power could produce good results.

Joint tenancies and tenancies by the entirety. The rules for disclaimers of interests in joint tenancies with right of survivorship and tenancies by the entirety made on or after December 31, 1997, are contained in Reg. § 25.2518-2(c)(4)(i). These rules provide that a disclaimer of an interest received in joint tenancy with right of survivorship or tenancies by the entirety must be made no later than nine months after the creation of the tenancy. Similarly, if a person receives a joint interest in property by operation of law upon the death of the first joint tenant to die, a disclaimer of the survivorship interest must be made no later than nine months after the death of the first joint tenant to die. The survivorship interest is generally deemed to be a one-half interest in the property regardless of the consideration provided by the individual making the disclaimer and regardless of the amount included in the decedent's gross estate under Code Sec. 2040. In general, all of the amount of a joint interest in property is included in a decedent's gross estate except to the extent of consideration provided by another person.[63] These rules under Reg. § 25.2518-2(c)(4)(i) apply regardless of whether the interest can be unilaterally severed under local law.

However, for interests in real estate held by spouses as joint tenancies with right of survivorship or as tenancies by the entirety created on or after July 14, 1988, the surviving spouse may disclaim any part of the joint interest that is includible in the decedent's gross estate under Code Sec. 2040.[64] Under Code Sec. 2040(b), one-half of the value of a joint interest in property held only by a married couple with right of survivorship or as tenants by the entirety is included in the decedent's gross estate. In addition, a special rule applies to joint bank accounts, brokerage accounts, and other investment accounts in which the transferor may unilaterally withdraw his or her own contributions without the consent of the other joint tenant.[65] Such contributions are revocable and therefore are not completed gifts for purposes of the gift tax.[66] For such accounts, the transfer creating the survivor's interest in the decedent's share of the joint account occurs on the date of the decedent's death. Thus, to be effective, a qualified disclaimer of such a joint account must occur no later than nine months after the date of the decedent's death. However, a surviving joint tenant may not disclaim any part of the account attributable to any consideration that he or she provided.

---

[63] Code Sec. 2040(a).

[64] Reg. § 25.2518-2(c)(4)(ii).

[65] Reg. § 25.2518-2(c)(4)(iii).

[66] Reg. § 25.2511-1(h)(4).

Planning pointer. When a client did not have the benefit of pre-death estate planning, estate planners frequently confront the problem of applicable credit amount (unified credit) bequests that are underfunded by reason of the ownership of substantial joint property by a spouse. Post-mortem planning might be necessary to salvage a defective estate plan and produce a larger nonmarital disposition. Thus, with the consent of the surviving spouse, the survivorship interest (i.e., the half interest deemed to belong to the predeceasing joint tenant) may be divested to other persons.

Disclaimer to favor charity. Code Sec. 2055(a) allows a deduction for a charitable transfer resulting from a disclaimer. Thus, if a decedent's will provides that a charity would receive a disclaimed bequest, a disclaimer might reduce estate taxes, while at the same time taking the bequest out of the disclaimant's estate. However, the beneficiary should consider income tax consequences before disclaiming a bequest. If the bequest is accepted and then given to charity, the legatee-donor will be entitled to an income tax deduction.[67] The value of the income tax deduction must be weighed against any higher estate taxes resulting from the acceptance of the bequest and the effect of such higher estate taxes on the legatee and others with whom he or she is concerned.

Income interest. Family income tax savings might play a part in motivating a disclaimer. For example, a family member in the highest income tax bracket who is given an income interest under a trust may wish to disclaim his or her interest if it places more income in the hands of family members in lower tax brackets. Also, diversion of income to family members in lower tax brackets might prevent loss of deductions or other tax breaks that are reduced or eliminated as adjusted gross income hits certain levels.

Mechanics of disclaimers. Code Sec. 2518 provides a single set of definitive rules for disclaimers for purposes of the estate, gift, and generation-skipping transfer taxes.

To be effective for tax purposes, a disclaimer must be qualified. A qualified disclaimer is an irrevocable and unqualified refusal to accept an interest in property. It must satisfy four requirements: (1) the refusal must be in writing; (2) the written refusal must be received by the transferor, his or her legal representative, or the holder of legal title to the property not later than nine months after the day on which the transfer is made (however, in any event,

---

[67] Code Sec. 170(a).

the period will not expire until nine months after the day on which a young person making a disclaimer attains age 21); (3) the person who disclaims must not have accepted the interest or any of its benefits before making the disclaimer; and (4) the interest disclaimed must pass to someone other than the person making the disclaimer without any direction on the part of the person making the disclaimer. (A valid disclaimer by a surviving spouse may be made even though the interest passes to a trust in which he or she has an income interest subject to an ascertainable standard.)

If any possibility exists that a disclaimer might be a useful post-mortem tool, the estate planner should advise the client to make provision for disclaimers in the will. This provision might include such details as the following:

- Disclaimers in whole or in part
- The requirement of a written statement to be delivered to the executor within the time limits imposed
- Provision for the disposition of the disclaimed bequest and details as to what is required to assure an effective disclaimer for federal tax purposes even though it may be ineffective under local law

The provision in the will that disposes of the disclaimed bequest is important to the one who is going to disclaim. The disclaimant cannot disclaim property in favor of anyone; the disclaimant can only refuse to accept the bequest and allow it to pass under that provision of the will.

.02 Election Against the Will

In many states, when a person's will does not give the surviving spouse a prescribed share of the testator's estate, the surviving spouse is given a right to take against the will. If the surviving spouse makes the election, he or she will receive a larger share of the estate. At the same time, the election might have the effect of increasing the marital deduction,[68] thereby reducing estate taxes.

In some circumstances, the election can also result in the allowance of a charitable deduction[69] not otherwise allowable. For example, the decedent's will puts the residue in trust to pay the income to the surviving spouse for life, with the remainder to a charity. The trust is not, however, in the form of an annuity trust or unitrust, and therefore, does not qualify for an estate tax charitable deduction. Assume that the surviving spouse's life interest does not

[68] Code Sec. 2056(a).

[69] Code Sec. 2055.

qualify for a marital deduction. On the survivor's election to take against the will, the life income interest fails and the charity receives an immediate interest that qualifies for an estate tax deduction.[70]

.03 Will Contest or Settlement

A will contest or settlement can result in a shift of property interests under the will from one beneficiary to another or from a beneficiary named in the will to a person not named. If the contest or settlement is bona fide and at arm's length, no gift occurs.[71]

The IRS does not challenge the estate tax deductibility of immediate payments to a charity in settlement of a bona fide will contest solely on the ground that the payments were made in lieu of a trust remainder interest that would not have been deductible because of failure to meet Code Sec. 2055(e)(2) requirements.[72] However, the IRS cautions that it will scrutinize settlements to ensure that they do not represent a collusive attempt to circumvent Code Sec. 2055(e)(2).

A 1993 U.S. Tax Court decision[73] addressed the impact on the marital deduction of a will clause permitting the executor to allocate administrative expenses between income and principal. The surviving spouse challenged the will on the ground of undue influence. The executor then claimed a marital deduction for the portion of the estate passing to the spouse under the agreement. The IRS argued that the agreement should be disregarded and the marital deduction should be equal to the amount passing to the spouse under the terms of the will. The U.S. Tax Court emphasized the settlement was reached in the context of a bona fide adversarial proceeding and allowed a marital deduction for the amount passing under the agreement.

¶ 1530 QUALIFIED TERMINABLE INTEREST PROPERTY (QTIP) ELECTION

An exception to the terminable interest rule permits qualifying terminable interest property (QTIP) to qualify for the marital deduction if the executor so elects.[74] Because the decision of whether to set up a QTIP trust is a pre-mortem one, the factors to be taken into account in deciding whether to make the election are discussed at ¶ 1210, where QTIP requirements are discussed generally.

---

[70] Rev. Rul. 78-152, 1978-1 CB 296, modified by Rev. Rul. 89-31, 1989-1 CB 277.

[71] *R.S. Righter, Exr.*, 66-2 USTC ¶ 12,427, 258 FSupp. 763, rev'd and rem'd on another issue, CA-8, 68-2 USTC ¶ 12,554, 400 F2d 344.

[72] Rev. Rul. 89-31, 1989-1 CB 277.

[73] *O. Hubert Est.*, 101 TC 314, CCH Dec. 49,342, aff'd CA-11, 95-2 USTC ¶ 60,209, aff'd SCt, 97-1 USTC ¶ 60,261.

[74] Code Sec. 2056(b)(7).

Part II

Special Situations

Chapter 16

Planning for the Executive

Overview .... ¶1601
Executive Compensation .... ¶1605
Lifetime and Estate Planning for Executive Benefits .... ¶1610
Use of Standard Techniques .... ¶1615
Total Financial Counseling for the Executive .... ¶1620
The Migratory Executive .... ¶1625

¶1601 OVERVIEW

Many corporate executives have a personal financial planning and estate planning position quite different from that of other individuals. They have pay packages that are bulging with fringe benefits, many of which they cannot take with them. Some fringe benefits, such as stock options, are often burdened with restrictions on current enjoyment. Other fringe benefits become available only on retirement or death.

Much of corporate executives' estates might be tied up in the stock of their employers. They are in need of diversification, but for tax and personal reasons, are locked into their employer's stock. They can be expected to have liquidity problems in life. Without adequate life insurance, their estates will also suffer liquidity problems.

In addition, corporate executives are often highly mobile, residing in different states or countries in the course of their careers. Rights and liabilities acquired in community property jurisdictions, for example, will frequently need to be examined. Different common law rights also could be called into question.

With compensation income taxed at a top rate of 35 percent through 2010, executives are always looking for fringe benefits that will enable them to live better and enjoy more without tax cost to them. If they are smart, they will look for fringe benefits with low after-tax cost to the company.

Some executives have little sense of capital or of saving. For them, the company provides and will continue to provide them financial security. However, many executives are becoming less sanguine in the face of takeovers, mergers, downsizings, business slowdowns, and adjustments.

An executive always faces business and social pressures to spend. Many executives have children who need or will need educating, often in private schools. Some children might already be in college or graduate schools.

These and other factors tend to create a great need for personal financial and estate planning on the part of corporate executives.

The emphasis in this chapter is on building the payroll estate and developing a feasible estate plan for the corporate executive. To help put things in focus, here is what a typical executive might look like and how his or her estate's balance sheet might shape up if he or she were to die today. The executive is 45; married; has three children ages 14, 17, and 19; and has a salary of $250,000.

Typical Executive Estate Balance Sheet

Assets	
Checking Account	$ 3,000
Savings Account (money market type)	20,000
Savings Account (joint with spouse ½ each)	10,000
Money Market Instruments	10,000
Listed Stock	55,000
Company Stock (restricted)	900,000
Unexercised Stock Options, 1,000 shares at $40 and current price $40	0
Home (joint with spouse ½ each)	625,000
Vacation Condominium (joint with spouse ½ each)	280,000
Unimproved Land	25,000
Tangible Personal Property	15,000
Deferred Compensation payable over 10 years after retirement or on death or termination of employment, present value	75,000
Vested Rights in Pension Plan	40,000
Vested Rights in Profit-Sharing Plan	554,000
Vested Rights in a Traditional IRA	6,000
Insurance	
Life Insurance (permanent—cash value $10,000, face value $50,000)	50,000
Group Life	100,000
Travel Accident Insurance ($50,000, but not figured in gross estate projection, because there is no way of knowing if the executive will die as a result of an accident)	
Total Assets	**$2,768,000**
Liabilities	
Home Mortgage	$ 220,000
Vacation Condominium Mortgage	60,000
Unimproved Land Mortgage	10,000
Company Stock Purchase Loan	100,000
Total Liabilities	$ 390,000
Net Worth	$ 2,378,000

The executive's spouse has no substantial assets of his or her own, except for a one-half interest in jointly held property of a value of $915,000. Without the $250,000 salary, the family's financial position, although not bad by the average person's standards, is not necessarily good. Without going into a detailed analysis, a few things are readily apparent. As far as the estate tax is concerned, the insurance policies are listed as part of the executive's assets so that $150,000 is includible in the gross estate (assuming $50,000 is not collected on the travel accident policy). The insurance policies might have been excluded from the gross estate if the executive had assigned the policies to a beneficiary other than the estate so that the executive retained no incidents of ownership at death.[1] Under Code Sec. 2040(b), only half of the jointly held property is includible in his or her gross estate.

With a gross estate of $2,310,500 (total assets of $2,768,000 minus one-half of the joint assets of $915,000 under Code Sec. 2040(b)) in 2006, and assuming that the mortgage debts and stock purchase debt are personal, amounting in all to $390,000 and adding say, $50,000 for administration expenses, the taxable estate is $1,870,500 (before application of the marital deduction). No federal estate tax is due as a result of the marital deduction[2] and the applicable exclusion amount of $2,000,000 (unified credit equivalent under Code Sec. 2010). But the estate needs $440,000 to pay administration expenses and debts. It has $150,000 in insurance proceeds and must gather the rest from the remaining assets available. The joint property is not available to the executor. The deferred compensation, if payable over a period of 10 years, will not be of much value, unless the company could be persuaded to pay the present value in a lump sum. The real estate does not appear to be a good source of ready cash, and the company stock might present some problems in view of the assumed restrictions. Spousal rights in the retirement benefits render them unavailable. Even if the savings account is drained and the listed securities sold, the estate does not have enough cash to pay off all of the debts and expenses. The family's position leaves much to be desired if existing living standards are to be maintained and the three children sent to college and graduate school.

A checklist of executive payroll benefits that an estate planner should consider as executive wealth builders follows. Special estate planning considerations and techniques for the executive are explored in this chapter.

---

[1] Code Sec. 2042.

[2] Code Sec. 2056(a).

¶1605 EXECUTIVE COMPENSATION

Salaries come first. To attract and retain good people, a company must pay competitive salaries. Indeed, to entice a good executive from another firm, a better-than-competitive salary, plus bonuses, is ordinarily required.

Salaries and cash bonuses are not everything. Capital-building benefits, such as qualified profit-sharing plans and stock bonus plans with their built-in capital accelerating mechanisms, are particularly attractive to executives. Executives are usually in high tax brackets and can benefit the most from the tax shelter. Tax-free current benefits such as, medical insurance, and life insurance, for example, are also popular. The executive whose company pays the premium on a $50,000 group-term life insurance policy receives the benefit tax free.[3] The company also receives benefits, in hard cash as well as intangible values. If the company is in a 35-percent tax bracket,[4] its after-tax cost of the group-term life insurance is only 65 percent of its cost.

Measuring company after-tax cost against the value of executive-employee benefits lies at the heart of most tax-favored compensation arrangements. However, it is not the whole story. For example, if it were, incentive stock options might not pass muster.

.01 Checklist of Executive Benefits

Here is a list of executive benefits and their income tax status along with an added cost/benefit analysis in many cases.

Qualified pension and profit-sharing plans and traditional IRAs. Executives are not taxed on employer contributions when made. Such plans also shelter the income from tax as long as it remains in the plan (see ¶905 for a detailed discussion of the qualified plan rules). Executives who are participants in qualified plans may also make contributions to traditional IRAs,[5] but the contributions will probably not be deductible (¶915).[6]

Qualified cash or deferred arrangements (401(k) plans). Employers are permitted to establish cash or deferred arrangements (CODAs) as part of a qualified plan (often referred to as 401(k) plans). Under a CODA, the executive and other employees have the choice of: (1) having the employer pay all (or part) of the employee's share of employer contributions in currently taxable cash, or (2) having payment made to the executive's or employee's account in a qualified

---

[3] Code Sec. 79(a).
[4] Code Sec. 11(b).
[5] Code Sec. 408.
[6] Code Sec. 219(g).

plan, with resulting income tax deferment. However, maximum annual elective deferrals are limited to $15,000 for 2006. The $15,000 limit is indexed for inflation in $500 increments beginning in 2007. In addition, individuals who are age 50 or older may contribute an additional $5,000 for 2006 and later years (see ¶ 925 for details).[7]

ESOPs. Employee stock ownership plans (ESOPs) generally take the form of a straight qualified stock bonus plan or one coupled with a qualified money-purchase pension plan (see ¶ 910 for a fuller discussion).[8]

As a tax-qualified plan, an ESOP enjoys all the tax advantages that qualified pension and profit-sharing plans enjoy. While there may be distributions of employer stock invested in an ordinary qualified profit-sharing plan, an ESOP must make a distribution of such stock if the participant or a beneficiary demands it.[9] However, an ESOP does not have to make a distribution of the stock if the charter or by-laws restrict the ownership of substantially all outstanding employer securities to employees or the ESOP.[10] The unrealized appreciation is not taxable to the executive on distribution, but only on a subsequent taxable transaction.

ESOPs offer added advantages to the company and its shareholders in that they may be used to raise capital by having the plan borrow to purchase stock from the company. The company's tax-deductible contributions to the plan enable it to pay off the loan. In effect the company pays off the loan with tax-deductible dollars. The ESOP might also provide a market for stock held by company shareholders. Other possible advantages of an ESOP to the company include its use as a financing vehicle in acquisitions, sales of part of the business, and buying out dissident shareholders.

ESOPs offer an opportunity to diversify tax free under a provision providing for nonrecognition of gain on a sale of company stock to an ESOP where the proceeds are invested in stocks of a publicly held company. The investment must occur within a certain time frame and certain other requirements must be met.[11]

For tax years beginning after December 31, 2001, and before January 1, 2011, a C corporation may deduct, at the election of plan participants or their beneficiaries, dividends paid to an ESOP and reinvested in qualified employer securities.[12] However,

[7] Code Secs. 402(g)(1) and 402(g)(5) and Cumulative Bulletin Notice 2000-66, IRB 2000-52, 600 (December 23, 2000).

[8] Code Sec. 409.

[9] Code Sec. 409(h)(1).

[10] Code Sec. 409(h)(2)(B).

[11] Code Sec. 401(a)(28)(B).

[12] Code Sec. 404(k)(2)(A).

such dividends are not deductible for alternative minimum tax purposes.

If the plan is to work, the company must be healthy, the employees must be interested in acquiring company stock, and the company and its shareholders must be willing to suffer the possible dilution of control. The latter might be especially important if the company is closely held, but might be manageable through the development of an acceptable repurchase plan.

ESOPs have received some negative publicity. Some well-known corporations abused ESOPs. In addition, the values of some ESOPs have decreased significantly. The IRS recently added abuses of ESOPs by S corporations to its list of abusive tax shelters.[13] Although an ESOP may be a shareholder in an S corporation, Code Sec. 409(p) prevents an S corporation from using an ESOP as a tax shelter for a small group of owners and executives. Rather, the ESOP must provide a meaningful benefit to rank-and-file employees.

The IRS allows an ESOP to direct a rollover of distributions of the S corporation stock to a participant's IRA without risking termination of the S election as long as the rollover meets all of the following conditions:

1. The ESOP must provide that the S corporation must repurchase the stock once the ESOP distributes the stock to the participant's IRA.
2. The S corporation must actually repurchase the stock on the same day of its distribution to the IRA.
3. No income, deduction, credit, or loss attributable to the stock is allocated to the participant's IRA.[14]

Because of the requirement for the S corporation to repurchase the stock the same day the ESOP distributes it to the participant's IRA, financial planners should urge the ESOP to make the distribution early in the day.

In addition, the Treasury has issued a temporary regulation[15] that addresses abusive situations where former S corporation owners receive (1) deferred compensation from a management company related to the S corporation or (2) special rights to acquire assets from the S corporation. These arrangements dilute the value of the S corporation stock in the ESOP. This type of deferred compensation and such special rights are treated as synthetic equity under the

---

[13] Rev. Rul. 2003-6, IRB 2003-3 (December 17, 2002).

[14] Rev. Proc. 2003-23, IRB 2003-11 (February 20, 2003).

[15] Temp. Reg. § 1.409(p)-1T.

temporary regulation. Treatment as synthetic equity results in income tax liability and excise tax liability for the recipients.

Incentive stock options. Incentive stock options (ISOs) are taxed in a favorable manner.[16] The granting of the option and its exercise are not taxable events.[17] Proceeds from the sale or exchange of the stock will be taxed as a capital gain, provided the stock is sold or exchanged after it has been held for at least two years from the date the option was granted *and* one year from the date it was exercised. If the stock is not held for the required period, the sale or exchange is treated as a disqualifying disposition and the employee is taxed at ordinary income tax rates on the difference between (1) the option price paid for the stock and (2) the lesser of the fair market value at the time of the option exercise or the sale price.[18] A number of requirements must be met for options to qualify as ISOs.[19] In addition, an annual $100,000 exercise limit applies.[20]

Final regulations[21] issued in 2004 revise key definitions related to ISOs, delete obsolete provisions, and clarify the tax treatment of disqualifying dispositions. In addition, the regulations make it clear any entity classified as a corporation for federal tax purposes is eligible to grant stock options. The final regulations took effect as of August 4, 2004, subject to special transitions rules that allowed taxpayers to rely on either prior final or earlier proposed regulations for certain options issued before January 1, 2006. However, compliance with the final regulations is required for all options as of January 1, 2006.[22]

An ISO is a stock option often granted to key employees. The grantee has the right to purchase stock without realizing income either when the corporation grants the option or when the employee exercises it. The grantee is first taxed when he or she sells or disposes of the stock. The grantee has either capital gain or loss.

Generally, an option must express the following:

- An offer to sell at the option price;
- The maximum number of shares acquirable under the option; and
- The time allowed to exercise the option.

The corporation must grant the ISOs under a shareholder-approved plan, which specifies the number of shares to be issued

[16] Code Sec. 422.

[17] Code Secs. 421(a) and 422(a).

[18] Code Sec. 422(c)(2).

[19] Code Sec. 422(b).

[20] Code Sec. 422(d).

[21] Reg. § 1.422-1, Reg. § 1.422-2, Reg. § 1.422-4, and Reg. § 1.422-5.

[22] TD 9144 (August 2, 2004).

and the class of employees who will receive the stock. Under the prior rules, the incentive stock option plan and the options themselves had to be in paper form. However, the final regulations allow them to be in electronic form. The corporation must grant an option within 10 years of the date the corporation adopts the plan or the date of its approval by shareholders. The grantee must exercise the option within 10 years from the date of grant.

The option price must be at least equal to the fair market value (FMV) of the stock when the corporation grants the option. The regulations explain that the corporation may determine the option price in any reasonable manner so long as the minimum price is not less than the FMV of the stock on the date of grant.

Generally, the grantee may not transfer the options to another party and keep the special tax treatment. The regulations carve a limited exception. Grantees may transfer options to a trust if they remain the beneficial owners. However, when a grantee transfers options under a divorce agreement, they lose their special tax status.

The regulations also identify three provisions that the corporation may include in an option, which do not render it defective. An ISO may contain the following provisions:

- Provide for a cashless exercise;
- Give the grantee the right to receive additional compensation when exercised; and
- Be subject to permissible conditions.

The regulations expand the definitions of option, corporation, and stock. Options now include warrants. Statutory option means an incentive stock option or an option granted under an employee stock purchase plan (ESPP). Corporation now includes a limited liability company (LLC) treated as a corporation for tax purposes.

When a grantee makes a disqualifying disposition of stock, the profit is treated as compensation income and not as capital gain. The compensation income generally equals the fair market value of the stock on the date the option was exercised minus the exercise price.

A special rule applies if the amount realized on a disqualifying disposition is less than the fair market value of the stock at the time the option was exercised. The amount included in the gross income of the grantee will not exceed the excess, if any, of the amount realized on the sale over the adjusted basis of each share. This rule applies only to dispositions where a loss (if sustained) would be recognized to the grantee. Thus, it does not apply if the stock is disposed of in a nonrecognition transaction or by gift.

For alternative minimum tax purposes, stock acquired by exercise of an ISO after 1987 is treated as though it were taxable under the Code Sec. 83 rules governing taxation of property given for services, rather than under the Code Sec. 421 rules that govern ISOs for regular income tax purposes.[23] Under the Code Sec. 83 rules, the difference between the value of ISO stock and the price paid for it by the employee on exercise is includible in AMT income when the stock is freely transferable or not subject to a substantial risk of forfeiture.[24] Under this rule, if a taxpayer acquires and disposes of ISO stock in the same tax year, the tax treatment under both the regular tax and the alternative minimum tax would be the same.[25] However, if a disqualifying disposition were to occur in a year after exercise, an AMT adjustment would be made in the year of exercise based upon the spread between the option price and the stock's fair market value (determined under Code Sec. 83 rules). Gross income would be recognized for regular tax purposes in the year of disposition.

Stock option plans generally are exempt from the $1 million annual deduction limit that applies to nonperformance-based compensation of top-paid officers of public corporations.[26] To be exempt, the options must not be issued with an exercise price below current market value at the time of the grant. In addition, certain shareholder approval and outside director oversight requirements must be met.[27]

Nonqualified options. Nonqualified options can be granted at bargain rates. Incentive options must be at 100 percent of fair market value at the time of grant. No tax consequences for either the executive or the company occur at the time of the grant of nonqualified options unless the option has a readily ascertainable value. The option would have a readily ascertainable value if the stock is actively traded on an established market, or its fair market value can otherwise be measured with reasonable accuracy.[28] However, on exercise of the option, the difference between the fair market value of the stock at the time and the option price (i.e., the bargain element) is taxable to the executive, with a corresponding deduction allowed to the company, unless the stock acquired is not transferable and is subject to a substantial risk of forfeiture.[29] In the latter case, the executive is taxed (and the company is allowed a deduction) when the stock becomes transferable or the risk ends,[30] unless the executive has elected to include the stock in his or her gross income

---

[23] Code Secs. 56(b)(3) and 83.
[24] Code Sec. 83(a).
[25] Code Secs. 422(c)(2) and 56(b)(3).
[26] Code Sec. 162(m)(1).
[27] Code Sec. 162(m)(4)(C).
[28] Reg. § 1.83-7(b).
[29] Code Sec. 83(a).
[30] Code Sec. 83(a).

in the year of the transfer.[31] If the executive makes the election, and he or she later forfeits his or her interest in the stock, no deduction is allowed for the loss.

If the option has a readily ascertainable value at the time of grant, the bargain element is immediately taxable to the executive and the company receives an equivalent deduction.

On exercise of the option, the executive will need cash or deferred payment financing. The Federal Reserve Board permits "cashless exercises" of stock options. Under this procedure, a broker buys the stock from the company at the exercise price, sells stock in the market sufficient to cover the purchase from the company, plus commissions and possible margin interest, and delivers the remaining stock to the executive.

If the executive is an officer, director, or 10-percent shareholder of the employer, he or she will be subject to the short-swing profits provision of the Securities and Exchange Act, Sec. 16(b), if he or she sells the stock within six months of acquiring it.

The executive must weigh the value of this form of cashless exercise against other forms of exercise of stock options that may be available with little or no cash involved: (1) a company loan at a low interest rate; and (2) swap of stock previously acquired for stock to be acquired. Both plans can be effected without payment of commissions and without any current tax liability. The first approach would have no Sec. 16(b) involvement. The second would qualify for a Sec. 16(b) exemption.

Cash bonuses. Payment of year-end bonuses may be timed so as to fall into the following tax year with a current compensation deduction for the employer and deferral of tax for the executive. An accrual basis corporation can take a deduction for its current tax year for a bonus not actually paid to an executive until the following tax year if all of the following requirements are met:

1. The executive doesn't own more than 50% in value of the corporation's stock,
2. The bonus is properly accrued on the corporation's books before the end of the current tax year, and
3. The bonus is actually paid within the first 2½ months of the following tax year.[32]

For an executive on the cash basis, the bonus won't be taxable income until the year in which it is paid.

---

[31] Code Sec. 83(b)(1).

[32] Reg. § 1.404(b)-1TQ&A2

If deferral of tax on a year-end bonus makes sense for an executive, the executive can request in advance that the employer delay payment until early in the following year. However, if the executive waits until a bonus is due and payable to request a deferral, the doctrine of constructive receipt will be triggered and the tax on the bonus will not be deferred. Also, if the deferral extends beyond 2½ months after the close of the taxable year, the bonus will be treated as nonqualified deferred compensation. Bonuses treated as deferred compensation are currently includible in income to the extent not subject to a "substantial risk of forfeiture" if the arrangement fails to meet certain distribution, acceleration of benefit, and election requirements (see below).

Performance shares. Performance shares are a variation of a bonus plan. The plan differs, however, in that it is apt to be geared to the long term. It attempts to match compensation with a unit's performance and with an individual's performance in relation to the unit's performance. The company sets targets. To the degree that those goals are met, the company gives awards. The final payout can be cash, stock, or both. Along the way, the company makes phantom awards. The executive is taxed on the final payout, and the company receives a corresponding tax deduction.

The claimed advantage over conventional stock plans is that performance shares are not so closely tied to the market, to some extent they reflect performance, and they do not require any payment by the executive.

To the extent that shares are awarded, the company faces dilution problems. Also, the value of the shares is a charge against earnings. Because of this factor, earnings must grow sufficiently to compensate for the charge while at the same time meeting the company's goals and objectives. Generally, plans of this type are not suitable for start-up companies, because they have difficulty in setting earnings goals.

Stock appreciation rights (SARs) and phantom stock. SARs and phantom stock are designed to provide the executive with a cash bonus measured by the appreciation in the value of the company's stock from the time the rights are granted over a set or determinable period. Like performance shares, SARs give an executive a stake in company growth without a cash investment. Payments made could include amounts equal to the dividends paid on the stock. The payments are treated the same as cash bonuses. They are taxable to the executive and deductible by the company.

Group term life insurance. Group term life insurance is tax free to the executive on coverage of up to $50,000,[33] subject to compliance with anti-discrimination rules.[34] For higher amounts of coverage, the executive receives a break on the portion of the employer-paid premium that is taxable.[35] The company receives a deduction for premiums paid regardless of the amount, if any, taxable to the executive, subject to the rules of reasonable compensation.[36]

Group permanent life insurance. Treasury regulations accept a single policy combining term insurance with permanent life insurance as being within the scope of Code Sec. 79 rules governing group term life insurance, provided many conditions are satisfied.[37] Complex formulas are provided for computing the amount taxable to the executive (¶ 945).

Split-dollar life insurance. Split-dollar life insurance is permanent insurance acquired under an arrangement by which the company and the executive split the premium cost. The company and the executive's beneficiaries also split the proceeds on an agreed basis. Either the company or the executive may own the policy. Under the endorsement method, the employer owns the policy and endorses an interest in the policy to the employee. Under the collateral assignment method, the employee owns the policy and assigns a security interest in the policy to the employer.

In a traditional split-dollar arrangement, the employer pays the portion of the annual policy premium that equals the increase in the policy's cash value for the year, and the employee pays the remainder of the premium. On the employee's death, the employer receives the cash surrender value of the policy (thus recouping most or all of its cost) and the employee's estate or beneficiary receives the remainder of the death benefit.

However, under an "equity" split-dollar arrangement, the death benefits that goes to the employee's estate or beneficiary is not limited to what is left over after the employee receives the cash value; the employee's estate or beneficiary receives a portion of the cash value as well. The employer generally recovers only an amount equal to the cumulative premiums it paid. The remainder of the death benefit goes to the employee's estate or beneficiary. During the life of the policy, when the cash value buildup exceeds the cumulative premiums paid by the employer, the employee is considered to

---

[33] Code Sec. 79(a).
[34] Code Sec. 79(d).
[35] Code Sec. 79(c).
[36] Code Sec. 162(a).
[37] Reg. § 1.79-1(b).

have an equity interest in the policy. If the policy is surrendered, the employee will receive a portion of the cash value.

On September 11, 2003, the IRS issued final regulations[38] on the treatment of all split-dollar life insurance arrangements. These regulations apply to split-dollar arrangements executed or materially modified after September 17, 2003. For split-dollar arrangements entered into on or before September 17, 2003, taxpayers may continue to rely on prior revenue rulings as described in Cumulative Bulletin Notice 2002-8, IRB 2002-4, 398 (January 3, 2002) as long as such arrangements are not materially modified.[39] Under the new regulations, the amount taxable to an individual under a traditional split-dollar arrangement with a company is generally determined as under prior law. This means the individual is taxed on the value of the death benefit coverage provided by the company, based on the cost of one year of term insurance. For split-dollar arrangements entered into before January 28, 2002, this cost may be determined using the PS 58 rates if a contractual arrangement between the company and the individual provides that those rates will be used.[40] For arrangements entered into on or after January 28, 2002, Table 2001 must be used to determine the cost of current life insurance protection.

While leaving the tax treatment of traditional split-dollar policies relatively intact, the final regulations substantially alter the tax treatment of equity split-dollar arrangements.

Under the final regulations, the tax consequences of a split-dollar life insurance arrangement depend on its classification under one of two alternative regimes: (1) the economic benefit regime or (2) the loan regime.

Under the economic benefit regime, the employer as owner of the insurance policy is deemed to provide economic benefits to the non-owner employee. The premiums paid by the employer are treated as compensation to the employee. In addition, any right or benefit in the insurance policy, such as in interest in the cash surrender value, is treated as additional compensation.

Under the loan regime, the employee owns the policy and the employer pays the premiums. The employer as the non-owner of the policy is deemed to loan the premium payments to the employee-owner of the policy. The loan regime applies where (1) the payment is made by the nonowner to the owner, (2) the payment

[38] Reg. § 1.61-22 and Reg. § 1.7872-15.

[39] Rev. Rul. 2003-105, IRB 2003-40 (September 11, 2003).

[40] Notice 2002-8, 2002-4 IRB 398 (January 3, 2002).

is a loan under the tax law or a reasonable person would expect the payments to be repaid and (3) the payment is made from or secured by the death benefit or the cash surrender value of the policy. Each premium payment is treated as a separate loan. If the loan under the split-dollar arrangement is not a below-market loan, the general rules for loans apply. The borrower may not deduct any interest paid on the split-dollar loan because it is personal interest. If the loan under the split-dollar arrangement is a below-market loan, the provisions of Code Sec. 7872 apply. However, the de minimis exception of Code Sec. 7872 does not apply to split-dollar loans. The imputed interest on a below-market loan to an employee under a split-dollar arrangement is usually taxable compensation to the employee.

The regulations do not affect the calculation of the amount included in an executive's gross income for group term life insurance that exceeds $50,000. The amount included in the executive's gross income in such cases is still determined under Reg. § 1.79-3(d)(2).

The company receives no deduction for premiums paid.[41] However, the company recovers the premiums paid tax free when the executive dies. The company would also recover the premiums paid tax free if and when the executive buys the policy or the company's lien against the policy while still alive.

Medical benefits. The company can provide medical benefits to executives and their dependents. The cost of the medical benefits generally will be tax deductible by the company[42] and tax free to the executive.[43] Medical benefits include (1) payment or reimbursement of accident and health insurance premiums, including major medical coverage and dental care; and (2) direct payment or reimbursement of medical or dental expenses.

If the executive were to pay his or her own medical expenses, they would be deductible only to the extent they exceeded 7.5 percent of the executive's adjusted gross income.[44] That floor on deductions makes employer-provided tax-free medical benefits particularly attractive.

As a general rule medical benefits are not subject to nondiscrimination requirements. Therefore, an employer can provide group health insurance only for key executives or other selected employees. However, if an employer provides health benefits under a discriminatory self-insured plan, benefits paid to highly compensated employees will be taxable to the extent they constitute "excess

[41] Code Sec. 264(a).
[42] Code Sec. 162(a).
[43] Code Secs. 105 and 106.
[44] Code Sec. 213(a).

reimbursements" over and above amounts received by non-highly compensated employees.[45]

An employer can deduct amounts paid or accrued during the tax year for medical benefits for employees, provided they qualify as ordinary and necessary expenses of the employer's business.[46]

An employee's own contributions for medical benefits are generally deductible as medical expenses, subject to the 7.5% deduction floor. However, employee contributions may be made on a pre-tax basis under a cafeteria plan. A cafeteria plan is an employer-provided plan that offers employees a choice between cash compensation and or more employee benefits, such as medical benefits. Employees who choose to receive medical benefits in lieu of cash compensation do not owe tax on the forgone compensation and the forgone compensation is not treated as wages for payroll tax purposes.[47]

Long-term care insurance. Group long-term care insurance is treated as accident and health insurance. Therefore, the value of employer-provided long-term care coverage is excludable from an employee's income as contributions to an accident and health plan.[48]

Long-term care insurance cannot, however, be offered as a benefit under a cafeteria plan.[49] Therefore, an employee's premiums for long-term care insurance cannot be paid on a pre-tax basis. Moreover, an employee's deductions for long-term care insurance premiums are subject to annual dollar limits based on the employee's attained age at the end of the taxable year of payment.[50] Moreover, the deduction for long-term care insurance premiums is subject to the overall 7.5 percent of adjusted gross income floor on medical expense deductions.

Health savings accounts. Health savings accounts (HSAs) are tax-exempt trusts or custodial accounts created exclusively to pay for the qualified medical expenses of the account holder and his or her spouse and dependents.[51] Contributions to an HSA can be made by "eligible individuals" or by their employers or both. Within limits, contributions to HSAs are deductible above-the-line in determining adjusted gross income if made by individuals and are excludable from gross income and taxable wages if made by their employers. Distributions from HSAs for qualified medical expenses are not includible in gross income. Distributions from an HSA for other purposes are includible in the account holder's gross income and are subject to

[45] Code Sec. 105(h)(1).
[46] Reg. § 1.162-10(a).
[47] Code Sec. 125.
[48] Code Sec. 106.
[49] Code Sec. 125(f).
[50] Code Sec. 213(d).
[51] Code Sec. 223.

an additional 10 percent penalty. However, the 10 percent penalty does not apply to distributions made after death, disability, or after the account holder attains age 65. Therefore, an HSA can serve as a tax-deferred retirement savings vehicle to the extent amounts in the account are not needed for current medical expenses.

An individual is eligible to make HSA contributions for any month if he or she (1) is covered under a high-deductible health plan as of the first day of that month and (2) is not covered under any other health plan that is not a high-deductible plan and that provides coverage for any benefit covered under the high deductible plan.

For 2006, high-deductible health plan must have a deductible of at least $1,050 for self-only coverage or $2,100 for family coverage, and an annual limit on out-of-pocket expenses (deductible, co-payments, etc.) of not more than $5,250 for self-only coverage or $10,500 for family coverage.

In the case of self-only coverage, the maximum contribution for 2006 is $2,700 or the amount of the annual deductible, if less. For family coverage, the maximum 2006 contribution is the lesser of the annual deductible or $5,450. An eligible individual who will be 55 or over before the close of 2006, can make an additional catch-up contribution of $600 for the year, regardless of the type of high-deductible coverage.

If an employer provides high-deductible health plan coverage coupled with an HSA and makes employer contributions to the HSAs, the employer must make available a comparable contribution on behalf of all employees with comparable coverage. Contributions are considered comparable if they are either of the same dollar amount or the same percentage of the deductible under the high-deductible plan. The comparability rule is applied separately to part-time employees (i.e., employees who are customarily employed for fewer than 30 hours per week). No restrictions are placed on the ability of the employer to offer different plans to different groups of employees

Archer medical savings accounts. Medical savings accounts (MSAs) were a precursor to HSAs designed for employees of small employers and self-employed individuals.[52]

Like an HSA, an MSA is a tax-exempt trust or custodial account that is set up to pay medical expenses in connection with a high-deductible health plan. Contributions to the account are deductible or excludable from an employee's income if made by an employer, and

---

[52] Code Sec. 220.

amounts in the account can be withdrawn tax-free to pay for out-of-pocket medical expenses. Amounts withdrawn for other purposes are taxable and subject to a 15 percent penalty unless the withdrawal is made after death, disability or Medicare eligibility.

Only self-employed individuals and employees of small employers (generally, those with 50 or fewer employees) were eligible to establish MSAs. MSAs were a pilot project that expired at the end of 2005. However, pending legislation may extend the availability of MSAs. In addition, contributions may continue to be made to MSAs established before the 2005 cutoff and existing accounts continue to qualify for tax-favored treatment.

For 2006, the high-deductible health plan supporting an MSA must have an annual deductible of not less than $1,800 and nor more than $2,700 in the case of self-only coverage, or not less than $3,650 and not more than $5,450 in the case of family coverage. Annual out-of-pocket expenses cannot exceed $3,650 for self-only coverage or $$6,650 for family coverage.[53] For individuals with self-only coverage, the maximum annual contribution is 65% of the deductible under the high-deductible plan; the maximum is 75% of the deductible for individuals with family coverage.

An employee can make contributions to his or her own MSA or contributions may be made by the employer sponsoring the high deductible plan, but not by both. As with HSAs, an employer that makes MSA contributions on behalf of employees must make comparable contributions for all employees with comparable coverage.

Death benefits. Death benefits are fully taxable to the recipient. Death benefits payable outside of qualified retirement plans are discussed in detail at ¶950.

Expense accounts. Business, travel, or entertainment expenses paid by the executive and reimbursed by the company under an accountable plan[54] will be tax free to the executive. However, only 50 percent of expenses for business meals and entertainment are deductible by the company,[55] subject to a number of relatively minor exceptions of limited application.[56]

Below-market interest loans. Below-market interest loans made by employers offer an attractive executive benefit. They can serve needs related to employment, such as the purchase of company stock under a stock purchase plan or stock option. They also can help

---

[53] Rev. Proc. 2005-70, 2005-47 IRB 979 (October 28, 2005).

[54] Reg. § 1.62-2.

[55] Code Sec. 274(n)(1).

[56] Code Sec. 274(n)(2).

with personal needs, such as providing college funds. However, loans to executive officers and directors of public companies are now prohibited by Sec. 402 of the Sarbanes-Oxley Act of 2002.

In the case of a demand loan, the employee has compensation income in the amount of the value of the use of the money lent and a deemed interest payment for the imputed interest.[57] The deemed interest payment is deductible only if it meets the requirements under Code Sec. 163. Generally, personal interest is not deductible.[58] The employer has imputed interest income and a corresponding compensation deduction. Term loans are less favorable to the executive, who is currently taxed on the value of the foregone interest for the entire term.[59] However, term loans can be structured to be treated as demand loans by making the benefit nontransferable and conditioned on future services.

If the executive is a shareholder, the employer is treated as having paid a dividend[60] or made a capital contribution equal to the foregone interest. The employer receives no deduction but the shareholder is treated as having paid interest to the employer. The deemed interest payment will be deductible if it meets the requirements of Code Sec. 163. The employer includes the deemed interest payment in gross income.

Company meals. Meals furnished by the company on its premises for its business convenience are tax free to the employees[61] and deductible by the company.[62]

Company lodging. Lodging furnished by the company for its business convenience that the employee is required to accept as a condition of employment is tax free to the employee[63] and deductible by the company.[64]

Education. Company-paid, business-related education designed to improve existing skills and not to prepare for a new occupation or profession is tax free to the employee[65] and deductible by the company.[66] No dollar limit applies to this fringe benefit. Graduate courses, undergraduate courses, and noncredit courses are eligible. In addition, an employee may exclude from gross income up to $5,250 of employer-paid educational assistance, whether or not the education is directly related to job performance. Benefits in excess of the

---

[57] Code Sec. 7872(a).
[58] Code Sec. 163(h).
[59] Code Sec. 7872(b).
[60] Code Sec. 301.
[61] Code Sec. 119(a).
[62] Code Sec. 162(a).
[63] Code Sec. 119(a).
[64] Code Sec. 162(a).
[65] Code Secs. 132(a)(3), 132(d), 162(a), and Reg. § 1.162-5.
[66] Code Sec. 162(a).

$5,250 limit are subject to income taxes and employment taxes unless the benefits may be excluded from gross income as a working condition fringe benefit under Code Sec. 132(h)(9).

To qualify for the exclusion for employer-provided educational assistance, the employer must furnish the assistance under a program described in Code Sec. 127(b). The program must be a separate written plan for the exclusive benefit of the employees, and it must not discriminate in favor of highly compensated employees. Not more than five percent of the educational benefits may be paid to the principal shareholders or owners. The program does not have to be funded, and the employees may not have the ability to choose other benefits instead of the educational assistance. The employer must provide reasonable notice of the availability and terms of the program to eligible employees.

Eligible expenses include tuition, fees, books, supplies, and equipment. Payments for room, board, transportation, and any equipment or supplies that a student will retain after the completion of the course are not eligible. Payments for recreational courses are not eligible for the exclusion. While at one time the exclusion was limited to education below the graduate level, current rules permit the exclusion to be claimed for graduate and professional courses beginning before January 1, 2011. Employers may provide different levels of benefits based on the grade a student earns in the class.[67] IRS Publication 970, "Tax Benefits for Education," provides additional information on employer-provided educational assistance programs.

Charitable contributions. Charitable contributions made by the company in the executive's name to charities designated by him are tax free to the executive. They are not deductible by the executive, but are deductible by the company.[68]

Financial counseling. Some companies provide legal, tax, investment, and estate planning services to executives through an outside counseling firm (see ¶ 1620 for details on the services). The amount paid is fully taxable to the executive,[69] but is deductible by him or her to the extent that the counseling involves tax advice, preparation of tax returns or investment advice,[70] subject to the two-percent floor under miscellaneous itemized deductions.[71]

Retirement planning. This exclusion covers any retirement planning advice or information provide to an employee or his or

---

[67] Code Sec. 127(c)(5).
[68] Code Sec. 170(a).
[69] Code Sec. 61(a).
[70] Code Sec. 212.
[71] Code Sec. 67.

her spouse if the employer maintains a qualified retirement plan. In addition to advice and information about the employer-provided plan, the services provided may include general advice and information on retirement. However, the exclusion does not apply to tax preparation, accounting, legal, or brokerage services. In addition, the exclusion does not apply to highly compensated employees unless the retirement planning services are available on substantially the same terms to each member of the group of employees who are normally provided with education and information regarding the employer's plan.[72]

Dependent care assistance. Code Sec. 129 allows expenses incurred for dependent care assistance under a written nondiscriminatory plan to be excluded from an employee's gross income, subject to an annual ceiling of $5,000 ($2,500 for a separate return made by a married person). Employers may claim a credit for providing child-care benefits to their employees. This credit is a part of the general business credit. The credit is equal to the sum of 25 percent of the qualified child-care expenses and 10 percent of the qualified child-care resources and referral expenditures. The total credit for any year may not exceed $150,000. This credit is effective for tax years beginning before January 1, 2011.[73]

Moving expenses. Company-paid qualified moving expenses are tax free to the executive[74] and deductible by the company.[75] Qualified moving expenses reimbursements[76] include expenses incurred for moving household goods and effects and the cost of traveling from the former residence to the new residence.[77] The distance between the executive's former recidence and the new place of work must be at least 50 miles farther than the distance between the executive's former residence and the former place of work.[78] The executive must also be employed for 39 weeks out of the 12-month period following the move.[79]

Cafeteria-style compensation. Under a cafeteria plan,[80] each executive may choose from among two or more benefits consisting of cash and qualified benefits (¶ 975).

Other fringe benefits. A company may provide a number of other fringe benefits tax free to executives. Certain categories of fringe benefits are accorded tax-free treatment, in some cases subject

[72] Code Sec. 132(m).
[73] Code Sec. 45F.
[74] Code Sec. 132(a)(6).
[75] Code Sec. 162(a).
[76] Code Sec. 132(g).
[77] Code Secs. 132(g) and 217(b)(1).
[78] Code Secs. 132(g) and 217(c)(1).
[79] Code Secs. 132(g) and 217(c)(2).
[80] Code Sec. 125.

to antidiscrimination rules. A detailed discussion of these rules appears at ¶985.

.02 Overcoming Limits on Benefits and Contributions

The maximum amount of annual additions to defined contribution plans, e.g., profit-sharing plans, is 100 percent of compensation, not to exceed $44,000 in 2006.[81] This amount is indexed for inflation in $1,000 increments. The maximum annual benefit payable under a defined benefit plan, e.g., the conventional pension plan, is $175,000 for 2006.[82] The maximum amount is indexed for inflation in $5,000 increments. The dollar limit is reduced if benefits begin before age 62 and increased for benefits beginning after age 65. Those individuals adversely affected by the limitations on contributions and benefits will want to consider the following:

- Excess benefit plans (see discussion below).
- Being elected to the board of directors of other corporations and receiving compensation for such service that may then become the basis of a contribution to a self-employed retirement plan. However, the U.S. Tax Court has held that fees earned by inside directors are not eligible for Keogh contributions,[83] since the IRS withdrew proposed regulations[84] under which such plans would have run afoul of the nondiscrimination rules.
- Setting up another plan (if the employer has only a single plan).
- Arranging for increased compensation (cash, stock, phantom stock, tax-favored fringe benefits, etc.) to make up, in whole or in part, for the reduction in benefits or contributions.
- Arranging for post-retirement consulting services.

.03 Deferred Compensation Plans

The objective of a deferred compensation agreement is to shift income from a year in which the executive is in a high tax bracket to a year in which the executive is expected to be in a lower tax bracket. Usually, the deferred compensation is expected to be paid after retirement.

Deferred compensation plans are commonly used to provide retirement benefits to highly compensated and other key employees,

---

[81] Code Secs. 415(c)(1) and 415(d)(1); Notice 2005-75, 2005-45 IRB 929 (November 3, 2005).

[82] Code Sec. 415(b)(1)(A); Notice 2005-75, 2005-45 IRB 929 (November 3, 2005).

[83] *P.H. Jacobs*, 66 TCM 1470, Dec. 49,444(M), TC Memo. 1993-570.

[84] Prop. Reg. § 1.414(o)-1(g).

often through an arrangement known as an "excess benefit" plan. An excess benefit plan is defined as a plan maintained by an employer solely for the purpose of providing benefits for certain employees in excess of the limitations on contributions and benefits imposed by Code Sec. 415. These plans are exempt from the minimum participation, funding, and vesting standards applicable to qualified plans generally.

Deferred compensation plans generally fall into two categories: funded and unfunded. An unfunded plan may simply involve a mere promise to pay an employee a certain amount at retirement. With a funded plan, amounts are set aside currently by the employer, typically in a trust or similar arrangement, to provide future benefits.

The American Jobs Creation Act of 2004[85] made major changes in the tax treatment of deferred compensation arrangements, including excess benefit plan. Prior to the Jobs Act, the precise tax treatment depended on whether a deferred compensation arrangement was funded or unfunded. A bare contractual promise of an employer to pay compensation at retirement or some other time in the future did not result in current taxable income to the employee. The IRS had ruled that there was no constructive receipt of income even if the employee's rights under the agreement were vested (nonforfeitable).[86] So an employee promised retirement benefits was taxed on the benefits when they were paid during retirement.

Under the prior rules for *funded* plans, an employee was not currently taxed on contributions to the plan, as long as the employee has no current access to the funds. However, an employee could be taxed on funds set aside in a trust or similar arrangement if he or she had a vested interest in the trust—even though benefits were not payable until retirement. This was known as the "economic benefit" doctrine.[87]

To avoid the economic benefit doctrine, funded deferred compensation plans were often set up in the form of a "rabbi trust" (the first IRS ruling permitting this arrangement involved a rabbi).[88] An employer's creditors could reach the assets of a rabbi trust. The economic benefit doctrine did not apply if the employee's control over the receipt of income was subject to substantial limitations or restrictions. The IRS ruled that trust funds were sufficiently restricted when they were subject to the claims of the employer's creditors.

[85] PL 108-357, 10/22/2004.

[86] Rev. Rul. 60-31, 1960-1 C.B. 174.

[87] Sproull v. Comm'r, 16 T.C. 244 (1951).

[88] PLR 8113107.

New rules under Section 409A. The American Jobs Creation Act of 2004 enacted Section 409A of the Internal Revenue Code which imposes new restrictions on deferred compensation arrangements.

Under Section 409A, all compensation deferred under a "nonqualified deferred compensation plan" is immediately includible in an employee's gross income if—

1. The compensation is not subject to a "substantial risk of forfeiture,"
2. The compensation was not previously included in gross income, or
3. The plan does not meet certain requirements for (a) distributions, (b) acceleration of benefits, and (c) elections (see below).[89]

Section 409A generally apples to amounts deferred after 2004.

A "nonqualified deferred compensation plan" is generally any nonqualified plan that provides for the deferral of the payment of compensation owed to an employee or other service provider to a time more than two and one half months after the end of the year in which the compensation ceases to be subject to a substantial risk of forfeiture. The term nonqualified deferred compensation plan does not include a qualified retirement plan, tax-deferred annuity, simplified employee pension or SIMPLE plan. It also does not include any bona fide vacation leave, sick leave, compensatory time, disability pay or death benefit plan or any Archer medical savings account, any health savings account, or any other medical reimbursement arrangement.[90]

The rights of a person to compensation are subject to a "substantial risk of forfeiture if the person's rights to such compensation are conditioned upon the performance of substantial services by any individual."[91] In other words, once an employee's rights to the plan's benefits become vested (they are not conditioned upon the performance of future services or subject to any other substantial risk of forfeiture), the benefits will generally be taxable to the employee unless the requirements of (3) above are met. If a nonqualified plan is not in compliance with or does not operate in compliance with these requirements at any time during a tax year, all amounts deferred under the plan for that tax year and all preceding tax years are included in gross income for that year to the extent not subject to a

[89] Code Sec. 409A(a)(1)(A).

[90] Prop. Reg. § 1.409A-1(a); Notice 2005-1, 2005-2 IRB 274.

[91] Code Sec. 83(c)(1).

substantial risk of forfeiture and not previously included in gross income.

The amount included in income also is subject to (1) interest (at the IRS's underpayment rate plus one percentage point) on the tax underpayments that would have occurred had the compensation been included in income for the tax year when first deferred, or if later, when not subject to a substantial risk of forfeiture; and (2) additional income tax equal to 20% of the compensation required to be included in gross income.[92]

Avoiding income inclusion. As noted above, where there is no substantial risk of forfeiture, three requirements must be met under Section 409A to avoid income inclusion.

1. *Distributions.* Distributions from a nonqualified deferred compensation plan may be allowed only upon an employee's separation from service or death, a specified time (or pursuant to a fixed schedule), change in control of a corporation, occurrence of an unforeseeable emergency, or if the employee becomes disabled. A nonqualified deferred compensation plan may not allow distributions other than upon the permissible distribution events.[93]

   In the case of a "specified employee" who separates from service, distributions may not be made earlier than six months after the date of the separation from service or upon death. "Specified employees" are key employees of publicly-traded corporations.[94]
2. *Acceleration of benefits.* No acceleration of distributions is generally allowed. Changes in the form of distribution that accelerate payments are subject to the rule prohibiting acceleration of distributions. However, this prohibition is not violated merely because a plan provides a choice between cash and taxable property if the timing and amount of income inclusion is the same regardless of the medium of distribution. For example, the choice between a fully taxable annuity contract and a lump-sum payment may be permitted.[95]
3. *Elections.* If a nonqualified deferred compensation plan provides that compensation can be deferred at the participant's election, the election must generally be made no later than the close of the preceding tax year.[96]

---

[92] Code Sec. 409A(a)(1)(B)(i).

[93] Code Sec. 409A(a)(2)(A).

[94] Code Sec. 409A(a)(2)(B)(i).

[95] Code Sec. 409A(a)(3).

[96] Code Sec. 409A(a)(4)(B).

A plan may permit subsequent elections to delay or change the form of payments under the plan. If it does permit such elections, a plan must require that the new election cannot take effect until at least 12 months after it is made. A subsequent election to further defer a distribution to be made after the participant's separation from service, on a predetermined date or schedule, or upon a change of ownership of the employer must defer any payment to which it applies (not just the first payment) for at least five years. A subsequent election relating to a payment to be made on a predetermined date or schedule cannot be made less than 12 months prior to the first scheduled payment.[97]

Employer's deduction. An employer can claim a deduction for payments made under a nonqualified deferred compensation plan only in the year they are includible in the gross income of the employee.[98]

¶1610 LIFETIME AND ESTATE PLANNING FOR EXECUTIVE BENEFITS

An executive's company benefits are likely to be a good part of the executive's total estate. This section considers the executive's lifetime choices in relation to various executive benefits and the disposition of benefits that become payable at death.

.01 Qualified Pension and Profit-Sharing Plans

The executive will often be a participant in a qualified pension or profit-sharing plan. If the company does not have a plan, the executive should press for one type or the other, or for an ESOP.

Whether or not the executive is an active participant in a qualified plan, the executive may set up a traditional IRA (individual retirement account) and contribute up to $4,000 for 2005, 2006, and 2007; and $5,000 for 2008, 2009, and 2010. The $5,000 limit is adjusted for inflation in 2009 and 2010.[99] In addition, individuals who are age 50 or older can make additional "catch-up" contributions. The additional contribution is $1,000 for 2006 through 2010.[100] A married individual who files a joint return may also contribute up to the annual limit for a spouse, assuming the spouse does not make his or her own contributions.[101] Executives who are participants in qualified plans are disallowed deductions for traditional IRA contributions if their income exceeds certain levels.[102]

---

[97] Code Sec. 409A(a)(4)(C).

[98] Code Sec. 404(a)(5).

[99] Code Sec. 219(b)(5)(A).

[100] Code Sec. 219(b)(5)(B).

[101] Code Sec. 219(c)(1).

[102] Code Sec. 219(g).

If the executive's adjusted gross income is below certain levels, he or she may contribute up to the maximum allowed each year (plus up to the same amount for the executive's spouse) to a Roth IRA instead of to a traditional IRA.[103] The amount that an executive may contribute to a Roth IRA begins to phase out at an adjusted gross income of $95,000 if single or $150,000 if married and filing a joint return. Contributions to Roth IRAs are not tax deductible,[104] but a taxpayer may make tax-free withdrawals of his or her contributions at any time.[105] Distributions from Roth IRAs are completely tax free after the taxpayer has held the account for five years if the taxpayer is at least age 59½, the taxpayer is disabled, the distribution is paid to a beneficiary after the taxpayer's death, or the distribution is used to pay for qualified expenses up to $10,000 of buying a home.[106]

If the company plan allows it, and the executive's budget allows, voluntary contributions to the company plan should be considered, for the tax shelter afforded on the income on the executive's own contributions. However, the executive should first compare returns from other tax-deferred or tax-free investments.

Profit-sharing plans, unlike pension plans, permit in-service withdrawal of vested amounts, subject to plan rules and restrictions and tax rules. Employer contributions withdrawn before age 59½, except for disability or death, are generally taxable as ordinary income and are generally subject to a 10-percent additional tax.[107] Although the 10-percent additional tax is often called a penalty, it is really an additional tax. Thus, a taxpayer cannot avoid the additional tax even for reasonable cause. The taxpayer must meet a statutory exception to avoid the additional tax. However, if a participant in a qualified plan changes jobs (or simply terminates his or her employment), a rollover-eligible distribution may be transferred directly tax free to a traditional IRA or to another qualified plan that accepts such contributions. If the participant receives the distribution, the participant may roll over the amount tax free to another qualified plan or a traditional IRA within 60 days of receiving the distribution.[108] The IRS may waive the 60-day limit for hardships such as a casualty or natural disaster for distributions made before 2011.[109] If such a distribution is made to the employee, rather than directly to another plan, it is subject to mandatory 20-percent income tax withholding, even if the employee intends to complete a rollover. Therefore, employees who want to transfer funds to another plan

[103] Code Sec. 408A(c)(2).
[104] Code Sec. 408A(c)(1).
[105] Reg. § 1.408A-6.
[106] Code Secs. 408A(d)(2), 408A(d)(5), 72(t)(2)(F), and 72(t)(8).
[107] Code Sec. 72(t).
[108] Code Sec. 402(c).
[109] Code Secs. 402(c)(3) and 408(d)(3).

or a traditional IRA should use the direct transfer method. (Note that distributions from traditional IRAs are not subject to 20-percent withholding.)

The full amount need not be rolled over but any amount retained will be taxable. See under the heading "Rollover of Qualified Plan Benefits," below.

On reaching the retirement age fixed in the plan, the executive usually has a choice of an annuity or a lump-sum distribution. If the executive is married and is a participant in a defined benefit plan (and under certain circumstances in the case of a profit-sharing plan), an automatic joint and survivor annuity is provided. The participant may elect out of such coverage only with his or her spouse's consent. The annuity payments will be treated for tax purposes the same as any other annuity taxable under Code Sec. 72.

In choosing between an annuity and a lump-sum distribution, one must weigh the income tax impact. Also, an annuity might cause Social Security benefits to be taxed each year, whereas a lump-sum distribution would not (Social Security benefits and Medicare at ¶ 3505). Investment factors also need to be considered. What is the projected after-tax return if the lump sum is invested by the executive? How does this return compare with the return if funds are left in the pension or profit-sharing trust?

Multiple individual or trust beneficiaries are allowed without losing the advantages of the income tax-favored lump-sum distribution rule. The distribution is taxed as though made to a single recipient, and the tax liability is then allocated to the recipients in proportion to their shares.

There are special advantages and special problems if distributions from the plan are in employer stock. Because the rules are the same as those under qualified stock bonus plans or ESOPs, these rules are explained in the paragraphs below specifically dealing with stock bonus plans and ESOPs.

See ¶ 905 for stretched out payout opportunities.

.02 Stock Bonus Plans and ESOPs

Stock bonus plans and ESOPs (employee stock ownership plans) generally contemplate a distribution of benefits in employer stock. However, an ESOP may bar a participant from demanding a distribution of employer securities if the employer's corporate charter or bylaws restrict the ownership of substantially all outstanding employer securities to employees or the ESOP. The ESOP must provide that participants denied stock have a right to cash.[110]

At some point, a participant might consider further holding of employer securities in his or her ESOP account as imprudent. Some relief is available for such a participant. Effective with respect to stock acquired after 1986, ESOPs must allow qualified participants (those who have attained age 55 and have completed 10 years of participation in the plan) to direct diversification of up to 25 percent of their account balances over a six-year period (50 percent in the sixth year).[111]

In the usual set-up, the employer securities are not publicly traded. If the employer securities are publicly traded, the market is often thin. Thus, participants must deal with a liquidity problem. The plan may not require that the distributee sell to the employer, but the distributee may have a right to put the stock distributed to him or her at a price determined by a fair valuation formula.[112] The position of a minority shareholder in a closely held corporation in which he or she is no longer employed is not usually a strong one. Therefore, the courts, and to a degree the IRS, allow discounts in valuing such interests.

If, however, the minority position is valuable and worth maintaining, the executive who receives a distribution in his or her employer's securities also receives tax advantages. If it is a lump-sum distribution, the entire net unrealized appreciation attributable to the part of the distribution that consists of employer securities is excluded in figuring the tax on the lump sum (unless the executive elects otherwise). The unrealized appreciation is taxable only on the disposition of the securities in a taxable transaction. If the executive holds the securities until death, one might expect that the recipient of the decedent's stock would have had his or her basis stepped up to the estate tax valuation. However, the IRS in Rev. Rul. 75-125[113] limits the step-up. Under this ruling, the recipient receives no increase in basis to the extent of the unrealized appreciation in employer securities at the time of distribution to the executive. The ruling offers this example of how the heirs, in this case the widow, compute gain on a sale of the securities. In addition, the total step-up in basis is limited to $1,300,000 plus $3,000,000 for property received by a surviving spouse for decedents who die in 2010.

> ***Example 16.1.*** Richard Hume, an executive, receives from the trust employer securities with a basis to the trust of $5,000

[110] Code Sec. 409(h)(2)(B).

[111] Code Sec. 401(a)(28)(B).

[112] Code Secs. 409(h)(1)(B) and 409(h)(4).

[113] 1975-1 CB 254.

and a fair market value at the time of distribution of $10,000. The securities have a value at his death of $12,000. They are sold by his widow, Jane, for $13,000. Her basis is $7,000, which is the value at death, $12,000, less the $5,000 in unrealized appreciation at the time of distribution to the executive. Thus, she realizes a gain of $6,000 on the sale at $13,000.

If the executive's estate or other beneficiary receives employer securities in a distribution that qualifies for favorable lump-sum treatment, the total unrealized appreciation (attributable to both employer and executive contributions) will not be taxable at that time. Rather, the gain is recognized when the securities are later disposed of in a taxable transaction (unless a contrary election is made). If the distribution does not qualify for lump-sum treatment, only the unrealized appreciation attributable to the executive's own nondeductible contributions is so treated. For further discussion of ESOPs, see ¶ 910.

.03 Rollover of Qualified Plan Benefits

The recipient of an eligible rollover distribution from a qualified plan may defer taxation of the distribution, either in whole or in part, by having all or some of the distribution transferred directly to another plan or to a traditional IRA, or by rolling over as much of the distribution attributable to employer contributions and deductible employee contributions (as were once permitted) as desired into another qualified plan or a traditional IRA within 60 days of the distribution.[114] A taxpayer may roll over an eligible distribution received before January 1, 2011, into a Code Sec. 457 deferred compensation plan. In addition, a taxpayer may roll over distributions received before January 1, 2011, from a Code Sec. 403(b) annuity into a traditional IRA, a 401k plan, a Code Sec. 457 deferred compensation plan, or another Code Sec. 403(b) annuity. Further, a taxpayer may roll over distributions received before January 1, 2011, from a qualified plan, traditional IRA, 401k plan, or Code Sec. 457 plan into a Code Sec. 403(b) annuity. As noted in detail at ¶ 905, mandatory 20-percent income tax withholding applies to eligible rollover distributions from qualified plans that are not transferred directly to another plan or to a traditional IRA.[115] Where property, such as employer securities, is included in the distribution, the recipient may roll it over. The recipient may also effect a bona fide sale of the property and roll over the proceeds, including any appreciation from the time of distribution. However, the recipient may not retain the property and roll over an amount of

[114] Code Sec. 402(c).

[115] Code Sec. 3405(c).

cash equal to the fair market value of the property.[116] If the distribution consists of cash and the proceeds of property or properties, and the recipient rolls over less than all, he or she must determine the amount, if any, of the cash rollover and the extent to which property proceeds have been rolled over. The recipient makes this determination by filing a designation not later than the date for filing an income tax return for the year of distribution. If no designation is filed, the rollover amount is allocated pro rata on the basis of the cash and the value of the property at the time of the distribution.

The spouse of a participant receiving an eligible rollover distribution from a qualified plan may effect a tax-free direct transfer, or a rollover into a traditional IRA, within 60 days of the distribution. The spouse of a participant who receives an eligible rollover distribution before January 1, 2011, may roll over the distribution to another qualified plan, a Code Sec. 403(b) annuity, a Code Sec. 457 plan, or a traditional IRA.[117]

.04 Simplified Employee Pension Plan Using an IRA

Code Sec. 408(k) provides for a simplified employee pension (SEP) plan making use of IRAs. An employee may participate in a SEP even though he or she is also a participant in a qualified plan, subject to Code Sec. 415 limits. Under a SEP, an employer makes contributions to a traditional individual retirement arrangement (called a SEP-IRA) set up by or for each eligible employee.[118] An employer does not have to make annual contributions to employees' SEP-IRAs, but if the employer does make contributions, it must not discriminate in favor of highly compensated employees. SEP-IRAs must cover all employees who have reached age 21, worked for the employee for at least three of the last five years, and received at least a minimum amount of compensation for the year. The minimum compensation level is $450 for 2006.[119]

Contributions to an employee's SEP-IRA are limited to the smaller of 25 percent of the employee's compensation or the annual dollar limit for additions to a defined contribution plan account. The dollar limit for defined contribution plan additions is $44,000 for 2006.[120] When computing SEP contributions, no more than $200,000 of an employee's compensation can be taken into account.

The employee may contribute a limited amount to his or her traditional IRA or Roth IRA in addition to the contributions the

[116] Rev. Rul. 87-77, 1987-2 CB 115.

[117] Code Sec. 402(c).

[118] Code Sec. 408(k).

[119] Notice 2005-75, 2005-45 IRB 929 (November 11, 2005).

[120] Notice 2005-75, 2005-45 IRB 929 (November 11, 2005).

employer makes to the SEP for the employee. For 2006 and 2007, the limit is $4,000; and for 2008, 2009, and 2010, the limit is $5,000. The $5,000 limit will be adjusted for inflation in 2009 and 2010. Individuals who are age 50 or older may contribute an additional $1,000 for 2006 through 2010. However, deductions for contributions to traditional IRAs and allowable contributions to Roth IRAs are phased out at certain income levels. For more information on SEPs, see ¶ 915.

.05 Incentive Stock Options

Incentive stock options are taxable in a favorable manner (¶ 1605). The exercise of the option by the executive eliminates any problems that might be associated with the valuation of an unexercised option as part of the executive's gross estate. Also, it invites consideration of lifetime gifts of the stock as a means of reducing the size of the executive's gross estate. Incidentally, the options themselves cannot be the subject of lifetime gifts. As a general rule, favorable tax treatment is available for an incentive stock option only if there is no disqualifying disposition of the stock within two years of the date of grant of the option or one year of the date of exercise. However, the holding period requirements do not apply to an option that is exercised after an employee's death by the employee's estate or by a person who acquired the right to exercise the option by reason of the employee's death.[121] If the option is exercised by the employee, but he or she dies before the expiration of the required holding period, the employee's estate or the person who acquired the stock by reason of the employee's death qualifies for favorable tax treatment even if the stock is sold before the expiration of the required holding period.[122]

.06 Nonqualified Options

At ¶ 1605 the tax treatment of nonqualified stock options is discussed at some length. This discussion is not repeated here except to note that the executive may elect to include in gross income, in the year of transfer, stock acquired under an option. The executive may make this election although the stock is not transferable and is subject to a substantial risk of forfeiture, so that tax otherwise would have been deferred. In addition to this election, the executive may be able to pay a tax on the grant of the option if the option has a readily ascertainable value at the time of grant, as defined in Reg. § 1.83-7(b).

Code Sec. 83, dealing generally with the tax on property transferred for the performance of services, provides in subsection (c)(2)

---

[121] Code Sec. 421(c)(1)(A); Reg. § 1.421-2(c)(1). [122] Reg. § 1.421-2(d).

that the rights of a person in property are transferable only if the rights in such property of any transferee are not subject to a substantial risk of forfeiture. The wholly gratuitous transfer of an unexercised option with no readily ascertainable fair market value at the time the option is granted does not give rise to any taxable income at the time of the transfer. The executive who transfers the option realizes gross income only when the option is exercised and property is transferred to the holder. This treatment applies although the option at the time of the grant has no ascertainable value but acquires such value before the option is transferred.[123]

The executive and an advisor might want to consider the transfer of options with no ascertainable value at the time of grant. Such a transfer would remove the option and the underlying stock from the executive's gross estate. The transfer has no current income tax consequences and low or no gift tax cost.

If the executive dies without having realized income from the transfer or exercise of the option, the executive's estate or beneficiary will, upon the exercise of the option or its transfer, be taxed on the income. This is treated as income in respect of a decedent,[124] and the party liable can deduct the estate tax attributable to the inclusion of the option in the executive's gross estate.[125]

Financing the exercise of the option is a matter of concern both from the point of view of exercise by the executive and by the executive's executor or beneficiary. The financing raises a number of questions. What is the source of the money? How much will it cost? How much value does the stock itself have as collateral if subject to restrictions and substantial conditions of forfeiture? If the stock is usable as collateral, what about margin requirements? What about the executor's authority to borrow? These and related questions must be weighed and answered.

.07 Letter Stock

Chances are the executive who holds letter stock will be familiar with the requirements that must be met to dispose of the stock. (Letter stock is privately placed common stock, so-called because the SEC requires a letter from the purchaser stating that the stock is not intended for resale.) Most likely the executive will want to dispose of it in compliance with SEC Rule 144, although that is not the only route open. Still, it is the safest route. Under it, publicly available current information about the company must exist, and a limitation

---

[123] Reg. § 1.83-7(a).

[124] Code Sec. 691(a).

[125] Code Sec. 691(c).

might apply to the number of shares that may be sold in any six-month period. Notice of intent to sell must be given to the SEC and to the exchange, if it is listed stock. The executive may not sell unless the stock is fully paid for and has been beneficially owned for at least two years.

However, special considerations apply if the executive's estate holds letter stock. The estate is not subject to the restrictions on the number of shares that may be sold in a six-month period, unless the estate itself is in the position of a control person. Also, the two-year holding period requirement is waived for the estate, unless it is a control person. If the estate is a control person, it can distribute the shares to legatees. They can sell the stock without regard to the holding period.

One must provide for full payment of the shares held, because that is a condition of sale under Rule 144.

.08 Deferred Compensation

An executive can do little about nonqualified deferred compensation before the right to it matures. A transfer of it will be ineffective, because it is an anticipatory assignment of income. That leaves the question of what to do with the right if the executive dies before receiving it.

Who should receive it from an income tax standpoint? Whoever receives it is going to have to report it as income in respect of a decedent.[126] The recipient may receive a deduction against the income received for the federal estate tax attributable to the inclusion of this item in the executive's gross estate.[127]

The executive could bequeath the deferred compensation to his or her spouse. The executive should consider the spouse's income tax situation under the estate plan being developed and the spouse's own separate estate or earnings, if any. If the surviving spouse will be in a fairly high combined federal, state, and local income tax bracket, bequeathing this additional income to the spouse will cause a sizable amount of it to go to the tax collectors. Also, if the executive bequeaths it to the surviving spouse and it qualifies for the marital deduction,[128] no increase in the estate tax will occur for its inclusion in the gross estate. Thus, the spouse will not be allowed an income tax deduction under Code Sec. 691(c). The spouse in addition to a marital bequest might also receive a nonmarital deduction bequest. If deferred compensation is made payable to the nonmarital deduction

[126] Code Sec. 691(a).

[127] Code Sec. 691(c).

[128] Code Sec. 2056(a).

bequest, the benefit of Code Sec. 691(c) may be available to help reduce the income tax liability.

The executive should also consider other possible beneficiaries. Children and grandchildren are often good possible beneficiaries. The executive should check the possible income tax consequences of a distribution to them or to a trust set up for their benefit.

An estate is allowed a deduction on its income tax return for distributions to beneficiaries of property in kind.[129] The IRS has ruled that this rule does not apply to a right to receive deferred compensation, because it is not a distribution of property in kind.[130]

.09 Life Insurance

Life insurance may be provided within limits, as an incident to a qualified pension or profit-sharing plan. The executive might be able to keep the proceeds of a life insurance policy out of his or her gross estate by transferring all incidents of ownership in the policy to a beneficiary other than the estate.[131]

However, the executive must be careful about transfers of the policy and premium payments within three years of death. Although Code Sec. 2035(a), as a general rule, excludes from the donor's estate gifts made within three years of death, this exclusion does not apply to gifts of life insurance.[132]

The exception of gifts of life insurance from the three-year rule of Code Sec. 2035 and whether gifts of premium money within three years of death are within the exception are discussed in some detail at ¶ 715. Generally, the payment of premiums within three years of death should not result in inclusion of the premiums, the policy proceeds, or any portion of the proceeds in the decedent's gross estate.

Normally one will want to keep life insurance proceeds out of the estate of the insured. To do so, the insured should assign the policy and all incidents of ownership and hope that he or she stays alive for at least three years.

However, the insured might not always want to keep the proceeds out of his or her gross estate. The estate might have liquidity needs which, if not satisfied, might conceivably result in a greater shrinkage of the value of the estate than the estate taxes resulting from inclusion of the proceeds. True, the insured may make the insurance proceeds payable to a beneficiary other than the estate, who would be expected to make the proceeds available to the estate

---

[129] Code Sec. 661(a) and Reg. § 1.661(a)-2.
[130] Rev. Rul. 68-195, 1968-1 CB 305.
[131] Code Sec. 2042.
[132] Code Secs. 2035(a)(2) and 2042.

by way of a loan or buy assets from the estate. However, the executive might not have confidence that the beneficiary would make the proceeds available to the estate. However, the insured cannot burden the beneficiary with a binding obligation because that would be interpreted as though the insured had named the estate as the beneficiary.

.10 Medical Savings Accounts and Health Savings Accounts

If the executive has an Archer medical savings account (MSA) under Code Sec. 220 or a health savings account (HSA) under Code Sec. 223, he or she does not have to withdraw anything from the MSA or HSA to pay or reimburse medical expenses incurred in the current year. Thus, the executive can use the MSA or HSA as an additional tax-qualified retirement account. The executive receives a current income tax deduction (within limits) and gains the advantage of tax-free investment build up on MSA or HSA funds not used for medical expenses.

.11 Contractual Death Benefits

The company may agree to pay an executive's surviving spouse or other beneficiary a death benefit if the executive dies on the job. The death benefit will not be taxable to the executive as income, but it will be taxable to the beneficiary. If includible in the executive's gross estate, the taxable portion is income in respect of a decedent,[133] and the estate tax attributable to that portion is deductible by the beneficiary.[134]

Whether a contractual death benefit is includible in the executive's gross estate depends on whether Code Sec. 2037 applies. The U.S. Tax Court has held, and the IRS concedes, that Code Sec. 2039(a), which would include in the gross estate an annuity or other payment receivable by any beneficiary surviving the executive, does not apply.[135] However, Code Sec. 2037, which would include in the gross estate transfers taking effect at death, might apply. For this section to apply, the following requirements are essential: (1) the executive makes a transfer of the benefits to a beneficiary during the executive's lifetime; (2) the beneficiary can receive the benefit only by surviving the executive; and (3) the executive retained a reversionary interest that exceeded five percent of the value of the payments immediately before the executive's death.[136]

---

[133] Code Sec. 691(a).

[134] Code Sec. 691(c).

[135] *H. Beal Est.*, 47 TC 269, CCH Dec. 28,204 (Acq.).

[136] *S. Bogley Est.*, CtCls, 75-1 USTC ¶ 13,068, 445 F2d 979; *H. Fried Est.*, 54 TC 805, CCH Dec. 30,065, aff'd CA-2, 71-2 USTC ¶ 12,796, 445 F2d 979, cert. denied, SCt, 404 US 1016.

The retention of a greater than five-percent reversionary interest can be a critical factor[137] and is determined under the IRS tables. The values vary with the age of the beneficiary, and the number of beneficiaries. Where a single beneficiary is named, the reversionary interest will rarely be found to be worth less than five percent. Hence, naming contingent beneficiaries is important if the primary beneficiary does not survive.

At one time, the IRS insisted that a contractual death benefit measured by an executive's salary in the year of death constituted a gift in the year of death. After losing on this in the courts, it has abandoned this position, but only if (1) the employee is automatically covered by the plan and has no control over its terms, (2) the employer retains the right to modify the plan, and (3) the employee's death is the event that first causes the value of the benefit to be ascertainable (see ¶ 950 for further discussion of this issue).[138]

.12 Voluntary Death Benefits

The company, although not willing to commit itself contractually, may make a voluntary payment to the surviving spouse or other beneficiary. The IRS believes that any amount would be taxable to the recipient and would not be excludable as a gift under Code Sec. 102.[139] However, the U.S. Tax Court noted that the key issue is the transferor's intent based on all the facts and circumstances. The U.S. Court of Appeals for the Ninth Circuit has held that payments made to the widow of an employee/stockholder were nontaxable gifts because the corporation received no economic benefits from the transfer and the employee had been fully compensated during his life for services he provided.[140] Whether a voluntary death benefit to a survivor is taxable or is a nontaxable gift will depend on the facts and circumstances of each case.

¶ 1615 USE OF STANDARD TECHNIQUES

An estate planner should have no doubt that the executive's estate requires special handling. However, the situation is not so special that the executive cannot utilize many of the standard estate planning techniques that are explained throughout this book. Indeed, many of them take on added importance for the executive primarily because the executive's estate might have more liquidity problems than most estates.

---

[137] Rev. Rul. 78-15, 1978-1 CB 289.

[138] *A. DiMarco Est.*, 87 TC 653, CCH Dec. 43,390; and Rev. Rul. 92-68, 1992-2 CB 257.

[139] *M.L. Sweeney*, 54 TCM 1003, Dec. 44,306(M) (1987).

[140] *L.H. Harper*, 72-1 USTC ¶ 9112, 454 F2d 222 (1971).

The use of the marital deduction alone[141] or in combination with available applicable credit amount (unified credit)[142] can save the executive's estate from federal estate tax liability. Nontax as well as tax considerations bear on the extent to which the marital deduction should be used, as discussed in ¶ 1215. Marriage is a prerequisite of the use of the marital deduction, and not all executives are married at the time of death.

Apart from federal estate tax liabilities and their discharge, the executive's estate from the very nature of its assets is apt to face liquidity problems. These liquidity problems might require life insurance solutions or a reordering of investments.

Gifts are often a useful way of minimizing estate tax liabilities. To minimize the estate tax through lifetime gifts, the executive should make full use of the annual gift tax exclusion ($12,000 for 2006, indexed for inflation).[143] If the donor is married, he or she may also use gift splitting,[144] i.e., making an election with the spouse's consent to have the gift treated as having been made half by each spouse, thus doubling the amount eligible for excusion. A gift of property that appreciates in value after the gift is made, even though subject to the gift tax, serves to exclude the appreciation from the gross estate of the donor. Gifts can also result in family income tax savings when income-producing property is the subject of the gift, subject to the special income tax rules for children under the age of 14. In selecting property for executive giving, one must be mindful of the rule that property passing from a decedent receives a basis stepped up to its value at the date of death (or six months later if the alternate valuation date is allowed and is elected by the executor).[145] The tax-free step up in basis eliminates any tax liability on appreciation up to the time of death (or six months later if the alternate valuation date is elected by the executor). However, for property received from decedents dying in 2010, the step up in basis is limited to $1,300,000 plus $3,000,000 for property received by a surviving spouse. No such step up rule applies to lifetime gifts. Rather, a donee obtains a basis in the gifted property equal to the donor's adjusted basis plus the gift tax attributable to the appreciation in the property.[146] One must also be especially careful of the estate's possible liquidity problems. Therefore, nonliquid assets might be prime candidates for giving. That same need for liquidity also suggests the possible use of the net gift technique in special circumstances. This technique involves having the donee pay the gift tax

[141] Code Sec. 2056(a).

[142] Code Sec. 2010.

[143] Code Sec. 2503(b).

[144] Code Sec. 2513.

[145] Code Sec. 1014(a).

[146] Code Sec. 1015.

tab as a means of preserving the executive's cash or cash equivalents (see ¶410, however, requiring exhaustion of donor's unified credit before any gift tax is payable by the donee and on possible income tax problems).

Gifts of low value life insurance are one possibility to be explored, taking into account the possible need for the policies to supply estate liquidity. Gifts to charity are another possibility because they not only reduce the executive's gross estate, but they also provide the executive with an income tax deduction.[147]

Creation of trusts is another major consideration. If parents are grantors of a trust, they will have difficulty avoiding being taxed on the trust income payable to their children. Apart from tax factors, trusts also provide protection against creditors of the grantor, control of the use of the trust funds by a fiduciary, and provide management of investments.

The effect of joint ownership of property, especially as it relates to joint ownership with the executive's spouse, needs to be explored.

As to joint tenancies between spouses, on the death of the first to die, only one-half of the value of the property is includible in the decedent's gross estate.[148] Only that half will generally get a step up in basis, regardless of the contributions made by either.[149] For this and other reasons, spouses may want to consider termination of interspousal joint tenancies. However, if the spouses hold the property as community property, all of the property receives a tax free step up in basis.[150]

On the other hand, under some circumstances the executive might want to maintain interspousal joint tenancies or to create new ones. The creation can be accomplished without gift tax consequences and removes one-half of the value from the gross estate for federal tax purposes of the first to die. Joint tenancy also excludes the full value of the property from the probate estate and reduces the costs of probate administration. A joint tenancy might also have some psychological benefits. An executive should not create a joint tenancy without considering long-term factors and contingencies. These factors include the impact on the estate of the survivor, the right of the survivor to dispose of the property without regard to the interests of children or others, the interest that the survivor's spouse on remarriage might acquire, the possibility that the marriage of the donor and donee spouse might terminate before the death of either.

---

[147] Code Sec. 170(a).

[148] Code Sec. 2040(b).

[149] Code Sec. 1014(a).

[150] Code Secs. 1014(a) and 1014(b)(6).

¶1620 TOTAL FINANCIAL COUNSELING FOR THE EXECUTIVE

Some companies furnish financial counseling services for their top executives, often employing outside firms. The cost may be as much as $3,000 to $4,000 or more per executive for the initial analysis and report, and $1,500 to $2,000 for an annual review and update. The cost paid by the company will be taxable to the executive. However, the portion of the amount includible in gross income that is allocable to the collection or production of income or to tax advice (including tax preparation) qualifies as an itemized deduction under Code Sec. 212, subject to the two-percent floor on miscellaneous itemized deductions.[151]

> **Note:** The value of retirement planning advice or information provided to an executive or his or her spouse is excludable from income if the employer maintains a qualified retirement plan, provided retirement planning services are available on substantially the same terms to each member of the group of employees who are normally provided with education and information regarding the employer's plan.[152]

The approach used by these firms can serve as a model for the estate planner engaged in putting together a financial and estate plan for an executive. The report issued by one of these counseling firms can run more than 100 double-spaced typewritten pages. Much of the report is boiler-plate, laying down pertinent general principles. However, the report also includes personalized comments and planning advice. The following is what a typical report might contain:

.01 Basic Data

This includes family relationships, personal objectives and considerations, a net worth statement, and a statement of family income and expenses.

.02 Analysis of Existing Plan

Existing wills of the executive and the executive's spouse, trusts, insurance policies, employee benefit plans, and beneficiary designations are analyzed. Property documents, bank accounts and securities holdings, and other relevant documents will be examined. Income and death tax consequences of the existing plan or documents will then be analyzed. Legal and tax weaknesses and strengths are noted. The general economic effect is set forth.

---

[151] Code Sec. 67.

[152] Code Sec. 132(m).

.03 General Recommendations

The report will recommend improvements. It might make recommendations as to lifetime gifts, with detailed suggestions as to amounts, the assets to be used, and the timing of the gifts. Gift tax considerations will be spelled out and recommendations will be made about the use of trusts or custodianships, if minors are involved. If a trust is to be used, the report will include details concerning the type of trust such as revocable, irrevocable, testamentary, or pourover. Charitable giving may also be considered if that appears to be an executive objective.

.04 Stock Options and Company Stock

The report will contain information on nonqualified stock and on stock acquired by the exercise of incentive stock options. Recommendations will be made as to their exercise, taking into account financing and tax consequences. Company stock holdings will be examined and recommendations will be made as to gifts, sales or exchanges, and bequests. Income and estate tax consequences will be noted, along with possible security law requirements.

.05 General Executive Benefits

The report will make recommendations regarding all employee benefits. The report will examine tax consequences and family considerations.

.06 Life Insurance

The report will make recommendations about existing policies. The report will note their strengths and weaknesses and make suggestions as to beneficiary designations. Estate and income tax considerations will be noted. The report might also suggest assignments of ownership of policies and the transfer of incidents of ownership. The report might make recommendations as to additional new insurance, with specifics as to the type of policy, premium payments, beneficiary designations, and settlement options.

.07 New Plan

The report will provide a new plan with specific details. These details will include, for example, the marital deduction bequest, with particular attention to the use of a QTIP, power of appointment, estate or portion trust for the marital deduction bequest, and the use of some form of credit shelter trust. The report will compare the new plan with the old plan in terms of tax and family considerations and the attainment of economic objectives.

.08 Investments

In some cases, the report will review existing investments and make recommendations concerning changes or professional investment counseling. Tax-favored investments will often merit special considerations. The impact of the passive loss rules[153] on particular types of investments may be explained.

.09 Budgets

Some firms become involved in the family budget and suggest areas in which the family can save money, or where reallocations are needed.

¶1625 THE MIGRATORY EXECUTIVE

Corporate executives, particularly those working for national and multinational companies, are more apt to move from one state or country to another.

The estate planner must have some appreciation of what these moves can mean and what past moves have meant in terms of property rights and any estate plan that is to be developed. Once the problems are recognized, the executive might be able to cope with them by marital agreements, revocable trusts, and good draftsmanship of wills. The following are some of the key problem areas and possible ways of handling them.

.01 Will Draftsmanship

Often in drafting a will, provisions can be omitted that are read into the will by virtue of the statutes or case law. Fiduciary powers and administrative provisions are often good candidates for omission. However, an attorney cannot afford to omit such provisions in preparing an executive's will because the executive is not certain where he or she might be located from one year or, perhaps, one month to the next. Dispositive provisions might also be affected by a move from one jurisdiction to another. For example, if the will provides for distributions to be made to children on their attaining the age of majority, one state's age limit might be higher or lower than the limit in another state. In addition, a bequest to children might include adopted children in one state and not in another state. The executive's will should therefore spell out fiduciary and administrative powers in particular. The will should not use terms affecting substantive matters that might be open to different interpretations from one jurisdiction to the next, without precisely defining them.

---

[153] Code Sec. 469.

.02 Community Property

Moves to and from community property jurisdictions involve special problems for married couples (¶ 325). Long after the couple has disposed of community property and acquired other property in another jurisdiction, the executive might find that the newly acquired property retains the character of community property.

To deal with many of the problems, the estate planner should consider recommending agreements between the spouses and the use of living trusts.

Anyone engaged in estate planning in a common-law state for an executive who has lived in, or might move to, a community property state should consult with a lawyer familiar with community property law. Community property laws can vary considerably from one state to another.

.03 Foreign Residence

The executive who resides in a foreign country might encounter various legal and tax problems. The executive's spouse and heirs might have rights under foreign law that may not be altered or, if alterable, could be difficult to understand and assert.

In these cases, the executive should keep the property in the foreign country to a minimum. The executive can do so by using a revocable trust set up in one of the states as a receptacle for assets that would otherwise follow the executive's residence. A joint account in the United States with the executive's spouse is another possibility, although joint accounts can present their own problems.

An executive residing in a foreign country should have two wills: one disposing of property located within the United States (as defined in the will) and the other disposing of property located in the foreign country. A marital agreement might be helpful in these circumstances.

Under Code Sec. 911, an individual meeting either a bona fide residency test or a specified physical presence test may elect to exclude up to $80,000[154] of foreign earned income attributable to the period of his or her residence in a foreign country for any tax year. The $80,000 amount will be indexed for inflation for years beginning after 2007.[155] The maximum annual exclusions are computed on a daily basis and, therefore, are reduced ratably for each day that a taxpayer is absent from a foreign country during the tax year.[156]

---

[154] Code Sec. 911(b)(2)(D)(i).

[155] Code Sec. 911(b)(2)(D)(ii).

[156] Code Sec. 911(b)(2)(A).

Chapter 17

Planning for the Professional

Overview ....¶1701
What Makes the Professional Special ....¶1705
Side Businesses ....¶1710
Corporate and Noncorporate Practice ....¶1715
Problems and Pitfalls in Corporate Operation ....¶1720
Planning for Shareholder-Professionals ....¶1725
Withdrawal and Expulsion ....¶1730

¶1701 OVERVIEW

Physicians, dentists, attorneys, accountants, and other professionals licensed by the state to practice their professions are a privileged class. They are subject to governmental regulations and bound by codes of ethics to which the ordinary business person is not held. Their licenses to practice, unlike licenses to operate taxis or buses, are not transferable.

¶1705 WHAT MAKES THE PROFESSIONAL SPECIAL

The paradoxical combination of privilege and regulatory restrictions makes financial and estate planning for the professional different. The restrictions to which the professional is subject make many of the estate planning techniques available to and commonly used for the handling of general business interests inapplicable. Because a professional may transfer his or her practice only to another professional, he or she cannot develop a family gift program involving business interests, as can other business owners. However, many professionals in increasing numbers are developing side businesses that make gift programs involving these businesses applicable (¶1710).

Professionals also have much more difficulty in building capital values by developing a practice because of the limitations on transferability. Professionals who own interests in side businesses are legally free to sell their other business interests to the highest bidder in a nonrestricted market, open to all types of bidders. A professional may usually sell an interest in a professional firm only to another professional. The buyer of a professional practice is very often a neophyte who is unable to pay a good price. There also is normally no assurance that the goodwill built up by the seller will pass to the buyer, which further limits the selling price.

Because of these and other factors, the decision-making process for the professional is often more difficult than is that confronting the ordinary business person.

The job of the financial and estate planner is to help the professional make rational choices where choice is possible and necessary. The financial and estate planner must also guide the professional in building and preserving income and wealth, and transmitting it to heirs and beneficiaries. The financial and estate plan should save taxes and be consistent with the professional client's personality, attitudes toward risk, and fundamental interests and desires.

To incorporate or not to incorporate or, if incorporated, to continue incorporation, is a question that many professionals face. This issue is addressed at ¶1715. The limited liability partnership has become a popular form of operating a professional practice. A partner in a limited liability partnership is not liable for the professional negligence or malpractice of another partner.

¶1710 SIDE BUSINESSES

Many professionals might develop businesses outside their established fields of practice. In many cases the side businesses may be related to their respective practices. A physician may, for example, establish a drug store or a medical testing lab where permitted; a dentist could set up a dental lab; accountants could begin a business consulting firm; attorneys could start an investment advisory or life insurance firm. All may hold real estate that they can rent to themselves for their professional practices or for their side businesses.

These side businesses, in addition to being independent of the practice in many cases and being transferable assets, may also furnish employment opportunities for members of the professional's family.

The legal form in which these businesses operate will vary sometimes in response to state laws and in some cases because of issues arising under some professional codes of ethics.

If the professional practice is incorporated, these side businesses may operate as subsidiaries of the parent firm or they may be set up as completely independent entities. They may be C corporations, S corporations, partnerships, limited liability companies, or sole proprietorships.

In many cases, in addition to functioning as separate profit centers, the side businesses may also operate to increase the profitability of the professional practices.

From a financial and estate planning point of view, such side businesses not only increase transferable wealth, but may also serve to increase the sale value of the professional practice if sold as a package with the practice.

¶ 1715 CORPORATE AND NONCORPORATE PRACTICE

Professionals in states that authorize the practice of their particular profession in corporate form can choose to practice in various legal and tax forms: as a regular or C corporation, as an S corporation (discussed in detail at ¶ 1945), as a regular partnership, as a limited liability partnership, or as a sole proprietorship. In addition, all states have adopted limited liability company acts. Some of these acts explicitly allow professionals to operate their practices as limited liability companies. The limited liability company is usually taxed as a partnership with the limited liability associated with the corporate form. However, limited liability companies may elect to be taxed as a corporation by filing Form 8832.[1] Limited liability companies are discussed at ¶ 2040.

Professionals should weigh a number of factors before deciding on one form or another. Operating as a partnership requires at least two partners. With the other forms one can maintain a solo practice. No limit exists on the number of shareholders a C corporation may have, but an S corporation may have no more than 100 shareholders.[2] However, a husband and wife are treated as one shareholder. In addition, certain family members may elect to be treated as one shareholder.[3] Also, for an entity to be respected as a corporation, corporate formalities must be strictly observed.

The professional's decision whether or not to incorporate is influenced by tax factors, although the tax advantages of incorporation now are derived mainly from the special treatment of some corporate fringe benefits. Issues formerly of concern, such as IRS

[1] Reg. § 301.7701-3.

[2] Code Sec. 1361(b)(1)(A).

[3] Code Sec. 1361(c)(1).

recognition of professional corporations and differences between corporate and noncorporate retirement plans, are no longer problematic. For a discussion of retirement plans, see ¶ 905.

Using the professional corporation as a tax shelter by retaining earnings taxed at corporate rates lower than the shareholder-owners' individual rates, taking advantage of the 70-percent dividends-received deduction,[4] and paying a top capital gains rate of only 15 percent[5] (through 2010) on a subsequent redemption or liquidation may provide some tax-saving opportunities for very high income professionals. However, personal service corporations do not benefit from graduated corporate income tax rates. Their income is taxed at a flat 35-percent rate.[6]

Planning pointer. There may be some advantage to retaining income in a personal service corporation and investing it in stock paying qualified dividends, if the shareholder intends to leave the stock and earnings there until death. The shareholder's heirs would receive a step-up in basis,[7] so that they could receive much of the appreciation in the value of the dividend-paying stock tax free. This strategy also rests partially on the assumption that Congress will not reduce the dividends-received deduction further. Congress has limited the tax-free step-up in basis as a price for eliminating the estate tax in 2010 only. The Economic Growth and Tax Relief Reconciliation Act of 2001[8] limited the step-up in basis to $1.3 million of assets transferred plus $3 million of assets transferred to a spouse in 2010 only.

For the purpose of the 35-percent flat tax, a personal service corporation is one substantially owned by its employees, retired employees, or their estates, and whose substantial activities involve the performance of services in the fields of health, law, engineering, architecture, accounting, actuarial science, performing arts, or consulting.[9]

The 35-percent flat rate should not necessarily create insurmountable tax problems for professionals who choose to incorporate. Because the corporation's income usually comes almost entirely from services performed by the professional shareholders, it can generally deduct compensation and benefits to the full extent of its income without running into reasonable compensation problems.[10] Thus, the corporation would have no tax liability. Some of the income of

[4] Code Sec. 243(a)(1).
[5] Code Sec. 1(h)(1)(C).
[6] Code Sec. 11(b)(2).
[7] Code Sec. 1014(a).
[8] H.R. 1836.
[9] Code Sec. 448(d)(2).
[10] Code Sec. 162(a).

a professional corporation with substantial investments in equipment or real estate could be attributable to those investments, but in most cases this income is more than offset by the expenses of maintenance and operation, and by depreciation (MACRS) deductions. However, the corporation must intend the payments to be compensation at the time of payment. If the payments were for a shareholder's benefit and later found not to be deductible, the corporation may not be able to deduct such payments as compensation.[11]

.01 Corporate Fringe Benefits

A regular C corporation (but not S corporations) may use tax-favored fringe benefits otherwise not available or available only to a limited extent under other forms of operation. These benefits include the following:

- The health and accident plan exclusion from income.[12]
- Employer payments to health and accident plan exclusion from income.[13]
- Group term life insurance exclusion from income.[14]
- Exclusion of the value of meals and lodgings provided for the convenience of the employer,[15] which is of limited value for most professionals, but possibly of value for some health services providers.

Benefits valued at $3,000, for example, if tax-free, are the equivalent of $4,000 taxable to an individual in a 25-percent tax bracket. If the corporation is in a zero tax bracket and the shareholder-professional is the sole shareholder and if the corporation does not have to provide benefits to other employees, the shareholder-professional would receive tax savings of $1,000. If the corporation is in an above-zero tax bracket, the after-tax cost to the corporation would be reduced, while the shareholder's savings would remain the same.

If the fringe benefit is one that must be made available to non-owner employees on a nondiscriminatory basis, the corporation must weight the cost of providing it to the other employees. To the extent that the cost of covering other employees serves to hold down direct compensation costs or promotes goodwill, loyalty, and productivity, the cost of coverage may well be offset.

If a sole practitioner dies, the executor or personal representative of the practitioner should return any records that belong to clients or

[11] *Neontology Associates, P.A. et al.*, 115 TC 43 (2000), *aff'd* 2002-2 USTC ¶50,550 (CA-3, 2002.).

[12] Code Sec. 105(b) and (c).

[13] Code Sec. 106.

[14] Code Sec. 79.

[15] Code Sec. 119.

patients. The estate will want to retain the professional's workpapers until the time for filing claims against the estate has expired. The estate might need the workpapers to defend a malpractice claim. The rules of the American Institute of Certified Public Accountants and several state boards of accountancy do not address the issue of a CPA's workpapers upon his or her death. Possibly, the state boards of accountancy in some states and the state licensing boards of other professions might address this issue. The executor of the estate should consult with the state licensing board as to the disposal of the professional's workpapers. If a professional in a partnership or professional corporation dies, the workpapers will usually remain with the firm.

.02 Health Coverage for Self-Employed Professionals

By employing his or her spouse and providing employees with health benefits (including coverage for spouses), a self-employed person may deduct all of the health insurance premiums (including the owner's premiums) on Schedule C.[16] This deduction would reduce the professional's income tax and his or her self-employment tax.

If the self-employed professional does not employ his or her spouse, the professional may deduct the cost of any health insurance provided to employees on Schedule C as an employee benefit program. However, the self-employed person may not deduct the cost of his or her own health insurance on Schedule C. Rather, the professional may deduct 100 percent of his or her own health insurance premiums as an above-the-line deduction on page 1 of Form 1040.[17] For this purpose, health insurance premiums include eligible long-term care premiums. Eligible long-term care premiums are those that would otherwise be deductible as a medical expense.[18]

This deduction reduces the professional's income tax, but not the self-employment tax.[19] The deduction is also limited to the professional's earned income.[20] In addition, the professional may not deduct any amount for health insurance on page 1 of Form 1040 for any month in which the professional is eligible to participate in any subsidized health plan maintained by any employer of the professional or his or her spouse.[21]

The financial planner will want to remind professionals of the need for disability income insurance. The ability of a professional to work in his or her profession is often the professional's most valuable

---

[16] Code Sec. 162(a), Reg. § 1.162-10(a), IRS Coordinated Issue Paper: All Industries, Health Insurance Deductibility for Self-Employed Individuals, UIL 162.35-02, March 29, 1999, Rev. Rul. 71-588, 1971-2 CB 91.

[17] Code Sec. 162(l)(1)(A).

[18] Code Secs. 162(l)(2)(C) and 213(d)(10).

[19] Code Sec. 162(l)(2)(C)(4).

[20] Code Sec. 162(l)(2)(A).

[21] Code Sec. 162(l)((2)(B).

asset. Yet, professionals might overlook the need for disability income insurance. The financial planner should advise the professional of the need for disability income insurance. The premiums for an individual disability income insurance policy are not deductible for income tax purposes, but any proceeds received are not taxable. However, if an employer pays the premiums for a disability income insurance policy, the employer may deduct the premiums as an employee benefit program.[22] The premiums paid by the employer for a group disability income insurance policy are tax free to the employee,[23] but any proceeds received will be taxable to the employee.[24] However, if the employer pays the premiums on the policy and treats the premiums as additional compensation, the employee may exclude any benefits received under the policy from his or her gross income.[25]

.03 Corporate Considerations

Some of these tax factors tend to favor S status and noncorporate forms of operation over the regular C corporate form of operation. Still, the opportunity to avoid double taxation by paying out all income in the form of compensation and benefits may cause many existing professional corporations to remain as such.

Whether the corporate operation is in C or S form, corporate limited liability follows. However, the corporate limited liability affords no protection to a shareholder-professional for a malpractice claim. In addition, a director or officer of a corporation is potentially subject to liability for breach of duty or wrongful acts as a director or officer. A director or officer should consider purchasing directors and officers liability insurance for these potential claims.

The rest of this chapter focuses on the professional corporation, that is, a C corporation, as the mode of practice. The limited liability company, partnership, and sole proprietorship forms are separately discussed in general terms in other chapters of this book.

¶1720 PROBLEMS AND PITFALLS IN CORPORATE OPERATION

Professionals should consider the disadvantages, problem areas, and pitfalls involved in a corporate operation. Many areas of concern involve tax matters, but the professional should also consider practical, legal, and ethical considerations. The list below briefly outlines these various considerations, all of which are discussed in greater detail later in this section.

---

[22] Code Sec. 162(a) and Reg. § 1.162-10(a).

[23] Code Sec. 106(a).

[24] Code Sec. 105(a).

[25] Code Sec. 105(a).

.01 Operating as a Corporation

To gain the tax and other advantages of corporate operation, the corporation must adhere to the formalities of corporate operation. Observing corporate formalities involves costs and expenditure of time and effort.

.02 Reasonable Compensation

A corporation may not deduct unreasonable compensation.[26] Even if the corporation believes the compensation paid is reasonable, the IRS may treat part of the payment received as a nondeductible dividend to the extent of the corporation's earnings and profits. However, the IRS may not treat the payment as a dividend solely by reason of the corporation's nonpayment of dividends out of its earnings and profits.[27]

.03 Tax Year

A personal service corporation must use the calendar year as its tax year unless the IRS consents to the use of a different year for business purposes or unless a fiscal year is elected under Code Sec. 444. Corporations making the election must make either "minimum distributions" to employee-owners before the end of the calendar year or must postpone deductions for some or all distributions to employee-owners.

.04 Limits on Use of Cash Method

C corporations, other than personal service corporations and corporations with annual gross receipts of $5 million or less, may not use the cash method of accounting.

.05 Personal Holding Company

If services are rendered on an individual patient or client-professional basis, a C corporation may have personal holding company problems, especially in one-owner corporations. However, the problems may be manageable under Rev. Ruls. 75-67, 75-249, and 75-250.[28] An S corporation is not subject to the personal holding company tax.

.06 Allocation of Income

Code Sec. 269A permits the IRS to allocate the income, deductions, and other items of a personal service corporation to more than

[26] Code Sec. 162(a).

[27] Rev. Rul. 79-8, 1979-1 CB 92.

[28] 1975-1 CB 169, 171 and 172.

10-percent shareholders if substantially all services are performed for only one other entity. There is a question under this provision whether an individual performing services for his or her personal service corporation is to be regarded as a separate entity so as to render the section applicable. Also, under Code Sec. 482, the IRS is empowered to allocate income between businesses controlled by the same interests (the stockholder-employee may be considered both a business and the controlling interest).

.07 Multiple Corporation Danger

Stockholder-employees of professional corporations sometimes own related corporations (e.g., a physician owns a medical service corporation and a corporation that owns his or her office building). The medical service corporation and building corporation may be a brother-sister controlled group and only a single $150,000 accumulated earnings credit is allowed. Also, special qualified retirement plan rules may come into play.

.08 Accumulated Earnings Tax

An accumulated earnings tax is imposed at a flat rate of 15 percent on the accumulated taxable income[29] of a corporation formed or availed of to avoid income tax on dividends by permitting earnings and profits to accumulate instead of being distributed to stockholders.[30] Every corporation is allowed to accumulate a minimum of $250,000[31] ($150,000 for certain service corporations under Code Sec. 535(c)(2)(B)) before the corporation must submit evidence that it has reasonable business needs for the accumulation. The corporation does not assess itself the accumulated earnings tax. Rather, the IRS may assess the tax on an audit of the corporation's income tax return.

.09 Converting Partnership to Corporate Form

Tax-free incorporation[32] may be jeopardized if partnership liabilities exceed the basis of the assets transferred to the corporation.[33] The liabilities to retired or deceased partners may also create special problems.

.10 Business Expense Deductions

If the IRS disallows an expense item taken by the corporation, corporate tax liability will be incurred or increased. If the corporation paid the amount disallowed to the professional, it may also be taxable

[29] Code Sec. 535.
[30] Code Sec. 531.
[31] Code Sec. 535(c)(2)(A).
[32] Code Sec. 351(a).
[33] Code Sec. 357(c).

to the professional (double taxation). The result is less corporate money for payment of compensation and hence a lower basis for corporate plan contributions.

.11 State and Local Taxes

State and local taxes may be imposed on corporations and not on unincorporated professional practices.

.12 Social Security Taxes

The incorporated professional picks up both the corporate and individual liability for Social Security taxes, although the corporation gets a tax deduction for the taxes it pays, including the 1.45-percent Medicare tax. The self-employed individual pays twice the individual rate,[34] but may deduct one-half of the self-employment tax as a deduction in computing adjusted gross income.[35]

.13 Balancing Interests of Different Professionals

If two or more professionals are shareholders, they may have different opinions on the important issues of how much income is to be deferred, what fringe benefits are appropriate, investment objectives of retirement plans, and other factors.

.14 Cost of Benefits

To the extent that the corporation must provide benefits on a nondiscriminatory basis and cover all employees, the tax benefits to shareholder-professionals will be offset by the after-tax cost of providing coverage to the other employees.

.15 Ethics

Some members of the legal profession perceive a question of ethics involved in a profit-sharing type of arrangement in which earnings of professionals (lawyers) are in effect split with nonprofessionals. However, some local bar associations have approved the status of nonlawyers as partners in law firms. Theoretically, a fee-splitting ethical question arises when younger professionals in effect split the amount they have earned for the corporation by way of higher corporate contributions on behalf of older shareholder-professionals participating in a defined-benefit pension plan. For accountants, the American Institute of CPAs' Code of Ethics permits organizing a professional corporation provided that the corporation complies with criteria spelled out in the Council Resolution

[34] Code Sec. 1401.

[35] Code Sec. 164(f).

contained in the Code of Professional Ethics. No serious ethical question of propriety is evident in the medical profession.

.16 Accrued Bonuses and Interest Payable to Owners

A personal service corporation may not deduct an accrued bonus or accrued interest payable to an employee-owner before the time the employee-owner would include the payment in income.[36]

¶1725 PLANNING FOR SHAREHOLDER-PROFESSIONALS

Financial and estate planning for the shareholder-owner of an interest in a professional corporation involves almost everything included in planning for the owner of a closely held corporation. Financial and estate planning considerations include the following:

- Lifetime giving
- Lifetime income tax planning
- Estate tax planning
- Estate liquidity
- Income tax planning for the estate and for the family
- Life insurance planning
- Beneficiary designations
- Settlement options for life insurance and for plan benefits
- Lifetime and testamentary trusts
- Will dispositions
- Forms of property ownership

The big difference in planning for the shareholder-professional is in the planning for the business interest itself. In this area the typical professional may be considered restricted in relation to the owner of a closely held business corporation. The latter has available all the techniques flowing from different forms of capitalization to programs revolving about gifts of shares of stock in the business to junior members of the family. Most of these planning techniques are not available to the owner of an interest in a professional corporation. The professional corporation does not have the same growth potential that a capital-oriented business corporation has. Planning for redemptions of stock to pay death taxes[37] would ordinarily be ruled out by the requirement that the stock be valued at more than 35 percent of the adjusted gross estate and the relatively small

[36] Code Sec. 267(a)(2).

[37] Code Sec. 303.

value of shares in a professional service corporation in relation to the estate owner's other assets.

Because of some areas in which the professional-shareholder may be viewed as restricted, the financial and estate planner might need to restore some balance to place the professional more nearly on par with the businessperson. One route is to look for ways to make the professional a businessperson. For example, the medical building that a physician owns or would like to own should be kept outside of the professional corporation and leased to it. The physician could then use the real estate to develop a gift program, which could produce tax savings and provide junior members with income for worthwhile purposes.

Leasing of equipment is another area to be explored. Even relatively inexpensive items of equipment, such as personal computers and word processors, may be fit candidates for developing an income, estate, and gift-tax-saving program for the professional's family. Of course, the lease arrangement must pass muster as the equivalent of an arm's-length transaction. The professional should support the lease arrangement by documenting it with a valid business purpose. Given such support, it should withstand IRS scrutiny.

Tax-favored investments, particularly tax-exempt bonds, may be of special interest.

.01 Shifting Income and Values Within the Professional Corporation

As a corporate practice ages and shareholders change, the way the practice divides profits might change. This change may produce tax consequences. Salary changes, while shifting income, do not have internal income tax consequences for the corporation and the group of professionals as a whole. When the practice shifts income, it may also want to shift relative ownership interests. Changes in stock ownership have tax consequences.

Usually, corporate profits will shift from senior members to junior members. This shift means that the junior members will be buying stock from the senior members. The latter will have a problem, most likely, of paying tax on the gain realized, and the younger members will have the problem of financing their purchases. The senior members will probably sell on credit.

A problem that may arise at the time of a sale of stock is valuation of the stock. Valuation problems are likely for accounts receivable, work in progress, and unbilled time. Because the professional corporation is usually on a cash basis, it is not taxed on the receivable until it collects it. A discount for the deferred tax should be allowed.

Another issue is the collectibility of the receivable. An additional discount should be allowed as an allowance for uncollectible accounts if the stock is to be fairly valued.

Of course, a professional corporation that buys the stock of a departing shareholder receives no tax deduction for the price paid. As a consequence, the corporation may prefer to pay the departing shareholder deductible severance pay in consideration of a conservatively valued stock price. However, the arrangement should not provide that the severance pay is in lieu of a higher value on the stock.

.02 Using Life Insurance in the Retirement Plan

A corporation can fund a qualified retirement plan partly with life insurance if the insurance is incidental to the main purpose of the plan, which is to provide retirement benefits. In the case of a pension plan, insurance is incidental if the pre-retirement death benefit does not exceed 100 times the monthly income to be provided by the pension at normal retirement age. The value of the pre-retirement survivor annuity required by Code Sec. 401(a)(11) must be taken into account in applying this test.

In the case of a profit-sharing plan, life insurance is incidental if less than 50 percent of the corporation's contribution credited to each employee's account is used to buy ordinary life insurance. This treatment holds, even though the total death benefit consists of the life insurance plus the amount credited to the participant's account at the time of death.[38] However, with a profit-sharing plan, if the life insurance, instead of being purchased with current contributions, is purchased by funds accumulated by the plan for at least two years, no limit applies to the amount of insurance that the plan can buy.

In both the pension plan and the profit-sharing plan, contributions attributable to life insurance protection result in current taxable income to the participants.

The life insurance in either type of plan can be very useful. It can provide the professional's beneficiary with cash, which can be received free of income taxes.[39] The professional may arrange to have the insurance proceeds excluded from his or her gross estate by complying with the requirements of Code Sec. 2042.

.03 Group-Term Life Insurance

The proceeds of a company-provided group-term life insurance policy will be includible in the professional's estate if, at the time of his or her death, he or she possesses any of the incidents of ownership

---

[38] Rev. Rul. 73-501, 1973-2 CB 127.

[39] Code Sec. 101(a)(1).

of the policy.[40] To remove the policy proceeds from his or her gross estate, the IRS requires, as spelled out in Rev. Rul. 69-54[41] that: (1) the policy be convertible to an individual policy on termination of the insured's employment; (2) the policy and state law permit absolute assignment by the employee of all incidents of ownership; and (3) the employee irrevocably assigns all his or her rights in the policy, including the conversion right. Note, though, that premiums in this arrangement may be gifts taxable to the employee.[42]

.04 Death or Retirement

Provisions should probably be made for the sale and purchase of a professional's shares upon death or retirement. The professional can do so via a corporate redemption or via a so-called cross-purchase agreement with the remaining shareholders.

The choice between a corporate redemption and a cross-purchase agreement rests on the same factors that apply in the case of any closely held business corporation, as fully discussed at ¶ 1935.

¶ 1730 WITHDRAWAL AND EXPULSION

Many state professional corporation statutes require that the corporation repurchase the shares of a professional shareholder who becomes disqualified. Disqualification usually means the loss of a license to practice; it does not cover the case of voluntary withdrawal or an expulsion.

The matter of withdrawal or expulsion must be covered by agreement of the parties. In either case, a termination of employment results. Determining whether an individual quit, was expelled, or was fired is often difficult. Therefore, as a practical matter, the agreement should probably treat withdrawal and expulsion similarly in terms of legal rights and obligations.

The board of directors will have the power to terminate the employment of any one of the professionals, with or without cause, unless they are protected by employment contracts.

In two-person professional corporations, the financial planner should consider what happens to the corporation, its assets, its liabilites, and its clients, if the shareholders no longer want to practice together.

[40] Code Sec. 2042.

[41] 1969-1 CB 221.

[42] Rev. Rul. 76-490, 1976-2 CB 300.

Chapter 18

Closely Held Businesses—Choice of Business Form

Overview .... ¶1801
Tax Factors .... ¶1805
Nontax Factors .... ¶1810

¶1801 OVERVIEW

Perhaps the most important question facing an owner of an interest in a closely held business is the choice of business form in which to operate, i.e., a regular C corporation, an S corporation, a partnership, a limited liability company (LLC), or a sole proprietorship. Owners of existing businesses periodically should reevaluate their form of operation. The following chapters discuss the various forms of business. This chapter examines the tax and nontax factors to consider in choosing the business form. Chapter 17 discusses choice-of-form considerations for professionals at ¶1715.

¶1805 TAX FACTORS

The income of S corporations, partnerships, limited liability companies taxed as partnerships, and sole proprietorships passes directly through to the individual owners. Limited liability companies may elect to be taxed either as corporations or as partnerships under rules discussed briefly below and in more detail at ¶2040. LLCs owned by one individual may elect to be treated as a disregarded entity, which means they are taxed as a sole proprietorship.[1]

.01 C Corporations

In considering the tax advantage of C corporations, the financial planner must consider the tax rate structure. The top individual

[1] Reg. § 301.7701-3(b)(1).

income tax rate is 35 percent through 2010, which is the same as the top corporate rate. A C corporation may be preferable if it meets both of the following two conditions: (1) the business is planning to retain earnings to fund growth, and (2) the business owners generally will be in higher tax brackets than would the business operated as a C corporation. Under Code Sec. 11, a C corporation is subject to the following tax rates:

Taxable Income	Tax Rate
First $50,000	15%
Over $50,000 but not over $75,000	25%
Over $75,000 but not over $100,000	34%
Over $100,000 but not over $335,000	39%
Over $335,000 but not over $10,000,000	34%
Over $10,000,000 but not over $15,000,000	35%
Over $15,000,000 but not over $18,333,333	38%
Over $18,333,333	35%

Another advantage of operating as a C corporation is that C corporations are subject to a lower alternative minimum tax (AMT) rate than are individuals. The AMT is equal to the tentative minimum tax over the regular tax.[2] The tentative minimum tax for a corporation is equal to 20 percent of the excess of the alternative minimum taxable income over the $40,000 exemption amount.[3] Individuals are subject to an alternative minimum tax rate as high as 28 percent.[4] Any alternative minimum foreign tax credit reduces the tentative minimum tax.[5] Alternative minimum taxable income is equal to the corporation's taxable income as modified for adjustments and tax preference items.[6]

Example 18.1. Robertson Corporation had taxable income of $689,000. Its regular tax liability is $234,260. It has adjustments and preferences for the alternative minimum tax of $800,000 in computing its alternative minimum taxable income. Thus, its alternative minimum taxable income is $1,489,000. Robertson Corporation does not qualify as a small corporation because its average annual gross receipts for the previous three years were $8,200,000. Robertson Corporation's tentative minimum tax is computed as follows: ($1,489,000 – $40,000) × 20% = $1,449,000 × 20% = $289,800. Robertson must pay regular tax of $234,260 and alternative minimum tax of $55,540 ($289,800 – $234,260).

[2] Code Sec. 55(a).
[3] Code Sec. 55(d)(2).
[4] Code Sec. 55(b)(1)(A)(i).
[5] Code Sec. 55(b)(1)(B).
[6] Code Sec. 55(b)(1)(B)(2).

In addition, small corporations, as defined in Code Sec. 56(e), are not liable for the AMT.[7] A corporation is not liable for the AMT in its first taxable year of existence.[8] For the first three years of a corporation's existence, it qualifies as a small corporation if its average annual gross receipts are $5,000,000 or less.[9] A corporation will continue to be a small corporation exempt from the AMT as long as its average annual gross receipts for the prior three-year period do not exceed $7,500,000.[10]

In determining whether a corporation is a small corporation, the corporation reduces its gross receipts for returns and allowances.[11] A corporation must annualize its gross receipts for any taxable year of less than 12 months for purposes of determining if it is a small corporation.[12] The Code provides that all entities treated as a single employer are treated as one corporation for the gross receipts test.[13]

The stock in a C corporation usually is a capital asset.[14] Thus, a gain on the sale of the shares in a C corporation results in a capital gain eligible for favorable tax treatment. If the stock is qualified small business stock held for more than five years, the shareholder may exclude 50 percent of the gain from his or her gross income.[15] However, the included gain is taxed at 28 percent. So the effective rate on the gain is 14%, only one percentage point less than the regular capital gains rate as long at that rate remains at 15 percent.[16] The shareholder must have obtained the stock directly from the corporation in exchange for money, property, or services.[17] A qualified small business is a C corporation with aggregate gross assets of less than $50,000,000.[18] However, certain businesses are not eligible.[19] Ineligible businesses include the following:

- Services firms such as law, accounting, and financial services
- Banks, investment firms, and insurance companies
- Any farming business
- Any natural resource business for which percentage depletion deduction is available
- Hotels, motels, and restaurants

Example 18.2. On August 6, 1995, Ray Kale invested $1,000,000 of his own money to start Kale Corporation, a

[7] Code Sec. 56(e).
[8] Code Sec. 56(e)(1)(C).
[9] Code Secs. 56(e)(1)(B), 56(e)(1)(D), and 448(c)(3)(A).
[10] Code Sec. 56(e)(1)(A).
[11] Code Secs. 56(e)(1)(D) and 448(c)(3)(C).
[12] Code Secs. 56(e)(1)(D) and 448(c)(3)(B).
[13] Code Secs. 56(e)(1)(D) and 448(c)(2).
[14] Code Sec. 1221.
[15] Code Sec. 1202(a).
[16] Code Sec. 1(h)(5).
[17] Code Sec. 1202(c)(1)(B).
[18] Code Sec. 1202(d).
[19] Code Sec. 1202(e)(3).

specialized manufacturing company. Ray received all of Kale Corporation's common stock in exchange for his investment. Kale Corporation was quite successful. On September 10, 2006, Ray sold all of his stock in Kale Corporation to Jonah Morris for $5,000,000. Ray Kale realized a gain of $4,000,000 ($5,000,000 – $1,000,000) on the sale of his stock. Ray invested the sales proceeds in mutual funds. Ray may exclude 50 percent of this $4,000,000 gain from his gross income. Ray's tax rate on the $2,000,000 included in his gross income is 28 percent.

The shareholder may elect to exclude from his or her gross income the gain on the sale of certain qualified small business stock to the extent he or she reinvests the proceeds in any qualified small business stock. The shareholder must have held the stock for more than six months and reinvest the sales proceeds within 60 days after the date of sale.[20] The gain not recognized reduces the basis of the new qualified business stock purchased.[21]

Example 18.3. Assume that Bob Cole invested $2,000,000 in a new company called Hy Performance Tools, Inc., which is qualified small business stock. Bob sold the stock to Mike Jones for $2,500,000 two years later and realized a $500,000 gain. Bob is not eligible to exclude 50 percent of the gain because he did not hold the stock for more than five years. Within 60 days after selling his stock, Bob invested $3,000,000 in Bob's Building Supplies Corporation in exchange for its stock. The stock is qualified small business stock. Bob will recognize no gain on the sale of his stock on Hy Performance Tools, Inc. However, his basis in his stock in Bob's Building Supplies Corporation would be $2,500,000 ($3,000,000 – $500,000).

If the stock qualifies, up to $50,000 a year ($100,000 for married joint) of a loss on the sale of the stock is deductible as an ordinary loss rather than as a capital loss.[22] The stock qualifies if it is Code Sec. 1244 stock. The stock is Code Sec. 1244 stock if the shareholder obtained it for money or other property from a corporation that was a small business corporation at the time of issue.[23] A small business corporation cannot have more than $1 million in contributed capital.[24] Any loss in excess of the $50,000 ($100,000 for married joint) annual limit will be a capital loss. Ordinary losses are fully deductible, but the Code states the maximum net capital loss deduction for an individual is $3,000 a year.[25]

---

[20] Code Sec. 1045(a).
[21] Code Sec. 1044(b)(3).
[22] Code Sec. 1244(b).
[23] Code Sec. 1244(c)(1).
[24] Code Sec. 1244(c)(3)(A).
[25] Code Sec. 1211(b).

Example 18.4. On October 5, 1998, John Veller invested $600,000 of cash and property in JV, Inc. in exchange for its stock. JV, Inc. did not do as well as John had hoped. On June 18, 2006, Veller sells half of his stock in JV, Inc. to Jim Highfill for $120,000. Veller realizes a loss of $180,000 ($120,000 – $300,000). Veller is married, and he files a joint return with his wife Cathy. They may deduct $100,000 as an ordinary loss. The remaining $80,000 loss is a long-term capital loss. They did not realize any capital gains during 2006. They may deduct $3,000 of the $80,000 capital loss and carry a $77,000 long-term capital loss forward to 2007.

The major disadvantage of operating as a C corporation is that the income of a C corporation is subject to double taxation. A C corporation pays taxes on its income at the corporate level. When a C corporation distributes its earnings as dividends, the shareholders pay individual income taxes on the dividends. The dividend distributions are not deductible by the corporation. However, the impact of this double taxation is minimized through 2010 because qualified dividends are taxed at the capital gain rate of no more than 15 percent.

.02 Personal Service Corporations

A personal service corporation is a C corporation that performs most of its activities as services in such fields as health, law, accounting, and consulting. In addition, the employees performing the services must own substantially all of the stock.[26] A personal service corporation may not use the graduated tax rate schedule that most C corporations use. Rather, a personal service corporation is subject to a flat tax rate of 35 percent.[27]

.03 S Corporations

The major tax advantage of operating as an S corporation is that the corporation generally pays no income tax. Rather, shareholders pay taxes on their pro rata share of the corporate income whether or not the corporation distributes it.[28] Shareholders of S corporations may deduct losses on their individual income tax returns to the extent of their basis in their S corporation stock and in their loans to the S corporation.[29] However, an S corporation shareholder does not receive any basis for the debts of the S corporation. The amount at risk rules[30] and the passive activity loss rules[31] may also limit any deduction for losses of the S corporation.

[26] Code Sec. 448(d)(2).
[27] Code Sec. 11(b)(2).
[28] Code Sec. 1366(a).
[29] Code Sec. 1366(d).
[30] Code Sec. 465.
[31] Code Sec. 469.

Distributions from the S corporation are generally tax free to the shareholders to the extent of the shareholder's basis in the S corporation stock.[32] Although basis in loans to the S corporation allows the deduction of losses, basis in loans to the S corporation does not prevent distributions from being taxable if the basis in the stock is zero. If the S corporation were ever a C corporation with earnings and profits, distributions not out of the accumulated adjustments account can be taxable as a dividend.[33]

Employee-owners of S corporations are not subject to self-employment tax on the corporation's earnings. Rather, salaries paid are subject to FICA taxes. Owner-employees of S corporations may not avoid all employment taxes by taking compensation solely in the form of distributions. The IRS will treat such distributions as salary to the extent of the fair market value of the employee's services.[34] S corporations can have qualified subsidiaries for business and legal purposes. The qualified subsidiaries are not a taxable entity for federal income tax purposes.

S corporations can have only one class of stock.[35] S corporations can have no more than 100 shareholders.[36] A husband and wife are treated as one shareholder. In addition, certain members of the same family may elect to be treated as one shareholder.[37]

.04 Partnerships

One of the major advantages for operating a business as a partnership is that a partnership does not pay federal income taxes.[38] However, a partnership must file an income tax return (Form 1065). The income of the partnership is taxed to the partners. Each partner includes his or her share of the partnership's net ordinary income and the partnership's separately stated items on the partner's individual income tax return.[39]

Unlike the limits on the number of S corporation shareholders, a partnership may have an unlimited number of partners. Also, partnerships have more flexibility in allocating income to partners than do S corporations in allocating income to shareholders. Generally, the partnership's income and loss is allocated to each partner based on the partnership agreement.[40] If the partnership has no agreement for sharing profits and losses, then the partner's distributive share of the partnership's income will be based on the partner's interest in the partnership.[41] The IRS may disregard the partnership's allocation if

[32] Code Sec. 1368(b)(1).
[33] Code Sec. 1368(c)(2).
[34] Rev. Rul. 74-44, 1974-1 CB 287.
[35] Code Sec. 1361(b)(1)(D).
[36] Code Sec. 1361(b)(1)(A).
[37] Code Sec. 1361(c)(1).
[38] Code Sec. 701.
[39] Code Sec. 702(a).
[40] Code Sec. 704(a).
[41] Code Sec. 704(b)(1).

it does not have substantial economic effect.[42] Special rules apply to contributed property to prevent the partners from assigning gains or losses that accrued on the property before the contribution to the partnership.[43]

A partner may deduct losses from the partnership to the extent of the partner's basis in the partnership.[44] The deduction for losses from the partnership may be further limited by the amount at risk rules[45] and the passive activity loss rules.[46] A partner's basis in the partnership includes the partner's share of the partnership's debts.[47] The ability to include the partnership's debts in the basis in the partnership is an advantage over operating as an S corporation. However, any reduction in the partner's share of the partnership's debts is a deemed distribution of cash to the partner.[48] Distributions from the partnership are tax free to the extent of the partner's basis in the partnership.[49]

General partners are subject to self-employment tax on their guaranteed payments and on their distributive share of the partnership's ordinary income.[50] Limited partners are subject to self-employment tax only on guaranteed payments received for services.[51]

.05 Limited Liability Companies (LLCs)

Limited liability companies operate under a charter granted by a state. LLCs have characteristics of corporations and partnerships. Owners of LLCs are called members. Members enjoy the limited liability features of a corporation and the ability to be taxed as a partnership. Most limited liability companies with more than one member file tax returns as partnerships to avoid double taxation.

Under the check-the-box regulations,[52] a limited liability company with two or more members may elect to be taxed as a partnership or as an association taxable as a corporation. A limited liability company with a single member may elect to be taxed as an association taxable as a corporation or be disregarded as a separate entity. If a limited liability company with a single member elects to be disregarded as a separate entity, the business will be treated as a sole proprietorship for federal income tax purposes. A limited liability company makes the election by filing Form 8832, "Entity Classification Election," with the Internal Revenue Service Center in

[42] Code Sec. 704(b)(2).
[43] Code Sec. 704(c).
[44] Code Sec. 704(d).
[45] Code Sec. 465.
[46] Code Sec. 469.
[47] Code Secs. 752(a) and 722.
[48] Code Sec. 752(b).
[49] Code Sec. 731(a)(1).
[50] Code Sec. 1402(a).
[51] Code Sec. 1402(a)(13).
[52] Reg. § 301.7701-3.

Philadelphia, Pennsylvania. The LLC should also attach a copy of Form 8832 to its tax return for the tax year of the election. If the law does not require the LLC to file a tax return for the year of the election, the owners should attach a copy of Form 8832 to their individual income tax returns for the year of the election. Each owner must treat items of income and deduction on his or her return consistent with the election.

If an LLC elects to be treated as an association taxable as a corporation and it wants to make an S election, it does not have to file Form 8832. Filing Form 2553 (Election by a Small Business Corporation) will be deemed to be an election to be taxed as an association.[53]

If a domestic limited liability company does not make the election, the IRS will treat the company as a partnership if it has two or more members. If the entity has one owner, the IRS will disregard the entity for federal income tax purposes.[54] The IRS will treat a foreign eligible entity as a partnership if it has two or more members and at least one member has unlimited liability. However, if all members have limited liability, the IRS will treat the entity as an association taxable as a corporation. If the foreign entity has a single owner who does not have limited liability, the IRS will disregard the entity.[55]

.06 Sole Proprietorships

A sole proprietorship is the simplest business form. A sole proprietorship does not pay income taxes as an entity. Rather, a sole proprietor reports the income and deductions of a sole proprietorship on his or her own individual income tax return (Form 1040) on Schedule C. The advantage of including the net income or net loss on Schedule C is that the sole proprietor may deduct any losses of the business subject only to the amount at risk rules[56], the passive activity loss rules[57], and the hobby loss rules.[58] The disadvantage of including all of the net income on Schedule C is that unlike a C corporation, a sole proprietor does not enjoy a graduated tax rate schedule for the business. The net income of a sole proprietorship is subject to tax at the owner's marginal income tax rate.

Sole proprietors must pay self-employment tax on the net income reported on Schedule C.[59] However, the law allows the self-employed taxpayer to deduct one-half of the self-employment tax liability as a deduction in arriving at adjusted gross income (adjustment to income) on Form 1040.[60] Sole proprietors may deduct all the ordinary

[53] Reg. § 301.7701-3T(c).
[54] Reg. § 301.7701-3(b)(1).
[55] Reg. § 301.7701-3(b)(2).
[56] Code Sec. 465.
[57] Code Sec. 183.
[58] Code Sec. 469.
[59] Code Secs. 1401 and 1402(a).
[60] Code Sec. 164(f).

and necessary business expenses of operating the business on Schedule C.[61] In addition, the law allows sole proprietors special deductions on page 1 of Form 1040 for health insurance premiums, contributions to medical savings accounts, and contributions for the owner to SEP, SIMPLE, and Keogh pension plans.

.07 Planning Considerations

S corporations, partnerships, and personal service corporations are subject to restrictions on the use of a fiscal year.[62] These restrictions, along with special elections allowing the use of a fiscal year for a price, are discussed in the following chapters. C corporations that are not personal service corporations are not subject to these restrictions on the use of a fiscal year.

S corporations and partnerships are not subject to the AMT. However, shareholders and partners are subject to the individual AMT on their share of pass-through items. The same is true for members of limited liability companies taxed as partnerships. Sole proprietors are subject to the individual AMT. A two-rate AMT structure applies to noncorporate taxpayers, subject to an exemption. Under the new Tax Increase Prevention and Reconciliation Act, the AMT exemption amount for 2006 is $62,550 on a joint return or a return of a surviving spouse, $42,500 for single or head of household, and $31,275 for married filing separately.

¶1810 NONTAX FACTORS

One should also consider a number of nontax factors in evaluating the choice of form of business. Certain universal concerns are common to all business plans: risk, finance, control, and continuity. If a business is risky with respect to tort liability or contract liability, the limited liability nature of a corporation or limited liability company makes these business forms more attractive. The limited liability consideration is especially important if the business owners have substantial wealth outside the business. However, a sole proprietorship or general partnership might be preferable if the business is relatively risk-free, offers little scope for expansion, and its owners have few assets. The formation, dissolution, and termination of a partnership is much easier than the comparable process for a corporation. The "red tape" required to start, operate, or terminate a noncorporate business is much less extensive than similar activities for a corporation.

---

[61] Code Sec. 162(a).

[62] Code Secs. 1378, 706(b)(1)(B) and 446(i)(1).

Often a corporation can borrow money more easily than can other business forms. A corporation also finds attracting and retaining talented employees and accumulating goodwill easier. A corporation can raise capital by selling shares of its stock and also use shares of stock to reward successful employees.

In a sole proprietorship, the sole proprietor controls the activities of the business. A partnership must decide how to share authority among the partners, who will make decisions, and what mechanisms the partnership will use when the partners disagree. A board of directors makes policy decisions for a corporation and delegates authority for operations to corporate officers and managers. In a corporation with few shareholders, serious conflicts can develop over control of the board.

A sole proprietorship dies with its owner. The death of a partner legally dissolves a partnership. However, with proper planning, the surviving partners can continue the business. A partnership terminates for federal income tax purposes when no business is carried on by any of the partners in a partnership or a sale or exchange of 50 percent or more of total interest in the partnership occurs within a 12-month period.[63] A corporation (whether S or C) has perpetual existence, and shareholders can sell or bequeath the stock freely.

[63] Code Sec. 708(b)(1).

Chapter 19

Planning for the Close Corporation Owner

Overview ....¶ 1901
Initially Planning the Business Structure ....¶ 1905
Recapitalization and Post-Organizational Planning ....¶ 1910
Obtaining Money from the Corporation Via Stock Redemptions ....¶ 1915
Using an Employee Stock Ownership Plan in Estate Planning for the Owners ....¶ 1920
Qualifying for Installment Payment of the Estate Tax ....¶ 1925
Keeping the Business in the Family ....¶ 1930
Buy-Sell Agreements—Questions and Answers ....¶ 1935
How Shares in Closely Held Corporations Are Valued ...¶ 1940
Electing S Corporation Status ....¶ 1945
Corporate-Owned Life Insurance and the Estate of a Controlling Shareholder ....¶ 1950

¶ 1901 OVERVIEW

Every owner of a substantial interest in a closely held corporation is a prime candidate for financial and estate planning services. The founder of a closely held corporation is a candidate for such services from the inception of the corporation. A financial planner can do a great deal in the initial planning of the business structure that will yield good financial planning results.

.01 Value of the Stock

Stock in the business is usually the principal asset of an owner of a close corporation. Thus, the stock is often the key element in financial planning.

Although the stock in the close corporation can be quite valuable, it is an illiquid asset. For estate and gift tax purposes, it can present difficult valuation problems. The real value of the stock might depend on the founder's talent and drive, which are qualities that valuation experts do not necessarily consider. The value attributable to the founder's work might not be apparent until years after the founder's death. The heirs might realize the value of the founder to the close corporation when its earnings begin to decline and the heirs try to sell their shares.

Special rules that apply for valuing intergenerational transfers of family businesses are discussed in Chapter 23.

.02 Key Areas the Financial Planner and Owner Must Address

Successor management. If the real value of the business derives from the current owner's talents, knowledge, contacts, and drive, the owner must plan to develop successor management. If successor management is not available within the family, then the owner must search outside the company or develop an employee within the company to assume management responsibilities. In any case, the financial planner must be prepared to assist in developing incentive compensation programs designed to recruit and/or retain talent. If the owner cannot find a suitable successor, then the owner must formulate a plan to dispose of the business.

Building a second estate. Having virtually everything invested in a business is generally not a good idea. The estate planner and the owner should seek to build a second estate to provide a cushion if the unexpected happens and the business fails or suffers a downturn. The financial planner must help the owner to create plans to take money out of the business. Techniques to take money out of the business include profit-sharing plans, a stock bonus plan, or an ESOP, with sales of stock to the trust; or stock redemptions. Another possibility is to give stock to charities to generate income tax deductions. The owner could then invest the tax savings. The business owner should also consider the benefits of life insurance.

Reserve fund for business. The financial planner should calculate how much extra cash the business may require when the owner dies, in terms of possible loss of key customers, tougher bank financing, and the need for more working capital to allow for successor management's inexperience. Accumulated earnings should be looked at with an eye to Code Secs. 531-537, with particular attention paid to the accumulated earnings credit of Code Sec. 535(c)(2), which sets the minimum credit at $250,000 ($150,000 for certain personal service corporations), and Code Sec. 537(b). The latter section permits accumulations for the purpose of Code Sec. 303 redemptions in the amount of administration expenses, federal estate taxes, and state death taxes. However, it applies only in the year in which the shareholder dies and the years thereafter. The corporation must have other reasonable business needs for prior accumulations.

Outside market. Does a market exist for the business? Where is the market? What can the business owner do to enhance marketability? Successor management and building funds within the business will help. What are the possibilities of a merger? Is there a possibility of going public? Should the business owner take steps to prepare the business for a possible public offering even though only a private offering appears likely?

Sale to insiders. The corporation can use an ESOP to dispose of a major stock interest with highly favorable income tax results (¶ 1920). Other possibilities include buy-sell agreements between any shareholder associates or with key employees capable of running the business. If a sale to associates is a possibility, and the associates are in a common age bracket with the client, the financial planner should consider whether to arrange a buy-sell at a moderate bargain price or to seek a higher price. If all associates agree, a bargain price could be to the client's advantage if co-owners and associates predecease the client. The buy-sell price will aid, if not control, the valuation for estate tax purposes, provided special rules contained in Code Sec. 2703 and discussed at ¶ 2310 are met.

Estate taxes. What will the owner's estate tax be under the present plan? To what extent is the client relying on the marital deduction[1] to reduce estate tax liabilities? What will happen if the spouse predeceases the client? What if the spouse survives and retains a significant stock interest until death? How much unified credit[2] is expected to be available? What steps are open to reduce the estate tax impact? Lifetime gifts? Charitable giving? Lifetime sale of the business? Life insurance? Fixing valuation? These are some of the questions that the estate planner should ask.

Estate liquidity. After the estate planner has determined the potential estate tax impact, the estate planner should calculate how much money the estate will need to pay debts, funeral expenses, administration expenses, federal and state death taxes, and cash bequests. How will the estate obtain the money required? What liquid assets will the estate likely have? What outside resources are available? Will individual heirs or trusts be in a position to lend funds to the estate or purchase illiquid assets? To what extent can the estate

[1] Code Sec. 2056.

[2] Code Sec. 2010.

rely on stock redemptions under Code Secs. 302 or 303 to meet liquidity needs? Will the corporation be in a position to effect the redemptions? If not, what steps can the business owner take to enable it to do so? Can the estate qualify for installment payments (¶ 1925)?

Stepped-up basis. Stock retained until death will receive a step-up in basis equal to its fair market value for estate tax purposes.[3] All income tax liability for prior appreciation will be eliminated leaving more money for the estate or heirs on a sale or redemption. This factor affects the choice between lifetime gifts of stock and testamentary dispositions. However, for property acquired from a decedent dying in 2010, the step up in basis is limited to $1,300,000 plus $3,000,000 for property received by a surviving spouse.

Valuation. What steps can the business owner take to fix the value of the stock for sale or estate tax purposes?

Recapitalization and restructuring. Recapitalizing to a mix of common and preferred stock offers a number of financial and estate planning advantages. Some of those strategies are discussed at ¶ 1910.

Executive benefits. To the extent that the client occupies the position of an executive in a closely held corporation, all of the planning considerations discussed in Chapter 16, "Planning for the Executive," apply.

¶ 1905 INITIALLY PLANNING THE BUSINESS STRUCTURE

Placing all business operations in one corporation is not always necessary or appropriate. The financial planner should not overlook the possibility of combining the corporate form with individual or partnership ownership of the elements of the business enterprise. The financial planner should also consider the use of multiple corporations. Multiple entities can open the door to many attractive estate planning possibilities.

For example, assume a business is engaged in the manufacture and sale of widgets. The business owner might set the business operations up as follows. The business owner uses a corporation for the operating part of the business—to do the manufacturing and selling, and to carry inventory and accounts receivable. The corporation receives a certain amount of working capital. The real estate and the plant in which the corporation operates, however, are owned by the shareholders individually or in partnership form and are

[3] Code Sec. 1014(a).

leased to the corporation. The corporation does not own the machinery and equipment it uses to manufacture the widgets. A limited partnership, in which the corporation is the general partner, owns the machinery and equipment. The shareholders are limited partners along with one or more trusts for the children of shareholders. The partnership leases the machinery to the corporation. If the business owner has extensive office equipment, computers, and fax machines, these too might be owned by the partnership or individual family members and leased to the corporation. Of course, the leasing arrangements must be fair and reasonable based on terms that might have been obtained in truly arm's-length transactions.

What has this structure accomplished? The shareholders, as owners of the real estate, might incur losses in the early years to offset their other income. However, the losses are losses from passive activities, which are business activities in which the taxpayer does not materially participate and the rental of any tangible property (irrespective of material participation).[4] A taxpayer may generally only use passive losses to offset income from passive activities[5] until the taxpayer disposes of the property in a taxable transaction to an unrelated party.[6] The taxpayer carries the disallowed passive activity losses forward to the next tax year.[7] Passive income does not include portfolio income (interest and dividends).[8] However, under a special exception for rental real estate in which an individual actively participates, the taxpayer may deduct up to $25,000 of losses against nonpassive income. The $25,000 loss allowance is phased out ratably between $100,000 and $150,000 of AGI.[9] Another exception permits closely held corporations to use passive losses to offset business income, but not portfolio income.[10]

Assuming that the shareholders have deducted the losses from the real estate, when the real estate begins to generate a net income, the shareholders can make gifts of the real estate to trusts for their children. These gifts produce income tax savings while removing the real estate from the shareholders' gross estates. In addition, the gifts provide the children with income to be used or accumulated for worthwhile purposes.

The rental income going to the limited partnership housing the machinery and equipment could be offset in part by depreciation deductions. If the partnership shows losses, the benefit of the depreciation deductions would be limited under the passive activity loss rules discussed above.

---

[4] Code Sec. 469(c).
[5] Code Sec. 469(d)(1).
[6] Code Sec. 469(g).
[7] Code Sec. 469(b).
[8] Code Sec. 469(e)(1).
[9] Code Sec. 469(i).
[10] Code Sec. 469(e)(2).

The fact that the corporation does not own the real estate or machinery or equipment might not have a material effect on the price obtainable on an eventual sale of the stock. Earnings are more likely to be the controlling factor in determining the value of the corporation.

Tremendous financial and estate planning opportunities exist in the initial structuring of the business through different forms of ownership and the use of different entities.

Planning opportunities are available in structuring the corporation itself. This chapter will not examine issues such as taxable or tax-free incorporation and other income tax factors. However, income tax factors are often related to estate planning.

Rather, this chapter will concentrate on the capital structure of the corporation. If the corporation has more than one-class-of-stock, it cannot be an S corporation.[11] Differences in voting rights alone, however, will not create a second class of stock for S corporation purposes.[12]

Under Subchapter S, corporate profits and losses are generally passed through to shareholders.[13] Thus, using an S corporation avoids the double taxation otherwise inherent in the corporate form. The S corporation election is discussed in detail at ¶ 1945.

Also, the financial planner should give some thought to the use of multiple corporations to multiply accumulated earnings credits[14] and split income between separate entities, and thereby have it taxed at lower rates. Using multiple corporations will provide tax savings only if the corporations are not controlled groups as defined in Code Sec. 1563.

Brother and sister controlled groups require that the total percentage of the least amount of stock owned by each of the shareholders in each of the corporations with common ownership be more than 50 percent. For example, corporations Ecks and Why would not be part of a controlled group under the definition based on the following stock ownership:

Shareholder	Ecks	Why	Minimum
Able	70%	15%	15%
Baker	15	15	15
Charles	15	70	15
	100%	100%	45%

[11] Code Sec. 1361(b)(1).

[12] Reg. § 1.1361-1(l)(1).

[13] Code Sec. 1366.

[14] Code Sec. 535(c).

However, the corporations would be a controlled group if Able owned 60 percent of Ecks and Charles owned 25 percent.

¶ 1910 RECAPITALIZATION AND POST-ORGANIZATIONAL PLANNING

At one time, recapitalizing a corporation with a mix of common and preferred stock offered financial and estate planning advantages with respect to intra-family transfers. Congress enacted Code Sec. 2036(c) in 1987 largely to eliminate these advantages, but Congress repealed this provision in 1990 and replaced it with new rules for valuing transfers of interests in family businesses. These rules are contained in Code Sec. 2701 and discussed in Chapter 23. The discussion below is a theoretical analysis related to recapitalizations of both family-owned companies and companies owned by unrelated parties. However, family companies must apply the Code Sec. 2701 rules to determine whether a recapitalization results in a gift. If a gift results, the family companies must determine the amount of the gift.

.01 Reasons for Recapitalization

Raising capital. When raising capital, one of the concerns of management is to retain control of the company. Raising capital from venture capitalists or other investors usually requires issuance of securities convertible into common stock, such as convertible debentures or convertible preferred stock. Depending on the negotiating power of each party, one possibility is to change the common stock into separate class A voting stock and class B nonvoting stock. Management would retain the class A stock, while reserving the class B stock for issuance to the investors on conversion. A variation, where allowed under applicable state law, might be some form of weighted voting stock with each class A share having 10 votes and each class B share having one vote.

Successor management. Hiring younger management is important to the continuity of any business. Senior management is concerned about maintaining control and having minority shareholders in the event a junior executive leaves the company. These concerns are usually covered by issuing nonvoting stock to junior executives, which they may convert to voting stock over time, with a buy-back agreement in the event of termination. Another alternative is to issue voting stock to junior management but restrict the voting rights of junior management for a specified period.

Retirement planning for senior management. A business owner might have a substantial portion of his or her assets invested in a closely held company. When approaching retirement, the business owner is concerned with converting the investment into a retirement fund to ensure sufficient liquidity during retirement and for estate tax purposes. Advance planning is important. Such planning should include an agreement among the shareholders for computing the price of the stock, how it is to be paid, and the security for the payment. In some instances, the shareholders may not want to convert the common stock into preferred stock or into debt with put and call options exercisable at various times.

Dissension among the owners. A solution to any dissension among the owners can take several forms such as a buyout, a division of the company, or a complete liquidation. Sometimes, the shareholders can provide for consequences of dissension in a buy-sell agreement. For instance, the agreement might provide a mechanism for triggering a put or call of the shares or for conversion into a nonvoting security.

Recapitalizations can take on many forms depending on the circumstances involved in each situation. A recapitalization provides management with flexibility.

.02 Sale-Leasebacks

In the initial structuring of a business, keeping the real estate and machinery out of the corporation can be desirable from a financial and estate planning point of view. Rather, individuals or a partnership of the shareholders or members of their families can own the real estate and machinery and lease them to the corporation. If the corporation owns the real estate and machinery from the outset, later the corporation might be able to enter a sale-leaseback arrangement with a shareholder, a partnership, or outside family members or trusts. However, the IRS watches such sale-leaseback transactions closely. The IRS might challenge the sale-leaseback on the ground that it is a sham transaction. However, if the arrangement is not a sham because it has the elements of an arm's-length transaction, and makes economic sense (for example, provides additional financing for the corporation), it may withstand an IRS challenge.

¶1915 OBTAINING MONEY FROM THE CORPORATION VIA STOCK REDEMPTIONS

Converting stock of a closely held corporation into cash without undue sacrifice of its real value can be one of the prime problems of the estate of a substantial shareholder. If the corporation has sufficient money, redemption of all or part of the stock held by the estate or its beneficiaries is a way of extracting the cash. If the estate is not careful, however, a redemption might be at the price of a deeper discount than if the estate had sold the stock to an existing shareholder or a stranger. The tax law might treat the stock redemption as a dividend,[15] instead of as a sale qualifying for capital gain taxation. While dividends are taxed at the same maximum 15 percent rate as capital gain, at least through 2010, qualifying the redemption as a sale is still preferable to dividend treatment. That's because a sale will allow the basis of the stock redeemed to be offset against the redemption proceeds, so that only the net difference is taxable. With dividend treatment, the entire redemption proceeds are taxable (to the extent of the corporation's earnings and profits). Also, if the stock passes from a decedent, its tax basis would be its fair market value at the date of death, or six months later at the alternate valuation date.[16] However, for property acquired from a decedent dying in 2010, the step up in basis to fair market value is limited to $1,300,000 plus $3,000,000 for property received by a surviving spouse.

Qualifying the redemption to be taxed as a sale or exchange and not as a dividend is very important. The Code provides two routes by which a shareholder may achieve this objective. One is Code Sec. 302, which deals with distributions in redemption of stock. The other is Code Sec. 303, which deals with distributions in redemption of stock to pay death taxes. Neither route is free from difficulty. However, Code Sec. 303 is usually the easier route.

If a redemption qualifies for sale or exchange treatment under Code Secs. 302 or 303, the amount distributed in excess of basis will be taxed as a long-term capital gain. The law deems capital assets acquired from a decedent to have been held long term, regardless of the actual holding period.[17] On the other hand, if a redemption does not qualify under either provision, the full amount received is taxed as a dividend if the corporation has sufficient earnings and profits.[18] Under 2006's Tax Increase Prevention Act, dividends will be taxed at a maximum rate of 15 percent through 2010. A net capital gain is the excess of a net long-term capital gain over any net short-term capital loss.[19] The tax rate for a net capital gain is the lower of the regular tax rate or the alternative tax rate.[20] The alternative tax rate for net capital gains consists of various layers. These layers can cause all or a part of a net capital gain, to be taxed at a rate of 5 percent, 15 percent, 25 percent, or 28 percent.[21] The rates of 5 percent and 15 percent apply through 2010, after which they will increase to 10 percent and 20 percent respectively. Discussing the complexities of calculating the tax on a net capital gain is beyond the scope of this

---

[15] Code Sec. 302(d).

[16] Code Sec. 1014(a).

[17] Code Sec. 1223(11).

[18] Code Secs. 301(c)(1) and 316(a).

[19] Code Sec. 1222(11).

[20] Code Sec. 1(h).

[21] Code Sec. 1(h).

chapter. A financial planner will find a good tax software program very helpful, if not essential, in advising clients on the tax treatment of net capital gains.

Apart from the rate differential, another incentive for qualifying for exchange treatment for stock acquired from a decedent is that the person acquiring the stock receives a stepped-up basis under Code Sec. 1014(a). The stepped-up basis eliminates any income tax on pre-death appreciation. For redemptions occurring shortly after the decedent's death, the step-up in basis will often mean little or no gain to recognize. However, for property acquired from a decedent dying in 2010, the step up in basis to fair market value is limited to $1,300,000 plus $3,000,000 for property received by a surviving spouse. Any actual gain qualifies for long-term capital gain treatment because Code Sec. 1223(11) treats all property acquired from a decedent as though it were held long term.

To take advantage of Code Sec. 303, the value of the stock in the decedent's gross estate must be more than 35 percent of the excess of the value of the gross estate over the deduction for expenses, claims, and casualty losses.[22] The redeeming shareholder will receive capital gains treatment only to the extent that the shareholder's interest is reduced directly (or through a binding obligation to contribute) by payment of death taxes or funeral or administration expenses.[23] Special rules apply if two or more separate corporations are involved, as noted below.[24]

The amount that the corporation may distribute without the distribution being taxed as a dividend is limited by the amount of estate and death taxes, and the amount of funeral and administration expenses allowable as deductions for federal estate tax purposes.[25] If the corporation exceeds the limits, the excess will be taxed as dividend income to the extent of the corporation's earnings and profits,[26] unless the distribution qualifies for capital gains treatment under Code Sec. 302.

To qualify under Code Sec. 303, the redemption must generally take place after the decedent's death and within the three-year period allowed for the assessment of estate tax. This period begins when the estate tax return is filed (normally within nine months of death), plus 90 days, or, if the estate files a petition with the U.S. Tax Court to challenge an IRS determination of estate tax, within 60 days of its final decision, whichever period is longer. However, if the executor has made an election to pay the estate tax in installments (¶ 1925), the

[22] Code Sec. 303(b)(2).
[23] Code Sec. 303(b)(3).
[24] Code Sec. 303(b)(2)(B).
[25] Code Sec. 303(a).
[26] Code Secs. 301(c) and 316(a).

time for redemption extends to the due date of the last installment.[27] However, in case of redemptions more than four years after death, capital gains treatment is limited to the lesser of (1) the aggregate amount of death taxes, funeral and administration expenses remaining unpaid immediately before the redemption; or (2) the total amount of such taxes and expenses paid within one year of the redemption.[28]

.01 Two or More Separate Corporations and Code Sec. 303

Often, a decedent owns stock in two or more closely held corporations. For example, a decedent might own an interest in a real estate corporation that leases property to an operating corporation in which the decedent holds an interest. In such case, if the gross estate includes 20 percent or more in value of the stock of each of two or more corporations, then the estate may consider the combined shares in determining whether it satisfies the 35-percent test of Code Sec. 303.[29]

.02 Important Considerations Affecting Use of Code Sec. 303

Code Sec. 303, despite its restrictions, is a way of extracting cash (and property) from a closely held corporation in a tax-favored way. The estate can use the cash to satisfy its liquidity needs. The estate can also use the cash to pay state death taxes, administration expenses, cash bequests, and funds for the family. However, the executor should consider the following negative factors.

Control of the business. If the stock to be redeemed represents the swing vote in the control of the business, the executor should weigh the loss of control against the benefits to be obtained. However, Rev. Rul. 87-132[30] offers a way of maintaining relative voting strength. In the case that gave rise to this ruling, a company had outstanding 300 shares of voting common stock owned equally by an estate and an individual who had no interest in the estate. The estate wanted to effect a Code Sec. 303 redemption but did not want to lose relative voting power. A proposed solution was to issue a stock dividend of 1,500 shares of new nonvoting common to each of the two shareholders and then to have the estate immediately redeem 1,000 of the new shares in a Code Sec. 303 redemption. The problem with the proposed solution was that, under existing IRS rulings, a stock distribution that is immediately redeemable is taxable rather than being tax free under Code Sec. 305. The IRS, recognizing that Code Sec. 303 is remedial and the time factors involved, carved out an

[27] Code Sec. 303(b)(1).
[28] Code Sec. 303(b)(4).
[29] Code Sec. 303(b)(2)(B).
[30] 1987-2 CB 82.

exception for Code Sec. 303 redemptions. In such a case, the stock dividend is tax free notwithstanding the immediate redemption.

In order to implement this type of solution, the redeeming shareholder might need to persuade the other shareholders to consent to the stock dividend and redemption. This consent may be necessary even where the party seeking the solution is in control under applicable state law or corporate charter provisions. This plan may require a greater-than-majority vote to effect such corporate action.

A corporation can use a recapitalization to achieve similar results. If the stock dividend and recapitalization solutions are not feasible, the shareholders should consider limiting the amount redeemed so that control will not be lost or relative voting strength will not be drastically weakened. Again, the shareholders must consider the effect of state law and corporate charter provisions.

Effect on business operations. How will taking cash or property for redemption purposes affect the operation of the business? Will working capital be depleted to an unreasonable degree? Will plans for replacement or expansion of plant and equipment be affected? What will the redemption do to the value of the shares, if any, retained? The shareholders should address these questions and similar questions.

Loss of deferred payment benefits. Code Sec. 6166 provides for deferred payment of estate taxes of 14 years when the estate includes a qualifying closely held business in the estate, as discussed at ¶ 1925. However, the estate might lose the benefits of installment payment of estate taxes if the estate or heirs divest themselves of 50 percent or more of the value of their interest in the business. The shareholders must exercise caution to keep any redemptions within the percentage limit or the redemption proceeds will have to be used to pay estate taxes.

Redemptions by different parties. Redemptions by different parties might pose some problems. As noted above, capital gain treatment is available to a redeeming shareholder only to the extent that the shareholder's interest is reduced directly (or through a binding obligation to contribute) by any payment of death taxes or funeral or administration expenses. This requirement obviously limits the number of shareholders able to take advantage of Code Sec. 303. A corporation might have two or more shareholders who qualify for redemption under Code Sec. 303, where the decedent's will bequeaths the stock to two or more persons. If two or more redemptions occur, the regulations take a first-come, first-served approach, regardless of whether the particular redemption might have qualified as an exchange under Code Sec. 302. To illustrate, the following is a condensed version of an example contained in Reg. § 1.303-2(g)(2).

> ***Example 19.1.*** An estate has Code Sec. 303 expenses of $225,000. The estate includes $450,000 in closely held stock, which is enough to meet the percentage test. During the first year, a beneficiary holding one-third of the shares redeems all his stock and receives $150,000. During the second year, the estate redeems another one-third and receives $150,000. Only $75,000 of the second redemption qualifies under Code Sec. 303. This result is correct even though the first $150,000 redemption might have qualified under Code Sec. 302.

Although the example relates to redemptions made in successive years, the rule would likely be no different for successive redemptions within the same year. The example clearly shows that if multiple redemptions occur, the corporation should attempt to qualify the redemptions under Code Sec. 302 in order not to waste the Code Sec. 303 limits. The discussion below addresses additional planning issues regarding Code Sec. 303 redemptions.

Valuation of stock. The redemption price will not necessarily be the same as the value that the IRS puts on the stock for estate tax purposes. If the redemption price exceeds the value for estate tax purposes, the former shareholder will realize a capital gain.

.03 Planning for Code Sec. 303 Redemptions

Advance planning is often required to take advantage of Code Sec. 303, with minimal or no adverse side effects. Some of the key factors to consider are as follows.

Meeting the 35-percent test. In some cases, the shareholders will have no problem in meeting the requirement that the stock includible in the gross estate is more than 35 percent of the value of the adjusted gross estate. However, if the client anticipates difficulty in satisfying this test, the estate planner might consider the following strategies:

- **Lifetime gifts.** Gifts of property other than stock made more than three years before death will reduce the estate and aid in meeting the 35-percent test. Gifts within the $12,000 annual exclusion limit (for 2006 and indexed for inflation) made within three years of death can also help in meeting the 35-percent test. However, other gifts made within three years of death will be includible in the gross estate for the purpose of the 35-percent test.[31] If a client

[31] Code Sec. 2035(c)(1).

owns stock in two or more closely held corporations, the client can retain the stock in the one which will be used for Code Sec. 303 redemption and give away the stock in the other(s) to improve the chances for meeting the 35-percent test.

Generally, if the client wants to make gifts, illiquid assets and those that do not show much appreciation potential are preferred. Gifts of appreciated property preclude stepped-up tax basis at death[32] and the escape from capital gains if the property were retained in the estate. In some circumstances, however, a better result would occur by forgoing the stepped-up basis available at death.

If the property shows little appreciation potential, a lifetime gift of the property will serve to remove future appreciation from the estate and not subject the donee to any serious erosion of basis.

- **Transfer of property to a corporation.** A shareholder may transfer property to a corporation tax free under Code Sec. 351 in exchange for more stock. For example, the shareholder might transfer property to the corporation, which he or she has been leasing to the corporation, in exchange for more corporate stock. The exchange increases the percentage of stock in the shareholder's estate.
- **Sale of nonbusiness assets.** A sale of nonbusiness assets and investment of the proceeds in the business will reduce the percentage of nonbusiness assets in the gross estate. In addition, the sale will increase the value of the stock.
- **Gift tax marital deduction planning.** Use of the estate tax marital deduction[33] will help in meeting the 35-percent test. In addition, the use of the gift tax marital deduction[34] will help if the shareholder makes the gifts more than three years before death. Although gifts within three years of death are generally not includible in the gross estate of the donor, such gifts (other than those qualifying for the annual exclusion) are includible for the purpose of determining Code Sec. 303 eligibility.[35]
- **Creation of spousal joint tenancies.** An individual who is not prepared to make an outright gift to a spouse to meet the 35-percent test should consider creating a joint tenancy with the spouse. An individual may create a joint tenancy with his or her spouse with no gift tax consequences because of the unlimited marital deduction.[36] Only one-half of the property that a decedent holds in joint tenancy with a spouse is includible in the decedent's gross estate.[37]

[32] Code Sec. 1014(a).

[33] Code Sec. 2056.

[34] Code Sec. 2523.

[35] Code Sec. 2035(c)(1).

[36] Code Sec. 2523.

[37] Code Sec. 2040(b).

Generally, only the half that is includible in the decedent's gross estate receives a stepped-up basis at the decedent's death. However, both halves of community property receive a tax-free step up in basis if the decedent's gross estate includes at least half of the value of the property.[38] The step up in basis to fair market value for property acquired from a decedent dying in 2010 is limited to $1,300,000 plus $3,000,000 for property received by a surviving spouse.

- **Multiple corporations.** If the client holds stock in two or more corporations and is unable to meet the 35-percent rule because of the multiple corporation 20-percent rule, a merger or consolidation of the corporations might serve to meet the qualifying tests. The client could also set up a holding company to hold the stock of the separate corporations. The stock of the holding company might then meet the Code Sec. 303 tests. Establishing an independent business purpose for the holding company is important to avoid the requirement to make dividend distributions to avoid personal holding company tax under Code Sec. 541. However, despite possible difficulties, the personal holding company merits consideration if other means of satisfying the Code Sec. 303 tests are not feasible.

Preparing the corporation for redemptions. The corporation must have the money to redeem the stock. If the client is counting on the Code Sec. 303 redemption to satisfy the estate's liquidity needs, the corporation must have cash or cash equivalents on hand. If liquidity is not a big factor, then the corporation can distribute illiquid property in redemption of the stock. The corporation could distribute property that is used in the business and plan a leaseback arrangement that permits the corporation to continue to use the property.

In lieu of cash, the corporation may give a shareholder its note. The redemption will then be deemed to have been made when the corporation gives the note, not when it pays the note.[39] This option gives the corporation additional time to pay for the stock. If the stock is not publicly traded, the shareholder may recognize any gain realized on the redemption using the installment method.[40]

Life insurance carried by the corporation on the life of the shareholder-executive may also finance the redemption. The insurance proceeds will be received by the corporation tax free.[41] However, the proceeds will be included in the decedent's gross estate if the decedent had any incidents of ownership in the policy.[42] However,

---

[38] Code Secs. 1014(a) and 1014(b)(6).

[39] Rev. Rul. 65-289, 1965-2 CB 86.

[40] Code Sec. 453.

[41] Code Sec. 101(a)(1).

[42] Code Sec. 2042(2).

incidents of ownership are not attributed to the insured solely because the proceeds are payable to a corporation that he or she controls.[43] Nevertheless, life insurance proceeds payable to the corporation will be a factor in determining the value of the stock for estate tax purposes.[44] For these reasons, allowing a member of the decedent's family to own the policy to keep the proceeds out of the gross estate might be better. The policy owner could then lend the proceeds to the corporation in order to effect the redemption.

The corporation's accumulation of earnings to meet redemption needs exposes the corporation to the risk of the accumulated earnings tax.[45] However, accumulations to meet "the reasonable needs of the business" are permissible. Code Sec. 537(a) defines the quoted phrase so as to include Code Sec. 303 needs of the business, which in Code Sec. 537(b) are defined as to permit accumulation in the tax year of the corporation in which a shareholder dies, or any taxable year thereafter, of an amount needed, or reasonably anticipated to be needed, to redeem stock under and within the limits of Code Sec. 303. In other words, if the corporation starts accumulating funds for an eventual redemption under Code Sec. 303 in years before death occurs, it may be hit with an accumulated earnings tax when more than $250,000 has been accumulated ($150,000 in the case of certain personal service corporations). The corporation can reduce the risk of the accumulated earnings tax by documenting other reasonable business needs for accumulating earnings. In addition, S corporations are not subject to the accumulated earnings tax.

Maintaining control. Where there are outside interests, redemptions can shift the balance of control unless the shareholders do something about it. If the corporation has only common stock, one of the things to consider is recapitalization. In the recapitalization, the corporation would issue common stock and nonvoting preferred stock. The corporation could then redeem the preferred stock without affecting control. The common stock and preferred stock are combined in applying the 35-percent test. If preferred stock is authorized but unissued, a simple approach would be to issue preferred stock as a stock dividend (before death).

However, a dividend of preferred stock on common stock would constitute Code Sec. 306 stock. A shareholder usually realizes ordinary income on the sale of Code Sec. 306 stock to the extent of the stock's ratable share of the corporation's earnings and profits at the time the corporation distributed the Code Sec. 306 stock.[46] The stock is also Code Sec. 306 stock in the hands of a transferee if the

[43] Reg. § 20.2042-1(c)(6).

[44] Reg. § 20.2031-2(f).

[45] Code Sec. 531.

[46] Code Sec. 306(a)(1)(A).

transferee determines his or her basis in the stock by reference to the basis of any other person in the Code Sec. 306 stock.[47] Thus, Code Sec. 306 stock received as a gift retains its character as Code Sec. 306 stock.

However, Code Sec. 306 stock received from a decedent that has a basis equal to its fair market value at the date of the decedent's death or at the alternate valuation date will no longer be Code Sec. 306 stock.[48] Therefore, the corporation could redeem preferred stock that a taxpayer received from a decedent and Code Sec. 306 would not apply. Any excess of the amount realized over the stock's ratable share of the corporation's earnings and profits first reduces the basis of the Code Sec. 306 stock and then is treated as gain on the sale of the stock.[49] A shareholder may not recognize a loss on the sale of Code Sec. 306 stock.[50] However, if the shareholder transfers the Code Sec. 306 stock to the corporation as a redemption, the amount received in the redemption is treated as a dividend to the extent of the corporation's earnings and profits at the time of the redemption.[51] Any amount received in excess of the earnings and profits first reduces the basis in the stock[52] and then is treated as a gain on the exchange of the stock.[53]

An exception to the usual rules of Code Sec. 306 applies if the shareholder disposes of the Code Sec. 306 stock in a sale to an unrelated party that completely terminates his or her entire stock interest in the corporation.[54] If the shareholder disposes of his or her Code Sec. 306 stock in a redemption, the usual Code Sec. 306 rules will not apply if the redemption qualifies as an exchange under Code Sec. 302(b)(3) as a complete termination of interest, an exchange under Code Sec. 302(b)(4) as a partial liquidation, or an exchange under Code Sec. 331 in complete liquidation of the corporation.[55] In addition, the usual Code Sec. 306 rules will not apply where gain or loss is not recognized to the shareholder or where the transactions do not have a principal purpose of avoiding federal income tax.[56]

Another way to effect a Code Sec. 303 redemption without loss of relative voting power is suggested by Rev. Rul. 87-132,[57] in which a corporation distributed a stock dividend of new nonvoting common stock to each of two shareholders. The estate immediately redeemed some of the new shares. A stock dividend that is immediately redeemable is usually taxable. However, the IRS allowed an exception for

[47] Code Sec. 306(c)(1)(C).
[48] Reg. § 1.306-3(e).
[49] Code Sec. 306(a)(1)(B).
[50] Code Sec. 306(a)(1)(C).
[51] Code Secs. 306(a)(2), 301(c)(1), and 316(a).
[52] Code Sec. 301(c)(2).
[53] Code Sec. 301(c)(3)(A).
[54] Code Sec. 306(b)(1)(A).
[55] Code Secs. 306(b)(1)(B) and 306(b)(2).
[56] Code Sec. 306(b)(3) and (4).
[57] 1987-2 CB 82.

Code Sec. 303 redemptions. Thus, the stock dividend was tax free notwithstanding the immediate redemption. Of course, in order to implement this type of solution, the other shareholders might need to agree to the stock dividend and redemption.

Limiting redemption. All redemptions qualifying under Code Sec. 303 count against the Code Sec. 303 limit on redemptions, including those that would qualify as exchanges under Code Sec. 302. The corporation needs a plan to avoid wasting Code Sec. 302 redemptions on Code Sec. 303 and to avoid redemptions under Code Sec. 303 in excess of its limits. One approach might be a contract between the shareholders and the corporation under whose terms the corporation is bound to redeem only as much of a shareholder's stock as the decedent's executor deems necessary, appropriate, and fair to all concerned.

.04 Redemptions Under Code Sec. 302

Apart from Code Sec. 303, the general rule is that a corporate distribution to a shareholder out of earnings and profits, including a redemption, is to be treated as a dividend, and not as a payment in exchange for stock.[58] However, four principal exceptions under Code Sec. 302(b) apply to redemptions:

1. A redemption not essentially equivalent to a dividend
2. A substantially disproportionate redemption
3. A termination of the shareholder's interest
4. Redemptions from noncorporate shareholders in partial liquidation

A redemption is not essentially equivalent to a dividend if it results in a "meaningful" reduction of the shareholder's "interest" in the corporation. Under the regulations, a determination must be made on a case-by-case basis. For this reason, the focus is usually on the second and third exceptions where there are more definitive rules. However, Rev. Rul. 75-502,[59] Rev. Rul. 75-512,[60] and Rev. Rul. 78-401[61] provide some specific guidance on the availability of the first exception. The first ruling indicated the factors to be considered relating to the shareholder's right to vote and exercise control, to participate in current earnings and accumulated surplus, and to share in the net assets on liquidation. In the second ruling the IRS held that a reduction of a shareholder's interest from 57 percent to 50 percent, with the remaining 50 percent being held by an unrelated party, was meaningful. Rev. Rul. 78-401 held that a reduction of a

[58] Code Secs. 301(c)(1) and 302(d).
[59] 1975-2 CB 111.
[60] 1975-2 CB 112.
[61] 1978-2 CB 127.

shareholder's interest from 90 percent to 60 percent was not meaningful, because the shareholder retained the power to control the day-to-day operations of the company. This factor, rather than the shareholder's reduced interest in earnings and surplus or liquidation proceeds, was given controlling weight. The fact that some corporate actions might require more than a 60 percent vote was deemed to be of *no* consequence where the corporation did not show such actions to be imminent.

A substantially disproportionate redemption is one that reduces the shareholder's percentage of voting stock interest below 80 percent of what it was before redemption and which leaves the shareholder with less than 50 percent of the corporation's outstanding stock. The attribution or constructive ownership rules set out in Code Sec. 318 complicate the matter considerably. The thrust of these rules is that the redeeming shareholder is treated as owning not only the shares registered in his or her own name but also those owned by his or her spouse, children, grandchildren, parents, estates or trusts of which the shareholder is the beneficiary, partnerships of which he or she is a member, and corporations in which he or she owns a majority of the stock interest. Furthermore, stock owned directly or indirectly by a beneficiary of an estate is considered owned by the estate.

Because of these rules, satisfying the disproportionate distribution exception is often difficult, before or after the death of the shareholder of a closely held family corporation.

One possible way of getting around the attribution rules after death would be if a beneficiary of the estate holding stock has ceased to be a beneficiary at the time of the redemption. Reg. § 1.318-3(a) says that an individual is no longer a beneficiary when he or she has received all the property he or she is entitled to, no longer has a claim against the estate, and only a remote possibility exists that the estate will seek a return of the property or payment to satisfy claims against the estate or expense of administration. However, the IRS has ruled that the interest of a residuary legatee is not terminated until the estate is closed.[62] Even with a special legatee, as long as the valuation of the closely held stock remains open, the IRS might consider the special legatee as a beneficiary.

If a shareholder completely terminates the shareholder's interest in the corporation, the redemption may qualify for sale or exchange treatment. A complete termination may also meet the

---

[62] Rev. Rul. 60-18, 1960-1 CB 145.

disproportionate redemption rules discussed above. In a complete termination, the constructive ownership rules of Code Sec. 318(a)(1) do not apply provided that the redeeming shareholder (1) has no interest in the corporation, other than as a creditor, for at least 10 years after the redemption; (2) agrees to notify the IRS of any acquisition within the 10-year period; and (3) retains all records of the redemption for 10 years. The interests barred include a position as an officer, director, or employee of the corporation.[63] This provision allows the corporation to redeem all of the shareholder's stock using an installment note. If the stock is not publicly traded, the shareholder may recognize any gain realized using the installment method.[64] Redeeming the stock with an installment note might be an attractive option to corporations that lack sufficient cash to pay for the stock immediately.

The shareholder will lose the waiver of the constructive ownership rules in certain circumstances beyond those involved in the reacquisition of an interest within the 10-year period. This waiver does not apply if (1) any part of the stock redeemed was acquired from a related person within 10 years; or (2) any related person owns stock, at the time of the redemption, the ownership of which is attributable to the redeeming shareholder, and such person acquired any stock in the corporation from the redeeming shareholder within 10 years and the stock so acquired is not redeemed in the same transaction. However, these limitations do not apply if the acquisition or disposition of stock does not have as one of its principal purposes the avoidance of federal income tax.[65] Thus, the IRS might not consider gifts of stock to children as part of an ongoing gift program to have tax avoidance as a principal purpose.[66]

Code Sec. 302(c)(2)(C) specifically provides that entities may waive the family attribution rules. However, beneficiaries must join in the waiver and must agree to be jointly and severally liable with the entity for any deficiency resulting from an acquisition by any of them within the 10-year period discussed above. The term "entity" includes trusts, estates, partnerships, and corporations. No provision exists for a waiver of attribution to and from entities and their beneficiaries. To the extent that these attribution rules apply, essentially the same problems and solutions exist under this exception as exist under the disproportionate exception.

[63] Code Sec. 302(c)(2)(A).

[64] Code Sec. 453.

[65] Code Sec. 302(c)(2)(B).

[66] IRS Letter Ruling 8236023, June 8, 1982.

.05 Partial Liquidation

Under the safe harbor rule of Code Sec. 302(e), a distribution is a partial liquidation for the purposes of the fourth exception to dividend treatment in these cases:

- It is not essentially equivalent to a dividend (determined at the corporate level) and occurs in the year in which the corporation adopts a plan of partial liquidation (or in the following year).
- The distribution occurs under a plan to cease conducting a business that has been actively conducted for five years.
- The corporation did not acquire the business in a taxable transaction within five years.
- The corporation is actively engaged in another trade or business.

.06 Distributions of Property

The corporation recognizes gain[67] but not loss[68] on a distribution of property as if the corporation sold the property for its fair market value. However, the fair market value of the property may not be less than a liability on the property to which the property is subject or which the shareholder assumed.[69] Whether the redemption is treated as a dividend or as an exchange has no effect on the recognition of gain or loss by the corporation.

.07 Dividend Distributions

If a distribution does not qualify as a stock redemption under Code. Sec. 302 or 303, then it is treated as a dividend. Through 2010, dividends are generally taxed at the same 5 percent and 15 percent rates that apply to net capital gain. Absent Congressional legislation, dividends will once again be subject to ordinary income rates (a maximum of 35 percent) after 2010. However, dividends are taxed as ordinary income only to the extent of the corporation's current and accumulated earnings and profits.[70]

A distribution that exceeds earnings and profits is treated first as a tax-free recovery of the shareholder's basis for the stock.[71] Basis can only be reduced to zero. Any distribution that exceeds both earnings and profits and the shareholder's basis in the stock is treated as capital gain.[72]

---

[67] Code Sec. 311(b).
[68] Code Sec. 311(a).
[69] Code Sec. 311(c).
[70] Code Sec. 316(a).
[71] Code Sec. 301(c)(2).
[72] Code. Sec. 301(c)(3).

Stock redemptions treated as dividends. A stock redemption that is treated as a dividend differs from other types of dividend distributions because the shareholder has actually surrendered stock to the corporation for which he or she had a basis. Since the redemption is treated as a dividend, the shareholder cannot use the basis to offset the redemption proceeds. Instead, the basis of the shareholder's remaining stock is adjusted for the basis of the stock redeemed. When the redeeming shareholder owns no remaining stock, the basis is allocated to other shareholders whose stock ownership is attributed to the redeeming shareholder under Code Sec. 318.[73]

> **Note:** In 2002, the IRS proposed regulations that provided for a different method of dealing with the basis of stock redeemed in a dividend-type transaction. Under the proposed regulations, an amount equal to the adjusted basis of the redeemed stock would have been treated as a loss. The loss would have been taken into account in a later year under rules contained in the proposed regulations.[74] However, these regulations were withdrawn in 2006 for further review.[75]

¶ 1920 USING AN EMPLOYEE STOCK OWNERSHIP PLAN IN ESTATE PLANNING FOR THE OWNERS

Employee stock ownership plans (ESOPs) offer advantages for small business employers and their employees. ESOPs as an employee benefit were discussed at ¶ 1910. This chapter discusses ESOPs from the standpoint of their use for post-organizational planning for business interests.

At ¶ 1915, this book discussed the problems faced by the shareholder in a closely held corporation who undertakes to have the corporation redeem the shareholder's stock before his or her death, as well as the problems confronting the owner's estate. The corporation itself faces a major problem. It must accumulate the funds for a redemption, and it can accumulate those funds only out of after-tax dollars. The corporation can carry life insurance on a key shareholder-executive and the proceeds will not be taxable to the corporation for regular tax purposes.[76] However, the corporation may not deduct the premiums.[77] Insurance can help with redemptions after a shareholder's death only if the shareholder is insurable.

---

[73] Reg. § 1.302-2(c).

[74] Prop Reg. § 1.302-5(c)

[75] Prop Rule 71-75, 04/19/2006.

[76] Code Sec. 101(a)(1).

[77] Code Sec. 264(a).

A dramatic change takes place when a corporation uses an ESOP. The annual cash contributions a company makes to an ESOP are tax-deductible. If a shareholder dies and the ESOP has sufficient cash, it purchases the shareholder's stock from his or her estate. Thus, the ESOP has acquired the stock with pre-tax, not after-tax dollars, because each dollar the company contributed to the ESOP was tax-deductible.

.01 Tax-Free Rollover on Sale of Qualified Securities to ESOPs

When one of the founders of an ESOP-sponsoring business is ready to retire and surrender control, the founder might be concerned about lack of diversification, which is now out of his or her control. Code Sec. 1042 permits such an individual or his or her estate to sell employer securities to the ESOP and defer recognition of gain by reinvesting the proceeds in securities of domestic corporations meeting certain tests. However, such deferral is available only if the holder of the securities has held them for at least three years before the sale to the ESOP.

The basis of the stock acquired is reduced by the amount of the deferred gain so that if the shareholder sells the securities acquired, the shareholder will recognize the deferred gain.[78] If the shareholder holds the securities until death, the shares receive a step-up in basis[79] and all tax liability for pre-death appreciation is eliminated.[80] However, for property acquired from a decedent dying in 2010, the step up in basis is limited to $1,300,000 plus $3,000,000 for property received by a surviving spouse.

.02 Financing

Formerly, there was an exclusion for 50-percent of interest income on loans made to an ESOP or to an employer corporation, the proceeds of which are used by the plan to acquire employer securities. The exclusion, available to banks, insurance companies, other commercial lenders, and regulated investment companies, was generally repealed for loans made after August 20, 1996.[81] However, the exclusion continues to apply to such loans made under a written binding contract in effect before June 10, 1996.[82] The exclusion also continues to apply to certain loans made after August 20, 1996, to refinance loans made before August 21, 1996. Qualified refinancing loans must meet the requirements of Code Sec. 133 before

[78] Code Sec. 1042(e).

[79] Code Sec. 1014(a).

[80] Code Sec. 1042(e)(3).

[81] Code Sec. 133, repealed by the Small Business Job Protection Act of 1996 (P.L. 104-188).

[82] Small Business Job Protection Act of 1996 (P.L. 104-188, Act Sec. 1602(c)(3).

repeal, not increase the outstanding principal amount of the prior loan, and not extend the term of the original loan.

.03 Dividends

Dividends paid in accordance with plan provisions on securities held by an ESOP on the record date are deductible by the corporation if paid (1) in cash to the participants in the plan or their beneficiaries; (2) to the plan and distributed in cash to the participants in the plan or their beneficiaries; or (3) if used to make payments to repay stock acquisition loans but only if the dividends involved are on the stock acquired by the loan.[83]

¶ 1925 QUALIFYING FOR INSTALLMENT PAYMENT OF THE ESTATE TAX

The federal estate tax is payable nine months after death.[84] If the value of an interest in a closely held business exceeds 35 percent of the value of the adjusted gross estate (gross value reduced by allowable expenses, losses and debts[85]), the executor may elect to pay the estate taxes attributable to the business interest in two or more but not more than 10 annual installments. A closely held business means an interest as (1) a sole proprietorship; (2) a partner in a partnership (a) having 45 or fewer partners, or (b) in which the decedent owned 20 percent or more of the capital; or (3) an owner of stock in a corporation (a) having 45 or fewer shareholders, or (b) in which the decedent owned 20 percent or more of the voting stock.[86]

.01 Installment Requirements

The installment payments must be equal. If the executor makes the election to pay such estate taxes in installments, the first installment payment is due not more than 5 years after the prescribed date for paying estate taxes. The maximum payment period is 14 years, rather than 15 years, because the due date for the last payment of interest is the same date as the due date for the first installment payment of the tax.[87] This provision allows the estate to defer the estate taxes attributable to the business interest for up to 14 years with a special two-percent interest rate applicable to the estate taxes on the first $1,000,000[88] (indexed for inflation under Code Sec. 6601(j)(3)) in taxable value of the closely held business. The inflation-adjusted amount for the estate of a decedent dying in 2006 is $1,200,000. For the purpose of meeting the 20-percent

[83] Code Sec. 404(k).
[84] Code Secs. 6075(a) and 6151(a).
[85] Code Sec. 6166(b)(6).
[86] Code Sec. 6166(b)(1).
[87] Code Secs. 6166(a)(3) and 6166(f)(1).
[88] Code Sec. 6601(j)(1)(A).

requirement, corporate voting stock held by members of the decedent's family, as well as the decedent's own voting stock, are to be counted.[89] Family members are spouse, children and grandchildren, parents, brothers, and sisters.[90] These attribution rules are not applicable in determining the number of shareholders.

If the estate obtains this 14-year extension for payment of taxes, the estate must pay only interest annually during the first four years. The estate may pay the tax owed in annual installments with interest over the next 10 years. Interest is charged at the rate of only two percent on the estate tax attributable to the first $1,000,000 (indexed for inflation under Code Sec. 6601(j)(3)) in taxable value.[91] The inflation-adjusted amount for the estate of a decedent dying in 2006 is $1,200,000. However, if the amount of the estate tax extended under Code Sec. 6166 is less than this amount, only the lower amount qualifies for the special two-percent rate.[92] Any amounts deferred that are in excess of the amount that qualifies for the two-percent rate (called the "two-percent amount") are taxed at a rate equal to 45 percent of the rate that applies to underpayments of tax.[93] The two-percent amounts deferred under Code Sec. 6166 (for estates of decedents dying after December 31, 1997) are not deductible on the estate tax return[94] or on the estate's income tax return.[95]

For 2006, the two-percent portion is equal to the tentative tax computed on the value of a decedent's closely held business interest between $2,000,000 (the amount of the applicable exclusion amount under Code Sec. 2010(c)) and $3,200,000 ($1,200,000 + $2,000,000). The $1,200,000 is the inflation-adjusted amount for the $1,000,000 amount provided in Code Sec. 6601(j)(1)(A).

Example 19.2. Brenda Pittman dies in 2006, when the applicable exclusion amount is $2,000,000. The estate tax value of Pittman's closely held corporate interest is $4,000,000 and her executor elects, pursuant to Code Sec. 6166, to extend the time for payment of the estate taxes. The amount of estate tax attributable to the value of the corporation between $2,000,000 and $3,200,000 is eligible for the 2% interest rate. The 2% portion is $540,900, computed as follows: a $1,320,800 tentative estate tax on $3,200,000 minus $780,800 (the applicable credit amount for 2006). An interest rate of 45% of the rate applicable to underpayments of tax is assessed against the portion of the estate tax exceeding the $540,900 amount.

---

[89] Code Sec. 6166(b)(2)(D)

[90] Code Secs. 6166(b)(2)(D) and 267 (c)(4).

[91] Code Sec. 6601(j)(1)(A).

[92] Code Sec. 6601(j)(2).

[93] Code Sec. 6601(j)(1)(B).

[94] Code Sec. 2053(c)(1)(D).

[95] Code Sec. 163(k).

If the estate has undistributed net income for any taxable year after its fourth taxable year, the executor must apply it to the unpaid estate taxes.[96]

The 14-year extension can help overcome a cash squeeze, at the small price of low interest rates. In situations where an extension appears to be of possible use but there is some question as to whether the estate can meet percentage tests, then the estate planner should give some thought to strategies that will help satisfy the test. The client could either increase the size of the closely held corporate interest, reduce the size of the other parts of the estate, or both.

The number of shareholders for purposes of the 45-partner limitation is to be determined immediately before the decedent's death.[97] A husband and wife holding stock in any form are counted as one shareholder.[98] If a partnership, other corporation, or trust is a shareholder, the partners, other shareholders, and beneficiaries of the trust are counted as shareholders.[99] The latter provision is designed to prevent circumvention of the 45-shareholder limitation through the use of these other entities.

The maximum estate tax deferrable is the amount of estate tax attributable to the closely held business interest. This amount is determined by the ratio of the value of the closely held corporate interest to the adjusted gross estate.[100] In addition, if one-half or more in value of the corporate voting stock is sold, or if aggregate withdrawals (distributions) are made that equal one-half of the value of the corporate interest, there is immediate acceleration of the unpaid balance of the estate tax.[101] This rule suggests that the provision has practical value only in situations where the executor or heir will continue to hold the voting stock in the closely held corporation.

The executor or personal representative may make the deferral election with respect to certain qualified holding companies provided that the indirectly owned interest would meet the requirements had the decedent owned it directly.[102] But the four-percent interest rate and five-year deferral of principal are not available to holding companies. Also, the portion of the value of the business attributable to passive assets does not qualify.[103]

This 14-year extension for paying the estate tax is a good planning tool if the estate can meet the 35-percent test. The 14-year

---

[96] Code Sec. 6166(g)(2)(A).

[97] Code Sec. 6166(b)(2)(A).

[98] Code Sec. 6166(b)(2)(B).

[99] Code Sec. 6166(b)(1)(C).

[100] Code Sec. 6166(a)(2).

[101] Code Sec. 6166(g)(1)(A).

[102] Code Sec. 6166(b)(8).

[103] Code Sec. 6166(b)(9).

extension is not subject to a means test. Even very large estates may qualify for the 14-year extension for paying the estate tax attributable to a closely held business.

To meet the 35-percent test in borderline situations, the business owner should consider making lifetime gifts of nonbusiness assets, more than three years before death. The unlimited marital deduction for lifetime gifts[104] offers one possibility of reducing the business owner's estate. Lifetime gifts taking advantage of the $12,000 annual exclusion (for 2006),[105] which is indexed for inflation under Code Sec. 2503(b)(2), is another way to reduce the adjusted gross estate. Gift-splitting with one's spouse[106] would be another way to make gifts with favorable tax consequences to help the estate qualify for the installment payment of the estate tax. The sale of nonbusiness assets and the acquisition of additional business assets with the proceeds might be another way to help the estate qualify for the installment payment of estate taxes. Administration expenses, whether deducted on the estate tax return or the income tax return, will also help.

The estate tax, eligible for installment payments, is reduced by the amounts distributed in a Code Sec. 303 redemption under Code Sec. 6166(g)(1)(B) (¶ 1915). This reduction is a factor in determining whether to use a Code Sec. 303 stock redemption or the tax deferral offered by Code Sec. 6166.

To take advantage of the installment payment of estate taxes, the executor must make the election on or before the due date of the estate tax return or any extensions. The executor should make the decision well in advance of the deadline to allow time to resolve any questions.

In measuring the tax attributable to the closely held voting stock, one multiplies the estate tax by a fraction. The numerator is the value of the closely held voting stock, and the denominator is the adjusted gross estate.

.02 Reasonable Cause Extension

An estate may obtain a discretionary extension of the time for payment of estate tax from the IRS for up to 10 years for reasonable cause.[107]

The congressional intent in adopting the reasonable cause standard was to make obtaining an extension easier to obtain than a discretionary extension had been under the undue hardship test. Reg. § 20.6161-1(a)(1) contains four examples of reasonable cause,

---

[104] Code Sec. 2523(a).
[105] Code Sec. 2503(b)(1).
[106] Code Sec. 2513.
[107] Code Sec. 6161(a)(2).

including a situation in which an estate cannot readily sell its assets to pay estate taxes or the estate consists in large part of rights to receive payments in the future.

¶1930 KEEPING THE BUSINESS IN THE FAMILY

Is the business worth keeping in the family? That is the first question. At this point, the shareholders must weigh not only current earnings but also future earnings in the light of possible changes in the market, technology, capital requirements, competition, supplies, and labor. If patents, copyrights, licenses, leases, or other assets that can be classified as wasting assets are involved, the shareholders must also take their expiration into account.

If the business is worth retaining, the next question is "Who will manage the business?" The first place to look for management is within the family. A business owner must realize that the process of choosing and implementing a succession plan can be difficult. The owner is apt to face issues of control, sibling rivalries, equality, love, money, and taxes, not to mention the owner's own mortality.

The overlap of family and business relationships can make the task of grooming a successor from within the family much more difficult than grooming an outsider to take over. Fortunately, the business owner can take various steps to make the transition run smoothly.

The business owner might want to establish an outside board of directors or advisors who would help select and train a successor. The business owner should establish specific rules for hiring family members. The owner should go so far as to develop qualifications for positions. Anyone, even a family member, would have to meet the qualifications in order to be hired.

Creating a development plan for potential successors is essential. The business owner's unexpected death or sudden disability could leave the company without needed leadership in the absence of a plan. The plan must address how the successor will acquire the technical expertise and skills needed to take control. In addition, a mechanism should exist for an ongoing evaluation of the successor's performance during the transition phase.

The business owner must teach every aspect of the business to the successor. Before turning over the reins completely, the owner can let the successor manage a department and evaluate the successor's performance.

Sometimes personality conflicts make grooming a child to take over for a parent extremely difficult. In such a case, the parent should consider bringing in an outside mentor. The parent would need to consider cost factors.

The family can use counseling if an absolute stalemate develops. Alternatively, the business owner can establish a family council to resolve conflicts.

To recruit and retain competent management, the corporation must arrange special compensation. Executive compensation arrangements are discussed in ¶1605. Recapitalization is one route that offers management an equity interest while preserving family control. On the other hand, if vesting control in management seems wiser, the corporation can give the new management voting common stock, and give the family preferred stock, which can provide a steady income.

If broad-based employee participation in the ownership of the enterprise appears to afford a sounder basis for successful operation of the business, then the shareholders should consider an employee stock ownership plan (ESOP).

Depending on the circumstances of the particular case, efforts aimed at keeping the business in the family might be aided by the use of the special use valuation election (¶2210.01) and the election to defer payment of estate taxes (¶1925).

¶1935 BUY-SELL AGREEMENTS—QUESTIONS AND ANSWERS

The owner of a closely held corporation is naturally concerned about what will happen to the corporation upon his or her death. Although a corporation may exist in perpetuity, many practical problems must be solved to ensure the continuity of a business. A buy-sell agreement deals with some of the problems.

A buy-sell agreement is a contract providing for the sale of the corporate stock upon the happening of a specified event. Generally, this event is the death of one of the stockholders. However, the agreement can also provide for a sale upon the disability or retirement of one of the parties. Buy-sell agreements may establish value for transfer tax purposes if they meet the rules contained in Code Sec. 2703 (discussed at ¶2310).

The following questions and answers offer guidance in the practical lifetime structuring of buy-sell agreements. Planning before death can help avert two serious tax problems: (1) the value of the stock for estate tax purposes, and (2) the source of funds to pay the estate tax (this problem is particularly important because of the limited market for the stock of a closely held corporation).

Q. **What are the key advantages of a buy-sell agreement?**

A. In the absence of a buy-sell agreement, the corporate stock might be unmarketable. The agreement avoids a forced sale or the unwilling or unwelcome participation in the business of the decedent's surviving spouse or heirs.

If the decedent's estate receives cash in exchange for the corporation's stock, funds are available for payment of federal and state estate taxes and other purposes.

The agreement provides for corporate succession and control of the business according to the parties' desires.

The agreement dispels fears that the business will terminate on the death of one of the stockholders. It is also a morale booster for key employees who otherwise might fear loss of their jobs. The agreement eliminates the risk of the corporation being barred from an election by reason of a nonqualifying or nonconsenting stockholder.

Q. **How does a buy-sell agreement work?**

A. There are three types of buy-sell agreements:

1. The *cross purchase agreement* is a buy-sell agreement that exists among stockholders. Example: A corporation has two shareholders, A and B. A and B both agree that, upon either's death, the decedent's estate must sell, and the survivor must purchase the decedent's stock.
2. The *stock redemption agreement* is an agreement to which the corporation and the shareholders are parties. The corporation agrees to buy (redeem) the decedent's stock. Example: A corporation has two shareholders, A and B. Both agree that their estates will sell or tender for redemption the shares they owned (see ¶1915 for a discussion of stock redemptions generally).
3. In a *hybrid or combination agreement*, the corporation and the stockholders agree to buy the decedent's stock. Such an agreement consists of both a cross purchase and a redemption agreement. Example: A corporation has two shareholders; each owns 100 shares of stock. There is a cross purchase agreement for 50 shares of stock and a stock redemption agreement for the remaining 50. Unless the surviving stockholders buy their agreed portion before the redemption by the corporation, the redemption

proceeds may be taxable as a dividend to the estate. Therefore, the surviving stockholders must take extreme care that the redemption does not occur first.

Q. **How can funds be obtained to pay for the stock?**

A. Funding with life insurance is generally used. Where the shareholders use the cross purchase approach, each stockholder owns an insurance policy on the life of every other stockholder. If the agreement provides for redemption of the stock by the corporation, the corporation carries a life insurance policy on each stockholder whose stock is to be purchased. Upon the death of a stockholder, the corporation or the surviving stockholder (depending upon the type of agreement) collects the insurance proceeds. The surviving stockholders or the corporation then uses the proceeds to purchase the stock of the deceased stockholder. The stockholders can use existing policies if a stockholder is now uninsurable. Where a corporation has only two stockholders, use of a single first-to-die policy covering both stockholders should be less costly than using two separate policies (¶ 705).

Making periodic contributions to a sinking fund is a method that is particularly valuable where a stockholder is uninsurable. However, the corporation must exercise care to avoid the accumulated earnings tax.[108]

Q. **What are the tax consequences of a cross purchase agreement?**

A. Insurance premiums paid by the shareholders are not deductible.[109]

Insurance proceeds paid to the surviving stockholder are exempt from income tax if the policy is acquired directly from an insurance company.[110] If the policy is acquired from another stockholder, proceeds are excluded only to the extent of consideration and premiums and other amounts paid by the transferee.[111] This is the so-called "transfer for value rule," which can be avoided by having the insurance policies owned by a partnership.[112]

Transfer of shares between the shareholders has no tax effect upon the corporation.

Sale of the decedent's stock by the heirs or estate will result in taxable gain to the extent that the sale proceeds exceed basis[113]

---

[108] Code Secs. 531-537.

[109] Code Sec. 264(a).

[110] Code Sec. 101(a)(2).

[111] Code Sec. 101(a)(2).

[112] IRS Letter Ruling 9012063, December 28, 1989.

[113] Code Sec. 1001.

(i.e., a stepped-up basis equal to the value of the stock for estate tax purposes under Code Sec. 1014(a)). The step up in basis for property acquired from a decedent dying in 2010 is limited to $1,300,000 plus $3,000,000 for property received by a surviving spouse. See ¶ 1005 for further details.

Sellers of the decedent's stock must include in gross income any interest they receive on the deferred part of the selling price.[114]

The basis of the surviving shareholders in the additional corporate shares they buy is equal to the share's purchase price.[115]

Q. **What are the tax consequences of a stock redemption agreement?**

A. Insurance premiums paid by the corporation to fund the redemption of shares are not deductible.[116]

The investment of corporate funds in insurance policies to fund a buy-sell agreement does not incur the penalty on unreasonable accumulation of earnings if the accumulation serves a valid corporate purpose rather than an individual shareholder's purpose.[117]

Insurance proceeds received by the corporation upon death of a stockholder are not subject to regular income tax,[118] but they may be subject to the alternative minimum tax by virtue of the adjustment for current earnings (ACE).[119]

The premiums paid on a policy insuring a stockholder are probably not taxable as dividends to the stockholder if the corporation is the owner and beneficiary and retains the incidents of ownership of the policy.

The premiums paid on an insurance policy covering the life of one stockholder are not taxable as dividends to the other stockholders.

Redemption of the deceased stockholder's stock generally has no tax consequences to the surviving shareholders; the basis of their stock is unchanged. However, for property acquired from a decedent dying in 2010, the step up in basis is limited to $1,300,000 plus $3,000,000 for property received by a surviving spouse.

A redemption resulting in a complete termination of the shareholder's interest generally results in sale or exchange treatment (¶ 1915).[120]

---

[114] Code Sec. 61(a).
[115] Code Sec. 1012.
[116] Code Sec. 264(a)(1).
[117] Code Sec. 533 and Reg. § 1.533-1(a).
[118] Code Sec. 101(a).
[119] Code Sec. 56(g).
[120] Code Sec. 302(b)(3).

A corporation realizes no gain from the redemption unless it distributes property with a greater value than its adjusted basis (appreciated property).[121] A corporation may not recognize any loss on a distribution of property with a value less than its adjusted basis.[122] The estate acquires a cost basis in the property distributed.[123] However, the estate should generally recognize little, if any, gain because the stock has a basis equal to its fair market value at the date of the decedent's death, or the alternative valuation date, except as limited for estates of decedents dying in 2010 as noted above.[124]

Q. **Which type of buy-sell agreement should the shareholders select?**

A. Each type of agreement has its advantages and disadvantages. Some key factors to consider are as follows.

Cross purchase agreement:

1. Surviving stockholders must pay for the deceased's stock with after-tax dollars.
2. This type of agreement is relatively simple and is quite satisfactory when the number of shareholders is small. It can become burdensome, however, when the corporation has many stockholders. For example, if a corporation has five shareholders at the time they execute a buy-sell agreement, the last survivor would have to purchase the shares of the four stockholders who predeceased him or her.
3. The obligation to purchase shares generally falls upon younger, minority-interest shareholders, who often are the least financially able to buy the shares.
4. This type of agreement generally results in fewer legal problems and less complicated tax consequences.

Stock redemption agreement:

1. Such an agreement has the virtue of simplicity when the corporation has several stockholders.
2. The corporation, not the stockholders, pays the life insurance premiums if the agreement is funded. The benefit is that the premiums are paid with money that has been taxed only to the corporation. When the shareholders pay the premiums in a cross purchase plan, the premiums are paid with money that might have been taxed both to the corporation and to the stockholders (as dividends).

---

[121] Code Sec. 311(b).
[122] Code Sec. 311(a).
[123] Code Sec. 1012.
[124] Code Sec. 1014(a).

3. Despite the use of the corporation's earnings and profits for the stockholders' benefit, no dividend treatment results.
4. If the corporation does not use insurance as a funding device, the corporation might not have sufficient money to redeem the shares when the deceased stockholder's shares are tendered for redemption.
5. If the corporation lacks sufficient money to redeem the decedent's shares, it can use installment payments of the purchase price and still waive the family attribution rules.[125] However, the debt creates a problem of security and interest.

Q. **How is valuation of the stock determined?**

A. Generally, the parties use one of the following four methods:

1. Book value at date of death or end of preceding accounting period. This method is often unrealistic.
2. Fixed price provided for in the agreement and agreed upon by the stockholders. This method is sound only if the stockholders review and update it periodically.
3. Price fixed by appraisal after death. The disadvantage of this method is the delay in choosing and then obtaining able appraisers. Consequently, the stockholders might not know the price for a significant time. Delay is a normal experience under this method.
4. Self-adjusting formula set forth in the agreement. The stockholders can use a variety of formulas, e.g., (a) book value at close of the preceding accounting period plus a fixed sum, or (b) a formula giving one weight to book value and another to the value indicated by the capitalization of earnings (see ¶ 1940 for further details on these methods and other valuation factors).

Q. **Is valuation binding for federal estate taxes?**

A. For the valuation to be binding for federal estate taxes, the agreement must state that the shareholders cannot freely dispose of or encumber their stock during their lifetimes. In the absence of a restriction on transferability, the government will not be bound even by a bona fide valuation. The IRS generally scrutinizes the valuation provided in a buy-sell agreement. The stockholders should determine the price through arm's-length bargaining and negotiations. Agreements entered into after October 8,

[125] Code Secs. 302(b)(3) and 302(c)(2)(A).

1990, must meet special requirements in order to fix value. These requirements are discussed in ¶ 2310.

Q. **What are disability buy-sell agreements?**

A. Although buy-sell agreements generally include death provisions, disability can and does disrupt many businesses. Therefore, these agreements often contain disability buyout provisions. The stockholders can use disability insurance policies for funding and can use the disability definition in the insurance policy as the definition of disability in the buy-sell agreement. The agreement can provide for the acquisition of the stock of the disabled stockholder after a period of six months or one year of disability. Normally, after this period, the stockholder will know whether the disability is permanent.

Q. **What are the tax consequences of such an agreement?**

A. The disabled stockholder will realize a gain or loss on the sale of his or her stock.[126]

The corporation may deduct the premiums paid on the disability income insurance policies.[127] However, unless the premiums are included in the gross income of the employee-stockholder, the disability income insurance proceed will be included in the stockholder's gross income.[128] However, once the disability insurance proceeds are treated as payment for the redemption of the stock, the corporation may not deduct the premiums and the stockholder will treat the payments as amounts received for the sale of his or her stock.

¶ 1940 HOW SHARES IN CLOSELY HELD CORPORATIONS ARE VALUED

For tax purposes, what are the shares of a closely held corporation worth? Many owners lack knowledge of their value. Yet, the determination of the value of the stock can have substantial tax consequences. Valuation of the shares of a closely held corporation can be especially important in the area of estate and gift taxes, but it can also have relevance for income taxes. Special valuation rules apply when a senior family member transfers common stock to junior family members while retaining preferred stock (¶ 2305).

How is value determined? A properly drafted buy-sell agreement ensures that a disabled shareholder or the estate of a deceased shareholder will receive a fair price for the shares of stock. Agreements

[126] Code Sec. 1001.

[127] Code Sec. 162(a).

[128] Code Secs. 61(a) and 105(a).

entered into after October 8, 1990, must meet special requirements in order to fix value. These requirements are discussed in ¶ 2310. If the stockholders do not have a controlling buy-sell agreement, then the Internal Revenue Code, Treasury regulations, revenue rulings, and court decisions offer guidance for determining value for tax purposes.

In practice, if the IRS challenges the values used by the taxpayer, the IRS and the taxpayer arrive at the valuation by a process of negotiation and compromise. The taxpayer usually tries for a low valuation, while the IRS seeks a high valuation. However, this is not always true. The taxpayer will want a high valuation, for example, if seeking a charitable contribution deduction or other income tax advantages.

Each side draws upon Treasury regulations, revenue rulings, and court decisions to support its position. In the course of negotiation, the gap is narrowed until the parties reach an acceptable compromise.

If the taxpayer is unwilling to accept the valuation determined by the IRS, the taxpayer may challenge it in the U.S. Tax Court or may pay the tax and sue for a refund in a U.S. district court or the U.S. Court of Federal Claims. Generally, in tax litigation, the burden is on the taxpayer to show that the determination by the IRS is incorrect. However, effective for court proceedings arising in connection with examinations commencing after July 22, 1998, the taxpayer may shift the burden of proof to the IRS by introducing credible evidence with respect to any factual issue.[129] In addition, the taxpayer must prove that he or she has complied with the requirements to substantiate any item, has maintained all records required, and has cooperated with reasonable requests by the IRS.[130] Corporations and partnerships whose net worth exceeds $7,000,000 or that have more than 500 employees may not shift the burden of proof to the IRS. The net worth of an estate is determined on the date of the decedents' death. The net worth of a trust is determined on the last day of the tax year, which is the subject of the dispute.[131] In practice, courts are likely to find a compromise value for the stock, between the valuations of IRS experts and those of the taxpayer. Valuation understatements beyond certain limits must be avoided at risk of penalty,[132] as discussed at ¶ 1005. The IRS has the burden of proof for the imposition of any penalty on an individual.[133] Other taxpayers have the burden of proof that the IRS should not impose a penalty on them.

Estates often litigate disputes concerning valuation issues. Unless the potential estate tax savings exceed the expense of litigation and the executor is reasonably confident of victory, the

---

[129] Code Sec. 7491(a).

[130] Code Sec. 7491(b).

[131] Code Secs. 7491(a)(2)(C) and 7430(c)(4)(A)(ii).

[132] Code Sec. 6662.

[133] Code Sec. 7491(c).

executor should not rush to the courts. An executor who litigates and loses may be liable for a surcharge unless the executor obtains the consent and approval of the beneficiaries.

For example, if an executor is dealing with a $10,000 difference in value taxable at 46 percent in 2006, the possible estate tax savings are not likely to justify the expense of litigation. The prudent solution would be to settle for a valuation somewhat higher than what the executor believes is the correct valuation. An estate planner should consider the possibility of valuation disputes in the planning stage. The estate planner should consider possibly higher valuations in computing estate taxes and planning for the estate's liquidity needs and other related matters.

No single formula applies to all valuation situations. The IRS, however, has issued guidelines to value closely held shares. (Rev. Rul. 59-60[134] enumerates factors for valuing such stocks for estate and gift tax purposes. Under Rev. Rul. 65-192,[135] these factors are equally applicable for income tax purposes.) The IRS *Valuation Training for Appeals Officers* coursebook provides a discussion of Rev. Rul. 59-60 and further insight as to how the IRS values closely held securities. The factors mentioned in these guides are not all-inclusive. Because valuation is not an exact science, the estate planner should consider all relevant factors affecting fair market value in the planning stage. The executor should consider these factors in resolving valuation disputes with the IRS.

.01 Factors to Consider

The following discussion is an analysis of the fundamental factors for valuing closely held shares.

FACTOR NO. 1
Nature and History of the Enterprise from Its Inception

The history of the business is important in establishing its past stability or instability, its growth or lack of growth, and its diversity or lack of diversity. These are some of the facts needed to ascertain the degree of business risk. The history should highlight the nature of the business, its products and/or services, its operating and investment assets, its capital structure, its plant facilities, and its sales records.

[134] 1959-1 CB 237.

[135] 1965-2 CB 259.

FACTOR NO. 2

Economic Outlook and the Condition of the Specific Industry

Knowledge and consideration of overall economic conditions are essential to appraise closely held stock. The company's progress in relation to its competitors and the industry's ability to compete are significant. Although courts will undoubtedly take judicial notice of the current economic situation, information on existing business and economic conditions can be useful.

FACTOR NO. 3

Book Value of the Stock and Financial Condition of the Business

Balance sheets, and necessary supplementary schedules, should be obtained for at least two years preceding the appraisal date. This date usually will disclose the liquid position of the enterprise, the book value of the assets (for a discussion of valuation of business real estate, see the end of ¶ 1940, herein), working capital, long-term indebtedness, capital structure, and net worth. These factors are customarily regarded as significant in evaluating a business. Separate consideration should be given to nonoperating investments such as securities and real estate. Book value (assets minus liabilities) might be significant, but book value generally bears no direct relationship to fair market value. Even where the IRS or the taxpayer contends that the fair market value approximates the book value, the courts seldom rely on book value. However, where the taxpayer made an attempt to show a lower value by using a capitalization-of-earnings method, the Claims Court required use of a book value method.[136]

FACTOR NO. 4

Earning Capacity of the Company

Although determining the most significant factor affecting the fair market value of stock is often difficult, earnings are generally deemed to be most important. Detailed income statements for a period (at least five years) immediately before the appraisal date are also important. (Of course, if the corporation has been in business for less than five years, a shorter period must be used.) The use of prior earnings records is recommended because they are usually the most reliable guide to expected future earning power.

The earnings for a prior period are not merely averaged in order to predict future earnings. Trends (rate of growth, static earnings, declining earnings) must be taken into account. Clearly, if past

[136] *A. Luce, Jr.*, Cls. Ct., 84-1 USTC ¶ 13,549.

earnings were materially affected by nonrecurring factors (e.g., unusual capital gains or losses), adjustments should be made for them. Because of the unique relationship of major shareholders to their closely held corporations (these shareholders are often officers and/or employees of the corporation), adjustments to reported earnings might have to be made for salaries. A determination should be made whether the same salaries would be paid to nonshareholders with the same ability and performing the same duties. The loss of a key executive can have a depressing effect on value, particularly if the corporation has no trained and capable employees to succeed to the management position. On the other hand, the loss of a key employee might not seriously impair the business because of adequate life insurance coverage or the availability of competent management. Although the extent of the loss and the consequent reduction in the value of the stock are difficult to establish, the estate planner should consider the type of business and the role of the key executive.

Even when future earning power has been computed, one of the most difficult problems remains. This problem is the determination of the proper multiple to apply to these earnings. No standard table of capitalization rates applies to closely held corporations. Perhaps the best guide to finding the appropriate capitalization rate is to ascertain that of comparable companies whose shares are publicly traded, making an appropriate adjustment downward because the closely held stock is not publicly traded. The following are among the most important factors to consider in deciding upon a capitalization rate in a particular case: (1) the nature of the business; (2) the risk involved; and (3) the stability or irregularity of earnings. Without attempting to be definitive, multiples of between 5 and 20 have been applied to the adjusted average annual earnings in many cases. During bear market conditions, the stocks of many publicly traded companies have sold at price-earnings (P/E) ratios ranging from one to four.

FACTOR NO. 5
Dividend-Paying Capacity

Another important factor is the dividend-paying capacity of the business, rather than the dividends actually paid in the past. However, the dividend-paying factor is probably a less reliable indication of fair market value than are other factors. In a closely held corporation, the controlling stockholder(s) can substitute salaries and bonuses for dividends, thereby reducing net income and understating the capacity of the corporation to pay dividends. In such enterprises, the payment of dividends is often based upon the financial and tax needs of the controlling stockholder or group in control. The IRS acknowledges the necessity of retaining a reasonable portion of profits in the business to meet competition; it thus recognizes that a publicly held company has more access to credit and at more reasonable terms than does a closely held corporation.

Where an actual or effective controlling interest is being valued, the dividend factor is *not* a material factor because the dividend payment is discretionary with controlling stockholders.

FACTOR NO. 6
Whether or Not the Enterprise Has Goodwill or Other Intangible Value

Goodwill is based primarily upon earning capacity. The presence and value of goodwill depend upon the excess of net earnings over and above a fair return on net tangible assets. Elements of goodwill include the prestige and renown of the business enterprise, the ownership of a brand or trade name, and a record of successful operation over a prolonged period in a particular locality.

No single method exists for valuing goodwill. The above-mentioned factors should be considered and when all else fails (i.e., there is not better basis available) the IRS suggests a formula approach described in Rev. Rul. 68-609.[137]

FACTOR NO. 7
Sales of the Stock and Size of the Block to Be Valued

Prior sales of stock of closely held corporations are meaningful and useful if they were arm's-length transactions. Such sales are closely scrutinized. Forced or isolated small sales do not generally reflect fair market value. Because prevailing market prices are not available, no adjustment or discount is made for "blockage." (Under the "blockage" theory, a "blockage discount" from the market price is allowable if the block of stock is so large that if it were placed on the market over a reasonable period of time, it would depress the price.) However, the size of the block of stock is relevant and should be considered. Valuing a large block of stock at a discount might be appropriate because of the general difficulty of disposing of it. (Because the suggested discount is predicated upon an insufficiency of buyers, no discount should apply if a buyer seeking control of the business is available.)

FACTOR NO. 8
Market Price of Stocks of Similar Corporations

In valuing unlisted securities, the value of securities of corporations in the same or a similar line of business, listed on an exchange,

[137] 1968-2 CB 327.

should be considered with other pertinent factors. However, if sufficient comparable companies whose stocks are so listed are not available, the appraiser might use a comparison with actively traded over-the-counter stocks. Although precise comparability is generally not attainable, some stocks might be reasonably similar.

.02 Weight of Factors

Depending upon the circumstances in each case, some factors might carry more weight than others. Earnings might be the most important criterion of value in some situations, whereas asset value will be more significant in others. Generally, the IRS accords primary consideration to earnings when valuing stock of companies selling products or services. Conversely, in an investment or real estate holding company, the IRS might give the greatest weight to the assets underlying the securities being valued.

Other factors considered include condition of plants and equipment; adequacy of accumulated depreciation; effect of legal restrictions and limitations; environmental hazards; contingent liabilities; union relations; employee relations; efficiency of management, employees and plant; dependence on major customers, suppliers and products; cash flow projections; and interest rates.

.03 Discount for Lack of Marketability

A substantial discount might be available on the basis that the stock lacks marketability, i.e., an absence of a ready or existing market for the sale or purchase of the securities being valued. In its *Valuation Training for Appeals Officers* coursebook, the IRS recognizes that if owners of closely held stock should try to list a block of securities on a stock exchange for sale to the public, they probably would have to make the offerings through underwriters, incurring costs for registration, distribution, and underwriters' commissions. The courts have upheld the use of such costs to determine lack of marketability. However, where securities law restrictions on unregistered stock owned by a decedent terminated on his death, the shares of stock were valued at their date-of-death value, unrestricted by a discount relating to the expired restrictions.[138]

.04 Minority Interests

A minority stock interest in a closely held corporation, owned by a person not related to the holders of the majority of the stock, will normally be valued for estate and gift tax purposes at a substantial discount from what would otherwise be its fair market value.

---

[138] *C.K. McClatchy Est.*, 106 TC 206, CCH Dec. 51,277.

In 1993, the IRS reversed its position that minority discounts generally are not permitted on intrafamily transfers of stock if the family in the aggregate has either voting control or de facto control at the time of the transfer. In Rev. Rul. 93-12,[139] the IRS announced its acceptance of court decisions holding that shares owned by family members are not attributed to another family member for determining the value of that individual's shares. The new position facilitates the transfer of greater amounts of stock at low or no gift-tax cost.

The U.S. Court of Appeals for the Tenth Circuit has held that a minority interest discount and a special use valuation (¶ 1005) are not mutually exclusive, provided that the minority discount is applied first.[140]

.05 Controlling Interests

The courts have recognized that an additional element of value might be present in a block of stock representing a controlling interest for valuation purposes. The taxpayer and the IRS might be at odds at times in the application of this rule. The IRS might be disposed to have "premium value" used where it will enhance revenue and might oppose its use where it will reduce revenue. The taxpayer, on the other hand, will favor use of the premium where it will reduce taxes, such as where the controlling interest is shielded from tax by the marital deduction or by unified credit, and oppose the premium where higher taxes will result.

.06 Key Person Discount

The IRS recognizes the fact that, in many types of business, the loss of a key individual can have a depressing effect on value.[141] Some courts have accounted for this depressing effect on value by applying a key person discount.

Where a taxpayer seeks a key person discount, the taxpayer should present evidence of special expertise and current significant management decisions.

.07 Valuation of Business Real Estate

Under Code Sec. 2032A, if certain conditions are met, the executor may elect to value real property included in the decedent's gross estate, which is devoted to closely held business use, on the basis of the property's value in the closely held business, rather than at its fair market value determined on the basis of its highest and best use.[142]

---

[139] 1993-1 CB 202.

[140] *C. Hoover Est.*, CA-10, 95-2 USTC ¶ 60,217.

[141] Rev. Rul. 59-60, 1959-1 CB 237.

[142] Code Sec. 2032A.

For the special valuation rule to apply, the deceased owner and/or a member of the owner's family must materially participate in the operation of the business.

For a discussion of how the provision is to be applied when business real estate is held directly by the decedent and of the conditions attached to the election, see ¶2110.

¶1945 ELECTING S CORPORATION STATUS

Many closely held corporations will want to consider electing exemption from corporate taxes under Subchapter S.[143] The S election offers these added advantages:

- Facilitating income-splitting within the family by way of gifts of stock.
- Permitting shareholders to deduct their share of corporate losses against outside income.[144] This ability is especially useful in start-up situations where the shareholders expect losses. However, the shareholder must materially participate in the business to deduct losses,[145] and the business must not consist of the rental of property.
- Reducing problems of unreasonable compensation.
- Avoiding penalty taxes on accumulated earnings or on personal holding companies.

S corporations compute their taxable income in the same manner as individuals with a few exceptions.[146] The dividends received deduction and corporation tax preferences generally do not apply to S corporations. Each shareholder takes into account a pro rata share of income, deductions, and credits.[147] Basis adjustments to stock are made in the same way as adjustments to basis of partnership interests.[148] Losses that are passed through and unused because of lack of basis[149] may be carried over to subsequent tax years until sufficient basis is acquired.[150]

In considering whether to operate as an S corporation, the corporate and the individual tax rates should be considered: the top individual rate is 35 percent, through 2010.[151] The top individual income tax rate of 35 percent is equal to the top corporate rate of 35 percent applicable to regular (C) corporations.[152] If a business is planning to retain earnings to fund growth, the owners might prefer

---

[143] Code Sec. 1363(a).
[144] Code Sec. 1366(a)(1).
[145] Code Secs. 469(a) and 469(c)(1).
[146] Code Sec. 1363(b).
[147] Code Sec. 1366.
[148] Code Sec. 1367.
[149] Code Sec. 1366(d)(1).
[150] Code Sec. 1366(d)(2).
[151] Code Sec. 1.
[152] Code Sec. 11(b).

to operate it as a regular corporation as opposed to operating it as an S corporation. The decision turns on whether the owners generally will be in higher income tax brackets than would the business, if the business were operated as a regular corporation.

An S corporation may not have more than 100 shareholders.[153] All members of a family, as well as their estates and spouses, are treated as one shareholder for purposes of determining if the 100-shareholder limit.[154] There is no need to make an affirmative election to have this rule apply. An S corporation may not have more than one class of stock, but differences in voting rights are permitted.[155]

New shareholders are bound by a prior election unless more than 50 percent of the shares of the stock consent to a revocation of the election.[156] An S corporation must use a calendar year unless it can show a valid business purpose for the use of a fiscal year to the satisfaction of the IRS or unless it makes a special election under Code Sec. 444. Under Code Sec. 444, an S corporation that would otherwise have to adopt a calendar year under the above rules may elect to adopt or change to a tax year with a deferral period not longer than three months (or the deferral period of the year from which the change is made, if that deferral period is shorter than three months).

S corporations that elect fiscal years must make "required payments" approximating the amount of tax the shareholders would have paid on income during the deferral period if the corporation had been on a calendar year.

Tax-favored fringe benefits of any employee owning more than two percent of the stock of an S corporation are treated in the same manner as those of a partner in a partnership. Thus, such benefits are taxable to the shareholders, but the corporation receives a deduction for the payment of the benefits. This treatment is less favorable than the treatment available to C corporation shareholder-employees.

An accrual-method S corporation may not deduct interest or an expense item payable to any shareholder until it makes payment and the shareholder includes it in income.[157] This rule applies to all shareholders;[158] it is not limited to those who own more than two percent of the S corporation's stock.

.01 Planning Opportunities

Some additional planning opportunities are discussed below. They are not necessarily listed in the order of importance because

[153] Code Sec. 1361(b)(1).

[154] Code Sec. 1361(c)(1)(A)(ii), as amended by the Gulf Zone Opportunity Act of 2005 (P.L. 109-135)).

[155] Reg. § 1.1361-1(l)(1).

[156] Code Sec. 1362(d)(1).

[157] Code Sec. 267(a)(2).

[158] Code Sec. 267(e).

the importance can vary with the circumstances of the individuals directly involved.

100 shareholders. The 100-shareholder rule allows broad-based equity financing and family income-splitting, without loss of control through the use of nonvoting common stock.

Nonvoting common. The use of nonvoting common stock enables those holding voting common stock to retain control. At the same time, the use of nonvoting common stock might affect valuation for gift and estate tax purposes.

Debt instruments. A debt instrument providing interest geared to an index such as the prime rate may be used without necessarily creating a second class of stock.[159]

New shareholders. Although new shareholders cannot terminate S corporation status by refusing to consent, they may do so by transferring stock to a nonqualified shareholder(s) unless contractually barred.

Passive income. Corporations with income that consists largely, if not entirely, of passive income are not disqualified as they once were. (Corporations with accumulated earnings and profits from regular corporate years are subject to a 25-percent of gross receipts passive income limitation.[160]

Foreign source income. Corporations with gross receipts from foreign sources might want to elect S status.

Election after termination. In general, a corporation may not make a new election within five years of a prior terminated or revoked election without the consent of the IRS.[161] If the termination was inadvertent, the S corporation and its shareholders may take steps to cure the problem and ask the IRS to disregard the inadvertent termination.[162]

Gifts of stock. Shareholders can use gifts of S corporation stock to achieve family income-splitting and tax savings. Income is allocable to shareholders on a per share, per day basis.[163]

.02 Trusts as S Shareholders

Trusts are not eligible shareholders subject to the following exceptions.

---

[159] Code Sec. 1361(c)(5).

[160] Code Sec. 1362(d)(3).

[161] Code Sec. 1362(g).

[162] Code Sec. 1362(f).

[163] Code Sec. 1366(a)(1).

Electing small business trusts. Stock in an S corporation may be held by certain electing small business trusts.[164] Any portion of such a trust that consists of S corporation stock will be treated as a separate trust[165] and will be taxed at the highest rate of tax for estates and trusts.[166] For a small business trust to be an eligible S corporation shareholder, no interest in the trust may be acquired by "purchase" (i.e., acquired with a cost basis).[167] Rather, the interests must be acquired by gift, bequest, or other nonpurchase acquisition.

The Committee Reports to the Small Business Job Protection Act of 1996[168] note that these trusts will facilitate family financial planning by allowing an individual to establish a trust to hold S corporation stock to spread income among family members or other trust beneficiaries.

A nonresident alien may be an eligible beneficiary of an electing small business trust.[169] However, the S election terminates on the date that a nonresident alien becomes a potential current beneficiary of an electing small business trust.[170] If the termination was inadvertent, the S corporation and its shareholders may take steps to cure the problem and ask the IRS to disregard the inadvertent termination.[171]

Grantor trusts. A trust, the grantor of which is treated as the owner under the rules of Code Secs. 671-677, may be a shareholder.[172] A grantor trust may remain an eligible shareholder for a two-year period following the death of the grantor, provided the entire corpus of the trust is includible in the grantor's gross estate.[173] However, a grantor trust is an eligible shareholder only if the grantor would be eligible, i.e., is a citizen or resident of the United States.[174]

Voting trusts. Voting trusts are eligible S shareholders.[175]

Code Sec. 678 trusts. Trusts in which a person other than the grantor is treated as the owner for income tax purposes under Code Sec. 678 are eligible shareholders. Code Sec. 678 provides that a person other than the grantor is to be treated as the owner if such person has the power exercisable solely by himself or herself to vest the corpus or the income therefrom in himself or herself.[176]

"Qualified subchapter S trust." A qualified subchapter S trust is a trust (1) with only one current income beneficiary;

---

[164] Code Sec. 1361(c)(2)(A)(v).
[165] Code Sec. 641(c)(1)(A).
[166] Code Secs. 641(c)(1)(B) and 641(c)(2).
[167] Code Sec. 1361(e)(1)(A)(ii).
[168] P.L. 104-188.
[169] Prop. Reg. § 1.1361-1(m)(1)(E).
[170] Prop. Reg. § 1.1361-1(m)(5)(iii).
[171] Code Sec. 1362(f).
[172] Code Sec. 1361(c)(2)(A)(i).
[173] Code Sec. 1361(c)(2)(A)(ii).
[174] Code Sec. 1361(c)(2)(A)(i).
[175] Code Sec. 1361(c)(2)(A)(iv).
[176] Code Sec. 1361(c)(2)(A)(i).

(2) any corpus to be distributed during the life of the current income beneficiary is to go only to such beneficiary; (3) the income interest of the current income beneficiary is to terminate on the earlier of the beneficiary's death or termination of the trust; and (4) on the termination of the trust during the life of the current beneficiary the trust is to distribute all of its assets to such beneficiary.[177] The beneficiary must elect to be subject to Code Sec. 678.[178]

Certain exempt organizations. Qualified retirement plan trusts described in Code Sec. 401(a) and charitable organizations described in Code Sec. 501(c)(3) are allowed to be S corporation shareholders.[179]

Many trusts commonly used in financial or estate planning will or can be made to fall within the rules allowing them to be shareholders of an S corporation.

.03 Other S Corporation Considerations

Time of election. The election may be made at any time during the prior tax year or on or before the fifteenth day of the third month of the tax year.[180]

S corporations allowed to have subsidiaries. An S corporation is allowed to own 80 percent or more of the stock of a C corporation. However, an S corporation may not elect to file a consolidated return with its affiliated C corporations.[181] In addition, an S corporation may own a qualified S corporation subsidiary.[182]

Some financial institutions may now elect S corporation status. The following types of financial institutions, which do not use the reserve method of accounting for bad debts, may elect S corporation status: (1) domestic building and loan associations, (2) any mutual savings bank, and (3) any cooperative bank without capital stock organized and operated for mutual purposes and without profit.[183]

¶1950 CORPORATE-OWNED LIFE INSURANCE AND THE ESTATE OF A CONTROLLING SHAREHOLDER

The Treasury regulations[184] provide that where the economic benefits of a life insurance policy on a decedent's life are reserved

[177] Code Sec. 1361(d)(3).
[178] Code Sec. 1361(d)(1)(B).
[179] Code Sec. 1361(c)(6).
[180] Code Sec. 1362(b).
[181] House Committee Report to the Small Business Job Protection Act of 1996 (P.L. 104-188).
[182] Code Sec. 1361(b)(3).
[183] Code Sec. 1361(b)(2)(A).
[184] Reg. § 20.2042-1(c)(6).

to a corporation of which the decedent is the sole or controlling stockholder, the corporation's incidents of ownership will not be attributed to the stockholder because of his or her stock ownership if the proceeds are payable to the corporation. Thus, the proceeds would not be included in the decedent's gross estate.[185] However, if the proceeds of an insurance policy the corporation owns on a sole or *controlling* stockholder's life are *not* payable to the corporation (or to a third party for a valid corporate business purpose), the incidents of ownership will be attributed to the insured through his or her stock ownership. Thus, the proceeds would be included in the decedent's gross estate.[186]

.01 Who Is a Controlling Stockholder?

An insured will not be treated as a controlling stockholder under the regulation unless the insured owns stock possessing more than 50 percent of the total combined voting power of the corporation at the time of death. However, if an insured individual owns as little as 51 percent of the outstanding voting stock, 100 percent of the life insurance proceeds on a policy owned by the corporation and not payable to the corporation will be included in the decedent's gross estate.[187]

One way to avoid this result is for the controlling stockholder to make gifts of enough voting shares to reduce his or her voting power to 50 percent or less.

.02 Weighing the Cost of Inclusion

The controlling shareholder will normally be in a position to control whether the insurance proceeds are to be payable to the corporation or to another beneficiary, in whole or in part. If the proceeds are payable in their entirety to the corporation, no part of the proceeds will be includible in the controlling shareholder's gross estate. However, the insurance payable to the corporation increases the value of the insured's shares and of all other shareholders. This result might be better for family members than if the insurance proceeds are made payable to them and includible in the controlling shareholder's gross estate.

If the shareholder decides to retain full control of the corporation but wants the insurance proceeds payable to a named beneficiary other than the corporation or his or her estate, and if the stockholder wants to exclude the insurance proceeds from estate taxation,

---

[185] Code Sec. 2042(2).

[186] Code Sec. 2042(2).

[187] Code Sec. 2042(2).

the corporation must surrender all incidents of ownership in the policy.

If shareholder wants to retain control, he or she might wish to purchase the policy from the corporation (or have the policy distributed as a dividend) and then transfer it and all incidents of ownership in it to a trust or a family member.

Chapter 20

Planning for the Partner

Overview .... ¶2001
The Family Partnership .... ¶2005
Family Limited Partnerships (FLPs) .... ¶2010
Death, Retirement, or Disability of Partner and Disposition of Partnership Interest .... ¶2015
Alternatives for Planning Partnership Successions and Terminations .... ¶2020
Income in Respect of a Decedent Partner .... ¶2025
Valuation of Partnership Interests for Estate Tax Purposes .... ¶2030
Installment Payment of Estate Taxes .... ¶2035
Limited Liability Companies (LLCs) .... ¶2040

¶2001 OVERVIEW

Tax law changes in the late 1980s operated to make partnerships the preferred form for conducting many businesses that traditionally had been conducted in corporate form. These changes included the following:

- The reduction of the top rate of tax for individuals below that of the top rate for regular (C) corporations.
- The repeal of the *General Utilities* doctrine and the resulting tax on corporate liquidations (by comparison, the liquidation of partnerships is usually tax free).
- A tough corporate alternative minimum tax.
- Limitations on the use of cash basis accounting by corporations.

Partnerships may no longer be the preferred form of doing business. The top individual income rate of 35 percent is now equal to the top corporate income tax rate. However, partnerships continue to offer some of the advantages over corporations that are mentioned above, as well as the following:

- Under Code Sec. 721, partners generally recognize no gain on the transfer of property to a partnership (with no requirement, as there is under Code Sec. 351 pertaining to corporations, that transferors own 80 percent of the business to be eligible for nonrecognition of gain).
- The basis of the partner's interest includes the partner's share of the partnership liabilities[1] (not so in either a C or an S corporation).
- Special allocation is permitted for items of income, gain, loss, deductions or credits (not so in either an S or C corporation).[2]
- Partnership interests may reflect different economic interests (not so in an S corporation, which is limited to one class of stock).
- Control can be placed in a preferred group (in an S corporation, the only difference is between voting and nonvoting stock).
- An S corporation cannot have more than 100 shareholders[3] (husband and wife counting as one under Code Sec. 1361(c)(1)). Members of a family may elect to be treated as one shareholder of an S corporation. A partnership is not so limited.
- Partners may receive nontaxable distributions to the extent of their basis in the partnership.[4]

A partnership is not a taxpayer, but it is a pass-through entity under Code Sec. 701. The partnership income is taxed, and the tax is paid at the partner level, even if it is not distributed under Code Sec. 702.

In any case, a partnership must file an income tax return (Form 1065).[5] It must also withhold and remit income, FICA, FUTA, and worker's compensation taxes and other amounts from the wages and salaries of its common-law employees. Partners are jointly and severally liable for any deficiencies and penalties. However, the partners are subject to self-employment tax rather than FICA, income tax withholding, and FUTA.

[1] Code Secs. 752(a) and 722.
[2] Code Sec. 704.
[3] Code Sec. 1361(b)(1).
[4] Code Sec. 731(a).
[5] Reg. § 1.6031-1(a)(1).

Further, audits and challenges to partnership characterizations of items are generally made at the partnership level, not individually with partners. However, a partnership with 10 or fewer partners, all natural persons or estates, is not covered by this provision unless it elects to be.

A partnership generally may not use a fiscal year as its tax year absent a business purpose[6] or the making of required payments under an election discussed at ¶ 1945 in connection with S corporations.[7] The election works the same way for partnerships as it does for S corporations.

.01 Negative Aspects of Partnerships

Probably the greatest disadvantage of a partnership is the liability exposure of the partners. The extent of this liability exposure depends in large part on the nature of the business operations. Insurance is generally available to cover the risk exposure. The partners can also take other steps to reduce the exposure.

Partners might also suffer in the area of employee benefits in comparison with corporate employees. Partners are not generally entitled to the tax-favored benefits accorded corporate employees, except for what may be the most important tax benefit of all, qualified retirement plans. Partners may be participants in Keogh (HR-10) plans as well as a variety of other qualified retirement plans. (¶ 2105). Such plans enjoy essential parity with corporate plans. Partners (and all self-employed persons) are entitled to deduct 100 percent of their health insurance costs.[8] (¶ 1715).

.02 Planning Matters

The family partnership offers opportunities for family income-splitting and estate and gift planning benefits. These benefits are explored below at ¶ 2005.

The most important area in which the financial planner can help the partner is in planning for the continuance or disposition of the partner's partnership interest on death, retirement, or disability. However, the tax provisions dealing with partnerships are among the most complex in the entire Code.

These areas, along with related questions affecting estate tax valuation of partnership interests and the concept of income in respect of a decedent,[9] as applied to partnership interests, are the main components of this chapter.

---

[6] Code Sec. 706(b)(1).
[7] Code Sec. 441(f)(3).
[8] Code Sec. 162(l).
[9] Code Sec. 691(a).

¶ 2005 THE FAMILY PARTNERSHIP

A partnership can be an effective way of splitting income among family members (children, parents, and others). Income splitting can be accomplished either directly or through a trust. (Trusts are favored where there are minor children.) Gifts of partnership interests can also reduce the gross estate of the donor.

Usually, no problems arise with a family partnership where each partner contributes services or capital to the business. Difficulties can arise, however, where a child or other relative who acquired a partnership interest by gift from a partner and who contributes little or nothing in the way of services is a partner. In these cases, if the business is a personal service business in which capital is not a material factor in producing income, the IRS and the courts, generally, refuse to recognize the partnership. They both look upon the arrangement as an attempt to assign income to "separate the fruit from the tree," as the courts sometimes phrase it. The tax law generally does not allow assignment of income.

On the other hand, Code Sec. 704(e)(1) specifically recognizes as a partner a person who *owns a capital interest* in a partnership in which *capital is a material income-producing factor* whether that person purchased the interest or received it by gift. Code Sec. 704(e)(3) states that an interest purchased by one member of a family from another is to be treated as created by gift from the seller, and the fair market value of a purchased interest is to be considered donated capital. Code Sec. 704(e)(3) goes on to say that the "family" of any individual includes the individual's spouse, ancestors, descendants, and any trusts for the primary benefit of such persons.

Code Sec. 704(e)(2) states that, where a partnership interest is created by gift, the donee includes the donee's distributive share of partnership income in gross income, less an allowance for reasonable compensation for services rendered to the partnership by the donor.

The Code provisions clearly sanction the use of family partnerships under certain terms and conditions. Nevertheless, the partnership must prove that it is genuine; that the partner in fact owns a partnership interest; that it is a capital interest; and that capital is a material income-producing factor.

.01 Trusts as Partners

Code Sec. 704(e)(3) expressly includes trusts for family members as permissible partners for tax purposes. Still, the trust may not be recognized for tax purposes unless the trustee actually functions as a fiduciary and administers the trust solely for the beneficiary's best interest.

The state in which the partnership is to be set up must be one of the great majority that permits a trust to be a partner in a business enterprise.

For tax purposes, the same tests used in determining the reality of an individual partner's interest are applied, coupled with special trust factors. In one case, a sole proprietor executed partnership and trust agreements whereby he transferred 15 percent of the business assets to himself as sole trustee of a trust for the benefit of his 10-year-old daughter. The IRS determined, and the courts agreed, that the trust was not a bona fide partner.[10]

.02 Special Rules

Some special rules affecting family partnerships are discussed below.

Contributions of property or money. A partner contributing property will be taxed on built-in gain or loss as of the time of contribution when the property is disposed of by the partnership.[11] Similar rules apply to contributions by a cash-method partner of accounts payable and other accrued but unpaid items.[12]

Character of gain or loss on contributed property. Generally, the character (capital or ordinary) of any gain or loss on the disposition of property by a partnership is determined at the partnership level. However, there are some far-reaching exceptions to this rule to prevent the conversion of ordinary income into capital gain, and capital losses into ordinary deductions, through a contribution of property to a partnership.[13]

Disguised sales. At one time, taxes on the transfer of property could be avoided or deferred, in some cases, if the transfer was accomplished through a contribution to a partnership followed by a tax-free distribution to the contributing partner to the extent of the partner's basis in the partnership. Now, however, a transfer of money or property by a partner to a partnership, when combined with a related transfer of money or property to the contributing partner or another partner, is outside the partnership rules and is treated as a sale between the partner and partnership or two or more partners, as appropriate.[14]

---

[10] *L. Ginsberg*, CA-6, 74-2 USTC ¶9660, 502 F2d 965, aff'g 32 TCM 1019, CCH Dec. 32,168(M), TC Memo. 1973-220.

[11] Code Sec. 704(c)(1).

[12] Code Sec. 704(c)(3).

[13] Code Sec. 724.

[14] Code Sec. 707(a)(2)(B).

.03 S Corporation as an Alternative

In many cases, a client can obtain the tax advantages of splitting income among family members by using an S corporation as an alternative to a family partnership (¶ 1945).

¶ 2010 FAMILY LIMITED PARTNERSHIPS (FLPS)

The family limited partnership (FLP) has had some success—and even more notoriety—in garnering estate, gift, and asset protection advantages. However, the IRS has been fighting the perceived abuses of FLPs. The IRS sees many of the tax breaks claimed in connection with FLPs as inappropriate.

Before suggesting a client use an FLP, the financial planner should exercise great caution, should become thoroughly familiar with the use of the FLP strategy, and should know the most recent applicable decisions and rulings. How successful the IRS will be in a particular case depends on the facts and circumstances. The financial planner should always warn clients about the possible dangers associated with the use of FLPs. Then, if the client decides to proceed in light of these dangers, it will be his or her decision.

.01 Advantages

Reasons advanced for setting up FLPs include the following:

- Favorable estate and gift tax treatment, primarily a result of valuation discounts claimed with respect to the partnership interests.
- Protection from creditors for assets held in the FLP.
- Ease of probate, including the possibility to avoid ancillary probate for out-of-state real property.
- Ability of the transferors (who are typically parents) to retain control over the transferred assets.

.02 Disadvantages

Reasons for caution when setting up FLPs include the following:

- High legal, accounting, and asset appraisal fees, amounting to thousands (or tens of thousands) of dollars.
- Loss of stepped-up basis that would have been available had the transferor parents retained their property until death under Code Sec. 1014(a), because in an FLP transaction, assets are transferred during lifetime, rather than at death. However, for property acquired from a decedent

dying in 2010, the step up in basis is limited to $1,300,000 plus $3,000,000 for property received by a surviving spouse.

- The spirited advancement of several legal theories to defeat or lessen the tax advantages of FLPs.

Discussing all the possible advantages and disadvantages of FLPs is beyond the scope of this chapter. Instead, this chapter will focus on the most important—and most contentious—claimed advantages relating to FLPs: the estate and gift tax breaks and the ability to put partnership assets beyond the reach of creditors.

.03 FLP Basics

Although there are different variations of the FLP, the FLP technique typically involves a husband and wife contributing assets to a limited partnership in exchange for interests in the partnership. Each spouse might receive a very small general partnership interest (equal to one percent of the value of the transferred assets) and a larger limited partnership interest (valued at 49 percent of the value of the transferred assets). They each retain their general partnership interests, but transfer a large portion of the limited partnership interests to their children (each of whom typically only receives a minority interest).

Despite transferring most of the partnership interests, the parents' retention of the general partnership interests gives them control over the operation of the partnership.

.04 Estate and Gift Tax Advantages

Applying valuation principles generally applicable throughout the Internal Revenue Code, the limited partnership interests transferred to the children would be worth significantly less for estate and gift tax purposes than would the same proportionate interest in the underlying assets. The holder of the minority limited partnership interest cannot make decisions about how the partnership is run, demand distributions, or force a liquidation of the partnership. In addition, an interest in a family partnership might be far less marketable than an interest in the underlying assets of the business. Because of these limitations, minority interest and lack of marketability discounts have been allowed on the transfer of interests in an FLP. The combined discount for a minority interest and of marketability has been in the 20 percent to 40 percent range, but in some cases, has been even higher. See, for example, *S. LeFrak Est.*[15] and *J. Barudin Est.*[16]

[15] 66 TCM 1297, CCH Dec. 49,396(M), TC Memo. 1993-526.

[16] 72 TCM 488, CCH Dec. 51,526(M), TC Memo. 1996-395.

.05 The IRS Fights Back

In battling FLPs, the IRS has employed several arguments, usually aimed at disallowing the claimed valuation discounts. Summarized below are some of the legal theories that the IRS may raise in a dispute involving an FLP.

Swing vote premium. An FLP arrangement will normally involve one or more of the transferor's children, each holding minority limited partnership interests. While this fact is central to the FLP's ability to generate a minority discount for such transferred interests, the IRS has raised the issue[17] that the children could combine their interests to create a "swing vote." If a swing vote is possible, the IRS believes the value of each of their limited partnership interests must reflect this power to control the partnership.

Code Sec. 2701 issue. This code section applies if a person transfers an interest in a partnership to or for the benefit of a family member and the transferor or an "applicable family member" retains an interest in the same partnership. If Code Sec. 2701 is applicable, the value of any partnership interest retained by the donor is valued at zero.

> **Planning pointer.** Fortunately for FLPs, Code Sec. 2701 includes an important exception. If the interest retained by the donor is proportionate to the transferred interest, without regard to nonlapsing differences with respect to management and limitations on liability, the zero value rule does not apply. Thus, an FLP agreement should give the same proportional rights to the transferors and the transferees with respect to income, gain, loss, and deductions.[18]

Code Sec. 2703 and the sham transaction doctrine. In IRS Technical Advice Memorandum 9719006, the IRS launched a major attack on FLPs. This ruling involved a transferor who held assets in a revocable trust. When she died, the trust property, as well as the property in a marital trust established by her predeceased husband, was to be divided equally between her son and daughter. The property of both of these trusts would be included in the transferor's gross estate at her death.

An FLP was formed two days before the transferor's death when she was terminally ill and had been taken off life support. The transferor's son and daughter each contributed about $33,000

[17] IRS Technical Advice Memorandum 9436005, May 26, 1994.

[18] Code Sec. 2701(a)(2).

in cash for a one-percent general partnership interest each. The transferor's revocable trust and her marital trust contributed over $2,259,000 to acquire the 98 percent limited partnership interests.

Immediately after formation of the partnership, the marital trust transferred two 30-percent limited partnership interests, one to each of the transferor's children, in exchange for $10,000 cash and a 30-year promissory note for $486,000.

On the deceased transferor's estate tax return, a 40-percent discount was applied to the promissory notes from the children. The partnership interests held by the transferor's trusts on the date of her death were valued at about 70 percent of the value of the underlying partnership assets. The result was that assets having a value of about $2,259,000 on one date were valued at only $1,177,000 two days later.

The IRS first disallowed the valuation discounts based on the sham transaction doctrine. Here, the IRS pointed out that because the son and daughter were the only beneficiaries under their mother's two trusts, they would have received all of the assets transferred into the partnership. Likewise, their promissory notes would be distributed to them, as trust beneficiaries, in effect canceling them. The IRS concluded that nothing of substance changed by reason of the FLP transaction. Thus, the FLP was to be disregarded for transfer tax purposes.

The second argument that the IRS invoked to disallow the claimed discounts was based on Code Sec. 2703. This section provides that the value of property is determined without regard to any option, agreement, or other restriction on the right to sell or use such property. Within this context, the partnership agreement was deemed to be a restriction within the meaning of Code Sec. 2703. Therefore, any reduction in value caused by the partnership agreement was to be disregarded unless the bona fide business arrangement exception of Code Sec. 2703(b) applied.

Under Code Sec. 2703(b), the general rule of Code Sec. 2703 does not apply to any option, agreement, right, or restriction that (1) is a bona fide business arrangement, (2) is not a device to transfer property to members of the transferor's family for less than full and adequate consideration, and (3) has terms comparable to those in similar arrangements entered into by persons in arm's-length transactions.

Not surprisingly, the IRS ruled that the bona fide business arrangement exception did not apply to the facts in Technical Advice Memorandum 9719006. The IRS concluded that even if the taxpayer had a legitimate business purpose for the FLP transaction (such as creditor protection), the facts showed that the transaction was entered into primarily for the purpose of artificially reducing the value of the transferor's gross estate. Thus, it was to be regarded as a device to transfer property to members of the transferor's family for less than adequate consideration in money or money's worth.

Application of Code Sec. 2704. The IRS has also raised objections to FLP valuation discounts based on subsections (a) and (b) of Code Sec. 2704. The Code Sec. 2704(a) trap is the easier one for planners to avoid. Financial planners can avoid this trap by making sure that the partnership agreement does not contain any lapsing voting or liquidation rights. (If it does, the FLP-related transfers will be subject to transfer tax, if the transferor and members of the transferor's family control the partnership before and after the lapse.)

Code Sec. 2704(b) provides that if a transfer of an interest in a partnership to a member of the transferor's family occurs and immediately after the transfer the transferor and members of the transferor's family control the entity, any applicable restriction is disregarded in determining the value of the transferred interest. For this purpose, an applicable restriction is defined as one that effectively limits the ability of the partnership to liquidate and with respect to which the transferor or any member of the transferor's family has the right after the transfer to remove, in whole or in part, the restriction.

The IRS applied Code Sec. 2704(b) to deny FLP valuation discounts in IRS Technical Advice Memorandum 9725002 and Letter Ruling 9723009 where the applicable restriction was a partnership provision that restricted partners from withdrawing from the partnership. Application of Code Sec. 2704(b) to such a situation turns on whether a limited partner's ability to liquidate his or her interest is to be equated with a partnership liquidation. The estates in the rulings argued "no." Rejecting their contentions, the IRS pointed to Reg. § 25.2704-2(b), which defines an applicable restriction as a limitation on the ability to liquidate an entity in whole or in part. Citing Example 5 of Reg. § 25.2704-2(d), the IRS concluded that a restriction on the rights of individual partners to liquidate was a limitation on the entity to liquidate in part.

Inclusion of interest in gross estate. Even if the FLP-related lifetime transfers withstand IRS scrutiny or attack, the IRS might still assert that the transferred interests should be included in the transferor's gross estate at death. Code Sec. 2036(a) mandates inclusion in the donor's gross estate of lifetime transfers that are not for full and adequate consideration in money or money's worth in which the donor retains for life or for a period which does not, in fact, end before his or her death: (1) the possession or enjoyment of, or the right to the income from, the property, or (2) the right to designate the persons who are to possess or enjoy the property or the income therefrom.[19]

If structured properly, the donor in an FLP situation can probably be given a substantial amount of control over the partnership business without the donee's interests' being includible in the donor's gross estate at death. However, if the controls retained by the donor are not commonly found in normal business relationships, the donee's interests will likely be includible in the donor's gross estate under the rules of Code Sec. 2036(a).

Code Sec. 2036(a) will also apply if an express or implied understanding exists at the time of the transfer that the transferor will retain the economic benefits of the partnership property. A number of appellate courts have recently required inclusion of FLP assets in the donor's gross estates on the grounds that an implied agreement existed under which the donor retained lifetime enjoyment and economic benefit of the assets.[20]

.06 Investment FLPs

The viability of FLPs funded by investment property, rather than by business property, is in doubt. First, whether the valuation discounts that have been allowed with respect to FLPs housing business interests will also apply to investment FLPs is unclear. The investment FLP would also seem vulnerable to IRS attack based on its failing the business purpose test required for partnership treatment under the tax law.

Transfers of business property to a partnership in exchange for partnership interests are generally tax free.[21] However, if the partnership is such that it would be treated as an investment company under Code Sec. 351 if it were incorporated, gain or loss will be recognized on such transfers for partnership interests.[22]

All of the other arguments discussed under the heading "The IRS Fights Back" (¶ 2010.05) would also apply to investment FLPs.

---

[19] *A. Strangi Est.*, 115 TC 478 (2000), aff'd in part, rev'd in part, rem'd in part, 2002-2 USTC ¶ 60,441 (CA-5, 2002); *Harper Est.*, 83 TCM 1641 (2002); *D. A. Kimbrell, Sr.* et al. (DC N.Tex., 2003).

[20] *Est. of Thompson*, CA-3,94 AFTR 2d 2004–5764 (September 9, 2004); gulig, CA-5, 96 AFTR 2d 2005-5048 (July 15, 2005); *Est. of Abraham*, CA-1, 95 AFTR 2d 2005-1018 (May 25, 2005);.

[21] Code Sec. 721(a).

[22] Code Sec. 721(b).

.07 Protection Against Creditors

Although the matter varies greatly with applicable local law, an FLP stands to impede a creditor's ability to reach the underlying partnership assets. At a minimum, the expected delays and legal fees might give the FLP partners the ability to negotiate a better deal with their creditors. Where local partnership and debt collection provisions are particularly debtor-friendly, the creditor may never be able to reach the assets, at least not on terms that would be economically worthwhile. A creditor might be able to obtain only a charging order, which gives the creditor rights to any distributions made by the partnership to the limited partner. The IRS treats a creditor with a charging order as a substituted partner.[23] Therefore, the holder of the charging order will receive a Schedule K-1 for the holder's distributive share of the partnership's income. Thus, the creditor is taxed on income that the creditor might never receive.

The shield of the FLP is certainly not complete, and the financial planner should warn clients already in financial distress about contributing assets to an FLP in hopes of avoiding creditor collections.[24]

¶2015 DEATH, RETIREMENT, OR DISABILITY OF PARTNER AND DISPOSITION OF PARTNERSHIP INTEREST

The death or retirement of a partner because of age or disability will usually have important human and economic consequences. Death or disability of a partner can also have profound legal and tax consequences. Under state law, unless the partnership agreement otherwise provides, the death or retirement of a partner terminates the partnership and requires a distribution of the partnership's assets to the partners or their successors in interest. This process of dissolution and liquidation of the partnership can result in a severe loss in values through forced sales, dissipation of going concern value and goodwill, and loss of jobs for the survivors. Dissolution of the partnership is clearly something that most clients will want to avoid. The partners may agree to continue the partnership in the event of the death or retirement of a partner.

---

[23] Rev. Rul. 77-137, 1977-1 CB 178, *D.L. Evans*, CA-7, 71-2 USTC ¶9597, 447 F.2d 547, aff'g 54 TC 40.

[24] See *In re Tai*, BC-DC Fla., 96-2 USTC ¶50,547.

The four basic alternatives on the death or retirement of a partner are as follows:

1. A sale of the deceased or retiring partner's interest to the remaining partners.
2. A sale of the interest to a new partner.
3. A distribution to the deceased partner's estate (or successor in interest) or to the retiring partner in liquidation of the partnership interest. This really amounts to a sale to the partnership, but it has vastly different tax consequences.
4. The estate or successor in interest of a deceased partner may continue as a partner.

The partnership should consider certain practical factors in choosing among these alternatives. Can a new partner be found to buy the interest? Will a newcomer be able to handle a partner's responsibilities? Will the new partner fit in with the remaining partners? If the executor is to continue holding an interest in the partnership, similar questions of competency apply. Also, the executor's holding of a partnership interest can only be a temporary solution, assuming the executor is willing to assume the personal responsibility and liability involved. An heir or successor in interest who continues to hold a partnership interest involves even more difficult questions of competency, personality, and responsibility.

The estate planner should not overlook or minimize these practical considerations. However, the estate planner must also look at tax considerations.

The estate planner must consider estate tax consequences and income tax consequences. This paragraph treats estate tax consequences only incidentally, but they are examined in greater detail in ¶ 2020.

If the retiring partner, the estate, or the successor in interest of a deceased partner sells the partnership interest to the remaining partners, the tax law treats the sale as a sale of a capital asset.[25] The retiring partner receives capital gain or loss treatment on the sale of the partnership interest, except to the extent of payments for unrealized receivables or inventory items.[26]

In case of death, a deceased partner's estate or successor in interest receives the same treatment. On death, the tax basis of the interest of the deceased partner is stepped up to its fair market

[25] Code Sec. 741.

[26] Code Sec. 741.

value at the date of death (or the alternate valuation date).[27] However, for property acquired from a decedent dying in 2010, the step up in basis is limited to $1,300,000 plus $3,000,000 for property received by a surviving spouse.

.01 Complete Liquidation of Interest of Retiring or Deceased Partner

A complete liquidation of the retiring or deceased partner's interest usually has entirely different tax consequences under rules contained in Code Sec. 736. Under Code Sec. 736(a), payments made in liquidation of the interest of a partner who has retired or died are generally treated as a distributive share of the partnership's income or as a guaranteed payment. The payments are a distributive share of the partnership's income if they are based on the partnership's income. The payments are treated as guaranteed payments if the partnership determines the payments without regard to the income of the partnership. However, under Code Sec. 736(b)(2), liquidation payments for goodwill and unrealized receivables generally are treated as made in exchange for the partner's interest in partnership property and not as a distributive share or guaranteed payment that could give rise to a deduction or its equivalent. This rule does not apply to payments made to a general partner in a service-type partnership, such as a medical, legal, accounting, or architectural firm, and the change does not affect the deductibility of compensation paid to a retiring partner for past services.[28]

Rules for unrealized receivables. Payments made for unrealized receivables (other than unbilled amounts and accounts receivable) are treated as made in exchange for the partner's interest in partnership property. Thus, for example, a payment for depreciation recapture is treated as made in exchange for an interest in partnership property and not as a distributive share or guaranteed payment that could give rise to a deduction or its equivalent.[29]

> **Planning pointer.** The special treatment of liquidation payments made for goodwill and unrealized receivables provides a great deal of planning flexibility for payments made to a general partner in a service partnership. In such situations, the parties can determine the extent to which payments for goodwill are to be treated as ordinary income or as capital gain. If the remaining partners are in the top income tax bracket, they may prefer to have the payments treated as deductible ordinary income. On the

[27] Code Sec. 751(a).
[28] Code Sec. 736(b)(3).
[29] Code Secs. 736(b)(2) and 751(c).

other hand, departing partners might prefer to have payments specifically allocated to goodwill. Such payments would not be taxable as ordinary income to the retiree, a deceased partner's estate, or successor and would not be deductible by the partnership, but would be taxed as capital gain. For payments to an estate, the estate is able to take advantage of a basis step-up on the death of the departing partner.[30] However, for property acquired from a decedent dying in 2010, the step up in basis is limited to $1,300,000 plus $3,000,000 for property received by a surviving spouse.

.02 Gain or Loss Attributable to Unrealized Receivables and Inventory Items

Money or property received in exchange for all or part of a partnership interest attributable to unrealized receivables or inventory items is treated as an amount realized from the sale or exchange of property that is not a capital asset. Thus, the sale or exchange of such property will result in ordinary income or loss under Code Sec. 751(a). The value is measured by the difference between the amount realized for the partnership interest allocated to these items and the portion of the selling or liquidating partner's basis attributable to these items.

Generally, the portion of the total amount realized that the parties allocate to these items in an arm's-length agreement will be regarded as correct.[31]

Unrealized receivables are rights to payment for goods or services, delivered or rendered or to be delivered or rendered.[32] However, unrealized receivables also include depreciation on real and personal property subject to recapture under Code Secs. 1250 and 1245. Such amounts are treated as made in exchange for the partner's interest in partnership property.[33] The term "inventory" includes not only stock in trade but also accounts receivable.[34]

.03 Fixing a Price for Sale or Liquidation

Valuing a partnership interest and fixing a price for a buy-sell agreement or partnership buy-out by liquidation are difficult. Reciting the factors the estate tax regulations take into account is easy. Reg. § 20.2031-3 says to look for the net amount a willing buyer would pay to a willing seller, both having reasonable knowledge of all

[30] Code Sec. 1014(a).

[31] Reg. § 1.751-1(a)(2).

[32] Reg. § 1.751-1(c).

[33] Code Sec. 751(c).

[34] Reg. § 1.751-1(d)(2)(ii).

relevant factors including a fair appraisal of the assets, tangible and intangible, including goodwill, the economic outlook of the industry, proceeds of life insurance, earning capacity, and other items.

However, different partners can look at all of the relevant factors, and each one will probably have a different opinion of value. Fixing the value or price among the partners becomes a matter of negotiation. The parties might negotiate one price on death, another on retirement, and still another on disability on the basis of different needs.

Buy-sell agreements may establish value for transfer tax purposes if they meet rules contained in Code Sec. 2703 (discussed at ¶2310).

Because of the possibility of wide-ranging fluctuations of value, the partners might give some thought to providing a disabled partner or a deceased partner's widow(er) with some participation in the recovery of earnings, if cyclical low earnings produce an unrealistically low price. These and other considerations specially tailored for the particular firm should be on the negotiating table. Provisions for periodic review of a stated value run the risk of delay by those satisfied with the last price fixed. The partners can supplement such provisions with an independent arbitration to decide any disagreement.

.04 Disability

Any agreement among the partners themselves or with the partnership for the sale or liquidation of their interests on death or retirement should normally also provide for disposition of the interest on disability. Disability calls for special attention in these following key areas:

- Defining disability.
- When transfer is to take place.
- Effect of recovery and recurrence.
- Removal from management.
- Price—Price may be the same as on death or retirement. What is the date of valuation? When does disability begin? When does the transfer take place?
- Death before completion of payments.
- Funding—If insurance is used, the funding will follow the pattern of the sale or liquidation on the death of a partner. It will either be a cross-purchase type of arrangement or an entity arrangement.
- Death or disability of two or more partners—If the partnership is small, and a key partner dies while another is out on disability, the partners should consider a dissolution of the partnership.

.05 Use of Insurance to Fund Agreement

Insurance funding will commonly play a part in whatever form of agreement is used to buy or liquidate a partnership interest. In some agreements, insurance is employed simply to furnish funds to the remaining partners or the partnership to make the acquisition. Any excess insurance may be retained by the partnership or the remaining partners or be paid to the estates of the deceased partners. In some cases, the insurance proceeds are made payable to the estate or beneficiary of the deceased partner. A partner might also hold a policy on his or her own life naming the remaining partners as beneficiaries, so that they will have funds with which to purchase the deceased partner's interest. The comparison of planning alternatives at the end of this section describes and evaluates the effects of various common insurance arrangements.

Financial planners should keep the following general considerations in mind in planning insurance:

- With a cross-purchase agreement, usually each partner buys a separate policy on the life of each of the other partners and pays the premiums, which are not tax deductible.[35] The younger members of the partnership bear a heavy premium burden unless some adjustment is made.
- With a partnership buy-out or liquidation agreement, the partnership usually buys a separate policy on the life of each partner and pays the premiums, which are not tax deductible.[36]
- The policy proceeds, in either case, are normally received free of income tax.[37]
- If the policy proceeds are made payable to the estate of the deceased partner, the financial planner should consider the matter of a possible excess or deficiency of the proceeds in relation to the fixed price for the interest to be acquired. Also, the financial planner should consider a possible attempt on the part of the IRS to include both the insurance proceeds and the value of the partnership interest in the gross estate of the deceased partner. Proper draftsmanship, making clear that the insurance proceeds are in payment for the partnership interest under a binding agreement with lifetime restrictions on transfer, will prevent double inclusion.
- The insured could own the policy with the proceeds payable to the surviving partners or the partnership. In such a case,

[35] Code Sec. 264.

[36] Code Sec. 264.

[37] Code Sec. 101(a).

the financial planner should exercise great caution to be sure that the insured is divested of all incidents of ownership in the policy to avoid having the proceeds includible in the insured's gross estate under Code Sec. 2042.[38]

- To reduce costs, term insurance and loans against cash policies can be used. If loans are to be used, the financial planner should be mindful of the rule barring deduction of interest payments generally[39] unless four of the first seven annual premiums are paid without borrowing.[40] Effective for contracts purchased after June 20, 1986, a taxpayer may deduct only the interest paid or accrued on the first $50,000.[41] And for "modified endowment" contracts[42] entered into after June 20, 1988, loans are treated as distributions taxable on a last-in-first-out (LIFO) basis,[43] and generally subject to a 10 percent additional tax if made before age 59½.[44]

A trust might help to hold down a partner's cost of carrying insurance on the lives of the other partners. The partner could, for example, buy a policy on partner A's life and transfer it to a trust along with sufficient income-producing property to generate enough income to pay the premiums. The partner should not be the insured or beneficiary of the policy, because Code Sec. 677 would treat the trust's income as taxable to the partner.

.06 Provision for Payment of Share of Post-mortem Profits

Sometimes an agreement will provide that the estate of a deceased partner be paid a share of the partnership's profits following death. This agreement might be the exclusive basis of payment or it might supplement other payments. Unless the agreement provides for the payment for goodwill, these payments would be taxable as income in respect of a decedent.[45] Apparently, these payments would also be includible in the gross estate to the extent of their value on the date of the decedent's death.[46] If the payments are to be paid over a period of years, difficult valuation problems arise.

.07 Adjusting Basis of Partnership Assets

By making a special election under Code Sec. 754, a partnership can adjust the basis of its assets when a change in partnership

[38] Reg. § 20.2042-1(c), IRS Letter Ruling 8610068 (December 11, 1985), *B. L. Fuchs Est.*, 47 TC 199 (1966), *Noel Est.*, 380 U.S. 678 (1965).

[39] Code Sec. 264(a).

[40] Code Sec. 264(d).

[41] Code Sec. 264(e)(1).

[42] Code Sec. 7702A(a).

[43] Code Sec. 72(e).

[44] Code Sec. 72(v).

[45] Code Sec. 691(a).

[46] Code Sec. 2031(a).

interests occurs. However, this adjustment will affect only the partner to whom an interest is transferred, not the other partners. If the election is in force, the adjusted basis of the partnership assets is increased by any excess of the adjusted basis to the transferee of the interest acquired over the partner's share of the adjusted basis of all partnership assets.[47]

> ***Example 20.1.*** Assume that Carrie Thomas pays $30,000 for Albert Jones' 50-percent interest in a partnership, which has assets with a basis of $40,000. Thomas has paid $10,000 [$30,000 – ($40,000 × 50%)] in excess of the basis for a share of partnership assets. This $10,000 is added to the basis of partnership assets for the benefit of Thomas only.

The election may be made even after a partnership has been terminated on account of the sale of a 50-percent interest, provided the election is made on a timely filed return for the final year.[48]

If the election is in effect and the adjusted basis of partnership property exceeds the transferee's basis for the partnership interest, then basis is to be reduced in a similar manner.[49] Therefore, the partnership should make the special election only after careful consideration of its potential advantages and disadvantages.

¶ 2020 ALTERNATIVES FOR PLANNING PARTNERSHIP SUCCESSIONS AND TERMINATIONS

This chapter has examined the income tax considerations affecting planning for partnership successions by way of sale or liquidation of partnership interests and insurance programs. However, this chapter has not discussed estate tax considerations to any considerable extent. Neither has this chapter discussed the alternatives to dissolution of the partnership or the continuance of the partnership by the executor or heir of a deceased partner.

The key factors affecting each of the basic approaches suggested at the outset as the basis of an overall comparison are discussed below.

.01 Purchase of the Decedent's Interest by the Surviving Partners—Unfunded Agreement

The surviving partners are apt to provide the best market for the interest of one of the partners. The agreement should be made in advance for the best tax and practical results.

---

[47] Code Sec. 743(b).

[48] Rev. Rul. 88-42, 1988-1 CB 265.

[49] Code Sec. 743(b).

Estate tax consequences. The buy-sell agreement fixing the sale price should determine the estate tax value, provided the agreement contains a lifetime restriction on transfer and meets rules contained in Code Sec. 2703 (discussed at ¶ 2310).

Income tax consequences. The tax year of a partner terminates on the date that the partner's interest in the partnership terminates, whether by death, sale, or otherwise.[50] However, the partnership itself does not terminate unless the partnership no longer carries on a business or there is a sale or exchange of at least 50 percent or more of the total interest in the partnership within a 12-month period.[51]

The estate of the decedent will usually not realize any gain on the sale of the decedents's partnership interest to the surviving partners. The basis of the interest is stepped up to the estate tax valuation,[52] and the amount the estate receives will be the estate tax valuation of the interest. However, Code Sec. 1014(c) does not allow the step up in basis for any property that represents income in respect of a decedent under Code Sec. 691(a) (¶ 2025). In addition, for property acquired from a decedent dying in 2010, the step up in basis is limited to $1,300,000 plus $3,000,000 for property received by a surviving spouse.

The survivors must use their own funds to buy the decedent's interest. The amount they pay increases their basis in the partnership.[53] In addition, if the surviving partners share of the partnership's liabilities increases, their bases in their respective partnership interests will likewise increase.[54] If the payment to the estate results in the estate's relinquishing its interest in appreciated assets, the survivors may elect, under Code Secs. 743(b) and 754, to increase the adjusted basis of the partnership property by the amount paid for the decedent's interest in excess of the decedent's proportionate share of the partnership's basis for its assets.

> ***Example 20.2.*** Assume that the Abel Baker Campo partnership has $10,000 in cash and an asset with a tax basis of $5,000 which is worth $20,000. Assume that Baker dies and Abel and Campo pay Baker's estate $10,000 for Baker's interest, or $5,000 over the tax basis of the partnership assets. Abel and Campo, by making the required election, may increase the tax basis of the partnership assets by $5,000.

---

[50] Code Sec. 706(c)(2)(A).
[51] Code Sec. 708(b)(1).
[52] Code Sec. 1014(a).
[53] Code Sec. 1012.
[54] Code Secs. 722 and 752(a).

If the estate's interest in the partnership is 50 percent or more, a sale to the surviving partners will cause a termination of the partnership for income tax purposes.[55]

.02 Purchase of Decedent's Interest by the Surviving Partners—Funded Agreement

The buy-out agreement may be funded in various ways, but insurance is almost always the medium. When the partners use insurance, a variety of alternatives exists as to ownership of the policies, beneficiaries, and payment of premiums. Three possible variants are as follows.

Policy owned by surviving partners and proceeds payable to them. The estate tax consequences and income tax consequences discussed above in connection with an unfunded buy-sell agreement apply here as well. The survivors increase the basis of their interests by the amount paid to the estate and by any increase in their share of the partnership's liabilities.[56] Only the value of the partnership interest should be includible in the decedent's gross estate, not the insurance proceeds.

Policy owned by the survivors and the estate is the beneficiary. The partnership agreement or cross-purchase agreement among the partners might provide that the partnership interest is to be transferred for the insurance proceeds and no further payment is to be made.

One of the advantages of this approach is that the proceeds are payable directly to the estate without going through the survivor's hands, thus seemingly removing the risk of diversion of the funds to other purposes. Doubt exists whether the survivors can increase their income tax basis in this way.

Survivors own the policy with the proceeds payable to an heir. In this method, the insurance proceeds would be payable directly to the decedent's heir. Whether or not this approach would succeed remains undecided, and estate planners should carefully consider its consequences before recommending it to clients.

.03 Insurance Funding of Payments in Liquidation of a Deceased Partner's Interest

Example 20.3. Assume that a three-partner law firm carries $60,000 in term insurance on Jake Shaw's life payable to the partnership. If, on Shaw's death, his surviving spouse receives

[55] Code Sec. 708(b)(1)(B).

[56] Code Sec. 1012.

$35,000 for his interest, the partnership, instead of obtaining an after-tax cost of $35,000 on the payments made to Shaw's surviving spouse, would show a $25,000 "profit," less its investment in the insurance premiums. If the agreement were to provide that the insurance proceeds were to be allocated to the capital accounts of the surviving partners, each of the two surviving partners would increase the basis of his or her partnership interest by $30,000. The partnership could also allocate a portion of the proceeds to the deceased partner's account, say one-third, or $20,000. This allocation would serve to decrease the Code Sec. 736(a) payments and increase the Code Sec. 736(b) payments. Furthermore, the partnership agreement could allow payment for goodwill, which would affect the allocations under Code Sec. 736(a) and (b).

If the partnership owns the policy and the estate is the beneficiary, the decedent's gross estate might include both the insurance proceeds and the value of the partnership interest. However, this potential double inclusion should be manageable with a properly drawn agreement that clearly provides that the insurance proceeds are in full liquidation of the decedent's interest.

Other problems of this plan include determining whether the survivors' bases may be increased by their share of the proceeds. If the premiums have all been charged to the decedent's capital account, then Code Sec. 736 is completely avoided. The proceeds would be includible in the decedent's gross estate, but there would be no income tax. The surviving partners would not be able to increase the bases of their interests. If the partnership allocated the premiums paid to the capital accounts of each partner, the survivors should be able to increase their bases by an allocable portion of the proceeds.

.04 Estate, Heir, or Successor Continuing as Partner

With this approach, no formula fixes the value of the decedent's interest. Thus, one can expect the IRS to argue for a high valuation for estate tax purposes. The IRS would likely add goodwill to net asset value and value the business as a going concern, unless the interest qualifies for the marital deduction.

Furthermore, using this approach does not result in any income tax consequences for either the surviving partners, the estate, or other successors to the decedent's interest, except as the estate or other successors receive a stepped-up basis for the interest acquired (limited for property acquired from a decedent dying in 2010 as noted previously).

.05 Dissolution of the Partnership

From an estate tax point of view, an estate planner might argue that, on dissolution, only the net asset value of the decedent's share should be valued. However, the IRS looks at the value of the business as a going concern, which is the price a willing buyer would pay and a willing seller would accept for the assets, goodwill, and demonstrated earning capacity of the interest.

From an income tax standpoint, enjoying the flexibility allowed by Code Sec. 736 upon liquidation of the decedent's interest is not possible. Any excess over basis, received by the decedent's estate or other successor is treated as capital gain under Code Secs. 731 and 732, except for unrealized receivables and inventory items, which are taxable as ordinary income under Code Sec. 751. The partnership may elect under Code Sec. 754 to make the optional adjustments to basis permitted under Code Sec. 743. This election permits the partnership to increase the basis of partnership property by the excess of the basis of the decedent's interest in the partnership over the decedent's proportionate share of the adjusted basis of the partnership property.

¶ 2025 INCOME IN RESPECT OF A DECEDENT PARTNER

Because most individuals are on the cash basis method of accounting, they cannot report income until they have received it. If an individual dies before receiving income, the person who receives the income realized by the decedent must include the amount in gross income as income in respect of a decedent (IRD) under Code Sec. 691(a).

In a partnership setting, IRD includes payments considered as a distributive share or guaranteed payment in liquidation of a deceased partner's interest within the reach of Code Sec. 736(a). IRD may also include payments for goodwill in such liquidations, if no special allocation is made for goodwill, and payments for unrealized receivables and inventory items. Income in respect of a decedent would also encompass a share in the partnership profits earned after the partner's death and payable under a pre-death agreement.

IRD is thus includible in the income tax return of the estate or the eventual recipient. It is also includible in the decedent's estate tax return.[57] However, the person taxable on this income is allowed a full income tax deduction for the estate tax attributable to the inclusion of

[57] Code Sec. 2031(a).

the income in the gross estate.[58] The method of computing this deduction is set out in Code Sec. 691(c)(2). The deduction is of value only to the recipient and not to other beneficiaries of the estate who might be the ones who bear the burden of the estate taxes.

An estate planner can recommend a number of important steps to soften the impact of IRD:

- Consider the prospective income tax position of the possible recipients of IRD. Consider giving the IRD or some part of it to family members in lower income tax brackets, spreading it among multiple beneficiaries.
- The choice of a charity as recipient saves both estate taxes and income taxes.
- If the executor is to receive IRD, the decedent's will should give the executor the right to distribute IRD before receiving it to spread it among recipients in low income tax brackets.
- Consider making a specific bequest of the partnership interest and having the bequest distributed before the end of the estate's taxable year, or provide in the partnership agreement that specific beneficiaries, rather than the estate, are to succeed to the interest.
- If the IRD is payable to the estate, the estate's choice of a fiscal year can prevent bunching of income where the estate anticipates that certain IRD payments will be received in one month and other IRD payments in later months.

¶ 2030 VALUATION OF PARTNERSHIP INTERESTS FOR ESTATE TAX PURPOSES

Valuation of a partnership interest for the purpose of fixing a price for a buy-sell or buy-out agreement is difficult. If the agreement is binding on all parties, and they are not free to dispose of their interests during life, the price stated in the agreement should be used as the basis for estate tax valuation. Agreements entered into after October 8, 1990, must meet special requirements in order to fix value. These requirements are discussed in ¶ 2310.

Absent an agreement, the executor must determine the fair market value of the interest at the date of death or the alternate valuation date. The executor must weigh all relevant factors, such as the nature of the business, general economic outlook in the industry, book value, financial condition, proven earning capacity, and intangibles such as goodwill.

[58] Code Sec. 691(c)(1).

Even though dissolution and discontinuance of the partnership business is the route chosen, one might think the IRS would look solely to net asset value, without regard to going concern value or goodwill. However, the IRS wants to value the partnership interest at its fair market value or the price that a willing buyer would pay and a willing seller accept.[59]

In CCH's *IRS Valuation Training for Appeals Officers* coursebook, the IRS says that the appraisal of partnership interests does not vary greatly from the valuation of closely held stock (¶ 1940), except for certain accounting distinctions.

.01 Valuation of Business Real Estate

Under certain conditions, the executor may elect to value real property included in the decedent's gross estate, which is devoted to closely held business use, based on use of the property in the closely held business, rather than at its fair market value based on its highest and best use.[60] There is a limit on the aggregate decrease in the value of qualified real property resulting from the election to use the special use valuation method.[61] For the estate of a decedent dying in calendar year 2006, the aggregate decreased in value may not exceed $900,000.[62]

This section requires that the owner or a member of the owner's family materially participate in the operation of the business for specified periods, both before and after the decedent's death. A surviving spouse's active participation in management will suffice.[63]

The Secretary of the Treasury is directed to prescribe regulations for the application of this rule to situations involving real estate held by a partnership. As to the decedent, a partnership is a closely held business as defined in Code Sec. 6166(b)(1), if 20 percent or more of the total capital interest in the partnership is included in the decedent's gross estate. In addition, a partnership which has no more than 45 partners is a closely-held business for purposes of Code Sec. 2032A.

The Treasury regulations provide that, in applying the requirement of material participation to partnerships, activities in the management and operation of the real estate component of the business as a whole are determinative.[64] The time and manner of making the special election are the subject of a Treasury regulation.[65]

---

[59] Code Sec. 2031(a) and Reg.§ 20.2031-3.

[60] Code Sec. 2032A.

[61] Code Sec. 2032A(a)(2) and (3).

[62] Rev. Proc. 2005-70, 2005-47 IRB 979 (October 28, 2005).

[63] Code Sec. 2032A(b)(1).

[64] Reg. § 20.2032A-3(f)(2).

[65] Reg. § 20.2032A-8.

For a discussion of how this provision is to be applied when business real estate is held directly by the decedent and of the conditions attached to the election, see ¶2110.

¶2035 INSTALLMENT PAYMENT OF ESTATE TAXES

If the value of an interest in a closely held business exceeds 35 percent of the value of the adjusted gross estate (gross value reduced by allowable expenses, losses and debts),[66] the executor may elect to pay the estate taxes attributable to the business interest in 2 or more but not more than 10 annual installments. The installment payments must be equal. If the executor makes the election to pay such estate taxes in installments, the first installment payment is due not more than 5 years after the prescribed date for paying estate taxes. The maximum payment period is 14 years, rather than 15 years, because the due date for the last payment of interest is the same date as the due date for the first installment payment of the tax.[67] This provision allows the estate to defer the estate taxes attributable to the business interest for up to 14 years with a special two-percent interest rate applicable to the estate taxes on the first $1,000,000[68] (indexed for inflation after 1998 under Code Sec. 6601(j)(3)) in taxable value of the closely held business. For the estate of a decedent dying in 2006, the inflation-adjusted amount is $1,200,000. In the case of a partnership interest, in addition to the 35-percent test, the partnership must have no more than 45 partners *or* 20 percent or more of the total capital interest in the partnership must be included in the decedent's gross estate.[69] For the purpose of meeting the 20-percent requirement, partnership interests held by members of the decedent's family, as well as the decedent's own interest, are to be counted.[70] Family members are spouse, children and grandchildren, parents, brothers and sisters.[71] These attribution rules are not applicable in determining the number of partners.

If the estate obtains this 14-year extension for payment of taxes, the estate must pay only interest annually during the first four years. The estate may pay the tax owed in annual installments with interest over the next 10 years. Interest is charged at the rate of only two percent on the estate tax attributable to the first $1,000,000 (indexed for inflation after 1998 under Code Sec. 6601(j)(3)) in taxable value.[72] The inflation-adjusted amount for the estate of a decedent dying in 2006 is $1,200,000. However, if the amount of the estate tax extended

[66] Code Sec. 6166(b)(6).

[67] Code Secs. 6166(a)(3) and 6166(f)(1).

[68] Code Sec. 6601(j)(1)(A).

[69] Code Sec. 6166(b)(1)(B).

[70] Code Sec. 6166(b)(2)(D).

[71] Code Secs. 6166(b)(2)(D) and 267(c)(4).

[72] Code Sec. 6601(j)(1)(A).

under Code Sec. 6166 is less than this amount, only the lower amount qualifies for the special two-percent rate.[73] Any amounts deferred that are in excess of the amount that qualifies for the two-percent rate (called the "two-percent amount") are taxed at a rate equal to 45 percent of the rate that applies to underpayments of tax.[74] The two-percent amounts deferred under Code Sec. 6166 are not deductible on the estate tax return[75] or on the estate's income tax return.[76]

For 2006, the two-percent portion is equal to the tentative tax computed on the value of a decedent's partnership interest between $2,000,000 the amount of the applicable exclusion amount under Code Sec. 2010(c)) and $3,200,000 ($1,200,000 + $2,000,000). The $1,200,000 is the inflation-adjusted amount provided in Code Sec. 6601(j)(1)(A).

> ***Example 20.4.*** Bob Putnam dies in 2006, when the applicable exclusion amount is $2,000,000. The estate tax value of Putnam's partnership interest is $4,000,000 and his executor elects, pursuant to Code Sec. 6166, to extend the time for payment of the estate taxes. The amount of estate tax attributable to the value of the partnership between $2,000,000 and $3,200,000 is eligible for the 2% interest rate. The 2% portion is $540,900 computed as follows: a $1,320,800 tentative estate tax on $3,200,000 minus $780,800 (the applicable credit amount for 2006). An interest rate of 45% of the rate applicable to underpayments of tax is assessed against the portion of the estate tax exceeding the $540,000 amount.

If the estate has undistributed net income for any taxable year after its fourth taxable year, the executor must apply it to the unpaid estate taxes.[77]

The 14-year extension can help overcome a cash squeeze, at the small price of low interest rates. In situations where an extension appears to be of possible use but there is some question as to whether the estate can meet the percentage tests, then the estate planner should give some thought to strategies that will help satisfy the test. The client could either increase the size of the partnership interest, reduce the size of the other parts of the estate, or both.

The number of partners for purposes of the 45-partner limitation is to be determined immediately before the decedent's death.[78] A husband and wife holding an interest in any form are counted as

---

[73] Code Sec. 6601(j)(2).

[74] Code Sec. 6601(j)(1)(B).

[75] Code Sec. 2053(c)(1)(D).

[76] Code Sec. 163(k).

[77] Code Sec. 6166(g)(2)(A).

[78] Code Sec.166(b)(2)(A).

one partner.[79] If a corporation or other partnership or trust is a partner, the shareholders, other partners, and beneficiaries of the trust are counted as partners.[80] The latter provision is designed to prevent circumvention of the 45-partner limitation through the use of these other entities.

The maximum estate tax deferrable is the amount of estate tax attributable to the partnership interest. This is determined by the ratio of the value of the partnership interest to the adjusted gross estate.[81] In addition, if one-half or more in value of the interest is sold, or if aggregate withdrawals are made that equal one-half of the value of the partnership interest, there is immediate acceleration of the unpaid balance of the estate tax.[82] This rule suggests that the provision has practical value only in situations where the executor or heir will continue to hold the partnership interest.

The value of a partnership for Code Sec. 6166 purposes includes only assets used to carry on the business. Passive assets are not included.[83]

¶ 2040 LIMITED LIABILITY COMPANIES (LLCs)

The limited liability company (LLC) is another form of operation for conducting a small business that is now available in all 50 states and in the District of Columbia. Limited liability companies address many of the shortfalls of the other forms of business organization.

LLCs are hybrid business entities that can provide their members with both the limited liability characteristics of corporations and the pass-through tax treatment of partnerships. LLCs, like limited partnerships and corporations, are creatures of statute. The members of an LLC enjoy the same freedom from personal liability for obligations of the business as do shareholders of a corporation.

Pursuant to the "check-the-box" regulations,[84] an LLC with two or more members that is not required to be classified as a corporation generally can choose to be taxed as either a partnership or as an association taxable as a corporation. In addition, a single-member LLC may be treated as an association (taxed as a corporation) or disregarded as an entity separate from its owner (taxed as a sole proprietorship or branch). An LLC makes the election under Reg. § 301.7701-3(b)(1) by filing Form 8832, "Entity Classification Election."

---

[79] Code Sec. 6166(b)(2)(B).
[80] Code Sec. 6166(b)(1)(C).
[81] Code Sec. 6166(a)(2).
[82] Code Sec. 6166(g)(1)(A).
[83] Code Sec. 6166(b)(9).
[84] Reg. § 301.7701-3(b)(1).

.01 Advantages of LLCs

Members of LLCs enjoy the same protections from personal liability for business obligations as shareholders of a corporation or limited partners in a limited partnership. Unlike the limited partnership form, which requires at least one general partner who is personally liable for all of the debts of the business, no such requirement exists for an LLC.

An LLC with two or more members that is not required to be a corporation generally may be classified as a partnership for tax purposes. Thus, the LLC is not a separate taxable entity unless it elects to be treated as an association taxable as a corporation.

One person may form and own an LLC. If the LLC is owned by only one person, the entity is generally ignored for federal tax purposes. Thus, if an individual owns an LLC, the individual will be treated as a sole proprietor unless he or she elects to have the LLC treated as an association taxable as a corporation. If a corporation owns an LLC, the LLC will be treated as a division of the corporation.

LLCs, S corporations, and partnerships all provide for the pass-through of income and loss to their owners. LLCs, however, can be used in a wider range of circumstances than can S corporations. For example, S corporations may have no more than 100 shareholders.[85] (For this purpose, a husband and wife are treated as one shareholder. In addition, certain members of a family may elect to be treated as one shareholder of an S corporation.) With limited exceptions for certain trusts, shareholders in S corporations must be individuals. Other types of investors, such as corporations and partnerships, are not eligible to be S corporation shareholders. In addition, S corporations may issue only a single class of stock.[86] LLCs are not subject to any of these restrictions.

LLC members have flexibility to allocate income or loss on a basis other than each member's percentage interest in the LLC. By contrast, in the case of an S corporation, all such allocations must be based strictly on each shareholder's stock ownership.[87]

An LLC treated as a partnership for tax purposes is eligible to elect under Code Sec. 754 to adjust the tax bases of its assets after a change of ownership of a membership interest. In addition, such an LLC can use debt to increase a member's basis in the member's interest.

[85] Code Sec. 1361(b).

[86] Code Sec. 1361(b)(1).

[87] Code Sec. 1366(a).

.02 Disadvantages of LLCs

The most frequently cited disadvantage of LLCs has been uncertainty resulting from the lack of legal precedent for LLC disputes. Corporations, partnerships, and limited partnerships have been around for some time, while LLCs are relative newcomers. A Uniform Limited Liability Company Act has been adopted by an increasing number of states. Nonetheless, LLC acts can differ materially from state to state.

The cost of forming an LLC may be more substantial than establishing a sole proprietorship or partnership. Moreover, for motion is likely to entail extensive paperwork, requiring legal assistance.

State tax treatment of LLCs varies. Most state laws provide that the classification of LLCs will follow the federal tax classification. However some states apply entity-level taxes regardless of the federal tax classification of an LLC.

.03 Conversion of a Partnership into an LLC

A partnership may be converted into an LLC without adverse tax consequences, whether or not the limited liability company is formed in the same state as the partnership.[88] Thus, converting a partnership into an LLC will not cause the partners to recognize gain or loss. The LLC is treated as a continuation of the partnership.

[88] Rev. Rul. 95-37, 1995-1 CB 130.

Chapter 21

Planning for the Sole Proprietor

Overview .... ¶2101
Alternatives Available to the Sole Proprietor .... ¶2105
Disposition of the Business upon Retirement or Death ...... ¶2110

¶2101 OVERVIEW

The sole proprietor has the same basic financial problems as a businessperson operating through a closely held corporation or partnership, but the sole proprietor's problems are likely to be more severe. The sole proprietor has no partner to help shoulder the burden if disability strikes. Usually, no one is standing in immediate line of succession, ready to take over, run the business, and preserve its value on the sole proprietor's death. When a sole proprietor dies or becomes disabled, without some contingency planning, virtually everything that the sole proprietor has built up can be wiped out in short order. That is the central problem.

¶2105 ALTERNATIVES AVAILABLE TO THE SOLE PROPRIETOR

A sole proprietor should explore several alternative financial and estate planning methods.

.01 Business Entity

Probably the first question the sole proprietor should ask is whether the sole proprietorship form of doing business really makes sense over time. The sole proprietor should consider a switch to the corporate form of business. A one-person corporation will not solve the successor problem immediately, but it can facilitate its ultimate solution by giving the sole proprietor incentives to recruit and retain successors. At the same time, the corporate form can open up a whole new world of wealth-building possibilities not available to a sole proprietor: the world of executive benefits. In addition, the corporate form opens important wealth-transferring possibilities by transfers of stock to family members.

If the regular corporate form is not practical, the sole proprietor might want to consider an S corporation, which is generally taxed similar to a partnership, as discussed at ¶1945. Another possibility is to operate as a partnership or limited liability company (LLC). A partnership can provide some measure of insurance against the hazards of disability and precipitous loss of value on death. However, finding a partner and maintaining a partnership relationship has its own problems. Perhaps the sole proprietor is not ready for a regular partnership. If so, a family partnership might be the answer. In this case, the sole proprietor does not form a partnership with a stranger but with family members. The sole proprietor can still be the boss. The family members can be silent partners. Trusts for minor members of the family may also be partners. The family partnership can produce immediate income tax savings by way of income splitting. It will also serve to decrease the ex-sole proprietor's gross estate for estate tax purposes. In the course of time, if not immediately, it may be the source of successor management and permit continuance of the business in the family or a sale at a better price than would otherwise be obtainable. The subject of family partnerships is discussed at ¶2005.

.02 Tax Shelter

If the sole proprietor remains unconvinced of the need for a change in the form of doing business, the next item on the agenda should be how to obtain a business-related tax shelter.

If the sole proprietor does not already have one, a SIMPLE plan, a Keogh (HR-10) plan, or a simplified employee pension (SEP) can serve to shelter retirement savings from income taxes. Sole proprietors and other self-employed individuals can enjoy essentially the same qualified plan benefits as corporate employees. Under Code Sec. 219(g)(3), participation in a qualified plan will deprive the sole proprietor of deductions for IRA contributions if adjusted gross income exceeds the following amounts for the tax years and filing statuses indicated:

Tax Year	Married Filing Jointly	Single or Head of Household
2006	$75,000	$50,000
2007 and later	$80,000	$50,000

For the filing status of married filing jointly, deductible IRA contributions for taxpayers covered by a qualified plan begin to phase out at $0 of adjusted gross income.[1] However, even if so deprived, the sole proprietor can still make a nondeductible contribution. As long as the sole proprietor is not an active participant in a qualified plan, IRA contributions would be deductible no matter how high adjusted gross income is. For a detailed discussion of the qualified plan and IRA rules, see ¶ 905 and ¶ 915, respectively.

If a qualified plan or a regular SEP is too expensive, taking into account required coverage of employees, then the sole proprietor might want to take a look at the Roth IRA for the sole proprietor and any other favored employees, the sole proprietor's spouse included.

.03 Disability Insurance

After considering the above forms of tax shelter, the sole proprietor can go back to the problem of disability. Sole proprietorships, can deal in personal services or engage in manufacturing, retailing, or wholesaling.

The latter type will probably be able to keep the business in operation for a while if the sole proprietor is disabled. The end result, however, is likely to be a shutdown. With a personal service business, the end result is the same, only it comes about more dramatically. When the sole proprietor is disabled, the business cannot provide services to realize earnings. The accounts receivable might carry the disabled service provider for a short time. However, unless the sole proprietor returns to work, the business will fail.

The sole proprietor in either case should consider disability income insurance protection and a certain amount of overhead insurance. The proprietor of a personal service business is not going to close the office, terminate the lease, and fire employees the moment disability strikes as long as there is a chance business will resume before too long. Even a proprietor who is convinced that the disability is permanent will want to stay open for a time, at least to collect the accounts receivable and arrange for the termination of the business. If it is a capital-based business, the business might continue with employees running it for a short while. The sole proprietor will still want to think about overhead insurance. The premiums on overhead insurance are tax deductible, but the proceeds are taxable. The premiums for disability income insurance are not tax

[1] Code Sec.219(g)(3)(iii).

deductible, but the proceeds of the disability income insurance are not taxable.

¶2110 DISPOSITION OF THE BUSINESS UPON RETIREMENT OR DEATH

The next question is: What is to be done with the business when the owner reaches retirement age or dies? Liquidation is the ultimate solution if the sole proprietor can find no other solution. However, the sole proprietor should avoid liquidation if at all possible because it means severe shrinkage of value. Liquidation means a sale of assets at forced-sale prices, sacrifice of goodwill, discounting accounts receivable, and elimination of what had been a continuing source of income. If this shrinkage takes place on the death of the owner, life insurance can be a means of making up the difference between going-concern and liquidation value.

.01 Control by Executor

As an alternative to liquidation, the sole proprietor might consider having the executor (or personal representative) carry on the business, but this is not a long-term, viable solution. The executor will rarely be in a position to be ready, able, and willing to undertake the job and assume personal liability and all that is entailed in running the business. Even more important, all of the assets of the estate will be exposed to the liabilities of the proprietorship. If an executor can be found to take on the job, the chances are, with the prospect of beneficiaries of the estate and their counsel second-guessing him or her, the executor will err on the side of ultra-conservatism. On the other hand, by the time the executor is able to obtain court authorization, serious shrinkage in value might already have taken place and the executor might feel pressured to be more aggressive, which could be even worse. This alternative is possibly better than liquidation, but it is rarely feasible and hardly a good choice. However, it may win by default.

If the sole proprietor chooses to have the executor carry on the business, the executor must decide what to do with the business interest. The executor should make an immediate survey of liability insurance coverage and obtain additional protection, if necessary. Then the executor will have to determine whether the estate can sell the interest as a going concern at a value higher than its liquidation value. If the interest has going-concern value and the executor decides to keep it, the executor's job becomes more difficult than if the estate liquidated the interest. The executor will have to evaluate management and make any necessary changes. The executor will then want to consider the future ownership form of the business. Incorporation is the clear solution for the liability exposure that the estate and the fiduciary face by continued operation in an unincorporated form. Incorporation not only reduces liability, but it also facilitates transfer of the business. The double taxation inherent in a corporate operation is a factor the executor should consider, along with the escape available through the S election. The executor might also consider operating the business as a limited liability company.

If the executor decides to incorporate the business, he or she faces a decision as to which assets to place in the corporation and which to keep out. The executor might find that he or she should keep ownership of the business real estate out of the corporation. Rather, the estate could own the real estate directly and lease it to the corporation. In forming the corporation, the executor will have all the pre-incorporation opportunities for planning discussed in planning for closely held corporations (Chapters 18 and 19).

.02 Family

Another possibility, of course, is to give the business to a family member—a son, a daughter, or the surviving spouse. Unless they have been in close touch with the business and understand it, they start out with two disadvantages: their inexperience and a serious difficulty in establishing credit, leading to a cash crunch. This approach could be better or worse than having the executor try to run the business. Obviously, the decision will depend on the individuals involved, their background, experience, credibility, and their willingness to work.

If the business interest and other estate assets would subject the estate to federal estate taxes, the sole proprietor should consider a bequest of the business interest to the surviving spouse, rather than to a younger family member. A bequest of the business interest to the surviving spouse would shield the business interest from federal estate taxes because of the marital deduction.[2] The surviving spouse could then employ the younger family member to operate the business. One of the possibilities the sole proprietor should consider is the use of a QTIP trust to house the business interest. The younger family member, as trustee or under a contract with an independent trustee, might operate the business during the surviving spouse's lifetime. The income from the business would be payable to the surviving spouse at least annually. On the spouse's death, the interest would pass to the younger family member.

[2] Code Sec. 2056.

.03 Sale

The sole proprietor should consider forming a family partnership, especially if coupled with a sale of part of the partnership to someone capable of running the business. Key employees are the most likely candidates for a purchase agreement. This approach removes the specter of liquidation and makes possible a purchase at lower cost than if the full interest were being sold. If the business owner forms a family limited partnership during his or her lifetime, an easier transfer of leadership is possible, with standby assistance available for the new managers. Lifetime gifts of partnership interests to family members and/or gifts of the sale proceeds by the owner will reduce any estate tax liabilities, taking into account the available unified credit and the marital deduction. Consumption of sale proceeds also reduces the estate. In addition, gifts of partnership interests will reduce the owner's income tax liabilities. If the purchase is designed to take place at death, the agreement might establish the value of the interest for estate tax purposes. Agreements entered into after October 8, 1990, must meet special requirements in order to fix value. These requirements are discussed at ¶ 2310.

Of course, if the business owner does not desire this approach or if it is not feasible, a sale of the business to capable employees is another alternative. The business owner could arrange for the sale to take effect on retirement, death, or at some other time.

The chief problem in consummating a sale of the business to employees is often financing. If the purchase is to take place at death, then life insurance on the life of the sole proprietor can be used to fund the purchase. Of course, the sole proprietor must be insurable. The employees will own the policy or policies and pay the premiums. Payments could be a problem if an ordinary life policy were to be used. Term insurance premiums would cost less than the premiums for an ordinary life policy, but the cost would become prohibitive should the owner live too long. In any case, the premiums paid are not tax deductible,[3] and one may anticipate some difficulty in financing them.

Also, the owner might be called on to pay the premiums, with provisions for reimbursement to the estate on the owner's death. This plan raises a question as to whether the premiums paid are to be regarded as a loan or as taxable compensation. The outcome is uncertain, depending on a number of variables.

---

[3] Code Sec. 264(a).

Insurance can also be used to fund a purchase that is to take place on the owner's retirement. In such a case, the business owner would use some form of policy that would provide sufficient cash when payment is to be made. Again, premium costs become a factor for the employees.

Policy proceeds at death can be made payable to the purchasing employees, the executor of the deceased sole proprietor, or a trust. If the business owner will use cash values to fund a lifetime purchase, the business owner might arrange to have a direct interest in the policy's cash value.

If the proceeds are made payable to the employees, the business owner incurs a risk that the proceeds might never be applied to their intended purposes. If the proceeds are payable to the executor, the business owner incurs a possible risk that both the policy proceeds and the value of the interest to be purchased would be includible in his or her gross estate. This risk should be manageable, however, with proper draftsmanship based on principles similar to those discussed in ¶2015 in connection with partnerships.

On the whole, payment of the proceeds to a trust might be best. However, the financial planner should ascertain the fees and costs involved. Payment of the proceeds to a trust would assure payment without delay and without the possible risk of double estate tax inclusion when payable to the executor.

If the sole proprietor is uninsurable but holds policies obtained while insurable, the sole proprietor should consider selling these policies to the employees. Because of the insured's present uninsurability, the value of the policies could be open to dispute. They should be worth more than their current cash value. How much more might depend on an evaluation of the insured's health and his or her actual life expectancy. However, the sole proprietor should evaluate the adverse income tax consequences resulting from a transfer of an insurance policy for value. Under Code Sec. 101(a)(2), the proceeds in excess of the consideration paid by the employees, and the subsequent premiums paid and other amounts subsequently paid, will be taxable to the employees. However, Code Sec. 101(a)(2) provides an exception in the case of transfers to "partners" that might be worth exploring.

The sole proprietor should explore other means of financing apart from insurance funding, or, in addition to insurance funding. For example, instead of selling the business intact, the sole proprietor might arrange to sell the operating part of the business only. The sole proprietor, the estate, or heirs would retain the property, plant, and equipment and lease it to the purchasers. Another possibility would be to sell the business for a down payment and a note. The seller could negotiate to retain a portion of the earnings in return for favorable financing terms. Other options include selling the business to a family member for a private annuity or self-canceling installment note.

A sole proprietor might desire to sell the business to his or her children. However, the children might not have sufficient cash to purchase the business. The sole proprietor could sell the business to the children for a self-canceling installment note. The business would provide the cash flow for the installment payments. If the seller dies before the note is paid in full, the children's liability on the note ends. Thus, the note has no value on the date of the seller's death, and the unpaid balance is not included in the seller's gross estate. The estate might have to recognize the deferred gain on the note for income tax purposes.[4] In addition, the buyer usually will have to reduce the basis in property acquired by the note by the unpaid balance on the note.[5]

The IRS closely scrutinizes notes that are automatically canceled when the lender dies. That's because a bona fide self-canceling note is not subject to estate tax since the lender's interest is extinguished at death. Courts have held that such a note between family members is presumed to be a gift and not a bona fide transaction. However, this presumption can be rebutted if there is a clear showing that the parties intended to create a true debtor-creditor relationship. For example, one federal court of appeals recently upheld the validity of a self-canceling installment note used by a son to buy his father's business even though the father's death canceled the note shortly after its execution. The court ruled that transaction was bona fide and should not be treated as a taxable gift.[6]

A sole proprietor could also sell the business to the children in exchange for a private annuity. A private annuity would provide the seller with income for his or her life. A sale for a private annuity removes the business assets from the seller's gross estate without the transfer being treated as a gift as long as the annuity provides adequate consideration. At the death of the seller, the buyers' obligation to make payments on the annuity ceases. Using a private annuity allows the buyers to purchase the business without needing a great deal of cash or having to qualify for a loan. The buyers use the cash generated by the business to make the annuity payments. A sale

[4] Code Sec. 691(a)(5).

[5] Code Sec. 108(e)(5).

[6] *Est. of Costanza*, 320 F.3d 595, (6th Cir. 2003).

for a private annuity does not require the estate to recognize any gain for income tax purposes on the death of the seller. Using a private annuity, however, is often complex.

.04 Valuation for Estate Tax Purposes

A binding buy-sell agreement, negotiated at arm's length, may fix the valuation for estate tax purposes. Each asset should be valued on its own merits. For example, even though receivables are collectible, the time element involved in collection justifies a discount. Obsolescence and deterioration can be important factors in inventory valuation.

.05 Valuation of Qualified Business Real Estate

Under Code Sec. 2032A, if certain conditions are met, the executor may elect to value real property used in a closely held business or as a farm on the basis of its value in the business, rather than its fair market value determined on the basis of its highest and best use. However, this special use valuation cannot reduce the decedent's gross estate by more than $900,000 for a decedent dying in calendar year 2006. This amount is indexed for inflation.[7]

> **Planning pointer.** The executor may make a protective election with a timely filed estate tax return if the executor is not certain that the property meets the requirements for special use valuation. Once the executor determines that the property qualifies for special use valuation, the executor must file an additional notice of election within 60 days of the determination.[8]

To qualify for the special use valuation, the decedent must have been a citizen or resident of the United States at the time of death and the following conditions must be met:

- The value of the closely held business assets in the decedent's estate, including both real and personal property (but reduced by debts attributable thereto) must be at least 50 percent of the decedent's gross estate (reduced by debts and expenses);
- At least 25 percent of the adjusted value of the gross estate must be qualified closely held business real property;
- The real property qualifying for special use valuation must pass to a qualified heir;

[7] Code Sec. 2032A(a)(3).

[8] Reg. § 20.2032A-8(b).

- Such real property must have been owned by the decedent or a member of his family and used or held for use as a closely held business for five of the last eight years prior to the decedent's death;
- The decedent or a member of his or her family must have materially participated in the operation of the closely held business in five years out of the eight years immediately preceding the date the decedent died, became disabled or retired (active management by the surviving spouse will satisfy the requirement); and
- The executor must elect current use valuation on the first estate tax return filed by the estate and attach to the return information specified in Reg. § 20.2032A-8(b), including copies of written appraisals of the fair market value of the real property, and an agreement by each person having an interest in the property consenting to liability for any recapture tax that may be imposed.

A relief provision applies in certain instances where the estate did not comply with technical requirements timely. The estate may perfect defective special use elections without regard to whether the estate's original estate tax return evidenced "substantial compliance" with the technical rules for making the election. If the executor submits a timely notice of election and recapture agreement, but the election does not contain all the required information or signatures, the executor may supply the missing information or signatures within 90 days of being notified by the IRS.

For purposes of the 50-percent and 25-percent tests, the value of property is determined without regard to its special use value. The term "qualified heir" means a member of the decedent's family, including the decedent's spouse, parents, brothers, sisters, children, stepchildren, and spouses and lineal descendants of those individuals. Only the property that passes or is deemed to pass from a decedent is eligible for special use valuation. Property considered to have so passed includes property purchased from a decedent's estate by a qualified heir as well as property received by bequest, devise, or inheritance, or in satisfaction of a right to a pecuniary bequest. Property passing to a qualified heir as a result of a qualified disclaimer is considered as passing from the decedent.[9]

Trust property is deemed to have passed to a qualified heir to the extent that the qualified heir has a present interest in the trust. Property that meets the other requirements for special use can be specially valued if it passes to a discretionary trust. No beneficiary of

---

[9] Rev. Rul. 82-140, 1982-2 CB 208.

the trust can have a present interest because of discretion in the trustee to determine the amount to be received by any individual beneficiary. In addition, all potential beneficiaries of the trust must be qualified heirs.

Property transferred within three years of death is included in the adjusted gross estate for purposes of meeting the 50-percent test where the property continued to be qualified real property until the date of death. However, such property is not taken into account for purposes of the 25-percent test (¶ 2210).[10]

The mere passive renting of property will not qualify. However, the property will qualify where a related party leases the property and conducts farming or other business activities on the property. Leasing to a nonfamily member may qualify if the rental is substantially dependent on production.

If within 10 years after the decedent's death, but before the death of the qualified heir, the property is disposed of to nonfamily members or ceases to be used for the originally qualified use, then the estate must recapture the estate tax benefits resulting from the special use valuation. (However, a two-year grace period applies immediately following death when failure of the qualified heir to make qualified use of the property will not result in recapture). In addition, recapture does not apply if the disposition results from the death of the qualified heir.

Recapture is not triggered by a net cash rental of specially valued property by a surviving spouse or lineal descendants of the decedent to a member of the decedent's family (see ¶ 2210 for more details).

A transfer by a qualified heir to a member of the heir's family is not subject to recapture.[11] However, a transfer to an individual who is not a member of the qualified heir's family is subject to recapture even though the transferee is a member of the decedent's family.[12] The law extends the statute of limitations for the assessment and collection of any recaptured tax. A special lien also continues for as long as the potential liability may exist. However, the IRS may waive the lien if it finds that the interests of the United States are adequately protected.

In planning to take advantage of the special use valuation provision, the financial planner should take into account the possible effect the lower valuation can have on the tax basis of the property and on the future income tax liability of the heirs. Use of the lower

---

[10] Rev. Rul. 87-122, 1987-2 CB 221.

[11] Code Sec. 2032A(c)(1)(A).

[12] Rev. Rul. 89-22, 1989-2 CB 276.

special use value for estate tax purposes will give the heirs a lower tax basis for income tax purposes than would a highest and best use value. The lower basis would ultimately result in a higher income tax on disposition of the property by the heirs. The financial planner should also consider the effect of a higher valuation on death tax costs.

Of course, the sole proprietor may be married and eligible to take advantage of the unlimited marital deduction possibly in combination with the maximum use of the available unified credit. In such a case, the sole proprietor's estate will not have any federal estate tax liability, and special use valuation is not a factor. In such circumstances, a valuation based on highest and best use will provide a higher basis for the property passing from the decedent. A higher basis will usually produce better income tax results on a taxable disposition of the property.

If the sole proprietor is not sure of meeting the 50-percent and 25-percent requirements and wants to take advantage of the special use provision, he or she should consider lifetime gifts of nonqualified property or gifts of the proceeds of the sale of such property. To be effective for purposes of the 50-percent test, the business owner must make the gifts more than three years before death.

No special use valuation applies to lifetime gifts of qualifying real estate. The absence of special use valuation for such gifts means that the business owner must consider retaining closely held business real estate to take advantage of the special use provision at death. If the property has good appreciation potential, however, the business owner might save transfer taxes by paying a gift tax based on current fair market value rather than paying estate taxes at death based on appreciated value, even allowing for a special use discount.

Fundamentally, the purpose of the special use valuation provision is to reduce the tax burden on the decedent's estate and heirs. However, the reduction in estate taxes might be at the expense of increased income taxes. Thus, its use does not guarantee an overall reduction in both estate and income taxes.

The financial planner should also consider the recapture potential. In this connection, the life expectancy of the qualified heir becomes a factor because the death of the qualified heir eliminates recapture.

The special use provision introduces complexities in before- and after-death planning, the costs of which need to be taken into account. Also, these complexities might require a different executor than the sole proprietor might otherwise choose. Further, preparing to meet the requirements of the special valuation methods calls for extensive record keeping.

See also ¶2210 for a discussion of the qualified family-owned business deduction.

.06 Joint Ownership of Business Realty and Personalty with Spouse

If the sole proprietor and spouse own real estate and tangible personal property used in the business as joint tenants, 50 percent of the value of such property will be excluded from the gross estate of the first to die under Code Sec. 2040(b) (¶315.02) regardless of the contribution of the survivor.

.07 Installment Payments of Estate Tax

If the value of the business interest includible in the proprietor's gross estate is equal to at least 35 percent of the adjusted gross estate, the executor may elect to pay part or all of the estate tax attributable to the business interest in 2 to 10 equal annual installment payments.[13] The first installment payment is due not more than 5 years after the prescribed payment date.[14] The discussion of this topic in ¶2035 in connection with partnerships applies equally here.

[13] Code Sec. 6166(a).

[14] Code Sec. 6166(a)(3).

Chapter 22

Planning for the Farmer and Rancher

Overview ....¶2201
Keeping the Property Intact ....¶2205
Minimizing Death Taxes ....¶2210
Liquidity ....¶2215
Income Averaging for Farmers ....¶2220
Providing for Heirs Who Have Left the Farm ....¶2225

¶2201 OVERVIEW

Farmers and ranchers differ in many ways, but they are generally grouped together for tax purposes. This chapter will follow the same pattern. Unless making a distinction is important, both are referred to as farmers. In addition,"farms"include ranches.

¶2205 KEEPING THE PROPERTY INTACT

Farms represent a substantial investment in land, equipment, and buildings. Although a farmer's net worth can be substantial, the farmer's estate is apt to be highly illiquid. The prices of the things the farmer buys can go up at a far faster rate than the prices of the things the farmer sells. Rising labor costs have made increased mechanization a competitive necessity, which further increases the farmer's debt and interest charges.

The farmer often wants to remain a farmer, involve the children in farm operations, keep the farm together and pass it on to the family. However, taxes and agri-economics can make doing so very difficult without careful planning. Without the marital deduction, keeping a farm intact if the estate is without liquid assets to pay federal estate taxes is difficult. Under current rules, estate taxes can be up to 45 percent of the market value of the farm in excess of the applicable exclusion amount. The liquidity problem is worse if the farm is mortgaged.

One solution is to sell part of the farm to pay the death taxes. However, that solution might be infeasible with a ranch. Another problem is dealing fairly with the children who remain farmers and the children who leave the farm. Often, the family can solve this problem only by the farming part of the family buying out the interests of the others. This solution can create difficulties for both buyers and sellers.

Against this background, the three things a financial plan should do for a farmer are as follows:

1. Minimize death taxes.
2. Provide sufficient liquidity for the farm operation to continue.
3. Adjust in a satisfactory manner the interests of the heirs who remain and those who have left the farm.

Code Sec. 2032A (discussed at ¶ 2210) provides some estate tax relief for farmers by permitting actual use valuation of the farm, instead of valuation based on highest and best use.

¶ 2210 MINIMIZING DEATH TAXES

Minimizing death taxes is a very broad subject which much of this book addresses. Some techniques that might be especially useful in planning for the farmer are discussed below.

.01 Valuation of Qualified Real Estate Used in Farming or Other Closely Held Business

Under Code Sec. 2032A, if certain conditions are met, the executor may elect to value real property included in the decedent's estate, used in a closely held business or as a farm on the basis of the property's value as a farm or its value in the closely held business, rather than its fair market value determined on the basis of its highest and best use. However, this special use valuation cannot reduce the decedent's gross estate by more than $900,000 for a decedent dying in calendar year 2006.[1] This $870,000 figure is indexed for inflation.[2]

To qualify for the special use valuation, the decedent must have been a citizen or resident of the United States at the time of death and

---

[1] Rev. Proc. 2005-70, 2005-47 IRB 979 (October 28, 2005).

[2] Code Sec. 2032A(a)(3).

the following conditions must be met: (1) the value of the farm or closely held business assets in the decedent's estate, including both real and personal property (but reduced by debts attributable thereto), must be at least 50 percent of the decedent's gross estate (less debts and expenses); (2) at least 25 percent of the adjusted value of the gross estate must be qualified farm or closely held business real property; (3) the real property qualifying for special use valuation must pass to a qualified heir; (4) such real property must have been owned by the decedent or a member of his family and used or held for use as a farm or closely held business for five of the last eight years prior to the decedent's death; (5) the decedent or a member of his or her family must have materially participated in the operation of the farm or closely held business in five out of the eight years preceding the date the decedent died, became disabled or retired; (6) the executor must attach to a timely filed estate tax return a notice of election containing certain information specified in Reg. § 20.2032A-8(b), including copies of written appraisals of the fair market value of the real property, and an agreement, signed by each person having an interest in the property, consenting to the tax treatment provided for dispositions and for failure to use for qualified purpose.

Active management by a surviving spouse satisfies the material participation requirement.

For purposes of the 50-percent and 25-percent tests, the value of property is determined without regard to its special use value. The term"qualified heir"means a member of the decedent's family, including his spouse, parents, brothers, sisters, children, stepchildren, and spouses and lineal descendants of those individuals.

Only property that has passed from a decedent is eligible for special use valuation. However, property purchased from a decedent's estate by a qualified heir as well as property received by bequest, devise, or inheritance, or in satisfaction of a right to a pecuniary bequest is considered to have so passed. Property passing to a qualified heir as a result of a qualified disclaimer is considered as passing from the decedent.[3]

In general, trust property is deemed to have passed to a qualified heir to the extent that the qualified heir has a present interest in the trust. Property that meets the other requirements for special use can be specially valued if it passes to a discretionary trust. No beneficiary of the trust can have a present interest because of discretion in the

[3] Rev. Rul. 82-140, 1982-2 CB 208.

trustee to determine the amount to be received by any individual beneficiary. In addition, all potential beneficiaries of the trust must be qualified heirs.

The mere passive renting of property will not qualify. However, the property will qualify where a related party leases the property and conducts farming or other business activities on the property. Leasing to a nonfamily member may even qualify if the rental is substantially dependent on production.

A relevant question is whether the property is used as a"farm or for farming purposes."Code Sec. 2032A(e) contains a long list of farming activities.

Salvaging special use valuation. Code Sec. 2032A(d)(3) provides for"perfection"of elections of special use valuation within 90 days of a request by the IRS. Defective special use elections may be perfected without regard to whether the estate's original estate tax return evidenced"substantial compliance"with the technical rules for making the election. If the executor submits a timely notice of election and recapture agreement, but the election does not contain all the required information or signatures, the executor may supply the missing information or signatures within 90 days of being notified by the IRS.

Special valuation methods. Under Code Sec. 2032A(e)(7), if an estate and a farm or real estate used for farming qualifies for Code Sec. 2032A special use valuation, their value is to be determined by dividing:

1. The excess of the average annual gross cash rental (the use of net-share rentals is permitted if cash rentals for comparable land in the same locality are not available) for comparable land used for farming purposes and located in the locality of such farm over the average annual state and local real estate taxes for such comparable land by
2. The average annual effective interest rate for all new Federal Land Bank Loans.

However, Code Sec. 2032A(e)(7)(C) provides that this special farm valuation rule does not apply:

1. Where it is established that there is no comparable land from which the average annual gross rental may be determined.
2. Where the executor elects to have the value of the farm determined by applying the following factors from Code Sec. 2032A(e)(8) (these factors would also apply in the

case of qualified closely held business real property other than property devoted to farming):

a. The capitalization of income that the property can be expected to yield for farming or closely held business purposes over a reasonable period of time under prudent management using traditional cropping patterns for the area, taking into account soil capacity, terrain configuration, and similar factors.

b. The capitalization of the fair rental value of the land for farmland or closely held business purposes.

c. Assessed land values in a state which provides a differential or use value assessment law for farmland or closely held businesses.

d. Comparable sales of other farm or closely held business land in the same geographical area far enough removed from a metropolitan or resort area so that nonagricultural use is not a significant factor in the sales price.

e. Any other factor which fairly values the farm or closely held business value of the property.

See Reg. § 20.2032A-4 for further details on the method of valuing farm realty.

Recapture rules. Under Code Sec. 2032A(c)(1), if within 10 years after the decedent's death, but before the death of the qualified heir, the property is disposed of to nonfamily members or ceases to be used for the originally qualified use (Code Sec. 2032A(c)(7) provides a two-year"grace"period for nonuse), then the estate tax benefits resulting from the special use valuation will be recaptured. Also, certain qualified heirs are treated as materially participating in the farm or other business operation during the recapture period when such heir engages in the active management of the farm or business.

Recapture is not triggered by a net cash rental of specially valued property by a surviving spouse or lineal descendants of the decedent to a member of the decedent's family.

A transfer by a qualified heir to a member of his or her family is not subject to recapture.[4] However, a transfer to an individual who is not a member of the qualified heir's family is subject to recapture even though the transferee is a member of the decedent's family.[5]

The grant of a conservation easement in property subject to special use valuation is not considered to be a disposition of the property for purposes of the recapture tax.

[4] Code Sec. 2032A(c)(1)(A).

[5] Rev. Rul. 89-22, 1989-1 CB 276.

Planning considerations. Use of the marital deduction and the available unified credit can avoid all estate taxes, at least on the death of the first spouse. In such a case, valuation at fair market value based on the highest and best use might be preferable to special use valuation. In planning to take advantage of the special use valuation provision, the financial planner should take into account the possible effect the lower valuation can have on the tax basis of the property and the future income tax liability of the heirs.

Taxpayers who are uncertain of meeting the 50-percent and 25-percent requirements but want to take advantage of the special use provision will want to consider making lifetime gifts of nonqualified property or the proceeds of the sale of such property. To be effective for this purpose, the gifts must be made more than three years before death.[6]

No special use valuation applies to lifetime gifts of qualifying real estate. Thus, the client must consider retaining farm interests or closely held business real estate to take advantage of the special use provision at death. On the other hand, if the property has good appreciation potential, a lifetime gift of the property might be a good tax planning strategy. The gift tax based on current fair market value might be less than the estate tax at death based on appreciated value, even allowing for the special use discount.

Fundamentally, the purpose of the special use valuation provision is to reduce the estate tax burden of the decedent's estate and heirs. However, the reduction in estate taxes might be at the expense of higher income taxes on the disposition of the property. Thus, the special use valuation provision does not guarantee an overall reduction in estate and income taxes.

The financial planner should consider the recapture potential. Thus, the life expectancy of the qualified heir becomes a factor, because the death of the qualified heir eliminates recapture. The heir can avoid personal liability for recapture by posting a bond that meets certain requirements. A procedure also exists for subordinating the government's lien for recapture. This provision helps the heirs to obtain credit based on the value of the realty.

The special use provision can involve complex planning, before and after death. Further, preparing to meet the requirements of the special valuation methods calls for extensive record keeping.

---

[6] Code Sec. 2035(c)(1).

.03 Joint Ownership with Spouse

Under Code Sec. 2040(b), generally only one-half of the jointly held property with a right of survivorship is includible in the gross estate of the first spouse to die. This rule applies regardless of the contribution or lack of contribution by either spouse (see ¶ 315.02 for a detailed discussion of this provision). The one-half that passes to the survivor qualifies for the marital deduction under Code Sec. 2056 and receives a tax-free step-up in basis under Code Sec. 1014. The step up in basis is limited to $1,300,000 plus $3,000,000 for property acquired by a surviving spouse from a decedent dying in 2010. The other one-half, already possessed by the survivor, generally receives no step-up in basis. Rather, the other half carries over or continues its original basis. This rule can be an important factor against the use of joint ownership of highly appreciated property where the spouse who is expected to die first holds or can be given sole ownership. However, if the couple owned the property as community property, all of the property is deemed to have been acquired from the decedent.[7] Therefore, all of the property would receive a step up in basis to fair market value.[8]

.04 Management Powers

The estate planner will want to think about giving the surviving spouse or trustee certain powers to facilitate management. For example, the estate planner might consider the power to lease for a period extending beyond the surviving spouse's lifetime, the power to deal with mineral interests in the land, and the power to make soil conservation improvements and enter into any necessary arrangements with the Department of Agriculture.

.05 Form of Operation

A trust is not usually a good vehicle for operating a farm. Therefore, for this and other reasons, a financial planner should recommend a corporation or a partnership as the entity for holding the farm assets.

.06 Private Annuity

A transfer of a farm to a descendant in exchange for a joint and survivor annuity for the farmer and the farmer's spouse effectively removes the property transferred from the farmer's estate if the rules governing private annuities, as discussed in Chapter 8, are met.

---

[7] Code Sec. 1014(b)(6).

[8] Code Sec. 1014(a).

.07 Lifetime Gifts

Lifetime gifts of nonfarm assets are one way of minimizing the size of the gross estate. The high gift tax rate schedule makes for greater reliance on the gift tax annual exclusion and gift splitting in developing a gift program. Such a program makes possible a fairly rapid reduction of an estate, given a sufficient number of donees. Farm assets are not suitable for gifts because of the need to retain operational control of the farm as a going concern.

.08 Incorporation

Incorporation of the farm might prove of great value for estate planning purposes. A corporation lends itself to planning for the reduction of estate tax values by gifts of corporate securities, while at the same time permitting retention of operational control. The operation of the farm can remain uninterrupted by the probate process. Redemptions of stock under Code Sec. 303 become possible. The redemption is treated as a sale or exchange, and not as a dividend. Gain is realized only to the extent that the redemption proceeds exceed the recipient's basis under the step-up to estate tax value under Code Sec. 1014 (¶ 1005). However, a Code Sec. 303 redemption to pay death taxes can have an adverse effect on special use valuation.[9]

Corporate stock can be used to make gifts to the family. If gifts are made over a span of years, in amounts within the annual gift tax exclusion, estate tax values can be greatly lowered without gift tax consequences. If the senior family member's stock ownership is reduced to the point that stock holdings represent a minority interest in terms of control, the value of the holdings will be further decreased for estate tax purposes. In addition, the special farm valuation method, discussed above, will be available even though the farm is held in corporate form.[10]

A farmer can operate a farm as a regular or C corporation, or as an S corporation (¶ 1945). An S corporation may have both voting and nonvoting stock without violating the one-class-of-stock rule. An S corporation may also have a form of safe-harbor debt that will not be deemed a second class of stock.

When the farmer uses the regular corporate form, the shareholder-employees may enjoy fringe benefits not available to partners, sole proprietors, or S corporation shareholders. However, parity exists between corporate and noncorporate retirement plans.

---

[9] Rev. Rul. 85-73, 1985-1 CB 325.

[10] Reg. § 20.2032(A)-(3)(b).

One corporate fringe benefit that might be of special value to the farmer or rancher is meals and lodging for the convenience of the employer. Under Code Sec. 119, an employee may exclude meals and lodging from gross income if furnished for the convenience of the employer.

The U.S. Tax Court applied the Code Sec. 119 exclusion in a case involving a dairy farm.[11] The issue in the case was whether meals and lodging furnished to shareholder-employees were excludable from gross income. In determining whether the lodging was excluded from gross income, the Court concluded that"dairy farming is simply not a nine-to-five business."It pointed to the possibility of escaped cattle, broken-down milk coolers, calf-birth, and bleeding udders as requiring personnel on hand at all times.

The cost of gas and electricity furnished to the residence would also be excluded from the gross income of the shareholder-employees as part of the lodging expenses. Telephone service might also be excluded if an allocation were made to business use.

The U.S. Tax Court has allowed the exclusion in other cases in which the taxpayer was required to reside on the farm as a condition of employment and the taxpayer had to be available for duty at all times.[12] In another case, the U.S. Tax Court did not allow the exclusion. However, the U.S. Court of Appeals for the Ninth Circuit reversed the decision and allowed the exclusion because taxpayers were required to be available for duty at all times.[13]

Any farming operation involving the care and maintenance of livestock or the storage of farm produce, especially if refrigeration or heat is required, and other operations calling for nighttime supervision, may qualify. This exclusion can provide a substantial benefit to shareholder-employees.

Whether or not a partnership may receive the benefits of Code Sec. 119 is the subject of conflicting opinions. The IRS does not consider a sole proprietor his or her own employee for purposes of Code Secs. 119 or 162.

In short, corporate operation seems the safest route to ensure the availability of the tax benefits. However, other tax factors may weigh against use of the corporate form, unless all or nearly all corporate income is paid out in the form of salary and benefits.

---

[11] *J. Harrison*, 41 TCM 1384, CCH Dec. 37,869(M), TC Memo. 1981-211.

[12] *J. Grant Farms, Inc.*, 49 TCM 1197, CCH Dec. 42,016(M), TC Memo 1985-174, and *D.L. Johnson*, 49 TCM 1203, CCH Dec. 42,017(M), TC Memo 1985-175.

[13] *M. Caratan*, CA-9, 71-1 USTC ¶9353, 442 F2d 606 (1971), *rev'g* 52 TC 960 CCH Dec. 29,738.

.09 Family Partnership

The family partnership discussed in ¶ 2005 can also be valuable in estate planning for a farmer who is unwilling or unable to incorporate.

¶ 2215 LIQUIDITY

If one individual owns all the stock of a farming corporation, the stock is highly illiquid. Moreover, the stated objective of keeping the farm in the family could obviously not be attained by selling the stock to outsiders. Even if the securities were not illiquid, those same factors and the economics of farm operation in general would decrease liquidity. The marital deduction is one way of solving the liquidity problem insofar as funds to pay estate taxes might otherwise be needed. Insurance is another method of solving this problem, providing funds not only for the payment of any taxes but also to pay cash legacies, debts and expenses, living and operating expenses. The practical reality is that only a small percentage of farmers take advantage of insurance benefits. If the farmer used the corporate form, group-term or group-permanent life insurance might prove to be enough of a bargain to gain greater acceptance of insurance benefits. Also, if the farmer used qualified retirement plans, incidental insurance benefits might also be available. Those individuals covered by qualified plans may also make contributions to their own individual retirement accounts (¶ 915).

Liquidity can also be furnished by the development of investment programs. Even if the farm is to be operated as a sole proprietorship, the farmer should consider a qualified plan and an IRA in conjunction with a qualified plan. The financial planner should pay attention to the special methods of computing self-employment income of farmers. Special rules apply to dealing with government payments, farm rentals, and share-farmers.

Crops and livestock are other sources of liquidity, but developing a savings or investment program is preferable.

¶ 2220 INCOME AVERAGING FOR FARMERS

An individual engaged in a farming business may elect to average farm income over three years.[14] The tax imposed in any tax year will equal the sum of the tax computed on taxable income reduced by "elected farm income"plus the increase in tax that would result if taxable income for each of the three prior tax years were increased by an amount equal to one-third of the elected farm income.[15]

[14] Code Sec. 1301(a).

[15] Code Sec. 1301(a).

Elected farm income means the amount of taxable income attributable to any farming business that is specifically subject to this three-year averaging election.[16] Gain from the sale or disposition of property, other than land, regularly used by the farmer for a substantial period in such a farming business is treated as attributable to a"farming business."[17]

The averaging provision is not available to trusts or estates.[18] In addition, it does not apply for employment tax or alternative minimum tax purposes.[19]

¶2225 PROVIDING FOR HEIRS WHO HAVE LEFT THE FARM

The farmer has three basic choices if he or she wants to keep the farm intact and operational: (1) provide cash legacies in an amount which, if invested, would give the legatees roughly as much as those operating the farm could expect to receive on their investment; (2) give the absentees an interest in the farm or stock of the farm corporation, but give the farm operators or corporation an option to purchase their interest at a fair price; and (3) find some way in which the absentees could participate in the farm profits either as landlords, debtors, or security holders.

---

[16] Code Sec. 1301(b)(1)(A).

[17] Code Sec. 1301(b)(1)(B).

[18] Code Sec. 1301(b)(2).

[19] Conference Committee Report to the Taxpayer Relief Act of 1997 (P.L. 105-34).

Chapter 23

Impact of Freeze Rules on Intra-Family Transfers

Overview ....¶ 2301
Business Valuation Rules ....¶ 2305
Options and Buy-Sell Agreements ....¶ 2310
Transfers of Trust Interests ....¶ 2315
Lapsing Rights and Restrictions ....¶ 2320

¶ 2301 OVERVIEW

A traditional estate tax freeze was a technique used to limit the value of business interests in a decedent's gross estate. The technique worked by passing on any appreciation in the value of the business to the next generation. In the typical estate tax freeze, a parent would cause a closely held corporation to recapitalize its stock into two classes. The parent would keep a class of preferred stock that was limited in value using a fixed dividend preference. The children would receive common stock that would grow in value as the value of the corporation grew. In another type of estate tax freeze, the parent would retain an interest for a term of years or a life estate in a trust or property for the ultimate benefit of the children. This technique would effectively shift future appreciation in the property to the children. Under a third type of estate freeze technique, a corporate buy-sell agreement, a parent would grant to a child an option to purchase property at a fixed price or a formula price on the parent's death.

The typical business freeze involved a parent retaining preferred stock and making a gift of common stock. Over the years, Congress wrestled with legislation to curb the abuses arising from estate freezes. It enacted a cumbersome rule under which the value of the common stock was brought back into the donor's gross estate. However, Congress retroactively repealed that rule as though it had never been enacted. Congress replaced it with four separate Code sections, which are discussed in the balance of this chapter. These sections deal with valuation of preferred interests in corporations and partnerships (¶ 2305), options in buy-sell agreements (¶ 2310), interests in trusts (¶ 2315), and lapsing rights and restrictions (¶ 2320).

¶ 2305 BUSINESS VALUATION RULES

Special rules contained in Code Sec. 2701 and the regulations thereunder can come into play when an individual transfers an interest in a corporation or partnership to a family member and retains certain rights (or an applicable family member possesses such rights). These rules determine whether and to what extent the transfer is a gift. The underlying premise behind these rules is that the value of a residual interest in a corporation or partnership is determined by subtracting the value of the retained interest from the value of the entire entity, with an adjustment to reflect the actual fragmented ownership.[1]

Specific rules apply for determining the value of retained rights. Under these rules, retained rights might have no or low value, thereby pushing up the value of the transferred residual interest. This result is to be contrasted with the traditional recapitalization. In a traditional recapitalization, most of the value of the company is loaded into the retained preferred interest, and very little value assigned to the transferred common interest. This result is no longer possible for family transfers subject to the Code Sec. 2701 rules.

.01 Transfers Subject to the Rules

The rules apply to the transferor of a residual interest to or for the benefit of a member of the family. A member of the family is, with respect to the transferor, the transferor's spouse, a lineal descendant of the transferor or the transferor's spouse, and the spouse of any such descendant.[2]

Transfer defined. For purposes of the special valuation rules, the term "transfer" has a specific meaning. For example, a transfer for full and adequate consideration is a transfer for purposes of these rules although the transfer is not a taxable gift for gift tax purposes. Any redemption, recapitalization, contribution to capital, or other change in the capital structure of a corporation or partnership is

[1] Reg. § 25.2701-1(a)(2).

[2] Code Sec. 2701(e)(1).

treated as a transfer of an interest in the entity if the transferor or applicable family member:

- Receives a retained right affected by these provisions
- Surrenders a junior equity interest and receives property other than an applicable retained interest
- Surrenders a senior equity interest and the fair market value of an applicable retained interest already held by that individual increases[3]

A termination of an interest held through a corporation, partnership, estate, trust, or other entity, or a contribution to capital by an entity to the extent an individual indirectly holds an interest in the entity, is also treated as a transfer if the indirectly held property either: (1) would have been includible in the gross estate of the individual if the individual had died at the time of the termination, or (2) is in a grantor trust of which the indirect holder is treated as the owner.[4]

Exceptions. The rules do not apply in the following circumstances:

- To any right conferred by a retained interest for which market quotations are readily available on an established securities market.
- To a retained interest that is of the same class as the transferred interest.
- When the rights in the retained interest are of a class that is proportionally the same as all of the rights in the transferred interests in the business, other than nonlapsing differences in voting power. In the case of a partnership, the rules do not apply to nonlapsing differences with respect to management and limitations on liability, including differences between classes attributable to nonlapsing provisions necessary to comply with partnership allocation requirements.
- To rights to convert into a fixed number or a fixed percentage of the shares of the same class as the transferred stock if the rights are nonlapsing, subject to proportionate adjustment for splits, combinations, reclassification, and similar changes in the capital stock, and adjusted for accumulated dividends not paid on a timely basis (a similar exception applies to rights in partnerships).
- A transfer to a member of the transferor's family to the extent the transfer results in a proportionate reduction in

[3] Code Sec. 2701(e)(5) and Reg. § 25.2701-1(b). [4] Reg. § 25.2701-1(b)(2)(C)(1).

each class of interest held by the transferor and all applicable family members in the aggregate.[5]

.02 Retained Rights Generally

Valuation rules apply to two types of retained rights. The first kind of right is an extraordinary payment right, which is defined as any liquidation, put, call, or conversion right, any right to compel liquidation or similar right, the exercise or nonexercise of which affects the value of the transferred interest.[6] A call right includes any option, warrant, or other right to acquire an equity interest. An extraordinary payment right is valued at zero, unless the holder of that right must exercise it at a specific time and at a specific amount.

The other type of right is a retained distribution right. A retained distribution right that is noncumulative or lacks a preference upon liquidation is valued at zero if immediately before the transfer, the transferor and applicable family members control the entity.

A distribution right generally is a right to distributions with respect to stock of a corporation or a partnership interest. A distribution right does not include any right to receive distributions with respect to an interest that is either of the same class as, or a class that is subordinate to, the transferred interest. A distribution right also does not include any right in a junior equity interest; any liquidation, put, call, or conversion right; or a guaranteed payment determined without regard to income.[7]

A retained distribution right that consists of a qualified payment right is not valued at zero under these rules.[8] A qualified payment right is a dividend payable under cumulative preferred stock, or a comparable payment under a partnership interest, to the extent the payment is determined at a fixed rate.[9]

Example 23.1. Brenda Harris holds all of the voting common stock of a corporation and all of the Series 1, 3, and 4 Class A preferred stock. The Series 2 Class A preferred stock is owned by a trust, the beneficiaries of which are Brenda's children. Brenda transfers all of the Series 3 and 4 Class A preferred stock to the trust. The Series 1 Class A stock is entitled to cumulative dividends at a fixed rate. The Series 1 Class A preferred stock is an applicable retained interest, but it is valued at its fair market value, rather than at zero because it carries a distribution right that is a qualified payment right.

---

[5] Code Sec. 2701(a)(2) and 2701(c)(2)(C); and Reg. § 25.2701-1(c).

[6] Reg. § 25.2701-2(b)(2).

[7] Reg. § 25.2701-2(b)(3).

[8] Reg. § 25.2701-2(a)(2).

[9] Reg. § 25.2701-2(b)(6).

Applicable family member. An applicable family member is, with respect to any transferor, the transferor's spouse, ancestors of the transferor and the spouse, and spouses of such ancestors.

Control. For a corporation, control is defined as holding, before the transfer, at least 50 percent, by vote or value, of the stock of the corporation. For a partnership, control generally means holding at least 50 percent of either the capital or profits interest in the partnership. In addition, any general partner in a limited partnership is deemed to have control. In determining control, the interests of the transferor, applicable family members and lineal descendants of the parent transferor or the transferor's spouse are included.[10] In addition, individuals are treated as holding interests held indirectly through corporations, partnerships, estates, trusts, or other entities.[11]

Excluded rights. Rights expressly excluded from application of the valuation rules are mandatory payment rights, liquidation participation rights, rights of a partner to guaranteed payments of a fixed amount, and nonlapsing conversion rights. Mandatory payment rights include the right to receive a specific amount payable at death and a mandatory redemption right in preferred stock requiring that the stock be redeemed at a specified date at par value. Liquidation participation rights are valued either without regard to the ability to compel liquidation or under a rule requiring that all rights are exercised in a manner that results in the lowest value for all the rights.

.03 Extraordinary Payment Rights Combined with Distribution Rights

A retained interest that confers both (1) a liquidation, put, call, or conversion right, and (2) a distribution right that consists of the right to receive a qualified payment, is valued on the assumption that each right is exercised in a manner resulting in the lowest total value for all of these rights.[12] A qualified payment is defined as a dividend payable on a periodic basis at a fixed rate, including a rate that bears a fixed relationship to a specified market interest rate, under cumulative preferred stock or a comparable payment under a partnership agreement.

> ***Example 23.2.*** Frank Anderson is a father who retains cumulative preferred stock in a transfer to which these valuation rules apply. The cumulative dividend is $100 per year and the stock may be redeemed at any time after 2 years for $1,000. The

[10] Code Sec. 2701(b)(2)(C).

[11] Reg. § 25.2701-6.

[12] Reg. § 25.2701-2(a)(3).

value of the cumulative preferred stock is the lesser of (1) the present value of 2 years of $100 in dividends plus the present value of the redemption for $1,000 in year 2, or (2) the present value of $100 paid every year in perpetuity.

Example 23.3. Edward Davis holds all 1,000 shares of Ex Corporation's preferred stock bearing an annual cumulative dividend of $100 per share and all 1,000 shares of Ex's voting common stock. Edward has the right to put all the preferred stock to Ex at any time for $900,000. Edward transfers the common stock to his daughter Leah, while holding the preferred stock. Assume that the fair market value of Ex at the time of the transfer is $1.5 million, and the fair market value of the dividend right is $1 million. The preferred stock confers both an extraordinary payment right (the put right) and a qualified payment right (the right to receive cumulative dividends). Therefore, the value of these rights is determined as if the put right will be exercised in a manner that results in the lowest total value being determined for the rights, that is, by assuming that the put will be exercised immediately. The value of Davis's preferred stock is $900,000 (the lower of $1 million or $900,000).

A transferor or applicable family member may elect not to treat all rights of the same class to dividends, or comparable payments, as qualified payment rights. In addition, a transferor or applicable family member may elect to treat a distribution right as a qualified payment right to be paid in the amounts and at the times specified in the election.[13]

Example 23.4. Tim West and his daughter, Debra Kale, are partners in a partnership to which West contributes an existing business. West is entitled to 80% of the net cash receipts of the partnership until he receives $1 million, after which he and Kale will each receive 50% of the partnership's cash flow. West's liquidation preference equals $1 million. The retained right to $1 million is valued at zero unless West elects to treat it as a right to receive qualified payments in the amounts and at the times specified in the election. Amounts not paid at the times specified in the election are subject to the rules regarding the transfer tax treatment of accumulated distributions.

Applicable family members subject to special rule. Applicable family members holding qualified payment rights are subject to these valuation rules even though they have not made a transfer. As a result, these individuals would be subject to a compounding rule for

[13] Code Sec. 2701(c)(3)(C).

missed payments (as discussed below), which could increase their future estate and gift tax liability. To avoid this result, any qualified payment made to an applicable family member is treated as a nonqualified payment unless the family member elects to treat the payment, or consistent portion thereof, as a qualified payment.

Making elections. The elections to treat payments as qualified or nonqualified payments must be made by attaching a statement to the Form 709, "Federal Gift Tax Return," filed by the transferor. Regulations set forth the information to be provided on the statement. Once made, these elections are revocable only with the consent of the IRS.

.04 Subtraction Method

The amount of the gift resulting from a transfer to which the special valuation rules apply is determined using a subtraction method of valuation. Generally, the amount of the gift is determined by subtracting the values of all family-held senior equity interests from the value of all family-held interests in the entity immediately before the transfer. The balance is then allocated among the transferred interests and other family-held subordinate equity interests. Family-held interests are interests held by the transferor, applicable family members, and lineal descendants of the parents of the transferor or his spouse. A senior equity interest is an equity interest that has a right to income or principal distributions that is preferred as compared to the transferred interest. A subordinate equity interest is an interest as to which the retained interest is senior. The regulations prescribe a four-step subtraction method.[14]

.05 Transfer Tax Treatment of Accumulated Distributions

If a transferor retains cumulative preferred stock valued under the rule pertaining to the treatment of distribution rights combined with liquidation rights, the amount of the transferor's taxable gifts or taxable estate is increased by a certain amount. The amount of the increase is determined as follows:

1. The value of the distributions payable during the period beginning on the date of the transfer and ending on the date the interest of the prior interest holder terminated, determined as if all such distributions were paid on the date payment was due and all such distributions were reinvested by the transferor as of the date of payment at a yield equal to the discount rate used in determining the value of the applicable retained interest, over

[14] Reg. § 25.2701-3.

2. The value of the distributions paid during such period computed on the basis of the time when such distributions were actually paid, including the earnings on the payments determined as if each payment were reinvested as of the date paid at a yield equal to the discount rate used in determining the value of the distribution right, and to the extent required to prevent double tax, including any amount otherwise included in the gift or estate tax base.

This increase is intended to compensate for late or unpaid qualified payments that could have been reinvested by the recipient had the payments been made as due.

For purposes of this computation, a qualified payment includes payment in the form of a debt instrument, the term of which does not exceed four years, that bears compound interest at a rate no less than the appropriate discount rate payable from the due date of the qualified payment.[15]

The amount of the increase determined under this provision, however, is limited to an amount equal to the following:

1. The excess of the fair market values of equity interests that are junior to any retained preferred interests at the date of the later transfer plus any amounts paid to redeem a subordinate equity interest, over those values as of the date of the prior transfer of the junior interest, multiplied by
2. A fraction (determined immediately before the later transfer), the numerator of which is the number of shares of preferred interests held by the transferor, and the denominator of which is the number of all shares of the same class of preferred interest.[16]

.06 Minimum Value of Junior Equity Interest

A minimum value is established for a junior equity interest in a corporation or partnership. The minimum value is not less than a pro rata portion of 10 percent of the sum of the total equity in the corporation or partnership, plus any debt that the corporation or partnership owes to the transferor or members of his or her family. Debt does not include the following:

- Short-term indebtedness incurred to conduct the entity's trade or business, such as amounts payable for current services

[15] Reg. § 25.2701-4(c).

[16] Reg. § 25.2701-4(c)(6).

- Loan guarantees by the transferor or an applicable family member
- Amounts permanently set aside in a qualified deferred compensation arrangement
- A lease of property if the lease payments represent full and adequate consideration for the use of the property

This minimum value is intended to reflect the option value of the right of the residual interest to future appreciation.[17]

.07 Adjustments to Mitigate Double Taxation

In the case of retained rights valued pursuant to these special valuation rules, the possibility exists that rights given a zero value will be subject to double taxation on a subsequent transfer or inclusion in the gross estate of the transferor. To avoid this result, final regulations generally allow an adjustment in the computation of the transferor's gift tax if either the transferor or an applicable family member transfers an applicable retained interest to or for the benefit of an individual other than the transferor or applicable family member.[18] In addition, if the applicable retained interest had not been so transferred before the death of the transferor, the executor of his or her estate is entitled to make the adjustment in computing the transferor's estate tax. However, the executor must be able to demonstrate the fair market value of the applicable retained interest as of the date of death of the transferor.

The actual adjustment mechanism is complicated and difficult to describe. Nevertheless, the following example should serve to demonstrate how the adjustment works for a lifetime transfer of an applicable retained interest.

> ***Example 23.5.*** Donald Smith holds 1,500 shares of $1,000 par value preferred stock of Widget, Inc. (bearing an annual noncumulative dividend of $100 per share that may be put to Widget at any time for par value) and all 1,000 shares of voting common stock of Widget. On January 15, 2002, when the total FMV of the preferred stock is $1.5 million and the total FMV of the common stock is $500,000, Donald transfers all of the common stock to his daughter, Jill Jones. Under Code Sec. 2701, the value of the preferred stock is zero and the gift of the common stock is $2 million. On October 1, 2005, at a time when the value of Smith's preferred stock is $1.4 million, he transfers all of it to Jones.

[17] Code Sec. 2701(a)(4).

[18] Reg. § 25.2701-5.

Under the adjustment mechanism, Smith reduces the amount on which his tentative gift tax is computed under Code Sec. 2502 by $1.4 million so that no gift tax is paid on the transfer. The $1.4 million is the lesser of $1.5 million (the amount by which the initial gift of the common stock was increased as a result of Code Sec. 2701) or $1.4 million (the duplicated amount). The duplicated amount is 100% (the portion of the Code Sec. 2701 subsequently transferred) times $1.4 million, the amount by which the gift tax value of the preferred stock exceeds zero (the Code Sec. 2701 value of the preferred stock at the time of the initial transfer).

¶ 2310 OPTIONS AND BUY-SELL AGREEMENTS

When valuing any property for estate, gift, and generation-skipping transfer tax purposes, the value is determined without regard to any option, agreement, or other right to acquire or use the property at less than fair market value, or any restriction on the right to sell or use such property, unless the option, agreement, right, or restriction meets three requirements.[19] These requirements are that the option, agreement, right, or restriction: (1) is a bona fide business arrangement, (2) is not a device to transfer such property to members of the decedent's family for less than full and adequate consideration in money or money's worth, and (3) is comparable to similar arrangements entered into by persons in an arm's-length transaction.

Also, although not in Code Sec. 2703, under long-standing principles that continue to apply according to applicable Committee reports, an agreement must have lifetime restrictions in order to be binding upon death. Under the Code Sec. 2703 rules, the mere showing that the agreement is a bona fide business arrangement does not establish that the agreement is not a device to transfer property to members of the decedent's family for less than full and adequate consideration.

The requirements are considered to be met if more than 50 percent by value of the property subject to the right or restriction is owned by persons who are not members of the transferor's family. Family members include the transferor, applicable family members (as discussed in ¶ 2305 in connection with the rules for business interests), any lineal descendants of the parents of the transferor or the transferor's spouse, and any other individual who is the natural object of the transferor's bounty.[20]

[19] Code Sec. 2703.

[20] Reg. § 25.2703-1(b)(3).

These requirements apply to any restriction, however created. For example, they apply to restrictions implicit in the capital structure of the partnership or contained in a partnership agreement, articles of incorporation, corporate bylaws, or a shareholder's agreement. A lease is a right or restriction that is subject to these requirements. These requirements do not, however, apply to perpetual restrictions on the use of real property that qualified for either the gift or estate tax charitable deduction.[21]

The requirements apply to agreements, options, rights, or restrictions entered into or granted after October 8, 1990, and those that are substantially modified after October 8, 1990.[22] A right or restriction that is substantially modified is treated as being created on the date of the modification. A modification resulting in other than a de minimis change in the quality, value, or timing of the rights of any party with respect to property subject to a right or restriction is a substantial modification. The addition of a family member as a party to the right or restriction in a generation no lower than the lowest generation occupied by persons already party to the right or restriction is not a substantial modification. However, the IRS held in Letter Ruling 9620017[23] that a pre-October 8, 1990, shareholder agreement was substantially modified where a proposed change to the agreement allowed the controlling shareholder to transfer stock to members of his family.

A substantial modification does not include mandatory changes under a right or restriction or a change to a right or restriction to approximate the fair market value more closely. Thus, the IRS has ruled that a grandfathered buy-sell agreement was not substantially modified by changing the strike price to fair market value, or by providing a reciprocal arrangement so that at the death of one of three shareholders, the remaining two would have equal buyout rights.[24] A substantial modification also does not include amendments to a corporation's articles of incorporation and bylaws that change the number of directors and the indemnity and immunity provisions for directors and officers, and increase the number of shares to effectuate a stock split.[25]

Family limited partnerships. The IRS has taken the position that valuation discounts on the creation of a family limited partnership and the transfer of interests in the partnership just before a

[21] Code Secs. 2522 and 2055.

[22] Reg. § 25.2703-2.

[23] February 15, 1996.

[24] IRS Letter Ruling 9417007, January 13, 1994.

[25] Reg. § 25.2703-1(c).

decedent's death could be denied. The IRS could deny the valuation discounts on the theory that the steps to accomplish the transfer should be disregarded for estate tax valuation purposes as a sham transaction, or under the rules of Code Sec. 2703.[26] The IRS may also seek to include the transferred interest in the decedent's gross estate under Code Sec. 2036. In such cases, the IRS may argue that the decedent made the transfer for less than full or adequate consideration in money or money's worth.[27]

According to the IRS, under the circumstances of the transaction, the children really received the underlying partnership assets, subject to the partnership agreement. Thus, the partnership agreement itself was an agreement within the meaning of Code Sec. 2703, and any reduction in value caused by the partnership agreement could be disregarded.

Even if the steps of the transaction were not collapsed and the partnership interests, rather than the underlying assets, were treated as the subject of the transfers, the IRS argued that Code Sec. 2703 would still apply. It pointed out that, under Reg. § 25.2703-1(a)(3), a restriction could either be contained in a partnership agreement or implicit in the capital structure of the partnership. Under the facts of the ruling, the partnership agreement and state law implicitly imposed several restrictions on the ability of the beneficiaries to sell their interests. The IRS said that these restrictions could be disregarded in valuing the partnership interests. More about family limited partnerships and the special valuation rules appears at ¶ 2010.

¶ 2315 TRANSFERS OF TRUST INTERESTS

Code Sec. 2702 provides special valuation rules for transfers of interests in trusts to or for the benefit of members of the transferor's family made after October 8, 1990.

Family members are broadly defined to include the transferor's spouse, lineal descendants of the transferor or his or her spouse, spouses of those descendants, the transferor's ancestors, siblings, and the spouses of any of them.[28] As broad as this definition is, it omits nieces, nephews, and cousins. Thus, a taxpayer could form a pre-Code Sec. 2036(c) grantor retained income trust (GRIT) with

---

[26] IRS Technical Advice Memorandum 9719006, January 14, 1997.

[27] *A. Strangi Est.*, 115 TC 478 (2000), aff'd in part, rev'd in part, and rem'd in part, 2002-2 USTC ¶ 60,441 (CA-5, 2002); *Harper Est.*, 83 TCM 1641 (2002); *D.A. Kimbell, Sr.*, et al. (D.C. N. Texas, 2003).

[28] Code Sec. 2702(e), which picks up the family definition in Code Sec. 2704(c)(2).

these extended family members and other nonfamily members, including a live-in companion.

If a taxpayer is going to make a transfer to a trust for a family member, Code Sec. 2702, with certain exceptions, provides that for gift tax purposes any retained interest other than a qualified retained interest, i.e., a grantor retained annuity or unitrust (a GRAT or a GRUT), is valued at zero. Consequently, any gift of a remainder interest would be valued at the full value of the property transferred to the trust.

Exceptions. Code Sec. 2702 contains two express exceptions: (1) incomplete gifts; and (2) transfers of an interest in trust if all the property in the trust consists of a residence to be used as a personal residence by persons holding term interests in the trust (a qualified personal residence trust or QPRT).[29]

An incomplete gift means any transfer that would not be treated as a gift, whether or not consideration was received for the transfer. A transfer to a revocable trust, for example, would be treated as an incomplete gift.

The exception for the personal residence is discussed below at ¶ 315.03.

In addition to these two express exceptions, the law also provides an implicit exception for transfers to trusts for nonfamily members, which may take the form of grantor retained income trusts, as discussed at ¶ 315.02. Further, special rules apply to transfers of certain tangible property and undeveloped land. These rules are discussed at ¶ 315.04 below in connection with the treatment of nontrust property.

The Code Sec. 2702 rules also apply to joint purchases of property, as discussed at ¶ 315.05.

.01 The General Rule

Code Sec. 2702 is concerned with the valuation for gift tax purposes of transfers in trust to or for the benefit of a member of the transferor's family and the valuation of retained interests of the transferor or any applicable family member.

Code Sec. 2702 provides that any retained interest that is not a qualified interest and not subject to an exception is valued at zero. If the retained interest is a qualified interest, its value generally is to be determined under Code Sec. 7520 and the applicable IRS tables.

---

[29] Code Sec. 2702(a)(3).

Code Sec. 2702 further provides that a qualified interest is (1) a right to receive fixed amounts payable at least annually, (2) a right to receive amounts payable at least annually, which are a fixed percentage of the trust's assets determined annually, or (3) a noncontingent remainder interest if all the other interests in the trust consist of interests described in (1) and (2).

A trust of the first type can be likened to an annuity, although it may be for a term of years and not necessarily for life. For that reason, it has come to be known as a grantor retained annuity trust, with the acronym GRAT. The second type can be likened to a unitrust, and for that reason, it has come to be known as a GRUT.

With a common law grantor retained income trust (GRIT), which generally is no longer allowed except for transfers to nonfamily members and trusts that take advantage of the residence exception, use of the IRS valuation tables frequently results in the retained income interest being overvalued and the remainder interest being undervalued. For example, if low-dividend, high-growth stock is transferred to the trust, use of the table causes the retained interest to be valued on the basis of an assumed income or interest rate. Use of the table can result in a much higher valuation than if the actual yield were used.

The qualified interest rules preclude this technique. The annuity or unitrust amount must be paid regardless of the actual yield of the trust assets. Because the trust is a grantor trust, the grantor will be taxed on all of the trust's income,[30] even if it exceeds the amount needed to pay the annuity or unitrust amount. This result is better than having the trust income taxed under the highly compressed brackets that apply for trusts.

GRATs and GRUTs are not limited as to duration. The longer the term interest, the lower the value of the remainder for gift tax purposes. However, if the transferor dies before the expiration of the term, the full value of the trust would be includible in his or her gross estate under Code Sec. 2036(a)(1). This rule operates as a practical limitation on the duration of the trust. It should be significantly shorter than the transferor's life expectancy under mortality tables or, more importantly, the transferor's actual life expectancy based on his or her medical condition.

The IRS has taken the position that a GRAT established with a revocable spousal interest, giving the spouse a contingent right to receive the property if the grantor died prematurely, was not a qualified interest.[31] Accordingly, the value of the spousal interest could

---

[30] Code Sec. 671.

[31] IRS Technical Advice Memorandum 9707001, October 25, 1996.

not be taken into account in valuing the property transferred to the GRAT.

.02 Common Law GRITs

Code Sec. 2702 leaves little room for common law grantor retained income trusts (GRITs), because the retained interest in a GRIT would generally be valued at zero under the provision. However, Code Sec. 2702 is only concerned with transfers in trust to or for the benefit of a member of the transferor's family. A member of the family is rather broadly defined by Code Sec. 2704(c)(2) (picked up in Code Sec. 2702) as an individual's (1) spouse, (2) ancestor or lineal descendant of the individual or his spouse, (3) brother or sister, or (4) or any spouse of an individual in (2) or (3).

Broad as it is, this definition leaves out many others, some of whom may be close family members. For example, nieces and nephews, and others with no blood or legally recognized relationship such as a friend or companion are not included.

Common law GRITs may be set up for such individuals. Such GRITs generally have an advantage over GRATs and GRUTs in that the retained interest might be overvalued, resulting in the remainder interest being undervalued. For example, a GRIT may be funded with low-dividend paying, high-growth stocks. The stock might produce dividends, for example, of only one or two percent of the value of the stock. Yet, the retained interest might be valued on the assumption that it will provide the grantor with a yield of six percent or so annually. The result is a higher value for the retained interest than the actual yield warrants. Also, the low yield makes for smaller income taxable to the grantor.

These common law GRITs have no fixed period of duration. Thus, with longer durations, the value of a gift of remainder interests can be kept lower. However, as a practical matter, duration should be safely short of the grantor's life expectancy, because if he or she dies during the term of the trust, the corpus of the trust will be includible in his or her gross estate.

Code Sec. 2702 also expressly excepts personal residences from its reach. This exception is separately discussed at ¶ 2315.03 below.

.03 The Exception for Residences

Code Sec. 2702 excepts personal residences from the general rule valuing retained interests in certain transferred property at zero unless the retained interest is a qualified interest. This exception creates important opportunities for tax-saving, intra-family wealth transfers.

As an intra-family wealth transfer vehicle, the exception is most useful where the family home is expected to appreciate significantly in value over the term of the trust. The Code Sec. 2702 zero value rules do not apply to a transfer of an interest in a personal residence trust or a qualified personal residence trust.[32] The latter was created by the Treasury regulations to address certain practical problems. However, it involves a tradeoff, as explained below.

Personal residence trust. A personal residence trust is a trust the governing instrument of which prohibits, for the original duration of the term interest, the holding of any asset other than one residence used or held for use as a personal residence of the term holder and qualified proceeds. A personal residence is the term holder's principal residence, one other residence, or an undivided fractional interest in either. A co-op qualifies as a personal residence.[33] The residence must not be occupied by anyone other than the term holder, his or her spouse and dependents, and must be available at all times for use as a personal residence by the term holder.

A personal residence may include appropriate structures used for residential purposes and adjacent land that is reasonably appropriate for residential purposes. The IRS has allowed a tract of land as large as 43 acres to be considered as reasonably appropriate for residential purposes.[34] However, estate planners should exercise caution in similar cases because the result depends on all the facts and circumstances of a particular case. Further, a personal residence may be subject to a mortgage. The term holder may use a portion of the residence for business purposes, but may not provide transient lodging, such as a hotel or bed and breakfast, or provide substantial services in connection with lodging.

The trust may not hold personal property, such as household furnishings. Qualified proceeds, which may be held by the trust, are amounts held by the trust for no longer than two years that were received as a result of damage, destruction, or involuntary conversion of the personal residence.

One's spouse who holds an interest in the same residence may transfer his or her interest to the same personal residence trust, but only if the governing instrument prohibits anyone other than one's spouse from holding a concurrent term interest.[35]

---

[32] Code Sec. 2702(a)(3) and Reg. § 25.2702-5.

[33] IRS Letter Ruling 9448035, September 2, 1994.

[34] IRS Letter Ruling 9639064, June 27, 1996.

[35] Reg. § 25.2702-5(b).

Qualified personal residence trust. A qualified personal residence trust (QPRT) is similar to a personal residence trust, except that a QPRT may also hold limited amounts of cash for payment of trust expenses, sale proceeds, insurance on the residence, and insurance proceeds. However, the governing instrument of a QPRT must prohibit distribution of trust income to anyone other than the term holder. The trust instrument must also provide that any income of the trust be distributed to the term holder not less frequently than annually. In addition, the governing instrument must provide that on cessation of use of the residence as a personal residence, either the trust terminates and all trust assets are distributed to the term holder, or the term interest is converted to a qualified annuity interest. The trustee may be given sole discretion to choose either option. The distribution or conversion must occur within 30 days of the date on which the trust ceases to be a qualified personal residence trust. Excess sale proceeds that are not reinvested in a new personal residence may be converted to a qualified annuity interest.[36] The IRS has provided an annotated sample declaration of trust and alternate provisions that meet the requirements of Code Sec. 2702(a)(3)(A) and Reg. § 25.2702-5(c).[37]

The Treasury regulations provide additional guidance on the tax treatment of QPRTs. These regulations are generally effective for trusts created after May 16, 1996. Reg. § 25.2702-5(c)(9) requires that the governing instrument of the trust include a provision prohibiting the trust from selling or transferring the residence (whether directly, or indirectly) to the grantor, the grantor's spouse, or an entity controlled by either. This prohibition would have to apply during the original term interest of the trust, and to any time after the original term interest that the trust was a grantor trust. For purposes of this requirement, a sale or transfer to another grantor trust of the grantor or the grantor's spouse is considered a sale or transfer to the grantor or the grantor's spouse.

This requirement prohibiting a sale or transfer prevents families using personal residence trusts or QPRTs from realizing large income tax savings. If the grantor leaves the residence in trust until expiration of its term, the remainder beneficiaries will acquire the property with a carryover basis[38] from the grantor, often leaving them with a large built-in gain. On the other hand, if the grantor were allowed to repurchase the residence just before the end of the trust term, more favorable tax results could be obtained. No gain would be recognized to the grantor on the repurchase,[39] and at the end of the

---

[36] Reg. § 25.2702-5(c).

[37] Rev. Proc. 2003-42, IRB 2003-23 (June 9, 2003).

[38] Code Sec. 1015.

[39] Rev. Rul. 85-13, 1985-1 CB 184.

trust term, the beneficiaries would receive flat-basis cash. Further, the residence would return to the grantor, would be included in the grantor's gross estate, and would receive a stepped-up basis under Code Sec. 1014. The total step up in basis is limited to $1,300,000 plus $3,000,000 for property received by a surviving spouse from a decedent dying in 2010.

However, the prohibited sale rule of Reg. § 25.2702-5(c)(9) does not apply to a distribution for no consideration after the grantor's death and before expiration of the term interest to any person pursuant to the provisions of the trust or pursuant to exercise of a power retained by the grantor under the trust provisions. Nor does it apply to a distribution for no consideration to the grantor's spouse after the expiration of the trust term pursuant to the language of the trust.

Reg. § 25.2702-5(a)(2) provides that a trust that failed to qualify for the personal residence trust or QPRT exception to the zero value rule may be modified to bring it into compliance. Such a modification must be commenced within 90 days after the due date (including extensions) for filing the gift tax return reporting the transfer of the residence, and must be completed within a reasonable time thereafter. If the reformation is not completed by the due date (including extensions) for filing the gift tax return, the grantor or the grantor's spouse must attach a statement to this return, stating that the reformation has been commenced or will be commenced within the 90-day period. For trusts created before January 1, 1997, the reformation must have commenced before March 24, 1998, and must be completed within a reasonable time after commencement.

.04 Treatment of Property Not Held in Trust

Under Code Sec. 2702(c), the transfer of a term interest in property not held in trust is treated like the retention of an interest in trust. Thus, for example, if a father gives a remainder interest in stock to his son, he is deemed to make a gift of 100 percent of the value of the stock, not merely the actuarial value of the remainder interest.

However, Code Sec. 2702(d) provides a special rule for the valuation of a term interest in certain tangible property. This section provides that if the nonexercise of rights in tangible property would not have a substantial effect on the valuation of the remainder interest in such property, the value of such term interest would not be zero under the general rule. In this case, the value would be the amount that the holder establishes an unrelated person would pay for such interest in an arm's-length transaction.

The Senate Finance Committee, in discussing the special rules for tangible property, makes reference to a joint purchase of paintings and undeveloped land as within the ambit of these special rules. Joint purchases are discussed at ¶ 2315.05 below.

.05 Joint Purchases

Intra-family joint purchases of property had a fairly long vogue as estate planning devices. A parent and child would purchase income producing property from a third person. The parent would receive a life income or term interest, and the child would receive a remainder interest. Each would pay the actuarial value for each interest, computed under IRS tables. The goal was to buy property with good appreciation potential. No gift tax would be due on the acquisition of the property because each party paid the full value of the interest acquired. Nothing would be includible in the parent's gross estate on his or her death, even though the parent held a life income interest. Code Sec. 2036(a), which drew into the gross estate of a decedent property that the parent had transferred during his or her lifetime in which the parent retained a life income interest or an interest that did not in fact end until his or her death, did not apply. The reason was that the parent had not made a lifetime transfer and had not retained an interest in the property transferred.

Now, a joint purchase of property is treated as the acquisition of the entire property by the holder of the term interest followed by a transfer of the remainder interest. The Senate Finance Committee stated, "Thus, for purposes of determining the amount of the gift, the bill [the law] effectively treats the purchaser of a life estate pursuant to a joint purchase as making a transfer of the entire property less the consideration paid by the remainderman."

¶ 2320 LAPSING RIGHTS AND RESTRICTIONS

Code Sec. 2704 deals with the tax treatment of certain restrictions and lapsing rights upon the value of an interest in a partnership or corporation. It is intended to prevent results similar to those in *D. Harrison Est.*,[40] in which the lapse of Harrison's right to liquidate his interest in partnership with his sons upon his death resulted in a drastic reduction in the value of his partnership interest at death by over $20 million.

Code Sec. 2704(a) provides that the lapse of voting or liquidation rights in a family-controlled corporation or partnership results in a transfer by gift or an inclusion in the gross estate. The amount of the transfer is the value of all the interests in the entity held by the

[40] 52 TCM 1306, CCH Dec. 43,609(M), TC Memo. 1987-8.

transferor immediately before the lapse (assuming the right was nonlapsing) over the value of the interests immediately after the lapse.

Code Sec. 2704(b) provides that any restriction that effectively limits the ability of a corporation or partnership to liquidate is ignored in valuing a transfer among family members if (1) the transferor and family members control the corporation or partnership immediately before the transfer, and (2) the restriction either lapses after the transfer or can be removed by the transferor or members of his or her family, either alone or collectively.

For purposes of Code Sec. 2704, the definition of family-controlled is a broad one, and family members include the transferor's (1) spouse, (2) ancestors, lineal descendants, or the spouse of such persons, (3) brothers and sisters, and (4) any spouse of individuals in (2) and (3).

These rules apply to restrictions or rights (or limitations on rights) created after October 8, 1990.

The IRS has applied Code Sec. 2704 to the valuation of interests transferred in family limited partnerships (FLPs). For example, IRS Letter Ruling 9723009[41] involved the transfer of an interest in an FLP whose partnership agreement provided that no partner could withdraw from the partnership. Under applicable state law, however, absent the restriction in the partnership agreement, the transferee could have withdrawn and liquidated with six-month's notice. Because the prohibition on the decedent's right to liquidate her interest was more restrictive than state law, it was an applicable restriction and was disregarded for purposes of valuing the transferred stock.

[41] February 24, 1997.

Chapter 24

Planning for Marriage, Divorce, or Separation

Overview ....¶ 2401
The Premarital Agreement ....¶ 2405
Special Planning for Subsequent Marriages ....¶ 2410
Marriage Versus Living Together Outside of Marriage ....¶ 2415
Divorce and Separation ....¶ 2420
Alimony ....¶ 2425
Child Support ....¶ 2430
Property Settlements ....¶ 2435
Legal Expenses ....¶ 2440
Division of Retirement Benefits ....¶ 2445

¶ 2401 OVERVIEW

Preparing financially for marriage, divorce, or separation requires careful planning and full consideration of the options available.

¶ 2405 THE PREMARITAL AGREEMENT

A financial planner should consider the use of premarital agreements (also known as prenuptial agreements or antenuptial agreements) whenever one of the parties is contemplating making a substantial gift to the other in consideration of the marriage. Another use of a prenuptial agreement is to limit the statutory, common law, or community property rights of each party to the other party's property or to limit or eliminate other claims of one against the other. Couples often use this type of agreement only where there is a substantial disparity in the wealth of the parties. However, a couple might also use a prenuptial agreement where each party has substantial wealth and the parties wish to maintain their financial independence. Another situation in which couples often use a prenuptial agreement is where one or both of the parties have had prior marriages that confer on them continuing rights or impose on them continuing duties (¶ 2410).

In its common form, the prenuptial agreement involves a transfer, or the promise of a transfer, of property from the more affluent individual to the other. The transaction is either outright or in trust, in exchange for a release of all rights and claims the other individual might have for support or against the transferor's property or estate.

The National Conference of Commissioners on Uniform State Laws adopted the Uniform Premarital Agreement Act in 1983. This Act provides assistance for couples who want to make agreements before marriage regarding such things as alimony and property dispositions in the event of separation, divorce, or death. The District of Columbia and the following 26 states have adopted some form of this Act:

Arizona	Nebraska
Arkansas	Nevada
California	New Jersey
Connecticut	New Mexico
Delaware	North Carolina
Hawaii	North Dakota
Idaho	Oregon
Illinois	Rhode Island
Indiana	South Dakota
Iowa	Texas
Kansas	Utah
Maine	Virginia
Montana	Wisconsin

States that have not adopted this Act often have similar laws. However, the laws vary somewhat among the states. A financial planner should urge a couple considering a premarital agreement to consult a competent attorney in the state where they plan to live.

A financial planner should consider a prenuptial agreement as part of the financial and estate plan of both parties. He or she should evaluate it in terms of its estate, gift, and income tax consequences; legal considerations; and other matters as discussed below.

.01 Validity in General

As a general rule, for a premarital agreement involving property rights to be valid under state law, it must be fair, reasonable, and equitable. In order to meet this test, both parties must make a full and fair disclosure of all their income and property.

.02 Release of Support Obligations

Most states adhere to the view that a prenuptial agreement cannot relieve a spouse of his or her support obligation. The U.S. Supreme Court held that a statute that provides that husbands, but not wives, can be required to pay alimony on divorce is unconstitutional, because alimony rests on need and need is gender neutral.[1] Thus, if the marriage fails, an individual might remain liable for support unless relieved of this obligation by a legal separation agreement, divorce, or the subsequent remarriage of his or her divorced spouse. However, all states prohibit couples from making binding agreements about obligations for child support payments.

.03 Alimony Rights

An individual may challenge the validity of alimony provisions in a premarital agreement in many states as against public policy. However, under the current trend of authority, many states will not deem such provisions to be contrary to public policy if they take into account the adequacy of the spouse's means of support, or if the support obligation is subject to increase or decrease under changed conditions.

.04 Governing Law

If the possibility exists that the parties might change their domicile and move to another jurisdiction, the prenuptial agreement should address governing law. Addressing the governing law is particularly important if the change is from or to states with conflicting public policy views (paragraph .03, above) or involves moving from common law to community property states.

.05 Community Property Law

If the parties are residents of a community property state or might become residents of a community property state, the agreement should address their community and separate property rights and obligations.

---

[1] *N. Orr*, 440 US 268, 99 SCt 1102.

.06 Income Tax Consequences

If an individual transfers property to a spouse or to a former spouse incident to a divorce as part of a premarital settlement in consideration of the release of the support obligation, the transferor recognizes no gain or loss.[2] The transferee's adjusted basis in the property is the same as the transferor's adjusted basis.[3]

.07 Gift Tax Consequences

A transfer of property to a current spouse is not subject to gift tax because of the unlimited marital deduction.[4] A transfer of property to a former spouse in satisfaction of marital or property rights is a taxable gift to the extent that the value of the property transferred exceeds the actuarial value of any support obligation or other consideration in money or money's worth.[5] The gift is subject to the $12,000 annual exclusion (for 2006),[6] which is indexed to inflation.[7] However, the transfer will not be a taxable gift if it complies with the requirements of Code Sec. 2516.[8] Code Sec. 2516 applies when a husband and wife enter into a written agreement concerning their marital and property rights and they divorce within the three-year period beginning on the date one year before they make the agreement. A transfer of property pursuant to the agreement in settlement of marital rights, property rights, or support for minor children is not subject to gift tax. Such transfers are considered made for a full and adequate consideration in money or money's worth.

.08 Estate Tax Consequences

A lifetime transfer made by an individual can be includible in his or her gross estate under Code Secs. 2035-2038, except in the case of a bona fide sale for adequate and full consideration in money or money's worth. Code Sec. 2043(a) governs transfers for a consideration in money or money's worth where the consideration is less than adequate and full. In such a case, the decedent's gross estate includes only the fair market value at the time of death of the transferred property exceeding the value of the consideration received by the decedent. Code Sec. 2043(b) also provides that a relinquishment of marital rights in the decedent's property or estate is not to be regarded in any degree as a consideration in money or money's

[2] Code Sec. 1041(a) and Temp. Reg. § 1.1041-1T(a).

[3] Code Sec. 1041(b).

[4] Code Sec. 2523(a).

[5] Code Sec. 2043(b) and Rev. Rul. 68-379, 1968-2 CB 414.

[6] Code Sec. 2503(b)(1).

[7] Code Sec. 2503(b)(2).

[8] House Committee Report on P.L. 98-369 (Deficit Reduction Act of 1984).

worth unless the transfer complies with the requirements of Code Sec. 2516 (discussed in .07 above).

Therefore, the prenuptial agreement must first be tested against the cited Code sections. Code Sec. 2035, dealing with transfers within three years of death and their includibility in the gross estate of the transferor, should pose no problem unless the transfer is of a life insurance policy on the life of the transferor. Code Sec. 2036 applies only if the donor retains a life estate, which is not likely. Code Sec. 2037 can be more troublesome. In order to escape its reach, the transfer must be one that takes effect in the present, or at least at some future time before death. If it is to take effect at death, it must not provide for the retention of a reversionary interest exceeding five percent of the value of the property transferred. To avoid attack under Code Sec. 2038, the transfer must not be subject to revocation or amendment.

Assuming that the parties can structure the transfer under the prenuptial agreement to avoid inclusion under these sections, whether or not the transfer is for full and adequate consideration in money or money's worth becomes immaterial. The transfer is not includible in the transferor's gross estate.

Even though the transaction is within reach of one of these sections and consideration in money or money's worth is important in determining whether the transfer is includible in the transferor's gross estate, the value of the transferred property will not be includible in the transferor's gross estate to the extent that it is in release of support rights. This result occurs because the IRS and the courts distinguish between support rights and marital rights or inheritance rights. The renunciation of marital rights is consideration, while renunciation of inheritance rights is not.[9]

.09 Claims Against the Transferor's Estate

Whether or not the estate may deduct a claim against the estate[10] based on a premarital agreement depends primarily on whether the claim is supported by consideration. If the claim is based on giving up the marital rights, it generally will not be deductible because marital rights are generally not consideration in money or money's worth.[11] However, the estate may deduct property transferred in satisfaction of a claim pursuant to an agreement that complies with the provisions of Code Sec. 2516 (discussed in .07 above). Thus, if a transferor dies before completing the transfers under a written agreement that

[9] Rev. Rul. 68-379, 1968-2 CB 414.

[10] Code Sec. 2053(a)(3).

[11] Code Sec. 2043(b).

meets the requirements of Code Sec. 2516, the estate may deduct the value of the property transferred in satisfaction of the claim.[12]

If a transfer or payment was to be made under a prenuptial agreement in consideration of the release of support rights, the claim made against the estate should be deductible.

.10 Claims Against the Transferee's Estate

If the surviving spouse is given a greater interest than the prenuptial agreement provided, to the detriment of a descendant, the payment of any claim made by the latter against the estate of the surviving spouse may be deductible by the estate.[13]

.11 Release of Right to Retirement Benefits

A married individual has an interest under federal law in the retirement benefits belonging to his or her spouse.

.12 Structuring the Agreement

In setting up a prenuptial agreement, using a trust instead of an outright transfer is often advisable. With an irrevocable trust, the property will generally be kept out of the settlor's gross estate even if the trust is set up within three years of death. A transferor might give his or her spouse a life interest, with the possible right to invade the principal (corpus) in accordance with a defined standard, with a remainder going to the children or other beneficiaries. In such a case, the trust property can be kept out of the spouse's gross estate. In general, a trust arrangement has all its usual advantages.

The agreement does not have to be in any particular form. It should be in writing; it should name the parties; and it should describe the property to be transferred and the time at which the transfer is to take place (i.e., before marriage, after marriage, or on the death of the groom). It should also recite the promises to marry, the considerations for the transfer(s), the rights relinquished, and special provisions to be included in wills or trusts of one or both parties. The parties should consider the danger of mutual wills and the possible loss of the marital deduction.

.13 Breach of Agreement

A party might decide to terminate the agreement and call off the wedding. Therefore, the agreement should provide that the parties are then restored to the status quo before the agreement. Because the

---

[12] House Committee Report on P.L. 98-369 (Tax Reform Act of 1984).

[13] *M.K. Patterson Est.*, 46 TCM 618, CCH Dec. 40,243(M), TC Memo. 1983-381.

parties might have undertaken obligations in connection with the marriage (such as wedding plan expenses, apartment rental, gifts to each other and from third parties), the agreement might also specify who keeps what gifts and who provides for payment and/or reimbursement of expenses.

¶2410 SPECIAL PLANNING FOR SUBSEQUENT MARRIAGES

In a subsequent marriage, special considerations apply where one or both parties to the subsequent marriage have children by a prior marriage. The situation is further complicated where the couple plans to have children of their own.

.01 Termination of a Prior Marriage

Whether or not a prior marriage has been legally terminated can pose problems. No problem occurs if the termination is by death and there is actual proof of death. However, in the rare situation where termination by death is to be established on the basis of a presumption of death through prolonged absence without communication or other evidence of survival, problems can arise. The more common problem involves the validity of a prior divorce. For example, the court that granted the divorce might subsequently declare it invalid. Moreover, a problem can arise where a divorce obtained in one state or in a foreign country is later declared invalid in another state.

The validity or invalidity of a prior divorce (and common law marriage) can affect the parties' eligibility to file joint income tax returns, their estate and gift tax marital deduction, and their Social Security benefits. In those states that recognize a common law marriage, the couple may file a joint tax return.[14] The Social Security Act (SSA) recognizes a common law marriage if valid under state law for payment of widow's benefits. The SSA also recognizes an invalid ceremonial marriage for payment of benefits, but it does not recognize an invalid common law marriage.

The IRS will not generally question the validity of any divorce decree until a court of competent jurisdiction has declared it to be invalid. However, where a state court declares the prior divorce to be invalid, the IRS will usually follow the later court decision, rather than the prior divorce decree.[15]

From a planning standpoint, the safe course is to accept the IRS approach as stated in Rev. Rul. 67-442. Any departure from that rule would require a careful study of applicable judicial decisions that

[14] Rev. Rul. 83-183, 1983-2 CB 220.

[15] Rev. Rul. 67-442, 1967-2 CB 65.

might be relied on to uphold the validity of the marriage despite a state decree declaring a prior divorce invalid.

.02 Children of a Prior Marriage

If either or both parties to a marriage have children by a prior marriage, protection of the children requires special attention. The parties can provide such protection by a premarital agreement, outright gifts to the children, living trusts, custodial accounts, testamentary bequests, and testamentary trusts. A QTIP trust merits special consideration.

The parties should also consider acquiring additional life insurance by the parent or the child on the parent's life, naming the child as beneficiary. The child might also be named as beneficiary of existing policies. New policies might be obtained to provide added coverage for the new spouse and/or that individual's children by a prior marriage. Generally, the child should purchase life insurance policies on the life of a parent, rather than the parent purchasing the policy. In the latter case, the policy would be an asset of the parent and the policy proceeds would be includible in the parent's gross estate.[16] If the child is not old enough to purchase insurance, the purchase might possibly be made through the use of a custodial account, or by a trustee of an irrevocable life insurance trust (ILIT) for the benefit of the child.

The latter is the preferred method of providing for children of a prior marriage where the parent has sufficient assets with which to fund the trust. If the trust is created before marriage, the property transferred to it will generally not be included in determining the common law, statutory, or other interest of the transferor's spouse upon subsequent marriage. However, state law differs as to the effect of the creation of a premarital revocable trust on the interests created by state law in favor of a spouse. Therefore, a financial planner should check applicable state law.

.03 Prenuptial Agreements

Couples use prenuptial agreements more frequently where one or both parties have been previously married than where the marriage is the first for both. Prenuptial agreements are especially common where one or both parties have children from prior marriages. Such agreements can play a special role where two elderly individuals plan to marry. In such a case, family members of one or both parties might fear that the legal rights and obligations flowing

[16] Code Sec. 2042(2).

from what promises to be a short-term relationship might operate to the family members' disadvantage. This concern is particularly true where the assets of one of the parties include a family business. Family anxieties can also exist where there is a great disparity in the ages of the parties to the contemplated marriage.

.04 Tax Consequences

The tax consequences of a prenuptial agreement in connection with a second or subsequent marriage involving a transfer of property in consideration of a release of marital or support rights are the same as those for a first marriage (¶2405), except for factual differences in the two situations.

.05 Will Provisions

The couple and financial planner should consider emotional factors in ordering the disposition of property by will if one or both parties was previously married to someone else. These factors are not present in connection with a first marriage. This consideration is particularly important where the prior marriage ended in divorce. In addition, the couple must consider the children—his, hers, and theirs. A will that bequeaths everything to the survivor or a typical two-trust arrangement might be inappropriate, even where the couple has no children or where provisions for the children have already been made. Siblings, parents, and other related parties might be potential beneficiaries. Even an ex-spouse might merit consideration or might demand recognition by virtue of a property settlement or court decree.

In many cases, the bequest to the surviving spouse will be limited to the statutory, common law, or other interest required by law.

As suggested in 2, above, in connection with the discussion of children, a QTIP bequest merits special consideration from the standpoint of providing for a surviving spouse and deferring payment of estate taxes while at the same time protecting other intended beneficiaries.

¶2415 MARRIAGE VERSUS LIVING TOGETHER OUTSIDE OF MARRIAGE

The practice of couples living together outside of marriage has become quite common in recent years. Thus, the financial planner whose client is an individual cohabiting with another outside of marriage should advise the client of the probable legal and financial consequences (see also Chapter 25). Unless the relationship establishes a common law or informal marriage in a state that recognizes such marriages, the relationship by itself does not create rights similar to those of husband and wife. However, a contractual agreement concerning property rights between the parties may be enforceable.

Although a written contract might not be essential, prudence suggests the need for a written contract to avoid the difficulties involved in proving an oral contract. If a written contract does not appear to be feasible, then a financial planner should consider advising the client to keep a diary in which he or she would record any oral agreement(s) or conversations that might result in an enforceable contract. A financial planner should refer any legal questions involving such a contract to a competent attorney.

Various tax factors can affect a decision to marry or to live together outside of marriage. A two-earner couple generally pays more in income taxes if they are married than if they are living together. This phenomenon is known as the marriage penalty. Also, the couple should consider the following factors.

.01 Passive Activity Losses

Generally, a taxpayer may use losses from passive activities to offset income from passive activities only.[17] A taxpayer may not use losses from passive activities to offset portfolio income such as interest or dividends[18] or active income from employment and business activities in which the taxpayer materially participates.[19] A taxpayer carries forward any unused passive activity loss to the next tax year.[20] A taxpayer may deduct any unused passive activity loss against portfolio income and/or active income when the taxpayer disposes of the activity in a taxable transaction.[21] If a taxpayer disposes of a passive activity through death, the unused passive activity loss, limited to the step up in basis under Code Sec. 1014(a), is allowed as a deduction on the decedent's final income tax return.[22] However, a taxpayer may use up to $25,000 of losses from real estate activities in which the investor actively participates to offset active income and portfolio income.[23] The active participation threshold is lower than the material participation standard.[24] The $25,000 ceiling applies to single taxpayers and to married couples. Also, the $25,000 is phased out by $1 for every $2 that adjusted gross income exceeds $100,000.[25] Thus, the ceiling is fully phased out at an adjusted gross income of $150,000. These figures apply to single taxpayers and to married couples. These amounts are not indexed for inflation.

[17] Code Secs. 469(d)(1) and 469(a).
[18] Code Sec. 469(e)(1)(A).
[19] Code Secs. 469(e)(2)(B) and 469(e)(3).
[20] Code Sec. 469(b).
[21] Code Sec. 469(g)(1).
[22] Code Sec. 469(g)(2)(A).
[23] Code Sec. 469(i).
[24] Code Sec. 469(i)(6).
[25] Code Sec. 469(i)(3)(A).

.02 Personal and Dependency Exemptions

The deduction for personal and dependency exemptions is $3,300 in 2006, and it is indexed to inflation in future years.[26] However, the deduction for personal and dependency exemptions is phased out at the rate of two percent for each $2,500 of adjusted gross income in excess of $225,750 for joint returns, $188,150 for heads of household, $150,500 for single taxpayers, and $112,875 for married taxpayers filing separately.[27] These amounts are indexed to inflation.[28] For tax years 2006 and 2007, a taxpayer will lose only two-thirds of the amount that would be lost under the general phase-out rule; for 2008 and 2009, only one-third of the amount will be lost. The phase-out will be repealed for tax year 2010 only.[29]

.03 Limitation on Itemized Deductions

Itemized deductions (excluding medical expenses, investment interest and casualty losses) are reduced by three percent of adjusted gross income in excess of a threshold amount.[30] The threshold amounts for 2006 are $150,500 for joint returns and single filers and $75,250 for married persons filing separately,[31] with a maximum reduction of 80 percent of otherwise allowable itemized deductions.[32] These amounts are indexed for inflation.[33] For tax years 2006 and 2007, a taxpayer will lose only two-thirds of the amount that would be lost under the general phase-out rule; for 2008 and 2009, only one-third of the amount will be lost.[34] The limitation will be repealed for tax year 2010 only.[35]

.04 Standard Deduction

In 2006, the basic standard deduction is $5,150 for single taxpayers, $7,550 for heads of household, $10,300 for married couples filing jointly, and $5,150 for a married taxpayer filing separately.[36] For 2006, the additional standard deduction for blindness or being age 65 or over is $1,000 for each married taxpayer and $1,250 for a single taxpayer or head of household.[37] The basic standard deduction and the additional standard deduction are indexed for inflation.[38]

.05 Transfers Between Parties

In general, gain or loss is not recognized on an outright transfer of property from one spouse to another and the recipient spouse does

[26] Code Secs. 151(d)(1) and 151(d)(4)(A).
[27] Code Sec. 151(d)(3).
[28] Code Sec. 151(d)(4)(B).
[29] Code Sec. 151(d)(3)(E).
[30] Code Sec. 68(a).
[31] Code Sec. 68(b)(1).
[32] Code Sec. 68(a)(2).
[33] Code Sec. 68(b)(2).
[34] Code Sec. 68(f).
[35] Code Sec. 68(g).
[36] Code Sec. 63(c)(2).
[37] Code Secs. 63(c)(3) and 63(f).
[38] Code Sec. 63(c)(4).

not recognize income as a result of the transfer.[39] Furthermore, the transfer is made free of gift tax by virtue of the unlimited marital deduction.[40] The foregoing does not apply to transfers to nonresident alien spouses; gain would be recognized with respect to such transfers.[41] However, the transferor would not recognize any loss realized because it would be a sale or exchange to a related party.[42]

If the parties are not married, the transferor will recognize gain or loss unless the transfer qualifies as a gift under Code Sec. 102. If the transfer is compensation for any services rendered, the transferor will recognize gain on any property transferred, but the transferor may be entitled to a deduction under Code Sec. 162(a) if the compensation represents an ordinary and necessary business expense. The transferee would recognize gross income for any property received as compensation to the extent of the property's fair market value.[43] Gifts in excess of the amount of the $12,000 annual exclusion[44] (for 2006) would be subject to gift tax. The $12,000 annual exclusion is indexed to inflation.[45]

.06 Deductible IRA Contributions

An individual will not be considered to be an active participant in an employer-sponsored retirement plan merely because his or her spouse is a participant. The ability of such a nonparticipant spouse to claim an IRA deduction is phased out when the couple's combined adjusted gross income exceeds $150,000.[46] The deduction is denied in full when their adjusted gross income exceeds $160,000.[47] These amounts are *not* indexed to inflation.

> **Planning pointer.** To provide security to the less wealthy of the parties and to ensure that the payment will be excluded from the recipient's gross income, the parties should consider entering into an prenuptial-type agreement even though they might not plan to get married. However, the wealthier party would incur a gift tax liability on any transfer, and gift tax rates are generally higher than income tax rates. Of course, the transferor may use any available unified credit[48] to reduce or avoid any gift tax. However, such use of the unified credit might be at the expense of later estate and gift taxes. For gifts made through 2009, the applicable exclusion amount for gift tax purposes is $1,000,000. This amount is not indexed for inflation.

---

[39] Code Sec. 1041.
[40] Code Sec. 2523(a).
[41] Code Sec. 1041(d).
[42] Code Secs. 267(a)(1), 267(b)(1), and 267(c)(4).
[43] Code Sec. 61(a) and Reg. § 1.61-2(d).
[44] Code Sec. 2503(b)(1).
[45] Code Sec. 2503(b)(2).
[46] Code Sec. 219(g)(7)(A).
[47] Code Sec. 219(g)(7)(B).
[48] Code Sec. 2505.

¶ 2420 DIVORCE AND SEPARATION

Few individuals contemplate divorce or separation when they get married. However, many marriages end in divorce. A financial planner must carefully consider the financial results of a potential separation or divorce. Alimony, child support, and property settlements all have tax consequences that a financial planner should consider when advising a married couple contemplating divorce or an unmarried couple contemplating marriage.

Tax factors and state law affect alimony, child support, and property settlements in divorce. Most states have enacted equitable distribution laws under which all assets acquired during a marriage by either spouse, other than those acquired through inheritance, personal injury settlements, or a gift from someone other than the spouse, are to be divided equitably, not necessarily equally, by the divorce court.

Generally, the court may take into account many factors in determining an equitable distribution of assets, including the length of the marriage, the contributions of both spouses, the future earning capacities of each spouse, and any children.

The equitable distribution laws increase the responsibilities of matrimonial lawyers. They must carefully evaluate all assets in a marriage, including pensions, business assets, stocks and bonds, real estate, savings accounts, and marital gifts. A license to practice a profession (such as public accounting, medicine, law, and architecture) and an academic degree might be considered marital property under state law. Lottery winnings might also be subject to equitable distribution. The matrimonial lawyer must attempt to discover hidden assets. Accountants and appraisers might become part of the process.

The increased responsibilities of divorce attorneys result in longer trials where issues are contested. Couples often negotiate the settlement of contested issues because of cost factors and the uncertainty in predicting how a court might decide the issues.

Division of retirement benefits is separately discussed at ¶ 2445.

.01 Community Income of Separated Spouses

Code Sec. 66 provides rules for the tax treatment of certain types of community income where the spouses live apart during the entire calendar year and do not file a joint return for the year.

For the Code Sec. 66 rule to apply, one or both spouses must have earned income for the calendar year that is community income, no portion of which has been transferred directly or indirectly between the spouses, except for de minimis amounts and payments made solely to satisfy support obligations for dependent children.

If the couple qualifies, earned income (other than trade or business income or a partner's distributive share of partnership income) is treated as the income of the spouse who earned it, for federal income tax purposes. Trade or business income (other than partnership income) is treated as the income of the spouse who owns the business unless the other spouse exercises substantially all of the management and control of the trade or business.[49] In the case of a partnership, the income is taxed to the spouse who has a distributive share of the partnership profits.[50]

The Code Sec. 66 rule applies to situations where a spouse establishes that he or she did not know, or have reason to know, of an item of community income, and including the item in that spouse's income would be inequitable. In addition, the IRS has the power to disallow the benefits of any community property law to a taxpayer if the taxpayer acts as if he or she is solely entitled to the income and the taxpayer failed to notify his or her spouse of that income.[51]

.02 Kiddie Tax

For 2006, the unearned income of a child in excess of $1,700 is taxed at the higher of the parent's marginal tax rate or the child's marginal tax rate (this subject is dealt with in detail at ¶ 3205).[52] Under the 2006 Tax Increase Prevention and Reconciliation Act, the triggering age for the kiddie tax has been raised. Under prior law, the kiddie tax applied to children under age 14; under the new law, it applies to children under age 18 beginning with 2006.[53] Special rules apply for children of divorced or separated parents.

If the child's parents are divorced, legally separated, or have lived apart for the last six months of the year, only the taxable income of the custodial parent is taken into account.[54] If the custodial parent remarries and files a joint return with someone who is not the child's parent, the total income shown on the joint return is taken into account. Where the parents are still married but choose to file separate returns (as may be the case before a divorce settlement), the marginal tax rate of the parent with the larger taxable income is used.[55]

---

[49] Code Sec. 1402(a)(5)(A), incorporated by reference.

[50] Code Sec. 1402(a)(5)(B).

[51] Code Sec. 66(b).

[52] Code Sec. 1(g).

[53] Code Sec. 1(g)(2)(A) , as amended by 2006 Tax Increase Prevention and Reconciliation Act Sec.510(a)).

[54] Code Sec. 1(g)(5)(A).

[55] Code Sec. 1(g)(5)(B).

If the parent or parents subsequently report greater income that causes the parent's income to be taxed at a higher marginal bracket, the parent could recalculate the kiddie tax and file an amended return. The parent is obligated to file the child's return. In the case of divorced parents, this responsibility falls on the custodial parent.

When a parent cannot obtain the necessary information before the due date of the child's return, the parent can file the kiddie tax form (Form 8615) using reasonable estimates. The parent can file an amended return when the parent obtains the information.

.03 Joint Return Considerations

A financial planner advising a separated couple or couple contemplating divorce must deal with the issue of whether the couple will file a joint tax return. A financial planner may want to consider an indemnity agreement, particularly where the client is concerned about whether his or her spouse has declared all of his or her income or overstated deductions. Often, when a divorce is imminent, the parties will want to file separate returns. Both parties are jointly and severally liable for the tax due on a joint return, including any deficiencies assessed later.[56] A spouse can avoid liability for the tax assessed on a joint return only if the spouse proves that he or she is an innocent spouse.[57] If the parties are no longer married, are legally separated, or are no longer living together, then a party may elect to limit his or her liability to his or her allocable share of the income.[58] All joint filers may seek relief from liability if the party did not know or have reason to know of an understatement in tax and holding the individual liable for the additional tax would be inequitable.[59]

Often the higher-income spouse will want the other spouse to sign the joint return. However, he or she might refuse to sign a joint return. No one can be forced to sign a joint return. However, a line of U.S. Tax Court cases might provide some help.

In one case, the U.S. Tax Court considered a return as a joint return, even though neither spouse signed the return; it contained only the typed names of the spouses and the signature of the tax return preparer. However, evidence indicated that the wife had intended to file a joint return but had refused to sign the return in an attempt to extract concessions in the midst of a divorce proceeding.[60] However, if the other spouse files a separate return, nothing can be done.[61]

---

[56] Code Sec. 6013(d)(3).

[57] Code Sec. 6015.

[58] Code Secs. 6015(a)(2) and 6015(c).

[59] Code Sec. 6015(b).

[60] *V. Riportella*, 42 TCM 869, CCH Dec. 38,189(M), TC Memo. 1981-463.

[61] *J. Springmann*, 54 TCM 592, CCH Dec. 44,208(M), TC Memo. 1987-474.

In addition, if one spouse signs the other spouse's name to a joint return, the IRS might deem the other spouse to have consented to the joint return unless the other spouse files a separate return. In case a divorce appears imminent, a financial planner should advise the client of the joint and several liability associated with a joint return and the potential adverse consequences of not filing a return. In most of these cases, the spouses should file separate returns. The timing of the divorce decree is important because for filing purposes, the marital status is determined on the last day of the tax year.[62]

¶2425 ALIMONY

Alimony, for tax purposes, is generally a payment made by an individual to or on behalf of his or her former spouse under a divorce or separation instrument.[63] Alimony can have income, estate, and gift tax consequences.

Code Secs. 71 and 215 permit alimony payments to be made taxable to the recipient[64] and deductible by the payor[65] in computing adjusted gross income[66] or tax free to the recipient and nondeductible by the payor.[67] Normally, the parties choose the first alternative because the payor is usually in a higher tax bracket than the recipient. In these circumstances, the payor can pay more at lower after-tax costs. On the other hand, if the payor is in a relatively low tax bracket, or has no taxable income, but expects to make the payments out of capital, the tax deduction is of little value. Moreover, the fact that the recipient can receive tax-free payments normally allows that individual to accept smaller payments with the same after-tax result as higher payments made taxable to the recipient.

.01 Requirements for Alimony Treatment

Cash. Payments must be in cash and be received by, or on behalf of, the payee spouse.[68]

Divorce or separation instrument. Payments must be made under a decree of divorce or separate maintenance or under a written instrument incident to the divorce, a written separation agreement, or a decree requiring support or maintenance payments.[69]

Living apart. Where the parties are divorced or legally separated, they may not be members of the same household at the time payments are made.[70]

---

[62] Code Sec. 7701(a)(3).

[63] Code Sec. 71(b)(1).

[64] Code Sec. 71(a).

[65] Code Sec. 215(a).

[66] Code Sec. 62(a)(10).

[67] Code Sec. 71(b)(1)(B).

[68] Code Sec. 71(b)(1)(A).

[69] Code Sec. 71(b)(2).

[70] Code Sec. 71(b)(1)(C).

Death of payee. The payor must have no liability to make any payment for any period after the death of the payee.[71] The divorce decree might not address the issue of whether the payments cease after the death of the payee. In that case, state law determines whether the payments cease on the death of the payee.[72]

Treatment by parties. The parties must not designate the payments as not being alimony. The option to designate payments as not being alimony, and the related planning considerations are separately discussed below.[73]

Front-loading. If the alimony payments in the first year exceed the average payments in the second and third year by more than $15,000, the excess amounts are recaptured in the third year by requiring the payor to include the excess in income and allowing the payee who previously included the alimony in income a deduction for that amount in computing adjusted gross income.[74] A similar rule applies to the extent that the payments in the second year exceed the payments in the third year by more than $15,000.[75] This rule is intended to prevent individuals whose divorce occurs near the end of the year from making a deductible property settlement at the beginning of the next year. Recapture is not required if either party dies or if the payee spouse remarries by the end of the calendar year which is two years after the payments began and payments cease by reason of that event.[76] Also, the rule does not apply to temporary support payments or to payments that fluctuate as a result of a continuing liability to pay, for at least three years, a fixed portion or portions of income from the earnings of a business, property, or services.[77]

> ***Example 24.1.*** Assume that Bill West makes alimony payments to his former wife, Jean West, of $50,000 in the first year and no payments in the second or third year. He must recapture $35,000, assuming none of the exceptions apply. If, instead, he made payments of $50,000 in the first year, $20,000 in the second year, and nothing in the third year, he would recapture $5,000 from the second year (the excess over $15,000) and $27,500 for the first year (the excess of $50,000 over the sum of $15,000 and $7,500). (The $7,500 is the average of payments for years two and three after reducing the payments by the $5,000 recaptured from year two.)

---

[71] Code Sec. 71(b)(1)(D).

[72] *A.R. Zinsmeister*, TC Memo 2000-364, 80 TCM 774 (2000) *aff'd* CA-8 (unpublished opinion) 2001-2 USTC ¶50,717.

[73] Code Sec. 71(b)(1)(B).

[74] Code Sec. 71(f).

[75] Code Sec. 71(f)(1).

[76] Code Sec. 71(f)(5).

[77] Code Sec. 71(f)(5)(C).

.02 Reduced Payments Geared to Contingency Involving Child

If alimony payments are to be reduced on the happening of a contingency relating to a child, then an amount equal to the amount of the reduction will be treated as child support rather than as alimony.[78] For example, if payments are to be reduced by $100 a month when a child reaches age 18, then $100 of each monthly payment will be treated as child support from the outset.

Other examples of contingencies include marrying, dying, or leaving school.[79] The rule will also apply where payments will be reduced at a time that can clearly be associated with such a contingency.[80]

Temporary Reg. § 1.71-1T states that there are only two situations in which payments that would otherwise qualify as alimony will be presumed to be reduced "at a time clearly associated with the happening of a contingency relating to a child of the payor." The first situation is where the payments are to be reduced no more than six months before or after the date the child is to attain the age of 18, 21, or local age of majority. The second situation is where the payments are to be reduced on two or more occasions that occur not more than one year before or after a different child of the payor spouse attains a certain age (which must be the same age for each such child) between the ages of 18 and 24, inclusive. The presumptions created by the regulation are rebuttable.

In all other situations, reductions in payments will not be treated as clearly associated with the happening of a contingency relating to a child of the payor.

Planning pointer. A financial planner might be able to avoid the first of the two situations described above and provide the client with a tax deduction for what are in substance child support payments.

Example 24.2. Assume that Donald McElroy proposes to pay Claire McElroy additional deductible alimony intended to be used by Claire for the eventual college education of their 14-year-old child, Nell. The divorce instrument could reduce alimony at a fixed time that occurs more than six months after Nell attains age 21, carefully avoiding any specific mention of Nell's age or needs. Claire might not use the added alimony,

---

[78] Code Sec. 71(c)(2).
[79] Code Sec. 71(c)(2)(A).
[80] Code Sec. 71(c)(2)(B).

less the tax liability incurred, for the intended purpose. In addition, Nell may not attend college. Donald must weigh these risks before providing extra alimony. If Donald finds the risks acceptable, the benefits of an income tax deduction to Donald might make the suggested approach attractive.

.03 Nonalimony Treatment by Agreement

The parties can agree to have payments not treated as alimony and, thus, as not taxable to the payee or deductible by the payor.[81]

Planning pointer. In some cases, this rule may afford tax savings opportunities for the payee spouse. As a practical matter, the payee spouse would be required to share the savings with the payor spouse in the form of reduced payments. For example, assume that for the next two years the payor spouse will have no taxable income and that the payee spouse will be in the 45-percent (combined federal and state) tax bracket. If the payments are $1,000 a month and the parties choose nonalimony treatment, the payee spouse will save $10,800 ($24,000 × 45%) in taxes over two years. The payee spouse could share the savings with the payor to persuade the payor to agree to nonalimony treatment.

.04 Compliance

The payee must furnish the payor with his or her Social Security number and the payor must furnish the name and Social Security number of the payee to the IRS,[82] subject in either case to a $50 penalty for failure to comply.[83]

.05 Divorce Trusts

A financial planner might consider using a Code Sec. 682 trust.

Example 24.3. Assume that Pablo Estrada transfers income-producing property to the Code Sec. 682 trust. The payments made to his former wife, Teresa Estrada, are taxable to her under the usual trust rules. Pablo may not deduct the payments, but they are not taxable to him even though they might otherwise be deemed taxable to him under the grantor trust rules of Code Secs. 671-677. The trust gives Teresa a measure of security that she might be willing to pay for in terms of lower alimony payments. From an income tax standpoint, Pablo might be in the same position, or better off, than he would have been in if he

---

[81] Code Sec. 71(b)(1)(B) and Reg. § 1.71-1T(b) Q-A-8.

[82] Code Sec. 215(c) and Temp. Reg. § 1.215-1T.

[83] Code Sec. 6723.

made the alimony payments directly and received a deduction. For example, assume that Pablo has income-producing property yielding $10,000 per year and he uses all of it to pay alimony. The alimony deduction offsets the income. When he transfers that property to the trust, the income is no longer taxable to him. Pablo's income tax situation is the same, but he no longer holds title to the property. He could be better off with the trust by, in effect, achieving deductions for payments that would not be deductible if paid outright because of the six-year rule discussed above. If Pablo retains a reversionary interest or creates a remainder interest to take effect on termination of alimony obligations, the transfer of legal title may be regarded as temporary. If he retains a reversionary interest, it will be includible in his gross estate under Code Sec. 2037. If Pablo creates a remainder interest, he might have a gift-tax liability. If the interest is in favor of persons other than his estate, however, it will not be includible in his gross estate.

¶ 2430 CHILD SUPPORT

Child support is excluded from the gross income of the recipient,[84] and it is not deductible by the payor.[85] However, if alimony payments are to be reduced on the happening of a contingency involving a child, a portion of the payments will not qualify as alimony (¶ 2425).[86]

Special rules apply for claiming the exemption for a dependent child whose parents are divorced or separated. The parent having custody for the greater portion of the year is entitled to the exemption,[87] unless that parent waives his or her right to claim the exemption in a written declaration and the noncustodial parent attaches the declaration to his or her return.[88] The taxpayer must use Form 8332, "Release of Claim to Exemption for Child of Divorced or Seperated Parents," or a document that is substantially similar. Financial planners should urge their clients not to rely solely on the divorce decree. Furthermore, the general rule does not apply in the case of multiple support agreements.[89]

These rules apply to parents not living together during the last six months of the calendar year, as well as those divorced or separated under a written separation agreement.[90]

---

[84] Code Sec. 71(c)(1).
[85] Temp. Reg. § 1.71-1T.
[86] Code Sec. 71(c)(2).
[87] Code Sec. 152(e)(1).
[88] Code Sec. 152(e)(2).
[89] Code Sec. 152(e)(3).
[90] Code Sec. 152(e)(1)(A).

Support provided by the spouse of a remarried parent is treated as support provided by that parent.[91]

Any agreement or decree dealing with child support should state the specific age at which the obligation is to terminate, instead of using a general term such as the age of majority. This term can raise questions of interpretation if the legislature of the state where the child lives alters the age of majority while the decree or agreement is still in force.

A financial planner should also evaluate the income and gift tax effects if the state lowers the age of majority, to the extent that the change relieves a parent of the support obligation. Payments made to the child after the child reaches the age of majority might be considered gifts rather than a discharge of a support obligation.

The IRS may seize an income tax refund to pay a parent's delinquent child support obligation.[92] If the parent files a joint return, the nonobligated spouse may file a claim as an injured spouse to avoid having the refund attributable to his or her income from being seized. To do so, the nonobligated spouse must write "Injured Spouse" in the upper left corner of Form 1040 and attach Form 8379, "Injured Spouse Allocation." The IRS will determine how much of the refund to which the nonobligated spouse is entitled.[93]

.01 Medical Expense Deductions

A child is treated as a dependent of both parents for medical expense deduction purposes, regardless of which parent is entitled to the dependency exemption.[94]

.02 Disabled Individual

Qualification for a dependency exemption is to be determined without regard to any income received by an individual who is permanently and totally disabled for services performed at a sheltered workshop school operated by a charity or the government.[95]

.03 Trusts

Trusts for child support are not particularly advantageous because trust income used for support would be taxable to the settlor-parent under Code Sec. 677(b).

---

[91] Code Sec. 152(e)(5).

[92] Code Secs. 6305 and 6402(c), and Reg. § 301.6305-1(b)(4)(iii).

[93] Rev. Rul. 80-7, 1908-1 CB 296.

[94] Code Sec. 213(d)(5).

[95] Code Sec. 151(c)(5).

¶ 2435 PROPERTY SETTLEMENTS

Matrimonial settlements can include partition of co-owned property, property exchanges, and property settlements, independently of equitable distribution statutory provisions or under such provisions as noted at ¶ 2420. These adjustments might have income, estate, and gift tax consequences. If the obligor files for bankruptcy, serious questions arise as to dischargeability (see the discussion below).

.01 Income Tax Aspects

A transfer of property between spouses incident to a divorce in settlement of their marital rights is a nontaxable transaction, subject to certain exceptions.[96] The transfer is treated as a gift for income tax purposes, and the transferee receives the transferor's adjusted basis.[97] Tax-free treatment is accorded whether the transfer is for cash, property, the relinquishment of marital rights, the assumption of liabilities in excess of basis, or other consideration. The parties have up to one year after a divorce to make the transfer.[98] Code Sec. 1041 does not apply if the transferee is a nonresident alien.[99]

Annuity. A transferee of an annuity is taxed under the usual annuity rules[100] and recovers the transferor's investment in the contract,[101] notwithstanding that the annuity is alimony or is in discharge of a support obligation.

Life insurance. A transferee of a life insurance contract will not be taxed on the proceeds under the transfer-for-value rule.[102]

Series E, Series EE, and Series I bonds. Code Sec. 1041 does not apply to Series E, EE, or I bonds. Thus, the transferor must include the deferred, accrued interest in gross income in the year of the transfer.[103] The transferee spouse takes the transferor's adjusted basis, which reflects the increase for the interest includible in the transferor's gross income.

Transfers to trusts. Code Sec. 1041(a) does not apply to transfers to trusts of installment obligations and property with liabilities in excess of basis.[104] The transferee's adjusted basis is increased for any gain recognized.

> **Planning pointer.** Property settlements generally do not trigger gain to the transferor. However, tax considerations can

---

[96] Code Sec. 1041(a).
[97] Code Sec. 1041(b).
[98] Code Sec. 1041(c).
[99] Code Sec. 1041(d).
[100] Code Sec. 72.
[101] Code Sec. 1041(b).
[102] Code Secs. 1041(b), 101(a)(1), and 101(a)(2)(A).
[103] Rev. Rul. 87-112, 1987-2 CB 207, Code Sec. 454(c), and Reg. § 1.454-1(a).
[104] Code Sec. 1041(e).

play an important role in the selection of the properties to be transferred because of the carryover basis rules

Example 24.4. Assume that David Nash is negotiating a property settlement incident to a divorce with his wife Sara Nash. David owns stock of X Corporation worth $100,000 and having an adjusted basis of $20,000. David also owns stock of Y Corporation worth $100,000 and having an adjusted basis of $80,000. Assume that both spouses agree that each is entitled to $100,000 worth of stock. A transfer of the X stock would be highly advantageous to David because the X stock has a built-in gain of $80,000 and the Y stock David retains has a built-in gain of only $20,000. A more equitable approach would be for each spouse to take $50,000 worth of each of the two stocks.

Dividing properties with equal bases is not always possible. For example, a wife might want or be awarded the residence, which might have a lower adjusted basis than property the husband will receive. In such a case, the parties might agree to provide the wife with additional property to compensate her for the greater tax liability that she will face on a sale of the residence than the husband will face on a sale of the property he receives. However, if a sale of the residence by the wife would qualify for the $250,000 exclusion of gain under Code Sec. 121, perhaps no adjustment would be warranted or possibly an adjustment to the husband would be appropriate. Thus, while the parties can select property for division without concern for immediate tax consequences, the parties should consider future tax consequences.

The American Jobs Creation Act of 2004 changed the way certain suspended losses from an S corporation are treated in a transfer to a spouse or former spouse incident to a divorce. Annulments or marriages treated as void from the beginning are considered as divorces for purposes of Code Sec. 1041.[105] If a shareholder in an S corporation transfers stock in the S corporation to his or her spouse or to his or her former spouse incident to a divorce, any suspended losses due to the shareholder's insufficient adjusted basis in the S corporation's stock and debt are treated as having been incurred by the transferee.[106] The transferor recognizes no gain or loss on the transfer of the stock in the S corporation to his or her spouse or to his or her former spouse incident to a divorce.[107] Code Secs.1041 and 1366(d)(2) apply to a transfer to a spouse whether or not a divorce occurs.[108]

---

[105] Temp. Reg. § 1.1041-1T Q&A 8.

[106] Code Sec. 1366(d)(2).

[107] Code Sec.1041(a).

[108] Temp. Reg. § 1.1041-1T Q&A 2.

Example 24.5. Harmon King was a shareholder in Crown Wholesale, Inc., which is an S corporation. Harmon has $24,000 in suspended losses from the S corporation because the losses exceed his basis in his S corporation stock and in the loans he made to the S corporation. In 2006, Harmon and his wife Wanda are divorced. As a part of the divorce settlement, Harmon transfers his stock in Crown Wholesale, Inc. to Wanda. The law treats the $24,000 in suspended losses as having been incurred by Wanda.

The American Jobs Creation Act of 2004 does not specifically state what happens to suspended losses when a shareholder transfers some, but not all, of the shares owned in an S corporation to a spouse or former spouse incident to a divorce. Shareholders of an S corporation take items of income, deduction, credit, and loss into account on a pro rata basis.[109] Therefore, allocating the suspended loss between the shareholder and the transferee based on the number of shares owned after the transfer might be a reasonable way to allocate the suspended losses.

If a shareholder of an S corporation has enough basis to deduct a loss but does not have enough amount at risk, the shareholder may not deduct the loss.[110] The shareholder carries forward the loss indefinitely until the shareholder has enough amount at risk.[111]

The amendment to Code Sec. 1366 did not state what happens to losses suspended because of insufficient amount at risk. Under prior law, if the taxpayer transferred his or her shares in a transaction where the transferee determined his or her basis in whole or in part by reference to the adjusted basis of the transferor, the suspended loss due to the taxpayer's insufficient amount at risk was added to the taxpayer's adjusted basis in the activity solely for the purpose of the transferee determining his or her adjusted basis.[112] In a transfer to a spouse or former spouse incident to a divorce, the transferee determines his or her adjusted basis in the shares by reference to the basis of the transferor.[113] A financial planner can reasonably assume that prior law still applies. Thus, the suspended loss due to insufficient amount at risk would be added to the transferee's adjusted basis in the shares of the S corporation.

If the suspended loss is a passive activity loss, the shareholder may deduct the loss only to the extent of passive income.[114] The shareholder carries over to the next tax year any losses allocated to

[109] Code Sec. 1366(a)(1).
[110] Code Sec. 465(a)(1).
[111] Code Sec. 465(a)(2).
[112] Prop. Reg. § 1.465-67.
[113] Code Sec. 1041(b).
[114] Code Secs. 469(a)(1) and (d)(1).

the shareholder that the shareholder may not deduct in the current year.[115]

The amendment to Code Sec. 1366 does not address what happens to losses suspended because of the passive activity loss rules when a shareholder in an S corporation transfers shares to a spouse or to a former spouse incident to a divorce. Assuming that the prior law continues to apply, the suspended passive loss would increase the adjusted basis of the stock in the hands of the transferor immediately before the transfer.[116] The increase in the basis of the stock in the hands of the transferor increases the basis of the transferee in a transfer to a spouse or to a former spouse incident to a divorce because the adjusted basis of the transferor becomes the adjusted basis of the transferee.[117]

If the transferor could not deduct the loss because of insufficient basis in the S corporation stock and loans to the S corporation, the transferee must have sufficient basis in the S corporation stock and debt and sufficient amount at risk to deduct the loss.[118] If the loss is a loss from a passive activity, the transferee will also need sufficient passive income to be able to deduct the suspended loss.[119]

.02 Estate Tax Aspects

In general, Code Secs. 2036–2038 and 2043, discussed at the beginning of the chapter in connection with prenuptial agreements, can also have a substantial impact on property settlements. The property settlement must be measured against the basic requisites for inclusion under the cited sections. The transfer is not problematic if it does not fall within their limitations. If the transfer falls within one of these sections, then the estate planner must ask whether the transfer meets the exception for bona fide sales or exchanges for adequate and full consideration in money and money's worth. If the transfer meets the exception, it will not be included in the decedent's gross estate. If the transfer is for a consideration in money or money's worth that is less than adequate and full, the amount included in the decedent's gross estate is the value at the time of death of the property transferred in excess of the consideration received.[120] Relinquishment of marital rights in the property or the decedent's estate is not to be treated as consideration in money or money's worth unless the relinquishment complies with the requirements of Code Sec. 2516.

---

[115] Code Sec. 469(b).

[116] Code Sec. 469(j)(6).

[117] Code Sec. 1041(b).

[118] Code Secs. 465(a)(1) and 1366(d).

[119] Code Sec. 469(a)(1).

[120] Code Sec. 2043(a).

In this connection, the distinction between marital property rights and support rights comes into play. A relinquishment of support rights is consideration in money or money's worth to the extent of the value of the rights released. A relinquishment of marital rights or property rights is not consideration in money or money's worth[121] unless it meets the requirements of Code Sec. 2516.[122] If the transfer does not satisfy the Code Sec. 2516 requirements, the parties may rely on a U.S. Supreme Court decision that ruled that a transfer of property in exchange for a release of marital property rights is deemed to be for full and adequate consideration where the exchange has been approved and made part of a court decree.[123] The IRS says that to come within the boundaries of this decision, the court that approves the settlement must also have the power to change it.[124] The U.S. Court of Appeals for the Second Circuit has rejected this notion, holding that it was sufficient that the court merely had the power to approve it.[125]

.03 Gift Tax Aspects

Code Sec. 2516 provides that transfers of property made under the terms of a written agreement between spouses in settlement of their marital or property rights incident to divorce are deemed to be for an adequate and full consideration in money or money's worth (and thus are exempt from gift tax), if the spouses obtain a final decree of divorce within two years after entering into the agreement or enter into an agreement within one year after divorce. If the transfer is treated as a gift and is completed while the parties remain married, the unlimited gift tax marital deduction is available.[126]

.04 Bankruptcy of Obligor

Obligations for alimony or child support are not dischargeable in bankruptcy.[127] In addition, the financial planner should bear in mind the treatment of debts arising from a property settlement in bankruptcy. Debts incurred in a property settlement incident to a divorce or separation are not dischargeable in bankruptcy unless the debtor does not have the ability to pay the debt from the debtor's income or property not reasonably necessary for the support of the debtor or his or her dependent or if the debtor operates a business, for the payment of necessary business expenses.[128] This test is known as the ability test. The U.S. Bankruptcy Court often relies on the debtor's

[121] Code Sec. 2043(b)(1) and Rev. Rul. 68-379, 1968-2 CB 414.

[122] Code Sec. 2043(b)(2).

[123] *C. Harris*, CA-2, 50-2 USTC ¶10,786, 71 SCt 181.

[124] Rev. Rul. 60-160, 1960-1 CB 374.

[125] *D. Natchez*, CA-2, 83-1 USTC ¶13,519.

[126] Code Sec. 2523(a).

[127] 11 U.S.C. 523(a)(5).

[128] 11 U.S.C. 523(a)(15)(A).

disposable income[129] and earning potential in deciding whether the debtor satisfies the ability test. If the debtor proves that he or she does not have the ability to pay the debt, the debtor must then satisfy the fairness test for the debt to be dischargeable. Under the fairness test, the debt is dischargeable only if the benefit to the debtor is greater than the detriment to the debtor's spouse, former spouse, or child.[130] The U.S. Bankruptcy Court usually considers all relevant facts and circumstances in rendering a decision on the fairness test.

¶2440 LEGAL EXPENSES

One spouse generally cannot deduct personal legal expenses, or those of a spouse, incurred to obtain a divorce because these expenses are personal expenses.[131] However, an individual may deduct the fees paid for personal tax advice[132] incident to the divorce. However, an individual may not deduct fees paid for tax advice for his or her spouse. Fees paid for one's personal tax advice are deductible only as miscellaneous itemized deductions[133] subject to the two-percent adjusted gross income floor.[134] However, if the tax advice relates to a business, the fees for such tax advice would be deductible in arriving at adjusted gross income[135] as a business expense.[136] Rev. Rul. 72-545[137] shows how one spouse can allocate legal fees in divorce proceedings to deductible tax advice, because legal expenses per se are not deductible. One way is to hire a separate tax advisor for each spouse rather than relying on the attorney handling the divorce for tax advice. If one law firm handles both tax and family law aspects, then the firm can make an allocation of the legal fees based on time spent on each aspect and comparable fees in the locality.

The other spouse may deduct fees not only for tax counsel but also for services that produce taxable alimony or other taxable income.[138] Fees incurred to produce taxable alimony income are deductible only as miscellaneous itemized deductions,[139] subject to the two-percent adjusted gross income floor.[140] The expenses of obtaining the divorce, separation, or property settlement are personal expenses and not deductible by the spouse.[141]

Rather than have one spouse pay the full amount of the fees of his or her spouse's lawyers, apportioning the fees between alimony and

[129] 11 U.S.C. 1325(b)(2).
[130] 11 U.S.C. 523(a)(15)(B).
[131] Code Sec. 262(a).
[132] Code Sec. 212.
[133] Code Sec. 67(b).
[134] Code Sec. 67(a).
[135] Code Sec. 62(a)(1).
[136] Code Sec. 162(a).
[137] 1972-2 CB 179.
[138] Code Sec. 212.
[139] Code Sec. 67(b).
[140] Code Sec. 67(a).
[141] Code Sec. 262(a) and Reg. § 1.262-1(b)(7).

tax advice and separating the nondeductible items might be preferable. The other spouse would then pay for the items that he or she would be able to deduct. Because the spouse would be relieved of a nondeductible expense, he or she might then raise the amount of tax-deductible alimony to help the other spouse pay the deductible items.

Code Sec. 67 imposes a two-percent floor on aggregate miscellaneous itemized deductions. Code Sec. 68 reduces certain itemized deductions, including miscellaneous itemized deductions, by three percent of adjusted gross income in excess of $150,500 for joint returns and single filers, and $75,250 for married couples filing separately (2006 figures). These amounts are indexed to inflation.[142] The maximum reduction is 80 percent of the itemized deductions subject to the phaseout. The three-percent limitation applies to miscellaneous itemized deductions in excess of two percent of AGI. Itemized deductions not subject to the three-percent phaseout include medical expenses, investment interest, and casualty and theft losses.[143] However, for tax years beginning after December 31, 2005, and before January 1, 2010, the limitation on certain itemized deductions will be reduced every two years.[144] The limitation is repealed for 2010 only.[145]

¶ 2445 DIVISION OF RETIREMENT BENEFITS

The Internal Revenue Code permits qualified retirement plan and Code Sec. 403(b) annuity benefits to be transferred for the purpose of meeting alimony, property division, or child support obligations, provided the transfers are pursuant to a qualified domestic relations order (QDRO).[146]

A qualified domestic relations order is an order, judgment, or decree that relates to child support, alimony, or property rights of a spouse or former spouse, child, or dependent of the participant made pursuant to a state domestic relations law.[147]

The order must clearly specify the amount or percentage of the participant's benefits to be paid to the alternate payee and the number of payments or the period for which the payments are to be made.[148]

For income tax purposes, the basic rule is that the alternate payee is treated as a distributee of plan benefits.[149] However, payments to an alternate payee under a QDRO before the participant

142 Code Sec. 68(b)(2).

143 Code Sec. 68(c).

144 Code Sec. 68(f).

145 Code Sec. 68(g).

146 Code Secs. 401(a)(13)(B), 402(e)(1), and 414(p).

147 Code Sec. 414(p).

148 Code Sec. 414(p)(2).

149 Code Secs. 72(m)(10) and 402(e).

attains age 59½ are not subject to the 10-percent additional income tax that might otherwise apply.[150]

Payments made to a child as an alternate payee are taxable to the participant.

Special rules apply for certain distributions to alternate payees who are spouses or former spouses of the participant. In particular, if a distribution of the balance to the credit of the employee would constitute a lump-sum distribution, then a distribution of the balance of the credit of the alternative payee constitutes a lump-sum distribution.

Any portion of a total distribution to an alternate payee may be rolled over tax free to a traditional IRA, whether or not the distribution qualifies for lump-sum treatment under the rule discussed above. Amounts not rolled over are taxed under the annuities rules of Code Sec. 72.

The transfer of an IRA to a spouse pursuant to a divorce decree or a written instrument incident to a divorce is not a taxable transfer by the transferor.[151]

[150] Code Sec. 72(t)(2)(C).

[151] Code Sec. 408(d)(6).

Chapter 25

Planning for Couples Living Together

Overview ....¶ 2501
Unmarried Couples Living Together ....¶ 2505

¶ 2501 OVERVIEW

In recent years, living together outside of marriage and domestic partnerships have become increasingly common. Financial planners must focus on the special problems that these relationships create in order to develop a successful plan for the client. Individuals involved in such arrangements are also more concerned about their rights and asserting such rights at the time of death, separation, disability, and retirement.

¶ 2505 UNMARRIED COUPLES LIVING TOGETHER

Each relationship has its special problems, and financial strategies that may be appropriate for one relationship may not be appropriate for another relationship. For instance, the needs of a retired, unmarried couple living together differ considerably from a young couple living together. The older couple may be concerned about the loss of Social Security benefits, negotiating a marital agreement, and dealing with family problems brought on by a possible remarriage. Younger couples in the prime of their relationship have other concerns.

.01 Role of the Financial Planner

The financial planner should take an active role in obtaining information from the client in the same manner that the planner obtains such information from married couples or from singles who live alone. The financial planner does not have to play moralist.

The only concern of the financial planner should be to obtain the information necessary to advise the client properly.

As in the case of planning for married couples, the financial planner may want to interview both parties in the nonmarital situation. However, each of the parties may want to have separate attorneys advising them as to their respective rights. At a minimum, the financial planner should provide full disclosure of potential conflicts of interest.

.02 Legal Background

Every jurisdiction has extensive laws governing the marital relationship. However, few laws exist that govern couples living together outside of marriage. Some exceptions exist such as in the states that recognize common-law marriages. Simply because a couple is living together does not mean the couple has a common-law marriage. Couples must satisfy state law requirements as to residence and to holding themselves out to the public as husband and wife.

The palimony cases are another exception. The common law of contracts, rather than statutes, is the foundation for these cases. One party asserts a claim for support from the other party in return for having provided services or some other form of consideration.

Several states and local governments have adopted laws prohibiting discrimination based on sexual orientation. Of particular interest is the right to continue to dwell in the mutual residence after the tenant-partner has died. In April 2000, the state of Vermont passed the Act Relating to Civil Unions that took effect on July 1, 2000. This law allows gay couples to join in civil unions similar to marriage. The state of Vermont enacted this legislation after the Vermont Supreme Court reversed a lower court's ruling that upheld the constitutionality of the state's marriage statutes.[1]

On April 20, 2005, Connecticut became the second state to allow civil unions when the Governor signed into law, "An Act Concerning Civil Unions" (Chapter 246, P.L. 2003). The law became effective October 1, 2005. The law allows partners in a civil union the same basic rights as married couples have under Connecticut law.

The domestic partner law in California (A.B. 205, California Family Code Sec. 297) was signed into law in October 2003 and became effective on January 1, 2005. It allows same-sex couples who are at least 18 years old and unmarried opposite-sex couples

[1] *Stan Baker et al. v. State of Vermont*, Docket No. 98-302 (December 20, 1999).

who are at least 62 years old to enter into domestic partnerships. It gives domestic partners most of the same rights and responsibilities as married couples have under California law.

The state of New Jersey approved a Domestic Partnership Act on January 12, 2004. It became effective on July 10, 2004. The law allows same-sex couples who are at least 18 years old or unmarried opposite-sex couples who are at least 62 years old to register with the state as domestic partners and enjoy many of the same rights as do married couples.

Hawaii has recognized domestic partnerships since 1997. Maryland enacted a law allowing domestic partnerships in 2005. Maine passed a law allowing domestic partnerships on April 28, 2004 (P.L. 1995, c469 Chapter 672, H.P. 1152—L.D. 1579). It became effective on July 30, 2004. The Maine law allows limited rights to domestic partners. The District of Columbia has recognized domestic partnerships since 2002.

On November 18, 2003, the Massachusetts Supreme Judicial Court ruled that the statute banning same-sex marriage violated the Massachusetts Constitution.[2] The Court delayed the ruling for 180 days to allow the legislature to enact legislation in accordance with the Court's decision. The law allowing same-sex marriage went into effect in Massachusetts on May 17, 2004.

Under the federal Defense of Marriage Act (P.L. 104-199),[3] other states do not have to recognize same-sex marriages performed in Massachusetts, despite the full faith and credit clause of the U.S. Constitution. The federal government recognizes marriages only between a man and a woman. Therefore, same-sex married partners may not file a joint federal income tax return. Neither do same-sex couples qualify for the unlimited exclusion for transfers to one's spouse for gift tax purposes nor the unlimited marital deduction for estate tax purposes.

Same-sex marriage became legal all across Canada on July 20, 2005, with the enactment of the Civil Marriage Act (Bill C-38). Same-sex marriage was already legal in many of the provinces based on court decisions.

.03 Wills and Intestacy

Upon the death of an unmarried partner, the other partner has no automatic rights in property owned by the other partner.

---

[2] *Goodridge el al. v. Dept. of Public Health*, 798 N.E. 2d 941 (Mass, 2003).

[3] 1 U.S.C. 7.

The decedent may transfer property to the partner only by will, trust, lifetime gift, or joint ownership. Because a testator may revoke a will provision at any time before death, a provision in a will might not be entirely satisfactory to the partner-beneficiary. The property acquired by one partner on the other partner's death, whether by will or as the beneficiary of a living trust, will be subject to estate tax (except for decedents dying in 2010 because Congress repealed the estate tax for that year only). Property that the unmarried couple held as joint tenants with right of survivorship will pass to the surviving partner by operation of law. Property held as joint tenants with right of survivorship will be included in the decedent's gross estate unless the survivor can prove that the property belonged to the survivor or the survivor acquired the property for adequate consideration in money or money's worth.[4] An unmarried partner is not entitled to the unlimited marital deduction that a married individual receives.[5]

Because the partners can easily terminate the relationship at any time, the testator might want to provide that the bequest or devise is effective only if the parties are living together at the time of the testator's death. Similarly, if the testator nominates the partner as a fiduciary (executor or trustee), the testator might want to provide that the nomination is contingent upon the parties living together at the date of the testator's death. The testator should nominate a contingent fiduciary in the event the parties were not living together at the date of the testator's death.

.04 Lifetime Arrangements

A revocable trust can be an effective financial and estate planning tool. If the partner is a beneficiary of the trust, the partner can enjoy benefits currently and receive the property in the trust upon the grantor's death. The grantor maintains control and can revoke the trust at any time. The grantor could use an irrevocable trust, but then the grantor might want the partner's enjoyment conditioned on the parties continuing to live together. In that event, the trust would have to provide for an alternative beneficiary. Accordingly, the irrevocable trust is probably not a useful planning device in a nonmarital relationship.

Other forms of lifetime arrangements include outright gifts and the creation of co-ownership interests in property. These transfers involve potential gift tax liability. If one partner owns property or purchases property and then conveys title to the property to each

---

[4] Code Sec. 2040(a).

[5] Code Sec. 2056(a).

partner as joint tenants, the donor has made a taxable gift equal to half the value of the property.[6] However, the donor may reduce or avoid the gift tax by the annual gift tax exclusion[7] and by the applicable credit amount.[8] An unmarried partner may not transfer an unlimited amount of property to the other partner free of gift tax as can a married couple.[9]

Co-ownership can either be as joint tenants with right of survivorship or as tenants in common. Joint tenants with right of survivorship means that upon the death of one joint tenant, the property goes to the survivor. With respect to bank accounts, the joint owner can withdraw the funds at any time (¶ 315.01). The creation of a joint account does not result in any gift tax because the gift is not complete until the recipient withdraws the funds.[10]

Life insurance may be useful in several respects. It provides a benefit to the partner at a modest cost and is a transfer outside of probate. To avoid estate and gift tax on the life insurance, the financial and estate planner could suggest that the client form an irrevocable life insurance trust or have the beneficiary be the owner of a new policy. If the beneficiary is the owner of the policy, the arrangement might also have psychological benefits. The partner could also be the beneficiary of IRAs and pension plans. However, the value of IRAs and pension plans will be included in the decedent's gross estate.[11] In addition, the beneficiary will be subject to income tax on the amounts as income in respect of a decedent.[12] Unlike a spouse, the unmarried partner cannot roll the decedent's IRA into his or her own IRA.[13]

.05 Children

The existence of children complicates the problems of couples living together outside of marriage. The parent, whether natural or adoptive, will want to make provisions for children. The financial and estate planning process will be more complex if the children are from a prior relationship. In such cases, the financial and estate planner must exercise even greater care.

The legal problems of parenting can be acute when the relationship between the parents dissolves. For instance, when a couple breaks up, is a nonbiological parent entitled to visitation or even custody of the children? Courts and legislatures will have to contend with the handling of these matters with a view to redefining the term

---

[6] Reg. § 25.2511-1(h)(5).

[7] Code Sec. 2503(b).

[8] Code Secs. 2505(a) and 2010.

[9] Code Sec. 2523(a).

[10] Reg. § 25.2511-1(h)(4).

[11] Code Sec. 2031(a).

[12] Code Sec. 691(a).

[13] Code Sec. 408(d)(3)(c).

"parent" so as not to deny rights to one who acted as a de facto parent. Technical advances in the fields of in vitro fertilization and artificial insemination pose additional complicating factors if the donors and surrogates assert rights to the children.

The U.S. Supreme Court ruled that a Washington state court erred when it granted extensive visitation rights to a child's paternal grandparents over the objections of the child's mother.[14] The Supreme Court noted that the state of Washington's statute allowing anyone to petition for visitation rights at any time was "breathtakingly broad." The Court did not address the issue of whether all nonparental visitation laws had to show harm or potential harm to a child to satisfy a parent's Constitutional rights. Although this decision does not nullify state laws granting visitation rights to third parties, it might influence decisions involving custody and visitation claims of third parties. This decision adds even more weight to the need for careful planning for couples who live together with children of which only one partner is a legal parent.

.06 Agreement Between the Parties

The unmarried couple living together may want to sign a written agreement that sets forth their respective rights and obligations. The agreement could include provisions relating to household, vacation, and other living expenses as well as ownership of cars, furniture, and household assets. The agreement could be more extensive and include matters usually covered in a marital agreement. The purpose of such an agreement would be to avoid the expensive litigation encountered in a palimony suit.

In those states that recognize same-sex domestic partnerships, civil unions, or same-sex marriage, state law confers certain rights and obligations on the partners. However, those rights and obligations may not be recognized by other states. Moreover, private agreements between same-sex partners may not be recognized under state law. For example, the state of Virginia prohibits private contracts that confer marital benefits on same-sex partners and denies recognition to contractual arrangements entered into in other states. Therefore, financial planners should carefully research state law when planning for same-sex partners.

---

[14] *Troxel et vir. v. Granville*, Docket No. 99-138 aff'g 137 Wash.2d 1, 969 P.2d 21 (June 5, 2000).

.07 Powers of Attorney

Unmarried couples might want to execute durable powers of attorney that give the other partner the power to act on his or her behalf in the event of the individual's incapacity. A divorce usually terminates a durable power of attorney in which the spouse is the attorney-in-fact. However, the power would not automatically terminate if an unmarried partner serves as the attorney-in-fact. The unmarried principal should name a successor or contingent attorney-in-fact in case the partner is unable or unwilling to serve. Making the power of attorney contingent upon the couple's living together at the time of its exercise might seem wise. However, third parties would not want to investigate the living status of the couple before relying on the power. Thus, a better strategy is to revoke the power upon a separation.

Financial planners should alert an unmarried couple to the need for preparing for medical emergencies and incapacity. The financial planner should advise the couple about the need for living wills, durable powers of attorney for health care, and health care proxies (¶ 2905).

In states that recognize domestic partnerships, civil unions, or gay marriage, one partner may have the legal right to make medical decisions when the other partner becomes incapacitated. However, those rights may not be recognized by other states absent a medical power of attorney.

.08 What If the Couple Separates?

Financial planners should advise unmarried couples to consider how they would divide their property upon a separation. If the couple maintains separate ownership of various items of property, the division of property upon separation should be relatively easy. Each partner would take his or her own property. However, if the couple owns property as joint tenants with the right of survivorship or as tenants in common, the division of property on separation becomes more problematic. Another factor that unmarried couples should consider is that they cannot avoid tax on a distribution from a qualified plan as can a married couple using a qualified domestic relations order (QDRO).[15] In addition, exchanges of property upon separation are not tax free as they are in a divorce of a married couple.[16] The couple might make an agreement that sets forth their property rights upon a separation. The financial planner will usually advise the couple to seek assistance of an attorney with expertise in family

[15] Code Secs. 401(a)(13) and 414(p).

[16] Code Sec. 1041.

law and property law. Couples might not want to contemplate a separation because of emotional factors. Therefore, the financial planner will need to approach the issue of possible separation delicately.

.09 Filing Status

An unmarried couple may not file a joint federal income tax return. In addition, if one partner is not the legal parent of a child in the household, that parent may not file as head of household unless that partner may claim a dependency exemption for the child.[17] If a partner is not the legal parent of the child, he or she may claim a dependency exemption for the child only if the child lives in the same household for the entire year.[18] In addition, the partner must meet all other requirements for claiming the child as a dependent. A partner with a child may file as head of household if that partner provides more than half the cost of maintaining the household.[19]

The IRS chief counsel has concluded that California community property law does not apply to California domestic partners for federal tax purposes.[20] Therefore, an individual who is a registered domestic partner in California must report all of his or her earned income for federal tax purposes. By contrast, a husband and wife in a community property may each report one-half of the community income on a separate return.[21] California law provides that registered domestic partners cannot file joint tax returns and that a partner's earned income cannot be treated as community property income for state tax purposes. However, California community property laws do apply to registered domestic partners for other purposes.

[17] Code Sec. 2(b)(1)(A)(ii).

[18] Code Sec. 152(a)(9).

[19] Code Sec. 2(b)(1)(A)(i).

[20] Chief Counsel Advice 20060838.

[21] Poe v. Seaborn, 28 US 101 (November 24, 1930).

Chapter 26

Planning for the Elderly and Disabled

Overview .... ¶ 2601
The Elderly and Disabled .... ¶ 2605
The Mentally Impaired .... ¶ 2610

¶ 2601 OVERVIEW

The law of the elderly and disabled has become increasingly complex in recent years, and developments in this area demand the attention of financial and estate planners and their clients. As with most problems in the broad area of financial and estate planning, advance planning can alleviate, if not completely solve, many of the financial difficulties confronting elderly and disabled clients.

¶ 2605 THE ELDERLY AND DISABLED

Financial planners have a number of tools at their disposal in developing financial plans for clients who are elderly or disabled:

- A durable power of attorney can give the agent authority to manage the financial affairs of an elderly or disabled client and eliminate the need for the appointment of a guardian, committee, or conservator.
- Financial planners can use a springing durable power of attorney to bring into effect the authority when needed as determined by one or more triggering events.
- A revocable living trust can also provide for management of financial affairs including investments and payment of bills.
- In certain circumstances, financial planners can use an irrevocable trust to protect assets. In some cases, financial planners can use an irrevocable trust to help an individual

qualify for Medicaid. The financial planner should exercise caution because of rules that seemingly criminalize Medicaid planning (¶ 3515). However, in *New York State Bar Association v. Janet Reno, et al.*,[1] the U.S. District Court for the Northern District of New York declared unconstitutional the law that made the knowing and willful counsel of an individual, for a fee, to dispose of assets to become eligible for Medicaid to be a criminal act.[2] Attorney General Janet Reno agreed that the law was unconstitutional because it violated the First Amendment right of free speech.

- Financial planners can suggest a living will, health care proxy, or durable health care power of attorney (including a springing power) to allow an elderly person to provide guidance and legal protection for health care surrogates.
- In some cases, the financial planner can suggest joint bank accounts or accounts in trust for another (Totten trusts).
- Life insurance assignments may be useful in some situations.
- Lifetime gifts may also be appropriate.
- Long-term care insurance may be suitable for the elderly and any disabled individuals who are insurable. Nursing home care can easily cost over $50,000 a year. A variety of policies is available.

.01 Dealing with Limitations on Use of Planning Tools

Implementation of these tools depends on the client's being mentally competent to authorize their use at the time of the grant. Having expert witnesses and disinterested lay witnesses on hand at the time of the grant is wise. These witnesses can attest to and document the client's competency. Some states may require that a notary public attest to certain documents.

Durable powers. All states now recognize durable powers of attorney that survive the principal's incapacity. Clients must observe state formalities in creating the power. The client who grants the power is the principal and the individual to whom the principal grants the power is the holder or attorney-in-fact. Because the power may be revocable by the principal, third parties may be unwilling to act on the power unless it states that revocation shall be ineffective.

A durable power of attorney ends upon the death of the principal. In addition, the principal may revoke the durable power of attorney.

---

[1] 97 CV 1768-TMJ-DRE, (1998).

[2] Section 1128B(a)(6) of the Social Security Act, 42 U.S.C. § 1320-7(b)(a)(6).

If one's spouse is the attorney-in-fact, a divorce automatically terminates the durable power of attorney in some states. The durable power of attorney also terminates if the attorney-in-fact is unable or unwilling to serve. Principals may want to name successor attorneys-in-fact in case the designated attorney-in-fact predeceases the principal or is unable or unwilling to serve.

An attorney should draft the power in explicit terms broad enough to accomplish the client's desired objectives, including those related to estate planning. Although no one may delegate the authority to make or revoke a will, the principal may want to delegate the following powers:

- The power to make gifts in defined amounts to persons specified or to named charities
- The power to deal with retirement plans, IRAs, life insurance, and buy-sell agreements
- The power to fund living trusts

Springing powers. Springing powers are now widely sanctioned under either the statutory or judicial law of many states. However, some states may not approve springing powers. Thus, the financial planner should check the state law. The power must carefully define the triggering event, which ordinarily is incompetency, along with procedures for establishing its existence. Written certification by one or more physicians who have examined the principal will ordinarily be sufficient. The triggering event could conceivably be temporary physical disability or absence from the country as standby trusts sometimes provide, with provisions for termination of the power upon completion of the event. The springing power should carefully define the power granted considering the objectives sought, including those related to financial and estate planning.

Revocable living trusts. A revocable living trust can provide a great deal of flexibility. The settlor may revoke or amend a revocable living trust as long as he or she is competent. Initially, the settlor may only nominally fund the trust, but the settlor can fund the trust for any amount he or she chooses. The settlor may serve as trustee to keep down costs. However, a revocable living trust will still cost more than setting up a power of attorney. Upon determination of incompetency, the trust will become irrevocable for the benefit of the incompetent and the designated beneficiaries. The named successor trustee will take over. The settlor can use a durable power of attorney to pour all of his or her property into the trust upon the settlor's incompetency. The trust must contain provisions for determining incompetency, preferably by two physicians, as in connection with a springing power. The trust should give the trustee the authority to do things that the settlor would be disposed to do if he or she were not disabled.

While the settlor remains competent, the income, estate and gift tax consequences will be the same as with any revocable trust. The settlor will be taxable on the income, have no gift tax liability, and the value of the trust will be includible in the settlor's gross estate at death. Upon disability, if the settlor retains an income interest, as will normally be the case, the settlor will be taxable on the income and the trust will be includible in his or her gross estate.[3] In addition, a completed gift of the remainder interest will occur, unless the settlor, by will or proxy, retains certain powers over the disposition of the remainder.

Irrevocable living trusts. An irrevocable living trust ordinarily will involve gift tax costs for the transfer to the beneficiaries. The settlor can use the unified credit to offset any gift tax liability to the extent that the settlor has any remaining unified credit. With proper planning, an irrevocable living trust can be useful in enabling the settlor to qualify for Medicaid. These trusts are often called supplemental needs trusts or special needs trusts. The funds for these trusts can come from a third party such as a son or daughter or from the individual's own funds. The laws governing these trusts vary among the states. Financial planners would be wise to consult an attorney with expertise in elder law to discuss the creation of these trusts.

Living wills and health care proxies. Living wills and health care durable powers and proxies (¶ 2905) can be extremely useful in carrying out an individual's desires with respect to medical decisions when he or she is unable to make them. Generally, an individual may refuse extraordinary medical care to prolong life when competent. If the individual is incompetent, the attorney-in-fact or proxy may likewise refuse extraordinary medical care for the grantor of the power. Living wills and health care powers of attorney and proxies are virtually universally recognized under state laws.

Other planning tools. The elderly and potentially disabled can use the financial and estate planning tools generally used for young and healthy individuals. These tools include joint bank accounts, assignment of life insurance, lifetime giving, and other financial and estate planning tools. The only prerequisite is that the elderly or potentially disabled must take any action at a time when he or she is competent to act either directly in the use of these tools or by the appointment of surrogates with full authority to carry out the individual's directions.

---

[3] Code Sec. 2036(a).

.02 When Financial Planning Opportunities Are Neglected

Not everyone is foresighted enough to use the planning tools discussed above. In some cases, a wholly unforeseen accident or medical condition that totally incapacitates an individual may occur before the individual planned for it. Consequently, a need may arise for the appointment of a guardian, committee, or conservator.

The financial planner will want to be acquainted with the basics of these forms of surrogacy. Guardianships, for example, have been around for centuries. In many cases, guardianships have become encrusted with cumbersome rules designed to protect the ward, but which in their complexity may act to deplete the ward's assets.

States originally enacted conservatorships to provide a simplified method of securing authority to manage the financial affairs of incompetent persons. Since their institution, many states have expanded conservatorships to some degree, to assume the functions of a guardian of the ward.

Questions may arise under various laws as to whether a guardian or conservator can make health care decisions or engage in what amounts to financial and estate planning for the client. The Uniform Probate Code, which has been adopted in a number of states, gives the conservator the authority to do estate planning.

The bottom line from the standpoint of both the financial planner and the client is to consider the advantages of financial planning discussed above. A financial planner who fails to seize the opportunity to help an elderly or potentially incompetent client, may later face a malpractice claim.

¶ 2610 THE MENTALLY IMPAIRED

Five important vehicles or devices by which one person can hold and manage property for the benefit of another individual who is mentally impaired or otherwise unable to manage his or her property are as follows:

1. Trusts
2. Guardianships
3. Conservatorships
4. Custodianships
5. Powers of attorney

The main concern in this chapter is whether those who hold or manage property for another individual can engage in some forms of estate planning for the ward or principal. For example, can such an individual make gifts of property of the ward to achieve estate planning objectives?

The sections that follow examine this question under two conditions: (1) under the Uniform Probate Code, which has been enacted in 18 states and accepted in part in most of the remaining states, and (2) independently of the Probate Code.

.01 Under the Probate Code

Under the Uniform Probate Code, guardians are without specific power to engage in estate planning for their wards. One can assume that they are without implied powers in view of the specific powers conferred on conservators. The law specifically authorizes conservators to make gifts, such as the ward would make, not to exceed 20 percent of the annual income. In addition to the specific statutory powers that the Probate Code confers on the conservator, the court may confer such powers as the court itself could exercise.

The Probate Code specifically provides that the conservator and the court in exercising any powers should take into account any known estate plan of the ward. The known estate plan of the ward includes the ward's will, any revocable trust, and any contract, transfer, or joint ownership arrangement which the ward may have originated.

.02 Independently of the Probate Code

An elementary principle of law is that a donor must have donative intent to make an effective gift. A comatose individual obviously lacks donative intent. Yet, under the doctrine of substituted judgment, courts have been willing to allow guardians acting on behalf of comatose individuals, or other severely mentally impaired individuals, to make gifts.

Two premises serve as the foundation for this doctrine:

1. The individual must have adequate funds so that the gifts will not adversely affect the donor's maintenance and support. The court looks to the assets of the individual and projected income requirements.
2. A likelihood exists that the disabled individual would have made the gifts if capable of doing so. The court looks to prior actions with respect to gifts and estate planning strategies.

.03 Durable Power of Attorney

Where incapacity strikes later in life, an attorney-in-fact may make gifts on behalf of the principal without court intervention, provided the principal executed a properly drawn durable power of attorney. Generally, the durable power of attorney should specifically authorize the attorney-in-fact to make gifts according to the principal's instructions.

In addition to authorizing gifts, the financial planner should consider these possible limitations on the authority of the attorney-in-fact:

- Restricting gifts to the annual exclusion to ensure that transfers are free of gift tax and to preclude any use of the unified credit. The annual exclusion is $10,000 per donee, but it is indexed for inflation.[4] For calendar year 2006, the annual exclusion is $12,000 per donee.
- Specifying to whom the attorney-in-fact can make gifts or cannot make gifts. For example, can the attorney-in-fact make gifts to himself or herself and his or her family?
- Requiring equal or unequal gifts to grandchildren.

If a holder makes gifts not specifically authorized, the gifts may be includible in the gross estate of the principal as revocable transfers.[5] However, an exception may apply if applicable state law authorizes holders of durable powers to make gifts in accordance with their principal's personal history of gift giving. Gifts made by the power holder in conformance with such history have been held not includible in the decedent's gross estate.[6]

---

[4] Code Sec. 2503(b).

[5] Code Sec. 2038, *O. Casey Est.*, CA-4, 91-2 USTC ¶ 60,091.

[6] *J. Ridenour Est.*, CA-4, 1994-2 USTC ¶ 60,180.

Chapter 27

Planning for Generation-Skipping Transfers

Overview ....¶ 2701
Generation-Skipping Transfers ....¶ 2705

¶ 2701 OVERVIEW

This chapter reviews the generation-skipping transfer (GST) tax and its technical requirements. This chapter also suggests planning techniques to minimize exposure and to take advantage of exemptions and exclusions.

¶ 2705 GENERATION-SKIPPING TRANSFERS

Every individual has a substantial lifetime GST tax exemption under Code Sec. 2631, but this does not mean that planning for the GST tax is limited to the very wealthy. Through 2009, the GST tax exemption is equal to the estate tax applicable exclusion amount.[1] Therefore, the GST tax exemption is $2,000,000 in 2006, 2007, and 2008, and $3,500,000 in 2009.[2]

With even limited inflation over many years, many individuals of relatively modest wealth might find themselves subject to the tax without having properly planned for it. Estate planners must be prepared to address GST tax planning not only for the very wealthy, but also for individuals of more modest means.

.01 Flat-Rate Tax

The GST tax rate is equal to the product of the maximum federal estate tax rate, and the inclusion ratio for the transfer.[3] The

[1] Code Sec. 2631(c)

[2] Code Sec. 2010(c).

[3] Code Sec. 2641(a).

maximum federal estate tax rate is 46 percent in 2006, and 45 percent in 2007, 2008, and 2009. The estate tax and GST tax are repealed in 2010. The inclusion ratio is equal to 1 minus the applicable fraction.[4] The numerator of the applicable fraction is the amount of the GST tax exemption allocated to the trust that makes the transfer or to the property transferred in a direct skip. The denominator of the applicable fraction is the value of the property transferred minus any federal estate tax or state death tax recovered from the trust.

.02 When and How the Tax Is Levied

The GST tax is levied on direct skips, taxable terminations, and taxable distributions[5] to"skip"persons.[6] A skip person is an individual who is two or more generations below the generation of the transferor.[7] The GST tax rules generally apply to transfers made after October 22, 1986. However, certain transfers from trusts that were irrevocable before this date are not subject to the GST tax. If the estate planner is confronted with such a trust, he or she must take great care to comply with the complex and detailed exceptions to the general effective date, lest exemption from the GST be lost.[8]

For a direct skip that is not from a trust, the transferor is liable for the GST tax.[9] The GST tax on a direct skip is determined on a tax-exclusive basis, i.e., the tax base does not include the GST tax to be paid. A transferor computes the GST tax on a direct skip in a manner similar to that used to compute the gift tax.

On a taxable distribution, the base for the GST tax is the value of the property received by the transferee minus expenses incurred by the transferee with respect to the determination of the GST tax.[10] In the case of a taxable distribution, the transferee is liable for the GST tax.[11] If a taxable distribution consists of income for trust income tax purposes, the transferee may deduct the GST tax paid in computing his or her taxable income. However, the amount of the GST tax that the transferee may deduct may not exceed the amount of the distribution included in his or her gross income.[12] If the trust pays any of the GST tax, the law treats the tax payment as an additional taxable distribution.[13] The GST tax on a taxable distribution is determined on a tax-inclusive basis because the

[4] Code Sec. 2642(a)
[5] Code Sec. 2611(a).
[6] Code Sec. 2613(a).
[7] Code Sec. 2613(a)(1).
[8] See Reg. § 26.2601-(b).
[9] Code Sec. 2603(a)(3).
[10] Code Sec. 2621(a).
[11] Code Sec. 2603(a)(1).
[12] Code Sec. 164.
[13] Code Sec. 2621(b).

GST tax is to be paid out of the distributed property unless the governing instrument specifically directs otherwise.[14] If the trustee pays the GST tax on the taxable distribution, the law treats the tax payment as an additional taxable distribution.[15]

For a taxable termination or a direct skip from a trust, the trustee is liable for the GST tax.[16] On a taxable termination, the base for the GST tax is the value of the property minus a deduction for expenses, indebtedness, and taxes, attributable to the property.[17] The GST tax on a taxable termination is determined on a tax-inclusive basis because the GST tax is to be paid out of the distributed property unless the governing instrument specifically directs otherwise.[18]

Direct skips. A direct skip is a transfer to a skip person who is subject to estate or gift tax.[19] For example, a direct skip will occur if a parent makes a gift or leaves a legacy to a grandchild of $2.5 million. The transfer will be subject to both gift or estate tax and the GST tax. The GST tax on direct skips is computed by multiplying the full value of the property[20] by the applicable rate.[21] The applicable rate is computed by multiplying the maximum federal estate tax rate[22] by the inclusion ratio.[23] The inclusion ratio is equal to 1 minus the applicable fraction.[24] The applicable fraction for a direct skip is determined as follows: the numerator is the amount of the GST tax exemption allocated to the property transferred in the direct skip. Its denominator is the value of the property involved in the direct skip reduced by the value of the property transferred that is a nontaxable gift.[25] A nontaxable gift is the portion of the gift not subject to gift tax because of the annual exclusion or the exclusion for certain transfers for educational expenses or medical expenses.[26] The inclusion ratio for a direct skip becomes final when no additional GST tax can be assessed with respect to the direct skip.[27]

Example 27.1. Assume that Janet Smith died in 2006 and bequeathed $4,000,000 directly to her grandson, Steve Williams. Her will provided that this transfer is not to be reduced by estate, death, or GST taxes. Thus, Williams receives the entire $4,000,000. At the time of the transfer, $1,000,000 of the GST

[14] Code Sec. 2603(b).
[15] Code Sec. 2621(b).
[16] Code Sec. 2603(a)(2).
[17] Code Sec. 2622.
[18] Code Sec. 2603(b).
[19] Code Sec. 2612(c)(1).
[20] Code Sec. 2623.
[21] Code Sec. 2602.
[22] Code Sec. 2001(c)(1).
[23] Code Sec. 2641(a).
[24] Code Sec. 2642(a)(1).
[25] Reg. § 26.2642-1(c)(1).
[26] Reg. § 26.2642-1(c)(3).
[27] Reg. § 26.2642-5(a).

tax exemption is allocated to this bequest. The calculation of the GST tax would be as follows:

1. Determination of the applicable fraction: ($1,000,000 of the GST tax exemption divided by $4,000,000 in property equals the applicable fraction of 0.25),
2. Determination of the inclusion ratio: subtract the applicable fraction from 1. Thus, the inclusion ratio is 1 minus 0.25, or 0.75.

The GST tax rate is the product of the inclusion ratio—in this case, 0.75—and the maximum federal estate tax rate at the time of the transfer—46 percent. Thus, the rate of tax on this transfer is 34.5 percent. The GST tax due would be $1,380,000. ($4,000,000 × 34.5%)

Example 27.2. Assume that in 2006 Jeffrey Kauffman makes a lifetime gift of $3,212,000 to his granddaughter, Leah Cohen. Kauffman allocates $800,000 of his GST tax exemption to the transfer. Kauffman excludes $12,000 of the transfer under the annual exclusion rules for gift tax[28] and for the GST tax.[29] The calculation of the GST tax would be as follows:

1. Determination of the applicable fraction: divide the $800,000 of the GST tax exemption by the $3,212,000 in property minus the $12,000 annual exclusion ($800,000 ÷ $3,200,000). Therefore, the applicable fraction is 0.25,
2. Determination of the inclusion ratio: subtract the applicable fraction from 1. Thus, the inclusion ratio is 1 minus 0.25, or 0.75.

The GST tax rate is the product of the inclusion ratio—in this case, 0.75—and the maximum federal estate tax rate at the time of the transfer—46 percent. Thus, the rate of tax on this transfer is 34.5 percent. The GST tax due would be $1,104,000 ($3,200,000 × 34.5%). The GST tax paid by the donor or on a lifetime gift is treated as an additional gift for gift tax purposes, but not for GST tax purposes.[30] Thus, the amount subject to gift tax in this example is $4,304,000 ($3,212,000 − $12,000 + $1,104,000).

Taxable terminations. A taxable termination occurs when an interest in property held in trust terminates.[31] However, a taxable termination does not occur if: (1) a nonskip person has an interest in

[28] Code Sec. 2503(b).
[29] Code Sec. 2642(c).
[30] Code Sec. 2515.
[31] Code Sec. 2612(a).

the trust property immediately after the termination,[32] or (2) no distribution can be made, at any time after the termination, from the trust to a skip person.[33] For example, if a parent has created a trust for the benefit of his or her child, with the remainder to his or her grandchild, a taxable termination will occur on the death of the child. The GST tax on taxable terminations is levied (after deduction of certain expenses) on the full value of the property transferred and is payable by the trustee.[34] The applicable fraction for a taxable termination is determined by dividing the GST tax exemption allocated to the property by the value of the property reduced by any estate tax or state death tax recovered from the trust with respect to the property and any deduction for charitable contributions allowed with respect to the property.[35]

Taxable distributions. A taxable distribution is a distribution of income or principal from a trust to a skip person unless the distribution is a taxable termination or a direct skip.[36] For example, a taxable distribution occurs when the trustee of a trust created by a parent that permits distributions of income and principal to any descendant of the settlor during the lifetime of his or her child makes a distribution of income to a great-grandchild. In such a case, the GST tax on taxable distributions is levied (after deduction of certain expenses) on the full value of property received by the transferee and is payable by the beneficiary who receives the distribution.[37] If the trust pays the GST tax, the payment will be treated as a taxable distribution.[38] The applicable fraction for a taxable distribution is determined by dividing the GST tax exemption allocated to the property by the value of the property reduced by any estate tax or state death tax recovered from the trust with respect to the property and any deduction for charitable contributions allowed with respect to the property.[39]

.03 Avoiding a Direct Skip

The GST tax is imposed on every direct skip. An example of a direct skip is a transfer directly to or in trust for a grandchild, while the parent of the grandchild is living. Assuming the transferor has used the GST tax exemption, one way to avoid the immediate imposition of the tax is to have an interest held by a nonskip person.[40] For instance, a parent could transfer a life income interest to his or her child and a remainder interest to his or her grandchildren.

[32] Code Sec. 2612(a)(1)(A).
[33] Code Sec. 2612(a)(1)(B).
[34] Code Sec. 2622.
[35] Code Sec. 2642(a)(2).
[36] Code Sec. 2612(b).
[37] Code Sec. 2621(a).
[38] Code Sec. 2621(b).
[39] Code Sec. 2642(a)(2).
[40] Code Sec. 2621(a)(1)(A).

.04 Gross Up of Taxable Gifts for the GST Tax

Under Code Sec. 2515, persons who make lifetime direct skips will be liable for gift tax that is grossed up by the amount of the GST tax.

> ***Example 27.3.*** Assume that Juan Cruz has exhausted his lifetime GST tax exemption. He makes a gift of $1,000,000 in 2006 to his grandson Mario Rodriguez. He is allowed the $12,000 per donee annual exclusion. The GST tax on this gift is $454,480 [($1,000,000 – $12,000) × 46%] making the total taxable gift $1,442,480 ($1,000,000 – $12,000 + $454,480), on which the gift tax (without reference to the donor's available unified credit and assuming that the entire value of the gift is taxed in the 46% bracket) is $663,540 ($1,442,480 × 46%). Accordingly, the total transfer taxes on the gift of $1,000,000 are $1,118,020 ($454,480 + $663,540).

.05 GST Lifetime Exemption

The GST tax exemption through 2009 is equal to the estate tax applicable exclusion amount.[41] Married couples may elect to split the use of their GST tax exemptions for lifetime gifts[42] if they also elect gift splitting in computing the gift tax.[43] The use of the GST tax exemption will reduce the inclusion ratio of property subject to tax. A complicated set of rules governs the election of property to be covered by the exemption, allocation of the exemption if the transferor does not elect to apply it, and the taxation of property only partially covered by the exemption.

Strategic use of the lifetime exemption will permit potentially large sums to escape taxation. Once a transferor elects the exemption, property covered by the exemption will be exempt from taxation, even during multiple future skips.[44] Thus, a taxpayer should use assets with the greatest potential for appreciation to fund GST tax-exempt trusts.

As with the estate and gift tax unified credit, individuals seeking maximum GST tax savings should arrange their assets to make full use of the GST tax exemption. A married individual, with greater wealth than his or her spouse, should give assets to his or her spouse sufficient to permit use of that spouse's exemption. Such gifts ensure that the opportunity to exclude an amount equal to twice the statutory GST tax exemption will not be lost if the less wealthy spouse dies first.

---

[41] Code Sec. 2631(c).

[42] Code Sec. 2652(a)(2).

[43] Code Sec. 2513.

[44] Committee Reports on P.L. 99-514 (Tax Reform Act of 1986) 1986-3 CB (Vol. 2) 826.

.06 Inclusion Ratio

If a generation-skipping transfer consists of exempt and non-exempt property, computing the GST tax requires a calculation of the inclusion ratio with respect to such property. This ratio is the difference between "1"and the applicable fraction as shown by the following example.[45]

Example 27.4. On Audry Parker's death in 2006, after payment of the estate taxes, $2,500,000 is transferred to a trust for the benefit of her grandchildren. Her will specifically provides that the estate will pay the GST tax out of the residue of the estate. The full $2,000,000 GST tax exemption is allocated to this trust. Assuming no permitted deductions apply, the applicable fraction, the inclusion ratio, and tax rate are determined as follows:

$$\frac{\$2{,}000{,}000 \text{ exemption}}{2{,}500{,}000 \text{ property}} = 0.80$$

$1 - 0.80 = 0.20 \times 46\%$ (tax) $= 9.2\%$ (GST tax rate)

For individuals faced with a GST tax, using multiple trusts with each trust either totally exempt or subject to tax would be best.

Under Reg. § 26.2663-2, the GST tax can apply to lifetime and testamentary direct skips by nonresident aliens, but only to the extent that such transfers are subject to U.S. estate or gift tax. Thus, the GST tax will generally not apply to transferred property that does not have a situs in the United States.

.07 Annual Per Donee Exclusion and Gifts for Educational and Medical Expenses

Excluded from the GST tax are any amounts paid on behalf of an individual for educational and medical expenses.[46] This exclusion is the same one that applies for gift tax purposes under Code Sec. 2503(e). Similarly, the annual gift tax exclusion also applies for the GST tax.[47]

These transfers are referred to as nontaxable gifts in Code Sec. 2642(c). Under Code Sec. 2642(c)(1), a direct skip that is a nontaxable gift would not be subject to GST tax because such gifts always have an inclusion ratio of zero.

In the case of a transfer of a nontaxable gift to a trust, the interest of the beneficiary must be vested to be exempt from GST tax.

[45] Code Sec. 2642.

[46] Code Sec. 2611(b)(1).

[47] Code Sec. 2642(c)(3).

To accomplish vesting, two conditions must be satisfied: (1) no part of the principal or income may be distributed to or for the benefit of any person other than the beneficiary, and (2) if the trust does not terminate before the death of the beneficiary, the trust assets will be included in the beneficiary's gross estate.[48]

> **Planning pointer.** To receive the maximum GST tax exemption benefit for educational and medical expenses, a non-exempt (i.e., subject to GST tax) trust for a child should contain broad powers of invasion for educational and medical expenses for the child's offspring. Because such payments are nontaxable gifts with a zero inclusion ratio, such payments convert non-exempt property into exempt property.

If an individual uses the annual gift tax exclusion for a grandchild or great-grandchild through contributions to a trust, the interest of the beneficiary must be vested as noted above. The trust should be a totally GST tax-exempt trust.

.10 Reverse QTIP Election

Qualified terminable interest property (QTIP) is property that passes from a donor or decedent to his or her spouse who receives the income from the property for life. The income must be payable at least annually, and no person may appoint any of the property to anyone other than the spouse during the spouse's lifetime. The property in the QTIP trust is included in the spouse's gross estate upon his or her death.[49]

Property a decedent or donor transfers that is qualified terminable interest property is treated as the surviving spouse's property for purposes of the GST tax. This treatment could result in a potential waste of part of the GST tax exemption if the decedent's allowable GST exemption exceeds the value of property the unified credit shields from the estate tax. Code Sec. 2652(a)(3) allows the estate of the decedent for the purposes of the GST tax to elect to treat all property in a QTIP trust as though the QTIP election had not been made. In addition, for the purposes of the GST tax, a donee spouse may elect to treat a life estate received from his or her spouse for which a QTIP election has been made as though the QTIP election had not been made. The election is irrevocable.[50] If the estate or donee spouse makes the election, it must apply to all property in the trust subject to the QTIP election.[51] The purpose of this election is to treat

[48] Code Sec. 2642(c)(2) and Committee Reports on P.L. 100-647 (Technical and Miscellaneous Revenue Act of 1988).

[49] Code Sec. 2044.

[50] Reg. § 26.2652-2(a).

[51] Reg. § 26.2652-2(a).

the decedent, instead of the surviving spouse, as the transferor of the QTIP trust.

For purposes of the GST tax, the portions of a trust resulting from transfers from different transferors are treated as separate trusts.[52] Similar and independent shares of different beneficiaries in a trust are also treated as separate trusts for purposes of the GST tax.[53] In addition, if a trust is included in a decedent's gross estate or is created by the decedent's will, the severance of the trust into two or more trusts will be recognized for GST tax purposes if the severance is based on a provision in the will or trust that directs that the trust be severed on the death of the transferor or the trust is severed based on discretion granted by the governing instrument or local law. If the trusts are severed, the terms of the new trusts must provide for the same succession of interests and beneficiaries in the aggregate as under the old trust. The severance must occur before the due date for filing the estate tax return, including extensions allowed. The severance must occur on a fractional basis or if the governing instrument requires severance on the basis of a pecuniary amount, the separate share requirements for individuals must be met.[54] However, if the trusts are severed using fractional amounts, the new trusts do not have to receive a pro rata portion of each asset. The new trusts could receive assets that reflect the fair market value of all the assets in the old trust. If a court has not ordered a trust to be severed by the time the executor files the estate tax return, the executor must attach a statement describing any proceeding commenced to sever a trust and attach a copy of the severance petition.[55] The executor or trustee may allocate the individual's GST tax exemption to the separate trusts based on his or her discretion.[56]

To minimize total transfer taxes, a will should include a provision that allows the executor the discretion to sever a trust into two or more trusts in accordance with Reg. § 26.2654-1(b)(1). The will could also direct the executor to pay any taxes due from trusts that are not exempt from the GST tax. When an executor may sever a trust, the executor should place sufficient funds in a separate trust to use the remaining amount of the decedent's GST exemption. If the executor does not sever the trust, the executor must either: (1) make a reverse QTIP election for an amount larger than necessary with the result that upon the death of the surviving spouse, the executor of his or her estate will not be able to use any remaining GST tax exemption to the

[52] Code Sec. 2654(b)(1).
[53] Code Sec. 2654(b)(2).
[54] Reg. § 26.2654-1(b)(1).
[55] Reg. § 26.2654-1(b)(1).
[56] Reg. § 26.2654-1(b)(1)(C)(3).

QTIP trust; or (2) not make a reverse QTIP election and lose some of the decedent's GST tax exemption.

.11 Personal and Family Considerations

GST tax savings can present personal and family problems. Clients might wish to give their children outright use of funds, even at the cost of extra estate taxes on the death of the children. The estate planner should disclose possible GST tax savings, explain the pros and cons of exempt trusts to achieve such savings, and let the client make an informed decision. The estate planner should make and file a written memorandum of the discussion with the client.

Chapter 28

Planning for a Personal Residence

Overview .... ¶ 2801
Purchasing a Home .... ¶ 2805
Home Financing and Interest Deductions .... ¶ 2810
Deductibility of Home Mortgage Interest .... ¶ 2815
Exclusion of Gain on Sale of Residence .... ¶ 2820
Business Use of Home .... ¶ 2830
Vacation Homes .... ¶ 2835

¶ 2801 OVERVIEW

Ownership of one or more residences involves consideration of a number of tax and nontax factors. A list of some of the key factors follows, with cross-references to a more detailed discussion of particular factors, where applicable.

- **Purchasing a home.** An individual or family that is purchasing a home should consider several important factors. These factors include the structural integrity of the home, appreciation potential, quality of neighborhood schools, crime rate, transportation, legal considerations, use of a real estate agent, and financing.
- **Home financing and refinancing.** Understanding the various types of financing available to purchase or improve a residence is an important consideration for any prospective home buyer. Existing homeowners may want to know about refinancing options, including home equity loans and home equity lines of credit (HELOC). Deductibility of interest is apt to be of prime concern (¶ 2810).
- **Exclusion of gain.** Code Sec. 121 allows each taxpayer to exclude up to $250,000 of gain from the sale of a principal residence (¶ 2820). On a joint return, a couple may exclude

up to $500,000 of gain on the sale of a principal residence.[1] The taxpayer must meet certain ownership and use requirements.

- **Business and rental use of home.** A special provision is made for the disallowance of certain expenses in connection with the business use of a home and the rental of vacation homes (¶ 2830 and ¶ 2835, respectively).
- **Joint ownership by spouses.** A variety of special rules, involving both gift and estate tax consequences, becomes applicable when a residence is jointly owned by spouses (see Chapter 3 for discussion of co-ownership generally).
- **Joint ownership by unmarried individuals.** The pros and cons of joint ownership of a residence by unmarried individuals require careful consideration (see Chapter 3 for discussion of co-ownership generally).
- **Ownership in community property jurisdictions.** There are special rules to be considered if the residence is situated in a community property jurisdiction (see ¶ 325 for discussion of community property generally).
- **Placing residence in trust.** One of the options open to an individual owning a residence is to place it in trust and permit the spouse or others to use it on terms provided in the trust (see Chapter 6 for discussion of trusts generally). A grantor retained income trust (GRIT) can be funded with one's residence and achieve special estate planning benefits under an exception to the Code Sec. 2702 rules that normally limit the benefits of GRITs (¶ 2320). A residence placed in a trust for one's spouse may qualify for the marital deduction if the trust is set up to meet the requirements of a qualified terminable interest property (QTIP) or general power of appointment trust (¶ 1220).
- **Gift of a residence.** A gift of a residence, in some circumstances, may provide favorable financial and estate planning results and possibly other practical benefits (¶ 410).
- **Charitable contribution deduction.** A charitable contribution deduction is available for a remainder interest in a personal residence or farm (¶ 515.03). A charitable contribution deduction may also be available for a gift of a scenic easement appurtenant to a residence (¶ 535).
- **Title insurance.** Title insurance operates to protect a buyer and a lender against unforeseen or unknown title defects.
- **Special use valuation.** If a decedent's estate includes farm or business property that qualifies for special use

[1] Code Sec. 121(b)(2).

valuation, residential buildings thereon may be so valued (¶ 2210).

- **Purchases from nonresident alien.** A purchase of a residence from a nonresident alien may trigger a withholding obligation.
- **Casualty losses.** Casualty losses may be deductible to the extent they exceed $100 per event and 10 percent of adjusted gross income for all casualties and thefts.[2] In this connection, Code Sec. 1033(h) provides relief provisions for people whose principal residences (and/or contents) are involuntarily converted as a result of a Presidentially declared disaster. Under this provision, a taxpayer does not recognize any gain for insurance proceeds for personal property unless the property was scheduled property on the insurance policy. The owner may avoid recognizing any gain on the home if the taxpayer incurs cost for similar property, equal to the amount realized, within four years of the end of the tax year in which the taxpayer realized the gain.[3]
- **Real estate taxes.** Real estate taxes are deductible as an itemized deduction.[4]
- **Two or more homes.** For the individual who has two or more residences, there are special considerations:
  - Which home is to be the individual's principal residence? This issue becomes important in terms of meeting the $250,000 ($500,000 on a joint return) gain exclusion rule. It may also be important in terms of establishing domicile and governing law for purposes of the individual's estate plan.
  - If the individual has more than two residences, the mortgage interest deduction is limited to only two of the residences.[5]
  - If the residences are situated in different states, some consideration must be given to the requirement of ancillary administration of the estate and what steps, if any, might be taken to eliminate the problem.

¶ 2805 PURCHASING A HOME

Owning a home is part of the American dream. Owning a home provides an individual or family with a place to live, a valuable asset, tax benefits, and pride of ownership. A home is the largest investment

[2] Code Sec. 165(h).
[3] Code Sec. 1033(h)(1) and Code Sec. 1033(a)(2)(B).
[4] Code Sec. 164(a).
[5] Code Sec. 163(h)(4)(A).

that many people will make. Before purchasing a home, an individual or family should consider several important factors.

.01 Structural Integrity

A purchaser should ensure that the home is structurally sound. Of special interest are the foundation and roof. A financial planner would be wise to recommend that a client have the home inspected by a well-qualified inspector. New homes may come with a warranty. The purchaser should understand the terms of the warranty. Often the warranty will cover some things for one year, but cover the foundation for as long as ten years. Purchasers might want to have the home inspected again before the warranty coverage expires.

.02 Appreciation Potential

Although the tax law considers a home as a personal use asset, a client often treats his or her home as an investment. Many people move every five to ten years. A financial planner should advise a client to consider the appreciation potential of the home. This consideration is especially important because the tax law provides a generous exclusion for the gain realized on the sale or exchange of the home (¶ 2820).

.03 Quality of Neighborhood Schools

If the purchaser has children who are in school, the purchaser should consider the quality of the neighborhood schools the children would attend. The quality of the schools can vary considerably within a city. The financial planner should advise the client to obtain information on the quality of the schools. Visiting the schools before a purchase decision might be enlightening.

.04 Crime Rate

The purchaser would be wise to investigate the crime rate of a neighborhood before purchasing a home. Also, the purchaser should learn if the neighborhood has a citizen crime watch program.

.05 Transportation

The purchaser should check the roads that serve the neighborhood. If the area is a new area, the purchaser should learn what plans the local government has for expanding access. Of particular concern to many clients will be the ease of getting to and from the place where the client will work. Ease of transportation to shopping areas, the post office, and schools would also be important to many purchasers.

.06 Legal Considerations

Under the statute of frauds, a contract to purchase real estate must be in writing to be enforceable. Although real estate agents often have standard contracts that one can use to make an offer on a home, the purchaser does not have to use these standard contracts. In addition, the purchaser may modify the standard contracts. A purchaser would be wise to have an offer to purchase real estate reviewed by an attorney. Purchasers should be aware of restrictive covenants and easements. Usually, having a survey of the property performed by a registered land surveyor is a good idea. A purchaser would be wise to have his or her own attorney present at the closing to review all documents. The new homeowner should have the title to the property reviewed by an attorney and receive the attorney's opinion on the title and/or obtain title insurance.

.07 Use of a Real Estate Agent

Although some purchasers buy a home without using a real estate agent, the use of a real estate agent is common. Purchasers should remember that real estate agents generally represent the seller and owe a fiduciary duty to the seller. However, in many areas, buyer's brokers are available who represent the buyer's best interest. Purchasers should give serious consideration to employing a buyer's broker.

.08 Financing

Financing is a most important aspect of purchasing a home because few people pay for a home entirely out of their available funds. The next paragraph discusses home financing and interest deductions in detail.

¶ 2810 HOME FINANCING AND INTEREST DEDUCTIONS

The focus of this section is on financing. Deductions for interest are separately considered at ¶ 2815.

The two basic types of mortgages are fixed rate mortgages and adjustable rate mortgages. Variations of both types are separately considered below.

.01 Fixed Rate Mortgages

As the name implies, a fixed rate mortgage carries an interest rate that is fixed (generally at the loan closing) and remains constant until the loan is retired. Virtually all fixed rate home mortgages require level monthly payments and are self-amortizing, that is, at the end of the loan term, the principal balance will be zero. The total amount of interest paid on the mortgage increases with its term, which generally ranges from 15 years to 30 years. However, mortgage terms of 10 years or 20 years are becoming more popular. A lender may retain the loan in its portfolio or sell it on the secondary mortgage market and continue to earn servicing fees on the outstanding loan balance.

The outstanding feature of a fixed rate mortgage, from the borrower's standpoint, is the certainty that payments will not increase over the life of the loan, even if rates increase substantially. Also on the plus side is the possibility of payments in cheaper dollars due to inflation. On the minus side is the possibility that interest rates may decline during ownership. The only way to capitalize on lower rates would be to refinance the loan, a transaction that involves additional fees.

.02 Adjustable Rate Mortgages (ARMs)

Adjustable rate mortgages (ARMs) play an important part in home financing. The ARM is designed to transfer to borrowers some or all of the risk that lenders may encounter in connection with long-term mortgage loans in a climate of rising interest rates. The ARM may be presented to the borrower when mortgage interest rates are high as a means of passing along some of the benefits of an interest drop. Still, borrowers may be reluctant to start out with a high rate on the prospect of a future drop. As a result, ARMs, at least in their initial year, feature lower interest rates than fixed rates, in part to compensate the borrower for accepting more risk. In general, the greater the risk the borrower finds acceptable, the lower the interest rate. A typical ARM will include most, and possibly all, of the following features.

Index. This rate is the benchmark that the lender uses to adjust the rate. Common indexes are the rate on U.S. Treasury securities (six-month, one-, three- or five-year maturities) and the average cost of funds for savings institutions insured by the Savings Association Insurance Fund (SAIF).

Margin. The margin, also known as the spread, is the amount that the lender may add to the index value used in the agreement.

Initial rate and adjusted effective rate. The initial rate is the interest rate upon which the borrower's initial payments are based. Typically, the rate is lower than the amount that would be payable on a fixed rate mortgage. If the initial rate is much lower, it is said to be a "teaser," an artificially low rate designed to induce the borrower to enter into the arrangement. An easy way to see if the initial rate is artificially low in the first year is to figure out what the rate would be under the then applicable index, plus the margin, and compare this rate with the initial rate.

When rate adjustments occur, the adjusted effective rate is the index value used plus the margin. For example, if the index value is six percent and the margin is two percent, the adjusted effective rate is eight percent. The effective rate is not to be confused with the Annual Percentage Rate (APR), which takes into account the points levied when the loan is closed.

Adjustment period. This period is simply the time when payments or interest rates can change. They may change, for example, every six months, every year, or every three years.

Caps. Several caps may apply, including the following:

- **Payment cap.** This cap limits the increase in monthly payments at each adjustment period. For example, payment increases may be capped at 7.5 percent.
- **Interest adjustment cap.** The interest rate that monthly payments are based on cannot increase (or decrease) by more than a set percentage at each adjustment period. The cap is usually one or two percent.
- **Lifetime caps.** There may be one or several ceilings specified in the note. An ARM must by law carry an interest rate ceiling that limits the maximum interest that the lender may charge during the life of the loan. Lifetime interest caps usually are five or six percentage points higher than the initial rate. For example, if the initial effective rate is 5.5 percent, the rate can go no higher than 11.5 percent during the loan term if the lifetime interest cap is 6 percent. A lifetime payment cap places a percentage limit on the amount by which principal and interest payments can increase during the loan term. The note also may carry a cap on negative amortization.

Negative amortization. This condition occurs when the borrower's payments are less than the amount necessary to pay interest on the outstanding debt. As a result, the lender adds the unpaid interest to the loan principal.

.03 Other Kinds of Mortgages

Variations of the basic fixed rate and adjustable rate mortgages discussed above include the following.

Seven-year balloon mortgage. A seven-year balloon mortgage calls for fixed monthly payments based on a 30-year amortization of the mortgage. At the end of seven years, the borrower must pay the balance due on the loan. However, if the borrower meets certain conditions, he or she may refinance the loan at maturity with a 23-year fixed rate mortgage.

Graduated-payment mortgage (GPM). With a GPM, payments begin at a lower level than with a conventional mortgage and increase in fixed steps over the first several years. The borrower may usually choose between different rates of increase and different periods of increase. For example, the borrower may choose to have payments increase 5 percent each year or 2.5 percent each year for 10 years.

The major disadvantage of a GPM is that the borrower pays substantially more interest than under a conventional mortgage because of the slower amortization. If the home is resold before monthly payments have caught up with those under a conventional mortgage, the mortgage principal will have grown. As a result, the owner will have a smaller equity for the next home than at the inception of the mortgage if the appreciation of the home is less than the increase in the mortgage principal.

Graduated-payment adjustable mortgage (GPAM). This form of mortgage is a combination variable rate mortgage (VRM) and GPM. It starts out as a GPM, with lower payments increasing by steps, and, when payments reach the point where they would level off under a GPM, interest rates may move up or down as under a VRM. The complexity of the GPAM explains its less frequent use than VRMs or GPMs.

Price level adjusted mortgage (PLAM). With a PLAM, the lender sets the initial rate of interest at the prevailing real rate of interest (rate without any adjustment for inflation). At the end of each year, the principal balance is adjusted to keep pace with inflation (or deflation), so that it reflects the real purchasing power of the dollars initially borrowed. PLAMs involve many trade-offs for the borrower, the main one of which is negative amortization.

Another is that equity increases will not significantly increase the homeowner's ability to use the home as a source of additional borrowing. Finally, if inflation outpaces the borrower's income, the borrower may find keeping up with the monthly payments to be difficult.

Renegotiable-rate mortgage (RRM). The RRM is a series of short-term loans of possibly three, four, or five years secured by a long-term mortgage of perhaps 25 or 30 years. Each time the short-term loan is renewed, the interest rate changes in accordance with the formula fixed in the agreement. Federally chartered savings institutions make RRMs, using the Federal Housing Finance Board interest rate index, which is published monthly.

Lenders are required to renew the loan at the end of each short-term period, but the borrower may pay it off without penalty.

Shared-appreciation mortgage (SAM). With a SAM, the borrower gets a below-market interest rate for a designated period in exchange for giving the lender a share of the appreciation of the home's value over the period designated or on resale, whichever comes first.

If the borrower does not sell the home, he or she must pay the lender what is designated as "contingent interest," equal to the lender's share of the appreciation as determined by an independent appraisal. To protect the owner against the possibility of having to pay the lender a large sum at the time specified, the lender ordinarily guarantees to refinance at the interest rate then prevailing.

The SAM is more speculative for both parties than are the other types of mortgages discussed above. If, for example, inflation were to continue at a rate of nine percent a year for an indefinite period, the value of the house would double in eight years. The owner, even though guaranteed refinancing, might find carrying the home with the much greater mortgage difficult if not impossible. The lender, on the other hand, would receive a good return. The exact amount of cost to one and benefit to the other would depend on their relative shares in the appreciation. The relative shares in the appreciation would be affected by the extent to which the interest rate is below market. Typically, the interest rate will be one-third below market and the lender will get one-third of the appreciation.

Zero rate mortgage (ZRM). A ZRM is a mortgage that makes no express provision for interest. If it is a purchase money mortgage, interest is imputed to the mortgagee-seller (and the principal amount of the debt is reduced for the imputed interest) under either Code Sec. 483 or 1274, depending on the sale price and the stated note principal. However, the mortgagor-buyer of a personal residence does not adjust note principal, and is not entitled to a deduction for imputed interest if the debt instrument is given in consideration for the sale of the property.[6]

Flexible loan insurance program (FLIP). The FLIP is known as the pledged-account mortgage (PAM) because it makes

[6] Code Sec. 1275(b)(1); Reg. § 1.1275-2(f)(1).

use of a pledged savings account. It operates to provide graduated payments for the borrower and level payments for the lender.

The amount that the purchaser would ordinarily use as a down payment is placed in an interest-bearing savings account with the lending bank. The borrower pledges the account as additional security for the loan. Each month the lender withdraws an amount from the savings account which, when added to the reduced payment afforded the borrower, will equal the normal payment on a conventional mortgage. The borrower's payments increase periodically. As they increase, the payments from the savings account decrease. The computation is such that the savings account is normally completely used up at the end of five years.

Growing-equity mortgage (GEM). While all self-amortizing mortgages increase the mortgagor's equity, GEMs do so at a faster pace through gradually increasing principal payments. The interest rate remains constant. Because of the accelerated principal payments, the mortgagee is able to offer a lower interest rate than with a conventional mortgage. This factor, plus the shorter period before the principal is paid, along with the fixed interest rate, may make the GEM attractive to a borrower. However, the GEM runs counter to the conventional wisdom that, from a borrower's standpoint, the longer the term of the mortgage the better in that, with continuing inflation, future payments may be discharged with ever cheaper dollars. The basic factor to be weighed is whether the after-tax benefit of the lower interest rates saves as much as (or more than) the savings under a conventional mortgage with higher interest rates but a longer term.

Fixed rate with refinancing option. A so-called reduction-option loan gives the homeowner/mortgagor a built-in option to refinance without the usual closing costs of refinancing if rates drop at least two percentage points. Typically, the refinancing option may only be exercised between the 13th and 59th month of the mortgage. The cost of exercising the option will vary from lender to lender. Some lenders charge $100 plus 0.25 percent of the principal ($350 on a $100,000 loan). The cost of the option is an initial interest rate that is about a quarter of a percent higher than a comparable 30-year fixed rate mortgage without such an option.

Bi-weekly mortgages. The homeowner/mortgagor makes a mortgage payment bi-weekly (every two weeks) in an amount equal to half of what the payment would be on a conventional monthly payment mortgage. Interest figures to be at the same rate as on a conventional monthly. As a result, the borrower annually pays the equivalent of 13 conventional monthly payments. The mortgage is paid off sooner running anywhere from 17 to 20 years, depending on terms, rather than 30 years. This reduction in the term of the loan results in far lower aggregate interest payments. On the other hand, the opportunity to benefit by inflation by paying off with cheaper dollars is reduced.

Fixed-payment ARM. The lender adjusts the interest rate annually but the amount of monthly payments remains fixed by lengthening or shortening the term of the loan.

40-year mortgage. Some lenders offer 40-year loans. The differential in the monthly payments is not great but the difference on aggregate payments over the term of the loan is substantial.

Reverse mortgages. In a reverse mortgage (also called a home equity conversion) a homeowner borrows against the equity in his or her home by receiving the loan in monthly installments. Thus, the loan balance grows each month. However, the borrower does not have to make a payment as long as he or she lives. A reverse mortgage is a financial planning tool that older clients can use to convert the equity in their home to cash without having to move or risk losing their home.

¶2815 DEDUCTIBILITY OF HOME MORTGAGE INTEREST

A taxpayer may deduct home mortgage interest only if it constitutes qualified residence interest,[7] i.e., interest on either acquisition indebtedness, home equity debt, or both.[8] The total debt that can give rise to a deduction for qualified residence interest is $1.1 million—$1 million for acquisition debt and $100,000 for home equity debt.[9]

Besides the dollar limits, the major difference between the two categories is that acquisition debt qualifies only if the taxpayer uses it for purposes specified in the statute, such as the construction, acquisition, or substantial improvement of a qualifying residence.[10] By contrast, interest on qualifying home equity debt generally is deductible without regard to how the borrower used the funds.[11] For example, the interest is deductible even though the borrower used the funds to buy a car or boat or to finance a child's education. On the other hand, if the taxpayer used the loan proceeds to buy tax-exempt securities,[12] the deduction would be barred.

---

[7] Code Sec. 162(a) and Code Sec. 163(h)(2)(D).
[8] Code Sec. 163(h)(3).
[9] Code Sec. 163(h)(3).
[10] Code Sec. 163(h)(3)(B).
[11] Code Sec. 163(h)(3)(C).
[12] Code Sec. 265(a).

.01 Limitation on Itemized Deductions

Code Sec. 68 reduces allowable itemized deductions (excluding medical deductions, investment interest, casualty losses and wagering losses to the extent of wagering gains) by an amount equal to three percent of adjusted gross income (AGI) in excess of an annually adjusted amount. The reduction may not exceed 80 percent of allowable deductions. This reduction reduces the tax benefits of home ownership because both interest and real estate taxes are included in the reduction.

For tax years beginning after 2005 and before 2010, the overall limitation on itemized deductions is reduced.[13] For 2006 and 2007, the reduction of itemized deductions is limited to two-thirds of the otherwise applicable reduction. For 2008 and 2009, the reduction is limited to one-third of the otherwise applicable amount. The limitation on itemized deduction will not apply for 2010.[14]

For 2006, itemized deductions are reduced if AGI exceeds $150,500 ($72,250 for marrieds filing separately).[15]

> ***Example 28.1.*** Bill and Joan Steele file a joint return for 2006 with AGI of $221,200 and itemized deductions consisting only of real estate taxes and home mortgage interest of $40,000. Three percent of AGI in excess of $150,500 is $2121. However, for 2006 the reduction of itemized deductions is limited to two-thirds of that amount, or $1414. Therefore, the steels' itemized deductions are reduced to $38,586 ($40,000 – $1,414).

.02 Acquisition Debt

A loan is treated as acquisition debt and thus gives rise to deductible interest only if the following tests are met:[16]

- **Use of proceeds.** The taxpayer must use the loan proceeds to acquire, construct or substantially improve a qualified residence, or to refinance debt used for these purposes.
- **Security for debt.** The loan must be secured by the qualified residence.
- **Use of residence.** Code Sec. 163(h)(4)(A)(i) defines a qualified residence as the taxpayer's principal residence within the meaning of Code Sec. 121 and/or one other home considered used as residence under Code Sec. 280A(d)(1). Under the latter, a home qualifies if the taxpayer uses it

---

[13] Code Sec. 68(f).

[14] Code Sec. 68(g).

[15] Rev. Proc. 2005-70, 2005-47 IRB 979 (October 28, 2005).

[16] Code Sec. 163(h)(3)(B).

personally for more than the greater of 14 days or 10 percent of the days it is rented.

- **Dollar cap.** The aggregate amount of acquisition debt does not exceed $1 million.

IRS Notice 88-74[17] adds yet another requirement. Acquisition debt cannot exceed the cost of the residence (including the cost of improvements).

.03 Home Equity Debt

Like acquisition debt, home equity debt must be properly secured by a qualified residence in order to be deductible.[18] However, that is where the similarity ends. Interest on home equity debt generally is deductible regardless of how the taxpayer used the loan proceeds. Thus, a taxpayer can obtain a home equity loan to purchase a car or other personal assets and thereby convert nondeductible personal interest into fully deductible qualified residence interest.

.04 Limitation

Home equity debt cannot exceed the difference between the home's fair market value when the loan is obtained less the outstanding acquisition debt at that time.[19] Thus, the deduction for mortgage interest would be further limited on a 125-percent home loan to the interest on the portion of the loan secured by the value of the property at the time of the loan.

In addition, interest is not deductible to the extent the average outstanding equity debt exceeds $100,000 ($50,000 for marrieds filing separately).[20]

.05 Grandfathered Debt

A grandfather rule applies to debt incurred on or before October 13, 1987, and secured by a qualified residence on that date and at all times thereafter before the interest is paid or accrued. Such debt automatically is treated as acquisition debt, regardless (generally) of how the proceeds are used. Grandfathered debt is not subject to the otherwise applicable $1 million ceiling.[21] Any outstanding grandfathered debt reduces the $1 million limit on acquisition debt, but not below zero.

---

[17] 1988-2 CB 385.

[18] Code Sec. 163(h)(3)(C)(i).

[19] Code Sec. 163(h)(3)(C)(i).

[20] Code Sec. 163(h)(3)(C)(ii).

[21] Code Sec. 163(h)(3)(D).

.06 Residence

A residence includes a house, co-op, condominium, mobile home, boat, or house trailer that contains sleeping space and toilet and cooking facilities.[22] Time-share units also qualify as residences.[23] A time-sharing plan is an arrangement between two or more people that limits their interests in the property or limits their right to use it to a certain portion of the year (e.g., two weeks).

.07 Points

A lender may impose a variety of charges in connection with a home mortgage. Typically, one of the largest charges is for points, a one-time payment that increases the lender's yield on the loan. A point is one percent of the loan amount.

Generally, because points represent prepaid interest, a cash-basis taxpayer must deduct the interest expense ratably over the term of the loan. However, Code Sec. 461(g)(2) carves out an exception for points paid in connection with debt incurred to buy or improve a principal residence and secured by the residence. Such points are deductible as interest in the year paid (subject to the restrictions of Code Sec. 163(h)) as long as the payment of points is an established business practice in the area where the debt is incurred and the points levied are not in excess of the amount generally charged in the area.

Points paid in connection with refinancing a principal residence, or obtaining a home equity credit line secured by the home, are currently deductible only to the extent that the loan amount is used to improve the residence.[24] A taxpayer may amortize points that are not currently deductible over the life of the loan. The taxpayer may deduct any unamortized points at the time he or she pays off the loan.

A purchaser may deduct points paid by the seller on a mortgage loan obtained to purchase the taxpayer's principal residence. The purchaser treats the points paid by the seller as a reduction in the basis of the property.[25]

---

[22] Temp. Reg. § 1.163-10T(p)(3)(C)(ii).

[23] Temp. Reg. § 1.163-10T(p)(6).

[24] Rev. Rul. 87-22, 1987-1 CB 146.

[25] Rev. Proc. 94-27, 1994-1 CB 613.

.08 Alternative Minimum Tax (AMT) Factors

For AMT purposes, the deduction for qualified residence interest is not the same as it is for regular tax purposes; the following special rules apply:[26]

- Otherwise eligible acquisition debt does not give rise to an AMT deduction if the taxpayer uses the proceeds to build, buy, or substantially improve a boat or a mobile home used on a transient basis.
- Interest on home-equity debt is not allowed. The AMT deduction is limited to interest paid or accrued on acquisition debt and the refinancing of such debt.

The second rule, above, does not apply to qualified residence interest paid or accrued on a debt incurred before July 1, 1982.

When the debt was incurred, it must have been secured by a:

- Principal residence of the taxpayer; or
- Home, apartment, condominium or nontransient-use mobile home used by the taxpayer or by his brother, sister, spouse, ancestor, or lineal descendant.

.09 Mortgage for Business Loan

Code Sec. 163(h) limits deduction for personal interest. It allows a taxpayer to deduct interest on acquisition debt up to $1 million and home equity debt up to $100,000. However, Code Sec. 163(h) does not limit the deduction for interest incurred for loans used for business purposes.[27] If a taxpayer borrows against his or her home equity and uses the proceeds for business purposes, the taxpayer may deduct the interest on the appropriate form on the tax return (e.g., Schedule C for sole proprietors and Schedule F for farmers). The taxpayer may deduct the interest on a business loan even if the loan exceeds the value of the home such as on the well-advertised 125 percent loans. Taxpayers should be aware of the tracing rules to ensure a deduction for business interest.[28]

¶ 2820 EXCLUSION OF GAIN ON SALE OF RESIDENCE

An individual may generally exclude up to $250,000 ($500,000 on a joint return) of gain realized on the sale or exchange of a principal residence. To qualify for the $250,000 exclusion, the individual must have owned and occupied the home as a principal residence for an

[26] Code Sec. 56(e).

[27] Code Sec. 163(h)(2)(A).

[28] Temp Reg. § 1.163-8T.

aggregate of at least two of the five years before the sale or exchange. The exclusion applies to only one sale or exchange every two years. For tax year 2010 only, the exclusion of gain from the sale of a principal residence will apply to a decedent's principal residence that is sold by (1) the decedent's estate, (2) any individual who acquired the residence from the decedent as a result of his or her death, or (3) a trust established by the decedent that was a qualified revocable trust immediately before the decedent's death.[29]

.01 Married Individuals

The amount of excludable gain is increased to $500,000 for married individuals filing jointly if (1) either spouse meets the ownership test, (2) both spouses meet the use test, and (3) neither spouse is ineligible for exclusion because of having made a sale or exchange of a residence within two years.

When married couples file a joint tax return, they will be eligible for the exclusion (or a prorated part of it) if either spouse meets the ownership and use requirements.

.02 Gain Recognized to Extent of Depreciation

The exclusion does not apply, and gain is recognized, to the extent of any depreciation allowable with respect to the rental or business use of a principal residence after May 6, 1997.[30] Except for the gain due to depreciation recapture, the portion of the home used for business purposes is eligible for the $250,000 (or $500,000) exclusion.[31] However, if the taxpayer used a separate structure on the property for business purposes, any gain allocated to the separate structure is not eligible for the exclusion.[32]

.03 Exclusion Prorated

If a taxpayer does not meet the ownership or residence requirements, a pro rata amount of the $250,000 or $500,000 exclusion applies if the sale or exchange is due to a change in place of employment, health, or unforeseen circumstances. In such cases, the amount of the available exclusion is equal to $250,000 (or $500,000) multiplied by the portion that the shorter of (1) the aggregate periods during which the ownership and use requirements were met during the five-year period ending on the date of sale, or (2) the period after the date of the most recent sale or

---

[29] Code Sec. 121(d)(9).
[30] Reg. § 1.121-1(d).
[31] Reg. § 1.121-1(e).
[32] Reg. § 1.121-1(e).

exchange to which the exclusion applied bears to two years. The following example illustrates the proration formula.

> ***Example 28.2.*** On September 1, 2005, Al and Lisa Jackson purchase a townhouse in Boston for $450,000. Lisa receives an offer of employment in Atlanta, and on July 1, 2006, the Jacksons sell their townhouse for $480,000 and purchase a home in a suburb of Atlanta for $350,000. The Jacksons realize a $30,000 capital gain on their townhouse. Their exclusion is limited to $208,333 ($500,000 × 10 ÷ 24). Because their allowable exclusion exceeds their realized gain, they may exclude all of the $30,000 gain from their gross income.

.04 Less Need for Recordkeeping?

One of the stated reasons behind the enactment of the $250,000/$500,000 residential sale exclusion was eliminating the need for many homeowners to keep detailed records with respect to their residential purchases and sales. However, a financial planner should advise clients to keep records of capital improvements if there is any possibility that the client might be required to recognize any gain upon the sale of a home. Such a situation may arise under any of the following circumstances:

- The homeowners intend to live in the residence for a long period of time.
- The residence is rapidly appreciating in value.
- The homeowners may some day claim a depreciation deduction for a home office or rental use of the residence.
- There is a possibility that the owners may not use or own the residence long enough to qualify for the exclusion.

.05 Ownership and Use of Prior Residences

In determining the period of ownership and use of a current residence, a taxpayer may include periods that he or she owned and used previous residences for which gain was rolled over to the current residence under Code Sec. 1034.

.06 Incapacitated Homeowners

If a homeowner becomes physically or mentally incapable of self-care, the homeowner will be considered to use a home as a principal residence while he or she resides in a licensed care facility, such as a nursing home. For this rule to apply, the homeowner must have owned and used his or her residence as a principal residence for at least one year during the five years preceding the sale.

.07 Divorced and Widowed Homeowners

If a residence is transferred to a taxpayer incident to a divorce, the time during which the taxpayer's spouse or former spouse owned the residence is added to the taxpayer's period of ownership. A taxpayer who owns a residence is deemed to use it as a principal residence while the taxpayer's spouse or former spouse is given use of the residence under the terms of a divorce or separation.

A widowed taxpayer's period of ownership in a residence includes the period in which a deceased spouse owned the residence.

.08 Remainder Interests

The residential gain exclusion provision applies to gain on the sale or exchange of a remainder interest in a principal residence, provided that the person acquiring the residence is not a member of the taxpayer's family or other related person.[33]

.09 Claiming a Home Sale Loss

An individual's personal residence is a capital asset. Thus, if the requirements for exclusion of gain are not met, the taxpayer must recognize a capital gain on its sale or exchange. However, a taxpayer may not recognize a loss on the sale of a personal residence.[34]

When faced with the possibility of a loss on the sale of a principal residence, one strategy is to convert the residence into rental property before the sale. In such cases, a loss is computed on the difference between the amount realized from the sale and the lesser of (1) the fair market value of the property at the time of the conversion, or (2) the property's adjusted basis for loss at the time of the conversion, determined under Reg. § 1.1011-1. Accordingly, if the fair market value of the property as of the conversion is less than the adjusted basis of the property, the fair market value becomes the adjusted basis for purposes of calculating a loss.

¶ 2830 BUSINESS USE OF HOME

Code Sec. 280A bars the deduction of expenses attributable to a taxpayer's use of his or her home for business purposes, except for such expenses that are attributable to the portion of the home used exclusively and on a regular basis as:

- The principal place of any business of the taxpayer.

[33] As defined by Code Sec. 267(b) or 707(b). [34] Code Sec. 165(c).

- A place of business that is used by patients, clients, or customers in meeting or dealing with the taxpayer in the normal course of trade or business.

A home office will also qualify as a taxpayer's principal place of business if the taxpayer meets the following conditions:

- The office is used by the taxpayer to conduct administrative or management activities of the taxpayer's trade or business; and
- There is no other fixed location where the taxpayer conducts substantial administrative or management activities of the business.

In addition to allowing affected taxpayers to deduct a portion of residential interest, real estate taxes, utility charges, etc., many taxpayers may deduct the cost of traveling to and from their homes to other locations at which they conduct business.[35]

Caution. The definition of a taxpayer's principal place of business does not affect the requirement that home office expenses are deductible only if the office is used by the taxpayer exclusively on a regular basis as a place of business. Also, if the taxpayer is an employee, the taxpayer's use of the home office must be for the convenience of the employer.

There are two specific exceptions to the exclusive use rule which may be of value. One deals with the storage of inventory and product samples, and the other with the use of the home as a day-care facility under a state license. Another exception to the Code Sec. 280A rules that may be of importance to homeowners who take in overnight guests is found in the section's definition of "dwelling unit" so as to exclude the portion of a unit which is used exclusively as a hotel, motel, inn or similar establishment.[36] This exception is apt to be of particular importance to many owners of large homes in various parts of the country who operate a "bed and breakfast" out of their home.

The amount of a home office deduction (other than expenses which are deductible without regard to business use, such as taxes) is limited to the gross income from the activity, reduced by all other deductible expenses attributable to the activity but not allocable to the use of the unit itself. The taxpayer may carry forward disallowed deductions indefinitely, subject to the limitation, which will continue to apply even if the unit is not used as a residence.

---

[35] Rev. Rul. 99-7, IRB 1999-5, 4 (January 15, 1999).

[36] Code Sec. 280A(f)(1)(B).

Generally, a principal or second residence is not considered a qualified residence for purposes of the deduction for qualified residence interest (as discussed at ¶ 2810) to the extent the home is used for trade or business purposes or for rental. Thus, for example, an attorney who uses part of his or her home to meet or deal with customers or clients in the ordinary course of business cannot treat all of his or her otherwise qualifying interest expenses as residence interest. The taxpayer must allocate interest expense in the same way he or she allocates other expenses.

¶ 2835 VACATION HOMES

A vacation home does not pose any special tax problems if the taxpayer uses it solely for personal reasons. The primary issue is whether interest paid on debt secured by the vacation home is qualified residence interest. There also are no tax implications if the taxpayer rents the home for less than 15 days during a year. Under Code Sec. 280A(g), the income from this limited rental period is not taxable and no deductions are allowed with respect to the rental period.

Many vacation home owners rent the property for more than two weeks during the year. In such cases, the tax rules become a veritable quagmire.

The main issues are as follows:

- Whether the vacation home is considered to be the taxpayer's residence or investment property.
- Which expenses are deductible in connection with rental use of the home.
- How expenses are allocated between personal use and rental use.
- How to treat expenses in excess of income.

.01 Character of Vacation Home

Code Sec. 280A(d)(1) uses a mechanical test to determine the tax character of a vacation home. A dwelling unit is considered the owner's residence for a tax year if personal use exceeds the greater of (a) 14 days, or (b) 10 percent of the days the unit is rented out.[37] If personal use does not exceed the test, then the vacation home is considered held as an investment property, although the taxpayer still must allocate expenses between personal and investment use.

[37] Code Sec. 280A(d)(1).

.02 Consequences of Residence v. Investment Use

The tax character of the home determines how the taxpayer deducts interest expense, how much expense the taxpayer may deduct currently, and how the taxpayer must treat expenses in excess of income. The consequences are summarized in the following table.

Vacation Home Used as Residence	Vacation Home Held as Investment Property
Interest paid generally is not subject to the interest allocation rules of Reg. § 1.163-8T.	Interest paid is subject to the interest allocation rules of Reg. § 1.163-8T.
Interest allocable to personal use of residence is deductible as qualified residence interest, assuming all conditions of Code Sec. 163(h) are met.	Interest allocable to personal use of home is personal interest.
Currently deductible expenses limited to gross rental income.	Currently deductible expenses are not limited to gross income, but may be limited by the hobby loss rules or the passive loss rules.
Expenses in excess of income may be carried over to future years. When property is sold, unused carryovers are lost.	Expenses not currently deductible because of the passive loss rules may be carried over to future years; unused carryovers are deductible when property is sold, but carryover may be barred by the Code Sec. 183 hobby loss rule.

Chapter 29

Medical Care by Proxy

Overview ....¶ 2901
Planning Devices ....¶ 2905

¶ 2901 OVERVIEW

Living wills, durable powers of attorney, and health care proxies are tools that enable individuals to have some say about their medical treatment when they are unable to speak for themselves. Each in its own way shares the common problem of overcoming the common law rule that the authority of an agent expires when the principal's legal capacity to act expires. Statutory provisions overcome this problem.

These statutory provisions also serve to overcome two other common problems. First, physicians and hospitals are under a legal and ethical duty to preserve life. (The statutes provide some relaxation of their legal duties and liabilities.) Second, suicide and attempted suicide are usually illegal. Statutes providing for living wills, durable powers of attorney, and health care proxies allow individuals to have some say about their own health and medical care without risking the state charging them with attempted suicide.

¶ 2905 PLANNING DEVICES

The following discussions consider each of the three planning devices.

.01 Living Wills

Most states now recognize living wills. Living wills allow an individual who is permanently unconscious or whose death is imminent to direct physicians and hospitals to refrain from using certain life-sustaining medical treatment, such as respirators and feeding tubes.

Usually, a living will becomes effective only when two physicians certify in writing that the individual is permanently unconscious or is terminally ill. However, physicians and other health care providers are under no obligation to follow the directives of a living will. A living will might be of little benefit if its terms are too vague.

The Patient Self-Determination Act of 1990[1] requires that health care providers furnish adult patients with written information concerning their rights under state law to make decisions about medical care. These rights include the right to accept or refuse care and the right to formulate an advance directive. An advance directive is a written instruction, recognized under state law, which provides direction regarding the individual's health care if the individual becomes incapacitated. An advance directive includes a living will or durable power of attorney.

> **Planning pointer.** The emphasis on state law reminds financial planners that a client with residences in more than one state should provide appropriate directives for each state of residence. In addition, a directive aimed at universal usage is desirable, especially if the client travels frequently to other states. An individual with a living will may want to carry in his or her wallet or purse a card that identifies who has a copy of the living will. Individuals with a living will may also want to register them with a free registry service on the Internet.

> ***Example 29.1.*** Dora Woods is a widow who lives in Corinth, Mississippi. She has one son, John Woods, who lives nearby in Tupelo, Mississippi. John has a copy of her living will. She carries a card in her purse stating that John has a copy of her living will. The card also provides John's address and telephone number. Dora has also registered her living will with a living will registry on the Internet.

> ***Example 29.2.*** Jane Ferguson is a widow. She lives in Littleton, New Hampshire, during the spring and summer. She also travels throughout New England during the summer, and sometimes goes to Golden, Colorado, to see her son, Michael Ferguson. She lives in Jupiter, Florida, with her daughter, Beth Jenkins, during the fall and winter months. Jane should prepare an advance directive that complies with New Hampshire law and another advance directive that complies with Florida law. In addition, because Jane travels often, she should prepare another advance directive aimed at universal usage.

[1] P.L. 101-508.

.02 Durable Powers of Attorney

The individual who signs a durable power of attorney is the principal. The individual who holds the power is the attorney-in-fact or agent. An attorney-in-fact does not have to be an attorney-at-law. Depending upon state law, the principal must sign the durable power of attorney before witnesses, a notary public, or both. A durable power of attorney ends upon the death of the principal. In addition, the principal may revoke the durable power of attorney. If one's spouse is the attorney-in-fact, a divorce automatically terminates the durable power of attorney in some states. The durable power of attorney also terminates if the attorney-in-fact is unable or unwilling to serve.

The durable power of attorney should include several important clauses. It does not have to specify the desired medical treatment, but it should acknowledge that the principal has communicated his or her wishes to the attorney-in-fact. Still, the principal may want to describe in the durable power of attorney nonexclusive permitted specifics as a means of providing comfort. The physician or hospital called upon to implement the specifics will appreciate such authorization. Principals may want to name successor attorneys-in-fact in case the designated attorney-in-fact predeceases the principal or is unable or unwilling to serve. The durable power of attorney can also include a clause providing if a health care provider refuses to recognize the durable power of attorney that the principal wants his or her health care transferred to another physician or facility. Another important clause states that the principal wants his or her wishes carried out even if they conflict with the desires of relatives or the policies of health care providers.

Durable powers of attorney have far broader uses than health care. Confined to health care, durable powers of attorney are appropriate in situations in which the principal is not in imminent danger of death.

A variation of the durable power of attorney is the springing power of attorney. A springing power of attorney does not become effective until the happening of a specific event, such as the incapacity of the principal for a specific period (e.g., 60 days). A springing power of attorney may require that one or more physicians certify that the principal is incapacitated. An individual with a durable power of attorney may want to carry a card in his or her wallet or purse identifying who holds his or her durable power of attorney for health care.

> ***Example 29.3.*** Alfred Fisher signs a springing power of attorney. It provides that his son, Andrew Fisher, will have a durable power of attorney to make all decisions regarding his health care upon the notarized statements of two licensed

physicians. Alfred carries a card in his wallet that states that Andrew holds a springing power of attorney. The card also provides Andrew's address and telephone number.

.03 Health Care Proxies

Some states specifically provide for health care proxies. A health care proxy is essentially a durable power of attorney for medical matters. A number of other states allow them as a part of their living will statutes. Typically, the proxy merely names the individual to act under the statutory authority. Health care proxies may be more adaptable to a wider range of circumstances compared to a living will. However, the financial planner should check the governing state statute because it may contain limitations.

.04 Importance of Periodic Review

A financial planner should review a client's documents related to medical care periodically. The review should ensure that the documents still reflect the client's wishes. In addition, the financial planner should make sure that the documents have not been made obsolete by changes in state law. For example, the state of California created a new document called the Advance Health Care Directive that made durable powers of attorney for health care obsolete if they were executed before 1992.[2]

[2] California Probate Code Secs. 4700-4701.

Chapter 30

College Planning

Overview ....¶ 3001
Hope Scholarship and Lifetime Learning Credits ....¶ 3005
Qualified Tuition Programs ....¶ 3010
Interest on Education Loans ....¶ 3015
Coverdell Education Savings Accounts ....¶ 3020
Deduction for Higher Education Expenses ....¶ 3025

¶ 3001 OVERVIEW

College planning is a major area of financial planning. Amassing the financial resources for, and paying for, higher education expenses continues to be one of the major drains on a family's (or individual's) ability to attain other economic goals, such as retirement. While inflation rates in recent years have been tame, the yearly increases in higher educational expenses have typically far outstripped (and sometimes been double) the general inflation rate. These increases are not only felt when a family sends its children to college, but increasingly also when family wage earners themselves find going back to school necessary or advantageous. Financial planners should encourage their clients to begin planning for their children's college education when the children are still young.

Financial planners should discuss the financial aid that might be available to defray some of the higher education costs likely to be incurred by the children of their clients. Federal financial aid programs include the following:

- Federal Direct and FFEL Stafford Loans
- Federal Direct and FFEL Plus Loans (for parents)
- Federal Perkins Loans
- Federal Pell Grants

- Federal Supplemental Educational Opportunity Grants
- Federal Work Study

Information about federal financial aid programs is available at the following Web site: *www.studentaid.ed.gov.* To apply for federal financial aid, a student must complete the Free Application for Federal Student Aid (FAFSA). A student may complete the application on the Internet at *www.fafsa.ed.gov.* The student might also qualify for various scholarships and financial aid programs provided by the states. In addition, many students pay for part of their college education by working part-time while attending college and full time during the summer.

While the cost increases for higher education are certainly anything but good news, the tax law provides some worthwhile incentives for higher education. Seemingly like almost everything else about the tax law, these incentives carry with them certain conditions and requirements. Many of them will be useful only if the taxpayers are under certain income caps, and if the taxpayers—almost assuredly with the help of professional advisors—are willing to sort through the maze of complexity that attends these potential tax breaks.

Listed below are some of the more useful, and more commonly available, tax breaks in the Code, with any applicable cross references to sections in the book where they are discussed in greater detail:

- **Withdrawals from qualified plans.** Qualified educational expenses of the taxpayer, spouse, children, and grandchildren can be paid for from penalty-free withdrawals from qualified retirement plans (¶ 905).
- **Withdrawals from Coverdell Education Saving Accounts.** Education expense withdrawals from nondeductible Coverdell Education Savings Accounts can be tax free (¶ 915).
- **Credits for higher education tuition.** Two tax credits—the Hope scholarship credit and the lifetime learning credit—are available for payment of higher education or vocational training tuition (¶ 3005).
- **Qualified tuition programs.** The federal tax treatment of qualified state tuition programs has been clarified and expanded to benefit more individuals (¶ 3010). For tax years through 2010, qualified tuition programs include eligible private institutions that satisfy the Code Sec. 529 requirements.
- **Educational assistance loans.** Individuals are able to deduct interest paid on qualified education loans subject to a phaseout based on modified adjusted gross income (¶ 3015).

- **Business deduction.** A taxpayer may deduct as business expenses the cost of education that maintains or improves a skill required in the taxpayer's current line of business, or is incurred to meet express employer or legal requirements.[1]
- **U.S. Savings Bonds.** Taxpayers can exclude interest earned on Series EE and Series I bonds where bond proceeds are used to pay higher education expenses (¶ 315.03).
- **Scholarships.** Degree candidates can exclude from gross income qualified scholarships used for tuition, fees, and books at any primary, secondary, or postsecondary educational institution.[2]
- **Gift tax educational exclusion.** An unlimited gift tax exclusion is available for tuition payments made directly to an educational institution (¶ 405).
- **Student loan cancellations.** Where it is contingent upon a student working for a specified period in certain professions, the cancellation of educational debt by governmental, educational, or tax-exempt charitable organization, will be excluded from gross income.[3]
- **Deduction for higher education expenses.** Taxpayers can claim an "above-the-line" deduction for up to $4,000 of qualified tuition and related expenses (¶ 3035).

¶ 3005 HOPE SCHOLARSHIP AND LIFETIME LEARNING CREDITS

Two credits for tuition and related expenses can reduce an individual's tax liability. Low and middle income individuals can elect these credits for tuition expenses incurred by students pursuing college or graduate degrees or vocational training.[4] For 2006, the Hope scholarship credit provides a maximum allowable credit of $1,650 per student for each of the first two years of postsecondary education. The lifetime learning credit allows a credit of 20 percent of qualified tuition expenses paid by the taxpayer for any year the taxpayer does not claim the Hope credit. More specifically, for 2006 the Hope scholarship credit initially allows taxpayers a 100-percent credit per eligible student for the first $1,100 of tuition expenses (but not for room, board, or books) and a 50-percent credit for the second $1,100 of tuition paid. These amounts are indexed for inflation.[5] A taxpayer computes the 20-percent lifetime learning credit on the tuition paid

---

[1] Code Sec. 162.
[2] Code Sec. 117.
[3] Code Sec. 108(f).
[4] Code Sec. 25A.
[5] Code Sec. 25A(h).

by the taxpayer. The first $10,000 is the maximum eligible base for the lifetime learning credit.

Both credits are available for qualified expenses incurred for the taxpayer, spouse, and dependents. The $1,650 maximum Hope credit for 2006 is allowed per student. However, the maximum lifetime learning credit is calculated per taxpayer and does not vary depending on the number of students in the taxpayer's family.

If qualified tuition expenses are paid by the taxpayer during a tax year for an academic period which begins during the first three months following that tax year, the credits are claimed in the tax year in which the expenses are paid.[6]

> **Note.** Although the Hope scholarship credit and the lifetime learning credit are two distinct credits, because they share many common rules,[7] this chapter will generally discuss them together under this numbered paragraph. For convenience of discussion, the "two credits" or simply "the credits," mean the Hope credit and the lifetime learning credit. The following discussion points out where a rule only applies to one or the other credit.

.01 Hope Scholarship Credit

The Hope credit is available only for the first two years of post-secondary education. Further, a taxpayer may elect the credit for two tax years with respect to one student. In order to qualify for the Hope credit, the student must be taking at least one-half the normal course load of a full-time student. Regardless of whether a taxpayer claims the Hope credit with respect to a year when a student is only carrying a one-half course load, the credit is available only for the first two years.

Unlike the lifetime learning credit, a taxpayer may claim the Hope credit only if the student is enrolled in a program leading to a degree, certificate or other recognized educational credential.

.02 Lifetime Learning Credit

The lifetime learning credit is allowed for 20 percent of qualified tuition and fees paid by the taxpayer with respect to one or more students, up to $10,000. The credit is allowed only for tax years in which the taxpayer does not claim the Hope credit with respect to the same student's tuition. While the lifetime learning credit shares

---

[6] 6 Reg. § 1.25A-5(e)(2)(i).

[7] Code Sec. 25A.

many of the same rules that apply to the Hope credit, the lifetime learning credit is different in the following respects:

- The lifetime learning credit does not vary with the number of students in a taxpayer's household.
- The lifetime learning credit is available for an unlimited number of years.
- The lifetime learning credit is available for both undergraduate, postgraduate, and professional degree expenses.
- The lifetime learning credit may be claimed for any course at an eligible institution that helps an individual acquire or improve his or her job skills. (Thus, CPE credit and noncredit professional seminars may qualify for the credit, if provided by an eligible institution.)

.03 Income Limitations

In 2006, the allowable amount of both credits is reduced for taxpayers who have modified adjusted gross income (AGI) above $45,000 or above $90,000 for joint filers. The benefits of the credits are completely lost once individuals reach the $55,000 AGI level and joint filers reach the $111,000 AGI level. Neither credit is available for married filing separately.

In determining modified AGI for purposes of the credits, a taxpayer's AGI is increased by income earned outside the United States (amounts otherwise excluded from gross income under Code Secs. 911, 931, and 933). Income earned in Puerto Rico and U.S. possessions is considered to be earned abroad.

The income ranges for the phaseout of the credits are indexed for inflation.

.04 Double Tax Benefits Not Allowed

In computing the amount of qualified educational expenses for which a taxpayer may claim the Hope credit or lifetime learning credit, the following items reduce the amount of qualified educational expenses:

- Employer-paid educational expenses excluded from an employee's gross income under Code Sec. 127
- Scholarships and fellowships received tax free under Code Sec. 117
- Amounts the student deducts as a business expense under Code Sec. 162
- Amount of educational assistance excludable from the gross income of either the student or the taxpayer claiming the credit

- Payments for the student's educational expenses excludable from gross income under any U.S. law

For purposes of these rules, the credit is not reduced by educational expenses paid by reason of gift or inheritance.

Planning pointer. The credits are allowed only to a parent who both pays qualified education expenses and is allowed to claim the student as a dependent. If the parents are divorced and one parent pays the tuition and the other claims the dependency exemption under a support agreement, the credit will be lost. To prevent the loss of the credits, support agreements should provide that the parent paying the tuition also claims the dependency exemption.

.05 Credit and Exclusion

A taxpayer may claim a Hope credit or lifetime learning credit for a tax year and exclude from gross income amounts distributed from Coverdell Education Savings Account on behalf of the same student. However, the distribution must be used for different educational expenses from those for which the credit is claimed. If a taxpayer claims a Hope credit with respect to a student, then the lifetime learning credit will not be available for that same student for that year. However, the lifetime credit may be available with respect to that student for later years.

.06 Interaction with Qualified State Tuition Program Distributions

A taxpayer may claim the Hope or lifetime learning credit even if a distribution from a qualified state tuition program (¶ 3010) is used to pay qualified tuition and fees. Similarly, a taxpayer may claim the credits for payments of qualified education expenses made in kind from a state tuition program.

¶ 3010 QUALIFIED TUITION PROGRAMS

States may adopt tax-exempt, prepaid tuition savings programs. Such programs are now known as 529 plans because they are authorized under Code Sec. 529. They allow a person either (1) to purchase, in cash, tuition credits or certificates on behalf of a designated beneficiary, which entitles the beneficiary to the waiver or payment of qualified higher educational expenses, or (2) to make contributions to an account established on behalf of such a person solely for the purpose of paying for qualified higher education expenses. The law imposes several strictures designed to make sure that contributors are not able to the manipulate programs to gain a tax shelter on contributions in excess of those necessary to fund a higher education. The benefits of a qualified tuition program also extend to prepaid tuition programs of eligible private institutions that satisfy the Code Sec. 529 requirements. These 529 plans have become a popular tool for planning for the costs of children's college education.

.01 Qualified Higher Education Expenses

Qualified higher education expenses include tuition and fees paid to eligible education institutions, as well as certain room and board expenses.

Distributions of earnings, or educational benefits provided that exceed the value of contributions made, are taxed under the Code Sec. 72 annuity rules to the beneficiary (to the extent used to pay for or provide education), or to the contributor (to the extent refunded thereto).

The income tax liability normally triggered by a distribution from a qualified tuition program does not apply if, within 60 days, the taxpayer rolls over the amount distributed to the benefit of another family member (defined to include sons, daughters, brothers, sisters, nephews, nieces, certain in-laws, and the spouses of those relations).

.02 Interaction with Hope and Lifetime Learning Credits

To the extent that a distribution from a qualified tuition program is used to pay for qualified tuition and fees, the distributee will be able to claim the Hope credit or lifetime learning credit under Code Sec. 25A. Similarly, a taxpayer may take these credits for payments of qualified education expenses made in kind from the qualified tuition program.

.03 Coordination with Education Savings Bonds

Taxpayers are entitled to redeem U.S. Savings Bonds and exclude the earnings under Code Sec. 135 (as if the proceeds were used to pay higher education expenses) for redemption proceeds contributed to the program. When this occurs, the beneficiary's basis in the bond proceeds contributed on his behalf will be the contributor's basis in the bonds (that is, the original purchase price).

.04 Estate and Gift Tax Implications

Contributions to qualified tuition programs are completed gifts when made. Such contributions qualify for the gift tax annual exclusion and are excludable for purposes of the generation-skipping transfer tax, provided that they do not exceed the $12,000 (for 2006 and indexed for inflation) gift tax annual exclusion amount ($24,000 for 2006 if gift splitting). A contributor making a contribution in excess of the gift tax annual exclusion limit may elect to have the contribution treated as if made ratably over five years. If a contributor who has made this election dies during the five-year period, the portion of the contribution that has not been allocated is included in the contributor's gross estate.

If a beneficiary's interest is rolled over to another beneficiary, there is no gift or generation-skipping transfer tax liability, provided that the two beneficiaries are of the same generation. If, however, the beneficiary's interest is rolled over to someone in a lower generation, the five-year averaging rule may be applied to exempt up to $55,000 from generation-skipping transfer tax liability.

¶ 3015 INTEREST ON EDUCATION LOANS

Individuals may claim interest paid on qualified education loans as a deduction in computing adjusted gross income under Code Sec. 221. Thus, the deduction is available whether or not the taxpayer itemizes deductions. However, no deduction is allowed for interest on qualified education loans if the amount is allowed as a deduction under another Code section. For example, if a homeowner takes out a home equity loan to pay an educational expense, he would not be able to take both a deduction for mortgage interest and a deduction for educational expense paid.

.01 Deduction Limits

The maximum deduction allowed under Code Sec. 221 is $2,500. To be deductible, the interest must be paid with respect to qualified higher education expenses incurred in attending college or certain vocational schools. These costs include tuition, fees, room and board, books, and supplies, reduced by the following amounts excluded from gross income:

- Employer provided educational assistance[8]
- U.S. savings bond interest used to pay higher education costs[9]
- Coverdell Education Savings Accounts[10]

---

[8] Code Sec. 127.

[9] Code Sec. 130.

[10] Code Sec. 530.

- Excludable educational expenses (such as scholarships under Code Sec. 117) that are not gifts or inheritances

.02 Phaseout of Deduction

For tax year 2006, the education interest deduction is phased out beginning with modified AGI of $50,000 for single taxpayers and $105,000 on a joint return. The deduction is completely phased out at $65,000 for single taxpayers and at $135,000 for a married couple filing a joint return. These income phase-out ranges will be adjusted annually for inflation.

Planning pointer. The phaseout of the deduction for educational interest expenses begins at levels that will make the deduction unavailable to many middle-income (and all high-income) taxpayers. However, where it is available, a taxpayer can utilize its benefits in addition to the Hope or lifetime learning credits.

¶ 3020 COVERDELL EDUCATION SAVINGS ACCOUNTS

.01 Contributions

Taxpayers may contribute each year to a Coverdell Education Savings Account for any child under age 18. A taxpayer may contribute to a Coverdell Education Savings Account for children with special needs who are age 18 or older. The contributor does not have to be the parent of the child. Anyone, including the child, may contribute to the child's Coverdell Education Savings Account. The law does not allow contributions of securities or other property to a Coverdell Education Savings Account. Taxpayers must make all contributions to the Coverdell Education Savings Account in cash. The maximum annual contribution is $2,000. Taxpayers may not circumvent this limit by using multiple Coverdell Education Savings Accounts.

Phaseout rules reduce the annual limit if the taxpayer's modified adjusted gross income (AGI) exceeds certain threshold amounts.[11] For tax years through 2010, the $2,000 maximum annual contribution is phased out for married couples filing a joint return who have modified AGI greater than or equal to $190,000 and less than $220,000. The phaseout rules apply to other filers with modified AGI greater than or equal to $95,000 and less than $110,000. Taxpayers with modified AGI greater than or equal to the phaseout limits

[11] Code Sec. 530(c).

may not make any contributions to a Coverdell Education Savings Account on behalf of anyone. The annual contribution limit applies to each child, but the phaseout rules apply to each contributor. Thus, if a parent's maximum allowable contribution to a Coverdell Education Savings Account is less than the annual contribution limit, another family member or friend could make up the difference.

When the modified AGI reaches the threshold, the taxpayer must reduce the maximum annual contribution by an amount that bears the same ratio to the maximum annual contribution (i.e. $2,000) as the amount by which the contributor's modified AGI for the tax year exceeds the amount at which the threshold begins.[12]

> ***Example 30.1.*** Sara Jenkins, a single parent, has modified AGI for tax year 2006 of $104,000. Under the contribution phaseout provision, her annual contribution to the Coverdell Education Savings Account established for her son, Joseph, is limited to $800. To arrive at this amount, Jenkins must do the following:
>
> 1. Compute the excess of her modified AGI of $104,000 over $95,000 ($104,000 – $95,000 = $9,000)
> 2. Compute the ratio that the excess amount of $9,000 bears to $15,000 ($9,000/$15,000 = .6)
> 3. Compute the reduction amount by multiplying the maximum amount of $2,000 by .6 ($2,000 × .6 = $1,200)
> 4. Subtract the reduction amount of $1,200 from the maximum amount of $2,000 to arrive at her annual contribution limit of $800 ($2,000 – $1,200 = $800)
>
> Another contributor (including Jenkins' ex-husband) who does not file a joint return and has modified AGI of $95,000 or less may contribute up to $1,200 to Jenkins' son's Coverdell Education Savings Account for tax year 2006. If Jenkins remarries and files a joint return, any contribution by Jenkins and her new spouse will begin phasing out at modified AGI of $190,000 for 2006.

Modified AGI is the taxpayer's adjusted gross income for the tax year, increased by any amount excluded from gross income under Code Sec. 911 (relating to foreign earned income), Code Sec. 931 (relating to income sources within Guam, American Samoa, or the Northern Mariana Islands), and Code Sec. 933 (relating to income from sources within Puerto Rico).[13]

---

[12] Code Sec. 520(c)(1).

[13] Code Sec. 530(c)(2).

Although a taxpayer may not deduct contributions to a Coverdell Education Savings Account from gross income, the amounts grow on a tax-deferred basis. The law does not allow contributions to a Coverdell Education Savings Account during a year in which anyone contributes to a qualified tuition program on behalf of the child.[14]

.02 Excess Contributions

Code Sec. 4973 imposes a six-percent excise tax on excess contributions to a Coverdell Education Savings Account. The first item treated as an excess contribution is any excess over the maximum annual contribution amount per beneficiary. If the contributor's allowable contribution for the year is reduced based on the modified AGI phaseout,[15] then the excess contribution is the sum of the contributions minus the allowable reduced contributions.[16]

In addition, any contributions to a qualified tuition program[17] for the benefit of the same beneficiary covered by the Coverdell Education Savings Account are treated as excess contributions to the Coverdell Education Savings Account.[18] The excise tax is applicable in each year in which an excess contribution remains in a Coverdell Education Savings Account, not just the year in which the excess contribution is originally made.[19]

.03 Distributions

A taxpayer may exclude withdrawals from Coverdell Education Savings Accounts from gross income to the extent used to pay for qualified education expenses of the designated beneficiary in the year of withdrawal.[20] Qualified education expenses include tuition, fees, books, supplies, and equipment required for the enrollment or attendance of a designated beneficiary at an eligible institution.[21] Room and board expenses also qualify if the designated beneficiary is enrolled for at least one-half the normal full-time course load in a program leading to a degree or certificate. Amounts paid for a beneficiary for credits or certificates under qualified tuition programs are qualified education expenses.[22] However, a taxpayer must reduce the qualified expenses by any tax-free scholarship and other tax-free payments received for education expenses, except payments received by gift or inheritance.[23]

[14] Conference Committee Report to P.L. 105-34.

[15] Code Sec. 530(c)(1).

[16] Code Sec. 4973(e)(1)(A).

[17] Code Sec. 529.

[18] Code Sec. 4973(e)(1)(B).

[19] Code Sec. 4973(e)(1)(C).

[20] Code Sec. 530(d)(2)(A).

[21] Code Secs. 529(e)(3)(A) and 530(b)(2)(A).

[22] Code Sec. 530(b)(2)(B).

[23] Code Secs. 25A(g)(2) and 530(b)(2)(A).

A taxpayer may waive the exclusion from gross income for withdrawals from a Coverdell Education Savings Account.[24] A taxpayer might do so to claim the Hope credit or lifetime learning credit based on the qualified education expenses. A taxpayer who excludes amounts received from a Coverdell Education Savings Account may not claim one of these credits based on the same expenses.[25] Thus, the law allows the taxpayer to waive the exclusion from gross income for the distributions from a Coverdell Education Savings Account and claim one of the credits based on the eligible expenses.

An eligible educational institution includes accredited, postsecondary educational institutions offering credit toward a degree or other recognized postsecondary credential.[26] Proprietary and postsecondary vocational institutions, as defined under 20 U.S.C. § 1088, also qualify as eligible educational institutions. In addition, the educational institution must also be eligible to participate in the Department of Education student aid program. Qualified education expenses also include elementary and secondary education expenses (kindergarten through grade 12). The school may be a public, private, or religious school. Qualified elementary and secondary school expenses include expenses for tuition; fees; books; supplies; equipment; academic tutoring; the purchase of computer technology or equipment; Internet access or related services; and expenses for room and board, uniforms, transportation, and supplementary items and services, such as extended day programs, as required or provided by the school.

If distributions exceed the qualified education expenses for the year, the taxpayer computes the taxable portion of the distributions under the Code Sec. 72 annuity rules.[27] Thus, distributions would consist of a tax-free return of capital and taxable earnings.[28] A taxpayer computes the tax-free portion of a distribution by multiplying the distribution by the ratio of the total contributions to the account balance at the time of the distribution.[29]

> ***Example 30.2.*** Lisa Williams receives a $2,000 distribution from her Coverdell Education Savings Account in a year in which she did not incur any qualified education expenses. On the date of the distribution, her account balance is $10,000, and contributions made to the account total $4,000. The amount of the tax-free distribution from contributions is $800 ($2,000 × ($4,000/

[24] Code Sec. 530(d)(2)(C).

[25] Code Sec. 25A(e)(2).

[26] Code Sec. 530(b)(3) and 520(e)(5).

[27] Code Sec. 530(d)(1).

[28] Code Secs. 72(e)(2)(B) and 72(e)(9).

[29] Code Secs. 72(e)(8) and 72(e)(9).

$10,000)). Lisa will include $1,200 ($2,000 – $800) in her gross income.

A beneficiary could incur qualified education expenses during the year but receive distributions from a Coverdell Education Savings Account exceeding the qualified expenses. In that case, the law treats the qualified education expenses as paid from a pro rata share of both contributions and earnings on the account.[30] Thus, the taxpayer computes the portion of earnings excludable from gross income based on the ratio that the qualified education expenses bear to the total distributions. The beneficiary includes the remainder of the earnings in his or her gross income.

Example 30.3. Bruce Meek receives a $1,000 distribution from his Coverdell Education Savings Account. The distribution consists of $200 of contributions and $800 of earnings. Bruce pays $750 in qualified education expenses for the year. Bruce excludes $600 ($800 × ($750/$1,000)) from his gross income. Bruce includes the remaining $200 from earnings in his gross income.

The distribution from a Coverdell Education Savings Account included in gross income is generally subject to an additional 10-percent tax.[31] The additional 10-percent tax does not apply to distributions made on account of the beneficiary's death or disability, waiver of exclusion of distributions from gross income,[32] to the extent of a scholarship, or the return of excess contributions and earnings.[33]

The balance remaining in a Coverdell Education Savings Account must be distributed within 30 days after a beneficiary reaches age 30 unless the beneficiary is a special needs beneficiary.[34]

In addition, the account balance must be distributed within 30 days after the death of a beneficiary under age 30.[35] In the event of a required distribution, the account balance is deemed to be distributed at the end of the 30-day period,[36] and the beneficiary must include the earnings portion of the distribution in his or her gross income.[37]

.04 Loans and Other Prohibited Transactions

A person may not use a Coverdell Education Savings Account as collateral for a loan. Other prohibited transactions include the use of

[30] Code Sec. 530(d)(2)(B).
[31] Code Sec. 530(b)(4).
[32] Code Sec. 530(d)(4)(B)(iv).
[33] Code Sec. 530(d)(4)(B).
[34] IRS Restructuring and Reform Act of 1998, Conference Committee Report on P.L. 105-206.
[35] Code Sec. 530(b)(1)(E).
[36] Code Sec. 530(b)(8).
[37] Code Sec. 530(d)(1).

the assets in the Coverdell Education Savings Account by the beneficiary or a fiduciary.[38]

.05 Community Property Laws

For tax purposes, community property laws do not apply to Coverdell Education Savings Accounts.[39]

.06 Rollovers

Before a beneficiary attains age 30, the balance of a Coverdell Education Savings Account may be transferred or rolled over to a Coverdell Education Savings Account for a family member to defer or possibly avoid any tax liability on the earnings in the account. A beneficiary of a Coverdell Education Savings Account may receive distributions from a Coverdell Education Savings Account and roll them over into a Coverdell Education Savings Account for a member of the beneficiary's family.[40] Family members include ancestors, descendants, brothers, sisters, nephews, nieces, certain in-laws, and the spouses of these relatives. Stepparents, stepsiblings and stepchildren are also considered members of the family.[41] The beneficiary does not include these distributions in his or her gross income, provided that the beneficiary rolls the funds over within 60 days of the distribution. Similarly, any change in the beneficiary of a Coverdell Education Savings Account does not constitute a distribution for tax purposes if the new beneficiary is a member of the family of the original beneficiary as defined in Code Sec. 520(e)(2). The new beneficiaries in these circumstances must be under age 30 as of the date of the distribution or change in beneficiary.[42] Rollover contributions do not count against the annual limit on contributions.

The rollover provisions allow families to roll funds not needed by one child into a Coverdell Education Savings Account for the benefit of another child.

> ***Example 30.4.*** Paco and Elena Martinez set up a Coverdell Education Savings Account for their son, Juan. Paco and Elena determine that their daughter, Belita, will need more financial assistance with her education than will Paco. They roll $3,000 from the Coverdell Education Savings Account set up for Juan into a Coverdell Education Savings Account for Belita. The rollover is tax free.

Taxpayers may also roll over amounts in a Coverdell Education Savings Account into another Coverdell Education Savings Account

[38] Code Sec. 4975(c).
[39] Code Sec. 530(f)(1).
[40] Code Sec. 530(d)(5).
[41] Code Secs. 529(e)(2) and 152(a).
[42] Code Sec. 530(d)(5) and (6).

for the benefit of the same beneficiary. A taxpayer might effect such a rollover to obtain greater investment diversification.

.07 Estate and Gift Tax Considerations

For gift tax purposes, a contribution to a Coverdell Education Savings Account is a completed gift of a present interest at the time of the contribution.[43] Therefore, the contribution is eligible for the annual gift tax exclusion ($12,000 for 2006 and indexed for inflation).[44] The contribution is also excluded in computing the generation-skipping transfer tax.[45]

The Code generally does not treat distributions from a Coverdell Education Savings Account as taxable gifts. Also, if a taxpayer rolls over a beneficiary's interest in a Coverdell Education Savings Account to another beneficiary or changes the beneficiary, no gift or generation-skipping transfer tax consequences result, provided the two beneficiaries are of the same generation. If a beneficiary's interest is rolled over to a beneficiary in a lower generation (e.g., parent to child or uncle to niece), the five-year averaging rule may apply to exempt up to $60,000 of the transferred amount. An interest in a Coverdell Education Savings Account is not includible in the gross estate of any individual except with respect to amounts distributed on account of the death of the designated beneficiary.

The divorce of the designated beneficiary does not have to cause a taxable distribution to the spouse or ex-spouse. The transfer of a beneficiary's interest in a Coverdell Education Savings Account to a spouse or ex-spouse under a divorce or separation agreement is not a taxable transfer. After the transfer, the tax law treats the interest in the account as belonging to the spouse/ex-spouse.[46]

If a spouse or family member acquires a beneficiary's interest in a Coverdell Education Savings Account at the death of the beneficiary, the tax law views the spouse or family member as the account beneficiary of the Coverdell Education Savings Account. However, if a person other than a spouse or family member is the designated beneficiary, the Coverdell Education Savings Account terminates at death. In these circumstances, the account balance is includible in the beneficiary's gross income as of the date of death (or, if the beneficiary is the estate, on the decedent's final income tax return).

[43] Code Sec. 530(d)(3) and Sec. 529(c)(2)(A).

[44] Code Sec. 2503(b).

[45] Code Secs. 530(d)(3) and 529(c).

[46] Code Secs. 530(d)(7) and 220(f).

¶ 3025 DEDUCTION FOR HIGHER EDUCATION EXPENSES

A deduction can be claimed for qualified tuition and related expenses for tax years beginning after December 31, 2001, and before January 1, 2006.[47] Legislation pending in Congress may extend this legislation.

A taxpayer may claim this deduction in computing his or her adjusted gross income. Therefore, a taxpayer does not have to itemize deductions on Schedule A to claim the deduction. In 2005, the maximum deduction is $4,000 for taxpayers with adjusted gross income not more than $130,000 on a joint return and $65,000 on other returns. Taxpayers whose adjusted gross income exceeds the limits but which does not exceed $160,000 on a joint return or $80,000 on other returns may deduct up to $2,000 in qualified expenses.[48] However, a married individual who files a separate return may not claim the deduction for any year in any amount.[49] A taxpayer who is a nonresident alien for any part of the tax year may claim the deduction only if he or she is treated as a resident alien due to an election under Code Secs. 6013(g) or 6013(h).

The adjusted gross income limit is determined without regard to the foreign earned income exclusion and the exclusion for foreign housing costs and income of residents of Guam, American Samoa, the Northern Mariana Islands, and Puerto Rico. However, the following items are taken into account in computing adjusted gross income solely for determining eligibility for the deduction for qualified higher education expenses:

- Taxable Social Security benefits
- Exclusion for certain savings bond interest used to pay higher education expenses
- Exclusion for employer-provided adoption assistance
- The deduction for retirement savings (traditional IRAs)
- Student loan interest payments
- The disallowance of passive activity losses

Taxpayers may not receive a double benefit by deducting their qualified higher education expenses and receive another tax benefit for the same expenses.[50] In addition, an individual who may be claimed as a dependent on another taxpayer's return, may not deduct qualified higher education expenses.[51]

---

[47] Code Sec. 222.
[48] Code Sec. 222(b).
[49] Code Sec. 222(d)(4).
[50] Code Sec. 222(c)(1).
[51] Code Sec. 222(c)(3).

The taxpayer must identify on his or her tax return the name and Social Security number of the student for whom qualified tuition and related expenses were paid.[52]

Qualified tuition and related expenses include tuition and fees required for the enrollment or attendance of the taxpayer, the taxpayer's spouse, or any dependent for whom the taxpayer is entitled to deduct a dependency exemption, at an eligible educational institution for courses of instruction. Eligible educational institutions include accredited public, nonprofit, or proprietary post-secondary institution.

The deduction is allowed for expenses paid during an eligible tax year, in connection with enrollment during the year or in connection with an academic term beginning during the year or the first three months of the following year.[53]

[52] Code Sec. 222(d)(2).

[53] Code Sec. 222(d)(3).

Part III

Building the Estate

Chapter 31

Investment and Financial Planning Strategies and Vehicles

Overview .... ¶3101
Saving More as a Means of Coping with Low Yields .... ¶3105
Tax-Exempt Government Obligations .... ¶3110
Like-Kind Property Exchanges .... ¶3115
Investments in Securities .... ¶3120
Capital Gains Exclusion for Qualified Small Business Stock .... ¶3125
Deferral for Investment in Specialized Small Business Investment Companies .... ¶3130
U.S. Government Securities .... ¶3135
Mutual Funds .... ¶3140
Money Market Investments and Strategies .... ¶3145
Ginnie Maes, Fannie Maes, and Freddie Macs .... ¶3150
Commodities Futures Funds .... ¶3155
Original Issue Discount and Zero Coupon Bonds .... ¶3160
Stripping Coupon Interest from Bonds .... ¶3165
Options as a Gains Hedge .... ¶3170
Junk Bonds .... ¶3175
Real Estate Investing .... ¶3180
Brokerage Accounts .... ¶3185
Commissions and Investment Charges .... ¶3190
Debt Consolidation .... ¶3195

¶3101 OVERVIEW

Investors are concerned about (1) how tax factors affect their investments or prospective investments, and (2) how economic risks affect their investments and prospective investments. These considerations are discussed at ¶3101.01 and ¶3101.03, respectively.

Both the investor and the financial planner should have a basic familiarity with securities laws as they affect investments. Having a knowledge of securities laws is especially important because recent scandals have increased government scrutiny of corporations and securities transactions (¶3101.04).

In addition, the Sarbanes-Oxley Act of 2002 has added to the legal complexity. This Act created the Public Company Accounting Oversight Board to regulate accountants. This Act also increased financial reporting requirements for publicly held companies. In addition, the CEO and CFO must prepare a statement to accompany the audit report to certify the appropriateness and accuracy of the financial statements and disclosures.

Specific investments, other investment considerations, and other financial planning matters are discussed in the balance of this chapter.

.01 Investments and Taxation

Investments and investors are in one way or another affected by three federal taxes—income, estate, and gift—but principally by the income tax. State and local taxes also affect investments, but the focus of this chapter is at the federal level.

Most investors are aware of the tax factors affecting their investments, at least in a general sort of way. Nevertheless, they and some of their financial advisors might profit by the following primer on basic tax principles.

The catchall. All income and gain from whatever source derived is includible in gross income (subject to tax) unless specifically exempted.[1]

Tax-free income. Generally, the interest earned on obligations of a state or subdivision thereof, or of any U.S. territory or possession, or any subdivision thereof, or of the District of Columbia, is exempt from federal income tax,[2] but may nevertheless be includible in the gross income base for determining tax on an individual's Social Security benefits.[3]

---

[1] Code Sec. 61(a).

[2] Code Sec. 103.

[3] Code Sec. 86(b)(2)(B).

Return of capital. Amounts received as a return of capital or investment are not taxable as income.

The Internal Revenue Code provides for the tax-free return of capital through depreciation[4] and depletion[5] deductions and deduction of a portion of annuity payments.[6]

When property is sold or exchanged, the Code permits recovery of the investment and treats only the excess as realized gain.[7]

Open transactions. Where property is sold and the fair market value of property received by the seller is not reasonably ascertainable, the transaction may be deemed open. In such cases, the seller will not be taxed on the unascertainable amount until it becomes ascertainable. However, the IRS will recognize transactions as open only in rare and extraordinary circumstances.

In an open transaction, the cash and any property received that has an ascertainable fair market value are applied against the seller's basis and any excess is treated as gain realized.

Capital gains and losses. Although the tax rates have changed over time, the rate of tax on net capital gains is less than the rate of tax on ordinary income. Qualified dividends are subject to a maximum tax rate of 15 percent, which is the same maximum tax rate imposed on most long-term capital gains realized after May 5, 2003. Taxpayers in the 10-percent or 15-percent marginal tax rate bracket for ordinary income are subject to a 5-percent tax rate on qualified dividends and a 5-percent tax rate on most long-term capital gains realized after May 5, 2003. These rates apply through 2010.

High-income individuals benefit substantially if a particular transaction gives rise to a long-term capital gain as opposed to ordinary income. An even better tax result can be achieved if the individual can utilize losses to offset capital gains. In addition, if the losses exceed gains, the first $3,000 ($1,500 for married couples filing separately) may be used to offset ordinary income.[8] The disallowed losses are carried forward indefinitely.[9]

An exclusion for 50 percent of the gain on the sale or exchange of qualified small business stock held for more than five years[10](¶ 3125) and a deferral mechanism for investment in specialized small business investment companies[11](¶ 3130) also aid small businesses.

---

[4] Code Sec. 167.
[5] Code Sec. 611.
[6] Code Sec. 72(b).
[7] Code Sec. 1001(a).
[8] Code Sec. 1211.
[9] Code Sec. 1212.
[10] Code Sec. 1202.
[11] Code Sec. 1045.

Deferring tax on gain. An individual can be viewed as becoming wealthier as his or her property appreciates in value. However, the gain is not taxed until the gain has been realized through a sale or exchange.[12]

Involuntary conversions. A taxpayer's voluntary action is usually a prerequisite to the realization of gain or loss. The Code prescribes nonrecognition for gains on involuntary conversions of property (i.e., destruction in whole or in part, theft, seizure, condemnation or sale under threat of condemnation) under certain conditions.[13] Generally, qualified replacement property must be acquired within two years after the end of the tax year of the conversion.[14] However, the period for the replacement of property involuntarily converted due to a Presidentially declared disaster ends four years (instead of the regular two years) after the close of the first tax year in which any part of the gain upon conversion is realized.[15] For condemned real estate, a taxpayer has three years from the end of the tax year in which the conversion occurred to obtain qualified replacement property.[16] Losses on the involuntary conversion of business or investment property are recognized.

Like-kind exchanges. No gain or loss is recognized on an exchange of property held for productive use in a trade or business or for investment solely for other property of a like-kind to be held for business or investment.[17] If the taxpayer also receives money or nonqualified property in the exchange, the gain is taxable to the extent of such money and the fair market value of the disqualified property.[18] Such money and disqualified property are called boot. The property received in exchange must be received within certain time limits to qualify for nonrecognition.[19] Most like-kind exchanges are of real estate. Most of these exchanges are not simultaneous exchanges. Rather, the vast majority of like-kind exchanges are deferred exchanges made through a qualified intermediary.

Installment sales. The installment method of reporting, when available, generally permits delaying the reporting of gains until payments are received.[20] The installment method is not available for sales of stocks and bonds traded on an established securities market.[21] On a sale of depreciable property, any recapture of depreciation must be reported in the year of sale.[22] Receipt of a purchaser's

---

[12] Code Sec. 1001(a).
[13] Code Sec. 1033.
[14] Code Sec. 1003(a)(2)(B).
[15] Code Sec. 1033(h)(1)(B).
[16] Code Sec. 1033(g)(4).
[17] Code Sec. 1031(a).
[18] Code Sec. 1031(b).
[19] Code Sec. 1031(a)(3).
[20] Code Sec. 453(a)(1).
[21] Code Sec. 453(k)(2).
[22] Code Sec. 453(i).

obligation that is payable on demand or that is readily marketable, i.e., traded on an exchange, is treated as cash.[23] Special rules govern installment sales of nonfarm real estate having a sales price in excess of $150,000 if the seller's deferred payments for all such real property sales exceed $5 million.[24]

Investment expenses. Code Sec. 212 permits the deduction of all ordinary and necessary expenses connected with the production or collection of income, or for the management or maintenance of property held for the production of income, or for the determination, collection, or refund of any tax. However, Code Sec. 212 deductions generally are part of the pool of miscellaneous itemized deductions that are subject to a floor of two percent of adjusted gross income.[25] Code Sec. 212 deductions attributable to rents and royalties are deductible in computing adjusted gross income (above the line) and are not subject to the floor. Also, the following itemized deductions are not subject to the floor: interest, taxes, certain losses, expenses in connection with personal property used in a short sale, deduction relating to annuity payments that cease before the annuitant recovers his or her investment, amortizable bond premium, and deductions by cooperative housing corporation tenant-shareholders.[26] Some of these deductions may also be subject to the overall limitation on itemized deductions, which has been repealed for tax year 2010 only.[27]

Deduction of investment interest. The deduction is limited to the amount of investment income.[28] Interest paid to acquire or carry tax-exempt bonds is not deductible.[29] Amortizable bond premium is treated as an offset to interest income on the bond, rather than as a separate interest deduction subject to the investment interest limitation.[30] Most dividends are no longer included in investment income for the purpose of calculating the limit on the deduction for investment interest because dividends are taxed at a maximum rate of 15 percent through 2010. However, a taxpayer may elect to include dividends in investment income for purposes of calculating the limit on the investment interest deduction. However, any dividends the taxpayer elects to include in investment income are taxed as ordinary income and subject to a maximum tax rate of 35 percent. A taxpayer makes the election on Form 4952, "Investment Interest Expense Deduction."

---

[23] Code Sec. 453(f)(4).
[24] Code Sec. 453A.
[25] Code Sec. 67.
[26] Code Sec. 67(b).
[27] Code Sec. 68.
[28] Code Sec. 163(d)(1).
[29] Code Sec. 265(a)(2).
[30] Code Sec. 171(e).

Net capital gain from investment property generally is not counted as investment income for purposes of figuring the investment interest limit.[31] However, taxpayers may elect to treat net capital gain from investment property as investment income. If the taxpayer makes the election on Form 4952, the net capital gain is taxed as ordinary income.[32]

Passive losses. In general, salary, active business income, and portfolio income (interest, dividends, annuities, gains from the disposition of property held for investment) may not be offset by losses from passive activities.[33] Losses generated by a passive activity, i.e., a tax shelter, may only be used against income from a passive activity.[34] Unused passive losses are carried forward indefinitely and can be used to offset passive income. In addition, the unused passive losses are allowed on a fully taxable disposition of the property involved.[35]

An activity is passive if it involves the conduct of a trade or business in which the taxpayer does not materially participate in the activity.[36] A passive activity also includes any rental activity.[37] No interest in a limited partnership will be treated as involving material participation.[38] Material participation requires regular, continuous and substantial participation in the activities of the business.[39]

Some relief from the passive loss rules is provided for real estate professionals,[40] as discussed at ¶3180. In addition, individuals who actively participate in rental real estate activities may deduct up to $25,000 of losses from such activities against active income and portfolio income.[41] Active participation requires a lower level of participation than does material participation. The $25,000 maximum amount is phased out by 50 percent of the amount by which the taxpayer's adjusted gross income exceeds $100,000.[42] The taxpayer's adjusted gross income for this purpose is computed before the rental real estate loss and without regard to certain other items.[43]

Taxes. Almost all state, local, and U.S. possessions taxes are deductible under Code Sec. 164, except sales and use taxes. However, sales taxes paid on depreciable property are added to the basis of the property and depreciated. Sales taxes paid on items deductible as business expenses, such as office supplies, are treated as an additional cost of such items. Taxes deductible as itemized deductions are

---

[31] Code Sec. 163(d)(4)(B)(iii).
[32] Code Sec. 1(h)(3).
[33] Code Sec. 469(a).
[34] Code Secs. 469(a) and 469(d)(1).
[35] Code Sec. 469(g)(1).
[36] Code Sec. 469(c)(1).
[37] Code Sec. 469(c)(2).
[38] Code Sec. 469(h)(2).
[39] Code Sec. 469(h)(1).
[40] Code Sec. 469(c)(7).
[41] Code Secs. 469(i)(1) and 469(i)(2).
[42] Code Sec. 469(i)(3).
[43] Code Sec. 469(i)(3)(e).

subject to the overall limitation on itemized deductions, which has been repealed for tax year 2010 only.[44]

Losses. Losses on the sale or exchange of investment property are deductible above the line in computing adjusted gross income.[45] Thus, such losses are not an itemized deduction and hence are not subject to the two-percent floor. Personal theft and casualty losses for individuals are itemized deductions that are subject to a reduction of $100 per casualty event[46] and a 10-percent adjusted gross income (AGI) floor for all theft and casualty losses.[47] However, theft losses due to an investment in a fraudulent investment scheme are not subject to the $100 floor or the 10-percent AGI floor.[48]

Individual alternative minimum tax. After calculation of an individual's regular tax, he or she might be required to compute the tentative alternative minimum tax (AMT). If the latter is higher, he or she must pay regular tax and the AMT.[49] Exemptions apply that vary with the taxpayer's filing status. The exemption for a joint return or surviving spouse is $62,550 for a tax year beginning in 2006. The exemption for a head of household or single taxpayer is $42,500 for a tax year beginning in 2006. The exemption for a married taxpayer who files a separate return is $31,275 for a tax year beginning in 2006.[50] These exemption amounts are not indexed to inflation. In addition these exemptions are subject to a phaseout rule based on the individual's alternative minimum taxable income (AMTI). These exemptions must be reduced by 25 percent of the AMTI in excess of $150,000 in the case of a joint return or a return of a surviving spouse, $112,500 in the case of a single taxpayer or head of household, and $75,000 in the case of a married taxpayer filing a seperate return. Thus, as a taxpayer's income increases over time, avoiding the alternative minimum tax becomes more difficult. In addition, a taxpayer must use special rules in computing alternative minimum taxable income.[51] A two-tiered set of tax rates applies to the excess of the alternative minimum taxable income over the exemption amount. A 26-percent rate applies to the first $175,000 of this excess, and a 28-percent rate applies to the remainder.[52]

Limitation on itemized deductions. Code Sec. 68 reduces allowable itemized deductions (excluding medical deductions, investment interest, casualty losses and wagering losses to the extent

---

[44] Code Sec. 68.

[45] Code Sec. 62(a)(3).

[46] Code Sec. 165(h)(1).

[47] Code Sec. 165(h)(2).

[48] Reg. § 1.165-7(c).

[49] Code Sec. 55(a)(1).

[50] Code Secs. 55(d)(1), as amended by the Tax Increase Prevention and Reconciliation Act of 2005 (P.L. 109-222).

[51] Code Secs. 55(b)(2), 56, 57, and 58.

[52] Code Sec. 55(b)(1)(A).

of wagering gains) by an amount equal to two percent of adjusted gross income (AGI) in excess of $150,500 ($72,250 for married persons filing separately) for 2006. The reduction in itemized deductions will remain at two percent for tax years beginning in 2007 and will drop to one percent for tax years beginning in 2008 and 2009. The limitation will be repealed for 2010 only. The reduction threshold is indexed annually for inflation.

The reduction may not exceed 80 percent of allowable deductions. This reduction reduces the tax benefits of most itemized deductions such as mortgage interest, real estate taxes, and state and local income taxes.

.02 Capital Gain Tax Breaks

Net capital gains are generally taxed at lower rates than is ordinary income.[53] A net capital gain is the excess of a net long-term capital gain over any net short-term capital loss.[54] A net long-term capital gain is the excess of long-term capital gains over long-term capital losses.[55] A net short-term capital loss is the excess of short-term capital losses over short-term capital gains.[56] Long-term capital gains and losses result from the sale or exchange of capital assets held for more than one year.[57] Short-term capital gains and losses result from the sale or exchange of capital assets held one year or less.[58] In some cases, the Code deems a sale or exchange to occur. For example, a worthless security is deemed sold for zero on the last day of the tax year in which it becomes worthless.[59] Financial assets such as stocks and mutual funds that emphasize long-term capital appreciation conveniently are usually capital assets[60] with the potential for favorable capital gains treatment. Although land used in a business and depreciable assets used in a trade or business are not capital assets as many people believe,[61] gains on the sale or exchange of such assets have the potential for long-term capital gain treatment under Code Sec. 1231(a)(1). Although the tax rates on net capital gains are quite favorable, an individual or a married couple filing a joint return may not deduct more than $3,000 a year of a net capital loss against ordinary income.[62] The taxpayer may carry the remaining net capital loss forward indefinitely.[63]

So what types of investments do the special tax rates for net capital gains and qualified dividends discourage? Certainly, these rates discourage investments in assets that pay out their benefits

[53] Code Sec. 1(h)(1).
[54] Code Sec. 1222(11).
[55] Code Sec. 1222(7).
[56] Code Sec. 1222(6).
[57] Code Secs. 1222(3) and 1222(4).
[58] Code Secs. 1222(1) and 1222(2).
[59] Code Sec. 165(g)(1).
[60] Code Sec. 1221(a).
[61] Code Sec. 1221(a)(2).
[62] Code Secs. 165(f) and 1211(b).
[63] Code Sec. 1212(b)(1).

in the form of interest. Interest is taxed as ordinary income and subject to a tax rate as high as 35 percent.[64]

The prime examples of investments that pay interest include time deposits, bonds, and bond mutual funds. Rental properties held primarily for their rental income, rather than for their appreciation potential might also be less attractive than are stocks.

Also, investments that derive advantage from tax deferral (such as qualified plans and tax-deferred annuities) are less attractive at lower tax rates on net capital gains. However, tax-deferred investments that also provide tax-deductible opportunities (such as traditional IRAs) should remain popular.

Collectibles[65] are generally subject to a capital gains tax rate of up to 28 percent.[66]

The planning strategy of making charitable contributions of appreciated property through split-interest trusts (e.g., CRATS and CRUTs) to avoid capital gains is less beneficial the lower the tax rates on net capital gains.

> **Note.** In determining how long an asset was held, the taxpayer begins counting on the date after the day the property was acquired. The same date of each following month is the beginning of a new holding period month, regardless of the number of days in the preceding month. For example, if property was acquired on June 1, 2006, the taxpayer's holding period began on June 2, 2006. The date the asset is disposed of is part of the holding period.

Tax rates on net capital gains. Generally, net capital gains are subject to a tax rate of 15 percent.[67] This rate is reduced to 5 percent for individuals in the 10-percent or 15-percent ordinary income tax brackets.[68] These capital gain rates apply through 2010.

The alternative capital gains rates apply not only to individuals, but also to estates and trusts.[69] In addition, the rates apply when the taxpayer is determining the alternative minimum tax.[70]

Depreciable real estate. The Code Sec. 1231 gain from the sale or exchange of depreciable real property that is treated as a long-term capital gain but which would be treated as ordinary income if the property were depreciable personal property (that is, Code Sec. 1245 property) is taxed at a maximum rate of 25 percent.[71] The

[64] Code Sec. 1.
[65] Code Sec. 408(m).
[66] Code Sec. 1(h)(4).
[67] Code Sec. 1(h)(1)(C).
[68] Code Sec. 1(h)(1)(B).
[69] Code Sec. 641(b).
[70] Code Sec. 55(b)(3).
[71] Code Sec. 1(h)(7)(A).

balance of the remaining Code Sec. 1231 gain treated as a long-term capital gain is taxed at a maximum rate of 15 percent.[72]

> ***Example 31.1.*** In 2006, Joe Green sold a building for $125,000. Green had originally paid $50,000 for the building a number of years ago. Over the years that he owned the building, Green had deducted $50,000 depreciation. Thus, his adjusted basis in the building was zero at the time of sale. Of his $125,000 recognized gain, he would pay a maximum rate of 25% on $50,000 (the amount that had been allowable as depreciation) and a maximum rate of 15% on the remaining $75,000.

Collectibles. As a general rule, collectibles do not qualify for the 5-percent or 15-percent rates on net capital gains. For example, gain from the sale of stamps, antiques, gems, and most coins are taxed at the maximum rate of 28 percent.[73] However, certain newly minted gold and silver coins issued by the federal government and coins issued under state law qualify for the lower capital gains rates, even though such coins generally would fall within the definition of collectibles.[74]

Small business stock. When a taxpayer sells or exchanges certain small business stock (that is, Code Sec. 1202 stock) that the taxpayer has held for more than five years, 50 percent of the gain may be excluded from the taxpayer's gross income.[75] If the small business stock qualifies for this 50-percent exclusion, any recognized gain from its sale or exchange will be taxed at the maximum rate of 28 percent.[76] Therefore, the effective tax rate on such gains is 14 percent (50% × 28%), and the maximum tax rate on most long-term capital gains is 15 percent through 2010. However, if the gain is large, even a one-percentage point reduction in the tax rate can result in significant savings.

Pass-through entities. An individual's capital gains include his or her share of capital gains from a pass-through entity (such as a mutual fund, S corporation, partnership, estate or trust), and the entity may pass through capital gains to their shareholders or beneficiaries.

.03 How Economic Risk Affects Investment

The one certainty about the stock market is that prices will fluctuate; its direction is never completely certain. If it were, every person could be rich beyond dreams of avarice.

---

[72] Code Sec. 1(h)(1)(C).

[73] Code Sec. 1(h)(5).

[74] Code Secs. 1(h)(6)(A) and 408(m)(3).

[75] Code Sec. 1202(a).

[76] Code Secs. 1(h)(4)(A)(ii) and 1(h)(7).

Risk of loss can be minimized through diversification and asset allocation. The goal of asset allocation is to tailor a portfolio of stocks, bonds, money market investments, foreign securities, precious metals, and other investments in a mix that recognizes the client's risk/return preferences and also hedges against big drops in the stock market such as the drop in the NASDAQ of over 60 percent from its high in 2000 to April 2001. Asset allocation involves choosing the right *categories* of assets for the investor, and a willingness to sacrifice a maximum gain in good times in order to avoid the worst in bad times.

Asset allocation comes highly recommended but is not without its potential drawbacks. It might promote a passive attitude toward true value investing where the emphasis is to buy good investments and hold them for a long time, maximizing values while minimizing trading and transaction costs. Asset allocation also relies on an investor profile, which can change if the investor's preference for risk and return also changes over time. Any reallocation of assets is likely to involve transaction costs. Asset allocation also involves the periodic readjustment of assets. This periodic readjustment might be integral to the asset allocation strategy, if percentage holdings in one category rise above a certain level. Formal application of the strategy calls for a sale of the surplus asset and the purchase of an asset that is under-represented in the portfolio. This process can again trigger annual or more frequent activity in a portfolio, raising transaction costs. All of these factors should lead the investor to some skepticism and the avoidance of false hopes. Asset allocation has the hopeful air of science about it. However, its successful performance, unlike a scientific experiment, will not always be replicated in the real world.

.04 Investments and Securities Laws

Federal and state securities laws affect investments. In many respects such laws are highly complex. The CCH FEDERAL SECURITIES LAW REPORTER runs to eight heavy volumes and its BLUE SKY LAW REPORTER contains another six volumes. The securities law obviously contains many statutes and case law, along with administrative regulations and rulings in these volumes. All this law is grist for securities law specialists, but contains a body of knowledge that is much more than an investor or the issuer of investment securities would need to know about securities laws. However, the average buyer or seller of securities should be familiar with some aspects of the federal and state securities laws.

Common law fraud. Long before the enactment of our current federal securities laws (the Securities Exchange Act of 1934 and the Securities Act of 1933) and state counterparts of the '34 Act, common law principles of fraud and contract were applicable to transactions involving the sale, purchase, or issuance of securities.

Statutory fraud. The 1933 Act deals with the issuance and registration of securities and concerns issuers. Portions of the 1934 Act as they affect buyers and sellers of securities are the primary concern here.

The 1934 Act built on common law fraud concepts and expanded them. Section 10(b) of the Act and SEC Rule 10b-5, briefly stated, made the following acts unlawful in the sale or purchase of a security through the mail or other means of interstate commerce:

- Use of any device or scheme to defraud
- Making a material misstatement or omission of fact
- Commission of any act that operates as an attempt to defraud or deceive an individual

The omissions provision makes unlawful and fraudulent what was not such at common law. It applies to omissions of material fact that make the representations misleading.

The misstatement and omission provision has given rise to more litigation and rulings than the other parts of the rule. It applies to securities transactions, generally, whether conducted face to face or through brokers. It applies to unregistered securities and those exempt from registration under the 1933 Act, including the stock of closely held corporations. Many, if not most, state blue sky securities laws contain provisions similar to Rule 10b-5.

Materiality. As previously noted, to come within Rule 10b-5, the misstatement or omission must be of a material fact (opinion will not suffice). What is material in this context? Basically, it is something a reasonable investor would take into consideration in making an investment decision. However, ascertaining what a reasonable investor would do will usually not be an easy task.

Nonpublic information about a firm's financial condition, a proposed cut or increase in dividends, a stock split or a new product or discovery will ordinarily qualify as material. Preliminary merger talks might qualify, depending on the particular circumstances, even though they have not reached the point of an agreement in principle. The proximity or remoteness of the occurrence of a particular fact can affect its materiality.

This rule is often invoked in insider trading cases. The rule can apply to individuals having no direct relationship with the corporation. For example, an employee of a law firm that has been retained in connection with a planned tender offer tells a friend or relative about a planned tender offer being processed by the law firm. This scenario illustrates a relationship between a tipper and a tippee. The tippee buys stock of the target company. When the tender offer becomes public, the tippee sells the stock at a profit.

The tipper in this example is not a buyer or seller of stock of the target company. He or she may nevertheless be held liable as having engaged in an unlawful transaction under Rule 10b-5 under a theory developed by some courts and upheld on appeal by an equally divided U.S. Supreme Court in *U.S. v. Carpenter*.[77] The tipper is held liable on the ground that he or she has misappropriated confidential information belonging to his or her employer and the employer's client. The law in this area is not clear. The tipper and tippees of the primary tippee who buy and sell securities on the basis of the tip can also be held liable.[78] If the tippee did not know of the confidential nature of the tipped information, he or she might avoid liability.[79]

Rule 10b-5 is used most frequently against true corporate insiders, such as officers, directors, and 10-percent shareholders and their tippees who trade on good or bad nonpublic information about the tippers' companies. Such insiders can be held personally liable even though they derive no direct profit. The profits of the tippee will be considered profits of the insider-tipper.

To invoke the rule, a purchase or sale of securities must occur. The rule may not be invoked if an individual might have bought or sold securities but for the fraud charged. If a purchase and sale does occur, the connection between the fraud and the purchase or sale might be quite tenuous. The rule's application is not limited to transactions in publicly traded securities. One of the first cases that applied the rule involved closely held stock.

Short swing profits. Insiders in a narrower sense than discussed above, namely officers, directors, and 10-percent shareholders of a corporation whose stock is publicly traded, are subject to Section 16(b) of the 1934 Act. It provides that if such individuals buy and sell or sell and buy their company's stock within a six-month period, they

[77] 108 SCt 316.

[78] *SEC v. Musella*, CCH Federal Securities Law Reports ¶ 93,589.

[79] *Chestman*, CA-2, 903 F2d 75 and *Willis*, DC NY, 737 F.Supp. 269.

must disgorge any profits made and pay over the profits to their corporation.

This provision is operative even though the insider is not shown to have traded on inside information. Thus, an irrebuttable presumption is that the purchase and sale or sale and purchase was made on the basis of inside information.

Certain exemptions apply for stock acquired under employee benefit plans, subject to certain conditions. Company counsel should be called upon to provide details.

¶3105 SAVING MORE AS A MEANS OF COPING WITH LOW YIELDS

In times of low interest rates, many individuals have sought alternative investments to boost returns. A less risky way to accumulate more cash is to save more money regularly.

A financial planner can suggest other ways to help the client increase returns and wealth. For example, a financial planner can sit down with the client and create a financial plan for him or her. This plan will help the client to achieve better money management, which, in turn, will increase savings and wealth. The process of developing the plan might reveal that the client is spending too much on certain items. For example, the client might be eating out too frequently. The client might realize substantial savings by eating planned meals at home on a regular basis.

Other benefits of a financial plan include helping the client to avoid late charges on mortgage payments and fees for bouncing checks. As an added bonus, the plan might help the client reduce total interest and finance charges on credit card debt.

A financial planner should not overlook traveling as a means of savings. Clients who routinely book flights near their actual travel dates can realize big discounts by booking well in advance, where feasible.

The following are some other steps that can help increase wealth:

- Moving funds from money market accounts into mutual funds invested in intermediate or short-term Treasuries. This change should result in higher yields without substantially increasing risk. Further, the income will not be subject to state and local income taxes.
- Taking full advantage of any opportunity to participate in a company 401(k) plan, especially if the plan provides matching employer contributions. The client's contribution will

save income taxes, and the tax on earnings on the funds in the account will be deferred.

- Paying credit card balances or transferring credit card debt to lenders who charge lower interest.
- Buying mutual fund shares in equal amounts at regular intervals to dollar cost average, rather than making sporadic purchases.
- Participating in a company automatic savings plan. Some companies offer these plans. Deductions from paychecks are automatically transferred to brokerage accounts or IRAs at regular intervals.

¶ 3110 TAX-EXEMPT GOVERNMENT OBLIGATIONS

Under Code Sec. 103(a), gross income does not include interest on any state (D.C. and possessions included) or local (any political subdivision of a state) bonds, subject to the exceptions in subsection (b). The latter excepts (1) any private activity bond that is not a qualified bond, (2) any arbitrage bond, and (3) any bond that is not registered.

Private activity bonds are generally taxable. A bond is a private activity bond if (1) a trade or business use test and a security or payment test is satisfied, or (2) a private loan restriction is satisfied.[80] A number of private activity bonds qualify for exemption including a relatively new category of exempt facility bonds, qualified enterprise zone facility bonds to help finance property located in an empowerment zone, or enterprise community.[81] In general, the regular tax-exempt bond rules apply. However, proceeds of these bonds may be used for acquiring both new and used property (i.e., use is not limited to the acquisition of new property). Also, more than 25 percent of net bond proceeds may be used to finance the acquisition of land. The Taxpayer Relief Act of 1997 created a new type of financing bonds—empowerment zone bonds. These bonds are similar to enterprise zone bonds, except that empowerment zone bonds: (1) are not private activity bonds under Code Sec. 146 and thus are not subject to the value cap on such bonds, and (2) are not subject to the $3 million per empowerment zone limit.[82]

The foregoing is simply an overview of very complex special rules directly affecting tax-exempt bonds. Financial planners and investors cannot be expected to master the intricate rules dealing with tax

[80] Code Sec. 141.

[81] Code Sec. 1394.

[82] Code Sec. 1394(f).

exempt securities. However, both must be aware of the possible alternative minimum tax (AMT) consequences of investments in private activity bonds.[83] In addition, both must be sure that any private activity bonds acquired on the basis that they are exempt do, in fact, qualify for the exemption and/or that their qualification is guaranteed by a responsible issuer or independent guarantor. Finally, both should be aware that the characterization of a particular issue as exempt from all taxation does not provide an exemption from estate tax.[84]

A prospective investor in tax-exempt bonds must be concerned with factors that are truly beyond his or her control. The future trend of interest rates and the interrelated factor of inflation can have a great bearing on the ultimate success of a tax-exempt investment. The investor who is fairly convinced that interest rates and inflation will increase will not want to hold long-term bonds. Their value will decrease if interest rates rise and significant inflation takes place.

.01 The Minimum Tax and Tax-Exempt Bonds

Interest on private activity tax-exempt bonds is a preference item subject to the alternative minimum tax (AMT).[85]

AMT bonds yield a higher rate of interest than comparable issues of fully exempt bonds, i.e., 1/4 to 1/2 percent more. Many clients will not face the AMT. Careful investors can obtain higher yields with AMT bonds than with fully exempt bonds.

.02 Investment Vehicles

The investor has three basic ways to invest in tax-exempt obligations: individual purchases, purchase of shares in a unit trust, and purchase of shares in a mutual bond fund.

Individual bonds. Factors bearing on the purchase of individual bonds are that bonds issued by the investor's own state or a subdivision thereof will usually be exempt from state and local taxes, as well as from federal income taxes. Bonds with good ratings are readily saleable. The cost of buying and selling bonds is usually less than the cost of stock transactions. Nevertheless, dealers prefer to deal in round lots and several points can be lost in odd lots. Placing an order for a few thousand dollars of tax-exempt bonds is difficult. Bearer bonds are more marketable than registered bonds, although bonds issued after June 1983 must be registered to be eligible for federal tax exemption.[86] Many bonds are callable. The issuer of

[83] Code Sec. 57(a)(5)(A).

[84] *Wells Fargo Bank*, SCt, 88-1 USTC ¶ 13,759.

[85] Code Sec. 57(a)(5)(A).

[86] Code Sec. 149(a)(1).

registered bonds will directly contact the holder. With bearer bonds, the call is made through public announcements. The holder of a callable bond must be on the alert for a call.

Unit trusts. Most municipal bond funds are unit trusts, consisting of a fixed portfolio of long-term bonds to be held until maturity or until called by the issuers. The unit trust is not a managed fund and is appropriate for the investor who is willing to buy and hold a trust portfolio.

Unit trusts offer the investor a means of profiting from declining interest rates and rising bond prices. They can also involve a loss of value before maturity with a rise in interest rates.

Most trusts charge no redemption fee but do carry a sales charge, to be paid at once.

Mutual funds. Mutual funds are managed funds (unlike unit trusts) in which fund managers adjust the fund portfolio to meet changing market conditions. For their services mutual funds Charge an annual management fee that generally ranges from 1.5 to 2 percent of the amount invested. In addition to the management fee, if the fund is an open-end type of fund, with shares being continually sold, the fund might charge a sales charge, ranging from one percent to as much as 8.5 percent of the amount invested. Many no load mutual funds are available that charge no sales charge but may have exit fees.

Closed end funds do not continually offer new shares. Once they have made their initial offering of shares, sales by the fund are closed. Investors must buy and sell their shares in the over-the-counter market. Closed-end funds can trade at, below, or above net asset value.

.03 Tax-Exempt Zero Coupon Bonds

A tax-exempt zero coupon bond is sold at a deep discount from its face value. It pays no current interest, as would a coupon bond. As with other forms of zero coupon securities, tax-exempt zeros provide the investor with a chance to lock in favorable rates of interest over the long term without having to suffer reinvestment risks each time an interest payment would be made. Of course, the long-term benefits of tax-exempt zeros can be undercut by call provisions in the bonds, or payment at maturity in dollars whose value has been eroded by inflation. Tax-exempt zeros can be a particularly good way for parents to avoid the kiddie tax, which subjects unearned income in excess of $1,700 for 2006 of a child under age 18 to income tax at the higher of the child's rate or the parents' rate (¶3205).[87]

[87] Code Sec. 1(g), as amended by the Tax Increase Prevention and Reconciliation Act of 2005 (P.L. 109-222).

Code Sec. 1286(d) provides special rules for stripped tax-exempt securities.

¶ 3115 LIKE-KIND PROPERTY EXCHANGES

For the person holding appreciated property who wants to dispose of it and replace it with other property, a like-kind exchange (1031 exchange) can be an effective way of doing so without incurring a current tax liability. Recognition of the gain on the appreciation is deferred until the property received in the exchange is disposed of in a taxable transaction during the recipient's life. Recognition may be indefinitely postponed so long as the property is held by the recipient or is exchanged in one or more subsequent like-kind exchanges during the recipient's lifetime. If the recipient holds the replacement property until his or her death, the untaxed pre-death appreciation will permanently escape income tax because of the step-up in basis.[88] However, for property acquired from a decedent dying in 2010, the step up in basis is limited to $1,300,000 plus $3,000,000 for property received by a surviving spouse.

Before a client enters into a like-kind exchange, the financial planner should help the client explore the following:

- The extent of the gain on a sale. With the low capital gains rates available (15-percent maximum rate for capital assets held for more than one year), the question of whether or not a capital asset or a Code Sec. 1231 asset should be sold outright deserves reconsideration.
- Whether the property owner has realized losses that may offset any gains that he or she would realize on a sale of the property.
- Whether a sale can be made using the installment method of reporting provided by Code Sec. 453. If an installment sale is possible, the financial planner should compare the cost of such disposition to a Code Sec. 1031 exchange. The financial planner should remember the rule that any depreciation recapture income must be recognized in the year of an installment sale, even though no payments are received in that year.[89]
- How a sale of the property and reinvestment of the proceeds in other property, with possibly higher depreciation

[88] Code Sec. 1014(a).

[89] Code Sec. 453(i).

deductions and lower taxes on a resale of the replacement property, compares with a like-kind exchange.

- The current tax bracket of the owner and any possible changes therein within the foreseeable future.
- Whether the property owner will retain the replacement property indefinitely and whether it will be included in the owner's estate and receive a stepped-up basis.[90] The step up in basis is limited to $1,300,000 plus $3,000,000 for property received by a surviving spouse for decedents dying in 2010.

The basic requirement for a tax-deferred like-kind exchange is that the exchange be of like-kind properties and otherwise satisfy the requirements of Code Sec. 1031.

.01 Requirements of a Like-Kind Exchange

The requirements of a like-kind exchange as set out in Code Sec. 1031 are as follows:

1. Both the property exchanged and that received in exchange be held for productive use in a trade or business or for investment.[91]
2. The properties exchanged must be of like kind.[92]
3. The property to be received in the exchange must be identified as such within 45 days after the property relinquished in the exchange is transferred.[93]
4. The property must be received no later than the earlier of:
   a. 180 days after the property relinquished in the exchange is transferred,[94] or
   b. The due date of the taxpayer's return, determined with regard to extensions.[95]

The Code expressly excludes from eligibility stock in trade or other property held primarily for sale; stocks, bonds, notes or other securities or evidences of indebtedness; certificates of trust or beneficial interest; and rights that can be enforced by legal action, e.g., debts or tort actions.[96] Otherwise, Code Sec. 1031 applies to both real and personal property, although most exchanges involve real estate.

---

[90] Code Sec. 1014(a).
[91] Code Sec. 1031(a)(1).
[92] Code Sec. 1031(a)(1).
[93] Code Sec. 1031(a)(3)(A).
[94] Code Sec. 1031(a)(3)(B)(i).
[95] Code Sec. 1031(a)(3)(B)(ii).
[96] Code Sec. 1031(a)(2).

.02 Partnerships

Generally partnership interests are not eligible for like-kind exchanges.[97] Partnership interests in partnerships electing to be excluded from subchapter K are treated as interests in the assets of the partnership. Such interests would therefore be eligible for like-kind exchange treatment.

.03 Like-Kind Property

For purposes of Code Sec. 1031, like-kind property is property of the same character, nature, or class.[98] One kind or class of property may not be exchanged on a tax-deferred basis for property of a different kind or class.[99] Real estate may not be exchanged for personal property, for example. However, as a general rule, an exchange of any parcel of real estate for another will qualify as a like-kind exchange without regard to its location or use. This rule permits raw land to be exchanged on a tax-deferred basis for an office building, and a farm for urban rental property or for timberland. However, foreign real property is never considered of a like kind to U.S. real property;[100] likewise, foreign personal property is never considered of a like kind to U.S. personal property.[101]

.04 Receipt of Cash and Other Forms of Boot

Often in an exchange onc party will be called upon to make cash payments, to assume a mortgage or take the property subject to a mortgage, or to deliver property of a different kind in order to equalize values. The cash payments, debt relief, and property of a different kind are called boot. If a transferor assumes a mortgage on the property received or receives property subject to a mortgage, such mortgage will reduce the boot received from debt relief on the transferred property. However, the debt incurred may not offset other forms of boot such as cash.[102] The receipt of boot will have no effect on whether the exchange of properties is entitled to nonrecognition of gain. However, the party who receives the boot must recognize any gain realized to the extent of the boot received.[103] The gain not recognized is the gain deferred. The basis in the new like-kind property is equal to its fair market value minus the gain deferred. The basis of any property of a different kind received is its fair market value at the time of receipt.[104] Losses are never recognized on like-kind exchanges even if boot is received or paid.[105] If a loss is realized on a like-kind

[97] Code Sec. 1031(a)(2)(D).

[98] Reg. §§ 1.1031(a)-1(b) and 1.1031(a)-2.

[99] Reg. § 1.1031(a)-1(b).

[100] Code Sec. 1031(h)(1).

[101] Code Sec. 1031(h)(2)(A).

[102] Reg. §§ 1.1031(b)-1(c) and 1.1031(d)-2.

[103] Code Sec. 1031(b).

[104] Code Sec. 1031(d).

[105] Code Sec. 1031(a)(1).

exchange, the basis of the new like-kind property is its fair market value plus the loss realized on the exchange.[106]

¶ 3120 INVESTMENTS IN SECURITIES

Investment in securities has always involved a strong element of risk in assessing a company's prospects. Economic considerations, diversification, and asset allocation are discussed at ¶ 3101.03. Here, the primary concern is tax factors.

.01 In General

Before- and after-tax earnings are elements to consider, along with a host of other factors, internal and external. Also, consider the after-tax costs of realizing any capital appreciation. See ¶ 3101.01 for discussion of the tax treatment of capital gains and losses. Year-end planning for securities transactions is discussed at ¶ 3310.

.02 Short Selling

Most individuals buy stocks with the hope that the stocks will go up in value and they will make money on the appreciation. In addition, the investor might possibly receive dividends. An owner of stock is said to be long in the stock. Individuals who feel that particular stocks are overpriced and will go down in value sometimes attempt to make money by short selling. With short selling, an individual actually sells the stock before he or she owns it. An individual must use a margin account to sell stock short.

Example 31.2. Stock of Widget, Inc., is currently selling at $60 a share. Frank Smith thinks the Widget stock is overvalued and will go down in price. He tells his broker that he wants to sell 200 shares of Widget short.

What actually happens is that Smith's broker lends him 200 shares of Widget. Smith then immediately sells them for $60 a share leaving the $12,000 (less selling expenses) on deposit with the broker. Smith then waits for the price of the stock to go down.

The stock goes down to $30 a share. Smith thinks the price has hit bottom. So he buys 200 shares at $30 a share at a total cost of $6,000 (plus commission). He uses these shares to pay back the shares he borrowed from his broker. The broker then gives Smith the $12,000 (less selling expenses) from the broker. Thus, Smith has made $6,000 (less transaction costs) by correctly predicting that the stock would decrease in value.

[106] Code Sec. 1031(d).

Risks and costs. In times when stocks appear to be grossly overvalued, individuals might be very tempted to try to make money by selling short. However, a financial planner should warn his or her clients of the risks of short selling.

With a long position, the most that the client can lose is the amount he or she paid for the stock. With a short sale, the client theoretically has unlimited risk in that the client could be wrong and the price of the stock could soar. The client eventually has to buy the shares and return them to the broker. If the client covers the short position at a time when the stock has appreciated in value from the time he or she sold the stock borrowed from the broker, the client will lose money.

The market can be very volatile and prices can rise or fall rapidly. Sometimes, a flurry of short covering in and of itself will contribute greatly to the quick rises in value of particular stocks. Going back to the example above, assume that a few days after Smith shorted the stock, its price jumped to $80 a share. If he immediately covered (i.e., bought 200 shares at $80 per share), he will be out $4,000 (plus transaction costs). Also, if the price increases before the short seller covers, he or she has to deposit additional funds with the broker. Furthermore, the short seller must pay any dividends on the borrowed stock until he or she covers.

Shorting against the box. With this technique, the individual sells short shares that he or she already owns. Frequently, this is done at the end of a year when an investor wants to lock in his or her gain currently but not have to recognize it until the following year. A short sale against the box is a hedged position. If the stock appreciates, the investor gains on the stock he or she owns, but loses the same amount on the short sale. If the stock declines in price, the reverse is true.

Short-against-the-box transactions are generally treated as constructive sales of the appreciated stock as of the date of the transaction. A safe harbor exists, however, for certain short-against-the-box transactions that are closed within 30 days after the end of the year that the transaction was opened.[107] The gain or loss is considered a capital gain or loss if the property used to close the sale is a capital asset in the hands of the selling taxpayer.

For transactions that meet certain safe harbor rules, no gain or loss is recognized until the short sale is closed by the delivery of the replacement stock to the lender. The gain or loss is the difference

---

[107] Code Sec. 1259.

between the proceeds received from the short sale and the cost of the property used to close it.

¶ 3125 CAPITAL GAINS EXCLUSION FOR QUALIFIED SMALL BUSINESS STOCK

The Internal Revenue Code provides a tax break that is designed to help qualifying small businesses raise capital by allowing a long-term noncorporate investor in original issue stock to exclude 50 percent of the gain from his or her gross income. The taxpayer must have held the stock for more than five years.[108] The taxable portion is a long-term capital gain, taxed at the maximum rate of 28 percent[109] (the 15-percent long-term rate[110] is not available where the seller qualifies for the 50-percent exclusion from gain[111]). Seven percent of the gain excluded from gross income is a tax preference item for AMT purposes.[112]

> ***Example 31.3.*** Gene Gray invests $100,000 in qualifying small business stock on June 2, 2000. His investment is very profitable, and he sells the stock 6 years later in June 2006 for $1.1 million. He has substantial gross income from other sources during the year of sale.
>
> If Gray is not subject to the AMT in the year of sale, his tax on the gain will be $140,000 [28% × ($1,000,000 – $500,000)]. If all of his gain were subject to tax, his tax rate would be 15%, and his tax would be $150,000 ($1,000,000 × 15%). Thus, the Code Sec. 1202 exclusion saved him $10,000 ($150,000 – $140,000). If Gray is subject to the top 28% AMT rate when he sells the stock, he will pay $149,800 of tax on his gain {[28% × ($500,000 × 7%)] + ($500,000 × 28%)}. Thus, his tax savings would be only $200 ($150,000 – $149,800).
>
> **Planning pointer.** The denial of the 15-percent capital gains rate where the 50-percent exclusion applies is designed keep a taxpayer from reaping a double tax benefit. However, if a taxpayer, after holding the small business stock for more than one year,[113] but less than five years, sells the stock, the gain would qualify for the 15-percent maximum rate.[114]

.01 Qualifying for the Break

The 50-percent capital gains exclusion applies only to gain on eligible stock: (1) originally issued by a qualifying corporation after

[108] Code Sec. 1202(a).
[109] Code Sec. 1(h).
[110] Code Sec. 1(h)(1)(C).
[111] Code Secs. 1(h)(5) and 1(h)(8).
[112] Code Sec. 57(a)(7).
[113] Code Sec. 1222(3).
[114] Code Sec. 1(h)(C).

August 10, 1993, and (2) held for more than five years. Generous cumulative limits apply to the gain that may be excluded.[115]

.02 Eligible Stock

The exclusion generally applies only with respect to:

- Stock that was acquired by the taxpayer at its original issue after August 10, 1993. The stock can be acquired directly or through an underwriter.
- Stock acquired in exchange for money or other property (other than stock), or as compensation for services provided to the corporation (other than acting as the stock's underwriter).[116]

The tax break applies to preferred stock (including convertible preferred) as well as common stock, assuming the taxpayer meets all the requirements.

.03 Ineligible Stock

The exclusion does not apply to a taxpayer's stock if either of two conditions exists:

1. The issuing corporation directly or indirectly buys *any* of its own shares from the taxpayer or persons related to the taxpayer within a four-year period that begins two years before the stock's original issue date. Related persons are determined under the rules of Code Sec. 267(b) (e.g., close family members) or Code Sec. 707(b) (e.g., a person and his or her more than 50-percent controlled partnership).
2. The issuing corporation redeems, within a two-year period beginning one year before the stock's issuance, more than five percent by value of its stock as of the beginning of the two-year period. A corporation that redeems stock through a related corporation under Code Sec. 304(a) is considered to have bought its own stock in the amount of the deemed redemption distribution under Code Sec. 304(a).[117]

.04 Issuer Qualifications

The exclusion does not apply unless the corporation issuing the stock is a qualifying entity that (1) meets an active business test, (2) is engaged in a qualifying business, and (3) passes a gross assets test.[118]

---

[115] Code Sec. 1202(b).

[116] Code Sec. 1202(c).

[117] Code Sec. 1202(c)(3).

[118] Code Sec. 1202(d).

.05 Tax-Free Transfers

Although the law does not allow the exclusion to a post-issuance purchaser of otherwise qualified stock, the tax break is preserved for those who receive such stock as a gift or due to the death of the original purchaser. The transferor's holding period also carries over to the transferee. Similarly, qualified stock distributed by a partnership to its partners keeps its tax character intact as long as the partners held their partnership interests when the stock was acquired, but only to the extent their shares of the partnership have not changed since the stock was bought. The partnership holding period for the qualified stock also carries over to the distributee-partners.[119]

.06 Maximum Excludable Amount

For each eligible corporation, a shareholder can exclude gain only to the extent the gain does not exceed the greater of (1) 10 times the taxpayer's adjusted basis in the stock disposed of during the tax year (post-issuance additions to basis are disregarded), or (2) $10 million gain ($5 million for married taxpayers filing separately) reduced by gain excluded in earlier years from sales of stock in the corporation.[120]

.07 Special Basis Rules

If property (other than money or stock) is transferred to a corporation in exchange for its stock, the basis of the stock received is treated as not less than the fair market value of the property exchanged. If the qualified stock's basis is later increased by the holder's additional capital contributions, the contributed property's basis at that time is at least equal to its FMV at that time. These rules assure that only gains that accrue after the transfer are eligible for the exclusion.[121]

.08 Rollover of Gain on Sales of Qualified Small Business Stock (Code Sec. 1045)

For sales of qualified small business stock, a taxpayer other than a corporation may elect to roll over capital gain from sales of such stock held for more than six months if the taxpayer purchases other small business stock within 60 days of the stock sale. Accordingly, gain is recognized only to the extent that the amount realized on the sale exceeds the cost of the replacement stock, as reduced by the portion of such cost, if any, that was previously taken into account.[122]

---

[119] Code Sec. 1202(h).

[120] Code Sec. 1202(b).

[121] Code Sec. 1202(i).

[122] Code Sec. 1045(a).

To the extent that capital gain is not recognized, that amount will reduce the basis of the replacement stock.[123] The rollover break is only available to taxpayers other than a corporation.[124] Partnerships and S corporations are eligible to make the election if at all times during the tax year all the interests in the partnership or S corporation were held by individuals, estates, and trusts with no corporate beneficiaries.[125] Prop. Reg. § 1.1045-1 explains how Code Sec. 1045 applies to partnerships, including tiered partnerships. C corporations are not eligible to make the election.

> **Planning pointer.** For investors who choose to have a certain portion of their portfolio always invested in qualified small business stock, this rollover provision will allow indefinite postponement of tax on small business stock gains.

¶ 3130 DEFERRAL FOR INVESTMENT IN SPECIALIZED SMALL BUSINESS INVESTMENT COMPANIES

Investors who sell publicly traded securities may elect to defer the recognition of any capital gain realized by purchasing an interest in a specialized small business investment company (SSBIC). The interest may be common stock or a partnership interest as long as the company qualifies as an SSBIC. The profit on such sales is not currently taxed to the extent that the stock-sale proceeds are reinvested within 60 days in an SSBIC.[126] An SSBIC is a company licensed under section 301(d) of the Small Business Investment Company Act of 1958 as in effect on May 13, 1993. Generally, an SSBIC is an investment company that finances small business concerns owned by disadvantaged persons.

.01 Basis Reduction

As with other rollovers, tax on the gain is deferred, not eliminated. The mechanism for deferral is a downward basis adjustment in the SSBIC stock or partnership interest, equal to the gain that is not currently taxed.[127]

Gain on the SSBIC stock may qualify for the 50-percent exclusion (¶ 3125).[128] However, if the SSBIC purchase qualifies as small business stock eligible for the 50-percent capital gain exclusion, basis in the SSBIC stock is not reduced for purposes of calculating the gain eligible for the exclusion.[129] This treatment prevents the deferred

[123] Code Sec. 1045(b)(3).

[124] Code Sec. 1045(a).

[125] Committee Reports on P.L. 105-206 (IRS Restructuring and Reform Act of 1998).

[126] Code Sec. 1044(a).

[127] Code Sec. 1044(d).

[128] Code Sec. 1202(a).

[129] Code Sec. 1044(d).

gain from qualifying for the exclusion but makes it available for appreciation occurring after the SSBIC stock is acquired.

.02 Rollover Limits

The amount of gain eligible for the rollover for a tax year generally is limited to the lesser of (1) $50,000, or (2) $500,000 reduced by previously excluded gain ($25,000 and $250,000 for married individuals filing separately). For corporations, the limits are $250,000 and $1,000,000.[130]

¶3135 U.S. GOVERNMENT SECURITIES

The Treasury Department currently offers Treasury bills, notes, and inflation-protected securities. In addition, the Treasury resumed issuing 30-year bonds in February 2006, after suspending issuance of such bonds in 2001. U.S. savings bonds, which are also issued by the Treasury Department, are separately discussed below.

Taken as a group, Treasury securities offer these advantages:

- **Safety.** They are the safest investments.
- **Liquidity.** They are highly liquid and readily marketable prior to maturity.
- **Yields.** Yields might be only slightly lower than on high-grade corporate bonds, ranging from one-third of a point to two points lower. When investors become concerned about the safety of corporate bonds, the spread increases.
- **Limited tax exemption.** The interest is exempt from all state and local income taxes, but not from federal income taxes.

Treasury (or "T") bills are issued with maturities of 4, 13, and 26 weeks. The minimum purchase is $1,000, but an investor may purchase a larger amount in multiples of $1,000 above the minimum. The maximum purchase on a noncompetitive basis is $5 million. The maximum purchase on a competitive basis is 35 percent of the offering amount. The Treasury sells them at a discount to their face value. They are issued in book-entry form, rather than as an engraved certificate. Book-entry securities protect the owner against loss, theft, and counterfeiting.

Treasury notes are issued in terms of 2, 3, 5, and 10 years, and are offered in multiples of $1,000. The price and interest rate of a note are determined at auction. The price may be greater than, less than, or equal to the note par value.

---

[130] Code Sec. 1044(b).

Treasury inflation-protected securities (TIPS) are issued in terms of 5, 10, and 20 years, and are offered in multiples of $1,000. The principal is adjusted according to the Consumer Price Index (CPI). With a rise in the index, or inflation, the principal increases; with a fall in the index, or deflation, the principal decreases. TIPS pay interest every six months. The interest rate is a fixed rate determined at auction. Though the rate is fixed, interest payments vary because the rate is applied to the adjusted principal. The amount of each interest payment is determined by multiplying the adjusted principal by one-half the interest rate.

Original issue Treasury securities may be purchased online at *www.treasurydirect.gov* through noncompetitive bidding. This Web site also has more complete information on Treasury bills and other Treasury securities. Previously issued securities must be purchased through commercial banks or securities dealers.

.01 Tax Treatment of T-Bills, Notes, and Bonds

In general, periodic inclusion of original issue discount is required of the holders of debt obligations. However, for T-bills, discount is not considered to accrue until the obligation is paid at maturity or otherwise disposed of.[131] In other words, a taxpayer can defer income by purchasing T-bills that mature in the next year. This practice was eliminated for banks, securities dealers, accrual-basis taxpayers, and certain others by requiring current accrual of income, effective for obligations acquired after July 18, 1984.[132]

While cash-basis investors were excepted from the accrual rule, the ability of a cash-basis investor to make leveraged purchases of T-bills as a device to defer tax on ordinary income is limited by Code Sec. 1282, which operates to defer interest deductions for such leveraged investments. However, this rule does not apply if the taxpayer elects to accrue the discount currently.

Gain on the sale of a T-bill (on which the discount has not been currently accrued) is treated as ordinary income to the extent of the"ratable share of acquisition discount" and any gain in excess of this amount is treated as short-term capital gain. Acquisition discount is the difference between the stated redemption price at maturity and the taxpayer's basis. The ratable share is the portion equal to the ratio of the number of days the T-bill is held to the number of days between the date of acquisition and the date of maturity. Loss on a sale is treated as a short-term capital loss.

---

[131] Code Sec. 454(b).

[132] Code Sec. 1281.

Notes return a fixed rate of interest and have maturities of not less than two years or more than 10 years. Usually, the issues with longer maturities carry greater interest. Notes may be purchased at *www.treasurydirect.gov* or through brokers or commercial banks for a fee. They are issued in a minimum amount of $1,000. Larger amounts are available in increments of $1,000. The maximum purchase is $5 million on a noncompetitive basis or 35 percent of the offering on a competitive basis.

Bonds have fixed rates of interest and have maturities of at least five years, but usually 30 years. The Treasury resumed issuing 30-year bonds in February 2006 after suspending such issues in October 2001. Previously issued 30-year Treasury bonds still trade in the market. Some may be subject to call.

Bonds may be purchased on margin, sometimes for as little as 10 percent, which encourages speculation. Large gains and losses are possible, depending on the fluctuation of interest rates, a factor usually very difficult to predict.

Treasury Inflation-Protected Securities (TIPS) were introduced in January, 1997 by the U.S. Treasury Department. The Treasury issues TIPS in terms of 5, 10, and 20 years, with the principal adjusted daily for inflation. The adjustment is payable at maturity, but has a current effect, because semiannual interest payments are determined as a fixed percentage of the inflation-adjusted principal at the time the interest is paid. An investor may purchase TIPS at *www.treasurydirect.gov* or through banks or brokers. The minimum purchase of TIPS is $1,000. Additional amounts are available in multiples of $1,000. The maximum purchase is $5 million on a noncompetitive basis or 35 percent of the offering amount on a competitive basis.

.02 Savings Bonds

Series EE/E bonds issued by the Treasury between May 1997 and before May 2005 earn a variable rate of interest based on the market. Series EE bonds issued on May 1, 2005, and thereafter earn a fixed rate of interest. The interest rate through October 2006 is 3.7 percent.

Available in denominations as low as $50 and as high as $10,000 for paper bonds, Series EE bonds lend themselves to systematic accumulation programs, either through payroll deduction arrangements or individual plans. When an investor purchases an EE bond electronically at *www.treasurydirect.gov*, the minimum purchase is $25 for an EE bond with a face value of $25. Paper bonds are issued at 50 percent of face value. The maximum purchase is $30,000, whether an investor purchases the Series EE electronically or in paper form.

No interest is paid until maturity, and the holder is not taxed until the bond is redeemed unless the holder makes an election to be taxed annually. Interest on the bonds is exempt from state and local taxes.

As of September 1, 2004, an investor may not exchange Series EE bonds for Series HH bonds. Series HH bonds paid interest semiannually. Owners who deferred reporting interest on the EE bonds given up in exchange for the HH bonds can continue to defer reporting such interest until the HH bonds are redeemed, disposed of, or reach final maturity. However, the interest on the HH bonds is currently reportable.

Series I bonds are savings bonds that offer protection against inflation. The Treasury issues them at face value. The minimum purchase is $25 for an I bond purchased electronically at *www.treasurydirect.gov.* The minimum purchase for a paper I bond is $50. The interest is indexed to inflation. The interest is added to the I bond each month and paid when the bondholder redeems the bond. Federal income taxes on the interest income can be deferred for up to 30 years.

> **Planning pointer.** Series EE (or Series I bonds) might be useful in dealing with the kiddie tax, which subjects unearned income of a minor under age 18 in excess of $1,700 for 2006 to tax at the higher of the child's rate or the parents' rate (¶ 3205).[133] The buildup of interest through Series EE bonds will not subject the minor to current tax. The Series EE bonds may be redeemed after the minor attains age 14 and the proceeds used for other investments.

¶ 3140 MUTUAL FUNDS

Mutual funds offer the investor the following advantages:

- Diversification of investment
- Professional research and management of investments
- Liquidity
- Pass-through of income and gains without tax at the fund level
- Governmental regulation of the industry

[133] Code Sec. 1(g).

Mutual funds also allow for greater financial flexibility than is available with purchases of individual stocks or bonds. For example, the amount paid for stocks is controlled by the price at which the stocks are trading. With a mutual fund, an individual merely needs to invest the minimum amount required by the fund, which in many cases is $1,000 or $2,500. Additional shares can be purchased in smaller increments.

Mutual funds include open-end funds and closed-end funds, but open-end funds are by far the most common. Open-end funds stand ready on any business day to sell additional shares and to redeem shares tendered by existing fund shareholders.

Closed-end funds have a fixed capitalization. After the initial offering, the shares trade in the open market or on an exchange. Unlike open-end fund shares, shares in closed-end funds are not redeemable by the fund. Occasionally, additional shares may be distributed to existing shareholders as stock dividends and sometimes may be offered to existing shareholders of record.

Closed-end funds often trade at substantial discounts from their net asset value. No general agreement exists as to why this phenomenon occurs. One reason for their trading at a discount is that the funds will not redeem the shares. As a result, a shareholder who wishes to dispose of his or her shares must act through a broker, who in turn must find a buyer.

The size of the discount, if attributable to a marketability factor only, would vary with the lack of marketability. If the market is very thin, for example, the discount would be greater than if the shares had a ready market.

The brokerage rates charged in such transactions are also a factor. The usual rate will be the rate charged for equity trades of similar value for a similar type of customer. When making any comparison with open-end funds, the financial planner should remember that open-end funds might charge a redemption fee.

Some funds sell at a premium, that is, at a price above net asset value. The reason for the premium is more difficult to explain than discounts, which can be accounted for at least, in part, on the basis of marketability.

.01 The Rise of No-Loads; Comparison of Load and No-Load Funds

No-load funds (those without sales charges) now have greater acceptance than ever before vis-a-vis load funds (those with sales charges).

A financial planner can easily understand why an individual with $10,000 to invest would feel more comfortable with the full $10,000 invested. The investor in a load fund by way of contrast might have as much as $850 deducted from the $10,000 investment for sales charges. At first glance that $850 might be thought of as 8.5 percent of the amount invested. However, if the sales charge is applied to the $9,150 left for investment, the percentage jumps to 9.3 percent.

The investor in a load fund might have to wait a year or more before reaching the break-even point. If the investor earns less than 9.3 percent after taxes, the break-even point might take much longer.

The other factor is primarily a psychological one. Seldom can an investor easily walk away from a poor investment. However, walking away from a fund in which the investor has the full $10,000 invested when it is down $500, is easier than when the load fund is down to $8,650 and the investor stands to lose $1,350.

Despite sales charges, load funds do sell. A most important reason is that a large portion of the sales is made on a person-to-person basis. On the other hand, sales of no-loads primarily rely on advertisements in the financial and investment press.

The personal selling is most often done by emphasizing past performance and the potential of continued future performance. The registered representative might tell the investor that the investment should be looked upon as a long-term investment. Thus, if performance is good over the long term, the initial sales charge is of small consequence. Moreover, if the fund being sold is a member of a family of funds, the investment may be transferred without additional sales charges to a fund that holds higher promise or that better suits the needs of the investor at the time. No-load mutual funds also offer similar switching opportunities within their family of funds.

> **Planning pointer.** The investor should be mindful that commission-free switches between families of funds will not alter the usual tax consequences that attend a sale of a capital asset and the purchase of another. The seller will recognize gain or loss even though he or she invests in another fund in the same family.[134] To the extent that he or she wishes to reduce the gain occasioned by sale of fund shares, the best approach may be to make a commission-free sale of shares at a loss in another fund within the same family. For further details on the tax treatment of mutual funds, see the discussion below under the heading "Tax treatment and tax strategies."

[134] Code Sec. 1001(c).

Both types of funds charge management fees, which are not likely to vary greatly between the two types of funds. The investor should check whether the fund has a 12b-1 fee to cover marketing and promotional expenses. The investor should also check whether the fund has a deferred sales load, deducted either upon redemption or in installments over time, subject to specified conditions.

.02 SEC Fee Disclosure/Advertising Standards

Mutual funds must use specified standards in prospectuses and advertising. The standards apply to fee disclosure as well as periods for reporting past performance. Investors should benefit greatly from the ability to compare the fees of funds and to understand projected returns, but should not limit their inquiry to fee comparisons.

.03 Types of Funds and Fund Objectives

Many different types of mutual funds with different investment objectives are available, as listed below.

Aggressive growth funds emphasize rapid growth, which generally means speculative investment in new companies with high growth potentials.

Straight growth funds hold well-known blue-chip company stock with good capital growth records in order to obtain a safe, steady, and long-term increase in capital.

Growth funds normally invest in companies with long-term earnings that are expected to grow significantly faster than the averages of stocks in the major unmanaged stock averages.

Growth and income funds combine a growth of earnings objective with an income requirement for level or rising dividends.

Fixed income funds typically have more than 75 percent of their assets in fixed-income issues, such as money market instruments, bonds, and preferred stock.

Bond funds typically hold portfolios that consist primarily of corporate or municipal bonds, accent income rather than growth, and tend to be more conservative than income funds. Enhanced bond funds that invest primarily in U.S. government bonds might achieve still higher current returns through sales of options on bonds. However, the exercise of call options by purchasers will undermine the fund's ability to participate in increases in the bond market. Thus, over the long term, predicting whether these enhanced bond funds (which typically involve payment of a sales charge) will outperform no-load funds is difficult.

Income funds normally invest less than 75 percent in fixed income issues and less than 50 percent in equities in order to obtain their principal aim of generating income.

Balanced funds maintain a portfolio of stocks and bonds in a ratio of about 60/40 in order to achieve net asset stability.

Other types of mutual funds include the following:

- Small company growth funds
- International funds
- Natural resource funds
- Specialty funds
- Capital appreciation funds
- Gold-oriented funds (mining, finance houses, coins, or bullion)
- Equity income funds
- Junk bond funds
- Option income funds
- Money market funds
- Commodities futures funds (¶ 3155)
- Zero coupon mutual funds (see separate discussion below)
- Foreign bond mutual funds
- Tax-exempt plan-only funds
- Dual-purpose funds
- Multiple choice management funds
- Ethical investment funds
- Index funds

.04 Zero Coupon Mutual Funds

These funds have been created to capitalize on the advantages of the zero coupon concept, which is to reduce reinvestment risk for the holder (¶ 3160). By using the fund's superior buying power, the investor might be able to obtain zero coupon bonds (particularly in small denominations) at better rates than he or she could through a direct purchase. Dealer markups on direct purchases might be considerable. Zero coupon mutual funds permit easy redemptions and enable the investor to increase his or her investment through much smaller reinvestments than would ordinarily be allowed through direct purchase. Recordkeeping services are provided.

These funds appear to be more liquid than zero coupon bonds owned directly by the investor. The funds can be designed to provide target maturity dates every five years.

Although zero coupon mutual funds may be offered on a no-load basis, the share price for the fund will reflect the management fee and expenses paid to the fund's operator. The financial planner will have to check such prices to ascertain the real cost of investing through a zero coupon mutual fund. Also, because liquidity must exist to fund early redemptions and sales, a zero coupon mutual bond fund cannot be fully invested in such securities. The fund must contain some element of cash equivalents. Purchase of zero coupon bonds through a mutual fund cannot alter the risks inherent in the zero coupon concept: a rise in interest rates before the anticipated maturity date of the underlying bonds necessarily will cause the value of the underlying bonds to fall, which, in turn, will cause the value of the investor's mutual fund shares to drop. Accordingly, fund managers indicate that investors should hold their shares until maturity if possible.

.05 Tax Treatment and Tax Strategies

Mutual funds pass through their income, less expenses, to shareholders in the form in which it is received by the fund, that is, as ordinary income, capital gains, or tax-exempt income.

.06 Determination of Basis

Keeping track of basis can be difficult where fund shares are purchased over a long period and/or where dividends or capital gain distributions are used to purchase shares. However, under Reg. § 1.1012-1(e)(1), a taxpayer may elect to have basis determined by the use of one of two averaging methods if the shares: (1) are left in the custody of a custodian or agent in an account maintained for the acquisition or redemption of shares of the fund, and (2) were acquired at different prices or bases.

The two averaging methods are the double-category and single-category methods. Under the former, at the time of each sale, shares are divided into two categories: (1) those held more than one year, and (2) those held one year or less. The basis of a share in either category is the total basis of all shares in the category divided by the total number of shares in that category. The seller may specify to the custodian or agent from which category the shares are to be sold.

Under the single-category method, all shares are considered as a single category regardless of when acquired. The average basis of each share is the total basis of all shares in the account divided by the number of shares in the account. The shares sold are considered to be those shares first acquired.

Once chosen, a method may not be changed without IRS consent. Where neither of the averaging methods is used, basis is determined under the rules applicable for determining the basis of stock.

¶ 3145 MONEY MARKET INVESTMENTS AND STRATEGIES

A large percentage of America's savings is in money market instruments. These instruments include money market funds, unit investment trusts, money market annuities, and bank money market accounts. Bank certificates of deposit (CDs), broker CDs, and equity CDs can also be viewed as money market instruments along with Treasury bills (T-bills). The latter are discussed at ¶ 3135.

Money market instruments are suitable for investors seeking a high degree of liquidity, safety, better yields compared to with traditional passbook savings accounts, and no loss of principal (or gain) as a result of changes in interest rates. Specific features of the different instruments are considered in connection with the separate discussions of the various instruments.

Money market funds are mutual funds that invest in money market instruments of the kind indicated, along with commercial paper and repurchase agreements.

Unit investment trusts invest primarily in CDs and can be viewed as six-month money market funds. However, unit investment trusts do not have the checking privileges and other conveniences offered by money market funds. The rate of return is fixed. They usually are more aggressive than money market funds in their investments. Their CDs might include Eurodollar CDs, deposits of foreign banks in New York, and deposits in foreign banks. A slightly higher risk is involved in dealing with overseas funds, but most professionals discount it. Yields are likely to be higher than for bank CDs. The minimum investment is usually $1,000. Also, the amount invested can be withdrawn during the first four months, and some trusts may permit withdrawal during the last two months.

Interest rates vary almost daily, and money market instruments reflect these changes sooner or later. The investor must undertake to obtain the best return on his or her money whether interest rates go up or down.

.01 Strategies

In moving in and out of the money market and from one money market investment vehicle to another, the investor must be concerned about *safety*, *liquidity*, and *yield*.

Safety can be found in three ways, with some qualifications:

1. FDIC or similar government insurance, currently $100,000 per account. Within the same bank, all of a customer's different deposits are added together and insured in the aggregate for $100,000, although separate categories of accounts (e.g. single accounts, joint accounts, and self directed retirement accounts may be eligible for separate insurance coverage limits. Self-directed retirement accounts are currently insares for up to $250,000.
2. A diversified, professionally managed portfolio in a highly regulated industry. The investor can achieve further diversification by dividing his or her investments among different vehicles of the same class and different classes of vehicles.
3. The guarantee of a bank or other major financial institution.

Money funds and unit investment trusts provide liquidity. Bank-offered, long-term deposits of six months or more are generally lacking in liquidity. Some banks have permitted loans to be made against the deposit, with loss of interest on the amount withdrawn plus an added point or more of interest. Broker-offered bank CDs offer a secondary market that will provide liquidity before maturity of the underlying CD.

.02 Tax Factors

If T-bills are held by a money market fund, unit investment trust, or bank, the exemption from state and local income tax might not be passed through to the holders of interests in the fund, trust, or CD. The investor should check with the fund or trust on this account. If the fund is organized as a limited partnership, then the exemption from state and local taxes is passed through to the investor as a limited partner. In such situations, the investor will receive a Form K-1,"Partner's Share of Income, Credit, Deductions, Etc.," from the fund, which will show the exempt nature of the income on the form.

Some CDs do not pay accumulated interest until the certificate matures. In this respect, they are different from money market funds. Thus, in some situations, a certificate can provide a means of deferring tax. For example, if a calendar year taxpayer buys such a 26-week certificate in July, the interest earned will be includible in gross income for the following year.

Another factor to consider in connection with bank CDs is that the investor might incur penalties for early withdrawal of funds. The penalty for premature withdrawal is an allowable deduction from gross income in arriving at the depositor's adjusted gross income, i.e., it is deductible up front without itemizing.[135]

¶3150 GINNIE MAES, FANNIE MAES, AND FREDDIE MACS

The Government National Mortgage Association (GNMA or "Ginnie Mae"), Federal National Mortgage Association (FNMA or "Fannie Mae") and the Federal Home Loan Mortgage Corporation (FHLMC or "Freddie Mac") are three entities that pass through mortgage interest and principal on a pool of home mortgages to investors on a monthly basis. Investments in these mortgage pools might provide the investor with current yields that exceed the yield on money market funds with a high degree of safety of principal. Interest on Ginnie Maes, Fannie Maes, and Freddie Macs is subject to federal, state, and local income tax.

The securities offered by each of these entities have slightly different features. Ginnie Mae insures payment of principal and income from FHA and VA mortgages of the same coupon and maturity that are assembled by a mortgage banker who deposits them with a bank custodian. Ginnie Mae does not formally act as issuer of these securities. However, Ginnie Mae is an agency of the U.S. government and its guarantee is backed by the full faith and credit clause, as are U.S. Treasury bonds. Interest and principal are paid monthly to certificate holders on a modified passthrough basis. Thus, the interest and principal are passed through regardless of whether they have been collected on time. The modified passthrough is to be distinguished from a straight pass through, under which payments are passed through only as collected.

Although the original life of the mortgages in the pool might be 25 or 30 years, the average life of the pool of mortgages will be closer to 10 to 12 years. This reduction in the average life of the pool is due to prepayments as a result of sales, refinancing, and other factors inducing prepayment.

The minimum purchase requirement on these securities is $25,000 (see mutual funds and unit trusts permitting much smaller investments, below), with $1 increments above this amount.

---

[135] Code Sec. 62(a)(9).

The characteristics of Fannie Mae and Freddie Mac securities are quite similar to those of Ginnie Mae, with certain important differences. Unlike Ginnie Mae, these two entities actually issue mortgage-backed securities. Fannie Mae securities are not backed by a full faith and credit guarantee of the U.S. government. Rather, Freddie Mac is a semi-private corporation for which such an airtight guarantee is unavailable. These entities also have differing policies on pass-through. Fannie Mae, like Ginnie Mae, guarantees a modified pass-through. However, Freddie Mac will guarantee timely payment of interest only. It guarantees that principal will be repaid, but the repayment of principal can be up to a year late.

.01 Comparative Characteristics

The different characteristics of these three entities can yield somewhat different market results. The financial planner should consider the following:

- Ginnie Maes are safer than Fannie Maes or Freddie Macs because they offer a U.S. government guarantee of the timely payment of interest and principal.
- The cost of Ginnie Mae safety is that Fannie Mae and Freddie Mac securities cost slightly less for a comparable issue (translating into a higher yield).
- Ginnie Maes constitute the largest market for mortgage-backed securities and are more widely owned by individuals and mutual funds; securities of the other entities are not. This factor might result in greater liquidity (and higher price) for Ginnie Mae securities if the investor wishes to sell them before maturity.
- Notwithstanding the above factors, many comparable securities of these entities are trading very close in price. The yields of U.S. Treasury notes and bonds should be compared to these mortgage-backed securities.

.02 Advantages of Mortgage-Backed Securities

Taken collectively, Ginnie Maes, Fannie Maes, and Freddie Macs offer several advantages:

- Liquidity (especially in the case of Ginnie Maes and holdings in Ginnie Mae mutual funds) is attractive, particularly when compared to single issues of municipal bonds.
- Even Fannie Mae and Freddie Mac issues, which are not backed by a U.S. government guarantee, are safer than other high-yielding securities, such as corporate debt, preferred stock, and municipal bonds.

- Individual investors can participate in relatively high-yielding mortgage-backed investments without the administrative burden and legal expenses attending conventional mortgage-backed investments.
- Because part of the principal is returned with each monthly interest payment, these securities may have special utility in providing income for those who are retired.

.03 Disadvantages

The following are the possible disadvantages to be weighed:

- Substantial portions of the pooled mortgages may be prepaid. A sharp fall in interest rates from the rate at which the mortgage was written is almost certain to result in large-scale prepayments. While prepayments might be good news for an investor who bought securities at a discount (see above), the investor who bought at par or at a premium will face these possible results:
- He or she might not receive the yield anticipated, even though he or she might have anticipated an average maturity of 10 to 12 years;
- If he or she paid a premium for the high-interest rate initially in effect, prepayment of a mortgage will result in a partial loss of the investment.
- If interest rates go up, an investor's sale of his or her investment before maturity will result in a partial loss of his or her investment.
- If inflation continues, as it almost certainly will at some level, interest and principal payments will be made in dollars worth less in terms of purchasing power than the dollars invested.
- The investor must realize that these securities are not bonds, although their sensitivity to interest rates makes them act similar to bonds. Individual investors might misunderstand that the initial yield is not guaranteed, that these securities can easily be sold at a loss, and that interest charges and prepayments can turn what began as a desirable investment into an undesirable one. Before investing, the prospective buyer must consider whether the initial yield advantage that mortgage-backed securities offer over U.S. Treasury notes or bonds (for example) is worth the risk that such yields might not be payable in the future. The individual buyer should also realize that he or she will be investing in a market dominated by large financial institutions.

Some of the adverse factors listed above are not unique to mortgage-backed securities but will affect almost any type of fixed-debt obligation, although not necessarily in the same way. Mortgage interest rates might change more rapidly than the rate on corporate debentures, for example. In a period of rising interest rates, mortgage interest rates might rise faster than those on conventional fixed-debt securities. Thus, on a sale of a mortgage-backed security certificate, the investor might realize a larger capital loss.

.04 Hedging Against the Prepayment Risk

The investor can hedge against the prepayment risk and/or a drop in yield of the Ginnie Mae (GM) by simultaneously purchasing long-term zero-coupon Treasury bonds.

.05 Mutual Funds

Some Ginnie Mae and Freddie Mac mutual funds allow initial investments of as little as $1,000. The mutual funds represent shares in an ever-changing pool of Ginnie Mae mortgage certificates. The investor should learn what sales charge and other fees that the fund charges.

The character of the pools in these mutual funds changes. Thus, an investor will probably have more difficulty predicting prepayment in the case of mutual funds than in the case of the unit trusts discussed below. However, the fund's investment goals can provide some clue as to prepayments. A fund that invests in high interest rates is likely to experience a high rate of prepayments as interest rates decline and refinancing becomes feasible.

.06 Unit Trusts

Unit trusts give the investor participation in a fixed pool of mortgages. The initial investment in these trusts may be as low as $1,000. Some include a check writing privilege. The investor should ask what fees and charges he or she will incur for investing in these trusts.

The investor might be offered two types of trusts: (1) a trust with a relatively high interest rate and selling at a premium; and (2) a discount trust.

The former, while providing a higher interest rate, involves a higher risk of prepayment. The latter provides a lower interest rate with capital gain potential if held until maturity.

In choosing between the two, the investor must take into account his or her objectives and tax posture after examining the goals and portfolios of the trusts involved.

¶3155 COMMODITIES FUTURES FUNDS

Commodities futures funds offer investors the potential to realize substantial profits through leverage but without the unlimited risk that direct trading in commodities futures involves. The investor's risk is limited to the initial investment with the funds, which also offer diversity. However, these funds incur substantial indirect costs that are passed on to investors.

- **Registration.** Public funds can incur legal, accounting, and printing costs of up to $500,000 in registering with the Securities and Exchange Commission and the Commodity Futures Trading Commission. Because these costs are charged against the fund's equity, the value of an investor's unit in the fund can decline even before the first trade is executed.
- **Trading advisor fees.** Trading advisors typically are paid an annual fee of four percent of the fund's equity, plus a percentage of profits. By way of comparison, fees paid to managers of mutual funds range from 0.5 to 0.75 percent of the fund's equity.
- **Commissions.** The high volume trading triggered by the limited life of futures contracts and the volatile nature of the market generates substantial commissions that can cost from 10 to 35 percent of the average annual equity in the fund.

These indirect costs will no doubt bear on a decision of whether to invest in a commodities futures fund. A particular fund's track record will be an even more important consideration.

¶3160 ORIGINAL ISSUE DISCOUNT AND ZERO COUPON BONDS

Bonds issued at a price lower than the redemption price are original issue discount bonds. The investor's return consists of periodic interest paid on the bond, plus the spread between the issue price and the redemption price.

Some original issue discount bonds do not provide for the payment of periodic interest. In effect, the issuer borrows both the principal and the interest for the term of the bond. These bonds are known as zero coupon bonds.

Code Sec. 1272 provides a method of amortizing original discount in a way that parallels the manner in which interest accrues through borrowing with interest-bearing, nondiscount bonds. The computation begins with a determination of the yield to maturity of the discount obligation using annual compounding. The yield so determined is then applied to the value of the obligation at the date of issuance and at the end of each one-year period ending with the anniversary of the date of issue. The computed value of the obligation will increase each year by the portion of the yield due to original discount, but not by any portion attributable to a coupon payment.

Any excess of a subsequent purchaser's cost over the adjusted issue price is amortized over the remaining maturity period of the bond on a straight-line basis and reduces OID income.

The rules apply not only to corporate bonds but also to bonds issued by any government or political subdivision, except short-term government bonds or U.S. savings bonds. Bonds issued by individuals and tax-exempt bonds are not subject to the rules.[136]

.01 Investment Feature of Zero Coupon Bonds

A key investment feature of zero coupon bonds is that they provide the investor with the assurance of a set yield throughout the term. The lock-in feature is desirable if interest rates decline, is of no special value if interest remains the same, and has negative value if rates increase. However, another form of investment risk with zero coupon bonds is the risk of default at maturity, which is discussed below.

.02 Risk of Default at Maturity

All bonds, coupon bonds issued at par, coupon bonds issued at a discount, and zero coupon bonds involve some risk of default at maturity. With coupon bonds issued at a discount, the risk is somewhat greater than with coupon bonds issued at par. With coupon bonds issued at par, the holder prior to maturity will be receiving the stipulated coupon interest, which he or she will also receive with OID bonds, although most likely at a lesser rate. He or she might also have imputed interest included in his or her gross income, unless the holder is tax-exempt or not taxable. Any resulting tax on the interest will further reduce yield. With zero coupon bonds, the holder's loss on default at maturity will necessarily be even greater because he or she will not have received any interest before maturity. Zero coupon insured certificates of deposit, discussed below, are designed to provide FDIC insurance against default. Also, the mock zero coupon bonds developed with stripped long-term Treasury bonds, are calculated to provide a U.S. Treasury guarantee against default.

---

[136] Code Sec. 1272(a)(2).

.03 Zero Coupon Insured CDs

Bank certificates of deposit have the same advantages and disadvantages as other zero coupon debt obligations. If the bank is a member of the FDIC, depositors have government insurance up to the regular $100,000 ceiling ($250,000 for self-directed retirement accounts) per account to assure payment of principal at maturity (a financial planner should watch for possible changes in FDIC coverage). Banks are not permitted to repurchase their own certificates under a Federal Reserve Board regulation. Hence, the investor should consider the possibility of disposing of the certificates before maturity, if circumstances arise that require early disposition.

Some certificates that have been issued are nonnegotiable. Such certificates would lock the investor in until maturity, which might not prove to be too great a burden if maturity is relatively soon. Other certificates are negotiable. However, without a secondary market, they might be difficult to dispose of before maturity except at sacrifice prices. A brokerage house offering these certificates might make a secondary market and agree to buy them back at the market price prevailing at the time of repurchase. This factor should be considered by the prospective investor.

> **Planning pointer.** Zero coupon bonds are useful as a means of locking in good interest rates prevailing at the time of purchase and avoiding the reinvestment risk involved with coupon bonds.

The usefulness of zero coupon bonds is limited to three principal categories:

1. **Tax-sheltered accounts.** Zero coupon bonds can produce high yields in qualified retirement plans in which the participant may direct investments, or in participant-directed investments in Keogh plans, individual retirement accounts (IRAs), tax-sheltered annuities, and other tax-deferred retirement plans.
2. **Minors and low-bracket taxpayers.** Zero coupon bonds can also be useful in providing funds for a minor or other person likely to be taxed at a low rate on the imputed interest, if taxed at all. However, investors should remember that the kiddie tax, causes the unearned income in excess of $1,700 for 2006 of a minor under the age of 18 to be taxed at the higher of the child's rate or the parents' rate.[137]

---

[137] Code Sec. 1(g).

3. **Tax-exempt zero coupon bonds.** Such bonds can be useful for avoiding tax by persons in top tax brackets and for avoiding tax at the parents' rate by a minor under the age of 14 (¶ 3205).

When taxable zero coupon bonds are owned by persons who are subject to tax, such persons should consider the fact that even higher amounts of interest will be imputed as the security nears maturity. If the security is negotiable, a transfer at a point when the imputed interest becomes burdensome to a trust for a number of low-income family members might be considered as a means of splitting the imputed income among separate taxpayers. The value for gift tax purposes necessarily would take into account the tax burden that the security carries as it reaches maturity. The tax burden would also be considered in fixing a sale price if the security were to be sold.

The fundamental problem with corporate zero coupon bonds, especially those of the long-term variety, remains the possibility of default in payment at maturity. Also, STRIPS (Separate Trading at Registered Interest and Principal Securities) might prove attractive because they are direct obligations of the U.S. government and are backed by its full faith and credit. The Treasury does not issue STRIPS. The Treasury allows holders of Treasury notes and bonds to separate them into their interest and principal components. STRIPS can be held and traded in the commercial book-entry system. Holders may also reconstitute the separate interest and principal components into whole notes or bonds.

The demand for long-term Treasury zero coupon bonds has stemmed from their ability to lock in interest yields by avoiding reinvestment risk if interest rates fall. This feature is a plus when yields are high but not when interest rates are low and are expected to increase.

As sales commissions charged on zero coupon bonds appear to be considerably higher than those charged on conventional Treasury obligations, the prospective investor might wish to weigh commission costs in determining whether to buy zero coupon bonds. The STRIPS zero coupon bond program (¶ 3165) could provide a low-cost means for buying zero coupon bonds.

One may wish to reverse conventional wisdom about zero coupon bonds and buy zero coupon bonds with relatively short maturities (where yields exceed conventional Treasury bonds) and to invest in conventional Treasury bonds for the long term. The latter securities also have a better established secondary market and appear to suffer less if interest rates rise than do zero coupon bonds.

¶3165 STRIPPING COUPON INTEREST FROM BONDS

The seller who strips coupons and then disposes of either the bond or the coupons must allocate basis to each in proportion to their relative fair market values at the time of sale. This basis allocation eliminates any artificial tax loss.

Further, any unreported interest accrued on the coupons before the disposition of either the bond or the coupons must be included in the seller's gross income and added to the basis allocated between the bond and the coupons.

The items not disposed of (the coupons, for instance) are to be treated as original issue discount bonds; they are subject to the OID rules discussed at ¶3160.

The purchaser of either the bond or the coupons must treat them as bonds issued at a discount and subject to the OID rules discussed at ¶3160. The result is that the purchaser must include the amount of OID in gross income over the remaining term of the bond, instead of being able to defer recognition of income until maturity or earlier disposition.

In the face of these rules, one might be disposed to pronounce coupon stripping dead. Such a pronouncement might be premature. Despite the rules, some leading brokerage houses have bought large amounts of long-term Treasury bonds, placed them in the hands of a custodian, and developed mock zero-coupon bond issues and separate issues of the stripped coupons. The use of a custodian is designed to avoid the difficulty that would exist if a brokerage house guaranteed that they would pay through all the funds. The use of Treasury bonds, instead of corporate bonds, is designed to guarantee payoff unless the government defaults.

Purchasers of these issues have been primarily tax-exempt trusts. They have purchased them with the idea of locking in higher returns. This strategy is ordinarily useful only when returns are higher at the time of purchase than at projected future rates.

Despite the fact that individual purchasers must pay taxes on the imputed interest that they do not receive, some individuals have invested in the bonds as a convenient way of receiving a lump-sum amount to make future balloon payments on mortgages. Another reason would be to build an educational fund for children.

These issues are sold with varying maturities with a view to meeting the particular needs of the investor. The principal problems in connection with these issues are likely to be overpricing and the absence of a secondary market.

.01 Tax-Exempt Bonds

The original issue discount (OID) inclusion rules do not apply to tax-exempt stripped bonds. Nevertheless, a seller of a tax-exempt stripped bond or coupons detached from the bond must allocate the basis of the bond with coupons attached between the items retained and the items disposed of.[138] Thus, as in the case of taxable obligations, the seller of a stripped tax-exempt obligation may not create an artificial loss because he or she must allocate basis to the retained coupons. In addition, if the taxpayer sells tax-exempt coupons separately, he or she might realize taxable gain on the sale or redemption of the retained stripped bond attributable to allocation of a portion of the seller's basis to the detached coupons.

For purchases or sales of stripped tax-exempt obligations or stripped coupons (subject to exceptions discussed below), a portion of the OID must be treated as if it comes from a tax-exempt obligation, while OID in excess of tax-exempt OID is treated as if it comes from an obligation that is not exempt from taxation.[139] The tax-exempt portion of the OID is the excess of a tax-exempt obligation's stated redemption price at maturity (or the amount payable on a coupon's due date) over an issue price that would produce a yield to maturity on the purchase date of a stripped bond or stripped coupon, equal to the lower of (1) the coupon rate of interest on the tax-exempt obligation from which the coupons were stripped, or (2) the actual yield to maturity (on the basis of the purchase price) of the stripped coupon or bond.[140] Instead of using the coupon rate in alternative (1), a purchaser may elect to use the original yield to maturity of the tax-exempt obligations.

.02 Gain on Disposition of Market Discount Bonds

Because of interest rate increases occurring after their issuance, bonds often sell below par value, but Congress considers market discounts on bond prices to be indistinguishable from original issue discount.

Code Sec. 1276 generally requires that gain on disposition be taxed as ordinary income to the extent of its accrued market discount, as defined in Code Sec. 1278(a)(2). Instead of recognizing income on disposition, the investor may elect to treat income as accruing annually during the life of the bond. Under Code Sec. 1278(b)(4), the taxpayer's basis in the bond is increased by the amount includible in gross income by virtue of the election.

---

[138] Code Sec. 1286(d)(1)(C).

[139] Code Sec. 1286(d)(1).

[140] Code Sec. 1286(d)(2).

Code Sec. 1277 contains complicated provisions limiting an investor's ability to take current income tax deductions for interest on debt incurred to purchase or carry a market discount bond. Any excess deductions are carried forward until the year of disposition of the bond.

The term "market discount bond" does not apply to short-term obligations (with maturities of less than one year), tax-exempt bonds purchased before May 1, 1993, U.S. savings bonds, installment obligations, or taxable bonds issued on or before July 8, 1984, and purchased before May 1, 1993.

¶ 3170 OPTIONS AS A GAINS HEDGE

An investor can use options to protect gains in stock already owned: (1) buy put options (the right to sell at a given price), and (2) sell call options (the right to buy at a given price). The examples that follow assume that the investor owns a corresponding amount of appreciated stock covered by the respective put or call and that the investor is not simply trading in the options themselves (referred to in options parlance as "naked trading"). The examples also assume that the stock held by the investor is publicly traded. In addition, for purposes of the examples that follow, the transaction costs of purchasing puts and selling calls are not taken into account (although investors should keep in mind that such costs are considerably greater than regular investment brokerage commissions).

.01 Buying Puts and Selling Calls

Buying puts and selling calls offer different kinds of protection against a decline in value of the appreciated security held by the investor. The two methods are also subject to different income tax rules.

Example 31.4. Carla Nelson is an investor who owns 100 shares of stock with a basis of $30 and a current market price of $70. She fears a decline in price, but does not want to sell. She buys a put option on the stock at $70, which is to last for six months. The price (or premium) for the put is $7 per share. By using a put option, Nelson gains the right to sell the stock at any time during the next six months at a price of $70. What Nelson has purchased is a kind of insurance policy for her gain, illustrated as follows:

Stock Basis	$3,000
Plus: Unrealized Appreciation	4,000
Value of Investment	$7,000

Minus: Cost of Put	$ 700
	$6,300
Minus: Stock Basis	3,000
PROTECTED GAIN	$3,300

If the price of the underlying stock declines during the six-month period, the decline will be protected, or hedged, by the put option, which gives Nelson the right to sell at $70 during this period. On the other hand, if the price for the underlying stock increases, Nelson will benefit fully from such increase and her only cost is the premium for the put. However, if the price of the stock does not fluctuate significantly during the six-month period, the option will expire and she will lose the entire investment in the put. Nevertheless, Nelson will have purchased almost complete protection against market decline during the finite period of the option.

The investor can obtain cash on the sale (or "writing," in options jargon) of a call option. Unlike the put buyer, the seller of call options receives a premium, because he or she is taking the risk of having to deliver stock to the buyer at a price above the market price sometime in the future. Selling a call option offers significantly less protection than that available to the put holder.

Example 31.5. To illustrate the effect of selling a call, the same stock basis and unrealized capital gain will be used as in the previous example, but a premium of $7 to Nelson, the call seller, will be assumed. The effects of both slight and significant market declines will then be illustrated.

I. *Decline of $3 in stock value during option period, with option held until expiration date:*

Stock Basis	$3,000
Plus: Unrealized Appreciation	4,000
Value of Investment	$7,000
Plus: Call Premium	$ 700
	$7,700
Decrease of Stock	300
Net Value of investment	$7,400

Accordingly, the sale of a call option under these circumstances does more than protect the unrealized capital gain on the stock. It actually results in a profit on the options transaction of $400.

II. *Decline of $20 in stock value during option period, with option held until expiration date:*

Stock Basis	$3,000
Plus: Unrealized Appreciation	4,000
Value of Investment	$7,000
Plus: Call Premium	$ 700
	$7,700
Decrease of Stock	2,000
Net Value of investment	$5,700

Where a stock significantly declines in value, the sale of a call option only protects the unrealized gain to the extent of the premium received by the investor ($700). Beyond that, the call seller, unlike the put buyer, is exposed to market risk. Here, $1,300 of price decline remains unprotected. Further, if the price of the stock rises, the call seller will not benefit, because the buyer will demand the underlying stock at the exercise price. This case can be contrasted with the situation of the put buyer, who receives no premium up front but who does stand to gain if the price of the stock increases beyond the price of the put.

The decision as to whether to buy puts or sell calls depends on such factors as the size of the premium to be received from the sale of a call, the relative risk involved, the level of pessimism of the investor, and the degree to which the investor wants to protect an unrealized capital gain.

.02 Stock Index Options and Index Futures

The investor in publicly traded stock faces two key risks: (1) company risk, and (2) market risk. The first category relates to the fortunes or misfortunes of the particular company. This risk is known as alpha risk or nonsystematic risk. The second recognizes that, no matter how well the particular company may perform, if the stock market as a whole shows a downtrend, it may carry the particular stock with it. This risk is known as beta risk or systematic risk.

A put option on a particular stock will protect the investor against both types of risk. If the investor holds a diversified portfolio of securities, the purchase of individual put options on each security might be too costly or cumbersome. The investor might feel that the principal risk is market risk rather than the risk attending the particular securities. In that case, the investor should consider an index option as a means of protecting against market risk.

Index options give the holder the option to buy or sell a specified value of an index by a specified time. Index futures contracts are also available. These futures contracts *obligate* the holder to buy or sell. An index future is subject to margin calls and theoretically has an unlimited risk, although as a practical matter the downside risk and upward movement of the index is limited.

The risk of a purchaser of an index option or an option on index futures is limited to the price of the option. Because of the high risk factors associated with futures, the primary focus of the discussion that follows is on index options.

Index options. Index options are traded in much the same manner as regular stock options, except that the settlement is in cash, rather than stock. In addition, the settlement is based on the difference between the exercise or strike price of the option and the index value at the close on the day of exercise, multiplied by a specified multiplier. Different indices are calculated in different ways.

> ***Example 31.6.*** John East holds a put option on a particular index exercisable at $80. If he exercises the option when the index drops to $75 and the particular index uses a multiplier of 100, he would be entitled to receive $500 [($80 – $75) × 100] in cash.

The amount received on settlement is not all profit. The cost of the option must be taken into account. The cost basically depends on the strike price and the period for which the option is good. The strike price might be above the current index value (in the money), at current value (at the money) or below current value (out of the money). With a put option, the higher the strike price in relation to current value, the higher the price of the option. With a call option, the higher the strike price in relation to current value, the lower the price of the option.

Options on index futures. Options on index futures are similar to index options in that they offer limited risk. However, unlike index options, options on index futures are not settled in cash. Rather, settlement involves transfer of the underlying futures contracts themselves. After settlement, the investor has the option of retaining the position acquired, with the risks and profit opportunities associated with it, or liquidating the position by making an offsetting transaction.

As with exercises of index options, exercises of options on index futures involve loss of whatever remaining time value the option might have. Thus, a sale is usually preferable. A sale also offers the opportunity to cash out immediately.

¶3175 JUNK BONDS

Junk bonds are high-yield corporate bonds with lower than investment grade ratings from Moody's or Standard & Poor's. The low ratings of junk bonds are often the product of unfavorable conditions at the issuing company, high debt/equity ratios, and other factors that tend to downgrade conventional estimates of their safety. In the case of the new junk bonds, the issuing corporation is forced to offer a higher rate of interest than would be necessary if the bonds enjoyed a higher rating. A company might use junk bonds to finance a leveraged buy-out.

If the rating services are correct, the purchase of junk bonds involves added risk for the investor over standard, high-grade corporate bonds. Proponents of these bonds, however, argue that the higher interest rate is ample recompense for the added risk.

Double-digit returns advertised for junk bond funds might attract much attention in an otherwise single-digit market. However, the advertised yields can be misleading in that junk bond funds typically carry higher load charges and/or redemption fees than other funds.

The funds are composed of bonds rated below triple B or unrated bonds. The low rating reflects the risk of default. Because the funds diversify, the risk might be reduced.

Not all junk bonds are the same, and the composition of the fund should be scrutinized. Corporate junk bonds issued by relatively new companies whose track records are untested could be reasonable risks. On the other hand, municipal junk bonds might be backed by a declining public sovereignty and could be a poor risk. However, unrated municipal bonds might be issued by small but sound governments and could be a good risk.

¶3180 REAL ESTATE INVESTING

In the past, real estate investments have had four key components of special potential benefit: leverage, cash flow, tax savings, and appreciation. The combination made real estate investments more attractive than most other investments. An investor could buy real estate with a down payment ranging from 10 to 25 percent of its price and have tax losses stemming from depreciation in amounts equal to 40 percent of the purchase price over the first five years. The real estate investment would produce high after-tax benefits for those in high income tax brackets.

Moreover, investors were often bailed out of poor investments by inflation that pushed up rents which, in turn, pushed up prices.

Investors and promoters made money quite handsomely. However, prices rose to artificial heights. In the rush to invest in real estate, investors often lost sight of economic reality. Buildings were constructed for tax reasons with little regard for demand. Willing lenders, eager developers, and tax-burdened investor/buyers combined to create a vast oversupply in many real estate markets. Banks contributed in no small way to the oversupply. Construction loans carry higher interest rates than permanent financing; deregulation and other factors boosted deposits; competition boosted rates on deposits, ergo an increased reliance on construction loans to support deposits.

.01 The Current Tax Picture

Depreciation. The 19-year accelerated depreciation in place before the Tax Reform Act of 1986 was replaced by 31.5-year (commercial property) and 27.5-year (residential) straight-line depreciation. RRA '93 increased the recovery period for nonresidential real property to 39 years, effective generally for property placed in service on or after May 13, 1993.

Dividends and Capital gains. Dividends and net capital gain are subject to a maximum tax of 15 percent through 2010.[141] On the other hand, the top ordinary income tax rate is 35 percent through 2010.

Leverage—at risk rules. The at risk rules apply to real estate,[142] with an exception for qualified nonrecourse financing by nonaffiliated lending institutions.[143]

Passive activity rules generally. Deductions from passive activities, to the extent that they exceed income from all such activities (exclusive of portfolio income, i.e., generally interest, dividends and royalties), usually may not be deducted against other income of the taxpayer.[144] Passive activities are defined to include trade or business activities in which the taxpayer does not materially participate[145] (e.g., a limited partnership interest in an activity) and rental activities.[146] In the case of rental real estate in which an individual actively participates, up to $25,000 of losses from all such activities may be taken each year against nonpassive income of the taxpayer.[147] This amount is, however, phased out ratably between $100,000 and $150,000 of adjusted gross income (AGI)

---

[141] Code Sec. 1(h)(1)(C).

[142] Code Sec. 465.

[143] Code Sec. 465(b)(6).

[144] Code Sec. 469(a)(1).

[145] Code Sec. 469(c)(1).

[146] Code Sec. 469(c)(2).

[147] Code Sec. 469(i).

(determined without regard to passive losses).[148] Suspended losses may be carried forward.[149]

Application of the $25,000 allowance is tricky. The $25,000 allowance is applied by first netting income and loss from all of the taxpayer's rental real estate activities in which he or she actively participates. If the taxpayer has a net loss for the year from such activities, net passive income (if any) from other activities is then applied against it in determining the amount eligible for the $25,000 allowance.[150]

For example, assume that a taxpayer has $25,000 of losses from a rental real estate activity in which he or she actively participates. If the taxpayer also actively participates in another rental real estate activity, from which he or she has $25,000 of gain, resulting in no net loss from rental real estate activities in which he or she actively participates, then no amount is allowed under the $25,000 allowance for the year. This result follows whether or not the taxpayer has net losses from other passive activities for the year.

Credits from passive activities. Credits from passive activities are generally limited to the tax allocable to the passive activities.[151] Suspended credits may be carried forward.[152]

Rehabilitation[153] and low-income housing credits[154] (but not losses from such activities except to the extent indicated above) may be used to offset tax on up to $25,000 of nonpassive income regardless of whether the taxpayer actively participates, subject to a phaseout between $200,000 and $250,000 of AGI.

Real estate professionals get relief from PAL rules. Taxpayers who are real estate professionals may treat losses from real estate activities in which they materially participate as nonpassive losses.[155] This relief applies for a tax year only if the taxpayer is a real estate professional who materially participates in the real estate activity that generates the passive activity loss (PAL).

A taxpayer is a "real estate professional" only if the taxpayer performs more than half of his or her trade-or-business personal services and spends more than 750 hours a year in real property trades or businesses in which the taxpayer materially participates.[156] Real property trades or businesses are broadly defined to include "any real property development, redevelopment, construction, reconstruction, acquisition, conversion, rental, operation, management, leasing, or brokerage trade or business."[157]

---

148 Code Sec. 469(i)(3).
149 Code Sec. 469(b).
150 Code Sec. 469(i)(1).
151 Code Sec. 469(d)(2).
152 Code Sec. 469(b).
153 Code Sec. 469(i)(3)(B).
154 Code Sec. 469(i)(3)(C).
155 Code Sec. 469(c)(7)(A).
156 Code Sec. 469(c)(7)(B).
157 Code Sec. 469(c)(7)(C).

Suspended passive activity losses (PALs) from a rental real property activity treated as nonpassive losses because of the relief provision are treated as losses from a former passive activity.[158] Suspended losses (from prior periods when the activity was treated as passive) can only offset income from the activity (no longer treated as passive due to the taxpayer's material participation). However, such suspended losses cannot offset other income. When the taxpayer disposes of his or her interest in the activity in a fully taxable transaction with an unrelated party, any remaining suspended PALs allocable to the activity from the time it was considered passive would be allowed in full.[159]

Limitation on investment interest. Investment interest is deductible only to the extent of net investment income.[160]

Rehabilitation credits. The law allows a 10-percent tax credit for rehabilitation expenditures of nonresidential buildings (other than certified historic structures) built before 1936 and a 20-percent tax credit for certified historic structures.[161] A taxpayer may use this credit to offset tax on any type of income, subject to a phaseout, as discussed above under credits from passive activities.

Low-income housing credit. The low-income housing credit[162] offers taxpayers one of the few true tax shelter investment opportunities available today. The credit is claimed over 10 years.

The credit is especially generous for high-income investors. Although tax credits and losses from low-income rental real estate are subject to the passive activity restrictions, the credit can offset tax each year on up to $25,000 of nonpassive income, such as wages, self-employment income, interest, or dividends. High-income investors generally do not qualify for this break for losses from most other rental real estate activities, for two reasons:

1. The $25,000 maximum allowance generally phases out between adjusted gross income of $100,000 and $150,000.[163] However, it is fully available for credits from qualified low-income housing investments, with no phaseout.[164]
2. The $25,000 exception to the passive-loss rules for most rental real estate losses and credits is available only to investors who actively participate in the management of the property.[165] However, low-income housing investors

[158] Reg. § 1.469-9(e)(2) and Code Sec. 469(f).
[159] Code Sec. 469(g)(1).
[160] Code Sec. 163(d)(1).
[161] Code Sec. 47(a).
[162] Code Sec. 42.
[163] Code Sec. 469(i)(3)(A).
[164] Code Sec. 469(i)(3)(C).
[165] Code Sec. 469(i)(1).

qualify for the exception even if they are totally uninvolved passive investors, such as limited partners.

Although the tax benefits of the low-income housing credit can be excellent, investors should also consider other factors. These investments generally are unsuitable for low-net-worth individuals who need current income from their investments. The return is generally provided by a combination of leverage and current tax advantages. Depending upon the kind of development, upon how well it is managed, and upon the long-term health of the real estate market, low-income housing investments might or might not also return a Code Sec. 1231 gain or long-term capital gain when later sold.

.02 Real Estate: Demand Will Remain

The demand for real estate is here to stay. However, real estate in some parts of the United States has increased in value so greatly that many analysts are warning of a potential collapse of the real estate market in those areas. Financial planners should exercise caution in advising clients about real estate investments in areas that have rapidly appreciated. Real estate remains the prime beneficiary of the law of supply and demand. Even moderate population and industry growth will in the longer term support higher real estate values, which means higher rents and prices. The appreciation potential remains. The United States might never again experience double-digit inflation, but real estate will remain a beneficiary of whatever inflation-induced price increases take place.

.03 Escape from Depreciation Limitations

An investor might consider using a ground lease to obtain rent deductions for land. In effect, the investor receives depreciation deductions for land.

Buyers on an installment basis might seek to reduce the price by offering higher interest. The higher interest would be deductible currently whereas depreciation would be stretched out for years. The seller with a low basis might prefer, however, for the payments to take the form of a Code Sec. 1231 gain or capital gain rather than interest, in order to have the benefit of the maximum capital gains rate (generally 15 percent for long term capital gains through 2010, although a maximum rate of 25 percent applies to gain that is attributable to allowable depreciation)[166] as against a top rate of 35 percent on interest through 2010.

---

[166] Code Sec. 1(h).

.04 Favored Investments

Real estate has an edge over traditional fixed income investments in that it stands to afford some long-term inflation protection by staying abreast of the Consumer Price Index (CPI), if not ahead of it.

The emphasis on income orientation generally means reduced leverage. Higher leverage makes for higher mortgage service and interest charges and reduces income. The unavailability of seller non-recourse financing also makes for reduced leverage. Larger down payments are called for. Still, with a 40-percent down payment, a 50-percent rise in the value of the property gives the investor a 125-percent profit (50/40) (before taxes).

Some promoters offer all-cash deals (no mortgages). They offer higher rates of return (not necessarily counting the investor's loss of use of the cash invested) than leveraged deals but require 100-percent appreciation for the investment to double (before taxes).

Health care facilities. Health care facilities operated as a trade or business can benefit from the ever-increasing demand for such facilities by the graying population. The primary source of income for investors is apt to be the services and care provided, rather than the housing.

Real estate investment trusts (REITs). REITs are not subject to the limitations reducing the tax benefits of limited partnerships. Neither are they subject to the corporate tax provisions or the alternative minimum tax. Moreover, REITs are not apt to be hurt by the longer depreciation schedules because they have generally always used longer schedules. Also, they have never been able to pass through losses. Still, taking into account the bad performance of REITs in the seventies, caution is advised.

¶ 3185 BROKERAGE ACCOUNTS

Investments in securities are generally made through a securities broker. The three basic elements in investing are selection, timing, and execution. The broker might give advice in connection with selection and timing. Full service brokers offer such services, but discount brokers do not. All participate in execution.

The focus of this paragraph is on execution techniques. An understanding of such techniques can help minimize trading costs. The use of discount brokers lowers commission charges. An understanding of the spread between bid and ask prices can also reduce costs. Trading on margin and the broker's holding of securities in street names will also be considered, along with Securities

Investor Protection Corporation (SIPC) protection and claims against brokers.

.01 Discount Brokers v. Full-Service Brokers

Many discount brokers offer savings in commissions over those charged by full-service brokers. The ranks of discount brokers include banks and savings and loans and some very large firms.

The most important difference between discount brokers and full-service brokers, apart from the commissions charged, is that the discount brokers do not offer regular advice or recommendations about investments. Also, they might not offer new issues.

However, they might offer some of the same nonadvisory services that full-service brokers offer. Most, for example, offer every kind of order, free safekeeping of securities, toll-free phone numbers, individual trade confirmations, and monthly statements. Many discount brokers also offer current news on securities, dividend reinvestment, and cash management accounts.

Commissions. The commission savings with discount brokers can be substantial. Commissions vary greatly from broker to broker and depend on the kind of trade. A typical full commission on a sale of 200 shares of a $40 stock might be $144. The commission of a discount broker for the same trade might be less than $10.

How are the discount brokers able to offer such savings? Most of the savings are achieved by eliminating the commissions paid to registered representatives; by utilizing the Internet; by reduction of overhead costs, i.e., eliminating a research department and services most customers do not use; and by high volume to some extent.

Full-service brokers might be willing to reduce commissions on request, based on the volume of trading an individual routinely maintains.

Almost all discount brokers have their own commission structures. Some will increase or reduce commissions depending on an individual's total trading volume, whether an order is placed before a certain time, whether a specified form of order is used, whether a purchase and sale are made on the same day, and whether other variations occur.

The schedules of a number of discount brokers should be obtained and examined from the standpoint of what appears to be best for the particular investor, taking into account his or her trading patterns and volume of trading.

Some discount brokers set their commissions on the basis of the value of the trade, others on the basis of the number of shares, without regard to value, and some use both methods. The share method is better for the investor buying high-priced stocks; the value method favors the individual generally trading in low-priced stocks.

With over-the-counter (OTC) stocks, the charge may be a markup instead of a commission. The markup might not always be disclosed on statements. The investor must inquire and compare the markup with the commission of discount brokers. Some full-service brokers might be able to buy OTC stocks from a broker that makes a market in the particular stock and sells it from inventory. In such a case, the investor might be able to buy the stock at a better price and lower commission with a full-service broker than with a discount broker.

On odd lots or transactions with a value of $2,000 or less, discount brokers, like full-service brokers, might have minimums. In such cases, the investor might not realize any savings with a discount broker.

Price is not the only consideration. An investor may prefer to deal with a large firm, one that is nearby or convenient, with a bank where he or she can combine brokerage with banking, or with a discount broker that offers services that the investor wants or needs.

When not to use discount brokers. The investor who wants or needs regular advice on investments and respects the advice of his or her full-service broker should most likely stay with that firm. Other reasons for staying with a full commission broker with whom the investor is satisfied include the following:

- Low frequency of trading and low value of trades so that savings with a discount broker would not warrant change.
- Trading initiated by a brokerage firm that has done well. (Trades initiated by an investor could be handled through a discount broker if savings would be significant.)
- The convenience of handling all transactions through a regular broker. Convenience is worth more than the savings with a discount broker for some transactions.

.02 Trading on Margin

Borrowing through a margin account to purchase securities obviously permits the purchase of a larger block of stock than would otherwise be possible. Thus, buying on margin magnifies potential gains and losses.

Margin accounts require an initial margin and a maintenance margin. The initial margin is regulated by the Federal Reserve. Currently, for common stocks, convertible securities, and short sales, the investor must put up 50 percent of the value and can only borrow on margin the remaining 50 percent.

Stock exchanges and brokerage houses set maintenance margins. The New York Stock Exchange maintenance margin is 25 percent. Most brokerage houses require at least 30 percent. If the value falls below the maintenance level, the investor receives a call for more margin. If the investor fails to respond, the stock is sold, and the broker credits the proceeds against the margin debt. The investor receives any remaining proceeds.

If the value of the stock rises above the initial margin requirement, the investor may be able to withdraw the excess if the margin account is not restricted. A restricted account is one where the sum of all securities and margin debt produces an overall margin that is between the initial margin and the maintenance margin.

The investor incurs an interest charge on the amount borrowed. The rate is geared to the call money rate, the charge on loans to brokers on stock exchange collateral, and is usually one and one-half to two points over that rate. This call rate varies from time to time. The larger brokerage houses might offer a lower rate than smaller houses. The investor should ask the brokerage house about its interest rate on margin debt.

Short sales. Short sales are also subject to margin requirements. In short selling, the investor borrows the securities that he or she sells. The broker retains the proceeds of the sale. Generally, no interest is paid. The broker will ordinarily invest the money in money market funds and keep the earnings.

In addition to the proceeds, the short seller must deposit cash or securities as initial margin. Initially, the short seller puts up margin equal to 50 percent of the value of the securities borrowed. If the securities borrowed go up in value, he or she must deposit more cash to maintain the percentage level.

> ***Example 31.7.*** Sam Cole sells short 100 shares of borrowed stock at \$50 per share. The proceeds of the sale, \$5,000, are kept by the broker. In addition, Cole must deposit 50% of the value of the stock, or \$2,500, to maintain the initial margin.
>
> Assuming that the maintenance margin is 30%, he will get a margin call when the price of the stock rises by a percentage equal to 1 plus the initial margin times the purchase price

(\$50) divided by 1 plus the maintenance margin times the purchase price (\$50), i.e., $\{[(1+.50)\times\$50]\div[(1+.30)\times\$50]\}=\$75\div\$65=115.38\%$; $115.38\%\times\$50=\$57.69$. In this case, the price will be just below \$58.

In a short sale, any cash dividends from the shorted stock must be paid to the broker. Stock can be shorted only on an uptick, i.e., when the price is higher than on the previous trade.

.03 Use of Street Name or Customer's Name

Securities may be left by the owner in the broker's custody and name, that is, a street name. The use of street names facilitates transactions in the securities owned, obviating the need for the owner to execute a transfer. Traders often leave all of their securities in street names as a matter of convenience. Investors who intend to hold securities on a long-term basis also sometimes leave their holdings in street names. However, to leave the securities in a street name for any considerable length of time involves a dual risk for the owner. This risk extends to the trader as well where there is a fair time period between trades. The risks are as follows:

- The risk of bankruptcy or financial failure on the part of the broker
- If a customer enters into a short sale, the risk that the broker might lend the securities to the short seller with the adverse result discussed separately below

In the event of the broker's bankruptcy, the trustee must reduce to money all securities that are part of the bankrupt's estate, except customer securities. In other words, securities held in street names are sold, consistent with good market practice, and the proceeds become part of the estate. As to customer name securities, the trustee must deliver such securities to the customer, unless the customer has a negative net equity.[167]

The customer whose securities are left in a street name is protected by the Securities Investor Protection Corporation (SIPC). Still, the customer could reduce this risk by having securities registered in his or her own name.

.04 Securities Investor Protection

SIPC grew out of the voluntary liquidations, mergers, receiverships, and bankruptcies of many brokerage houses in the early seventies.

---

[167] See Bankruptcy Act Sections 748 and 751.

SIPC extends protection to securities customers of SIPC member firms in the following manner:

- First, customers of a failed firm will receive securities registered in their names or in the process of such registration. No dollar limit applies to the value of the securities.
- Second, the customers will receive, on a pro rata basis, all remaining cash and customers' securities held by the firm. Again, no dollar limit applies to the value of the property returned.
- Third, SIPC funds will be available to satisfy the remaining claims of each customer up to $500,000, except that claims for cash, instead of securities, are limited to a maximum of $100,000.
- Finally, any remaining assets after payment of liquidation expenses may be available to satisfy any remaining customer claims on a pro rata basis.

The dollar limits of protection apply to accounts with each SIPC member. A customer may have accounts with the same SIPC member in different capacities and still be protected to the dollar limit on each separate account.

Investors should be aware of the dollar limitations, as to both cash and securities. At the same time, the investor should remember that in the event of broad-scale failures in the brokerage industry, the SIPC might not be able to provide full indemnification up to the $500,000/$100,000 limits for each customer.

Protection against failure. The best protection against broad-scale failures would seem to be to have securities in the customer's name only and to limit cash on deposit with the brokerage house at any time to amounts substantially below the $100,000 limit. The investor should transfer the proceeds of sales to an insured bank account or insured S&L accounts as soon as feasible.

To minimize the risk to the customer of failure of an individual firm or firms, registration of securities in the customer's name would seem best, along with withdrawal of excess cash. Separate accounts in different capacities with the same firm or the use of different firms should also be considered.

Claims against brokers. The typical brokerage account agreement with a customer calls for the settlement of all claims against the broker by arbitration. The U.S. Supreme Court has upheld the validity and enforceability of such arbitration clauses even as applied to fraud claims under Rule 10b-5 and RICO claims.[168] The U.S. Supreme Court has held that investors' claims arising under the Securities Act of 1933 are subject to arbitration pursuant to a predispute agreement.[169]

.05 Asset Management Accounts

Asset management accounts set up by brokerage firms, banks, and insurance companies under various names permit customers to coordinate and conduct their financial activities in one place. Minimum deposit requirements and services available vary from company to company. A financial planner should consider whether a client's financial needs would be served better by using these accounts or by using different companies for different services.

Services provided. Individual accounts, such as checking, a money market fund, and a brokerage account, are linked together. Money can be transferred freely from account to account. A customer can transfer excess checking account cash into money market funds to assure the highest yield on the money. Conversely, a margin loan can be automatically transferred into a checking account to prevent a check from bouncing. If the account is with a brokerage firm, dividends on securities can be credited immediately to a money market or other designated mutual fund. Financial services firms might also provide credit cards, debit cards, and a personal line of credit with these accounts.

Financial activities of the account are reported each month in a consolidated statement. Most brokerage firms do not return canceled checks without request and the payment of a fee.

Assessing desirability of asset management funds. Whether such accounts make sense must be answered on a client-by-client basis. For a client who regularly buys or sells securities with a brokerage firm in excess of required account minimums anyway, the additional annual fee may be inconsequential compared with the services it engenders. The client might have other reasons for opening an asset management account.

> ***Example 31.8.*** Owen Hyde is an investor in Brandon, Florida, with a sizable municipal bond portfolio. He would prefer to keep the bonds in a safe deposit vault and clip the coupons himself. However, some banks in Florida charge a fee of $3 each time coupons are clipped. If he holds the bonds in an asset management account, he incurs no clipping fee. Moreover, the coupon

[168] *Shearson/American Express, Inc. v. McMahon*, 47 CCH U.S. SUPREME COURT BULLETIN B3013 (6/8/87).

[169] *Rodriguez de Quijas v. Shearson/American Express, Inc.*, U.S. SCt, CCH FEDERAL SECURITIES LAW REPORTS ¶ 94,407 (1989).

interest can be transferred to whatever investment medium he desires.

.06 American Depositary Receipts (ADRs)

Increased interest in foreign securities has led sophisticated investors to search for a convenient way to own them. While a U.S. investor can buy foreign stocks through foreign exchanges or U.S. brokers who have overseas affiliates, the U.S. investor might find that direct ownership is inconvenient. The investor could encounter legal, transfer tax, and probate difficulties inherent in ownership of foreign property. Dividends are often paid in foreign currency, and information about the company itself is often difficult to obtain.

American Depositary Receipts, popularly known as ADRs, are a convenient alternative to direct ownership of foreign securities. An ADR is a negotiable certificate, issued by a U.S. bank, evidencing that shares of the foreign company's stock (or the company's bonds) are on deposit in the bank. The bank, and not the ADR holder, is the owner of record of the underlying security and is charged with relieving the ADR holder of the burdensome task of ownership of the security.

The principal advantages of ADR investments over direct ownership are as follows:

- **Ease of transfer.** The transfer of these certificates is relatively uncomplicated, especially when probate and foreign inheritance tax proceedings are considered.
- **Bearer form.** Many foreign securities, including stocks, are issued in bearer form. Announcement of dividends is made by publication in a foreign newspaper, and the physical presentation of share certificates is necessary to obtain the dividend. This procedure is greatly simplified through the ADR system, because the bank has an organized way to collect dividends.
- **U.S. dollars.** ADR holders are paid in U.S. dollars and not in foreign currency, which saves the holder the costs of currency conversion.
- **Current information.** While direct investors in foreign securities might have difficulty in obtaining current information about the foreign company, banks routinely obtain such information. In the case of sponsored ADRs, where the foreign issuer pays some or all of the costs of the bank's management of the ADR account, the ADR holder can receive information directly from the issuer or through the bank.

- **Liquidity.** ADRs are registered securities on U.S. markets and are traded on U.S. exchanges (most often over the counter). As such, they provide the holder with more liquidity than direct ownership of foreign securities.

Under a sponsored ADR, the holder is relieved of some or all of the costs of maintaining the account (aside from brokerage). Nonsponsored ADRs involve transaction costs to the investor upon creation of the account (where, for example, the investor makes a direct purchase of a foreign security, but then arranges for an ADR account at a bank). The costs of creating an account run from $3 to $5 per hundred shares, depending on the price per share. Nonsponsored ADR accounts also charge the holder a fee upon dividend or interest payments (in the case of foreign stocks, for only a few cents per share).

Planning pointer. While ADRs make ownership of foreign securities easier than direct ownership, investment in any foreign company can pose problems for a U.S. investor. Foreign companies are not subject to U.S. corporation or securities laws. Also, as with any individual investment, the stock exchange index in which the foreign security is traded may soar, but the security represented by the ADR might not rise.

Choosing a reputable international mutual fund whose managers presumably have current information and insights about fund investments might be safer for the investor.

¶3190 COMMISSIONS AND INVESTMENT CHARGES

The financial planner and client will want to know the costs of buying and selling an investment, including approaches that offer the prospect of reducing the costs of investment.

The costs of investment might include commissions, fees, and other compensation for persons who advise the client and/or sell the investment to the client. However, the client would appear to have no reason to pay for services that he or she does not need or use. If the client, without the aid of the organization or its sales personnel, can analyze the facts connected with the investment and can make the investment decision alone, the client has less need to compensate outsiders for a service. Instead, the client is free to buy or sell the investment through the least costly medium.

The client might have less freedom to make a low-cost sale in some classes of investments than in others. Discount brokerage opportunities exist for stocks, bonds, and commodities transactions. As with other assets, the nature of the investment (for example, tax shelters) or contractual provisions (as in the case of "back-end load" mutual funds) might limit the client's options in buying or selling the asset at the best price.

In many cases, buying or selling an investment at the best price can more than compensate for added costs paid to the broker, agent, or other person. This potential savings holds particularly true when a large dollar amount is involved.

In addition to purchase and sales charges, the financial planner should also be alert to management fees, which may be charged to the client's account for as long as he or she owns the investment or maintains the account.

.01 Commission or Load Arrangements

In most cases, the person buying or selling an investment will have to pay up-front charges for his or her investment activity. These charges can take the form of commissions, the payment of which reduces the client's account or causes direct out-of-pocket expense. The charges can also take the form of loads, by which the client is not directly charged. Instead, less than his or her full amount paid will be invested. The difference is the load.

Limited partnership interests. Purchase of a limited partnership interest will generally involve the payment of a load or commission to the agent who brought about the purchase, as well as to other persons connected with the sponsorship and offering of the investment. Such loads are not out-of-pocket charges. Instead, the prospectus will show that a percentage of the purchase price for a unit will not go to the actual acquisition of the asset. Rather, the difference will constitute sales and distribution expenses to compensate the agent, sponsor, and others for selling the investment to the client. The prospectus will reveal the amount of such commissions.

Sale of limited partnership investments presents a difficult problem for the financial planner. A nonpublic interest is likely to be hard to sell. Public limited partnership interests are more readily salable, but the client usually will have little opportunity to know the amount of brokerage costs in advance. However, a few exchanges assist in the sale of shelters, both public and nonpublic.

Stocks. Brokerage commissions are charged on stock purchases and sales when the firm is acting as an agent for the purchaser or seller. Transactions in over-the-counter (OTC) stocks, where the broker makes a market in the security, might be made on a markup basis, with some markups being very high and undisclosed to the account holder.

While the commissions on many stock transactions are competitive or negotiated, as opposed to the fixed commission system that previously prevailed, full service brokerage houses claim to provide more services in the form of investment research and advice than discount brokers. Under the system of negotiated rates, a major client might be able to negotiate for lower rates. The client's success will have much to do with his or her market power.

The client who wishes to reduce his or her commissions can have two accounts: a full service account, in which he or she seeks investment advice, and a discount account to handle situations in which he or she performs the investment analysis.

For a further discussion of fee arrangements comparing full-service and discount brokers, see ¶3185.

Bonds. Bond investments are generally sold at fairly low commissions, at least when compared to stocks. The broker obtains his compensation because of a spread or markup on the bond. This markup will cause the investor to pay more for bonds yielding a specified amount on purchase and will cause the investor to receive less than he or she might expect upon sale of the bond. Zero-coupon bonds may be sold on a markup basis to the investor, based on a percentage of their ultimate face value and not of their initial discounted price. The unaided investor might have difficulty in determining the amount of the markup. However, he or she might be able to obtain more attractive prices on larger transactions.

A person may invest in U.S. government securities directly through a Federal Reserve Bank, at no cost.

Commodities. Like stocks and bonds, commodities brokers include full-service firms charging higher commissions for a range of services and discount brokers that charge only for execution of trades.

Mutual funds. Mutual funds are often sold on a load basis with higher loads of eight percent or more for smaller lots. The load varies with the number of shares purchased. The prospectus will reveal the amount of the sales commission, both as a percentage of the asked price and as a percentage of the bid price or net asset value. For example, 8.5 percent of the asked price is 9.3 percent of the bid price. As with stock and bond investments, the client who has a firm grip on investment information, is willing to perform investment analysis, and is confident of his or her decision might choose a no-load mutual fund. The client would see no reason to buy a load fund, which compensates salespersons who were not instrumental in bringing about the purchase.

Both load and no-load funds charge annual management fees, which are often comparable.

For a further comparison between load and no-load funds, see ¶ 3140.

.02 No-Load Arrangements

Investors have shown increased interest in arrangements that will eliminate up-front sales commissions in order to maximize the amount of money actually invested. No-load arrangements are not in any sense free. No-load arrangements might be sponsored by organizations that can market their products without an expensive outside sales force. However, the sponsors of no-load funds will receive income from annual or more frequent maintenance charges and other fees.

The client who is interested in acquiring a no-load investment should ascertain the extent to which the investment in question is no-load or whether the equivalent of a load will be charged later, rather than simply relying on the no-load label. Outstanding investment performance by a fund with a back-end load can counterbalance the apparent handicap of redemption and distribution charges.

¶ 3195 DEBT CONSOLIDATION

Clients with several different debts might be able to reduce interest costs by consolidating their debts, especially if the new debt will be a home equity loan or credit line that gives rise to tax deductible interest.[170] Having only one bill to pay monthly also eases paperwork burdens.

The client could have other financial planning reasons for consolidating debts. For example, such a move might be advisable if a client needs more time to pay debts.

.01 Types of Consolidation Loans

Banks generally allow individuals to borrow against the equity in their residence. Interest on the first $100,000 of such loans generally is deductible for income tax purposes.[171]

Home equity loans differ somewhat from home equity lines of credit. Home equity loans charge a fixed rate of interest and extend for a term selected by the borrower. Home equity lines of credit have a variable rate and a revolving line of credit.

---

[170] Code Sec. 163.

[171] Code Sec. 163(h)(3)(C).

Home equity loans. Many lenders offer two types of home-equity loans. One type has these features: maximum loan amount of $50,000, no application fee or prepayment penalties, mortgage recording fee and, in some cases, a mortgage tax. In many cases, paying a slightly higher interest rate avoids such closing costs.

The second type of home equity loan allows far greater amounts to be borrowed. However, as a general rule, the borrower will have to pay an application fee, attorney fees, title insurance, recording fees, mortgage tax, and points.

Home equity lines of credit. With a home equity line of credit (HELOC), the homeowner receives a revolving line of credit using his or her home as collateral. The interest rate is variable and typically is based on an index, such as the prime rate, plus two or three percentage points. One can usually obtain such credit lines without paying application fees or closing costs unless it is a very large credit line. In some cases, an individual can effectively use a home equity line of credit to refinance a first mortgage loan. This technique is useful if the balance on the first mortgage is relatively low and the interest rate on it is relatively high.

Unsecured loans. A client also can use an unsecured loan to consolidate debts, but such loans often carry very high interest rates. In addition, the interest will not be deductible if the proceeds are used for personal purposes.[172]

.02 Other Factors

Clients should not consolidate debts carrying no interest in the absence of other factors favoring immediate payment. For example, bills owed to professionals might not carry interest and generally should be paid under their regular payment schedule. Of course, if the physician, dentist, or lawyer will not complete services until the bill is paid, then such debts should be consolidated.

Also, clients must be made to realize that they will lack flexibility when they consolidate their debts. Clients will have no opportunity to choose which debt or debts to pay in times of extreme cash flow problems, as would be the case if they did not consolidate their debts.

Moreover, a financial planner should impress upon clients that they should not view consolidation as meaning that their financial

---

[172] Code Sec. 163(h).

condition has improved so greatly that they can now go on a spending spree. Clients might wish the payment on their consolidated debt to be smaller than the total payments on their unconsolidated debts. A financial planner should advise these clients that a smaller payment will result in an increase in interest costs.

Chapter 32

Family Income-Splitting Techniques

Overview ....¶ 3201
Unearned Income of Children Under Age 14 ....¶ 3205
Transfers That Avoid the Kiddie Tax ....¶ 3210
Transfers to Other Family Members ....¶ 3215
"Defective" Grantor Trusts ....¶ 3220
Gift-Leaseback of Business Property ....¶ 3225
Splitting Business Income with Family ....¶ 3230
Gifts of Property in Anticipation of Sale ....¶ 3235
The Private Annuity ....¶ 3240

¶ 3201 OVERVIEW

The individual who buys a ticket in a $500,000 lottery and writes in the names of his four children on the ticket along with his own may not be fully aware of some of the fine points of family income-splitting. The income tax on $500,000 is significantly more than the income tax on $100,000 for five individuals combined. However, he or she has captured the basic idea that each dollar of added income a person receives is taxed at that person's marginal tax rate. Thus, by diverting income to children or other members of the family with little or no income of their own, one can increase the family's overall after-tax income.

For 2006, a 25-percent spread exists between the 35-percent top rate and the 10-percent bottom rate. In addition, an 18-point spread exists between the 33-percent bracket and the 15-percent bracket. These spreads provide a strong incentive for income-shifting as a means of reducing overall family income tax rates. However, taxpayers are subject to a maximum tax rate of 15 percent on most net capital gains through the end of tax year 2010. The top capital gains rate on collectibles is 28 percent, and the tax rate on unrecaptured Code Sec. 1250 gains (dealing with depreciation recapture on realty) is 25 percent.[1]

Of course, if income-splitting is to succeed, it is usually not quite as simple as the lottery example might have indicated. The parent must have made a completed gift of a share in the ticket before the drawing. In all cases, one must do more than simply split income. No one can avoid tax on dividends, interest, or other income merely by instructing the payer of the income to pay or credit all or part of it to children or other family members. That would be separating the fruit from the tree, which the courts and the IRS state is something that taxpayers cannot do because of the assignment of income doctrine,[2] to avoid being taxed on the fruit. Unless the taxpayer transfers the tree, the source of the income along with the fruit, there is no effective income shifting or splitting.

This limitation should cause one to pause. It is not a serious limitation when all that is being given away is an interest in a $2 lottery ticket before the drawing. It is a different story, however, if stock or other property of far greater present value and present income-producing capacity is to be the vehicle for income splitting. The rest of this chapter will explore a variety of family income-splitting techniques that might be of practical use in building family resources. Many of these techniques have been developed in other portions of this book, and the treatment here will be concise.

¶ 3205 UNEARNED INCOME OF CHILDREN UNDER AGE 18

Despite popular conceptions to the contrary, a family can still achieve intra-family savings by shifting income-producing assets to children, even if they are subject to the kiddie tax.[3]

.01 Kiddie Tax Basics

The kiddie tax separates a child's unearned income into three slices. For 2006, assuming the child has no earned income and no itemized deductions. The breakdown looks like this:

100% tax-free income: Unearned income up to $850, sheltered by child's special $850 standard deduction ...	$850
Income subject to tax at the child's rate	$850

[1] Code Sec. 1(h).

[2] Code Sec. 73 and *Lucas v. Earl*, 2 USTC ¶ 496, 50 S. Ct. 241 (USSC, 1930).

[3] Code Sec. 1(g).

	Unearned income over
Net unearned income subject to tax at parental rate	$1,700

Assuming a young child has no other income, and his parents are in a higher tax bracket, the transfer of assets that produce $1,600 in income saves the family federal income taxes. If the child invests the money in a savings account with a low interest rate, a parent or other family member can make a fairly large gift of assets without coming close to the $1,600 limit.

If the child's unearned income already is substantially above the net unearned income limit, it is still possible to cut overall family income taxes by making gifts of property designed to produce income or profit in the future, when the child is no longer subject to the kiddie tax. Such gifts include the following:

- Growth stock or growth mutual funds that have low current dividends but that one hopes will increase in value (and dividend yield) over the long term
- Stock in the family business, which the corporation can redeem after the child is no longer subject to the kiddie tax
- Assets that produce no income currently but may pay off handsomely years down the road (e.g., prime undeveloped land)
- Series EE or Series I bonds, on which the child can defer the tax on the accrued interest until the child redeems the bonds

.02 Age Limitation

Not all children with investment income are subject to the kiddie tax. In the past, it applied only to children under the age of 14 at the close of the tax year. The Tax Increase Prevention and Reconciliation Act of 2005 expanded the kiddie tax coverage. The minimum age at which a child is exempt from the kiddie tax has been increased from age 14 to age 18. This change is effective for tax years beginning after December 31, 2005.[4]

Since the age increase is effective for tax year 2006, the change has immediate impact. For example, parents who had planned to sell a child's college stock portfolio in 2006 when the child reaches 14 now have to wait for more years if they intend to take advantage of the

[4] Code Sec. 1(g)(2)(A) as amended by the Tax Increase Prevention and Reconciliation Act of 2005 (P.L. 109-222).

child's lower tax rate. If the parents plan to postpone a sale until 2008 when the child's capital gains rate could be zero, then they may have to wait longer—if the child is not yet age 18 in 2008. Otherwise, the gain will still be taxed at the parent's presumably higher rate.

Under the new law, the investment income of a child who is under age 18 and married is not subject to the kiddie tax if the child files a joint return for the tax year. However, the child's eligibility to file a joint return is not enough to avoid application of the kiddie tax. The child must actually file a joint return for the tax year.

.03 Election Out of Kiddie Tax

Parents may elect to include directly on their return the income of certain children who are subject to the kiddie tax. A child who is under age 18 is not required to file a return if his or her parents elect to include the child's gross income on the parent's return. Parents make the election by attaching Form 8814, "Parents' Election To Report Child's Interest and Dividends," to the parents' income tax return. The parents may make the election only if the child's income was more than $850 but less than $8,500 (for 2006) and consists of only interest, dividends, and Alaska Permanent Fund dividends. In addition, the child must not have made estimated tax payments and not be subject to backup withholding (see instructions to IRS Form 8814 for additional requirements). In addition to being taxed on the child's interest and dividends in excess of $1,700, the parents who make this election must increase their tax liability directly by an amount equal to the lesser of $85 (for 2006) or 10 percent of the excess of the child's interest and dividends over $850 (for 2006). All of the relevant figures relating to the election out of the kiddie tax are adjusted each year for inflation.

Planning pointer. Electing out of the kiddie tax simplifies tax filing chores, but apart from that, it may not be a good move taxwise. Including the child's interest and dividends on the parents' return will increase the parents' adjusted gross income. This increase in adjusted gross income could cost the family deductions and loss of other tax breaks under various limits based on adjusted gross income. For example, the following itemized deductions are deductible only to the extent that they exceed the specified percentages of adjusted gross income:

- Medical expenses (7.5%)[5]
- Casualty and theft losses (10%)[6]
- Miscellaneous itemized deductions (2%)[7]

---

[5] Code Sec. 213(a).

[6] Code Sec. 165(h)(2).

[7] Code Sec. 67.

Thus, an increase in the parents' adjusted gross income will reduce the amounts of any of these deductions. In addition, the election may increase the family's state income tax.

¶ 3210 TRANSFERS THAT AVOID THE KIDDIE TAX

A parent can give investment property to his or her minor children in a variety of ways, with the advantage that the property and the income are kept within the family. A parent can avoid having the income taxed at the parent's rate only if the child is age 18 or older or the expected income does not exceed $1,700 (for 2006). Since the parents' tax rate could be as much as 35 percent and could rise even higher taking into account state and local taxes, shifting income to children that are not hit with the kiddie tax can result in substantial income tax savings for the family.

Although the emphasis is on regular income tax savings, parents should also consider the effects on possible alternative minimum tax (AMT), estate and gift tax consequences, and legal considerations. If the donor is within range of the AMT, a transfer to a child of property that generates tax preference items has added advantages for the family provided the minor is not within range of AMT. The discussion that follows lists several methods of making gifts to children when the child is age 18 or over or the child's income will not exceed $1,700 (for 2006). Not all of them result in shifting income, but those that do not are included by showing "how not to shift income." In all instances, the various pros and cons are discussed. The discussion assumes that the child is age 14 or older, unless otherwise indicated.

.01 Outright Gift

Income is shifted. The property is taken out of the parent's estate. The annual gift tax exclusion is available ($12,000 or $24,000 if the other parent consents under Code Sec. 2503(b) (for 2006 and adjusted for inflation). There is generally no legal problem in transferring the property to the minor, but he or she will have legal problems in dealing with the property and the income. As a general rule, the child cannot make an effective will. If the child dies, the property normally reverts to the parent under the intestacy law.

.02 Joint Ownership

Income tax consequences vary, as do gift tax consequences, with the property involved. Usually there is no gift on the creation of a joint bank account. The gift occurs when the child withdraws and uses the money in the account.[8] With securities, there is an immediate gift when the securities are registered in joint names.[9] The income tax consequences follow the gift tax rules. When the child receives a gift, the child becomes taxable on the income attributable to the child's interest in the property, and the parent is relieved of tax on that part. Even though the transfer is a completed gift, the property is nevertheless includible in the parent's gross estate.[10] There is no legal problem on the initial transfer. While the property remains in joint ownership, each party may have a veto over a sale.

.03 Revocable Trust

The parent gives property to a revocable trust for the benefit of the child. There are no income, estate, or gift tax consequences as a result of the mere transfer. If the parent dies without revoking the trust, then it becomes irrevocable and results in income and estate tax consequences. While the parent is alive, the trust provides management and protection, with the parent retaining the ultimate control.

.04 Totten Trust

This trust is merely a sort of revocable trust in a type of joint bank account that exists in some states. When the parent dies, the balance passes to the child.

.05 U.S. Savings Bonds

The parent buys Series EE or Series I bonds in the child's name. Interest will be taxable to the child. However, the child can defer tax until the bonds mature unless he or she elects to report the interest income each year. Because the child's income can be expected to increase, the child would probably be better off not deferring the tax (assuming the child is age 18 or the annual income will not exceed $1,700 (for 2006)). The annual gift tax exclusion and gift-splitting are available. Also, the bond is excluded from the parent's gross estate and includible in the child's gross estate. The child may redeem at any time if he or she is old enough to act. If the bond is not delivered to the child, the income, estate, and gift tax consequences are not clear. Using this method is usually not best, therefore, except for small amounts.

.06 Custodial Account

These special accounts are authorized by the various states' Gifts to Minors Acts. Many states are in the process of adopting a new

[8] Reg. § 25.2511-1(h)(4).
[9] Reg. § 25.2511-1(h)(5).
[10] Code Sec. 2040(a).

Uniform Transfers to Minors Act (UTMA), which replaces the Uniform Gifts to Minors Act. UTMA lifts the property limitations and makes other favorable changes, as discussed at ¶ 425. Even though a child must be age 18 to avoid the kiddie tax, a custodial account may still make tax sense in some situations. For example, in some states the "turnover" age for custodial accounts is age 21. Also, the kiddie tax will not be a factor even when the child is under age 18 if the annual income expected from the account does not exceed $1,700 (for 2006). Income from the account that is used to satisfy the parent's obligation of support becomes taxable to the parent. The annual gift tax exclusion and gift-splitting are available. On the child's death, the account is includible in the child's gross estate. If the parent is the donor and is the custodian and dies during the child's minority, the account is included in the parent's gross estate. Custodial accounts have gained favor relative to trusts that accumulate income, as discussed at paragraph .07, below.

.07 Special Trust for Minors

Code Sec. 2503(c) recognizes a special type of trust designed with gift tax considerations in mind. This trust qualifies for the annual gift tax exclusion and gift-splitting provided its conditions are met, i.e., the "property" and income must be expendable on behalf of the child before he or she reaches age 21 and must pass to the child when he or she reaches age 21 ("property" does not necessarily include corpus). A special form of trust may hold S corporation stock (¶ 1945). Income will be taxed to the parent only to the extent used for the child's support. The trust property is taken out of the parent's gross estate (if the parent is not the trustee) and is includible in the child's gross estate. Income will be taxable under the usual trust rules. Income distributed to or on behalf of the child will be taxable to the child, and income accumulated in the trust will be taxable to the trust. Because of the sharp compression of the trust tax brackets, trusts have become very unattractive vehicles for accumulating income for minors. For example, for tax years beginning in 2006, the 15-percent rate applies to taxable income up to $2,050, the 25-percent rate applies to taxable income between $2,050 and $4,850, the 28-percent rate applies to taxable income between $4,850 and $7,400, the 33-percent rate applies to taxable income between $7,400 and $10,050, and the 35-percent rate applies to taxable income over $10,050. Trusts are not eligible for the 10-percent rate allowed to individuals. In many cases, custodial accounts may be preferred to Code Sec. 2503(c) minor's trusts. With a custodial account, the income is taxed at the child's rate (assuming the child is age 18 or the income does not exceed $1,700 (for 2006)). Income accumulated in a trust, on the other hand, would be subject to the highly compressed brackets set out above.

.08 Irrevocable Trust

Usually, the trustee is given direction to use principal and income for the benefit of the minor. Income is not taxable to the parent, except as used for support, but is taxable under the usual trust rules (see paragraph .06, above). Those rules can make accumulating income in trusts quite costly, as discussed at paragraph .07, above. No annual gift tax exclusion is available because the gift to the trust is not of a present interest in property.[11] Property is removed from the parent's gross estate (if the parent is not the trustee). However, the parent loses complete control of the property upon the creation of the trust.

.09 Charitable Remainder Annuity Trust (CRAT) or Unitrust (CRUT)

The parent transfers property to a trust to pay a certain sum to the child (no less than five percent of the value of the property transferred) or a fixed percentage (no less than five percent) of the value of the property determined at least annually for a specific number of years (no more than 20) or for life. At the end of the term of years or at the child's death, the principal goes to charity. The income from the property is not taxable to the parent. The parent also receives a charitable contribution deduction for the present value of the charity's remainder interest.[12] The annual gift tax exclusion is available and the property is removed from the parent's gross estate.

¶ 3215 TRANSFERS TO OTHER FAMILY MEMBERS

Income may also be shifted to parents and other relatives as well as to minor children.

Of course, when an individual transfers income-producing property, the transfer might have gift tax consequences. The gift tax annual exclusion ($12,000 in 2006, or $24,000 with gift splitting under Code Sec. 2503(b) and adjusted for inflation) and applicable credit amount (unified credit)[13] can shelter the transfer from gift tax.

Families can use the private annuity (¶ 810) to split income with family members other than minors.

[11] Code Sec.2503(b)(1).

[12] Code Sec. 170.

[13] Code Sec. 2505.

¶ 3220 "DEFECTIVE" GRANTOR TRUSTS

Traditionally, the grantor trust rules (¶ 605) were viewed as a stumbling block to saving income taxes. However, in some cases, a family can realize tax savings by purposely causing the grantor trust rules to apply, resulting in a "defective" grantor trust. With this approach, the income will be taxed at the grantor's brackets. The income tax cost may be lower than if the income were taxed at the trust's rates. Also, payment of the income tax by the grantor will not be regarded as a taxable gift by the grantor to the beneficiary who directly benefits by the payment.

> **Planning pointer.** As noted above, sometimes setting up a trust in which income will be taxed to the grantor will be beneficial under the grantor trust rules. But doing so poses the danger that the trust property will be included in the grantor's gross estate. However, discrepancies between the grantor trust rules and the estate tax inclusion rules allow the income to be taxed to the grantor without the property being included in his or her gross estate. Carefully limiting a grantor's administrative control over a trust, making the grantor's spouse a discretionary beneficiary, and giving the grantor the power to substitute property of an equivalent value are techniques for achieving the desired result.

¶ 3225 GIFT-LEASEBACK OF BUSINESS PROPERTY

In a gift-leaseback of business property, a business owner transfers property used in his or her business or practice to a trust, usually set up for his children's benefit. However, the trust could be for the benefit of other family members. The trust then leases the property back to the settlor at a rental based on the property's fair rental value. The goal is for the settlor to get a deduction for the rent paid to the trust, which makes income available to members of the family in a lower tax bracket. The gift or sale and leaseback technique will generally not be available for an individual who needs or wants to get the property back. But the technique is viable for one willing to part with the property permanently, subject to the caveat that the technique will not shift income to a lower tax bracket in the case of a child beneficiary under the age of 18 who has unearned income in excess of $1,700 (2006). Taxpayers could still use the technique with distribution of principal to the child at the end of the trust or with remainder to a grandchild.

Other new uses may also develop. For example, an individual who is assisting his or her parents may want to give them an income interest for life with the remainder over to his or her children.

If a grandchild is named as remainder person, the generation-skipping transfer tax theoretically could come into play. In any event, no gift tax may result if the unified credit is available to offset the tentative gift tax. Also, annual exclusions will be available for gifts of present interests (i.e., the trust is one requiring the mandatory distribution of income at least annually, is one for a minor conforming to the requirements of Code Sec. 2503(c), or is one containing a *Crummey* power of withdrawal).

On the other side of the coin, with no reversionary interest, the property will not be brought back into the settlor's gross estate, assuming the settlor retains no prohibited controls.

The most frequently transferred property is an office building. Often, the transaction takes place when the settlor has begun to run out of depreciation deductions on the building and anticipates that the rent deductions will be substantially higher than any depreciation deductions.

Normally, the IRS will respect a gift-leaseback if the following conditions are met: (1) the donor does not maintain substantially the same control over the property that he or she had before; (2) the leaseback is in writing and requires a reasonable rental; (3) the leaseback (as distinguished from the gift) has a bona fide business purpose; and (4) the donor does not maintain an equitable interest in the trust.

¶ 3230 SPLITTING BUSINESS INCOME WITH FAMILY

To split business income with a family member, the business owner gives the member an interest in the business. If the business is in corporate form and has elected S corporation treatment, the owner is limited to gifts of the single class of stock allowed such corporations.[14] However, an S corporation may have voting and nonvoting common without violating the one-class-of-stock rule, as discussed at ¶ 1945. If it is a regular C corporation, the owner may give not only common stock but also preferred stock and debt securities if the capital structure permits.

If the business is a partnership, the family member receives a partnership interest and is recognized as a partner for tax purposes. This treatment applies though the new partner performs no services, as long as he or she owns an interest in the capital of the partnership and capital is important in producing partnership income (see ¶ 2005 for a discussion of family partnerships).

---

[14] Code Sec. 1361(b)(1).

If the business is a sole proprietorship, the owner could restructure the business as a family partnership.

Putting children to work in the family business and paying them is another way of splitting business income. A child who may be claimed as a dependent on the parents' return does not get a personal exemption deduction on his or her own tax return. Absent earned income, all but $850 of his or her $5,150 (for 2006) standard deduction would be wasted. Placing the child on the payroll avoids such waste and also enables the child to make deductible IRA contributions, even if the child is a participant in the retirement plan of the business, provided the child's income is below a certain level. Further, income not offset by the standard deduction and the IRA deduction will be taxed to the child at his or her low-bracket rate (10 percent on taxable income up to $7,550 for 2006). Another benefit is that if the child is under age 18 and employed by his or her parent as a sole proprietor or as a partnership consisting only of his or her parents, the child's wages are exempt from Social Security and Medicare tax.[15] In such cases, the child's wages expense would also reduce the parent's income tax and self-employment tax.[16] Wages paid to one's children must be reasonable for work actually performed.

¶ 3235 GIFTS OF PROPERTY IN ANTICIPATION OF SALE

If a high-tax-bracket family member holds property that he or she expects to sell at a profit, a better overall family tax result might be achieved by giving the property to a low-tax-bracket member of the family who then makes the actual sale. But a transfer to a child under age 18 will not achieve the desired result because the child's unearned income over $1,700 (2006) is taxed at the parents' top rate (¶ 3205).

A district court case sanctioned this approach. In so doing, it relied on charitable "bail out" cases that allow the owner of a closely held corporation to contribute stock to a charity with the specific intent of having the corporation redeem the stock from the charity. In these situations, the redemption is not treated as a redemption to the shareholder as long as the donor parts with all dominion and control over the stock and there is no written promise by the corporation that it will redeem the stock.[17]

In holding that the gain was taxable to the donee and not to the donor, the court said, "Though the facts in this case show a tax

---

[15] Code Sec. 3121(b)(3)(A).

[16] Code Sec. 162(a).

[17] *D. Palmer*, 62 TC 684, CCH Dec. 32,739 (Acq.), aff'd CA-8, 75-2 USTC ¶ 9726, 523 F2d 1308; Rev. Rul. 78-197, 1978-1 CB 83.

avoidance, they also show legal transactions not fictitious or so lacking in substance as to be anything different from what they purported to be . . ."[18] However, the parent would be wise not to negotiate the sale of the property before making the gift to avoid any chance of the IRS invoking the step-transaction and assignment of income doctrines.

A taxpayer cannot use this approach effectively if the gift is to be made in trust. Code Sec. 644 provides that if appreciated property is transferred to a trust and is sold within two years of transfer, the trust will be taxed as if the sale had been made by the grantor.

If a taxpayer uses this approach, the taxpayer should file a timely gift tax return (if the requisite amount is involved), and show clearly that the donor has surrendered all dominion and control. If the donor merely wishes to make a gift of the gain, the IRS may treat the transaction as a sale of the property by the donor followed by a gift of the amount of the gain.

¶ 3240 THE PRIVATE ANNUITY

The private annuity is another way of shifting income within a family unit. A private annuity often involves a transfer from a high-tax-bracket member to one in a lower bracket, but this type of transfer is not essential. The most common form of this type of annuity is where an aging parent transfers a substantial portion of his or her estate to a son or daughter in exchange for a promise to pay the parent an annuity for life.

The advantage of the private annuity in general and the circumstances under which it may be especially useful or contra-indicated are discussed at some length at ¶ 810.

---

[18] *J. Haley*, DC Ga., 75-1 USTC ¶ 9375, 400 FSupp. 111.

Chapter 33

Year-End and New Year Tax Planning

Overview .... ¶ 3301
Planning Methods .... ¶ 3305
Year-End Planning for Securities Transactions .... ¶ 3310
Year-End Planning Ideas .... ¶ 3315
Year-End Planning for Estimated Taxes .... ¶ 3320
New Year Planning .... ¶ 3325

¶ 3301 OVERVIEW

Year-end tax planning presents important tax-saving opportunities for financial planners and their individual and business clients. Usually the planning should begin early in the last quarter of the tax year. This time is usually late enough to have a good picture of the year. In addition, a financial planner will have a fair basis for predicting the client's income and deductions for the next year.

A common objective of year-end planning is to shift a part of this year's tax burden to the next year. A taxpayer shifts income to the next year by deferring receipt (or accrual) of some income until next year or by accelerating deductions from next year to this year, or both. The real advantage of the tax deferral is that it gives the taxpayer continued use of funds that would otherwise have gone to pay taxes. The use of the funds for a longer time can be a decided benefit.

However, a taxpayer must weigh the benefit of having the funds for a longer period against the cost of the strategies required to receive it.

If a client must postpone the receipt of cash or spend cash to get a tax deduction, the lost use of this money must be measured against the use of the tax money deferred. Of course, if the client can get a deduction without spending cash, the benefit is obvious. Examples include a bad-debt deduction or a loss on a securities transaction.

There are two other important points about tax deferral: (1) The client cannot assume that he or she is going to have the use of the tax dollars saved for the full year. The client should consider the impact of estimated taxes. Depending on various factors, the client might have to pay the tax dollars saved this year in quarterly installments next year. (2) If the effect of deferral is to push the client into a higher bracket next year, he or she might pay more in total taxes for the two years than if matters had been left alone.

The other key objective in year-end tax planning is to level out taxable income from one year to the next. In a progressive income tax system such as ours, the tax bite is minimized by keeping income level. If the client expects that next year's income will be higher, he or she should accelerate some of next year's income into this year and postpone some of this year's tax deductions until next year. If the client expects a drop in next year's income, then he or she should reverse the process, by postponing income while accelerating deductions.

As with the tax deferral approach, the client should perform a cost/benefit analysis. When the client is increasing cash income and postponing cash layouts, he or she is getting the use of more money. How much is that worth to the client and how much does he or she have to pay in added taxes to get it? How much will the leveling off save overall?

Another important objective of year-end planning is to reduce or avoid the penalty for underpayment of estimated taxes.

.01 Impact of Tax Legislation

One factor that can dramatically affect a decision to accelerate or postpone income or deductions is the passage of tax legislation. Most pieces of major tax legislation have provisions that will in some way significantly affect how taxpayers treat particular items of income and deduction. Some provisions in new tax legislation usually take effect on the first day of the year. Other provisions often take effect on specific dates. Where provisions take effect on the first of the year, the planner is presented with an unusually fertile ground for unearthing year-end planning strategies.

.02 Manipulating AGI

A taxpayer might need to accelerate income or defer it in order to meet adjusted gross income (AGI) limitations that accompany certain tax benefits. For example, a taxpayer may wish to lower his or her AGI to take advantage of several tax benefits tied to AGI, including the following based on limitations for the year 2006. Amounts adjusted for inflation are based on Rev. Proc. 2005-70.[1]

- **Roth IRA contributions.** Phased out beginning at AGI of $150,000 for married couples ($95,000 for single taxpayers).[2]
- **Contributions to Coverdell Education Savings Accounts.** Phased out beginning at AGI of $190,000 for married couples ($95,000 for single taxpayers).[3]
- **Hope scholarship credit and lifetime learning credit.** Phased out beginning at AGI of $90,000 for married couples ($45,000 for single taxpayers).[4] These amounts are indexed for inflation.[5]
- **Child tax credit.** Phased out beginning at AGI of $110,000 for married couples ($75,000 for single taxpayers and $55,000 for married filing separately).[6] These amounts are not adjusted for inflation.
- **Education loan interest deduction.** Phased out beginning at AGI of $105,000 for married couples ($50,000 for single taxpayers).[7] These amounts are adjusted for inflation.[8]
- **Deduction for higher education expenses.** A taxpayer may deduct a limited amount of qualified tuition and related expenses in computing AGI. The deduction is limited to $4,000 in 2006. This deduction is not allowed in 2006 and later years (unless Congress enacts an extension). The law allows the deduction for taxpayers with an AGI that does not exceed $130,000 on a joint return and $65,000 for a single taxpayer. The law allows a $2,000 deduction for taxpayers with an AGI that does not exceed $160,000 on a joint return and $80,000 for a single taxpayer for 2005.[9] A married taxpayer who files a separate return may not deduct higher education expenses.[10] A taxpayer who is a nonresident alien for any part of the tax year may deduct higher education expenses only if he or she is treated as a resident alien because of an election under Code Sec. 6013(g) or (h).[11] This provision does not affect education expenses that qualify as a business expense.

In addition to the above tax benefits, the following tax benefits (based on 2006 figures) are also tied to AGI:

- **Personal and dependency exemptions.** Phased out beginning at $225,750 for married couples filing jointly

[1] IRB 2005-47 (October 28, 2005).
[2] Code Sec. 408A(c)(3).
[3] Code Sec. 530(c)(1)(A)(i).
[4] Code Sec. 25A(d)(2)(A).
[5] Code Sec. 25A(h)(2)(A).
[6] Code Sec. 24(b).
[7] Code Sec. 221(b)(2)(B).
[8] Code Sec. 221(g).
[9] Code Sec. 222(b).
[10] Code Sec. 222(d)(4).
[11] Code Sec. 222(d)(5).

($150,500 for single taxpayers and $188,150 for heads of household).[12] The Economic Growth and Tax Relief Reconciliation Act of 2001 repealed the limit on deductions for personal and dependency exemptions for 2010 only. For tax years beginning after December 31, 2005, and before January 1, 2010, the limit on personal and dependency exemption deductions will be reduced every two years.

- **Certain itemized deductions.** Reduced by three percent of AGI over $150,500 (up to a maximum reduction of 80 percent) for both married couples filing jointly and single taxpayers. The threshold is $75,250 for married couples who file separately.[13] The Economic Growth and Tax Relief Reconciliation Act of 2001 repealed the limit on certain itemized deductions for 2010 only. For tax years beginning after December 31, 2005, and before January 1, 2010, the limit on certain itemized deductions will be reduced every two years.
- **IRA contributions for active qualified plan participants.** Phased out beginning at AGI of $75,000 for married couples filing jointly. This amount increases to $80,000 in 2007 and later years. The phase out is $50,000 for a single taxpayer in 2006 and later years.[14]
- **Social Security income.** Up to 85 percent includible in gross income if AGI exceeds certain amounts (based on certain formulas).[15]
- **Credit for household and dependent care services necessary for gainful employment.** Commonly called the child care credit, it decreases for AGI of more than $15,000 and levels out at AGI in excess of $43,000, for both married couples filing jointly and single taxpayers.[16]
- **Interest exemption for savings bonds used for qualified higher education expenses.** Phased out beginning at AGI of $94,700 for married couples filing jointly ($63,100 for other returns).[17]
- **Exception to the passive loss deduction limitation for active participants.** Phased out starting at AGI of $100,000 for both married couples filing jointly and single taxpayers (a higher limit applies if rehabilitation tax credits were utilized).[18]

[12] Code Sec. 151(d).
[13] Code Sec. 68.
[14] Code Sec. 219(g)(3)(B).
[15] Code Sec. 86.
[16] Code Sec. 21(a).
[17] Code Sec. 135.
[18] Code Sec. 469(i).

Itemized deductions not tied to the reduction for 3 percent of AGI in excess of the $150,500 ($75,250 for married filing separately) threshold (for 2006) include deductions for medical expenses, investment interest, casualty losses, and wagering losses (to the extent of winnings).[19]

Planning pointer. The 2-percent AGI floor for miscellaneous itemized deductions,[20] the 7.5-percent floor on medical expense deductions,[21] and the 10-percent floor on casualty and theft losses[22] decrease as AGI decreases. Thus, lowering AGI allows more expenses to be deductible. On the other hand, lowering AGI may reduce the charitable deduction because the deduction is limited to 50 percent of AGI (30 percent for capital gain property and for contributions to private foundations, 20 percent for capital gain property given to private foundations).[23]

.03 Alternative Minimum Tax Considerations

For those within range of the alternative minimum tax,[24] the need for year-end tax planning becomes particularly acute. Such individuals may find themselves in a situation where further deductions against their regular income only serve to expose them to alternative minimum tax liability. Thus, any additional deductions would be wasted. To avoid loss of these deductions, the client could shift the deductions, or part of them, to a year in which they would provide a tax benefit. Alternatively, the strategy might be to limit the deduction in the first place. For example, the client could use alternative depreciation, rather than regular depreciation (MACRS), in appropriate situations.[25]

If the client cannot avoid the alternative minimum tax, a different strategy can save taxes: accelerate income into the year when the alternative minimum tax is due. The rate of tax on extra income subject to AMT is either 26 percent or 28 percent,[26] compared to a regular tax top rate of 35 percent through 2010.[27]

¶ 3305 PLANNING METHODS

After the individual decides whether to postpone or accelerate income or deductions, he or she then looks for ways and means to accomplish the chosen objective.

---

[19] Code Sec. 68(c).
[20] Code Sec. 67.
[21] Code Sec. 213(a).
[22] Code Sec. 165(h).
[23] Code Sec. 170.
[24] Code Sec. 55.
[25] Code Sec. 168.
[26] Code Sec. 55(b)(1)(A)(i).
[27] Code Sec. 1.

.01 Postponing Income

The opportunities for an individual to postpone income are limited. Some key methods include the following:

- Postponing the sale of investments at a profit
- Making installment sales of property that qualifies for installment reporting, thereby pushing all or a portion of the gain over to subsequent years
- Deferring compensation under a plan
- Postponing the receipt of distributions from a pension or profit-sharing plan until next year or taking annuity payments
- Giving income-producing property to family members age 18 or over before the right to income ripens
- Billing customers or clients at the beginning of the new year
- Delaying the completion of sales and contracts, finishing construction jobs, etc.
- Purchasing Treasury bills, certificates of deposit, and other investments that will mature in the next year (provided that the taxpayer is a cash-basis taxpayer)
- Making additional contributions to qualified plans or IRAs, if available
- Making additional contributions to an Archer Medical Savings Account (MSA)[28] or health savings account.[29]

If the employer, for reasons of his or her own, defers payment of a year-end bonus until January, the employee recognizes the income in the new year. But the employer must not give the employee a choice as to when payment is to be made because he or she would then be deemed to be in constructive receipt when the choice is presented. In such cases, the employee would report the income in the old year when the employee constructively received it.[30]

.02 Accelerating Income

One of the practical ways an individual has to accelerate income is to make profitable sales of assets this year instead of next year.

A redemption of U.S. savings bonds can accelerate interest income. Distributions from traditional IRAs or qualified plans can be accelerated. Dividends can be taken out of a closely held corporation. Sending bills to clients early enough so collection during the

[28] Code Sec. 220.

[29] Code Sec. 223.

[30] Code Sec. 451 and Reg. § 1.451-2.

current year is expected might be an effective way to accelerate income. Similarly, completing sales, contracts, and construction jobs may help.

.03 Postponing Deductions

Here are the major ways of postponing deductions:

- Delay the sale of a loss investment.
- Delay payment of deductible items (if doing so does not impair credit standing or incur late charges).
- Postpone charitable contributions.

.04 Accelerating Deductions

An individual may accelerate into this year certain deductions he or she would otherwise take next year. He or she may accelerate deductions by doing the following:

- Double up on charitable contributions, making next year's and this year's currently; a pledge will not do.
- Take losses on investments.
- Prepay state or city income taxes. Where the taxing authority has the estimated tax system, this will generate a deduction. If the taxing authority does not have such a system, prepayment will be deductible if the authority accepts it as *payment*, not merely as a deposit against future tax.
- Prepay property taxes. The IRS will allow a deduction for prepayment of property taxes if the taxing authority accepts amounts tendered as *payment*, not as a deposit against future taxes.
- Incur above-the-line expenses early, such as moving expenses.

In general, a deduction for prepaid interest is allowable only in the tax year in which the interest is earned or accrued.[31]

¶ 3310 YEAR-END PLANNING FOR SECURITIES TRANSACTIONS

The tax rate for most net capital gains realized through the end of 2010 is 15 percent. For taxpayers in the 10-percent or 15-percent marginal rate for ordinary income, the tax rate for most net capital gains realized through the end of 2007 is 5 percent. For tax year's 2008 through 2010, the tax rate on net capital gains for taxpayers in

[31] Code Sec. 461(g).

the 10-percent or 15-percent marginal rate for ordinary income is 0 percent. For tax years beginning in 2011 and later, the tax rates of 20 percent and 15 percent on net capital gains that were in effect before the Jobs and Growth Tax Relief Reconciliation Act of 2003 will apply once again. A net capital gain is the excess of a net long-term capital gain over any net short-term capital loss. However, a rate of 28 percent applies to long-term capital gains from sales or exchanges of collectibles, and a rate of 25 percent applies to unrecaptured Code Sec. 1250 gain (depreciation recapture on real estate). Losses for each long-term tax-rate group will be used to offset gains within the group. If a long-term tax-rate group has a net loss, the loss will be used first to offset net gain for the highest long-term tax-rate group, then to offset the next highest tax-rate group, and so on.

> ***Example 33.1.*** Bob Smith has a net loss for the 15-percent tax-rate group. That net loss will be used first to offset any net gain in the 28-percent group, and then net gain in the 25-percent group (gains on depreciation recapture under Code Sec. 1250).

A carryover of a net long-term capital loss from a prior year can be used first to offset net gain for the long-term highest tax-rate group, and so on.

A net short-term capital loss (that is, a net loss from capital transactions involving holding periods of one year or less) can be used to first offset net gain for the highest long-term tax-rate group, and so on.

> ***Comment.*** Code Sec. 1(h) provides the tax rates on the various categories of capital gains. The IRS announced their interpretation of these rules in Notice 97-59.[32] Taxpayers could not get a much better interpretation of the rules on treatment of capital losses. From a year-end tax planning perspective, taxpayers who accelerate the recognition of a net loss in the 15-percent group can use it to offset net capital gains otherwise taxable at the 28-percent rate, rather than having to wait to use them to offset 15-percent rate gains in the next year.

¶ 3315 YEAR-END PLANNING IDEAS

Consider the following year-end financial or estate planning ideas before the close of December.

.01 Gifts

The client could make as many annual exclusion ($12,000 for 2006 and indexed to inflation) gifts to donees (double the amount

[32] 1997-2 CB 309.

of annual exclusion gifts if the client is married and the spouse consents to "split" the gifts) as he or she desires. The annual gift tax exclusion per donee is lost if not used before the end of the year.[33]

.02 Charities

Compute the maximum charitable income tax deduction that the client may be allowed for the year and advise the client to make charitable donations accordingly.[34]

.03 Losses

If a client wants to recognize a year-end loss, he or she should not sell securities to a family member. Such a loss will not be allowed on the income tax return. For this purpose, a family member means a spouse, brother, sister, ancestor or lineal descendant. However, a loss realized on a sale to an in-law, aunt, uncle, nephew, niece, cousin, or unrelated person will be recognized.[35]

.04 Spouse's Gains and Losses

If a client is married, he or she should double-check each spouse's capital gains and losses. Capital gains realized by one spouse may be offset by capital losses incurred by the other. This rule applies though each spouse owns securities in his or her own name.

.05 Basis

A client should not make a gift of stock or other property that has declined substantially in value since he or she bought it. If the client does so, the donee's basis for determining a loss is the lower of the donor's basis or the fair market value at the time of gift.[36] Thus, the client will probably do better if he or she sells the property, realizes a capital loss for tax purposes, and then makes a gift of the proceeds.

.06 Dividend Income

To shift some dividend income to a lower bracket member of the family, a client could make a gift of the dividend-paying security before the year-end dividend. It will then show up on the donee's income tax return, not the donor's. However, the client should keep in mind the income tax rules for minors under the age of 18. However, shifting dividend income might not be a good strategy in many cases. Qualified dividends received through December 31, 2010, are generally taxed at 15 percent. Qualified dividends are taxed at 5 percent for taxpayers in the 10-percent or 15-percent

[33] Code Sec. 2503(b) and Code Sec. 2513.

[34] Code Sec. 170.

[35] Code Sec. 267.

[36] Code Sec. 1015(a).

rate brackets. For tax year's 2008 through 2010, qualified dividends are taxed at 0 percent to taxpayers in the 10-percent or 15-percent rate brackets.

.07 Keogh and SEP Plans

For self-employed individuals, a Keogh plan must be set up before the end of the year. However, a self-employed individual may establish a SEP plan up to the extended due date of his or her income tax return. A self-employed individual may make contributions to either plan up to the filing of a timely return.

¶ 3320 YEAR-END PLANNING FOR ESTIMATED TAXES

Generally, a taxpayer may avoid the penalty for underpayment of estimated taxes by making timely payments of estimated taxes that exceed 90 percent of the current year's tax liability of 100 percent of the prior year's tax liability.[37] To use the 100 percent of the prior year's tax liability exception, the taxpayer must have filed a tax return for the prior taxable year. In addition, the prior taxable year must have been a 12-month taxable year. However, if the taxpayer's AGI was greater than $150,000 in the preceding year, the taxpayer must pay 110 percent of the prior year's tax liability in timely estimated payments to avoid the penalty.[38]

Also, the penalty does not apply if the gross tax liability minus withholding is less than $1,000.[39] In addition, the penalty will not apply if the taxpayer did not have any tax liability in the preceding tax year if the preceding tax year was a 12-month year and the taxpayer was a U.S. citizen or resident for the preceding tax year.[40] For this purpose, tax liability refers to gross tax liability rather than net tax due. The Code treats tax withheld as though paid in equal amounts on the due dates for estimated payments.[41]

Thus, a taxpayer may be able to reduce or avoid the penalty for underpayment of estimated tax by having tax withheld late in the year. A taxpayer who owns a corporation can pay a bonus to himself or herself and withhold tax to avoid or reduce the penalty. The bonus must qualify as reasonable compensation.[42]

¶ 3325 NEW YEAR PLANNING

Tax planning is not limited to a particular time of year, but it is something that requires consideration throughout the year. In fact,

[37] Code Sec. 6654(d)(1)(B).
[38] Code Sec. 6654(d)(1)(C).
[39] Code Sec. 6654(e)(1).
[40] Code Sec. 6654(e)(2).
[41] Code Sec. 6654(g)(1).
[42] Code Sec. 162(a).

the earlier the process begins, the easier the taxpayer can achieve maximum tax savings. A client should consider the following planning opportunities because they also represent wealth-building strategies.

.01 Reducing AGI

The reduction of adjusted gross income (AGI) can be important in the impact of Code Sec. 68, which, for 2006, reduces itemized deductions (except medical, casualty, theft, investment interest and wagering losses) by three percent of AGI in excess of $150,500 ($75,250 on separate returns by marrieds). This reduction of AGI is also important because of the phaseout of personal exemptions on AGI in excess of $225,750 on joint returns by marrieds ($188,150 for heads of household, $150,500 for singles and $112,875 for marrieds filing separately) at a rate of two percent on each unit of AGI of $2,500 in excess of the threshold amount (2006 figures). To reduce AGI, consider the following:

- IRA contributions (deductible and nondeductible)
- Salary reduction plans (401k plans and 403b plans)
- Keogh contributions
- SEP plan contributions
- SIMPLE plan contributions
- Use of pretax dollars to fund a flexible spending account, an Archer medical savings account, or a health savings account
- Voluntary contributions to a qualified plan (takes income earned on contributions out of an individual's gross income)
- Deferred compensation arrangement
- Tax-exempt income
- Converting taxable earned income into tax-favored fringe benefits, such as accident and health insurance, group-term life insurance, company below-market loans, legal services, educational assistance, and company services and products acquired at discounts

Note. The earlier in the year the taxpayer takes these steps, the greater the benefits.

.02 Family Gifts

A taxpayer can make gifts of income-producing property to family members to remove the income from the property from his or her gross income.

.03 Capital Gains

Income from most net capital gains realized through the end of 2010 is taxed at a maximum rate of 15 percent. However, for taxpayers in the 10 percent and 15 percent regular tax brackets, the capital gain rate is only 5 percent (zero percent for 2008 through 2010). Consider transferring capital asset held for more than one year to junior family members for tax at 5 (or zero) percent.

.04 Personal Interest

Convert nondeductible personal interest to deductible qualified residence interest.

.05 College Fund

The earlier in the year the client contributes to the fund, the better.

.06 Employment of Family Members

Owners of family businesses receive tax deductions on compensation paid to family members. In addition, wages paid to one's child under the age of 18 are exempt from FICA tax.[43] Senior family members under age 65 who receive Social Security benefits may have compensation tailored to minimize loss of benefits. Social Security recipients who are age 65 or older no longer lose Social Security benefits because of compensation.

.07 Minimum Distributions from Retirement Plans

Delaying the distributions until year-end allows the taxpayer to take full advantage of tax deferral.

.08 Use of Installment Sale

Can defer payment of tax and possibly reduce tax for those that will be eligible for the lowest capital gain tax rate when the payments are received.

.09 Dependency

Faced with loss of a dependent's exemption by phaseout, enabling the dependent to cease being a dependent allows the individual to become eligible for his or her own personal exemption and lower-bracket tax status, plus receive the full standard deduction.

---

[43] Code Sec. 3121(b)(3)(A).

Chapter 34

Maximizing Deductions and Reducing Taxes

Overview .... ¶ 3401
Exemptions .... ¶ 3405
Tax Credits .... ¶ 3410
Charitable Contributions .... ¶ 3415
Medical Expenses and Insurance .... ¶ 3420
Interest .... ¶ 3425
Bad Debts .... ¶ 3430
Estate Planning, Tax Advice, and Tax-Related Expenses .... ¶ 3435
Planning for the Limitation on Deductions for Itemized Expenses .... ¶ 3440
Employment Tax .... ¶ 3445
Adoption Credit and Exclusion .... ¶ 3450

¶ 3401 OVERVIEW

There are many ways to reduce income taxes. This chapter covers some of the various methods that can be used.

¶ 3405 EXEMPTIONS

The dependency exemption is $3,300 in 2006 (subject to indexing in future years). The primary concern is about exemptions for dependent children, but exemptions for other relatives are also addressed. Loss of exemptions for high-income individuals is considered, as is the impact of exemptions on a dependent's standard deduction. A taxpayer must include on the return the Social Security number of any dependent for whom an exemption is claimed.

.01 Children

Ensuring that the parent, who typically has a larger income than the child, receives the exemption is often the planning aim. However, the opposite may be true for higher income individuals, as separately discussed below. For a parent to claim the exemption for a "qualifying child," the child (1) must have the same principal place of abode as the parent for more than one-half of that tax year; (2) must not have attained age 19 or, if a student, age 24; and (3) must not have provided over one-half of his or her own support for the calendar year in which the taxpayer's tax year begins.[1] Scholarships received by a child are excluded from amounts spent for the child's support.[2] In most instances, whether a child furnishes more than half of his or her support is clear. However, when a child earns income through part-time employment, the parent should consider the support test carefully. For example, the parent may want to have the child save enough of his or her income so that the child is providing less than one-half of his or her support.

If the parents are divorced or separated, the parents together must provide over half the support of the child to claim a dependency exemption for the child.[3] The custodial parent generally gets the exemption deduction.[4] However, the custodial parent may waive the right to claim the exemption in favor of the other parent by filing Form 8332, "Release of Claim to Exemption for Child of Divorced or Separated Parents."[5] Financial planners should encourage their clients to use this form and not rely solely on the divorce decree.[6] The noncustodial parent might be able to negotiate a release of the claim for the exemption for the child.

.02 Other Relatives

An individual is entitled to a dependency exemption for a parent or almost any other relative, even in-laws, if the individual furnishes more than half of the relative's support, and the relative has gross income that is less than the exemption amount.[7]

.03 Impact on Standard Deduction

The standard deduction of an individual who may be claimed as a dependent on another taxpayer's return is limited to the greater of $850 or the sum of the individual's earned income and $300 for the

---

[1] Code Sec. 152(c)(1).

[2] Code Sec. 151(f)(5).

[3] Code Sec. 152(e)(1)(A).

[4] Code Sec. 152(e)(1).

[5] Code Sec. 152(e)(2).

[6] *M.R. Loffer*, TC Memo 2002-98, 84 TCM 618 (2002) and *M.S. Norwood and C.R. Norwood*, TC Memo 2003-63, 85 TCM 982 (2003).

[7] Code Sec. 152(a).

year 2006.[8] This limitation does not apply with respect to the additional standard deduction allowed to elderly or blind individuals.

.04 Reverse Planning for Higher Income Individuals

Individuals with substantial income may consider reverse planning for the dependency exemption because of the phaseout of the personal exemptions. For 2006, the exemption phases out at the rate of two percent for each $2,500 (or fraction thereof) of adjusted gross income (AGI) in excess of $225,750 for a joint return ($112,875 for married persons filing separately), $188,150 for a head of household, $150,000 for a single filer, and fully phases out when AGI exceeds $348,250 on a joint return, $310,650 for head of household, $273,000 for a single filer, and $174,125 for married individuals filing separately. For tax years beginning after December 31, 2005, and before January 1, 2010, the reduction in the allowable deduction for personal and dependency exemptions will be reduced every two years. The reduction is repealed for tax year 2010 only.

Individuals who may partially or fully lose the benefit of the exemption and who have dependents with incomes subject to tax, might want to ensure that each dependent is entitled to claim his or her own exemption. An added bonus is that the child's standard deduction would not be limited, as discussed above.

Consider the effect on state income taxes. Also, check that employee benefits that extend to dependents are not cut off by reverse planning. If the plan defines "dependent" with reference to the federal dependency exemption, reverse planning may be inadvisable.

.05 Reducing Adjusted Gross Income (AGI)

One method for avoiding loss of personal exemptions under the phaseout mechanism is to reduce AGI. Most deductions are not allowed in computing AGI. However, deductions for contributions to HR 10 (Keogh) plans, SEP plans, SIMPLE plans, traditional IRAs, Archer Medical Savings Accounts, and Health Savings Accounts are allowed in arriving at AGI.[9] Another device is to reduce compensation through deferred compensation plans and contributions to benefit plans. Employee contributions to 401(k) and 403(b) deferred compensation plans are excluded from gross income and thus are not included in AGI. Similarly, contributions by employees to qualified cafeteria plans[10] are also excluded from compensation and AGI.

---

[8] Code Sec. 63(c)(5).

[9] Code Sec. 62(a)(2).

[10] Code Sec. 125.

.06 Multiple Support Arrangements

Problems may arise where a person shares in the support of a dependent. This situation might occur if several adult children support an elderly parent. In this situation, instead of having each of the contributors fighting to claim the exemption, the individuals can enter into a multiple support agreement so that the contributors take turns claiming the dependency exemption. In the case of two or more contributors, any one contributor does not have to contribute more than half the dependent's support. However, all of the contributors together must contribute over half the dependent's support and meet all other requirements for claiming a dependency exemption. Those who contribute more than 10 percent of the dependent's support may agree on who is to get the exemption, and the rest must promise in writing that they will not claim the exemption. A taxpayer should use Form 2120 to claim a dependency exemption using a multiple support agreement.

¶ 3410 TAX CREDITS

.01 Child Care Credit

A parent may receive a tax credit for amounts paid for the care of a dependent child under age 13[11] to allow the parent to work or attend school full-time.[12] This credit is the credit for expenses for household and dependent care services necessary for gainful employment, but it is commonly called the child care credit.[13] A parent could shift income within the extended family by paying the child's grandparents for taking care of their grandchildren under age 13 while the parent is at work or attending school full-time, subject to the general rules governing the child care credit. However, payments to individuals who are dependents do not qualify for the credit.[14]

The base for the credit is the least of (1) the amount paid for eligible expenses, (2) the taxpayer's earned income if single or if married the lesser of the earned income of each spouse, and (3) the maximum amount allowed. For tax years through 2010, a parent who is a full-time student is deemed to have earned income of $250 per month for one eligible child or $500 per month for two or more eligible children for each month that the parent is a full-time student.[15] For these tax years, the maximum base for the credit is $3,000 for one qualifying child or dependent and $6,000 for two or more qualifying children or dependents.[16]

---

[11] Code Sec. 21(b)(1)(A).
[12] Code Sec. 21(d).
[13] Code Sec. 21.
[14] Code Sec. 21(d)(6).
[15] Code Sec. 21(d)(2).
[16] Code Sec. 21(c).

For taxpayers with adjusted gross income in excess of $43,000 for tax years through 2010, the credit is 20 percent of the expense.[17] The maximum credit for such taxpayers in tax years through 2010 is $600, or $1,200 if there are two or more children or dependents. The maximum amount of expenses eligible for the credit must be reduced by the amount excludable under a Code Sec. 129 employer-provided dependent care assistance plan.[18] Financial planners should inform their clients that as long as the payments include compensation for the care of a qualifying individual, that payments for household services, such as cleaning, qualify for the credit.[19]

.02 Child Tax Credit

In addition to the child care credit, taxpayers who have qualifying children under age 17 are entitled to a child tax credit.[20] The amount of the credit is $1,000 per child through 2010. In 2011, the child tax credit is reduced to $500 per child. The child tax credit is limited to the excess of the taxpayer's regular tax liability over the tentative minimum tax for the year.

At certain levels of modified adjusted gross income, the credit begins to be phased out at a reduction of $50 for every $1,000 above the threshold levels.[21] The threshold levels where the credit begins to be phased out are as follows:[22]

	Phase out begins at:
Joint filers	$110,000
Marrieds, filing separately	55,000
Singles	75,000

The level of modified adjusted gross income of which the child tax credit is completely phased out depends on the number of qualifying children. These threshold amounts are not adjusted for inflation.

Part of the child tax credit is refundable for all taxpayers with qualifying children regardless of the taxpayer's regular tax liability or alternative minimum tax liability. The credit is refundable to the extent of the taxpayer's earned income in excess of 15 percent of the taxpayer's earned income that exceeds $11,300 (in 2006 and indexed for inflation) up to the per child credit amount. Taxpayers with three or more children may calculate the refundable portion of the credit using the excess of their Social Security taxes and one half of their

[17] Code Sec. 21(a)(2).
[18] Code Sec. 21(c).
[19] Code Sec. 21(b)(2)(A).
[20] Code Sec. 24(a).
[21] Code Sec. 24(b)(1).
[22] Code Sec. 24(b)(2).

self-employment taxes over the earned income credit instead of the 15-percent amount if it results in a greater refundable credit.

Hurricane Katrina victims may elect to calculate the refundable child tax credit for a tax year that includes August 25, 2005, by using their earned income for 2004. If the taxpayer makes this election, the taxpayer must also use the earned income for 2004 to calculate the earned income credit.

> **Planning pointer.** The parent who is entitled to the dependency exemption for a child is the parent who may claim the child tax credit. Therefore the child tax credit is a major consideration in negotiating divorce agreements and multiple support agreements.

.03 Earned Income Credit

The earned income credit is a refundable tax credit for low income taxpayers.[23] A taxpayer with investment income over $2,800 (for 2006 and indexed for inflation) is not eligible for the credit.[24] The maximum amount of the credit for 2006 is $412 if the taxpayer has no qualifying children. If the taxpayer has one qualifying child, the maximum credit is $2,747. If the taxpayer has two or more qualifying children, the maximum credit is $4,536. A qualifying child includes natural children, stepchildren, siblings, and descendants of any of these qualifying children. In addition, qualifying children include eligible foster children.[25] The child must be under age 19 at the end of the year or a full-time student under age 24.[26] In addition, a child who is permanently and totally disabled at any time during the tax year is a qualifying child regardless of age.[27] The qualifying child must live with the taxpayer for more than half the year.[28] A taxpayer who does not have a qualifying child may claim the credit if the taxpayer or the taxpayer's spouse is at least age 25 but less than age 65 at the end of the tax year. The taxpayer must have lived in the United States for more than half the year and not be a dependent of another taxpayer.[29] The amount of the credit is based on the taxpayer's earned income.[30] A taxpayer who is married must file a joint return to claim the credit.[31]

---

[23] Code Sec. 32.
[24] Code Sec. 32(i).
[25] Code Sec. 32(c)(3).
[26] Code Sec. 32(c)(3)(C).
[27] Code Sec. 32(c)(3)(C).
[28] Code Sec. 32(c)(3)(A).
[29] Code Sec. 32(c)(1)(A).
[30] Code Sec. 32(a)(2)(B).
[31] Code Sec. 32(d).

The table below shows for the year 2005 the income necessary to receive the maximum credit, the income at which the maximum credit begins to be phased out, and the income at which the credit is eliminated for a filing status other than married filing jointly. These amounts and the maximum credit available are adjusted for inflation each year.[32]

Number of Children	Income to Receive Maximum Credit Available	Income at Which Phase-out Begins	Income at Which Credit Is Eliminated
0	$ 5,380	$ 6,740	$12,120
1	$ 8,080	$14,810	$32,001
2 or more	$11,340	$14,810	$36,348

The table below shows for the year 2006 the income necessary to receive the maximum credit, the income at which the maximum credit begins to be phased out, and the income at which the credit is eliminated for a filing status of married filing jointly. These amounts and the maximum credit available are adjusted for inflation each year.[33]

Number of Children	Income to Receive Maximum Credit Available	Income at Which Phase-out Begins	Income at Which Credit Is Eliminated
0	$ 5,380	$ 8,740	$14,120
1	$ 8,080	$16,810	$34,001
2 or more	$11,340	$16,810	$38,848

Earned income includes only taxable employee compensation and self-employment income.

.04 Credit for the Elderly and the Permanently and Totally Disabled

The law allows a nonrefundable credit for taxpayers who are age 65 or older by the end of the year or who are retired on disability because of permanent and total disability.[34] The credit is equal to 15 percent of a base amount less Social Security benefits, railroad retirement benefits and veteran's benefits excluded from gross income. Thus, if Social Security or similar benefits equal or exceed the base amount, the taxpayer is not eligible for the credit. The base

[32] Code Sec. 32(j).
[33] Code Sec. 32(j).
[34] Code Sec. 22(b).

amount is $5,000 for a single taxpayer or on a joint return where only one spouse qualifies, $7,500 on a joint return where both spouses qualify, and $3,750 on a married filing separately return. In addition, if the taxpayer is under age 65 at the end of the year, the base amount may not exceed the disability income received during the year.[35] Further, if the taxpayer's AGI exceeds a threshold amount, the taxpayer must reduce the base for the credit by half the AGI over the threshold amount. The threshold amount is $7,500 for a single filer, $10,000 on a joint return, and $5,000 for married filing separately.[36] The base amounts and threshold amounts are not adjusted for inflation. A married couple must file a joint return to claim the credit unless they lived apart for the entire year.[37] A nonresident alien may not claim the credit.[38]

> ***Example 34.1.*** Anthony and Maria Santucci are each age 65. During the year, they began to receive Social Security benefits. They received $2,000 in Social Security benefits during the year. In addition, they had $13,000 in interest income. They would compute their credit for the elderly as follows:

Base Amount	$7,500
Less: Excluded Social Security Benefits	(2,000)
Less: AGI Adjustment	
($13,000 – $10,000) × 50% =	(1,500)
Base for the Credit	$4,000
Rate	× 15%
Tentative Credit (Limited to Tax Liability)	$ 600

¶ 3415 CHARITABLE CONTRIBUTIONS

Chapter 5 offers a detailed treatment of charitable giving, from both income tax and estate tax points of view. There, giving on a major scale is discussed, including such matters as gifts of appreciated property, bargain sales of appreciated property, gifts of charitable remainders, pooled income funds, charitable remainders in a personal residence or farm, and contributions of future interests in tangible personal property (art, paintings, and the like). Chapter 5 also covers charitable annuities and gifts of life insurance as well as gifts of income. This chapter discusses charitable giving on a more everyday basis.

[35] Code Sec. 22(c).
[36] Code Sec. 22(d).
[37] Code Sec. 22(e)(1).
[38] Code Sec. 22(f).

.01 Contributions of $250 or More

A taxpayer who makes a contribution of $250 or more may not deduct it unless the gift is substantiated by a contemporaneous written acknowledgement from the charity.[39] A canceled check is not considered proof. "Contemporaneous" means on or before the earlier of the date the taxpayer files his or her return for the year in which the contribution is made or the due date plus extensions for the return.[40] From a practical standpoint, however, donors should get written acknowledgement from the charity as soon as they make each affected contribution.

The disallowance rule for unsubstantiated gifts of $250 or more applies separately to each gift.[41] Although gifts generally are not aggregated, the IRS warns that it is authorized to issue antiabuse rules to prevent avoidance "by taxpayers writing separate smaller checks on the same date."

There is no prescribed acknowledgement form. The charity's statement must, however, indicate the donor's name (the Social Security number or taxpayer ID is not necessary) and provide sufficient information to substantiate the amount of the contribution. Separate acknowledgements for each $250 contribution are not necessary; the charity can furnish periodic statements substantiating such contributions.[42]

The information that the donor must obtain from the charity depends on the type of donation:

- For gratuitous contributions of $250 or more in cash, the charity indicates the amount given, and that the donor received nothing in return.
- For gratuitous contributions of $250 or more in property (or cash and property), the charity must describe, but need not value, the property and also must state that the donor received nothing in return.[43]
- For contributions of $250 or more where the donor receives intangible religious benefits in exchange, the acknowledgement requirements generally are the same as for gratuitous contributions. However, the charity must state that the donor received an intangible religious benefit, although it need not value or describe it.[44] An intangible religious benefit is one provided by an organization exclusively for religious purposes and of a type that is not generally sold

[39] Code Sec. 170(f)(8)(A).
[40] Code Sec. 170(f)(8)(C).
[41] Reg. § 1.170A-13(f)(1).
[42] Code Sec. 170(f)(8)(C).
[43] Code 170(f)(8)(B)(i).
[44] Reg. § 1.170A-13(f)(2)(iv).

outside the donative context. An example of such an intangible religious benefit is admission to a religious ceremony.[45]

Under Reg. § 1-170A-13, goods or services that have insubstantial value as determined under annually indexed IRS guidelines need not be taken into account by the charity for purposes of the $250 rule. Also, this regulation addresses contributions by payroll and provides that for purposes of the $250 threshold, each paycheck is treated as a separate contribution.

.02 Quid Pro Quo Contributions

Charities that solicit or receive quid pro quo contributions in excess of $75 (i.e., payments that are partly contributions and partly consideration for goods or services from the charity, e.g., football tickets provided by a college, dinner supplied by a religious organization, or a compact disc supplied by a public television station) must supply the donor with a written statement that essentially makes a good faith estimate of the deductible portion of the payment. There is a de minimis exception and an exception for receipt of an intangible religious benefit. Charities that fail to comply are hit with penalties.[46]

.03 Gifts of Used Clothing, Furniture, Etc.

The important issue here is fair valuation. Some charities give the donor a written statement of value. Regardless of whether the charity gives such a statement, if a donor gives used items whose total valuation exceeds $500 in a taxable year, the donor must file Form 8283.[47] If the total deduction is over $5,000, the donor must obtain appraisals of the values of the donated property.[48]

.04 Wheelchairs and Medical Equipment

The patient who has recovered from an illness and who no longer requires a wheelchair, special bed, crutches, braces, or other special equipment may donate them to a hospital, and receive a deduction for their fair market value provided the taxpayer held such items for more than one year. The patient might have deducted these same items as medical expenses, and thus can generate double deductions. If the taxpayer held these items for one year or less, the deduction would be limited to the taxpayer's adjusted basis in the items donated.[49]

---

[45] S Rep No. 36, 103d Cong. 1st Sess. (1993).
[46] Code Sec. 6115.
[47] Reg. § 1.170A-13(b)(3).
[48] Reg. § 1.170A-13(c).
[49] Code Sec. 170(e).

.05 Scenic Views and Other Easements

Contributions of open-air or scenic easements by a property owner to the federal, state, or local government may be deducted. The value of the contribution is measured by the difference between the fair market value of the property before and after the granting of the easement.[50] An enforceable easement in perpetuity contributed to the state by the owner of a mansion declared to be a state landmark has qualified as a charitable contribution of a scenic easement.[51]

A right-of-way easement may also qualify. An easement along the edge of a person's property for use by the general public for hiking and skiing may also qualify.[52] An estate tax charitable deduction for qualified easements is also available.[53]

.06 Donations of Vehicles

If the taxpayer donates a vehicle worth over $500, the taxpayer must obtain a contemporaneous written acknowledgement from the charity. If the charitable organization sells the vehicle without any significant intervening use or significant improvement of the vehicle, the deduction will be limited to the gross proceeds from the sale. The acknowledgement must contain the taxpayer's name and taxpayer identification number, and the vehicle identification number or similar number. If the charitable organization sold the vehicle without any significant intervening use or improvements, the charitable organization must also state that it sold the vehicle in an arm's length transaction to an unrelated party, the gross proceeds from the sale, and state that the deductible amount may not exceed the amount of such gross proceeds.[54]

.07 Unreimbursed Expenses

If a person works for a charity, including service as an unsalaried federal, state, or local official, he or she may deduct as a charitable contribution unreimbursed commuting expenses, cost of uniforms, telephone calls, materials, supplies, stationery, stamps, and other items. Through 2006, a taxpayer may deduct $500 for each evacuee from Hurricane Katrina for whom the taxpayer provides housing in the taxpayer's principal residence for at least 60 consecutive days. The maximum deduction is $2,000. The taxpayer may claim it once for all tax years.

---

[50] Rev. Rul. 73-339, 1973-2 CB 68, as clarified in Rev. Rul. 76-376, 1976-2 CB 53.

[51] Rev. Rul. 75-358, 1975-2 CB 76.

[52] Rev. Rul. 74-583, 1974-2 CB 80.

[53] Code Sec. 2055(f).

[54] Code Sec. 170(f)(12).

If a taxpayer uses his or her car for charitable work, 14 cents per mile can be deducted.[55] No deduction is allowed for charitable travel expenses, such as the cost of a trip to attend an organization's national convention as a delegate of a local group (unless there is no significant element of personal pleasure or vacation time).[56] For miles driven on behalf of a charity for work related to Hurricane Katrina, the taxpayer may deduct 70 percent of the standard business mileage rate beginning on August 25, 2005, through December 31, 2006. The standard business mileage rate is for 2006 is 44.5 cents per mile. Therefore, the taxpayer may deduct 32 cents per mile for miles driven for charity work related to Hurricane Katrina during 2006.

.08 Certain Ordinary Income Business Property—Inventory

A corporation, other than an S corporation, may take a deduction for ordinary income property, such as inventory, in an amount that exceeds its tax basis, on certain conditions:

- The use of the property by the charity is related to its charitable purpose and the property is to be used solely for the care of the ill, needy, or infants;
- The property is not transferred by the donee;
- The corporation receives from the charity a written statement representing that its use and disposition of the property will be in accordance with paragraphs 1 and 2; and
- If the property is subject to regulation under the Federal Food, Drug, and Cosmetic Act, it meets the applicable requirements on the date of transfer and for 180 days prior to the transfer.

If *all* these conditions are met, then Code Sec. 170(e)(3) allows a deduction equal to the basis plus one-half of the appreciation of the property, in no event to exceed twice the basis of the property.

¶ 3420 MEDICAL EXPENSES AND INSURANCE

.01 Medical Expenses

Medical care expenses, subject to the 7.5-percent floor discussed below, are tax deductible. Code Sec. 213 defines "medical care" expenses to include amounts paid "for the diagnosis, cure, mitigation, treatment or prevention of disease for the purpose of affecting any structure or function of the body." The IRS interprets this as including the services of physicians, surgeons, psychiatrists, dentists,

[55] Code Sec. 170(i).

[56] Code Sec. 170(j).

optometrists, chiropractors, osteopaths, physiotherapists, podiatrists, psychologists, nurses, and Christian Science practitioners.

The IRS has ruled that expenses for certain weight-loss programs are deductible as medical expenses.[57] The taxpayer must have incurred the expenses for treatment of a specific disease, including obesity, diagnosed by a physician.

The Code further includes medical travel expenses and health insurance as deductible items. The Code's definitions have been the subject of much interpretation by the IRS and the courts. The definition might be broader than one thinks.

Capital improvements to a home for medical care such as elevators, inclinators, air conditioning, special ramps, intercom systems, a special motor-driven hospital bed, and other items may qualify to the extent that they do not increase the home's value.[58] Also, if a capital expenditure qualifies as a medical expense, the cost of maintenance will also qualify so long as the medical reason continues.

Code Sec. 213(d)(9) generally denies a medical deduction for cosmetic surgery. Exceptions apply for the removal of congenital defects. Cosmetic surgery to ameliorate a personal injury resulting from an accident or trauma or to ameliorate a disfiguring disease is also excepted. Cosmetic surgery includes any procedure aimed at improving a patient's appearance and that does not meaningfully promote the proper function of the body or prevent or treat disease or illness.[59]

The most serious limitation on the use of the medical expense deduction is found in the rule that restricts the amount to that over 7.5 percent of adjusted gross income.[60] The best way to avoid the 7.5-percent limitation is to pay for medical expenses through an Archer medical savings account[61] or flexible spending account.[62] The next best way to deal with the 7.5-percent limitation is to bunch as many medical expenses into a single year as possible without jeopardizing health. The expenses cannot always be accelerated or deferred, but some can be. For instance:

- Major home installations for medical reasons—air conditioning and other items already mentioned
- Stocking up on prescription drugs and insulin
- Deferred payment of a medical bill

---

[57] Rev. Rul. 2002-19, IRB 2002-16, 778 (April 2, 2002).

[58] Reg. § 1.213-1(e)(1)(iii).

[59] Code Sec. 213(d)(9)(B).

[60] Code Sec. 213(a).

[61] Code Sec. 220.

[62] Code Sec. 125.

- Timing elective surgery and other nonessential medical or dental work, advancing or postponing from one year to another
- Accident and health insurance premiums are deductible when paid

Generally a taxpayer may not deduct currently a prepayment of the expense for medical services to be performed next year.

The 7.5-percent floor makes employer-provided medical benefits[63] very attractive.

Medical expense deductions may be increased, in some cases, by married couples filing separate returns, with one spouse paying all of the medical expenses. The tax saving results from the fact that the smaller the adjusted gross income shown on the return, the larger the medical expenses deduction that can be taken above the 7.5-percent floor. It will only work out favorably, however, where both spouses have approximately equal incomes. This situation generally occurs automatically in community property states where spouses share in their earnings. In other states, of course, spouses do not automatically have equal incomes under state law. However, if both spouses are working or have separate sources of income in more or less equal amounts, the concept is applicable. Generally, the spouse with the larger income should pay and deduct not only medical expenses but also the greater part of other deductible items such as taxes and interest to equalize taxable incomes.

Unreimbursed amounts paid for qualified long-term care services provided to a taxpayer or to the taxpayer's spouse or dependents are treated as medical care for purposes of the medical expense deduction.[64]

Similarly, eligible long-term care insurance premiums that do not exceed certain limits (based on the insured's age) are treated as medical expenses for purposes of the medical expense deduction.[65]

.02 Health Savings Accounts

Health savings accounts (HSAs) are tax-exempt trusts or custodial accounts created exclusively to pay for the qualified medical expenses of the account holder and his or her spouse and dependents.[66] Contributions to an HSA can be made by "eligible individuals" or by their employers or both. Within limits, contributions to HSAs are deductible above-the-line in determining adjusted gross income if made by individuals and are excludable from gross

[63] Code Secs. 104, 105, and 106.

[64] Code Sec. 213(d)(1)(C).

[65] Code Sec. 213(d)(1)(D).

[66] Code Sec. 223.

income and taxable wages if made by their employers. Distributions from HSAs for qualified medical expenses are not includible in gross income. Distributions from an HSA for other purposes are includible in the account holder's gross income and are subject to an additional 10 percent penalty. However, the 10 percent penalty does not apply to distributions made after death, disability, or after the account holder attains age 65. Therefore, an HSA can serve as a tax-deferred retirement savings vehicle to the extent amounts in the account are not needed for current medical expenses.

An individual is eligible to make HSA contributions for any month if he or she (1) is covered under a high deductible health plan as of the first day of that month and (2) is not covered under any other health plan that is not a high-deductible plan and that provides coverage for any benefit covered under the high deductible plan.

For 2006, high-deductible health plan must have a deductible of at least $1,050 for self-only coverage or $2,100 for family coverage, and an annual limit on out-of-pocket expenses (deductible, co-payments, etc.) of not more than $5,250 for self-only coverage or $10,500 for family coverage.

In the case of self-only coverage, the maximum contribution for 2006 is $2,700 or the amount of the annual deductible, if less. For family coverage, the maximum 2006 contribution is the lesser of the annual deductible or $5,450. An eligible individual who will be 55 or over before the close of 2006, can make an additional catch-up contribution of $600 for the year, regardless of the type of high-deductible coverage.

If an employer provides high deductible health plan coverage coupled with an HSA and makes employer contributions to the HSAs, the employer must make available a comparable contribution on behalf of all employees with comparable coverage. Contributions are considered comparable if they are either of the same dollar amount or the same percentage of the deductible under the high deductible plan. The comparability rule is applied separately to part-time employees (i.e., employees who are customarily employed for fewer than 30 hours per week). No restrictions are placed on the ability of the employer to offer different plans to different groups of employees

.03 Archer Medical Savings Accounts

Archer medical savings accounts (MSAs) were a precursor to HSAs designed for employees of small employers and self-employed individuals.[67]

---

[67] Code Sec. 220.

Like an HSA, an MSA is a tax-exempt trust or custodial account that is set up to pay medical expenses in connection with a high-deductible health plan. Contributions to the account are deductible or excludable from an employee's income if made by an employer, and amounts in the account can be withdrawn tax-free to pay for out-of-pocket medical expenses. Amounts withdrawn for other purposes are taxable and subject to a 15 percent penalty unless the withdrawal is made after death, disability or Medicare eligibility.

Only self-employed individuals and employees of small employers (generally, those with 50 or fewer employees) were eligible to establish MSAs. MSAs were a pilot project that expired at the end of 2005. However, pending legislation may extend the availability of MSAs. In addition, contributions may continue to be made to MSAs established before the 2005 cutoff and existing accounts continue to qualify for tax-favored treatment.

For 2006, the high-deductible health plan supporting an MSA must have an annual deductible of not less than $1,800 and not more than $2,700 in the case of self-only coverage, or not less than $3,650 and not more than $5,450 in the case of family coverage. Annual out-of-pocket expenses cannot exceed $3,650 for self-only coverage or $6,650 for family coverage.[68] For individuals with self-only coverage, the maximum annual contribution is 65 percent of the deductible under the high-deductible plan; the maximums is 75 percent of the deductible for individuals with family coverage.

An employee can make contributions to his or her own MSA or contributions may be made by the employer sponsoring the high deductible plan, but not by both.

As with HSAs, an employer that makes MSA contributions on behalf of employees must make comparable contributions for all employees with comparable coverage.

.04 Long-Term Care Insurance

Qualified long-term care insurance for chronically ill individuals will be treated as an accident and health insurance contract.[69] Amounts received under contracts issued after December 31, 1996, will generally be excludable from gross income as amounts received for personal injuries and sickness. The excludable amount is capped at a rate of $250 per day for 2006 on per diem contracts.[70] This amount is indexed for inflation. Employer-provided long-term care insurance premiums are not excludable from an employee's

[68] Rev. Proc. 2005-70, 2005-47 IRB 979 (October 28, 2005).

[69] Code Sec. 7702B(a)(1).

[70] Code Sec. 7702B(d)(2).

income if provided through a cafeteria or other flexible spending arrangement.[71]

The deduction for 100 percent of health insurance expenses of self-employed individuals[72] applies to the portion of long-term care insurance premiums that would otherwise be deductible as medical expenses under Code Sec. 213(d)(10) based on the taxpayer's age. The portion of long-term care insurance premiums that would otherwise be deductible as a medical expense may be paid from an Archer medical savings account.[73]

¶ 3425 INTEREST

Various restrictions and limitations apply to deductions for interest. For example, personal interest (e.g., car loans, credit cards) is not deductible.[74] For this purpose, interest due on IRS deficiencies is considered personal interest.

Qualified residence interest[75] is fully deductible subject to the certain limitations on itemized deductions discussed at ¶ 3440. It is interest on debt secured by a qualified residence. A qualified residence includes the taxpayer's principal residence and a second residence of the taxpayer.[76] Subject to a grandfather rule, qualified residence interest includes: (1) interest on acquisition indebtedness up to a maximum amount of $1 million ($500,000 for married individuals filing separately)[77] and (2) interest on home equity indebtedness up to a maximum amount of $100,000 ($50,000 for married individuals filing separately).[78] Acquisition debt is debt incurred in acquiring, constructing, or substantially improving a principal or second residence (including a boat with cooking, sleeping, and toilet facilities).[79] Acquisition indebtedness is reduced as the debt principal is paid down and cannot be increased by refinancing. Pre-October 13, 1987, mortgage debt on a first or second residence is treated as acquisition debt, not subject to the $1 million limit, but it reduces the $1 million limit on new acquisition debt. For a more detailed discussion of home financing, see ¶ 2810.

Prepaid interest for periods beyond the taxable year is not currently deductible.[80] There is, however, an exception for "points" paid by a homeowner in connection with a mortgage to finance the purchase or improvement of a principal residence. The points are

[71] Code Sec. 106(c).
[72] Code Sec. 162(l)(2)(c).
[73] Code Sec. 220(d)(2)(B).
[74] Code Sec. 163(h).
[75] Code Sec. 163(h)(3).
[76] Code Sec. 163(h)(4)(A).
[77] Code Sec. 163(h)(3)(B).
[78] Code Sec. 163(h)(3)(C).
[79] Code Sec. 163(h)(3)(B).
[80] Code Sec. 461(g)(1).

deductible in the year paid and need not be deducted ratably over the period of the loan.[81] If the seller assumes payment of "points," he or she may deduct the amount paid from the sum realized on the sale, but he or she may not take an interest deduction. However, when the seller pays points on a loan for the buyer to acquire a principal residence, the buyer may deduct the points. The buyer treats the points paid by the seller as a reduction in the basis of the residence.[82] The exception generally does not apply to points paid when refinancing a mortgage unless the proceeds are used for improvements. Also, the exception does not apply to a second residence or to rental property. In such cases, the points are usually deducted ratably over the period of the new mortgage (see ¶2815 for a discussion). Of course, if the mortgage is paid off before its term, the remainder of the points may then be deducted.

Interest on investment debt is deductible only to the extent of net investment income (investment income net of investment expenses other than interest).[83] A client could consider buying stock on margin for which he or she could receive a deduction for the margin interest up to the amount of investment income. Buying stock on margin is a useful way to raise money because the interest rate on brokerage accounts is generally on the low side.

> **Planning pointer.** Nondeductible personal interest can be converted into deductible interest through a home equity loan. The home equity loan is used to pay outstanding personal loans or to finance new purchases. The interest on the home equity loan is deductible on home equity indebtedness up to $100,000, as noted above. However, some clients may have home loans where the total mortgage debts exceed the value of the home (e.g., the 125 percent of value loans). In that case, only the interest on the home equity debt up to $100,000 and secured by the value of the property is deductible.

¶3430 BAD DEBTS

In lending to a relative or friend, a taxpayer should observe loan formalities. The taxpayer should get a note, charge reasonable interest, and fix a due date. These elements are important in establishing the basis for a bad-debt deduction if the loan is not repaid and also in avoiding having the transaction treated as a taxable gift.

---

[81] Code Sec. 461(g)(2).

[82] Rev. Proc. 94-27 1994-1 CB 613.

[83] Code Sec. 163(d).

If it is a nonbusiness loan that is not repaid, it will be treated as a short-term capital loss.[84] The nonbusiness bad debt is deductible in the tax year in which it becomes worthless,[85] only up to the amount of net capital gains plus up to $3,000 of ordinary income.[86]

¶ 3435 ESTATE PLANNING, TAX ADVICE, AND TAX-RELATED EXPENSES

Expenses incurred in connection with tax matters are usually deductible only as a miscellaneous itemized deduction[87] and only to the extent that the total miscellaneous itemized deductions exceed two percent of adjusted gross income.[88] Such expenses are also subject to the limitations on itemized deductions discussed in ¶ 3440. Such expenditures include all ordinary and necessary expenses connected with preparing tax returns, determining or contesting tax liability, and in getting tax counsel. However, the costs of tax advice and preparation related to a business are deductible as business expenses. In addition, the costs of tax advice and preparation fees related to rental and royalty property are deductible against the rental and royalty income.[89]

Estate planning, of course, involves both legal and tax considerations. Personal legal expenses are generally not deductible. Therefore, only that portion of a fee charged for estate planning attributable to tax advice is deductible,[90] subject to the two-percent floor. The estate planner should break down any charge for estate planning services into tax and nontax advice.[91] The allocation must be reasonable and realistic.

Fees paid for investment advice are also deductible only if miscellaneous deductions exceed the two-percent floor. Services provided in relation to periodic planning sessions and the evaluation of potential investments to the extent needed to formulate an opinion regarding a particular investment fall under the heading of investment advice. However, investment fees paid for services in connection with the acquisition of investment vehicles, such as services used in negotiating purchase prices and creating the vehicles themselves, are not deductible.[92]

The two-percent floor on the deductibility of nontrade or business expenses renders investment and tax advice nondeductible for

---

[84] Code Sec. 166(d)(1).

[85] Code Sec. 166(d)(1).

[86] Code Sec. 1211(b).

[87] Code Sec. 212 and Code Sec. 67(b).

[88] Code Sec. 67(a).

[89] Rev. Rul. 92-29, 1992-1 CB 20.

[90] *S. Merians*, 60 TC 187, CCH Dec. 31,966.

[91] *H.C. Goldaper*, 36 TCM 1381, CCH Dec. 34,673(M), TC Memo. 1977-343.

[92] *R. Honodel*, 76 TC 351, CCH Dec. 37,686.

most clients who seek planning advice. Most individuals will pay these expenses with after-tax dollars. However, clients with a business or rental property receive the benefit of deducting tax planning advice related to those activities against the income from such activities.

¶ 3440 PLANNING FOR THE LIMITATION ON DEDUCTIONS FOR ITEMIZED EXPENSES

Code Sec. 68 imposes an overall limitation on the amount of allowable itemized deductions (not including the deductions for medical expenses, investment interest, casualty losses, and wagering losses to the extent of wagering income). Itemized deductions are reduced in 2006 by three percent of AGI in excess of the threshold amount of $150,500 for both married couples filing jointly and single taxpayers ($75,250 for married persons filing separately). The threshold is indexed for inflation.

The reduction may not be more than 80 percent of allowable itemized deductions and is disregarded in calculating the alternative minimum tax. The reduction applies only after application of the two-percent floor for miscellaneous deductions under Code Sec. 67, and under its terms any other limitation on deductions that may be applicable. For tax years beginning after December 31, 2005, and before January 1, 2010, the limitation on itemized deductions will be reduced every two years. The limitation is repealed for tax year 2010 only.

A basic strategy in offsetting the effect of the limitation on itemized deductions, as with the exemption phaseout, involves deferral of income and income shifting. Where a taxpayer has itemized deductions that are subject to the limitation, deferring income to another year or shifting income to other family members would effectively lower AGI with a corresponding decrease in the limitation on itemized deductions. Spreading capital gains over several years may be an effective means of shifting income to lower AGI, thereby lowering the limitation on deductions. In addition to strategies aimed at lowering AGI, a taxpayer could control the timing of deductions subject to the limitation by taking them in the year with the lower AGI. This strategy would likewise have the effect of reducing the limitation (see ¶ 3325 for additional strategies for reducing AGI).

¶ 3445 EMPLOYMENT TAX

A maximum wage/earnings base applies to the old age, survivors, and disability insurance (OASDI) portion of the Social Security tax.

For 2006, the maximum wage/earnings base subject to the 6.2-percent OASDI portion of the Social Security tax (which employer and employee each must pay) is $94,200. No ceiling exists on the Medicare hospital insurance (HI) portion of the Social Security tax. Thus, employers and employees each must pay 1.45 percent HI tax on every dollar of wages.

Self-employed taxpayers pay 12.4 percent for the OASDI portion of the self-employment tax subject to the $94,200 limit for 2006. However, the amount subject to the tax is the lesser of 92.35 percent of the net business income[93] or the $94,200 ceiling. The base for the HI portion of the tax is 92.35 percent of the net business income with no ceiling. Self-employed individuals now pay 2.90 percent in HI on this amount. Self-employed taxpayers are allowed an above-the-line income tax deduction for one-half of the self-employment taxes paid.[94]

> ***Example 34.2.*** In tax year 2006, Mary McNicoll, a self-employed person, has $200,000 of Schedule C income.
>
> Mary pays $17,037.10 in self-employment tax (taking into account that the 2006 OASDI wage/earnings base is $94,200). The net amount subject to tax on Schedule SE is $184,700 ($200,000 × .9235). Of that amount, $94,200 is subject to the OASDI portion and the entire $184,700 will be subject to the HI portion ($5,356.30). Mary may deduct $8,518.55 (half of $17,037.10) from her gross income to arrive at AGI.

The HI paid can also affect a high-earning self-employed's Keogh or SEP contribution. Half of the Schedule SE self-employment tax is subtracted from earned income to arrive at the net earned income base against which the Keogh/SEP contributions rate is applied.

There may be some opportunity to avoid these higher taxes by operating as an S corporation and setting one's salary at the low end of the range of acceptable salaries. However, an S corporation shareholder/employee may not avoid all employment taxes by receiving all payments as dividends.[95]

Another way to reduce the self-employment tax is to purchase equipment and take the maximum deduction allowed under Code Sec. 179.

---

[93] Code Sec. 1402(a)(12).

[94] Code Sec. 164(f).

[95] Rev. Rul. 74-44, 1974-1 CB 287.

¶3450 ADOPTION CREDIT AND EXCLUSION

.01 Credit for Adoption Expenses

Code Sec. 23 allows taxpayers a tax credit of up to $10,960 per child in 2006 for qualified adoption expenses, including reasonable and necessary adoption fees, court costs, adoption expenses, and other expenses directly related to the adoption of an eligible child. This amount is indexed for inflation. This same amount ($10,960 in 2006) is allowed for the adoption of a special needs child regardless of actual adoption expenses. The credit for the adoption of a special needs child is allowed in the year the adoption becomes final. The tax credit is allowed in the tax year in which the taxpayer pays or incurs the qualified adoption expenses. An eligible child is a child less than 18 years old, or an individual who is mentally or physically unable of self-care.[96]

In 2006, the credit for adoption expenses is phased out for taxpayers with modified adjusted income between $164,410 and $204,410.[97] The credit is not refundable, but a taxpayer may carry over any unused credit for up to five years.[98]

.02 Exclusion for Adoption Expenses

An employee's gross income does not include amounts paid by an employer for the employee's qualified adoption expenses pursuant to an adoption assistance program.[99] The income phaseout, and the effective dates for the provision, parallel the rules applicable to the credit for adoption expenses, above. An employee may not receive a double benefit by excluding adoption expenses paid by an employer and taking a credit based on the same amount.[100]

[96] Code Sec. 23(d)(2).
[97] Code Sec. 23(b)(2).
[98] Code Sec. 23(c).
[99] Code Sec. 137.
[100] Code Sec. 23(b)(3).

Chapter 35

Social Security Benefits, Medicare, and Medicaid

Overview ....¶ 3501
Tax Planning for Social Security Benefits ....¶ 3505
Medicare ....¶ 3510
Medicaid ....¶ 3515
Kinds of Social Security Benefits ....¶ 3520
Computation of Social Security Benefits ....¶ 3525
Avoiding Loss of Social Security Benefits ....¶ 3530

¶ 3501 OVERVIEW

This chapter discusses the benefits and rules of Social Security, Medicare, and Medicaid.

¶ 3505 TAX PLANNING FOR SOCIAL SECURITY BENEFITS

Under complex Social Security income inclusion rules, some taxpayers must pay tax on 85 percent of their Social Security benefits.[1] Many benefit recipients, however, are able to exclude all of their Social Security benefits from their gross income or pay tax on only half of their benefits. These rules drastically increase the marriage penalty for retired couples who are both receiving Social Security benefits.

However, the rule including 85 percent of Social Security benefits applies only to those with provisional income in excess of $44,000 for joint filers, $0 for a married individual filing separately who does

[1] Code Sec. 86.

not live apart from his or her spouse for all of the tax year, or $34,000 for all other filers.[2] For most people, provisional income is AGI plus tax-exempt interest, plus one-half of Social Security benefits.[3]

Mechanically, the inclusion rules for Social Security benefits are built on two tiers. The following discussion explains how the rules work for taxpayers other than marrieds filing separately who do not live apart from their spouses for the entire year.

.01 First Tier

The rules requiring 50 percent inclusion of Social Security benefits in gross income apply to those recipients whose provisional income bases are within the following dollar ranges: above $25,000 but not above $34,000 for unmarried taxpayers; and above $32,000 but not above $44,000 for marrieds filing jointly.[4] For such taxpayers, the maximum amount of Social Security benefits included in gross income is the lesser of (1) 50 percent of the benefits, or (2) 50 percent of the excess of the provisional income base over the applicable threshold amount ($25,000 or $32,000).

.02 Second Tier

For those who have provisional income bases above $34,000 or $44,000 (as appropriate), gross income includes the following:

- The smaller of (a) the amount of benefits included in the first tier, or (b) $6,000 for marrieds filing jointly or $4,500 for other taxpayers, plus
- 85 percent of the excess of the taxpayer's provisional income base over $44,000 for marrieds filing jointly or $34,000 for other taxpayers.

However, for recipients who fall in the second tier, the amount subject to tax is capped at 85 percent of the Social Security benefits.

.03 Marrieds Filing Separately

Taxpayers who are married at the close of a tax year, file separate returns, and did not live apart from their spouses for the entire year pay tax on 85 percent of each and every Social Security benefit dollar (or 85 percent of provisional income, if that is less). In *T.W. McAdams*,[5] the U.S. Tax Court ruled in a case of first impression that living apart means living in separate residences, not merely in separate bedrooms.

---

[2] Code Secs. 86(c)(1)(C) and 86(c)(2).
[3] Code Sec. 86(b).
[4] Code Sec. 86(c).
[5] 118 TC—, No. 24, Dec. 54,743 (May 15, 2002).

.04 Higher Inclusion Has Variable Effect

Social Security recipients with provisional income in excess of $44,000 or $34,000 (as appropriate) include more than 50 percent of their Social Security benefits in gross income. Depending on income and benefit levels, some pay tax on more than 50 percent but less than 85 percent of their benefits. Others pay tax on a full 85 percent of their benefits.

> ***Example 35.1.*** Each year, Mr. and Mrs. David English have $40,000 of income from pensions, dividends and tax-exempts and receive $12,000 of Social Security benefits, producing a provisional income base of $46,000 ($40,000 + $6,000).
>
> As a result, $7,700 of their income is taxed (roughly 64-percent). The couple's income is not high enough for the 85-percent-of-benefits cap to come into play.
>
> ***Example 35.2.*** Each year, Mr. John Bates and Mrs. Rose Piccoli Bates have $50,000 of income from pensions, dividends and tax-exempt bonds and receive $14,000 of Social Security benefits. They have provisional income of $57,000 ($50,000 + $7,000).
>
> As a result, $11,900 of Social Security income is taxed, which is a full 85-percent of their benefits.

.05 Marriage Penalty Impact

Some Social Security recipients will pay a very high price if they sanctify their union with marriage vows instead of simply living together.

> ***Example 35.3.*** Assume the same facts as in Example 35.2 except that Mr. John Bates and Ms. Rose Piccoli live together, instead of being married, and each has exactly half their combined income. Thus, each has $25,000 of income from pensions, dividends and tax-exempt bonds, and $7,000 of Social Security income.
>
> As a result, the amount of Social Security income included for the tax year is $1,750 for each person and a total of $3,500 for both. This amount is roughly 70-percent less than the $11,900 of Social Security benefits that would be subject to tax if they were married.

.06 Social Security Recipients Who Work Part-Time

For Social Security recipients under normal retirement age (age 65 to age 67 depending on date of birth), part-time, supplemental earnings may reduce benefit levels and cause more of what is left to be exposed to tax. For example, under the Social Security earnings test that applies to retirees under normal retirement age, a person can earn $12,480 in 2006 without having benefits reduced. Beyond that dollar level, however, one dollar is deducted from benefits for every two dollars earned over the exempt amount (see ¶ 3530 for further details). Between reduced benefits, a higher income inclusion on Social Security benefits that are paid, FICA taxes, and income taxes, a part-time earner who takes on more work could wind up losing a significant portion of his or her pay increase.

> ***Example 35.4.*** Jeff Solomon is a single 63-year-old who has $10,000 of salary from a part-time job, $16,940 of income from pensions and investments, and $7,000 of Social Security benefits. Jeff has been asked to work more hours at his part-time job in exchange for $5,000 more in pay. The year is 2006.
>
> If Jeff declines the offer from his employer, he will have provisional income of $30,440 ($10,000 + $16,940 + 50% of $7,000). He will include $3,500 of his Social Security benefits in income. Assuming Jeff is in the 15-percent bracket, he will pay $525 in tax on his benefits.
>
> If Jeff works more hours at his part-time job and is paid an additional $5,000, more than 45-percent ($2,298/$5,000) of the extra pay will be lost to taxes and benefit reductions.

Gross pay boost	$5,000.00
Reduction in benefits ($15,000 – $12,480) × 50%	(1,260.00)
FICA on $5,000 extra (7.65%)	(382.50)
Income tax on $5,000 of earnings (@ 15%)	(750.00)
Income tax saved on reduced benefits ($1,260 × 50% × 15%)	94.50
Net	$2,702.00

.07 Practice Aid for Calculating the Taxable Portion of Social Security Benefits

The following worksheet shows how taxpayers other than marrieds filing separately will compute the taxable portion of their Social Security benefits.*

FIRST TIER

1. 50 percent of Social Security benefits ________
2. Modified AGI (generally AGI plus tax-exempt income) ________
3. Total of Lines 1 and 2—Provisional income ________
4. Less $32,000 (joint filers) or $25,000 (all others) ________
5. Income over base ________
6. 50 percent of Line 5 ________
7. 50 percent of Social Security benefits ________
8. Enter smaller of Line 6 or 7 ________

   If Line 3 does not exceed $44,000 (joint filers) or $34,000 (other taxpayers), Line 8 amount = portion of Social Security benefit includible in gross income ________ ________

   If Line 3 exceeds $44,000 (joint filers) or $34,000 (other taxpayers), continue with Line 9

SECOND TIER

9. Enter smaller of Line 8 or $6,000 (marrieds filing jointly) or $4,500 (other taxpayers) ________
10. 85 percent of Line 3 less $44,000 (joint filers) or $34,000 (other taxpayers) ________
11. Line 9 plus Line 10 ________
12. 85 percent of Social Security benefits ________
13. Lesser of Line 11 or 12 = portion of Social Security benefit includible in income ________

* Marrieds filing separate returns who did not live apart from their spouses for the entire year pay tax on the lesser of (1) 85 percent of each and every Social Security benefit dollar, or (2) 85 percent of provisional income.

.08 Strategies for Dealing with Tax on Benefits

Retired people who are affected by the tax on Social Security benefits, especially those subject to the 85-percent inclusion rules, may be able to reduce their exposure by using the following techniques. However, taxes should never be the sole motivating factor behind any investment decision.

- Switching funds into investments that pay monthly checks that include a tax-free return of capital component. Annuities are prime examples of such investments. That part of each annuity payment representing the return of the purchaser's investment is not currently taxed and is not factored into the Social Security income inclusion. By contrast, interest (tax free or not) and dividends directly affect the amount of Social Security income that is taxed. Ginnie Maes are other investments that include a tax-free return of capital component.
- For those who are not expending all of their investment income for living expenses, deferral techniques might make sense. For example, Series EE and Series I bonds continue to offer an attractive yield plus tax deferral. The interest buildup in a Series EE or Series I bond is not taxed until the bondholder redeems it. Another alternative that may be appropriate would be a switch of some cash from income funds into growth funds.
- Where retirees have a choice, they should consider withdrawing interest from their municipal bond funds before withdrawing cash from IRAs for living expenses. This strategy is helpful because municipal bond interest is taken into account in computing the tax on Social Security benefits, but interest accruing in an IRA is not. In addition, usually withdrawing cash from non-IRA accounts before dipping into the IRAs will provide more tax benefits. Withdrawals of the principal from a money market account or mutual fund are not taxed (only the interest or dividend earnings are included in income). By contrast, each dollar withdrawn from a traditional IRA is included in gross income (unless the taxpayer made nondeductible contributions).
- Retirees should try to avoid selling appreciated assets because a large profit could subject a full 85 percent of their Social Security benefits to tax.

.09 Lump-Sum Social Security Benefits

A taxpayer could incur a large tax liability if the taxpayer receives a large lump-sum payment of Social Security benefits that the taxpayer should have received over several years. In such cases, a taxpayer may elect to include the Social Security benefits in gross income only to the extent of the sum of the amounts that would have been included in gross income if the taxpayer had received the payments in the years to which the payments are attributable.[6] The details on making the lump-sum election are contained in IRS Publication 915 "Social Security and Equivalent Railroad Retirement Benefits."

.10 Social Security Benefits in Lieu of Workers' Compensation Benefits

Workers' compensation benefits are generally excluded from gross income.[7] However, to the extent that workers' compensation benefits reduce Social Security benefits, the workers' compensation benefits will be taxable as Social Security benefits.[8]

¶ 3510 MEDICARE

Medicare is a federal health insurance program primarily designed for individuals entitled to Social Security who are age 65 or older (although younger individuals can also qualify, e.g., those receiving Social Security disability and those with end-stage renal disease). One may obtain more information about Medicare by calling (800) MEDICARE (633-4227) or by visiting its Web site www.medicare.gov.

.01 In General

Basic Medicare consists of two parts. Part A covers inpatient hospital services and services furnished by other institutional health care providers, such as skilled nursing homes, home health agencies, and hospices. Part B covers the services of doctors, suppliers of medical items and services, and various types of outpatient services.

Certain items and services are excluded from coverage under both parts. Also, services that involve "custodial care" (i.e., the type of services normally associated with long-term care patients, such as observation and help with daily living activities) are not covered. In addition, services determined by Medicare not to be reasonable are not covered.

The patient must pay a portion of the cost of some covered services because of deductible and coinsurance requirements.

[6] Code Sec. 86(e)(1).

[7] Code Sec. 104(a)(1).

[8] Code Sec. 86(d)(3).

.02 Enrollment

Part A coverage is automatically provided for persons entitled to Medicare. Part B coverage, however, must be paid for through monthly premiums. For 2006, the premium is $88.50 a month. Persons not automatically entitled to Medicare can voluntarily enroll in the program if they pay the $393 monthly Part A premium (for persons with 30-39 quarters of Social Security coverage, or, for persons married or formerly married to such a person for certain lengths of time, the monthly premium is reduced to $216.00) and also enroll in Part B.

.03 Part A Coverage and Limitations

Here is a brief summary of Part A coverage and limitations.

Covered services. Part A covers most hospital services including the following items and services furnished to an individual admitted to a hospital as an inpatient: room and board; drugs and biologicals; supplies, appliances, and equipment; diagnostic and therapeutic items and services; nursing services; the services of staff doctors not directly related to the personal treatment of individual patients; and the services of all interns, residents, and teaching physicians. Part A also covers certain home health services and hospice care.

Part A covers generally the same inpatient services provided in a participating skilled nursing facility as it covers in a hospital. However, the services must be "skilled" nursing services and not merely "custodial care."

Limitations. Part A is limited in terms of how long the program will pay for services, and it requires beneficiaries to share some of the costs. For example, inpatient hospital coverage expires after 90 days of benefits have been used per benefit period (although the beneficiary has an additional 60 "lifetime reserve days" that can be used only once.) A benefit period is a period of consecutive days that begins with a hospitalization and ends when the patient has not been an inpatient for 60 consecutive days.

Beneficiaries must pay a separate inpatient hospital deductible for each benefit period. The deductible is $952 for 2006. There are also coinsurance requirements. For example, there is a per-day coinsurance charge for inpatient hospital stays of more than 60 days in the same benefit period. The 2006 charge is $238 per day for the 61st day through the 90th day of an inpatient hospital stay (there is no coinsurance for the first 60 days) and, if lifetime reserve days (days 91-150) are used, the coinsurance is $476 per day.

.04 Part B Service and Limitations

Part B coverage is defined in terms of which specific services are involved. Only those services specifically listed as covered will be paid by Medicare, although some of the listed services are quite broad in scope. Not all of the covered services are listed here. However, covered services include such items as physicians' services; drugs that cannot be self-administered such as the flu vaccine; outpatient services; therapy services; diagnostic tests; etc. Many items are specifically excluded (e.g., routine checkups, glasses and hearing aids, most dental work, personal comfort items, etc.).

Medicare Part B also provides numerous preventive services. Medicare covers bone mass measurements once every 24 months for qualified individuals and more often if medically necessary. The individual's physician can determine if the individual is a qualified individual. Medicare also covers several different kinds of colorectal cancer screenings for covered individuals age 50 and older. These screenings include a fecal occult blood test once every 12 months and a flexible sigmoidoscopy once every 48 months. Medicare covers a colonoscopy for covered individuals regardless of age once every 24 months for individuals at high risk for colon cancer or once every 10 years for other individuals as long as the colonoscopy is not within 48 months of a screening flexible sigmoidoscopy. A physician may use a barium enema instead of a flexible sigmoidoscopy or a colonoscopy. Medicare also covers glucose monitors, test strips, and lancers for covered individuals with diabetes. Certain individuals with diabetes are also eligible for diabetes self-management training. Medicare covers a glaucoma screening once every 12 months for covered individuals who are at high risk for glaucoma. Medicare covers a mammogram screening once every 12 months for women age 40 and over. In addition, Medicare allows one baseline mammogram between ages 35 and 39 if the woman is covered by Medicare. All women with Medicare may receive a Pap test and pelvic examination once every 24 months. These preventive exams are allowed once ever 12 months for women who are at high risk for cervical or vaginal cancer or if the woman is of childbearing age and has had an abnormal Pap test in the previous 36 months. Medicare covers a prostate cancer screening, including a digital rectal examination and a prostate specific antigen (PSA) test once every 12 months for all covered men age 50 and older. Medicare covers an annual flu shot in the fall or winter for all covered individuals. In addition, Medicare covers one pneumonia shot and allows Hepatitis B shot for certain covered individuals who are at medium to high risk for Hepatitis B.

Part B has deductible and coinsurance requirements for most covered items. For example, the deductible is $124 per year and the coinsurance is generally 20 percent of the Medicare-approved charge.

.05 Medicare Part C

Medicare Part C known as Medicare+Choice is available to Medicare beneficiaries who are entitled to part A and enrolled in Part B. Medicare+Choice is either a managed care plan, a private fee-for-service plan, or a medicare preferred provider organization. Payments made under a contract with a Medicare+Choice provider replace the payments that Medicare would otherwise pay under Part A and Part B. These managed care plans are mostly health maintenance organizations (HMOs). Medicare+Choice plans generally must provide the same items and services, including preventive services, available to beneficiaries under Part A and Part B. Medicare+ Choice plan may provide additional benefits such as prescription drugs and more prevention and wellness programs. The only exception is MSAs. The enrollment criteria for a Medicare-managed care plan are as follows:

- The individual must be enrolled in Part B and continue to pay the Part B premium.
- The individual must live in the plan's service area.
- The individual cannot be receiving care in a Medicare-certified hospice.
- The individual cannot have permanent kidney failure.

Generally, an eligible individual may joint a Medicare+Choice plan at any time. Medicare-managed care plans must have open enrollment from November through December of each year. If an individual enrolls during that period, the coverage becomes effective on January 1 of the next year. However, some Medicare+Choice Plans limit the number of members in their plans. An individual who enrolls in a Medicare-managed care plan may return to regular Medicare at any time for any reason.

.06 Medicare Part D Prescription Drug Coverage

All Medicare beneficiaries are eligible for Medicare Part D prescription drug coverage beginning in 2006.

There are two ways to obtain Medicare prescription drug coverage. A beneficiary can join a Medicare prescription drug plan directly or enroll in a Medicare health plan that offers prescription drug coverage. Beneficiaries must pay a monthly premium, which varies by plan, and a yearly deductible (no more than $250 in 2006). Beneficiaries must also pay a part of the cost of prescriptions, including a co-payment or coinsurance. Costs will vary depending on the drug plan selected. Some plans may offer more coverage and additional drugs for a higher monthly premium. Beneficiaries with limited income and resources may qualify for extra help and may not have to pay a premium or deductible.

The initial enrollment period for Medicare Part D began November 15, 2005 and ended May 15, 2006. Eligible beneficiaries who did not enroll by May 15, 2006, may pay a penalty. The next enrollment period is from November 15, 2006 to December 31, 2006.

.07 Medigap Policies

Medicare beneficiaries should consider purchasing a Medicare supplement policy to fill gaps in the coverage provided by Medicare. These policies, called "Medigap" policies, must meet certain federal standards, which afford some measure of protection for the policy purchaser. For example, the insurance company may not cancel Medigap policies except for nonpayment of premiums.

¶ 3515 MEDICAID

Medicaid is a program of government-financed medical care for specified groups of poor people. A detailed discussion of it is beyond the scope of this chapter. Additional information about Medicaid is available at *http://cms.hhs.gov*, which is the Web site for the Centers for Medicare and Medicaid Services (formerly the Health Care Financing Administration) administered by the United States Department of Health and Human Resources. However, because many middle class individuals give their assets away in an attempt to qualify for Medicaid so that the costs of medical care will not wipe out their assets, this chapter provides some details on allowable income and resources. The treatment is brief and is not intended to be exhaustive.

The financial eligibility standards that govern Medicaid eligibility allow an individual, a couple, or a family to keep a small amount of income plus the following assets: a home, a car, personal and household items, and (within limits) property essential for self-support, life insurance, burial spaces, cash or cashable assets, and a few other resources. The government counts all additional income and resources in determining eligibility for Medicaid.

Most of the income that a single Medicaid recipient can keep while living at home becomes available to pay for nursing facility care if the individual enters a nursing facility. Medicaid covers long-term nursing facility care that Medicare rejects as "custodial."

.01 Spousal Impoverishment

A primary concern of a married couple with one spouse in a nursing facility is that they will use a substantial portion of their income and resources to pay the facility. Thus, very little will be left for the spouse who is not in the nursing facility.

Income. The law addresses this issue by allowing the community spouse (the spouse who does not live in the nursing facility) to keep enough of the couple's income to raise his or her income to at least 150 percent of the federal poverty line for a couple. The community spouse can keep even more income if the income is in his or her name. Community spouses with costly shelter and utility needs within specific limits can keep some additional monthly income. The total monthly income that a community spouse can keep ranges between $1,603.75 and $2,488.50 in 2006 unless a higher limit is established by a fair hearing or a court order.

Institutionalized spouses can keep monthly income of $30 or more (as determined by the state) as a personal allowance. They can also use some of their income to pay for noncovered or noninsured medical expenses that they incur and to maintain dependents.

Resources. The community spouse can keep a share of the couple's "countable resources" that is the greatest of (1) in 2006, a level between $19,908 and $99,540 established by the state, (2) one-half of the couple's countable resources if that half does not exceed $99,540 in 2006, or (3) a higher limit established by a fair hearing or a court order. This amount is called the Protected Resource Amount. The institutionalized spouse may transfer assets to the community spouse so he or she may obtain the greatest permissible share.

.02 Trusts

Individuals may think that they can use trusts to shelter assets that would render them ineligible for Medicaid. However, the law deems all of a trust's funds or payments that can be obtained by the individual, the individual's spouse, or anyone acting for the individual or the individual's spouse, to be available to pay for the individual's medical or nursing facility care, even if the funds or payments are not distributed. For such trusts established after August 10, 1993, any of the trust's funds or payments that are not available to pay for such care are deemed to have been transferred with a delay in Medicaid coverage as a result, except that a 60-month delay instead of a 36-month delay applies. Exceptions apply for trusts that contain assets of disabled individuals under age 65, specific retirement income trusts in certain states, and "pooled" trusts for disabled individuals.

.03 Transfer of Assets

The Health Insurance Portability and Accountability Act of 1996[9] cast a shadow over asset transfers made to qualify for Medicaid. Effective January 1, 1997, it was a criminal misdemeanor or felony to knowingly and willfully dispose of assets in order for an individual to qualify for Medicaid, or to assist in such transfers, within (1) 36 months of applying for Medicaid, in the case of an outright transfer, or (2) within 60 months of applying for Medicaid, in the case of a trust. Penalties included up to $25,000 in fines, up to five years in prison, and revocation of Medicaid eligibility for up to one year. These sanctions were to apply in addition to the delay of eligibility and recovery provisions discussed below. This provision was amended on August 5, 1997. The amended rule applied only to those who for a fee advised an individual to make such a transfer. The penalty was to be a maximum of one year in prison and a fine of up to $10,000. However, this provision was ruled as an unconstitutional infringement on the right of free speech under the First Amendment.[10]

Medicaid eligibility for nursing facility or home and community-based long-term care is delayed for an individual who disposes of assets for less than fair market value on or after a "look-back" date that is 36 months (60 months if the transfer is made through a trust) before the date on which the individual is both: (1) a Medicaid applicant, and (2) in an institution. Certain transfers are exempt from this rule.

¶ 3520 KINDS OF SOCIAL SECURITY BENEFITS

The benefits that most persons think of when they say "Social Security" are of four basic kinds: old-age or disability benefits for the worker; benefits for the dependents of retired or disabled workers; benefits for the survivors of a worker who has died; and the lump-sum death benefit. The following table describes these benefits in more detail, and indicates the insured status that the worker must have before he or she may receive the benefits.

[9] P.L. 104-191.

[10] *New York Bar Association v. Janet Reno et al.*, No. 97 CV 1760 (NDNY, 1997).

.01 Insured Status and Benefit Table

OLD-AGE OR DISABILITY BENEFITS

Monthly benefits can be paid to—	*If the worker—*
A retired worker age 62 or over.	Is fully insured.
A disabled worker under age 65.	Would have been fully insured had he or she attained age 62 in the month the disability began and (except in the case of a person disabled because of blindness) has 20 quarters of coverage out of the 40 calendar quarters ending with the quarter in which the disability began.
A worker disabled before age 31 who does not have sufficient quarters of coverage to meet above requirement.	Has quarters of coverage in one-half of the quarters elapsing in the period after attaining age 21 and up to and including the quarter of becoming disabled, but no fewer than 6, or, if disabled in a quarter before attaining age 24, he or she has 6 quarters of coverage in the 12 calendar-quarter period immediately before he or she became disabled.
(A worker may be disabled after age 31 if he or she had a period of disability prior to age 31.)	

DEPENDENTS OF RETIRED OR DISABLED WORKERS

Monthly benefits can be paid to—	*If the worker—*
The spouse of a person entitled to disability or retirement insurance benefits, if he or she is: (a) Age 62 or over (may be divorced spouse in certain circumstances); or (b) Caring for a child who is under age 16 or disabled and entitled to benefits.	Is fully insured or insured for disability benefits, whichever is applicable, as shown above.
An unmarried child or grandchild (if parents are deceased) of a person entitled to disability or retirement insurance benefits if the child or grandchild is: (a) Under age 18: or (b) Under age 19 if a full-time elementary or secondary school student: or (c) Age 18 or over and under a disability which began before the child or grandchild reached age 22.	Is insured for retirement or disability benefits, whichever is applicable, as shown above.

SURVIVORS BENEFITS

Monthly benefits can be paid to—	*If the worker—*
A widow or widower (may be surviving divorced spouse in certain circumstances) age 60 or over.	Is fully insured.
A widow or widower and, under certain conditions, a surviving divorced spouse, if the widow or widower or divorced spouse is caring for a child entitled to benefits if the child is under age 16 or disabled.	Is either fully or currently insured.
A disabled widow or widower (may be surviving divorced spouse in certain circumstances), age 50 or over but under age 60, whose disability began within a certain period.	Is fully insured.
An unmarried child or grandchild (if parents are deceased) of a deceased worker if the child or grandchild is: (a) Under age 18; or (b) Under age 19 if a full-time elementary or secondary school student; or (c) Age 18 or over and under a disability which began before the child or grandchild reached age 22.	Is either fully or currently insured.
A dependent parent, age 62 or over, of the deceased worker.	Is fully insured.

LUMP-SUM DEATH PAYMENT

The lump-sum death payment will be paid in the following order of priority—	*If the worker—*
(a) The widow(er) of the deceased wage earner who was living in the same household as the deceased wage earner at the time of death; (b) The widow(er) (excluding a divorced spouse) who is eligible for or entitled to benefits based on the deceased wage earner's record for the month of death; (c) Children who are eligible for or entitled to benefits based on the deceased wage earner's record for the month of death. If no surviving widow(er) or child as defined above survives, no lump sum is payable.	Is either fully or currently insured.

.02 "Fully Insured" and "Currently Insured" Status

Forty quarters of coverage assure "fully insured" status for life. If a person reached age 62 in 1984, 33 quarters of coverage will suffice, with 34 required if he or she reached age 62 in 1985, 35 if he or she reached age 62 in 1986, 36 if he or she reached age 62 in 1987, 37 if he or she reached age 62 in 1988, 38 if he or she reached age 62 in 1989, 39 if he or she reached age 62 in 1990, and 40 if he or she reached age 62 in 1991 or later.

Fully insured status means that an individual is entitled to full benefits, including retirement benefits.

If an individual is "currently insured," he may be entitled to disability benefits, and if he dies his family may be entitled to survivor benefits, but he will not be entitled to old-age retirement benefits. "Currently insured" status requires coverage in six quarters out of the 13 preceding disability or death.

¶ 3525 COMPUTATION OF SOCIAL SECURITY BENEFITS

The computation of benefits is quite complicated. The following steps are required:

1. Elapsed years. Count the calendar years after 1950 (or after attaining 21, if later) and before the year in which the worker will attain age 62. In figuring disability benefits, the count ends the year before disability.

2. Computation years. From the "elapsed years" deduct five years to get the "computation years." There are special rules for computing disability benefits.

3. Base years. List the worker's earnings for each year beginning with 1951 and ending with the year before the year in which the benefits will begin. The following table lists the maximum creditable amounts for each year.

Year	Amount	Year	Amount
1951-1954	$ 3,600	1978	17,700
1955-1958	4,200	1979	22,900
1959-1965	4,800	1980	25,900
1966-1967	6,600	1981	29,700
1968-1971	7,800	1982	32,400
1972	9,000	1983	35,700
1973	10,800	1984	37,800
1974	13,200	1985	39,600
1975	14,100	1986	42,000
1976	15,300	1987	43,800
1977	16,500	1988	45,000

1989	48,000	1998	68,400
1990	51,300	1999	72,600
1991	53,400	2000	76,200
1992	55,500	2001	80,400
1993	57,600	2002	84,900
1994	60,600	2003	87,000
1995	61,200	2004	87,900
1996	62,700	2005	90,000
1997	65,400	2006	94,200

4. Indexing. The earnings in step 3 must be indexed to national average earnings over the same period in accordance with the following listing of average earnings:

1951	$2,799.16	1978	10,556.03
1952	2,973.32	1979	11,479.46
1953	3,139.44	1980	12,513.46
1954	3,155.64	1981	13,733.10
1955	3,301.44	1982	14,531.34
1956	3,532.36	1983	15,239.24
1957	3,641.72	1984	16,135.07
1958	3,673.80	1985	16,822.51
1959	3,855.80	1986	17,321.82
1960	4,007.12	1987	18,426.51
1961	4,086.76	1988	19,334.04
1962	4,291.40	1989	20,099.55
1963	4,396.64	1990	21,027.98
1964	4,576.32	1991	21,811.60
1965	4,658.72	1992	22,935.42
1966	4,938.36	1993	23,132.67
1967	5,213.44	1994	23,753.53
1968	5,571.76	1995	24,705.66
1969	5,893.76	1996	25,913.90
1970	6,186.24	1997	27,426.00
1971	6,497.08	1998	28,861.44
1972	7,133.80	1999	30,469.84
1973	7,580.16	2000	32,154.82
1974	8,030.76	2001	32,921.92
1975	8,630.92	2002	33,252.09
1976	9,226.48	2003	34,064.95
1977	9,779.44	2004	35,648.55

The formula for indexing uses the worker's actual earnings for a given year, national average earnings in the "indexing year" (which is the second year before the "eligibility year"), and national average earnings in the year being indexed, as follows:

$$\text{Worker's Actual Earnings} \times \frac{\text{Average Earnings in Indexing Year}}{\text{Average Earnings in Year Being Indexed}}$$

5. Primary insurance amount (PIA). The next step involves the use of another formula to find the worker's Primary Insurance Amount (PIA). For the worker whose eligibility year is 2006, convert the Average Indexed Monthly Earnings (AIME) to a PIA by adding 90 percent of the first $656 or less of AIME, 32 percent of any AIME above $656 to $3,955, and 15 percent of any AIME above $3,995. The result rounded down to the next-lower multiple of 104 (if it is not already a multiple of 10¢) is the PIA.

The PIA is the amount payable to a retiree applying at normal retirement age (age 65 to age 67 depending on the year of birth) and is the basis for computing almost all benefits. For example, retirement benefits at age 62 are a percentage of the PIA.

The PIA is increased by cost-of-living adjustments for the three preceding years in the case of a worker whose benefits commence at normal retirement age (age 65 to age 67 depending on year of birth). On the other hand, the PIA amount of a worker whose benefits begin at age 62 would not be increased to reflect past cost-of-living adjustments.

Social Security benefit calculators can be found on the Social Security Administration website at www.ssa.gov.

.01 Increases in Benefits—COLA

Social Security benefits are subject to change to reflect increases of three percent or more in the Consumer Price Index (CPI).

If reserves in the old age and disability trust funds fall below 20 percent, the cost-of-living adjustment (COLA) will be based on the lower of the increase in the CPI or the average increase in wages. The increase for 2006 was 4.1 percent, starting with the January 2006, check.

.02 Delayed Retirement Credit

For each month a worker delays retirement past normal retirement age, the benefit he or she will get is increased based on a credit that varies depending on age. Workers born in the period 1917–1924 get ¼ ¼ of one percent per month (three percent per year). Persons born after 1924 get larger increases with a worker born after 1943 receiving a delayed retirement credit of eight percent per year. A surviving spouse's benefits are also increased under this rule, but other dependents' benefits are not affected.

In deciding whether to delay retirement and receive a larger benefit, the individual would have to consider the present state of his/her health and life expectancy to determine if more benefits will actually be received than at full retirement age. Other considerations would include availability of other funds for living purposes and spouse desires. Full retirement age is from age 65 to age 67 depending on the year of birth:

Year of Birth	Full Retirement Age
1937 or earlier	65
1938	65 and 2 months
1939	65 and 4 months
1940	65 and 6 months
1941	65 and 8 months
1942	65 and 10 months
1943–1954	66
1955	66 and 2 months
1956	66 and 4 months
1957	66 and 6 months
1958	66 and 8 months
1959	66 and 10 months
1960 and later	67

.03 Checking Status of Individual's Account

The Social Security Administration has a toll-free telephone number (1-800-772-1213) that can be used to obtain Form SSA-7004, "Request for Social Security Statement." Within a few weeks of mailing the completed form, an individual will receive a detailed packet of information called a "Social Security Statement." One may also request this statement from the Social Security Administration's Internet home page at www.ssa.gov. The Social Security Administration will mail a copy of an individual's Social Security Statement annually within three months of the individual's birthday. Checking the status of an individual's account each year is important to ensure that the Social Security Administration has credited the correct amount of earnings to the account.

.04 Deciding When to Begin Receiving Social Security Benefits

An individual needs 40 quarters of coverage to begin receiving Social Security benefits at age 62. If an individual begins receiving Social Security benefits at age 62, the amount is decreased by 5/9 of one percent for each month before full retirement age. Thus, if an individual's full retirement age is 65, the monthly benefits are 20 percent less than if the individual waited until age 65. If an individual's full retirement age is 67, the monthly benefits for starting benefits at 62 is about 30 percent less than they would be at age 67.

To decide when to begin receiving Social Security benefits, one must consider the increase in benefits from waiting, possible taxation of benefits, loss of benefits because of earnings before full retirement age, life expectancy, and the rate of return that the recipient could earn on investments. In many cases, if the recipient is not earning over the amount at which he or she would lose benefits, the recipient will be better to begin receiving benefits at age 62. However, the financial planner should evaluate each case on its own and consider all relevant facts to advise a client properly.

¶ 3530 AVOIDING LOSS OF SOCIAL SECURITY BENEFITS

.01 Working While Receiving Benefits

In 2006, a person under full retirement age can earn up to $12,480 ($1,040 per month) without loss of Social Security benefits. If the individual has reached full retirement age, he or she will not lose any Social Security benefits because of earnings. The loss of benefits for earnings in excess of the threshold amounts is one dollar for every two dollars in excess monthly earnings for retirees under full retirement age. Once the individual reaches full retirement age (age 65 to 67), he or she can earn an unlimited amount without loss of Social Security benefits.

In the first year of eligibility, a monthly test also applies to the months in the year before the individual attains full retirement age. A worker, who is under full retirement age for any month in 2006 and retires in 2006 after attaining full retirement age, is entitled to a full benefit for any month in which he or she neither earns more than $2,770 nor is substantially self-employed, regardless of his or her total earnings for the year. On the other hand, if the worker earns more than $2,770 in any month before reaching full retirement age, he or she will lose one dollar of benefits for every three dollars of excess earnings.

The earnings limitation for a Social Security recipient under full retirement age may create a substantial disincentive for work that provides significant earnings. The results will vary depending on several factors:

- The amount of benefits the individual would be entitled to if he or she did not continue to work
- In the case of a married participant, the amount of benefits, if any, that the individual's spouse would be entitled to
- The extent to which benefits would be taxed if they were not lost because of earnings

- The amount of earnings and Social Security taxes thereon
- The individual's income tax bracket
- The value of any delayed retirement credit

.02 Escape Hatch

Income from self-employment is counted in the year in which it is received except if it is paid in a year after one becomes entitled to Social Security and was earned before the recipient became entitled to Social Security.

On the other hand, the earnings of an employee are counted in the year in which they are earned regardless of when they are received.

If an individual eligible for Social Security benefits is legitimately self-employed and is able to work out a deferred compensation arrangement with the person for whom he or she performs services, the individual apparently will be able to have earnings in excess of the Social Security earnings limitations without losing benefits. If the deferred income is not actually or constructively paid until he or she attains full retirement age (65 to 67), no loss of benefits will result. Even a deferral for a year could prove helpful as enabling the individual to retain benefits for the year of deferral.

Part IV

Planning Aids

Appendix

Federal Income Tax Rates, Deductions, Exemptions, FICA and FUTA Taxes .... ¶5001
Annual Cost-of-Living Adjustments and Dollar Limitations for Employee Trusts .... ¶5005
Unified Federal Estate and Gift Tax Rates for Tax Years 2005 Through 2009 .... ¶5010
Reg. §1.72-9 Annuity and Life Expectancy Tables .... ¶5020
Growth of $1 at Interest .... ¶5025
How Much to Save to Have $1 in Future .... ¶5030
How Much $1 Saved Each Year Will Increase .... ¶5035
How Much $1 to Be Paid in the Future Is Currently Worth .... ¶5040
Valuation of Annuities, Life Estates, Remainders, Etc. ..... ¶5045

¶5001 FEDERAL INCOME TAX RATES, DEDUCTIONS, EXEMPTIONS, FICA AND FUTA TAXES

.01 2006 Income Tax Rate Schedules for Noncorporate Taxpayers

Married Individuals Filing Joint Returns and Surviving Spouses

If Taxable Income Is:	The Tax Is:
Not over $15,100	10% of the taxable income
Over $15,100 but not over $61,300	$1,510 plus 15% of the excess over $15,100
Over $61,300 but not over $123,700	$8,440 plus 25% of the excess over $61,300
Over $123,700 but not over $188,450	$24,040 plus 28% of the excess over $123,700
Over $188,450 but not over $336,550	$42,170 plus 33% of the excess over $188,450
Over $336,550	$91,043 plus 35% of the excess over $336,550

Heads of Households

If Taxable Income Is:	The Tax Is:
Not over $10,750	10% of the taxable income
Over $10,750 but not over $41,050	$1,075 plus 15% of the excess over $10,750
Over $41,050 but not over $106,000	$5,620 plus 25% of the excess over $41,050
Over $106,000 but not over $171,650	$21,857.50 plus 28% of the excess over $106,000
Over $171,650 but not over $336,550	$40,239.50 plus 33% of the excess over $171,650
Over $336,550	$94,656.50 plus 35% of the excess over $336,550

Unmarried Individuals (other than Surviving Spouse and Heads of Households)*

If Taxable Income Is:	The Tax Is:
Not over $7,550	10% of the taxable income
Over $7,550 but not over $30,650	$755 plus 15% of the excess over $7,550
Over $30,650 but not over $74,200	$4,220 plus 25% of the excess over $30,650
Over $74,200 but not over $154,800	$15,107.50 plus 28% of the excess over $74,200

If Taxable Income Is:	The Tax Is:
Over $154,800 but not over $336,550	$37,675.50 plus 33% of the excess over $154,800
Over $336,550	$97,653 plus 35% of the excess over $336,550

*For 2006, unearned income in excess of $1,700 of a child under age 18 is taxed at the higher of the child's rate or his or her parent's marginal rate.

Married Individuals Filing Separate Returns

If Taxable Income Is:	The Tax Is:
Not over $7,550	10% of the taxable income
Over $7,550 but not over $30,650	$755 plus 15% of the excess over $7,550
Over $30,650 but not over $61,850	$4,220 plus 25% of the excess over $30,650
Over $61,850 but not over $94,225	$12,020 plus 28% of the excess over $61,850
Over $94,225 but not over $168,275	$21,085 plus 33% of the excess over $94,225
Over $168,275	$45,521.50 plus 35% of the excess over $168,275

Estates and Trusts*

If Taxable Income Is:	The Tax Is:
Not over $2,050	15% of the taxable income
Over $2,050 but not over $4,850	$307.50 plus 25% of the excess over $2,050
Over $4,850 but not over $7,400	$1,007.50 plus 28% of the excess over $4,850
Over $7,400 but not over $10,050	$1,721.50 plus 33% of the excess over $7,400
Over $10,050	$2,596 plus 35% of the excess over $10,050

*The 10-percent rate that applies to individuals does not apply to estates and trusts.

.02 Standard Deduction

Tax Years Beginning in 2006

Joint return or surviving spouse	$10,300
Single (other than head of household or surviving spouse)	$ 5,150
Head of household	$ 7,550
Married filing separate returns	$ 5,150

For an individual who can be claimed as a dependent on another taxpayer's return, the basic standard deduction in 2006 cannot exceed the greater of $850 or the sum of $300 and the individual's earned income. The standard deduction for an individual who can be claimed as a dependent on another taxpayer's return may not exceed the general standard deduction amount. The additional standard deduction amount for the aged and blind is $1,000 in 2006. These amounts are increased to $1,250 in 2006 if the individual is also unmarried and not a surviving spouse.

.03 Personal Exemption

The personal exemption is $3,300 in 2006. Exemptions are phased out at the rate of two percent for each $2,500 or fraction thereof ($1,250 for married individuals filing separately) of adjusted gross income (AGI) in excess of certain threshold amounts. In 2006, these amounts are $225,750 for a joint return, $188,150 for a head of household, $150,500 for a single taxpayer, and $112,875 for married individuals filing separately.

The exemption is fully phased out when AGI exceeds the thresholds by more than $122,500 ($61,250 for married individuals filing separately).

.04 Itemized Deductions

An individual generally may not deduct personal interest.[1] However, an individual may deduct interest on acquisition indebtedness up to $1 million and interest on a home equity loan up to $100,000 on the taxpayer's principal residence and one other residence.[2]

A taxpayer's otherwise allowable itemized deductions (other than medical expenses, investment income, casualty losses and wagering losses to the extent of wagering income) must be reduced by an amount equal to three percent of AGI in excess of $150,500 ($75,250 for married persons filing separately) in 2006. The reduction may not be more than 80 percent of allowable itemized deductions (with the exceptions noted above). For 2006, the reduction is limited to ⅔ of the otherwise applicable amount.

[1] Code Sec. 163(h).

[2] Code Sec. 163(h)(3).

.05 Corporate Tax Rates

Taxable Income			
over	*but not over*	*the tax is*	*of the amount over*
0	$ 50,000	15%	0
$ 50,000	75,000	$ 7,500 + 25%	$ 50,000
75,000	100,000	13,750 + 34%	75,000
100,000	335,000	22,250 + 39%	100,000
335,000	10,000,000	113,900 + 34%	335,000
10,000,000	15,000,000	3,400,000 + 35%	10,000,000
15,000,000	18,333,333	5,150,000 + 38%	15,000,000
18,333,333	....	6,416,667 + 35%	18,333,333

Personal service corporations are denied the benefit of the graduated rate. Their income is taxed at a flat 35-percent rate.[3]

.06 Self-Employment Tax

A self-employed individual must pay self-employment tax in addition to the income tax. The self-employment tax is 15.3 percent: 12.4 percent for the old age survivors and disability insurance (OASDI) part[4] and 2.9 percent for the hospital insurance (HI) (Medicare) part.[5] The self-employment income is subject to a ceiling for the OASDI part that changes annually.[6] The ceiling is $94,200 for 2006. The HI part is not subject to a ceiling. A self-employed taxpayer may deduct the product of the net earnings from self-employment and one-half of the 15.3 percent self-employment tax rate in computing the tentative base for the self-employment tax.[7] Schedule SE simplifies this calculation by multiplying the unadjusted net earnings from self-employment by 92.35 percent. Any FICA wages the taxpayer earned during the year reduce the ceiling for the OASDI part.[8] After subjecting the 92.35 percent of self-employment income to the OASDI ceiling, the taxpayer computes the self-employment tax by multiplying the base by 12.4 percent for the OASDI part and by 2.9 percent for the HI part. The self-employment tax is the sum of the OASDI part and the HI part. One half of the self-employment tax liability is deductible in computing adjusted gross income on Form 1040.[9] One half of the self-employment tax is also subtracted from earned income to arrive at the net earned income base against which the Keogh/SEP contributions rate is applied.

[3] Code Sec. 11(b)(2).
[4] Code Sec. 1401(a).
[5] Code Sec. 1402(b).
[6] Code Sec. 1402(b).
[7] Code Sec. 1402(a)(12).
[8] Code Sec. 1402(b).
[9] Code Sec. 164(f).

.07 Social Security and Unemployment Taxes

Federal Insurance Contributions Act (FICA). A 6.2 percent tax is imposed on both employees and employers for Social Security (old age survivors and disability insurance) and hospital insurance (Medicare) purposes under the Federal Insurance Contributions Act (FICA). Both employers and employees pay the 1.45 percent HI tax on every dollar of wages. For 2006, the maximum wage base subject to the OASDI portion of the tax is $94,200.

The tax rate, the maximum wage base for the OASDI portion, and the maximum tax for OASDI are as follows:

Calendar Year	*Tax Rate*	*Maximum Wage Base**	*Maximum Tax for OASDI*
2006	6.2%	$94,200	$5,840.40

*As adjusted by the Secretary of Health and Human Services.

The 1.45 percent hospital insurance portion of the tax applies to all wages.

Unemployment Insurance (FUTA). The Federal Unemployment Tax Act (FUTA) rate is 6.2 percent through 2007 and 6.0 percent in 2008 and later years.[10] The employer's net federal tax for the year is normally 0.8 percent through 2007 because of credits granted for state unemployment tax.[11] The tax is on the first $7,000 of wages paid to an employee during the calendar year.[12]

¶ 5005 ANNUAL COST-OF-LIVING ADJUSTMENTS AND DOLLAR LIMITATIONS FOR EMPLOYEE TRUSTS

Reproduced below are the cost-of-living adjustments that apply for various qualified retirement plan purposes for calendar year 2006.

Code Sec. 415 provides for dollar limitations on benefits and contributions under qualified defined benefit pension plans. It also requires that the Commissioner annually adjust these limits for cost-of-living increases. In 2006, the maximum limitation for the annual benefit under Code Sec. 415(b)(1)(A) for defined benefit plans is $175,000.

---

[10] Code Sec. 3101.
[11] Code Sec. 3302.
[12] Code Sec. 3306(b).

The limitation for defined contribution plans under Code Sec. 415(c)(1)(A) is $44,000 for 2006.

The Code provides that various other dollar amounts are to be adjusted at the same time and in the same manner as the dollar limitation of Code Sec. 415(b)(1)(A) is adjusted. These dollar amounts and the adjusted amounts are discussed below.

The special limitation for qualified police or firefighters under Code Sec. 415(b)(2)(G) is not reduced where the benefit begins before the Social Security retirement age.

The limitation on the exclusion for elective deferrals under Code Sec. 402(g)(1) is $15,000 for 2006. Beginning in 2007, the $15,000 limit is indexed for inflation. Taxpayers who are age 50 or older may contribute an additional $5,000 for 2006 and later years. (The reference covers employee contributions to 401(k) plans and salary reduction SEPs under 408(k).)

The dollar amounts under Code Sec. 409(o)(1)(C)(ii) for determining the maximum account balance in an employee stock ownership plan subject to a five-year distribution period is $885,000 for 2006. The dollar amount for lengthening the five-year distribution period of that section for tax credit employee stock ownership plans is $175,000 for 2006.

The limitation used in the definition of a highly compensated employee under section 414(q)(1)(B) is $100,000 for 2006.

The annual compensation limit under Code Secs. 401(a)(17) and 404(l) is $220,000 for 2006 and is indexed for inflation.

The minimum compensation amount under Code Sec. 408(k)(2)(C) regarding simplified employee plans (SEPs) remains at $450 for 2006. The maximum SEP compensation amount under Code Sec. 408(k)(3)(C) is $220,000 for 2006.

The maximum contribution amount under Code Sec. 408(p)(2)(A) for SIMPLE retirement accounts is $10,000 for 2006. Beginning in 2006, it is indexed for inflation. Taxpayers who are age 50 or older may contribute an additional $2,500 for 2006 and later years.

¶ 5010 UNIFIED FEDERAL ESTATE AND GIFT TAX RATES FOR TAX YEARS 2005 THROUGH 2009

The benefit of the graduated rates and unified credit is phased out for large estates, as explained at ¶ 5010.01 in connection with the applicable credit amount (unified credit).

If the amount is: Over (1)	But not over (2)	Tax on (1)	Rate on Excess (1)
$ 0	$ 10,000	$ 0	18
10,000	20,000	1,800	20
20,000	40,000	3,800	22
40,000	60,000	8,200	24
60,000	80,000	13,000	26
80,000	100,000	18,200	28
100,000	150,000	23,800	30
150,000	250,000	38,800	32
250,000	500,000	70,800	34
500,000	750,000	155,800	37
750,000	1,000,000	248,300	39
1,000,000	1,250,000	345,800	41
1,250,000	1,500,000	448,300	43
1,500,000	2,000,000	555,800	45
2,000,000	2,500,000	780,800	47 in 2005 46 in 2006 45 in 2007-2009

.01 Unified Credit Against Federal Estate and Gift Taxes and Filing Requirements

Applicable credit amount. Code Sec. 2010 shows an applicable credit amount for the unified credit against federal estate and gift taxes. The amount of this credit is the amount of the tentative tax computed on the applicable exclusion amount (formerly called the "exemption equivalent"). The applicable exclusion amount for estate tax purposes is as follows:

Year	*Applicable Exclusion Amount*
2006, 2007, and 2008	2,000,000
2009	3,500,000

For gifts made through 2009, the applicable exclusion amount for gift tax purposes is $1,000,000. This amount is not indexed for inflation.

Filing requirements. An estate tax return must be filed if a decedent's gross estate, increased by post-1976 taxable gifts, exceeds the applicable exclusion amount for the year of the decedent's death.

.02 Estate Tax Worksheet

Here is an estate tax worksheet that can be used in estimating potential estate taxes.

Computation of Tentative Tax Base

1.	Client's property interests	$______
2.	Transfers with retained interests	______
3.	Annuities and life insurance proceeds	______
4.	General powers of appointment of property	______
5.	Property which qualified for a QTIP marital deduction in the decedent's spouse's estate	______
6.	Gift taxes paid on gifts within three years of death	______
7.	Gross estate	______
8.	Less: expenses, indebtedness, taxes, and losses	______
9.	Adjusted gross estate	______
10.	Less: (a) Marital deduction	______
	(b) Charitable deduction	______
11.	Taxable estate	______
12.	Adjusted taxable gifts	______
13.	Tentative tax base	$______

Computation of Estate Tax

14.	Tentative tax	$______
15.	Less: gift taxes	______
16.	Tentative estate tax before credits	______
17.	Less: unified credit	______
18.	Gross estate tax	______
19.	Estate tax before other credits	______
20.	Less: other credits	______
21.	Net estate tax	$______

Line 1. Include interests in property owned, as well as all or a share of jointly owned property in accordance with Code Sec. 2033 and other rules. For community property, exclude spouse's share. Watch for the special value rule for certain real property under Code Sec. 2032A.

Line 8. These are the deductions allowed under Code Secs. 2053 and 2054 and should include estimates of funeral and estate administration expenses. State death taxes are a deduction for estates of decedents who die through 2009.

Line 9. The concept of adjusted gross estate is important for purposes of determining qualifications for the Code Sec. 6166 14-year deferral of tax attributable to a business interest.

Line 10(a). The marital deduction for property passing to or for a surviving spouse is unlimited.[13]

Line 12. Adjusted taxable gifts means the total amount of taxable gifts made after 1976 other than gifts which are includible in the gross estate under other rules, such as those included at line 2, above.

Line 14. The rate schedule at Code Sec. 2001(c) is applied to the amount at line 12, above.

Line 15. The gift taxes to be subtracted are those on gifts made by the client after 1976 that are not includible in the gross estate.

Line 21. Other credits are those for any tax on prior transfers[14] and foreign death taxes.[15]

¶ 5020 REG. § 1.72-9 ANNUITY AND LIFE EXPECTANCY TABLES

In December 1986, the IRS issued final regulations that provided new annuity tables to be used to compute the portion of the amount received as an annuity that is includible in gross income and to compute required minimum distributions under qualified plans and IRAs.

The tables are gender neutral and are based on 1983 mortality tables, superseding gender-based tables that used 1937 mortality tables. The new table, which follows this discussion, is effective for investments made after June 30, 1986. For a discussion of how annuity payments are taxed, see ¶ 805–¶ 810. Benefits may be paid over the joint life expectancy of a qualified plan participant (or IRA owner) and a beneficiary. All of the life expectancy tables are contained in IRS Publication 939, "General Rule for Pensions and Annuities." IRS Publication 590, "Individual Retirement Arrangements (IRAs)," also contains life expectancy tables for use by IRA beneficiaries.

[13] Code Sec. 2056(a).

[14] Code Sec. 2013.

[15] Code Sec. 2014.

ORDINARY LIFE ANNUITIES ONE LIFE—EXPECTED RETURN MULTIPLES

Age	Multiple	Age	Multiple	Age	Multiple
5	76.6	42	40.6	79	10.0
6	75.6	43	39.6	80	9.5
7	74.7	44	38.7	81	8.9
8	73.7	45	37.7	82	8.4
9	72.7	46	36.8	83	7.9
10	71.7	47	35.9	84	7.4
11	70.7	48	34.9	85	6.9
12	69.7	49	34.0	86	6.5
13	68.8	50	33.1	87	6.1
14	67.8	51	32.2	88	5.7
15	66.8	52	31.3	89	5.3
16	65.8	53	30.4	90	5.0
17	64.8	54	29.5	91	4.7
18	63.9	55	28.6	92	4.4
19	62.9	56	27.7	93	4.1
20	61.9	57	26.8	94	3.9
21	60.9	58	25.9	95	3.7
22	59.9	59	25.0	96	3.4
23	59.0	60	24.2	97	3.2
24	58.0	61	23.3	98	3.0
25	57.0	62	22.5	99	2.8
26	56.0	63	21.6	100	2.7
27	55.1	64	20.8	101	2.5
28	54.1	65	20.0	102	2.3
29	53.1	66	19.2	103	2.1
30	52.2	67	18.4	104	1.9
31	51.2	68	17.6	105	1.8
32	50.2	69	16.8	106	1.6
33	49.3	70	16.0	107	1.4
34	48.3	71	15.3	108	1.3
35	47.3	72	14.6	109	1.1
36	46.4	73	13.9	110	1.0
37	45.4	74	13.2	111	.9
38	44.4	75	12.5	112	.8
39	43.5	76	11.9	113	.7
40	42.5	77	11.2	114	.6
41	41.5	78	10.6	115	.5

¶ 5025 GROWTH OF $1 AT INTEREST

The table shows what $1 will grow to when deposited at various rates of interest, compounded annually, and held for different periods.

YEAR	4.50%	5.00%	5.50%
1	1.045000	1.050000	1.055000
2	1.092025	1.102500	1.113025
3	1.141166	1.157625	1.174241
4	1.192519	1.215506	1.238825
5	1.246182	1.276282	1.306960
6	1.302260	1.340096	1.378843
7	1.360862	1.407100	1.454679
8	1.422101	1.477455	1.534687
9	1.486095	1.551328	1.619094
10	1.552969	1.628895	1.708144
11	1.622853	1.710339	1.802092
12	1.695881	1.795856	1.901207
13	1.772196	1.885649	2.005774
14	1.851945	1.979932	2.116091
15	1.935282	2.078928	2.232476
16	2.022370	2.182875	2.355263
17	2.113377	2.292018	2.484802
18	2.208479	2.406619	2.621466
19	2.307860	2.526950	2.765647
20	2.411714	2.653298	2.917757
21	2.520241	2.785963	3.078234
22	2.633652	2.925261	3.247537
23	2.752166	3.071524	3.426152
24	2.876014	3.225100	3.614590
25	3.005434	3.386355	3.813392

YEAR	6.00%	6.50%	7.00%	7.50%
1	1.060000	1.065000	1.070000	1.075000
2	1.123600	1.134225	1.144900	1.155625
3	1.191016	1.207950	1.225043	1.242297
4	1.262477	1.286466	1.310796	1.335469
5	1.338226	1.370087	1.402552	1.435629
6	1.418519	1.459142	1.500730	1.543302
7	1.503630	1.553987	1.605781	1.659049
8	1.593848	1.654996	1.718186	1.783478
9	1.689479	1.762570	1.838459	1.917239
10	1.790848	1.877137	1.967151	2.061032
11	1.898299	1.999151	2.104852	2.215609
12	2.012196	2.129096	2.252192	2.381780
13	2.132928	2.267487	2.409845	2.560413
14	2.260904	2.414874	2.578534	2.752444
15	2.396558	2.571841	2.759032	2.958877
16	2.540352	2.739011	2.952164	3.180793
17	2.692773	2.917046	3.158815	3.419353
18	2.854339	3.106654	3.379932	3.675804
19	3.025600	3.308587	3.616528	3.951489
20	3.207135	3.523645	3.869684	4.247851
21	3.399564	3.752682	4.140562	4.566440
22	3.603537	3.996606	4.430402	4.908923
23	3.819750	4.256386	4.740530	5.277092
24	4.048935	4.533051	5.072367	5.672874
25	4.291871	4.827699	5.427433	6.098340

YEAR	8.00%	8.50%	9.00%	9.50%
1	1.080000	1.085000	1.090000	1.095000
2	1.166400	1.177225	1.188100	1.199025
3	1.259712	1.277289	1.295029	1.312932
4	1.360489	1.385859	1.411582	1.437661
5	1.469328	1.503657	1.538624	1.574239
6	1.586874	1.631468	1.677100	1.723791
7	1.713824	1.770142	1.828039	1.887552
8	1.850930	1.920604	1.992563	2.066869
9	1.999005	2.083856	2.171893	2.263222
10	2.158925	2.260983	2.367364	2.478228
11	2.331639	2.453167	2.580426	2.713659
12	2.518170	2.661686	2.812665	2.971457
13	2.719624	2.687930	3.065805	3.253745
14	2.937194	3.133404	3.341727	3.562851
15	3.172169	3.399743	3.642482	3.901322
16	3.425943	3.688721	3.970306	4.271948
17	3.700018	4.002262	4.327633	4.677783
18	3.996019	4.342455	4.717120	5.122172
19	4.315701	4.711563	5.141661	5.608778
20	4.660957	5.112046	5.604411	6.141612
21	5.033834	5.546570	6.108808	6.725065
22	5.436540	6.018028	6.658600	7.363946
23	5.871464	6.529561	7.257874	8.063521
24	6.341181	7.084574	7.911083	8.829556
25	6.848475	7.686762	8.623081	9.668364

YEAR	10.00%	10.50%	11.00%
1	1.100000	1.105000	1.110000
2	1.210000	1.221025	1.232100
3	1.331000	1.349233	1.367631
4	1.464100	1.490902	1.518070
5	1.610510	1.647447	1.685058
6	1.771561	1.820429	1.870415
7	1.948717	2.011574	2.076160
8	2.143589	2.222789	2.304538
9	2.357948	2.456182	2.558037
10	2.593742	2.714081	2.839421
11	2.853117	2.999059	3.151757
12	3.138428	3.313961	3.498451
13	3.452271	3.661926	3.883280
14	3.797498	4.046429	4.310441
15	4.177248	4.471304	4.784589
16	4.594973	4.940791	5.310894
17	5.054470	5.459574	5.895093
18	5.559917	6.032829	6.543553
19	6.115909	6.666276	7.263344
20	6.727500	7.366235	8.062312
21	7.400250	8.139690	8.949166
22	8.140275	8.994357	9.933574
23	8.954302	9.938764	11.026267
24	9.849733	10.982335	12.239157
25	10.834706	12.135480	13.585464

YEAR	11.50%	12.00%	12.50%	13.00%
1	1.115000	1.120000	1.125000	1.130000
2	1.243225	1.254400	1.265625	1.276900
3	1.386196	1.404928	1.423828	1.442897
4	1.545608	1.573519	1.601807	1.630474
5	1.723353	1.762342	1.802032	1.842435
6	1.921539	1.973823	2.027287	2.081952
7	2.142516	2.210681	2.280697	2.352605
8	2.388905	2.475963	2.565785	2.658444
9	2.663629	2.773079	2.886508	3.004042
10	2.969947	3.105848	3.247321	3.394567
11	3.311491	3.478550	3.653236	3.835861
12	3.692312	3.895976	4.109891	4.334523
13	4.116928	4.363493	4.623627	4.898011
14	4.590375	4.887112	5.201580	5.534753
15	5.118268	5.473566	5.851778	8.254270
16	5.706869	6.130394	6.583250	7.067326
17	6.363159	6.866041	7.406156	7.986078
18	7.094922	7.689966	8.331926	9.024268
19	7.910838	8.612762	9.373417	10.197423
20	8.820584	9.646293	10.545094	11.523088
21	9.834951	10.803848	11.863231	13.021089
22	10.965971	12.100310	13.346134	14.713831
23	12.227057	13.552347	15.014401	16.626629
24	13.633169	15.178629	16.891201	18.788091
25	15.200983	17.000064	19.002602	21.230542

YEAR	13.50%	14.00%	14.50%	15.00%
1	1.135000	1.140000	1.145000	1.150000
2	1.288225	1.299600	1.311025	1.322500
3	1.462135	1.481544	1.501124	1.520875
4	1.659524	1.688960	1.718787	1.749006
5	1.883559	1.925415	1.968011	2.011357
6	2.137840	2.194973	2.253372	2.313061
7	2.426448	2.502269	2.580111	2.660020
8	2.754019	2.852586	2.954227	3.059023
9	3.125811	3.251949	3.382590	3.517876
10	3.547796	3.707221	3.873066	4.045558
11	4.026748	4.226232	4.434660	4.652391
12	4.570359	4.817905	5.077686	5.350250
13	5.187358	5.492411	5.613950	6.152788
14	5.887651	6.261349	6.656973	7.075706
15	6.682484	7.137938	7.622234	8.137062
16	7.584619	8.137249	8.727458	9.357621
17	8.608543	9.276464	9.992940	10.761264
18	9.770696	10.575169	11.441916	12.375454
19	11.089740	12.055693	13.100994	14.231772
20	12.586855	13.743490	15.000638	16.366537
21	14.286080	15.667578	17.175731	18.821518
22	16.214701	17.861039	19.666212	21.644746
23	18.403686	20.361585	22.517812	24.891458
24	20.888184	23.212207	25.782895	28.625176
25	23.708088	26.461916	29.521415	32.918953

YEAR	15.50%	16.00%	16.50%	17.00%
1	1.155000	1.160000	1.165000	1.170000
2	1.334025	1.345600	1.357225	1.368900
3	1.540799	1.560896	1.581167	1.601613
4	1.779623	1.810639	1.842060	1.873887
5	2.055464	2.100342	2.146000	2.192448
6	2.374061	2.436396	2.500089	2.565164
7	2.742041	2.826220	2.912604	3.001242
8	3.167057	3.278415	3.393164	3.511453
9	3.657951	3.802961	3.953059	4.108400
10	4.224933	4.411435	4.605314	4.806828
11	4.879798	5.117265	5.365191	5.623989
12	5.636166	5.936027	6.250447	6.580067
13	6.509772	6.885791	7.281771	7.698679
14	7.518787	7.987518	8.483263	9.007454
15	8.684199	9.265521	9.883002	10.538721
16	10.030250	10.748004	11.513697	12.330304
17	11.584938	12.467685	13.413457	14.426456
18	13.380604	14.462514	15.626678	16.878953
19	15.454598	16.776517	18.205080	19.748375
20	17.850060	19.460759	21.208918	23.105599
21	20.616820	22.574481	24.708389	27.033551
22	23.812427	26.186398	28.785273	31.629255
23	27.503353	30.376222	33.534843	37.006228
24	31.766372	35.236417	39.068093	43.297287
25	36.690160	40.874244	45.514328	50.657828

YEAR	17.50%	18.00%	18.50%	19.00%
1	1.175000	1.180000	1.185000	1.190000
2	1.380625	1.392400	1.404225	1.416100
3	1.622234	1.643032	1.664007	1.685159
4	1.906125	1.938778	1.971848	2.005339
5	2.239697	2.287758	2.336640	2.386354
6	2.631644	2.699554	2.768918	2.839761
7	3.092182	3.185474	3.281168	3.379315
8	3.633314	3.758859	3.888184	4.021385
9	4.269144	4.435454	4.607498	4.785449
10	5.016244	5.233836	5.459885	5.694684
11	5.894087	6.175926	6.469964	6.776674
12	6.925552	7.287593	7.666907	8.064242
13	8.137524	8.599359	9.085285	9.596448
14	9.561590	10.147244	10.766063	11.419773
15	11.234869	11.973748	12.757784	13.589530
16	13.200971	14.129023	15.117974	16.171540
17	15.511141	16.672247	17.914800	19.244133
18	18.225590	19.673251	21.229038	22.900518
19	21.415068	23.214436	25.156410	27.251616
20	25.162705	27.393035	29.810345	32.429423
21	29.566179	32.323781	35.325259	38.591014
22	34.740260	38.142061	41.860432	45.923307
23	40.819806	45.007632	49.604612	54.648735
24	47.963272	53.109006	58.781465	65.031994
25	56.356844	62.668627	69.656038	77.388073

YEAR	19.50%	20.00%
1	1.195000	1.200000
2	1.428025	1.440000
3	1.706490	1.728000
4	2.039255	2.073600
5	2.436910	2.488320
6	2.912108	2.985984
7	3.479969	3.583181
8	4.158563	4.299817
9	4.969482	5.159780
10	5.938531	6.191736
11	7.096545	7.430084
12	8.480371	8.916100
13	10.134044	10.699321
14	12.110182	12.839185
15	14.471668	15.407022
16	17.293643	
17	20.665903	
18	24.695754	
19	29.511426	
20	35.266154	
21	42.143055	
22	50.360950	
23	60.181336	
24	71.916696	
25	85.940452	

¶5030 HOW MUCH TO SAVE TO HAVE $1 IN FUTURE

The table shows how much to put aside at the end of each year in order to have $1 at different periods in the future, using different rates of interest compounded annually.

YEAR	4.50%	5.00%	5.50%
2	0.488998	0.487805	0.486618
3	0.318773	0.317209	0.315654
4	0.233744	0.232012	0.230294
5	0.182792	0.180975	0.179176
6	0.148878	0.147017	0.145179
7	0.124701	0.122820	0.120964
8	0.106610	0.104722	0.102864
9	0.092574	0.090690	0.088839
10	0.081379	0.079505	0.077668
11	0.072248	0.070389	0.068571
12	0.064666	0.062825	0.061029
13	0.058275	0.056456	0.054684
14	0.052820	0.051024	0.049279
15	0.048114	0.046342	0.044626
16	0.044015	0.042270	0.040583
17	0.040418	0.038699	0.037042
18	0.037237	0.035546	0.033920
19	0.034407	0.032745	0.031150
20	0.031876	0.030243	0.028679
21	0.029601	0.027996	0.026465
22	0.027546	0.025971	0.024471
23	0.025682	0.024137	0.022670
24	0.023987	0.022471	0.021036
25	0.022439	0.020952	0.019549

YEAR	6.00%	6.50%	7.00%	7.50%
2	0.485437	0.484262	0.483092	0.481928
3	0.314110	0.312576	0.311052	0.309538
4	0.228591	0.226903	0.225228	0.223568
5	0.177396	0.175635	0.173891	0.172165
6	0.143363	0.141568	0.139796	0.138045
7	0.119135	0.117331	0.115553	0.113800
8	0.101036	0.099237	0.097468	0.095727
9	0.087022	0.085238	0.083486	0.081767
10	0.075868	0.074105	0.072378	0.070686
11	0.066793	0.065055	0.063357	0.061697
12	0.059277	0.057568	0.055902	0.054278
13	0.052960	0.051283	0.049651	0.048064
14	0.047585	0.045940	0.044345	0.042797
15	0.042963	0.041353	0.039795	0.038287
16	0.038952	0.037378	0.035858	0.034391
17	0.035445	0.033906	0.032425	0.031000
18	0.032357	0.030855	0.029413	0.028029
19	0.029621	0.028156	0.026753	0.025411
20	0.027185	0.025758	0.024393	0.023092
21	0.025005	0.023613	0.022289	0.021029
22	0.023046	0.021691	0.020406	0.019187
23	0.021278	0.019961	0.018714	0.017535
24	0.019679	0.018398	0.017189	0.016050
25	0.018227	0.016981	0.015811	0.014711

YEAR	8.00%	8.50%	9.00%	9.50%
2	0.480769	0.479616	0.478469	0.477327
3	0.308034	0.306539	0.305055	0.303580
4	0.221921	0.220288	0.218669	0.217063
5	0.170456	0.168766	0.167092	0.165436
6	0.136315	0.134607	0.132920	0.131253
7	0.112072	0.110369	0.108691	0.107036
8	0.094015	0.092331	0.090674	0.089046
9	0.080080	0.078424	0.076799	0.075205
10	0.069029	0.067408	0.065820	0.064266
11	0.060076	0.058493	0.056947	0.055437
12	0.052695	0.051153	0.049651	0.048188
13	0.046522	0.045023	0.043567	0.042152
14	0.041297	0.039842	0.038433	0.037068
15	0.036830	0.035420	0.034059	0.032744
16	0.032977	0.031614	0.030300	0.029035
17	0.029629	0.028312	0.027046	0.025831
18	0.026702	0.025430	0.024212	0.023046
19	0.024128	0.022901	0.021730	0.020613
20	0.021852	0.020671	0.019546	0.018477
21	0.019832	0.018695	0.017617	0.016594
22	0.018032	0.016939	0.015905	0.014928
23	0.016422	0.015372	0.014382	0.013449
24	0.014978	0.013970	0.013023	0.012134
25	0.013679	0.012712	0.011806	0.010959
26	0.012507	0.011580	0.010715	0.009909
27	0.011448	0.010560	0.009735	0.008969
28	0.010489	0.009639	0.008852	0.008124
29	0.009619	0.008806	0.008056	0.007364
30	0.008827	0.008051	0.007336	0.006681

YEAR	10.00%	10.50%	11.00%
2	0.476190	0.475059	0.473934
3	0.302115	0.300659	0.299213
4	0.215471	0.213892	0.212326
5	0.163797	0.162175	0.160570
6	0.129607	0.127982	0.126377
7	0.105405	0.103799	0.102215
8	0.087444	0.085869	0.084321
9	0.073641	0.072106	0.070602
10	0.062745	0.061257	0.059801
11	0.053963	0.052525	0.051121
12	0.046763	0.045377	0.044027
13	0.040779	0.039445	0.038151
14	0.035746	0.034467	0.033228
15	0.031474	0.030248	0.029065
16	0.027817	0.026644	0.025517
17	0.024664	0.023545	0.022471
18	0.021930	0.020863	0.019843
19	0.019547	0.018531	0.017563
20	0.017460	0.016493	0.015576
21	0.015624	0.014707	0.013838
22	0.014005	0.013134	0.012313
23	0.012572	0.011747	0.010971
24	0.011300	0.010519	0.009787
25	0.010168	0.009429	0.008740

YEAR	11.50%	12.00%	12.50%	13.00%
2	0.4728132388	0.4716981132	0.4705882353	0.4694835681
3	0.2977763551	0.2963489806	0.2949308756	0.2935219701
4	0.2107738808	0.2092344363	0.2077079108	0.2061941974
5	0.1589817720	0.1574097319	0.1558540390	0.1543145434
6	0.1247912454	0.1232257184	0.1216797811	0.1201532321
7	0.1006550465	0.0991177359	0.0976030757	0.0961108038
8	0.0827990200	0.0813028414	0.0798321856	0.0783867196
9	0.0691259707	0.0676788888	0.0662600042	0.0648689020
10	0.0583772102	0.0569841642	0.0556217819	0.0542895558
11	0.0497514437	0.0484154043	0.0471122783	0.0458414545
12	0.0427142151	0.0414368076	0.0401943390	0.0389860847
13	0.0368953016	0.0356771951	0.0344958241	0.0333503411
14	0.0320300825	0.0308712461	0.0297507101	0.0286674959
15	0.0279243614	0.0268242396	0.0257637513	0.0247417797
16	0.0244323792	0.0233900180	0.0223883932	0.0214262445
17	0.0214425881	0.0204567275	0.0195124801	0.0186084385
18	0.0188681666	0.0179373114	0.0170487264	0.0162008548
19	0.0166405294	0.0157630049	0.0149281952	0.0141343943
20	0.0147047839	0.0138787800	0.0130957330	0.0123537884
21	0.0130164837	0.0122400915	0.0115067060	0.0108143279
22	0.0115392673	0.0108105088	0.0101246265	0.0094794811
23	0.0102431115	0.0095599650	0.0089193964	0.0083191328
24	0.0091030208	0.0084634417	0.0078659881	0.0073082605
25	0.0080980307	0.0074999698	0.0069434409	0.0064259276

YEAR	13.50%	14.00%	14.50%	15.00%
2	0.4683840749	0.4672897196	0.4662004662	0.4651162791
3	0.2921221947	0.2907314804	0.2893497588	0.2879769618
4	0.2046931901	0.2032047833	0.2017288719	0.2002653516
5	0.1527910955	0.1512835465	0.1497917481	0.1483155525
6	0.1186458704	0.1171574957	0.1156879076	0.1142369066
7	0.0946406583	0.0931923773	0.0917656994	0.0903603636
8	0.0769661101	0.0755700238	0.0741981278	0.0728500896
9	0.0635051669	0.0621683838	0.0608581379	0.0595740150
10	0.0529869780	0.0517135408	0.0504687376	0.0492520625
11	0.0446023222	0.0433942714	0.0422166937	0.0410689830
12	0.0378113211	0.0366693269	0.0355593835	0.0344807761
13	0.0322399012	0.0311636635	0.0301207919	0.0291104565
14	0.0276206298	0.0266091448	0.0256320815	0.0246884898
15	0.0237572163	0.0228089630	0.0218959329	0.0210170526
16	0.0205023244	0.0196154000	0.0187642550	0.0179476914
17	0.0177432135	0.0169154359	0.0161237596	0.0153668623
18	0.0153921647	0.0146211516	0.0138863402	0.0131862874
19	0.0133799284	0.0126631593	0.0119824868	0.0113363504
20	0.0116511339	0.0109860016	0.0103566708	0.0097614704
21	0.0101610103	0.0095448612	0.0089640464	0.0084167914
22	0.0088729970	0.0083031654	0.0077680465	0.0072657713
23	0.0077569775	0.0072308130	0.0067386033	0.0062783947
24	0.0067879502	0.0063028406	0.0058508096	0.0054298296
25	0.0059450182	0.0054984079	0.0050838993	0.0046994023

YEAR	15.50%	16.00%	16.50%	17.00%
2	0.4640371230	0.4629629630	0.4618937644	0.4608294931
3	0.2866130223	0.2852578731	0.2839114480	0.2825736811
4	0.1988141185	0.1973750695	0.1959481019	0.1945331137
5	0.1468548125	0.1454093816	0.1439791140	0.1425638643
6	0.1128042936	0.1113898702	0.1099934387	0.1086148021
7	0.0889761095	0.0876126771	0.0862698077	0.0849472428
8	0.0715255774	0.0702242601	0.0689458078	0.0676898916
9	0.0583156020	0.0570824868	0.0558742591	0.0546905102
10	0.0480630117	0.0469010831	0.0457657770	0.0446565967
11	0.0399505356	0.0388607515	0.0377990342	0.0367647916
12	0.0334327944	0.0324147333	0.0314258934	0.0304655819
13	0.0281318343	0.0271841100	0.0262664771	0.0253781386
14	0.0237774299	0.0228979733	0.0220492036	0.0212302181
15	0.0201712633	0.0193575218	0.0185748018	0.0178220950
16	0.0171645308	0.0164136162	0.0156938131	0.0150040103
17	0.0146434484	0.0139522494	0.0132920262	0.0126615693
18	0.0125195831	0.0118848526	0.0112807572	0.0107059953
19	0.0107232318	0.0101416556	0.0095901910	0.0090674523
20	0.0091987802	0.0086670324	0.0081647123	0.0076903593
21	0.0079013828	0.0074161691	0.0069595618	0.0065300350
22	0.0067945424	0.0063526353	0.0059383976	0.0055502493
23	0.0058483167	0.0054465820	0.0050714859	0.0047214054
24	0.0050379680	0.0046733862	0.0043343385	0.0040191703
25	0.0043429337	0.0040126153	0.0037066717	0.0034234282

YEAR	17.50%	18.00%	18.50%	19.00%
2	0.4597701149	0.4587155963	0.4576659039	0.4566210046
3	0.2812445069	0.2799238607	0.2786116780	0.2773078950
4	0.1931300037	0.1917386709	0.1903590154	0.1889909377
5	0.1411634882	0.1397778418	0.1384067820	0.1370501666
6	0.1072537641	0.1059101292	0.1045837031	0.1032742921
7	0.0836447254	0.0823619994	0.0810988095	0.0798549022
8	0.0664561840	0.0652443589	0.0640540919	0.0628850604
9	0.0535308333	0.0523948239	0.0512820801	0.0501922023
10	0.0435730482	0.0425146413	0.0414808893	0.0404713094
11	0.0357574364	0.0347763862	0.0338210645	0.0328909005
12	0.0295331132	0.0286278089	0.0277489990	0.0268960219
13	0.0245183074	0.0236862073	0.0228810735	0.0221021529
14	0.0204401277	0.0196780583	0.0189431510	0.0182345628
15	0.0170984119	0.0164027825	0.0157342570	0.0150919063
16	0.0143431211	0.0137100839	0.0131038628	0.0125234484
17	0.0120596999	0.0114852711	0.0109371677	0.0104143070
18	0.0101593036	0.0096394570	0.0091452695	0.0086755939
19	0.0085720996	0.0081028390	0.0076584229	0.0072376496
20	0.0072425665	0.0068199812	0.0064213045	0.0060452907
21	0.0061261256	0.0057464327	0.0053896170	0.0050543994
22	0.0051866820	0.0048462577	0.0045276075	0.0042294304
23	0.0043947980	0.0040901996	0.0038062232	0.0035415560
24	0.0037263162	0.0034542973	0.0032017187	0.0029672666
25	0.0031613074	0.0029188261	0.0026945919	0.0024872993

YEAR	19.50%	20.00%
2	0.4555808656	0.4545454545
3	0.2760124482	0.2747252747
4	0.1876343389	0.1862891207
5	0.1357078539	0.1343797033
6	0.1019817036	0.1007057459
7	0.0786300248	0.0774239263
8	0.0617369435	0.0606094224
9	0.0491247940	0.0480794617
10	0.0394854232	0.0385227569
11	0.0319853296	0.0311037942
12	0.0260682250	0.0252649649
13	0.0213487047	0.0206200011
14	0.0175514675	0.0168930552
15	0.0144748227	0.0138821198
16	0.0119678578	
17	0.0099156392	
18	0.0082293223	
19	0.0068393632	
20	0.0056907465	
21	0.0047395606	
22	0.0039504912	
23	0.0032949577	
24	0.0027497051	
25	0.0022957260	

¶5035 HOW MUCH $1 SAVED EACH YEAR WILL INCREASE

The table shows how much $1 put aside at the end of each year will increase at different rates of interest compounded annually for different periods.

YEAR	4.50%	5.00%	5.50%
1	1.000000	1.000000	1.000000
2	2.045000	2.050000	2.055000
3	3.137025	3.152500	3.168025
4	4.278191	4.310125	4.342266
5	5.470710	5.525631	5.581091
6	6.716892	6.801913	6.888051
7	8.019152	8.142008	8.266894
8	9.380014	9.549109	9.721573
9	10.802114	11.026564	11.256260
10	12.288209	12.577893	12.875354
11	13.841179	14.206787	14.583498
12	15.464032	15.917127	16.385591
13	17.159913	17.712963	18.286798
14	18.932109	19.598632	20.292572
15	20.784054	21.578564	22.408663
16	22.719337	23.657492	24.641140
17	24.741707	25.840366	26.996403
18	26.855084	28.132385	29.481205
19	29.063562	30.539004	32.102671
20	31.371423	33.065954	34.868318
21	33.783137	35.719252	37.786076
22	36.303378	38.505214	40.864310
23	38.937030	41.430475	44.111847
24	41.689196	44.501999	47.537998
25	44.565210	47.727099	51.152588

YEAR	6.00%	6.50%	7.00%	7.50%
1	1.000000	1.000000	1.000000	1.000000
2	2.060000	2.065000	2.070000	2.075000
3	3.183600	3.199225	3.214900	3.230625
4	4.374616	4.407175	4.439943	4.472922
5	5.637093	5.693641	5.750739	5.808391
6	6.975319	7.063728	7.153291	7.244020
7	8.393838	8.522870	8.654021	8.787322
8	9.897468	10.076856	10.259803	10.446371
9	11.491316	11.731852	11.977989	12.229849
10	13.180795	13.494423	13.816448	14.147087
11	14.971643	15.371560	15.783599	16.208119
12	16.869941	17.370711	17.888451	18.423728
13	18.882138	19.499808	20.140643	20.805508
14	21.015066	21.767295	22.550488	23.365921
15	23.275970	24.182169	25.129022	26.118365
16	25.672528	26.754010	27.888054	29.077242
17	28.212880	29.493021	30.640217	32.258035
18	30.905653	32.410067	33.999033	35.677388
19	33.759992	35.516722	37.378965	39.353192
20	36.785591	38.825309	40.995492	43.304681
21	39.992727	42.348954	44.865177	47.552532
22	43.392290	46.101636	49.005739	52.118972
23	46.995828	50.098242	53.436141	57.027895
24	50.815577	54.354628	58.176671	62.304987
25	54.864512	58.887679	63.249038	67.977862

YEAR	8.00%	8.50%	9.00%	9.50%
1	1.000000	1.000000	1.000000	1.000000
2	2.080000	2.085000	2.090000	2.095000
3	3.246400	3.262225	3.278100	3.294025
4	4.506112	4.539514	4.573129	4.606957
5	5.866601	5.925373	5.984711	6.044618
6	7.335929	7.429030	7.523335	7.618857
7	8.922803	9.060497	9.200435	9.342648
8	10.636628	10.830639	11.028474	11.230200
9	12.487558	12.751244	13.021036	13.297069
10	14.486562	14.835099	15.192930	15.560291
11	16.645487	17.096083	17.560293	18.038518
12	18.977126	19.549250	20.140720	20.752178
13	21.495297	22.210936	22.953385	23.723634
14	24.214920	25.098866	26.019189	26.977380
15	27.152114	28.232269	29.360916	30.540231
16	30.324283	31.632012	33.003399	34.441553
17	33.750226	35.320733	36.973705	38.713500
18	37.450244	39.322995	41.301338	43.391283
19	41.446263	43.665450	46.018458	48.513454
20	45.761964	48.377013	51.160120	54.122233
21	50.422921	53.489059	56.764530	60.263845
22	55.456755	59.035629	62.873338	66.988910
23	60.893296	65.053658	69.531939	74.352856
24	66.764759	71.583219	76.789813	82.416378
25	73.105940	78.667792	84.700896	91.245934

YEAR	10.00%	10.50%	11.00%
1	1.000000	1.000000	1.000000
2	2.100000	2.105000	2.110000
3	3.310000	3.326025	3.342100
4	4.641000	4.675258	4.709731
5	6.105100	6.166160	6.227801
6	7.715610	7.813606	7.912860
7	9.487171	9.634035	9.783274
8	11.435888	11.645609	11.859434
9	13.579477	13.868398	14.163972
10	15.937425	16.324579	16.722009
11	18.531167	19.038660	19.561430
12	21.384284	22.037720	22.713187
13	24.522712	25.351680	26.211638
14	27.974983	29.013607	30.094918
15	31.772482	33.060035	34.405359
16	35.949730	37.531339	39.189948
17	40.544703	42.472130	44.500843
18	45.599173	47.931703	50.395936
19	51.159090	53.964532	56.939488
20	57.274999	60.630808	64.202832
21	64.002499	67.997043	72.265144
22	71.402749	76.136732	81.214309
23	79.543024	85.131089	91.147884
24	88.497327	95.069854	102.174151
25	98.347059	106.052188	114.413307

YEAR	11.50%	12.00%	12.50%	13.00%
1	1.000000	1.000000	1.000000	1.000000
2	2.115000	2.120000	2.125000	2.130000
3	3.358225	3.374400	3.390625	3.406900
4	4.744421	4.779328	4.814453	4.849797
5	6.290029	6.352847	6.416260	6.480271
6	8.013383	8.115189	8.218292	8.322706
7	9.934922	10.089012	10.245579	10.404658
8	12.077438	12.299693	12.526276	12.757263
9	14.466343	14.775656	15.092061	15.415707
10	17.129972	17.548735	17.978568	18.419749
11	20.099919	20.654583	21.225889	21.814317
12	23.411410	24.133133	24.879125	25.650178
13	27.103722	28.029109	28.989016	29.984701
14	31.220650	32.392602	33.612643	34.882712
15	35.811025	37.279715	38.814223	40.417464
16	40.929293	42.753280	44.666001	46.671735
17	46.636161	48.883674	51.249252	53.739060
18	52.999320	55.749715	58.655408	61.725138
19	60.094242	63.439681	66.987334	70.749406
20	68.005080	72.052442	76.360751	80.946829
21	76.825664	81.698736	86.905845	92.469917
22	86.660615	92.502584	98.769075	105.491006
23	97.626586	104.602894	112.115210	120.204837
24	109.853643	118.155241	127.129611	136.831465
25	123.486812	133.333870	144.020812	155.619556

YEAR	13.50%	14.00%	14.50%	15.00%
1	1.000000	1.000000	1.000000	1.000000
2	2.135000	2.140000	2.145000	2.150000
3	3.423225	3.439600	3.456025	3.472500
4	4.885360	4.921144	4.957149	4.993375
5	6.544884	6.610104	6.675935	6.742381
6	8.428443	8.535519	8.643946	8.753738
7	10.566283	10.730491	10.697318	11.066799
8	12.992731	13.232760	13.477429	13.726819
9	15.746750	16.085347	16.431656	16.785842
10	18.872561	19.337295	19.814246	20.303718
11	22.420357	23.044516	23.687312	24.349276
12	26.447106	27.270749	28.121972	29.001667
13	31.017465	32.088654	33.199658	34.351917
14	36.204823	37.581065	39.013609	40.504705
15	42.092474	43.642414	45.670582	47.580411
16	48.774957	50.980352	53.292816	55.717472
17	56.359577	59.117601	62.020275	65.075093
18	64.968120	68.394066	72.013215	75.836357
19	74.738816	78.969235	83.455131	88.211811
20	85.828556	91.024928	96.556125	102.443583
21	98.415411	104.768418	111.556763	118.810120
22	112.701491	120.435996	128.732494	137.631638
23	128.916193	138.297035	148.396705	159.276384
24	147.319879	158.658620	170.916517	184.167841
25	168.208062	181.870827	196.699412	212.793017

YEAR	15.50%	16.00%	16.50%	17.00%
1	1.000000	1.000000	1.000000	1.000000
2	2.155000	2.160000	2.165000	2.170000
3	3.489025	3.505600	3.522225	3.538900
4	5.029824	5.066496	5.103392	5.140513
5	6.809447	6.877135	6.945452	7.014400
6	8.864911	8.977477	9.091451	9.206848
7	11.238972	11.413873	11.591541	11.772012
8	13.981013	14.240093	14.504145	14.773255
9	17.148070	17.518508	17.897329	18.284708
10	20.806020	21.321469	21.850388	22.393108
11	25.030954	25.732904	26.455702	27.199937
12	29.910751	30.850169	31.820893	32.823926
13	35.546918	36.786196	38.071341	39.403993
14	42.056690	43.671967	45.353112	47.102672
15	49.575477	51.659505	53.836375	56.110126
16	58.259676	60.925026	63.719377	66.648848
17	68.289926	71.673030	75.233075	78.979152
18	79.874864	84.140715	88.646532	93.405608
19	93.255468	98.603230	104.273210	110.284561
20	108.710066	115.379747	122.478289	130.032936
21	126.560126	134.840506	143.687207	153.138535
22	147.176945	157.414987	168.395596	180.172086
23	170.989372	183.601385	197.180869	211.801341
24	198.492725	213.977607	230.715713	248.807569
25	230.259097	249.214024	269.783805	292.104856

YEAR	17.50%	18.00%	18.50%	19.00%
1	1.000000	1.000000	1.000000	1.000000
2	2.175000	2.180000	2.185000	2.190000
3	3.555625	3.572400	3.589225	3.606100
4	5.177859	5.215432	5.253232	5.291259
5	7.083985	7.154210	7.225079	7.296598
6	9.323682	9.441968	9.561719	9.682952
7	11.955326	12.141522	12.330637	12.522713
8	15.047509	15.326996	15.611805	15.902028
9	18.680823	19.085855	19.499989	19.923413
10	22.949967	23.521309	24.107487	24.708862
11	27.966211	28.755144	29.567372	30.403546
12	33.860298	34.931070	36.037336	37.180220
13	40.765850	42.216663	43.704243	45.244461
14	48.923373	50.818022	52.789528	54.840909
15	58.484964	60.965266	63.555591	66.260682
16	69.719832	72.939014	76.313375	79.850211
17	82.920803	87.068036	91.431350	96.021751
18	98.431944	103.740283	109.346149	115.265884
19	116.657534	123.413534	130.575187	138.166402
20	138.072602	146.627970	155.731596	165.418018
21	163.235307	174.021005	185.541942	197.847442
22	192.801486	206.344785	220.867201	236.438456
23	227.541746	244.486847	262.727633	282.361762
24	268.361552	289.494479	312.332245	337.010497
25	316.324823	342.603486	371.113710	402.042491

YEAR	19.50%	20.00%
1	1.000000	1.000000
2	2.195000	2.200000
3	3.623025	3.640000
4	5.329515	5.368000
5	7.368770	7.441600
6	9.805680	9.929920
7	12.717788	12.915904
8	16.197757	16.499085
9	20.356319	20.798902
10	25.325802	25.958682
11	31.264333	32.150419
12	38.360878	39.580502
13	46.841249	48.496603
14	56.975293	59.195923
15	69.085475	72.035108
16	83.557143	
17	100.850785	
18	121.516689	
19	146.212443	
20	175.723869	
21	210.990024	
22	253.133078	
23	303.494029	
24	363.675364	
25	435.592060	

¶ 5040 HOW MUCH $1 TO BE PAID IN THE FUTURE IS CURRENTLY WORTH

The table shows how much $1 to be paid at various periods in the future is now worth, with interest at different rates compounded annually. Adding an annual inflation factor to the interest rate will help to compute real present value, i.e., assuming an interest rate of six percent and an annual inflation rate of three percent, the nine-percent interest rate would be used to determine present value.

YEAR	4.50%	5.00%	5.50%
1	0.956938	0.952381	0.947867
2	0.915730	0.907029	0.898452
3	0.876297	0.863838	0.851614
4	0.838561	0.822702	0.807217
5	0.802451	0.783526	0.765134
6	0.767896	0.746215	0.725246
7	0.734828	0.710681	0.687437
8	0.703185	0.676839	0.651599
9	0.672904	0.644609	0.617629
10	0.643928	0.613913	0.585431
11	0.616199	0.584679	0.554911
12	0.589664	0.556837	0.525982
13	0.564272	0.530321	0.498561
14	0.539973	0.505068	0.472569
15	0.516720	0.481017	0.447933
16	0.494469	0.458112	0.424581
17	0.473176	0.436297	0.402447
18	0.452800	0.415521	0.381466
19	0.433302	0.395734	0.361579
20	0.414643	0.376889	0.342729
21	0.396787	0.358942	0.324862
22	0.379701	0.341850	0.307926
23	0.363350	0.325571	0.291873
24	0.347703	0.310068	0.276657
25	0.332731	0.295303	0.262234

YEAR	6.00%	6.50%	7.00%	7.50%
1	0.943396	0.938967	0.934579	0.930233
2	0.889996	0.881659	0.873439	0.865333
3	0.839619	0.827849	0.816298	0.804961
4	0.792094	0.777323	0.762895	0.748801
5	0.747258	0.729881	0.712986	0.696559
6	0.704961	0.685334	0.666342	0.647962
7	0.665057	0.643506	0.622750	0.602755
8	0.627412	0.604231	0.582009	0.560702
9	0.591898	0.567353	0.543934	0.521583
10	0.558395	0.532726	0.508349	0.485194
11	0.526788	0.500212	0.475093	0.451343
12	0.496969	0.469683	0.444012	0.419854
13	0.468839	0.441017	0.414964	0.390562
14	0.442301	0.414100	0.387817	0.363313
15	0.417265	0.388827	0.362446	0.337966
16	0.393646	0.365095	0.388735	0.314387
17	0.371364	0.342813	0.316574	0.292453
18	0.350344	0.321890	0.295864	0.272049
19	0.330513	0.302244	0.276508	0.253069
20	0.311805	0.283797	0.258419	0.235413
21	0.294155	0.266476	0.241513	0.218989
22	0.277505	0.250212	0.225713	0.203711
23	0.261797	0.234941	0.210947	0.189498
24	0.246979	0.220602	0.197147	0.176277
25	0.232999	0.207138	0.184249	0.163979

YEAR	8.00%	8.50%	9.00%	9.50%
1	0.925926	0.921659	0.917431	0.913242
2	0.857339	0.849455	0.841680	0.834011
3	0.793832	0.782908	0.772183	0.761654
4	0.735030	0.721574	0.708425	0.695574
5	0.680583	0.665045	0.649931	0.635228
6	0.630170	0.612945	0.596267	0.580117
7	0.583490	0.564926	0.547034	0.529787
8	0.540269	0.520669	0.501866	0.483824
9	0.500249	0.479880	0.460428	0.441848
10	0.463193	0.442285	0.422411	0.403514
11	0.428883	0.407636	0.387533	0.368506
12	0.397114	0.375702	0.355535	0.336535
13	0.367698	0.346269	0.326179	0.307338
14	0.340461	0.319142	0.299246	0.280674
15	0.315242	0.294140	0.274538	0.256323
16	0.291890	0.271097	0.251870	0.234085
17	0.270269	0.249859	0.231073	0.213777
18	0.250249	0.230285	0.211994	0.195230
19	0.231712	0.212244	0.194490	0.178292
20	0.214548	0.195616	0.178431	0.162824
21	0.198656	0.180292	0.163698	0.148697
22	0.183941	0.166167	0.150182	0.135797
23	0.170315	0.153150	0.137781	0.124015
24	0.157699	0.141152	0.126405	0.113256
25	0.146018	0.130094	0.115968	0.103430

YEAR	10.00%	10.50%	11.00%
1	0.909091	0.904977	0.900901
2	0.826446	0.818984	0.811622
3	0.751315	0.741162	0.731191
4	0.683013	0.670735	0.658731
5	0.620921	0.607000	0.593451
6	0.564474	0.549321	0.534641
7	0.513158	0.497123	0.481658
8	0.466507	0.449885	0.433926
9	0.424098	0.407136	0.390925
10	0.385543	0.368449	0.352184
11	0.350494	0.333438	0.317283
12	0.318631	0.301754	0.285841
13	0.289664	0.273080	0.257514
14	0.263331	0.247132	0.231995
15	0.239392	0.223648	0.209004
16	0.217629	0.202397	0.188292
17	0.197845	0.183164	0.169633
18	0.179859	0.165760	0.152822
19	0.163508	0.150009	0.137678
20	0.148644	0.135755	0.124034
21	0.135131	0.122855	0.111742
22	0.122846	0.111181	0.100669
23	0.111678	0.100616	0.090693
24	0.101526	0.091055	0.081705
25	0.092296	0.082403	0.073608

YEAR	11.50%	12.00%	12.50%	13.00%
1	0.896861	0.892857	0.888889	0.884956
2	0.804360	0.797194	0.790123	0.783147
3	0.721399	0.711780	0.702332	0.693050
4	0.646994	0.635518	0.624295	0.613319
5	0.580264	0.567427	0.554929	0.542760
6	0.520416	0.506631	0.493270	0.480319
7	0.466741	0.452349	0.438462	0.425061
8	0.418602	0.403883	0.389744	0.376160
9	0.375428	0.360610	0.346439	0.332885
10	0.336706	0.321973	0.307946	0.294588
11	0.301979	0.287476	0.273730	0.260698
12	0.270833	0.256675	0.243315	0.230706
13	0.242900	0.229174	0.216280	0.204165
14	0.217847	0.204620	0.192249	0.180677
15	0.195379	0.182696	0.170888	0.159891
16	0.175227	0.163122	0.151901	0.141496
17	0.157155	0.145644	0.135023	0.125218
18	0.140946	0.130040	0.120020	0.110812
19	0.126409	0.116107	0.106685	0.098064
20	0.113371	0.103667	0.094831	0.086782
21	0.101678	0.092560	0.084294	0.076798
22	0.091191	0.082643	0.074928	0.067963
23	0.081786	0.073788	0.066603	0.060144
24	0.073351	0.065882	0.059202	0.053225
25	0.065785	0.058823	0.052624	0.047102

YEAR	13.50%	14.00%	14.50%	15.00%
1	0.881057	0.877193	0.873362	0.869565
2	0.776262	0.769468	0.762762	0.756144
3	0.683931	0.674972	0.666168	0.657516
4	0.602583	0.592080	0.581806	0.571753
5	0.530910	0.519369	0.508127	0.497177
6	0.467762	0.455587	0.443779	0.432328
7	0.412125	0.399637	0.387580	0.375937
8	0.363106	0.350559	0.338498	0.326902
9	0.319917	0.307508	0.295631	0.284262
10	0.281865	0.269744	0.258193	0.247185
11	0.248339	0.236617	0.225496	0.214943
12	0.218801	0.207559	0.196940	0.186907
13	0.192776	0.182069	0.172000	0.162528
14	0.169847	0.159710	0.150218	0.141329
15	0.149645	0.140096	0.131195	0.122894
16	0.131846	0.122892	0.114581	0.106865
17	0.116164	0.107800	0.100071	0.092926
18	0.102347	0.094561	0.087398	0.080805
19	0.090173	0.082948	0.076330	0.070265
20	0.079448	0.072762	0.066664	0.061100
21	0.069998	0.063826	0.058222	0.053131
22	0.061672	0.055988	0.050849	0.046201
23	0.054337	0.049112	0.044409	0.040174
24	0.047874	0.043081	0.038785	0.034934
25	0.042180	0.037790	0.033874	0.030378

YEAR	15.50%	16.00%	16.50%	17.00%
1	0.865801	0.862069	0.858369	0.854701
2	0.749611	0.743163	0.736798	0.730514
3	0.649014	0.640658	0.632444	0.624371
4	0.561917	0.552291	0.542871	0.533650
5	0.486508	0.476113	0.465983	0.456111
6	0.421219	0.410442	0.399986	0.389839
7	0.364692	0.353830	0.343335	0.333195
8	0.315751	0.305025	0.294708	0.284782
9	0.273377	0.262953	0.252969	0.243404
10	0.236690	0.226684	0.217140	0.208037
11	0.204927	0.195417	0.186387	0.177810
12	0.177426	0.168463	0.159989	0.151974
13	0.153615	0.145227	0.137329	0.129892
14	0.133000	0.125195	0.117879	0.111019
15	0.115152	0.107927	0.101184	0.094888
16	0.099698	0.093041	0.086853	0.061101
17	0.086319	0.080207	0.074552	0.069317
18	0.074735	0.069144	0.063993	0.059245
19	0.064706	0.059607	0.054930	0.050637
20	0.056022	0.051385	0.047150	0.043280
21	0.048504	0.044298	0.040472	0.036991
22	0.041995	0.038188	0.034740	0.031616
23	0.036359	0.032920	0.029820	0.027022
24	0.031480	0.028380	0.025596	0.023096
25	0.027255	0.024465	0.021971	0.019740

YEAR	17.50%	18.00%	18.50%	19.00%
1	0.851064	0.847458	0.843882	0.840336
2	0.724310	0.718184	0.712137	0.706165
3	0.616434	0.608631	0.600959	0.593416
4	0.524624	0.515789	0.507139	0.498669
5	0.446489	0.437109	0.427965	0.419049
6	0.379991	0.370432	0.361152	0.352142
7	0.323396	0.313925	0.304770	0.295918
8	0.275231	0.266038	0.257189	0.248671
9	0.234239	0.225456	0.217038	0.208967
10	0.199352	0.191064	0.183154	0.175602
11	0.169662	0.161919	0.154560	0.147565
12	0.144393	0.137220	0.130431	0.124004
13	0.122888	0.116288	0.110068	0.104205
14	0.104585	0.098549	0.092884	0.087567
15	0.089009	0.083516	0.078384	0.073586
16	0.075752	0.070776	0.066146	0.061837
17	0.064470	0.059980	0.055820	0.051964
18	0.054868	0.050830	0.047105	0.043667
19	0.046696	0.043077	0.039751	0.036695
20	0.039741	0.036506	0.033545	0.030836
21	0.033822	0.030937	0.028308	0.025913
22	0.028785	0.026218	0.023889	0.021775
23	0.024498	0.022218	0.020159	0.018299
24	0.020849	0.018829	0.017012	0.015377
25	0.017744	0.015957	0.014356	0.012922

YEAR	19.50%	20.00%
1	0.836820	0.833333
2	0.700268	0.694444
3	0.585998	0.578704
4	0.490375	0.482253
5	0.410356	0.401878
6	0.343394	0.334898
7	0.287359	0.279082
8	0.240468	0.232568
9	0.201228	0.193807
10	0.168392	0.161506
11	0.140914	0.134588
12	0.117919	0.112157
13	0.098677	0.093464
14	0.082575	0.077887
15	0.069101	0.064905
16	0.057825	
17	0.048389	
18	0.040493	
19	0.033885	
20	0.028356	
21	0.023729	
22	0.019857	
23	0.016616	
24	0.013905	
25	0.011636	

¶5045 VALUATION OF ANNUITIES, LIFE ESTATES, REMAINDERS, ETC.

The value of annuities, unitrust interests, life estates, remainders, and reversions is determined under tables issued by the IRS under Code Sec. 7520. Taxpayers use one set of tables, based on the 1990 census, to determine the value of an interest that has a valuation date after April 30, 1999. Another set of tables, based on the 1980 census, is used for valuation dates after April 30, 1989, and before May 1, 1999. The tables have two components: (1) a mortality component, and (2) an interest component.

Under the tables, the interest rates are adjusted monthly. The mortality component is based on the latest mortality tables, which are to be revised at least once every 10 years. The interest component is revised monthly geared to 120 percent of the applicable federal mid-term rate on Treasuries compounded annually (rounded to the nearest two-tenths of one percent). For charitable transfers, the interest rate for the month of the transfer or for either of the two preceding months may be used.

The Code Sec. 7520 tables are contained in IRS Publication 1457 "Actuarial Values, Book Aleph," Publication 1458 "Actuarial Values, Book Beth," and Publication 1459 "Actuarial Values, Book Gimel." Book Aleph contains tables of valuation factors, and examples that show how to compute other valuation factors, for determining the present value of annuities, life estates, terms of years, remainders, and reversions, measured by one or two lives. Taxpayers may also use these factors in the valuation of interests in a charitable remainder annuity trust (CRAT) and a pooled income fund. Book Beth contains term certain tables and tables of one and two life valuation factors for computing the present value of remainder interests in a charitable remainder unitrust (CRUT). Book Gimel has tables for calculating depreciation adjustment factors.

> **Planning pointer** As noted above, the interest factor under the valuation tables changes monthly. As a result, the value of a gift or the amount of a charitable deduction could be higher or lower in an earlier or later month depending on the type of interest being valued and the direction of interest rates. For transfers, any part of which qualify for an income, estate, or gift tax charitable deduction, a client may use the interest rate for the month of the transfer or for either of the two preceding months. No such flexibility is afforded for purely personal transfers. However, estate planners and their clients who can reasonably predict which direction interest rates are headed from one

month to the next may be able to reduce transfer tax costs. They can accelerate or defer a transfer to obtain the advantage of a higher or lower rate, as the case may be. A change in interest rates affects various interests as follows:

Type of Interest	*Effect of Increase in Rate on Value*	*Effect of Decrease in Rate on Value*
Life income	Increases	Decreases
Remainder after life income	Decreases	Increases
Reversion after life income	Decreases	Increases
Term income	Increases	Decreases
Remainder after term income	Decreases	Increases
Reversion after term income	Decreases	Increases
Life annuity	Decreases	Increases
Remainder after life annuity	Increases	Decreases
Reversion after life annuity	Increases	Decreases
Term annuity	Decreases	Increases
Remainder after term annuity	Increases	Decreases
Reversion after term annuity	Increases	Decreases
Unitrust interest	Unaffected	Unaffected
Remainder after unitrust interest	Unaffected	Unaffected

Index

References are to paragraph (¶) numbers

A

Accelerated charitable remainder trusts . . . 515.01

Accountant for estate, help for executor from . . . 1405

Accounting method, cash . . . 1720.04, 2001, 2025, 3305.01

Accounts receivable
- discounted upon death of sole proprietor . . . 2110
- included in inventory items . . . 2015.02

Accrued benefit for qualified retirement plan . . . 905.01
- adjusted if distributions are delayed past age 70½ . . . 905.02

Accumulated earnings credit . . . 1720.04, 1901.02
- multiple corporations to multiply . . . 1905

Accumulated earnings tax . . . 1720.08, 1915.03
- S corporation status to avoid . . . 1945

Accumulated taxable income of corporation, flat-rate tax on . . . 1720.08

Accumulation trusts . . . 605.01, 605.04, 615
- nontax benefits of . . . 660

Acquisition debt for home mortgage interest . . . 2815, 2815.02, 2815.05, 2815.08, 2815.09

Acquisition of property, checking mode of . . . 305

Act Relating to Civil Unions (Vermont) . . . 2505.02

Ademption of legacy . . . 1105.04

Adjustable life insurance policy . . . 705.02

Adjusted gross income (AGI)
- child's income reported on parents' return as raising their . . . 3205.02
- on IRS Form 1040 . . . 5001.06
- itemized deductions dependent on percentages of . . . 3205.02, 3301.02, 3420.01
- lowering, tax benefits that decrease by . . . 3301.02
- manipulating . . . 3301.02
- reducing . . . 3325.01, 3405.05
- tax benefits dependent on ceilings of, descriptions of . . . 3301.02

Adjusted gross income (AGI) used as ceiling
- for deductibility of IRA contributions . . . 915.01
- for itemized deductions . . . 901

Adoption expenses
- credit for . . . 3450.01
- exclusion for . . . 3450.02

Advance principal distribution to beneficiary . . . 660.02

Age of majority for children . . . 425.02
- distributing trusts funds upon . . . 425.04
- reducing alimony payments upon . . . 2425.02
- tax effects of state lowering . . . 2430

Aggressive growth mutual funds . . . 3140.03

Alimony
- compliance with reporting requirements for . . . 2425.04
- contingencies for . . . 2425.02
- deduction for fees that produce taxable . . . 2440
- front-loading payments of . . . 2425.01
- as gender neutral support . . . 2405.02
- not dischargeable in bankruptcy of obligor . . . 2435.04

Alimony—continued
- provisions in premarital agreement for, challenges to . . . 2405.03
- reduced on contingency relating to child . . . 2425.02, 2430
- requirements for payments to be treated as . . . 2425.01
- retirement benefits to make payments of . . . 2445
- state laws impacting . . . 2420
- taxable to recipient and deductible by payor . . . 2425

Alternate valuation date . . . 210.05

Alternative minimum tax (AMT)
- adjustment for current earnings (ACE) for . . . 1935
- application to estates and trusts of . . . 605.08
- consequences of investing in private activity bonds for . . . 3110–3110.01
- corporate . . . 2001
- deduction for qualified residence interest for, rules governing . . . 2815.08
- exemption from . . . 1805.07, 3101.01
- lower rate for C corporations of . . . 1805.01
- not applicable to charitable contributions of appreciated property . . . 505.09
- partnerships not subject to . . . 1805.07
- S corporations not subject to . . . 1805.07
- stock acquired by ISO for . . . 1605.01
- tax rates for . . . 3101.01
- transfers to minors older than 14 affecting parents' . . . 3210
- year-end planning for . . . 3301.03

American Council on Gift Annuities . . . 520

American Depositary Receipts (ADRs) . . . 3185.06

American Institute of Certified Public Accountants (AICPA) . . . 105, 1715.01
- Code of Ethics of . . . 1720.15

American Jobs Creation Act of 2004 . . . 2435.01

Annuitant
- of charitable gift annuity . . . 520
- of charitable remainder annuity trust . . . 515.01
- exclusion amount from gross income of . . . 805.03
- health of . . . 810.01
- remaining annuity basis as itemized deduction on final return of . . . 805.03
- guaranteed payments to . . . 801
- taxation of income of . . . 810.02
- terminally ill . . . 810.04

Annuities . . . 801–810. *See also* individual types
- advantages of . . . 805
- basis in . . . 805.02, 805.03
- commercial . . . 805–805.03
- death benefit, refund, or survivor income in . . . 1005.02
- insurance proceeds paid as . . . 710
- lifetime gift of . . . 410.01
- obligor of, taxable income for . . . 810.06
- paid by charities . . . 520
- portion includible in gross income of . . . 5020
- private . . . 810–810.06, 3240
- for proceeds of qualified plan . . . 1610.01
- qualifying as income interests . . . 405.02
- starting date after 1986 for . . . 805.03, 810.02
- taxation of . . . 805.03, 810, 905.02
- valuation of . . . 810.01

Annuity payments
components of . . . 810.02
deferring income using . . . 3305.01
gift tax on . . . 810.03
obligor's basis in property equaling . . . 810.06

Antiques as good for lifetime giving . . . 410.01

Appeals Division, IRS, appeal of IRS agent's determination with . . . 101

Appeals Officer, IRS, negotiating stock valuation with . . . 101

Applicable family member
definedfortransfersofresidualinterest . . . 2305.01–.04
transfer of applicable retained interest by . . . 2305.07

Appraiser responsibilities for developing qualified appraisal of large gift of property . . . 505.04

Appreciated property
bargain sales of . . . 505.10
contributions of . . . 505.08–.09, 3101.02
deferring tax on gain from . . . 3101.01
lifetime gifts of . . . 410.01–.02
like-kind exchanges of . . . 3115–3115.04
recognition of gain on . . . 3115

Archer medical savings accounts . . . 1605.01, 1610.10, 3305.01, 3325.01, 3420.02, 3425.03

Art appraisals . . . 505.04

Artwork
copyrighted . . . 535
giving museum right of possession and enjoyment of . . . 515.04
as good for lifetime giving . . . 410.01
partial interests in . . . 535

Asset allocation . . . 3101.03

Asset management accounts, services and fees for . . . 3185.05

Assets
of estate, valuation date for . . . 1520–1520.02
tax basis of . . . 210.05

Assignment of income doctrine . . . 3201

Assignment, written notice of insurance . . . 701.01

Athletic facilities as fringe benefit, on-premises . . . 985.06

Attorney
estate . . . 1405
ethics of splitting earnings with nonprofessionals for . . . 1720.15
matrimonial (divorce) . . . 2420
stipulation of guardian prepared by . . . 1415

Attorney's fees deducted from gross estate . . . 1005, 1005.03

Automatic savings plan through employer . . . 3105

B

Bad debts, establishing basis for deduction of . . . 3430

Balanced mutual funds . . . 3140.03

Bankruptcy
of broker . . . 3185.03–.04
of insurance company . . . 750.01
of obligor paying alimony or child support . . . 2435.04

Bargain sale
of appreciated property . . . 505.10
to charity . . . 501.01
as gift to donee . . . 410.06

***Barudin, Estate of J.* . . .** 2010.04

Basis
of estate property . . . 315.02
of lifetime gifts v. testamentary transfers . . . 410.02
of stock, decline in . . . 3315.01
of survivor in property held in joint tenancy . . . 310.04

Bed and breakfast operation in home . . . 2830

Below-market loans to employees . . . 970–970.02

Beneficiary of Coverdell Education Savings Account
changing . . . 3020.06, 3020.07
death of . . . 3020.07
distributions to . . . 3020.03
rollovers of balance by . . . 3020.06
transfer of interest of, under divorce agreement . . . 3020.07

Beneficiary of estate
adult, protecting incompetent . . . 1105.09
cash bequest v. residuary payment to . . . 1105.04, 1110.11
children of, receiving parent's share . . . 1105.07
conflict of interest between executor and . . . 1405
contingency . . . 1101, 1105.07
contractual death benefits received by . . . 1610.11
disclaimer of bequest by . . . 415, 1525.01
distributions as taxable to . . . 1515.07
estate borrowing from . . . 1510.03
estate tax as excise tax on . . . 1005
executor as making distributions from estate to . . . 1405
favoritism toward . . . 1515.01
income . . . 1105.06
minor, protecting . . . 1105.08
predeceasing testator . . . 1101, 1105.07
selected by law . . . 1101
survivorship issues for . . . 1105.15
unmarried partner as . . . 2505.03

Beneficiary of insurance policy, avoiding naming estate as . . . 610

Beneficiary of IRA . . . 915.01
distributions based on life expectancy of . . . 915.01
nonspousal . . . 955.01, 2505.04
spouse as, commencement of distributions for . . . 915.01

Beneficiary of life insurance
changing . . . 701.01
child from prior marriage as . . . 2410.02
estate as . . . 610
excluding insurance proceeds from gross income of . . . 710
guardian of children as . . . 1415
partners as . . . 2015.05
policy transferred to . . . 525.03, 715, 715.01, 1601
predeceasing insured . . . 525.03, 715.01, 735.01
selecting . . . 730
spouse as policy owner and . . . 725
unmarried partner as . . . 2505.04

Beneficiary of qualified retirement plan
contingent . . . 905.02
selecting . . . 905.02
spousal v. nonspousal . . . 955.01, 2505.04

Beneficiary of trust
adult child as . . . 605.05
for annuity v. unitrust . . . 515.01
as co-trustee . . . 660.02
Crummey power for . . . 615, 660.04
for death benefits . . . 950
delayed distribution to . . . 660.11
disinheriting . . . 660.10
distributed income taxable to . . . 605.01
DNI giving trust deductions to . . . 605.03

Beneficiary of trust—continued
effect of deductions on estate tax return v. estate income tax return as affecting . . . 1515.04
influencing conduct of . . . 660.09–.10
legally incompetent or disabled person as . . . 601, 660.05
life income interest of . . . 515.02, 3225
look-through rules for . . . 905.02
mandatory distribution of income to . . . 425.04
maturity of . . . 410.04
minor as . . . 405.05, 425.01, 425.04, 601
for pooled income fund, permanent . . . 515.02
power to withdraw trust principal by . . . 660.03, 660.04
qualified heir as . . . 2210.01
for short-term trust . . . 605.01
taxation of . . . 530, 601, 605.03
terminal illness of . . . 405.05
transfer of nonincome-producing property in trust to pay income to . . . 410.01
unmarried partner as . . . 2505.04

Benefits, executive
lifetime and estate planning for . . . 1610
overcoming limits on . . . 1605.02
types of . . . 1605.01. *See also* individual types

Bequest types . . . 1105.04, 1110.10, 1210, 1225.01

***Berzon* decision about present income interest** . . . 615

***Boggs v. Boggs*, qualified plan decision in** . . . 325.02

Bond mutual funds . . . 3140.03

Bond premiums as offset to interest income . . . 3101.01

Bond requirement for executors . . . 1405, 1410

Bonds
basis in . . . 3165.02
commissions and fees for transactions of . . . 3190.01
direct gift made by transfer of . . . 415
empowerment zone . . . 3110
enterprise zone . . . 3110
facility . . . 3110
individual . . . 3110.02
junk . . . 3175
market discount . . . 3165.02
municipal . . . 3175
mutual funds holding . . . 3110.02
private activity . . . 3110–3110.01
stripping coupon interest from . . . 3165–3165.02
tax-exempt . . . 3101.01, 3110–3110.03
tax-exempt stripped . . . 3165–3165.01
tax-exempt zero coupon . . . 3110.03, 3160.03
unit trusts of . . . 3110.02
U.S. Treasury . . . 3135–3135.01

Bonus to owner of corporation, timing of . . . 3320

Boot, receipt of . . . 3115.04

***Braun, F.C., Jr.* decision on trust income used for support** . . . 425.01

Brokerage accounts
arbitration clauses for . . . 3185.04
in asset management accounts . . . 3185.05
commissions paid for . . . 3185–3185.01, 3190–3190.01
full-service v. discount . . . 3185–3185.01, 3190, 3190.01
joint . . . 310.02, 315.05, 1525.01

Brokerage houses, IRAs offered by . . . 915.01

Burden of proof for IRS assessment, shifting . . . 101

Business expense, deduction of tax advice as . . . 2440

Business form choice
for closely held businesses . . . 1801–1810
nontax factors in making . . . 1810
planning for . . . 1805.07, 1905
for professional practice . . . 1715–1715.03

Business income split with family members . . . 3230

Business interests as good for lifetime giving . . . 410.01

Business operations
effect of redeeming closely held stock on . . . 1915.02
interest paid or incurred by estate in connection with . . . 1515.06

Business real property, valuation of . . . 1105.05

Business risk, ascertaining . . . 1940.01

Business travel as working condition fringe benefit . . . 985.03

Business use of home . . . 2801, 2820.04, 2830

Buy-sell agreements
in closely held corporations . . . 1901.02, 1910.01, 1935
valuing partnership interest and fixing price for . . . 2015.03, 2020.01, 2030
valuing property and modifications to . . . 2310
valuing sole proprietorship for estate tax purposes using . . . 2110.04

Bypass trust
estate taxes saved using . . . 640
purposes of . . . 1225, 1225.04

***Byrum, M.* decision for retention of voting rights** . . . 610.01

C

C corporation
as choice of business form . . . 1805.01
farm operated as . . . 2210.08
fringe benefits of, tax-favored . . . 1715.01
limits on use of cash method accounting for . . . 1720.04
partnership business form compared with . . . 2001
personal holding company problems of . . . 1720.05
splitting income with family members from . . . 3230
tax factors affecting S corporation v. . . . 1715.03
tax rate of . . . 1805.01, 2001
tax year of . . . 1720.03
unreasonable compensation not deductible by . . . 1720.02

Cafeteria plans for employee benefits . . . 975, 3420.03

Cafeteria-style compensation for executives . . . 1605.01

Capital gain property
contribution to foundations of . . . 505.09
deduction and tax treatment of . . . 505.09
percentage limitations for contributions of . . . 505, 505.02

Capital gains. *See also* Net capital gain
on bargain sales of appreciated property . . . 505.10
on C corporation stock shares . . . 1805.01
on lifetime gifts . . . 410.02
long- v. short-term . . . 3101.02
on lump-sum distributions . . . 905.02
on pass-through entity . . . 3101.02
on property held longer than five years . . . 3101.02
on qualified small business stock, exclusion for . . . 3125–3125.08
on real estate investments . . . 3180.01
of sale of partnership interest . . . 2015
of spouse . . . 3315.04

Capital gains—continued
tax rates for . . . 501, 505.09, 805.02, 3101.01, 3101.02, 3115, 3180.01 3201, 3310, 3325.03

Capital improvements to personal residence to offset gains on later sale . . . 2820.04

Capital loss
carryover from prior year of . . . 3310
maximum deduction for . . . 1805.01
to offset capital gains . . . 410.02, 3101.01, 3310
to offset ordinary income . . . 3101.01
on sale of partnership interest . . . 2015
on sale of qualified small business stock . . . 1805.01
of spouse . . . 3315.04
unabsorbed in year of death . . . 1505.01

Capital-building benefits for executives . . . 1605

Capitalization rate for closely held corporation . . . 1940.01

Cash bequests . . . 1105.04

Cash needs of survivor
joint ownership in planning for . . . 310
life insurance to provide for . . . 701
living trust to provide for . . . 1105.01

Cash refund annuity . . . 805

Cash surrender value of life insurance . . . 701.02

Cash value life insurance policy . . . 705.02
loans against . . . 2015.05
proceeds paid to beneficiary excludable from gross estate . . . 955.03

Cash year-end bonuses for executives . . . 1605.01

Casualty losses
AGI floor for deducting . . . 3205.02
estate's handling of . . . 1515

CATS (certificates of accrual on Treasury securities) for IRAs . . . 915.01

Centers for Medicare and Medicaid Services . . . 3515

Certificates of deposit (CDs)
deferring tax using . . . 3145.02
direct gift made by transfer of . . . 415
as money market instruments . . . 3145
as secondary market for money market instruments . . . 3145.01
zero coupon insured . . . 3160.02–.03

Certified Financial Planner Board of Standards . . . 105

Certified Financial Planner (CFP) . . . 105

Certified historic structure, preservation of . . . 535.02

Charitable "bail out" cases . . . 3235

Charitable contributions
of appreciated property . . . 505.08–.09, 3101.02
estate tax deductions for . . . 510–510.02
gratuitous, cash v. goods or services of . . . 505.04, 3415.01
intangible religious benefits in exchange for . . . 3415.01
of life insurance . . . 501.01, 525–525.03, 725
made in executives' names . . . 1605.01
made to maximize income tax deduction . . . 3315.02
maximizing deductions and reducing taxes using . . . 3415–3415.08
of miles driven for work related to Hurricane Katrina . . . 3415.07
overvaluation penalty for . . . 505.05
by payroll . . . 505.04
percentages limitations for . . . 505.02, 505.09
postponing or accelerating deductions between tax years by delaying or doubling up . . . 3305.03–.04

Charitable contributions—continued
of property having capital gain and ordinary income potential . . . 505.09
of property in anticipation of sale . . . 3235
of remainder interest in personal residence . . . 2801
substantiation requirements for . . . 505, 505.04
timing of deduction for . . . 505.06
of $250 or more . . . 3415.01
unreimbursed expenses deductible as . . . 3415.07
of used vehicles . . . 3415.06
written acknowledgment of . . . 3415.01

Charitable gift annuities . . . 520

Charitable giving . . . 501–535.03
checklist of income tax contribution deduction rules for, table of . . . 505.01
deductible portion of *quid pro quo* . . . 505, 3415.02
income tax deduction for . . . 505–505.10
questions arising about . . . 505
techniques for . . . 501.01. *See also* individual techniques
written substantiation of . . . 505, 505.04

Charitable lead trust . . . 501.01, 530

Charitable remainder annuity trust (CRAT) . . . 510.02, 515.01, 535, 3101.02, 3210.09, 5045

Charitable remainder trust . . . 501.01, 515.01
pooled income funds compared with . . . 515.02

Charitable remainder unitrust (CRUT) . . . 510.02, 515.01, 535, 3101.02, 3210.09, 5045

Charities
annuities paid by . . . 520
categories of Treasury list of approved . . . 505
charitable remainder in personal residence or farm granted to . . . 515.03
disclaimer of bequest to favor . . . 1525.01
gifts for conservation purposes to . . . 535.01–535.03
gifts of income to . . . 530
irrevocable remainder interests in pooled income fund of . . . 515.02
power to allocate income or corpus of trust among . . . 605.02
private . . . 505.01
public . . . 505.01
semipublic . . . 505.01
split gifts to spouse and . . . 515.01
written acknowledgment of contributions by . . . 3415.01
written statement for deductible portion of *quid pro quo* contributions to public . . . 505.01, 3415.02

Charity bailout of closely held stock . . . 505.09

Chartered Financial Consultant (ChFC) . . . 105

Child care credit
AGI ceiling and phaseout for . . . 3301.02
base for . . . 3410.01
maximum . . . 3410.01

Child support
alimony payment reductions treated as . . . 2425.02, 2430
delinquent, income tax refund seized to pay . . . 2430
excluded from gross income of recipient and nondeductible by payor . . . 2430
not dischargeable in bankruptcy of obligor . . . 2435.04
retirement benefits to make payments of . . . 2445
state laws impacting . . . 2420
transfer of property in settlement of . . . 2405.07
trusts for . . . 2430.03

Child tax credit . . . 3410.02

Children
as beneficiaries of estate, protecting . . . 1105.08
as beneficiaries of life insurance . . . 730, 735
Code Secs. 2503(b) and 2503(c) trusts for minor . . . 425.04
of couple living together, provisions for . . . 2505.05
deferred income of . . . 410.05
disinheriting . . . 210.08, 1110.17
distribution of trust principal to . . . 660.01
employment of . . . 3405.01
farm or ranch property kept intact and passed down to . . . 2205
gifts to . . . 405.05, 410.01, 425–425.04, 3201, 3305.01
kiddie tax on unearned income of . . . *See* Kiddie tax
less than age 14, taxable unearned income of . . . 315.01, 405.01
life insurance on life of parents purchased by . . . 2410.02
lifetime gifts to . . . 405.01, 405.05
limited partnership interests of FLP transferred to . . . 2010.03, 2010.05
older than 14, income shifting of investment property to . . . 3210
parents supported by adult . . . 3405.01
power of appointment in favor of . . . 1301
of primary beneficiaries receiving parent's share of estate . . . 1105.07
from prior marriage, protecting interests of . . . 1225, 2410.02
QTIP to guarantee interests of . . . 405.02, 2410.02
recapitalizing stock in closely held corporation for interests to give to . . . 2301
retirement benefit payments to, as alternate payees . . . 2445
sale of sole proprietorship to . . . 2110.03
standard deduction for . . . 3205.01, 3210, 3230, 3405
support requirements for dependency exemption of . . . 3405.01
tax returns of . . . 405.05
trusts established to benefit . . . 420, 425, 425.04, 601, 720, 735, 1101, 1225.04, 1415, 3210.07, 3225
U.S. savings bonds as attractive investment for college education of . . . 315.03
working in family business . . . 3230

Civil Marriage Act (Canada) . . . 2505.02

Client needs and objectives . . . 295

***Clifford* trusts** . . . 405.01, 405.05, 605.01, 605.07

Closely held businesses
advantages of joint tenancy for . . . 315.02
comparison of business form choices for . . . 1801–1810
estate holding interest in . . . 1510.04
farm valuation as . . . 2210.01
financial condition of, valuation process examining . . . 1940.01
installment payments of estate taxes for . . . 535.03
interest of, valued at more than 35 percent of adjusted gross estate . . . 310.04, 1925
interests in, as good for lifetime giving . . . 410.01
partnership interests as . . . 2030.01, 2035
private annuity for family members to transfer interests of . . . 810
real estate valuation for . . . 2110.05

Closely held corporation
balance of control in . . . 1915.03
business structure of . . . 1905
capital structure of . . . 1905
charitable "bail out" cases of gifts by . . . 3235
controlling interest in . . . 1940.05
disproportionate distribution exception for stock redemptions in . . . 1915.04

Closely held corporation—continued
dissension among owners of . . . 1910.01
distribution of property by . . . 1915.06
dividend-paying capacity of . . . 1940.01
earning capacity of . . . 1940.01
ESOP in . . . 910
executive benefits for . . . 1901.02
extracting cash in tax-favored way from . . . 1915.02
fair market value for stock in . . . 101
finding appropriate capitalization rate for . . . 1940.01
goodwill of . . . 1940.02
maintaining voting strength upon stock redemption in . . . 1915.02
minority stock interest in . . . 1940.04
number of shareholders in . . . 1925.01
outside board of directors or advisors for . . . 1930
outside market for . . . 1901.02
owner's estate for . . . 1901.02
planning for owner of . . . 1901–1950.02
prepared for redemptions of stock . . . 1915.03
recapitalizing and restructuring, stock types for . . . 1901.02, 1910–1910.02, 1915.02, 1915.03, 1930, 2301
reserve fund for . . . 1901.02
retirement planning for senior management of . . . 1910.01
rules for transfers of interest in . . . 1910
role of life insurance in planning for owner of . . . 701
sale of nonbusiness assets of . . . 1915.03
sale to insider of . . . 1901.02
shareholder in . . . 105
stock basis for . . . 1901.02, 1915
stock redemptions from . . . 1915–1915.05, 1940.02
stock valuation for . . . 101, 1901.01, 1901.02, 1940–1940.07
successor management of . . . 1901.02, 1910.01, 1930
termination of shareholder's interest in . . . 1915.04
transition to new management of . . . 1930

Closely held stock
book value of . . . 1940.01
charity bailout of . . . 505.09
comparable, market price of . . . 1940.01
controlling interest in corporation using . . . 1940.05
factors to consider in valuing . . . 1940.01
installment note to redeem . . . 1915.04
lack of marketability of, discount for . . . 1940.03
in multiple corporations . . . 1915.01
redemption under Code Secs. 302 and 303 of . . . 1915–1915.06, 1925.01
transferred to corporation as redemption . . . 1915.03
valuation different for estate tax and redemption price upon sale of . . . 1915.02
weight of factors in valuing . . . 1940.02

Code Sec. 403(b) annuities
limited deductibility of IRA contributions for participants in . . . 915.01
premature withdrawal penalty for . . . 905.02

Code Sec. 678 trusts . . . 1945.02

Code Sec. 682 (divorce) trust . . . 2425.05

Co-executors, reasons to use . . . 1405.02

Collectibles
capital gains tax rate for . . . 3101.02, 3201
penalties for IRAs investing in . . . 915.01

Commercial annuities . . . 805–805.03. *See also* individual types
private annuities compared with . . . 810

Commercial banks for IRA accounts . . . 915.01

Commodities, commissions for transactions of . . . 3190.01

Commodity futures funds . . . 3155

Common law fraud . . . 3101.04

Community property
document check of items held in . . . 305
estate and gift tax considerations of . . . 325.01
joint property v. . . . 325.01, 2210.03
life insurance issues for . . . 325.03, 715.03
newly acquired property retaining character of . . . 1625.02
personal residence as . . . 2801
premarital agreement to address rights and obligations for . . . 2405.05
premarital agreement to limit rights for . . . 2405
problems for executives with . . . 1625.02
qualified employee benefit plan issues for . . . 325.02
retained after parties move to noncommunity property state . . . 325.01
rules distinguishing between separate and . . . 325.01
separate property held in addition to . . . 325, 325.01
states having laws for, list of . . . 301, 325

Company car or airplane . . . 985.03

Company lodging for executives . . . 1605.01

Company meals for executives . . . 1605.01

Compensation for personal injuries in community property states as separate property . . . 325.01

Compensation for top-paid officers of public corporations, nonperformance-based . . . 1605.01

Complex trusts . . . 605.03

Conservation easement . . . 535.01–.03
exclusion from gross estate of 40 percent of value of land for . . . 535.03
income and estate tax deductions for . . . 535.01
objectives of . . . 535.02

Conservation purposes defined . . . 535.02

Conservatorships . . . 2605.02

Constructively received income of decedent . . . 1505.04

Consumer product testing by employees . . . 985.03

Contractual death benefits . . . 1610.11

Contributions of co-tenants to acquisition of property . . . 305

Controlled corporation, right to vote transferred stock in . . . 1005.02

Controlling shareholder
corporate-owned life insurance on . . . 1950
defined . . . 1950.01
estate of, weighing cost of inclusion in . . . 1950.02

Convenience joint bank accounts . . . 315.01

Convertible term insurance . . . 705.02

Co-ownership of property . . . 301–330, 2505.04

Corporate operation . . . 1720–1720.16

Corporate tax rates . . . 5001.05

Corporations *See also* **C corporation, Closely held corporation,** *and* **S corporations**
accumulated taxable income of . . . 1720.08
adhering to formalities of . . . 1720.01
advantages of . . . 1810
business expense deduction by . . . 1720.10
for closely held business . . . 1801
control of . . . 2305.02
danger of multiple . . . 1720.07
farm assets held by . . . 2210.05, 2210.08, 2215, 2225
fringe benefits of . . . 1715.01
limited liability companies taxed as partnerships or . . . 1715
limits on use of cash basis accounting by . . . 2001
one-person . . . 2105.01

Corporations—continued
property transfer in exchange for stock to . . . 3125.07
red tape of . . . 1810
shifting income and relative ownership interests in . . . 1725.01
state and local taxes imposed on . . . 1720.11
valuation of . . . 1905
withdrawal and expulsion of professional shareholders of . . . 1730

Cosmetic surgery, medical care expenses of . . . 3420.01

Cost of benefits for employees of professional . . . 1720.14

Co-trustees of trusts . . . 660.07, 665.01, 665.02
with no rights or powers for insurance trust . . . 735.01, 735.02

COUGARS (certificates on government receipts) for IRAs . . . 915.01

Couples living together, planning for . . . 2501–2505.09

Coverdell Education Savings Accounts . . . 915.01, 3001, 3005.05
contribution maximum and phaseout rules for . . . 3020.01, 3301.02
coordination with Hope or lifetime learning credit of . . . 3020.03
distributions from . . . 3020.03
excess contributions to, excise tax on . . . 3020.02
excluded from gross income . . . 3015.01

Credit card balances, paying off . . . 3105

Credit for elderly and permanently and totally disabled . . . 3410.04

Credit shelter trust, estate taxes saved using . . . 640

Creditors' claims
effect of sole v. joint ownership on . . . 310
family limited partnerships protected against . . . 2010.01, 2010.07
life insurance sheltered from . . . 701, 705.02
spendthrift provisions of trust to prevent . . . 601, 660.06
state rules about . . . 630

Crime rate around prospective personal residence, investigating . . . 2805.04

***Cristofani* decision** . . . 660.04

Cross purchase agreement
funding sale or liquidation of partnership interest through . . . 2015.04, 2015.05
key factors for . . . 1935
for life insurance of stockholders in closely held corporation . . . 1935
for sale and purchase of shares upon death of professional . . . 1725.04

***Crummey* power for trusts** . . . 405.02, 615, 660.04, 735.02, 1305

Custodial account for child
income shifted to minor using . . . 3210.06
to purchase life insurance on life of parent . . . 2410.02

Custodial parent
dependent deduction for . . . 2430, 3405.02
taxable income for kiddie tax of . . . 2420.02

Custodian
donor as custodian in . . . 425.02
donor's spouse as custodian in . . . 425.02

Custodianships
compared to other vehicles for gifts to minors . . . 425.04
estate tax aspects of accounts for . . . 425.02

Custodianships—continued
gift tax aspects of accounts for . . . 425.02
income tax aspects of accounts for . . . 425.02
minor taxed on income of . . . 325.04
restrictions on gifts causing formation of . . . 425
trusts v. . . . 420

D

***D.D. Palmer* decision** . . . 505.09
Data source list of estate owner . . . 1125
Day-care facility, home used as . . . 2830
De minimis fringe benefits . . . 985.04
Death benefits
for employees . . . 950
for executives . . . 1605.01
Death payment from Social Security Administration, lump-sum . . . 3520.01
Death Tax Elimination Act of 2000 . . . 1005, 1715
Death taxes
financial plan's goal to minimize . . . 2205, 2210
state . . . 705.02, 1215.08
Debt
acquisition . . . 2815, 2815.02, 2815.05, 2815.08, 2815.09, 3420.03
credit card, transferring . . . 3105
direct gift made by forgiveness of . . . 415
grandfathered . . . 2815.05
home equity . . . 2815, 2815.03–.04, 2815.08, 2815.09
owed by corporation or partnership to transferor or family members . . . 2305.06
for qualified residence interest, total deductible . . . 2815
Debt consolidation . . . 3195–3195.02
Debts of decedent
form for recording . . . 1125
provisions in will for . . . 1110.06
Declaration of trust, IRS sample . . . 2315.03
Deductions *See also* **Itemized deductions** *and* **individual deductions**
accelerated to current tax year . . . 3305.04
for charitable contributions, table of maximum . . . 505.01
for contributing used vehicles to a charitable organization . . . 3415.06
on income or estate tax return, items considered for . . . 1515–1515.12
limited for AMT . . . 3301.03
maximizing . . . 3401–3450.02
for miles driven on behalf of a charity for work related to Hurricane Katrina . . . 3415.07
postponed until following tax year . . . 3301.03, 3305.03
for providing housing for Hurricane Katrina evacuees . . . 3415.07
shifted between years . . . 3301.03, 3305.03–.04
split within family . . . 515.04
Defective special use valuation elections, perfecting . . . 2210.01
Defense of Marriage Act . . . 2505.02
Deferred annuities . . . 805.01
Deferred compensation
for employees . . . 1605.01
for executives . . . 1610.08
postponing income and reducing AGI using . . . 3305.01, 3325.01
Defined benefit plans
advantages of . . . 930
automatic survivor benefits of . . . 905.01
benefits determined at outset of participation in . . . 905.01
defined contribution plans v. . . . 905.01
dollar limitations on benefits and contributions under . . . 5005
funding . . . 905.01
as supplement to profit-sharing plan . . . 920.01
target plans compared to . . . 930.02
Defined contribution (money purchase) plans
automatic survivor benefits of some . . . 905.01
defined benefit plan features v. . . . 905.01
dollar limitations on benefits and contributions under . . . 5005
employer contributions to . . . 905.01
funding . . . 905.01
overcoming limits on . . . 1605.02
QDRO dividing account of . . . 905.02
Delayed completion of sales and contracts to postpone income between years . . . 3305.01
Delayed distribution to beneficiaries of trust . . . 660.11
Dependency exemption. *See also* **Custodial parent**
AGI phaseout of . . . 3301.02, 3405
for child of unmarried couple . . . 2505.09
for disabled person . . . 2430.02
eliminated so individual can use own personal exemption and lower tax rate . . . 3325.09
impact on standard deduction of . . . 3405.03
multiple support arrangements to alternate claims for . . . 3405.06
for parent or other relative . . . 3405.02
reverse planning for, higher income individuals using . . . 3405.04
support requirements for . . . 3405.01–.02
waiver of . . . 3405.01
Dependent care assistance
employer-provided . . . 975, 980
excluded from employee's gross income . . . 1605.01
Dependents of retired or disabled workers benefits from Social Security Administration . . . 3520.01
Depreciation
accelerated . . . 3180.01
alternative . . . 3301.03
limitations of, escaping . . . 3180.03
recapture of . . . 2820.02, 3101.01, 3115, 3201
for rental or business use of principal residence . . . 2820.02
straight-line . . . 3180.01
Depressed assets in trust . . . 1510.02
Designated beneficiary for retirement plan distributions . . . 905.02
Development plan for successor in closely held corporation . . . 1930
***Dickman, E.C.* decision on reading of gift tax** . . . 415
***Diedrich, V.P.* decision for net gift technique** . . . 410.07
***DiMarco, Estate of A.* decision on gift-on-death theory** . . . 950
Direct skips to skip persons . . . 2705.02
avoiding . . . 2705.03
GST tax applied to lifetime and testamentary . . . 2705.06
Directors and offiers liability insurance . . . 1715.03
Disability buy-sell agreements . . . 1935

Disability income insurance
proceeds of, as not taxable . . . 2105.03
for professionals . . . 1715.02
for sole proprietors . . . 2105.03
for stockholders in closely held corporation . . . 1935

Disabled people
competency to appoint surrogates of . . . 2605.01
dependency exemption for . . . 2430.02
homeownership period for exclusion of gain on sale by . . . 2820.06
planning for . . . 2601–2605.02
tax credit for . . . 3410.04
tools for protecting interests of . . . 2605–2605.01
as trust beneficiaries . . . 601, 660.05

Disaster, Presidentially declared . . . 2801, 3101.01

Disclaimer
of bequest or devise as gift . . . 415
mechanics of qualified . . . 1525.01
as post-mortem planning tool . . . 905.02, 1235, 1525.01
provided for in will . . . 1110.19

Disclosure
encouraging . . . 210
financial . . . 212.02
personal . . . 210.03

Discount brokers . . . 3185–3185.01

Discount trust . . . 3150.06

Disguised sales to partnership . . . 2005.02

Disinheriting children . . . 210.08

Disinheriting trust beneficiaries . . . 660.10

Distributable net income (DNI) of trust . . . 605.03

Distributions
from ESOPS . . . 910
from IRAs . . . 3305.02
in kind from estate . . . 1510.01
from qualified personal residence trust . . . 2315.03
from qualified plans . . . 905.02, 915.01, 3305.02, 3325.09
rollover-eligible . . . 905.02
from Roth IRAs . . . 915.04, 1610.01
from SEP plans . . . 905.02
transfer tax treatment of accumulated . . . 2305.05

Dividend distributions under Code Sec. 404(k), no early withdrawal penalty for . . . 905.02

Dividend income, year-end shift of property to donee in lower tax bracket for reporting . . . 3315.06

Dividends forgone as gift, preferred . . . 415

Dividends of closely held corporation, stock
distributions . . . 1915.04
immediately redeemable, taxation of . . . 1915.03
partial liquidation not treated as . . . 1915.05
redemption causing meaningful reduction of shareholder's interest not treated as . . . 1915.04
stock redemptions by estate or beneficiaries treated as . . . 1915
substituting salaries and bonuses for . . . 1940.01
taken to accelerate income to current tax year . . . 3305.02

Dividends of foreign stock . . . 3185.06

Dividends of life insurance . . . 701.01

Dividends of S corporations . . . 1945

Dividends of shorted stock . . . 3185.02

Divorce
conversion of joint tenancy between spouses to tenancy in common following . . . 315.02
of designated beneficiary of education IRA . . . 3020.07

Divorce—continued
ending durable power of attorney in some states . . . 2605.01, 2905.02
invalid, effects on subsequent marriage of . . . 2410.01
legal expenses to obtain . . . 2440
residence transferred incident to, homeownership period for . . . 2820.07
separate tax returns filed for spouses having imminent . . . 2420.03

Divorce instrument, alimony under . . . 2425–2425.01

Divorce settlement
income tax aspects of . . . 2435.01
state law impacting . . . 2420
transfer of beneficiary's interest in education IRA under . . . 3020.07

Divorce trusts (Code Sec. 682 trust) . . . 2425.05

Doctrine of substituted judgment . . . 2610.02

Document check by estate planner as first step in evaluating property ownership . . . 305

Documentation kept by financial planner . . . 110

Dollar cost averaging mutual fund purchases . . . 3105

Domestic Partnership Act (New Jersey) . . . 2505.02

Donations
Intellectual property . . . 505.09
vehicles, boats, and airplanes . . . 505.09

Double-category averaging method for determining basis in mutual fund . . . 3140.06

Double indemnity of life insurance . . . 701.01

Double taxation
adjustment to transfer of applicable retained interest to prevent . . . 2305.07
avoided by S corporation . . . 1905
of C corporation income . . . 1805.01

Durable power of attorney
gifts on behalf of principal using . . . 2610.03
for health care . . . 2605.01, 2901, 2905.02
in planning for elderly and disabled people . . . 2605, 2605.01
springing v 2605, 2605.01, 2905.02
for representative making deathbed gifts . . . 430.01
revoking . . . 2905.02
termination of . . . 2605.01, 2905.02
for unmarried partner . . . 2505.07

E

***E. Morris Trusts* decision for multiple trusts . . .** 605.05

Early withdrawal penalty
for CDs . . . 3145.02
for IRAs . . . 915.01, 915.04
for profit-sharing plans . . . 920.01
for qualified plans . . . 905.02, 2445
for SEP plans . . . 915.02

Earned income credit . . . 3410.03

Earnings
before- and after-tax . . . 3120.01
of spouses in community property states . . . 325.01

Easement in gross defined . . . 535.01

Easements donated to government . . . 3415.05

Economatic life insurance policy . . . 705.02

Economic Growth and Tax Relief Reconciliation Act of 2001 (EGTRRA) . . . 101, 110, 210.03, 310.03

Economic outlook in valuing closely held stock . . . 1940.01

Education costs
business deduction for taxpayer of . . . 3001
company-paid . . . 1605.01

Education IRAs. *See* **Coverdell Education Savings Accounts**
AGI ceiling and phaseout for . . . 3301.02
balance distributed when beneficiary reaches age 30 from . . . 3020.03, 3020.06
community property laws not applicable to . . . 3020.05
distributions to pay qualified higher education expenses from . . . 3020.03
estate tax consequences of . . . 3020.07
excise tax on excess contributions to . . . 3020.02
$500 maximum annual contribution to . . . 3020.01–.02
gift tax consequences of . . . 3020.07
not used as collateral for loans . . . 3020.04
rollover to member of family of balance in . . . 3020.06–.07
terminated upon death of beneficiary . . . 3020.07
waiving exclusion from gross income of distributions from . . . 3020.03

Educational assistance loans . . . 3001, 3015–3015.02, 3301.02

EGTRRA . . . 101, 110, 210.03, 310.03

Elderly and disabled people
competency to assign surrogates of . . . 2605.01
planning for . . . 2601–2605.02
tax credit for . . . 3410.04

Elected farm income defined . . . 2220

Electing small business trust
holding stock in S corporation . . . 1945.02
nonresident alien as beneficiary of . . . 1945.02
tax consequences of . . . 605.06

Elective deferrals from salary
$6,500 cap for SIMPLE plans using . . . 915.03, 925.02
$10,500 aggregate cap for . . . 925.01, 925.02
$10,500 SARSEP cap for . . . 915.02

Elective surgery, timing . . . 3420.01

Employee awards distinguished from disguised compensation . . . 960

Employee benefit program . . . 1715.12

Employee benefits . . . 901–985.07
employee expectation of receiving . . . 901
tax-favored treatment to employer and employee of . . . 901

Employee discounts as fringe benefit . . . 985.02

Employee Retirement Income Security Act of 1974 (ERISA)
in *Boggs v. Boggs* . . . 325.02
ESOP rules under . . . 910

Employee stock ownership plans (ESOPs) . . . 1605.01, 1610.02
advantages of . . . 910
deducting dividends on securities held by . . . 1920.03
disadvantages of . . . 910
distribution period of, lengthening . . . 5005
employee ownership of closely held corporation through . . . 1930
employer contributions as deductible for . . . 1920
in estate planning for small business owners . . . 1920–1920.03
loans to . . . 1920.02
to purchase shareholder's stock from estate . . . 1920
tax-free rollover on sale of qualified securities to . . . 1920.01
vesting in . . . 910

Employees of partnership, withholding paid for . . . 2001

Employees of professionals, cost of benefits for . . . 1720.14

Employer, deductions for
of contributions to qualified plans . . . 905
of contributions to thrift plans . . . 935
of employee awards . . . 960
of health plan payments . . . 965
of imputed compensation paid through employee loans . . . 970.01
of insurance premiums paid for employees . . . 1715.12

Employer securities for executive compensation . . . 1610.02

Employment tax 3445. *See also* Social security tax

Empowerment zone, financing property located in . . . 3110

Entity arrangement for liquidation of partnership interest . . . 2015.04

Equitable distribution laws . . . 2420

Equity interests
minimum value of junior . . . 2305.06
senior and subordinate . . . 2305.04

Equity-indexed annuity . . . 805

Estate. *See also* **Probate estate**
administration costs of . . . 1005, 1005.03, 1110.07–.08, 1510.05–1515.12
avoiding inclusion of trust assets in . . . 1225.05
as beneficiary of life insurance policy of partner . . . 2020.02–.03
borrowing from beneficiary or trust . . . 1510.03
casualty losses during administration of . . . 1005
of child . . . 3210.05
community property in . . . 325.01
compressed income tax rates for . . . 405.01, 1515.02, 5001.01
conserving, lifetime gifts for . . . 401
deducting claims against transferor's estate for property addressed in premarital agreement . . . 2405.09–.10
deducting debts and obligations of . . . 1005, 1105.04
disposing of bulk (residue) of . . . 1105.07
distributions from, effect on beneficiaries' tax brackets of . . . 1515.07
distributions from executor as making . . . 1405
executor's and attorney's fees related to size of . . . 625
full value of jointly held property included in . . . 310.01
hidden costs of . . . 101
income tax rates for . . . 1515
interest paid or incurred by . . . 1515.06
irrevocable trust to keep premarital agreement property out of spouse's . . . 2405.12
life insurance proceeds kept out of . . . 1610.09, 1725.03
life insurance to provide liquidity for . . . 701, 715, 730
liquidity for, planning . . . 1510–1510.05, 1615, 1901.02, 1915.02
litigating dispute concerning valuation issues for . . . 1940
named beneficiaries for life insurance . . . 730
net worth of . . . 1940
as partner to continue deceased partner's interest . . . 2015, 2020.04
partnership interest included in . . . 2015.05
partnership profits received post-mortem by . . . 2015.06
qualifying for special use valuation . . . 535.03
provisions in . . . 1125

Estate—continued
residuary, lapsed legacies becoming part of . . . 1110.12
retention of records belonging to clients or patients by professional's . . . 1715.01
second, building . . . 1901.02
selling expenses of . . . 1515.09
shrinkage problem for legacies of . . . 1105.04
special assets of, instructions outside of will for . . . 1125
state limitations on contributions to charity from . . . 525
tax year of . . . 1515.11, 2025
transfer of irrevocable insurance trust to . . . 735.01
trust lending money to . . . 1110.18

Estate attorney, help for executor from . . . 1405

Estate income tax return, deducting administration expenses and casualty losses on . . . 1515

Estate owner, sample blank forms to record assets and liabilities of . . . 1125

Estate plan
changing testator's . . . 1525–1525.03
distorted . . . 750.01
for executive . . . 1605.01, 1620–1620.09
insurance as just one component of . . . 740
taxes affecting . . . 101, 105

Estate planner *See* Financial and estate planner

Estate planning. *See also* **individual types**
for closely held corporation owner . . . 1901–1950.02
for couples living together . . . 2501–2505.09
defined . . . 101
for elderly and disabled people . . . 2601–2610.03
for executive . . . 1601–1625.03
for farmer and rancher . . . 2201–2225
for generation-skipping transfers . . . 2701–2701.11
for higher education incentives . . . 3001–3020.07
for marriage, divorce, or separation . . . 2401–2445
for medical care by proxy . . . 2901–2905.03
misconceptions about . . . 210.06
for partner . . . 2001–2040.03
for personal residence . . . 2801–2835.02
for professional . . . 1701–1730
for sole proprietor . . . 2101–2110.07
usefulness of private annuities for . . . 810

Estate tax benefit, preserving . . . 660.03

Estate tax consequences
of charitable contributions . . . 510, 1525.02–.03
of charitable lead trusts . . . 530
of charitable remainder trusts . . . 515.01
of Code Sec. 303 stock redemption . . . 1925.01
of Code Sec. 2503(c) trust . . . 425.04
of community v. separate property . . . 325.01
of co-ownership of U.S. savings bonds . . . 315.03
of custodianships for minors . . . 425.02
of death benefits . . . 950
of death of unmarried partner . . . 2505.02
of disclaimer of bequests . . . 415, 1525.01
of dissolution of partnership . . . 2020.05
of divorce settlement . . . 2435.02
of education IRA contributions . . . 3020.07
of executor's administrative fees . . . 1405.03
of family limited partnerships . . . 2010.01, 2010.04
of family partnerships . . . 2001.02
of gifts or corporate stock for incorporated farm property . . . 2210.08
of income in respect of decedent partner . . . 2025
of irrevocable insurance trust . . . 735.01
of irrevocable living trust . . . 625
of joint tenancies and tenancies by entirety . . . 315.02
of life insurance . . . 705.02, 715–715.03, 735, 1601
of life insurance proceeds payable to charity . . . 525.02
of lifetime gifts . . . 401, 405.04, 410.01, 410.04

Estate tax consequences—continued
of pourover trust . . . 645
of power of appointment . . . 1305
of private annuity . . . 810
of property contributed for conservation purposes . . . 535.01
of property transferred to minors older than 14 . . . 3210
of property transferred under terms of premarital agreement . . . 2405.08, 2410.04
of purchase of decedent's partnership interest by surviving partners . . . 2020.01
of QDOT . . . 1230.03
of qualified plan and IRA benefits . . . 955.02
of qualified state tuition savings programs . . . 3010.04
of redeeming closely held stock . . . 1915.02
of revocable living trust . . . 630, 2605.01
of sale of partnership interest . . . 2015
of securities owned jointly . . . 315.05
of sole proprietor's business interest bequeathed to family member . . . 2110.02
of special use valuation of farm or ranch property . . . 2210.01–.02
of sprinkling trust . . . 660.01
of testamentary trust . . . 640
of transfers of property at death . . . 1001–1005.02
of transfers to minors age 14 or older . . . 3210–3210.09
of trusts . . . 601, 610–610.02, 660.04

Estate tax, federal
allocation by testator for estate to pay . . . 1105.14
binding valuation in buy-sell agreements for . . . 1935
calculating . . . 1005
credits offsetting . . . 1001–1005.01
deadline for paying . . . 1925
deduction for administration expenses affecting . . . 1515.05
deduction for charitable contributions from . . . 510–510.02
deduction for medical expenses from . . . 1505.03
eliminating second . . . 730, 735
inclusion of property to be gifted in gross estate resulting in . . . 430.01
insurance proceeds for . . . 701
irrevocable insurance trust to avoid . . . 735.01
on qualified terminable interest property . . . 405.02
reasonable cause extension for paying . . . 1925.02
tax rates for . . . 1001–1005
regulations on life insurance for . . . 525.01
trust distributions exempt from . . . 1230.03

Estate tax return
administration expenses on . . . 1515.06
current use valuation elected on first . . . 2110.05
deducting administration expenses and casualty losses on . . . 1515
late-filed . . . 1520.02
special use valuation for farm property elected on . . . 2210.01
v. joint income tax return with surviving spouse . . . 1505.01

Estate tax freeze . . . 2301

Estate tax, state . . . 325.01

Estate tax worksheet for estimating potential estate taxes . . . 5010.02

Estate taxes
deferred payment for 14 years of . . . 1915.02, 1925.01
effect of termination of joint tenancies on . . . 310.04
estimating potential . . . 5010.02
extension of time to pay . . . 1515.06, 2035
on farm or ranch passed down to family members . . . 2205
installment payments of . . . 535.03, 1925–1925.02, 2035, 2110.07

Estate taxes—continued
interest payable on . . . 1515.06, 2035
on life insurance . . . 705.02, 715–715.03, 1601
for owner of closely held corporation, planning for . . . 1901.02
record keeping for bank accounts for . . . 315.01
valuation of partnership interests for . . . 2030–2030.01

Estate trust to benefit surviving spouse . . . 1105.10, 1225.03

Estimated tax payments
by child . . . 3205.02
for deferred income of previous year . . . 3301
estate's handling of . . . 1515, 1515.12
penalty for underpayment of . . . 1515.12, 3320
required from trusts . . . 605.01
year-end planning for . . . 3320

***Evanson, C.*, decision on taxation of lifetime gifts . . .** 1005

Excess benefit plan for executives . . . 1605.02–.03

Exclusion amount from estate tax . . . 105
rule for spouses involving . . . 301, 315.02

Executive
benefits for . . . 1605.01, 1901.02. *See also* individual benefits
effects of relocations of . . . 1625–1625.03
life insurance for . . . 701, 705.02
loss of key, effect on company value of . . . 1940.01, 1940.06
planning for . . . 1601–1625.03
total financial counseling for . . . 1605.01, 1620–1620.09
typical, estate balance sheet for . . . 1601

Executive compensation . . . 1605–1605.03. *See also* individual components

Executor
advancing funds to . . . 630
carrying on sole proprietorship of decedent . . . 2110.01
conflict of interest between beneficiary and . . . 1405
fees for . . . 1005, 1005.03, 1405.03, 1505.02
job of . . . 1105.16
letters testamentary giving power to . . . 1405
liability of . . . 1515.12, 1940
local laws for . . . 665
multiple . . . 1405.02
named beneficiary of life insurance . . . 730
powers of . . . 1105.16, 1110.18, 1225.01
QDOT election made by . . . 1230
responsibilities of . . . 1405
risk of liability of . . . 1105.16
selecting . . . 1101, 1105.11, 1405–1405.03
surviving spouse as . . . 1225.01, 1505.02
will provision for appointing . . . 1110.15

Expense accounts for executives . . . 1605.01

Expenses paid as indirect gift . . . 415

F

Family income-splitting techniques . . . 3201–3240. *See also* individual techniques
for business income . . . 3230
family partnership using . . . 2005
lifetime planning to reduce estate tax using . . . 1001
S corporation using . . . 1945, 1945.01
used for lifetime gifts . . . 410.01, 420

Family limited partnerships (FLPs) . . . 2010–2010.07
advantages of . . . 2010.01
Code Sec. 2701 issue with . . . 2010.05

Family limited partnerships (FLPs)—continued
Code Sec. 2703 and sham transaction doctrine for . . . 2010.05, 2310
Code Sec. 2704 applied to . . . 2010.05
disadvantages of . . . 2010.02
lifetime gifts of, to pass through business income to donees . . . 410.01
high fees for . . . 2010.02
investment . . . 2010.06
IRS campaign against . . . 2010, 2010.05
lifetime transfers of assets for . . . 2010.02
shield from creditors' claims of . . . 2010.01, 2010.07
for spouses . . . 2010.03
"swing vote" of combined children's interests in . . . 2010.05
valuation discounts for . . . 2010.05, 2310
valuation of interests transferred in . . . 2320

Family members, income shifting to . . . 3215, 3305.01, 3315.01, 3325.06

Family partnership
in estate planning of farmer . . . 2205, 2210.09
sole proprietor as forming . . . 2110.03
to split business income of sole proprietorship with family members . . . 3230

Family partnership interest created as gift . . . 415

Family-owned businesses. *See* Closely held businesses

Fannie Mae (Federal National Mortgage Association) . . . 3150–3150.03
advantages of . . . 3150.02
characteristics of . . . 3150
compared with other mortgage-backed securities . . . 3150–3150.01
disadvantages of . . . 3150.03
minimum purchase requirement for . . . 3150

Farm property
charitable remainder in . . . 515.03
form of operation for . . . 2210.05
heirs who leave, providing for . . . 2225
incorporation of . . . 2210.08, 2215
installment payments of estate taxes for . . . 535.03
kept intact to pass on to children . . . 2205, 2210.09, 2225
leased to nonfamily member . . . 2210.01
liquidity of stock in . . . 2215
meals and lodging in operation of . . . 2210.08
minimizing death taxes for . . . 2210–2210.09
partial interests in, gifts of . . . 535
planning for . . . 2201–2225
preservation of open space on . . . 535.02
profits of, participation of heirs in . . . 2225
recapture of estate tax benefits from special use valuation of . . . 2210.01
renting of . . . 2210.01
valuation of . . . 1105.05, 2210.01–.02, 2210.08, 2801

Farmers
income averaging for . . . 2220
IRAs and qualified plans for . . . 2215

FDIC insurance . . . 3145.01, 3160.03

Federal financial aid programs . . . 3001

Federal income tax rate
for capital gains . . . 501, 505.09, 805.02, 3101.01, 3101.02, 3115, 3180.01, 3201, 3310, 3325.03
marginal . . . 105
for trusts . . . 405.01, 420, 425.01, 601, 605.01–.02, 625, 735.01, 3210.07–.08

Federal Insurance Contributions Act (FICA) tax . . . 3325.06, 5001.07

Federal Reserve Bank, T-bills, notes, and bonds purchased from . . . 3135, 3135.01

Federal Trade Commission (FTC), right-to-use plan rules of . . . 330

Federal Unemployment Tax Act (FUTA) tax rate . . . 5001.07

Fiduciaries . . . 1401–1415. *See also* Executor *and* Trustees
- alternate or successor . . . 1410
- appointment of, as will provision . . . 1110.15
- contingent . . . 2505.03
- corporate v. individual . . . 1405.01
- grantors or settlors as . . . 610.02
- of qualified retirement plans, responsibility of . . . 905.01
- selecting . . . 1405–1405.03

Financed insurance . . . 745

Financial aid programs, federal . . . 3001

Financial and estate planner
- breadth of knowledge and experience for . . . 105
- communication of client and . . . 205
- considerations in developing plan of . . . 225
- determination of insurance needs of client by . . . 740
- helping client plan will . . . 1101
- human relations skills of . . . 105
- ways sought to make professional client a businessperson by . . . 1725
- ways to save more money explained to client by . . . 3105

Financial and Estate Planning Questionnaire, sample blank . . . 215, 220

Financial counseling for executives . . . 1605.01, 1620–1620.09

Financial plan
- benefits of . . . 3105
- created for client to save more money . . . 3105
- for executives . . . 1605.01, 1620–1620.09. *See also* Executive
- prerequisites for sound . . . 205

Financial planner. *See* Financial and estate planner

Financial planning
- areas included in . . . 210.01
- defined . . . 101
- strategies and vehicles for . . . 3101–3195.02

First-time homebuyer expenses, no early withdrawal penalty for IRA distributions to pay . . . 905.02

Fixed annuity . . . 805

Fixed income mutual funds . . . 3140.03

Flexible loan insurance program (FLIP) . . . 2810.03

Flexible spending accounts
- for employee benefits . . . 975, 3420.03
- reducing AGI by funding . . . 3325.01

Foreign death taxes, credit against estate tax of paid2 . . . 1005.01, 1220.03

Foreign earned income exclusion . . . 1625.03

Foreign laws applied to executives residing abroad . . . 1625.03

Foreign property
- kept to minimum for executive residing in foreign country . . . 1625.03
- used for marital bequest . . . 1220.03

Foreign securities, bank deposits of ADRs representing . . . 3185.06

Foreign trust . . . 625, 655
- trust throwback rules applicable to . . . 601

Form SSA-7004, "Request for Social Security Statement" to check status of account . . . 3525.03

Forms for estate owner, sample blank . . . 1125

Foster child, earned income credit for . . . 3410.03

401(k) plans
- advantages to employers and employees of . . . 925.01
- AGI reduced using . . . 3325.01
- as employee benefit . . . 925–925.02
- employer matching contributions to . . . 925.01, 925.02, 3105
- for executives . . . 1605.01
- salary reduction arrangement for . . . 925.01, 925.02
- SIMPLE . . . 925.02
- taking full advantage of matching contributions and income tax savings of . . . 3105
- top-heavy rules for . . . 925.01–.02

403b plans
- AGI reduced using . . . 3325.01
- annuity contributions as tax sheltered in . . . 805.03
- loans on annuities in . . . 805.02

Fractional bequests . . . 1105.04, 1105.07, 1225.01

Fractional interest rule for spouses' jointly owned property . . . 305, 310.01

Fractional residuary marital deduction trust . . . 1225

Fraud by executor . . . 1405

Freddie Mac (Federal Home Loan Mortgage Corporation) . . . 3150–3150.03, 3150.05

Freddie Mac mutual fund . . . 3150.05

Free Application for Federal Student Aid (FAFSA) . . . 3001

Freeze rules on intra-family transfers . . . 2301–2320

Fringe benefits. *See also* individual benefits
- Code Sec. 132 . . . 985–985.07
- reducing AGI using tax-favored . . . 3325.01

Full-service brokers . . . 3185–3185.01

Funeral arrangements, avoiding stipulations in will about . . . 1105.02, 1110.04

Funeral expenses
- deducted from gross estate . . . 1005
- provisions in will for . . . 1110.06

Future interests in tangible personal property . . . 405.02, 410.01, 515.04

Future tax laws . . . 110

Futures contracts . . . 3155

G

***G.A. Rauenhorst* decision . . .** 505.09

***Gallenstein* decision regarding joint tenancies . . .** 315.02

Gay couples, laws affecting . . . 2505.02. *See also* Living together

General partner
- self-employment tax on guaranteed payments and share of ordinary income of . . . 1805.04

General power of appointment
- for property of decedent . . . 1005.02
- for trusts . . . 610

***General Utilities* doctrine, repeal of . . .** 2001

Generation-skipping transfer tax . . . 640, 1520
- annual gift tax exclusion as applying for . . . 2705.07, 3010.04
- calculating . . . 2705.02
- disclosing tax savings for . . . 2705.11

Generation-skipping transfer tax—continued
as flat-rate tax . . . 2705.02
exclusions for educational and medical expenses from . . . 2705.07
gross-up of taxable gifts for . . . 2705.04
inclusion ratio for exempt and nonexempt property in . . . 2705.06
levying . . . 2705.02
$1,060,000 lifetime exemption from . . . 2705, 2705.05
use of full exemption from . . . 2705.10

Generation-skipping transfers . . . 601.02, 2701–2705.11

Generation-skipping trusts . . . 601.02

Gift. *See also* Charitable giving *and* Lifetime gifts
appreciation of . . . 310.01, 310.02, 430.01
of artwork . . . 515.04
of cash v. income property . . . 410
of charitable remainder . . . 515
by check . . . 405.06
child support payments after age of majority considered . . . 2430
to class in will provision . . . 1110.14
Code Sec. 2503(b) trust property treated as . . . 425.04
of corporate stock in farm property . . . 2210.08
deathbed . . . 430.01–.02
direct . . . 1110.14
donative intent for making . . . 2610.02
donor's death within three years of making . . . 430–430.02
durable power of attorney authorizing . . . 2610.03
to family member in lower tax bracket . . . 740, 3205.01, 3325.02
of future interest through trust . . . 410.01, 420, 625
of income only, qualification as gift of present interest of . . . 425.04
of income to charity using charitable lead trust . . . 530
incomplete . . . 405.06, 2315
increased reliance on lifetime . . . 1001
joint property acquired by . . . 310.01
joint, to child and child's spouse . . . 210.03

Gift. See also **Charitable giving *and* Lifetime gifts—**
of life estate with general power of appointment . . . 405.02
of life insurance . . . 430.01, 501.01, 525–525.03, 715, 715.02, 725, 1610.09
lifetime incentive stock option . . . 1610.05
lifetime interspousal . . . 1215.06
to minimize estate tax liabilities . . . 1615
to minors . . . 420, 425–425.04
of money as legacy . . . 1105.04
net . . . 410.07
nonaction causing . . . 415
of nonbusiness property to increase value of business interest as percentage of adjusted gross estate . . . 430
by note . . . 405.06
outright, to child . . . 3210.01
of partnership interest . . . 2005
of personal residence . . . 2801
possibility of reverter for . . . 405.06
promise of . . . 405.06
of property . . . 410–410.07
property acquired during marriage by . . . 325.01
of property designed to produce future income or profit . . . 405.05, 3205.01
of remainder interest and retention of life estate in property . . . 405.06
of remainder interest by settlor for trust of elderly or disabled person . . . 2605.01
of remainder interest in real estate, farm, or personal residence . . . 501.01
of S corporation stock . . . 1945, 1945.01

Gift—continued
secrecy of . . . 401
to spouse . . . 405.02, 410.01, 410.03
of stock . . . 505.06, 3315.05
tax law changes affecting . . . 110, 1005
tenancy in common for noncontributor as creating . . . 320
of term interest to spouse . . . 405.02
title transferred in making complete . . . 405.06
in trust . . . 405.06, 420
to trust as well as uniform gift to minor custodianship . . . 605.05
to trust, transfer of taxable . . . 2705.07
of used clothing, furniture, and noncash donations to charity . . . 3415.03

Gift tax
computing . . . 405.02
on creation of joint tenancy . . . 310.02
estate tax calculation including payable . . . 1005
exclusions from . . . 310.02, 405.01, 405.02
favorable tax consequences of paying . . . 310.02
on gifts made within three years of death . . . 101, 715.02
"gross-up" rule for . . . 430.01–.02, 1005
on life insurance proceeds . . . 720–720.03, 725, 735.02
on pre-1977 gifts . . . 1005–1005.01
regulations on life insurance for . . . 525.01
on trusts . . . 530, 615
unified rate schedule for . . . 405.02

Gift tax consequences
of annuity . . . 810.03
of bargain sale . . . 410.06
of charitable lead trusts . . . 530
of charitable remainder trusts . . . 515.01
of community v. separate property . . . 325.01
of co-ownership of U.S. savings bonds . . . 315.03
of custodianships for minors . . . 425.02
of divorce on joint tenancy . . . 315.02
of divorce settlement . . . 2435.03
of education IRA contributions . . . 3020.07
of family limited partnerships . . . 2010.01, 2010.04
of family partnerships . . . 2001.02
of gift of life insurance policy . . . 410.01, 715.02, 725
of irrevocable living trust . . . 625
of joint bank account . . . 315.01
of lifetime gift of property . . . 410.01, 410.04
of living together . . . 2415.05
of net gift . . . 410.07
of payments to child after age of majority . . . 2430
of power of appointment . . . 1305
of property transferred to minors older than 14 . . . 3210
of property transfers under terms of premarital agreement . . . 2405.07, 2410.04
of qualified plan annuity rights and beneficiaries . . . 955.01
of qualified state tuition savings programs . . . 3010.04
of revocable trust . . . 2605.01
of securities owned jointly . . . 315.05
of split gifts . . . 405.03
of support obligation addressed in premarital agreement . . . 2405.07
of transfers in trust . . . 2315–2315.03
of transfers of income-producing property . . . 3215
of transfers to minors age 14 or older . . . 3210–3210.09
of trusts . . . 601, 660.04

Gift tax educational exclusion . . . 410.01, 3001

Gift tax exclusion of $10,000 annually per recipient . . . 310.02, 425
applicable only for gifts of present interest . . . 615
applicable to contributions to education IRAs . . . 3020.07

Gift tax exclusion of $10,000 annually per recipient—continued
available when corpus of trust is not yet distributed . . . 425.04
Code Sec. 2503(b) establishing exception of future interests for . . . 405.02
doubled using split gifts . . . 405.02, 720.01
for each spouse . . . 325.01
for gift of present interest . . . 405.02, 720, 725
for gift to unmarried partner . . . 2505.04
indexed to Consumer Price Index . . . 405.02
life income interest qualifying for . . . 405.02
making full use of . . . 1615, 3315.01
not available for future interests in annuity of life insurance . . . 520, 720
power of withdrawal from trusts limited to . . . 660.04
for property exceeding value of support obligations . . . 2405.07
restricting gifts to amount of . . . 2610.03
unified credit used with . . . 405.03, 410.04
U.S. savings bond investments using . . . 3210.05

Gift tax liability, completed gifts creating . . . 310.04

Gift tax return, donor filing of . . . 405.02, 405.03, 3235

Gift tax, state, donee's assumption of . . . 410.07

Gift-leaseback of business property . . . 3225

Gift-splitting
in computing gift tax of lifetime gifts . . . 2705.05
to double annual gift tax exclusion . . . 405.02, 425.04, 660.04, 3010.04, 3315.01
between spouse and charities . . . 510.02, 515.01
transfer made in part by surviving spouse under . . . 1005
for U.S. savings bond investments . . . 3210.05

Ginnie Mae mutual fund . . . 3150.05

Ginnie Maes (Government National Mortgage Association) . . . 3150–3150.06
advantages of . . . 3150.01
compared to Fannie Maes and Freddie Macs . . . 3150.01
disadvantages of . . . 3150.03
hedging . . . 3150.04
liquidity of . . . 3150.02
mutual funds of . . . 3150.05

Government obligations, tax-exempt . . . 3110–3110.03

Government plan for retirement
limited deductibility of IRA contributions for participants in . . . 915.01

Governments prohibited from using 401(k) plans, state and local . . . 925.01

***Graegin, Estate of C.* decision for administration expense deduction . . .** 1515.06

Grandchildren
as remainder people for gift-leaseback of business property . . . 3225
as skip persons . . . 2705.02
trusts established to benefit . . . 601, 601.02

Grandparents
trust established by young adult to help support . . . 405.05
trusts funded by, avoiding support obligation using . . . 425.01
visitation rights of . . . 2505.05

Grantor
as fiduciary . . . 610.02
of living trust, taxation rules for . . . 601, 660.01
permanent severance from property of . . . 610
retention of beneficial enjoyment or management or administrative powers by . . . 610.01

Grantor—continued
taxed for five percent or more reversionary interest in corpus or income . . . 605.02
terminal illness of . . . 530
trustee replacement by . . . 610.01

Grantor retained annuity trust (GRAT) . . . 625, 650, 2315–2315.02

Grantor retained interest trust (GRIT) . . . 625, 650, 2315–2315.02
common law . . . 2315.02

Grantor retained unitrust (GRUT) . . . 625, 650, 2315–2315.02

Grantor trust
"defective" . . . 3220
S corporation as shareholder of . . . 605.06
as shareholder in S corporation . . . 1945.02

Grantor trust rules . . . 530, 605.02, 810.01
description of . . . 610
grantor with reversionary interest treated as owner of trust under revised . . . 405.05
for income tax . . . 660.01
overview of . . . 601
private annuity taxation under . . . 810.01
purposely causing application of . . . 3220

Gross estate
administration fees for estate deductible from . . . 1405.02
of annuitant granting gift of property . . . 810.05
closely held business interest exceeding 35 percent of . . . 310.04
closely held corporation stock value exceeding 35 percent of . . . 1915, 1915.03
deathbed gifts generally excluded from . . . 410.05
decedent's, for joint tenancies between spouses . . . 1615
deductions from . . . 405.02, 1005
election for decreasing value of . . . 1520
farm assets' percentage of . . . 2210.01
gift tax of gifts within three years of death as included in . . . 410.05, 410.07, 430
gifts made more than three years before death excluded from donor's . . . 310.02, 425.03
gifts to charities made within three years before death included in donor's . . . 525.02
holding interest in closely held business . . . 1510.04
inclusion of trust property in . . . 610, 610.01, 665, 665.03
of life insurance owner different from insured . . . 720.03
life insurance proceeds included in . . . 405.04, 715–715.03, 730, 735.01, 2410.02
lifetime gifts of nonfarm assets to reduce size of farmer's . . . 2210.07
lifetime gifts of stock to reduce size of . . . 1610.05
limiting value of business interests in . . . 2301
of minor . . . 425.02
property included in . . . 101, 410.01, 1005, 1005.02, 1305, 2310, 2705.10
qualified plan and IRA benefits included in . . . 955.02, 2505.04
removing half of nonbusiness property from . . . 315.02, 410.01
retained incidents or ownership or reversionary interest of life insurance included in . . . 525.03, 610, 640, 1005.02
retained life interest in trust assets throwing them into settlor's . . . 660.01
revocable transfers included in . . . 101, 2610.03
sole proprietorship's business assets kept out of . . . 2110.03
transfers to FLP includible in transferor's . . . 2010.05

Gross income
all income and gain not specifically exempted as includible in . . . 3101.01
amount excludable by annuitant from . . . 805.03, 810.02
cancellations of student loans excluded from . . . 3001
dependent care assistance by employer excludable from . . . 980
for determining tax on Social Security benefits . . . 3101.01
employee award exclusions from . . . 960
employer-paid educational assistance excluded from . . . 1605.01
income items to include in decedent's . . . 1505.04
interest on deferred part of selling price of decedent's stock included in . . . 1935
life insurance payments and cap for . . . 701.01
portion of annuity includible in . . . 5020
tax-exempt government bond interest excluded from . . . 3110–3110.03
trust corpus includible in beneficiary's . . . 660.02, 660.04
unreported interest accrued on bonds included in . . . 3165
value of insurance premiums paid by employer included in . . . 710

"Gross-up" rule
for estate tax . . . 430.01–.02, 1005
for generation-skipping transfer tax . . . 2705.04

Ground lease to obtain rent deductions for land . . . 3180.03

Group life insurance . . . 735.02
as employee benefit . . . 701

Growth and income mutual funds . . . 3140.03

Growth mutual funds . . . 3140.03

Guardian
appointed for minor children through will . . . 1101, 1105.08, 1415
court appointment of . . . 635, 1415
fees for . . . 630
income tax return of minor filed by . . . 425.03
of incompetent adult . . . 1105.09, 1415
as recipient of gift to minor . . . 425.03
selecting . . . 1415
sharing parents' values . . . 1415
trust provision for paying beneficiary's . . . 660.05

Guardianship
compared to other vehicles for gifts to minors . . . 425–425.04
conservatorship expanded to be . . . 2605.02
considered to be trust for Code Sec. 677(b).I . . . 425.03
to manage gifts to minors . . . 425
regarded as trusts under state law . . . 425.01
requirements and costs of . . . 425.03, 2605.02

H

Hanging power . . . 660.04

***Harrison, Estate of D.* decision of lapsed right to liquidate . . .** 2320

***Harrison, J.* . . .** 2210.08

Heads of households, tax rate schedule for . . . 5001.01

Health care facilities, investing in . . . 3180.04

Health care proxies . . . 2901, 2905.03

Health care surrogates or proxies, guidance and legal protection for . . . 2605, 2605.01

Health coverage for self-employed professionals . . . 1715.02

Health Insurance Act of 1996 . . . 965

Health Insurance Act of 1997 . . . 3420.02

Health insurance of employees . . . 3420.01
benefits of . . . 965, 975
COBRA requirements for . . . 965
by self-employed professional . . . 1715.02

Health Insurance Portability Act of 1996 . . . 3515.03

Health insurance premiums
deductions by participants of . . . 3420.01
deductions by partners of . . . 2001.01
distributions from IRA used to pay . . . 905.02

Health savings accounts (HSAs) . . . 1605.01, 1610.11, 3325.01, 3405.05, 3420.02

***Herr, A.I.* decision about annual gift tax exclusion . . .** 425.04

Hidden assets during divorce, matrimonial lawyer as discovering . . . 2420

Higher education . . . 3001–3020.07
tax breaks for . . . 3001
tax breaks for . . . 3001

Highly compensated employee
ceiling for participation in SARSEP of . . . 915.02
definition and income level of . . . 905.01
employee discount of . . . 985.02
limitation used for defining . . . 5005
nondiscrimination rules affecting . . . 925.01, 935, 975, 980
salary deferrals in 401(k) plan of, compared with nonhighly compensated employees . . . 925.01
working condition fringe benefits excluded from gross income by . . . 985.03

Highway commuting vehicle . . . 985.05

Hold-back provisions for distribution from trust . . . 660.09–.10

Home. *See* **Personal residence**

Home equity debt for home mortgage . . . 2815, 2815.03–.04, 2815.08, 2815.09

Home equity lines of credit . . . 3195.01

Home inspector . . . 2805.01

Home office. *See* **Business use of home**

Hope scholarship credit . . . 3001, 3005–3005.01
choice from among other incentives of . . . 3005.05, 3010.02
computing qualified educational expenses for . . . 3005.04
Coverdell Education Savings Account exclusion waived for year to use . . . 3020.03
income limitations for . . . 3005.03, 3301.02
interaction with qualified state tuition program distributions of . . . 3005.06

Hospital insurance (HI) self-employment tax . . . 3445, 5001.06
FICA tax for . . . 5001.07

***Hubert Estate of O.* . . . decision about administration expenses in . . .** 1110.08

Human relations skills of planners . . . 105

Hybrid annuity . . . 805

I

Immediate vesting in joint bank account . . . 315.01

Incentive stock options (ISOs) for executives . . . 1605.01, 1610.05

Income acceleration or deferral between years, planning . . . 3301–3315.07, 3440, 3505.08

Income averaging for farmers . . . 2220

Income in respect of decedent (IRD)
deductions . . . 1515.10
distributive share or guaranteed payment for deceased partner as . . . 2025
exercise of nonqualified options treated as . . . 1610.06

Income mutual funds . . . 3140.03

Income postponement methods . . . 3305.01, 3505.08

Income shifting
to family members . . . 3215
in gift to minors . . . 425.01, 3210–3210.09
to offset limitation on itemized deductions . . . 3440
in professional corporation . . . 1725.01
spread in tax rates as incentive for . . . 3201
tax savings from . . . 735.01, 3201
to trust . . . 420, 740

Income sprinkling clause in trust instrument . . . 660.01, 660.08

Income tax, consequences for
of annuities . . . 810.02, 810.06, 2435.01
of bequeathing deferred compensation . . . 1610.08
of charitable contribution of life insurance . . . 525.01
of charitable remainder trusts . . . 515.01
of Code Sec. 2503(c) trust . . . 425.04
of co-ownership of property . . . 305, 310.03, 310.04, 315.02
of cross purchase agreement . . . 1935
of custodianships for minors . . . 425.02
of death benefits . . . 950
of defective grantor trusts . . . 3220
of disclaimers of bequests . . . 1525.01
of dissolution of partnership . . . 2020.05
of divorce settlement . . . 2435.01
of executor's administrative fees . . . 1405.03
of distributions in kind from estate . . . 1510.01
of income in respect of decedent partner . . . 2025
of investments . . . 3101.01–.02
of irrevocable living trust . . . 625
of joint bank account . . . 315.01
of life insurance . . . 410.01, 705.02, 710, 2015.05, 2435.01
of lifetime gifts . . . 401–405.01, 405.05, 410, 410.01
of money market instruments . . . 3145.02
of mutual fund holdings . . . 3140.05
of mutual fund switches . . . 3140.01
of property contributed for conservation purposes . . . 535.01
of purchase of decedent's partnership interest by surviving partners . . . 2020.01
of qualified state tuition savings programs . . . 3010.01
of retirement plan funding . . . 1725.02
of revocable insurance trust . . . 735
of revocable living trust . . . 630
of securities owned jointly . . . 315.05
of sprinkling trust . . . 660.01
of stock redemptions . . . 1915–1915.05
of support obligation addressed in premarital agreement . . . 2405.06
of testamentary trust . . . 640
of transfers to minors age 14 or older . . . 3210–3210.09
of trusts . . . 601, 605–605.08, 2435.01
of U.S. savings bonds owned jointly . . . 310.03, 315.03
of U.S. savings bonds transferred in divorce settlement . . . 2435.01

Income tax, federal
deduction for charitable contributions from . . . 505–505.10
favorable treatment of life insurance for . . . 701
favorable treatment of life insurance for . . . 701
rates for . . . 1515, 2001

Income tax, local
deduction for charitable contributions from . . . 505
income shifting to minimize progressive . . . 425.01
paid by surviving spouse receiving deferred compensation bequest . . . 1610.08
U.S. government security interest exempt from . . . 3135

Income tax rate schedules for noncorporate taxpayers . . . 5001.01

Income tax refund seized to pay delinquent child support . . . 2430

Income tax return, decedent's final . . . 1505

Income tax, state
affected by including child's income on parents' return . . . 405.05, 3205.02
deduction for charitable contributions from . . . 505
deduction for IRA contributions for . . . 915.01
dependency exemption's consequences for . . . 3405.04
on donor of net gift . . . 410.07
income shifting to minimize progressive . . . 425.01
paid by surviving spouse receiving deferred compensation bequest . . . 1610.08
prepaid to accelerate deductions to previous year . . . 3305.02
U.S. government security interest exempt from . . . 3135

Incorporation
of farm property . . . 2210.08
of professional practice . . . 1715

Incorporation, tax-free . . . 1720.09

Incorporation-by-reference theory regarding trust and will . . . 645

Indemnity agreement for separated spouses . . . 2420.03

Index futures . . . 3170.03
options on . . . 3170.03

Index options . . . 3170.03

Indexing of earnings for social security benefits . . . 3525

Individual retirement accounts (IRAs). . . . *See also* **individual types**
AGI income limits for deductible contributions to . . . 915.01, 915.02, 2105.02, 2415.06, 3301.02
AGI reduced using . . . 3325.01
of child . . . 3230
custodians required to provide distribution information for . . . 915.01
distributions from . . . 915.01
as employee benefit . . . 915–915.04
estate planning factors for . . . 955–955.02
for farmers . . . 2215
minimum distributions from, rules for . . . 905.02, 915.01
multiple . . . 915.01
popularity of . . . 3101.02
postponing income by increasing contribution to . . . 3305.01
premature withdrawal penalty for . . . 905.02
QTIP election for . . . 1210.01
retirement benefits paid under QDRO rolled over tax-free into . . . 2445
self-directed . . . 915.01

Individual retirement accounts (IRAs)—continued
SEP plans using . . . 915.02, 1610.04
spousal . . . 915.01, 1610.01

Individual retirement annuities issued by life insurance company . . . 915.01

Inflation-indexed securities (IIS) of U.S. Treasury Department . . . 3135.01

Inflation
boost to real estate investments of . . . 3180, 3185.04
effect on mortgage payments and balances of . . . 3150.03

Inheritance
joint property acquired by . . . 310.01
property acquired during marriage by . . . 325.01

Inheritance tax, state . . . 325.01, 735.01, 1520.01. *See also* **State death taxes**

Innocent spouse rules for relief from joint and several liability . . . 1505.01

Inside directors, fees of . . . 1605.02

Insiders subject to Section 16(b) of Securities Exchange Act for short swing profits . . . 3101.04

Installment sales
deferring income using . . . 3305.01
deferring tax using . . . 3325.08
depreciation recapture for . . . 3115
gain on . . . 3101.01

Insurance companies for IRA accounts . . . 915.01

Insurance funding for partnership interest buyout or liquidation . . . 2015.05, 2020.02–.03

Insurance interest of applicant for life insurance on another's life . . . 525.03

Insurance plan, financial and estate planner as creating . . . 740

Insurance premiums
business deduction of . . . 710
deductible by self-employed person . . . 1715.02
employer recovery of paid . . . 705.02, 1605.01
flexible . . . 705.02, 755
investment of net . . . 705.02
options for . . . 701.01
rising, in term insurance . . . 705.01
for split-dollar life insurance . . . 705.02
trust income to pay . . . 735.01
vanishing . . . 705.02
waiver of . . . 701.02

Insurance proceeds
avoiding inclusion in insurer's estate of . . . 715–715.03, 1610.09
direct gift of . . . 415
exempt, pourover trust to receive . . . 645

Insurance trust . . . 720, 735–735.02

Intangible value of closely held corporation . . . 1940.01

Intellectual property donations . . . 505.09

***Inter vivos* trust.** *See* **Living trusts**

Interest, bank account . . . 315.01

Interest paid, restrictions and limitations on deductions of . . . 3425

Interest rates
of adjustable rate mortgages, initial and adjusted effective . . . 2810.02
bond values as falling with increases in . . . 3140.04
locked in with zero coupon bonds . . . 3160.03
monthly adjustments to IRS . . . 5045
mortgage-backed securities as sensitive to . . . 3150.03
reflected in money market instruments . . . 3145

Interest rates tables
for current value of $1 paid in future . . . 5040
for increase of $1 saved each year . . . 5035
for money growth at various rates . . . 5025
for savings required to earn $1 at different periods . . . 5030

International mutual funds . . . 3185.06

Interval estate as timesharing arrangement . . . 330

Intra-family transfers . . . 2301–2320
special valuation rules for . . . 2305–2305.07

Inventory items
deduction of . . . 3415.08
gain or loss attributable to unrealized receivables and . . . 2015.02
substantially appreciated . . . 2015, 2015.02

Investment advice as miscellaneous itemized deduction . . . 3435

Investment advisory fees paid by trust . . . 605.01

Investment expenses as deductible . . . 3101.01

Investment interest paid as deductible . . . 1515.06, 3101.01

Investment philosophy of testator . . . 1125

Investment planning defined . . . 101

Investment property, losses on sale or exchange of . . . 3101.01

Investment strategies and vehicles . . . 3101–3195.02

Investments
accelerating deductions to previous tax year by taking losses on . . . 3305.04
choices in times of low interest rates for . . . 915.01
commissions and investment charges for . . . 3190–3190.02
delaying sale of loss . . . 3305.03
diversification of . . . 3101.03, 3140
economic risk of . . . 3101, 3101.03
leveraged . . . 3135.01
life insurance as . . . 701
liquid . . . 3140
postponing income or capital gains from . . . 3305.01
postponing sale of . . . 3305.01
in securities . . . 3120–3120.02
securities laws and . . . 3101.04
in specialized small business investment companies . . . 3130–3130.02
transaction costs of . . . 3101.03

Involuntary conversion of property . . . 3101.01

IRAs. *See* **Individual retirement accounts (IRAs), Roth IRA,** *and* **Traditional IRA**

Irrevocable insurance trust . . . 405.02, 735.01–.02

Irrevocable life insurance trust (ILIT) . . . 2410.02

Irrevocable living trust . . . 601, 625, 660, 2605.01

Irrevocable trust
changes not possible for . . . 620, 645
for group-term insurance policy . . . 945.03
for minor . . . 3210.08
property not includible in settlor's gross estate from . . . 601
to qualify for Medicaid . . . 2605, 2605.01
to structure premarital agreement transfers . . . 2405.12
tax law changes affecting . . . 110

IRS *Examination Technique Handbook for Estate Tax Examiners* . . . 2110.04

IRS Form K-1, "Partner's Share of Income, Credit, Deductions, Etc." . . . 3145.02

IRS Form 706 . . . 1405

IRS Form 709, Federal Gift Tax Return
election to treat payments as qualified or nonqualified payments made on statement attached to . . . 2305.03
using . . . 405.02

IRS Form 709A, gift tax return filed using . . . 405.02

IRS Form 1040, deductions by professionals of health insurance premiums on . . . 1715.02

IRS Form 1041 . . . 1405, 1405.03

IRS Form 1065 . . . 1805.04, 2001

IRS Form 1099-INT to report interest . . . 315.01

IRS Form 4952, "Investment Interest Expense Deduction" . . . 3101.01

IRS Form 5305-SEP to establish SEP . . . 915.02

IRS Form 5305A-SEP to establish salary-reduction SEP . . . 915.02

IRS Form 8332, "Release of Claim to Exemption for Child of Divorced or Separated Parents" . . . 2430, 3405.01

IRS Form 8615 . . . 2420.02

IRS Form 8814, "Parents' Election To Report Child's Interest and Dividends" . . . 3205.02

IRS Form 8832, "Entity Classification Election" . . . 1715, 1805.05

IRS Publication 526, "Charitable Contributions" . . . 505.04

IRS Publication 561, "Determining the Value of Donated Property" . . . 505.03

IRS Publication 590, "Individual Retirement Arrangements (IRAs)" . . . 5020

IRS Publication 915, "Social Security and Equivalent Railroad Retirement Benefits" . . . 3510.09

IRS Publication 939, "General Rule for Pensions and Annuities" . . . 5020

IRS Publication 970, "Tax Benefits for Higher Education" . . . 1605.01

IRS Publication 1457, "Actuarial Values, Book Aleph," . . . 810.03, 5045

IRS Publication 1458, "Actuarial Values, Book Beth" . . . 515.01, 5045

IRS Publication 1459, "Actuarial Values, Book Gimel" . . . 5045

IRS Schedule C
deductions for self-employed person of . . . 1715.02
net income of sole proprietor reported on . . . 1805.06

IRS Schedule K-1, trust's income reported on . . . 605.01

IRS Schedule SE, computing self-employment tax base using . . . 5001.06

IRS Valuation Guide for Income, Estate and Gift Taxes, Valuation Training for Appeals Officers . . . 505.03

IRS valuation tables under Code Sec. 7520 . . . 810.03–.04

IRS *Valuation Training for Appeals Officers* coursebook . . . 1940, 1940.03, 2030

Itemized deductions
Code Sec. 68 reduction of . . . 2815.01
of home mortgage points . . . 2815.07, 3425
income deferral and shifting to offset limited . . . 3440
of qualified residence interest . . . 2815–2815.09
of mutual fund expenses . . . 3140.05
planning for limitation on . . . 3440
of real estate taxes . . . 2801, 2815.01

Itemized deductions—continued
reductions based on AGI more than threshold for joint and single filers on . . . 2415.02, 3101.01, 3301.02, 3325.01, 3440, 5001.04
two percent AGI floor for miscellaneous . . . 605.01, 1620, 2440, 3101.01, 3205.02, 3301.02, 3435

J

Jewelry as good for lifetime giving . . . 410.01

Jobs and Growth Tax Relief Reconciliation Act of 2003
capital gains rates reduced under . . . 3310

Joint and several liability on joint return
for decedent and surviving spouse . . . 1505.01
for divorcing spouses . . . 2420.03

Joint and survivor annuities . . . 405.02, 805, 905.01, 955.01, 1610.01

Joint bank accounts
community property . . . 325.01
death of one joint tenant of . . . 315.01
disadvantages of . . . 315.01
disclaiming interest in . . . 1525.01
for elderly or disabled people . . . 2605, 2605.01
exclusion from gift tax of . . . 310.02
for minor and parent . . . 3210.02, 3210.04
not accessed after death until state tax waivers are presented . . . 1105.01
potential dangers of . . . 315.01
as source of income to family during administration of will . . . 1105.01
survivorship feature of . . . 315.01
for unmarried partners . . . 2505.04

Joint brokerage accounts
disclaiming interest in . . . 1525.01
exclusion from gift tax of . . . 310.02
registration of . . . 315.05

Joint income tax return of decedent and surviving spouse . . . 1505.01

Joint lives insurance policy . . . 705.02

Joint ownership
advantages of . . . 310, 315.02
of business realty and real property by spouses in sole proprietorship . . . 2110.06
of farm or ranch property . . . 2210.03
income tax consequences of . . . 305, 310.03, 310.04
loss of full control of property under . . . 310
scope of . . . 310
sole ownership compared to . . . 310
terminating existing . . . 315.02
unwinding . . . 310

Joint purchases of property . . . 2315.05

Joint returns, federal income tax. *See also* **Joint and several liability on joint return**
excludable gain on sale of residence for . . . 2820.01
personal and dependency exemptions on . . . 2415.02
for separated spouses . . . 2420.03
tax rate schedules for . . . 5001.01
threshold amount for reducing itemized deductions on . . . 2415.03

Joint tenancy with right of survivorship
advantages for closely held business of . . . 315.02
advantages for executives of . . . 1615
created by spouses before 1977 . . . 305, 315.02
created to meet 35-percent test . . . 1915.03
creating, as taxable gift . . . 310.02
disclaimer for . . . 1525.01
document check of items held in . . . 305
ending unwanted . . . 310
estate tax consequences of . . . 315.02

Joint tenancy with right of survivorship—continued
exclusion from estate of first spouse to die of property held in. . . . *See* Exclusion amount from estate tax
property of decedent held in . . . 101, 1005.02, 1101
severance of interests in . . . 305
for unmarried couple's property . . . 2505.03–.04

Joint tenants
business realty and tangible personal property owned by spouses as . . . 2110.06
proving contribution of survivor to property of . . . 310.01
simultaneous death of . . . 310, 310.01
termination of relationship of . . . 310.04

Jointly held property
lifetime gifts of . . . 410.01
mortgaged . . . 310.01
spouses having . . . 410.01

Judgment, direct gift made by assignment of . . . 415

Junior family member
common stock transfers to . . . 1940
short-term trust established for . . . 605.01, 605.07

K

Keogh (HR-10) plan
contributions rate for . . . 5001.06
contributions to, AGI reduction using . . . 3325.02
contributions to, timing . . . 3315.07
employment tax affecting contributions to . . . 3445
as sole proprietor's tax shelter . . . 2105.02

Key employees
incentive stock options for . . . 1605.01
in top-heavy qualified plan . . . 905.01

Key person, effect on corporation value of losing . . . 1940.01, 1940.06

Key personal papers, blank form for recording . . . 1125

Kiddie tax . . . 405.01, 410
age limitation . . . 3205.02
avoiding, tax-exempt zero coupon bonds for . . . 3110.03, 3160.03
avoiding, Series EE U.S. savings bonds for . . . 3135.02
for children of divorced or separated parents . . . 2420.02
on Code Sec. 2503(b) trust distributions to minors . . . 425.04
election out of . . . 3205.03
savings by shifting assets to children despite . . . 3205
severe impact on gifts to minors of . . . 425, 425.02, 425.03
three parts of unearned income for . . . 405.05, 3205.01
TIPRA and . . . 405.01, 405.05

***King, J.* decision on savings clauses** . . . 405.02

***Kisling, Estate of E.* decision about exclusions of trust property from gross estate** . . . 430

***Kurz, Estate of E.* decision on contingent powers of appointment** . . . 1305

L

Lapsing rights in family-controlled corporation or partnership . . . 2320

Laws of intestacy . . . 1110.12

Lawyer. *See* **Attorney**

Leased employees . . . 930

Leasing
of equipment to professionals . . . 1725
of medical building to professional corporation . . . 1725

LeFrak Estate of S. . . . 2010.04

Legacies in wills . . . 1105.04, 1110.10
lapsed . . . 1110.12

Legal expenses of setting up trust . . . 735

Letter stock . . . 1610.07

Leverage
with commodities futures funds . . . 3155
with real estate . . . 3180.04

Liability, business form selections to manage . . . 1810

Licensing timesharing arrangements . . . 330

Life income interest in gift . . . 405.02, 410.01
terminating . . . 1225.04

Life insurance . . . 701–705
accelerated death benefits (living benefits) of . . . 701.01
amount of, considering factors for determining . . . 740
on annuitant taken by obligor . . . 810.01
assignment of . . . 2605, 2605.01
borrowing against . . . 525, 701, 701.01, 701.03, 705.01, 745
cash value or cash accumulation feature of . . . 701, 701.01, 705.02, 755
changing insurers or policies for . . . 945.02
for chronically v. terminally ill insured . . . 710
community property issues for . . . 325.03
comparison of types of policies for, table of . . . 705.02
contestable period for . . . 755
on controlling shareholder, corporate-owned . . . 1950–1950.02
conversion privileges of . . . 525
defined for tax purposes . . . 701.02
effect of unlimited marital deduction on disposition of . . . 405.02
estate tax on . . . 705.02, 715–715.03, 1601
for executive . . . 1605.01, 1620.06, 1915.03
to finance purchase of sole proprietorship . . . 2110.03
to finance stock redemption . . . 1915.03, 1920
form for recording . . . 1125
to fund buy-sell agreements . . . 1935
functions of . . . 701
gift tax on gift of . . . 720–720.03, 725
gift to charity of . . . 501.01, 525–525.03, 725
gift within three years of death of . . . 405.04, 430.01
group . . . 701, 735.02
group permanent . . . 945.04
group term . . . 430.01, 905.01, 945.01–945.03, 975, 1725.03
guaranteed insurability rider for . . . 701.01
held by trust . . . 720
incidental, for pension plan . . . 930.03
incidental, for profit-sharing plan . . . 920.02
integrating will provisions with policy arrangements for . . . 1105.13
investment yields from . . . 710
lifetime gifts of, types of . . . 410.01
modified endowment . . . 701.03
nonparticipating cash value . . . 701.01
ownership clause for . . . 701.01
of partners to enable buyout of interest or liquidation of partnership upon death . . . 2015.05, 2020.02–.03
payable to beneficiaries of employee participants in ECOP . . . 910
permanent, group . . . 1605.01
permanent v. term . . . 701.01, 701.02
for premature death . . . 801
premiums. . . . *See* Insurance premiums

Life insurance—continued
removing incidents of ownership in . . . 955.03
replacing existing . . . 755
in retirement plan . . . 1725.02
settlement options for . . . 750–750.02
for sole proprietor . . . 701, 2110
special handling of proceeds for spouse of . . . 1220.01
state exemptions for . . . 701
transfer of . . . 710, 715–715.03, 1610.09
types of policies for . . . *See also* individual types 705–705.02.
for unmarried couples . . . 2505.04

Life insurance contract, understanding provisions of . . . 701.01

Life insurance policy, gift of . . . 101
favorable income tax treatment of cash value policy proceeds as lifetime . . . 410.01
gift tax on . . . 410.01, 720–702.03, 725
to minor . . . 425.02
to spouse . . . 405.02

Life interest
premarital agreement structured with irrevocable trust giving spouse . . . 2405.12
property transfer with owner retaining . . . 310.04, 405.06

Lifetime gift program, ongoing . . . 410.04

Lifetime gifts . . . 401–430.02, 1001, 1005
to avoid probate . . . 401
bargain sale . . . 410.06
basic strategies for . . . 410–410.07
basis for income tax of . . . 410.02
to children and grandchildren who are minors . . . 425–425.04
choosing between testamentary transfers and . . . 410.02
direct and indirect . . . 415
for elderly or disabled people . . . 2605, 2605.01
of farm or ranch real estate . . . 2210.01
GST tax exemption for . . . 2705.03
interspousal . . . 405.02, 410.02, 1215.06
made within three years of death as includible in estate . . . 1915.03
to meet 35-percent test for closely held corporation stock . . . 1925.01
of nonfarm assets to reduce size of farmer's gross estate . . . 2210.07
of property with appreciation potential to avoid transfer tax . . . 405.02
of qualifying real estate . . . 2110.05
reasons to use . . . 401
to reduce size of estate . . . 1610.05, 1915.03
tax factors of . . . 405.01–405.06
in trust . . . 420

Lifetime learning credit . . . 3001, 3005, 3005.02
choice from among other incentives of . . . 3005.05, 3010.02
computing qualified educational expenses for . . . 3005.04
Coverdell Education Savings Account exclusion waived for year to use . . . 3020.03
income limitations for . . . 3005.03, 3301.02
interaction with qualified state tuition program distributions of . . . 3005.06

Lifetime withdrawals from life insurance policy, tax treatment of . . . 701.03

Like-kind exchanges of property . . . 3101.01, 3115–3115.04
losses not recognized in . . . 3115.04
partnership interests generally not eligible for . . . 3115.02
requirements of . . . 3115–3115.01

Like-kind property . . . 3115.03

Limited liability companies (LLCs)
advantages of . . . 2040.01
as alternative to sole proprietorship entity . . . 2105.01
conversion of partnership to . . . 2040.03
disadvantages of . . . 2040.02
election to become . . . 1805.05
freedom from personal liability of . . . 2040, 2040.01
pass-through of income and loss of . . . 2040.01
single-member . . . 2040.02
taxation of . . . 1715, 1805, 1805.05, 2040, 2040.02
timing of . . . 410.05

Limited liability partnership . . . 1705

Limited partner, money market instrument organized as limited partnership passing exemption to investor as . . . 3145.02

Limited partnership interests . . . 3190.01

Liquidity for estate
of closely held corporation owner . . . 1901.02
life insurance to provide . . . 701, 715, 730
planning for . . . 1510–1510.05, 1615

Living together, couple
bank accounts for . . . 2505.04
co-ownership of property for . . . 2505.04
division of joint and separate property by . . . 2505.08
durable powers of attorney for . . . 2505.07
filing status of . . . 2505.09
lifetime arrangements for . . . 2505.04
palimony cases for . . . 2505.02
planning for . . . 2501–2505.09
premarital-type agreement for . . . 2415.06
property transfers for . . . 2415.05
provisions for children of . . . 2505.05
revocable trusts as effective tool for . . . 2505.04
role of financial planner for . . . 2505.01
tax advantages of . . . *See also* Marriage penalty 3505.05.
written agreement for rights and obligations of . . . 2505.06

Living trusts . . . 530, 625
income sprinkling with . . . 660.01
interest in property of . . . 610
to provide liquid family income . . . 1105.01
sale of assets to . . . 1510.02
types of . . . *See also* Irrevocable living trust, Pourover trust, *and* Revocable living trust 601.

Living will
to guide health care surrogates . . . 2605, 2605.01
health care proxy v. . . . 2905.03
as planning device . . . 2905.01
uses of . . . 2901

Loans. . . . *See also* **Debt**
against annuity balances . . . 805.02
against cash value of life insurance . . . 525, 701, 701.01, 701.03, 705.01, 745, 755
below-market interest . . . 405.01, 970–970.02, 1605.01
business, mortgage proceeds for . . . 2815.09
consolidation . . . 3195.01
construction . . . 3180
deducting bad debts on . . . 3430
demand . . . 970.01–.02
educational assistance . . . 3001, 3015–3015.02, 3301.02
home . . . *See* Mortgages
informal, will provisions for . . . 1110.06
interest-free, as gift . . . 415
lender applying insurance proceeds against . . . 725
qualified education . . . 3001, 3015–3015.02
from qualified plan . . . 940
secured by residence, advantage of . . . 970.02
student . . . 3001
term . . . 970.01

Local taxes generally deductible from federal tax under Code Sec. 164 . . . 3101.01

Long-term capital gains, tax rate on . . . 105

Long-term care insurance for elderly or disabled people . . . 2605, 3420.01, 3420.04, 3430.03

Long-term care, Medicaid eligibility for . . . 3515.03

Long-term tax rate group, losses of . . . 3310

***Looney, J.* decision about death benefits** . . . 950

Loss property, donation of proceeds from selling . . . 505.07

Low-income housing credits . . . 3180.01

Lump-sum distributions
of employer securities . . . 1610.02
from qualified plan . . . 905.02, 1610.01

M

Machinery and equipment kept out of closely held corporation assets . . . 1905, 1910.02

***McNeely, H.* decision about exclusions of trust property from gross estate** . . . 430

Malpractice claims . . . 1715.03

Margin accounts, initial and maintenance margins for . . . 3185.02

Marital deduction . . . 1201–1240.02
for alien surviving spouse . . . 1230
for appreciated property exceeding unified credit . . . 410.02
for business real estate of sole proprietor . . . 2110.05
checking effect of wills on . . . 305
choice of returns for, as affecting marital bequest . . . 1515.03
community property qualifying for . . . 325.01
deathbed gifts without gift or estate tax to spouse under . . . 410.05
denial of . . . 1240.01
exclusion from gift tax resulting from . . . 310.02, 410.03
for executive's estate . . . 1615
extent of use of . . . 1215
farm or ranch property passed on using . . . 2205, 2210.01, 2210.03
federal estate tax reduced by . . . 1105.15
gift of life estate with general power of appointment qualifying for . . . 405.02
for gift made within three years of death, no gift tax on . . . 430.01
gross estate reduced by bequests qualifying for . . . 1005
to help meet 35-percent test . . . 1915.03
insurance for surviving spouse to cover loss of . . . 740
life insurance settlement options and . . . 735, 750.02
lifetime gifts less urgent because of applicable . . . 410.04
lifetime interspousal gifts not providing transfer tax savings because of . . . 405.02
lifetime use of . . . 405.02
not applicable to spouses who are not U.S. citizens . . . 405.01
for personal residence . . . 1105.05
for pooled income fund beneficiary . . . 515.02
qualifying for . . . 1205–1205.02
requirements for . . . 405.02
for settlor of trust . . . 610
for sole proprietor's business interest . . . 2110.02
for split gift to spouse and charity . . . 510.02, 515.01
survivorship important for . . . 1105.15, 1240
transmission expenses as reducing . . . 1110.08
unlimited . . . 315.02, 325.01, 405.02, 720.02, 1001–1005, 1515.05, 2405.07

Marital deduction bequest
disclaimer of . . . 1525.01
patterns of . . . 1220
QTIP election with . . . 1225.01, 1520.01

Marital deduction trust . . . 1225, 1525.01

Marriage, common law . . . 2410.01

Marriage penalty . . . 2415, 3505, 3505.06

Marriage, prior
children of, protecting . . . 2410.02–.03
termination of . . . 2410.01

Marriage, subsequent
premarital agreement for . . . 2410.03–.04
special planning issues for . . . 2410–2410.05
will provisions for . . . 2410.05
will provisions for . . . 2410.05

Marriage v. living together, financial factors of . . . 2415–2415.06
deductible IRA contributions as . . . 2415.06
deduction for personal and dependency exemptions as . . . 2415.02
income threshold reducing itemized deductions as . . . 2415.03
passive activity losses as . . . 2415.01
standard deduction as . . . 2415.04
transfers of property as . . . 2415.05

Married couples. *See* **Spouses**

Materiality of facts for SEC Rule 10b-5 . . . 3101.04

Matrimonial or marriage settlement. *See* **Divorce settlement**

Medicaid . . . 3515–3515.03
irrevocable trust to help person qualify for . . . 2605, 2605.01
planning techniques for . . . 105
spousal impoverishment for, income retained by spouses under . . . 3515.01
transfer of assets to qualify for . . . 3515.03
trust assets considered available to pay expenses by . . . 3515.02

Medical benefits for executives . . . 1605.01

Medical care directives
adult patient's rights to make . . . 2905.01
periodic review of . . . 2905.04

Medical care by proxy . . . 2605, 2605.01, 2901–2905.04

Medical care expenses. *See also* **Medicare**
of cosmetic surgery . . . 3420.01
of decedent, deduction of . . . 1505.03
of dependent of divorced parents, deduction of . . . 2430.01
deduction of . . . 3420.01
exclusions from generation-skipping transfer tax of payments of . . . 2705.07
no early withdrawal penalty on funds distributed to pay . . . 905.02
percentage of AGI required for deduction of . . . 3205.02, 3301.02, 3420.01
of retired or laid off employees . . . 965
salary reduction feature of cafeteria plans for . . . 975
travel for, deduction of . . . 3420.01
unlimited gift tax exclusion for payment of . . . 405.02

Medical equipment, deduction for donation to hospital of used . . . 3415.04

Medical reimbursement plans, self-insured . . . 965

Medical savings accounts (MSAs), Archer . . . 1605.01, 1610.10, 3305.01,3405.08 3325.01, 3405.05, 3420.02, 3420.03

Medicare . . . 3510–3510.06
enrollment in Part A and Part B . . . 3510.02
general functions of . . . 3510.01
Medigap policies to pay expenses not covered by . . . 3510.07
Part A coverage and limitations for . . . 3510.03
Part B services and limitations for . . . 3510.04
Part C (Medicare+Choice) . . . 3510.05
Part D (Prescription Coverage) . . . 3510.06

Medicare Prescription Drug, Improvement, and Modernization Act of 2003 . . . 965

Mentally impaired people
planning for . . . 2610–2610.03
standby trust for . . . 635

***Metzger, Estate of A.F.* decision about gift timing . . .** 405.06

Mineral interests in farm or ranch land, power to deal with . . . 2210.04

Mineral rights and surface mining retained in contribution of conservation easement . . . 535.03

Minors. . . . *See* **Children**

Modified AGI
for earned income credit . . . 3410.03
for phaseout of contribution to education IRA . . . 3020.01–.02

Modified endowment contract (MEC) . . . 701.03, 710

Modified whole life insurance policy . . . 705.02

Money market funds . . . 3145
in asset management account . . . 3185.05

Money market instruments
money moved into mutual funds from . . . 3105
safety of . . . 3145.01
strategies for using . . . 3145.01
tax factors of . . . 3145.02
types of . . . 3145

Money purchase plan as type of pension plan . . . 930, 930.01

Mortgage interest deduction on personal residences . . . 2805, 2815–2815.09

Mortgage-backed securities . . . 3150–3150.06
advantages of . . . 3150.02
disadvantages of . . . 3150.03
hedging against risks of . . . 3150.04
mutual funds of . . . 3150.05
types of . . . 3150–3150.01
unit trusts of . . . 3150.06

Mortgages
adjustable rate, features of . . . 2810.02
biweekly . . . 2810.03
for business loan . . . 2815.09
entities passing through interest and principal on . . . 3150
FHA . . . 3150
fixed-payment adjustable rate . . . 2810.03
fixed rate, 15- and 30-year . . . 2810.01
fixed rate with refinancing option . . . 2810.03
40-year . . . 2810.03
graduated-payment . . . 2810.03
graduated-payment adjustable . . . 2810.03
growing-equity . . . 2810.03
pledged-account . . . 2810.03
points charged on . . . 2815.07, 3425
pool of, investment in . . . 3150.06
prepaying . . . 3150.03–.04
price level adjusted . . . 2810.03
renegotiable-rate . . . 2810.03
reverse . . . 2810.03
seven-year balloon . . . 2810.03

Mortgages—continued
shared-appreciation . . . 2810.03
VA . . . 3150
zero rate . . . 2810.03

Moving expenses
as fringe benefit . . . 985.07
incurred early to accelerate deductions to previous year . . . 3305.04
as tax free to executive . . . 1605.01

Multiple corporations
merged to meet qualifying tests for closely held corporation stock . . . 1915.03
to multiply accumulated earnings credit . . . 1905

Multiple support agreements for child . . . 2430

Multiple trusts
avoiding Code Sec. 643(f) for . . . 605.05
benefits of . . . 605.01
for income sprinkling among siblings . . . 660.01
trust throwback rules applicable to . . . 601

Mutual funds . . . 3140–3140.06
advantages of . . . 3140
basis in, determining . . . 3140.06
brokerage fees for closed-end . . . 3140
dollar cost averaging purchases of . . . 3105
fee disclosure and advertising standards required by SEC for . . . 3140.02
for IRA accounts . . . 915.01, 915.04
load v. no-load . . . 3140.01, 3190.01
management fees of . . . 3140.01, 3140.04
open- v. closed-end . . . 3140
redemption fee for open-end . . . 3140
selling at premium . . . 3140
switching among same-family . . . 3140.01
tax treatment of . . . 3140.05
types of . . . *See also* individual types3140.03.
variable annuities v. . . . 805.02

N

Naked trading . . . 3170

National Association of Insurance Commissioners . . . 710

National Center for Home Equity Conversion . . . 2810.03

National Conference of Commissioners on Uniform State Laws . . . 2405

Net capital gain or loss
calculating . . . 3101.02
investment property . . . 3101.01
tax rates on . . . 3101.02
tax-deferred investments as less attractive for . . . 3101.02

Net gift technique
donee paying gift tax in . . . 410.07
for liquidity . . . 1615

Net investment income, investment interest paid deductible to extent of . . . 3180.01

New year
billing customers at beginning of, deferring taxes by . . . 3305.01
tax planning for . . . 3325–3325.09

***New York State Bar Association v. Janet Reno, et al.* decision about Medicaid planning . . .** 2605

***Newman, Estate of* decision including gift in gross estate . . .** 405.06

No-additional-cost service as fringe benefit . . . 985.01

No-load arrangements to eliminate front-end sales commissions . . . 3190.02
Nonalimony treatment of payments to spouse by agreement . . . 2425.03
Nondiscrimination rules for qualified plans . . . 905.01
Nonhighly compensated employees in qualified plans, coverage rules for . . . 905.01
Nonincome-producing property
lifetime gift of . . . 410.01
trust provisions for holding . . . 665.04
Nonmarital deduction bequest . . . 1610.08
Nonmarital trust . . . 1225.04
Nonqualified stock options for executive compensation . . . 1605.01, 1610.06
Notes or claims held by decedent included in federal gross estate . . . 1005.02

O

Old age or disability benefits from Social Security Administration . . . 3520.01–.02
Old age survivors and disability insurance (OASDI) rates . . . 5001.06, 3445
On-the-job training as employee fringe benefit . . . 985.03
Open space easement, gift of . . . 535.01–.03
Open space preservation . . . 535.02
Open transactions . . . 3101.01
Options
buying put and selling call . . . 3170.01
call, writing . . . 3170.01
as gains hedge . . . 3170–3170.02
index . . . 3170.03
on index futures . . . 3170.03
put . . . 3170.03
stock index . . . 3170.03
in valuing property for tax purposes . . . 2310
Ordinary income property, deduction for donor of . . . 505.09
Ordinary life annuities, expected return multiples for, table of . . . 5020
Organ donations . . . 1110.04
Original issue discount (OID) bonds . . . 3160, 3160.02
rules for . . . 3165, 3165.01
Out placement services . . . 985.03
Over-the-counter (OTC) stocks . . . 3190.01, 3195.01
Overhead insurance for sole proprietor . . . 2105.03
Overvaluation penalty for donated property . . . 505.05
Ownership of property, evaluating forms of . . . 305

P

Paid-up insurance . . . 701.01
Painting, giving museum right of possession and enjoyment of . . . 515.04
Palimony cases . . . 2505.02
Parents
accidents killing both, planning for possibility of . . . 1415
Parents—continued
child taking over closely held corporation from . . . 1930
guardian for. *See* Guardian
income of child included on tax return of . . . 601
income sprinkling decided by . . . 660.01
life insurance purchased by child on life of . . . 2410.02
multiple support arrangements to alternate dependency exemption for elderly . . . 3405.06
power of appointment in favor of . . . 1801
trusts established to benefit . . . 601
values of, guardians who share . . . 1415
Parking, employer-provided . . . 985.05
Partial liquidation of closely held corporation shareholder . . . 1915.05
Partners. . . . *See also* **General partner**
death of . . . 1810, 2015, 2015.01, 2015.04, 2020–2020.05
disability of . . . 2015, 2015.04
estate, heir, or successor in interest continuing as . . . 2015, 2020.04
health insurance premium deductions by . . . 2001.01
liabilities to retired or deceased . . . 1720.09
liability exposure of . . . 2001.01
nontaxable distributions to . . . 2001
partnership income taxed and paid by . . . 2001
planning for . . . 2001–2040.03
property or money contributed by . . . 2005.02
purchase of partnership interest by surviving . . . 2020.01
qualified retirement plans for . . . 2001.01
recognized when capital is material income-producing factor . . . 2005
retirement of . . . 2015, 2015.01
self-employment tax for . . . 2001
tax year of . . . 2020.01
tax-favored benefits generally unavailable to . . . 2001.01
trusts as . . . 2005.01
Partnership
adjusting basis of assets of . . . 2015.07, 2020.01
advantages of . . . 2001
as alternative to sole proprietorship entity . . . 2105.01
alternatives to dissolution of . . . 2020–2020.04
buyout by liquidation of . . . 2015.03
choice of business form between corporation and . . . 2001
Code Sec. 119 benefits applied to . . . 2210.08
control of . . . 2305.02
converted to corporation . . . 1720
converted to limited liability company . . . 2040.03
debts of . . . 1805.04
disadvantages of . . . 2001.01
dissolved with death of partner . . . 1810, 2015, 2015.04, 2020.05, 2030
employees of, withholding for . . . 2001
estate receiving profits of . . . 2015.05
family . . . *See also* Family limited partnerships (FLPs) 2001.02, 2005–2005.03, 2105.01, 2110.03.
farm assets held by . . . 2210.05
goodwill of . . . 2015.01, 2020.04
income from, for separated spouses . . . 2420.01
insurance policies owned by . . . 1935
liabilities of, partner's share of . . . 2001
like-kind exchanges generally not available to . . . 3115.02
limited liability company taxed as corporation, association, or . . . 1715, 1805, 1805.05, 2040
pass through of income and loss to partners of . . . 1805, 1805.04, 2040.01
as pass-through entity to partners . . . 2001
qualified stock distributed by . . . 3125.05
role of life insurance in planning for partner of . . . 701
splitting income with family members from . . . 3230

Partnership—continued
tax year of . . . 1805.07, 2001
termination of . . . 1810, 2020.01
transfer of property to . . . 2001
treated as investment company . . . 2010.06

Partnership agreement, provisions of . . . 2020.01, 2025

Partnership buy-out or liquidation agreement . . . 2015.05, 2020.02, 2030

Partnership interest
basis of . . . 2001, 2020.01
bequest of . . . 2025
continuance or disposition upon death, retirement, or disability of . . . 2001.02, 2015
distribution to estate of deceased partner of . . . 2015
fair market value of . . . 2030
gifts of . . . 2005
insurance to fund buy-out or liquidation of . . . 2015.05, 2020.02
liquidation of . . . 2015, 2015.01, 2015.03
sale to new partner of . . . 2015
unfunded agreement to purchase decedent's . . . 2020.01
valuation of . . . 2015.03, 2015.04, 2020.01, 2030–2030.01

Passive activity
credits from . . . 3180.01
defined . . . 3101.01, 3180.01

Passive activity losses (PALs)
of closely held corporation . . . 1905
deduction limit for . . . 105, 2415.01, 3301.02
to offset passive activity income . . . 3101.01
for real estate . . . 3101.01, 3180.01
suspended . . . 3180.01

Patient Self-Determination Act of 1990 . . . 2905.01

Payroll taxes, tax-free employee benefits generally not subject to . . . 901

Pecuniary marital deduction trust . . . 1225

Pecuniary nonformula bequest . . . 1225.01

Penalties, IRS
for distributions from education IRA not used for qualified higher education expenses . . . 3020.03
for overvaluation of donated property . . . 505.05

Pendant power . . . 660.04

Pension plans . . . 930–930.03 *See also* **individual types**
excise tax on reversions for . . . 930
factors affecting costs and benefits of . . . 930
incidental life insurance for . . . 930.03
postponing receipt of payments from . . . 3305.01
terminating . . . 930

Performance shares for executives . . . 1605.01

Permanent cash value insurance . . . 705.01

Perpetual care, will provisions for . . . 1110.05

Personal and dependency exemptions . . . 2415.02, 3325.09, 3405–3405.06

Personal exemption phaseout rates . . . 3301.02, 3405.05, 5001.03

Personal Financial Specialist (CPA/PFS) . . . 105

Personal holding company . . . 1720.05

Personal holding company tax . . . 740, 1720.05

Personal interest converted to deductible qualified residence interest . . . 3325.04

Personal liability
freedom of LLC members from . . . 2040, 2040.01
of sole proprietorship . . .

Personal property, gifts of . . . 410.01

Personal property in estate. *See* **Tangible personal property**

Personal residence . . . 2801–2835.02
appreciation potential of . . . 2805.02
business use of . . . 2801, 2820.04, 2830
capital improvements to, recordkeeping for . . . 2820.04
casualty losses on . . . 2801
charitable remainder in . . . 515.03, 2801
as community property . . . 2801
converted to rental property prior to sale at loss . . . 2820.09
crime rate around . . . 2805.04
depreciation for rental or business use of . . . 2820.04
in divorce settlement . . . 2435.01
exception to Code Sec. 2702 in valuing retained interests for . . . 2315, 2315.03
financing and refinancing . . . 2801, 2810.08, 2810–2810.03
gift of, benefits of . . . 2801
gift of future interest in . . . 405.02
gift of remainder interest in . . . 501.01
joint ownership by spouses of . . . 2801
joint ownership by unmarried individuals of . . . 2801
joint tenancy for spouses' . . . 310, 315.02
legal considerations of contract for . . . 2805.06
lifetime gift of . . . 410.01
loss on sale of . . . 2820.09
mortgage interest deduction for . . . 2815–2815.08, 2901
partial interests in, gifts of . . . 535
placed in trust . . . 2801
principal, selecting . . . 2801
purchasing . . . 2801, 2805–2805.08
quality of neighborhood schools for . . . 2805.03
real estate agent used in purchase of . . . 2805.07
refinancing . . . 2815.07
remainder interest in, sale or exchange of . . . 2820.08
rental use of . . . 2801, 2820.04
special use valuation of . . . 2801
structural integrity of . . . 2805.01
time in licensed care facility included in ownership requirements for . . . 2820.06
title insurance for . . . 2801
transportation and commute time for . . . 2805.05
$250,000 exclusion for each taxpayer from gain on sale of . . . 315.02, 410.01, 1105.05, 2801, 2805.02, 2820–2820.08
ways to bequeath . . . 1105.05
withholding obligation for . . . 2801

Personal residence trust . . . 2315.03

Personal service corporation
accounting method for . . . 1720.04
accrued bonuses and interest payable to owners of, deducting . . . 1720.16
allocation of income of . . . 1720.06
calendar year required for . . . 1720.03
tax year of . . . 1805.07
35-percent flat tax of . . . 1715, 1805.02

Phantom stock . . . 1605.01

Planner. *See* **Financial and estate planner**

Planner's Checklist, sample blank . . . 220

Points on home mortgage loan . . . 2815.07, 3425

Pooled income funds . . . 515.02, 535, 5045

Portability of benefits of SEP . . . 915.02

Portability of distributions from qualified plan using rollover . . . 905.02

Portion trust . . . 1105.10, 1225.05

Post-mortem planning . . . 1501–1530

Pourover trust . . . 625, 645
  assets transferred into . . . 601
Power of appointment checklist . . . 1305.01
Power of appointment of testator . . . 1110.13
Power of appointment trust . . . 660.12, 1105.10, 1225.02, 1305
  for surviving spouse . . . 1225.02, 1525.01
Power of attorney for unmarried partner . . . 2505.07
Power to invade corpus . . . 660.02
Powers of appointment . . . 1301–1305.02
  contingent . . . 1305
  exercising, considerations for . . . 1305.02
  lapse as release of . . . 1305
  general and special . . . 660.12, 1305–1305.02
  gift of life estate with general . . . 405.02
  as object of disclaimer . . . 1525.01
  for surviving spouse in power of appointment trust . . . 1225.02, 1525.01
  for survivor, in QTIP . . . 1225
Precatory language in will . . . 1105
Premarital agreement . . . 2405–2405.13
  alimony provisions in, challenges to . . . 2405.03
  breach of . . . 2405.13
  claims against transferee's estate based on . . . 2405.10
  claims against transferor's estate based on . . . 2405.09
  community and separate property rights and obligations coverage in . . . 2405.05
  disclosure of income and property for . . . 2405.01
  estate tax consequences of . . . 2405.08, 2410.04
  gift tax consequences of . . . 2405.07, 2410.04
  governing law coverage in . . . 2405.04
  income tax consequences of . . . 2405.06, 2410.04
  irrevocable trust with life interest to spouse for transfers in . . . 2405.12
  release of support obligations in . . . 2405.01
  retirement benefits in . . . 2405.11
  structuring . . . 2405.12
  for subsequent marriage . . . 2410.03
  validity test of . . . 2405.01
Premium-only plans (POP). *See* **Cafeteria plans for employee benefits**
Premiums, life insurance. *See* **Insurance premiums**
Prenuptial agreement. *See* **Premarital agreement**
Prepayment risk of mortgage-backed securities . . . 3150.03–.05
Presumption of death . . . 2410.01
Primary insurance amount (PIA)
  formula . . . 3525
  table listing, by age . . . 3525.04
Principal residence. *See* **Personal residence**
Principal of trust
  power of beneficiary to withdraw . . . 660.03
  use of . . . 660.02
Private annuity . . . 810–810.06
  benefits of . . . 810
  factors to consider in setting up . . . 810.01
  to remove farm property from farmer's estate . . . 2210.06
  sale of sole proprietorship in exchange for . . . 2110.03
  to split income with family members . . . 3215
Private charities . . . 505.01
Privileged and underprivileged status of professionals . . . 1701–1705, 1725
Probate
  costs of . . . 101, 430.01, 1005, 1005.03
  disadvantages of . . . 625
  double, avoiding . . . 1105.15
  gift of life insurance as avoiding . . . 525
  joint tenancies as avoiding . . . 310, 315.02
  lifetime gifts as avoiding . . . 401
  property disposed of outside of . . . 1101
  trusts as avoiding . . . 601, 625, 630, 735, 735.01
Probate estate
  decision about insurance beneficiary affecting inclusion of proceeds in . . . 730
  in a different state from revocable trust . . . 630
  value of gifts made within three years of death not includible in . . . 430.01
Professionals
  balancing interests of different . . . 1720.13
  as business people . . . 1725
  corporate and noncorporate practices of . . . 1715–1715.03
  double taxation of . . . 1720.10
  ethics of profit-sharing arrangements for . . . 1720.15
  financial and estate planning issues for shareholders who are . . . 1725–1725.04
  planning for . . . 1701–1730
  problems and pitfalls in corporate operation for . . . 1720–1720.16
  as shareholder in professional corporation . . . 1725–1725.04
  side businesses of . . . 1710
  social security taxes on . . . 1720.12
  special issues for . . . 1705
  withdrawal or expulsion from practice of . . . 1730
Professional practice
  buying and selling . . . 1705
  corporate v. noncorporate . . . 1715–1715.03
  incorporated, side businesses as subsidiaries of . . . 1710
Profit-sharing plans . . . 920–920.02
  benefits of defined benefit plans compared with . . . 930
  distribution in employer stock from . . . 920
  early withdrawal penalty for . . . 920.01
  incidental insurance with . . . 920.02
  increasing effectiveness of . . . 920.01
  postponing distributions from . . . 3305.01
  tax advantages of . . . 920
Promissory note, charitable contribution in form of . . . 505.06
Property divisions in divorce settlement . . . 2435.01
Property, lifetime gift of
  appreciated . . . 410.01
  bargain-sale . . . 410.06
  cash gift v. . . . 410
  factors affecting selection of . . . 410.01
  growth potential of . . . 410.01
  high income-producing . . . 410.01, 3305.01
  income tax basis rules for . . . 410.02
  net gift technique for . . . 410.07
  not readily subject to controlled testamentary disposition . . . 410.01
  not to be sold . . . 410.01
  ongoing program for . . . 410.04
  property with low gift tax value and high estate tax value as optimal . . . 410.01, 410.04
  to spouse . . . 410.03
  timing strategies for . . . 410.05
  types of . . . 410.01
Property settlements following divorce. *See* **Divorce settlement**
Property taxes prepaid in previous year to accelerate deductions . . . 3305.04

Propstra, J. **discount in valuing real estate in** . . . 325.01
Prudent investor rule (UPIA) . . . 1105.16
Prudent man rule, UPIA as change to . . . 1105.16
PS58 cost of life insurance . . . 701.02, 705.02
Public charities . . . 505.01
Public Company Accounting Oversight Board . . . 3101

Q

QTIP trust . . . 1210.01, 1225–1225.01, 2410.02
property in transfers from . . . 2705.10
severed using fractional amounts . . . 2705.10
Qualified adoption expenses . . . 3450.01–.02
Qualified appraisal of property for large gifts . . . 505.04, 505.05
Qualified cash or deferred 401(k) arrangements . . . 1605.01
Qualified conservation contribution . . . 535.01, 535.03
Qualified conservation easement . . . 535.03
Qualified disclaimers, rules for . . . 415
Qualified domestic relations order (QDRO)
interest in qualified plan part of . . . 325.02, 905.02
no premature withdrawal penalty for funds distributed under . . . 905.02
retirement benefits divided under . . . 2445
Qualified domestic trusts (QDOTs) . . . 1230–1230.04
conditions for . . . 1230
estate tax on . . . 1230.03
protective election for . . . 1230.01
security rules for . . . 1230.04
Qualified education loans . . . 3001, 3015–3015.02
deduction limits for interest on . . . 3015.01
interest paid as deduction for . . . 3015
phaseout of deduction for . . . 3015.02
Qualified employee benefit plan
pourover trust to receive benefits from . . . 645
property rights in community property state for . . . 325.02
Qualified enterprise zone facility bonds . . . 3110
Qualified family-owned business deduction . . . 315.02
deducted from gross estate . . . 405.02
for farms and ranches . . . 2205
Qualified heir
defined . . . 2110.05, 2210.01
real property having special use valuation passing to . . . 2210.01
Qualified higher education expenses
defined . . . 3010.01
education IRA withdrawals to pay . . . 3020.03
no early withdrawal penalty for IRA distributions to pay . . . 905.02
qualified state tuition savings programs to pay . . . 3010
U.S. savings bonds to pay . . . 410.01, 3001, 3010.03, 3301.02
Qualified interest rules for grantor trust . . . 2315.01
Qualified long-term care services . . . 3420.01
Qualified payment defined . . . 2305.05
Qualified payment right . . . 2305.02–.03
Qualified pension plans . . . 1605.01, 1610.01
Qualified personal residence trust (QPRT) . . . 2315.03
Qualified plans. *See* **Qualified retirement plans**
Qualified plan benefits, rollover of . . . 1610.01, 1610.03
Qualified profit-sharing plans . . . 1610.01
Qualified real estate used in farming . . . 2210.01
Qualified replacement property following involuntary conversion . . . 3101.01
Qualified residence interest
converting personal interest to . . . 3325.04
deduction of home mortgage interest for, maximum . . . 2815, 3425
for interest paid by estate . . . 1515.06
for vacation home debt . . . 2835, 2835.02
Qualified retirement plan trusts as S corporation shareholders . . . 1945.02
Qualified retirement plans. *See also* **individual types**
as available to partners . . . 2001.01
beneficiary for, selecting . . . 905.02
borrowing from . . . 940
ceilings on benefits and contributions under Code Sec. 415 for . . . 905.01
cost-of-living adjustments to . . . 5005
distributions from . . . 905.02, 940, 2505.08
estate planning factors for . . . 955–955.03
fundamental aspects of . . . 905.01
funds left to beneficiaries from . . . 905.02
higher education funded with withdrawals from . . . 3001
as largest employee benefit . . . 901
life insurance to fund . . . 1725.02
limited deductibility of IRA contributions for participants in . . . 915.01
participation in and eligibility for . . . 905.01
post-mortem beneficiary change for . . . 905.02
postponing income by increasing contributions to . . . 3305.01
premature withdrawal penalty for . . . 905.02
rules for . . . 905–905.02
termination of . . . 905.01
top-heavy . . . 905.01
vesting in . . . 905.01
voluntary contributions to, AGI reduction using . . . 3325.01
Qualified scholarships for higher education excluded from income . . . 3001
Qualified small business stock
capital gains exclusion for . . . 3125–3125.08
rollover of gain on sale of . . . 3125.08
sale of . . . 1805.01
Qualified state tuition programs . . . 3001, 3010–3010.04
contributions exceeding $11,000 treated as if made ratably over five years for . . . 3010.04
education U.S. savings bonds used with . . . 3010.03
estate and gift tax consequences of . . . 3010.04
interaction with Hope and lifetime learning credits of . . . 3010.02
qualified higher education expenses for payment by . . . 3010–3010.01
Qualified subchapter S trust, S corporation as shareholder of . . . 605.06, 1945.02
Qualified terminable interest property (QTIP)
annuities qualifying as . . . 405.02, 1210
election by executor for . . . 1210.01, 1225.01, 1520.01
election of, IRS nullification of . . . 1210
exception to terminable interest rule of . . . 405.02, 735, 750.02, 1530

Qualified terminable interest property (QTIP)—continued
income interest property of . . . 1005.02
marital deduction for value of . . . 515.02, 1105.10, 1405
for payment of death taxes, right of recovery waived for . . . 1105.14
qualifying for . . . 1210
to reduce risk of loss in gift . . . 405.02
regulations for . . . 1210.02
reverse election for . . . 2705.10
for surviving spouse in residence . . . 1105.05
transfers of terminable interests considered . . . 405.02

Qualified transportation fringe benefits . . . 985.05

Qualifying life income trust. *See* **QTIP trust**

Qualifying marital bequests, comparison of . . . 1210

Questionnaire for client information, sample . . . 215

***Quid pro quo* contributions to charities** . . . 505, 505.01, 3415.02

R

Ranch property, planning for . . . 2201–2225

Real estate
at risk rules applicable to . . . 3180.01
as both land and improvements . . . 1105.05
business, valuation of . . . 1940.07, 2030
demand for . . . 3180.02
disclaiming joint interest in . . . 1525.01
form for recording . . . 1125
gift for conservation purposes of . . . 501.01, 535.01
gifts of . . . 410.01
gifts to trust for children of . . . 1905
installment sales of nonfarm . . . 3101.01
investing in . . . 3180–3180.04
kept out of closely held corporation assets . . . 1905, 1910.02
powers specified in will over . . . 1110.18
rental . . . *See* Rental property
tax rate for depreciable . . . 3101.02
used by professional to develop gift program . . . 1725

Real estate agent, buyer's v. seller's . . . 2805.07

Real estate investment trusts (REITs) . . . 3180.04

Real estate taxes as itemized deduction . . . 2801, 2815.01

Real estate valuation . . . 325.01, 1940.07, 2030, 2110.35

Recapitalization of closely held corporation . . . 1901.02
reasons for . . . 1910.01, 1915.03, 1930
results of . . . 1915.02
rules for valuing transfers of interests in . . . 1910

Refinancing personal residence . . . 2815.07

Refund for bad debts or losses, statute of limitations for . . . 1505.07

Rehabilitation credits . . . 3180.01

Religious services, provisions in will for . . . 1110.05

Remainder interest of property
in charitable remainder trusts . . . 515.01
contingent, gift tax exclusions for . . . 660.04
gift of . . . 410.01, 501.01
joint purchase as acquisition by holder of term interest followed by transfer of . . . 2315.05
left in trust . . . 310.04
valuation of pooled income fund . . . 515.02

Remarriage, spouse's . . . 210.07
child support following . . . 2430
joint ownership as ruling out post-mortem control over property in cases of . . . 310
terminating income interest upon . . . 1225.04

Rental property
conversion of home to be sold at loss to . . . 2820.09
held for rental income v. appreciation . . . 3101.02
suspended passive activity losses (PALs) from . . . 3180.01

Report of financial counselor for executive's financial and estate plan
analysis of existing plan for . . . 1620.02
basic data for . . . 1620.01
budget of family analyzed in . . . 1620.09
comparing old plan and new in . . . 1620.07
general benefits for . . . 1620.05
general recommendations for . . . 1620.03
investments review in . . . 1620.08
life insurance for . . . 1620.06
stock options and company stock in . . . 1620.04

Required minimum distributions of retirement benefits . . . 905.02, 915.01, 915.03

Residual interests, transfers of . . . 2305.01

Residuary bequests . . . 1105.04, 1110.11

Residuary legatee's interest terminated when estate closes . . . 1915.04

Residuary unified credit trust . . . 1225

Restatement (Second) of Trusts (American Law Institute) . . . 1105.16

Restatement (Third) of Trusts (American Law Institute) . . . 1105.16

Retained rights
combined extraordinary and distribution . . . 2305.03
extraordinary payment rights as . . . 2305.02
retained distribution rights as . . . 2305.02
valuation rules for . . . 2305–2305.07

Retirement age, normal
for social security benefits . . . 3525.02
vesting in qualified plan triggered upon . . . 905.01

Retirement plans. *See* **Qualified retirement plans** *and* **individual types**

Return of capital not taxable as income . . . 3101.01

Revenue Reconciliation Act of 1993 (RRA '93)
liquidation of partnership interest under . . . 2015.01
repeal of special treatment of payments for unrealized receivables by . . . 2015.02

Reversionary interest. *See also* **Retained rights**
in any property given away during lifetime . . . 1005.02
in contractual death benefits . . . 1610.11
in death benefits . . . 950
in divorce trust property . . . 2425.05
in life insurance . . . 525.03, 715.01, 735.01
in property transferred under premarital agreement . . . 2405.08
in trust, grantor trust rules for . . . 405.05
in trust, less than five percent . . . 405.05, 605.02, 610

Revised Uniform Anatomical Gift Act . . . 1110.04

Revocable joint bank accounts . . . 315.01

Revocable living trust . . . 601, 625, 630
to provide for management of financial affairs of elderly or disabled . . . 2605, 2605.01

Revocable transfers of property in gross estate . . . 101

Revocable trusts
as alternative to joint ownership of property for survivor . . . 310
changes and adjustments possible for . . . 645, 660, 735
for child . . . 3210.03
for couples living together . . . 2505.04
limitations and disadvantages of . . . 310
probate avoided using . . . 625
to protect assets of elderly and disabled people . . . 2605
to qualify for Medicaid . . . 2605
revocation or revision of . . . 110, 735
settlor allowed to retain control over and use property in . . . 310

Risk for investments
company . . . 3170.03
default . . . 3160.02
economic . . . 3101, 3101.03
market . . . 3170.03
prepayment . . . 3150.03–.06
reinvestment . . . 3160.03

Rollover
of education IRA balance to family member or same beneficiary . . . 3020.06–.07
of gain on investment in specialized small business investment company . . . 3130.02
of gain on sales of qualified small business stock . . . 3125.08
of qualified plan benefits . . . 905.02, 915.01, 1610.01, 1610.03, 2445

***Rosen* decision about present income interest . . .** 615

Roth IRA
AGI ceiling for contributing to . . . 915.04, 1610.01, 3301.02
contribution to, in addition to employer SEP contributions . . . 1610.04
contributions after age 70-1/2 to . . . 915.04
holding period for . . . 915.04
no required minimum distributions from . . . 915.04
pros and cons of . . . 915.04
for sole proprietors and their employees . . . 2105.02
tax-free distributions from . . . 915.04, 1610.01
traditional IRA funds rolled over into . . . 915.04

S

S corporation election . . . 1945–1945.03
advantages of . . . 1945
as alternative to sole proprietorship entity . . . 2105.01
by financial institutions . . . 1945.03
for farm operations . . . 2210.08
following termination of S corporation status, rules for . . . 1945.02
pass-through of income and loss of . . . 2040.01
single class of stock permitted under . . . 2210.08, 3230
time of . . . 1945.03

S corporation stock
American Jobs Creation Act of 2004 and suspended losses from . . . 2435.01
gifts of . . . 1945.01
lifetime gifts of, to pass through corporate income to donees . . . 410.01
in trust treated separately for income taxation . . . 605.06

S corporations
abuses of ESOPs by . . . 1605.01
debt instruments used by . . . 1945.01
distributions from . . . 1605.01, 1805.03
double taxation of C corporations avoided by . . . 1905

S corporations—continued
foreign source income of . . . 1945.01
fringe benefits to employees owning more than 2 percent of . . . 1945
limited deduction for losses of . . . 1805.03
maximum of 100 shareholders in . . . 1945, 1945.01, 2001
nonvoting common stock in . . . 1945.01
one class of stock in . . . 2001
partnership business form compared with . . . 2001
pass through of income of . . . 1805
passive income of . . . 1945.01
planning opportunities for . . . 1945.01
qualified subsidiaries of . . . 1805.03
as shareholders, types of trust not nullifying election for . . . 630, 1945.02
single class of stock required for . . . 1905
subsidiaries allowed for . . . 1945.03
tax advantages of . . . 1805.03
tax year of . . . 1805.07, 1945
termination of . . . 1945.01
use of trusts by . . . 605.06
voting v. nonvoting stock in . . . 2001

Safe deposit boxes, joint . . . 315.04

Sale of property
to permit equal division among beneficiaries . . . 1105.07
prior to contribution of loss property . . . 505.07
tax law changes affecting . . . 110

Sale or exchange treatment of stock redemption . . . 1915–1915.05

Sale-leasebacks of closely held corporation real estate and machinery . . . 1910.02

Sales and use taxes . . . 3101.01

Sarbanes-Oxley Act of 2002 regulations . . . 3101, 1605.01

SARSEP as SEP through salary reduction . . . 915.02, 1610.04

Savings accounts, joint
benefits of . . . 315.01
disadvantages of . . . 315.01
income tax consequences of . . . 310.03
survivorship feature of . . . 315.01

Savings Association Insurance Fund (SAIF) . . . 2810.02

Savings clauses for gifts . . . 405.02

Savings plans . . . 935

***Schelberg, Estate of W.* decision about death benefits . . .** 950

Scenic easements, contributions to government of . . . 3415.05

Schools, visit before purchasing personal residence to neighborhood . . . 2805.03

SEC Rule 10b-5 . . . 3101.04

Securities
gifted at low points in stock market . . . 410.05
as good lifetime gifts . . . 410.01
held in investor's rather than street name . . . 3185.03–.04
investments in . . . 3120–3120.02
joint ownership of . . . 315.05
laws prohibiting minors from registering . . . 425
restriction of charitable remainder trusts to tax-exempt . . . 515.01
safety of . . . 3145.01, 3150.02
short selling . . . 3120.02
sold to family member . . . 3315.03
U.S. government . . . 3135–3135.02
valuation of . . . 505.03

Securities Act of 1933 . . . 3101.04
Securities Exchange Act of 1934 . . . 3101.04
Securities Investor Protection Corporation (SIPC)
insurance protection by . . . 315.05
protection and claims against brokers of . . . 3185, 3185.03–.04
Securities laws, investments and . . . 3101.04
Self-employed professionals, health coverage for . . . 1715.02
Self-employment income of farmers . . . 2215
Self-employment tax . . . 1715.02, 5001.06
for partners . . . 2001
Selling expenses of estate . . . 1515.09
Semipublic charities . . . 505.01
Senior family member, advantages and disadvantages of joint bank account for . . . 315.01
Separate returns for married individuals
to maximize deduction of medical expenses . . . 3420.01
tax on social security benefits for taxpayers filing . . . 3505.03
tax rate schedule for . . . 5001.01
Separated spouses
community income of . . . 2420.01
living apart required for alimony . . . 2425.01
Separation instrument, alimony under . . . 2425–2425.01
Series E, EE, and I U.S. savings bonds. ***See*** **U.S. savings bonds**
Settlement options of life insurance . . . 701
Seven-payment test for financed insurance . . . 745
Severance of joint interests, unilateral v. mutual consent . . . 305
Severance pay for departing corporate shareholder . . . 1725.01
Sexual orientation, laws prohibiting discrimination based on . . . 2505.02
Shareholder-professionals, financial and estate planning considerations for . . . 1725–1725.04
Short-selling stocks . . . 3120.02, 3185.02
Short-term trust, uses of . . . 605.01, 605.07
Side businesses of professionals . . . 1710
SIMPLE (savings incentive match plans for employers) plans
ceiling for number of employees for . . . 915.03, 925.02
comparison of IRA and 401(k) types of . . . 925.02
compensation amount used in . . . 5005
early withdrawal penalty for . . . 915.03
employer matching contributions to . . . 915.03, 925.02
as IRA . . . 915.03
maximum annual contributions to . . . 915.03, 925.02
as part of 401(k) arrangement . . . 925.02
to reduce AGI . . . 3325.01, 3405.05
Simple trusts . . . 605.03
Simplified employee pension (SEP) plan
advantages of . . . 915.02
cap on income in determining contributions or benefits of . . . 905.01
compensation amount used in . . . 5005
contributions after age 70-½ to . . . 915.02
contributions rate for . . . 5001.06
disadvantages of . . . 915.02
Simplified employee pension (SEP) plan—continued
distributions from . . . 905.02
employer deductions for contributions to . . . 915.02
employer required coverage of employees using . . . 915.02
employment tax affecting contributions to . . . 3445
limited deductibility of IRA contributions for participants in . . . 915.01
to reduce AGI . . . 3325.01, 3405.05
salary reduction . . . 915.02
for self-employed individuals . . . 3315.07
as sole proprietor's tax shelter . . . 2105.02
as supplement to profit-sharing plan . . . 920.01
using IRA . . . 915.02, 1610.04
vesting in . . . 915.02
Simultaneous death of joint tenants . . . 310, 310.01
Single-category averaging method for determining basis in mutual fund . . . 3140.06
Single-premium life insurance . . . 525.01, 705.02
Sinking fund for uninsurable corporate stockholders . . . 1935
Skip persons, direct skips to . . . 2705.02
Small Business Investment Company Act of 1958 . . . 3130
Small Business Job Protection Act of 1996
leased employees defined in . . . 930
lump-sum distribution taxation change under . . . 1610.01
Small business stock, 50-percent exclusion from gross income for gains on . . . 105, 3101.02
Small corporations not subject to AMT . . . 1805.01
Smith, Estate of C.**, decision for equalization of tax . . .** 1240.02
Smith, Estate of, F.**, decision on taxation of lifetime gifts . . .** 405.02, 1005
Snyder, E.W.**, indirect gift decision of . . .** 415
Social security
employer contributions to . . . 905.01
FICA tax for HI and . . . 5001.07
Social Security Act (SSA), common law marriage recognized under . . . 2410.01
Social Security Administration, checking status of benefits with . . . 3525.03
Social security benefits . . . 3505–3505.08
avoiding loss of . . . 3530.01–3530.02
computation of . . . 3525
cost-of-living adjustment (COLA) to . . . 3525.01
currently insured and fully ensured status for . . . 3525.02
deciding age to begin to receive . . . 3525.04
delayed retirement credit for . . . 3525.02
first and second tier inclusion rules for gross income of . . . 3505–3505.02, 3505.07
gross income for determining tax on . . . 3101.01
included in income . . . 3301.02, 3505.06, 3505.09
integrated pension plan using base of . . . 930
in lieu of workers' compensation benefits . . . 3505.10
lump-sum election for . . . 3505.09
no longer lost because of compensation . . . 3325.06
part-time employment of people receiving . . . 3505.06
practice aid for calculating taxable portion of . . . 3505.07
reduced rates for . . . 3505.06
self-employment to avoid loss of . . . 3530.02
strategies to reduce exposure for tax on . . . 3505.08
table of insured state required for various . . . 3520.01
tax planning for . . . 3505–3505.08
taxes paid on . . . 3505–3505.06

Social security benefits—continued
types of . . . *See also* individual benefits 3520–3520.02.
working while receiving . . . 3505.06, 3530.01

Social security tax
maximum wage/earnings base applied to . . . 3445
on professional corporation . . . 1720.12

Soil conservation improvements, power to make . . . 2210.04

Sole ownership of property, joint ownership compared to . . . 310

Sole proprietor
disability insurance for . . . 2105.03
disposition of business upon retirement or death of . . . 2110–2110.07
executor continuing business of . . . 2110.01
family continuing business of . . . 2110.02
goodwill of . . . 2110
income and tax factors for . . . 1805, 1805.06
disadvantages as business entity of . . . 2101, 2105.01
life insurance to fund purchase of business interest of . . . 2110.03
liquidation value of . . . 2110.01
nontax factors for . . . 1810
questions of business entity for . . . 2105.01
role of life insurance in planning for . . . 701, 2110
planning for . . . 2101–2110.07
retirement of . . . 2110.03
sale to children of . . . 2110.03
sale to employees of . . . 2110.03
splitting income with family members from . . . 3230
tax shelter for . . . 2105.02

***Soliman, N.E.*, decision about home office** . . . 2830

Special (supplemental) needs trust . . . 2605.01

Special use valuation
of farm real estate . . . 2210.01–.02, 2801
of personal residence . . . 2801
qualified conservation easement as not preventing . . . 535.03

Specialized small business investment company (SSBIC)
deferral for investment in . . . 3130–3130.02
stock of, tax on gain of . . . 3135.01

Spendthrift provision in trust preventing access to interest by creditors . . . 601, 660.06

Split-dollar life insurance policy . . . 705.02, 1605.01

Split-gift concept . . . 310.02, 510.02, 515.01
to double unified credit and annual gift exclusion . . . 410.05, 720.01
tax and unified credit savings using . . . 405.03

Split-interest trusts, charitable contributions of appreciated property through . . . 3101.02

Spousal joint and survivor annuity . . . 405.02, 520

Spousal life insurance . . . 705.02

Spousal remainder trusts . . . 405.01, 405.05, 605.01, 605.07

Spouses. *See also* **Separated spouses** *and* **Surviving spouse**
capital gains and losses of . . . 3315.04
community, under Medicaid . . . 3515.01
consent required for qualified beneficiary other than . . . 955.01
counted as one partner in partnership . . . 2035
counted as one shareholder in S corporation . . . 2001
deferred compensation bequeathed to . . . 1610.08
disinheritance of . . . 1110.17
earnings of, as community property . . . 325.01
estate of first to die between . . . 1005.02

Spouses—continued
exclusion from gift taxes for . . . 310.02
family limited partnerships created by . . . 2010.03
grantors as holding powers or interests of their . . . 605.02
interest in retirement benefits under federal law for . . . 2405.11
joint ownership of farm or ranch property between . . . 2210.03
lifetime gifts to . . . 405.02, 410.01, 410.03
living apart. *See* Separated spouses
named as beneficiary of life insurance . . . 730
nonalimony treatment of payments between . . . 2425.03
non-U.S. citizen, gift-tax exclusion for . . . 405.01, 405.02
of participants receiving eligible rollovers from qualified plan, direct transfer by . . . 1610.03
property owned by . . . 315.02
second-to-die insurance for . . . 1215.03
split gifts to charities and . . . 510.02, 515.01
transfer of education IRA interest to . . . 3020.07
transfer of insurance to . . . 1215.02
trusts established to benefit . . . 601

Springing power of attorney 2605, 2605.01, 2905.02

Sprinkling trust . . . 660.01

Standard deduction
impact of dependency exemption on . . . 3405.03
for single and joint filers . . . 2415.04, 5001.02

Standby trust . . . 601, 625, 635

Start-up companies, corporate loss deductions for . . . 1945

State death taxes . . . 705.02, 1215.08. *See also* **Death taxes** *and* **Estate taxes**
allocation by testator for estate to pay . . . 1105.14
apportionment acts by states for . . . 1105.14
credit against taxable estate of paid . . . 1005.01
inclusion of property to be gifted in gross estate resulting in . . . 430.01
irrevocable insurance trust to avoid . . . 735.01
property exemptions for homestead or household goods from some . . . 1005.02
will provision for payments of . . . 1110.07

State obligations, income exempt for federal income tax from . . . 3101.01

State rule against perpetuities of trusts . . . 601, 630

State taxes generally deductible from federal tax under Code Sec. 164 . . . 3101.01

Statutory fraud . . . 3101.04

Statutory timesharing arrangements . . . 330

Step transaction doctrine . . . 425.01

Stepchildren, earned income credit for . . . 3410.03

Stock appreciation rights (SARs) . . . 1605.01

Stock basis . . . 3315.05

Stock bonus plans for executives . . . 1610.02

Stock index options . . . 3170.03

Stock market, lifetime gifts of securities timed for low points in . . . 410.05

Stock redemption agreement . . . 1935

Stock redemptions from closely held corporations . . . 1915–1915.06, 1935

Stock trades. *See also* **Brokerage accounts**
on margin . . . 3185.02
protection for investors in . . . 3185, 3185.03–.04
street names for . . . 3185.03

Stock valuation for closely held corporations . . . 101, 1901.01, 1901.02, 1940–1940.07

Straight annuities . . . 805

Straight growth mutual funds . . . 3140.03

Street name for securities left in broker's custody . . . 3185.03

Subscriptions to publications as fringe benefit . . . 985.03

Subtraction method of valuation . . . 2305.04

Supplemental (special) needs trusts . . . 2605.01

Surviving spouse
actively managing farm to satisfy material participation requirement for special use valuation . . . 2210.01
alien . . . 1230–1230.04
business interest of sole proprietor as bequest to . . . 2110.02
bypass trust to provide life income while bequeathing part of owner's property to . . . 640
common disaster provision for . . . 1240.01
with dependent child, filing status of . . . 1505.01
disclaimer by . . . 1525.01
disclaimer used in favor of . . . 1235, 1525.01
as dower or courtesy or statutory substitute, value of interest of . . . 1005.02
election against will by . . . 1525.02
election of, applied to pourover trust . . . 645
equalization provisions for . . . 410.03, 1240.02
estate size of, decreasing . . . 810
as executor . . . 1225.01, 1505.02
half of jointly held property passing to . . . 2210.03
interest in personal residence of . . . 1105.05
IRA inherited by, treatment as survivor's own IRA of . . . 915.01
joint return tax rates used for two years after spouse's death by . . . 1505.01, 1505.06
joint tax return for decedent and . . . 1505.01
life insurance to cover loss of marital deduction for . . . 740, 750.02
management powers for farm or ranch given to . . . 2210.04
possible remarriage of . . . 735, 1301
power of appointment for . . . 1301
QTIP property treated as property of . . . 2705.10
QTIP trust to benefit . . . 1225.01
qualifying as . . . 1505.06
residue of estate to . . . 1105.07
right of election differences by state for . . . 630
rollover of lump-sum distribution from spouse's plan by . . . 905.02
of subsequent marriage, bequest to . . . 2410.05
surviving common disaster . . . 1240.01
survivor annuity paid to . . . 955.02
tax rates for . . . 5001.01
transfer exchange for private annuity to dispose of marital deduction property by . . . 810
trust to protect interest of . . . 1101, 1105.10
unified credit for . . . 1005
unlimited marital deduction to transfer entire estate to . . . 101

Survivors
ability to handle investment portfolio important for . . . 1301
attempts to change executor's plan by . . . 1501
community property in trust for . . . 325.01
gift of future interests to . . . 520
interest in decedent's share of joint account for . . . 1525.01
power of appointment for . . . 1225, 1225.02
proving contributions of . . . 310.01
purchase of partnership interest by . . . 2020.01–.02
qualifying as surviving spouse . . . 1505.06

Survivors—continued
taxation of, in joint tenancy . . . 310.04
voluntary death benefits to . . . 1610.12

Survivors benefits from Social Security Administration . . . 3520.01–.02

Survivorship
for marital deduction . . . 1240
will issues for order of death and . . . 1105.15, 1110.16

T

T. Hahn decision regarding joint tenancies . . . 315.02

Tangible personal property
form for recording . . . 1125
long-term gain for contributions of . . . 505.09
sold from residue of estate . . . 1105.03
taxation of legatees for receiving decedent's . . . 1105.02
will provisions for disposing of . . . 1105.03, 1110.09

Target plan as type of pension plan . . . 930, 930.02

Tax advice expenses
deductible as miscellaneous itemized deduction . . . 3435
incident to divorce, deductible for personal . . . 2440

Tax basis of assets . . . 210.05

Tax Court cases regarding joint returns for divorcing spouses . . . 2420.03

Tax credits . . . 3410–3410.04 *See also* **individual credits**

Tax deferral to following year, planning for . . . 3301

Tax equalization clause to minimize aggregate estate tax . . . 410.03, 1240.02

Tax incentives for higher education . . . 3001–3020.07

Tax Increase Prevention and Reconciliation Act (TIPRA) . . . 105
capital gain property and . . . 505.09
IRAs and . . . 915.04
kiddie tax and . . . 405.01, 2420.02

Tax law changes . . . 110, 3301.01

Tax Reform Act of 1984, alternate valuation under . . . 1520.02

Tax Reform Act of 1986, depreciation revised under . . . 3180.01

Tax shelter
life insurance as . . . 701, 750.01
professional corporation as . . . 1715
for sole proprietor . . . 2105.02

Tax year
accelerating income to current . . . 3301–3301.02, 3305.02–3305.03
of corporation . . . 1720.03
deferring income to following . . . 3301–3301.02
of estate, choice of . . . 1515.11, 2025
of partner . . . 2020.01
of partnership . . . 2001
postponing income to following . . . 3301–3301.02, 3305.04
of trust, calendar . . . 605.01, 1515.11

Tax-free transfer of qualified stock . . . 3125.05

Taxable distributions from trust to skip person . . . 2705.02

Taxable estate
costs of disputing tax assessment deductible from . . . 101
credits applied to . . . 1005–1005.01
as difference between gross estate and allowable deductions . . . 1005
income tax rates for . . . 1510.01

Taxable income, leveling out . . . 3301

Taxable termination of interest in property . . . 2705.02

Taxpayer identification number (TIN) of charity donor . . . 505.04

Taxpayer Relief Act of 1997 . . . 3301.01
empowerment zone bonds created by . . . 3110
higher education incentives under . . . 3001
revaluation of lifetime gifts under . . . 405.02
rules for accelerated charitable remainder trusts in . . . 515.01
rules for principal place of business deductions for home office in . . . 2830
"short-against-the-box" technique largely eliminated by . . . 3185.02

Teamwork for financial and estate planning . . . 105

Tenancy by entirety with right of survivorship . . . 301
document check of items held in . . . 305
estate tax consequences of . . . 315.02
as form of joint ownership . . . 310
for property of spouses acquired by gift or inheritance . . . 310.01, 310.02

Tenancy in common
conversion to, benefits of . . . 310.04
document check of items held in . . . 305
gift from . . . 320
income-shifting using . . . 320

Term life insurance . . . 701.01, 701.02, 705.01
gifting . . . 725
group . . . 710, 1605.01
for partners to enable buy-out or liquidation of partnership interest upon death . . . 2015.05

Termination of joint tenancies . . . 310.04

Testamentary trust . . . 530, 625
alternate or successor trustee important for . . . 665.03
changes in circumstances affecting . . . 660
as created by will . . . 601, 640
fees for . . . 665
look-through treatment for beneficiaries of . . . 905.02
remainder interest in . . . 535

Testator
domicile of . . . 1110.02
forms for use of, sample blank . . . 1125
identity in will of . . . 1110.01
revocation of prior wills and codicils by . . . 1110.03

Theft losses, AGI floor for deducting . . . 3205.02

Thrift and savings plans . . . 935

Thrift institutions, IRAs offered by . . . 915.01

Time span ownership (TSO) of property . . . 330

Timesharing of property . . . 330, 2815.06

Timing of payments from estate, date consideration in . . . 1515.08

TIPRA . . . 105
capital gain property and . . . 505.09
IRAs and . . . 915.04
kiddie tax and . . . 405.01, 2420.02

Totten trusts
for minor . . . 3210.04
for elderly or disabled people . . . 2605

Traditional IRA
contributions to, in addition to employer SEP contributions . . . 1610.04
for executives having qualified plan . . . 1610.01
general terms of . . . 915.01
limited deductibility of contributions to . . . 915.01
nondeductible contributions to, deferral of tax on earnings of . . . 915.01
rollovers from, to Roth IRA . . . 915.04
rollovers to . . . 1610.01, 1610.03

Transfer of all incidents of ownership of insurance proceeds . . . 715, 715.01, 1725.03

Transfer of property at death
costs of . . . 101, 1005–1005.03
includable in estate . . . 1001–1005.03
testamentary, to grandchildren . . . 310.01

Transfer of property by premarital agreement . . . 2405

Transfer of property in exchange for private annuity . . . 810

Transfer of property, lifetime . . . 1001, 1005

Transfer of property to charity in exchange for annuity . . . 501.01, 520

Transfer of property to corporation in exchange for more stock, tax-free . . . 1915.03

Transfer of property to partnership . . . 2001, 2005.02, 2010.06

Transfer of property to trust
describing assets in . . . 601
within three years of death as includible in gross estate . . . 610, 1005.03

Transfer of term interest in property not held in trust . . . 2315.04

Transfers of property within three years of death, value included in federal gross estate for all . . . 1005.03

Transit passes as fringe benefit . . . 985.05

Traveling as means of savings . . . 3105

Treasury bills (T-bills), notes, and bonds . . . 3135
acquisition discount of . . . 3135.01
long-term . . . 3160.03
as money market instruments . . . 3145
sales commissions on . . . 3160.03
tax treatment of . . . 3135.01, 3145.02

Triggering event for springing durable power of attorney . . . 2605.01

Trust income
conduit principle for distribution of . . . 605.03
decline in . . . 660.08
to pay insurance premiums . . . 735.01
payable to children of grantors . . . 1615
retained life or reversionary interest by settlor of . . . 610
spendthrift provisions to prevent assignment of . . . 601, 660.06
as taxable to settlor . . . 660.03, 665
used to discharge legal obligation of settlor or spouse . . . 605.02

Trust instrument
coordinated with will for revocable living trust . . . 630
drafted by lawyer . . . 601
provisions in . . . 601, 610.02, 620, 660–660.12, 2605.01

Trust throwback rules . . . 601

Trustees . . . 665–665.04
accepting appointment . . . 1225.05
as acting for insured in insurance trust . . . 735
corporate v. individual . . . 665.01–.02

Trustees—continued
fees paid to . . . 601, 630, 665–665.02, 735
for IRAs, banks or qualified people as . . . 915.01
management powers for farm or ranch given to . . . 2210.04
multiple . . . 660.07, 665.01, 665.02
named in trust . . . 601
naming alternate or successor . . . 601, 665.03
as parent substitute using income sprinkling clause . . . 660.01
powers of . . . 601, 665.04, 735.02, 1105.16, 1110.18
prudent investor rule for . . . 1105.16
replaced by grantor . . . 610.01
resignation of . . . 665.03
restrictions on investment types of . . . 515.01
selecting . . . 660.01, 665, 665.03, 1105.11
settlor as . . . 2605.01
successor or substitute, exemption of bond of . . . 601
to supply attributes missing in beneficiary . . . 1105.09

Trusts . . . 601–665. *See also* **individual types**
accumulated income taxable to . . . 605.01, 605.04, 615, 625, 640, 660, 660.11, 3210.07–.08
administration costs of . . . 605.01, 735
administration of. *See* Trustees
administrative powers over . . . *See also* Trustees 605.02.
analysis of existing . . . 1620.02
as beneficiaries of IRAs . . . 915.01
as beneficiaries of life insurance . . . 730, 735
for benefit of children . . . 420, 425, 425.04, 601, 720, 735, 1101, 1225.04, 1415, 3210.07, 3225
for benefit of settlor . . . 601
calendar year used by . . . 605.01, 1515.11
Code Sec. 2503(b), income distributed by . . . 425.04
Code Sec. 2503(c), income accumulation by . . . 425.04, 3210.07
community property in . . . 325.01
compared to other vehicles for gifts to minors . . . 425.04
compressed tax rates for . . . 405.01, 420, 425.01, 601, 605.01–.02, 625, 735.01, 3210.07–.08
costs of establishing and administering . . . 101, 735
created by will . . . 640
Crummey power for . . . 405.02, 615, 660.04, 735.02, 945.03, 1305
depressed assets placed in . . . 1510.02
for disabled or incompetent adult . . . 1105.09
disclaiming interest in . . . 1525.01
duration of . . . 601
estate borrowing from . . . 1510.03
estate taxes on . . . 610–610.02
estimated tax payments required for income tax from . . . 605.01
flexibility as important for . . . 660
gift taxes on . . . 615
gifts in . . . 415, 420
gifts to charity using . . . 501.01, 515–515.03, 530
income shifting to . . . 740
inflation- and recession-proofing . . . 660.08
influencing conduct of beneficiaries through . . . 660.09
to invest and distribute estate to surviving spouse and children . . . 1101
life insurance policy held by . . . 720, 735, 945.03, 2015.05
in marital deduction planning . . . 1225–1225.05
net worth of . . . 1940
as partners . . . 2005.01, 2105.01
power of appointment for . . . 610
power of revocation of . . . 605.02, 735
power to direct disposition of . . . 610
present interest of qualified heir in . . . 2110.05
principal of, use of . . . 660.02
provisions included in . . . 601, 620, 660–660.12, 1105.10

Trusts—continued
reformed to meet QDOT requirements . . . 1230.02
as S corporation shareholders . . . 630, 1945.02
settlor's safe harbors under Code Sec. 674 . . . 605.02
support of beneficiary using income of . . . 425.01
tax rate schedule for . . . 5001.01
tax rules for . . . 601
taxation of . . . 605.03–.04, 625, 735
termination of . . . 660.07
testamentary additions to . . . 645
transfers of interests in . . . 2315–2315.04
transfer of property without retaining life interest in . . . 310.04
types of . . . 620, 625
uses for . . . 410.04, 420, 620

Tuition credits or certificates for payment of higher education expenses . . . 3010

Tuition, unlimited gift tax exclusion for payment of . . . 405.02, 410.01, 3001

U

Undervaluation penalty for undervaluing property . . . 405.01

Underwriters for closely held stock transactions . . . 1940.03

Unearned income of children
kiddie tax on . . . 405.01, 405.05, 425.02, 425.03
transfers of property that generate little . . . 410.05

Unemployment insurance (FUTA) tax. *See* **Federal Unemployment Tax Act (FUTA) tax rate**

Unified credit
as alternative to marital deduction . . . 1001
annual $10,000 gift tax exclusion used with . . . 405.03
applicable exclusion amount for . . . 5010.01
calculating . . . 101
with community property in estate . . . 325.01
equivalent applicable exclusion for . . . 1215.01
exemption from estate taxes for many estates under . . . 105, 610
filing requirements for . . . 5010.01
in gift-leaseback of business property . . . 3225
lifetime gifts less urgent because of applicable . . . 410.04
in making gifts to children . . . 410.01, 410.02
in making gifts to unmarried partner . . . 2505.04
marital deduction used in conjunction with . . . 1615
maximum estate size and phaseout of . . . 1001, 1005, 5010.01
precluding use of . . . 2610.03
to reduce gift tax . . . 625, 1005
split gifts to double . . . 405.03, 720.01
stepped increases during future years of . . . 1001, 1005
table of phase-in amounts of . . . 405.02, 5010.01
table of phase-out amounts for . . . 5010
tax-free transfers to children or others using . . . 405.02
underfunded bequests for . . . 1525.01
used before gift tax is paid with net gift . . . 410.07
used to make lifetime gift with high appreciation potential . . . 405.04
for valuation of business real estate of sole proprietor . . . 2110.05
valuation of farm or ranch property for use of . . . 2210.01

Unified credit trust . . . 1225

Uniform Anatomical Gift Act . . . 1110.04

Uniform Gifts to Minors Act (UGMA) . . . 425.02, 3210.06

Uniform Lifetime Table for retirement benefit minimum distributions . . . 905.02
Uniform Limited Liability Company Act . . . 2040.02
Uniform Marital Property Act . . . 301, 325
Uniform Premarital Agreement Act, states adopting . . . 2405
Uniform Premium Table . . . 945.01
Uniform Probate Code . . . 625, 2605.02, 2610–2610.01
Uniform Prudent Investor Act (UPIA) (Uniform Law Commissioners) . . . 665.04, 1105.16
Uniform Simultaneous Death Act . . . 310.01, 1105.15, 1240.02
Uniform Testamentary Additions to Trust Act . . . 645
Uniform Transfers to Minors Act (UTMA) . . . 425.02, 3210.06
Unit investment trusts . . . 3145
Unit trusts of pooled mortgages . . . 3150.06
U.S. Court of Federal Claims, suing for refund in . . . 1940
U.S. government securities, advantages of investing in . . . 3135–3135.02. *See also* **individual types**
U.S. possessions taxes generally deductible from federal tax under Code Sec. 164 . . . 3101.01
U.S. savings bonds
co-ownership of . . . 315.03
deferring tax on interest of . . . 405.05
income tax benefits of purchasing . . . 310.03, 315.03
exclusion from gift tax of purchase of . . . 310.02
forms for recording . . . 1125
interest formula for . . . 3135.02
interest penalty upon redemption in less than five years of . . . 3135.02
lifetime gifts of . . . 410.01
minors deferring tax until maturity of . . . 3210.05
redeemed to pay college tuition, exclusion from income of . . . 410.01, 3001, 3010.03, 3301.02
reporting income on or increased value of . . . 1505.05, 2435.01
Series EE v. HH . . . 3135.02
Series I, interest and appreciation of . . . 315.03, 1505.05, 2435.01, 3135.02
U.S. Tax Court, challenge to stock share valuation in . . . 1940
U.S. Treasury STRIPS (Separate Trading of Registered Income and Principal Securities) for IRAs . . . 915.01
Universal life insurance policy . . . 705.02
Unmarried individuals, tax rate schedule for . . . 5001.01
Unrealized receivables
gain or loss attributable to inventory items and . . . 2015.02
RRA '93 rules for . . . 2015.01
Unreimbursed expenses as charitable contribution . . . 3415.07
Unwinding joint ownership . . . 310

V

Vacation homes
personal v. investment use of . . . 2835.01–.02
qualified residence interest for . . . 2835, 2835.02
sale of . . . 2835.02
Valuation date for estate assets
alternate . . . 410.02
selecting . . . 1520–1520.02
Valuation of annuities, life estates, and remainders . . . 5045
Valuation of business real estate . . . 1940.07, 2030
Valuation of conservation easement . . . 535.02
Valuation of family limited partnership interests . . . 2320
Valuation of farm . . . 2205, 2210.01
Valuation of partnership interest . . . 2015.03, 2015.04, 2020.01, 2030–2030.01
Valuation of preferred interests in corporations and partnerships . . . 2301–2305.07
Valuation of property contributions for charitable deductions . . . 505.03, 515.01
Valuation of qualified family-owned business . . . 2210.02
Valuation of retained rights . . . 2305–2305.07
Valuation of sole proprietorship . . . 2110.04
Valuation of stock for closely held corporation . . . 101, 1940–1940.07
four methods for . . . 1935
Valuation of used clothing, furniture, and other noncash gifts to charity . . . 3415.07
Valuation tables
of Code Sec. 7520 . . . 405.01
interest factor for charitable giving for . . . 501.02, 515.01
Values for assets provided by clients . . . 210.04
Vanishing premium life insurance policy . . . 705.02
Variable annuity
disadvantages of . . . 805, 805.02
mutual fund v. . . . 805.02
as tied to mutual fund . . . 805
Variable life insurance policy . . . 705.02
Variable universal life (Universal Life II) insurance . . . 705.02
Vesting
of beneficiary's interest in nontaxable gift transferred to trust . . . 2705.07
in ESOP . . . 910
in qualified retirement plans . . . 905.01
in SEP IRA . . . 915.02
in SIMPLE plan, immediate . . . 915.03, 925.02
Viatical settlement provider . . . 701.01, 710
Visitation laws . . . 2505.05
Voluntary death benefits . . . 1615.12
Voting trusts . . . 601
S corporation shareholders of . . . 605.06, 1945.02

W

Waiver of premiums for life insurance . . . 701.01
Wasting assets . . . 1930
Wealth, steps for increasing . . . 3105
Wheelchairs, donation to hospital of . . . 3415.04
***White, J.* reasonableness of estate administration expenses argued in** . . . 1005.03
Whole life insurance policy, conventional . . . 705.02
Widowed homeowners, ownership period of home by deceased spouse included for . . . 2820.07

Wills
abatement clause in . . . 1105.04
administration powers specified in . . . 1110.18
advantages of . . . 1101
analysis of existing . . . 1620.02
attestation of witnesses' signatures on . . . 1115.07
avoiding use of joint, mutual, and reciprocal . . . 1120
contest or settlement of . . . 1525.03
contribution of property for conservation purposes made by . . . 535.01
coordinated with trust instrument for revocable living trust . . . 630
date and place of execution of . . . 1115.05
declaration of . . . 1115.01
distribution of income in respect of decedent provided for in . . . 2025
effect for jointly owned property and marital deduction of . . . 305
equalization clause containing six-month survivorship clause in . . . 1240.02
execution of . . . 1115–1115.07
for executive, considerations for drafting . . . 1625.01
family income during administration of . . . 1105.01
forms for . . . 1110
guardian nominated in . . . 1415
instructions outside of . . . 1125
invalidated by technical errors . . . 1115.07
joint tenancies as no substitute for . . . 310
legal language of . . . 1125
living. *See* Living will
numbered pages used in . . . 1115.06
order of death important for executing terms of . . . 1105.15, 1110.12
pourover trust receiving funds established by . . . 645
provisions and components of . . . 1110.01–.19, 1525.11, 2410.05, 2505.03, 2705.10
as public documents . . . 625, 1125
questions of interpretation of . . . 1105
revoking or revising . . . 110, 1110.03
separate provisions for tangible personal property disposition within . . . 1105.03
signature or testator's mark on . . . 1115.02
state law effects on . . . 1625.01
surviving spouse election against . . . 1525.02
trusts created by . . . 640, 1510.02
two, for executives residing in foreign country . . . 1625.03
witnesses to execution of . . . 1115.03–.04, 1115.07

Withdrawals of employee contributions to profit-sharing plans . . . 1610.01

Withholding on qualified plan distributions . . . 905.02

Workers' compensation benefits, Social Security benefits in lieu of . . . 3505.10

Working condition fringe benefits . . . 985.03, 1605.01

Working Families Tax Relief Act of 2004 . . . 3420.02

Y

Year-end lifetime gifts to use entire gift tax exclusion . . . 410.05

Year-end tax planning . . . 3301–3320
AGI altered as part of . . . 3301.02
AMT considerations in . . . 3301.03
for estimated taxes . . . 3320
ideas for . . . 3315–3315.07
impact of tax legislation on . . . 3301.01
methods to adjust income and deductions for . . . 3305–3305.04
for securities transactions . . . 3310

Yield to maturity
of tax-exempt obligations . . . 3165.01
of zero coupon bonds . . . 3160–3160.01

Yields of U.S. government securities compared with corporate bonds . . . 3135

Z

Zero coupon bonds
default risk of . . . 3160.02
to insure CDs . . . 3160.02–.03
investment feature of . . . 3160.01
for IRAs . . . 915.01
lifetime gifts of . . . 410.01
long-term . . . 3150.04
mock . . . 3165
periodic interest not paid on . . . 3160
STRIPS . . . 3160.03, 3165
tax-exempt . . . 3110.03
tax-sheltered accounts for . . . 3160.03
trust for splitting income from . . . 3160.03

Zero coupon mutual funds . . . 3140.03–.04